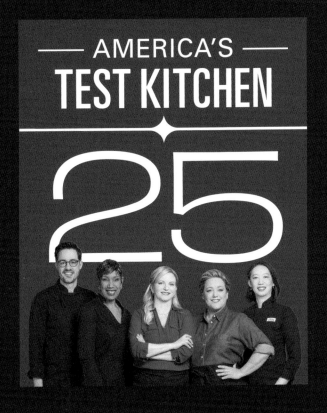

AMERICA'S TEST KITCHEN

25

500 RECIPES

THAT CHANGED THE WAY
AMERICA COOKS

25TH ANNIVERSARY COOKBOOK

Contents

Acknowledgments

Putting on a cooking show is no small feat. It literally takes an army. Doing it for 25 years, and making it the most successful and longest-running cooking show on TV is a milestone worthy of celebration. This special book is a love letter to the remarkable cast and crew that have brought ATK's recipes to life for millions of home cooks.

In addition to the 16 cast members you know, nearly 100 others work behind the scenes. Executive Producer Kaitlin Keleher conceived and developed each episode with help from Supervising Producer Caroline Rickert, Line Producer Diane Knox, Producer Alex Curran-Cardarelli, and Associate Producers TJ Johnson and Angelica Quintanilla. Special thanks to director Herb Sevush (our director for all 25 seasons) and director of photography Dan Anderson.

Along with the on-air crew, Director of Culinary Production Erin McMurrer and Culinary Producers Alli Berkey, Christie Morrison, and Janette Zepeda and Assistant Culinary Producer Mel Velasco helped plan and organize the 26 television episodes filmed in May 2023 and March 2024 and ran the "back kitchen," where all the food that appeared on camera originated. Chase Brightwell, Carolyn Grillo, Valerie Sizhe Li, Sawyer Phillips, Sarah Sandler, and Kate Shannon organized the ingredients and equipment segments. Senior Science Editor Paul Adams researched the science behind the recipes and wrote the science animations. Additional support was provided by our Production Coordinator Jennifer Cuciti. Producer Magdalena Bresson supported production of *America's Test Kitchen Celebrates 25 Years*.

During filming, chefs Graciel Caces, Mitchell Dalbey, Grier Hickman, Jami Samuelson-Kopec, and Lee Tan cooked all the food needed on set. Ashley Moore and Christine Tobin provided food styling. Manager of Procurement and Kitchen Facilities Rachel Applebaum, Ingredient Purchasing Coordinator Heather Tolmie, Ingredient Purchasing Specialist Crispin Lopez, Ingredient Receiving Specialist Christopher Miller, and Kitchen Facilities and Equipment Coordinator Ethan Rogers were charged with making sure all the ingredients and kitchen equipment we needed were on hand. Culinary Assistants Yesenia Grant, Skye Stanger, and Ethan Rogers helped coordinate the kitchen with the television set by readying props, equipment, and food. Deva Djaafar and Octavia Pidoux assisted with facilities management.

We also appreciate the hard work of the television crew including Ian Bishop, Jock Blaney, Mikaela Bloomberg, Nikki Bramley, Ian Buchanan, Fletcher Burns, Owen Cooper,

Lyris Darcy, Ryan Doris, Mike Duca, Mitchell Farias, Eric Fisher, Rose Fortuna, Mark Gardner, Eric Goddard, Brian Henderson, Amanda Hennessey, Samantha Hills, Lee Holloway, Harlem Logan, Lana Marks, Jay Maurer, Keith McManus, Michael Needleman, Anthony Phelps, Vikki Porter, Zach Robbins, Will Rogan, Kyle Sanville, Kyle Shea, Taylor Steele, and Jennifer Tawa. Dan Callahan, Jared Detsikas, Emilio Guido, Andrew Hobbs, Tom Killberg, Jimmy Martin, Clay Milneck, Ryan O'Donnell, and Lindsey Polevoy supported our remote shoots.

The show is edited by Steven Huffaker, Hamilton Jones, Nick Perlman, Sean Sandefur, Herb Sevush, and Edit House Productions, being overseen by Director of Post Production Chen Margolis with support from Assistant Editors Caroline Barry and Ben Mushinski. Motion graphics were provided by Neoscape. Yiorgos Tsvranidis managed the equipment.

We also would like to thank Hope Hennessey and Dani Cook at WETA for managing station relations, and the team at American Public Television that presents the show: Jim Dunford, Shawn Halford, Judy Barlow, Tom Davison, and Reina Roberts. Thanks also for production support from Zebra Productions, New York. Special thanks to Talamas.

Plugrà, American Cruise Lines, and Sur La Table sponsored the show, and we thank them for their support.

Welcome to America's Test Kitchen

This book has been tested, written, and edited by the folks at America's Test Kitchen, where curious cooks become confident cooks. Located in Boston's Seaport District in the historic Innovation and Design Building, it features 15,000 square feet of kitchen space including multiple photography and video studios. It is the home of *Cook's Illustrated* magazine and *Cook's Country* magazine and is the workday destination for more than 60 test cooks, editors, and cookware specialists. Our mission is to empower and inspire confidence, community, and creativity in the kitchen.

We start the process of testing a recipe with a complete lack of preconceptions, which means that we accept no claim, no technique, and no recipe at face value. We simply assemble as many variations as possible, test a half-dozen of the most promising, and taste the results blind. We then construct our own recipe and continue to test it, varying ingredients, techniques, and cooking times until we reach a consensus. As we like to say in the test kitchen, "We make the mistakes so you don't have to." The result, we hope, is the best version of a particular recipe, but we realize that only you can be the final judge of our success (or failure). We use the same rigorous approach when we test equipment and taste ingredients.

All of this would not be possible without a belief that good cooking, much like good music, is based on a foundation of objective technique. Some people like spicy foods and others don't, but there is a right way to sauté, there is a best way to cook a pot roast, and there are measurable scientific principles involved in producing perfectly beaten, stable egg whites. Our ultimate goal is to investigate the fundamental principles of cooking to give you the techniques, tools, and ingredients you need to become a better cook. It is as simple as that.

To see what goes on behind the scenes at America's Test Kitchen, check out our social media channels for kitchen snapshots, exclusive content, video tips, and much more. You can watch us work (in our actual test kitchen) by tuning in to *America's Test Kitchen* or *Cook's Country* on public television or on our websites.

Listen to *Proof* (AmericasTestKitchen.com/podcasts) to hear engaging, complex stories about people and food. Want to hone your cooking skills or finally learn how to bake—with an America's Test Kitchen test cook? Enroll in one of our online cooking classes.

However you choose to visit us, we welcome you into our kitchen, where you can stand by our side as we test our way to the best recipes in America.

 facebook.com/AmericasTestKitchen
 instagram.com/TestKitchen
 youtube.com/AmericasTestKitchen
 tiktok.com/@TestKitchen
 x.com/TestKitchen
 pinterest.com/TestKitchen

AmericasTestKitchen.com
CooksIllustrated.com
CooksCountry.com
OnlineCookingSchool.com

Join Our Community of Recipe Testers

Our recipe testers provide valuable feedback on recipes under development by ensuring that they are foolproof in home kitchens. Help the America's Test Kitchen book team investigate the how and why behind successful recipes from your home kitchen.

Our Story

Twenty-five years is a long time.

My favorite extra-vecchio balsamic vinegar from Modena (yes, I'm talking about the good stuff in tiny bottles) is aged that long. My prized cast-iron skillet with layers of seasoning was purchased at a flea market 25 years ago. And, yes, our television show is celebrating our silver anniversary. What accounts for our remarkable staying power, other than sheer determination?

***America's Test Kitchen* has always believed in the transformative power of home cooking.** Happy meals truly are made at home and we want you to cook often and successfully. From day one, our show has been engineered to provide home cooks with all the tools necessary for a delicious life in the kitchen.

The science segments explain the foundational principles so that you learn something every time you watch our show. The equipment reviews and taste tests ensure that you don't mess up before the oven is heated. But, at its heart, our show is about recipes. And, might I say, very good recipes. We've developed more than 13,000 dishes since that first episode in season 1. For this celebratory volume, we've selected the very best 500 recipes, from classics that have endured to exciting new dishes from recent seasons.

So what makes a game-changing recipe? First off, it has to be a recipe you make over and over. It can be something you make once a year but has become part of your family's culinary tapestry. My wife makes Perfect Pecan Pie (page 649) every November (times three, because it's Thanksgiving and the house is packed). Our children, nieces, and nephews can't imagine this holiday without this dessert. And neither can I.

A game-changing recipe can be something you make once a week, like Perfect Scrambled Eggs (page 59), with extra yolks and extra fat so they cook up super-tender and a novel folding technique so they turn out fluffy and light. Or maybe it's a recipe that becomes

your trademark, the dish all your friends and neighbors want you to make. For me, that's Paella on the Grill (page 473). My in-laws prefer that we visit them, but if I promise to make this showstopping dish they will leave their apartment in New Jersey, cross two New York bridges, and brave the infamous Long Island traffic to reach my backyard table.

Throughout the book, you'll find commentary from cast members recounting the dishes that have become personal game changers. And if you want to get started right now, see the list on page 5.

What unites all game-changing recipes is how they weave themselves into your life. They give you the confidence to think of yourself as a good cook. And because of our unique recipe development process that relies on input from thousands of home cooks across the country, we really do understand the realities of cooking at home. Our 60-plus test cooks and editors, many of whom you know from the television show, come to work every day with one goal: How can we help you? We hope this book, with the very best of our best recipes, inspires and empowers you.

Jack Bishop

CHIEF CREATIVE OFFICER

From the Beginning

HELLO FROM BRIDGET

I started working for *Cook's Illustrated* magazine
as a test cook in 1998. I'd been a subscriber, and I loved the idea of developing recipes for the no-frills/just-the-facts publication whose sole focus was helping people become better home cooks.

Back then, the test kitchen was comprised of a handful of people. As the newbie, my duties included grocery shopping, dishwashing, food prepping, and testing other people's recipes, but eventually I was green-lit to develop my own recipes. Julia joined the test kitchen a few months later, and our friendship developed almost immediately.

A short time later, there was talk about turning the test kitchen concept into a TV show, and if you were working in the test kitchen, you were going to be on the show. Talk about a baptism by fire! I was excited, but mostly terrified.

That first season of filming is almost a complete blur. I remember panicking before we rolled each morning, then relaxing a bit as I settled into doing what I knew—cooking—on camera. I quickly found out that cooking and talking in front of the camera is harder than it looks.

After that first season was wrapped, edited, and then aired, I watched an episode. It was different from any other cooking show I'd seen before. We weren't just showing great recipes; we were offering real-life tools to help people become better cooks. Would America like the show?

After 16 seasons as a test cook, I was paired with Julia to take over as co-hosts. This was new territory (we were allowed to look at the camera!) but I truly believe that our experience as test cooks on the show helped us settle into the role. The best part of hosting the show is getting to cook with so many of my colleagues—all of whom bring distinct points of view, enthusiasm, and real talent to the set each day.

Being co-host means that I get to cook with Julia. We have such a great time together that it's easy to forget there's a bank of cameras capturing our every move. And yes, I do make it my goal to make her break down with laughter at least once a season. Check out the sticky buns episode (season 17) if you want an idea of the fun we have together.

Really, that's what the show is all about. It's not flashy; we're not actors. We're just people who love to cook, teaching and learning from each other, and along the way, we're having a lot of fun. We've come a long way since that first season of *America's Test Kitchen*, but the mission has remained the same. I'm so thankful that somehow the viewers allowed us the grace to find our footing, and the folks at public television green-lit a second season, and another, and well, 25 seasons and counting. Here's to the next 25.

HELLO FROM JULIA

I started working at *Cook's Illustrated* magazine back in 1999 as a test cook. I did the grocery shopping, washed the dishes, and assisted the editors with their recipe projects. A few months later I developed my first test kitchen recipe for Chicken Marsala (page 214), and a year later I stood in front of the TV cameras for the first time on *America's Test Kitchen*. Since then, I've developed hundreds of recipes, edited dozens of cookbooks, and filmed a lot of TV shows. It's an absolute dream job and I've learned a ton over the past 25 years.

In the beginning, I focused primarily on the basics. Things such as "how to tell when a skillet is hot enough for searing" and "how to tell when a pork chop is perfectly cooked." (Answers: Add oil to the pan before heating and note how its texture changes, and cooked pork chops should register 140 degrees on an instant-read thermometer.) The recipes I showcased on the show were also fairly straightforward: pecan pie, glazed meatloaf, mashed potatoes. I started off with the classics.

But the food scene in America is always changing, and I've changed with it. Sous vide machines, air fryers, and multicookers are great examples of tools that weren't common 25 years ago. I now regularly use the multicooker and the air fryer during the week and pull out the sous vide for parties because it simplifies the timing of the main course. The same can be said for many ingredients that I now cook with, from gochujang to quinoa. In fact, many of the ingredients in my pantry today would be unrecognizable to my younger self.

I was humbled to take over the role of ATK co-host in 2017, alongside my dear friend Bridget, and we've been working hard to bring the show into a new era: incorporating new cast members, better explaining the science of cooking, and exploring new cultures through food. The change has been exciting and I'm happy to say that I'm still hungry for more.

5 GAME-CHANGING RECIPES TO GET YOU STARTED

- **For the newbie:** French Omelets (page 65)
  The cubed cold butter and chopsticks are genius

- **For the host:** Lumpiang Shanghai (page 41)
  Possibly the tastiest finger food on the planet

- **For the parent:** Deluxe Blueberry Pancakes (page 79)
  As much fun to make as to eat

- **For the weekend baker:** Perfect Sticky Buns (page 549)
  So good you will laugh yourself silly—just ask Bridget and Julia

- **For the lazy cook:** Red Lentil Soup with Warm Spices (page 126)
  Rarely is something so utterly easy so satisfying

Recipe Development

We Create Revolutionary Recipes That Work the First Time, and Every Time

BY KEITH DRESSER

Our unique, science-based recipe development process is the secret to our success. Here's how it works ⟶

5 REVOLUTIONARY RECIPE DISCOVERIES

- Never boil a hard-boiled egg (see page 27)
- Sear steak in a cold skillet (see page 307)
- Turn off the oven when roasting a chicken (see page 237)
- Roast turkey on a baking stone (see page 260)
- Let pizza dough rise for 3 days (see page 552)

It All Starts with Research

The recipe development process begins with our team of test cooks and food editors researching recipe ideas. We strive to create a collection of recipes from diverse cultures and cuisines that cater to a broad range of skills, accommodating both novices and seasoned home cooks alike. We also consider factors like seasonality, cooking techniques, and ingredient trends. Recipes are then assigned to a test cook, who thoroughly researches each recipe, consulting various sources and even interviewing chefs familiar with the dish to understand its history, cultural significance, ingredients, and preparation. Their research is distilled into a proposal that is shared with the rest of the team. The proposal acts as a roadmap for upcoming development, outlining the cook's envisioned path for the recipe.

The 5-Recipe Test Is Next

The first step in the kitchen, and probably the most important step in our development process, is the 5-recipe test. The cook chooses five existing recipes that represent the range of approaches to the same dish and prepares them exactly as written. We gather as a team of test cooks and editors to taste the five recipes and offer detailed feedback on factors like texture, seasoning, and appearance. The collaborative evaluation of these recipes helps to determine what makes a recipe good or bad and demonstrates how variations in techniques and ingredients impact the final outcome of a dish.

Single-Variable Testing Begins

The test cook takes the team's feedback and what they learned from cooking the five recipes to develop their own original recipe. This is the working recipe that the test cook will spend the next four weeks refining, revising, and testing every variable. They compare multiple variations and techniques to find the absolute best method, ensuring that the recipe is foolproof and reliable. There is a lot of trial and error and a test cook quickly learns that recipe development is never a straight line. Some years ago, I dedicated nearly six weeks to making more than 70 spice cakes in pursuit of the perfect recipe. That was an extreme case, but we might make our recipes 40, 50, up to 60 times until we get it right. It's this dedication to development that supports our mantra: "We make the mistakes so you don't have to."

Home Cooks Have the Final Say

Once we are satisfied with a recipe in the test kitchen, we pass it on to our volunteer at-home recipe testers for their feedback. This community of over 40,000 home cooks are integral contributors to the success of our recipes, and we involve them in the recipe development process because ultimately we are creating recipes that have to work at home. We learn from them what they didn't understand about the recipe, what they didn't like, and what they would change. We consider their feedback and then conduct further testing to update the recipe as needed. For recipes that don't pass muster, we go back into the kitchen and then survey again, but there are rare occasions when recipes won't result in publication, as in the case of our recipe for old-fashioned fudge. Even after six months of recipe development and 1,000 pounds of fudge, we never achieved a foolproof recipe worthy of a magazine article.

We Explain Why and Show How

Once a recipe is finalized, we write a narrative story about its development for publication. We do this to add context for the recipe and to show home cooks how we arrived at the recipe we did. The stories help to explain concepts, to teach new skills, and ultimately achieve our mission, which is to help curious cooks become confident cooks.

PASS

FAIL

The Science of Good Cooking

Let Science Be Your Sous Chef

BY DAN SOUZA

Understanding the science behind cooking has been an integral part of developing recipes at America's Test Kitchen since day one.

It's a critical component for both how we work and how we present our work. That's because when we talk about science in the kitchen we really mean two different kinds of science. The first is the scientific method—essentially controlled trial and error—which underpins our daily work in the test kitchen. We set up side-by-side tests altering just one variable so we can slowly, iteratively make our way to the best possible recipe. The second is scientific explanation. Science is happening in your food whether you want to observe it, pay attention to it, or completely ignore that it's there. We believe that when cooks focus on it, they gain confidence in the kitchen. That's why we teach the differences between salting and brining (and why salting leads to crispier poultry skin), the ins and outs of carryover cooking (and why you need to account for it to achieve perfectly cooked meats), and why pan sauces break (and how to fix them). We love recipes at America's Test Kitchen, but if you learn the science— the "why" behind cooking—you become less reliant on them. That's real confidence.

One of the best ways to bring food science to life is through big, visual demonstrations, like our TV science segments. Each segment helps explore an aspect of food science that directly impacts home cooks and we always provide a useful takeaway—each one offers a tip, trick, or technique that you can put to use in your cooking that very day.

We aim to make food science really practical and useful. But we also like to make it fun. One of my favorite science experiments involved Joe and a kids' bouncy castle. We wanted to explain what goes on when proofing a loaf of bread. With the castle revved up and full of air, Joe bounced around happily. But when we pulled the plug and cut the electricity the castle slowly deflated and ended up collapsing onto Joe. It was a light-hearted way to demonstrate what happens when yeasted dough proofs for too long and the yeast stops pumping out gas. (Joe has been our amiable crash test dummy for numerous other experiments and has since moved on to presenting recipes on the show rather than running on vats of cornstarch slurry or opening warm, explosive bottles of champagne.)

We have a single focus at America's Test Kitchen: to empower home cooks to make incredible food, gain confidence in the kitchen, and ultimately live happier lives. Science allows us to build failproof recipes and it can help you cook your best every day. By the transitive property that means science is the key to a happy life, right?

5 MEMORABLE SCIENTIFIC DISCOVERIES

- Most marinades don't tenderize meat, but salt does (see page 288)
- Baking soda helps ground meat remain tender (see page 101)
- Brining dried beans before cooking softens their skins so they don't blow out (see page 340)
- Make a flour paste in the microwave for the fluffiest-ever bread (see page 539)
- Temper chocolate in the microwave for the shiniest, snappiest coating (see page 580)

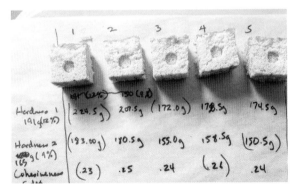

5 HIGHLIGHTS FROM THE ATK REVIEWS LAB

- Fill zipper-lock bags with marinara sauce and push them off the counter to see if the seals hold

- Saw coolers in half to reveal how much insulation there is (hint: low-rated models didn't have enough in the lid)

- Toast 1,095 consecutive slices of bread to challenge three top toasters

- Brew (and drink) more than 5,000 ounces of coffee to test 16 coffee makers

- Build a knife-wielding robot (with scientists' help!) to test the sturdiness and knife-friendliness of cutting boards

The Right Ingredients and Equipment Help Make You a Better Cook

BY LISA MCMANUS

Sure, we're known on *America's Test Kitchen* for delicious, thoroughly tested recipes that work. But that's only part of the story of successful cooking.

From the beginning at the test kitchen, we realized that having high-quality kitchen gear and ingredients actually makes a huge difference.

The best canned tomatoes taste velvety, sweet, and rich in tomato sauce, while the worst make a sauce that's watery and acidic. A good skillet resists warping and browns evenly; bad ones have hot spots that scorch your food. A well-made chef's knife—and an effective sharpener to maintain it—makes food prep simple, precise, and quick. A poorly made, dull knife? Misery.

Reviews have always been part of the DNA at America's Test Kitchen. Back in 1992, home cooks had no source of reviews focused on kitchen products. As Jack Bishop once put it, if you wanted to know which was the best food processor to buy, you had to ask your mom.

Well, no disrespect to moms everywhere, but we knew there had to be a better way.

Just as our test cooks do with recipes, we developed our own rigorous America's Test Kitchen approach to testing gear and tasting food. We will do whatever it takes to figure out the best kitchen products, whether we're banging skillets on concrete blocks to test their sturdiness, sampling 29 face-puckering vinegars, or sawing coolers in half to learn about their insulation. And because we've never accepted advertising or free product samples, we have always been free to tell you what we really think. Our goal has always been to give you solid advice on what's worth buying and using in your kitchen.

When *America's Test Kitchen* hit the TV airwaves 25 years ago, our first episode featured the Tasting Lab where a kid named Jack Bishop talked about how to choose the best canned tomatoes.

To this day, all of our product recommenda-tions—whether in a Tasting Lab segment with Jack, the Equipment Corner with Adam, or Gear Heads with Hannah and me—come from the test kitchen's original process of hands-on testing and scientific, unbiased tasting.

In between seasons of our television show, our Reviews team of testers works every day to test kitchen gear and taste food products that we can recommend to you. We also stock the winners of our testing process in the test kitchen, where ATK cooks use them every day. We want to know how the winning equipment holds up and whether top-ranked ingredients remain top-notch. In other words, we just don't tell you what to buy; we live with our choices, too. We've been doing this for more than 25 years—and we are never done learning and sharing what we know.

We know that if we do our job right, your cooking at home becomes easier, more successful—and more delicious.

Cast Q & A

Our ensemble cast comes from all over the country. Many of us worked in restaurant kitchens. Some of us learned from our mothers and grandmothers. We all love to cook and we all love to teach. In fact, we don't think of ourselves as television personalities. We are first and foremost educators, and here are our backstories.

Jack Bishop

THE OG

Taste-test guru for 25 years and part of the team that launched *Cook's Illustrated* **magazine in 1992**

When did you join the show and what do you remember about being on your first show?

We filmed a test episode in 1999 and then started shooting broadcast episodes in 2000. At the outset, I had no interest in doing TV. I was a writer and editor and had developed the tasting protocols we used to evaluate everything from olive oil to ice cream at *Cook's Illustrated*. But TV? No thanks. But after several seasons, I started to enjoy myself. My "how to succeed on TV" lessons—which I share with newer cast members—are as follows: (1) Focus on a small number of points that will help the viewer. (2) Have at least one unexpected talking point—something the viewer can share with a friend. (3) Smile even if you're terrified.

What's your favorite no-recipe recipe?

Pasta with garlic and olive oil. When I get home late and there's nothing to eat, there's always spaghetti, garlic, and high-quality olive oil. If there are fresh herbs in the garden or fridge, great. Or maybe I fry some capers or toast some panko bread crumbs. Nothing comforts or satisfies like this dish. And I never forget to finish with a sprinkle of Maldon, my favorite flaked sea salt from England.

What is your must-have kitchen tool?

Friends and family call me the salad whisperer. The salad spinner has transformed the chore of washing greens (yes, I'm old enough to remember salad before the spinner) into a pleasure. And my salads today are even better because the spinner removes more moisture than the old-fashioned kitchen towel method. No soggy greens in my salad bowl ... ever!

What question do fans ask you the most often?

Are Bridget and Julia really friends? And the happy answer is that they really are! Unlike other ensemble shows that bring together strangers who have been cast into their roles, the three of us (plus Adam) were all colleagues at *Cook's Illustrated* magazine before the television show started. Bridget and Julia worked together in the kitchen and had become friends well before the cameras rolled. And this applies to the rest of the team. Before she joined the cast, Becky was my colleague at the editors' table and she would help me advocate for more vegetarian recipes. Dan and I shared a love of science. I hired Lisa because I knew she'd make a great product reviewer. The camaraderie you see on air is real. We like each other, especially Bridget and Julia who have shared an amazing journey together for 25-plus years.

What's the best piece of cooking advice you've ever received?

Finish strong! Even if you're following a great ATK recipe, it might need some tweaking at the end. More salt, of course. But maybe more acid. It's amazing what a squirt of lemon juice will do to sauces, soups, stews, and pasta dishes. A drizzle of the finest extra-virgin olive (preferably olio nuovo from the most recent harvest). A sprinkle of chopped herbs for freshness. You get the idea. Taste your food and ask yourself how you can make it better. Then call everyone to the table.

Sam Block

FROM SURF TO TURF

Started her test kitchen journey teaching ATK classes on cruise ships but is happier cooking on terra firma

When did you join the show and what do you remember about being on your first show?

I joined the cast in 2022, season 24. I remember being a bundle of nerves! I came out on my first take with a lot of energy. Too much, in fact. But Julia looked at me, smiled, said "you got this," and the nerves washed away.

What was the first recipe you made on the show?

My first recipe was Red Lentil Kibbeh (page 520), which was a recipe I developed for *The Complete Plant-Based Cookbook*. Having made that recipe dozens of times, I was super-excited to kick off my TV debut with a recipe I felt so comfortable with.

What is your must-have kitchen tool?

My Microplane, hands down. I use it daily to grate garlic, citrus zest, Parmesan, nutmeg, and more.

What recipe made you the most proud to develop?

The chocolate-cardamom cake that I developed for our cookbook *Everything Chocolate*. It was my first big project recipe that took months to develop. I tested types of chocolate, pear preparation, oven temperature, rack location, leavening amounts, and so much more. The final result was a tea party stunner. Plus, my team and I got to eat a lot of cake.

Any funny moments/disasters/bloopers you would like to share?

The Red Lentil Kibbeh, served in a lettuce cup and dolloped with yogurt, has a porridge-like consistency. When it was time to eat I could hear my mom saying, "small bites, Sam." Let's just say my first mouthful got cut from the final episode. It's something I'm working on.

You've been rescued from a desert island; what do you want someone to cook for you?

A juicy smash burger with crispy shoestring fries. Or mac and cheese. Or a simple brick-oven margherita pizza. Really I'd imagine anything that doesn't involve coconut or raw fish.

What food/ingredient can you not get enough of?

Any and all fermented condiments. Some people put hot sauce on just about anything. For me, it's fish sauce.

Hannah Crowley
KITCHEN GEAR EXPERT

Leader of ATK Reviews, our nine-person team dedicated to testing equipment and evaluating supermarket ingredients

• •

When did you join the show and what do you remember about being on your first show?

Just in 2023. I'm a newbie. I come from YouTube where we film with like four of us in a room, very casual. Having so many people on the ATK set was overwhelming but the crew are all such pros and so nice, by the end of my first day I was having fun.

What is your must-have kitchen tool?

I love giving smaller rimmed baking sheets as gifts. I appreciate the half sheet pan size, too, but I cook so much in the toaster oven these days I find myself reaching for the one-eighth and quarter-sheet pan sizes more than my big pans. I also use them for serving plates (great for kids—unbreakable!), storage, and mising out ingredients or holding prepped food, like a salted steak. I own 14 sheet pans in these three sizes and I use them all regularly.

Any funny moments/disasters/bloopers you would like to share?

I remember trying to shoot with a digital thermometer and needing it to show a specific temperature. We were just boiling and cooling water on set, over and over again, while the crew waited and watched. Hot steam billowing, the temperature in the room rising. We could not get it to work. I was sweating bullets, literally and metaphorically. The next year we worked with Thermoworks to get a thermometer that you could set to a certain reading. Now if we just need to show a number for an educational purpose we can avoid steaming the whole joint up.

What question do fans ask you the most often?

Things they've been wondering about in their own personal kitchens. Is this thing worth buying? What's the best X? I love this and think of it as one of the best parts of my job. As humans we all have to cook and having this job immediately connects me to people and is such a great conversation starter. I never get tired of hearing what people are thinking about in the kitchen.

Keith Dresser

FROM BACK KITCHEN TO RECIPE STAGE

Behind-the-scenes kitchen majordomo turned recipe presenter extraordinaire

. . . .

When did you join the show and what do you remember about being on your first show?

I joined the ATK cast in season 17. Before that I was a culinary producer starting on season 3.

What was the first recipe you made on the show?

The first recipe I made was Really Good Garlic Bread.

What's your favorite no-recipe recipe?

Scrambled eggs. They are good any time of day and the combination of mix-ins is endless.

What is your must-have kitchen tool?

Sharp knives, emphasis on sharp.

What is your favorite recipe/episode so far?

Kimchi Bokkeumbap (page 338) in season 22. I love fast-moving recipes with a lot of knife work!

How do you prep for the show?

I usually walk or drive and cook through the recipe in my head.

You've been rescued from a desert island; what do you want someone to cook for you?

If someone has rescued me from a desert island, I'll make dinner for them! How about steak frites?

What's your ultimate comfort food?

Pasta with butter, grated Parmesan cheese, and black pepper.

What's the first recipe you learned how to cook?

Chocolate chip cookies. I remember the first time I could hold the mixer by myself.

Joe Gitter

SILENT PARTNER BECOMES ON-CAMERA TALENT

Debuted as Dan's "foil" for science segments, but now a seasoned recipe presenter— with such a lovely British accent

. . . .

When did you join the show and what do you remember about being on your first show?

I joined for season 24. I did both my recipes with Julia and I was blown away by her skill and professionalism. Bridget had caught Covid a couple of days before we were due to film our segment and Julia stepped in and had to do twice as many segments as she'd rehearsed for!

What's your favorite no-recipe recipe?

Fried rice. I always make extra rice so I have some on hand for a really quick and easy meal the whole family enjoys and it's so perfect for using up small amounts of leftover ingredients (ham, meat, veggies, onions).

What is your must-have kitchen tool?

My Thermapen: It's the key to cooking fish and meat skillfully.

How do you prep for the show?

I make the recipe at least five times in the runup to the show and narrate what I'm doing. On the morning of the show, I'll go for a run and I'll come to the set hungry. Hunger is the best seasoning and it'll make me extra excited for the tasting.

What was the hardest recipe you've had to make?

Vegan bacon for our *Vegan for Everybody* cookbook. I worked with making my own seitan out of bread flour but it required too much time and we had to cut the recipe.

What recipe made you the most proud to develop?

My recent small-batch focaccia that I'm working on for a forthcoming small-batch baking book. No bread offers a better reward-to-effort ratio.

You've been rescued from a desert island; what do you want someone to cook for you?

A full-on Peking duck.

Becky Hays

THE LONGEST-TENURED COOK ON THE SHOW

This cool-as-a-cucumber omnivore loves to make vegetable-forward dishes

• •

When did you join the show and what do you remember about being on your first show?

I joined the show in 2006 and debuted with black bean soup, which I grew up eating and find satisfying and comforting. I was nervous as heck, but once we wrapped, I could finally take a breath, and I was beyond thrilled. As a kid, I idolized Julia Child, so following in her footsteps was a true dream come true.

What's your favorite no-recipe recipe?

Vegetable soup. I start by sautéing a mirepoix (onion, carrot, and celery), then add a little tomato paste and garlic. In goes homemade broth, which I make and freeze whenever I have spare time in the kitchen. Next, I chop up all of the produce I can find in my fridge—everything goes, even leftover cooked veggies are fair game. At this point, I might also add canned beans, pasta, or rice. Freshen up each bowl with a few snips of garden herbs, and an easy, nourishing meal is served.

What is your favorite recipe/episode so far?

I had a blast with Julia making strawberry jam. Jam is a fun project, but it can be intimidating, so it was fun to show our viewers exactly how to do it—and that it's actually not hard at all. All those berries made the kitchen smell amazing, too.

How do you prep for the show?

Don't tell anyone, but I don't rehearse too much at all. I prepare the recipe once at home and then I casually review talking points while I'm having my hair and makeup done—in between lots of laughs with our beauty team. Everything feels more natural—and easier—if I mostly talk off the cuff.

What food/ingredient can you not get enough of?

Artichokes. In springtime, I enjoy them almost daily with lots of mayonnaise or melted butter with fresh tarragon. In the off-season, artichoke dip is where it's at!

Antoinette Johnson

THE NEWEST COOK ON THE SHOW

The winner of *ATK: The Next Generation*, Season 1, makes a splash with her practical style and Southern point of view

• •

When did you join the show and what do you remember about being on your first show?

I joined in 2022 after winning *America's Test Kitchen: Next Generation*. My first episode was a whirlwind of emotions. Despite the excitement of being on set, I was grappling with a thrilling secret—I had to keep my win under wraps until the Next Gen show aired.

What was the first recipe you made on the show or what was your first segment?

My signature dish from *Next Gen*: a whole fried branzino, a recipe I'd crafted and perfected over time without realizing its potential. Sharing it with the vast ATK audience was a surreal moment and a reminder that sometimes the dishes we take for granted can lead us to extraordinary places.

What is your favorite recipe/episode so far?

One that's deeply resonated with me is the Jamaican Stew Peas with Spinners (page 106). Beyond its exquisite flavors, this dish represents a culinary journey through the Black diaspora. It beautifully intertwines Jamaican and Southern influences, celebrating the rich tapestry of our shared heritage. It's a reminder that food is not just sustenance; it's a cultural connector.

What food/ingredient can you not get enough of?

Mustard is the unsung hero of my kitchen. It's like the Swiss Army knife of condiments—versatile, reliable, and always there when you need it. Whether it's slathered on a sandwich, mixed into a marinade, or whisked into a dressing, mustard adds that extra punch of flavor that takes a dish from good to great. Plus, with so many varieties to choose from, the possibilities are endless.

What's something you didn't know before you joined the ATK cast?

Imagine my surprise when I found out that those test cooks in the background were actually cooking for the show! I mean, I thought it was all culinary theater. But nope, they're the real deal and they get it right EVERY time.

Lan Lam

TECHNIQUE IS HER
MIDDLE NAME

Everyone's favorite teacher blends a deep knowledge of science with her passion for cooking

When did you join the show and what do you remember about being on your first show?

My first week at ATK was during the filming of season 12 and everyone told me, "When you're on set, pretend the cameras don't exist." Fast-forward to season 19 and you'd find me trying to calm my nerves by reminding myself that there were no cameras in front of me.

What's your favorite no-recipe recipe?

I learned to make rice from my grandmother and to this day, I use the same method: Rinse the rice until the water runs clear. Add water up to my knuckle. Bring to a simmer, cover and reduce the heat to low. Cook until rice is tender. Let rest for 5 minutes before fluffing.

What is your favorite recipe/episode so far?

I was lucky enough to chat with Martin Yan, a culinary hero of mine, when I was developing a version of Stir-Fried Beef and Gai Lan (page 317). He kindly shared his time and advice, giving me background information on key ingredients and sharing cooking tips. I was so pleased when I learned that I'd get to prepare that recipe on the show.

How do you prep for the show?

I jot down notes on index cards and use two different colored pens. One color is for the numbers that I need to memorize: 2 teaspoons of this, bake for 15 to 18 minutes, roll dough into 6-inch square, etc. The other is for the talking points that bring a recipe to life, like where the dish is from, why I chose a particular ingredient, etc.

What food/ingredient can you not get enough of?

I think the world can be divided into camps based on favorite starch. There are bread people, pasta/noodle people, potato people. Me? I'm a rice person. I love it in all forms.

What was the hardest recipe you've had to present on TV?

Working with laminated dough made me so nervous. It's made by enveloping a block of butter in a lean dough. I knew that under the hot studio lights, that butter was going to melt rapidly. I was so proud of myself for getting that portion of the filming down in one take.

Lisa McManus

**THE EPITOME OF
TEST KITCHEN RIGOR**

**No one is more thorough or
detail-oriented, which is why her
product reviews are so trusted**

*When did you join the show and what do you remember
about being on your first show?*

I started with the show in its 10th season, in 2010. I remember
being wracked with nerves for months ahead of time, but
everyone on the crew and cast was so incredibly nice to me
that once the cameras rolled, I was OK.

What was your first segment?

One of the first, and certainly one of the most memorable,
was cut-resistant gloves that protect your hands from
sharp objects like mandoline blades. I stuffed hot dogs into
the fingers and then sliced across the glove with a chef's
knife. (That was a test nobody was willing to do with their
own hands. I can't imagine why not!)

What is your must-have kitchen tool?

A very sharp chef's knife and a nice, roomy cutting board.

*Any funny moments/disasters/bloopers you would like
to share?*

That first year my segments were being taped on the very
last afternoon of the last day of filming for the season. We
shot one after the next, with minimal breaks for resetting.
And I made it to the last segment. This was it. Every single
one of us was ready to wrap. I was demonstrating the
winning electric wine opener. I just had to finish by saying,
"It's so easy," open a bottle and pour a glass, and we could
all go home. Absolute DOOM. I opened most of a case of
wine wrong. Bottle after bottle. Everyone would hold their
breath when I'd say once again, "It's SO EASY" and … nope.
I will never again say "It's so easy" on TV. I feel like it's cursed.

What's your safety blanket on set?

Our director, Herb Sevush. I just have to hear his inimitable
voice and I relax. He makes me laugh, and I completely
trust his instincts. Even when he walks up ONE SECOND
before we roll and rearranges the whole segment. Darn it,
he's always right. It's better.

What's your best advice for home cooks?

Don't be afraid of your kitchen gear; get in there and mess
it up and really use it. It's not kitchen decor, they're tools
to help you make great food.

Erin McMurrer

KITCHEN GENERAL

The leader of our kitchen operations team is incredibly organized and brings that same precision to her on-camera work

. . . .

When did you join the show and what do you remember about being on your first show?

I started on the *Cook's Country* show back in 2008. Julia was out on maternity leave, and I jumped in to help cover some of her episodes. It was a busy time: I was running the back kitchen and living upstairs from the set kitchen. I was terrified about being on camera and had many late nights practicing my lines and making the recipes, but I was also very excited for this rare opportunity and to take on this new challenge! In 2017, I switched shows and joined the cast of *America's Test Kitchen*.

What was the first recipe you made on the show?

My first recipes for *America's Test Kitchen* included Pear-Walnut Upside-Down Cake (page 593) and Red Lentil Soup with Warm Spices (page 126).

What's your favorite no-recipe recipe?

A savory galette. I always have pie dough in my freezer and will often create a galette with whatever I have on hand to make a versatile and satisfying meal.

What is your favorite recipe/episode so far?

I enjoy recipes that require a lot of hands-on work, such as Easy Apple Strudel (page 662), Rugelach (page 574), and Ultimate Flaky Buttermilk Biscuits (page 524) because I become engrossed in the process. I also really enjoy making powerhouse recipes that are easy to make, such as Red Lentil Soup with Warm Spices (page 126) and Rajas Poblanas con Crema (page 498).

What's your safety blanket on set?

Jitters are always there for me, so my safety blanket is remembering that it's not about me, but that it's about the food and sharing with the viewers everything that I know about the recipe.

You've been rescued from a desert island; what do you want someone to cook for you?

Roasted chicken, mashed potatoes, and a perfect simple salad.

Adam Ried

THE GUY YOU WANT TO CHECK WITH FIRST BEFORE YOU SHOP

Reliably telling viewers what to buy—and what to avoid—for 25 years

. . . .

When did you join the show and what do you remember about being on your first show?

Day one . . . the pilot. I believe there were some early-morning shots of bourbon to help calm the nerves.

What was your first segment?

Roasting racks.

What's your favorite no-recipe recipe?

Trick question. We're ATK; there are recipes for everything, except perhaps boiling water. But even then, it depends on what you're using the water for.

What is your must-have kitchen tool?

I actually have three: 12-inch tongs (OXO)—AND—a rasp-style grater (Microplane)—AND—ThermoWorks ChefAlarm Thermometer/Timer.

Any funny moments/disasters/bloopers you would like to share?

In the alley behind the old ATK office in Brookline, I shot a gas grill testing segment in a single take. An ATK staffer, whose brother was my neighbor, was watching and mentioned it to her brother. A couple of months later at our annual neighborhood block party, her brother told a few people on my street the story of my single-take segment, which earned me the neighborhood nickname "One Take."

You've been rescued from a desert island; what do you want someone to cook for you?

Some sort of simple snack cake: banana, apple, cardamom, olive oil, a fruit kuchen. Just about any kind will do.

What's the best piece of cooking advice you've ever received?

Stand facing the stove. (Sorry, I couldn't resist. A tip of the hat to Irma Rombauer.)

What's your ultimate comfort food?

Tuna noodle casserole (potato chip topping mandatory).

Elle Simone Scott

AN ENGAGING EDUCATOR WHO MAKES EVERYTHING BEAUTIFUL AND FUN

This food stylist and thought leader captures the joy of cooking in every photo and segment

. . . .

When did you join the show and what do you remember about being on your first show?

I joined the cast in April 2016 and I remember feeling an overwhelming sense of gratitude for the opportunity. I cried at my first cast photo shoot!

What was the first recipe you made on the show?

My first recipe was Shrimp Scampi (page 371)—voted America's favorite recipe.

What's your favorite no-recipe recipe?

Baked potatoes, of course!

What is your must-have kitchen tool?

A good chef's knife.

What question do fans ask you the most often?

Fans often ask me how I became a food stylist. I tell them that I apprenticed with more experienced food stylists for years before I got my own jobs and a lot of the hiring comes from networking.

What's the best piece of cooking advice you've ever received?

"A watched pot never boils."

What's the first recipe you learned how to cook?

My uncle taught me how to make omelets when I was about 8 years old.

What's your ultimate comfort food?

Any type of casserole or stew.

What recipe made you the most proud to develop?

Shrimp Mozambique is the recipe I'm most proud of; I developed it with Matthew Fairman for *Cook's Country*. I had an opportunity to do a deep cultural dive into the foundation of the recipe and had so much fun learning more food culture.

Dan Souza

SCIENTIST-IN-CHIEF

Despite having two jobs— science explainer and recipe presenter—you will never see him sweat

. . . .

When did you join the show and what do you remember about being on your first show?

2013. My first recipe was my Fresh Pasta Without a Machine (page 164). I remember thinking that I would be very nervous, but when I got up there and started making the recipe it was just fun!

What's your favorite no-recipe recipe?

I make a lot of tartines. Which is a fancy way of saying I make a lot of multicomponent open-faced sandwiches. I start with nice crusty bread that I griddle on one side. With that side facing down I build upwards with something creamy, like hummus or Greek yogurt seasoned with olive oil, then whatever tinned or smoked fish has my eye that day. Then it is a toppings bonanza: Pickled red onions, thin slices of preserved lemon, chopped nuts, flake salt, hot sauce, a squeeze of lemon or lime juice, fresh herbs—anything is fair game.

What is your must-have kitchen tool?

I really love my carbon-steel wok. It has a flat bottom so it works well on my stovetop, and I find myself reaching for it more than any other pan. It is adept at stir-frying, deep-frying, steaming, boiling, and nearly every cooking task in between.

What was the hardest recipe you've had to make?

Believe it or not, the most challenging recipe I've done on TV is holiday sugar cookies. Not because the recipe is difficult (which it is not), but because I am terrible at cookie decorating. I practiced for many days and still struggled to make them beautiful! In the end it's good to know your strengths and weaknesses.

You've been rescued from a desert island; what do you want someone to cook for you?

I'm likely to be both incredibly dehydrated and incredibly hungry. I'll take a large bowl of really good chicken noodle soup.

What question do fans ask you the most often?

Is Bridget really as funny as she seems on the show? Easy answer: funnier.

Erica Turner

The newest member of the *Cook's Illustrated* team excels at developing, and presenting, recipes from across the globe

When did you join the show and what do you remember about being on your first show?

I joined the show in 2022 and I remember a rush of energy for my first episode. I was so excited to dive right in and enjoy every moment of it and I really did have a lot of fun! I love doing TV and knowing that there's an audience on the other side of the screen watching. I really do hope that the home audience feels a part of the show and that they have fun with us.

What is your must-have kitchen tool?

I love spatulas! They're so versatile whether I'm cooking or baking. Whenever I've moved somewhere new and had to rebuild my kitchen supplies, a spatula is one of the first tools I buy.

What is your favorite recipe/episode so far?

My favorite episode so far is Pasta alla Zozzona (page 193). It was such a fun recipe to research, develop, and write. It's a rich and decadent pasta from the Roman countryside that's a combination of amatriciana and carbonara, plus a bunch of onions and sausage. It comes together rather quickly, making it a perfect meal for any day of the week.

What recipe made you the most proud to develop?

Kol böreği for *Cook's Illustrated* for sure. Börek are savory, flaky pastries found throughout the Mediterranean, Middle East, and Eastern Europe. I lived in Gaziantep, Turkey, and attended cooking school there. In Turkey, kol böreği is traditionally made with yufka, a thin dough comparable to phyllo, and filled with spinach and cheese, meat, or potatoes. I chose a spinach and cheese filling. To make it, layers of dough are filled and rolled and then wrapped around each other to create one big spiral. When it bakes, it's golden brown and so beautiful!

You've been rescued from a desert island; what do you want someone to cook for you?

Rice and beans with fresh avocado, sliced tomato, tostones, yuca with pickled red onions, and fresh juice. At the end of a long day, if I walk into my home and I smell rice and beans cooking, it immediately lifts my spirits and reminds me of my childhood.

Appetizers & Drinks

Photo: Baked Brie en Croûte

Classic Guacamole

Classic Guacamole

Makes 2 cups • **Total Time: 15 minutes**

Why This Recipe Works Guacamole is traditionally made in a molcajete, a three-legged Mexican mortar made of volcanic rock. To simulate the molcajete's coarse surface, we minced the onion and chile by hand with kosher salt; the coarse crystals broke down the aromatics, releasing their juices and flavors and transforming them into a paste that was easy to combine with the avocado and other ingredients. (The salt will also help the aromatics break down in a regular mortar and pestle.) A bit of lime zest added further brightness without acidity. We used a whisk to mix and mash the avocado into the paste, creating a creamy but still chunky dip. Chopped tomato and cilantro added fruity flavor and freshness.

> *For a spicier version, mince and add the serrano ribs and seeds to the onion mixture. A mortar and pestle can be used to process the onion mixture. Be sure to use Hass avocados here; Florida, or "skinny," avocados are too watery for dips.*

- 2 tablespoons finely chopped onion
- 1 serrano chile, stemmed, seeded, and minced
- 1 teaspoon kosher salt
- ¼ teaspoon grated lime zest plus 1½–2 tablespoons juice
- 3 ripe avocados, halved, pitted, and cut into ½-inch pieces
- 1 plum tomato, cored, seeded, and cut into ⅛-inch dice
- 2 tablespoons chopped fresh cilantro

Place onion, serrano, salt, and lime zest on cutting board and chop until very finely minced. Transfer onion mixture to medium bowl and stir in 1½ tablespoons lime juice. Add avocados and, using sturdy whisk, mash and stir mixture until well combined with some ¼- to ½-inch chunks of avocado remaining. Stir in tomato and cilantro. Season with salt and up to additional 1½ teaspoons lime juice to taste. Serve.

Ultracreamy Hummus

Makes 3 cups • **Total Time: 45 minutes**

Why This Recipe Works This hummus is velvety-smooth and creamy, with a satisfyingly rich, balanced flavor. To achieve a perfectly smooth texture, we simmered canned chickpeas with water and baking soda for 20 minutes and then quickly removed their grainy skins by gently swishing them under a few changes of water. Tahini is a major source of richness and flavor in hummus. To avoid the bitter flavors that can come from tahini made with heavily roasted sesame seeds, we chose a light-colored tahini, which indicated that the seeds were only gently roasted. For balanced garlic flavor, we steeped the garlic in lemon juice and salt to extract its flavor and deactivate alliinase, the enzyme that gives this allium its harsh bite. Finally, we added ample fresh lemon juice to give the hummus a bright flavor.

> *The hummus will thicken slightly over time; add warm water, 1 tablespoon at a time, as needed to restore its creamy consistency. Serve with crudités and pita bread or crackers. If desired, you can omit the parsley, reserved chickpeas, and extra cumin in step 5 and top with our Baharat-Spiced Beef Topping for Hummus or Spiced Walnut Topping for Hummus (recipes follow).*

- 2 (15-ounce) cans chickpeas, rinsed
- ½ teaspoon baking soda
- 4 garlic cloves, peeled
- ⅓ cup lemon juice (2 lemons), plus extra for seasoning
- 1 teaspoon table salt
- ¼ teaspoon ground cumin, plus extra for garnish
- ½ cup tahini, stirred well
- 2 tablespoons extra-virgin olive oil, plus extra for drizzling
- 1 tablespoon minced fresh parsley

1. Combine chickpeas, baking soda, and 6 cups water in medium saucepan and bring to boil over high heat. Reduce heat and simmer, stirring occasionally, until chickpea skins begin to float to surface and chickpeas are creamy and very soft, 20 to 25 minutes.

2. While chickpeas cook, mince garlic using garlic press or rasp-style grater. Measure out 1 tablespoon garlic and set aside; discard remaining garlic. Whisk lemon juice, salt, and reserved garlic together in small bowl and let sit for 10 minutes. Strain garlic-lemon mixture through fine-mesh strainer set over bowl, pressing on solids to extract as much liquid as possible; discard solids.

3. Drain chickpeas in colander and return to saucepan. Fill saucepan with cold water and gently swish chickpeas with your fingers to release skins. Pour off most of water into colander to collect skins, leaving chickpeas behind in saucepan. Repeat filling, swishing, and draining 3 or 4 times until most skins have been removed (this should yield about ¾ cup skins); discard skins. Transfer chickpeas to colander to drain.

4. Set aside 2 tablespoons whole chickpeas for garnish. Process garlic-lemon mixture, ¼ cup water, cumin, and remaining chickpeas in food processor until smooth, about 1 minute, scraping down sides of bowl as needed. Add tahini and oil and process until hummus is smooth, creamy, and light, about 1 minute, scraping down sides of bowl as needed. (Hummus should have pourable consistency similar to yogurt. If too thick, loosen with water, adding 1 teaspoon at a time.) Season with salt and extra lemon juice to taste.

5. Transfer to serving bowl and sprinkle with parsley, reserved chickpeas, and extra cumin. Drizzle with extra oil and serve. (Hummus can be refrigerated in airtight container for up to 5 days. Let sit, covered, at room temperature for 30 minutes before serving.)

TOPPINGS
Baharat-Spiced Beef Topping for Hummus
Makes 2 cups • Total Time: 35 minutes

Baharat is a warm, savory Middle Eastern spice blend. Ground lamb can be used in place of the beef, if desired. Toast the pine nuts in a dry skillet over medium-high heat until fragrant, 3 to 5 minutes. Serve the topping over hummus, garnishing with additional pine nuts and chopped fresh parsley.

- 2 teaspoons water
- ½ teaspoon table salt
- ¼ teaspoon baking soda
- 8 ounces 85 percent lean ground beef
- 1 tablespoon extra-virgin olive oil
- ¼ cup finely chopped onion
- 2 garlic cloves, minced
- 1 teaspoon hot smoked paprika
- 1 teaspoon ground cumin
- ¼ teaspoon pepper
- ¼ teaspoon ground coriander
- ⅛ teaspoon ground cloves
- ⅛ teaspoon ground cinnamon
- ¼ cup pine nuts, toasted
- 2 teaspoons lemon juice

1. Combine water, salt, and baking soda in large bowl. Add beef and toss to combine. Let sit for 5 minutes.

2. Heat oil in 12-inch nonstick skillet over medium heat until shimmering. Add onion and garlic and cook, stirring occasionally, until onion is softened, 3 to 4 minutes. Add paprika, cumin, pepper, coriander, cloves, and cinnamon and cook, stirring constantly, until fragrant, about 30 seconds. Add beef and cook, breaking up meat with wooden spoon, until beef is no longer pink, about 5 minutes. Add pine nuts and lemon juice and toss to combine.

Spiced Walnut Topping for Hummus
Makes ¾ cup • Total Time: 15 minutes

Do not overprocess; the topping should remain coarse-textured. Serve the topping over hummus.

- ¾ cup extra-virgin olive oil
- ⅓ cup walnuts
- ¼ cup paprika
- ¼ cup tomato paste
- 2 garlic cloves, peeled
- 1 teaspoon ground turmeric
- ½ teaspoon ground cumin
- ½ teaspoon ground allspice
- ½ teaspoon table salt
- ¼ teaspoon cayenne pepper

Process all ingredients in food processor until uniform coarse puree forms, about 30 seconds, scraping down sides of bowl halfway through processing. (Topping can be refrigerated for up to 5 days.)

Curry Deviled Eggs with Easy-Peel Hard-Cooked Eggs

Makes 12 eggs • Total Time: 25 minutes

Why This Recipe Works Getting the shells off all the eggs for deviled eggs can be a real hassle. If you start boiled eggs in cold water, the proteins in the egg white set slowly, giving them time to fuse to the surrounding membrane, so when you remove the shell, parts of the white come with it. For frustration-free peeling, we placed cold eggs directly into hot steam (in a steamer basket set over boiling water in a saucepan), which rapidly denatured the outermost egg white proteins, causing them to form a solid gel that shrank and pulled away from the membrane. The shells slipped off easily to reveal smooth, unblemished hard-cooked eggs. Using steam to cook the eggs also helped us avoid chalky or green-tinged yolks. Because the eggs never touched the water, they didn't lower the water temperature, making it easy to determine the optimum cooking time for consistently perfect results.

To slice, lay the egg on its side and sweep the blade cleanly down the center. Wipe the knife after each egg. You may use either regular or reduced-fat mayonnaise. If preferred, use a pastry bag fitted with a large plain or star tip to fill egg halves.

- 1 recipe Easy-Peel Hard-Cooked Eggs (recipe follows)
- 3 tablespoons mayonnaise
- 1 tablespoon minced fresh parsley, plus 12 small whole parsley leaves for garnishing
- 1½ teaspoons lemon juice
- 1 teaspoon Dijon mustard
- 1 teaspoon curry powder
  Pinch cayenne pepper

1. Slice each egg in half lengthwise with paring knife. Transfer yolks to bowl; arrange whites on serving platter. Mash yolks with fork until no large lumps remain. Add mayonnaise and use rubber spatula to smear mixture against side of bowl until thick, smooth paste forms, 1 to 2 minutes. Add minced parsley, lemon juice, mustard, curry powder, and cayenne and mix until fully incorporated.

2. Transfer yolk mixture to small heavy-duty plastic bag. Press mixture into 1 corner and twist top of bag. Using scissors, snip ½ inch off filled corner. Squeezing bag, distribute yolk mixture evenly among egg white halves. Garnish each egg half with parsley leaf and serve.

VARIATION
Bacon and Chive Deviled Eggs

Cook 2 slices bacon, chopped fine, in 10-inch skillet over medium heat until crisp, 5 to 7 minutes. Using slotted spoon, transfer bacon to paper towel–lined plate. Reserve 1 tablespoon fat. To thick, smooth yolk paste add reserved bacon fat, 1 tablespoon minced fresh chives, 2 teaspoons distilled white vinegar, ⅛ teaspoon salt, and pinch cayenne and mix until fully incorporated. Stir in three-quarters of bacon. Distribute yolk mixture evenly among egg white halves. Omit parsley leaf garnish. Sprinkle each egg half with remaining bacon and serve.

Easy-Peel Hard-Cooked Eggs

Makes 6 eggs • Total Time: 40 minutes
Be sure to use large, cold eggs that have no cracks. You can cook fewer than six eggs without altering the timing, or more eggs as long as your pot and steamer basket can hold them in a single layer. If you don't have a steamer basket, use a spoon or tongs to gently place the eggs in the water; it does not matter if the eggs are above the water or partially submerged. Unpeeled cooked eggs can be stored in the refrigerator for up to three days.

- 6 large eggs

1. Bring 1 inch water to rolling boil in medium saucepan over high heat. Place eggs in steamer basket. Transfer basket to saucepan. Cover, reduce heat to medium-low, and cook eggs for 13 minutes.

2. When eggs are almost finished cooking, combine 2 cups ice cubes and 2 cups cold water in medium bowl. Using tongs or spoon, transfer eggs to ice bath; let sit for 15 minutes. Peel before using.

Spanish Tortilla with Roasted Red Peppers and Peas

Serves 4 to 6 • **Total Time: 1 hour**

Why This Recipe Works This classic Spanish omelet is immensely appealing, but can be greasy, dense, and heavy if prepared incorrectly. Typical recipes call for up to 4 cups of extra-virgin olive oil to cook the potatoes, which can lead to an overly oily—and expensive—tortilla. We wanted an intensely rich, velvety, melt-in-your-mouth egg-and-potato omelet that didn't require using a quart of oil.

We first stuck with the traditional volume of olive oil until we could determine the proper type and ratio of ingredients. We chose starchy russet potatoes, thinly sliced, and standard yellow onions, which had a sweet, mellow flavor. We also settled on a ratio of eggs to potatoes that allowed the tortilla to set firm and tender, with the eggs and potatoes melding into one another. Unfortunately, when we reduced the amount of oil in the pan, half the potatoes were frying while the other half were steaming. We started over with slightly firmer, less starchy Yukon Golds. With a fraction of the oil in the skillet, they were a winner: starchy enough to become meltingly tender as they cooked, but sturdy enough to stir and flip halfway through cooking with few breaks. Finally, we had to determine the best way to flip the omelet. To do this, we simply slid the tortilla out of the pan and onto one plate. Then, placing another plate upside down over the tortilla, we easily flipped the whole thing and slid the tortilla back in the pan, making a once-messy task easy and foolproof.

> *Spanish tortillas are often served warm or at room temperature with olives, pickles, and Garlic Mayonnaise (recipe follows) as an appetizer. They may also be served with a salad as a light entrée. For the most traditional tortilla, omit the roasted red peppers and peas.*

- 6 tablespoons plus 1 teaspoon extra-virgin olive oil, divided
- 1½ pounds (3 to 4 medium) Yukon Gold potatoes, peeled, quartered, and cut into ⅛-inch-thick slices
- 1 small onion, halved and sliced thin
- 1 teaspoon table salt, divided
- ¼ teaspoon pepper
- 8 large eggs
- ½ cup jarred roasted red peppers, rinsed, dried, and cut into ½-inch pieces
- ½ cup frozen peas, thawed
  Garlic Mayonnaise (optional; recipe follows)

1. Toss ¼ cup oil, potatoes, onion, ½ teaspoon salt, and pepper in large bowl until potato slices are thoroughly separated and coated in oil. Heat 2 tablespoons oil in 10-inch nonstick skillet over medium-high heat until shimmering. Reduce heat to medium-low, add potato mixture to skillet, and set bowl aside (do not rinse). Cover and cook, stirring occasionally with heat-resistant rubber spatula, until potatoes offer no resistance when poked with paring knife, 22 to 28 minutes (some potato slices may break into smaller pieces).

2. Meanwhile, whisk eggs and remaining ½ teaspoon salt in reserved bowl until just combined. Using heat-resistant rubber spatula, fold hot potato mixture, red peppers, and peas into eggs until combined, making sure to scrape all of potato mixture out of skillet. Return skillet to medium-high heat, add remaining 1 teaspoon oil, and heat until just beginning to smoke. Add egg-potato mixture and cook, shaking pan and folding mixture constantly for 15 seconds; smooth top of mixture with heat-resistant rubber spatula. Reduce heat to medium, cover, and cook, gently shaking pan every 30 seconds, until bottom is golden brown and top is lightly set, about 2 minutes.

3. Using heat-resistant rubber spatula, loosen tortilla from pan, shaking it back and forth until tortilla slides around. Slide tortilla onto large plate. Invert tortilla onto second large plate and slide it, browned side up, back into skillet. Tuck edges of tortilla into skillet. Return pan to medium heat and continue to cook, gently shaking pan every 30 seconds, until second side is golden brown, about 2 minutes longer. Slide tortilla onto cutting board; let cool for at least 15 minutes. Cut tortilla into cubes or wedges and serve with garlic mayonnaise, if using.

VARIATION

Spanish Tortilla with Chorizo and Scallions
Use a cured, Spanish-style chorizo for this recipe. Portuguese linguiça is a suitable substitute.

In step 1, heat 4 ounces Spanish-style chorizo, cut into ¼-inch pieces, with 1 tablespoon oil (reduced from 2 tablespoons) in 10-inch nonstick skillet over medium-high heat, stirring occasionally, until chorizo is browned and fat has rendered, about 5 minutes. Add potato mixture to skillet with chorizo and rendered fat and cook as directed. Proceed with step 2, omitting red peppers and peas and folding 4 thinly sliced scallions into eggs.

GAME CHANGER

Less Oil but More Luxe Any Time of Day

"This Spanish tortilla is my go-to for an easy brunch or dinner. The tortillas I've made in the past were always pretty greasy because the traditional recipes I found used lots of olive oil (up to several cups). This recipe, however, only uses about 6 tablespoons, which I appreciate. Also, I've made them with different types of potatoes over the years and agree that Yukon Golds are the best choice because they have a buttery flavor and silky texture. Traditional recipes for tortilla often omit the roasted red peppers and peas, but I think they are nice additions here. The tortilla tastes terrific both warm and at room temperature, and adding a simple green salad turns it into dinner. Be sure to serve it with the garlic mayo."

—Julia

Garlic Mayonnaise
Makes 1¼ cups • Total Time: 15 minutes

 2 large egg yolks
 2 teaspoons Dijon mustard
 2 teaspoons lemon juice
 1 garlic clove, minced
 ¾ cup vegetable oil
 1 tablespoon water
 ¼ cup extra-virgin olive oil
 ½ teaspoon table salt
 ¼ teaspoon pepper

Process yolks, mustard, lemon juice, and garlic in food processor until combined, about 10 seconds. With machine running, slowly drizzle in vegetable oil, about 1 minute. Transfer mixture to medium bowl and whisk in water. Whisking constantly, slowly drizzle in olive oil, about 30 seconds. Whisk in salt and pepper. (Mayonnaise can be refrigerated in airtight container for up to 4 days.)

SEASON 3

Cheesy Nachos with Guacamole and Salsa

Serves 4 to 6 • Total Time: 1 hour

Why This Recipe Works Prepackaged cheese and guacamole and jarred salsa can transform nachos into bland fast food. We wanted nachos with hot, crisp tortilla chips, plentiful cheese and toppings, and the right amount of spicy heat. To ensure that all of the chips would be cheesy and spicy, we layered tortilla chips with a full pound of shredded cheddar and sliced jalapeños. Layering the jalapeños with the cheese also helped the chiles stick to the chips. We prepared a quick homemade salsa and chunky guacamole to spoon around the edges of the hot nachos. Spoonfuls of sour cream and chopped fresh scallions provided the final touches. Served with lime wedges, this fresh take on nachos is light-years beyond any fast-food version.

 8 ounces tortilla chips
 1 pound cheddar cheese, shredded (about 4 cups)
 2 large jalapeño chiles, sliced thin (about ¼ cup)
 2 scallions, sliced thin
 ½ cup sour cream
 1 recipe One-Minute Salsa (recipe follows)
 1 recipe Classic Guacamole (page 25)
 Lime wedges

Adjust oven rack to middle position and heat oven to 400 degrees. Spread half of chips in even layer in 13 by 9-inch baking dish. Sprinkle chips evenly with 2 cups cheddar and half of jalapeño slices. Repeat with remaining chips, cheddar, and jalapeños. Bake until cheese is melted, 7 to 10 minutes. Remove nachos from oven and sprinkle with scallions. Along edge of the baking dish, drop scoops of sour cream, salsa, and guacamole. Serve immediately, passing lime wedges separately.

ACCOMPANIMENT
One-Minute Salsa
Makes 1 cup • Total Time: 10 minutes
This quick salsa can be made with either fresh or canned tomatoes. If you like, replace the jalapeño with ½ chipotle chile in adobo sauce, minced.

 2 tablespoons chopped red onion
 2 tablespoons fresh cilantro leaves
 2 teaspoons lime juice
 ½ small jalapeño chile, stemmed and seeded (about 1½ teaspoons)
 1 small garlic clove, minced (about ½ teaspoon)
 ¼ teaspoon table salt
 Pinch pepper
 2 small ripe tomatoes, each cored and cut into eighths, or one (14.5-ounce) can diced tomatoes, drained

Pulse onion, cilantro, lime juice, jalapeño, garlic, salt, and pepper in food processor until minced, about 5 pulses, scraping down sides of workbowl as necessary. Add tomatoes and pulse until coarsely chopped, about 2 pulses.

Albóndigas en Salsa de Almendras

Makes 24 meatballs • Total Time: 1¼ hours

Why This Recipe Works These tender, bite-size meatballs cloaked in a rich, almond-based sauce appear on tapas menus in Spain. To make them at home, we started by pulsing ground pork, garlic, parsley, egg, and a panade of bread and water in a food processor. After shaping the mixture into 1-inch balls, we skipped browning, instead cooking the meatballs in a mixture of white wine, chicken broth, and softened onion flavored with paprika and saffron. This gentler method quickly cooked the meatballs through. For the picada, which thickens and flavors the sauce, we ground blanched almonds and bread until fine and then fried them in oil. We then mixed in minced garlic and parsley before stirring the picada into the sauce. A splash of sherry vinegar and a sprinkling of fresh parsley at the end added brightness to balance the flavors.

Sometimes fully cooked ground pork retains a slightly pink hue; trust your thermometer. These meatballs can be served as an appetizer with toothpicks or as a main course alongside a vegetable and potatoes or rice.

Picada
- ¼ cup slivered almonds
- 1 slice hearty white sandwich bread, torn into 1-inch pieces
- 2 tablespoons extra-virgin olive oil
- 3 tablespoons minced fresh parsley
- 2 garlic cloves, minced

Meatballs
- 1 slice hearty white sandwich bread, torn into 1-inch pieces
- 1 large egg
- 2 tablespoons water
- 2 tablespoons chopped fresh parsley, divided
- 2 garlic cloves, minced
- 1 teaspoon table salt
- ½ teaspoon pepper
- 1 pound ground pork
- 1 tablespoon extra-virgin olive oil
- ½ cup finely chopped onion
- ½ teaspoon paprika
- 1 cup chicken broth
- ½ cup dry white wine
- ¼ teaspoon saffron threads, crumbled
- 1 teaspoon sherry vinegar

GAME CHANGER

No-Fry Meatballs

"The first time I made albóndigas was for my book Boards: Stylish Spreads for Casual Gatherings. *I was excited to build a tapas board that would reflect my love for travel and global food scenes. This recipe was a reminder that while some foods are similarly approached around the world, the variations of ways to cook them are actually endless. Not only are these meatballs tender and delicious but they're a tad easier than meatballs that require either to be pan-roasted or fried for browning. Instead, these meatballs are cooked gently in a mixture of white wine, chicken broth, and softened onion flavored with paprika and saffron, making this a fairly hands-off meatballs recipe. Finally, the picada, which thickens and flavors the sauce, adds a few more herbaceous notes. And there you have the most tender small bite that is a lovely addition to your own tapas spread or as a light snack with a great bottle of Spanish wine."*

— Elle

1. **For the picada:** Process almonds in food processor until finely ground, about 20 seconds. Add bread and process until bread is finely ground, about 15 seconds. Transfer almond-bread mixture to 12-inch nonstick skillet. Add oil and cook over medium heat, stirring often, until mixture is golden brown, 3 to 5 minutes. Transfer to bowl. Stir in parsley and garlic and set aside. Wipe skillet clean with paper towels.

2. **For the meatballs:** Process bread in now-empty processor until finely ground, about 15 seconds. Add egg, water, 1 tablespoon parsley, garlic, salt, and pepper and process until smooth paste forms, about 20 seconds, scraping down sides of bowl as necessary. Add pork and pulse until combined, about 5 pulses.

3. Remove processor blade. Using your moistened hands, form generous 1 tablespoon pork mixture into 1-inch round meatball and transfer to plate; repeat with remaining pork mixture to form 24 meatballs.

4. Heat oil in now-empty skillet over medium heat until shimmering. Add onion and cook, stirring occasionally, until softened, 4 to 6 minutes. Add paprika and cook until fragrant, about 30 seconds. Add broth and wine and bring to simmer. Stir in saffron. Add meatballs and adjust heat to maintain simmer. Cover and cook until meatballs register 160 degrees, 6 to 8 minutes, flipping meatballs once.

5. Stir in picada and continue to cook, uncovered, until sauce has thickened slightly, 1 to 2 minutes longer. Off heat, stir in vinegar. Season with salt and pepper to taste. Transfer to platter, sprinkle with remaining 1 tablespoon parsley, and serve.

SEASON 23

Crispy Cacio e Pepe Bites

Makes 49 croquettes • Total Time: 50 minutes, plus 2 hours 20 minutes cooling and chilling

Why This Recipe Works We picked up the technique for these fried squares of tapioca deliciousness from John and Beverly Clark at Parachute Restaurant in Chicago. At the restaurant they were served as a snack: four bites of Pecorino-heavy fried tapioca, dusted in nori powder. They're cheesy and gooey like good arancini (Italian fried rice balls, often filled with mozzarella cheese) but the tapioca creates an appealing lighter, stretchier texture. They are a nod to the classic Roman dish cacio e pepe. We upped the amount of Pecorino and folded in a lot of black pepper. The result, which we dubbed tapiocacio e pepe, is a dead-simple, gluten-free, cheesy party bite.

Tapioca pearls are the same pearls used for tapioca pudding. Do not use minute tapioca. This recipe is heavy on black pepper—if you generally prefer less pepper, reduce to 1 tablespoon. If you aren't concerned with keeping these gluten-free, cornstarch or all-purpose flour may be substituted for the tapioca starch. In step 1, constant stirring guarantees that the tapioca pearls do not stick to the bottom of the saucepan. The mixture will become more difficult to stir the longer it cooks. Don't be alarmed. Keep calm and stir on.

1 quart whole milk
2 cups small tapioca pearls
3½ ounces Pecorino Romano, grated fine (1¾ cups), plus extra for serving
5 teaspoons pepper
2½ teaspoons kosher salt
½ cup tapioca starch, plus extra as needed
1 quart vegetable oil, for frying

1. Grease 8-inch square baking pan with vegetable oil spray. Bring milk to boil in large saucepan over medium-high heat. Add tapioca pearls and cook, stirring occasionally, until milk returns to boil, 30 to 60 seconds. Reduce heat to medium and simmer, stirring constantly, until tapioca plumps and exterior turns translucent (very center will remain white) and mixture is thickened, 6 to 8 minutes.

2. Off heat, fold in Pecorino, pepper, and salt. Working quickly, using rubber spatula, transfer tapioca mixture to prepared pan and spread into even layer. Let cool for 20 minutes. Cover and refrigerate until firm, at least 2 hours or up to 24 hours.

3. Place ½ cup tapioca starch in shallow dish; lightly dust cutting board with extra tapioca starch. Invert tapioca square onto cutting board. Cut tapioca into 49 squares (7 rows by 7 rows), wiping knife with damp dish towel as needed to prevent sticking. Roll cubes in tapioca starch, shaking off excess, and transfer to baking sheet. (Cut, dusted cubes can be refrigerated in airtight container for up to 3 days.)

4. Heat oil in large saucepan over high heat to 375 degrees. Add one-third of cubes and fry, stirring frequently, until golden brown, 2 to 4 minutes, adjusting heat as necessary to maintain oil between 350 and 375 degrees. Transfer to paper towel–lined baking sheet or plate and blot to remove excess oil; season lightly with salt. Repeat with remaining cubes in 2 batches. Transfer croquettes to serving platter, dust generously with Pecorino, and serve.

SEASON 4

Frico

Makes 8 large wafers • Total Time: 25 minutes

Why This Recipe Works As an accompaniment to cocktails or eaten just as a snack, frico is a simple, crisp wafer of flavorful cheese, usually Montasio, that has been melted and browned. We wanted to find the secret behind great frico, and then determine the best substitute for Montasio cheese, which isn't available in many supermarkets. Cheese simply grated into a hot pan could turn into a sticky mess, but we found that using a nonstick skillet allowed us to cook the frico without adding butter or oil. We discovered that it was easy to turn the frico to the other side once the first side was browned if we first took the skillet off the heat; the slightly cooled cheese didn't stretch or tear when we flipped it. Turning the heat down to cook the second side gave the best results; a pan that was too hot turned the cheese bitter. Many recipes suggest Parmesan as a substitute for Montasio, but we found Asiago cheese to be a better stand-in—though the real thing is even better.

Serve frico with drinks and a bowl of marinated olives or marinated sun-dried tomatoes. Frico is also good crumbled into a salad, crouton-style.

1 **pound Montasio or aged Asiago cheese, grated fine (about 8 cups)**

1. Sprinkle 2 ounces (about 1 cup) of grated cheese over bottom of 10-inch nonstick skillet set over medium-high heat. Use heat-resistant rubber spatula or wooden spoon to tidy lacy outer edges of cheese. Cook, shaking pan occasionally to ensure even distribution of cheese over pan bottom, until edges are lacy and toasted, about 4 minutes. Remove pan from heat and allow cheese to set for about 30 seconds.

2. Using fork on top and heat-resistant spatula underneath, carefully flip cheese wafer and return pan to medium heat. Cook until second side is golden brown, about 2 minutes. Slide cheese wafer out of pan and transfer to plate. Repeat with remaining cheese. Serve within 1 hour.

SEASON 23

Baked Brie en Croûte

Serves 8 to 10 • Total Time: 35 minutes, plus 50 minutes chilling and cooling

Why This Recipe Works The combination of warm, creamy Brie encased in a flaky puff pastry crust with sweet fruit topping sets a rich, refined tone for this appetizer. And while this cheese plate centerpiece is impressive, it could hardly be easier to prepare. Working with a firm wheel of cheese promised gooey cheese that still held its shape. Freezing the pastry-wrapped Brie for 20 minutes kept it from melting too much during baking. Adding the preserves after baking kept the flavor bright.

To thaw frozen puff pastry, let it stand either in the refrigerator for 24 hours or on the counter for 30 minutes to 1 hour. The Brie can be prepared through step 1 (but do not freeze) and refrigerated, wrapped tightly in plastic wrap, for up to 24 hours. Freeze for 20 minutes before continuing with step 2. Serve with sliced baguette or crackers.

1 (9 by 9½-inch) sheet frozen puff pastry, thawed
1 large egg, lightly beaten
1 (8-ounce) wheel firm Brie cheese
¼ cup apricot preserves or hot pepper jelly

1. Roll puff pastry into 12-inch square on lightly floured counter. Using pie plate or other round guide, trim pastry to 9-inch circle with paring knife. Brush edges lightly with beaten egg. Place Brie in center of pastry circle and wrap it in pastry. Brush exterior of pastry with beaten egg and transfer it to parchment paper–lined baking sheet. Freeze for 20 minutes.

2. Adjust oven rack to middle position and heat oven to 425 degrees. Bake cheese until exterior is deep golden brown, 20 to 25 minutes.

3. Transfer to wire rack. Spoon preserves into exposed center of Brie. Let cool for about 30 minutes. Serve with crackers or bread.

Wrapping Brie in Pastry

1. Lift pastry up over cheese, pleating it at even intervals and leaving opening in center where Brie is exposed.

2. Press pleated edge of pastry up to form rim.

SEASON 25

Bouyourdi

Serves 4 to 6 • **Total Time: 55 minutes**

Why This Recipe Works Warm, creamy feta quells the blaze of chiles in this crowd-pleasing taverna classic. To make this beloved Thessalonian meze, we started with Greek sheep's milk feta; ripe in-season tomatoes; and grassy, mild bell pepper. To double down on spiciness, we added both fresh chiles and dried chile flakes to create just enough heat to balance the creamy dairy. A hearty dose of extra-virgin olive oil enhanced the dish's overall richness and unified its components. We served the bouyourdi out of its earthenware baking dish with crusty bread alongside.

Use feta made from sheep's milk. If possible, purchase feta sold in brine, which will be more moist. Do not use precrumbled feta; it will become tough and dry in the oven. If your block of feta is thicker than 1 inch, slice it into 1-inch slabs before using. This dish is meant to be spicy. Bukovo pepper flakes are traditional, but any red pepper flakes can be used. Use an 8-inch square broiler-safe baking dish or a shallow earthenware dish or cazuela to mimic the clay vessel traditionally used for this dish. Serve with thick slices of crusty or toasted bread.

1 large tomato, cored
1 longhorn chile or ½ jalapeño chile, stemmed
¼ green bell pepper, cut into ¼-inch pieces
3 tablespoons extra-virgin olive oil, divided
1½ teaspoons dried oregano, divided
1 (7-ounce) block feta cheese
½ teaspoon bukovo or red pepper flakes

1. Adjust oven rack to upper-middle position and heat oven to 350 degrees.

2. Slice two ¼-inch rounds from tomato and set aside. Chop remaining tomato into ½-inch pieces and place in small bowl. Cut longhorn chile in half crosswise (reserve 1 half for other use). Slice two ¼-inch rings from longhorn chile half and set aside. Mince remaining longhorn chile and add to chopped tomatoes along with bell pepper, 2 tablespoons oil, and 1 teaspoon oregano. Stir to combine, pour into baking dish, and smooth into even layer.

3. Center feta block on top of vegetables. Arrange tomato slices and longhorn chile rings in single layer on top of feta. Drizzle with remaining 1 tablespoon oil and sprinkle with remaining ½ teaspoon oregano. Cover dish tightly with aluminum foil and bake until diced vegetables have softened and tomato slices are beginning to soften at edges, about 25 minutes.

4. Remove foil and return dish to oven. Turn on broiler. Broil until edges of tomato and longhorn chile slices are browned, 4 to 7 minutes. Remove dish from oven, sprinkle with bukovo, and serve.

Pa amb Tomàquet

Serves 4 to 6 • Total Time: 30 minutes

Why This Recipe Works Pa amb tomàquet—Catalan bread with tomato—is as simple as cooking gets, but the crunchy yet tender toasted bread and ripe tomato pulp make for an unbeatable combination, especially when seasoned with coarse salt and lavished with fruity olive oil. Ciabatta mimicked the airy, open structure of traditional pan de cristal. Halving the loaf laterally, opening it like a book, and cutting the halves into slices maximized its surface area for optimal toastiness. Toasted dry under the broiler, the bread charred lightly and quickly, so its interior crumb remained tender—a textural contrast that was just right for both supporting and absorbing the tomatoes' liquid. Rubbing a garlic clove over the toasts infused them with subtle savoriness. Halving and grating ripe round tomatoes on a box grater yielded loads of sweet, skin-free pulp that could be uniformly seasoned and spooned onto the toasts.

If possible, use ripe local tomatoes here. Avoid plum tomatoes; they're not juicy enough. If ciabatta is unavailable, substitute a crusty baguette, cut into 4-inch pieces. Use a fresh, robust, high-quality olive oil here. Serve as an appetizer or as an accompaniment to any meal.

  2 large ripe tomatoes, halved through equator
 ½ teaspoon table salt
  1 loaf ciabatta, halved horizontally and sliced crosswise 2 inches thick
  1 large garlic clove, peeled and halved crosswise
  3 tablespoons extra-virgin olive oil, plus extra for serving
     Flake sea salt

1. Place box grater in medium bowl. Rub cut side of tomatoes against large holes of grater until tomato flesh is reduced to pulp (skins should remain intact). Discard skins. (You should have about 1½ cups pulp.) Stir in table salt.

2. Adjust oven rack 6 inches from broiler element and heat broiler. Set wire rack in rimmed baking sheet and arrange bread slices cut side up on rack. Broil until browned, crisp, and starting to char at edges, 2 to 4 minutes. Rub toasts with cut side of garlic (apply more pressure for more-potent flavor; rub lightly for delicate flavor).

3. Arrange toasts on serving plate. Distribute tomato pulp evenly among toasts and spread to edges. Drizzle with oil and season lightly with flake sea salt. Serve immediately, passing extra oil and sea salt separately.

Cōngyóubǐng

Serves 4 to 6 • **Total Time: 1¼ hours, plus 30 minutes resting**

Why This Recipe Works The best cōngyóubǐng (scallion pancakes) are crispy and browned on the outside and flaky and delicately chewy inside. For our version, we opted for a boiling-water dough that stretched easily but did not spring back. To form alternating layers of dough and fat, we rolled the dough into a large, thin round; brushed it with a mixture of oil and flour; and sprinkled it with salt and scallions before rolling it into a cylinder. We coiled the cylinder into a spiral and then rolled it out into a round again. Making a small slit in the center of the pancake prevented steam from building up, so it laid flat and cooked evenly. A stir-together sauce complemented the richness of the pancakes.

For this recipe we prefer the steady, even heat of a cast-iron skillet. A heavy stainless-steel skillet may be used, but you may have to increase the heat slightly. To make the pancakes ahead of time, stack the uncooked pancakes between layers of parchment paper, wrap them tightly in plastic wrap, and refrigerate for up to 24 hours or freeze for up to 1 month. If frozen, thaw the pancakes in a single layer for 15 minutes before cooking. These pancakes may be served as a side dish or appetizer.

Dipping Sauce
- 2 tablespoons soy sauce
- 1 scallion, sliced thin
- 1 tablespoon water
- 2 teaspoons rice vinegar
- 1 teaspoon honey
- 1 teaspoon toasted sesame oil
  Pinch red pepper flakes

Pancakes
- 1½ cups (7½ ounces) plus 1 tablespoon all-purpose flour, divided
- ¾ cup boiling water
- 7 tablespoons vegetable oil, divided
- 1 tablespoon toasted sesame oil
- 1 teaspoon kosher salt, divided
- 4 scallions, sliced thin, divided

1. For the dipping sauce: Whisk all ingredients together in small bowl; set aside.

2. For the pancakes: Using wooden spoon, mix 1½ cups flour and boiling water in bowl to form rough dough. When cool enough to handle, transfer dough to lightly floured counter and knead until tacky (but not sticky) ball forms, about 4 minutes (dough will not be perfectly smooth). Cover loosely with plastic wrap and let rest for 30 minutes.

3. While dough is resting, stir together 1 tablespoon vegetable oil, sesame oil, and remaining 1 tablespoon flour. Set aside.

4. Place 10-inch cast-iron skillet over low heat to preheat. Divide dough in half. Cover 1 half of dough with plastic wrap and set aside. Roll remaining dough into 12-inch round on lightly floured counter. Drizzle with 1 tablespoon oil-flour mixture and use pastry brush to spread evenly over entire surface. Sprinkle with ½ teaspoon salt and half of scallions. Roll dough into cylinder. Coil cylinder into spiral, tuck end underneath, and flatten spiral with your palm. Cover with plastic and repeat with remaining dough, oil-flour mixture, salt, and scallions.

5. Roll first spiral into 9-inch round. Cut ½-inch slit in center of pancake. Place 2 tablespoons vegetable oil in skillet and increase heat to medium-low. Place 1 pancake in skillet (oil should sizzle). Cover and cook, shaking skillet occasionally, until pancake is slightly puffy and golden brown on underside, 1 to 1½ minutes. (If underside is not browned after 1 minute, turn heat up slightly. If it is browning too quickly, turn heat down slightly.) Drizzle 1 tablespoon vegetable oil over pancake. Use pastry brush to distribute over entire surface. Carefully flip pancake. Cover and cook, shaking skillet occasionally, until second side is golden brown, 1 to 1½ minutes. Uncover skillet and continue to cook until bottom is deep golden brown and crispy, 30 to 60 seconds longer. Flip and cook until deep golden brown and crispy, 30 to 60 seconds. Transfer to wire rack. Repeat with remaining 3 tablespoons vegetable oil and remaining pancake. Cut each pancake into 8 wedges and serve, passing dipping sauce separately.

Shaping Cōngyóubǐng

1. Roll dough into 12-inch round.

2. Brush round with oil-flour mixture; sprinkle with salt and scallions.

3. Roll up round into cylinder.

4. Coil cylinder, tucking end underneath, then flatten.

5. Roll out flattened spiral into 9-inch round; cut slit.

SEASON 23

Pakoras

Makes 15 pakoras • Total Time: 1 hour

Why This Recipe Works Pakoras are spiced vegetable fritters from the Indian subcontinent that are made with a thick batter of besan (flour milled from skinned and split brown chickpeas) and water. These crispy, craggy fritters make a cozy, satisfying snack. For vegetable-forward pakoras, we used a 4:1 ratio of chopped and shredded vegetables—a colorful trio of spinach, potato, and red onion worked nicely—to batter. Pakoras are often generously spiced, and ours are no exception, with liberal doses of cumin, coriander, turmeric, Kashmiri chile powder, fenugreek, and ajwain (an ingredient frequently added as a digestive aid). A serrano chile added bright, zingy heat. Baking powder kept the pakoras light and fluffy on the inside, and frying just five at a time in hot oil created evenly cooked interiors that weren't greasy.

Use the large holes of a box grater to shred the potato. For the best texture, we recommend measuring the prepped onion and potato by weight. Besan (also known as gram flour) is made by milling skinned and split brown chickpeas. To substitute standard chickpea flour (made from white chickpeas), add an additional 2 tablespoons of water to the batter. Besan, along with ajwain and Kashmiri chile powder, can be found in South Asian markets. If ajwain is unavailable, substitute dried thyme. If fenugreek is unavailable, it can be omitted. Use a Dutch oven that holds 6 quarts or more. Serve with Carrot-Tamarind Chutney (recipe follows).

1 large red onion, halved and sliced thin
(1½ cups/5 ounces)

1 large russet potato, peeled and shredded
(1½ cups/6½ ounces)

1 cup baby spinach, chopped

1 serrano chile, stemmed and minced

1 teaspoon ground cumin

1 teaspoon ground coriander

1 teaspoon ajwain

½ teaspoon table salt

½ teaspoon Kashmiri chile powder

¼ teaspoon ground fenugreek

¾ cup besan

1 teaspoon baking powder

½ teaspoon ground turmeric

¼ cup water

2 quarts canola oil for frying

1. In large bowl, combine onion, potato, spinach, serrano, cumin, coriander, ajwain, salt, chile powder, and fenugreek. Toss vegetables until coated with spices. Using your hands, squeeze mixture until vegetables are softened and release some liquid, about 45 seconds (do not drain).

2. In small bowl, mix together besan, baking powder, and turmeric. Sprinkle over vegetable mixture and stir until besan is no longer visible and mixture forms sticky mass. Add water and stir vigorously until water is well incorporated.

3. Adjust oven rack to middle position and heat oven to 200 degrees. Set wire rack in rimmed baking sheet. Add oil to large Dutch oven until it measures about 1½ inches deep and heat over medium-low heat to 375 degrees.

4. Transfer heaping tablespoonful of batter to oil, using second spoon to ease batter out of spoon. Stir batter briefly and repeat portioning until there are 5 pakoras in oil. Fry, adjusting burner, if necessary, to maintain oil temperature of 370 to 380 degrees, until pakoras are deep golden brown, 1½ to 2 minutes per side. Using spider skimmer or slotted spoon, transfer pakoras to prepared rack and place in oven. Return oil to 375 degrees and repeat with remaining batter in 2 batches. Serve immediately.

ACCOMPANIMENT
Carrot-Tamarind Chutney
Makes 1 cup • Total Time: 15 minutes
Tamarind juice concentrate can be found in South Asian markets.

½ cup chopped peeled carrot

¼ cup chopped red onion

3 tablespoons tamarind juice concentrate

2 tablespoons water

1 tablespoon lemon juice

2 teaspoons sugar

½ teaspoon ground cumin

½ teaspoon ground coriander

½ teaspoon table salt

Process carrot and onion in food processor until finely chopped, about 20 seconds, scraping down sides of bowl halfway through processing. Add tamarind concentrate, water, lemon juice, sugar, cumin, coriander, and salt and process until combined, about 20 seconds, scraping down sides of bowl halfway through processing (mixture will not be completely smooth). Transfer to bowl. (Chutney can be refrigerated for up to 3 days.)

SEASON 21
Gỏi Cuốn

Serves 4 • Total Time: 1¾ hours

Why This Recipe Works Springy noodles, crisp lettuce, an abundance of fresh herbs, and a bit of protein for heft make traditional gỏi cuốn (Vietnamese summer rolls) a pleasure to eat. Building them yourself requires a lot of prep work but we streamlined the process without sacrificing any flavor or texture. We put our own spin on the traditional practice of cooking the shrimp in the same water used to cook the pork: We used indirect rather than direct heat to ensure that the shrimp stayed tender. We found that briefly dunking the rice paper wrappers in cold water and transferring them to the counter while still stiff left them with enough surface moisture to hydrate them perfectly. This made the wrappers easier to work with and elastic enough to contain a generous amount of filling. Combining three different herbs and adding them to the rolls in a measured amount saved time. A spicy peanut sauce and a traditional fish sauce and lime mixture called nuớc chấm complemented the delicate flavors of the rolls.

If desired, omit the pork, double the amount of shrimp (use the same timing and amounts of water and salt), and place three shrimp halves on top of the scallions. If Thai basil is unavailable, increase the mint and cilantro to 1½ cups each. A wooden surface will draw moisture away from the wrappers, so assemble the rolls directly on your counter or on a plastic cutting board. If part of the wrapper starts to dry out while you are forming the rolls, moisten it with your dampened fingers. One serving (three rolls) makes a light meal, but these rolls can also be halved crosswise using a sharp, wet knife and served as an appetizer. These rolls are best served immediately. If you like, serve Nuớc Chấm (Vietnamese Dipping Sauce) (recipe follows) along with the peanut-hoisin sauce.

Gỏi Cuốn

Peanut-Hoisin Sauce

- 1 Thai chile, sliced thin
- 1 garlic clove, minced
- 1 teaspoon kosher salt
- 2/3 cup water
- 1/3 cup creamy peanut butter
- 3 tablespoons hoisin sauce
- 2 tablespoons tomato paste
- 1 tablespoon distilled white vinegar

Summer Rolls

- 6 ounces rice vermicelli
- 10 ounces boneless country-style pork ribs, trimmed
- 2 teaspoons kosher salt
- 18 medium-large shrimp (31 to 40 per pound), peeled, deveined, and tails removed
- 1 cup fresh mint leaves
- 1 cup fresh cilantro leaves and thin stems
- 1 cup Thai basil leaves
- 12 (8½-inch) round rice paper wrappers
- 12 leaves red or green leaf lettuce, thick ribs removed
- 2 scallions, sliced thin on bias

1. For the peanut-hoisin sauce: Using mortar and pestle (or on cutting board using flat side of chef's knife), mash Thai chile, garlic, and salt to fine paste. Transfer to medium bowl. Add water, peanut butter, hoisin, tomato paste, and vinegar and whisk until smooth.

2. For the summer rolls: Bring 2 quarts water to boil in medium saucepan. Stir in noodles. Cook until noodles are tender but not mushy, 3 to 4 minutes. Drain noodles and rinse with cold water until cool. Drain noodles again, then spread on large plate to dry.

3. Bring 2 quarts water to boil in now-empty saucepan. Add pork and salt. Reduce heat, cover, and simmer until thickest part of pork registers 150 degrees, 8 to 12 minutes. Transfer pork to cutting board, reserving water.

4. Return water to boil. Add shrimp and cover. Let stand off heat until shrimp are opaque throughout, about 3 minutes. Drain shrimp and rinse with cold water until cool. Transfer to cutting board. Pat shrimp dry and halve lengthwise. Transfer to second plate.

5. When pork is cool enough to handle, cut each rib crosswise into 2-inch lengths. Slice each 2-inch piece lengthwise ⅛ inch thick (you should have at least 24 slices) and transfer to plate with shrimp. Tear mint, cilantro, and Thai basil into 1-inch pieces and combine in bowl.

6. Fill large bowl with cold water. Submerge 1 wrapper in water until wet on both sides, no longer than 2 seconds. Shake gently over bowl to remove excess water, then lay wrapper flat on work surface (wrapper will be fairly stiff but will continue to soften as you assemble roll). Repeat with second wrapper and place next to first wrapper. Fold 1 lettuce leaf and place on lower third of first wrapper, leaving about ½-inch margin on each side. Spread ⅓ cup noodles on top of lettuce, then sprinkle with 1 teaspoon scallions. Top scallions with 2 slices pork. Spread ¼ cup herb mixture over pork.

7. Bring lower edge of wrapper up and over herbs. Roll snugly but gently until long sides of greens and noodles are enclosed. Fold in sides to enclose ends. Arrange 3 shrimp halves, cut side up, on remaining section of wrapper. Continue to roll until filling is completely enclosed in neat cylinder. Transfer roll to serving platter, shrimp side up, and cover with plastic wrap. Repeat with second moistened wrapper. Repeat with remaining wrappers and filling, keeping completed rolls covered with plastic. Uncover and serve with sauce. (Leftovers can be wrapped tightly and refrigerated for up to 24 hours, but wrappers will become chewier and may break in places.)

Rolling a Summer Roll

1. Bring lower edge of wrapper up and over herbs.

2. Roll snugly but gently until greens and noodles are enclosed.

3. Fold in sides to enclose ends.

4. Arrange 3 shrimp halves, cut side up, on remaining wrapper.

5. Continue to roll until filling is completely enclosed in neat cylinder.

Nước Chấm

Makes 1 cup • Total Time: 10 minutes

Hot water helps the sugar dissolve into the sauce.

3	tablespoons sugar, divided
1	small Thai chile, stemmed and minced
1	garlic clove, minced
⅔	cup hot water
5	tablespoons fish sauce
¼	cup lime juice (2 limes)

Using mortar and pestle (or on cutting board using flat side of chef's knife), mash 1 tablespoon sugar, Thai chile, and garlic to fine paste. Transfer to medium bowl and add hot water and remaining 2 tablespoons sugar. Stir until sugar is dissolved. Stir in fish sauce and lime juice.

SEASON 23

Lumpiang Shanghai with Seasoned Vinegar

Makes 18 to 20 lumpia • Total Time: 1½ hours

Why This Recipe Works Lumpiang Shanghai (often referred to as "lumpia") are relatives of Chinese egg rolls, a staple at Filipino holidays and celebrations. Our lumpiang Shanghai feature a savory pork and vegetable filling flavored with soy sauce, pepper, garlic, and ginger. We pulsed the vegetables and aromatics in a food processor until they were finely chopped before pulsing in the pork along with 2 tablespoons of beaten egg. The vegetable juices freed by the whirring blades of the processor, along with the egg, moistened and softened the filling, making it easy to pipe into neat strips on the wrappers. We rolled up the filling carefully, making sure to work out any air pockets. This prevented the lumpia from floating as they cooked, which can cause them to cook and crisp unevenly. We sealed the lumpia with beaten egg and then fried them in 350-degree oil until their exteriors were golden brown and crispy. We paired the rolls with white cane vinegar seasoned with garlic, pepper, and soy sauce.

Sukang maasim is a common Filipino vinegar made from sugarcane. It boasts a balanced, versatile tart-sweetness but you can substitute distilled white vinegar. Look for spring roll wrappers or lumpia wrappers in the frozen foods section of an Asian market. Use a Dutch oven that holds 6 quarts or more. Crisp leftover lumpia by baking them in a 425-degree oven for 8 to 10 minutes. When removed from the oven, the rolls will be soft; they will crisp as they cool.

GAME CHANGER

When It Comes to Fillings, Less Is More

"The biggest mistake dumpling newbies make is to overstuff them, which is the best way to cause the wrapper to split open during the cooking process. I've learned the hard way to resist the temptation to use too much filling. Instead, make sure that the filling is very well seasoned, almost over-seasoned. Remember, that wrapper is very bland. In this recipe, the food processor grinds the ingredients into a concentrated paste flavored with ginger, garlic, and soy. In addition to being more concentrated, a smooth paste is also less likely to tear delicate wrappers.

I don't like to fry when I have guests over. I prefer more hands-off cooking so I can pay attention to my guests. This recipe can be fried in advance and then crisped up in the oven—now that's a party game changer for me. I love way the flavor-packed fruity ketchup clings to the crispy wrapper. Or make both sauces and ask guests which one they prefer. Double dipping is allowed in my house."

—*Jack*

Serve warm or at room temperature. Instead of the dipping sauce, you can serve the lumpia with a store-bought sweet chili sauce or banana ketchup (recipe follows).

Dipping Sauce

- ⅔ cup sukang maasim
- 1 tablespoon soy sauce
- 1½ teaspoons pepper
- 1 teaspoon sugar
- 1 garlic clove, minced
- Pinch table salt

Lumpia

- ½ cup chopped onion
- ⅓ cup chopped carrot
- ⅓ cup chopped celery
- 4 garlic cloves, peeled
- 1 (½-inch) piece ginger, peeled
- 1 large egg
- 1 pound ground pork
- 1 tablespoon soy sauce
- 1 teaspoon pepper
- ¼ teaspoon table salt
- 18–20 (8-inch) square lumpia wrappers or spring roll wrappers
- 1½ quarts vegetable oil for frying

1. For the dipping sauce: Stir all ingredients together in bowl. Let stand at room temperature for at least 30 minutes to let flavors meld or refrigerate for up to 4 days.

2. For the lumpia: Process onion, carrot, celery, garlic, and ginger in food processor until finely chopped, scraping down sides of bowl as needed, about 20 seconds. Beat egg in small bowl until homogeneous. Add 2 tablespoons beaten egg to food processor, reserving remainder. Add pork, soy sauce, pepper, and salt and process until combined, scraping down sides of bowl as needed, 10 to 15 seconds. Transfer mixture to large heavy-duty zipper-lock bag and snip 1 corner to create 1-inch opening. Peel wrappers apart to separate; stack neatly and cover with very lightly dampened dish towel.

3. Place 1 wrapper on counter so 1 corner points to edge of counter. Pipe 5 by ¾-inch strip of filling parallel to counter, just below center of wrapper. Using pastry brush, apply light layer of egg wash onto upper 1½ inches of top corner of wrapper, making sure to brush all the way to edges. Fold bottom corner of wrapper over filling and press gently along length of filling to remove air pockets. Fold side corners over to enclose filling snugly and gently roll to form tight cylinder. Transfer, egg-washed corner down, to rimmed baking sheet or large platter. (Do not stack.) Wipe any excess egg from counter and repeat with remaining wrappers and filling, filling two at a time if you feel comfortable with it. (Lumpia can be refrigerated in single layer in airtight container for up to 24 hours. Alternatively, freeze in single layer and then stack in airtight container and freeze for up to 1 month. Do not thaw before frying.)

4. Heat oil in Dutch oven over medium heat to 350 degrees. Set wire rack in rimmed baking sheet. Line rack with paper towels. Using tongs, transfer 6 lumpia to oil and fry, adjusting burner, if necessary, to maintain oil temperature of 340 to 360 degrees, until lumpia are golden brown, 5 to 7 minutes (frozen lumpia will take 1 to 2 minutes longer). Transfer to prepared rack. Repeat with remaining lumpia in 2 batches. Let cool for at least 5 minutes before serving with dipping sauce.

Rolling Lumpia

1. Pipe even 5 by ¾-inch strip of filling just below center of wrapper.

2. Apply light layer of egg wash onto top corner of wrapper with pastry brush, making sure to brush all the way to edges.

3. Fold bottom corner of wrapper over filling and gently press along length of filling to remove air pockets.

4. Fold side corners over to enclose filling and gently roll to form tight cylinder.

Banana Ketchup

Makes 1 cup • Total Time: 25 minutes

This sauce can be used like traditional ketchup but is especially good with lumpia.

- 1 tablespoon vegetable oil
- 1 small shallot, minced
- 3 garlic cloves, minced
- 2 teaspoons grated fresh ginger
- 3 tablespoons tomato paste
  Pinch cayenne pepper
- 1/3 cup water
- 1/4 cup sukang maasim or distilled white vinegar
- 2 tablespoons sugar
- 1/4 teaspoon table salt
- 1 very ripe banana (6 ounces), peeled and chopped

1. Heat oil in small saucepan over medium heat until shimmering. Add shallot, garlic, and ginger and cook until fragrant, about 2 minutes. Add tomato paste and cayenne and cook, stirring constantly, until dark brown bits form on bottom of saucepan, about 1 minute. Stir in water, vinegar, sugar, and salt, scraping up any browned bits. Stir in banana; bring to simmer; and cook until banana is broken down, 5 to 7 minutes.

2. Transfer mixture to food processor and process until completely smooth, about 1 minute, scraping down sides of bowl as needed. Strain ketchup through fine-mesh strainer set over bowl, pressing on solids to extract as much ketchup as possible; discard solids. Season with salt to taste. Let cool completely before serving. (Ketchup can be refrigerated for up to 4 days; let come to room temperature before serving.)

SEASON 21

Cóctel de Camarón

Serves 4 to 6 • Total Time: 45 minutes

Why This Recipe Works This popular Mexican dish consists of cooked shrimp tossed with chopped vegetables in a bright tomato sauce. For shrimp that were tender, not rubbery, we cooked them using residual heat. Bringing the cooking water to a full boil before adding the shrimp ensured that there was enough heat in the saucepan to cook them through. Cutting the shrimp into bite-size pieces made them easier to eat. For a sauce that wasn't too sweet,

we used a combination of savory V8 juice and ketchup plus lime juice and hot sauce. V8's slightly viscous consistency, along with the ketchup, gave the sauce body to nicely coat the shrimp. Cucumber and red onion added crunch, avocado added creaminess, and cilantro added freshness.

We prefer untreated shrimp, but if your shrimp are treated with salt or additives such as sodium tripolyphosphate, do not add the salt in step 1. The balanced flavor of Valentina, Cholula, or Tapatío hot sauce works best here. If using a spicier, vinegary hot sauce such as Tabasco, start with half the amount called for and adjust to your taste after mixing. Saltines are a traditional accompaniment, but tortilla chips or thick-cut potato chips are also good. Serve this dish as an appetizer or light meal.

- 1 1/4 pounds large shrimp (26 to 30 per pound), peeled, deveined, and tails removed
- 1/4 teaspoon table salt, plus salt for cooking shrimp
- 1 cup V8 juice, chilled
- 1/2 cup ketchup
- 3 tablespoons lime juice (2 limes), plus lime wedges for serving
- 2 teaspoons hot sauce, plus extra for serving
- 1/2 English cucumber, cut into 1/2-inch pieces
- 1 cup finely chopped red onion
- 1 avocado, halved, pitted, and cut into 1/2-inch pieces
- 1/4 cup chopped fresh cilantro
  Saltines

1. Bring 3 cups water to boil in large saucepan over high heat. Stir in shrimp and 1 tablespoon salt. Cover and let stand off heat until shrimp are opaque, about 5 minutes, shaking saucepan halfway through. Fill large bowl halfway with ice and water. Transfer shrimp to ice bath and let cool for 3 to 5 minutes. Once cool, cut each shrimp crosswise into 3 pieces.

2. Combine V8 juice, ketchup, lime juice, hot sauce, and salt in medium bowl. Add cucumber, onion, and shrimp and stir until evenly coated. Stir in avocado and cilantro. Portion cocktail into individual bowls or glasses and serve immediately, passing saltines, lime wedges, and extra hot sauce separately.

SEASON 23

Roasted Oysters on the Half Shell with Mustard Butter

Serves 4 to 6 • Total Time: 55 minutes

Why This Recipe Works Roasting is a great option if you're nervous about shucking or eating raw oysters or if you simply want a new way to serve them on the half shell. Warming the oysters in a hot oven made them easier to shuck; we placed them on a baking sheet covered in a layer of crumpled aluminum foil to steady them and ensure that they didn't tip over and spill their flavorful liquor. After shucking them, we dolloped the oysters with mustard butter and returned them to the oven to cook through. After just a few minutes, they emerged plump, tender, and dressed with a punchy sauce.

You'll need an oyster knife and a large serving platter for this recipe. Using oysters that are 2½ to 3 inches long ensures that they will cook evenly.

- 5 tablespoons unsalted butter, softened
- 3 tablespoons minced fresh parsley, divided
- 1 tablespoon whole-grain mustard
- 24 oysters, 2½ to 3 inches long, well scrubbed
  Lemon wedges

1. Adjust oven rack to middle position and heat oven to 450 degrees. Stir butter, 2 tablespoons parsley, and mustard in bowl until well combined. Gently crumple and uncrumple two 24-inch lengths of aluminum foil. Place 1 piece in 18 by 13-inch rimmed baking sheet and second piece on large serving platter; cover foil on platter with dish towel for presentation, if desired. Nestle oysters, cupped side down, into foil on prepared sheet and bake until oysters open slightly, about 5 minutes. (It's OK to eat oysters that don't open.) Let oysters rest until cool enough to handle, about 5 minutes.

2. Shuck 1 oyster and discard top shell. Return oyster to foil, being careful not to spill much liquid. Repeat with remaining oysters.

3. Distribute mustard butter evenly among oysters, about ¾ teaspoon per oyster. Bake until thickest part of largest oyster registers 160 to 165 degrees, 5 to 8 minutes. Let rest for 5 minutes. Using tongs, carefully transfer oysters to prepared platter, nestling them into foil or towel to hold them level. Sprinkle remaining 1 tablespoon parsley over oysters. Serve, passing lemon wedges separately.

SEASON 22

Rhode Island–Style Fried Calamari

Serves 4 • Total Time: 55 minutes

Why This Recipe Works This version of fried calamari features tender, lightly springy squid and sliced banana peppers encased in a crispy, lacy, golden-brown crust, and garnished with more peppers straight from the jar. Slicing the squid bodies into ¾-inch-thick rings prolonged tenderness during frying. Dipping the squid in milk helped just enough of the dredge cling; proteins in the milk also encouraged browning when the milk soaked into the flour. Salting the milk bath, not the dredge or the fried pieces, seasoned the squid and peppers evenly. Dredging them in all-purpose flour (which contains proteins that brown) ensured that the coating turned deep golden brown before the squid had a chance to toughen. Adding baking powder to the dredge lightened the texture of the coating, and shaking off excess dredge prevented the coating from clumping. Letting the coated pieces rest while the oil heated gave the coating time to hydrate, preventing a dusty film from forming on the exterior. Frying in two batches prevented the oil temperature from dropping too much, so the pieces browned and crisped quickly.

GAME CHANGER

The Best Tool for Shucking Oysters Is Your Oven

"Eating raw oysters on the half shell is one of my life's true pleasures. So when my dear colleague Lan Lam was developing a technique for roasting oysters, I was deeply skeptical. Not of her ability, of course, but of the very concept of cooking these precious bivalves. Raw oysters display an incredible range of flavors, from cucumber and melon to seaweed and rich minerality. Roasting flattens some of these delicate characteristics, but as Lan proved, it also transforms oysters into true comfort food. She adds a dollop of mustard-parsley butter to each oyster and that sharp richness mingles with their natural brine to create a savory elixir. But there's a whole other reason to roast oysters—it's the safest and easiest way to get them open. Shucking raw oysters at home is hard work that can end in bruised and battered fingers. But popping oysters into a hot oven for just 5 minutes opens them naturally, making shucking a breeze. What's more pleasurable than that?"

—Dan

If desired, serve the calamari with Quick Marinara Sauce or Spicy Mayonnaise (recipes follow); make the sauce before preparing the squid. Use a Dutch oven that holds 6 quarts or more for this recipe. Precut squid will not cook up quite as tender as whole bodies that you cut yourself, but they are acceptable. If desired, you can double this recipe and fry the calamari in four batches; the amount of oil remains the same. We tested this recipe with King Arthur Gluten-Free Multi-Purpose Flour, and the results were acceptable.

- ½ cup milk
- 1 teaspoon table salt
- 1½ cups all-purpose flour
- 1 tablespoon baking powder
- ½ teaspoon pepper
- 1 pound squid, bodies sliced crosswise ¾ inch thick, any extra-long tentacles trimmed to match length of shorter ones
- 1½ cups jarred sliced banana peppers
- 2 quarts vegetable oil for frying
  Lemon wedges

1. Set wire rack in rimmed baking sheet. Set second rack in second sheet and line with triple layer of paper towels. Heat oven to 200 degrees.

2. Whisk milk and salt together in medium bowl. Combine flour, baking powder, and pepper in second medium bowl. Add squid to milk mixture and toss to coat. Using your hands or slotted spoon, remove half of squid, allowing excess milk mixture to drip back into bowl, and add to bowl with flour mixture. Using your hands, toss to coat evenly. Gently shake off excess flour and place coated squid in single layer on unlined rack. Repeat with remaining squid.

Add 1 cup banana peppers to flour mixture and toss with your hands to coat evenly. Gently shake off excess flour mixture and sprinkle peppers evenly among squid. Let sit for 10 minutes.

3. While squid and peppers rest, heat oil in large Dutch oven over high heat to 350 degrees. Carefully add half of squid and peppers and fry for exactly 3 minutes (squid will be golden brown). Using slotted spoon or spider skimmer, transfer calamari and peppers to paper towel–lined rack and place in oven to keep warm. Return oil to 350 degrees and repeat with remaining squid and peppers. Transfer calamari and peppers to platter, top with remaining peppers, and serve immediately with lemon wedges.

Frying Calamari

1. Slice squid bodies into ¾-inch-thick rings. Cut any long tentacles to match size of shorter ones.

2. Rest dredged squid on wire rack to allow flour to fully hydrate, preventing dusty film from forming on fried calamari.

3. Fry squid in 2 batches to prevent oil temperature from dropping too much, so pieces brown and crisp quickly.

4. Use spider skimmer or slotted spoon to transfer first batch of calamari to paper towel–lined rack and transfer to oven to keep warm.

Quick Marinara Sauce

Makes 1½ cups • Total Time: 15 minutes

  2 tablespoons extra-virgin olive oil
  1 garlic clove, minced
  1 (14.5-ounce) can crushed tomatoes
  1 tablespoon chopped fresh basil leaves
  ⅛ teaspoon sugar

Heat oil and garlic in 10-inch skillet over medium heat, stirring frequently, until fragrant but not browned, about 2 minutes. Stir in tomatoes and simmer until slightly thickened, about 5 minutes. Stir in basil and sugar and season with salt to taste.

Spicy Mayonnaise

Makes 1¼ cups • Total Time: 5 minutes

  1 cup mayonnaise
  2 tablespoons sriracha
  2 teaspoons grated lime zest plus 2 tablespoons juice
  ½ teaspoon smoked paprika

Whisk all ingredients together in bowl.

SEASON 23

Gravlax

Makes 1 pound salmon
Total Time: 15 minutes, plus 3 days chilling

Why This Recipe Works Gravlax might just be the perfect make-ahead party appetizer. Compared with its cousins smoked salmon, lox, and nova, which are all usually brined and then smoked, gravlax relies on a one-step process. The name, derived from "gravad lax" (Swedish for "buried salmon"), alludes to covering the fish with a salt-and-sugar cure (and typically dill). We used skin-on salmon because it made slicing the cured fish easier. A splash of brandy added flavor, helped the cure adhere, and assisted in the preserving process. Most recipes use granulated sugar, but we opted for brown sugar because its more complex flavor complemented the salmon. Pressing the salmon under a few cans helped it release moisture and gave the fillet a firmer, more sliceable texture. We basted the salmon with the released liquid once a day to help speed up the curing process and to keep it from drying out.

GAME CHANGER

You Don't Need an Ailment to Benefit from a Cure

"Long before I had a clue about IKEA, I grew up in a house with a mid-century modern, Scandinavian design aesthetic. That rubbed off on me, as I've always felt drawn to all things Scandinavian, including the fish-heavy cuisine. Over the years, gravlax, which is cured salmon, has become something of a staple for me, so much so that I've even organized and taught a class on it. The cure in question is a simple mixture of salt, sugar, and seasonings that you rub all over raw salmon, which is then wrapped, weighted, and rested for a couple of days. The cure draws liquid from the salmon, helping to preserve it and giving the flesh a tight, silky texture. Thin slices of gravlax on small toasts or Scandinavian crispbread, with a dollop of classic mustard-dill sauce, never cease to be a luxurious treat (and they're equally good on a bagel with cream cheese, à la cold-smoked salmon)."

—Adam

Serve the gravlax on crackers or rye bread topped with crème fraîche, shallot, and herbs (or other garnishes).

⅓ cup packed light brown sugar
¼ cup kosher salt
1 (1-pound) skin-on salmon fillet
3 tablespoons brandy
1 cup coarsely chopped fresh dill

1. Combine sugar and salt in bowl. Place salmon, skin side down, in 13 by 9-inch baking dish. Drizzle entire surface with brandy. Rub salmon evenly with sugar mixture, pressing firmly to adhere. Cover with dill, pressing firmly to adhere.

2. Cover salmon loosely with plastic wrap; top with square baking dish or pie plate; and weight with several large, heavy cans. Refrigerate until salmon feels firm, about 3 days, basting salmon with liquid released into dish once a day.

3. Scrape off dill. Remove salmon from dish and pat dry with paper towels. Slice thin and serve. (Gravlax can be wrapped tightly in plastic and refrigerated for up to 1 week. Don't slice until ready to serve.)

SEASON 5

Spiced Pecans with Rum Glaze

Makes 2 cups • Total Time: 45 minutes, plus 20 minutes cooling

Why This Recipe Works Most spiced nuts are made with a heavily sugared syrup that causes the nuts to clump awkwardly and leaves your hands in a sticky mess. We wanted to get maximum flavor and balanced sweetness with minimum mess.

We tried two popular methods—boiling the nuts in syrup and tossing them in butter—and eliminated both straight off. The former made the nuts sticky, and the latter dulled their flavor. A third method, coating the nuts with an egg white mixture, pretty much overwhelmed them with a candy-like coating. What finally worked was a light glaze made from very small amounts of liquid (we like either rum or water), sugar, and butter, which left the nuts just tacky enough to pick up an even, light coating of dry spices.

The spiced nuts can be stored in an airtight container at room temperature for up to five days.

2 cups raw pecan halves

Spice Mix
2 tablespoons sugar
¾ teaspoon table salt
½ teaspoon ground cinnamon
⅛ teaspoon ground cloves
⅛ teaspoon ground allspice

Rum Glaze
1 tablespoon rum, preferably dark, or water
1 tablespoon unsalted butter
2 teaspoons vanilla extract
1 teaspoon light or dark brown sugar

1. Adjust oven rack to middle position and heat oven to 350 degrees. Line rimmed baking sheet with parchment paper and spread pecans on it in even layer; toast until fragrant and color deepens slightly, about 8 minutes, rotating sheet halfway through baking. Transfer sheet with the nuts to wire rack.

2. For the spice mix: While nuts are toasting, combine all ingredients in medium bowl; set aside.

3. For the rum glaze: Bring all ingredients to boil in medium saucepan over medium-high heat, whisking constantly. Stir in pecans and cook, stirring constantly with wooden spoon, until almost all of liquid has evaporated, about 1½ minutes.

4. Transfer glazed pecans to bowl with spice mix; toss well to coat. Return glazed spiced pecans to parchment-lined baking sheet to cool before serving.

Holiday Eggnog

Serves 12 to 16 • Total Time: 45 minutes, plus 3 hours chilling

Why This Recipe Works The rich creamy flavor of a really fine eggnog is too good to pass up. It's well worth knowing how to make this indulgent treat; the homemade version beats store-bought by a mile. We started by tinkering with a standard custard recipe (six eggs to 4 cups milk to ½ cup sugar). To enhance the custard's flavor and richness, we added two extra egg yolks, a little more sugar, and a bit of salt. Many eggnog recipes call for the milk to be added to the beaten eggs very gradually; we found that this did indeed make for a smoother texture. Last, but not least, were the flavorings. Call us traditionalists, but in the end we felt that nothing beat vanilla extract and nutmeg for true holiday eggnog flavor.

Adding the milk to the eggs in small increments and blending after each addition helps ensure a smooth custard. To prevent curdling, do not heat the custard beyond 165 degrees. If it does begin to curdle, remove it from the heat immediately, pour it into a bowl set over a larger bowl of ice water to stop the cooking, and proceed with the recipe. You can omit the brandy to make a nonalcoholic eggnog, but you should also decrease the cream to ¼ cup to keep the right consistency. For the same reason, increase the cream to ¾ cup if you add another ½ cup alcohol for a high-test eggnog.

    6 large eggs plus 2 large yolks
    ½ cup plus 2 tablespoons sugar
    4 cups whole milk
    ¼ teaspoon table salt
    ½ cup brandy, bourbon, or dark rum
    1 tablespoon vanilla extract
    ½ teaspoon freshly grated nutmeg,
        plus extra for serving
    ½ cup heavy cream

1. Whisk eggs, yolks, and sugar in medium bowl until thoroughly combined, about 30 seconds; set aside. Bring milk and salt to simmer in large saucepan over medium-high heat, stirring occasionally.

2. When milk mixture comes to simmer, remove from heat and, whisking constantly, slowly pour into yolk mixture to temper. Return milk-yolk mixture to saucepan. Place over medium-low heat and cook, stirring constantly, until mixture reaches 160 to 165 degrees, 2 to 5 minutes.

3. Immediately pour custard through fine-mesh strainer into large bowl; stir in liquor, vanilla, and nutmeg. Cover with plastic wrap and refrigerate until well chilled, at least 3 hours or up to 3 days.

4. Just before serving, using stand mixer fitted with whisk attachment, whip cream on medium-low speed until foamy, about 1 minute. Increase speed to high and whip until soft peaks form, 1 to 3 minutes. Whisk whipped cream into chilled eggnog. Serve, garnished with extra nutmeg.

ATK 25

Makes 2 cocktails • Total Time: 20 minutes, plus 30 minutes cooling

Why This Recipe Works Behold: the ATK 25. Bridget developed this cocktail recipe for our 25th anniversary TV show. It represents our unique methodology in developing and presenting recipes to viewers. While testing, she, Julia, Jack, Adam, and Becky toasted to 25 more years to come. Julia is a Champagne aficionado, and Bridget adores a great gin cocktail, so the elegant French 75 cocktail, which is simply gin, simple syrup, lemon juice, and Champagne, became the starting point. Ruby-red grenadine added tart and sweet notes and reflected our signature red color. Our homemade grenadine is worth making as it brings added complexity. After shaking the gin, pomegranate and lemon juices, and grenadine together, we topped the glass with a very dry Champagne to counter the sweetness.

We strongly prefer Champagne for this cocktail, but you can use another sparkling wine as long as it is labeled extra brut. Use a channel knife to make the lemon twist.

Grenadine

- ¾ cup sugar
- 5 ounces unsweetened 100 percent pomegranate juice
- 8 allspice berries, lightly crushed
- ½ teaspoon pomegranate molasses (optional)

Cocktail

- 2 ounces London Dry gin
- 1¼ ounces unsweetened 100 percent pomegranate juice
- 1 ounce lemon juice, plus lemon twist for garnishing
- 1 ounce grenadine
- 4 ounces extra-dry Champagne, chilled

1. For the grenadine: Heat sugar; pomegranate juice; allspice berries; and pomegranate molasses, if using, in small saucepan over medium-low heat, whisking often, until sugar has dissolved, 2 to 4 minutes; do not boil. Let cool completely, about 30 minutes, then strain through fine-mesh strainer into airtight container. (Grenadine can be refrigerated for up to 1 month. Shake gently before using.)

2. For the cocktail: Add gin, pomegranate juice, lemon juice, and grenadine to cocktail shaker, then fill with ice. Shake mixture until fully combined and well chilled, about 15 seconds. Double-strain cocktail into 2 chilled flute glasses. Add 2 ounces Champagne to each glass and garnish with lemon twist. Serve.

Making a Lemon Twist

1. To make citrus zest twist, use channel knife to remove 3- to 4-inch strand, working around circumference of citrus in spiral pattern to ensure continuous piece.

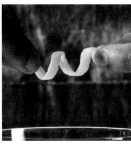

2. To garnish with citrus twist, curl strand tightly to establish uniform twist, then place in cocktail or on edge of glass.

New Englander

Makes 1 nonalcoholic cocktail
Total Time: 25 minutes, plus 30 minutes cooling

Why This Recipe Works A tart, vivid red New Englander is the perfect thing to serve alongside the rich fare so many of us gravitate toward in wintertime: It's elegant, festive, and sure to perk up your taste buds. The star of the drink is our cranberry shrub syrup. Cranberries are the ideal fruit to receive the sweet-tart shrub treatment; the syrup's luscious flavor shines when mixed with seltzer and a bit of lime juice. We found that the syrup had just the right sweetness. This recipe makes enough shrub syrup for up to four cocktails. To make additional cocktails, increase the lime juice and seltzer accordingly and repeat step 3.

Cranberry Shrub Syrup

- 2 cups fresh or frozen cranberries
- 1 cup sugar
- 6 ounces water
- 1 ounce white wine vinegar

New Englander

- ¼ ounce lime juice, plus lime twist for garnishing
- 6 ounces seltzer, chilled

1. For the cranberry shrub syrup: Bring cranberries, sugar, and water to boil in large saucepan over high heat. Reduce heat to medium-low, cover, and simmer until cranberries are beginning to break down, about 5 minutes.

2. Remove saucepan from heat and use potato masher to crush cranberries. Set fine-mesh strainer over medium bowl and line with triple layer of cheesecloth that overhangs edges. Transfer cranberry mixture to prepared strainer and let drain until liquid no longer runs freely and mixture is cool enough to touch, about 30 minutes. Pull edges of cheesecloth together to form pouch, then gently squeeze pouch to extract as much syrup as possible; discard solids. Whisk in vinegar. (Shrub syrup can be stored in airtight container for up to 1 month. Shake well before using.)

3. For the New Englander: Fill chilled collins glass halfway with ice. Add 2 ounces shrub syrup and lime juice and stir to combine using bar spoon. Add seltzer and, using spoon, gently lift shrub mixture from bottom of glass to top to combine. Top with additional ice and garnish with lime twist. Serve.

VARIATION
New Englander with Vodka
Add 1 ounce vodka to glass with shrub syrup.

For Sublime Margaritas, Start with Lime Zest

"Getting the assignment more than twenty-some years ago to develop a recipe for one of the most well-known, and well-loved, cocktails in all of human history was like learning that I had won the lottery and had to give a public speech in front of thousands of people—thrilling and terrifying. Lucky for me, I'd (ahem) done some prior research on the drink for a few years, and knew the better ones started with fresh citrus juice, not pre-bottled sour mixes, which often contain artificial flavors and high-fructose corn syrup. I ditched the bottled mix and grabbed the citrus reamer instead, squeezing limes by the case, and eventually adding lemon juice to the homemade mix to emphasize that fresh citrus punch. The test kitchen was filled with the unmistakable perfume of lemon and lime, a product of the scented oils from the fruit peels that became airborne with each squeeze. Knowing that lime zest is full of flavor—even more complex than that found in the lime juice—I let the finely grated zest soak with the juice and sugar for several hours and then strained the bright-colored potion. Once mixed with the right ratio of quality blanco or reposado tequila and a fine triple sec (avoid the artificially flavored dreck and seek a dry curaçao or Cointreau instead), the resulting recipe was bold, balanced, and incredibly refreshing. I'm happy to know that it's stood the test of time as well."

—*Bridget*

SEASON 25

Fresh Margaritas

Makes 1 quart • Total Time: 15 minutes, plus 4 hours chilling

Why This Recipe Works Poorly crafted margaritas tend to be slushy concoctions made with little more than ice, tequila, and artificially flavored corn syrup. We wanted a margarita with a balanced blend of fresh citrus flavors and tequila. We found that the key was using equal parts alcohol and citrus juice. For a mellow, delicate flavor, we preferred reposado tequila, made from 100 percent blue agave, which is aged about 12 months. Unaged tequilas gave our margaritas a raw, harsh flavor. And those made with superpremium tequilas, which are aged up to 6 years, tasted smooth, but their distinct tannic taste dominated the cocktail. As for orange-flavored liqueurs, a lower-alcohol liqueur, such as triple sec, worked best. Mixes and bottled citrus juice had no place in our cocktail—instead we steeped lemon and lime zest in their own juice for deep citrus flavor. With a bit of easy-to-dissolve superfine sugar and crushed ice, our margaritas were complete.

The longer the zest and juice mixture is allowed to steep, the more developed the citrus flavors will be in the finished margaritas. We recommend steeping for the full 24 hours, although the margaritas will still be great if the mixture is steeped for only the minimum 4 hours.

If you're in a rush and want to serve margaritas immediately, omit the zest and skip the steeping process altogether. If you can't find superfine sugar, process an equal amount of regular sugar in a food processor for 30 seconds.

- 4 teaspoons grated lime zest plus ½ cup juice (4 limes)
- 4 teaspoons grated lemon zest plus ½ cup juice (3 lemons)
- ¼ cup superfine sugar
  Pinch table salt
- 2 cups crushed ice, divided
- 1 cup 100 percent agave tequila, preferably reposado
- 1 cup triple sec

1. Combine lime zest and juice, lemon zest and juice, sugar, and salt in large liquid measuring cup; cover with plastic wrap and refrigerate until flavors meld, 4 to 24 hours.

2. Divide 1 cup crushed ice among 4 or 6 margarita or double old-fashioned glasses. Strain juice mixture into 1-quart pitcher or cocktail shaker. Add tequila, triple sec, and remaining 1 cup crushed ice; stir or shake until thoroughly combined and chilled, 20 to 60 seconds. Strain into ice-filled glasses and serve immediately.

SEASON 23
Rosé Sangria

Makes 12 cocktails • Total Time: 15 minutes, plus 2 hours chilling

Why This Recipe Works From its humble—and ancient—roots in Spain, sangria's popularity has spread worldwide. While sangria is traditionally made with red wine, other types can be used; here we opted for pretty pink rosé and updated the mix-ins to match its lighter flavor profile for a refreshing twist on the classic that really allowed the rosé's flavor to shine. This meant choosing our mix-ins judiciously, so after some experimentation we stuck to adding only a couple cups of mixed berries. A few ounces of delicately floral elderflower liqueur highlighted these fresh flavors, and pomegranate juice deepened the color of the sangria and complemented the berries. A splash of simple syrup rounded out the drink with a subtle sweetness.

The longer sangria rests before serving, the smoother and mellower it will taste. Give it an absolute minimum of 2 hours and up to 8 hours if possible.

- 2 (750-ml) bottles rosé wine
- 2 cups mixed berries
- 8 ounces pomegranate juice
- 4 ounces elderflower liqueur
- 4 ounces Simple Syrup (recipe follows)

1. Combine all ingredients in serving pitcher or large container. Cover and refrigerate until flavors meld and mixture is well chilled, at least 2 hours or up to 8 hours.

2. Stir sangria to recombine, then serve in chilled wine glasses half-filled with ice, garnishing individual portions with macerated berries.

Simple Syrup
Makes 8 ounces • Total Time: 15 minutes

- ¾ cup sugar
- 5 ounces warm tap water

Whisk sugar and warm water in bowl until sugar has dissolved. Let cool completely, about 10 minutes, before transferring to airtight container. (Syrup can be refrigerated for up to 1 month. Shake well before using.)

Sangria

Serves 4 • **Total Time: 10 minutes, plus 2 hours chilling**

Why This Recipe Works Many people mistake sangria for an unruly collection of fruit awash in a sea of overly sweetened red wine. We wanted a robust, sweet-tart wine punch. After trying a variety of red wines, we found that inexpensive wine works best. (Experts told us that the sugar and fruit called for in sangria throw off the balance of any wine used, so why spend a lot on something that was carefully crafted?) We experimented with untold varieties of fruit to put in our sangria and concluded that simpler is better. We preferred the straightforward tang of citrus in the form of oranges and lemons. And we discovered that the zest and pith as well as the fruit itself make an important contribution to flavor. Orange liqueur is standard in recipes for sangria, and after experimenting we found that here, as with the wine, cheaper was just fine, this time in the form of triple sec. What we wanted, and what we now had, was a light, refreshing drink.

Although this punch hails from Spain, it has become a mainstay on Mexican restaurant menus and pairs well with the country's spicy dishes. The longer sangria sits before drinking, the more smooth and mellow it will taste. A full day is best, but if that's impossible, give it an absolute minimum of two hours to sit. Use large, heavy, juicy oranges and lemons for the best flavor. If you can't find superfine sugar, process an equal amount of regular sugar in a food processor for 30 seconds. Doubling or tripling the recipe is fine, but you'll have to switch to a large punch bowl in place of the pitcher. An inexpensive Merlot is the best choice for this recipe.

- 2 large juice oranges, washed (1 sliced, 1 juiced)
- 1 large lemon, washed and sliced
- ¼ cup superfine sugar
- 1 (750-milliliter) bottle inexpensive, fruity, medium-bodied red wine, chilled
- ¼ cup triple sec

1. Add sliced orange, lemon, and sugar to large pitcher. Mash fruit gently with wooden spoon until fruit releases some juice, but is not totally crushed, and sugar dissolves, about 1 minute. Stir in orange juice, wine, and triple sec; refrigerate for at least 2 hours or up to 8 hours.

2. Before serving, add 6 to 8 ice cubes and stir briskly to distribute settled fruit and pulp; serve immediately.

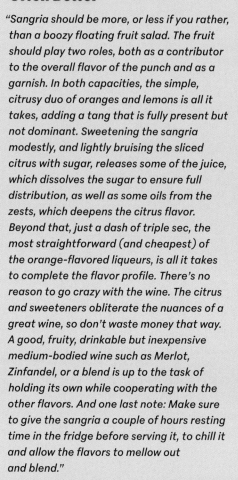

GAME CHANGER

Another Reminder That Simpler Is Often Better

"Sangria should be more, or less if you rather, than a boozy floating fruit salad. The fruit should play two roles, both as a contributor to the overall flavor of the punch and as a garnish. In both capacities, the simple, citrusy duo of oranges and lemons is all it takes, adding a tang that is fully present but not dominant. Sweetening the sangria modestly, and lightly bruising the sliced citrus with sugar, releases some of the juice, which dissolves the sugar to ensure full distribution, as well as some oils from the zests, which deepens the citrus flavor. Beyond that, just a dash of triple sec, the most straightforward (and cheapest) of the orange-flavored liqueurs, is all it takes to complete the flavor profile. There's no reason to go crazy with the wine. The citrus and sweeteners obliterate the nuances of a great wine, so don't waste money that way. A good, fruity, drinkable but inexpensive medium-bodied wine such as Merlot, Zinfandel, or a blend is up to the task of holding its own while cooperating with the other flavors. And one last note: Make sure to give the sangria a couple of hours resting time in the fridge before serving it, to chill it and allow the flavors to mellow out and blend."

—Adam

Sangria

Eggs & Breakfast

Photo: Green Shakshuka

Details Matter Most for Simple Recipes

"Scrambled eggs was one of the first dishes I tackled as a kid in the kitchen. I loved the process of cracking the shells and whipping the eggs with a fork. But more than anything, I liked that no matter what I did at the stovetop, I got to watch a sunny yellow pool magically transform into curds that I could stab with a fork and eat. In that sense scrambled eggs are easy—just apply heat and eat. But if you want something specific out of your scrambled eggs—say big, fluffy, tender curds, every time—you have to pay close attention to the details.

That's just what I did when developing this recipe. I tested everything—how much to whip the eggs, when to add salt, which dairy to include in the mix. But the most profound lesson I learned during the testing process was this: The key to big fluffy curds is to use your rubber spatula like a snow shovel, and slowly and methodically scrape cooked egg from the surface of the pan. Each pass of the spatula frees big, tender curds. And it's still a thrill to watch."

—Dan

Perfect Scrambled Eggs

Serves 4 • **Total Time: 10 minutes**

Why This Recipe Works For foolproof rich scrambled eggs with fluffy, moist curds that were creamy and light, we used a combination of high and low heat. The first step was to add salt to the uncooked eggs; salt dissolved some of the egg proteins so they were unable to bond when cooked, creating more tender curds. Beating the eggs until just combined, using the gentle action of a fork rather than a whisk, ensured that our scramble didn't turn tough. For intense creaminess, we chose half-and-half over milk; it produced rich, clean-tasting curds that were both fluffy and stable. To replicate the richer flavor of farm-fresh eggs, we added extra yolks. Finally, we started the eggs on medium-high heat to create puffy curds and then finished them over low heat so they wouldn't overcook. A 10-inch skillet kept the eggs in a thicker layer, trapping more steam and producing heartier curds.

It's important to follow the visual cues in this recipe, as pan thickness will affect cooking times. If using an electric stove, heat one burner on low heat and a second on medium-high heat; move the skillet between burners when it's time to adjust the heat. If you don't have half-and-half, substitute 8 teaspoons of whole milk and 4 teaspoons of heavy cream. To dress up the dish, add 2 tablespoons of chopped parsley, chives, basil, or cilantro or 1 tablespoon of dill or tarragon to the eggs after reducing the heat to low.

- 8 large whole eggs
- 2 large yolks
- ¼ cup half-and-half
- ⅜ teaspoon table salt
- ¼ teaspoon pepper
- 1 tablespoon unsalted butter, chilled

1. Beat eggs, yolks, half-and-half, salt, and pepper with fork until eggs are thoroughly combined and color is pure yellow; do not overbeat.

2. Heat butter in 10-inch nonstick skillet over medium-high heat until fully melted (butter should not brown), swirling to coat pan. Add egg mixture and, using heatproof rubber spatula, constantly and firmly scrape along bottom and sides of skillet until eggs begin to clump and spatula just leaves trail on bottom of pan, 1½ to 2½ minutes. Reduce heat to low and gently but constantly fold eggs until clumped and just slightly wet, 30 to 60 seconds. Immediately transfer eggs to warmed plates and season with salt to taste. Serve immediately.

Timing Scrambled Eggs

When spatula just leaves trail through eggs, turn the dial from medium-high to low.

Scrambled Eggs with Asparagus, Smoked Salmon, and Chives

Serves 4 • **Total Time: 25 minutes**

Why This Recipe Works When you want a heartier take on scrambled eggs, it's tempting to round up whatever leftover cooked vegetables are stashed in the refrigerator, toss them in a hot skillet with beaten eggs, and stir until curds form. But we wanted hearty scrambled eggs that were foolproof. We nixed spinach and Swiss chard: They tended to weep after cooking, making the eggs watery. Superdelicate greens were also out: They liked to clump, which made them difficult to disperse evenly. We settled on fresh asparagus, chives, and luxurious smoked salmon. The test kitchen likes to add dairy to beaten eggs, which makes fantastic classic scrambled eggs. But for this fresher take, we wanted to use extra-virgin olive oil for its grassy savoriness. Using oil would also reduce the amount of moisture we were adding to the eggs, ensuring that the asparagus would not get soggy. We beat some oil into the eggs, along with chives, salt, and pepper, and also used the oil, instead of butter, to cook the eggs. Just before they were fully cooked we added the asparagus, which we had quickly rendered crisp-tender first in a skillet. We then transferred our dish to a serving platter, draped it with glossy pieces of smoked salmon, and added more fresh chives.

If you can't find thin asparagus, peel the bottom halves of the spears until the white flesh is exposed and then halve each spear lengthwise, before cutting it into ½-inch pieces. If desired, all ingredient amounts can be halved; use a 10-inch skillet.

8 large eggs
3 tablespoons extra-virgin olive oil, divided
2 tablespoons minced fresh chives, divided
¼ teaspoon table salt
¼ teaspoon pepper
1 garlic clove, minced
8 ounces thin asparagus, trimmed and cut into
   ½-inch lengths
2 tablespoons water
2 ounces smoked salmon, torn into ½-inch strips

1. In medium bowl, beat eggs, 2 tablespoons oil, 1 table-spoon chives, salt, and pepper with fork until no streaks of white remain. Heat 1 teaspoon oil and garlic in 12-inch nonstick skillet over medium heat until fragrant, about 1 minute. Add asparagus and water, cover, and cook, stirring occasionally, until asparagus is crisp-tender, 3 to 4 minutes. Uncover and continue to cook until moisture has evaporated, about 1 minute longer. Transfer asparagus mixture to small bowl and set aside. Wipe skillet clean with paper towels.

2. Heat remaining 2 teaspoons oil in now-empty skillet over medium-high heat until shimmering. Add egg mixture and, using rubber spatula, constantly and firmly scrape along bottom and sides of skillet until eggs begin to clump and spatula just leaves trail on bottom of skillet, 30 to 60 seconds. Reduce heat to low and gently but constantly fold eggs until clumped and just slightly wet, 30 to 60 seconds. Fold in asparagus mixture. Transfer to serving dish, top with salmon, sprinkle with remaining 1 tablespoon chives, and serve.

VARIATIONS
Scrambled Eggs with Pinto Beans and Cotija Cheese
Serves 4 • Total Time: 20 minutes
If cotija cheese is unavailable, you can substitute feta cheese. This recipe can be easily halved, if desired; use a 10-inch skillet. We like to serve these eggs with warm tortillas and hot sauce.

8 large eggs
3 tablespoons extra-virgin olive oil, divided
¼ teaspoon table salt
¼ cup jarred sliced jalapeños, chopped coarse
2 garlic cloves, minced
1 (15-ounce) can pinto beans, rinsed
¼ cup chopped fresh cilantro, divided
1 ounce cotija cheese, crumbled (¼ cup)

1. In medium bowl, beat eggs, 2 tablespoons oil, and salt with fork until no streaks of white remain. Heat 1 teaspoon olive oil, jalapeños, and garlic in 12-inch nonstick skillet over medium heat until fragrant, about 1 minute. Add beans and 3 tablespoons cilantro and cook, stirring frequently, until moisture has evaporated, about 1 minute. Transfer bean mixture to small bowl and set aside. Wipe skillet clean with paper towels.

2. Heat remaining 2 teaspoons oil in now-empty skillet over medium-high heat until shimmering. Add egg mixture and, using rubber spatula, constantly and firmly scrape along bottom and sides of skillet until eggs begin to clump and spatula just leaves trail on bottom of skillet, 30 to 60 seconds. Reduce heat to low and gently but constantly fold eggs until clumped and just slightly wet, 30 to 60 seconds. Fold in bean mixture. Transfer to serving dish, sprinkle with cotija and remaining 1 tablespoon cilantro, and serve.

Scrambled Eggs with Shiitake Mushrooms and Feta Cheese
Serves 4 • Total Time: 30 minutes
This recipe can be easily halved, if desired; use a 10-inch skillet. Oyster or cremini mushrooms can be substituted for the shiitake mushrooms, if desired; to prepare the oyster or cremini mushrooms, trim the stems but do not remove them. Precrumbled feta is often coated with cellulose to keep it from caking. For the best results, buy a block of feta and crumble it yourself.

8 large eggs
3 tablespoons extra-virgin olive oil, divided
¼ teaspoon table salt, divided
¼ teaspoon pepper

1 shallot, minced
1 teaspoon minced fresh thyme
8 ounces shiitake mushrooms, stemmed and
   sliced thin
¼ cup water
1 ounce feta cheese, crumbled (¼ cup)

1. In medium bowl, beat eggs, 2 tablespoons oil, ⅛ teaspoon salt, and pepper with fork until no streaks of white remain. Heat 1 teaspoon oil, shallot, thyme, and remaining ⅛ teaspoon salt in 12-inch nonstick skillet over medium heat, stirring occasionally, until shallot is softened and beginning to brown, 2 to 3 minutes. Add mushrooms and water, cover, and cook, stirring frequently, until mushrooms are softened, 5 to 8 minutes. Uncover and continue to cook until moisture has evaporated, 2 to 3 minutes longer. Transfer mushroom mixture to small bowl and set aside. Wipe skillet clean with paper towels.

2. Heat remaining 2 teaspoons oil in now-empty skillet over medium-high heat until shimmering. Add egg mixture and, using rubber spatula, constantly and firmly scrape along bottom and sides of skillet until eggs begin to clump and spatula just leaves trail on bottom of skillet, 30 to 60 seconds. Reduce heat to low and gently but constantly fold eggs until clumped and just slightly wet, 30 to 60 seconds. Fold in mushroom mixture. Transfer to serving dish, sprinkle with feta, and serve.

SEASON 23

Xīhóngshì Chǎo Jīdàn

Serves 4 • Total Time: 25 minutes

Why This Recipe Works This classic Chinese stir-fry featuring pillowy egg curds enrobed in a chunky, savory-sweet tomato sauce is often the first thing Chinese children learn how to make. Typically served with plenty of steamed white rice, it's soothing, homey comfort food. We started by beating eggs with a little Shaoxing wine and toasted sesame oil to add savory notes as well as tenderness—the liquid and oil diluted the egg proteins and kept them from bonding too closely and turning tough. Quickly cooking the eggs over medium-high heat promoted airier curds. For the tomato base, garlic, ginger, and scallions provided savoriness while canned tomatoes gave us year-round consistency. Simmering the tomatoes with a measured amount of sugar made the base taste concentrated and rich before we combined it with the eggs.

| *Serve the stir-fry with steamed white rice.*

4 scallions, white parts sliced thin, green parts
   cut into 1-inch lengths
3 tablespoons vegetable oil, divided
3 garlic cloves, sliced thin
2 teaspoons grated fresh ginger
8 large eggs
2 tablespoons Shaoxing wine or dry sherry
1 teaspoon toasted sesame oil
1 teaspoon table salt, divided
1 (28-ounce) can whole peeled tomatoes, drained
   with juice reserved, cut into 1-inch pieces
2 teaspoons sugar

1. Combine scallion whites, 1 tablespoon vegetable oil, garlic, and ginger in small bowl; set aside. Whisk eggs, Shaoxing wine, sesame oil, and ½ teaspoon salt together in separate bowl.

2. Heat remaining 2 tablespoons vegetable oil in 12-inch nonstick or carbon-steel skillet or 14-inch flat-bottomed wok over medium-high heat until shimmering. Add egg mixture. Using rubber spatula, slowly but constantly scrape along bottom and sides of pan until eggs just form cohesive mass, 1 to 2 minutes (eggs will not be completely dry); transfer to clean bowl.

3. Add garlic mixture to now-empty pan and cook over medium heat, mashing mixture into pan, until fragrant, about 30 seconds. Add tomatoes and their juice, sugar, and remaining ½ teaspoon salt and simmer until almost completely dry, 5 to 7 minutes. Stir in egg mixture and scallion greens and cook, breaking up any large curds, until heated through, about 1 minute. Serve.

Breakfast Tacos: Scrambled Eggs, Migas, and Charred Tortillas

Serves 4 to 6 • **Total Time: 45 minutes**

Why This Recipe Works A breakfast taco spread, with creamy scrambled eggs wrapped in softly charred tortillas and showered with flavorful toppings, makes a fun way to cook breakfast for a crowd. We used a really long serving board for an assembly-line presentation, with tortillas and eggs first, followed by toppings and, finally, sauces. Because nothing is worse than cold eggs, we saved the scrambling for last. First, we got the toppings set up; we liked scallions, avocados, salsa, pickled jalapeños, Monterey Jack cheese, hot sauce, and lime wedges. Next, we charred the tortillas and wrapped them up to keep them warm. Finally we scrambled the eggs, called everyone to the table, and served the scramble right from the skillet. If you like, level up your board by adding an easy bean sauté (recipe follows) and browned chorizo.

Scrambled Eggs

Be sure to follow the visual cues when making the eggs, as your pan's thickness will affect the cooking time. If you're using an electric stovetop, heat a second burner on low and move the skillet to it when it's time to adjust the heat.

- 12 large eggs
- ½ teaspoon table salt
- ¼ teaspoon pepper
- 2 tablespoons unsalted butter

1. Whisk eggs, salt, and pepper in bowl until thoroughly combined and mixture is pure yellow, about 1 minute. Melt butter in 12-inch nonstick skillet over medium heat. Add egg mixture and, using heat-resistant rubber spatula, constantly and firmly scrape along bottom and sides of skillet until eggs begin to clump and spatula leaves trail on bottom of skillet, 1½ to 2½ minutes.

2. Reduce heat to low. Gently but constantly fold egg mixture until clumped and slightly wet, 30 to 60 seconds. Season with salt and pepper to taste. Serve immediately.

Migas

Omit butter. Heat 3 tablespoons vegetable oil in 12-inch nonstick skillet over medium-high heat until shimmering. Cut six 6-inch corn tortillas into 1 by ½-inch strips, then add to pan and cook, stirring occasionally, until golden brown, 4 to 6 minutes. Add 1 finely chopped onion, 1 finely chopped bell pepper, and 1 tablespoon minced jalapeño and cook until vegetables are softened, 5 to 7 minutes. Add egg mixture to tortilla mixture and proceed with recipe as directed. Before serving, gently fold in ⅓ cup shredded Monterey Jack and 1 tablespoon chopped fresh cilantro.

Sautéed Poblanos, Beans, and Corn

Makes 3 cups • **Total Time: 15 minutes**

Perfect for adding heft to your taco or even replacing eggs for vegan guests, this bean sauté comes together quickly and without a whole lot of planning thanks to canned beans and frozen corn.

- 1 tablespoon vegetable oil
- 2 poblano chiles, stemmed, seeded, and chopped
- 1 (15-ounce) can pinto beans, rinsed
- 1 cup frozen corn
- ½ cup chopped onion
- 2 teaspoons chili powder
- ¼ teaspoon table salt

Heat oil in 12-inch nonstick skillet over medium heat until shimmering. Add poblanos, beans, corn, onion, chili powder, and salt and cook until softened, 6 to 8 minutes.

Charring Tortillas

1. If you have a gas stove, hold 1 tortilla with tongs over flame, turning every few seconds to get even char. If you have an electric stove, heat a little oil in a skillet and warm tortilla over medium-high heat, turning every few seconds.

2. Wrap tortillas in clean dish towel to keep warm. Or, get a tortilla warmer (look for the brand Imusa's cloth version).

A Breakfast Spread That Even Vegans Will Love

"If you're anything like me, you have friends from all walks of life so when I'm entertaining, I have to be prepared for any and all varieties of food needs. The task becomes making sure that everyone is considered and eating well when planning a menu. My vegan and vegetarian friends expect the same level of culinary savoir faire as the ones who eat anything I put on the table. That's why I love making a breakfast taco spread with all the fixings. The Spanish migas with fried eggs is definitely geared towards my eat-all friends: It's bready, it's filling, and it's packed with traditional flavors. The poblanos, beans, and corn are just as hearty but offer flavorful beans brilliantly combined with corn and fresh salsa roja. Beans are the strong protein on deck providing everyone with a robust breakfast option."

— *Elle*

Salsa Roja

Makes 1½ cups • Total Time: 25 minutes

This drizzle-able, slightly spicy, tomatoey sauce—meant to be served warm—brings breakfast tacos to life. To make the salsa spicier, reserve and add the jalapeño seeds to the blender before processing. Make sure to drain the tomatoes after microwaving them so that the salsa does not become too watery.

- 1 pound plum tomatoes, cored and chopped
- 2 garlic cloves, chopped
- 1 jalapeño chile, stemmed, seeded, and chopped
- 2 tablespoons chopped fresh cilantro
- 1 tablespoon lime juice
- 1 teaspoon table salt
- ¼ teaspoon red pepper flakes

1. Combine tomatoes and garlic in bowl and microwave, uncovered, until steaming and liquid begins to pool in bottom of bowl, about 4 minutes. Transfer tomato mixture to fine-mesh strainer set over bowl and let drain for 5 minutes.

2. Combine jalapeño, cilantro, lime juice, salt, pepper flakes, and drained tomato mixture in blender. Process until smooth, about 45 seconds. Season with salt to taste. Serve warm. (Salsa can be refrigerated for up to 3 days; cover and microwave briefly to rewarm before serving.)

SEASON 14

Fluffy Omelets

Serves 2 • Total Time: 25 minutes

Why This Recipe Works: A different breed than French-style rolled omelets or diner-style omelets folded into half-moons, fluffy omelets are made by baking whipped eggs in a skillet until they rise above the lip of the pan. We love their impressive height and delicate texture. But most recipes result in oozing soufflés or dry, bouncy rounds—or eggs that barely puff up at all. To give our omelet lofty height without making it tough, we folded butter-enriched yolks into stiffly whipped whites stabilized with cream of tartar. The whipped whites gave the omelet great lift while the yolks and butter kept it tender and rich-tasting. We chose light but flavorful fillings that satisfied without weighing down the omelet.

A teaspoon of white vinegar or lemon juice can be used in place of the cream of tartar, and a hand mixer or a whisk can be used in place of a stand mixer. We recommend using the fillings that accompany this recipe; they are designed not to interfere with the cooking of the omelet.

- 4 large eggs, separated
- 1 tablespoon unsalted butter, melted, plus 1 tablespoon unsalted butter
- ¼ teaspoon table salt
- ¼ teaspoon cream of tartar
- 1 recipe filling (recipes follow)
- 1 ounce Parmesan cheese, grated (½ cup)

1. Adjust oven rack to middle position and heat oven to 375 degrees. Whisk egg yolks, melted butter, and salt together in bowl. Place egg whites in bowl of stand mixer and sprinkle cream of tartar over surface. Fit stand mixer with whisk and whip egg whites on medium-low speed until foamy, 2 to 2½ minutes. Increase speed to medium-high and whip until stiff peaks just start to form, 2 to 3 minutes. Fold egg yolk mixture into egg whites until no white streaks remain.

2. Heat remaining 1 tablespoon butter in 12-inch ovensafe nonstick skillet over medium-high heat, swirling to coat bottom of pan. When butter foams, quickly add egg mixture, spreading into even layer with spatula. Remove pan from heat and gently sprinkle filling and Parmesan evenly over top of omelet. Transfer to oven and cook until center of omelet springs back when lightly pressed, 4½ minutes for slightly wet omelet and 5 minutes for dry omelet.

3. Run spatula around edges of omelet to loosen, shaking gently to release. Slide omelet onto cutting board and let stand for 30 seconds. Using spatula, fold omelet in half. Cut omelet in half crosswise and serve immediately.

Asparagus and Smoked Salmon Filling

Makes ¾ cup   •   Total Time: 20 minutes

- 1 teaspoon olive oil
- 1 shallot, sliced thin
- 5 ounces asparagus, trimmed and cut on bias into ¼-inch lengths
  Pinch table salt
- 1 ounce smoked salmon, chopped
- ½ teaspoon lemon juice

Heat oil in 12-inch nonstick skillet over medium-high heat until shimmering. Add shallot and cook until softened and starting to brown, about 2 minutes. Add asparagus, pinch salt, and pepper to taste, and cook, stirring frequently, until crisp-tender, 5 to 7 minutes. Transfer asparagus mixture to bowl and stir in salmon and lemon juice.

Mushroom Filling

Makes ¾ cup   •   Total Time: 20 minutes

- 1 teaspoon olive oil
- 1 shallot, sliced thin
- 4 ounces white or cremini mushrooms, trimmed and chopped
- ⅛ teaspoon table salt
- 1 teaspoon balsamic vinegar

Heat oil in 12-inch nonstick skillet over medium-high heat until shimmering. Add shallot and cook until softened and starting to brown, about 2 minutes. Add mushrooms and salt and season with pepper to taste. Cook until liquid has evaporated and mushrooms begin to brown, 6 to 8 minutes. Transfer mixture to bowl and stir in vinegar.

Artichoke and Bacon Filling

Makes ¾ cup   •   Total Time: 20 minutes

- 2 slices bacon, cut into ¼-inch pieces
- 1 shallot, sliced thin
- 5 ounces frozen artichoke hearts, thawed, patted dry, and chopped
- ⅛ teaspoon table salt
- ½ teaspoon lemon juice

Cook bacon in 12-inch nonstick skillet over medium-high heat until crisp, 3 to 6 minutes. Using slotted spoon, transfer bacon to paper towel–lined plate. Pour off all but 1 teaspoon fat from skillet. Add shallot and cook until softened and starting to brown, about 2 minutes. Add artichokes and salt and season with pepper to taste. Cook, stirring frequently, until artichokes begin to brown, 6 to 8 minutes. Transfer artichoke mixture to bowl and stir in bacon and lemon juice.

SEASON 10

French Omelets

Serves 2   •   Total Time: 40 minutes

Why This Recipe Works The French omelet is a pristine rolled affair. Our perfect French omelet recipe had to give us golden yellow eggs with an ultracreamy texture rolled around minimal filling. Instead of a classic black carbon steel omelet pan and a fork, a nonstick skillet and bamboo skewers and wooden chopsticks gave us small curds with a silky texture. Preheating the pan for 10 minutes over low heat eliminated any hot spots. For a creamy texture, we added very cold butter to the beaten eggs. To keep the omelet light, we avoided excessive beating. The omelet cooked so quickly it was hard to judge when it was done, so we turned off the heat when the eggs were still runny and covered the pan to finish cooking them. For an easy rolling method, we slid the omelet onto a paper towel and used the towel to roll the omelet into the sought-after cylinder.

Because making these omelets is such a quick process, make sure to have all your ingredients and equipment at the ready. If you don't have skewers or chopsticks to stir the eggs in step 3, use the handle of a wooden spoon. Warm the plates in a 200-degree oven.

- 2 tablespoons unsalted butter, cut into 2 pieces
- ½ teaspoon vegetable oil
- 4 large eggs plus 2 large egg yolks, cold, divided
- ¼ teaspoon table salt, divided
- ⅛ teaspoon black pepper, divided
- 2 tablespoons shredded Gruyère cheese, divided
- 4 teaspoons minced fresh chives, divided

1. Cut 1 tablespoon butter in half. Cut remaining 1 tablespoon butter into small pieces, transfer to small bowl, and place in freezer while preparing eggs and skillet, at least 10 minutes. Meanwhile, heat oil in 8-inch nonstick skillet over low heat for 10 minutes.

2. Crack 2 eggs into medium bowl and separate third egg; reserve white for another use and add yolk to bowl. Add ⅛ teaspoon salt and pinch pepper. Break yolks with fork, then beat eggs at moderate pace, about 80 strokes, until yolks and whites are well combined. Stir in half of frozen butter cubes.

3. When skillet is fully heated, use paper towels to wipe out oil, leaving thin film on bottom and sides of skillet. Add half of reserved 1 tablespoon butter to skillet and heat until melted. Swirl butter to coat skillet, add egg mixture, and increase heat to medium-high. Use 2 chopsticks or wooden skewers to scramble eggs using quick circular motion to move around skillet, scraping cooked egg from side of skillet as you go, until eggs are almost cooked but still slightly runny, 45 to 90 seconds. Turn off heat (remove skillet from heat if using electric burner) and smooth eggs into even layer using heatproof rubber spatula. Sprinkle omelet with 1 tablespoon Gruyère and 2 teaspoons chives. Cover skillet with tight-fitting lid and let sit, 1 minute for runnier omelet and 2 minutes for firmer omelet.

4. Heat skillet over low heat for 20 seconds, uncover, and, using heatproof rubber spatula, loosen edges of omelet from skillet. Place folded square of paper towel onto warmed plate and slide omelet out of skillet onto paper towel so that omelet lies flat on plate and hangs about 1 inch off paper towel. Roll omelet into neat cylinder and set aside. Return skillet to low heat and heat for 2 minutes before repeating instructions for second omelet starting with step 2. Serve.

Rolling a French Omelet

Slide finished omelet onto paper towel–lined plate. Use paper towel to lift omelet and roll it up.

SEASON 19

Broccoli and Feta Frittata

Serves 4 to 6 • **Total Time: 40 minutes**

Why This Recipe Works The frittata is sometimes called a lazy cook's omelet. After all, it contains the same ingredients but doesn't require folding the eggs around the filling, a skill that takes practice to master. But even the practical frittata requires a little know-how, lest the bottom turn rubbery or the center end up loose and wet. We wanted to uncover the keys to a tender, evenly cooked, cohesive frittata, and we wanted it to be big and hearty enough to serve at least four for dinner. We started with a well-seasoned filling made with bold ingredients and combined it with a dozen eggs to make a substantial dinner. To ensure that the frittata was cohesive, we chopped the filling ingredients small so that they could be surrounded and held in place by the eggs. To help the eggs stay tender even when cooked to a relatively high temperature, we added milk and salt. The liquid diluted the proteins, making it harder for them to coagulate and turn the eggs rubbery, and salt weakened the interactions between proteins, producing a softer curd. Finally, for eggs that were cooked fully and evenly, we started the frittata on the stovetop, stirring until a spatula left a trail in the curds, and then transferred the skillet to the oven to gently finish.

This frittata can be served warm or at room temperature. When paired with a salad, it can serve as a meal.

12 large eggs

⅓ cup whole milk

¾ teaspoon table salt, divided

1 tablespoon extra-virgin olive oil

12 ounces broccoli florets, cut into ½-inch pieces (4 cups)

Pinch red pepper flakes

3 tablespoons water

½ teaspoon grated lemon zest plus ½ teaspoon juice

4 ounces feta cheese, crumbled into ½-inch pieces (1 cup)

1. Adjust oven rack to middle position and heat oven to 350 degrees. Whisk eggs, milk, and ½ teaspoon salt in bowl until well combined.

2. Heat oil in 12-inch ovensafe nonstick skillet over medium-high heat until shimmering. Add broccoli, pepper flakes, and remaining ¼ teaspoon salt; cook, stirring frequently, until broccoli is crisp-tender and spotty brown, 7 to 9 minutes. Add water and lemon zest and juice; continue to cook, stirring constantly, until broccoli is just tender and no water remains in skillet, about 1 minute longer.

3. Add feta and egg mixture and cook, using rubber spatula to stir and scrape bottom of skillet until large curds form and spatula leaves trail through eggs but eggs are still very wet, about 30 seconds. Smooth curds into even layer and cook, without stirring, for 30 seconds. Transfer skillet to oven and bake until frittata is slightly puffy and surface bounces back when lightly pressed, 6 to 9 minutes. Using rubber spatula, loosen frittata from skillet and transfer to cutting board. Let stand for 5 minutes before slicing and serving.

VARIATIONS

Asparagus and Goat Cheese Frittata

This recipe works best with thin and medium-size asparagus.

Substitute 1 pound asparagus, trimmed and cut into ¼-inch lengths, for broccoli and ¼ teaspoon pepper for pepper flakes. Reduce cooking time in step 2 to 3 to 4 minutes. Omit water. Substitute goat cheese for feta and add 2 tablespoons chopped fresh mint to eggs with cheese.

Chorizo and Potato Frittata

Be sure to use Spanish-style chorizo, which is dry-cured and needs only to be heated through.

Substitute 1 pound Yukon Gold potatoes, peeled and cut into ½-inch pieces, for broccoli and ¼ teaspoon ground cumin for pepper flakes. In step 2, cook potatoes until half are lightly browned, 8 to 10 minutes. Substitute 6 ounces Spanish-style chorizo sausage, cut into ¼-inch pieces, and 1 teaspoon sherry vinegar for lemon zest and juice. Substitute ½ cup chopped fresh cilantro for feta.

Shiitake Mushroom Frittata with Pecorino Romano

While the shiitake mushrooms needn't be cut into exact ½-inch pieces, for a cohesive frittata, make sure that no pieces are much larger than ¾ inch.

Substitute 1 pound shiitake mushrooms, stemmed and cut into ½-inch pieces, for broccoli and ¼ teaspoon pepper for pepper flakes. Reduce water to 2 tablespoons and substitute 2 minced scallion whites, 1 tablespoon sherry vinegar, and 1½ teaspoons minced fresh thyme for lemon zest and juice. Substitute ¾ cup shredded Pecorino Romano for feta and add 2 thinly sliced scallion greens to eggs with cheese.

SEASON 7

Huevos Rancheros

Serves 2 to 4 • **Total Time: 1¾ hours**

Why This Recipe Works Roughly translated as "rancher's eggs" or "country eggs," this Mexican egg dish was devised to use up leftover salsa and tortillas for a quick but filling breakfast. Over the years it's become a popular brunch dish in the United States. For our version, we examined each component of the dish to produce a satisfying meal. The salsa is a crucial element, and we know from experience that jarred salsa can't compare to freshly made, so we looked for ways to maximize the flavor of our supermarket tomatoes. We found that roasting plum tomatoes turned them more flavorful, and we thought roasting the onion and jalapeños improved their flavor as well. It was difficult to get fried eggs from the skillet onto the tortillas neatly (and without breaking the yolks), so we turned to poaching the eggs for a tidier presentation. We made things even easier by poaching them right in the simmering salsa, saving ourselves a pot to clean in the bargain. To pep up the supermarket tortillas, we brushed them with a little oil, sprinkled them with salt, and toasted them in the oven. Crisp tortillas, creamy eggs, and fiery salsa combined for a great version of this Mexican classic.

To save time, make the salsa the day before and store it in the refrigerator. If you like, serve with Refried Beans (recipe follows).

2. Brush both sides of each tortilla lightly with remaining 1 tablespoon oil, sprinkle both sides with salt, and place on clean baking sheet. Bake until tops just begin to color, 5 to 7 minutes; flip tortillas and continue to bake until golden brown, 2 to 3 minutes more.

3. Meanwhile, bring salsa to gentle simmer in 12-inch nonstick skillet over medium heat. Remove from heat and make 4 shallow wells in salsa with back of large spoon. Break 1 egg into cup, then carefully pour egg into well in salsa; repeat with remaining 3 eggs. Season each egg with salt and pepper, then cover skillet and place over medium-low heat. Cook to desired doneness: 4 to 5 minutes for runny yolks, 6 to 7 minutes for set yolks.

4. Place tortillas on serving plates; gently scoop 1 egg onto each tortilla. Spoon salsa around each egg, covering tortillas but leaving portion of eggs exposed. Sprinkle with remaining 1 tablespoon cilantro and serve with lime wedges.

ACCOMPANIMENT
Refried Beans
Makes 3 cups • Total Time: 35 minutes

- 2 (15-ounce) cans pinto beans, rinsed, divided
- 3/4 cup chicken broth
- 1/2 teaspoon table salt
- 3 slices bacon, chopped fine
- 1 small onion, chopped fine
- 1 large jalapeño chile, stemmed, seeded, and minced
- 1/2 teaspoon ground cumin
- 2 garlic cloves, minced
- 2 tablespoons minced fresh cilantro
- 2 teaspoons lime juice

1. Process all but 1 cup of beans with broth and salt in food processor until smooth, about 15 seconds, scraping down sides of workbowl with rubber spatula if necessary. Add remaining beans and pulse until slightly chunky, about 10 pulses.

2. Cook bacon in 12-inch nonstick skillet over medium heat until bacon just begins to brown and most of fat has rendered, about 4 minutes. Transfer to small bowl lined with strainer; discard bacon and add 1 tablespoon fat back to skillet. Increase heat to medium-high; add onion, jalapeño, and cumin; and cook until softened and just starting to brown, 3 to 5 minutes. Stir in garlic and cook until fragrant, about 30 seconds. Reduce heat to medium, stir in pureed beans, and cook until thick and creamy, 4 to 6 minutes. Off heat, stir in cilantro and lime juice.

- 3 jalapeño chiles, halved, seeds and ribs removed, divided
- 1½ pounds ripe plum tomatoes (about 6 medium), cored and halved
- ½ onion, cut into ½-inch wedges
- 3 tablespoons vegetable oil, divided
- 1 tablespoon tomato paste
- 2 garlic cloves, peeled
- 1 teaspoon table salt
- ½ teaspoon ground cumin
- ⅛ teaspoon cayenne pepper
- 3 tablespoons minced fresh cilantro, divided
- 1–2 tablespoons lime juice, plus lime wedges for serving
- 4 (6-inch) corn tortillas
- 4 large eggs

1. Adjust oven rack to middle position and heat oven to 375 degrees. Mince 1 jalapeño and set aside. In medium bowl, combine tomatoes, remaining 2 jalapeños, onion, 2 table-spoons oil, tomato paste, garlic, 1 teaspoon salt, cumin, and cayenne; toss to mix thoroughly. Place vegetables, cut side down, on rimmed baking sheet. Roast until tomatoes are tender and skins begin to shrivel and brown, 35 to 45 minutes; cool on baking sheet for 10 minutes. Increase oven temperature to 450 degrees. Using tongs, transfer roasted onion, garlic, and jalapeños to food processor. Process until almost completely broken down, about 10 seconds, pausing halfway through to scrape down sides of workbowl with rubber spatula. Add tomatoes and process until salsa is slightly chunky, about 15 seconds more. Add 2 tablespoons cilantro and reserved minced jalapeño and season with salt, pepper, and lime juice to taste.

Eggs Benedict with Perfect Poached Eggs and Foolproof Hollandaise

Serves 4 • Total Time: 1 hour

Why This Recipe Works To produce poached eggs with tender, tidy whites, we drained the eggs in a colander. We also deposited them into the boiling water one by one to prevent them from being jostled. Salted water with vinegar helped the whites set up quickly. Using a Dutch oven filled with 6 cups of water left plenty of headspace so that steam fully cooked the gooey portion of the white. Our unconventional technique for hollandaise required whisking softened butter and egg yolks in a double boiler, creating an emulsion stable enough to be chilled and reheated. We served our perfect eggs atop toasted English muffins and bacon, topped with our velvety hollandaise.

> *For the best results, be sure to use the freshest eggs possible. Cracking the eggs into a colander will rid them of any watery, loose whites and result in perfectly shaped poached eggs. The hollandaise can be refrigerated in an airtight container for three days. Reheat in the micro-wave on 50 percent power, stirring every 10 seconds, until heated through, about 1 minute. You will need an instant-read thermometer to make this recipe.*

Hollandaise
- 8 tablespoons unsalted butter, cut into 8 pieces and softened
- 4 large egg yolks
- ⅓ cup boiling water
- 2 teaspoons lemon juice
- Pinch cayenne pepper

Eggs
- 1 tablespoon distilled white vinegar
- Table salt, for cooking eggs
- 8 large eggs

- 4 English muffins, split
- 8 slices Canadian bacon

1. For the hollandaise: Whisk butter and egg yolks in large heat-resistant bowl set over medium saucepan filled with ½ inch of barely simmering water (don't let bowl touch water). Slowly add boiling water and cook, whisking constantly, until thickened and sauce registers 160 to 165 degrees, 7 to 10 minutes.

2. Off heat, stir in lemon juice and cayenne; season with salt. Cover and set aside in warm place until serving time.

3. For the eggs: Bring 6 cups water to boil in Dutch oven over high heat, and add vinegar and 1 teaspoon salt. Fill second Dutch oven halfway with water and heat over high heat until water registers 150 degrees; adjust heat as needed to maintain 150 degrees.

4. Crack 4 eggs, one at a time, into colander. Let stand until loose, watery whites drain away from eggs, 20 to 30 seconds. Gently transfer eggs to 2-cup liquid measuring cup. Remove first pot with added vinegar from heat. With lip of measuring cup just above surface of water, gently tip eggs into water, one at a time, leaving space between them. Cover pot and let stand until whites closest to yolks are just set and opaque, about 3 minutes. If after 3 minutes whites are not set, let stand in water, checking every 30 seconds, until eggs reach desired doneness. (For medium-cooked yolks, let eggs sit in pot, covered, for 4 minutes, then begin checking for doneness.)

5. Using slotted spoon, carefully lift and drain each egg over Dutch oven, then transfer to pot filled with 150-degree water and cover. Return Dutch oven used for cooking eggs to boil and repeat steps 4 and 5 with remaining 4 eggs.

6. Adjust oven rack 6 inches from broiler element and heat broiler. Arrange English muffins, split side up, on baking sheet and broil until golden brown, 2 to 4 minutes. Place 1 slice bacon on each English muffin and broil until beginning to brown, about 1 minute. Remove muffins from oven and transfer to serving plates. Using slotted spoon, carefully lift and drain each egg and lay on top of each English muffin. Spoon hollandaise over top and serve.

Çılbır

Çılbır

Serves 4 • **Total Time: 40 minutes**

Why This Recipe Works Çılbır, a hot meze and light meal cooked in homes all over Turkey, consists of a just-set egg, garlicky yogurt, and swirls of spiced butter. To make it, we started with a base of strained yogurt, which provided a plush, creamy bed for the poached egg. Grated garlic mixed seamlessly with the yogurt. For perfect poached eggs, we drained the loose whites before dropping the eggs into water seasoned with salt and vinegar. This helped the whites set up quickly, ensuring that the yolks would still be liquid, as did gently cooking the eggs off the heat. For the finishing touch, we melted butter until it started to sizzle and turn nutty before adding fruity red pepper flakes, which turned the butter bright red.

Strained yogurt has had some of the whey removed so that it's thicker than regular yogurt. Turkish strained yogurt is ideal for çılbır, but if you can't find it, Greek yogurt works well, too; do not use labneh, which is too thick for this recipe. A rasp-style grater makes quick work of turning the garlic into a paste. We strongly recommend seeking out the mild Turkish red pepper flakes pul biber or Aleppo pepper; however, ½ teaspoon of paprika can be substituted. For the tidiest presentation, use the freshest eggs possible. Çılbır can be eaten at any time of day; we like to pair it with a salad when serving it for lunch or dinner.

- 1 cup plain whole-milk strained yogurt
- ½ teaspoon garlic, minced to paste
- ⅛ teaspoon table salt, plus salt for cooking eggs
- 4 large eggs
- 1 tablespoon distilled white vinegar
- 2 tablespoons unsalted butter
- 1 teaspoon pul biber or ground dried Aleppo pepper
- ¼ teaspoon dried mint (optional)
  Pita, flatbread, or crusty bread

1. Stir yogurt, garlic, and salt in medium bowl until just combined. Divide yogurt mixture evenly among 4 serving plates or shallow bowls, spreading each portion with small spatula or back of spoon to make flat bed large enough to hold 1 poached egg. Set aside plates and allow yogurt to warm up while you prepare eggs.

2. Bring 1½ quarts water to boil in Dutch oven over high heat. Meanwhile, crack eggs, one at a time, into colander. Let stand until loose, watery parts of whites drain away from eggs, 20 to 30 seconds. Gently transfer eggs to 2-cup liquid measuring cup.

Change the Way You Eat Poached Eggs

"Whether perched atop a toasted English muffin and enrobed in buttery hollandaise or nested in a tangle of dressed bitter greens and crispy lardons, poached eggs always seem to land in rarefied company. I think part of the reason is that they have a reputation for being tricky to cook. The techniques in this recipe make poaching eggs easy and foolproof. Which is a good thing, because once you try poached eggs the Turkish way you'll want them in your regular rotation.

The key to poached eggs that emerge from the pot looking like perfect mounds of fresh mozzarella—free of wispy, messy strands— is to crack them into a colander before cooking. This step allows the thinner portion of the egg white to simply slip away. After poaching, the eggs are ready to land on a creamy swoop of strained yogurt seasoned with fresh garlic and salt. The final touch is a drizzle of butter infused with fruity, mildly spicy Turkish red pepper flakes and a sprinkle of dried mint. Rarefied company, indeed."

—Dan

3. Add vinegar and 1 teaspoon salt to boiling water. Remove pot from heat. With lip of measuring cup just above surface of water, gently tip eggs into water, one at a time, leaving space between them. Cover pot and let stand until whites closest to yolks are just set and opaque, about 3 minutes. If after 3 minutes whites are not set, let stand in water, checking every 30 seconds, until eggs reach desired doneness.

4. While eggs cook, heat butter in small saucepan over medium heat until it sputters, 2 to 3 minutes. Stir in pepper flakes (butter will foam) and remove from heat.

5. Using slotted spoon, carefully lift and drain 1 egg over pot. Pat bottom of spoon dry with paper towel and gently place egg on yogurt bed. Repeat with remaining eggs. Drizzle butter evenly over eggs. Sprinkle each serving with pinch dried mint, if using, and season with salt and pepper to taste. Serve immediately, passing pita separately.

Soft-Cooked Eggs

Serves 4 • Total Time: 15 minutes

Why This Recipe Works Traditional methods for making soft-cooked eggs are hit or miss. We wanted one that delivered a set white and a fluid yolk every time. Calling for fridge-cold eggs and boiling water has two advantages: It reduces temperature variables, which makes the recipe more foolproof, and it provides the steepest temperature gradient, which ensures that the yolk at the center stays fluid while the white cooks through. Using only ½ inch of boiling water instead of several cups to cook the eggs means that the recipe takes less time and energy from start to finish. Because of the curved shape of the eggs, they actually have very little contact with the water, so they do not lower the water temperature when they go into the saucepan. This means that you can use the same timing for anywhere from one to six eggs without altering the consistency of the finished product.

Be sure to use large eggs that have no cracks and are cold from the refrigerator. Because precise timing is vital to the success of this recipe, we strongly recommend using a digital timer. You can use this method for one to six large, extra-large, or jumbo eggs without altering the timing. If you have one, a steamer basket makes lowering the eggs into the boiling water easier. We recommend serving these eggs in eggcups and with buttered toast for dipping, or you may simply use the dull side of a butter knife to crack the egg along the equator, break the egg in half, and scoop out the insides with a teaspoon.

4 large eggs

1. Bring ½ inch water to boil in medium saucepan over medium-high heat. Using tongs, gently place eggs in boiling water (eggs will not be submerged). Cover saucepan and cook eggs for 6½ minutes.

2. Remove cover, transfer saucepan to sink, and place under cold running water for 30 seconds. Remove eggs from pan and serve, seasoning with salt and pepper to taste.

VARIATIONS

Soft-Cooked Eggs with Salad
Serves 2

Be sure to run the soft-cooked eggs under cold water for 30 seconds before peeling.

Combine 3 tablespoons olive oil, 1 tablespoon balsamic vinegar, 1 teaspoon Dijon mustard, and 1 teaspoon minced shallot in jar, seal lid, and shake vigorously until emulsified, 20 to 30 seconds. Toss with 5 cups assertively flavored salad greens (arugula, radicchio, watercress, or frisée). Season with salt and pepper to taste, and divide between 2 plates. Top each serving with 2 peeled soft-cooked eggs, split crosswise to release yolks, and season with salt and pepper to taste.

Soft-Cooked Eggs with Sautéed Mushrooms
Serves 2

Be sure to run the soft-cooked eggs under cold water for 30 seconds before peeling.

Heat 2 tablespoons olive oil in large skillet over medium-high heat until shimmering. Add 12 ounces sliced white or cremini mushrooms and pinch salt and cook, stirring occasionally, until liquid has evaporated and mushrooms are lightly browned, 5 to 6 minutes. Stir in 2 teaspoons chopped fresh herbs (chives, tarragon, parsley, or combination). Season with salt and pepper to taste, and divide between 2 plates. Top each serving with 2 peeled soft-cooked eggs, split crosswise to release yolks, and season with salt and pepper to taste.

Soft-Cooked Eggs with Steamed Asparagus
Serves 2

Be sure to run the soft-cooked eggs under cold water for 30 seconds before peeling.

Steam 12 ounces asparagus (spears about ½ inch in diameter, trimmed) over medium heat until crisp-tender, 4 to 5 minutes. Divide between 2 plates. Drizzle each serving with 1 tablespoon extra-virgin olive oil and sprinkle each serving with 1 tablespoon grated Parmesan. Season with salt and pepper to taste. Top each serving with 2 peeled soft-cooked eggs, split crosswise to release yolks, and season with salt and pepper to taste.

Green Shakshuka

Serves 4 • **Total Time: 1 hour**

Why This Recipe Works For a vibrant, earthy green shakshuka, we replaced the robust tomato and pepper sauce from red shakshuka with a mix of leafy greens and herbs: savory, mineral-y Swiss chard; tender baby spinach; and a bunch of fresh parsley. We started by softening the thinly sliced stems of the chard with onion and garlic in olive oil and then added cumin and coriander before wilting the chard leaves, parsley, and spinach. Next, we pureed a portion of the cooked greens with water and bread. The bread helped bind some of the water so that the puree was thick and homogenous. The puree provided a smooth consistency for evenly transferring heat to the eggs, which helped them cook at the same rate, while the portion of unblended greens provided a sturdy bed for the eggs. Cooking the eggs covered allowed them to be heated from above and below.

> *If sumac, which adds brightness, is unavailable, omit it in the steps and serve with lemon wedges (lemon juice may dull the color of the greens). Use a glass lid if you have one. If not, peek at the eggs frequently as they cook. Serve with hot sauce and garnish with Microwave-Fried Garlic (recipe follows).*

6 tablespoons extra-virgin olive oil
1 pound Swiss chard, stems sliced ¼ inch thick (2 cups), leaves cut into 1½- to 2-inch pieces (8 cups)
1 onion, chopped fine
8 garlic cloves, sliced thin
1 teaspoon table salt, divided
2 teaspoons ground coriander
2 teaspoons ground cumin
2 cups plus 2 tablespoons chopped fresh parsley leaves and stems, divided
1 pound (16 cups) baby spinach
1 ounce country-style bread, cut into ½-inch pieces (½ cup), plus bread for serving
1¼ cups water
1½ teaspoons ground sumac, divided
8 large eggs
1 ounce goat cheese or feta cheese, crumbled (¼ cup)

1. Heat oil in 12-inch nonstick skillet over medium heat until shimmering. Add chard stems, onion, garlic, and ½ teaspoon salt. Cook, stirring occasionally, until vegetables are soft and lightly browned, 8 to 10 minutes.

2. Add coriander and cumin and cook until fragrant, about 1 minute. Add chard leaves and 2 cups parsley. Adjust heat to medium-low and cook, covered, stirring occasionally, until greens are just wilted but still bright green, 2 to 3 minutes.

3. Add half of spinach, cover, and cook until just wilted. Add remaining spinach and cook, covered, stirring occasionally, until all spinach is wilted but still bright green, 3 to 5 minutes. Off heat, transfer 1½ cups greens mixture to blender. Add bread, water, 1 teaspoon sumac, and remaining ½ teaspoon salt. Process until smooth puree forms, about 1 minute, scraping sides of blender jar as needed. Stir puree into skillet and smooth into even layer.

4. Using back of spoon, make 8 shallow indentations (about 1 inch wide) in surface of greens (seven around perimeter and one in center). Crack 1 egg into each indentation (which will hold yolk in place but not fully contain egg). Spoon greens over edges of egg whites so whites are partially covered and yolks are exposed.

5. Bring to simmer over medium heat. Cover and cook until yolks film over, 3 to 5 minutes, adjusting heat to maintain gentle simmer. Continue to cook, covered, until whites are softly but uniformly set (if skillet is shaken lightly, each egg should jiggle as single unit), 1 to 2 minutes longer. Off heat, sprinkle with goat cheese, remaining 2 tablespoons parsley, and remaining ½ teaspoon sumac. Season with salt to taste and serve, passing bread separately.

Microwave-Fried Garlic

Makes ½ cup • Total time: 20 minutes

½ cup thinly sliced garlic
½ cup vegetable oil
1 teaspoon confectioners' sugar

1. Stir garlic into oil in medium bowl.

2. Microwave for 3 minutes. If garlic hasn't begun to brown, stir and microwave 90 seconds longer.

3. Repeat stirring and microwaving in 30-second increments until slices are golden brown, keeping in mind that garlic will continue to darken and crisp as it cools.

4. Using slotted spoon, transfer garlic to paper towel–lined plate. Dust garlic with sugar (to offset any bitterness) and season it with salt to taste. (Fried garlic can be stored in airtight container at room temperature for up to 2 days.)

SEASON 23

Simple Cheese Quiche

Serves 6 to 8 • Total Time: 1½ hours, plus 1½ hours chilling and resting

Why This Recipe Works Our ideal quiche has a tender, buttery pastry case embracing a velvety-smooth custard that is neither too rich nor too lean. We tested numerous combinations of dairy and eggs to find the perfect combination. The baking temperature was equally important; 350 degrees was low enough to set the custard gently and hot enough to brown the top before the filling dried out and became rubbery. To keep the crust from becoming soggy, we parbaked it before adding the filling. To avoid spilling the custard, we set the parbaked crust in the oven before pouring the custard into the pastry shell. For perfectly baked quiche every time, we pulled it out of the oven when it was still slightly soft and allowed it to set up as it cooled.

> *Be sure to add the custard to the pie shell while the crust is still warm so that the quiche will bake evenly. You can substitute other fresh herbs, such as thyme, tarragon, marjoram, or parsley, for the chives.*

1 recipe single-crust pie dough (page 630), rolled into 12-inch round
5 large eggs
2 cups half-and-half

¼ teaspoon table salt
¼ teaspoon pepper
4 ounces cheddar cheese, shredded (1 cup)
1 tablespoon minced fresh chives

1. Adjust oven rack to middle position and heat oven to 375 degrees. Grease 10-inch cast-iron skillet. Roll crust loosely around rolling pin and gently unroll it onto prepared skillet. Ease crust into skillet by gently lifting and supporting edge of dough with your hand while pressing into skillet bottom and corners with your other hand. Tuck ½ inch of dough underneath itself to form tidy, even edge that lies against sides of skillet. Press tucked edge against sides of skillet using index finger to create attractive fluted rim. Wrap skillet loosely in plastic wrap and freeze until dough is firm, about 30 minutes.

2. Line pie crust with double layer of aluminum foil, covering edges, and fill with pie weights. Transfer skillet to oven and bake until pie dough looks dry and is pale in color, 25 to 30 minutes. Using pot holders, transfer skillet to wire rack and remove weights and foil. Reduce oven temperature to 350 degrees.

3. Beat eggs, half-and-half, salt, and pepper with fork in 4-cup liquid measuring cup. Stir in cheddar. Being careful of hot skillet handle, return skillet to oven. Carefully pour egg mixture into shell until it reaches about ½ inch from top edge of crust (you may have extra egg mixture).

4. Bake quiche until center is set and knife inserted 1-inch from edge comes out clean, about 30 minutes. Let quiche cool for at least 1 hour before sprinkling with chives and serving.

Breakfast Strata with Spinach and Gruyère

Serves 6 • **Total Time: 2½ hours, plus 1 hour 20 minutes chilling and standing**

Why This Recipe Works A classic breakfast dish, strata is easy to prepare, presents a variety of flavors, can feed a crowd and, perhaps best of all, can (and indeed should) be made ahead of time. Too often, though, it is overloaded with fillings; we wanted a savory bread pudding with a balanced, well-seasoned filling. Recipes recommend all kinds of bread to use; we liked supermarket French or Italian loaves, which were neutral in flavor but had a sturdy texture. Rather than cubing the bread, which is often recommended, we sliced it to retain the layered quality of the dish and let the slices dry slightly (stale bread held up better than fresh). We used whole eggs and half-and-half for the custard, with a tad more dairy than eggs, and increased the amount of custard to saturate the bread more fully. A surprisingly successful addition to the custard was white wine, which we reduced to evaporate the alcohol; it brightened all the flavors. A key to ensuring cohesiveness in the strata was weighting it while it rested for at least 1 hour; this way, every piece of bread absorbed some custard. We kept our fillings minimal so they wouldn't overwhelm the bread and custard, and we sautéed the filling ingredients before adding them to the casserole to keep moisture from turning the dish watery.

> *To weigh down the assembled strata, use two 1-pound boxes of sugar, laid side by side over the plastic-covered surface. To double this recipe, use a 13 by 9-inch baking dish greased with 1½ tablespoons butter and increase the baking time in step 5 to 1 hour and 20 minutes.*

8–10 (½-inch-thick) slices supermarket French or Italian bread

5 tablespoons unsalted butter, softened, divided

4 shallots, minced (about ½ cup)

1 (10-ounce) package frozen chopped spinach, thawed and squeezed dry

½ cup dry white wine

6 ounces Gruyère cheese, shredded (1½ cups), divided

6 large eggs

1¾ cups half-and-half

1 teaspoon table salt

Pinch pepper

1. Adjust oven rack to middle position and heat oven to 225 degrees. Arrange bread in single layer on rimmed baking sheet and bake until dry and crisp, about

40 minutes, turning slices over halfway through baking time. (Alternatively, leave slices out overnight to dry.) Let bread cool completely, then spread butter evenly over 1 side of each bread slice, using 2 tablespoons butter; set aside.

2. Heat 2 tablespoons butter in 10-inch nonstick skillet over medium heat. Add shallots and cook until softened, about 3 minutes. Add spinach and season with salt and pepper; cook until spinach is warm, about 2 minutes. Transfer to medium bowl and set aside. Add wine to skillet, increase heat to medium-high, and simmer until reduced to ¼ cup, 2 to 3 minutes; set aside.

3. Butter 8-inch square baking dish with remaining 1 tablespoon butter; arrange half of bread slices, buttered side up, in single layer in dish. Sprinkle half of spinach mixture, then ½ cup Gruyère, evenly over bread slices. Arrange remaining bread slices in single layer over cheese; sprinkle remaining spinach mixture and ½ cup Gruyère evenly over bread. Whisk eggs in medium bowl until combined; whisk in reduced wine, half-and-half, salt, and pepper. Pour egg mixture evenly over bread layers.

4. Wrap strata tightly with plastic wrap, pressing wrap against surface of strata. Weigh strata down and refrigerate for at least 1 hour or up to 24 hours.

5. Remove dish from refrigerator and let stand at room temperature for 20 minutes. Meanwhile, adjust oven rack to middle position and heat oven to 325 degrees. Uncover strata and sprinkle remaining ½ cup Gruyère evenly over surface; bake until both edges and center are puffed and edges have pulled away slightly from sides of dish, 50 to 55 minutes. Let cool on wire rack for 5 minutes and serve.

French Toast

Serves 4 • **Total Time: 1½ hours**

Why This Recipe Works When it comes to French toast, the results can be hardly worth the trouble. The bread is soggy, too eggy, or just plain bland. We wanted to come up with French toast that's crisp on the outside and soft and puffy on the inside, with rich, custard-like flavor every time. We first focused on determining which type of bread fared best in a typical batter made with milk and eggs. Tasters eliminated French and Italian breads for being chewy. We then turned to white sandwich bread, which comes in two kinds: regular and hearty. Regular bread was gloppy both inside and out. Hearty bread crisped up nicely on the outside, but still had mushiness. Drying out the bread in a low oven, however, produced French toast that was crisp on the outside and velvety on the inside. As for flavor, tasters thought the French toast tasted overly eggy. We recalled a recipe that required bread dipped in milk mixed with just yolks, versus whole eggs. The yolks-only soaking liquid made a huge difference, turning the taste rich and custard-like. Research revealed that most of the flavor in eggs comes not from the yolk but from the sulfur compounds in the whites, so problem solved. For flavorings, we settled on cinnamon, vanilla, and brown sugar. For nutty butter flavor, we incorporated melted butter into the soaking liquid, warming the milk first to prevent the butter from solidifying. A final bonus—the recipe worked just as well with challah.

For best results, choose a firm sandwich bread, such as Arnold Country White or Pepperidge Farm Farmhouse Hearty White, or a good challah. Thomas' English Muffin Toasting Bread also works well. To prevent the butter from clumping during mixing, warm the milk in a microwave or small saucepan until warm to the touch (about 80 degrees). The French toast can be cooked all at once on an electric griddle, but may take an extra 2 to 3 minutes per side. Set the griddle temperature to 350 degrees and use the entire amount of butter for cooking. Serve with warm maple syrup.

8 large slices high-quality hearty white sandwich bread or challah
1½ cups whole milk, warmed
3 large egg yolks
3 tablespoons light brown sugar
2 tablespoons unsalted butter, melted, plus 2 tablespoons for cooking
1 tablespoon vanilla extract
½ teaspoon ground cinnamon
¼ teaspoon table salt

1. Adjust oven rack to middle position and heat oven to 300 degrees. Place bread on wire rack set over rimmed baking sheet. Bake bread until almost dry throughout (center should remain slightly moist), about 16 minutes, flipping slices halfway through cooking. Remove bread from rack and let cool for 5 minutes. Return baking sheet with wire rack to oven and reduce temperature to 200 degrees.

2. Whisk milk, egg yolks, sugar, 2 tablespoons melted butter, vanilla, cinnamon, and salt in large bowl until well blended. Transfer mixture to 13 by 9-inch baking pan.

3. Soak bread in milk mixture until saturated but not falling apart, 20 seconds per side. Using firm slotted spatula, pick up 1 bread slice and allow excess milk mixture to drip off; repeat with remaining slices. Place soaked bread on another baking sheet or platter.

4. Melt ½ tablespoon of butter in 12-inch skillet over medium-low heat. Use slotted spatula to transfer 2 slices of soaked bread to skillet and cook until golden brown, 3 to 4 minutes. Flip and continue to cook until second side is golden brown, 3 to 4 minutes longer. (If toast is cooking too quickly, reduce heat slightly.) Transfer to baking sheet in oven. Wipe out skillet with paper towels. Repeat cooking with remaining bread, 2 pieces at a time, adding ½ tablespoon more butter for each batch. Serve warm.

Easy Pancakes

Makes sixteen 4-inch pancakes
Total Time: 45 minutes

Why This Recipe Works Everyone loves sitting down to a plate of fluffy, golden, flavorful pancakes, but making them is another matter. Nobody wants to run out for buttermilk before the first meal of the day, never mind haul out (and then clean) their stand mixer to whip egg whites. That's where box mixes come in, but their convenience is hardly worth the results they deliver: rubbery pancakes with a Styrofoam-like flavor. We wanted tender, fluffy, flavorful pancakes that were simple to make using pantry-friendly ingredients and basic kitchen tools. To make them tall and fluffy, we prepared a thick batter by using a relatively small amount of liquid and lots of baking powder. We also mixed the batter minimally to ensure that lumpy pockets of flour remained, and we let the batter rest briefly, allowing the flour pockets to hydrate slightly. Sugar, vanilla, and baking soda provided sweetness, depth, and saline tang, respectively.

> *The pancakes can be cooked on an electric griddle set to 350 degrees. They can be held in a preheated 200-degree oven on a wire rack set in a rimmed baking sheet. Serve with salted butter and maple syrup or with a flavored butter (recipes follow).*

  2   cups (10 ounces) all-purpose flour
  3   tablespoons sugar
  4   teaspoons baking powder
  ½   teaspoon baking soda
  1   teaspoon table salt
  2   large eggs
  ¼   cup plus 1 teaspoon vegetable oil, divided
  1½ cups milk
  ½   teaspoon vanilla extract

1. Whisk flour, sugar, baking powder, baking soda, and salt together in large bowl. Whisk eggs and ¼ cup oil in second medium bowl until well combined. Whisk milk and vanilla into egg mixture. Add egg mixture to flour mixture and stir gently until just combined (batter should remain lumpy with few streaks of flour). Let batter sit for 10 minutes before cooking.

2. Heat ½ teaspoon oil in 12-inch nonstick skillet over medium-low heat until shimmering. Using paper towels, carefully wipe out oil, leaving thin film on bottom and sides of skillet. Drop 1 tablespoon batter in center of skillet. If pancake is pale golden brown after 1 minute, skillet is ready. If it is too light or too dark, adjust heat accordingly.

3. Using ¼-cup dry measuring cup, portion batter into skillet in 3 places, leaving 2 inches between portions. If necessary, gently spread batter into 4-inch round. Cook until edges are set, first sides are golden brown, and bubbles on surface are just beginning to break, 2 to 3 minutes. Using thin, wide spatula, flip pancakes and continue to cook until second sides are golden brown, 1 to 2 minutes longer. Serve. Repeat with remaining batter, using remaining ½ teaspoon oil as necessary.

BUTTERS
Orange-Almond Butter
Makes ½ cup   •   Total Time: 10 minutes
Do not use buckwheat honey; its intense flavor will overwhelm the other flavors.

  8   tablespoons unsalted butter, cut into
      ¼-inch pieces, divided
  2   teaspoons grated orange zest
  2   teaspoons honey
  ¼   teaspoon almond extract
  ⅛   teaspoon table salt

Microwave 2 tablespoons butter in medium bowl until melted, about 1 minute. Stir in orange zest, honey, almond extract, salt, and remaining 6 tablespoons butter. Let mixture stand for 2 minutes. Whisk until smooth. (Butter can be refrigerated for up to 3 days.)

Ginger-Molasses Butter
Makes ½ cup   •   Total Time: 10 minutes
Do not use blackstrap molasses; its intense flavor will overwhelm the other flavors.

  8   tablespoons unsalted butter, cut into
      ¼-inch pieces, divided
  2   teaspoons molasses
  1   teaspoon grated fresh ginger
  ⅛   teaspoon table salt

Microwave 2 tablespoons butter in medium bowl until melted, about 1 minute. Stir in molasses, ginger, salt, and remaining 6 tablespoons butter. Let mixture stand for 2 minutes. Whisk until smooth. (Butter can be refrigerated for up to 3 days.)

Deluxe Blueberry Pancakes

Deluxe Blueberry Pancakes

Makes 12 pancakes • **Total Time: 45 minutes**

Why This Recipe Works To take lazy summer breakfasts to a new level of luxury, we paired sweet-tart, high-season blueberries with sweet, malty pancakes that had plenty of cushiony fluff. A combination of buttermilk and malted milk powder upgraded the batter's flavor and complexity. The former added tang and interacted with the baking soda to provide better lift; the latter boosted the lactic sweetness and contributed a faint roasty note that complemented the bursts of punchy, tart berries. Stirring melted butter (rather than vegetable oil) into the batter and frying the pancakes in more butter made for rich-tasting pancakes with lightly crispy edges. Folding the berries into the batter rather than dropping them onto the portioned pancakes ensured that they were encased in the crumb instead of sitting on the surface, where they might burn when the pancakes were flipped.

This recipe requires the viscosity of buttermilk. You can substitute ⅔ cup of plain Greek yogurt (any fat level) and 1⅓ cups of water for the buttermilk; do not use buttermilk powder or a mixture of milk and lemon juice. For the best results, weigh the flour. An electric griddle set at 325 degrees can be used in place of a skillet; if using a large griddle, cook six pancakes at a time in 1 tablespoon of butter. We like serving these pancakes with salted butter and maple syrup.

 2 tablespoons unsalted butter, plus 3 tablespoons melted and cooled slightly
 2 cups (10 ounces) all-purpose flour
 3 tablespoons malted milk powder
 2 tablespoons sugar
 2 teaspoons baking powder
 ½ teaspoon baking soda
 ½ teaspoon table salt
 2 cups buttermilk
 1 large egg
 7½ ounces (1½ cups) blueberries
 ½ teaspoon vegetable oil

1. If planning on serving all pancakes at once, set wire rack in rimmed baking sheet and heat oven to 200 degrees. Cut 2 tablespoons butter into ½-tablespoon pieces and set aside. Whisk flour, milk powder, sugar, baking powder, baking soda, and salt together in medium bowl. Whisk buttermilk, egg, and melted butter together in second medium bowl (it's OK if butter forms clumps). Make well in center of flour mixture and add buttermilk mixture; whisk until just combined (a few lumps should remain). Fold in blueberries.

2. Heat oil in 12-inch nonstick skillet over medium-low heat until shimmering. Using paper towels, carefully wipe out oil, leaving thin film on bottom and sides of skillet. Drop 1 tablespoon batter in center of skillet. If pancake is pale golden brown after 1 minute, skillet is ready. If it is too light or too dark, adjust heat accordingly. Discard pancake.

3. Melt ½ tablespoon butter in now-empty skillet and use spatula to spread over surface. When butter is sizzling, use ⅓-cup dry measuring cup or slightly mounded 2-ounce (#16) portion scoop to portion batter into skillet in 3 places. Using back of cup or scoop, gently spread each portion into 4½-inch round. Cook until edges are set and first side is deep golden brown (coloring will not be even), 2 to 3 minutes. Using thin, wide spatula, flip pancakes and continue to cook until bottoms are just set, about 1 minute longer. Gently slide pancakes around skillet to collect butter. Cook until second sides are deep golden brown, 1 to 1½ minutes. Serve pancakes immediately, or transfer to prepared wire rack and place in oven to keep warm. Repeat with remaining butter and batter in 3 batches.

100 Percent Whole-Wheat Pancakes

Makes 15 pancakes • **Total Time: 45 minutes**

Why This Recipe Works Most recipes for whole-wheat pancakes call for a mix of white and whole-wheat flours, and a host of extra flavorings. Why not just whole-wheat flour? We discovered that using all whole-wheat flour actually delivers light, fluffy, and tender pancakes—not the dense cakes you'd imagine—because whole-wheat flour contains slightly less gluten-forming protein than white flour and because the bran in whole-wheat flour cuts through any gluten strands that do form. Recipes for pancakes made with white flour advise undermixing to avoid dense, tough pancakes, but with whole-wheat flour we were guaranteed light and tender cakes even as we whisked our batter to a smooth consistency. We saw no need to cover up whole wheat's natural flavor with other add-ins; its earthy, nutty taste proved to be the perfect complement to maple syrup.

An electric griddle set at 350 degrees can be used in place of a skillet. If substituting buttermilk powder and water for fresh buttermilk, use only 2 cups of water to prevent the pancakes from being too wet. To ensure the best flavor, use either recently purchased whole-wheat flour or flour that has been stored in the freezer for less than 12 months. Serve with maple syrup and butter.

2 cups (11 ounces) whole-wheat flour
2 tablespoons sugar
1½ teaspoons baking powder
½ teaspoon baking soda
¾ teaspoon table salt
2¼ cups buttermilk
5 tablespoons plus 2 teaspoons vegetable oil, divided
2 large eggs

1. Adjust oven rack to middle position and heat oven to 200 degrees. Spray wire rack set in rimmed baking sheet with vegetable oil spray; place in oven.

2. Whisk flour, sugar, baking powder, baking soda, and salt together in medium bowl. Whisk buttermilk, 5 tablespoons oil, and eggs together in second medium bowl. Make well in center of flour mixture and pour in buttermilk mixture; whisk until smooth. (Mixture will be thick; do not add more buttermilk.)

3. Heat 1 teaspoon oil in 12-inch nonstick skillet over medium heat until shimmering. Using paper towels, carefully wipe out oil, leaving thin film on bottom and sides of pan. Using ¼-cup dry measuring cup or 2-ounce ladle, portion batter into pan in 3 places. Gently spread each portion into 4½-inch round. Cook until edges are set, first side is golden brown, and bubbles on surface are just beginning to break, 2 to 3 minutes. Using thin, wide spatula, flip pancakes and continue to cook until second side is golden brown, 1 to 2 minutes longer. Serve pancakes immediately or transfer to wire rack in oven. Repeat with remaining batter, using remaining 1 teaspoon oil as necessary.

SEASON 18

German Pancake

Serves 4 • Total Time: 50 minutes

Why This Recipe Works The German pancake, sometimes called a Dutch baby, is a study in contrasts: The edge of the skillet-size breakfast specialty puffs dramatically to form a tall, crispy rim with a texture similar to that of a popover while the base remains flat, custardy, and tender, like a thick crepe. Our German pancake achieves its

dramatic appearance and contrasting textures thanks to a few test kitchen tricks. First, we mixed up a simple batter containing just the right amounts of eggs, flour, and milk to produce a pancake with crispy yet tender edges and a custardy center. To produce a tall, puffy rim and an even, substantial center, we started the pancake in a cold oven and then turned the heat to 375 degrees. This allowed the center of the pancake to begin to set up before the rim got hot enough to puff up. Finally, we put fruit on as a topping rather than baking it into the pancake. Without fruit to weigh things down, the pancake puffed dramatically and its texture remained delicate.

A traditional 12-inch skillet can be used in place of the nonstick skillet; coat it lightly with vegetable oil spray before using. As an alternative to sugar and lemon juice, serve the pancake with maple syrup or our Brown Sugar–Apple Topping (recipe follows).

1¾ cups (8¾ ounces) all-purpose flour
¼ cup (1¾ ounces) sugar, divided
1 tablespoon grated lemon zest plus 1 tablespoon juice
½ teaspoon table salt
⅛ teaspoon ground nutmeg
1½ cups milk
6 large eggs
1½ teaspoons vanilla extract
3 tablespoons unsalted butter

1. Whisk flour, 3 tablespoons sugar, lemon zest, salt, and nutmeg together in large bowl. Whisk milk, eggs, and vanilla together in second bowl. Whisk two-thirds of milk mixture into flour mixture until no lumps remain, then slowly whisk in remaining milk mixture until smooth.

2. Adjust oven rack to lower-middle position. Melt butter in 12-inch ovensafe nonstick skillet over medium-low heat. Add batter to skillet, immediately transfer to oven, and set oven to 375 degrees. Bake until edges are deep golden brown and center is beginning to brown, 30 to 35 minutes.

3. Transfer skillet to wire rack and sprinkle pancake with lemon juice and remaining 1 tablespoon sugar. Gently transfer pancake to cutting board, cut into wedges, and serve.

TOPPING
Brown Sugar–Apple Topping
Makes 2 cups • Total Time: 25 minutes
You can substitute Honeycrisp or Fuji apples for the Braeburn apples, if desired.

- 2 tablespoons unsalted butter
- 1/3 cup water
- 1/4 cup packed (1¾ ounces) brown sugar
- 1/4 teaspoon ground cinnamon
- 1/8 teaspoon table salt
- 1¼ pounds Braeburn apples (3 to 4 apples), peeled, cored, halved, and cut into ½-inch-thick wedges, wedges halved crosswise

Melt butter in 12-inch skillet over medium heat. Add water, sugar, cinnamon, and salt and whisk until sugar dissolves. Add apples, increase heat to medium-high, and bring to simmer. Cover and cook, stirring occasionally, for 5 minutes. Uncover and continue to cook until apples are translucent and just tender and sauce is thickened, 5 to 7 minutes longer. Transfer to bowl and serve. (Topping can be refrigerated for up to 2 days.)

SEASON 11
Buttermilk Waffles

**Makes eight 7-inch round waffles
Total Time: 40 minutes**

Why This Recipe Works Most waffle recipes are time-consuming affairs. We wanted waffles with a crisp, golden-brown, dimpled crust surrounding a moist, fluffy interior, but for rushed morning schedules, we wanted this recipe to require little more than measuring out some flour and cracking an egg. To get crisp, the exterior of a waffle must first become dry, but moist steam racing past the crisping waffle as it cooks slows down the process. We needed a drier batter with plenty of leavening oomph. To do this, we took a cue from Japanese tempura batters, which often use seltzer or club soda in place of still water. The

tiny bubbles of carbon dioxide released from the water inflate the batter the same way as a chemical leavener—minus the metallic taste that baking soda and powder sometimes impart. We replaced the buttermilk in our pancake recipe with a mixture of seltzer and powdered buttermilk. These waffles were incredibly light, but not as crisp as we wanted. Because butter contains water, the melted butter in our batter was imparting moisture to the waffles, preventing them from crisping. When we replaced the melted butter with oil, the delicious result was a wonderfully crisp texture along with excellent flavor.

While the waffles can be eaten directly from the waffle iron, they will have a crispier exterior if rested in a warm oven for 10 minutes. Buttermilk powder is available in most supermarkets and is generally located near the dried milk products or in the baking aisle (leftover powder can be kept in the refrigerator for up to a year). Seltzer or club soda gives these waffles their light texture; use a freshly opened container for maximum lift. Avoid Perrier, which is not bubbly enough. Serve with butter and warm maple syrup.

- 2 cups (10 ounces) unbleached all-purpose flour
- 1/2 cup dried buttermilk powder
- 1 tablespoon sugar
- 3/4 teaspoon table salt
- 1/2 teaspoon baking soda
- 1/2 cup sour cream
- 2 large eggs
- 1/4 cup vegetable oil
- 1/4 teaspoon vanilla extract
- 1¼ cups unflavored seltzer water or club soda

1. Adjust oven rack to middle position and heat oven to 250 degrees. Set wire rack over rimmed baking sheet and place baking sheet in oven. Whisk flour, buttermilk powder, sugar, salt, and baking soda in large bowl to combine. Whisk sour cream, eggs, oil, and vanilla in medium bowl to combine. Gently stir seltzer into wet ingredients. Make well in center of dry ingredients and pour in wet ingredients. Gently stir until just combined. Batter should remain slightly lumpy with streaks of flour.

2. Heat waffle iron and bake waffles according to manufacturer's instructions (use about ⅓ cup for 7-inch round iron). Transfer waffles to rack in warm oven and hold for up to 10 minutes before serving.

SEASON 21

Yeasted Waffles

Makes six 7-inch round waffles or four 9-inch square waffles • Total Time: 30 minutes, plus 12 hours rising

Why This Recipe Works Raised waffles sound old-fashioned and require advance preparation, but they are crisp, tasty, and easy to prepare. A tiny bit of planning makes our raised waffle recipe easy to have ready in the morning. We wanted yeasted waffles that were creamy and airy, tangy, and refined and complex. We settled on all-purpose flour, found the right amount of yeast to provide pleasant tang, and added a full stick of melted butter for rich flavor. Refrigerating the batter overnight kept the growth of the yeast under control and produced waffles with superior flavor. All we had to do in the morning was heat up the waffle iron.

The batter must be made 12 to 24 hours in advance. We prefer the texture of the waffles made in a classic waffle iron, but a Belgian waffle iron will work, though it will make fewer waffles. The waffles are best served fresh from the iron but can be held in an oven until all of the batter is used. As you make the waffles, place them on a wire rack set in a baking sheet, cover them with a clean dish towel, and place the baking sheet in a 200-degree oven. When the final waffle is in the iron, remove the towel to allow the waffles to crisp for a few minutes. These waffles are quite rich; buttering them before eating is not compulsory and, to some, may even be superfluous.

1¾ cups milk
8 tablespoons unsalted butter, cut into 8 pieces
2 cups (10 ounces) all-purpose flour
1 tablespoon sugar
1½ teaspoons instant or rapid-rise yeast
1 teaspoon table salt
2 large eggs
1 teaspoon vanilla extract

1. Heat milk and butter in small saucepan over medium-low heat until butter is melted, 3 to 5 minutes. Let mixture cool until warm to touch.

2. Whisk flour, sugar, yeast, and salt together in large bowl. In small bowl, whisk eggs and vanilla together. Gradually whisk warm milk mixture into flour mixture until smooth, then whisk in egg mixture. Scrape down bowl with rubber spatula, cover tightly with plastic wrap, and refrigerate for at least 12 hours or up to 24 hours.

3. Adjust oven rack to middle position and heat oven to 200 degrees. Set wire rack in rimmed baking sheet and place in oven. Heat waffle iron according to manufacturer's instructions. Remove batter from refrigerator when waffle iron is hot (batter will be foamy and doubled in size). Whisk batter to recombine (batter will deflate).

4. Cook waffles according to manufacturer's instructions (use about ½ cup batter for 7-inch round iron and about 1 cup batter for 9-inch square iron). Serve immediately or transfer to wire rack in oven to keep warm while cooking remaining waffles.

SEASON 25

Liège Waffles

Makes 8 waffles • Total Time: 1¼ hours, plus 9½ to 10 hours chilling and rising

Why This Recipe Works Unlike Brussels or American waffles, made from batter and typically eaten for breakfast, the Liège kind traditionally are handheld treats for eating any time of day. They're made from yeasted dough that's scented with vanilla, enriched with plenty of fat (usually butter), and studded with chunks of pearl sugar. As the waffle bakes, sugar near the surface melts and then caramelizes against the hot iron, forming a satisfyingly crunchy crust. Using minimal liquid in the dough ensured that the waffles stayed crisp, and resting the dough overnight encouraged gluten development that rendered the crumb properly feathery, with subtle elastic chew.

Dredging the risen dough portions in granulated sugar helped the waffles caramelize all over as they baked, and calibrating the iron temperature to 360 to 365 degrees ensured that the dough cooked through and browned simultaneously.

You'll need a Belgian waffle iron for this recipe. Belgian pearl sugar is available at some supermarkets or online; do not use smaller Swedish pearl sugar. Unlike American waffles, these are meant to be served warm as a snack or a dessert, not as breakfast. To serve them all at once, hold the waffles on a wire rack set in a rimmed baking sheet in a 200-degree oven while the others finish cooking.

- 2 cups (11 ounces) bread flour
- 1½ tablespoons granulated sugar plus ⅓ cup for coating dough
- 2 teaspoons instant or rapid-rise yeast
- 1 teaspoon table salt
- 12 tablespoons unsalted butter, cut into 12 pieces and softened
- ½ cup warm milk (110 degrees)
- 1 large egg
- 1 tablespoon vanilla extract
- 1 cup (5½ ounces) Belgian pearl sugar

1. Whisk flour, 1½ tablespoons granulated sugar, yeast, and salt together in bowl of stand mixer. Add butter, milk, egg, and vanilla. Fit stand mixer with dough hook and mix on low speed until all flour is moistened, about 1 minute. Increase speed to medium-low and continue to mix until dough is smooth and elastic, 12 to 15 minutes, scraping down bowl halfway through mixing (dough will be very soft and will stick to sides and bottom of bowl). Transfer to medium bowl. Cover and refrigerate for at least 8 hours or up to 48 hours.

2. Line rimmed baking sheet with parchment paper and spray lightly with vegetable oil spray. Transfer dough to counter and flatten to about 1 inch thickness (dough will be firm). Spread pearl sugar over dough and press into dough. Beginning with edge nearest you, roll dough into cylinder, enclosing sugar. Knead dough until sugar is evenly incorporated (a bench scraper is helpful for releasing dough from counter; if pieces of sugar pop out of dough, press them back in).

3. Divide dough into 8 equal portions (each should weigh just over 3½ ounces). Roll 1 portion between your hands to form 4-inch-long sausage shape. Pat into rough 4 by 2-inch oval. Transfer to prepared baking sheet. Repeat with remaining portions. Cover and let rise until puffy and room temperature, 1½ to 2 hours.

4. Heat Belgian waffle iron to 360 degrees (drop of water on iron will skitter across surface and take 4 to 5 seconds to evaporate). As iron heats, spread remaining ⅓ cup granulated sugar in small dish. Place 1 dough portion in sugar and turn to coat on all sides. Transfer to center of waffle iron and close lid so it rests on dough but do not press down or lock. Cook until waffle is deep golden brown and surface sugar is beginning to caramelize, about 2½ minutes. Using 2 forks, spear waffle on left and right sides; lift, and transfer to wire rack to cool (surface sugar will be hot; do not handle for at least 90 seconds). Repeat with remaining dough and serve.

SEASON 25

Crepes with Berries and Apricot Beurre Monté

Serves 4 • Total Time: 1 hour

Why This Recipe Works Beurre monté, emulsified melted butter, is a classic French preparation that gilds everything it's drizzled over, adding richness and a glossy appearance. It can also be used as a creamy sauce base for a range of savory or sweet seasonings. Vigorously whisking cold butter into simmering water broke up the butterfat into droplets that dispersed throughout the water, establishing a thick, creamy emulsion. Whisking apricot preserves, peach schnapps, and lemon juice into the beurre monté produced a rich, easy-to-make sauce that paired especially well with crepes and berries. Preheating the pan over a low flame ensured that it was thoroughly heated—a must for crepes that cook and brown properly. We poured the batter into the pan and used a tilt-and-shake method to help it distribute evenly across the cooking surface.

To allow for practice, this recipe yields 10 crepes; only eight are needed for serving. Remove the berries from the fridge at least 1 hour before serving. The beurre monté can be covered and kept warm over your stove's lowest setting for up to 1 hour; it will break if simmered for an extended period of time. Beurre monté cannot be cooled and reheated.

Crepes

- ½ teaspoon vegetable oil
- 1 cup (5 ounces) all-purpose flour
- 1 teaspoon sugar
- ½ teaspoon kosher salt
- 1½ cups milk
- 3 large eggs
- 2 tablespoons unsalted butter, melted and cooled

Beurre Monté

- 3 tablespoons water
- 8 tablespoons unsalted butter, cut into 8 pieces and chilled
- 1½ tablespoons apricot preserves
- 1½ teaspoons peach schnapps
- 1 teaspoon lemon juice
- ⅛ teaspoon kosher salt

- 4 ounces (1 cup) fresh raspberries, blackberries, or blueberries, room temperature

1. For the crepes: Place oil in 12-inch nonstick skillet and heat over low heat for at least 10 minutes. While skillet is heating, whisk flour, sugar, and salt together in medium bowl. In separate bowl, whisk together milk and eggs. Add half of milk mixture to dry ingredients and whisk until smooth. Whisk in melted butter. Whisk in remaining milk mixture until smooth.

2. Using paper towel, wipe out skillet, leaving thin film of oil on bottom and sides. Increase heat to medium and let skillet heat for 1 minute. After 1 minute, test heat of skillet by placing 1 teaspoon batter in center and cook for 20 seconds. If mini crepe is golden brown on bottom, skillet is properly heated. If it is too light or too dark, adjust heat accordingly and retest.

3. Pour ¼ cup batter into pan and tilt and shake gently until batter evenly covers bottom of pan. Cook crepe without moving it until top surface is dry and crepe starts to brown at edges, loosening crepe from side of pan with rubber spatula, about 25 seconds. Gently slide spatula underneath edge of crepe, grasp edge with your fingertips, and flip crêpe. Cook until second side is lightly spotted, about 20 seconds. Transfer cooked crepe to wire rack. Return pan to heat and heat for 10 seconds before repeating with remaining batter. As crepes are done, stack on wire rack. (Crepes can be covered and refrigerated for up to 2 days.)

4. For the beurre monté: Bring water to simmer in small saucepan over medium-high heat; reduce heat to maintain very gentle simmer. Add 1 piece butter and cook, whisking constantly, until butter is melted, 20 to 30 seconds. Continue to cook, whisking in butter 1 piece at a time until all butter is incorporated and sauce has consistency of thin gravy, 3 to 4 minutes. Whisk in preserves, schnapps, lemon juice, and salt. Reduce heat to lowest possible setting and cover to keep warm.

5. To serve: Transfer crepes to large plate and cover with second plate. Microwave until crepes are warm, 30 to 45 seconds. Arrange crepes on serving plates. Scatter berries over crepes. Whisk sauce vigorously to blend in any butterfat that has collected on surface. Spoon sauce over crepes and serve immediately.

SEASON 23

Congee

Serves 4 to 6 • Total Time: 1 hour

Why This Recipe Works Great congee (Chinese rice porridge) features soft, barely intact grains gently bound by their silky, viscous cooking liquid; the result should be fluid but thick and creamy enough to suspend any toppings. Our formula started with a 13:1 ratio of liquid to long-grain white rice, which produced an appropriately loose porridge (we cut the water with a little chicken broth to give our congee clean flavor with a savory backbone). Then we simmered the rice vigorously to encourage the grains to break down in about 45 minutes (instead of a more typical

Easy-Peel Jammy Eggs

Makes 1 to 6 eggs • Total Time: 15 minutes

This method will yield eggs with runny yolks and fully set whites. Be sure to use large eggs that have no cracks and are cold from the refrigerator and to use a pot that is large enough to hold the eggs in a single layer.

1–6 large eggs

Bring ½ inch water to boil in medium saucepan over medium-high heat. Using tongs, gently place up to 6 eggs in boiling water (eggs will not be submerged). Cover and cook for 8 minutes. Transfer saucepan to sink and run cold water over eggs for 30 seconds to stop cooking. Peel before using.

Microwave-Fried Shallots

Makes ½ cup • Total Time: 20 minutes

Fried shallots deliver bursts of crunch and savory flavor to Congee but they're easy to overcook and require constant stirring. The microwave solves all that.

3 shallots, sliced thin
½ cup vegetable oil

Combine shallots and oil in medium bowl. Microwave for 5 minutes. Stir and continue to microwave 2 minutes longer. Repeat stirring and microwaving in 2-minute increments until beginning to brown, 4 to 6 minutes. Repeat stirring and microwaving in 30-second increments until deep golden brown, 30 seconds to 2 minutes. Using slotted spoon, transfer shallots to paper towel–lined plate; season with salt to taste. Let drain and crisp, about 5 minutes.

90-minute gentle simmer), partially covering the pot to help the contents cook quickly while minimizing evaporation. To prevent the congee from boiling over, we rinsed excess starch from the raw rice and wedged a wooden spoon between the lid and the side of the pot, giving the water bubbles a chance to escape.

For vegetarian congee, substitute water for the chicken broth. Jasmine rice can be substituted for conventional long-grain white rice; do not use basmati. We prefer the distinctive flavor of Chinese black vinegar here; look for it in Asian supermarkets. Congee provides a subtle savory background for flavorful toppings.

¾ cup long-grain white rice
1 cup chicken broth
¾ teaspoon table salt
   Scallions, sliced thin on bias
   Fresh cilantro leaves
   Dry-roasted peanuts, chopped coarse
   Chili oil
   Soy sauce
   Chinese black vinegar

1. Place rice in fine-mesh strainer and rinse under cold running water until water runs clear. Drain well and transfer to Dutch oven. Add broth, salt, and 9 cups water and bring to boil over high heat. Reduce heat to maintain vigorous simmer. Cover pot, tucking wooden spoon horizontally between pot and lid to hold lid ajar. Cook, stirring occasionally, until mixture is thickened, glossy, and reduced by half, 45 to 50 minutes.

2. Serve congee in bowls, passing scallions, cilantro, peanuts, oil, soy sauce, and vinegar separately.

Ten-Minute Steel-Cut Oatmeal

Serves 4 • Total Time: 20 minutes, plus 8 hours soaking

Why This Recipe Works Most oatmeal fans agree that the steel-cut version of the grain offers the best flavor and texture, but many balk at the 40-minute cooking time. We decreased the cooking time to only 10 minutes by stirring the oats into boiling water the night before; the grains hydrated and softened overnight. In the morning, we added more water (or fruit juice or milk) and simmered the mixture for 4 to 6 minutes, until thick and creamy. A brief resting period off the heat ensured the perfect consistency.

The oatmeal will continue to thicken as it cools. If you prefer a looser consistency, thin the oatmeal with boiling water. Customize your oatmeal with toppings such as brown sugar, toasted nuts, maple syrup, or dried fruit.

4 cups water, divided
1 cup steel-cut oats
¼ teaspoon table salt

1. Bring 3 cups water to boil in large saucepan over high heat. Remove pan from heat; stir in oats and salt. Cover pan and let stand overnight.

2. Stir remaining 1 cup water into oats and bring to boil over medium-high heat. Reduce heat to medium and cook, stirring occasionally, until oats are softened but still retain some chew and mixture thickens and resembles warm pudding, 4 to 6 minutes. Remove pan from heat and let stand for 5 minutes. Stir and serve, passing desired toppings separately.

VARIATIONS

Apple-Cinnamon Steel-Cut Oatmeal
Increase salt to ½ teaspoon. Substitute ½ cup apple cider and ½ cup whole milk for water in step 2. Stir ½ cup peeled, grated sweet apple, 2 tablespoons packed dark brown sugar, and ½ teaspoon ground cinnamon into oatmeal with cider and milk. Sprinkle each serving with 2 tablespoons coarsely chopped toasted walnuts.

Carrot-Spice Steel-Cut Oatmeal
Increase salt to ¾ teaspoon. Substitute ½ cup carrot juice and ½ cup whole milk for water in step 2. Stir ½ cup finely grated carrot, ¼ cup packed dark brown sugar, ⅓ cup dried currants, and ½ teaspoon ground cinnamon into oatmeal with carrot juice and milk. Sprinkle each serving with 2 tablespoons coarsely chopped toasted pecans.

SEASON 14

Almond Granola with Dried Fruit

Makes 9 cups • Total Time: 1¼ hours, plus 1 hour cooling

Why This Recipe Works Store-bought granola suffers from many shortcomings. It's often loose and gravelly and/or infuriatingly expensive. We wanted to make our own granola at home, with big, satisfying clusters and crisp texture. The secret was to firmly pack the granola mixture into a rimmed baking sheet before baking. Once baked, we had a granola "bark" that we could break into crunchy lumps of any size.

Chopping the almonds by hand is the first choice for superior texture and crunch. If you prefer not to hand chop, substitute an equal quantity of slivered or sliced almonds. (A food processor does a lousy job of chopping whole nuts evenly.) Use a single type of your favorite dried fruit or a combination. Do not use quick oats.

⅓ cup maple syrup
⅓ cup packed (2⅓ ounces) light brown sugar
4 teaspoons vanilla extract
½ teaspoon table salt
½ cup vegetable oil
5 cups (15 ounces) old-fashioned rolled oats
2 cups (10 ounces) raw almonds, chopped coarse
2 cups raisins or other dried fruit, chopped

1. Adjust oven rack to upper-middle position and heat oven to 325 degrees. Line rimmed baking sheet with parchment paper.

2. Whisk maple syrup, brown sugar, vanilla, and salt in large bowl. Whisk in oil. Fold in oats and almonds until thoroughly coated.

3. Transfer oat mixture to prepared baking sheet and spread across sheet into thin, even layer (about ⅜ inch thick). Using stiff metal spatula, compress oat mixture until very compact. Bake until lightly browned, 40 to 45 minutes, rotating pan once halfway through baking. Let cool on wire rack to room temperature, about 1 hour. Break cooled granola into pieces of desired size. Stir in dried fruit. (Granola can be stored in airtight container for up to 2 weeks.)

VARIATIONS

Spiced Walnut Granola with Dried Apple
Add 2 teaspoons ground cinnamon, 1½ teaspoons ground ginger, ¾ teaspoon ground allspice, ½ teaspoon freshly grated nutmeg, and ½ teaspoon pepper to maple syrup mixture in step 2. Substitute coarsely chopped walnuts for almonds. After granola is broken into pieces, stir in 2 cups chopped dried apples.

Hazelnut Granola with Dried Pear
Substitute coarsely chopped skinned hazelnuts for almonds. After granola is broken into pieces, stir in 2 cups chopped dried pears.

Pecan-Orange Granola with Dried Cranberries
Add 2 tablespoons finely grated orange zest and 2½ teaspoons ground cinnamon to maple syrup mixture in step 2. Substitute coarsely chopped pecans for almonds. After granola is broken into pieces, stir in 2 cups dried cranberries.

Granola with Bark and Bite

"It's hard to believe that a granola recipe can be a game changer, but this recipe has ruined all other granola for me. From overly sweet and expensive store-bought options to dry, pebbly homemade versions, none compare. With big, satisfying clusters of toasty oats and nuts, and a crisp texture that shatters when bitten, this granola checks all the boxes. The key to the likable crispness is the balance of oil and liquid sweetener (in this case maple syrup). When the water in the syrup evaporates in the heat of the oven, the sugars left behind develop into a thin coating on the oats and nuts. But without any fat, the sugar coating will become brittle and dry. A half cup of oil provides a pleasantly crisp coating with a sense of moistness without being greasy. Another important step is the press. Firmly packing the granola mixture into a tight, compact layer before baking creates a single sheet of granola once it is baked. The end result is more of a granola 'bark' that can be broken into clumps of any size."

– Keith

Soups & Stews

Photo: Hot Ukrainian Borscht

Classic Chicken Noodle Soup

Serves 6 to 8 • **Total Time: 2 hours**

Why This Recipe Works Chicken noodle soup is one of the all-time great comfort foods, and homemade broth is a must. We wanted to make it the old-fashioned way—starting with a whole chicken. We began by cutting the chicken, minus the breast, into small pieces to be browned in batches. Cutting the bones exposed more bone marrow, key for both flavor and body. To develop additional flavor, we sweated the browned pieces in a covered pot with an onion, then simmered them for less than half an hour. Now we had a broth that just needed some salt and bay leaves to round out its flavor. We reserved some of the skimmed fat from the broth to sauté aromatics and carrots for the soup, and we added in tender chicken breast pieces that had already been poached in the broth. For extra flavor, we cooked the egg noodles right in the soup pot so they could absorb meaty flavor from the broth. With a final sprinkling of chopped parsley, our chicken noodle soup was complete: rich, homemade broth; moist pieces of chicken; tender vegetables; and perfectly cooked noodles.

> *Make sure to reserve the chicken breast pieces until step 2; they should not be browned. If you use a cleaver, you will be able to cut up the chicken parts quickly. A chef's knife or kitchen shears will also work. Be sure to reserve 2 tablespoons of chicken fat for sautéing the aromatics in step 4; however, if you prefer not to use chicken fat, vegetable oil can be substituted.*

Stock

- 1 tablespoon vegetable oil
- 1 (4-pound) whole chicken, breast removed, split, and reserved; remaining chicken cut into 2-inch pieces
- 1 onion, chopped
- 2 quarts boiling water
- 2 teaspoons table salt
- 2 bay leaves

Soup

- 2 tablespoons chicken fat, reserved from making stock, or vegetable oil
- 1 onion, chopped
- 1 large carrot, peeled and sliced ¼ inch thick
- 1 celery rib, sliced ¼ inch thick
- ½ teaspoon dried thyme
- 3 ounces egg noodles (about 2 cups)
- ¼ cup minced fresh parsley leaves

1. For the stock: Heat oil in Dutch oven over medium-high heat until shimmering. Add half of chicken pieces and cook until lightly browned, about 5 minutes per side. Transfer cooked chicken to bowl and repeat with remaining chicken pieces; transfer to bowl with first batch. Add onion and cook, stirring frequently, until onion is translucent, 3 to 5 minutes. Return chicken pieces to pot. Reduce heat to low, cover, and cook until chicken releases its juices, about 20 minutes.

2. Increase heat to high; add boiling water, reserved chicken breast pieces, salt, and bay leaves. Reduce heat to medium-low and simmer until flavors have blended, about 20 minutes.

3. Remove breast pieces from pot. When cool, remove skin and bones from breast pieces and discard. Shred meat with your fingers or 2 forks and set aside. Strain stock through fine-mesh strainer into container, pressing on solids to extract as much liquid as possible; discard solids. Allow liquid to settle for about 5 minutes and skim off fat; reserve 2 tablespoons, if desired. (Shredded chicken, strained stock, and fat can be refrigerated in separate airtight containers for up to 2 days.)

4. For the soup: Heat reserved chicken fat in large Dutch oven over medium-high heat. Add onion, carrot, and celery and cook until softened, about 5 minutes. Add thyme and reserved stock and simmer until vegetables are tender, 10 to 15 minutes.

5. Add noodles and reserved shredded chicken and cook until just tender, 5 to 8 minutes. Stir in parsley, season with salt and pepper to taste, and serve.

Tortilla Soup

Serves 6 • Total Time: 1½ hours

Why This Recipe Works   This intensely flavored tortilla soup is our quicker version of the traditional dish. We broke the soup down to its three classic components—the flavor base, the chicken stock, and the garnishes—and devised techniques and substitute ingredients that streamlined the recipe. We achieved maximum flavor by composing a puree made from chipotles, tomatoes, onions, garlic, jalapeños, and epazote, and then frying the puree in oil. We then added the puree to canned chicken broth after poaching chicken in it. We easily oven-toasted lightly oiled tortilla strips instead of frying them and served the soup over them topped with a range of traditional garnishes.

> *Despite its somewhat lengthy ingredient list, this recipe is very easy to prepare. To make ahead, complete the soup short of adding the shredded chicken to the pot at the end of step 3. Return the soup to a simmer over medium-high heat before proceeding. The tortilla strips and the garnishes are best prepared the day of serving.*

Tortilla Strips

- 8 (6-inch) corn tortillas, cut into ½-inch-wide strips
- 1 tablespoon vegetable oil

Soup

- 2 bone-in, skin-on split chicken breasts (about 1½ pounds) or 4 bone-in, skin-on chicken thighs (about 1¼ pounds), skin removed and trimmed
- 8 cups chicken broth
- 1 very large white onion (about 1 pound), peeled and quartered, divided
- 4 garlic cloves, peeled, divided
- 2 sprigs fresh epazote or 8 to 10 sprigs fresh cilantro plus 1 sprig fresh oregano
- ½ teaspoon plus ⅛ teaspoon table salt, divided
- 2 tomatoes, cored and quartered
- ½ jalapeño chile
- 1 chipotle chile in adobo sauce, plus up to 1 tablespoon adobo sauce
- 1 tablespoon vegetable oil

Garnishes

- Lime wedges
- Avocado, peeled, pitted, and diced fine
- Cotija cheese, crumbled, or Monterey Jack cheese, diced fine
- Fresh cilantro leaves
- Jalapeño chile, minced
- Crema Mexicana or sour cream

1. **For the tortilla strips:** Adjust oven rack to middle position and heat oven to 425 degrees. Spread tortilla strips on rimmed baking sheet; drizzle with oil and toss until evenly coated. Bake until strips are deep golden brown and crisped, about 14 minutes, rotating pan and shaking strips (to redistribute) halfway through baking. Season strips lightly with salt; transfer to plate lined with several layers of paper towels.

2. **For the soup:** While tortilla strips bake, bring chicken, broth, 2 onion quarters, 2 garlic cloves, epazote, and ½ teaspoon salt to boil over medium-high heat in large saucepan; reduce the heat to low, cover, and simmer until chicken is just cooked through, about 20 minutes. Using tongs, transfer chicken to large plate. Pour broth through fine-mesh strainer; discard solids in strainer. When cool enough to handle, shred chicken into bite-size pieces; discard bones.

3. Puree tomatoes, jalapeño, chipotle chile, 1 teaspoon adobo sauce, remaining 2 onion quarters, and remaining 2 garlic cloves in food processor until smooth, about 20 seconds. Heat oil in Dutch oven over high heat until shimmering; add tomato-onion puree and remaining ⅛ teaspoon salt and cook, stirring frequently, until mixture has darkened in color, about 10 minutes. Stir strained broth into tomato mixture, bring to boil, then reduce heat to low and simmer to blend flavors, about 15 minutes. Taste soup; if desired, add up to 2 teaspoons more adobo sauce. Add shredded chicken and simmer until heated through, about 5 minutes. To serve, place portions of tortilla strips in bottom of individual bowls and ladle soup into the bowls; pass garnishes separately.

The Secret Flavor Booster You've Been Washing Down the Drain

"If you've ever soaked a stew pot in the sink overnight before scrubbing away the browned ring clinging to the sides of the pan, you're guilty of washing away some serious flavor. It's OK! I've been guilty of it too. It wasn't until I was developing my recipe for chicken stew that I had a moment of clarity and saw the error of my ways. Just like the ultrasavory brown bits clinging to the bottom of a pot after you sear meat or aromatics, that ring of brown is a concentrated source of flavor. The ring occurs when water evaporates from the soup or stew and leaves behind proteins and sugars that undergo the Maillard reaction. We like to call it side fond, and you can reclaim it by simply scraping it off the walls and into the food. The benefit is twofold: Your stew is more flavorful and you need less elbow grease to clean the pot. That's a tasty combination."

—Dan

Best Chicken Stew

Serves 6 to 8 • **Total Time: 2½ hours**

Why This Recipe Works While recipes for chicken stew are few and far between, the ones we've come across are either too fussy or too fancy, or seem more soup than stew, with none of the complexity and depth we expect from the latter. We wanted to develop a chicken stew recipe that would satisfy like the beef kind—one with succulent bites of chicken, tender vegetables, and a truly robust gravy. To start, we created an ultraflavorful gravy using chicken wings, which we later discarded. Browning the wings lent deep chicken flavor to the stew, and since wings are more about skin and bones than about meat, discarding them after they'd enriched the gravy didn't seem wasteful. Browning the wings in rendered bacon fat lent porky depth and just a hint of smoke. Soy sauce and anchovy paste, though unusual for chicken stew, lent more savory depth (without making the stew taste salty or fishy). Reducing the liquid at the beginning of cooking and then cooking the stew uncovered further concentrated the flavor. To finish our stew, we added white wine for brightness and a sprinkle of parsley for freshness.

Mashed anchovy fillets (rinsed and dried before mashing) can be used instead of anchovy paste. Use small red potatoes measuring 1½ inches in diameter.

- 2 pounds boneless, skinless chicken thighs, halved crosswise and trimmed
- 3 slices bacon, chopped
- 1 pound chicken wings, halved at joint
- 1 onion, chopped fine
- 1 celery rib, minced
- 2 garlic cloves, minced
- 2 teaspoons anchovy paste
- 1 teaspoon minced fresh thyme
- 5 cups chicken broth, divided
- 1 cup dry white wine, plus extra for seasoning
- 1 tablespoon soy sauce
- 3 tablespoons unsalted butter, cut into 3 pieces
- ⅓ cup all-purpose flour
- 1 pound small red potatoes, unpeeled, quartered
- 4 carrots, peeled and cut into ½-inch pieces
- 2 tablespoons chopped fresh parsley

1. Adjust oven rack to lower-middle position and heat oven to 325 degrees. Arrange chicken thighs on baking sheet and lightly season both sides with salt and pepper; cover with plastic wrap and set aside.

2. Cook bacon in Dutch oven over medium-low heat, stirring occasionally, until crispy, 6 to 8 minutes. Using slotted spoon, transfer bacon to medium bowl. Add chicken wings to pot, increase heat to medium, and cook until well browned on both sides, 10 to 12 minutes; transfer wings to bowl with bacon.

3. Add onion, celery, garlic, anchovy paste, and thyme to fat in pot; cook, stirring occasionally, until dark fond forms on pan bottom, 2 to 4 minutes. Increase heat to high; stir in 1 cup broth, wine, and soy sauce, scraping up any browned bits; and bring to boil. Cook, stirring occasionally, until liquid evaporates and vegetables begin to sizzle again, 12 to 15 minutes. Add butter and stir to melt; sprinkle flour over vegetables and stir to combine. Gradually whisk in remaining 4 cups broth until smooth. Stir in wings and bacon, potatoes, and carrots; bring to simmer. Transfer to oven and cook, uncovered, for 30 minutes, stirring once halfway through cooking.

4. Remove pot from oven. Use wooden spoon to draw gravy up sides of pot and scrape browned fond into stew. Place over high heat, add thighs, and bring to simmer. Return pot to oven, uncovered, and continue to cook, stirring occasionally, until chicken offers no resistance when poked with fork and vegetables are tender, about 45 minutes longer. (Stew can be refrigerated for up to 2 days.)

5. Discard wings and season stew with up to 2 tablespoons extra wine. Season with salt and pepper to taste, sprinkle with parsley, and serve.

Chicken and Sausage Gumbo

Serves 6 • **Total Time: 2 hours**

Why This Recipe Works Most recipes for the beloved Louisiana soup, gumbo, start with a wet roux, a cooked paste of flour and fat that can take an hour or more to make. We streamlined this process by using a dry roux of oven-toasted flour, which gave the same effect as a wet roux but without the oil. To flavor our gumbo we used easy-to-work-with boneless, skinless chicken thighs and andouille sausage, rounding out the dish with garlic, thyme, bay leaves, and spices. We stirred in white vinegar rather than hot sauce at the end for acidity without adding heat to an already well-seasoned dish.

This recipe is engineered for efficiency: Get the flour toasting in the oven and then prep the remaining ingredients before you begin cooking. We strongly recommend using andouille, but in a pinch, kielbasa can be substituted. The salt level of the final dish may vary depending on the brand of sausage, so liberal seasoning with additional salt at the end may be necessary. Serve over white rice.

- 1 cup all-purpose flour
- 1 tablespoon vegetable oil
- 1 onion, chopped fine
- 1 green bell pepper, chopped fine
- 2 celery ribs, chopped fine
- 3 garlic cloves, minced
- 2 bay leaves
- 1 tablespoon minced fresh thyme
- 1 teaspoon paprika
- ½ teaspoon cayenne pepper
- ¼ teaspoon table salt
- ¼ teaspoon pepper
- 4 cups chicken broth, divided
- 2 pounds boneless, skinless chicken thighs, trimmed
- 8 ounces andouille sausage, sliced into ¼-inch-thick half-moons
- 6 scallions, sliced thin
- 1 teaspoon distilled white vinegar
  Hot sauce

1. Adjust oven rack to middle position and heat oven to 425 degrees. Place flour in 12-inch ovensafe skillet and bake, stirring occasionally, until color of ground cinnamon or dark brown sugar, 40 to 55 minutes. (As flour approaches desired

color it will take on a very nutty aroma that will smell faintly of burnt popcorn and it will need to be stirred more frequently.) Transfer flour to medium bowl and cool. (Toasted flour can be stored in airtight container for up to 1 week.)

2. Heat oil in Dutch oven over medium heat until shimmering. Add onion, pepper, and celery and cook, stirring frequently, until softened, 5 to 7 minutes. Stir in garlic, bay leaves, thyme, paprika, cayenne, salt, and pepper and cook until fragrant, about 1 minute. Stir in 2 cups broth. Add chicken thighs in single layer (they will not be completely submerged by liquid) and bring to simmer. Reduce heat to medium-low, cover, and simmer until chicken is fork tender, 15 to 17 minutes. Transfer chicken to plate.

3. Slowly whisk remaining 2 cups broth into toasted flour until thick, batter-like paste forms. (Add broth in small increments to prevent clumps from forming.) Return pot to medium heat and slowly whisk flour paste into gumbo, making sure each addition is incorporated before adding next. Stir sausage into gumbo. Simmer, uncovered, until gumbo thickens slightly, 20 to 25 minutes.

4. Once cool enough to handle, shred chicken into bite-size pieces. Stir chicken and scallions into gumbo. Remove pot from heat and stir in vinegar and season with salt to taste. Discard bay leaves. Serve, passing hot sauce at table. (Gumbo can be refrigerated in airtight container for up to 24 hours).

SEASON 8

White Chicken Chili

Serves 6 to 8 • Total Time: 1½ hours

Why This Recipe Works Chili made with chicken has become popular as a lighter, fresher alternative to the red kind. Though many recipes produce something more akin to chicken and bean soup, we thought there was potential to develop a rich stew-like chili with moist chicken, tender beans, and a complex flavor profile. Ground chicken had a spongy texture and crumbly appearance, so we chose bone-in, skin-on breasts, later shredding the meat and discarding the skin and bones, and used the fat rendered from searing them to cook the aromatics. A single type of chile was one-dimensional; we used a combination of jalapeño, Anaheim, and poblano chiles, which have distinct characteristics that complement one another. Simply sautéing the chiles with the other aromatics left them flat-tasting and too crisp, so we covered the pot and cooked them longer to soften them and deepen their flavors. Using canned cannellini beans circumvented the hassle of dried beans and tasted just as good. We tried thickening the chili with masa harina, which we had used as a thickener in other chili recipes, but the texture and flavor didn't work well here. Instead, we pureed some of the chili mixture, beans, and broth, which made the chili thicker without compromising its flavor. To finish, a minced raw jalapeño stirred in before serving provided a shot of fresh chile flavor.

> *Adjust the heat in this dish by adding the minced ribs and seeds from the jalapeño as directed in step 6. If Anaheim chiles cannot be found, add an additional poblano and jalapeño to the chili. This dish can also be successfully made by substituting chicken thighs for the chicken breasts. If using thighs, increase the cooking time in step 4 to about 40 minutes or until the chicken registers 175 degrees on an instant-read thermometer. Serve the chili with sour cream, tortilla chips, and lime wedges.*

- 3 pounds bone-in, skin-on chicken breast halves, trimmed
- ¾ teaspoon table salt, divided
- ½ teaspoon pepper
- 1 tablespoon vegetable oil
- 3 jalapeño chiles
- 3 poblano chiles, stemmed, seeded, and cut into large pieces
- 3 Anaheim chiles, stemmed, seeded, and cut into large pieces
- 2 onions, cut into large pieces
- 6 garlic cloves, minced
- 1 tablespoon ground cumin
- 1½ teaspoons ground coriander
- 2 (15-ounce) cans cannellini beans, rinsed, divided
- 3 cups chicken broth, divided
- ¼ cup minced fresh cilantro leaves
- 3 tablespoons lime juice (2 limes)
- 4 scallions, white and light green parts sliced thin

1. Sprinkle chicken evenly with ½ teaspoon salt and pepper. Heat oil in Dutch oven over medium-high heat until just smoking. Add chicken, skin side down, and cook without moving until the skin is golden brown, about 4 minutes. Using tongs, turn chicken and lightly brown other side, about 2 minutes. Transfer chicken to plate; remove and discard skin.

2. While chicken is browning, remove and discard ribs and seeds from 2 jalapeños; mince flesh. In food processor, pulse half of poblanos, Anaheims, and onions until consistency of chunky salsa, 10 to 12 pulses, scraping down sides of

workbowl halfway through. Transfer mixture to medium bowl. Repeat with remaining poblanos, Anaheims, and onions; combine with first batch (do not wash food processor blade or workbowl).

3. Pour off all but 1 tablespoon fat from Dutch oven (adding more vegetable oil if necessary) and reduce heat to medium. Add minced jalapeños, chile-onion mixture, garlic, cumin, coriander, and remaining ¼ teaspoon salt. Cover and cook, stirring occasionally, until vegetables soften, about 10 minutes. Remove pot from heat.

4. Transfer 1 cup cooked vegetable mixture to now-empty food processor workbowl. Add 1 cup beans and 1 cup broth and process until smooth, about 20 seconds. Add vegetable-bean mixture, remaining 2 cups broth, and chicken breasts to Dutch oven and bring to boil over medium-high heat. Reduce heat to medium-low and simmer, covered, stirring occasionally, until chicken registers 160 degrees (175 degrees if using thighs), 15 to 20 minutes (40 minutes if using thighs).

5. Using tongs, transfer chicken to large plate. Stir in remaining beans and continue to simmer, uncovered, until beans are heated through and chili has thickened slightly, about 10 minutes.

6. Mince remaining jalapeño, reserving and mincing ribs and seeds, and set aside. When cool enough to handle, shred chicken into bite-size pieces, discarding bones. Stir shredded chicken, cilantro, lime juice, scallions, and minced jalapeño (with seeds if desired) into chili and return to simmer. Season with salt and pepper to taste, and serve.

Beef and Vegetable Soup

Serves 4 to 6 • **Total Time: 1¼ hours**

Why This Recipe Works Rich and hearty beef and vegetable soup with old-fashioned flavor is a snap to make—if you have a few hours free and several pounds of beef and bones hanging around. This version develops the same flavors and textures in under an hour. We knew the key to this recipe would be finding the right cut of meat, one that had great beefy flavor and that would cook up tender in a reasonable amount of time. Tender cuts, like strip steak and rib eye, became tough, livery, and chalky when simmered in soup. Sirloin tip steak was the best choice—when cut into small pieces, the meat was tender and offered the illusion of being cooked for hours; plus, its meaty flavor imparted richness to the soup.

In place of labor-intensive homemade beef broth, we doctored store-bought beef broth with aromatics and lightened its flavor profile with chicken broth. To further boost the flavor of the beef, we added cremini mushrooms, tomato paste, soy sauce, and red wine, ingredients that are rich in glutamates, naturally occurring compounds that accentuate the meat's hearty flavor. To mimic the rich body of a homemade meat stock (made rich through the gelatin released by the meat bones' collagen during the long simmering process), we relied on powdered gelatin. Our beef and vegetable soup now had the same richness and flavor as cooked-all-day versions in a whole lot less time.

Choose whole sirloin tip steaks over ones that have been cut into small pieces for stir-fries. If sirloin tip steaks are unavailable, substitute blade or flank steak, removing any hard gristle or excess fat. White mushrooms can be used in place of the cremini mushrooms, with some trade-off in flavor. If you like, add 1 cup of frozen peas, frozen corn, or frozen cut green beans during the last 5 minutes of cooking. For a heartier soup, add 10 ounces of red potatoes, cut into ½-inch pieces (2 cups), during the last 15 minutes of cooking.

1 pound sirloin tip steaks, trimmed and cut into ½-inch pieces
2 tablespoons soy sauce
1 teaspoon vegetable oil
1 pound cremini mushrooms, trimmed and quartered
1 large onion, chopped
2 tablespoons tomato paste
1 garlic clove, minced
½ cup red wine
4 cups beef broth
1¾ cups chicken broth
4 carrots, peeled and cut into ½-inch pieces
2 celery ribs, cut into ½-inch pieces
1 bay leaf
1 tablespoon unflavored gelatin
½ cup cold water
2 tablespoons minced fresh parsley leaves

1. Combine beef and soy sauce in medium bowl; set aside for 15 minutes.

2. Heat oil in Dutch oven over medium-high heat until just smoking. Add mushrooms and onion; cook, stirring frequently, until onion is browned and dark bits form on pan bottom, 8 to 12 minutes. Transfer vegetables to bowl.

3. Add beef and cook, stirring occasionally, until liquid evaporates and meat starts to brown, 6 to 10 minutes. Add tomato paste and garlic; cook, stirring constantly, until fragrant, about 30 seconds. Add red wine, scraping bottom of the pot with wooden spoon to loosen any browned bits, and cook until syrupy, 1 to 2 minutes.

4. Add beef broth, chicken broth, carrots, celery, bay leaf, and browned mushrooms and onion; bring to boil. Reduce heat to low, cover, and simmer until vegetables and meat are tender, 25 to 30 minutes. While soup is simmering, sprinkle gelatin over cold water in small bowl and let sit until gelatin softens, about 5 minutes.

5. When soup is finished, turn off heat. Discard bay leaf. Add gelatin mixture and stir until completely dissolved. Stir in parsley, season with salt and pepper to taste, and serve.

Best Beef Stew

Serves 6 to 8 • **Total Time: 3¾ hours**

Why This Recipe Works The taste of beef stew is rarely as complex as its rich aroma would lead you to believe. We wanted a rich-tasting but approachable beef stew with tender meat, flavorful vegetables, and a rich brown gravy that justified the time it took to prepare. After browning the beef (chuck-eye is our preferred cut for stew), we caramelized the usual choices of onions and carrots, rather than just adding them raw to the broth. To mimic the luxurious, mouth-coating texture of beef stews made with homemade stock (provided by the collagen in bones that is transformed into gelatin when simmered), we included powdered gelatin and flour. We added frozen pearl onions toward the end of cooking along with some frozen peas.

Use a good-quality medium-bodied wine, such as a Côtes du Rhône or Pinot Noir, for this stew. Try to find beef that is well marbled with white veins of fat. Meat that is too lean will come out slightly dry. Four pounds of blade steaks, trimmed of gristle and silver skin, can be substituted for the chuck-eye roast. While the blade steak will yield slightly thinner pieces after trimming, it should still be cut into 1½-inch pieces. Look for salt pork that looks meaty and is roughly 75 percent lean.

2 garlic cloves, minced
4 anchovy fillets, minced fine (about 2 teaspoons)
1 tablespoon tomato paste
1 (4-pound) boneless chuck-eye roast, trimmed and cut into 1½-inch pieces
2 tablespoons vegetable oil, divided
1 large onion, halved and sliced ⅛ inch thick
4 carrots, peeled and cut into 1-inch pieces
¼ cup unbleached all-purpose flour
2 cups red wine
2 cups chicken broth
4 ounces salt pork, rinsed of excess salt
2 bay leaves
4 sprigs fresh thyme
1 pound Yukon Gold potatoes, unpeeled, cut into 1-inch pieces
1½ cups frozen pearl onions, thawed
2 teaspoons unflavored gelatin
½ cup water
1 cup frozen peas, thawed
Table salt and ground black pepper

1. Adjust oven rack to lower-middle position and heat oven to 300 degrees. Combine garlic and anchovies in small bowl and press mixture with back of fork to form paste. Stir in tomato paste and set mixture aside.

2. Pat meat dry with paper towels (do not season meat). Heat 1 tablespoon vegetable oil in Dutch oven over high heat until just starting to smoke. Add half of beef and cook until well browned on all sides, about 8 minutes total, reducing heat if oil begins to smoke or fond begins to burn. Transfer beef to large plate. Repeat with remaining 1 tablespoon vegetable oil and remaining beef, leaving second batch of meat in pot after browning.

3. Reduce heat to medium and return first batch of beef to pot. Add onion and carrots to pot and stir to combine with beef. Cook, scraping bottom of pan to loosen any browned bits, until onion is softened, 1 to 2 minutes. Add garlic mixture and cook, stirring constantly, until fragrant, about 30 seconds. Add flour and cook, stirring constantly, until no dry flour remains, about 30 seconds.

4. Slowly add wine, scraping bottom of pan to loosen any browned bits. Increase heat to high and allow wine to simmer until thickened and slightly reduced, about 2 minutes. Stir in broth, salt pork, bay leaves, and thyme. Bring to simmer, cover, transfer to oven, and cook for 1½ hours.

5. Remove pot from oven. Discard bay leaves and salt pork. Stir in potatoes, cover, return pot to oven, and cook until potatoes are almost tender, about 45 minutes.

6. Using large spoon, skim any excess fat from surface of stew. Stir in pearl onions. Cook over medium heat until potatoes and onions are cooked through and meat offers little resistance when poked with fork (meat should not be falling apart), about 15 minutes. Meanwhile, sprinkle gelatin over water in small bowl and let sit until gelatin softens, about 5 minutes.

7. Increase heat to high and stir in softened gelatin mixture and peas. Simmer until gelatin is fully dissolved and stew is thickened, about 3 minutes. Season with salt and pepper to taste. Serve. (Stew can be cooled, covered tightly, and refrigerated for up to 2 days. Reheat gently before serving.)

SEASON 17

Alcatra

Serves 6 • Total Time: 4½ hours

Why This Recipe Works Alcatra, a simple and meaty Portuguese beef stew, features tender chunks of beef braised in wine with onions, garlic, and spices. Unlike beef stews that require searing the beef to build savory flavor or adding flavor boosters like tomato paste and anchovies, this recipe skips those steps and ingredients, highlighting the warm and bright flavors of the spices and wine as much as the meatiness of the beef. We used beef shank because it is lean (which means the cooking liquid doesn't need to be skimmed) and full of collagen, which broke down into gelatin and gave the sauce full body. Submerging the sliced onions completely in the liquid under the meat caused them to form a meaty-tasting compound that amped up the savory flavor of the broth. Slices of smoky-sweet Spanish chorizo sausage matched up perfectly with the other flavors in the stew.

> *Beef shank is sold both crosscut and long-cut (with and without bones). We prefer long-cut since it has more collagen. You can substitute 4 pounds of bone-in crosscut shank if that's all you can find. Remove the bones before cooking and save them for another use. Crosscut shank cooks more quickly, so check the stew for doneness in step 2 after 3 hours. A 3½- to 4-pound chuck roast, trimmed of fat and cut into 2½-inch pieces, can be substituted for the shank. Serve this dish with crusty bread or boiled potatoes.*

3 pounds boneless long-cut beef shanks
1 teaspoon table salt
5 garlic cloves, peeled and smashed
5 allspice berries
4 bay leaves
1½ teaspoons peppercorns
2 large onions, halved and sliced thin
2¼ cups dry white wine
¼ teaspoon ground cinnamon
8 ounces Spanish-style chorizo sausage, cut into ¼-inch-thick rounds

1. Adjust oven rack to middle position and heat oven to 325 degrees. Trim away any fat or large pieces of connective tissue from exterior of shanks (silverskin can be left on meat). Cut each shank crosswise into 2½-inch pieces. Sprinkle meat with salt.

2. Cut 8-inch square of triple-thickness cheesecloth. Place garlic, allspice berries, bay leaves, and peppercorns in center of cheesecloth and tie into bundle with kitchen twine. Arrange onions and spice bundle in Dutch oven in even layer. Add wine and cinnamon. Arrange shank pieces in single layer on top of onions. Cover and cook until beef is tender, about 3½ hours.

3. Remove pot from oven and add chorizo. Using tongs, flip each piece of beef over, making sure that chorizo is submerged. Cover and let stand until chorizo is warmed through, about 20 minutes. Discard spice bundle. Season with salt and pepper to taste. Serve.

SEASON 7

Carbonnade à la Flamande

Serves 6 • Total Time: 3½ hours

Why This Recipe Works In Belgian carbonnade, the heartiness of beef melds with the sweetness of sliced onions in a lightly thickened broth that is rich, deep, and satisfying, with the malty flavor of beer. This version keeps things simple by drawing out maximum flavor from our three main ingredients. We found that top blade steak, which has a fair amount of marbling, provided the best texture and a "buttery" flavor that worked well alongside the onions and beer. White and red onions were too sweet in our stew; yellow onions worked better. Because overcaramelization caused the onions to disintegrate, we made sure just to brown them lightly. Tomato paste gave the stew depth, as did garlic. Fresh thyme and bay leaves provided seasoning, and a splash of cider vinegar added the right level of acidity.

A Hands-Off Approach Makes a Stellar Stew

"Stews are one of my favorite things to make; I think they are borderline magic for the home cook. The ingredients are slow-simmered and somewhere along the way they combine into something much better than the sum of their parts. Alcatra, the elegant beef stew from Portugal, pushes the magic trick even more. Somehow the parsimonious ingredient list is turned into something quite extraordinary. This recipe also takes a hands-off approach. Onions are piled into the pot. A bundle of allspice, garlic, and peppercorns goes in with the onions. White wine—the only liquid—is poured over the onions along with cinnamon. Finally, collagen-rich beef shanks top the pile. Lid goes on... pot goes in the oven... and I go about my day for a few hours.

A flavor powerhouse, Spanish chorizo, is added to the pot near the end of cooking to permeate the broth with the flavors of paprika and pork. It's as good as it gets; the beef falls apart with the slightest prodding of a fork and the broth is both complex and clean. The only necessary addition is some crusty bread to mop up every last drop of stew."

—Bridget

Beer is a staple of Belgian cooking, and we found that it's less forgiving than wine when used in a stew. The light lagers we tried resulted in pale, watery stews; better were dark ales and stouts. But beer alone often made for bitter-tasting stew, so we included some broth; a combination of chicken and beef broth gave us more solid and complex flavor.

Top blade steaks (also called blade or flat-iron steaks) are our first choice, but any boneless roast from the chuck will work. If you end up using a chuck roast, look for the chuck-eye roast, an especially flavorful cut that can easily be trimmed and cut into 1-inch pieces. Buttered egg noodles or mashed potatoes make excellent accompaniments to carbonnade.

3½ pounds top blade steaks, 1 inch thick, trimmed of gristle and fat and cut into 1-inch pieces
1¼ teaspoons table salt, divided
¾ teaspoon pepper
3 tablespoons vegetable oil, divided
2 pounds yellow onions, halved and sliced ¼ inch thick
1 tablespoon tomato paste
2 garlic cloves, minced
3 tablespoons unbleached all-purpose flour
¾ cup chicken broth
¾ cup beef broth
1½ cups (12-ounce bottle or can) dark beer or stout
4 sprigs fresh thyme, tied with kitchen twine
2 bay leaves
1 tablespoon cider vinegar

1. Adjust oven rack to the lower-middle position and heat oven to 300 degrees. Dry beef thoroughly with paper towels, then sprinkle with ¾ teaspoon salt and pepper. Heat 2 teaspoons oil in Dutch oven over medium-high heat until beginning to smoke; add one-third of beef to pot. Cook without moving until well browned, 2 to 3 minutes; using tongs, turn each piece and continue cooking until second side is well browned, about 5 minutes longer. Transfer browned beef to medium bowl. Repeat with 2 teaspoons oil and half of remaining beef. (If drippings in bottom of pot are very dark, add ½ cup chicken or beef broth and scrape pan bottom with wooden spoon to loosen browned bits; pour liquid into bowl with browned beef, then proceed.) Repeat once more with 2 teaspoons oil and remaining beef.

2. Add remaining 1 tablespoon oil to now-empty Dutch oven; reduce heat to medium-low. Add onions, tomato paste, and remaining ½ teaspoon salt; cook, scraping the bottom of pot with wooden spoon to loosen browned bits, until onions have released some moisture, about 5 minutes. Increase heat to medium and continue to cook, stirring occasionally, until onions are lightly browned, 12 to 14 minutes. Stir in garlic and cook until fragrant, about 30 seconds. Add flour and stir until onions are evenly coated and flour is lightly browned, about 2 minutes. Stir in broths, scraping pan bottom to loosen any browned bits; stir in beer, thyme, bay leaves, vinegar, browned beef with any accumulated juices, and salt and pepper to taste. Increase heat to medium-high and bring to full simmer, stirring occasionally; cover partially, then place pot in oven. Cook until fork inserted into beef meets little resistance, 2 to 2½ hours.

3. Discard thyme and bay leaves. Season with salt and pepper to taste, and serve. (Stew can be cooled and refrigerated in airtight container for up to 4 days; reheat over medium-low heat.)

Trimming Blade Steaks

To trim blade steaks, halve each steak lengthwise, leaving gristle on 1 half. Then simply cut gristle away.

Best Ground Beef Chili

Serves 8 to 10 • **Total Time: 3¼ hours**

Why This Recipe Works Our ground beef chili can hold its own against the traditional chunky beef kind. We used 85 percent lean ground beef for flavor and tenderness. To protect the meat from dryness, we treated it with salt and baking soda. Both ingredients helped the meat hold on to moisture so the whole 2 pounds of beef could be browned in one batch. Simmering the meat for 90 minutes gave its collagen enough time to break down. We made a homemade chili powder for potent spicy flavor, and we used tortilla chips to add both bulk and corn flavor. Shortly before serving, we stirred any flavorful orange fat collected on the top back into the chili.

Diced avocado, sour cream, and shredded Monterey Jack or cheddar cheese are also good options for garnishing. This chili is intensely flavored and should be served with tortilla chips and/or plenty of steamed white rice.

    2   pounds 85 percent lean ground beef
    2   tablespoons plus 2 cups water, divided
 1½   teaspoons table salt
   ¾   teaspoon baking soda
    6   dried ancho chiles, stemmed, seeded,
        and torn into 1-inch pieces
    1   ounce tortilla chips, crushed (¼ cup)
    2   tablespoons ground cumin
    1   tablespoon paprika
    1   tablespoon garlic powder
    1   tablespoon ground coriander
    2   teaspoons dried oregano
    2   teaspoons pepper
   ½   teaspoon dried thyme
    1   (14.5-ounce) can whole peeled tomatoes
    1   tablespoon vegetable oil
    1   onion, chopped fine
    3   garlic cloves, minced
 1–2   teaspoons minced canned chipotle chile in
        adobo sauce
    1   (15-ounce) can pinto beans, undrained
    2   teaspoons sugar
    2   tablespoons cider vinegar
        Lime wedges
        Coarsely chopped cilantro
        Chopped red onion

1. Adjust oven rack to lower-middle position and heat oven to 275 degrees. Toss beef with 2 tablespoons water, salt, and baking soda in bowl until thoroughly combined. Set aside for 20 minutes.

2. Meanwhile, place anchos in Dutch oven set over medium-high heat; toast, stirring frequently, until fragrant, 4 to 6 minutes, reducing heat if anchos begin to smoke. Transfer to food processor and let cool.

3. Add tortilla chips, cumin, paprika, garlic powder, coriander, oregano, pepper, and thyme to food processor with anchos and process until finely ground, about 2 minutes. Transfer mixture to bowl. Process tomatoes and their juice in now-empty workbowl until smooth, about 30 seconds.

4. Heat oil in now-empty pot over medium-high heat until shimmering. Add onion and cook, stirring occasionally, until softened, 4 to 6 minutes. Add garlic and cook until fragrant, about 1 minute. Add beef and cook, stirring with wooden spoon to break meat up into ¼-inch pieces, until beef is browned and fond begins to form on pot bottom, 12 to 14 minutes. Add ancho mixture and chipotle; cook, stirring frequently, until fragrant, 1 to 2 minutes.

5. Add beans and their liquid, sugar, tomato puree, and remaining 2 cups water. Bring to boil, scraping bottom of pot to loosen any browned bits. Cover, transfer to oven, and cook until meat is tender and chili is slightly thickened, 1½ to 2 hours, stirring occasionally to prevent sticking.

6. Remove chili from oven and let stand, uncovered, for 10 minutes. Stir in any fat that has risen to top of chili, then add vinegar and season with salt to taste. Serve, passing lime wedges, cilantro, and chopped onion separately. (Chili can be refrigerated for up to 3 days.)

Simple Beef Chili with Kidney Beans

Simple Beef Chili with Kidney Beans

Serves 8 to 10 • **Total Time: 2¾ hours**

Why This Recipe Works We wanted an easy recipe for a basic chili, made with supermarket staples, that would have some heat and great flavors—chili that would please almost everyone. To start, we added the spices with the aromatics (bell pepper, onions, and lots of garlic) to get the most flavor, and used commercial chili powder with a boost from more cumin, oregano, cayenne, and coriander. For the meat, we found that 85 percent lean beef gave us full flavor. A combination of diced tomatoes and tomato puree gave our chili a well-balanced saucy backbone. We added canned red kidney beans with the tomatoes so that they absorbed flavor. For a rich, thick consistency, we cooked the chili with the lid on for half of the cooking time.

Good choices for condiments include diced fresh tomatoes, diced avocado, sliced scallions, chopped red onion, chopped cilantro leaves, sour cream, and shredded Monterey Jack or cheddar cheese. If you are a fan of spicy food, consider using a little more of the red pepper flakes or cayenne—or both. The flavor of the chili improves with age; if possible, make it a day or up to three days in advance and reheat before serving. Leftovers can be frozen for up to one month.

- 2 tablespoons vegetable oil
- 2 onions, chopped fine
- 1 red bell pepper, stemmed, seeded, and chopped
- 6 garlic cloves, minced
- ¼ cup chili powder
- 1 tablespoon ground cumin
- 2 teaspoons ground coriander
- 1 teaspoon red pepper flakes
- 1 teaspoon dried oregano
- ½ teaspoon cayenne pepper
- 2 pounds 85 percent lean ground beef
- 2 (15-ounce) cans dark red kidney beans, rinsed
- 1 (28-ounce) can diced tomatoes
- 1 (28-ounce) can tomato puree
- ½ teaspoon table salt
  Lime wedges

1. Heat oil in Dutch oven over medium heat until shimmering but not smoking. Add onions, bell pepper, garlic, chili powder, cumin, coriander, red pepper flakes, oregano, and cayenne and cook, stirring occasionally, until the vegetables are softened and beginning to brown, about 10 minutes.

GAME CHANGER

Worth Making 100 Times

"I first made this wonderful chili several years ago, when I was testing Dutch ovens. Whenever we're testing kitchen products on the ATK Reviews team, we comb through dozens of our recipes using that product. We try to choose the most typical and, frankly, the easiest to make—because we are going to have to do it over and over and over, exactly the same way, in every product of the testing lineup. That's one of the ways we can make fair comparisons of all of the products' performance, handling, and cleanup. But that also means we're going to spend a day or two completely immersed in that recipe, right up to our eyebrows. Well, I can honestly say that after making dozens of batches of this simple, delicious chili, I still wanted to eat it. And I still make it at home regularly. It's that good, and easy. Everyone loves it, especially since they can customize their bowls with their preferred toppings. It's even better the next day if you have leftovers. It freezes beautifully, and is terrific for tailgates and potlucks. As recipes go, this one's a classic and a keeper."

—Lisa

Increase heat to medium-high and add half of beef. Cook, breaking up pieces with wooden spoon, until no longer pink and just beginning to brown, 3 to 4 minutes. Add remaining beef and cook, breaking up pieces with wooden spoon, until no longer pink, 3 to 4 minutes.

2. Add beans, tomatoes with juice, tomato puree, and ½ teaspoon salt. Bring to boil, then reduce heat to low and simmer, covered, stirring occasionally, for 1 hour. Remove lid and continue to simmer for 1 hour longer, stirring occasionally (if chili begins to stick to bottom of the pot, stir in ½ cup water and continue to simmer), until beef is tender and chili is dark, rich, and slightly thickened. Season with salt to taste. Serve with lime wedges.

SEASON 21

Chile Verde con Cerdo

Serves 6 to 8 • Total Time: 2¾ hours, plus 1 hour salting

Why This Recipe Works Our new-school approach to making stew brings every element of this tangy, fragrant, meaty Mexican classic to its full potential. To make a vibrant chile verde, we started by salting chunks of fat-and-collagen-rich pork butt roast for an hour, which ensured that the meat cooked up well seasoned and juicy. Gently braising the pork in the oven allowed the meat's fat and collagen to thoroughly break down, making it supple. Browning the pork trimmings (chopped coarse to maximize their surface area) instead of the chunks built a savory fond without drying out the surface of the meat. Broiling the tomatillos, poblanos, jalapeño, and garlic concentrated their flavors and imbued them with a touch of smokiness. Seasoning the chili with warm spices and sugar softened its acidity and heat. Omitting broth and/or water minimized the amount of liquid in the pot, so that the salsa—the only source of liquid—reduced to a tight, flavorful sauce that clung nicely to the meat.

> *Pork butt roast is often labeled Boston butt in the supermarket. If your jalapeño is shorter than 3 inches long, you may wish to use two. If fresh tomatillos are unavailable, substitute three 11-ounce cans of tomatillos, drained, rinsed, and patted dry; broil as directed. Serve with white rice and/or warm corn tortillas.*

1 (3½- to 4-pound) boneless pork butt roast, trimmed and cut into 1½-inch pieces, trimmings reserved
1 tablespoon plus 1 teaspoon kosher salt, divided
1 cup water
1½ pounds tomatillos, husks and stems removed, rinsed well and dried
5 poblano chiles, stemmed, halved, and seeded
1 large onion, peeled, cut into 8 wedges through root end
5 garlic cloves, unpeeled
1 jalapeño chile, stemmed and halved
1 tablespoon vegetable oil
1 teaspoon dried oregano
1 teaspoon ground cumin
⅛ teaspoon ground cinnamon
Pinch ground cloves
2 bay leaves
2 teaspoons sugar
1 teaspoon pepper
½ cup minced fresh cilantro, plus extra for serving
Lime wedges

1. Toss pork pieces with 1 tablespoon salt in large bowl. Cover and refrigerate for 1 hour. Meanwhile, chop pork trimmings coarse. Transfer to Dutch oven. Add water and bring to simmer over high heat. Cook, adjusting heat to maintain vigorous simmer and stirring occasionally, until all liquid evaporates and trimmings begin to sizzle, about 12 minutes. Continue to cook, stirring frequently, until dark fond forms on bottom of pot and trimmings have browned and crisped, about 6 minutes longer. Using slotted spoon, discard trimmings. Pour off all but 2 tablespoons fat; set aside pot.

2. Adjust 1 oven rack to lower-middle position and second rack 6 inches from broiler element and heat broiler. Line rimmed baking sheet with aluminum foil. Place tomatillos, poblanos, onion, garlic, and jalapeño on prepared sheet and drizzle with oil. Arrange chiles skin side up. Broil until chile skins are blackened and vegetables begin to soften, 10 to 13 minutes, rotating sheet halfway through broiling. Transfer poblanos, jalapeño, and garlic to cutting board.

3. Turn off broiler and heat oven to 325 degrees. Transfer tomatillos, onion, and any accumulated juices to food processor. When poblanos, jalapeño, and garlic are cool enough to handle, remove and discard skins (it's OK if some small bits of chile skin remain). Remove seeds from jalapeño and reserve. Add poblanos, jalapeño, and garlic to processor. Pulse until mixture is roughly pureed, about 10 pulses, scraping down sides of bowl as needed. If spicier chili is desired, add reserved jalapeño seeds and pulse 3 times.

4. Heat reserved fat in Dutch oven over medium heat until just shimmering. Add oregano, cumin, cinnamon, and cloves and cook, stirring constantly, until fragrant, about 30 seconds. Stir in tomatillo mixture, bay leaves, sugar, pepper, and remaining 1 teaspoon salt, scraping up any browned bits. Stir in pork and bring to simmer. Cover, transfer to oven, and cook until pork is tender, about 1½ hours, stirring halfway through cooking.

5. Remove pot from oven and let sit, covered, for 10 minutes. Discard bay leaves. Using heatproof rubber spatula, scrape browned bits from sides of pot. Stir in any fat that has risen to top of chili. Stir in cilantro; season with salt and pepper to taste. Serve, passing lime wedges and extra cilantro separately.

Caldo Verde

Serves 6 to 8 • **Total Time: 1 hour**

Why This Recipe Works This soup of sausage, potatoes, and hearty greens is a staple in many Portuguese households. While the flavors are rich, it's not a heavy soup. Without changing the soup's essentially light character, we wanted to create a slightly heartier result—something that could function as a main course. To start, we replaced the Portuguese linguica sausage with widely available Spanish-style chorizo, which boasts a similar garlicky profile. We sautéed the sausage right in the Dutch oven in just 1 tablespoon of olive oil, eliminating the need to dirty an extra skillet. For deeper flavor, we split the water with an equal amount of chicken broth. Collard greens offered a more delicate sweetness and a meatier bite than kale, and chopping the leaves into bite-size pieces made them more spoon-friendly. Finally, we swapped out starchy russet potatoes for sturdy Yukon Golds, which held their shape during cooking. Pureeing some of the potatoes and a few tablespoons of olive oil into our soup base made a creamier, heartier dish. A bit of white wine vinegar brightened the pot.

We prefer collard greens, but kale can be substituted. Serve this soup with hearty bread and, for added richness, a final drizzle of extra-virgin olive oil.

  ¼ cup extra-virgin olive oil, divided
 12 ounces Spanish-style chorizo sausage, cut into ½-inch pieces
  1 onion, chopped fine
  4 garlic cloves, minced
 1¼ teaspoons table salt
  ¼ teaspoon red pepper flakes
  2 pounds Yukon Gold potatoes, peeled and cut into ¾-inch pieces
  4 cups chicken broth
  4 cups water
  1 pound collard greens, stemmed and cut into 1-inch pieces
  2 teaspoons white wine vinegar

1. Heat 1 tablespoon oil in Dutch oven over medium-high heat until shimmering. Add chorizo and cook, stirring occasionally, until lightly browned, 4 to 5 minutes. Transfer chorizo to bowl and set aside. Reduce heat to medium and add onion, garlic, salt, and pepper flakes and season with pepper to taste. Cook, stirring frequently, until onion is translucent, 2 to 3 minutes. Add potatoes, broth, and water; increase heat to high and bring to boil. Reduce heat to medium-low and simmer, uncovered, until potatoes are just tender, 8 to 10 minutes.

2. Transfer ¾ cup solids and ¾ cup broth to blender jar. Add collard greens to pot and simmer for 10 minutes. Stir in chorizo and continue to simmer until greens are tender, 8 to 10 minutes longer.

3. Add remaining 3 tablespoons oil to soup in blender and process until very smooth and homogeneous, about 1 minute. Remove pot from heat and stir pureed soup mixture and vinegar into soup. Season with salt and pepper to taste, and serve. (Soup can be refrigerated for up to 2 days.)

Jamaican Stew Peas with Spinners

Serves 6 to 8 • **Total Time: 3 hours, plus 8 hours soaking**

Why This Recipe Works In order to replicate this homey Jamaican stew using ingredients easily found in American supermarkets, we made some simple substitutions. We started by swapping in dried small red beans for the Jamaican dried red peas, which can be difficult to source in the United States. Instead of salted pig tails or salted beef, we used smoked ham hocks, which, though not traditional, was not a huge leap since some cooks make stew peas using the leftover bone from a Christmas ham. Fine-tuning the spices and aromatics—allspice berries, garlic, garlic powder, celery, thyme, and a Scotch bonnet chile—gave the stew rich, nuanced flavor, and a combination of chicken broth and coconut milk added savoriness and sweet creaminess. To make the dish even more satisfying, we finished by adding the rustic flour-and-water dumplings known as spinners.

Small dried dark-red beans (usually labeled "small red beans") are similar to the dried red peas used in Jamaica and have a creamy texture when cooked, but you can substitute dried red kidney beans, if desired. If you don't have any coconut oil on hand, you can substitute vegetable oil. If you can't find a Scotch bonnet chile, use a habanero. For the best results, use full-fat coconut milk. Serve with steamed long-grain white rice.

1 pound (about 2 cups) small dried red beans, picked over and rinsed
6 cups plus 3 tablespoons water, divided
4 sprigs fresh thyme, plus 1 tablespoon chopped, divided
1 Scotch bonnet chile, pierced once with tip of paring knife
1 bay leaf
1 teaspoon whole allspice berries
1 tablespoon unrefined coconut oil
1 onion, chopped
1 green bell pepper, stemmed, seeded, and chopped
1 large celery rib, chopped (¾ cup)
3 tablespoons minced garlic
2 teaspoons garlic powder
1¼ teaspoons table salt, divided
½ teaspoon pepper
2 (12-ounce) smoked ham hocks
2 cups chicken broth
1 (14-ounce) can coconut milk
½ cup all-purpose flour
6 scallions, chopped

1. Combine beans and 6 cups water in large container and soak at room temperature for at least 8 hours or up to 24 hours.

2. Bundle thyme sprigs, Scotch bonnet, bay leaf, and allspice in cheesecloth; secure with kitchen twine; and set aside. Heat oil in large Dutch oven over medium heat until shimmering. Add onion, bell pepper, celery, garlic, garlic powder, ½ teaspoon salt, and pepper and cook, stirring occasionally, until onion is translucent, 6 to 8 minutes.

3. Add beans and their soaking liquid, ham hocks, chicken broth, cheesecloth bundle, and ½ teaspoon salt. Increase heat to high and bring to boil. Lower heat to maintain vigorous simmer. Cook uncovered, stirring occasionally, until beans start to soften and liquid is slightly reduced, about 1½ hours. Stir in coconut milk and continue to cook until beans are completely soft (it's OK if some skins crack) and sauce thickens, about 30 minutes longer.

4. While stew simmers, combine flour and remaining ¼ teaspoon salt in bowl. Make well in mixture. Gradually add remaining 3 tablespoons water, stirring until shaggy mass forms. Knead in bowl until dough clears sides of bowl and forms tight ball (if dough seems too dry to shape, add up to 2 teaspoons water, ½ teaspoon at a time). Pinch off about 1 teaspoon dough and roll between your palms to form 3-inch-long dumpling with tapered ends. Transfer to plate and repeat with remaining dough (you should have 14 to 16 dumplings).

5. Taste stew; adjust spiciness, if desired, by pressing cheesecloth bundle against side of pot with back of spoon to release juice of Scotch bonnet. Discard bundle and transfer ham hocks to plate to cool slightly. Gently drop dumplings into stew. Simmer, without stirring, until dumplings are set, about 5 minutes. While dumplings cook, debone ham hocks and cut meat into ½-inch pieces (you'll have ½ to ⅔ cup meat); discard bones, skin, and fat. Stir meat, scallions, and chopped thyme into stew. Season with salt and pepper to taste. Simmer until flavors have melded and scallions have softened slightly, 10 to 15 minutes. Serve.

Making Spinners

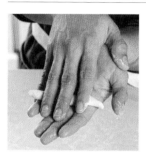

These dumplings are an essential component of stew peas. As they poach, some of the flour sloughs off, giving the broth body. To make one, pinch off about 1 teaspoon of dough and roll it between your palms to form 3-inch-long dumpling with tapered ends.

SEASON 24

Hot Ukrainian Borscht

Serves 6 to 8 • Total Time: 3¾ hours

Why This Recipe Works The markers of classic Ukrainian borscht include beets for their earthy sweetness and vivid color, as well as green cabbage, carrots, onions, and potatoes—staple crops that grow abundantly in Ukrainian soil. Pork, the cuisine's default protein, builds up a meaty backbone, and a souring agent such as vinegar, lemon juice, or tomatoes invigorates the broth. We cooked collagen-rich pork butt slowly to yield a full-bodied broth with succulent meat for the soup. Shredding the beets and carrots helped the hard roots cook efficiently and varied their texture from the chunkier potatoes. We also separately sautéed the beets and carrots before simmering them; the high heat helped them soften quickly and intensified their savory sweetness. Loads of tomato paste, briefly sautéed with the beets to deepen its flavor, plus a last-minute shot of lemon juice, brightened the earthy, meaty broth. Letting the soup rest as long as possible before serving gave the flavors time to meld.

Pork butt roast is often labeled Boston butt in the supermarket. For efficiency, prep the vegetables while the broth cooks, or make the broth ahead. In step 2, the chilled fat hardens on the surface of the broth and is easy to remove with a spoon. This soup benefits from being made in advance—at least a few hours before eating and up to three days. Serve with bread. Garnish with sour cream, if desired.

Broth
- 10 cups water
- 1 (2-pound) boneless pork butt roast, well trimmed and cut in half
- 1 onion, halved
- 1 large carrot, sliced 1 inch thick
- 2 bay leaves
- ½ teaspoon table salt

Soup
- 1 pound Yukon Gold potatoes, peeled and cut into 1-inch pieces
- ½ small head green cabbage, halved, cored, and sliced thin crosswise (5 cups)
- 1½ teaspoons table salt, divided
- ¼ cup vegetable oil
- 1 onion, chopped fine
- 8 ounces beets, trimmed, peeled, and shredded (2 cups)
- 2 carrots, peeled and shredded (1½ cups)
- 1 (6-ounce) can tomato paste
- ⅓ cup chopped fresh dill, plus more for garnish
- 1 tablespoon lemon juice, plus more for serving

1. For the broth: Combine all ingredients in Dutch oven and bring to boil over high heat. Adjust heat to simmer and cook, covered, until pork is tender, about 2 hours, occasionally skimming foam off surface.

2. Transfer pork to large plate or cutting board. Discard onion, carrot, and bay leaves. When pork is cool enough to handle, cut into bite-size pieces (it's OK if meat starts to shred). Skim fat from surface of broth. (Alternatively, let broth cool completely and refrigerate overnight. Refrigerate pork separately.)

3. For the soup: Reserve ½ cup broth. In Dutch oven, bring remaining broth to boil over high heat. Add potatoes, cabbage, and ½ teaspoon salt. Adjust heat to maintain gentle simmer and cook, covered, until potatoes are just tender, 8 to 10 minutes.

4. Meanwhile, heat oil in 12-inch skillet over medium heat until shimmering. Add onion and cook, stirring frequently, until softened, about 5 minutes. Add beets, carrots, and ½ teaspoon salt and cook, stirring frequently, until softened, 3 to 5 minutes. Stir in tomato paste (mixture will be thick) and cook until fragrant and tomato paste is slightly darkened in color, 1 to 2 minutes. Slowly add reserved broth, scraping bottom of pan to loosen any browned bits.

5 Add beet mixture to Dutch oven and stir gently to combine. Cover and simmer for 5 minutes. Stir in pork, dill, lemon juice, and remaining ½ teaspoon salt. Season with salt, pepper, and lemon juice to taste. Portion borscht into bowls and garnish each serving with more dill. Serve. (Borscht can be refrigerated for up to 3 days or frozen for up to 4 months.)

New England Clam Chowder

Serves 6 • **Total Time: 1 hour**

Why This Recipe Works Good traditional chowder can be daunting for the home cook. The biggest hurdle is a finicky ingredient that most people don't know how to work with—clams. We wanted to come up with a clam chowder that was economical, could be prepared quickly, and provided a simple method for working with the star ingredient. We tested a variety of clams and found that medium-size hard-shell clams guaranteed the most clam flavor. Rather than shucking the raw clams and adding them to the pot, we easily steamed the clams to open them, then used the steaming liquid as our broth. The steamed clams had to be pulled from the pot when they had just opened; allowing them to open completely meant they would overcook quickly when returned to the soup to heat through. Waxy red potatoes were the best choice for our creamy chowder and bacon added great smoky flavor. As for the creaminess factor, using a modest amount of heavy cream instead of milk meant that we could use less dairy for a rich chowder that tasted distinctly of clams.

> *Don't skip the step of scrubbing the clams; many clams have bits of sand embedded in their shells that can ruin a pot of chowder. To remove the sand, simply scrub them under cold, running water using a soft brush.*

7 pounds medium-size hard-shell clams, such as cherrystones, washed and scrubbed clean

3 slices thick-cut bacon, cut into ¼-inch pieces

1 large onion, chopped

2 tablespoons all-purpose flour

1½ pounds red potatoes, unpeeled, cut into ½-inch chunks

1 bay leaf

1 teaspoon fresh thyme or ¼ teaspoon dried thyme

1 cup heavy cream

2 tablespoons minced fresh parsley leaves

1. Bring 3 cups water to boil in Dutch oven. Add clams and cover with tight-fitting lid. Cook for 5 minutes, uncover, and stir with wooden spoon. Quickly cover pot and steam until clams just open, 2 to 4 minutes. (Don't let clams open completely.) Transfer clams to large bowl and let cool slightly; reserve broth. Open clams with paring knife, holding clams over bowl to catch any juices. With knife, sever muscle that attaches clam to bottom shell and transfer meat to cutting board; discard shells. Mince clams and set aside. Pour clam broth into large bowl, holding back last few tablespoons of broth in case of sediment; set clam broth aside. (You should have about 5 cups. If not, add bottled clam juice or water to make this amount.) Rinse and dry pot, then return pot to burner.

2. Cook bacon in pot over medium heat until crispy, 5 to 7 minutes. Add onion and cook, stirring occasionally, until softened, about 5 minutes. Add flour and stir until lightly colored, about 1 minute. Gradually whisk in reserved clam broth. Add potatoes, bay leaf, and thyme and simmer until potatoes are tender, about 10 minutes. Add clams, cream, parsley, and salt and pepper to taste; bring to simmer. Discard bay leaf, and serve.

Cioppino

Serves 4 to 6 • **Total Time: 1¼ hours**

Why This Recipe Works Brought to San Francisco by Italian immigrants, the earliest versions of cioppino were uncomplicated affairs made by fishermen with the day's catch. We wanted a restaurant-worthy cioppino in which every component was perfectly cooked but which could be on the table quickly and with minimal fuss. First, we scaled down the seafood. For the fish, halibut fillets worked perfectly—they were tender and had just enough heft. As for the shellfish, a combination of briny littleneck clams and savory-sweet mussels had the flavors we were looking for. The only way to perfectly cook three varieties of seafood was to cook each one separately and bring them all together in the hot broth to serve. We poached the halibut in the broth while the clams and mussels steamed in a separate pan. Removing them as they opened ensured ideal doneness for each one. We used white wine to steam the mussels and clams, and then added the briny cooking liquid to the stew for a boost of intense seafood flavor. Replacing the water in the broth with bottled clam juice improved the broth even further.

Any firm-fleshed, ¾- to 1-inch-thick whitefish (such as cod or sea bass) can be substituted for halibut. Discard clams or mussels with unpleasant odors, cracked shells, or shells that won't close. If littlenecks are not available, substitute Manila or mahogany clams, or use 2 pounds of mussels. If using only mussels, skip step 3 and cook them all at once with the butter and wine for 3 to 5 minutes.

¼ cup vegetable oil
2 large onions, chopped fine
½ teaspoon table salt
½ teaspoon pepper
¼ cup water
4 garlic cloves, minced
2 bay leaves
1 teaspoon dried oregano
⅛–¼ teaspoon red pepper flakes
1 (28-ounce) can whole peeled tomatoes, drained with juice reserved, chopped coarse
1 (8-ounce) bottle clam juice
1 (1½-pound) skinless halibut fillet, ¾ to 1 inch thick, cut into 6 pieces
1 pound littleneck clams, scrubbed
1¼ cups dry white wine
4 tablespoons unsalted butter
1 pound mussels, scrubbed and debearded
¼ cup chopped fresh parsley
Extra-virgin olive oil

1. Heat vegetable oil in Dutch oven over medium-high heat until shimmering. Add onions, salt, and pepper; cook, stirring frequently, until onions begin to brown, 7 to 9 minutes. Add water and cook, stirring frequently, until onions are soft, 2 to 4 minutes. Stir in garlic, bay leaves, oregano, and pepper flakes and cook for 1 minute. Stir in tomatoes and reserved juice and clam juice and bring to simmer. Reduce heat to low, cover, and simmer for 5 minutes.

2. Submerge halibut in broth, cover, and simmer gently until fish is cooked through, 12 to 15 minutes. Remove pot from heat and, using slotted spoon, transfer halibut to plate; cover with aluminum foil and set aside.

3. Bring clams, wine, and butter to boil in covered 12-inch skillet over high heat. Steam until clams just open, 5 to 8 minutes, transferring them to pot with tomato broth as they open.

4. Once all clams have been transferred to pot, add mussels to skillet; cover; and cook over high heat until mussels have opened, 2 to 4 minutes, transferring them to pot with tomato broth as they open. Pour cooking liquid from skillet into pot, being careful not to pour any grit from skillet into pot. Return broth to simmer.

5. Stir parsley into broth and season with salt and pepper to taste. Divide halibut among serving bowls. Ladle broth over halibut, making sure each portion contains both clams and mussels. Drizzle with olive oil and serve immediately.

Cataplana

Serves 4 to 6 • **Total Time: 1 hour**

Why This Recipe Works This stunning one-pot stew is named after the clamshell-shaped copper pot in which it's traditionally cooked. Popular in Portugal's Algarve region, cataplanas are used to cook and serve a number of dishes; our recipe takes inspiration from the classic dish amêijoas na cataplana (clams in a cataplana). To mimic the steamy cooking environment of a cataplana, we cooked our version in a Dutch oven with a tight-fitting lid. We added clams and shrimp at the very end of cooking, preserving their delicate textures and rendering them plump, juicy, and tender. The inclusion of clam juice in addition to wine not only boosted the seafood flavor of the dish but also ensured that it had ample, flavorful broth to soak up crusty bread.

We prefer untreated shrimp, but if your shrimp are treated with salt or additives such as sodium tripolyphosphate (STPP), do not add the salt in step 1. Look for small littleneck or Manila clams that are all about 2 inches across so that they cook at the same rate. If you've had past problems with gritty clams or this is your first time cooking clams, you may wish to purge them before cooking. We call for linguica sausage, but if it's unavailable, you can substitute chouriço or Spanish chorizo. Most linguica sausages are about 1½ inches thick; if yours are narrower, cut them into ¼-inch coins. Serve with crusty bread.

12   ounces extra-large shrimp (21 to 25 per pound), peeled, deveined, and cut in half crosswise
¾   teaspoon table salt, divided
 2   tablespoons extra-virgin olive oil
12   ounces linguica sausage, quartered lengthwise and sliced ¼ inch thick
 2   garlic cloves, minced
¾   teaspoon smoked paprika
½   teaspoon red pepper flakes
 1   large onion, halved and sliced thin
 1   fennel bulb, stalks discarded, bulb halved, cored, and sliced thin lengthwise
 1   red bell pepper, stemmed, seeded, and cut into ¼-inch-wide strips
 1   (28-ounce) can whole peeled tomatoes, drained and chopped coarse
 1   (8-ounce) bottle clam juice
½   cup dry white wine
 3   pounds littleneck or Manila clams, scrubbed
½   cup chopped fresh parsley
     Lemon wedges

1. Combine shrimp and ¼ teaspoon salt in bowl; refrigerate until needed. Heat oil in large Dutch oven over medium-high heat until shimmering. Add linguica and cook, stirring occasionally, until browned and fat is slightly rendered, about 4 minutes. Stir in garlic, paprika, and pepper flakes and cook until fragrant, about 30 seconds.

2. Add onion, fennel, bell pepper, and remaining ½ teaspoon salt and cook, stirring occasionally, until vegetables are softened, 8 to 10 minutes. Stir in tomatoes, clam juice, and wine. Bring to simmer and cook, stirring occasionally, until thickened slightly, about 5 minutes.

3. Increase heat to high and bring mixture to boil. Stir in clams; cover and cook until clams have opened, 5 to 7 minutes, stirring halfway through cooking. Off heat, stir in shrimp. Cover and let stand off heat until shrimp are opaque and just cooked through, about 5 minutes. Discard any unopened clams. Stir in parsley and season with salt to taste. Transfer to serving bowl, if desired, and serve, passing lemon wedges separately.

Scrubbing Clams

Before cooking clams, use a soft brush to scrub them well to remove any sand and grit.

Guay Tiew Tom Yum Goong

Serves 4 to 6 • **Total Time: 1¼ hours**

Why This Recipe Works The hot and sour soup called tom yum features vibrant flavors in every sip. The heat comes from chiles and galangal (Thai ginger), the sour from lime juice and tamarind (a dark, tart fruit). But tom yum also serves up saltiness courtesy of fish sauce and sweetness via a touch of sugar. Lemongrass, makrut lime leaves, cilantro, and Thai basil round out the fragrant bowl. There are many versions of tom yum soup, but one of our favorites, known as guay tiew tom yum goong, is chock-full of shrimp, rice noodles, and sometimes mushrooms and/or tomatoes and topped with nam prik pao, a deeply savory, sweet, and spicy chili jam (so called because of its jammy consistency).

We chose chicken broth as our starting point and infused it with aromatics, which we had sliced and lightly smashed to release their flavorful oils. The broth developed a heady perfume after just 15 minutes of simmering. Sugar and fish sauce rounded things out with sweetness and saltiness. To bulk up the soup, we stirred in fresh oyster mushrooms and the grassy green parts of the scallions. Next, we slipped a pound of peeled large shrimp into the steaming broth off the heat. The residual heat ensured that the shrimp gently cooked through with little risk of turning rubbery. Halved cherry tomatoes added pops of color and another layer of acidity and sweetness, and a healthy squeeze of lime juice delivered the sour flourish that is a hallmark of guay tiew tom yum goong. We first soaked rice noodles in boiling water and then ladled the fragrant soup over them. For a finishing touch, we topped each bowl with a crimson dollop of nam prik pao.

Whole shrimp are traditional in this soup, but you can halve them crosswise before cooking to make them easier to eat. If galangal is unavailable, substitute fresh ginger. Makrut lime leaves add a lot to this soup. If you can't find them, substitute three 3-inch strips each of lemon zest and lime zest. We prefer vermicelli made from 100 percent rice flour to varieties that include a secondary starch such as cornstarch. If you can find only the latter, soak them longer—up to 15 minutes.

4 ounces rice vermicelli

2 lemongrass stalks, trimmed to bottom 6 inches

4 scallions, trimmed, white parts left whole, green parts cut into 1-inch lengths

6 makrut lime leaves, torn if large

2 Thai chiles, stemmed (1 left whole, 1 sliced thin), divided, plus 2 Thai chiles, stemmed and sliced thin, for serving (optional)

1 (2-inch) piece fresh galangal, peeled and sliced into ¼-inch-thick rounds

8 cups chicken broth

1 tablespoon sugar, plus extra for seasoning

8 ounces oyster mushrooms, trimmed and torn into 1-inch pieces

3 tablespoons fish sauce, plus extra for seasoning

1 pound extra-large shrimp (21 to 25 per pound), peeled, deveined, and tails removed

12 ounces cherry tomatoes, halved

2 tablespoons lime juice, plus extra for seasoning, plus lime wedges for serving

½ cup fresh cilantro leaves

¼ cup fresh Thai basil leaves, torn if large (optional)

1 recipe Nam Prik Pao (optional)(recipe follows)

1. Bring 4 quarts water to boil in large pot. Remove from heat, add vermicelli, and let sit, stirring occasionally, until vermicelli are fully tender, 10 to 15 minutes. Drain, rinse with cold water, drain again, and distribute evenly among large soup bowls.

2. Place lemongrass, scallion whites, lime leaves, whole Thai chile, and galangal on cutting board and lightly smash with meat pounder or bottom of small skillet until mixture is moist and very fragrant. Transfer lemongrass mixture to Dutch oven. Add broth and sugar and bring to boil over high heat. Reduce heat and simmer for 15 minutes. Using slotted spoon, remove solids from pot and discard.

3. Add mushrooms, fish sauce, scallion greens, and sliced Thai chile and simmer for 3 to 4 minutes. Stir in shrimp. Cover and let sit off heat until shrimp are opaque and cooked through, 4 to 5 minutes. Stir in tomatoes and lime juice. Season with extra sugar, extra fish sauce, and extra lime juice to taste.

4. Ladle soup into bowls of noodles; sprinkle with cilantro and Thai basil, if using. Serve, drizzled with nam prik pao, if using, and passing lime wedges and extra sliced Thai chiles, if using, separately.

Nam Prik Pao

Makes ¾ cup • Total Time: 30 minutes

This sweet, savory, and spicy condiment is the classic garnish for guay tiew tom yum goong, but it's too good to be relegated to a single use. Thai cooks also use it on fried eggs, noodles, and white rice; in stir-fries; or even as a sandwich spread. Slice the shallots to a consistent thickness to ensure even cooking. For a spicier jam, add more chile seeds.

- ½ cup vegetable oil
- 2 large shallots, sliced thin
- 4 large garlic cloves, sliced thin
- 10 dried arbol chiles, stemmed, halved lengthwise, and seeds reserved
- 2 tablespoons packed brown sugar
- 3 tablespoons lime juice, plus extra for seasoning (2 limes)
- 2 tablespoons fish sauce, plus extra for seasoning

1. Set fine-mesh strainer over heatproof bowl. Heat oil and shallots in medium saucepan over medium-high heat, stirring frequently, until shallots are deep golden brown, 10 to 14 minutes. Using slotted spoon, transfer shallots to second bowl. Add garlic to hot oil and cook, stirring constantly, until golden brown, 2 to 3 minutes. Using slotted spoon, transfer garlic to bowl with shallots. Add arbols and half of reserved seeds to hot oil and cook, stirring constantly, until arbols turn deep red, 1 to 2 minutes. Strain oil through prepared strainer into bowl; reserve oil and transfer arbols to bowl with shallots and garlic. Do not wash saucepan.

2. Process shallot mixture, sugar, and lime juice in food processor until thick paste forms, 15 to 30 seconds, scraping down sides of bowl as needed.

3. Return paste to now-empty saucepan and add fish sauce and 2 tablespoons reserved oil. Bring to simmer over medium-low heat. Cook, stirring frequently, until mixture is thickened and has jam-like consistency, 4 to 5 minutes. Off heat, season with extra lime juice, extra fish sauce, and salt to taste. (Jam can be refrigerated for up to 1 month.)

SEASON 12

Broccoli-Cheese Soup

Serves 6 to 8 • **Total Time: 1¼ hours**

Why This Recipes Works We were after a soup with pure broccoli flavor that wasn't hiding behind the cream or the cheese. Overcooked broccoli has a sulfurous flavor, but we discovered when we cooked our broccoli beyond the point of just overcooked—for a full hour—those sulfur-containing compounds broke down, leaving behind intense, nutty broccoli. Its texture was fairly soft, but that was perfect for use in a soup. Adding baking soda to the pot sped up the process, shortening the broccoli's cooking time to a mere 20 minutes. A little spinach lent bright green color to the soup without taking over the flavor. After adding cheddar and Parmesan, we had a soup so full of flavor and richness that it didn't even need the typical cream. Serve with buttery croutons, if desired.

> *To make a vegetarian version of this soup, substitute vegetable broth for the chicken broth.*

- 2 tablespoons unsalted butter
- 2 pounds broccoli, florets chopped into 1-inch pieces, stems peeled and sliced ¼ inch thick
- 1 onion, chopped coarse
- 2 garlic cloves, minced
- 1½ teaspoons dry mustard
- 1 teaspoon table salt
- Pinch cayenne pepper
- 3–4 cups water, divided
- ¼ teaspoon baking soda
- 2 cups chicken broth
- 2 ounces baby spinach (about 2 cups)
- 3 ounces sharp cheddar cheese, shredded (¾ cup)
- 1½ ounces Parmesan cheese, grated fine (¾ cup), plus extra for serving

Unexpected Ingredients Bring Big Flavor and Color

"My fondest memory of this soup is the time when we had a winter nor'easter a few years back and lost power. Thankfully, we had a wood burning stove to keep us warm, and soon our house filled up with family and friends who were all looking for a warm place to congregate. Once we were all settled in and had the small generator working to keep our phones charged and a couple of lights on, it occurred to me that I happened to have the ingredients on hand to make a big batch of soup. In less than an hour, we were all enjoying hot bowls of a simple yet satisfying meal. The generator allowed me to power up the hot plate to cook the soup and the blender to puree it. Along with some crusty bread, it was the perfect (and unexpected) meal to have during a blustery storm.

I particularly love this soup not only because it's quick to make, but also because the broccoli flavor is at the forefront and isn't masked with large amounts of cheese like so many other broccoli-cheese soups. The flavor is enhanced by a modest amount of cheddar, Parmesan, and also a small amount of spinach, which helps to give it a vibrant green color."

— Erin

1. Melt butter in Dutch oven over medium-high heat. Add broccoli, onion, garlic, mustard, salt, and cayenne and cook, stirring frequently, until fragrant, about 6 minutes. Add 1 cup water and baking soda. Bring to simmer, cover, and cook until broccoli is very soft, about 20 minutes, stirring once during cooking.

2. Add broth and 2 cups water and increase heat to medium-high. When mixture begins to simmer, stir in spinach and cook until wilted, about 1 minute. Transfer half of soup to blender, add cheddar and Parmesan, and process until smooth, about 1 minute. Transfer soup to medium bowl and repeat with remaining soup. Return soup to Dutch oven, place over medium heat and bring to simmer. Adjust consistency of soup with up to 1 cup water. Season with salt and pepper to taste. Serve, passing extra Parmesan.

Silky Butternut Squash Soup

Serves 4 to 6 • Total Time: 1¾ hours

Why This Recipe Works The best butternut squash soup strikes a perfect balance between nuttiness and sweetness. Getting that balance right depends on selecting just a few key ingredients so the sweet squash flavor can take center stage. We found our answer to intense squash flavor in the squash's seeds and fibers. We sautéed them with shallots and butter, simmered them in water, and then used the liquid to steam the unpeeled quartered squash. Once the squash had cooled, we scooped out the flesh and pureed it with the steaming liquid for a perfectly smooth texture. Dark brown sugar intensified the sweetness of the squash. Finally, we enriched the soup with heavy cream and a pinch of nutmeg to round out the rich flavors.

Lightly toasted pumpkin seeds, drizzles of balsamic vinegar, or sprinklings of paprika or cracked black pepper make appealing accompaniments to this soup.

4 tablespoons unsalted butter
1 large shallot, minced (about ¼ cup)
3 pounds butternut squash (about 1 large squash), cut in half lengthwise, each half cut in half widthwise; seeds and fibers scraped out and reserved
6 cups water
1½ teaspoons table salt
½ cup heavy cream
1 teaspoon dark brown sugar
Pinch grated nutmeg

1. Melt butter in Dutch oven over medium-low heat. Add shallot and cook, stirring frequently, until translucent, about 3 minutes. Add seeds and fibers from squash and cook, stirring occasionally, until butter turns saffron color, about 4 minutes.

2. Add water and salt to pot and bring to boil over high heat. Reduce heat to medium-low, place squash, cut side down, in steamer basket, and lower basket into pot. Cover and steam until squash is completely tender, about 30 minutes. Take pot off heat and use tongs to transfer squash to rimmed baking sheet. When cool enough to handle, use large spoon to scrape flesh from skin. Reserve squash flesh in bowl and discard skin.

3. Strain steaming liquid through fine-mesh strainer into second bowl; discard solids in strainer. (You should have 2½ to 3 cups liquid.) Rinse and dry pot.

4. Working in batches and filling blender jar only halfway for each batch, puree squash, adding enough reserved steaming liquid to obtain smooth consistency. Transfer puree to clean pot and stir in remaining steaming liquid, cream, and brown sugar. Warm soup over medium-low heat until hot, about 3 minutes. Stir in nutmeg, season with salt to taste, and serve. (Soup can be refrigerated in airtight container for up to 2 days. Warm over low heat until hot; do not boil.)

Super Greens Soup with Lemon-Tarragon Cream

Serves 4 to 6 • **Total Time: 1¾ hours**

Why This Recipe Works We wanted a deceptively delicious, silky-smooth soup that delivered a big dose of healthy greens. It should be packed with all the essential nutrients of hearty greens and boast a deep, complex flavor brightened with a garnish of lemon and herb cream. First, we built a flavorful foundation of sweet caramelized onions and earthy sautéed mushrooms. We added broth, water, and lots of leafy greens (we liked a mix of chard, kale, arugula, and parsley), and simmered until the greens became tender before blending them smooth. We were happy with the soup's depth of flavor, but it was watery and too thin. Many recipes we found used potatoes as a thickener, but they lent an overwhelmingly earthy flavor. Instead, we used Arborio rice: The rice's high starch content thickened the soup to a velvety, lush consistency without clouding its bright, vegetal flavors. For a vibrant finish, we whisked together heavy cream, sour cream, lemon zest, lemon juice, and tarragon and drizzled it over the top.

| *Our favorite brand of Arborio rice is RiceSelect.*

- ¼ cup heavy cream
- 3 tablespoons sour cream
- ½ teaspoon plus 2 tablespoons extra-virgin olive oil, divided
- 1¼ teaspoons table salt, divided
- ½ teaspoon minced fresh tarragon
- ¼ teaspoon finely grated lemon zest plus ½ teaspoon juice
- 1 onion, halved through root end and sliced thin
- ¾ teaspoon light brown sugar
- 3 ounces white mushrooms, trimmed and sliced thin
- 2 garlic cloves, minced
  Pinch cayenne pepper
- 3 cups water
- 3 cups vegetable broth
- ⅓ cup Arborio rice
- 12 ounces Swiss chard, stemmed and chopped coarse
- 9 ounces kale, stemmed and chopped coarse
- ¼ cup fresh parsley leaves
- 2 ounces (2 cups) baby arugula

1. Combine cream, sour cream, ½ teaspoon oil, ¼ teaspoon salt, tarragon, and lemon zest and juice in bowl. Cover and refrigerate until ready to serve.

2. Heat remaining 2 tablespoons oil in Dutch oven over medium-high heat until shimmering. Stir in onion, sugar, and remaining 1 teaspoon salt and cook, stirring occasionally, until onion releases some moisture, about 5 minutes. Reduce heat to low and cook, stirring often and scraping up any browned bits, until onion is deeply browned and slightly sticky, about 30 minutes. (If onion is sizzling or scorching, reduce heat. If onion is not browning after 15 to 20 minutes, increase heat.)

3. Stir in mushrooms and cook until they have released their moisture, about 5 minutes. Stir in garlic and cayenne and cook until fragrant, about 30 seconds. Stir in water, broth, and rice, scraping up any browned bits, and bring to boil. Reduce heat to low, cover, and simmer for 15 minutes.

4. Stir in chard, kale, and parsley, 1 handful at a time, until wilted and submerged in liquid. Return to simmer, cover, and cook until greens are tender, about 10 minutes.

5. Off heat, stir in arugula until wilted. Working in batches, process soup in blender until smooth, about 1 minute per batch. Return pureed soup to clean pot and season with salt and pepper to taste. Drizzle individual portions with lemon-tarragon cream and serve.

Cauliflower Soup

Serves 4 to 6 • **Total Time: 1 hour**

Why This Recipe Works For a creamy cauliflower soup that tasted first and foremost of cauliflower, we did away with the distractions—no cream, flour, or overpowering seasonings. Cauliflower, simmered until tender, produced a creamy, velvety smooth puree, without the aid of any cream, due to its low insoluble fiber content. For the purest flavor, we cooked it in salted water (instead of broth), skipped the spice rack entirely, and bolstered it with sautéed onion and leek. We added the cauliflower to the simmering water in two stages so our soup offered the grassy flavor of just-cooked cauliflower and the sweeter, nuttier flavor of long-cooked cauliflower. Finally, we fried a portion of the florets in butter until both the cauliflower and butter were golden brown and used each as a separate, richly flavored garnish.

White wine vinegar may be substituted for the sherry vinegar. For best flavor and texture, trim the core thoroughly of green leaves and leaf stems, which can be fibrous and contribute to a grainy texture in the soup.

1 head cauliflower (2 pounds)
8 tablespoons unsalted butter, cut into 1-tablespoon pieces, divided
1 leek, white and light green parts only, halved lengthwise, sliced thin, and washed thoroughly
1 small onion, halved and sliced thin
1½ teaspoons table salt
4½ cups water
½ teaspoon sherry vinegar
3 tablespoons minced fresh chives

1. Pull off outer leaves of cauliflower and trim stem. Using paring knife, cut around core to remove; thinly slice core and reserve. Cut heaping 1 cup of ½-inch florets from head of cauliflower; set aside. Cut remaining cauliflower crosswise into ½-inch-thick slices.

2. Melt 3 tablespoons butter in large saucepan over medium-low heat. Add leek, onion, and salt; cook, stirring frequently, until onion is softened but not browned, about 7 minutes.

3. Increase heat to medium-high; add water, sliced core, and half of sliced cauliflower; and bring to simmer. Reduce heat to medium-low and simmer gently for 15 minutes.

Add remaining sliced cauliflower, return to simmer, and continue to cook until cauliflower is tender and crumbles easily, 15 to 20 minutes longer.

4. While soup simmers, melt remaining 5 tablespoons butter in 8-inch skillet over medium heat. Add reserved florets and cook, stirring frequently, until florets are golden brown and butter is browned, 6 to 8 minutes. Remove skillet from heat and use slotted spoon to transfer florets to small bowl. Toss florets with vinegar and season with salt to taste. Pour browned butter in skillet into small bowl and reserve for garnishing.

5. Process soup in blender until smooth, about 45 seconds. Rinse out pan. Return pureed soup to pan and return to simmer over medium heat, adjusting consistency with up to ½ cup water as needed (soup should have thick, velvety texture, but should be thin enough to settle with a flat surface after being stirred) and seasoning with salt to taste. Serve, garnishing individual bowls with browned florets, drizzles of browned butter, and chives and seasoning with pepper to taste.

Wild Rice and Mushroom Soup

Serves 6 to 8 • **Total Time: 2¼ hours, plus 20 minutes resting**

Why This Recipe Works For a rich, earthy, nutty-tasting soup, we had to figure out how to make wild rice and mushrooms do more than just add bulk. Fresh cremini mushrooms provided a meaty texture, and dried shiitakes, ground into a powder and added to the broth, ensured full-bodied mushroom flavor. Simmering the wild rice with baking soda decreased the cooking time and brought out its complex flavor. Cooking the rice in the oven, instead of on the stovetop, made it tender with a pleasant chew. To infuse the entire soup with wild rice flavor, we replaced some of the water in the soup with the rice's leftover cooking liquid. Including tomato paste and soy sauce amplified the nutty, earthy flavor profile. A final addition of cornstarch helped suspend the rice in the broth to give our soup a velvety texture.

White mushrooms can be substituted for the cremini mushrooms. We use a spice grinder to process the dried shiitake mushrooms, but a blender also works.

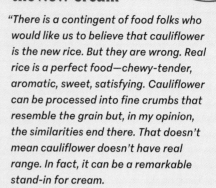

3. Melt butter in Dutch oven over high heat. Add cremini mushrooms, onion, tomato paste, pepper, minced garlic, and remaining ¾ teaspoon salt. Cook, stirring occasionally, until vegetables are browned and dark fond develops on bottom of pot, 15 minutes. Add sherry, scraping up any browned bits, and cook until reduced and pot is almost dry, about 2 minutes. Add ground shiitake mushrooms, reserved rice cooking liquid, broth, and soy sauce and bring to boil. Reduce heat to low and simmer, covered, until onion and mushrooms are tender, about 20 minutes.

4. Whisk cornstarch and remaining ¼ cup water together in small bowl. Stir cornstarch slurry into soup; return to simmer; and cook until thickened, about 2 minutes. Remove pot from heat and stir in cooked rice, cream, chives, and lemon zest. Cover and let stand for 20 minutes. Season with salt and pepper to taste, and serve.

¼	ounce dried shiitake mushrooms, rinsed
4¼	cups water, divided
1	sprig fresh thyme
1	bay leaf
5	garlic cloves, peeled (1 whole, 4 minced)
1½	teaspoons table salt
¼	teaspoon baking soda
1	cup wild rice
4	tablespoons unsalted butter
1	pound cremini mushrooms, trimmed and sliced ¼ inch thick
1	onion, chopped fine
1	teaspoon tomato paste
1	teaspoon pepper
⅔	cup dry sherry
4	cups chicken broth
1	tablespoon soy sauce
¼	cup cornstarch
½	cup heavy cream
¼	cup minced fresh chives
¼	teaspoon finely grated lemon zest

1. Adjust oven rack to middle position and heat oven to 375 degrees. Grind shiitake mushrooms in spice grinder until finely ground (you should have about 3 tablespoons).

2. Bring 4 cups water, thyme sprig, bay leaf, whole garlic clove, ¾ teaspoon salt, and baking soda to boil in medium saucepan over high heat. Add rice and return to boil. Cover saucepan, transfer to oven, and bake until rice is tender, 35 to 50 minutes. Strain rice through fine-mesh strainer set in 4-cup liquid measuring cup; discard thyme sprig, bay leaf, and garlic clove. Add enough water to reserved cooking liquid to measure 3 cups.

SEASON 9

Best French Onion Soup

Serves 6 • Total Time: 4¾ to 5¼ hours

Why This Recipe Works The ideal French onion soup combines a satisfying broth redolent of sweet caramelized onions with a slice of toasted baguette and melted cheese. We wanted a foolproof method for achieving extraordinarily deep flavor from the humble onion—the star of this classic soup. The secret to a rich broth was to caramelize the onions fully. Caramelizing the onions, deglazing the pot, and then repeating this process dozens of times kept ratcheting up the flavor. The bad news was what a laborious, hands-on process this proved to be. Fortunately, we found that if we first cooked the onions, covered, in a hot oven, we only needed to deglaze the onions on the stovetop three or four times. Just one type of onion (yellow) was sufficient, but a combination of three different liquids (water, chicken broth, and beef broth) added maximum flavor. For the topping, we toasted the bread before floating it on the soup to ward off sogginess and added only a modest sprinkling of nutty Gruyère so the broth wasn't overpowered.

Sweet onions, such as Vidalia or Walla Walla, will make this dish overly sweet. Be patient when caramelizing the onions in step 2; the entire process takes 45 to 60 minutes. Use broiler-safe crocks and keep the rims of the bowls 4 to 5 inches from the heating element to obtain a proper gratinée of melted, bubbly cheese. If using ordinary soup bowls, sprinkle the toasted bread slices with Gruyère and return them to the broiler until the cheese melts, then float them on top of the soup.

For the best flavor, make the soup a day or two in advance. Alternatively, the onions can be prepared through step 1, cooled in the pot, and refrigerated for up to three days before proceeding with the recipe.

Soup

- 3 tablespoons unsalted butter, cut into 3 pieces
- 4 pounds onions, halved and sliced through root end ¼ inch thick
- 1½ teaspoons table salt, divided
- 2 cups water, divided, plus extra for deglazing
- ½ cup dry sherry
- 4 cups chicken broth
- 2 cups beef broth
- 6 sprigs fresh thyme, tied together with kitchen twine
- 1 bay leaf

Cheese Croutons

- 1 small baguette, cut on bias into ½-inch slices
- 8 ounces Gruyère cheese, shredded (2 cups)

1. For the soup: Adjust oven rack to lower-middle position and heat oven to 400 degrees. Generously spray inside of large (at least 7-quart) Dutch oven with vegetable oil spray. Add butter, onions, and 1 teaspoon salt to pot. Cook, covered, for 1 hour (onions will be moist and slightly reduced in volume). Remove pot from oven and stir onions, scraping bottom and sides of pot. Return pot to oven with lid slightly ajar and continue to cook until onions are very soft and golden brown, 1½ to 1¾ hours longer, stirring onions and scraping bottom and sides of pot after 1 hour.

2. Carefully remove pot from oven and place over medium-high heat. Cook onions, stirring frequently and scraping bottom and sides of pot, until liquid evaporates and onions brown, 15 to 20 minutes, reducing heat to medium if onions are browning too quickly. Continue to cook, stirring frequently, until pot bottom is coated with dark crust, 6 to 8 minutes, adjusting heat as necessary. (Scrape any browned bits that collect on spoon back into onions.) Stir in ¼ cup water, scraping pot bottom to loosen crust, and cook until water evaporates and pot bottom has formed another dark crust, 6 to 8 minutes. Repeat process of deglazing 2 or 3 more times, until onions are very dark brown. Stir in sherry and cook, stirring frequently, until sherry evaporates, about 5 minutes.

3. Stir in 2 cups water, chicken broth, beef broth, thyme sprigs, bay leaf, and remaining ½ teaspoon salt, scraping up any final bits of browned crust on bottom and sides of pot. Increase heat to high and bring to simmer. Reduce heat to low, cover, and simmer for 30 minutes. Discard thyme sprigs and bay leaf, then season with salt and pepper to taste.

4. For the croutons: While soup simmers, heat oven to 400 degrees. Arrange baguette slices in single layer on rimmed baking sheet and bake until dry, crisp, and golden at edges, about 10 minutes. Set aside.

5. Adjust oven rack 6 inches from broiler element and heat broiler. Set individual broiler-safe crocks on baking sheet and fill each with about 1¾ cups of soup. Top each bowl with 1 or 2 baguette slices (do not overlap slices) and sprinkle evenly with Gruyère. Broil until cheese is melted and bubbly around edges, 3 to 5 minutes. Let cool for 5 minutes; serve.

SEASON 21

Ultimate Cream of Tomato Soup

Serves 3 to 4 • **Total Time: 1½ hours**

Why This Recipes Works Canned cream of tomato soup is a childhood favorite. But grown-up tastes deserve something better; the canned soup's overly sweet flavors are just not all that appealing today. We wanted a well-balanced cream of tomato soup, one with rich color, great tomato flavor, and a silky texture. Right away, we turned to canned tomatoes; fresh tomatoes are at their best just a few months out of the year and we didn't want to restrict our soup-making to just one season. To coax the most flavor from our canned whole tomatoes, it was essential to roast them in the oven. The intense dry heat worked to evaporate surface liquids and concentrate the flavor, and a sprinkling of brown sugar encouraged caramelization.

For a Better Tomato Soup, Concentrate, Don't Condense

"There are lots of styles of tomato soups out there, but when we're talking about cream of tomato soup, what immediately comes to mind? Perhaps a red-and-white-labeled can of the condensed soup? Yeah, that's what I think of too. That velvety, red soup was positively comfort-in-a-bowl when I was a kid, but my mature taste buds demand something … well, for lack of a better term, less ketchup-y.

Because this is a soup most often served in the colder months, we quickly nixed relying on quality summer tomatoes. Reliably flavorful canned plum tomatoes became the backbone ingredient. The problem was, as flavorful as they were right out of the can, once blended with the necessary water or broth, their tomato flavor became quite muted. Our solution was to roast the drained whole plum tomatoes with just a little brown sugar until the tomatoes were a little browned, shriveled, and so sticky that they became candy-like. The tomato flavor was exponentially concentrated and deepened, and the resulting soup reflected this. The tomato juices were used as the main liquid in the recipe, with a little cream (and brandy) added at the end to give plushness to the soup, and warmth to the belly. Even after all these years, this remains my favorite soup."

—*Bridget*

We cooked our roasted tomatoes with shallots, chicken broth, and reserved tomato juice to develop robust flavor, then pureed the tomatoes (with broth) to keep the deep flavor of the tomato broth intact. Finished with heavy cream and a splash of brandy, this cream of tomato soup will satisfy everyone at the table.

Make sure to use canned whole tomatoes that are not packed in puree; you will need some of the juice to make the soup.

2 (28-ounce) cans whole tomatoes (not packed in puree), drained, 3 cups juice reserved, tomatoes seeded
1½ tablespoons dark brown sugar
4 tablespoons unsalted butter
4 large shallots, minced
1 tablespoon tomato paste
Pinch ground allspice
2 tablespoons unbleached all-purpose flour
1¾ cups chicken broth
½ cup heavy cream
2 tablespoons brandy or dry sherry
Cayenne pepper

1. Adjust oven rack to upper-middle position and heat oven to 450 degrees; line rimmed baking sheet with aluminum foil. Spread tomatoes in single layer on foil, and sprinkle evenly with brown sugar. Bake until all liquid has evaporated and tomatoes begin to color, about 30 minutes. Let tomatoes cool slightly, then peel them off foil; transfer to small bowl and set aside.

2. Heat butter over medium heat in medium nonreactive saucepan until foaming; add shallots, tomato paste, and allspice. Reduce heat to low, cover, and cook, stirring occasionally, until shallots are softened, 7 to 10 minutes. Add flour and cook, stirring constantly, until thoroughly combined, about 30 seconds. Whisking constantly, gradually add broth; stir in reserved tomato juice and roasted tomatoes. Cover, increase heat to medium, and bring to boil; reduce heat to low and simmer, stirring occasionally, to blend flavors, about 10 minutes.

3. Strain mixture through fine-mesh strainer set over medium bowl. Process solids from strainer and 1 cup strained liquid in blender until smooth, 1 to 2 minutes. (Soup can be refrigerated for up to 3 days or frozen for up to 2 months. Reheat over low heat before proceeding with step 4.)

4. Return pureed mixture and remaining strained liquid to clean saucepan. Stir in cream and heat over low heat until hot, about 3 minutes. Off heat, stir in brandy. Season with salt and cayenne to taste, and serve.

Soupe au Pistou

Serves 6 • Total Time: 55 minutes

Why This Recipes Works Provençal vegetable soup is a classic French summer soup with a delicate broth that is intensified by a dollop of pistou, the French equivalent of Italy's pesto. We wanted a simple version that focused on fresh seasonal vegetables. Leeks, green beans, and zucchini all made the cut; we like their summery flavors, different shapes, and varying shades of green. We added canned white beans (which were far more convenient than dried in this quick-cooking soup) and orecchiette for its easy-to-spoon shape. Using the liquid from the canned beans added much-needed body to the broth. For the pistou, we just whirred basil, Parmesan, olive oil, and garlic together in our food processor.

For the best flavor, we prefer broth prepared from our Vegetable Broth Base (page 130), but you can use store-bought broth.

Pistou
¾ cup fresh basil leaves
1 ounce Parmesan cheese, grated (½ cup)
⅓ cup extra-virgin olive oil
1 garlic clove, minced

Soup
1 tablespoon extra-virgin olive oil
1 leek, white and light green parts only, halved lengthwise, sliced ½ inch thick, and washed thoroughly
1 celery rib, cut into ½-inch pieces
1 carrot, peeled and sliced ¼ inch thick
½ teaspoon table salt
2 garlic cloves, minced
3 cups vegetable broth
3 cups water
½ cup orecchiette or other short pasta
8 ounces haricots verts or green beans, trimmed and cut into ½-inch lengths
1 (15-ounce) can cannellini or navy beans, undrained
1 small zucchini, halved lengthwise, seeded, and cut into ¼-inch pieces
1 large tomato, cored, seeded, and cut into ¼-inch pieces

1. For the pistou: Process all ingredients in food processor until smooth, scraping down sides of bowl as needed, about 15 seconds. (Pistou can be refrigerated for up to 4 hours.)

2. For the soup: Heat oil in Dutch oven over medium heat until shimmering. Add leek, celery, carrot, and salt and cook until vegetables are softened, 8 to 10 minutes. Stir in garlic and cook until fragrant, about 30 seconds. Stir in broth and water and bring to simmer.

3. Stir in pasta and simmer until slightly softened, about 5 minutes. Stir in haricots verts and simmer until bright green but still crunchy, 3 to 5 minutes. Stir in cannellini beans and their liquid, zucchini, and tomato and simmer until pasta and vegetables are tender, about 3 minutes. Season with salt and pepper to taste. Serve, topping individual portions with generous tablespoon pistou.

SEASON 6
Black Bean Soup

Serves 6 • Total Time: 3 hours

Why This Recipe Works Black bean soup is full of robust earthy flavor. Our easy-to-make recipe results in a soup rich with sweet, spicy, smoky flavors and brightened with fresh garnishes. Dried beans imparted good flavor to the broth as they simmered, and we didn't have to soak them first. A touch of baking soda in the cooking water kept the beans from turning gray. Homemade stock is great here but we added flavor to prepared broth. Ham steak provided the smoky pork flavor of a ham hock and more meat as well. We spiced up the aromatics with lots of cumin and some red pepper flakes. For a chunky texture in our soup, we pureed it only partially, thickening it further with a slurry of cornstarch and water. Lastly lime juice added brightness.

Dried beans tend to cook unevenly, so be sure to taste several beans to determine their doneness in step 1. For efficiency, you can prepare the soup ingredients while the beans simmer and the garnishes while the soup simmers. Though you do not need to offer all of the garnishes listed, do choose at least a couple; garnishes are essential for this soup, as they add not only flavor but texture and color as well. Leftover soup can be refrigerated in an airtight container for up to three days; reheat it in a saucepan over medium heat until hot, stirring in additional chicken broth if it has thickened beyond your liking.

Beans

- 1 pound (2 cups) dried black beans, rinsed and picked over
- 4 ounces ham steak, trimmed of rind
- 2 bay leaves
- 5 cups water
- ⅛ teaspoon baking soda
- 1 teaspoon table salt

GAME CHANGER

The Joy of Dried Black Beans

"I grew up eating black bean soup that my mom made following a recipe from her mother's 1938 edition of The Joy of Cooking. *It's a terrific recipe that results in a fancy pureed soup that's finished with a drizzle of sherry (this 'adult' garnish thrilled me as a child), paper-thin slices of lemon, and chopped hard-boiled egg. It's outstanding.*

I still make that soup, but I'm also very fond of this more rustic version that I developed years ago. It starts with dried black beans, which are economical and develop rich earthy flavor as they simmer. I flavor the broth with a standard mirepoix (onion, celery, and carrot) along with plenty of garlic, cumin, bay leaves, and a ham steak. A pinch of baking soda ensures that the soup develops a rich, dark color. You can use any or all of the following garnishes (I'm not happy unless I have every last one in my bowl): sour cream, lime wedges, avocado, diced red onion, and cilantro. Each brings color and vibrancy to the thick, flavorsome soup."

Soup

- 3 tablespoons olive oil
- 2 large onions, minced
- 3 celery ribs, chopped fine
- 1 large carrot, chopped
- ½ teaspoon table salt
- 5–6 garlic cloves, minced (about 2 tablespoons)
- 1½ tablespoons ground cumin
- ½ teaspoon red pepper flakes
- 6 cups chicken broth
- 2 tablespoons cornstarch
- 2 tablespoons water
- 2 tablespoons lime juice

  Lime wedges
  Minced fresh cilantro leaves
  Red onion, diced fine
  Avocado, peeled, pitted, and diced medium
  Sour cream

1. For the beans: Place beans, ham, bay leaves, water, and baking soda in large saucepan with tight-fitting lid. Bring to boil over medium-high heat; using large spoon, skim foam as it rises to surface. Stir in salt, reduce heat to low, cover, and simmer briskly until beans are tender, 1¼ to 1½ hours (if necessary, add 1 cup more water and continue to simmer until beans are tender); do not drain beans. Discard bay leaves. Remove ham steak (ham steak darkens to color of beans), cut it into ¼-inch cubes, and set aside.

2. For the soup: Heat oil in large Dutch oven over medium-high heat until shimmering but not smoking; add onions, celery, carrot, and salt and cook, stirring occasionally, until vegetables are soft and lightly browned, 12 to 15 minutes. Reduce heat to medium-low and add garlic, cumin, and red pepper flakes; cook, stirring constantly, until fragrant, about 3 minutes. Stir in beans, bean cooking liquid, and chicken broth. Increase heat to medium-high and bring to boil, then reduce heat to low and simmer, uncovered, stirring occasionally, to blend flavors, about 30 minutes.

3. To finish the soup: Ladle 1½ cups beans and 2 cups liquid into food processor or blender, process until smooth, and return to pot. Stir cornstarch and water in small bowl until combined, then gradually stir half of cornstarch mixture into soup; bring to boil over medium-high heat, stirring occasionally, to fully thicken. If soup is still thinner than desired once boiling, stir remaining cornstarch mixture to recombine and gradually stir mixture into soup; return to boil to fully thicken. Off heat, stir in lime juice and reserved ham; ladle soup into bowls and serve immediately, passing garnishes separately.

Acquacotta

Serves 8 to 10 • Total Time: 1½ hours

Why This Recipe Works Don't let the name acquacotta, meaning "cooked water" in Italian, deceive you. In this Tuscan soup, water, vegetables, beans, and fresh herbs are transformed into a supremely satisfying meal when egg yolks are whisked into the broth before it's ladled over toasted bread. We used chicken broth and amped up the flavor with a soffritto, a mixture of sautéed onion, celery, and garlic. A food processor made quick work of finely chopping these ingredients as well as the canned tomatoes that flavor the broth. Aromatic parsley, oregano, and fennel fronds gave our soup its distinctive taste. Finally, we thickened the broth with a mixture of the bean canning liquid and egg yolks before serving our finished soup over toasted slices of crusty bread.

If escarole is unavailable, you can substitute 8 ounces of kale. We prefer Pecorino Romano's salty flavor, but Parmesan can be substituted, if desired. If your cheese has a rind, slice it off the wedge and add it to the pot with the broth in step 3 (remove it before serving). We like to serve this soup the traditional way, with a poached or soft-cooked egg spooned on top of the toast before the broth is ladled into the bowl.

Soup

- 1 large onion, chopped coarse
- 2 celery ribs, chopped coarse
- 4 garlic cloves, peeled
- 1 (28-ounce) can whole peeled tomatoes
- ½ cup extra-virgin olive oil
- ¾ teaspoon table salt
- ⅛ teaspoon red pepper flakes
- 8 cups chicken broth
- 1 fennel bulb, 2 tablespoons fronds minced, stalks discarded, bulb halved, cored, and cut into ½-inch pieces
- 2 (15-ounce) cans cannellini beans, drained with liquid reserved, rinsed
- 1 small head escarole (10 ounces), trimmed and cut into ½-inch pieces (8 cups)
- 2 large egg yolks
- ½ cup chopped fresh parsley
- 1 tablespoon minced fresh oregano
  Grated Pecorino Romano cheese
  Lemon wedges

Toast

- 10 (½-inch-thick) slices thick-crusted country bread
- ¼ cup extra-virgin olive oil

Hearty Ham and Split Pea Soup with Potatoes

Serves 6 • **Total Time: 3¾ to 4¼ hours**

Why This Recipe Works Split pea soup tends to show up on the home cook's menu only when the previous meal (usually a holiday celebration) featured a big ham—and the leftovers are begging to be made into soup. We wanted a recipe for an old-fashioned ham and split pea soup that could be made anytime, with a readily available cut of ham that would also provide enough meat for really hearty soup. We found that we could get good, meaty ham stock with a picnic shoulder, a small, inexpensive cut that adds great flavor and provides plenty of meat for the soup (and some leftovers too). While it was easy enough to cook the peas in the ham stock, our vegetables benefited from a sauté in a separate pan. We found that caramelized vegetables gave this straightforward soup a richness and depth of flavor that had been missing—it was well worth the time spent washing an extra pan. Adding a few red potatoes with the carrots, celery, and onions turned our soup into a truly satisfying meal.

Use an entire small 2½-pound smoked picnic portion ham if you can find one. Otherwise, buy a half-picnic ham and remove some meat, which you can roast and use in sandwiches, salads, or omelets. To remove the meat, loosen the large comma-shaped muscles on top of the ham with your fingers, then use a knife to cut the membrane separating the comma-shaped muscles from the rest of the ham.

2½ pounds smoked ham, bone-in
4 bay leaves
12 cups water
1 pound (2 cups) green split peas, picked over and rinsed
1 teaspoon dried thyme
2 tablespoons extra-virgin olive oil
2 onions, chopped
2 carrots, peeled and chopped
2 celery ribs, chopped
1 tablespoon unsalted butter
2 garlic cloves, minced
 Pinch sugar
3 small red potatoes (about 8 ounces), unpeeled, cut into ½-inch chunks
 Minced red onion (optional)
 Balsamic vinegar

1. For the soup: Pulse onion, celery, and garlic in food processor until very finely chopped, 15 to 20 pulses, scraping down sides of bowl as needed. Transfer onion mixture to Dutch oven. Add tomatoes and their juice to now-empty processor and pulse until tomatoes are finely chopped, 10 to 12 pulses; set aside.

2. Stir oil, ¾ teaspoon salt, and pepper flakes into onion mixture. Cook over medium-high heat, stirring occasionally, until light brown fond begins to form on bottom of pot, 12 to 15 minutes. Stir in tomato mixture, increase heat to high, and cook, stirring frequently, until mixture is very thick and rubber spatula leaves distinct trail when dragged across bottom of pot, 9 to 12 minutes.

3. Add broth and fennel bulb to pot and bring to simmer. Reduce heat to medium-low and simmer until fennel begins to soften, 5 to 7 minutes. Stir in beans and escarole and cook until fennel is fully tender, about 10 minutes.

4. Whisk egg yolks and reserved bean liquid together in bowl, then stir into soup. Stir in parsley, oregano, and fennel fronds. Season with salt and pepper to taste.

5. For the toast: Adjust oven rack about 5 inches from broiler element and heat broiler. Place bread on aluminum foil–lined rimmed baking sheet, drizzle with oil, and season with salt and pepper. Broil until bread is deep golden brown.

6. Place 1 slice bread in bottom of each individual bowl. Ladle soup over toasted bread. Serve, passing Pecorino and lemon wedges separately.

1. Place ham in large Dutch oven, add bay leaves and water, cover, and bring to boil over medium-high heat. Reduce heat to low and simmer until meat is tender and pulls away from bone, 2 to 2½ hours. Remove ham meat and bone from pot and set aside.

2. Add split peas and thyme and simmer, uncovered, until peas are tender but not dissolved, about 45 minutes. Meanwhile, shred meat into bite-size pieces and set aside. Discard rind and bone.

3. Heat oil in large skillet over medium-high heat until shimmering. Add onions, carrots, and celery and sauté, stirring frequently, until most of liquid evaporates and vegetables begin to brown, 5 to 6 minutes. Reduce heat to medium-low and add butter, garlic, and sugar. Cook vegetables, stirring frequently, until deeply browned, 30 to 35 minutes; set aside.

4. Add sautéed vegetables, potatoes, and shredded ham to pot with split peas. Simmer until potatoes are tender, peas dissolve, and soup thickens to consistency of light cream, about 20 minutes. Season with pepper to taste. Discard bay leaves and ladle soup into bowls. Sprinkle with red onion, if using, and serve, passing balsamic vinegar separately. (Soup, minus garnishes, can be refrigerated in airtight container for up to 2 days. Warm over low heat until hot; do not boil.)

Harira

Serves 6 to 8 • **Total Time: 1½ hours**

Why This Recipes Works A popular Moroccan soup, harira features a hearty mix of legumes flavored with warm spices and fresh herbs. Like countless other regional dishes, harira's exact ingredients vary from region to region and even from family to family. For our version, we carefully reduced the ingredient list and altered the technique to deliver harira's flavors in less time. We decided to omit the meat (lamb, chicken, or beef is common) in this soup—with all the other robust flavors and textures in the mix, the meat wasn't missed. To save time, we opted for convenient canned chickpeas rather than dried beans, plus quick-cooking lentils. We pared down the number of spices to a key five available in most supermarkets. For more depth of flavor, we also replaced half the water with chicken broth. Using large amounts of just two herbs made for quicker prep and a more efficient use of fresh ingredients. Finishing the

dish with fresh lemon juice helped focus all the flavors. This wonderfully complex-tasting, spice-filled soup, made almost entirely from pantry ingredients, brought humble lentils to a whole other level.

For a vegetarian version, substitute vegetable broth for the chicken broth and water. We like to garnish this soup with a small amount of harissa, a fiery North African chili paste.

⅓ cup extra-virgin olive oil
1 large onion, chopped fine
2 celery ribs, chopped fine
5 garlic cloves, minced
1 tablespoon grated fresh ginger
2 teaspoons ground coriander
2 teaspoons smoked paprika
1 teaspoon ground cumin
½ teaspoon ground cinnamon
⅛ teaspoon red pepper flakes
¾ cup minced fresh cilantro, divided
½ cup minced fresh parsley, divided
4 cups chicken broth
4 cups water
1 (15-ounce) can chickpeas, rinsed
1 cup brown lentils, picked over and rinsed
1 (28-ounce) can crushed tomatoes
½ cup orzo
4 ounces Swiss chard, stemmed and cut into ½-inch pieces
2 tablespoons lemon juice, plus lemon wedges for serving

1. Heat oil in large Dutch oven over medium-high heat until shimmering. Add onion and celery and cook, stirring frequently, until translucent and starting to brown, 7 to 8 minutes. Reduce heat to medium, add garlic and ginger, and cook until fragrant, 1 minute. Stir in coriander, paprika, cumin, cinnamon, and pepper flakes and cook for 1 minute. Stir in ½ cup cilantro and ¼ cup parsley and cook for 1 minute.

2. Stir in broth, water, chickpeas, and lentils; increase heat to high and bring to simmer. Reduce heat to medium-low, partially cover, and simmer gently until lentils are just tender, about 20 minutes.

3. Stir in tomatoes and pasta and simmer, partially covered, for 7 minutes, stirring occasionally. Stir in chard and continue to cook, partially covered, until pasta is tender, about 5 minutes longer. Off heat, stir in lemon juice, remaining ¼ cup cilantro, and remaining ¼ cup parsley. Season with salt and pepper to taste. Serve, passing lemon wedges separately.

SEASON 17

Red Lentil Soup with Warm Spices

Serves 4 to 6 • Total Time: 55 minutes

Why This Recipe Works Red lentils are one of our favorite legumes. They cook quickly and don't require any presoaking or brining like other beans. One of their best qualities, however, is that they disintegrate when cooked, forming a creamy, thick puree—perfect for a satisfying soup. Their mild flavor does require a bit of embellishment, so we started by sautéing onions in butter and used the warm mixture to bloom some fragrant spices found in North African cooking. Tomato paste and garlic completed the base before the addition of the lentils, and a mix of chicken broth and water gave the soup a full, rounded character. After only 15 minutes of cooking, the lentils were soft enough to be pureed with a whisk. A generous dose of lemon juice brought the flavors into focus, and a drizzle of spice-infused butter and a sprinkle of fresh cilantro completed the transformation of commonplace ingredients into a comforting soup.

Pair this soup with a salad and bread for lunch or a light supper.

  4 tablespoons unsalted butter, divided
  1 large onion, chopped fine
  1 teaspoon table salt
  ¾ teaspoon ground coriander
  ½ teaspoon ground cumin
  ¼ teaspoon ground ginger
  ¼ teaspoon pepper
  ⅛ teaspoon ground cinnamon
     Pinch cayenne pepper
  1 tablespoon tomato paste
  1 garlic clove, minced
  4 cups chicken broth
  2 cups water
10½ ounces (1½ cups) red lentils, picked over and rinsed
  2 tablespoons lemon juice, plus extra for seasoning
1½ teaspoons dried mint, crumbled
  1 teaspoon paprika
  ¼ cup chopped fresh cilantro

1. Melt 2 tablespoons butter in large saucepan over medium heat. Add onion and salt and cook, stirring occasionally, until softened but not browned, about 5 minutes. Add coriander, cumin, ginger, pepper, cinnamon, and cayenne and cook until fragrant, about 2 minutes. Stir in tomato paste and garlic and cook for 1 minute. Stir in broth, water, and lentils and bring to simmer. Simmer vigorously, stirring occasionally, until lentils are soft and about half are broken down, about 15 minutes.

2. Whisk soup vigorously until it is coarsely pureed, about 30 seconds. Stir in lemon juice and season with salt and extra lemon juice to taste. Cover and keep warm. (Soup can be refrigerated for up to 3 days. Thin soup with water, if desired, when reheating.)

3. Melt remaining 2 tablespoons butter in small skillet over medium-low heat. Remove from heat and stir in mint and paprika. Ladle soup into individual bowls, drizzle each portion with 1 teaspoon spiced butter, sprinkle with cilantro, and serve.

Quinoa and Vegetable Stew

Serves 6 to 8 • Total Time: 1 hour

Why This Recipe Works Quinoa stews are common in many South American regions. Traditional recipes call for annatto powder and Andean varieties of potatoes and corn. We found that paprika has a similar flavor profile to annatto powder; we rounded it out with cumin and coriander. Red bell pepper, tomatoes, red potatoes, sweet corn, and frozen peas were a nice mix of vegetables. We added the quinoa after the potatoes had softened and cooked it until it released starch to help give body to the stew. Finally, we added the traditional garnishes: queso fresco, avocado, and cilantro.

We like the convenience of prewashed quinoa. If you buy unwashed quinoa (or are unsure whether it's washed), be sure to rinse it before cooking to remove its bitter protective coating (called saponin). This stew tends to thicken as it sits; add additional warm vegetable broth to loosen. Do not omit the garnishes; they are important to the flavor of the stew.

2 tablespoons vegetable oil
1 onion, chopped
1 red bell pepper, stemmed, seeded, and cut into ½-inch pieces
5 garlic cloves, minced
1 tablespoon paprika
2 teaspoons ground coriander
1½ teaspoons ground cumin
6 cups vegetable broth
1 pound red potatoes, unpeeled, cut into ½-inch pieces
1 cup prewashed white quinoa
1 cup fresh or frozen corn
2 tomatoes, cored and chopped coarse
1 cup frozen peas
8 ounces queso fresco or feta cheese, crumbled (2 cups)
1 avocado, halved, pitted, and diced
½ cup minced fresh cilantro

1. Heat oil in Dutch oven over medium heat until shimmering. Add onion and bell pepper and cook until softened, 5 to 7 minutes. Stir in garlic, paprika, coriander, and cumin and cook until fragrant, about 30 seconds. Stir in broth and potatoes and bring to boil over high heat. Reduce heat to medium-low and simmer gently for 10 minutes.

2. Stir in quinoa and simmer for 8 minutes. Stir in corn and simmer until potatoes and quinoa are just tender, 5 to 7 minutes. Stir in tomatoes and peas and let heat through, about 2 minutes.

3. Off heat, season with salt and pepper to taste. Sprinkle individual portions with queso fresco, avocado, and cilantro before serving.

VARIATION

Quinoa and Vegetable Stew with Eggs
Serving this stew with a cooked egg on top is a common practice in Peru.

Crack 6 large eggs evenly over top of stew after removing from heat and seasoning with salt and pepper in step 3; cover and let eggs poach off heat until whites have set but yolks are still soft, about 4 minutes. To serve, carefully scoop cooked eggs and stew from pot with large spoon.

Pasta e Piselli

Serves 4 • Total Time: 45 minutes

Why This Recipe Works Like its better-known cousins pasta e fagioli and pasta e ceci, the traditional Italian dish pasta e piselli combines a legume, peas, with small pasta to form a hearty soup. For a one-pot meal, we cooked the pasta in a broth flavored with sautéed onion and savory pancetta, simultaneously infusing the pasta with savoriness and thickening the rich, silky broth. Then we added the peas (we used frozen petite peas) and immediately took the pot off the heat to preserve their tenderness and color. A sprinkle of Pecorino Romano contributed richness and tangy depth. Last-minute additions of minced herbs and extra-virgin olive oil punched up the aroma and flavors of the dish.

3. Stir in peas and remove saucepan from heat. Stir in parsley, Pecorino, and mint. Season with salt and pepper to taste. Serve, drizzling with extra oil and passing extra Pecorino separately.

SEASON 25

Hong Kong–Style Wonton Noodle Soup

Serves 4 to 6 • Total Time: 1 hour

Why This Recipe Works The wontons in Hong Kong–style noodle soup are characterized by square yellow wrappers, juicy pork, and large pieces of shrimp. To achieve a cohesive filling, we agitated ground pork to release its sticky myosin proteins before seasoning it with scallion, Shaoxing wine, sesame oil, oyster sauce, and soy sauce and combining it with a piece of halved shrimp in each wrapper. For a flavorful seafood broth, we used the shells reserved from the shrimp as well as pungent flounder powder—a crucial part of this soup's Hong Kong identity. Dried flounder powder contributed savoriness and concentrated fish flavor. A splash of soy sauce and a pinch of white pepper rounded out the broth. Bright green bok choy and thin, fresh wonton noodles perfectly complemented the bouncy wontons and the savory seafood broth. To make the wontons, this mixture is divided among 24 wonton wrappers and the shrimp pieces are pressed on top. Be sure to leave the ends of wontons open.

If you'd prefer to substitute small pasta such as tubetti, ditali, elbow macaroni, or small shells for the ditalini, do so by weight, not by volume. We prefer frozen petite peas (also labeled as petits pois or baby sweet peas) because they are sweeter and less starchy than fresh peas or regular frozen peas, but you can substitute regular frozen peas. Do not defrost the peas before using them. For a vegetarian version, omit the pancetta, substitute vegetable broth for the chicken broth, and add an extra 2 tablespoons of grated cheese. Pecorino Romano adds a welcome sharpness; do not substitute Parmesan.

- 2 tablespoons extra-virgin olive oil, plus extra for drizzling
- 1 onion, chopped fine
- 2 ounces pancetta, chopped fine
- ½ teaspoon table salt
- ½ teaspoon pepper
- 2½ cups chicken broth
- 2½ cups water
- 7½ ounces (1½ cups) ditalini
- 1½ cups frozen petite peas
- ⅓ cup minced fresh parsley
- ¼ cup grated Pecorino Romano cheese, plus extra for serving
- 2 tablespoons minced fresh mint

1. Heat oil in large saucepan over medium heat until shimmering. Add onion, pancetta, salt, and pepper and cook, stirring frequently, until onion is softened, 7 to 10 minutes.

2. Add broth and water and bring to boil over high heat. Stir in pasta and cook, stirring frequently, until liquid returns to boil. Reduce heat to maintain simmer; cover; and cook until pasta is al dente, 8 to 10 minutes.

Look for freshly ground pork, which is typically sold in bulk at the butcher's counter, where it has a higher percentage of fat and a coarser texture than prepackaged pork. We prefer homemade chicken broth; however, store-bought broth can be substituted. If flounder powder is unavailable, it can be omitted, though the soup will not be as full-bodied. Do not substitute flounder fish seasoning (which contains added salt and flavorings) or powders made from other varieties of fish. Serve with Chinese red vinegar, a finishing vinegar with a hint of sweetness.

- 1 teaspoon vegetable oil
- 12 large shrimp (26 to 30 per pound), peeled, deveined, tails removed, and shells reserved
- 4 cups Chicken Broth (page 130)
- 2 cups water
- ¼ teaspoon plus ⅛ teaspoon table salt, divided
- 1 teaspoon dried flounder fish powder, divided
- 1 tablespoon soy sauce, divided
- ¼ teaspoon white pepper, divided
- 4 ounces ground pork

1 scallion, minced
1 tablespoon Shaoxing wine
2 teaspoons oyster sauce
½ teaspoon toasted sesame oil, plus extra
   for serving
24 (3-inch) square Hong Kong–style
   wonton wrappers
2 heads baby bok choy (4 ounces each),
   greens separated
6 ounces fresh thin wonton noodles

1. Heat vegetable oil in large saucepan over high heat until shimmering. Add reserved shrimp shells and cook, stirring frequently, until shells begin to turn spotty brown, about 2 minutes. Add broth, water, and ¼ teaspoon salt and bring to boil. Off heat, stir in ½ teaspoon flounder powder and let steep for 15 minutes. Strain broth through fine-mesh strainer and return to now-empty saucepan. Stir in 2 teaspoons soy sauce and ⅛ teaspoon pepper. Cover and keep warm.

2. Halve each shrimp crosswise; set aside. Using wooden spoon or 4 bundled chopsticks, vigorously stir pork in medium bowl until it has stiffened and started to pull away from sides of bowl and has slightly lightened in color, about 5 minutes. Stir in scallion, Shaoxing wine, oyster sauce, sesame oil, remaining ⅛ teaspoon salt, remaining ½ teaspoon flounder powder, remaining 1 teaspoon soy sauce, and remaining ⅛ teaspoon pepper until well combined.

3. Lightly dust parchment paper–lined rimmed baking sheet with flour. Place 6 wrappers on sheet, place heaping ½ teaspoon pork filling in center of each wrapper, then top with 1 piece of shrimp and gently press into filling. Form wontons by gathering corners of wrapper around filling and pinching

dough tightly just above filling to seal; leave ends of wrapper unsealed. Transfer wontons to prepared sheet, cover with damp dish towel, and repeat with remaining wrappers and filling in 3 batches. (Wontons can be refrigerated for up to 24 hours or frozen on sheet until solid, then transferred to zipper-lock bag and stored in freezer for up to 1 month. Do not thaw frozen dumplings before cooking; increase simmer time to about 6 minutes.)

4. Meanwhile, bring 4 quarts water to boil in Dutch oven. Add bok choy and cook until tender, about 1 minute. Using spider skimmer or slotted spoon, transfer bok choy to plate. Return water to boil, add wonton noodles, and cook until just tender. Using spider skimmer, transfer noodles to colander and rinse thoroughly; divide noodles among serving bowls. Return water to boil, add wontons, and cook until wontons turn translucent and tender and float to the top, about 4 minutes. Using spider skimmer, divide wontons among bowls and top with bok choy.

5. Return broth to boil over high heat, then ladle over bok choy, noodles, and dumplings. Serve, passing extra sesame oil separately.

Making Wontons

1. Place heaping ½ teaspoon pork filling in center of each wrapper, then top with 1 piece of shrimp and gently press into filling.

2. Form wontons by gathering corners of wrapper around filling.

3. Pinch dough tightly just above filling to seal; leave ends of wrapper unsealed.

Vegetable Broth Base

Makes 1¾ cups base; enough for 7 quarts broth
Total Time: 20 minutes

Why This Recipe Works Homemade broth enlivens any dish, but for vegetarian cooking, an overpowering broth can be ruinous. For our base, we focused on mild but impactful vegetables. Mirepoix, a mix of chopped onions, celery, and carrots, is a classic combination; we started there, swapping in leeks for their mild onion flavor and minimal moisture content. Celery root had a creamier, more complex celery taste than celery ribs. Dried minced onions reinforced the leeks, and carrots contributed pleasant sweetness. Tomato paste and soy sauce bolstered the savory qualities, and parsley added brightness. Kosher salt seasoned the broth while keeping it convenient: Salt lowers water's freezing point, so the concentrate would remain easy to scoop. Even better, our base had less salt than most store-bought broths. Creating the base was easy: We pulsed the ingredients in a food processor and froze the paste.

For the best balance of flavors, measure the prepped vegetables by weight. Kosher salt aids in grinding the vegetables. The broth base contains enough salt to keep it from freezing solid, making it easy to remove 1 table-spoon at a time. To make 1 cup of broth, stir 1 tablespoon of fresh or frozen broth base into 1 cup of boiling water. If particle-free broth is desired, let the broth steep for 5 minutes and then strain it through a fine-mesh strainer.

- 2 leeks, white and light green parts only, chopped and washed thoroughly (2½ cups or 5 ounces)
- 2 carrots, peeled and cut into ½-inch pieces (⅔ cup or 3 ounces)
- ½ small celery root, peeled and cut into ½-inch pieces (¾ cup or 3 ounces)
- ½ cup (½ ounce) parsley leaves and thin stems
- 3 tablespoons dried minced onions
- 2 tablespoons kosher salt
- 1½ tablespoons tomato paste
- 3 tablespoons soy sauce

Process leeks, carrots, celery root, parsley, minced onions, and salt in food processor, scraping down sides of bowl frequently, until paste is as fine as possible, 3 to 4 minutes. Add tomato paste and process for 1 minute, scraping down sides of bowl every 20 seconds. Add soy sauce and continue to process 1 minute longer. Transfer mixture to airtight container and tap firmly on counter to remove air bubbles. Press small piece of parchment paper flush against surface of mixture and cover. Freeze for up to 6 months.

Chicken Broth

Makes 8 cups • Total Time: 5½ hours

Why This Recipe Works Good homemade chicken broth is liquid gold. In this recipe we coaxed out rich flavor and full body by using chicken wings, which are convenient as well as gelatin-rich, giving the broth a luscious consistency. Minimal additions ensure the broth tastes as chicken-y as possible. Chicken wings are readily available but we also like to think ahead and put other resources to good use. We like to hold on to leftover trimmings and carcasses from roasted or poached poultry in our freezer. Once we have about a pound or more, we substitute them for an equal amount of wings.

If you have a large pot (at least 12 quarts), you can easily double this recipe to make 1 gallon.

- 4 pounds chicken wings
- 3½ quarts water
- 1 (1-inch) piece ginger, sliced into ¼-inch-thick rounds
- 2 scallions, cut into 2-inch lengths
- 1½ teaspoons table salt

1. Bring chicken and water to boil in large stockpot or Dutch oven over medium-high heat, skimming off any scum that comes to surface. Reduce heat to low and simmer gently for 3 hours.

2. Add ginger, scallions, and salt and continue to simmer for 2 hours. Strain broth through fine-mesh strainer into large pot or container, pressing on solids to extract as much liquid as possible; discard solids. Let broth settle for about 5 minutes, then, using wide, shallow spoon, skim excess fat from surface. (Cooled broth can be refrigerated for up to 4 days or frozen for up to 1 month.)

VARIATION
Pressure-Cooker Chicken Broth
Total Time: 1½ hours
Add all ingredients to 6- or 8-quart electric pressure cooker. Lock lid in place and close pressure release valve. Select high pressure cook function and cook for 1 hour. Turn off pressure cooker and let pressure release naturally for 15 minutes. Quick-release any remaining pressure, then carefully remove lid, allowing steam to escape away from you. Strain broth as directed. (If using stovetop pressure cooker, bring cooker to high pressure over medium-high heat. As soon as indicator signals that pot has reached high pressure, reduce heat to medium-low and cook, adjusting heat as needed to maintain high pressure. Remove cooker from heat before allowing pressure to release.)

GAME CHANGER

Making Liquid Gold

"While I love the convenience of store-bought chicken broth, the real thing made from scratch is worlds better. And making it in a pressure cooker (or Instant Pot) extracts full, rich, intense chicken flavor from a handful of ingredients in record time. I find it's a great project for a rainy cold day, making the house smell wonderful. I first used this recipe while testing pressure cookers, making the identical recipe in every product over and over. At the end of the day, I was very popular in the test kitchen, because everyone got to take broth home. (We all know the value of homemade stock!) I like to divide up the batch into containers and pop them in the freezer, ready to enhance homemade soups, gravies, and sauces."

—Lisa

Salads

Photo: Kale Caesar Salad

1. Combine vinegar, shallot, mayonnaise, mustard, salt, and pepper to taste in small nonreactive bowl. Whisk until mixture is milky in appearance and no lumps of mayonnaise remain.

2. Place oil in small measuring cup so that it is easy to pour. Whisking constantly, very slowly drizzle oil into vinegar mixture. If pools of oil are gathering on surface as you whisk, stop adding oil and whisk mixture well to combine, then resume whisking in oil in a slow stream. Vinaigrette should be glossy and lightly thickened, with no pools of oil on its surface.

VARIATIONS

Foolproof Lemon Vinaigrette
This vinaigrette is best for dressing mild greens.

Follow recipe for Foolproof Vinaigrette, substituting lemon juice for vinegar, omitting shallot, and adding ¼ teaspoon finely grated lemon zest and pinch sugar along with salt and pepper.

Foolproof Balsamic-Mustard Vinaigrette
This vinaigrette is best for dressing assertive greens.

Follow recipe for Foolproof Vinaigrette, substituting balsamic vinegar for wine vinegar, increasing mustard to 2 teaspoons, and adding ½ teaspoon chopped fresh thyme along with salt and pepper.

Foolproof Walnut Vinaigrette
Follow recipe for Foolproof Vinaigrette, substituting 1½ tablespoons roasted walnut oil and 1½ tablespoons regular olive oil for extra-virgin olive oil.

Foolproof Herb Vinaigrette
Follow recipe for Foolproof Vinaigrette, adding 1 tablespoon minced fresh parsley leaves or chives and ½ teaspoon minced fresh thyme, tarragon, marjoram, or oregano leaves to vinaigrette just before use.

SEASON 11

Foolproof Vinaigrette

Makes ¼ cup, enough to dress 8 to 10 cups lightly packed greens • Total Time: 10 minutes

Why This Recipe Works Vinaigrettes often seem a little slipshod—harsh and bristling in one bite, dull and oily in the next. We were determined to nail down a formula for the perfect vinaigrette, one that would consistently yield a homogeneous, harmonious blend of bright vinegar and rich oil in every forkful. For starters, we found that top-notch ingredients are crucial. Balsamic vinegar worked best with more assertive greens. We liked fruity extra-virgin olive oil as an all-purpose oil option, and walnut oil for nuttier vinaigrettes. As for mixing methods, whisking together the ingredients only gets you so far. We used a key ingredient—mayonnaise—to emulsify (bind together) the oil and vinegar for a stabilized, smooth dressing.

Red wine, white wine, or champagne vinegar will work in this recipe; however, it is important to use high-quality ingredients. This vinaigrette works with nearly any type of green (as do the walnut and herb variations). For a hint of garlic flavor, rub the inside of the salad bowl with a cut clove of garlic before adding the lettuce.

　1　tablespoon wine vinegar
1½　teaspoons very finely minced shallot
　½　teaspoon mayonnaise
　½　teaspoon Dijon mustard
　⅛　teaspoon table salt
　3　tablespoons extra-virgin olive oil

SEASON 23

Lao Hu Cai

Serves 4 • Total Time: 25 minutes

Why This Recipe Works This vibrant Chinese salad, called tiger salad for its bold flavors and textures, is traditionally served to stimulate the appetite at the beginning of a meal or to reset the palate between courses. We balanced the bracing vinaigrette (a combination of unseasoned rice vinegar, sugar, salt, soy sauce, and sesame oil), piquant scallions, and hot chiles with the herbal freshness of cilantro

and the juicy crunch of sliced celery, which together made up the salad's vegetable base. The earthy sweetness of chopped roasted peanuts and toasted sesame seeds and the rich sesame oil added further layers of texture and flavor to the dish.

For a spicier salad, include the chile seeds. For less spice, substitute half of a small green bell pepper (cut into 2-inch-long matchsticks) for the serrano.

- 1 tablespoon unseasoned rice vinegar
- 1 teaspoon sugar
- ½ teaspoon table salt
- ½ teaspoon soy sauce
- ¾ teaspoon toasted sesame oil
- 1 Thai chile, stemmed, halved, seeded, and sliced thin
- 3½ cups fresh cilantro leaves and tender stems, chopped into 2-inch lengths
- 4 celery ribs, sliced on bias ¼ inch thick
- 3 scallions, white and green parts sliced thin on bias
- 1 serrano chile, stemmed, quartered, seeded, and sliced thin
- 2 teaspoons sesame seeds, toasted
- 2 tablespoons chopped salted dry-roasted peanuts

1. In small bowl, stir vinegar, sugar, salt, and soy sauce until sugar and salt are completely dissolved. Add oil and Thai chile and stir to combine.

2. In large bowl, combine cilantro, celery, scallions, and serrano. Sprinkle with sesame seeds and dressing and toss to combine.

3. Transfer salad to platter, sprinkle with peanuts, and serve immediately.

Kale Caesar Salad

Serves 4 • Total Time: 1 hour, plus 40 minutes cooling and chilling

Why This Recipe Works We weren't willing to sacrifice flavor in order to make a healthier version of classic Caesar salad. It had to include a rich, creamy dressing, but we did want to eliminate some of the usual fat. We tried both mayonnaise-based and egg-based dressings and found that the heartier kale really needed a thicker mayonnaise base to stand up to it. Using that as a starting point, we cut out half the mayonnaise, replacing it with low-fat yogurt. We found we only needed a half cup of Parmesan to get the satisfying, nutty flavor so essential to Caesar dressing. The addition of anchovy fillets provided rich umami notes. A 10-minute soak in warm water tenderized the kale. We swapped the usual white bread croutons for croutons made from whole-grain bread, as the hearty greens paired well with the more rustic croutons.

- 12 ounces curly kale, stemmed and cut into 1-inch pieces (16 cups)
- 3 ounces rustic whole-grain bread, cut into ½-inch cubes (1½ cups)
- 2 tablespoons extra-virgin olive oil, divided
- ⅛ teaspoon plus ½ teaspoon table salt, divided
- ⅛ teaspoon plus ½ teaspoon pepper, divided
- 3 tablespoons mayonnaise
- 3 tablespoons plain low-fat yogurt
- 1 ounce Parmesan cheese, grated (½ cup), divided
- 1 tablespoon lemon juice
- 2 teaspoons white wine vinegar
- 2 teaspoons Worcestershire sauce
- 2 teaspoons Dijon mustard
- 3 anchovy fillets, rinsed and minced
- 1 garlic clove, minced

1. Adjust oven rack to middle position and heat oven to 350 degrees. Place kale in large bowl and cover with warm tap water (110 to 115 degrees). Swish kale around to remove grit. Let kale sit in warm water bath for 10 minutes. Remove kale from water and spin dry in salad spinner in multiple batches. Pat leaves dry with paper towels if still wet.

2. Toss bread, 1 tablespoon oil, ⅛ teaspoon salt, and ⅛ teaspoon pepper together in bowl. Spread on rimmed baking sheet and bake until golden and crisp, about 15 minutes. Let croutons cool completely on sheet. (Cooled croutons can be stored in airtight container at room temperature for up to 24 hours.)

3. In large bowl whisk mayonnaise, yogurt, ¼ cup Parmesan, lemon juice, vinegar, Worcestershire sauce, mustard, anchovies, garlic, remaining ½ teaspoon salt, and remaining ½ teaspoon pepper until well combined. Whisking constantly, drizzle in remaining 1 tablespoon oil until combined.

4. Toss kale with dressing and refrigerate for at least 20 minutes or up to 6 hours. Toss dressed kale with croutons and remaining ¼ cup Parmesan. Serve.

SEASON 22

Horiatiki Salata

Serves 4 to 6 • Total Time: 25 minutes, plus 30 minutes salting

Why This Recipe Works Imagine bites of sweet tomatoes, briny olives, savory onion, crunchy cucumber, and tangy feta—without any lettuce filler—and you've got horiatiki salata, the real Greek salad. Ripe tomatoes are loaded with juice that can flood the salad, so we tossed halved wedges (perfect for chunky but manageable bites) with salt and let them drain in a colander for 30 minutes. Soaking the onion slices in ice water lessened their hot bite while maintaining their fresh, crisp texture. A creamy Greek feta, which must be made with at least 70 percent fatty sheep's milk, brought richness to the vegetables. When we tried subbing in fresh oregano for the traditional dried, we understood why the dried herb is preferred: Its more delicate flavor complemented—but didn't upstage—the vegetables. Vinaigrette isn't traditionally used to dress horiatiki salata, but we did tweak the custom of drizzling the salad separately with oil and vinegar by tossing the vegetables with each component, ensuring that the mixture was lightly but evenly dressed.

> Soaking the sliced onion in ice water tempers its heat and bite. Use only large, round tomatoes here, not Roma or cherry varieties, and use the ripest in-season tomatoes you can find. A fresh, fruity, peppery olive oil works well here if you have it. We prefer to use feta by Real Greek Feta or Dodoni in this recipe. The salad can be served with crusty bread as a light meal for four.

1¾ pounds tomatoes, cored
¾ teaspoon table salt, plus salt for salting tomatoes
½ red onion, sliced thin
2 tablespoons red wine vinegar
1 teaspoon dried oregano, plus extra for seasoning
½ teaspoon pepper
1 English cucumber, quartered lengthwise and cut into ¾-inch chunks

GAME CHANGER

Make a Meal of Summer Produce (and Cheese)

"I tend to get a wee bit lazy when it's hot and steamy outside, but that doesn't mean that my appetite wanes. Ever since my colleague Steve Dunn developed this picture-perfect, satisfying recipe for horiatiki salata, it's become my go-to sultry-weather dinner. I grow green bell peppers, heirloom tomatoes, red onion, and a few varieties of cucumber in my vegetable garden, so half of the ingredient list is already growing in my backyard. For the rest, I make sure to keep my cupboard stocked with good-quality kalamata olives, briny capers, grassy extra-virgin olive oil, red wine vinegar, and dried Greek oregano. Then, when it's time for a no-fuss, low-effort late July or August lunch or dinner, all I need to do is procure a thick block of sheep's milk feta. After that, it's just a matter of sauntering out to the garden, harvesting the necessary veggies, and putting together this hearty main course salad. With a loaf of rustic bread and an icy glass of wine, there is no better al fresco dinner."

—*Becky*

1   green bell pepper, stemmed, seeded,
    and cut into 2 by ½-inch strips
1   cup pitted kalamata olives
2   tablespoons capers, rinsed
5   tablespoons extra-virgin olive oil, divided
1   (8-ounce) block feta cheese, sliced into
    ½-inch-thick triangles

1. Cut tomatoes into ½-inch-thick wedges. Cut wedges in half crosswise. Toss tomatoes and ½ teaspoon salt together in colander set in large bowl. Let drain for 30 minutes. Place onion in small bowl, cover with ice water, and let sit for 15 minutes. Whisk vinegar, oregano, pepper, and salt together in second small bowl.

2. Discard tomato juice and transfer tomatoes to now-empty bowl. Drain onion and add to bowl with tomatoes. Add vinegar mixture, cucumber, bell pepper, olives, and capers and toss to combine. Drizzle with ¼ cup oil and toss gently to coat. Season with salt and pepper to taste. Transfer to serving platter and top with feta. Season each slice of feta with extra oregano to taste. Drizzle feta with remaining 1 tablespoon oil. Serve.

Mediterranean Chopped Salad

Serves 4 to 6 • **Total Time: 40 minutes**

Why This Recipe Works Chopped salads are often little better than a random collection of cut-up produce from the crisper drawer exuding moisture that turns the salad watery and bland. We wanted a lively, thoughtfully chosen composition of lettuce and vegetables—cut into bite-size pieces—with supporting players like beans and cheese contributing hearty flavors and chunky textures. Salting the cucumber and tomatoes to remove excess moisture was an important first step. As for the dressing, we found that an assertive blend of equal parts oil and vinegar delivered the bright, acidic kick this salad needed. We also found that marinating the bell peppers and onions in the dressing for 5 minutes before adding the cheese and other tender components brought a welcome flavor boost.

1   cucumber, peeled, halved lengthwise, seeded, and cut into ½-inch dice (about 1¼ cups)
1   pint grape tomatoes, quartered (about 1½ cups)
    Table salt for salting vegetables
3   tablespoons extra-virgin olive oil
3   tablespoons red wine vinegar

1   garlic clove, minced
1   (15-ounce) can chickpeas, drained and rinsed
½   cup pitted kalamata olives, chopped
½   small red onion, minced (about ¼ cup)
½   cup chopped fresh parsley
1   romaine lettuce heart, cut into ½-inch pieces (about 3 cups)
4   ounces feta cheese, crumbled (1 cup)

1. Combine cucumber, tomatoes, and 1 teaspoon salt in colander set over bowl and drain for 15 minutes.

2. Whisk oil, vinegar, and garlic together in large bowl. Add drained cucumber and tomatoes, chickpeas, olives, onion, and parsley. Toss and let stand at room temperature to blend flavors, 5 minutes.

3. Add romaine and feta and toss to combine. Season with salt and pepper to taste, and serve.

Salade Lyonnaise

Serves 4 • **Total Time: 45 minutes**

Why This Recipe Works With an Italian assist, our version of this iconic salad of crisp bitter greens, poached egg, and salted cured pork would be at home in any French bistro. Choosing a mix of bitter greens—frisée and chicory—gave this classic French salad enough volume, structure, and flavor to stand up to the richer elements of bacon and egg.

2. Pour off all but 2 tablespoons fat from skillet, leaving pancetta in skillet. Add shallot and cook, stirring frequently, until slightly softened, about 30 seconds. Off heat, add vinegar and mustard and stir to combine.

3. Drizzle vinaigrette over frisée in large bowl and toss thoroughly to coat. Add chicory and toss again. Season with salt and pepper to taste. Divide salad among 4 plates. Gently place 1 egg on top of each salad, then season with salt and pepper to taste. Serve immediately.

ACCOMPANIMENT
Perfect Poached Eggs
Makes 4 eggs • Total Time: 35 minutes
Use the freshest eggs possible for this recipe.

4 large eggs
1 tablespoon distilled white vinegar
Table salt for poaching eggs

1. Bring 6 cups water to boil in Dutch oven over high heat. Meanwhile, crack eggs, one at a time, into colander. Let stand until loose, watery whites drain away from eggs, 20 to 30 seconds. Gently transfer eggs to 2-cup liquid measuring cup.

2. Add vinegar and 1 teaspoon salt to boiling water. Remove pot from heat. With lip of measuring cup just above surface of water, gently tip eggs into water, one at a time, leaving space between them. Cover pot and let stand until whites closest to yolks are just set and opaque, about 3 minutes. If after 3 minutes whites are not set, let stand in water, checking every 30 seconds, until whites are set.

3. Using slotted spoon, carefully lift and drain each egg over Dutch oven. Season with salt and pepper to taste, and serve.

To keep the flavor true to the French original, we called for pancetta rather than American bacon since it is unsmoked, salt cured, and rolled just like ventreche (also known as French pancetta). Making a bold, warm vinaigrette in the skillet not only infused the salad with richer bacon flavor but also allowed us to gently tenderize the frisée. Poached eggs delivered both runny yolks and tender whites that easily melded into the salad, which was critical to the success of the dish.

Order a ½-inch-thick slice of pancetta at the deli counter; presliced or diced pancetta is likely to dry out or become tough. If you can't find chicory or escarole, dandelion greens make a good substitute. If using escarole, strip away the first four or five outer leaves and reserve them for another use. Serve this salad with crusty bread as a light lunch or dinner.

1 (½-inch-thick) slice pancetta (about 5 ounces)
2 tablespoons extra-virgin olive oil
1 tablespoon minced shallot
2 tablespoons red wine vinegar
4 teaspoons Dijon mustard
1 head frisée (6 ounces), torn into bite-size pieces
5 ounces chicory or escarole, torn into bite-size pieces (5 cups)
1 recipe Perfect Poached Eggs (recipe follows)

1. Cut pancetta vertically into thirds, then cut each third crosswise into ¼-inch-wide pieces. Combine pancetta and 2 cups water in 10-inch nonstick or carbon-steel skillet and bring to boil over medium-high heat. Boil for 5 minutes, then drain. Return pancetta to now-empty skillet. Add oil and cook over medium-low heat, stirring occasionally, until lightly browned but still chewy, 4 to 6 minutes.

SEASON 25
Salade Niçoise

Serves 2 • Total Time: 1¼ hours

Why This Recipe Works Cooking the potatoes for our salade Niçoise in heavily salted water ensured that they were well seasoned; using that same water for the green beans was not only efficient but also meant that some of the calcium ions in the beans' cell walls were displaced by plentiful sodium ions, breaking the links between the pectin molecules in the beans. This effect caused the beans to soften quickly while remaining a brilliant green.

Breaking with tradition, we flattened the cooked potatoes and crisped their exteriors in a hot skillet while our eggs cooked to a jammy, not hard-cooked, consistency. The mixture of hot and cold and crisp and creamy elements made the salad more interesting to eat, and the punchy, lemon-heavy vinaigrette, spiked with anchovies to enhance its savoriness, complemented the hearty components perfectly. A final sprinkling of briny capers and olives gave our salad traditional Mediterranean flair.

> *This recipe moves quickly, so be sure to have all your ingredients in place before starting. You can substitute 1 teaspoon of anchovy paste for the anchovies. A high-quality oil-packed tuna such as Tonnino Tuna Fillets in Olive Oil works well here. If Niçoise olives are unavailable, substitute chopped pitted kalamatas. We like jammy eggs, with a consistency halfway between soft- and hard-cooked, in this salad. If you prefer soft-cooked eggs, cook them for 7 minutes; if you prefer hard-cooked eggs, cook them for 12 minutes.*

Vinaigrette

- 3 tablespoons extra-virgin olive oil
- 2 tablespoons lemon juice
- 1 tablespoon minced shallot
- 1 teaspoon minced fresh thyme
- 1 teaspoon Dijon mustard
- 2 anchovies, rinsed and minced
- ¼ teaspoon table salt
- ⅛ teaspoon pepper

Salad

- 5 ounces grape tomatoes, halved lengthwise
- ¼ teaspoon sugar
- ⅛ teaspoon table salt, plus salt for cooking vegetables
- 12 ounces small red potatoes, 1 to 2 inches in diameter
- 6 ounces green beans, trimmed
- 3 tablespoons extra-virgin olive oil
- 3 large eggs
- 1 (5- to 7-ounce) jar/can olive oil–packed tuna, drained and broken into bite-size pieces with fork
- 2 tablespoons chopped pitted Niçoise olives
- 1 tablespoon capers

1. For the vinaigrette: Whisk all ingredients together in small bowl.

2. For the salad: Stir together tomatoes, sugar, and salt in small bowl. Bring 6 cups water to boil in medium saucepan over medium-high heat. Add potatoes and 3 tablespoons salt and cook until potatoes are easily pierced with paring knife, 12 to 15 minutes. Using tongs, transfer potatoes to cutting board, leaving water in saucepan.

3. Return water to boil. Add green beans and cook until just tender, 4 to 5 minutes. While green beans cook, fill medium bowl halfway with ice and water. Using tongs, transfer green beans to ice water, leaving water in saucepan. Let beans cool, about 5 minutes. While green beans cool, gently flatten each potato with side of chef's knife to ½- to ¾-inch thickness (it's OK if some potatoes crumble).

4. Heat oil in 10-inch nonstick skillet over medium-high heat until shimmering. Add potatoes and cook until brown and lightly crisped on both sides, 2 to 3 minutes per side. Meanwhile, return water to boil over medium-high heat. Add eggs, cover, and cook for 8 minutes (eggs needn't be submerged).

5. Line cutting board with double layer of paper towels. Transfer crisped potatoes to half of paper towel and season with salt to taste. Transfer green beans to remaining half of paper towel to drain, leaving cold water in bowl.

6. Divide tomatoes, tuna, and beans between 2 plates, piling them in separate mounds. Transfer cooked eggs to cold water to chill for 30 seconds. Peel and halve eggs and place 3 halves on each plate. Divide potatoes between plates. Drizzle each salad with 2 tablespoons vinaigrette. Sprinkle salads with olives and capers and serve, passing extra vinaigrette.

VARIATION

Salad Niçoise for Four

You'll need a large cutting board for draining the potatoes and beans; alternatively, use a large rimmed baking sheet.

To serve four, double all ingredients except water and salt used for cooking the potatoes, eggs, and beans. Fry potatoes in 12-inch skillet.

Classic Tuna Salad

Classic Tuna Salad

**Makes 2 cups, enough for 4 sandwiches
Total Time: 15 minutes**

Why This Recipe Works Tuna salads have been given a bad name by their typically mushy, watery, and bland condition. We wanted a tuna salad that was evenly textured, moist, and well seasoned. We learned that there are three keys to a great tuna salad. The first is to drain the tuna thoroughly in a colander; don't just tip the water out of the can. Next, break up the tuna with your fingers for a finer, more even texture. Finally, season the tuna before adding the mayonnaise for maximum flavor. Some additions to tuna salad are a matter of taste, but we thought that small amounts of garlic and mustard added another dimension, and minced pickle was a piquant touch. In addition to classic tuna salad, we developed a tuna with balsamic vinegar and grapes, another with curry powder and apples, and a third with lime and horseradish.

> *Our favorite canned tuna is American Tuna Pole Caught Wild Albacore.*

- 2 (6-ounce) cans solid white tuna in water
- 1 small celery rib, minced (about ¼ cup)
- 2 tablespoons lemon juice
- 2 tablespoons minced red onion
- 2 tablespoons minced dill or sweet pickles
- 2 tablespoons minced fresh parsley
- ½ small garlic clove, minced
- ½ teaspoon table salt
- ¼ teaspoon ground black pepper
- ½ cup mayonnaise
- ¼ teaspoon Dijon mustard

Drain tuna in colander and shred with your fingers until no clumps remain and texture is fine and even. Transfer tuna to medium bowl and mix in celery, lemon juice, onion, pickles, parsley, garlic, salt, and pepper until evenly blended. Fold in mayonnaise and mustard until tuna is evenly moistened. (Tuna salad can be refrigerated in airtight container for up to 3 days.)

VARIATIONS

Tuna Salad with Balsamic Vinegar and Grapes

Omit lemon juice, pickles, garlic, and parsley. Add 2 tablespoons balsamic vinegar, 6 ounces halved red seedless grapes (about 1 cup), ¼ cup lightly toasted slivered almonds, and 2 teaspoons minced thyme to tuna along with salt and pepper.

GAME CHANGER

Another Reminder That Success Is in the Details

"Everyone has their favorite comfort food—think mac and cheese, soups of many stripes (chicken noodle, and creamy tomato, especially with a grilled cheese sandwich riding shotgun, rank high), spaghetti with meatballs, toast with butter—you get the idea. One of my favorites is the ubiquitous tuna salad sandwich. To be honest, I find that even a bad rendition, containing just the tuna and mayo, can soothe life's rough edges for me, but carefully made tuna salad is a dramatic step up. When most people make tuna salad from water-packed canned tuna, they may not drain out that water thoroughly. It's worth taking a little care here: Add the tuna to a colander and press it gently to expel all the water. But don't stop there. Using your fingers to break up the tuna until the texture is fine and even, with no large lumps, ensures a pleasing texture and even seasoning in the finished salad. The next step is perhaps even more important: Add lemon juice, salt and pepper, and other seasonings to the tuna and mix them in before adding the mayo. This order may seem like a small detail, but you'll taste the difference because the tuna itself will be so well seasoned."

—*Adam*

Curried Tuna Salad with Apples and Currants

Omit pickles, garlic, and parsley. Add 1 medium firm, juicy apple, cut into ¼-inch dice (about 1 cup), ¼ cup currants, and 2 tablespoons minced fresh basil to tuna along with lemon juice, salt, and pepper; mix 1 tablespoon curry powder into mayonnaise before folding into tuna.

Tuna Salad with Lime and Horseradish

Omit lemon juice, pickles, and garlic. Add 2 tablespoons lime juice, ½ teaspoon grated lime zest, and 3 tablespoons prepared horseradish to tuna along with salt and pepper.

Classic Chicken Salad

Serves 4 to 6 • Total Time: 45 minutes, plus 30 minutes cooling

Why This Recipe Works Recipes for chicken salad are only as good as the chicken itself. If the chicken is dry or flavorless, no amount of dressing or add-ins will camouflage it. To ensure juicy and flavorful chicken, we used a method based on sous vide cooking (submerging vacuum-sealed foods in a temperature-controlled water bath). Our ideal formula was four chicken breasts and 6 cups of cold water heated to 170 degrees and then removed from the heat, covered, and left to stand for about 15 minutes. This yielded incomparably moist chicken that was perfect for chicken salad.

To ensure that the chicken cooks through, don't use breasts that weigh more than 8 ounces or are thicker than 1 inch. Make sure to start with cold water in step 1. We like the combination of parsley and tarragon, but 2 tablespoons of one or the other is fine. This salad can be served in a sandwich or spooned over leafy greens.

Table salt for cooking chicken
4 (6- to 8-ounce) boneless, skinless chicken breasts, no more than 1 inch thick, trimmed
½ cup mayonnaise
2 tablespoons lemon juice
1 teaspoon Dijon mustard
¼ teaspoon pepper
2 celery ribs, minced
1 shallot, minced
1 tablespoon minced fresh parsley
1 tablespoon minced fresh tarragon

1. Dissolve 2 tablespoons salt in 6 cups cold water in Dutch oven. Submerge chicken in water. Heat pot over medium heat until water registers 170 degrees. Turn off heat, cover pot, and let stand until chicken registers 165 degrees, 15 to 17 minutes.

2. Transfer chicken to paper towel–lined baking sheet. Refrigerate until chicken is cool, about 30 minutes. While chicken cools, whisk mayonnaise, lemon juice, mustard, and pepper together in large bowl.

3. Pat chicken dry with paper towels and cut into ½-inch pieces. Transfer chicken to bowl with mayonnaise mixture. Add celery, shallot, parsley, and tarragon; toss to combine. Season with salt and pepper to taste. Serve. (Salad can be refrigerated for up to 2 days.)

VARIATIONS
Waldorf Chicken Salad
Add ½ teaspoon ground fennel seeds to mayonnaise mixture in step 2. Substitute 1 teaspoon minced fresh thyme for parsley and add 1 peeled Granny Smith apple, cut into ¼-inch pieces, and ½ cup coarsely chopped toasted walnuts to salad with celery.

Curried Chicken Salad with Cashews
Microwave 1 teaspoon vegetable oil, 1 teaspoon curry powder, and ⅛ teaspoon cayenne pepper together, uncovered, until oil is hot, about 30 seconds. Add oil mixture to mayonnaise and substitute lime juice for lemon juice and 1 teaspoon grated fresh ginger for mustard in step 2. Substitute 2 tablespoons minced fresh cilantro for parsley and tarragon, and add ½ cup coarsely chopped toasted cashews and ⅓ cup golden raisins to salad with celery.

Chicken Salad with Red Grapes and Smoked Almonds
Add ¼ teaspoon grated lemon zest to mayonnaise mixture in step 2. Substitute 1 teaspoon minced fresh rosemary for tarragon, and add 1 cup quartered red grapes and ½ cup coarsely chopped smoked almonds to salad with celery.

Panzanella

Serves 4 • Total Time: 1¼ hours, plus 20 minutes cooling

Why This Recipe Works In the best Italian bread salad panzanella, the sweet juice of tomatoes mixes with a bright vinaigrette, moistening chunks of crusty bread until they're soft and just a little chewy. We toasted fresh bread in the oven, rather than using the traditional day-old bread. The bread lost enough moisture to absorb the dressing without getting waterlogged. A 10-minute soak in the dressing yielded perfectly moistened, nutty-tasting bread ready to be tossed with the tomatoes, which we salted to intensify their flavor. Cucumber and shallot for crunch and bite plus plenty of chopped fresh basil perfected our salad.

The success of this recipe depends on high-quality ingredients, including ripe, in-season tomatoes and fruity olive oil. Fresh basil is also a must. Your bread may vary in density, so you may not need the entire loaf for this recipe.

1	(1-pound) loaf rustic Italian or French bread, cut or torn into 1-inch pieces (about 6 cups)
½	cup extra-virgin olive oil, divided
¾	teaspoon table salt, divided
1½	pounds tomatoes, cored, seeded, and cut into 1-inch pieces
3	tablespoons red wine vinegar
¼	teaspoon pepper
1	cucumber, peeled, halved lengthwise, seeded, and sliced thin
1	shallot, sliced thin
¼	cup chopped fresh basil

1. Adjust oven rack to middle position and heat oven to 400 degrees. Toss bread pieces with 2 tablespoons oil and ¼ teaspoon salt; arrange bread in single layer on rimmed baking sheet. Toast bread pieces until just starting to turn light golden, 15 to 20 minutes, stirring halfway through baking. Set aside and let cool to room temperature.

2. Gently toss tomatoes and remaining ½ teaspoon salt in large bowl. Transfer to colander set over bowl; set aside to drain for 15 minutes, tossing occasionally.

3. Whisk vinegar, pepper, and remaining 6 tablespoons oil into tomato juices. Add bread pieces, toss to coat, and let stand for 10 minutes, tossing occasionally.

4. Add tomatoes, cucumber, shallot, and basil to bowl with bread pieces and toss to coat. Season with salt and pepper to taste, and serve immediately.

Fattoush

Serves 4 • Total Time: 50 minutes

Why This Recipe Works The Levantine salad fattoush combines fresh, flavorful produce with crisp pita and bright herbs. We skipped the step of seeding and salting the cucumbers and tomatoes, favoring the crisp texture of the cucumber (the English variety, which has fewer seeds) and the flavorful seeds and jelly of the tomato. We fended off soggy bread by making the pita moisture-repellent, brushing its craggy sides with plenty of olive oil before baking. The oil prevented the pita chips from absorbing the salad's moisture while still allowing them to take on some of its flavor. A summery blend of mint, cilantro, and peppery arugula comprised the salad's greenery, and a lemony vinaigrette lent it a bright finish.

The success of this recipe depends on ripe, in-season tomatoes. A rasp-style grater makes quick work of turning the garlic into a paste.

2	(8-inch) pita breads
3	tablespoons plus ¼ cup extra-virgin olive oil, divided
3	tablespoons lemon juice
¼	teaspoon garlic, minced to paste
¼	teaspoon table salt
1	pound tomatoes, cored and cut into ¾-inch pieces
1	English cucumber, peeled and sliced ⅛ inch thick
1	cup arugula, chopped coarse
½	cup chopped fresh cilantro
½	cup chopped fresh mint
4	scallions, sliced thin

1. Adjust oven rack to middle position and heat oven to 375 degrees. Using kitchen shears, cut around perimeter of each pita and separate into 2 thin rounds. Cut each round in half. Place pita bread, smooth side down, on wire rack set in rimmed baking sheet. Brush 3 tablespoons oil over surface of pita. (Pita does not need to be uniformly coated. Oil will absorb and spread as it bakes.) Season with salt and pepper to taste. Bake until pita is crisp and pale golden brown, 10 to 14 minutes.

2. While pita toasts, whisk lemon juice, garlic, and ¼ teaspoon salt together in small bowl. Let stand for 10 minutes.

3. Place tomatoes, cucumber, arugula, cilantro, mint, and scallions in large bowl. Break pita into ½-inch pieces and place in bowl with vegetables. Add lemon-garlic mixture and remaining ¼ cup oil and toss to coat. Season with salt and pepper to taste. Serve immediately.

SEASON 21

Beet Salad with Spiced Yogurt and Watercress

Serves 6 • **Total Time: 55 minutes**

Why This Recipes Works For a stunning beet salad plated with panache, we use a yogurt-lime dressing as an ultracreamy landing pad for beets and watercress. A swipe through this salad is a cool, creamy, earthy, tangy treat. Beets are very dense, so roasting whole ones can take up to 2 hours. Instead, we peeled and cut the beets into small chunks and microwaved them in a covered bowl with a small amount of water. Peeling them before cooking cut out the wait time for them to cool. Cutting them into pieces exposed much more surface area so they cooked faster, and cooking them in the microwave (as opposed to on the stovetop) caused water molecules inside the beets to boil rapidly and intensely, so they cooked through in less than 30 minutes. Beets work well in any side dish, particularly in a salad with greens and nuts. Instead of tossing the components together, we used the yogurt as an anchor for the other ingredients by thinning it with lime juice and water, spreading it on a platter, and topping it with lightly dressed beets and greens as well as toasted pistachios for crunch.

Be sure to wear gloves when peeling and dicing the beets to prevent your hands from becoming stained. The moisture content of Greek yogurt varies, so add the water slowly in step 2. We like to make this salad with watercress, but baby arugula can be substituted, if desired. For the best presentation, use red beets here, not golden or Chioggia beets.

2 pounds beets, trimmed, peeled, and cut into ¾-inch pieces
1 teaspoon plus 2 pinches table salt, divided
1¼ cups plain Greek yogurt
¼ cup minced fresh cilantro, divided
3 tablespoons extra-virgin olive oil, divided
2 teaspoons grated fresh ginger
1 teaspoon grated lime zest plus 2 tablespoons juice, divided, plus extra juice for seasoning (2 limes)
1 garlic clove, minced
½ teaspoon ground cumin
½ teaspoon ground coriander
¼ teaspoon pepper
5 ounces (5 cups) watercress, torn into bite-size pieces
¼ cup shelled pistachios, toasted and chopped, divided

1. In largest bowl your microwave will accommodate, stir together beets, ⅓ cup water, and ½ teaspoon salt. Cover with plate and microwave until beets can be easily pierced with paring knife, 25 to 30 minutes, stirring halfway through microwaving. Drain beets in colander and let cool.

2. In medium bowl, whisk together yogurt, 3 tablespoons cilantro, 2 tablespoons oil, ginger, lime zest and 1 tablespoon juice, garlic, cumin, coriander, pepper, and ½ teaspoon salt.

Slowly stir in up to 3 tablespoons water until mixture has consistency of regular yogurt. Season with salt, pepper, and extra lime juice to taste. Spread yogurt mixture over serving platter.

3. In large bowl, combine watercress, 2 tablespoons pistachios, 2 teaspoons oil, 1 teaspoon lime juice, and pinch salt and toss to coat. Arrange watercress mixture on top of yogurt mixture, leaving 1-inch border of yogurt mixture. Add beets to now-empty bowl and toss with remaining 1 teaspoon oil, remaining 2 teaspoons lime juice, and remaining pinch salt. Place beet mixture on top of watercress mixture. Sprinkle salad with remaining 2 tablespoons pistachios and remaining 1 tablespoon cilantro and serve.

VARIATION
Beet Salad with Goat Cheese and Arugula

    2 pounds beets, trimmed, peeled,
       and cut into ¾-inch pieces
    ½ teaspoon plus ⅛ teaspoon plus
       2 pinches table salt, divided
    4 ounces goat cheese, crumbled (1 cup)
    2 tablespoons minced fresh chives, divided
    ½ teaspoon grated lemon zest plus 5 teaspoons juice,
       divided, plus extra juice for seasoning
    ½ teaspoon caraway seeds
    ¼ teaspoon pepper
    5 ounces (5 cups) baby arugula
    ¼ cup sliced almonds, toasted, divided
    1 tablespoon extra-virgin olive oil, divided

1. In largest bowl your microwave will accommodate, stir together beets, ⅓ cup water, and ½ teaspoon salt. Cover with plate and microwave until beets can be easily pierced with paring knife, 25 to 30 minutes, stirring halfway through microwaving. Drain beets in colander and let cool.

2. In medium bowl, use rubber spatula to mash together goat cheese, 1 tablespoon chives, lemon zest and 2 teaspoons juice, caraway seeds, pepper, and ⅛ teaspoon salt. Slowly stir in up to ⅓ cup water until mixture has consistency of regular yogurt. Season with salt, pepper, and extra lemon juice to taste. Spread goat cheese mixture over serving platter.

3. In large bowl, combine arugula, 2 tablespoons almonds, 2 teaspoons oil, 1 teaspoon lemon juice, and pinch salt and toss to coat. Arrange arugula mixture on top of goat cheese mixture, leaving 1-inch border of goat cheese mixture. Add beets to now-empty bowl and toss with remaining 2 teaspoons lemon juice, remaining 1 teaspoon oil, and remaining pinch salt. Place beet mixture on top of arugula mixture. Sprinkle salad with remaining 2 tablespoons almonds and remaining 1 tablespoon chives and serve.

Broccoli Salad with Creamy Avocado Dressing

Serves 4 to 6 • Total Time: 25 minutes

Why This Recipe Works This dynamic salad combines crisp broccoli, dried fruit, nuts, and a creamy dressing. We made a lush but light dressing by replacing the mayonnaise with avocado and olive oil, buzzing them in a food processor with garlic and lemon for a bright and savory flavor. We balanced the sweet tang of dried fruit and rich toasty flavors of the nuts by adding shallot and tarragon. Blanching and shocking the broccoli softened its raw edge and brightened its color. To ensure that the florets and stems cooked evenly, we layered them strategically in the pot.

| *Be sure to use a fully ripe Hass avocado here.*

    1   cup water
    ¾   teaspoon table salt, plus salt for cooking broccoli
    1½   pounds broccoli, florets cut into 1-inch pieces, stalks
          peeled, halved lengthwise, and sliced ¼ inch thick
    1   avocado, halved, pitted, and cut into ½-inch pieces
    2   tablespoons extra-virgin olive oil
    1   teaspoon grated lemon zest,
          plus 3 tablespoons juice
    1   garlic clove, minced
    ¼   teaspoon pepper
    ½   cup dried cranberries
    ½   cup sliced almonds, toasted
    1   shallot, sliced thin
    1   tablespoon minced fresh tarragon

1. Bring water and ½ teaspoon salt to boil in large sauce-pan over high heat. Add broccoli stalks, then place florets on top of stalks so that they sit just above water. Cover and cook until broccoli is bright green and crisp-tender, about 3 minutes. Meanwhile, fill large bowl halfway with ice and water. Drain broccoli well, transfer to ice water, and let sit until just cool, about 2 minutes. Transfer broccoli to triple layer of paper towels and dry well. Dry bowl and set aside.

2. Process avocado, oil, lemon zest and juice, garlic, salt, and pepper in food processor until smooth, about 30 seconds, scraping down sides of bowl as needed. Season with salt and pepper to taste.

3. Combine broccoli, dressing, cranberries, almonds, shallot, and tarragon in now-empty large bowl until evenly coated. Season with salt and pepper to taste. Serve.

Brussels Sprouts Salad with Warm Mustard Vinaigrette

Serves 6 • Total Time: 50 minutes

Why This Recipe Works Though most often sautéed or roasted, raw brussels sprouts make a great salad green and here they play a starring role. We dressed our brussels sprout salad in a warm mustard vinaigrette that gently tenderized the sprouts while letting them retain their fresh flavor. Bites of quick pickled shallot and dried apricots added pop to this elegant salad, while ricotta salata cheese, chopped toasted pistachios, and watercress added rich-ness, flavor, and a touch of bitterness. We dressed the salad in the skillet before transferring it to a serving bowl.

A food processor's slicing blade can be used to slice the brussels sprouts, but the salad will be less tender.

5 tablespoons white wine vinegar
1 tablespoon whole-grain mustard
1 teaspoon sugar
¼ teaspoon table salt
1 shallot, halved through root end and sliced thin crosswise
¼ cup dried apricots, chopped
5 tablespoons vegetable oil
⅓ cup shelled pistachios, chopped

1½ pounds brussels sprouts, trimmed, halved, and sliced thin
1½ ounces (1½ cups) watercress, chopped
4 ounces ricotta salata, shaved into thin strips using vegetable peeler

1. Whisk vinegar, mustard, sugar, and salt together in bowl. Add shallot and apricots, cover tightly with plastic wrap, and microwave until steaming, 30 to 60 seconds. Stir briefly to submerge shallot. Let cool to room temperature, about 15 minutes.

2. Heat oil in 12-inch skillet over medium heat until shimmering. Add pistachios and cook, stirring frequently, until pistachios are golden brown, 1 to 2 minutes. Off heat, whisk in shallot mixture. Add brussels sprouts and toss with tongs until dressing is evenly distributed and sprouts darken slightly, 1 to 2 minutes. Transfer to serving bowl. Add watercress and ricotta salata and toss to combine. Season with salt and pepper to taste, and serve immediately.

VARIATION
Brussels Sprout Salad with Warm Bacon Vinaigrette

¼ cup red wine vinegar
1 tablespoon whole-grain mustard
1 teaspoon sugar
¼ teaspoon table salt
1 shallot, halved through root end and sliced thin crosswise
4 slices bacon, cut into ½-inch pieces
1½ pounds brussels sprouts, trimmed, halved, and sliced thin
1½ cups finely shredded radicchio, long strands cut into bite-size lengths
2 ounces Parmesan cheese, shaved into thin strips using vegetable peeler
¼ cup sliced almonds, toasted

1. Whisk vinegar, mustard, sugar, and salt together in bowl. Add shallot, cover tightly with plastic wrap, and microwave until steaming, 30 to 60 seconds. Stir briefly to submerge shallot. Cover and let cool to room temperature, about 15 minutes.

2. Cook bacon in 12-inch skillet over medium heat, stirring frequently, until crispy, 6 to 8 minutes. Off heat, whisk in shallot mixture. Add brussels sprouts and radicchio and toss with tongs until dressing is evenly distributed and sprouts darken slightly, 1 to 2 minutes. Transfer to serving bowl. Add Parmesan and almonds and toss to combine. Season with salt and pepper to taste, and serve immediately.

Give Thanks for Raw Sprouts

"My family's holiday table is pretty traditional for where I'm from. Turkey, gravy, mashed potatoes, stuffing, etc. Delicious but all cooked, and in various shades of brown and off-white. After I watched this recipe's development in the test kitchen, I brought it as my contribution to the table that year. It was a revelation! As people who enjoy salads and eat them readily, somehow something this fresh had never been included in our Thanksgiving spread. It was just the ticket to add some tangy crunch alongside all of the richness. It's great in fall while brussels sprouts are in season, big and vibrant and crunchy, sometimes sold still on the stalk. Yet importantly for me, in this recipe Lan figured out how to gentle the supercrunchy nature of brussels sprouts into something that tastes bright and fresh but won't break your jaw after a few bites. The watercress adds light crunch and elegance. The toasty pistachios, tangy pickled shallots, salty ricotta salata, and sunny apricots combined hit every note, earning this salad a recurring spot on our holiday table."

—Hannah

Creamy Buttermilk Coleslaw

Serves 4 • Total Time: 20 minutes, plus 1 hour salting

Why This Recipe Works Order barbecue down South and you'll likely get buttermilk coleslaw on the side. Unlike all-mayonnaise coleslaw, buttermilk coleslaw is coated in a creamy and refreshingly tart dressing. This recipe showcases the best attributes of this slaw : a pickle-crisp texture and a tangy dressing that clings to it. To prevent watery coleslaw, we salted, rinsed, and dried the shredded cabbage. As the salted cabbage sat, moisture was pulled out of it, wilting it to the right crispy texture. For a tangy dressing that clung to the cabbage, we supplemented the buttermilk with mayonnaise and sour cream. Adding shredded carrot contributed color and sweetness while the mild flavor of shallot was a welcome addition. Sugar, mustard, and cider vinegar amped up the slaw's tanginess.

To serve the coleslaw immediately, rinse the salted cabbage in a large bowl of ice water, drain it in a colander, pick out any ice cubes, then pat the cabbage dry before dressing.

- 1 pound red or green cabbage (about ½ medium head), shredded (about 6 cups)
- ¼ teaspoon table salt, plus salt for salting cabbage
- 1 medium carrot, peeled and shredded
- ½ cup buttermilk
- 2 tablespoons mayonnaise
- 2 tablespoons sour cream
- 1 small shallot, minced (about 1 tablespoon)
- 2 tablespoons minced fresh parsley
- ½ teaspoon cider vinegar
- ½ teaspoon sugar
- ¼ teaspoon Dijon mustard
- ⅛ teaspoon pepper

1. Toss cabbage with 1 teaspoon salt in colander set over medium bowl. Let stand until cabbage wilts, at least 1 hour or up to 4 hours. Rinse cabbage under cold running water (or in large bowl of ice water if serving immediately). Press, but do not squeeze, to drain; pat dry with paper towels. Transfer cabbage to large bowl; add carrot.

2. Combine buttermilk, mayonnaise, sour cream, shallot, parsley, vinegar, sugar, mustard, pepper, and salt in small bowl. Pour buttermilk dressing over cabbage and carrot and toss to coat. Serve chilled or at room temperature. (Coleslaw can be refrigerated in airtight container for up to 2 days.)

Shredding Cabbage

1. Cut cabbage into quarters, then trim and discard hard core.

2. Separate cabbage into small stacks of leaves that flatten when pressed.

3. Use chef's knife to cut each stack of cabbage leaves into thin shreds.

Esquites

Serves 6 to 8 • **Total Time: 45 minutes**

Why This Recipe Works This recipe provides a simpler route to enjoying elote (Mexican street corn) in salad form (esquites) that doesn't require firing up the grill. First, we cooked the kernels in a little oil in a covered skillet on the stovetop. The kernels browned and charred while the lid prevented the kernels from popping out of the hot skillet. It also trapped steam, which helped to cook the corn. We cooked the corn in two batches, which allowed more kernels to have contact with the skillet. Once the corn was perfectly toasted, we used the hot skillet to bloom chili powder and cook minced garlic, which tempered its bite. To tie everything together, we made a simple crema, which we tossed with the charred corn and spices before adding crumbled cotija, chopped cilantro, and sliced scallions.

If desired, substitute plain Greek yogurt for the sour cream. We like serrano chiles here, but you can substitute a jalapeño chile that has been halved lengthwise and sliced into ⅛-inch-thick half-moons. Adjust the amount of chiles to suit your taste. If cotija cheese is unavailable, substitute feta cheese.

- 3 tablespoons lime juice, plus extra for seasoning (2 limes)
- 3 tablespoons sour cream
- 1 tablespoon mayonnaise
- 1–2 serrano chiles, stemmed and cut into ⅛-inch-thick rings
- ¾ teaspoon table salt, divided
- 2 tablespoons plus 1 teaspoon vegetable oil, divided
- 6 ears corn, kernels cut from cobs (6 cups)
- 2 garlic cloves, minced
- ½ teaspoon chili powder
- 4 ounces cotija cheese, crumbled (1 cup)
- ¾ cup coarsely chopped fresh cilantro
- 3 scallions, sliced thin

1. Combine lime juice, sour cream, mayonnaise, serrano(s), and ¼ teaspoon salt in large bowl. Set aside.

2. Heat 1 tablespoon oil in 12-inch nonstick skillet over high heat until shimmering. Add half of corn and spread into even layer. Sprinkle with ¼ teaspoon salt. Cover and cook, without stirring, until corn touching skillet is charred, about 3 minutes. Remove skillet from heat and let stand, covered, for 15 seconds, until any popping subsides. Transfer corn to bowl with sour cream mixture. Repeat with 1 tablespoon oil, remaining ¼ teaspoon salt, and remaining corn.

3. Return now-empty skillet to medium heat and add remaining 1 teaspoon oil, garlic, and chili powder. Cook, stirring constantly, until fragrant, about 30 seconds. Transfer garlic mixture to bowl with corn mixture and toss to combine. Let cool for at least 15 minutes.

4. Add cotija, cilantro, and scallions and toss to combine. Season salad with salt and up to 1 tablespoon extra lime juice to taste. Serve.

Pai Huang Gua

Serves 4 • **Total Time: 35 minutes**

Why This Recipe Works Pai huang gua, smashed cucumbers, is a Sichuan dish that is typically served with rich, spicy food. We started with English cucumbers, which are nearly seedless and have a thin, crisp skin. Placing them in a zipper-lock bag and smashing them into large, irregular pieces sped up a salting step that helped to expel excess water. The craggy pieces also did a better job of holding on to the dressing. Using black vinegar, an aged rice-based vinegar, added a mellow complexity to the soy sauce and sesame dressing.

We recommend using Chinese Chinkiang (or Zhenjiang) black vinegar in this dish because of its complex flavor. If you can't find it, you can substitute 2 teaspoons of rice vinegar and 1 teaspoon of balsamic vinegar. A rasp-style grater makes quick work of turning the garlic into a paste.

2 (14-ounce) English cucumbers
    Kosher salt for salting cucumbers
4 teaspoons Chinese black vinegar
1 teaspoon garlic, minced to paste
1 tablespoon soy sauce
2 teaspoons toasted sesame oil
1 teaspoon sugar
1 teaspoon sesame seeds, toasted

1. Trim and discard ends from cucumbers. Cut cucumbers crosswise into 3 equal lengths. Place pieces in large zipper-lock bag and seal bag. Using small skillet or rolling pin, firmly but gently smash cucumbers until flattened and split lengthwise into 3 or 4 spears. Tear spears into rough 1- to 1½-inch pieces and transfer to colander set in large bowl. Toss pieces with 1½ teaspoons salt and let stand for at least 15 minutes or up to 30 minutes.

2. While cucumber sits, whisk vinegar and garlic together in small bowl; let stand at least 5 minutes or up to 15 minutes.

3. Whisk soy sauce, sesame oil, and sugar into vinegar mixture until sugar has dissolved. Transfer cucumber pieces to medium bowl and discard any extracted liquid. Add dressing and sesame seeds to cucumbers and toss to combine. Serve immediately.

SEASON 21

Green Bean Salad with Cherry Tomatoes and Feta

Serves 4 to 6 • Total Time: 40 minutes

Why This Recipe Works Cooking vegetables until they're soft enough to be speared with a fork generally means you've got to boil the living color out of them—not to mention all their fresh, grassy flavor. To make the beans in this salad tender, bright green, and deeply flavored, we blanched them in heavily salted water (¼ cup of salt to 2 quarts of water). This quickly softened the pectin in the beans' skins, so they became tender before losing their vibrant color; it also seasoned them inside and out and gave them a meaty, highly seasoned, and intensely green-beany flavor—without making them overly salty. We made these flavorful green beans the star ingredient in a Mediterranean composition using cherry tomatoes, briny feta cheese, mint, and parsley and also created a French-style version with capers and tarragon.

If you don't own a salad spinner, lay the green beans on a clean dish towel to dry in step 2. The blanched, shocked, and dried green beans can be refrigerated in a zipper-lock bag for up to two days.

1½ pounds green beans, trimmed and cut into
      1- to 2-inch lengths
¼ teaspoon table salt, plus salt for blanching
12 ounces cherry tomatoes, halved
¼ cup extra-virgin olive oil
2 tablespoons chopped fresh mint
2 tablespoons chopped fresh parsley
1 tablespoon lemon juice
¼ teaspoon pepper
2 ounces feta cheese, crumbled (½ cup)

1. Bring 2 quarts water to boil in large saucepan over high heat. Add green beans and ¼ cup salt, return to boil, and cook until green beans are bright green and tender, 5 to 8 minutes.

2. While green beans cook, fill large bowl halfway with ice and water. Drain green beans in colander and immediately transfer to ice bath. When green beans are no longer warm to touch, drain in colander and dry thoroughly in salad spinner.

3. Place green beans, tomatoes, oil, mint, parsley, lemon juice, pepper, and salt in bowl and toss to combine. Transfer to platter, sprinkle with feta, and serve.

Green Bean Salad with Shallot, Mustard, and Tarragon

- 1 shallot, sliced thin
- 1 tablespoon white wine vinegar
- ¼ teaspoon table salt, plus salt for blanching
- 1½ pounds green beans, trimmed and cut into 1- to 2-inch lengths
- 3 tablespoons extra-virgin olive oil
- 1 tablespoon Dijon mustard
- 1 tablespoon capers, rinsed and minced
- 2 teaspoons minced fresh tarragon
- ¼ teaspoon pepper

1. Place shallot, vinegar, and salt in large bowl and toss to combine; set aside. Bring 2 quarts water to boil in large saucepan over high heat. Add green beans and ¼ cup salt, return to boil, and cook until green beans are bright green and tender, 5 to 8 minutes.

2. While green beans cook, fill large bowl halfway with ice and water. Drain green beans in colander and immediately transfer to ice bath. When green beans are no longer warm to touch, drain in colander and dry thoroughly in salad spinner.

3. Add green beans, oil, mustard, capers, tarragon, and pepper to bowl with shallot mixture and toss to combine. Transfer to platter and serve.

French Potato Salad

Serves 6 • Total Time: 45 minutes

Why This Recipe Works French potato salad, served warm or at room temperature, is composed of sliced potatoes glistening with olive oil, white wine vinegar, and plenty of fresh herbs. The potatoes should be tender but not mushy, and the flavor of the vinaigrette should penetrate the relatively bland potatoes but not be oily or dull. To prevent torn skins and broken slices, we had to slice the potatoes before boiling them. To tone down the flavor of harsh garlic, we blanched it before mixing the vinaigrette. A little extra vinegar added a pleasing sharpness, while some reserved potato water added just the right amount of moisture and saltiness to the salad. Dijon mustard combined with strong herbs also perked things up. Pouring the vinaigrette over the warm potatoes on a sheet pan, then folding in the other ingredients, kept the slices intact.

If fresh chervil isn't available, substitute an additional ½ tablespoon minced parsley and an additional ½ teaspoon minced tarragon. For best flavor, serve the salad warm, but to make ahead, follow the recipe through step 2, cover with plastic wrap, and refrigerate. Before serving, bring the salad to room temperature, then add the shallot and herbs.

- 2 pounds red potatoes (about 6 medium or 18 small), unpeeled, sliced ¼ inch thick
  Table salt for cooking potatoes
- 1 medium garlic clove, peeled and threaded on skewer
- ¼ cup extra-virgin olive oil
- 1½ tablespoons champagne vinegar or white wine vinegar
- 2 teaspoons Dijon mustard
- ½ teaspoon pepper
- 1 small shallot, minced (about 1 tablespoon)
- 1 tablespoon minced fresh chervil
- 1 tablespoon minced fresh parsley
- 1 tablespoon minced fresh chives
- 1 teaspoon minced fresh tarragon

1. Place potatoes, 6 cups cold water, and 2 tablespoons salt in a large saucepan. Bring to boil over high heat, then reduce heat to medium. Lower skewered garlic into simmering water and blanch, about 45 seconds. Immediately run garlic under cold tap water to stop cooking process; remove garlic from skewer and set aside. Simmer potatoes, uncovered, until tender but still firm (paring knife can be slipped into and out of center of potato slice with no resistance), about 5 minutes. Drain potatoes, reserving ¼ cup cooking water. Arrange hot potatoes close together in single layer on rimmed baking sheet.

2. Press garlic through garlic press or mince by hand. Whisk garlic, reserved potato cooking water, oil, vinegar, mustard, and pepper in small bowl until combined. Drizzle dressing evenly over warm potato slices; let stand for 10 minutes.

3. Meanwhile, toss shallot, chervil, parsley, chives, and tarragon gently together in small bowl. Transfer potatoes to large serving bowl. Add shallot-herb mixture and mix lightly with rubber spatula to combine. Serve immediately.

SEASON 3

All-American Potato Salad

Serves 4 to 6 • **Total Time: 40 minutes, plus 1 hour 20 minutes cooling and chilling**

Why This Recipe Works For an extra-flavorful potato salad, we took advantage of our discovery that seasoning the potatoes while they're hot maximizes flavor. We tossed hot potatoes with white vinegar and found russet potatoes to be more flavorful than other potato varieties treated the same way. Russets do crumble a bit when mixed, but we found this quality charming, not alarming. Just ½ cup of mayonnaise dressed 2 pounds of potatoes perfectly.

Note that this recipe calls for celery seeds, not celery salt; if only celery salt is available, use the same amount but omit the addition of salt in the dressing. When testing the potatoes for doneness, simply taste a piece; do not overcook the potatoes or they will become mealy and will break apart. The potatoes must be just warm, or even fully cooled, when you add the dressing. If you find the potato salad a little dry for your liking, add up to 2 tablespoons more mayonnaise.

- 2 pounds russet potatoes (3 to 4 medium), peeled and cut into ¾-inch cubes
- ½ teaspoon table salt, plus salt for cooking potatoes
- 2 tablespoons distilled white vinegar
- ½ cup mayonnaise
- 1 celery rib, chopped fine
- 3 tablespoons sweet pickle relish
- 2 tablespoons minced red onion
- 2 tablespoons minced fresh parsley
- ¾ teaspoon dry mustard
- ¾ teaspoon celery seeds
- ¼ teaspoon pepper
- 2 Easy-Peel Hard-Cooked Eggs (page 27), peeled and cut into ¼-inch cubes (optional)

1. Place potatoes in large saucepan and add water to cover by 1 inch. Bring to boil over medium-high heat; add 1 tablespoon salt, reduce heat to medium, and simmer, stirring once or twice, until potatoes are tender, about 8 minutes.

2. Drain potatoes and transfer to large bowl. Add vinegar and, using rubber spatula, toss gently to combine. Let stand until potatoes are just warm, about 20 minutes.

3. Meanwhile, in small bowl, stir together mayonnaise, celery, relish, onion, parsley, dry mustard, celery seeds, pepper, and salt. Using rubber spatula, gently fold dressing and eggs, if using, into potatoes. Cover with plastic wrap and refrigerate until chilled, about 1 hour; serve. (Potato salad can be covered and refrigerated for up to 1 day.)

SEASON 22

Watermelon Salad with Cotija and Serrano Chiles

Serves 4 to 6 • **Total Time: 20 minutes**

Why This Recipe Works Melon salads are prone to some common pitfalls: namely, watered-down dressings and garnishes that slide to the bottom of the salad bowl. Because watermelons vary in sweetness, we started by tasting our watermelon to determine how much sugar to incorporate into our dressing. To counter the abundant water contributed by the watermelon, we made an intense dressing with assertive ingredients such as lime juice, scallions, serrano chiles, and fresh cilantro, but we skipped the oil, which would only be repelled by the water on the surface of the watermelon. Instead we added richness with chopped roasted pepitas and cotija cheese, which adhered to the surface of the watermelon pieces and held on to the dressing. To avoid watering down the dressing, we left the watermelon in large chunks, which freed less juice and accentuated the contrast between the well-seasoned exterior and the sweet, juicy interior.

Taste your melon as you cut it up: If it's very sweet, omit the sugar; if it's less sweet, add the sugar to the dressing. Jalapeños can be substituted for the serranos. If cotija cheese is unavailable, substitute feta cheese. This salad makes a light and refreshing accompaniment to grilled meat or fish.

GAME CHANGER

Timing Makes All the Difference

"*I adore the cold, creamy comfort of potato salad—and when it's perfectly made, I can eat tubs of it, either all by itself as a satisfying snack or alongside grilled or barbecued meats. While developing other potato salad recipes, we found that seasoning the potatoes with vinegar while they're hot is transformative, giving them a lightly tangy flavor that beautifully complements the earthiness of the starchy potatoes. So when I developed this salad, I started by boiling russet potatoes, draining them, and spreading them out on a baking sheet so that I could season them with lots of white vinegar. I found that russets soaked up the vinegar better than less starchy varieties such as Yukon Gold or Red Bliss potatoes treated the same way. (Russets do crumble a bit when mixed, but that's perfectly fine with me.) Just ½ cup of mayonnaise spiked with sweet pickle relish, chopped red onion, and dry mustard coats 2 pounds of potatoes with a lively dressing. Another secret ingredient is celery seed: Its lightly spicy, herbal flavor backs up the fresh chopped celery that's also in the mix. And, if you like them, chopped hard-cooked eggs bring sunny, yolky color and richness.*"

—*Becky*

⅓ cup lime juice (3 limes)

2 scallions, white and green parts separated and sliced thin

2 serrano chiles, stemmed, halved, seeded, and sliced thin crosswise

1–2 tablespoons sugar (optional)

¾ teaspoon table salt

6 cups 1½-inch seedless watermelon pieces

3 ounces cotija cheese, crumbled (¾ cup), divided

5 tablespoons chopped fresh cilantro, divided

5 tablespoons chopped roasted, salted pepitas, divided

Combine lime juice, scallion whites, and serranos in large bowl and let sit for 5 minutes. Stir in sugar, if using, and salt. Add watermelon, ½ cup cotija, ¼ cup cilantro, ¼ cup pepitas, and scallion greens and stir to combine. Transfer to shallow serving bowl. Sprinkle with remaining ¼ cup cotija, remaining 1 tablespoon cilantro, and remaining 1 tablespoon pepitas and serve.

VARIATIONS
Cantaloupe Salad with Olives and Red Onion
Serves 4 to 6

Taste your melon as you cut it up: If it's very sweet, omit the honey; if it's less sweet, add the honey to the dressing. We like the gentle heat and raisiny sweetness of ground dried Aleppo pepper here, but if it's unavailable, substitute ¾ teaspoon of paprika and ¼ teaspoon of cayenne pepper. This salad makes a light and refreshing accompaniment to grilled meat or fish and couscous or steamed white rice.

½ red onion, sliced thin

⅓ cup lemon juice (2 lemons)

1–3 teaspoons honey (optional)

1 teaspoon ground dried Aleppo pepper

½ teaspoon table salt

1 cantaloupe, peeled, halved, seeded, and cut into 1½-inch chunks (6 cups)

5 tablespoons chopped fresh parsley, divided

5 tablespoons chopped fresh mint, divided

¼ cup finely chopped pitted oil-cured olives, divided

Combine onion and lemon juice in large bowl and let sit for 5 minutes. Stir in honey, if using; Aleppo pepper; and salt. Add cantaloupe, ¼ cup parsley, ¼ cup mint, and 3 table-spoons olives and stir to combine. Transfer to shallow serving bowl. Sprinkle with remaining 1 tablespoon parsley, remaining 1 tablespoon mint, and remaining 1 tablespoon olives and serve.

GAME CHANGER

A Salad Dressing That Actually Sticks

"My 4th of July weekends on the Jersey shore would be nothing without a cold beer, burgers on the grill, and a refreshing melon salad. I've always been on salad duty. For many years, I used the classics: watermelon, feta, fresh mint, and a vinaigrette. It did the job, though I noticed my family constantly scooping out the dressing and goodies that fell to the bottom. They didn't mind, but I did. So last summer I changed the menu. This recipe was the opposite of everything I'd been doing all these years! The simple assertive dressing full of lime juice, scallions, serranos, and cilantro purposefully omits oil to ensure that it clings. Crunchy pepitas and savory cotija adhered so tightly to the melon you'd think I used a glue gun. I placed the bowl next to the burgers, and watched my family ogle. Before I knew it, every bite of this flavor-overloaded salad was gone in record time. When cleanup commenced, I grabbed the bowl and stared at the bottom. The empty bottom. What a beautiful sight."

—Sam

Honeydew Salad with Peanuts and Lime
Serves 4 to 6

Taste your melon as you cut it up: If it's very sweet, omit the sugar; if it's less sweet, add the sugar to the dressing. This salad makes a light and refreshing accompaniment to grilled meat or fish and steamed white rice.

⅓ cup lime juice (3 limes)
1 shallot, sliced thin
2 Thai chiles, stemmed, seeded, and minced
1 garlic clove, minced
½ teaspoon table salt
1–2 tablespoons sugar (optional)
1 tablespoon fish sauce
1 honeydew melon, peeled, halved, seeded, and cut into 1½-inch chunks (6 cups)
5 tablespoons chopped fresh cilantro, divided
5 tablespoons chopped fresh mint, divided
5 tablespoons salted dry-roasted peanuts, chopped fine, divided

1. Combine lime juice and shallot in large bowl. Using mortar and pestle (or on cutting board using flat side of chef's knife), mash Thai chiles, garlic, and salt to fine paste. Add chile paste; sugar, if using; and fish sauce to lime juice mixture and stir to combine.

2. Add honeydew, ¼ cup cilantro, ¼ cup mint, and ¼ cup peanuts and toss to combine. Transfer to shallow serving bowl. Sprinkle with remaining 1 tablespoon cilantro, remaining 1 tablespoon mint, and remaining 1 tablespoon peanuts and serve.

SEASON 8

Cool and Creamy Macaroni Salad

Serves 8 to 10 • Total Time: 45 minutes

Why This Recipe Works Macaroni salad seems simple enough—toss elbow macaroni and seasonings with a mayo-based dressing. So why does this salad often fall short? We set out to make a picnic-worthy macaroni salad with tender pasta and a creamy, well-seasoned dressing. First we had to get the pasta texture just right. To do this, we didn't drain the macaroni as thoroughly as we could have; any excess water was absorbed by the pasta as it sat, which prevented the finished salad from drying out. We also cooked the macaroni to a point where it still had some bite so the pasta wouldn't get too soft when mixed with the mayonnaise. For the most flavor, we seasoned the

pasta first—before adding the mayo—so that the seasonings could penetrate and flavor the macaroni. Garlic powder added flavor (fresh garlic was too harsh), and lemon juice and Dijon mustard enlivened the creamy dressing.

Don't drain the macaroni too well before adding the other ingredients—a little extra moisture will keep the salad from drying out. If you've made the salad ahead of time, simply stir in a little warm water to loosen the texture before serving.

Table salt for cooking pasta
1 pound elbow macaroni
½ small red onion, minced
1 celery rib, chopped fine
¼ cup minced fresh parsley
2 tablespoons lemon juice
1 tablespoon Dijon mustard
⅛ teaspoon garlic powder
Pinch cayenne pepper
1½ cups mayonnaise

1. Bring 4 quarts water to boil in large pot. Stir 1 tablespoon salt and pasta into boiling water and cook, stirring often, until nearly tender, about 5 minutes. Drain pasta and rinse with cold water until cool, then drain briefly so that macaroni remains moist. Transfer to large bowl.

2. Stir in onion, celery, parsley, lemon juice, mustard, garlic powder, and cayenne and let sit until flavors are absorbed, about 2 minutes. Add mayonnaise and let sit until salad is no longer watery, 5 to 10 minutes. Season with salt and pepper to taste, and serve. (Salad can be refrigerated in airtight container for up to 2 days.)

Antipasto Pasta Salad

Serves 6 to 8 • Total Time: 1 hour, plus 30 minutes cooling

Why This Recipe Works We love a traditional antipasto platter, chock-full of cured meats, cheese, and pickled vegetables. It's a full-flavored and satisfying dish—and something that we thought would translate well to a hearty pasta salad. We quickly decided that short, curly pasta was the best shape to use, as its curves held on to the salad's other components, making for a more cohesive dish. Quickly rendering the fat from the meats in the microwave helped to keep this salad from becoming greasy. We used an increased ratio of vinegar to oil in the dressing—the sharp, acidic flavor cut the richness of the meats and cheese for a brighter-tasting salad. For well-seasoned pasta, we tossed the hot pasta with the dressing—hot pasta absorbs dressing better than cold pasta. Slicing the meat into thick strips meant that its hearty flavor wasn't lost among the other ingredients. And grating the cheese, rather than cubing it, made for evenly distributed sharp flavor throughout the salad.

We also liked the addition of 1 cup chopped pitted kalamata olives or 1 cup jarred artichokes, drained and quartered, to this salad.

- 8 ounces sliced pepperoni, cut into ¼-inch strips
- 8 ounces thick-sliced soppressata or salami, halved and cut into ¼-inch strips
- 10 tablespoons red wine vinegar
- 6 tablespoons extra-virgin olive oil
- 3 tablespoons mayonnaise
- 1 (12-ounce) jar pepperoncini, drained (2 tablespoons liquid reserved), stemmed, and chopped coarse
- 4 garlic cloves, minced
- ½ teaspoon table salt, plus salt for cooking pasta
- ½ teaspoon pepper
- ¼ teaspoon red pepper flakes
- 1 pound short, curly pasta, such as fusilli or campanelle
- 1 pound white mushrooms, trimmed and quartered
- 4 ounces aged provolone cheese, grated (1 cup)
- 1 (12-ounce) jar roasted red peppers, drained, patted dry, and chopped coarse
- 1 cup chopped fresh basil

1. Bring 4 quarts water to boil in large pot. Place pepperoni on large paper towel–lined plate. Cover with second paper towel and place soppressata on top. Cover with another paper towel and microwave on high power for 1 minute. Discard paper towels and set pepperoni and soppressata aside.

2. Whisk 5 tablespoons vinegar, oil, mayonnaise, pepperoncini liquid, garlic, salt, pepper, and pepper flakes together in medium bowl.

3. Stir 1 tablespoon salt and pasta into boiling water and cook, stirring often, until pasta is just past al dente. Drain pasta and return it to pot. Pour ½ cup of dressing and remaining 5 tablespoons vinegar over pasta and toss to combine; season with salt and pepper to taste. Spread pasta in single layer on rimmed baking sheet and let cool to room temperature, about 30 minutes.

4. Meanwhile, bring remaining dressing to simmer in large skillet over medium-high heat. Add mushrooms and cook until lightly browned, about 8 minutes. Transfer to large bowl and cool to room temperature.

5. Add meat, provolone, peppers, basil, and pasta to mushrooms and toss to combine. Season with salt and pepper to taste, and serve.

Chilled Soba Noodles with Cucumber, Snow Peas, and Radishes

Serves 4 to 6 • Total Time: 40 minutes

Why This Recipe Works Soba noodles, made from buckwheat flour or a buckwheat-wheat flour blend, have a chewy texture and nutty flavor and are often enjoyed chilled. For a refreshing cold noodle salad, we cooked soba noodles in unsalted boiling water until tender but still resilient and rinsed them under cold running water to remove excess starch and prevent sticking. We then tossed the soba with a miso-based dressing, which clung to and flavored the noodles without overpowering their distinct taste. To help keep the vegetables from collecting at the bottom of the bowl, we cut them into shapes and sizes that would get entwined in the noodles, so they'd incorporate nicely while adding crunch and color. Sprinkling strips of toasted nori over the top added more texture. Their understated briny taste was the perfect finishing touch to the earthy, perfectly cooked noodles; sweet-savory dressing; and cool, crunchy vegetables.

Sheets of nori, a dried seaweed that adds a subtle briny umami flavor and crisp texture to this salad, can be found in packets at Asian markets or in the Asian section of the supermarket. Plain pretoasted seaweed snacks can be substituted for the toasted nori, and yellow, red, or brown miso can be substituted for the white miso, if desired. Our favorite soba noodles are Shirakiku Soba Japanese Style Buckwheat Noodle. This dish isn't meant to be overtly spicy, but if you prefer more heat, use the full ½ teaspoon of red pepper flakes. These chilled noodles pair nicely with salmon, shrimp, tofu, or chicken for lunch or a light dinner.

- 8 ounces dried soba noodles
- 1 (8-inch square) sheet nori (optional)
- 3 tablespoons white miso
- 3 tablespoons mirin
- 2 tablespoons toasted sesame oil
- 1 tablespoon sesame seeds
- 1 teaspoon grated fresh ginger
- ¼–½ teaspoon red pepper flakes
- ⅓ English cucumber, quartered lengthwise, seeded, and sliced thin on bias
- 4 ounces snow peas, strings removed, cut lengthwise into matchsticks
- 4 radishes, trimmed, halved, and sliced into thin half-moons
- 3 scallions, sliced thin on bias

1. Bring 4 quarts water to boil in large pot. Stir in noodles and cook according to package directions, stirring occasionally, until noodles are cooked through but still retain some chew. Drain noodles and rinse under cold water until chilled. Drain well and transfer to large bowl.

2. Grip nori sheet, if using, with tongs and hold about 2 inches above low flame on gas burner. Toast nori, flipping every 3 to 5 seconds, until nori is aromatic and shrinks slightly, about 20 seconds. If you do not have a gas stove, toast nori on rimmed baking sheet in 275-degree oven until it is aromatic and shrinks slightly, 20 to 25 minutes, flipping nori halfway through toasting. Using scissors, cut nori into four 2-inch strips. Stack strips and cut crosswise into thin strips.

3. Combine miso, mirin, oil, 1 tablespoon water, sesame seeds, ginger, and pepper flakes in small bowl and whisk until smooth. Add dressing to noodles and toss to combine. Add cucumber; snow peas; radishes; scallions; and nori, if using, and toss well to evenly distribute. Season with salt to taste, and serve.

SEASON 13

Lentil Salad with Olives, Mint, and Feta

Serves 4 to 6 • **Total Time: 1¼ hours, plus 1 hour soaking**

Why This Recipe Works The most important step in making a lentil salad is cooking the lentils so they maintain their shape and firm-tender bite. We found two keys to ensuring the ideal texture. First, we brined the lentils in warm salt water. With brining, the lentils' skins softened, which led to fewer blowouts. Second, we cooked the lentils in the oven, which heated them gently and uniformly. We paired our perfectly cooked lentils with a tart vinaigrette and bold mix-ins.

French green lentils, or lentilles du Puy, are our preferred choice for this recipe, but it works with any type of lentil except red or yellow. Brining helps keep the lentils intact, but if you don't have time, they'll still taste good without it. The salad can be served warm or at room temperature.

- 1 cup lentils, picked over and rinsed
- ½ teaspoon table salt, plus salt for soaking lentils
- 6 cups water
- 2 cups chicken broth
- 5 garlic cloves, lightly crushed and peeled
- 1 bay leaf
- 5 tablespoons extra-virgin olive oil
- 3 tablespoons white wine vinegar
- ½ cup pitted kalamata olives, chopped coarse
- ½ cup minced fresh mint
- 1 large shallot, minced
- 1 ounce feta cheese, crumbled (¼ cup)

1. Place lentils and 1 teaspoon salt in bowl. Cover with 4 cups warm water (about 110 degrees) and soak for 1 hour. Drain well. (Drained lentils can be refrigerated for up to 2 days before cooking.)

2. Adjust oven rack to middle position and heat oven to 325 degrees. Combine drained lentils, remaining 2 cups water, broth, garlic, bay leaf, and salt in ovensafe medium saucepan. Cover and bake until lentils are tender but remain intact, 40 minutes to 1 hour. Meanwhile, whisk oil and vinegar together in large bowl.

3. Drain lentils well; discard garlic and bay leaf. Add drained lentils, olives, mint, and shallot to dressing and toss to combine. Season with salt and pepper to taste. Transfer to serving dish, sprinkle with feta, and serve.

VARIATIONS
Lentil Salad with Spinach, Walnuts, and Parmesan Cheese
Substitute sherry vinegar for white wine vinegar. Place 4 ounces baby spinach and 2 tablespoons water in bowl. Cover and microwave until spinach is wilted and volume is halved, 3 to 4 minutes. Remove bowl from microwave and keep covered for 1 minute. Transfer spinach to colander; gently press to release liquid. Transfer spinach to cutting board and chop coarse. Return to colander and press again. Substitute chopped spinach for olives and mint and ¾ cup coarsely grated Parmesan cheese for feta. Sprinkle with ⅓ cup coarsely chopped toasted walnuts before serving.

Lentil Salad with Hazelnuts and Goat Cheese
Substitute red wine vinegar for white wine vinegar and add 2 teaspoons Dijon mustard to dressing in step 2. Omit olives and substitute ¼ cup chopped parsley for mint. Substitute ½ cup crumbled goat cheese for feta and sprinkle with ⅓ cup coarsely chopped toasted hazelnuts before serving.

Lentil Salad with Carrots and Cilantro
Substitute lemon juice for white wine vinegar. Toss 2 carrots, peeled and cut into 2-inch-long matchsticks, with 1 teaspoon ground cumin, ½ teaspoon ground cinnamon, and ⅛ teaspoon cayenne pepper in bowl. Cover and microwave until carrots are tender but still crisp, 2 to 4 minutes. Substitute carrots for olives and ¼ cup minced fresh cilantro for mint. Omit shallot and feta.

Wheat Berry Salad with Radicchio, Dried Cherries, and Pecans

Serves 4 to 6 • **Total Time: 1¾ hours**

Why This Recipe Works: The earthy, nutty flavor and firm chew of whole grains make them an ideal choice for a hearty side dish or light main course. Though many recipes call for cooking whole grains in a measured amount of water until all the liquid is absorbed, we found that cooking the wheat berries like pasta—simply simmering them in an abundance of water until they were tender but still chewy—yielded faster and more consistent results. Soaking the wheat berries overnight, while optional, helped to further shorten the cooking time and prevented the grains from blowing out. Parsley and radicchio added color and fresh bite to the salad, and chewy, sweet dried cherries; crunchy toasted pecans; and creamy, pungent blue cheese crumbles contributed welcome textural interest.

If using refrigerated grains, let them come to room temperature before making the salad. Any whole grain can be substituted for the wheat berries. Any variety of radicchio can be used.

- 3 tablespoons extra-virgin olive oil
- 2 tablespoons red wine vinegar
- 1 small shallot, minced
- ½ teaspoon table salt
- ½ teaspoon pepper
- 2¾ cups cooked wheat berries
- 1 cup chopped Chioggia radicchio
- 1 cup fresh parsley leaves
- ½ cup pecans, toasted and chopped coarse, divided
- ¼ cup dried cherries
- 1 ounce blue cheese, crumbled (¼ cup)

Whisk oil, vinegar, shallot, salt, and pepper together in large bowl. Add wheat berries, radicchio, parsley, half of pecans, and cherries to dressing and toss to combine. Season with salt and pepper to taste. Transfer to serving bowl and sprinkle with blue cheese and remaining pecans. Serve.

Wheat Berry Salad with Radicchio, Dried Cherries, and Pecans

Pasta, Noodles & Dumplings

Photo: Japchae

Pasta with Garlic and Oil

Serves 4 to 6 • **Total Time: 50 minutes**

Why This Recipe Works Nothing sounds easier than pasta with olive oil and garlic, but too often this dish turns out oily or rife with burnt garlic. We were after a flawless version of this quick classic, with bright, deep garlic flavor and no trace of bitterness or harshness. For a mellow flavor, we cooked most of the garlic over low heat until sticky and straw-colored; a modest amount of raw garlic added at the end brought in some potent fresh garlic flavor. Extra-virgin olive oil and reserved pasta cooking water helped to keep our garlic and pasta saucy. A splash of lemon juice and sprinkling of red pepper flakes added some spice and brightness to this simple, yet complex-flavored recipe.

For a twist on pasta with garlic and oil, try sprinkling toasted fresh bread crumbs over individual bowls, but prepare them in advance. Simply pulse two slices of high-quality white sandwich bread, torn into quarters, in a food processor to coarse crumbs. Combine with 2 tablespoons extra-virgin olive oil; season with salt and pepper; and bake on a rimmed baking sheet at 375 degrees until golden brown, 8 to 10 minutes.

1 pound spaghetti
1¼ teaspoons table salt, divided, plus salt for cooking pasta
6 tablespoons extra-virgin olive oil, divided
12 garlic cloves, minced, divided
3 tablespoons chopped fresh parsley
2 teaspoons lemon juice
¾ teaspoon red pepper flakes
½ cup grated Parmesan cheese (optional)

1. Bring 4 quarts water to boil in large pot. Add pasta and 1 tablespoon salt and cook, stirring often, until al dente; reserve ⅓ cup cooking water, then drain pasta and return it to pot.

2. Meanwhile, heat 3 tablespoons oil, 3 tablespoons garlic, and ½ teaspoon salt over low heat in 10-inch nonstick skillet. Cook, stirring constantly, until garlic is sticky and straw-colored, 10 to 12 minutes. Off heat, stir in parsley, lemon juice, pepper flakes, 2 tablespoons reserved pasta cooking water, and remaining garlic.

3. Transfer drained pasta to warm serving bowl; add remaining 3 tablespoons oil and remaining reserved pasta cooking water and toss to combine. Add garlic mixture and remaining ¾ teaspoon salt; toss to combine. Serve, sprinkling individual bowls with Parmesan, if desired.

Pasta Cacio e Uova

Serves 4 • **Total Time: 35 minutes**

Why This Recipe Works This cheese and egg pasta, called cas' e ov in its native Naples, makes its way to the table in a flash. The method is simple: Mix beaten eggs and cheese with garlic-infused lard, hot pasta, and some of its starchy cooking water. While we liked this with olive oil, cacio e uova made with lard not only tasted fuller and richer, it also heightened the cheese flavor and felt cleaner on the palate. To keep our sauce from scrambling, we mixed the sauce and pasta together off the heat. This melted the cheese and brought the eggs up to temperature gently.

Tubetti is traditionally used for this dish, but you can substitute 8 ounces (2 cups) of elbow macaroni. Lard contributes an incomparably rich, savory flavor to the sauce. Look for it in the meat section, or near the shortening, or near the butter. Our favorites are U.S. Dreams Lard and John Morrell Snow Cap Lard. Because this dish is very rich, we recommend serving it in small portions.

3 tablespoons lard or extra-virgin olive oil
2 garlic cloves, lightly crushed and peeled
2 large eggs
1 ounce Parmesan cheese, grated (½ cup)
1 ounce Pecorino Romano cheese, grated (½ cup)
2 tablespoons minced fresh parsley
¼ teaspoon table salt, plus salt for cooking pasta
¼ teaspoon pepper
8 ounces (1½ cups) tubetti

1. Melt lard in 8-inch skillet over medium-low heat. Add garlic and cook, swirling skillet and flipping garlic occasionally, until garlic is pale golden brown, 7 to 10 minutes. (Tiny bubbles will surround garlic, but garlic should not actively fry. Reduce heat if necessary.) Turn off heat, but leave skillet on burner. Discard garlic.

2. While garlic cooks, bring 2 quarts water to boil in large saucepan. Beat eggs in medium bowl until very few streaks of white remain. Stir in Parmesan, Pecorino, parsley, salt, and pepper and set aside.

3. Stir pasta and 1½ teaspoons salt into boiling water and cook, stirring often, until pasta is tender (slightly past al dente). Reserve ¼ cup cooking water, then drain pasta and return it to saucepan. Immediately add lard, egg mixture, and 1 tablespoon reserved cooking water to pasta and stir until cheese is fully melted. Adjust consistency with remaining reserved cooking water, 1 tablespoon at a time, as needed. Serve immediately.

Pasta in a Flash

"Pasta is my ultimate comfort food, so when Pasta Cacio e Uova was developed, I was an immediate fan. This dish is a perfect blend of simplicity and flavor, with small pasta cradled in a velvety, ultrasmooth egg-cheese sauce. It's a quick and delicious fare that requires only a handful of common ingredients, making it perfect for whipping up on a moment's notice.

While the sauce for Cacio e Uova seems straightforward—mix beaten eggs and cheese with fat, hot pasta, and some of its cooking water—the mixture can turn out grainy and curdled if it overheats. To keep the sauce from scrambling, the sauce ingredients and the hot pasta are quickly mixed together off the heat. The cheese melts and the eggs come up to temp and thicken using only the residual heat of the pasta and saucepan, which means there is little risk of overcooking. To build flavor in the sauce without overwhelming the subtle egg flavor, we gently toast a couple of crushed garlic cloves in the fat to add a subtle bite. A cheesy blend of tangy Pecorino Romano and nutty Parmesan highlight the richness of the silky-smooth sauce."

— Keith

Fresh Pasta Without a Machine

Makes 1 pound • Total Time: 1½ hours, plus 1 hour resting

Why This Recipe Works Not everyone has a pasta machine, and rolling out pasta dough by hand is no easy task. For an easy-to-roll pasta dough (that would still cook up into delicate, springy noodles), we added six extra egg yolks and a couple of tablespoons of olive oil to our dough. In addition, we incorporated an extended resting period to allow the gluten network to relax. To roll and cut the pasta, we first divided the pasta into smaller manageable pieces, then used a rolling pin to roll the dough and a sharp knife to cut the dough into noodles.

If using a high-protein all-purpose flour like King Arthur brand, increase the number of egg yolks to seven. The longer the dough rests in step 2, the easier it will be to roll out. When rolling out the dough, avoid adding too much flour, which may result in excessive snapback. Serve with Walnut Cream Sauce (recipe follows) or a sauce of your choice.

2 cups (10 ounces) all-purpose flour, plus extra as needed

2 large eggs, plus 6 large yolks

2 tablespoons extra-virgin olive oil

Table salt for cooking pasta

1. Process flour, eggs and yolks, and oil in food processor until mixture forms cohesive dough that feels soft and is barely tacky to touch, about 45 seconds. (If dough sticks to your fingers, add up to ¼ cup flour, 1 tablespoon at a time, until barely tacky. If dough doesn't become cohesive, add up to 1 tablespoon water, 1 teaspoon at a time, until it just comes together; process 30 seconds longer.)

2. Transfer dough to clean surface and knead by hand to form smooth, uniform ball, 1 to 2 minutes. Shape dough into 6-inch-long cylinder. Wrap with plastic wrap and set aside at room temperature to rest for at least 1 hour or up to 4 hours.

3. Cut cylinder crosswise into 6 equal pieces. Working with 1 piece of dough (rewrap remaining dough), dust both sides with flour, place cut side down on clean counter, and press into 3-inch square. Using heavy rolling pin, roll into 6-inch square. Dust both sides of dough lightly with flour.

4A. For strand pasta: Starting at center of square, roll dough away from you in 1 motion. Return rolling pin to center of dough and roll toward you in 1 motion. Repeat steps of rolling until dough sticks to counter and measures roughly 12 inches long. Lightly dust both sides of dough with flour and continue rolling dough until it measures roughly 20 inches long and 6 inches wide, lifting dough frequently to release it from counter. (You should be able to easily see outline of your fingers through dough.) If dough firmly sticks to counter and wrinkles when rolled out, dust dough lightly with flour. Transfer pasta sheet to clean dish towel and let sit, uncovered, until firm around edges, about 15 minutes; meanwhile, roll out remaining dough. Starting with 1 short end, gently fold pasta sheet at 2-inch intervals until sheet has been folded into flat, rectangular roll. With sharp chef's knife, slice crosswise into ³⁄₁₆-inch-wide strands. Use your fingers to unfurl pasta and transfer to baking sheet. Repeat folding and cutting remaining sheets of dough. Cook pasta within 1 hour.

4B. For garganelli: Starting at center of square, roll dough away from you in 1 motion. Return rolling pin to center of dough and roll toward you in 1 motion. Repeat steps of rolling until dough sticks to counter and measures roughly 12 inches long. Lightly dust both sides of dough with flour and continue rolling dough until it measures roughly 15 inches long and 6 inches wide, lifting dough frequently to release it from counter. If dough firmly sticks to counter and wrinkles when rolled out, dust dough lightly with flour. Transfer pasta sheet to clean dish towel and let sit, uncovered, until firm around edges, about 15 minutes; meanwhile, roll out remaining dough. Using sharp knife or pizza cutter, cut 1 air-dried pasta sheet into 1½-inch squares; discard scraps.

Lay 1 square of pasta diagonally on counter or, to create ridges in pasta, on top of garganelli or gnocchi board, inverted fork, or wire rack. Wrap 1 corner of pasta square around ⅜-inch dowel (or pencil), and with gentle pressure roll away from you until pasta is completely wrapped around dowel and seam is sealed. Slide shaped pasta off dowel onto lightly floured rimmed baking sheet and repeat with remaining pasta squares and sheets.

5. Bring 4 quarts water to boil in large pot. Add pasta and 1 tablespoon salt and cook until tender but still al dente, about 3 minutes. Reserve 1 cup cooking water. Drain pasta and toss with sauce; serve immediately.

To make ahead: Follow recipes through step 4, transfer baking sheet of pasta to freezer, and freeze until pasta is firm. Transfer to zipper-lock bag and store for up to 2 weeks. Cook frozen pasta straight from freezer as directed in step 5.

SAUCE
Walnut Cream Sauce
Makes 2 cups; enough for 1 pound pasta
Total Time: 25 minutes

1½ cups walnuts, toasted, divided
¾ cup dry white wine
½ cup heavy cream
1 ounce Parmesan cheese, grated (½ cup)
¼ teaspoon table salt
½ teaspoon pepper
¼ cup minced fresh chives

1. Process 1 cup walnuts in food processor until finely ground, about 10 seconds. Transfer to small bowl. Pulse remaining ½ cup walnuts in food processor until coarsely chopped, 3 to 5 pulses. Bring wine to simmer in 12-inch skillet over medium-high heat; cook until reduced to ¼ cup, about 3 minutes. Whisk in cream, ground and chopped walnuts, Parmesan, salt, and pepper. Remove pan from heat and cover to keep warm.

2. To serve, return pan to medium heat. Add pasta, ½ cup reserved cooking water, and chives; toss to combine. Season with salt and pepper to taste, and add remaining cooking water as needed to adjust consistency. Serve immediately.

Rolling, Cutting, and Shaping Pasta Dough by Hand

1. Shape dough into 6-inch cylinder; wrap in plastic wrap and let rest for at least 1 hour. Divide into 6 equal pieces. Reserve 1 piece; rewrap remaining 5.

2. Working with reserved piece, dust both sides with flour, then press cut side down into 3-inch square. With rolling pin, roll into 6-inch square, then dust both sides again with flour.

3. Roll dough to 12 by 6 inches, rolling from center of dough 1 way at a time, then dust with flour. Continue rolling to desired size, lifting frequently to release from counter. Transfer dough to clean dish towel and air-dry for about 15 minutes.

4. Using sharp knife or pizza cutter, cut dried pasta sheet into 1½-inch squares. Lay 1 square diagonally on counter or, to create ridges in pasta, on top of a garganelli or gnocchi board, inverted fork or wire rack.

5. Wrap 1 corner of pasta square around ⅜-inch dowel (or pencil), and with gentle pressure roll away from you until pasta is completely wrapped around dowel and seam is sealed.

6. Slide shaped pasta off dowel onto lightly floured rimmed baking sheet and repeat with remaining pasta squares and sheets.

Pasta with Burst Cherry Tomato Sauce and Fried Caper Crumbs

Serves 4 to 6 • Total Time: 50 minutes

Why This Recipe Works Cherry tomatoes are the perfect choice for a quick fresh tomato sauce. You can toss them directly into the pan without any prep, and they don't need lengthy cooking to concentrate their flavor or thicken into a sauce. That's because they're naturally more flavorful than the bigger varieties used in sauce, and they're full of soluble pectin that breaks down readily to a saucy consistency. To ensure that some of the cherry tomatoes remained intact and would pop in the mouth with their characteristic flood of juices, we cooked them for 10 minutes in a covered saucepan, where only the tomatoes in contact with the bottom of the pan burst and those on top steamed more gently in the released juices. To keep the sauce bright and tomato-focused, we sautéed the tomatoes with garlic, pepper flakes, and a touch of sugar, along with anchovies that melded into the mix without fishiness. Butter tossed with the pasta brought a light, creamy richness to the dish. We finished it with fresh basil and a topping of fried bread crumbs and capers.

> *Be sure to use cherry tomatoes; grape tomatoes won't break down as much and will produce a drier sauce. Our topping contributes crunch and depth, but you can substitute 1 cup (2 ounces) of grated Parmesan cheese, if desired. For a spicier dish, use the larger amount of red pepper flakes.*

Topping

- 2 tablespoons extra-virgin olive oil
- ¼ cup capers, rinsed and patted dry
- 1 anchovy fillet, rinsed, patted dry, and minced
- ½ cup panko bread crumbs
- ⅛ teaspoon table salt
- ⅛ teaspoon pepper
- ¼ cup minced fresh parsley
- 1 teaspoon grated lemon zest

Pasta

- ¼ cup extra-virgin olive oil
- 2 garlic cloves, sliced thin
- 2 anchovy fillets, rinsed and patted dry
- 2 pounds cherry tomatoes
- 1½ teaspoons table salt, plus salt for cooking pasta
- ¼ teaspoon sugar
- ⅛–¼ teaspoon red pepper flakes
- 12 ounces penne rigate, orecchiette, campanelle, or other short pasta
- 2 tablespoons unsalted butter, cut into 2 pieces and chilled
- 1 cup fresh basil leaves, torn if large

1. For the topping: Heat oil in 10-inch skillet over medium heat until shimmering. Add capers and anchovy and cook, stirring frequently, until capers have darkened and shrunk, 3 to 4 minutes. Using slotted spoon, transfer caper mixture to paper towel–lined plate; set aside. Leave oil in skillet and return skillet to medium heat. Add panko, salt, and pepper to skillet and cook, stirring constantly, until panko is golden brown, 4 to 5 minutes. Transfer panko to medium bowl. Stir in parsley, lemon zest, and reserved caper mixture.

2. For the pasta: Bring 4 quarts water to boil in large pot. While water is coming to boil, heat oil, garlic, and anchovies in large saucepan over medium heat. Cook, stirring occasionally, until anchovies break down and garlic is lightly browned, 4 to 5 minutes. Add tomatoes, salt, sugar, and pepper flakes to saucepan and stir to combine. Cover and increase heat to medium-high. Cook, without stirring, for 10 minutes.

3. Meanwhile, add pasta and 1 tablespoon salt to boiling water. Cook, stirring often, until al dente. Reserve ½ cup cooking water, then drain pasta and return it to pot. Off heat, add butter and tomato mixture to pasta and stir gently until oil, butter, and tomato juices combine to form light sauce, about 15 seconds. Adjust consistency with reserved cooking water as needed, adding 2 tablespoons at a time. Stir in basil and season with salt to taste. Serve, passing topping separately.

Marinara Sauce

Makes 4 cups • Total Time: 55 minutes

Why This Recipe Works Making a tomato sauce with deep, complex flavor usually requires hours of simmering. We wanted to produce a multidimensional marinara sauce in under an hour, perfect for any night of the week. Our first challenge was picking the right tomatoes. We found canned whole tomatoes, which we hand-crushed to remove the hard core, to be the best choice in terms of both flavor and texture. We boosted tomato flavor by sautéing the tomato pieces until they glazed the bottom of the pan, after which

Little Tomatoes Make a Big-Flavored Sauce

"I first tasted pasta sauce made with cherry tomatoes in the test kitchen more than 20 years ago, and it's been my go-to method ever since. I love how the sweet-acidic flavor of the cherry tomatoes gives the sauce a clean flavor and that they require no prep beyond a quick wash.

When I started teaching my daughter how to cook, this was the first thing I taught her. The method is simple and relatively hands off, but the transformation of the little fresh tomatoes into a flavorful sauce in just 10 minutes using a covered pot is fun—it feels a bit like kitchen alchemy. The method also lends itself nicely to variations: You can easily add other flavors to the pot depending on your mood, or as my daughter taught me, use an immersion blender at the end to make the sauce smooth.

The new thing that this recipe taught me was how to make a zippy fried caper and bread-crumb topping, which has become somewhat of a standard topping in our house. It adds incredible flavor and texture to lots of dishes beyond pasta."

—Julia

we added their liquid. We shortened the simmering time by using a skillet instead of a saucepan (the greater surface area of a skillet encourages faster evaporation and flavor concentration). Finally, we added just the right amount of sugar, red wine (we especially liked Chianti and Merlot), and, just before serving, a few uncooked canned tomatoes for texture, fresh basil for fresh herbal flavor, and olive oil for richness.

You can figure on about 3 cups of sauce per pound of pasta. Chianti or Merlot works well for the dry red wine. Because canned tomatoes vary in acidity and saltiness, it's best to add salt, pepper, and sugar to taste just before serving. If you prefer a chunkier sauce, give it just three or four pulses in the food processor in step 4.

2 (28-ounce) cans whole tomatoes
3 tablespoons extra-virgin olive oil, divided
1 onion, chopped fine
2 garlic cloves, minced
½ teaspoon dried oregano
⅓ cup dry red wine
3 tablespoons chopped fresh basil
   Sugar

1. Pour tomatoes into strainer set over large bowl. Open tomatoes with your hands and remove and discard fibrous cores; let tomatoes drain excess liquid, about 5 minutes. Remove ¾ cup tomatoes from strainer and set aside. Reserve 2½ cups tomato juice and discard remainder.

2. Heat 2 tablespoons oil in 12-inch skillet over medium heat until shimmering. Add onion and cook, stirring occasionally, until softened and golden around edges, 6 to 8 minutes. Add garlic and oregano and cook, stirring constantly, until garlic is fragrant, about 30 seconds.

3. Add tomatoes from strainer and increase heat to medium-high. Cook, stirring every minute, until liquid has evaporated and tomatoes begin to stick to bottom of pan and browned bits form around pan edges, 10 to 12 minutes. Add wine and cook until thick and syrupy, about 1 minute. Add reserved tomato juice and bring to simmer; reduce heat to medium and cook, stirring occasionally and scraping up any browned bits, until sauce is thickened, 8 to 10 minutes.

4. Transfer sauce to food processor and add reserved tomatoes; pulse until slightly chunky, about 8 pulses. Return sauce to skillet; add basil and remaining 1 tablespoon oil; and season with salt, pepper, and sugar to taste. Serve. (Sauce can be refrigerated in airtight container for up to 3 days or frozen for up to 1 month.)

SEASON 18

Meatless "Meat" Sauce with Chickpeas and Mushrooms

Makes 6 cups; enough for 2 pounds pasta
Total Time: 1 hour

Why This Recipe Works This vegetarian version of tomato-meat sauce boasts a rich, savory flavor, and hearty, unctuous body—the qualities we wanted most in a quick meat sauce. We started with cremini mushrooms and tomato paste—both rich sources of savory flavor. We let the food processor do the work for us, using it to chop up our mushrooms, onions, and chickpeas, which added hearty texture. Extra-virgin olive oil did double duty, cooking the mushrooms and the classic Italian aromatics of garlic, dried oregano, and red pepper flakes and enriching the sauce. To loosen the sauce without diluting its flavor, we added vegetable broth. Chopped fresh basil added a bright finish.

Make sure to rinse the chickpeas after pulsing them in the food processor or the sauce will be too thick. Our favorite canned chickpeas are from Goya, our favorite crushed tomatoes are from San Merican, and our favorite tomato paste is from Cento.

10 ounces cremini mushrooms, trimmed
 6 tablespoons extra-virgin olive oil, divided
 1 teaspoon table salt
 1 onion, chopped
 5 garlic cloves, minced
1¼ teaspoons dried oregano

¼ teaspoon red pepper flakes
¼ cup tomato paste
1 (28-ounce) can crushed tomatoes
2 cups vegetable broth
1 (15-ounce) can chickpeas, rinsed
2 tablespoons chopped fresh basil

1. Pulse mushrooms in 2 batches in food processor until chopped into ⅛- to ¼-inch pieces, 7 to 10 pulses, scraping down sides of bowl as needed. (Do not clean workbowl.)

2. Heat 5 tablespoons oil in Dutch oven over medium-high heat until shimmering. Add mushrooms and salt and cook, stirring occasionally, until mushrooms are browned and fond has formed on bottom of pot, about 8 minutes.

3. While mushrooms cook, pulse onion in food processor until finely chopped, 7 to 10 pulses, scraping down sides of bowl as needed. (Do not clean workbowl.) Transfer onion to pot with mushrooms and cook, stirring occasionally, until onion is soft and translucent, about 5 minutes. Combine garlic, oregano, pepper flakes, and remaining 1 tablespoon oil in bowl.

4. Add tomato paste to pot and cook, stirring constantly, until mixture is rust-colored, 1 to 2 minutes. Reduce heat to medium and push vegetables to sides of pot. Add garlic mixture to center and cook, stirring constantly, until fragrant, about 30 seconds. Stir in tomatoes and broth; bring to simmer over high heat. Reduce heat to low and simmer sauce for 5 minutes, stirring occasionally.

5. While sauce simmers, pulse chickpeas in food processor until chopped into ¼-inch pieces, 7 to 10 pulses. Transfer chickpeas to fine-mesh strainer and rinse under cold running water until water runs clear; drain well. Add chickpeas to pot and simmer until sauce is slightly thickened, about 15 minutes. Stir in basil and season with salt and pepper to taste. (Sauce can be refrigerated for up to 2 days or frozen for up to 1 month.)

SEASON 20
Pasta alla Norma

Serves 6 to 8 • Total Time: 1¼ hours

Why This Recipe Works Pasta alla norma is Sicily's most iconic pasta dish. It consists of a lively combination of tender eggplant and robust tomato sauce, which is seasoned with herbs, mixed with al dente pasta, and finished with shreds of salty, milky ricotta salata. The dish gets its name

from the epic opera *Norma*; just as the opera is associated with perfection, so too is the hearty pasta. We salted and microwaved the eggplant to quickly draw out its moisture so that it wouldn't absorb too much oil, and we added a secret ingredient, anchovies, to our tomato sauce to give it a deep, savory flavor without any fishiness. We waited until the last minute to combine the eggplant and sauce; this prevented the eggplant from becoming soggy.

If coffee filters are not available, food-safe, undyed paper towels can be substituted when microwaving the eggplant. Be sure to remove the eggplant from the microwave immediately so that the steam can escape. For a spicier dish, use the larger amount of pepper flakes.

1½ pounds eggplant, cut into ½-inch pieces
½ teaspoon table salt, plus salt for cooking pasta
¼ cup extra-virgin olive oil, divided
4 garlic cloves, minced
2 anchovy fillets, rinsed, patted dry, and minced
¼–½ teaspoon red pepper flakes
1 (28-ounce) can crushed tomatoes
6 tablespoons chopped fresh basil
1 pound ziti, rigatoni, or penne
3 ounces ricotta salata, shredded (1 cup)

1. Toss eggplant with salt in bowl. Line entire surface of plate with double layer of coffee filters and lightly spray with vegetable oil spray. Spread eggplant in even layer on coffee filters; wipe out and reserve bowl. Microwave until eggplant is dry and shriveled to one-third of its original size, 8 to 15 minutes (eggplant should not brown). Transfer eggplant immediately to paper towel–lined plate. Let cool slightly.

2. Transfer eggplant to now-empty bowl, drizzle with 1 tablespoon oil, and toss gently to coat; discard coffee filters and reserve plate. Heat 1 tablespoon oil in 12-inch nonstick skillet over medium-high heat until shimmering. Add eggplant and cook, stirring occasionally, until well browned and fully tender, about 10 minutes. Remove skillet from heat and transfer eggplant to now-empty plate.

3. Add 1 tablespoon oil, garlic, anchovies, and pepper flakes to now-empty skillet and cook using residual heat, stirring constantly, until fragrant and garlic becomes pale golden, about 1 minute (if skillet is too cool to cook mixture, set it over medium heat). Add tomatoes and bring to simmer over medium-high heat. Cook, stirring occasionally, until slightly thickened, 8 to 10 minutes.

4. Gently stir in eggplant and cook until heated through and flavors meld, 3 to 5 minutes. Stir in basil and remaining 1 tablespoon oil. Season with salt to taste.

5. Meanwhile, bring 4 quarts water to boil in large pot. Add pasta and 1 tablespoon salt and cook, stirring often, until al dente. Reserve ½ cup cooking water, then drain pasta and return it to pot. Add sauce and toss to combine. Adjust consistency with reserved cooking water as needed. Serve, passing ricotta salata separately.

SEASON 15

Pasta with Pesto, Potatoes, and Green Beans

Serves 6 • Total Time: 1¼ hours

Why This Recipe Works We hadn't thought of putting pasta and potatoes in the same dish until we learned that it's the preferred way to serve pesto in Liguria, Italy—the birthplace of the basil sauce. But our initial attempts at the dish needed work. The sauce was slightly grainy and the sharp, raw garlic dominated. Timing was another issue: When everything was cooked together, the green beans could be jarringly crisp and the pasta way too soft—or vice versa. How could we get all the elements of this dish to cook perfectly? The traditional method called for cutting the potatoes into chunks and then, once cooked, vigorously mixing them with the pesto, pasta, and green beans. The agitation sloughed off their corners, which dissolved into the dish, pulling the pesto and cooking water together to form a simple sauce. Simply trading out starchy russets for creamy, waxy red potatoes eliminated graininess and made

our sauce smooth. We cooked the potatoes fully, then used the starchy water to cook the pasta. As for the pesto, we toasted the garlic and pine nuts for warm, mellow flavor (then used the same skillet to quickly steam the green beans). We used plenty of pasta water to bring the sauce together. Two tablespoons of butter made it even silkier, and a splash of lemon juice brought all the flavors into focus.

> *If gemelli is unavailable, penne or rigatoni make good substitutes. Use large red potatoes measuring 3 inches or more in diameter.*

- ¼ cup pine nuts
- 3 garlic cloves, unpeeled
- 1 pound large red potatoes, peeled and cut into ½-inch pieces
- ½ teaspoon table salt, plus salt for cooking vegetables
- 12 ounces green beans, trimmed and cut into 1½-inch lengths
- 2 cups fresh basil leaves
- 1 ounce Parmesan cheese, grated (½ cup)
- 7 tablespoons extra-virgin olive oil
- 1 pound gemelli
- 2 tablespoons unsalted butter, cut into ½-inch pieces and chilled
- 1 tablespoon lemon juice
- ½ teaspoon pepper

1. Toast pine nuts and garlic in 10-inch skillet over medium heat, stirring frequently, until pine nuts are golden and fragrant and garlic darkens slightly, 3 to 5 minutes. Transfer to bowl and let cool. Peel garlic and chop coarse.

2. Bring 3 quarts water to boil in large pot. Add potatoes and 1 tablespoon salt and cook until potatoes are tender but still hold their shape, 9 to 12 minutes. Using slotted spoon, transfer potatoes to rimmed baking sheet. (Do not discard water.)

3. Meanwhile, bring ½ cup water and ¼ teaspoon salt to boil in now-empty skillet over medium heat. Add green beans, cover, and cook until tender, 5 to 8 minutes. Drain green beans and transfer to sheet with potatoes.

4. Process basil, Parmesan, oil, pine nuts, garlic, and salt in food processor until smooth, about 1 minute.

5. Add pasta to water in large pot and cook, stirring often, until al dente. Set colander in large bowl. Drain pasta in colander, reserving cooking water in bowl. Return pasta to pot. Add butter, lemon juice, pepper, potatoes and green beans, pesto, and 1¼ cups reserved cooking water and stir vigorously with rubber spatula until sauce takes on creamy appearance. Add additional cooking water as needed to adjust consistency and season with salt and pepper to taste. Serve immediately.

While we prefer linguine or spaghetti, any pasta shape will work here. You may substitute ½ teaspoon of red wine vinegar and ¼ teaspoon of red pepper flakes for the pepperoncini.

SEASON 10

Pasta alla Trapanese

Serves 4 to 6 • Total Time: 40 minutes

Why This Recipe Works In the Sicilian village of Trapani, there's a very different kind of pesto—it's basically pesto crossed with tomato sauce. Almonds replace pine nuts, but the big difference is the appearance of fresh tomatoes—not as the main ingredient, but as a fruity, sweet accent. For a clean, bright version of this uncooked sauce, fresh tomatoes were best. Cherry and grape tomatoes proved equal contenders, sharing a similar brightness and juiciness that was far more reliable than that of their larger cousins. We processed the tomatoes with a handful of basil, garlic, and toasted almonds. The almonds contributed body and thickened the sauce while retaining just enough crunch to offset the tomatoes' pulpiness; using blanched, slivered almonds avoided the muddy flavor often contributed by papery skins. We added a scant amount of hot vinegar peppers for zing, then drizzled in olive oil in a slow, steady stream to emulsify the pesto. As a finishing touch, we stirred grated Parmesan into the pasta along with our light, bright, and texturally satisfying pesto.

1 pound linguine or spaghetti
1 teaspoon table salt, plus salt for cooking pasta
¼ cup slivered almonds, toasted
12 ounces cherry or grape tomatoes
½ cup packed fresh basil leaves
1 garlic clove, minced
1 small pepperoncini, stemmed, seeded, and minced (about ½ teaspoon)
Pinch red pepper flakes (optional)
⅓ cup extra-virgin olive oil
1 ounce Parmesan cheese, grated (½ cup), plus extra for serving

1. Bring 4 quarts water to boil in large pot. Add pasta and 1 tablespoon salt and cook, stirring often, until al dente. Reserve ½ cup cooking water, then drain pasta and return it to pot.

2. Meanwhile, process almonds; tomatoes; basil; garlic; pepperoncini; salt; and pepper flakes, if using, in food processor until smooth, about 1 minute, scraping down sides of bowl as needed. With machine running, slowly drizzle in oil, about 30 seconds.

3. Add pesto and Parmesan to pasta and adjust consistency of sauce with reserved pasta cooking water as needed. Serve immediately, passing extra Parmesan separately.

¼ teaspoon red pepper flakes
2 (15-ounce) cans chickpeas, undrained
2 cups water
1 teaspoon table salt
8 ounces (1½ cups) ditalini
1 tablespoon lemon juice
1 tablespoon minced fresh parsley
1 ounce Parmesan cheese, grated (½ cup)

1. Process pancetta in food processor until ground to paste, about 30 seconds, scraping down sides of bowl as needed. Add carrot, celery, and garlic and pulse until finely chopped, 8 to 10 pulses. Add onion and pulse until onion is cut into ⅛- to ¼-inch pieces, 8 to 10 pulses. Transfer pancetta mixture to large Dutch oven. Pulse tomatoes in now-empty food processor until coarsely chopped, 8 to 10 pulses. Set aside.

2. Add oil to pancetta mixture in Dutch oven and cook over medium heat, stirring frequently, until fond begins to form on bottom of pot, about 5 minutes. Add rosemary, anchovy, and pepper flakes and cook until fragrant, about 1 minute. Stir in tomatoes, chickpeas and their liquid, water, and salt and bring to boil, scraping up any browned bits. Reduce heat to medium-low and simmer for 10 minutes. Add pasta and cook, stirring frequently, until tender, 10 to 12 minutes. Stir in lemon juice and parsley and season with salt and pepper to taste. Serve, passing Parmesan and extra oil separately.

Pasta e Ceci

Serves 4 to 6 • **Total Time: 1 hour**

Why This Recipe Works Pasta e ceci, a sibling of pasta e fagioli, is a hearty and fast one-pot meal that's simple to prepare, yet packed full of satisfying flavor. To keep the cooking time to under an hour, we used canned chickpeas—along with their starchy liquid—to add even more body and flavor to the dish. Cooking the chickpeas and ditalini in the same pot blended the dish, and the additional starch released by the pasta created a silky texture. We simmered the chickpeas before adding the pasta, in order to achieve the perfect creamy softness. Using a food processor produced a finely minced soffritto of onions, garlic, carrot, celery, and pancetta, an addition that gave the dish a meaty backbone. And we achieved depth of flavor by adding anchovy, tomatoes, and Parmesan. Parsley and lemon juice provided a bright contrast just before serving.

Another short pasta, such as orzo, can be substituted for the ditalini, but make sure to substitute by weight and not by volume.

2 ounces pancetta, cut into ½-inch pieces
1 small carrot, peeled and cut into ½-inch pieces
1 small celery rib, cut into ½-inch pieces
4 garlic cloves, peeled
1 onion, halved and cut into 1-inch pieces
1 (14-ounce) can whole peeled tomatoes, drained
¼ cup extra-virgin olive oil, plus extra for serving
2 teaspoons minced fresh rosemary
1 anchovy fillet, rinsed, patted dry, and minced

Linguine allo Scoglio

Serves 6 • **Total Time: 1¾ hours**

Why This Recipe Works To create a seafood pasta dish with rich, savory seafood flavor in every bite (not just in the pieces of shellfish), we made a sauce with clam juice and four minced anchovies, which fortified the juices shed by the shellfish. Cooking the shellfish in a careful sequence—precooking hardier clams and mussels first and then adding the shrimp and squid during the final few minutes of cooking—ensured that every piece was plump and tender. We parboiled the linguine and then finished cooking it directly in the sauce; the noodles soaked up flavor while shedding starches that thickened the sauce so that it clung well to the pasta. Fresh cherry tomatoes, lots of garlic, fresh herbs, and lemon made for a bright, clean, complex-tasting sauce.

For a simpler version of this dish, you can omit the clams and squid and increase the amounts of mussels and shrimp to 1½ pounds each; you'll also need to increase the amount of salt in step 2 to ¾ teaspoon.

If you can't find fresh squid, it's available frozen at many supermarkets and typically has the benefit of being precleaned. Bar Harbor makes our favorite clam juice.

- 6 tablespoons extra-virgin olive oil, divided
- 12 garlic cloves, minced
- ¼ teaspoon red pepper flakes
- 1 pound littleneck clams, scrubbed
- 1 pound mussels, scrubbed and debearded
- 1¼ pounds cherry tomatoes (half of tomatoes halved, remaining left whole)
- 1 (8-ounce) bottle clam juice
- 1 cup dry white wine
- 1 cup minced fresh parsley, divided
- 1 tablespoon tomato paste
- 4 anchovy fillets, rinsed, patted dry, and minced
- 1 teaspoon minced fresh thyme
- ½ teaspoon table salt, plus salt for cooking pasta
- 1 pound linguine
- 1 pound extra-large shrimp (21 to 25 per pound), peeled and deveined
- 8 ounces squid, sliced crosswise into ½-inch-thick rings
- 2 teaspoons grated lemon zest, plus lemon wedges for serving

1. Heat ¼ cup oil in large Dutch oven over medium-high heat until shimmering. Add garlic and pepper flakes and cook until fragrant, about 1 minute. Add clams, cover, and cook, shaking pan occasionally, for 4 minutes. Add mussels, cover, and continue to cook, shaking pan occasionally, until clams and mussels have opened, 3 to 4 minutes longer. Transfer clams and mussels to bowl, discarding any that haven't opened, and cover to keep warm; leave any broth in pot.

2. Add whole tomatoes, clam juice, wine, ½ cup parsley, tomato paste, anchovies, thyme, and salt to pot and bring to simmer over medium-high heat. Reduce heat to medium and cook, stirring occasionally, until tomatoes have started to break down and sauce is reduced by one-third, about 10 minutes.

3. Meanwhile, bring 4 quarts water to boil in large pot. Add pasta and 1 tablespoon salt and cook, stirring often, for 7 minutes. Reserve ½ cup cooking water, then drain pasta.

4. Add pasta to sauce in Dutch oven and cook over medium heat, stirring gently, for 2 minutes. Reduce heat to medium-low, stir in shrimp, cover, and cook for 4 minutes. Stir in squid, lemon zest, halved tomatoes, and remaining ½ cup parsley; cover and continue to cook until shrimp and squid are just cooked through, about 2 minutes longer. Gently stir in clams and mussels. Remove pot from heat, cover, and let stand until clams and mussels are warmed through, about 2 minutes. Season with salt and pepper to taste, and adjust consistency with reserved cooking water as needed. Transfer to large serving dish, drizzle with remaining 2 tablespoons oil, and serve, passing lemon wedges separately.

SEASON 15

Rigatoni with Beef and Onion Ragu

Serves 6 to 8 • **Total Time: 2¾ to 3¼ hours**

Why This Recipe Works This thrifty yet supremely satisfying meat sauce, known as alla genovese, was born in 16th-century Naples. It began as a combination of beef and aromatic vegetables that were cooked down to make two meals: a savory sauce for pasta and another, separate meal of cooked beef. Later, most of the vegetables took a back seat to onions, which became the foundation of this deeply flavorful sauce. To make the ultrasavory recipe work in a modern context, we turned all the elements into one substantial sauce by shredding the meat into the sauce. To eliminate the need for stirring and monitoring during cooking, we moved the process from the stovetop to the even heat of the oven. A surprising ingredient—water—proved essential to extracting maximum flavor from the onions. We also added tomato paste for extra flavor and color. To encourage the sauce to cling to the pasta, we vigorously stirred them together so that the starch from the pasta added body to the sauce. A bit of grated Pecorino brought the flavors together.

If marjoram is unavailable, substitute an equal amount of oregano. Pair this dish with a lightly dressed salad of assertively flavored greens.

1 (1- to 1¼-pound) boneless beef chuck-eye roast, cut into 4 pieces and trimmed of large pieces of fat

1 teaspoon kosher salt, plus salt for cooking pasta

½ teaspoon pepper

2 ounces pancetta, cut into ½-inch pieces

2 ounces salami, cut into ½-inch pieces

1 small carrot, peeled and cut into ½-inch pieces

1 small celery rib, cut into ½-inch pieces

2½ pounds onions, halved and cut into 1-inch pieces

2 tablespoons tomato paste

1 cup dry white wine, divided

2 tablespoons minced fresh marjoram, divided

1 pound rigatoni

1 ounce Pecorino Romano cheese, grated (½ cup), plus extra for serving

1. Sprinkle beef with salt and pepper and set aside. Adjust oven rack to lower-middle position and heat oven to 300 degrees.

2. Process pancetta and salami in food processor until ground to paste, about 30 seconds, scraping down sides of bowl as needed. Add carrot and celery and process 30 seconds longer, scraping down sides of bowl as needed. Transfer paste to Dutch oven and set aside. Pulse onions in processor in 2 batches, until ⅛- to ¼-inch pieces form, 8 to 10 pulses per batch.

3. Cook pancetta mixture over medium heat, stirring frequently, until fat is rendered and fond begins to form on bottom of pot, about 5 minutes. Add tomato paste and cook, stirring constantly, until browned, about 90 seconds. Stir in 2 cups water, scraping up any browned bits. Stir in onions and bring to boil. Stir in ½ cup wine and 1 tablespoon marjoram. Add beef and push into onions to ensure that it is submerged. Transfer to oven and cook, uncovered, until beef is fully tender, 2 to 2½ hours.

4. Transfer beef to carving board. Place pot over medium heat and cook, stirring frequently, until mixture is almost completely dry. Stir in remaining ½ cup wine and cook for 2 minutes, stirring occasionally. Using 2 forks, shred beef into bite-size pieces. Stir beef and remaining 1 tablespoon marjoram into sauce and season with salt and pepper to taste. Remove from heat, cover, and keep warm.

5. Bring 4 quarts water to boil in large pot. Add pasta and 2 tablespoons salt and cook, stirring often, until just al dente. Drain pasta and add to warm sauce. Add Pecorino and stir vigorously over low heat until sauce is slightly thickened and rigatoni is fully tender, 1 to 2 minutes. Serve, passing extra Pecorino separately.

SEASON 1

Pasta with Rustic Slow-Simmered Tomato Sauce with Meat

Serves 4 • Total Time: 2½ to 3 hours

Why This Recipe Works Slow-simmered Italian meat sauce—the kind without meatballs—relies on pork for rich flavor. But the pork found in supermarkets is so lean, we needed an option that could provide enough fat and flavor to create a flavorful meat sauce with fall-off-the-bone-tender meat. We used readily available fattier boneless pork butt roast, which turned meltingly tender when cooked for a long time and added meaty flavor. Boneless beef short ribs can also be used, but they need to cook a little longer. Red wine accentuated the meatiness of the sauce, which was built on a simple combination of sautéed onion and canned whole tomatoes.

2. Return meat and any accumulated juices to skillet; add tomatoes and reserved juice. Bring to boil, then reduce heat to low; cover; and simmer gently, turning meat several times, until meat is very tender, 1½ to 2 hours for pork and 2 to 2½ hours for beef. (If beef isn't tender after 2 hours, add ¼ cup water and continue to cook until tender.)

3. Transfer meat to clean plate. Using 2 forks, shred meat into bite-size pieces, discarding any large pieces of fat or connective tissue. Return meat to skillet. Return sauce to simmer over medium heat and cook, uncovered, until slightly thickened, about 5 minutes. Season with salt and pepper to taste.

4. Bring 4 quarts water to boil in large pot. Add pasta and 1 tablespoon salt and cook, stirring often, until al dente. Reserve ½ cup cooking water, then drain pasta and return to pot. Add sauce to pasta and toss to combine, adjusting consistency with reserved cooking water as needed. Serve. (Sauce can be refrigerated for up to 4 days or frozen for up to 2 months.)

This sauce can be made with either beef or pork. Pork butt roast is often labeled Boston butt in the super-market. To prevent the sauce from becoming greasy, trim the meat well and drain off most of the fat from the skillet after browning. This thick, rich, robust sauce is best with tubular pasta, such as ziti, rigatoni, or penne. Pass grated Pecorino Romano (especially nice with pork) or Parmesan cheese at the table.

- 1 tablespoon extra-virgin olive oil
- 1½ pounds boneless pork butt roast or boneless beef short ribs, trimmed and cut into 1½-inch pieces
- ¾ teaspoon table salt, divided, plus salt for cooking pasta
- ½ teaspoon pepper
- 1 onion, chopped fine
- ½ cup red wine
- 1 (28-ounce) can whole peeled tomatoes, drained with juice reserved, chopped fine
- 1 pound short tubular pasta

1. Heat oil in 12-inch skillet over medium-high heat until shimmering. Sprinkle meat with ½ teaspoon salt and pepper and brown on all sides, turning occasionally with tongs, 5 to 7 minutes. Transfer meat to large plate; pour off all but 1 teaspoon fat from skillet. Add onion and remaining ¼ teaspoon salt and cook until softened, 2 to 3 minutes. Add wine and simmer briskly, scraping up any browned bits, until wine reduces by half, about 2 minutes.

Ragu alla Bolognese

Makes about 6 cups • Total Time: 2½ hours

Why This Recipe Works Unlike meat sauces in which tomatoes dominate, Bolognese sauce is about the meat, with the tomatoes in a supporting role. We wanted a traditional recipe for this complexly flavored sauce, with rich meatiness up front and a good balance of sweet, salty, and acidic flavors. We also wanted a velvety texture that would lightly cling to the noodles. For an ultrameaty version, we used six different types of meat: ground beef, pork, and veal; pancetta; mortadella; and chicken livers. These meats and the combination of red wine and tomato paste gave us a rich, complex sauce with balanced acidity. The addition of gelatin lent the sauce a silky texture.

This recipe makes enough sauce for 2 pounds of pasta. Eight teaspoons of gelatin is equivalent to one (1-ounce) box of gelatin. If you can't find ground veal, use an additional 12 ounces of ground beef.

1 cup chicken broth
1 cup beef broth
8 teaspoons unflavored gelatin
1 onion, chopped coarse
1 large carrot, peeled and chopped coarse
1 celery rib, chopped coarse
4 ounces pancetta, chopped
4 ounces mortadella, chopped
6 ounces chicken livers, trimmed
3 tablespoons extra-virgin olive oil
¾ pound 85 percent lean ground beef
¾ pound ground veal
¾ pound ground pork
3 tablespoons minced fresh sage
1 (6-ounce) can tomato paste
2 cups dry red wine
1 pound pappardelle or tagliatelle
   Table salt for cooking pasta
   Grated Parmesan cheese

1. Combine chicken broth and beef broth in bowl; sprinkle gelatin over top and set aside. Pulse onion, carrot, and celery in food processor until finely chopped, about 10 pulses, scraping down bowl as needed; transfer to separate bowl. Pulse pancetta and mortadella in now-empty food processor until finely chopped, about 25 pulses, scraping down bowl as needed; transfer to second bowl. Process chicken livers in now-empty food processor until pureed, about 5 seconds; transfer to third bowl.

2. Heat oil in Dutch oven over medium-high heat until shimmering. Add beef, veal, and pork; cook, breaking up pieces with wooden spoon, until all liquid has evaporated and meat begins to sizzle, 10 to 15 minutes. Add pancetta mixture and sage; cook, stirring frequently, until pancetta is translucent, 5 to 7 minutes, adjusting heat as needed to keep fond from burning. Add chopped vegetables and cook, stirring frequently, until softened, 5 to 7 minutes. Add tomato paste and cook, stirring constantly, until rust-colored and fragrant, about 3 minutes.

3. Stir in wine, scraping up any browned bits. Simmer until sauce has thickened, about 5 minutes. Stir in broth mixture and return to simmer. Reduce heat to low and cook at bare simmer until thickened (wooden spoon should leave trail when dragged through sauce), about 1½ hours.

4. Stir in pureed chicken livers, bring to boil, and remove from heat. Season with salt and pepper to taste; cover and keep warm.

5. Bring 4 quarts water to boil in large pot. Add pasta and 1 tablespoon salt and cook, stirring often, until al dente. Reserve ¾ cup cooking water, then drain pasta and return it to pot. Add half of sauce and reserved cooking water to pasta and toss to combine. Transfer to serving bowl and serve, passing Parmesan separately. (Leftover sauce can be refrigerated for up to 3 days or frozen for up to 1 month.)

SEASON 18

Weeknight Tagliatelle with Bolognese Sauce

Serves 4 to 6 • **Total Time: 1¾ hours**

Why This Recipe Works To create a Bolognese sauce that could come together quickly on a busy weeknight but rival the depth and richness of a long-cooked version, we started by browning the aromatic vegetables (but not the ground beef, which would dry out and toughen if seared) to develop a flavorful fond; we also treated the ground beef with a baking soda solution to ensure that it stayed tender. Adding pancetta, which we ground and browned deeply with the aromatic vegetables, boosted the sauce's meaty flavor, and a healthy dose of tomato paste added depth and brightness. We also added Parmesan cheese, usually reserved for serving, directly to the sauce as it cooked for its umami richness. To develop concentrated flavor and a consistency that nicely coated the pasta, we boiled beef broth until it was reduced by half and added it to the sauce, which then needed to simmer only 30 minutes longer. Finally, we intentionally made the sauce thin because the eggy noodles (traditionally tagliatelle or pappardelle) absorb a lot of liquid; once they soaked up some of the sauce, it coated the noodles beautifully.

3. Pulse pancetta in food processor until finely chopped, 15 to 20 pulses. Add onion, carrot, and celery and pulse until vegetables are finely chopped and mixture has paste-like consistency, 12 to 15 pulses, scraping down sides of bowl as needed.

4. Heat butter and oil in large Dutch oven over medium-high heat until shimmering. Add pancetta-vegetable mixture and remaining ¼ teaspoon pepper and cook, stirring occasionally, until liquid has evaporated, about 8 minutes. Spread mixture in even layer in bottom of pot and continue to cook, stirring every couple of minutes, until very dark browned bits form on bottom of pot, 7 to 12 minutes longer. Stir in tomato paste and cook until paste is rust-colored and bottom of pot is dark brown, 1 to 2 minutes.

5. Reduce heat to medium, add beef, and cook, using wooden spoon to break meat into pieces no larger than ¼ inch, until beef has just lost its raw pink color, 4 to 7 minutes. Stir in wine, scraping up any browned bits, and bring to simmer. Cook until wine has evaporated and sauce has thickened, about 5 minutes. Stir in broth and Parmesan. Return sauce to simmer; cover, reduce heat to low, and simmer for 30 minutes (sauce will look thin). Remove from heat and season with salt and pepper to taste.

6. Rinse pot that held broth. While sauce simmers, bring 4 quarts water to boil in now-empty pot. Add pasta and 1 tablespoon salt and cook, stirring occasionally, until al dente. Reserve ¼ cup cooking water, then drain pasta. Add pasta to pot with sauce and toss to combine. Adjust sauce consistency with reserved cooking water as needed. Transfer to platter or individual bowls and serve, passing extra Parmesan separately.

If you use our recommended beef broth, Better Than Bouillon Roasted Beef Base, you can skip step 2 and make a concentrated broth by adding 4 teaspoons paste to 2 cups water. To ensure the best flavor, be sure to brown the pancetta-vegetable mixture in step 4 until the fond on the bottom of the pot is quite dark. The cooked sauce will look thin but will thicken once tossed with the pasta. Tagliatelle is a long, flat, dry egg pasta that is about ¼ inch wide; if you can't find it, you can substitute pappardelle. Substituting other pasta may result in a too-wet sauce.

1 pound 93 percent lean ground beef
½ teaspoon pepper, divided
¼ teaspoon baking soda
4 cups beef broth
6 ounces pancetta, chopped coarse
1 onion, chopped coarse
1 large carrot, peeled and chopped coarse
1 celery rib, chopped coarse
1 tablespoon unsalted butter
1 tablespoon extra-virgin olive oil
3 tablespoons tomato paste
1 cup dry red wine
1 ounce Parmesan cheese, grated (½ cup), plus extra for serving
1 pound tagliatelle
Table salt for cooking pasta

1. Toss beef with 2 tablespoons water, ¼ teaspoon pepper, and baking soda in bowl until thoroughly combined. Set aside.

2. While beef sits, bring broth to boil over high heat in large pot (this pot will be used to cook pasta in step 6) and cook until reduced to 2 cups, about 15 minutes; set aside.

Pork, Fennel, and Lemon Ragu with Pappardelle

Serves 4 to 6 • **Total Time: 2¾ hours**

Why This Recipe Works This white ragu, known as ragù bianco, skips tomatoes in favor of bright lemon and rich cream. This version features shreds of meltingly tender braised pork punctuated by tart lemon, licorice-y fennel, and salty Pecorino Romano cheese. We ensured plenty of savoriness in the ragu by creating fond twice. We first browned finely chopped pancetta, onion, and fennel in a Dutch oven and then added water and a touch of cream to create a braising liquid. A pork shoulder, which we halved crosswise to make cooking faster and shredding

A Ragu Without Tomatoes Is a Very Good Thing

"I grew up on a steady diet of Italian American cooking prepared by my nana, Katherine Pizzarello. Let's just say there were tomatoes involved. Don't get me wrong; tomatoes are my favorite vegetable, in part because they are at once sweet, acidic, and rich with umami. But tomatoes are not subtle. This white ragu is the perfect demonstration of the 'less is more' principle. Strip away excess ingredients, remove the tomatoes that are omnipresent in other slow-simmered Italian pasta sauces, and you can really taste the two kinds of pork in this meaty sauce. The sweet, licorice notes of the fennel come to the fore and the lemon balances out the richness of the pork and the cream. And while it's easy to think that ragus are all about the tomatoes and slow cooking, this sauce reminds me that a ragu is about humble ingredients being transformed into something greater than the sum of those parts. And you don't need tomatoes to make that happen."

—Jack

easier, simmered in this liquid in the oven, where a second fond formed on the sides of the pot. After scraping this second fond into the sauce, we brightened its flavor with plenty of lemon juice before adding the pasta.

> *Pork butt roast is often labeled Boston butt in the supermarket. To ensure that the sauce isn't greasy, be sure to trim the roast of all excess surface fat. You can substitute tagliatelle for the pappardelle, if desired.*

    4   ounces pancetta, chopped
    1   large onion, chopped fine
    1   large fennel bulb, 2 tablespoons fronds
        chopped, stalks discarded, bulb halved,
        cored, and chopped fine
    4   garlic cloves, minced
    2   teaspoons finely chopped fresh thyme
 1½   teaspoons table salt, plus salt for cooking pasta
    1   teaspoon pepper
  ⅓   cup heavy cream
    1   (1½-pound) boneless pork butt roast,
        well trimmed and cut in half across grain
 1½   teaspoons grated lemon zest plus ¼ cup juice
        (2 lemons)
  12   ounces pappardelle
    2   ounces Pecorino Romano cheese, grated (1 cup),
        plus extra for serving

1. Adjust oven rack to middle position and heat oven to 350 degrees. Cook pancetta and ⅔ cup water in Dutch oven over medium-high heat, stirring occasionally, until water has evaporated and dark fond forms on bottom of pot, 8 to 10 minutes. Add onion and fennel bulb and cook, stirring occasionally, until vegetables soften and start to brown, 5 to 7 minutes. Stir in garlic, thyme, salt, and pepper and cook until fragrant, about 30 seconds.

2. Stir in cream and 2 cups water, scraping up any browned bits. Add pork and bring to boil over high heat. Cover, transfer to oven, and cook until pork is tender, about 1½ hours.

3. Transfer pork to large plate and let cool for 15 minutes. Cover pot so fond will steam and soften. Using spatula, scrape browned bits from sides of pot and stir into sauce. Stir in lemon zest and juice.

4. While pork cools, bring 4 quarts water to boil in large pot. Using 2 forks, shred pork into bite-size pieces, discarding any large pieces of fat or connective tissue. Return pork and any juices to Dutch oven. Cover and keep warm.

5. Add pasta and 1 tablespoon salt to boiling water and cook, stirring occasionally, until al dente. Reserve 2 cups cooking water, then drain pasta and add it to Dutch oven. Add Pecorino and ¾ cup reserved cooking water and stir until sauce is slightly thickened and cheese is fully melted, 2 to 3 minutes. If desired, stir in remaining reserved cooking water, ¼ cup at a time, to adjust sauce consistency. Season with salt and pepper to taste and sprinkle with fennel fronds. Serve immediately, passing extra Pecorino separately.

SEASON 2

Spaghetti and Meatballs

Serves 4 to 6   •   Total Time: 1½ hours

Why This Recipe Works One of the problems with meatballs is that they're thought of as smaller, rounder versions of hamburgers. This would be fine if meatballs were cooked to rare or medium-rare, as most hamburgers are, but meatballs are usually cooked to well-done. This can leave them flavorless, dry, and dense, so they need some help to lighten their texture. What we were after was nothing short of great meatballs: crusty and dark brown on the outside and soft and moist on the inside. White bread soaked in buttermilk added as a binder gave the meatballs a creamy texture and an appealing tang. Using an egg was also important for texture and flavor; its fats and emulsifiers added moistness and richness. An egg yolk alone worked best and kept the meatballs moist and light; the white just made the mixture sticky and hard to handle, with no benefits. Adding some ground pork to the usual ground beef enhanced the flavor. Broiling dried out the meatballs; pan-frying was the best way to brown the meatballs and kept the interior moist. Finally, building the tomato sauce on top of the browned bits left in the pan after frying the meatballs made for a hearty, robust-tasting sauce.

> *The shaped meatballs can be covered with plastic wrap and refrigerated for several hours ahead of serving time; fry the meatballs and make the sauce at the last minute. If you don't have buttermilk, you can substitute 6 tablespoons of plain yogurt thinned with 2 tablespoons of milk.*

Meatballs

- 2 slices hearty white sandwich bread, crusts removed, torn into small pieces
- ½ cup buttermilk
- 12 ounces 85 percent lean ground beef
- 4 ounces ground pork
- ¼ cup grated Parmesan cheese
- 2 tablespoons minced fresh parsley
- 1 large egg yolk
- 1 garlic clove, minced
- ¾ teaspoon table salt
- ⅛ teaspoon pepper
- Vegetable oil for pan-frying

Tomato Sauce and Pasta

- 2 tablespoons extra-virgin olive oil
- 1 garlic clove, minced
- 1 (28-ounce) can crushed tomatoes
- 1 tablespoon chopped fresh basil
- 1 pound spaghetti
- Table salt for cooking pasta
- Grated Parmesan cheese

Making Meatballs

1. Use fork to mash bread and buttermilk into smooth paste.

2. Working with 3 tablespoons meatball mixture at a time, form mixture into 1½-inch ball by gently rolling it between your palms.

3. Fry meatballs, turning every so often, until crusty golden brown all over.

1. For the meatballs: Mash bread and buttermilk to smooth paste in large bowl. Let stand for 10 minutes.

2. Add beef, pork, Parmesan, parsley, egg yolk, garlic, salt, and pepper to mashed bread; stir gently until uniform. Gently form into 1½-inch round meatballs (about 14 meatballs). (When forming meatballs use light touch; if you compact meatballs too much, they can become dense and hard.)

3. Pour oil into 12-inch skillet until it measures depth of ¼ inch. Heat over medium-high heat until shimmering. Add meatballs in single layer and cook until well browned on all sides, about 10 minutes. Transfer meatballs to paper towel–lined plate and discard oil left in skillet.

4. For the sauce: Add oil and garlic to now-empty skillet and cook over medium heat, scraping up any browned bits, until fragrant, about 30 seconds. Add tomatoes with their juice; bring to simmer; and cook until sauce thickens, about 10 minutes. Stir in basil and season with salt and pepper to taste. Add meatballs and simmer, turning them occasionally, until heated through, about 5 minutes.

5. For the pasta: Meanwhile, bring 4 quarts water to boil in large pot. Add pasta and 1 tablespoon salt and cook, stirring often, until al dente. Reserve ½ cup cooking water, then drain pasta and return it to pot. Add several large spoonfuls of tomato sauce (without meatballs) to pasta and toss to coat. Adjust consistency of sauce with reserved pasta cooking water as needed. Serve immediately, topping individual bowls with more tomato sauce and several meatballs and passing Parmesan separately.

Italian-Style Turkey Meatballs

Serves 4 to 6 • **Total Time: 1½ hours**

Why This Recipe Works Ground turkey is a great choice when you want to eat less red meat, but using it to make meatballs presents some challenges. Our turkey meatballs rival those made from beef or pork, thanks to a few test kitchen tricks. We started with 85 or 93 percent lean turkey; these fattier options produced moister meatballs. Next, we added an egg and fresh bread crumbs to help bind the meatballs. And a stint in the fridge was key to firming up the gelatin and creating juicy texture. To boost meaty flavor, we added glutamate-rich ingredients such as Parmesan cheese, anchovies, tomato paste, and dried shiitake mushrooms. Braising the meatballs in a quick tomato sauce gave them time to soak up extra flavor.

| *Serve with spaghetti.*

    1 cup chicken broth
 ½ ounce dried shiitake mushrooms
    2 slices hearty white sandwich bread,
      torn into 1-inch pieces
    1 ounce Parmesan cheese, grated (½ cup),
      plus extra for serving
    1 tablespoon chopped fresh parsley
 1½ teaspoons unflavored gelatin
    1 teaspoon table salt

 ½ teaspoon pepper, divided
    4 anchovy fillets, rinsed, patted dry,
      and minced, divided
 1½ pounds 85 or 93 percent lean ground turkey
    1 large egg, lightly beaten
    4 garlic cloves, minced, divided
    1 (14.5-ounce) can whole peeled tomatoes
 ½ teaspoon dried oregano
 ⅛ teaspoon red pepper flakes
    3 tablespoons extra-virgin olive oil
    2 tablespoons tomato paste
 ¼ cup chopped fresh basil
      Sugar

1. Microwave broth and mushrooms in covered bowl until steaming, about 1 minute. Let sit until softened, about 5 minutes. Drain mushrooms in fine-mesh strainer and reserve liquid.

2. Pulse bread in food processor until finely ground, 10 to 15 pulses; transfer bread crumbs to large bowl (do not wash processor bowl). Add Parmesan, parsley, gelatin, salt, and ¼ teaspoon pepper to bowl with bread crumbs and mix until thoroughly combined. Pulse mushrooms and half of anchovies in food processor until chopped fine, 10 to 15 pulses. Add mushroom mixture, turkey, egg, and half of garlic to bowl with bread-crumb mixture and mix with your hands until thoroughly combined. Divide mixture into 16 portions (about ¼ cup each). Using your hands, roll each portion into ball; transfer meatballs to plate and refrigerate for 15 minutes.

3. Pulse tomatoes and their juice in food processor to coarse puree, 10 to 15 pulses. Combine oregano, pepper flakes, remaining ¼ teaspoon pepper, remaining anchovies, and remaining garlic in small bowl; set aside.

4. Heat oil in 12-inch nonstick skillet over medium-high heat until shimmering. Add meatballs and cook until well browned all over, 5 to 7 minutes. Transfer meatballs to paper towel–lined plate, leaving fat in skillet.

5. Add reserved anchovy mixture to skillet and cook, stirring constantly, until fragrant, about 30 seconds. Increase heat to high; stir in tomato paste, reserved mushroom liquid, and pureed tomatoes; and bring to simmer. Return meatballs to skillet, reduce heat to medium-low, cover, and cook until meatballs register 160 degrees, 12 to 15 minutes, turning meatballs once. Transfer meatballs to platter, increase heat to high, and simmer sauce until slightly thickened, 3 to 5 minutes. Stir in basil and season with sugar, salt, and pepper to taste. Pour sauce over meatballs and serve, passing extra Parmesan separately.

Foolproof Spaghetti Carbonara

Serves 4 • Total Time: 1 hour

Why This Recipe Works This quintessential Roman pasta dish is made with simple ingredients, but the results can be disappointing. The finicky egg-based sauce (made from either whole eggs or just yolks, plus finely grated cheese) relies on the heat of the warm pasta to become lush and glossy, but that rarely happens without the addition of tons of fat. We wanted to make a classic carbonara that was foolproof but not so rich that eating a full serving was impossible. We started by replacing the guanciale, or cured pork jowl, with readily available American bacon. To approximate the meaty chew of guanciale, we cooked the bacon with a little water, which produced tender-chewy pieces. We used just a touch of the rendered fat in our sauce for consistent bacon flavor in every bite. To make a richly eggy sauce that wouldn't become dry and clumpy when mixed with the pasta, we used three eggs and an extra yolk for richness. But the real secret here was adding starch in the form of pasta water. Boiling the pasta in half the usual amount of water gave us extra starchy water to coat the proteins and fats in the cheese, preventing them from separating or clumping, and making for a perfectly velvety sauce. Tossing the spaghetti with the sauce in a warm serving bowl allowed the warm pasta to gently "cook" the carbonara sauce without overcooking the eggs.

It's important to work quickly in steps 2 and 3. The heat from the cooking water and the hot spaghetti will "cook" the sauce only if used immediately. Warming the mixing and serving bowls helps the sauce stay creamy. Use a high-quality bacon for this dish; our favorite is Vande Rose Applewood Smoked Artisan Dry Cured Bacon.

> 8 slices bacon, cut into ½-inch pieces
> ½ cup water
> 3 garlic cloves, minced
> 2½ ounces Pecorino Romano, grated (1¼ cups)
> 3 large eggs plus 1 large yolk
> 1 teaspoon pepper
> 1 pound spaghetti
>   Table salt for cooking pasta

1. Bring bacon and water to simmer in 10-inch nonstick skillet over medium heat; cook until water evaporates and bacon begins to sizzle, about 8 minutes. Reduce heat to medium-low and continue to cook until fat is rendered and bacon browns, 5 to 8 minutes longer. Add garlic and cook, stirring constantly, until fragrant, about 30 seconds. Strain bacon mixture through fine-mesh strainer set in bowl. Set aside bacon mixture. Measure out 1 tablespoon fat and place in medium bowl. Whisk Pecorino, eggs and yolk, and pepper into fat until combined.

2. Meanwhile, bring 2 quarts water to boil in Dutch oven. Set colander in large bowl. Add pasta and 1 teaspoon salt to pot; cook, stirring frequently, until al dente. Drain pasta in colander set in bowl, reserving cooking water. Pour 1 cup cooking water into liquid measuring cup and discard remainder. Return pasta to now-empty bowl.

3. Slowly whisk ½ cup reserved cooking water into Pecorino mixture. Gradually pour Pecorino mixture over pasta, tossing to coat. Add bacon mixture and toss to combine. Let pasta rest, tossing frequently, until sauce has thickened slightly and coats pasta, 2 to 4 minutes, adjusting consistency with remaining reserved cooking water if needed. Serve immediately.

Warming the Bowl

To help sauced pasta stay creamy longer, warm mixing bowl (and serving bowls). Drain cooked spaghetti in colander set in large serving bowl. Water will heat bowl, and some of it can be reserved for sauce.

Potato Gnocchi with Browned Butter and Sage Sauce

Serves 4 • Total Time: 1¾ hours, plus 1 hour straining

Why This Recipe Works Good potato gnocchi are something of a culinary paradox; light, airy pillows created from dense, starchy ingredients. The method is simple: Knead mashed potatoes into a dough with a minimum of flour; shape; and boil for a minute. And yet the potential pitfalls are numerous (lumpy mashed potatoes, too much or too little flour, a heavy hand when kneading, and bland flavor). We wanted a foolproof recipe for impossibly light gnocchi with unmistakable potato flavor. Baking russets (parcooked in the microwave for speed and ease) produced intensely flavored potatoes—an excellent start to our gnocchi base. To avoid lumps, which can cause gnocchi to break apart during cooking, we turned to a ricer for a smooth, supple mash. While many recipes offer a range of flour to use, which ups the chances of overworking the dough (and producing leaden gnocchi), we used an exact amount based on the ratio of potato to flour so that our gnocchi dough was mixed as little as possible. And we found that an egg, while not traditional, tenderized our gnocchi further, delivering delicate pillow-like dumplings.

Gnocchi, like many baking recipes, require accurate measurement to achieve the proper texture; it's best to weigh the potatoes and flour. After processing, you may have slightly more than the 3 cups (16 ounces) of potatoes required for this recipe; do not be tempted to use more than 3 cups. Instead of the browned butter sauce try Gorgonzola Cream Sauce, Parmesan Sauce with Pancetta and Walnuts, and Porcini Mushroom Broth (recipes follow).

Potato Gnocchi

- 2 pounds russet potatoes, unpeeled
- 1 large egg, lightly beaten
- ¾ cup plus 1 tablespoon (4 ounces) all-purpose flour
- 1 teaspoon table salt, plus salt for cooking gnocchi

Browned Butter and Sage Sauce

- 4 tablespoons unsalted butter, cut into 4 pieces
- 1 small shallot, minced
- 1 teaspoon minced fresh sage
- 1½ teaspoons lemon juice
- ¼ teaspoon table salt

1. For the gnocchi: Adjust oven rack to middle position and heat oven to 450 degrees. Poke each potato 8 times with paring knife over entire surface. Place potatoes on plate and microwave until slightly softened at ends, about 10 minutes, flipping potatoes halfway through cooking. Transfer potatoes directly to oven rack and bake until skewer glides easily through flesh and potatoes yield to gentle pressure, 18 to 20 minutes.

2. Hold potato with pot holder or dish towel and peel with paring knife. Process potato through ricer or food mill onto rimmed baking sheet. Repeat with remaining potatoes. Gently spread riced potatoes into even layer and let cool for 5 minutes.

3. Transfer 3 cups (16 ounces) warm potatoes to large bowl. Using fork, gently stir in egg until just combined. Sprinkle flour and salt over potato mixture. Using fork, gently combine until no pockets of dry flour remain. Press mixture into rough dough, transfer to lightly floured counter and gently knead until smooth but slightly sticky, about 1 minute, lightly dusting counter with flour as needed to prevent sticking.

4. Line 2 rimmed baking sheets with parchment paper and dust liberally with flour. Cut dough into 8 pieces. Lightly dust counter with flour. Gently roll 1 piece of dough into ½-inch-thick rope, dusting with flour to prevent sticking. Cut rope into ¾-inch lengths. Hold fork, with tines facing down, in your hand and press side of each piece of dough against ridged surface with your thumb to make indentation in center; roll dough down and off tines to form ridges. Transfer formed gnocchi to prepared sheets and repeat with remaining dough.

5. **For the sauce:** Melt butter in 12-inch skillet over medium-high heat, swirling occasionally, until butter is browned and releases nutty aroma, about 1½ minutes. Off heat, add shallot and sage, stirring until shallot is fragrant, about 1 minute. Stir in lemon juice and salt and cover to keep warm.

6. Bring 4 quarts water to boil in large pot. Add 1 table-spoon salt. Using parchment paper as sling, add half of gnocchi and cook until firm and just cooked through, about 90 seconds (gnocchi should float to surface after about 1 minute). Remove gnocchi with slotted spoon, transfer to skillet with sauce, and cover to keep warm. Repeat with remaining gnocchi and transfer to skillet. Gently toss gnocchi with sauce to combine; serve.

Making Ridges on Gnocchi

To make ridges on gnocchi, hold fork with tines facing down. Press each dough piece (cut side down) against tines with your thumb to make indentation. Roll dumpling down tines to create ridges on sides.

SAUCES
Gorgonzola Cream Sauce
Makes 1 cup • Total Time: 10 minutes
Adjust the consistency of the sauce with up to 2 tablespoons cooking water before adding the gnocchi to it.

  ¾ cup heavy cream
  ¼ cup dry white wine
  4 ounces Gorgonzola cheese, crumbled (1 cup)
  2 tablespoons minced fresh chives

Bring cream and wine to simmer in 12-inch skillet over medium-high heat. Gradually add Gorgonzola while whisking constantly and cook until melted and sauce is thickened, 2 to 3 minutes. Stir in chives and season with salt and pepper to taste. Remove from heat and cover to keep warm.

Parmesan Sauce with Pancetta and Walnuts
Makes 1 cup • Total Time: 25 minutes
Serve gnocchi prepared with this sauce with extra grated Parmesan cheese on the side.

  ½ cup chicken broth
  1 ounce Parmesan cheese, grated (½ cup)
  ¼ cup heavy cream
  2 large egg yolks
  ⅛ teaspoon pepper
  2 teaspoons extra-virgin olive oil
  3 ounces pancetta, chopped fine
  ½ cup walnuts, chopped coarse

Whisk broth, Parmesan, cream, egg yolks, and pepper in bowl until smooth. Heat oil in 12-inch skillet over medium heat until shimmering. Add pancetta and cook until crisp, 5 to 7 minutes. Stir in walnuts and cook until golden and fragrant, about 1 minute. Off heat, gradually add broth mixture, whisking constantly. Return skillet to medium heat and cook, stirring often, until sauce is thickened slightly, 2 to 4 minutes. Season with salt to taste. Remove from heat and cover to keep warm.

Porcini Mushroom Broth
Makes 1¼ cups • Total Time: 35 minutes
Serve gnocchi with this sauce and grated Parmesan cheese.

  1¾ cups chicken broth
  ½ ounce dried porcini mushrooms, rinsed
  3 tablespoons extra-virgin olive oil
  1 small shallot, minced
  2 garlic cloves, sliced thin
  ⅓ cup dry white wine
  2 tablespoons minced fresh parsley

1. Microwave broth and mushrooms in covered bowl until steaming, about 1 minute. Let stand until softened, about 5 minutes. Drain mushrooms through fine-mesh strainer lined with coffee filter, reserving liquid and chopping porcini.

2. Heat 1 tablespoon oil in 12-inch skillet over medium heat until shimmering. Add chopped mushrooms, shallot, and garlic and cook until lightly browned, 2 to 4 minutes. Stir in reserved porcini soaking liquid, wine, and remaining 2 tablespoons oil, scraping up any browned bits. Bring mix-ture to boil and cook, whisking occasionally, until reduced to 1¼ cups, 6 to 9 minutes. Stir in parsley and season with salt and pepper to taste. Remove from heat and cover to keep warm.

Tomato Sauce

- 2 (28-ounce) cans diced tomatoes
- 2 tablespoons extra-virgin olive oil
- 3 garlic cloves, minced
- ½ teaspoon red pepper flakes (optional)
- ½ teaspoon table salt
- 2 tablespoons chopped fresh basil

Cheese Filling and Pasta

- 1½ pounds (3 cups) part-skim ricotta cheese
- 4 ounces Parmesan cheese, grated (2 cups), divided
- 8 ounces whole-milk mozzarella cheese, shredded (2 cups)
- 2 large eggs, lightly beaten
- 2 tablespoons chopped fresh parsley
- 2 tablespoons chopped fresh basil
- ¾ teaspoon table salt
- ½ teaspoon pepper
- 16 no-boil lasagna noodles

1. For the sauce: Adjust oven rack to middle position and heat oven to 375 degrees. Pulse 1 can tomatoes with their juice in food processor until coarsely chopped, 3 to 4 pulses. Transfer to bowl. Repeat with remaining can of tomatoes.

2. Heat oil; garlic; and pepper flakes, if using, in large saucepan over medium heat until fragrant but not brown, 1 to 2 minutes. Stir in tomatoes and salt and simmer until slightly thickened, about 15 minutes. Stir in basil; season with salt to taste.

Filling Baked Manicotti

1. Using spoon, spread about ¼ cup of filling evenly over bottom three-quarters of each noodle, leaving top quarter of noodles exposed.

2. Starting at bottom, roll each noodle up around filling, and lay in prepared baking dish, seam side down.

Baked Manicotti

Serves 6 to 8 • Total Time: 2 hours

Why This Recipe Works Manicotti is composed of a straightforward collection of ingredients (pasta, cheese, and tomato sauce), but it can be surprisingly fussy to prepare. Blanching, shocking, draining, and stuffing slippery pasta requires patience and time. We wanted an easy-to-prepare recipe that produced great-tasting manicotti. Our biggest challenge was filling the slippery manicotti tubes. We solved the problem by discarding the tubes and spreading the filling onto a pliable lasagna noodle, which we then rolled up. No-boil lasagna noodles were ideal for this method. We used part-skim ricotta as the base of our filling; eggs, Parmesan, and mozzarella cheese added richness, flavor, and structure to the ricotta filling. For a quick and bright sauce, we pureed canned diced tomatoes and simmered them with sautéed garlic and red pepper flakes; then we finished the sauce with fresh basil.

We prefer Barilla no-boil lasagna noodles for their delicate texture resembling fresh pasta. Note that Pasta Defino and Ronzoni brands contain only 12 no-boil noodles per package; the recipe requires 16 noodles. The manicotti can be prepared through step 5, covered with a sheet of parchment paper, wrapped in aluminum foil, and refrigerated for up to three days or frozen for up to one month. (If frozen, thaw the manicotti in the refrigerator for one to two days.) To bake, remove the parchment, replace the aluminum foil, and increase the baking time to 1 to 1¼ hours.

3. For the cheese filling and pasta: Combine ricotta, 1 cup Parmesan, mozzarella, eggs, parsley, basil, salt, and pepper in medium bowl; set aside.

4. Pour 2 inches boiling water into 13 by 9-inch broiler-safe baking dish. Slip noodles into water, one at a time, and let them soak until pliable, about 5 minutes, separating them with tip of knife to prevent sticking. Remove noodles from water and place in single layer on clean dish towels. Discard water and dry baking dish.

5. Spread bottom of baking dish evenly with 1½ cups sauce. Using spoon, spread ¼ cup cheese mixture evenly onto bottom three-quarters of each noodle (with short side facing you), leaving top quarter of noodle exposed. Roll into tube shape and arrange in baking dish, seam side down. Top evenly with remaining sauce, making certain that pasta is completely covered.

6. Cover baking dish tightly with aluminum foil and bake until bubbling, about 40 minutes. Remove baking dish from oven and remove foil. Adjust oven rack 6 inches from broiler element and heat broiler. Sprinkle manicotti evenly with remaining 1 cup Parmesan. Broil until cheese is spotty brown, 4 to 6 minutes. Cool for 15 minutes; cut into pieces and serve.

SEASON 10
Baked Ziti

Serves 8 to 10 • Total Time: 2 hours, plus 20 minutes cooling

Why This Recipe Works Our ideal baked ziti has al dente pasta, a rich and flavorful sauce, and melted cheese in every bite. For a sauce with big flavor and light prep, we cooked sautéed garlic with canned diced tomatoes and tomato sauce. Fresh basil and dried oregano added aromatic flavor. Just when the tomato sauce seemed perfect, we added ricotta, and a familiar problem reared its head: Rather than baking up creamy and rich, the ricotta was grainy and dulled the sauce. Cottage cheese was the best choice for a replacement—its curds have a texture similar to ricotta, but are creamier and tangier. For more flavor, we combined the cottage cheese with eggs, Parmesan, and heavy cream thickened with cornstarch. Adding this milky mixture to the tomato sauce made the sauce bright, rich, and creamy. When it came to the pasta, we undercooked it and then baked it with a generous amount of sauce for perfectly al dente pasta and plenty of sauce left to keep our baked ziti moist. As for the mozzarella, we cubed instead of shredding it, which dotted the finished casserole with gooey bits of cheese.

We prefer baked ziti made with heavy cream, but whole milk can be substituted by increasing the amount of cornstarch to 2 teaspoons and increasing the cooking time in step 3 by 1 to 2 minutes. Our preferred brand of mozzarella is Polly-O. Part-skim mozzarella can also be used.

1 pound (2 cups) whole-milk or 1 percent cottage cheese
2 large eggs, lightly beaten
3 ounces Parmesan cheese, grated (1½ cups), divided
1 pound ziti or other short tubular pasta
  Table salt for cooking pasta
2 tablespoons extra-virgin olive oil
5 garlic cloves, minced
1 (28-ounce) can tomato sauce
1 (14.5-ounce) can diced tomatoes
1 teaspoon dried oregano
½ cup plus 2 tablespoons chopped fresh basil, divided
1 teaspoon sugar
1 cup heavy cream
¾ teaspoon cornstarch
8 ounces whole-milk mozzarella cheese, cut into ¼-inch pieces (1½ cups), divided

1. Adjust oven rack to middle position and heat oven to 350 degrees. Whisk cottage cheese, eggs, and 1 cup Parmesan together in medium bowl; set aside. Bring 4 quarts water to boil in large pot. Add pasta and 1 tablespoon salt and cook, stirring occasionally, until pasta begins to soften but is not yet cooked through, 5 to 7 minutes. Drain pasta and leave in colander (do not wash pot).

2. Meanwhile, heat oil and garlic in 12-inch skillet over medium heat until garlic is fragrant but not brown, about 2 minutes. Stir in tomato sauce, diced tomatoes, and oregano; simmer until thickened, about 10 minutes. Off heat, stir in ½ cup basil and sugar; season with salt and pepper to taste.

3. Stir cream and cornstarch together in small bowl; transfer mixture to now-empty pasta pot set over medium heat. Bring to simmer and cook until thickened, 3 to 4 minutes. Remove pot from heat and add cottage cheese mixture, 1 cup tomato sauce, and ¾ cup mozzarella; stir to combine. Add pasta and stir to coat thoroughly with sauce.

4. Transfer pasta to 13 by 9-inch baking dish and spread remaining tomato sauce evenly over pasta. Sprinkle remaining ¾ cup mozzarella and remaining ½ cup Parmesan over top. Cover baking dish tightly with aluminum foil and bake for 30 minutes.

5. Remove foil and continue to cook until cheese is bubbling and beginning to brown, about 30 minutes longer. Let cool for 20 minutes. Sprinkle with remaining 2 tablespoons basil and serve.

It Is Possible to Improve on Nana's Recipe

"To be clear, no one in my life has ever cooked like Katherine Pizzarello. Not Dan. Not Julia. Not Lan. My nana made the best Italian food. Full stop.

So why am I writing about improving on Nana's recipe? Well, sometimes heritage recipes don't age well. When I make Nana's baked ziti, it's not as good as I remember. Part of the problem is that I'm scaling down her recipe and baking it in a standard 13-by-9 casserole dish. But this test kitchen recipe illuminated the other problem. During my childhood, I'm pretty sure Nana was using better ricotta than what I can easily buy 50-plus years later. Nana's ricotta was fresher, creamier, and richer than today's supermarket offerings. Her ricotta was good enough to eat on a spoon, perhaps sprinkled with a little powdered sugar. While you can still find artisan-quality ricotta at cheese shops, most supermarket ricotta will bake up grainy and dry in ziti recipes like this. To avoid this, the test kitchen found that pillowy whole-milk cottage cheese was a better base. The large curds don't dry out and turn grainy. Enriching the bland cottage cheese with lots of Parm makes it taste good. And a generous pour of heavy cream provides richness.

My kids have come to love this recipe so much that I made it for Christmas last year. Who needs a fancy roast when you can celebrate with a perfectly cooked pasta casserole? I know Nana would agree."

—Jack

1 (28-ounce) can diced tomatoes
  Water
1 tablespoon extra-virgin olive oil
1 onion, chopped fine
½ teaspoon table salt
3 garlic cloves, minced
⅛ teaspoon red pepper flakes
1 pound meatloaf mix
10 curly-edged lasagna noodles, broken into
  2-inch lengths
1 (8-ounce) can tomato sauce
1 ounce Parmesan cheese, grated (½ cup),
  divided, plus extra for serving
8 ounces (1 cup) ricotta cheese
3 tablespoons chopped fresh basil

1. Pour tomatoes and their juice into 4-cup liquid measuring cup. Add water until mixture measures 4 cups.

2. Heat oil in 12-inch nonstick skillet over medium heat until shimmering. Add onion and salt and cook until onion begins to brown, 6 to 8 minutes. Stir in garlic and pepper flakes and cook until fragrant, about 30 seconds. Add meatloaf mix and cook, breaking apart meat, until no longer pink, about 4 minutes.

3. Scatter noodles over meat but do not stir. Pour diced tomato mixture and tomato sauce over noodles. Cover and bring to simmer. Reduce heat to medium-low and simmer, stirring occasionally, until noodles are tender, about 20 minutes.

4. Remove skillet from heat and stir in all but 2 tablespoons Parmesan. Season with salt and pepper to taste. Dot with heaping tablespoons of ricotta, cover, and let stand off heat for 5 minutes. Sprinkle with basil and remaining 2 tablespoons Parmesan. Serve.

Skillet Lasagna

Serves 4 to 6 • Total Time: 55 minutes

Why This Recipe Works Lasagna isn't usually a dish you can throw together at the last minute. Even with no-boil noodles, it takes a good amount of time to get the components just right. Our goal was to transform traditional baked lasagna into a stovetop skillet dish without losing any of its flavor or appeal. We built a hearty, flavorful meat sauce with onions, garlic, red pepper flakes, and meatloaf mix (a more flavorful alternative to plain ground beef). Canned diced tomatoes along with tomato sauce provided juicy tomato flavor and a nicely chunky texture. We scattered regular curly-edged lasagna noodles, broken into pieces, over the top of the sauce (smaller pieces are easier to eat). We then diluted the sauce with a little water so that the noodles would cook through. After a 20-minute simmer with the lid on, the pasta was tender, the sauce was properly thickened, and it was time for the cheese. Stirring Parmesan into the dish worked well, but we discovered that the sweet creaminess of ricotta was lost unless we placed it in heaping tablespoonfuls on top of the lasagna. Letting the cheese warm through for several minutes was the final step for this supereasy one-pan dish.

Meatloaf mix is a combination of ground beef, pork, and veal, sold prepackaged in many supermarkets. If it's unavailable, use ground beef. A skillet with a tight-fitting lid works best for this recipe. To make this dish a bit richer, sprinkle the lasagna with additional shredded cheese, such as mozzarella or provolone, along with the Parmesan in step 4.

Spinach Lasagna

Serves 8 to 10 • Total Time: 2 hours

Why This Recipe Works Traditional spinach lasagna combines layers of homemade pasta, fresh spinach, béchamel (white sauce), and cheese. For an easier spinach lasagna, we ditched the mozzarella, added cottage cheese, and used no-boil noodles. As for the fresh spinach, the mature curly variety easily stood up to the heat of the oven. Blanching and shocking the spinach allowed it to keep its verdant color and pure flavor. To infuse our luxurious white

sauce with flavor, we sautéed a cup of minced shallots and plenty of garlic in butter before whisking in the flour for the roux. Cottage cheese provided pleasing tang and extra creaminess, while nutty fontina replaced bland mozzarella. The real key to our recipe's success was that we parcooked the no-boil noodles by soaking them in boiling water. This cut the baking time down to 20 minutes, which helped the spinach maintain its vibrancy.

Italian fontina cheese works best in this dish. If it is not available, substitute whole-milk mozzarella. If your baking dish is not broiler-safe, brown the lasagna at 500 degrees for about 10 minutes.

Sauce

- 1¼ pounds curly-leaf spinach, stemmed
- ½ teaspoon table salt, plus salt for cooking vegetables
- 5 tablespoons unsalted butter
- 6 shallots, minced
- 4 garlic cloves, minced
- ¼ cup all-purpose flour
- 3½ cups whole milk
- 2 bay leaves
- ¾ teaspoon ground nutmeg
- ¼ teaspoon pepper
- 3 ounces Parmesan cheese, grated (1½ cups), divided

Cheese Filling and Pasta

- 8 ounces (1 cup) whole-milk cottage cheese
- 1 large egg
- ¼ teaspoon table salt
- 12 no-boil lasagna noodles
- 8 ounces Italian fontina cheese, shredded (2 cups)

1. For the sauce: Bring 4 quarts water to boil in large pot. Fill large bowl halfway with ice and water. Add spinach and 1 tablespoon salt to boiling water and cook, stirring often, until spinach is just wilted, about 5 seconds. Using slotted spoon, transfer spinach to ice bath and soak until completely cool, about 1 minute; drain spinach and transfer to clean dish towel. Wrap towel tightly around spinach to form ball and wring until dry. Chop spinach and set aside.

2. Melt butter in medium saucepan over medium heat. Add shallots and garlic and cook, stirring frequently, until shallots are softened, about 4 minutes. Add flour and cook, stirring constantly, until thoroughly combined, about 1½ minutes; mixture should not brown. Gradually whisk in milk; increase heat to medium-high and bring to boil, whisking often. Stir in bay leaves, nutmeg, pepper, and salt; reduce heat to low; and simmer, whisking occasionally, for 10 minutes. Discard bay leaves, then whisk in ½ cup Parmesan until completely melted. Reserve ½ cup sauce in small bowl; press plastic wrap directly against surface and set aside. Transfer remaining sauce to second bowl and stir in spinach, mixing well to break up any clumps; press plastic directly against surface and set aside.

3. For the cheese filling: Process cottage cheese, egg, and salt in food processor until very smooth, about 30 seconds.

4. For the pasta: Adjust oven rack to middle position and heat oven to 425 degrees. Pour 2 inches boiling water into 13 by 9-inch broiler-safe baking dish. Slip noodles into water, one at a time, and soak until pliable, about 5 minutes, separating noodles with tip of paring knife to prevent sticking. Remove noodles from water and place in single layer on clean dish towels; discard water. Dry and grease dish.

5. Spread reserved sauce evenly over bottom of prepared dish. Arrange 3 noodles in single layer on top of sauce. Spread 1 cup spinach mixture evenly over noodles, sprinkle remaining 1 cup Parmesan over spinach mixture, and top cheese with 3 noodles. Spread 1 cup spinach mixture evenly over noodles, sprinkle 1 cup fontina over spinach mixture, and top with 3 noodles. Spread 1 cup spinach mixture evenly over noodles, followed by cheese filling. For final layer, arrange remaining 3 noodles over cheese filling, then cover noodles with remaining spinach mixture. Sprinkle remaining 1 cup fontina over spinach mixture.

6. Cover dish tightly with aluminum foil that has been sprayed with vegetable oil spray and bake until edges are just bubbling, about 20 minutes, rotating dish halfway through baking. Remove dish from oven and remove foil. Adjust oven rack 6 inches from broiler element and heat broiler. Broil lasagna until cheese on top becomes spotty brown, 4 to 6 minutes. Let lasagna cool for 15 minutes before serving.

adding ½ cup to the ziti in step 4, ½ cup to the béchamel, and the remaining ½ cup to the top of the béchamel. We strongly recommend using a spider skimmer to transfer the pasta to the baking dish, but a slotted spoon will work. To accommodate all the components, use a baking dish that is at least 2¼ inches tall.

Meat Sauce
- ¾ teaspoon table salt
- ¼ teaspoon baking soda
- 1 tablespoon plus ½ cup water, divided
- 8 ounces 93 percent lean ground beef
- 1 tablespoon vegetable oil
- ½ cup finely chopped onion
- 3 garlic cloves, minced
- 1¼ teaspoons ground cinnamon
- 1 teaspoon dried oregano
- 1 teaspoon dried mint
- 1 teaspoon paprika
- ⅛ teaspoon red pepper flakes
- ⅛ teaspoon pepper
- ¼ cup red wine
- ⅓ cup tomato paste

Béchamel and Pasta
- 2 tablespoons unsalted butter
- 2 tablespoons all-purpose flour
- 1 garlic clove, minced
- ½ teaspoon table salt
- ¼ teaspoon grated nutmeg
- ⅛ teaspoon pepper
- 4 cups whole milk
- 8 ounces (2½ cups) ziti
- 4 ounces kasseri cheese, shredded (1 cup), divided
- 1 large egg, lightly beaten

1. **For the meat sauce:** Mix salt, baking soda, and 1 tablespoon water in bowl. Add beef and toss until thoroughly combined. Set aside.

2. Heat oil in medium saucepan over medium heat until shimmering. Add onion and cook, stirring frequently, until softened, about 3 minutes. Stir in garlic, cinnamon, oregano, mint, paprika, pepper flakes, and pepper and cook until fragrant, 1 to 2 minutes. Add wine and cook, stirring occasionally, until mixture is thickened, 2 to 3 minutes. Add tomato paste, beef mixture, and remaining ½ cup water and cook, breaking up meat into pieces no larger than ¼ inch with wooden spoon, until beef has just lost its pink color, 3 to 5 minutes. Bring to simmer; cover; reduce heat to low; and simmer for 30 minutes, stirring occasionally. Off heat, season with salt to taste. (Meat sauce can be refrigerated in airtight container for up to 3 days. Heat through before proceeding with step 3.)

Pastitsio

Serves 6 • **Total Time: 2½ hours, plus 20 minutes cooling**

Why This Recipe Works In the best renditions of this Greek meat and macaroni casserole, the components—tubular pasta, ground meat and tomato sauce, and a plush blanket of béchamel—are impressively stratified. We started by treating ground beef with baking soda before cooking, which altered its chemistry and made it better able to hold on to moisture. We skipped the usual browning step to avoid toughening the meat's exterior, which also saved time. Cinnamon, oregano, dried mint, and paprika made the flavor profile distinctly Greek. A minimal amount of red wine plus lots of tomato paste added brightness and savoriness. We further streamlined the method by parcooking the ziti (the closest substitute for authentic Greek "number 2" macaroni) in the hot béchamel; doing so hydrated the pasta just enough to ensure that it would be fully cooked after baking, and the pasta's starches helped thicken the béchamel. We then thickened the rest of the béchamel by whisking in cheese and an egg until it was spreadable. Sprinkling more cheese over the top encouraged the surface to brown.

Don't use ground beef that's less than 93 percent lean or the dish will be greasy. We like the richness of whole milk for this dish, but you can substitute 2 percent low-fat milk, if desired. Do not use skim milk. Kasseri is a semifirm sheep's-milk cheese from Greece. If it's unavailable, substitute a mixture of 1½ ounces (¾ cup) grated Pecorino Romano and 3 ounces (¾ cup) shredded provolone,

3. For the béchamel and pasta: Adjust oven rack to middle position and heat oven to 375 degrees. Spray 8-inch square baking dish with vegetable oil spray and place on rimmed baking sheet. Melt butter in large saucepan over medium heat. Add flour, garlic, salt, nutmeg, and pepper and cook, stirring constantly, until golden and fragrant, about 1 minute. Slowly whisk in milk and bring to boil. Add pasta and return to simmer, stirring frequently to prevent sticking. When mixture reaches simmer, cover and let stand off heat, stirring occasionally, for 15 minutes (pasta will not be fully cooked).

4. Using spider skimmer, transfer pasta to prepared dish, leaving excess béchamel in saucepan. Sprinkle ⅓ cup kasseri over pasta and stir to combine. Using spatula, gently press pasta into even layer. Add ⅓ cup kasseri to béchamel and whisk to combine. Whisk egg into béchamel. Spread meat sauce over pasta and, using spatula, spread into even layer. Top with béchamel. Sprinkle remaining kasseri over béchamel. Bake until top of pastitsio is puffed and spotty brown, 40 to 50 minutes. Let cool for 20 minutes. Serve.

Stovetop Macaroni and Cheese

Serves 4 • Total Time: 20 minutes

Why This Recipe Works Everyone loves macaroni and cheese with its smooth and creamy sauce. We wanted a quick stovetop version with an ultracreamy texture and authentic cheese flavor—so good that it would satisfy everyone at the table. We based our sauce on American cheese which has plenty of emulsifier to keep it smooth but not a lot of flavor. So we combined it with more-flavorful extra-sharp cheddar. A bit of mustard and cayenne pepper added piquancy. We cooked the macaroni in a smaller-than-usual amount of water (along with some milk), so we didn't have to drain it; the liquid that was left after the elbows were hydrated was just enough to form the base of the sauce. Rather than bake the mac and cheese, we sprinkled crunchy, cheesy toasted panko bread crumbs on top—the final touch to this easy-to-prepare family favorite.

> *Because the macaroni is cooked in a measured amount of liquid, we don't recommend using different shapes or sizes of pasta. Use a 4-ounce block of American cheese from the deli counter rather than presliced cheese.*

1½ cups water
 1 cup milk
 8 ounces elbow macaroni
 4 ounces American cheese, shredded (1 cup)
 ½ teaspoon Dijon mustard
    Small pinch cayenne pepper
 4 ounces extra-sharp cheddar cheese, shredded (1 cup)
 ⅓ cup panko bread crumbs
 1 tablespoon extra-virgin olive oil
 ⅛ teaspoon table salt
 ⅛ teaspoon pepper
 2 tablespoons grated Parmesan cheese

1. Bring water and milk to boil in medium saucepan over high heat. Stir in macaroni and reduce heat to medium-low. Cook, stirring frequently, until macaroni is soft (slightly past al dente), 6 to 8 minutes. Add American cheese, mustard, and cayenne and cook, stirring constantly, until cheese is completely melted, about 1 minute. Off heat, stir in cheddar until evenly distributed but not melted. Cover saucepan and let stand for 5 minutes.

2. Meanwhile, combine panko, oil, salt, and pepper in 8-inch nonstick skillet until panko is evenly moistened. Cook over medium heat, stirring frequently, until evenly browned, 3 to 4 minutes. Off heat, sprinkle Parmesan over panko mixture and stir to combine. Transfer panko mixture to small bowl.

3. Stir macaroni until sauce is smooth (sauce may look loose but will thicken as it cools). Season with salt and pepper to taste. Transfer to warm serving dish and sprinkle panko mixture over top. Serve immediately.

Pasta alla Zozzona

Pasta alla Zozzona

Serves 4 • **Total Time: 1 hour**

Why This Recipe Works Pasta alla zozzona is a fusion of two Roman classics, amatriciana and carbonara, with pork sausage and onions added in to send the pasta over the top. "Zozzona," a Roman dialect word for "dirty," references the dish's rich flavor and the unusual mash-up of ingredients. To create a meaty, creamy, and decadent pasta that reflects the true tradition of pasta alla zozzona, we used equal parts guanciale and Italian sausage to double down on pork flavor and to create significant amounts of pork fat that emulsified into the passata and created a creamy, not greasy, sauce. Egg yolks and Pecorino Romano imparted further creaminess to the sauce.

> Because this pasta is quite rich, serve it in slightly smaller portions with a green vegetable or salad. Guanciale (cured pork jowl) adds savory depth and richness to this dish. If guanciale is unavailable, use the highest-quality pancetta you can find; be sure to buy a 5-ounce chunk and not presliced or prediced. Do not use bacon; its smoky flavor will overpower the dish. Passata is an uncooked tomato puree usually found near the other tomato products in the grocery store; if you're buying the Pomì brand it may be labeled "strained tomatoes." If you cannot find passata, you can use tomato puree instead.

- 5 ounces guanciale
- 1 tablespoon extra-virgin olive oil
- 5 ounces sweet Italian sausage, casings removed, broken into 1-inch pieces
- ½ cup finely chopped onion
- ¾ cup passata
- 8 ounces rigatoni
  Table salt for cooking pasta
- 1 ounce Pecorino Romano cheese, grated fine (½ cup), plus extra for serving
- 2 large egg yolks
- ¼ teaspoon pepper

1. Slice guanciale into ¼-inch-thick strips, then cut each strip crosswise into ¼-inch pieces. Heat guanciale and oil in 10-inch nonstick skillet over medium heat, stirring frequently, until fat is rendered and guanciale is starting to brown, 4 to 6 minutes.

2. Add sausage and onion and cook, using wooden spoon to break meat into pieces no larger than ½ inch, until sausage is no longer pink, 8 to 10 minutes. Stir in passata; reduce heat to medium-low; and simmer, covered, stirring occasionally, until fat is fully incorporated, 2 to 4 minutes.

GAME CHANGER

Simple Indulgence with Pork Fat

"We all have those days when we want to indulge, and pasta alla zozzona doesn't disappoint. Zozzona pushes the limits of traditional Roman pasta dishes, combining the flavors of amatriciana and carbonara, and adding sausage and onions for a pasta upgrade. Perfectly al dente rigatoni cradles pockets of meat and creamy tomato sauce that gush with flavor. Saturated with porky goodness, our zozzona contains equal parts guanciale and Italian sausage (greater in weight than the actual pasta itself) that envelop each silky bite. There's truly something magical about cooking this recipe and watching how the sauce transforms in a matter of seconds into a silky, glossy blend. It's a fun one to quickly whip up for friends and family. I like to serve it with a fresh green salad and a brisk, postmeal walk, to balance the indulgence. Fun fact: Developing this recipe literally inspired my trip to Rome, Italy, a couple of months later for my birthday. Every time I make this recipe it takes me back to the fun I had developing it and then eating my way through the city and Roman countryside."

— *Erica*

3. Meanwhile, bring 2 quarts water to boil in large pot. Add pasta and 1 teaspoon salt and cook, stirring often, until al dente. Reserve 1 cup cooking water, then drain pasta and return it to pot. Add tomato-meat sauce to pasta. Set pot over medium-low heat and stir until pasta is well coated, about 1 minute.

4. Whisk Pecorino, egg yolks, and pepper in medium bowl until combined. Slowly whisk ½ cup of reserved cooking water into egg yolk mixture (mixture will not be smooth). Off heat, stir egg yolk mixture into pasta until sauce looks glossy and is slightly thickened, about 1 minute. Adjust sauce consistency with remaining reserved cooking water as needed. Transfer pasta to platter and serve immediately, passing extra Pecorino separately.

Pappardelle with Duck and Chestnut Ragu

Serves 4 • **Total Time: 3 hours**

Why This Recipe Works We found inspiration in the Veneto area of Italy for our robust ragu that pairs duck with sweet, creamy chestnuts. Slowly browning duck legs produced plenty of flavorful fat for cooking aromatics. Assertive rosemary and acidic red wine cut through the duck's richness to make a flavorful, lustrous sauce that clung beautifully to wide noodles such as pappardelle. Chestnuts not only thickened the sauce but also appeared in the crispy bread crumb topping.

You can find fresh chestnuts seasonally in markets, but they must be roasted before use and are difficult to peel. We prefer to purchase the roasted peeled chestnuts that are sold jarred or vacuum-packed in many supermarkets near other nuts. Don't substitute water chestnuts, which belong to an entirely different plant family.

2 cups (9 ounces) peeled cooked chestnuts, divided
1 large onion, chopped coarse
1 carrot, peeled and chopped coarse
1 celery rib, chopped coarse
2 (12- to 14-ounce) duck leg quarters, trimmed
1 teaspoon table salt, plus salt for cooking pasta
1½ teaspoons minced fresh rosemary, divided
1 cup dry red wine
2½ cups chicken broth
¼ cup panko bread crumbs
1 teaspoon red wine vinegar
1 pound fresh pappardelle (recipe follows)

1. Adjust oven rack to middle position and heat oven to 300 degrees. Pulse chestnuts in food processor until finely chopped, 10 to 12 pulses, scraping down sides of bowl as needed; transfer to bowl. Pulse onion, carrot, and celery in now-empty processor until finely chopped, 10 to 12 pulses; set aside.

2. Using metal skewer, poke 15 to 20 holes in skin of each duck leg quarter, then pat dry with paper towels. Place duck skin side down in Dutch oven and cook over medium heat until well browned on first side and fat has rendered, 15 to 20 minutes. Flip duck and continue to cook until well browned on second side, about 3 minutes; transfer to plate. Pour off and reserve all but 2 tablespoons fat from pot.

3. Add vegetable mixture and salt to fat left in pot and cook over medium heat until vegetables are softened, 5 to 7 minutes. Stir in 1 teaspoon rosemary and cook until fragrant, about 30 seconds. Stir in wine, scraping up any browned bits, and cook until reduced slightly, about 1 minute.

4. Stir in broth and half of chestnuts. Nestle duck into pot with any accumulated juices and bring to simmer. Cover, transfer pot to oven, and cook until duck is very tender and falling off bones, about 2 hours.

5. While duck cooks, heat 1 tablespoon reserved fat in 10-inch skillet over medium heat until shimmering (discard remaining fat or reserve for another use). Add panko and cook, stirring frequently, until light golden brown, 2 to 3 minutes. Stir in remaining chestnuts and remaining ½ teaspoon rosemary and cook until fragrant and deep golden brown, about 2 minutes; set aside.

6. Remove pot from oven. Transfer duck to cutting board, let cool slightly, then shred meat into bite-size pieces using 2 forks; discard skin and bones. Bring sauce to simmer over medium-high heat and cook until thickened slightly, 3 to 5 minutes. Stir in shredded meat and vinegar and season with salt and pepper to taste.

7. Meanwhile, bring 4 quarts water to boil in large pot. Add pasta and 1 tablespoon salt and cook, stirring often, until al dente. Reserve ½ cup cooking water, then drain pasta and return it to pot. Add sauce and toss to combine. Adjust consistency with reserved cooking water as needed. Season with salt and pepper to taste. Sprinkle individual portions with chestnut-panko mixture before serving.

Fresh Pappardelle

Makes 1 pound • Total Time: 1½ hours, plus 30 minutes resting

Use this tender, easy-to-roll dough for strand pasta. Six egg yolks, in addition to two whole eggs and a couple tablespoons of olive oil, make the dough incredibly supple while also adding great flavor. The addition of olive oil is a debated topic in Italy, but we find that it makes the dough easier to roll while still keeping it springy and delicate. You can roll this dough with a manual pasta machine or by hand. Resting the dough for at least 30 minutes before rolling allows the gluten—the protein network that forms when flour and liquid interact and that makes doughs chewy—time to relax and minimizes contraction. If using a high-protein all-purpose flour, such as King Arthur, increase the number of egg yolks to seven.

- 2 cups (10 ounces) all-purpose flour, plus extra as needed
- 2 large eggs plus 6 large yolks
- 2 tablespoons extra-virgin olive oil

1A. For mixing and kneading with a machine: Process flour, eggs and yolks, and oil in food processor until mixture forms cohesive dough that feels soft and is barely tacky to touch, about 45 seconds. (If dough sticks to your fingers, add up to ¼ cup flour, 1 tablespoon at a time, until barely tacky. If dough doesn't become cohesive, add up to 1 tablespoon water, 1 teaspoon at a time, until it just comes together; process 30 seconds longer.)

1B. For mixing and kneading by hand: Place flour in large bowl. Using fork, mix eggs, egg yolks, and oil together in separate bowl, then stir into flour. Using your hands, knead dough in bowl until mixture forms cohesive dough that feels soft and is barely tacky to touch, about 3 minutes. (If dough sticks to your fingers after 3 minutes, add up to ¼ cup flour, 1 tablespoon at a time, until barely tacky. If dough doesn't become cohesive, add up to 1 tablespoon water, 1 teaspoon at a time, until it just comes together; knead 1 minute longer.)

2. Transfer dough to clean surface and knead by hand to form smooth, uniform ball, 1 to 2 minutes. Shape dough into 6-inch-long cylinder. Wrap with plastic wrap and set aside at room temperature to rest for at least 30 minutes or up to 4 hours.

3. Transfer dough to clean counter, divide into 3 pieces, and cover with plastic wrap. Flatten 1 piece of dough into ½-inch-thick disk. Using pasta machine with rollers set to widest position, feed dough through rollers twice. Bring tapered ends of dough toward middle and press to seal. Feed dough seam side first through rollers again. Repeat feeding dough tapered ends first through rollers set at widest position, without folding, until dough is smooth and barely tacky.

4. Narrow rollers to next setting and feed dough through rollers twice. Continue to progressively narrow rollers, feeding dough through each setting twice, until dough is thin and semitransparent. Transfer sheet of pasta to liberally floured sheet of parchment paper. Cover with second sheet of parchment, followed by damp dish towel to keep pasta from drying out. Repeat rolling with remaining 2 pieces of dough, stacking pasta sheets between floured layers of parchment.

5. Cut 1 air-dried pasta sheet in half crosswise. Starting with short end, gently fold each half-sheet at 2-inch intervals to create flat, rectangular roll.

6. Using sharp knife, slice pasta rolls crosswise into 1-inch-wide sections. Use your fingers to unfurl pasta strands, then liberally dust strands with flour and transfer them to lightly floured rimmed baking sheet. Repeat with remaining pasta sheets.

Cutting Pappardelle by Hand

1. Cut 1 air-dried pasta sheet in half crosswise. Starting with short end, gently fold each half-sheet at 2-inch intervals to create flat, rectangular roll.

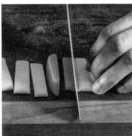

2. Using sharp knife, slice pasta rolls crosswise 1 inch wide. Use your fingers to unfurl pasta, then liberally dust strands with flour and transfer them to lightly floured rimmed baking sheet. Repeat with remaining pasta sheets.

Japchae

Serves 4 • Total Time: 1½ hours

Why This Recipe Works Japchae, one of Korea's most popular noodle dishes, is a celebration of colorful vegetables, each of which is cut thin and then lightly sautéed and seasoned separately to preserve its texture and bright color. Briefly blanching and squeezing the spinach and shiitakes before sautéing helped them shed some of their abundant water and collapsed the mushrooms so that they didn't pick up too much oil. Japchae also often includes a bit of beef or pork; thinly slicing, marinating, and sautéing well-marbled boneless short ribs added bites of savory, meaty richness. Dangmyeon, Korea's beloved sweet potato starch noodles, soaked up all the salty-sweet dressing while still retaining their unique springy chew.

Dangmyeon, Korean sweet potato starch noodles, are sometimes labeled as japchae noodles or sweet potato starch vermicelli. Do not substitute other noodles or use frozen spinach instead of fresh. Halve lengthwise any scallions wider than ½ inch. To streamline assembly, cut, cover, and refrigerate the vegetables in advance. Serve this dish warm or at room temperature.

- 8 ounces boneless beef short ribs, trimmed
- 2 teaspoons plus ¼ cup soy sauce, divided
- 2 tablespoons plus ¼ teaspoon sugar, divided
- 2¼ teaspoons minced garlic, divided
- 1 teaspoon pepper, divided
- 4¼ teaspoons toasted sesame oil, divided
- 1¾ teaspoons kosher salt, divided
- 1 (10-ounce) bag curly-leaf spinach
- 6 ounces shiitake mushrooms, stemmed and sliced ¼ inch thick
- 8 ounces dangmyeon
- 1¾ teaspoons vegetable oil, divided
- 1 small onion, halved and sliced thin
- 3 scallions, cut into 2-inch pieces
- 2 carrots, peeled and cut into 2- to 2½-inch-long matchsticks (1 cup)
- 1 small red bell pepper, stemmed, seeded, and cut into ⅛-inch-wide strips
- 2 tablespoons sesame seeds, toasted, divided

1. Bring 2 quarts water to boil in large pot. Slice beef crosswise ¼ inch thick. Cut slices into ¼-inch-thick strips. Toss beef, 2 teaspoons soy sauce, 2 teaspoons sugar, 2 teaspoons garlic, and ½ teaspoon pepper in bowl until well combined. Add 2 tablespoons soy sauce, 2 teaspoons sugar, 2 teaspoons sesame oil, ½ teaspoon salt, and remaining ½ teaspoon pepper to large bowl.

2. Add spinach to boiling water and cook until leaves are just wilted, 5 to 10 seconds. Using spider skimmer or slotted spoon, transfer spinach to colander. Rinse under cold running water until leaves are cool enough to handle, about 30 seconds. Squeeze spinach dry and transfer to cutting board. Return water to boil. Add mushrooms and cook until tender and pliant, about 30 seconds. Using spider skimmer or slotted spoon, transfer mushrooms to colander. Rinse under cold running water until mushrooms are cool, about 1 minute. Squeeze dry and transfer to cutting board.

3. Return water to boil. Add dangmyeon and cook, stirring occasionally, until noodles are cooked through but still very chewy, 5 to 8 minutes. Drain noodles in colander and shake to remove excess water. Lift about one-quarter of noodles with tongs and use kitchen shears to cut noodles 8 inches below tongs. Repeat 3 more times with remaining noodles. Transfer noodles to large bowl with soy sauce mixture and toss until noodles are evenly coated. Add spinach to small bowl and use your clean hands to break up into small clumps. Add ¼ teaspoon sesame oil, ¼ teaspoon salt, and remaining ¼ teaspoon garlic and toss with spinach until well combined. Transfer spinach to bowl with noodles.

4. Heat ¼ teaspoon vegetable oil, ¼ teaspoon salt, and mushrooms in 10-inch nonstick skillet over medium heat. Cook, stirring frequently, until warmed through but not browned, about 1 minute. Transfer to bowl with noodles. Add onion, scallions, ¼ teaspoon salt, and ½ teaspoon vegetable oil to now-empty skillet and cook, stirring often, until vegetables have lost their raw bite and are crisp but not browned, 3 to 4 minutes. Transfer to bowl with noodles.

5. Add carrots, ⅛ teaspoon salt, and ¼ teaspoon vegetable oil to now-empty skillet and cook, stirring constantly, until carrots have lost their raw bite and are crisp but not browned, about 3 minutes. Transfer to bowl with noodles. Add bell pepper, ⅛ teaspoon salt, and ¼ teaspoon vegetable oil to now-empty skillet and cook, stirring constantly, until bell pepper has lost its raw bite and is crisp but not browned, about 1 minute. Transfer to bowl with noodles.

6. Increase heat to medium-high and add remaining ½ teaspoon vegetable oil to now-empty skillet. When oil shimmers, add beef and cook, stirring frequently, until cooked through, 3 to 4 minutes. Transfer to bowl with noodles. Let beef rest for 5 minutes. Add 1½ tablespoons sesame seeds, remaining 2 tablespoons soy sauce, remaining 2¼ teaspoons sugar, remaining 2 teaspoons sesame oil, and remaining ¼ teaspoon salt to bowl with noodles. Using your clean hands, toss everything to combine. Mound on serving platter, sprinkle with remaining 1½ teaspoons sesame seeds, and serve.

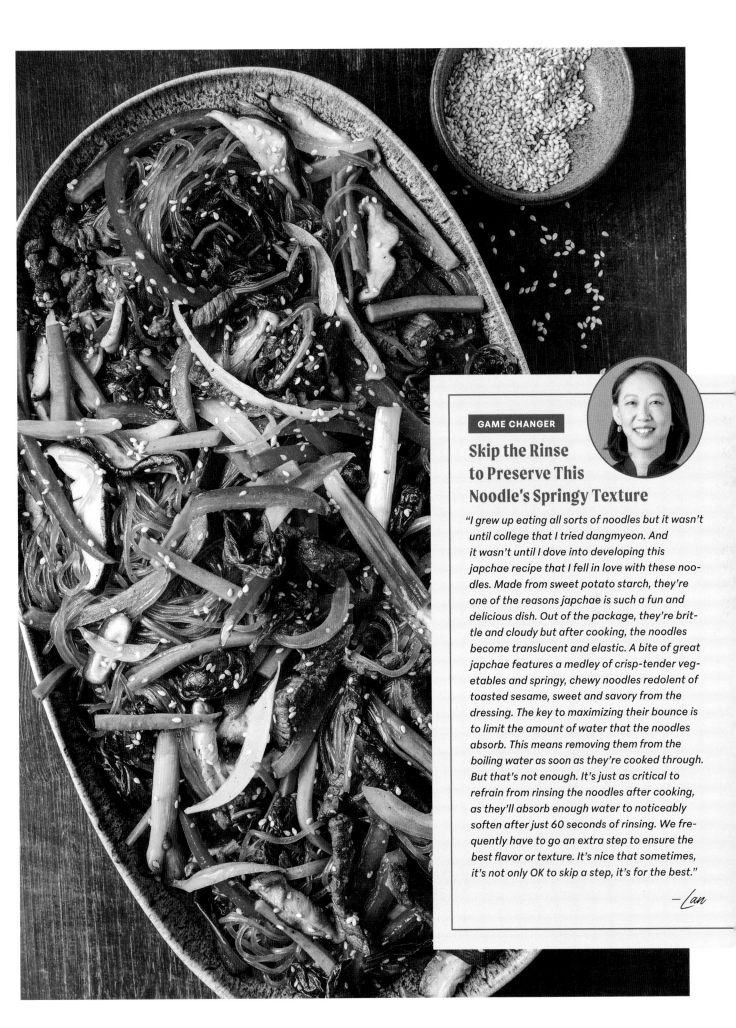

Skip the Rinse to Preserve This Noodle's Springy Texture

"I grew up eating all sorts of noodles but it wasn't until college that I tried dangmyeon. And it wasn't until I dove into developing this japchae recipe that I fell in love with these noodles. Made from sweet potato starch, they're one of the reasons japchae is such a fun and delicious dish. Out of the package, they're brittle and cloudy but after cooking, the noodles become translucent and elastic. A bite of great japchae features a medley of crisp-tender vegetables and springy, chewy noodles redolent of toasted sesame, sweet and savory from the dressing. The key to maximizing their bounce is to limit the amount of water that the noodles absorb. This means removing them from the boiling water as soon as they're cooked through. But that's not enough. It's just as critical to refrain from rinsing the noodles after cooking, as they'll absorb enough water to noticeably soften after just 60 seconds of rinsing. We frequently have to go an extra step to ensure the best flavor or texture. It's nice that sometimes, it's not only OK to skip a step, it's for the best."

—Lan

Beef Ho Fun

Serves 4 to 6 • **Total Time: 30 minutes, plus 30 minutes marinating**

Why This Recipe Works Beef ho fun is a foundational recipe in Cantonese cooking, the kind taught in semester one of cooking school. For such a simple dish of noodles, there are a lot of things to get right. We tossed the beef in a cornstarch slurry to keep it velvety and tender when cooked, and we stirred together a simple but balanced sauce of soy sauce, oyster sauce, Shaoxing wine, a bit more cornstarch, and pepper. To keep all the components from sticking together in a gummy mass, we cooked them all separately: first the beef; then the vegetables; and finally the noodles, which we tossed over high heat to achieve the perfect amount of char. This dish is everything you'd want in a stir-fried noodle: savory rice noodles, crunchy veg, and tender wok-fried beef, served up hot and fast.

> *Fresh ho fun noodles (sometimes labeled chow fun) are wide, flat rice noodles and are critical to this dish; do not substitute other types of fresh or dried noodles. If ho fun noodles are stuck together out of the package, place them on a plate and cover with a wet paper towel. Microwave at 50 percent power 20 seconds at a time until the noodles pull apart.*

  6   ounces flank steak, trimmed
  1   tablespoon water
  ¼   teaspoon baking soda
  5   teaspoons soy sauce, divided
  1   tablespoon oyster sauce, divided
  1   tablespoon Shaoxing wine, divided
  1   teaspoon cornstarch
  ¼   teaspoon white pepper
  2   teaspoons dark soy sauce
 12   ounces fresh ho fun noodles
  2   tablespoons vegetable oil, divided
  6   ounces (3 cups) bean sprouts
  ½   small onion, sliced ¼ inch thick
  2   garlic cloves, minced
  1   teaspoon grated fresh ginger
  3   scallions, green parts only, cut into 1½-inch pieces

1. Cut beef with grain into 2½- to 3-inch-wide strips. Transfer to plate and freeze until firm, about 15 minutes. Slice strips crosswise against grain ¼ inch thick. Combine water and baking soda in medium bowl. Add beef and toss to coat; let sit for 5 minutes.

2. Whisk 2 teaspoons soy sauce, 1 teaspoon oyster sauce, 1 teaspoon Shaoxing wine, cornstarch, and white pepper together in large bowl. Add beef mixture, toss to coat, and let sit at room temperature for 30 minutes.

3. Whisk remaining 1 tablespoon soy sauce, remaining 2 teaspoons oyster sauce, remaining 2 teaspoons Shaoxing wine, and dark soy sauce together in small bowl. Using fingers, unfurl noodles and transfer to rimmed baking sheet; set sauce and noodles aside.

4. Heat empty 14-inch flat-bottomed wok over high heat until just beginning to smoke. Drizzle 1 tablespoon oil around perimeter of wok and heat until just smoking. Add beef mixture and cook, tossing slowly but constantly, until just beginning to brown, about 2 minutes; transfer to clean bowl. Wipe wok clean with damp paper towels.

5. Heat now-empty wok over high heat until just beginning to smoke. Drizzle 1½ teaspoons oil around perimeter of wok and heat until just smoking. Add bean sprouts, onion, garlic, and ginger and cook, tossing slowly but constantly, until vegetables begin to soften and lightly char, about 1 minute; transfer to bowl with beef.

6. Heat now-empty wok over high heat until just beginning to smoke. Drizzle remaining 1½ teaspoons oil around perimeter of wok and heat until just smoking. Add noodles and cook, tossing gently but constantly, until beginning to char, about 1 minute. Add beef mixture and scallions and toss gently to combine. Drizzle reserved soy sauce mixture around perimeter of hot wok and cook, tossing gently to coat noodles, about 30 seconds. Serve.

Dan Dan Mian

Serves 4 • Total Time: 1¼ hours

Why This Recipe Works Sichuan's most popular street food consists of chewy noodles bathed in a spicy, fragrant chili sauce and topped with crispy, savory bits of pork and plump lengths of baby bok choy. Gently heating Sichuan chili powder, ground Sichuan peppercorns, and cinnamon in vegetable oil yielded a flavorful chili oil base for the sauce. For ultracrispy pieces of pork, we smeared ground pork into a thin layer across the wok, broke it up into bits, and gave it a hard sear. Stirring in minced garlic and grated ginger, plus a big scoop of the Sichuan pickle called ya cai, added unique tang and complexity. Blanching baby bok choy brightened its color and gave the vegetable its juicy, palate-cleansing effect. We trimmed and halved the bulbs lengthwise to create bite-size pieces that softened at the same rate. Saving the blanching water to boil the noodles was efficient, and thoroughly rinsing the noodles after they were cooked washed away surface starch that would have caused them to stick together.

If you can't find Sichuan chili powder, substitute Korean red pepper flakes (gochugaru). Sichuan peppercorns provide a tingly, numbing sensation that's important to this dish; find them in the spice aisle at Asian markets. We prefer the chewy texture of fresh, eggless Chinese wheat noodles here. If they aren't available, substitute fresh lo mein or ramen noodles or 8 ounces of dried lo mein noodles. Ya cai, Sichuan preserved mustard greens, gives these noodles a savory and pungent boost; you can buy it online or at an Asian market. If ya cai is unavailable, omit it and increase the soy sauce in step 2 to 2 teaspoons. This dish can be served warm or at room temperature.

Sauce
- ¼ cup vegetable oil
- 1 tablespoon Sichuan chili powder
- 2 teaspoons Sichuan peppercorns, ground fine
- ¼ teaspoon ground cinnamon
- 2 tablespoons soy sauce
- 2 teaspoons Chinese black vinegar or balsamic vinegar
- 2 teaspoons sweet wheat paste or hoisin sauce
- 1½ teaspoons Chinese sesame paste or tahini

Noodles
- 8 ounces ground pork
- 2 teaspoons Shaoxing wine or dry sherry
- 1 teaspoon soy sauce
- 2 small heads baby bok choy (3 ounces each)
- 1 tablespoon vegetable oil, divided

- 3 garlic cloves, minced
- 2 teaspoons grated fresh ginger
- 1 pound fresh Chinese wheat noodles
- ⅓ cup ya cai
- 2 scallions, sliced thin on bias

1. For the sauce: Heat oil, chili powder, peppercorns, and cinnamon in 14-inch wok or 12-inch nonstick skillet over low heat for 10 minutes. Using rubber spatula, transfer oil mixture to bowl (do not wash wok). Whisk soy sauce, vinegar, wheat paste, and sesame paste into oil mixture. Divide evenly among 4 shallow bowls.

2. For the noodles: Bring 4 quarts water to boil in large pot. While water comes to boil, combine pork, Shaoxing wine, and soy sauce in medium bowl and toss with your hands until well combined. Set aside. Working with 1 head bok choy at a time, trim base (larger leaves will fall off) and halve lengthwise through core. Rinse well.

3. Heat 2 teaspoons oil in now-empty wok over medium-high heat until shimmering. Add reserved pork mixture and use rubber spatula to smear into thin layer across surface of wok. Break up meat into ¼-inch chunks with edge of spatula and cook, stirring frequently, until pork is firm and well browned, about 5 minutes. Push pork mixture to far side of wok and add garlic, ginger, and remaining 1 teaspoon oil to cleared space. Cook, stirring constantly, until garlic mixture begins to brown, about 1 minute. Stir to combine pork mixture with garlic mixture. Remove wok from heat.

4. Add bok choy to boiling water and cook until leaves are vibrant green and stems are crisp-tender, about 1 minute. Using slotted spoon or spider skimmer, transfer bok choy to plate; set aside. Add noodles to boiling water and cook, stirring often, until almost tender (center should still be firm with slightly opaque dot). Drain noodles. Rinse under hot running water, tossing with tongs, for 1 minute. Drain well.

5. Divide noodles evenly among prepared bowls. Return wok with pork to medium heat. Add ya cai and cook, stirring frequently, until warmed through, about 2 minutes. Spoon equal amounts of pork topping over noodles. Divide bok choy evenly among bowls, shaking to remove excess moisture as you portion. Top with scallions and serve, leaving each diner to stir components together before eating.

Making a Crispy Pork Topping

Smear ground pork into thin layer across wok with rubber spatula; jab at it with tool's edge to break it up into bits, and sear it hard—really hard for fine bits of pork with crispy edges.

Chinese Pork Dumplings

Makes 40 dumplings • Total Time: 1½ hours

Why This Recipe Works Chinese dumplings are as much fun to make as they are to eat. Our dough has just two ingredients—boiling water and flour—and is easy to roll out and remains moist. For the filling, we started with ground pork, mixing in vegetable oil and sesame oil to provide richness to the lean meat. Soy sauce, ginger, Shaoxing wine, hoisin sauce, and white pepper added flavor to the meat, and cabbage and scallions contributed subtle crunch. Mixing the filling in the food processor was quick and tidy; it also developed myosin, a protein that helped the filling hold together when cooked. To shape the dumplings, we developed a simpler two-pleat approach that achieved the appearance and functionality of a traditional multipleat crescent. To ensure even browning, we brushed a cold nonstick skillet with oil and snugly arranged 20 dumplings in it before turning on the heat.

For dough that has the right moisture level, we strongly recommend weighing the flour. For an accurate measurement of boiling water, bring a full kettle of water to a boil and then measure out the desired amount. To ensure that the dumplings seal completely, use minimal flour when

kneading, rolling, and shaping so that the dough remains slightly tacky. Keep all the dough covered with a damp towel except when rolling and shaping. There is no need to cover the shaped dumplings. A shorter, smaller-diameter rolling pin works well here, but a conventional pin will also work.

Dough

2½ cups (12½ ounces) all-purpose flour
1 cup boiling water

Filling

5 cups 1-inch napa cabbage pieces
1 teaspoon table salt, divided
12 ounces ground pork
1½ tablespoons soy sauce, plus extra for dipping
1½ tablespoons toasted sesame oil
1 tablespoon vegetable oil, plus 2 tablespoons for pan-frying (optional)
1 tablespoon Shaoxing wine or dry sherry
1 tablespoon hoisin sauce
1 tablespoon grated fresh ginger
¼ teaspoon white pepper
4 scallions, chopped fine
Chinese black vinegar or unseasoned rice vinegar
Chili oil

1. For the dough: Place flour in food processor. With processor running, add boiling water. Continue to process until dough forms ball and clears sides of bowl, 30 to 45 seconds longer. Transfer dough to counter and knead until smooth, 2 to 3 minutes. Wrap dough in plastic wrap and let rest for 30 minutes.

2. For the filling: While dough rests, scrape any excess dough from now-empty processor bowl and blade. Pulse cabbage in processor until finely chopped, 8 to 10 pulses. Transfer cabbage to medium bowl and stir in ½ teaspoon salt; let sit for 10 minutes. Using your hands, squeeze excess moisture from cabbage. Transfer cabbage to small bowl and set aside.

3. Pulse pork, soy sauce, sesame oil, 1 tablespoon vegetable oil, Shaoxing wine, hoisin, ginger, white pepper, and remaining ½ teaspoon salt in now-empty food processor until blended and slightly sticky, about 10 pulses. Scatter cabbage over pork mixture. Add scallions and pulse until vegetables are evenly distributed, about 8 pulses. Transfer pork mixture to small bowl and, using rubber spatula, smooth surface. Cover with plastic and refrigerate.

4. Line 2 rimmed baking sheets with parchment paper. Lightly dust with flour and set aside. Unwrap dough and transfer to counter. Roll dough into 12-inch cylinder and cut cylinder into 4 equal pieces. Set 3 pieces aside and cover with plastic. Roll remaining piece into 8-inch cylinder. Cut cylinder in half and cut each half into 5 equal pieces. Place dough pieces on 1 cut side on lightly floured counter and lightly dust with flour. Using palm of your hand, press each dough piece into 2-inch disk. Cover disks with damp towel.

5. Roll 1 disk into 3½-inch round (wrappers needn't be perfectly round) and re-cover disk with damp towel. Repeat with remaining disks. (Do not overlap disks.)

6. Using rubber spatula, mark filling with cross to divide into 4 equal portions. Transfer 1 portion to small bowl and refrigerate remaining filling. Working with 1 wrapper at a time (keep remaining wrappers covered), place scant 1 table-spoon filling in center of wrapper. Brush away any flour clinging to surface of wrapper. Lift side of wrapper closest to you and side farthest away and pinch together to form 1½-inch-wide seam in center of dumpling. (When viewed from above, dumpling will have rectangular shape with rounded open ends.) Lift left corner farthest away from you and bring to center of seam. Pinch to seal. Pinch together remaining dough on left side to seal. Repeat pinching on right side. Gently press dumpling into crescent shape and transfer to prepared sheet. Repeat with remaining wrappers and filling in bowl. Repeat dumpling-making process with remaining 3 pieces dough and remaining 3 portions filling.

7A. To pan-fry: Brush 12-inch nonstick skillet with 1 table-spoon vegetable oil. Evenly space 16 dumplings, flat sides down, around edge of skillet and place four in center. Cook over medium heat until bottoms begin to turn spotty brown, 3 to 4 minutes. Off heat, carefully add ½ cup water (water will sputter). Return skillet to heat and bring water to boil. Cover and reduce heat to medium-low. Cook for 6 minutes. Uncover, increase heat to medium-high, and cook until water has evaporated and bottoms of dumplings are crispy and browned, 1 to 3 minutes. Transfer dumplings to platter, crispy sides up. (To cook second batch of dumplings, let skillet cool

for 10 minutes. Rinse skillet under cool water and wipe dry with paper towels. Repeat cooking process with remaining 1 tablespoon vegetable oil and remaining dumplings.)

7B. To boil: Bring 4 quarts water to boil in large Dutch oven over high heat. Add 20 dumplings, a few at a time, stirring gently to prevent them from sticking. Return to simmer, adjusting heat as necessary to maintain simmer. Cook dumplings for 7 minutes. Drain well.

8. Serve dumplings hot, passing vinegar, chili oil, and extra soy sauce separately for dipping.

To make ahead: Freeze uncooked dumplings on rimmed baking sheet until solid. Transfer to zipper-lock bag and freeze for up to 1 month. To pan-fry, increase water to ⅔ cup and covered cooking time to 8 minutes. To boil, increase cooking time to 8 minutes.

Assembling Chinese Pork Dumplings

1. Place scant 1 tablespoon filling in center of wrapper.

2. Seal top and bottom edges to form 1½-inch-wide seam.

3. Bring far left corner to center of seam and pinch together.

4. Pinch rest of left side to seal. Repeat process on right side.

5. Gently press dumpling into crescent shape.

Shu Mai

Makes 40 dumplings • **Total Time: 1½ hours**

Why This Recipe Works Our goal was to create an exemplary version of shu mai (steamed Chinese dumplings)—one that boasted a tender, thin skin and a moist, flavorful filling. Our favorite shu mai rely on coarse-ground pork and shrimp. To ensure proper flavor and texture, we chopped the pork (boneless country-style spareribs) in a food processor rather than relying on supermarket ground pork, which is often inconsistent. To prevent the meat from drying out, we mixed in a little powdered gelatin dissolved in soy sauce. We added the shrimp to the food processor, too. Dried shiitake mushrooms, cilantro, fresh ginger, and water chestnuts helped round out the flavorful filling. We chose widely available egg roll skins and cut them into rounds with a biscuit cutter. Once we added the filling and gathered up the edges of the wrappers, we steamed the dumplings in a steamer basket.

Do not trim the excess fat from the spareribs, as the fat contributes flavor and moistness. Use any size shrimp except popcorn shrimp; there's no need to halve shrimp smaller than 26 to 30 per pound before processing. The dumplings may be frozen for up to 3 months; cook straight from the freezer for about an extra 5 minutes. Shu mai are traditionally served with a spicy chili oil (recipe follows), or use store-bought.

2 tablespoons soy sauce

½ teaspoon unflavored gelatin

1 pound boneless country-style pork spareribs, cut into 1-inch pieces, divided

½ pound shrimp, peeled, deveined, tails removed, and halved lengthwise

¼ cup chopped water chestnuts

4 dried shiitake mushroom caps (about ¾ ounce), soaked in hot water for 30 minutes, squeezed dry, and cut into ¼-inch dice

2 tablespoons cornstarch

2 tablespoons minced fresh cilantro

1 tablespoon toasted sesame oil

1 tablespoon Shaoxing wine or dry sherry

1 tablespoon unseasoned rice vinegar

2 teaspoons sugar

2 teaspoons grated fresh ginger

½ teaspoon table salt

½ teaspoon pepper

1 (1-pound) package 5½-inch square egg roll wrappers

¼ cup finely grated carrot (optional)

1. Combine soy sauce and gelatin in small bowl. Set aside to allow gelatin to bloom, about 5 minutes.

2. Meanwhile, place half of pork in food processor and pulse until coarsely ground into pieces that are about ⅛ inch, about 10 pulses; transfer to large bowl. Add shrimp and remaining pork to food processor and pulse until coarsely chopped into pieces that are about ¼ inch, about 5 pulses.

Filling and Forming Shu Mai

1. Place heaping 1 tablespoon filling in center of wrapper. Pinch 2 opposing sides of wrapper with your fingers. Rotate dumpling 90 degrees, and pinch again.

2. Continue to pinch dumpling until you have 8 equidistant pinches around circumference of dumpling.

3. Gather up sides of dumpling and squeeze gently at top to create "waist."

4. Hold dumpling in your hand and gently but firmly pack filling into dumpling with butter knife.

ACCOMPANIMENT

Quick Chili Oil

Makes ½ cup

Total Time: 15 minutes, plus 1 hour cooling

  1 tablespoon soy sauce

  2 teaspoons sugar

  ½ teaspoon table salt

  ½ cup peanut oil

  ¼ cup red pepper flakes

  2 garlic cloves, peeled

Combine soy sauce, sugar, and salt in small bowl; set aside. Heat oil in small saucepan over medium heat until just shimmering and registers 300 degrees. Remove pan from heat and stir in pepper flakes, garlic, and soy mixture. Let cool to room temperature, stirring occasionally, about 1 hour. Discard garlic before storing.

Transfer to bowl with coarsely ground pork. Stir in soy sauce mixture, water chestnuts, mushrooms, cornstarch, cilantro, oil, Shaoxing wine, vinegar, sugar, ginger, salt, and pepper until well combined.

3. Line large baking sheet with parchment paper. Divide egg roll wrappers into 3 stacks (six to seven per stack). Using 3-inch biscuit cutter, cut two 3-inch rounds from each stack of egg roll wrappers (you should have 40 to 42 rounds). Cover rounds with moist paper towels to prevent drying.

4. Working with 6 rounds at a time, brush edges of each round lightly with water. Place heaping 1 tablespoon filling in center of each round. Form dumplings by pinching 2 opposing sides of wrapper with your fingers. Rotate dumpling 90 degrees and, again, pinch opposing sides of wrapper with your fingers. Continue to pinch dumpling to form 8 equidistant pinches around circumference. Gather up sides of dumpling and squeeze gently at top to create rounded and open shape with "waist." Gently but firmly pack down filling with back of spoon or butter knife. Transfer to prepared baking sheet, cover with damp kitchen towel, and repeat with remaining wrappers and filling. Top center of each dumpling with pinch of grated carrot, if using.

5. Cut piece of parchment paper slightly smaller than diameter of steamer basket and place in basket. Poke about 20 small holes in parchment to allow steam to pass through and lightly coat with vegetable oil spray. Place batches of dumplings on parchment, making sure they are not touching. Set steamer basket over simmering water and cook, covered, until no longer pink, 8 to 10 minutes. Serve immediately.

SEASON 25

Har Gow

Makes 24 dumplings • Total Time: 1¼ hours, plus 30 minutes chilling and resting

Why This Recipe Works The meticulously crafted Cantonese crystal shrimp dumplings called har gow are one of the great joys of a dim sum feast. Making them at home lets you truly appreciate their gifts. The recipe begins with preparing a wheat starch and tapioca starch dough in a food processor to produce a lightly springy, translucent wrapper. We added boiling water to the starches and let the starch briefly gelatinize to give the dough structure; we then drizzled in melted lard to make an extensible dough that was easy to flatten into thin rounds and pliable enough to pleat around a filling. We also used the food processor to chop and mix the shrimp for the filling. This agitation extracted the protein myosin, which bound with water and fat during cooking to keep the filling moist. We added melted lard to the filling for richness, along with modest amounts of ginger, garlic, and Shaoxing wine. Minced bamboo shoots or water chestnuts contributed a bit of crunch. Dim sum chefs use the wide side of a cleaver to smear pieces of dough into round wrappers, but we used a tortilla press, which is easier for novices. Finally, we pleated the dough around small mounds of filling to form the classic pleated purse shape of har gow before steaming them in a bamboo steamer.

A bamboo steamer is traditional for steaming the dumplings. We developed this recipe with Red Lantern wheat starch and Bob's Red Mill tapioca starch. We strongly recommend weighing the starches. For an accurate measurement of boiling water, bring a kettle of water to a boil and then measure out the desired amount. You can substitute vegetable oil for the lard. Any size shrimp can be used; the larger the shrimp, the more pulses will be required to chop them in step 2. Canned water chestnuts can be substituted for the bamboo shoots. If you don't own a tortilla press, flatten the dough with a 6-inch cake pan or another similar-size clean, flat surface. Serve with Chili Oil (recipe follows).

Dough
- 1 cup plus 2 tablespoons (5¼ ounces) wheat starch
- ¼ cup plus 3 tablespoons (1¾ ounces) tapioca starch
  Pinch table salt
- ½ cup plus 1 tablespoon boiling water
- 4 teaspoons lard, melted

Filling
- 6 ounces shrimp, peeled, deveined, and tails removed
- 2 tablespoons finely chopped canned bamboo shoots
- 1 tablespoon lard, melted and cooled
- 1 teaspoon Shaoxing wine
- ½ teaspoon grated fresh ginger
- ½ teaspoon minced garlic
- ¼ teaspoon sugar
- ¼ teaspoon table salt
- ¼ teaspoon white pepper
- ¼ teaspoon soy sauce

1. For the dough: Process wheat starch, tapioca starch, and salt in food processor until combined, about 3 seconds. Add boiling water and let rest for 5 seconds. Pulse once. Add melted lard and process until dough forms ball that clears sides of processor bowl, about 1 minute (if dough does not come together, add up to 2 teaspoons hot water, ½ teaspoon at a time, processing for 10 seconds between additions, until dough ball forms). Transfer to lightly greased counter and knead for 1 minute. Dough should be slightly tacky. Shape dough into ball and cover with plastic wrap.

2. For the filling: In clean, dry workbowl, pulse all filling ingredients until shrimp is finely ground, 10 to 20 pulses. Transfer to bowl; cover; and refrigerate until filling is well chilled, about 20 minutes.

3. To shape, divide dough into 4 equal portions. On lightly greased counter, roll 1 portion of dough into 6-inch rope. Divide rope into 6 equal pieces. Cover all pieces with plastic wrap. Use lightly oiled tortilla press to press 1 piece of dough into 3¼-inch round.

4. Place dough round on fingers of your nondominant hand. Place heaping ½ tablespoon of filling in center of dough. To create first pleat, use thumb and index finger of your other hand to pinch dough just above pinky and lift pleat toward top of filling.

5. Using index finger of hand holding dumpling, push dough toward pinched portion to begin forming second pleat. Use index finger of pleating hand to position second pleat against first pleat. Repeat pleating motion, rotating dough with each pleat, until all of dough is pleated and dumpling has rounded shape.

6. Hold dumpling pleated side up, and use your thumb and index finger to press pleats together just above filling to seal dumpling. Gently tear excess dough from dumpling. Place dumpling pleated side up on counter and cover with plastic wrap. Repeat with remaining dough and filling, lightly oiling tortilla press and counter as needed.

7. To steam, bring 4 cups water to boil in 14-inch flat-bottomed wok or 12-inch skillet. Meanwhile, lightly grease two 8-inch parchment rounds. Place rounds in two 10-inch bamboo steamer baskets. Arrange dumplings on prepared parchment so that they are not touching; stack baskets and cover. Reduce heat to maintain simmer and set steamer in wok. Steam until har gow wrappers are translucent, about 8 minutes. Off heat, remove steamer from wok and let rest, covered, for 10 minutes. Serve.

Shaping Har Gow

1. To create first pleat, use your thumb and index finger to pinch dough.

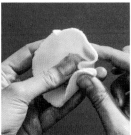

2. Use index finger of your other hand to push dough to begin second pleat.

3. Position second pleat against first pleat.

4. Repeat, rotating with each pleat, until dumpling has rounded shape.

5. Press pleats above filling to seal.

6. Gently tear off excess dough.

Chili Oil

Makes 1¾ cups
Total Time: 1 hour, plus 1½ hours cooling

Chili oil, neutral oil infused with aromatics and spices and tinted vibrant red by Sichuan chili flakes, features in many traditional Chinese dishes. It also can be used at the table to add color and moderate heat to noodles, soups, or dumplings such as Har Gow. If Sichuan chili flakes are unavailable or you'd prefer a less spicy chili oil, you can substitute gochugaru (Korean chili flakes).

- 1¼ cups vegetable oil
- 1 shallot, sliced into ¼-inch rings
- 1 (2-inch) piece ginger, peeled and sliced into ¼-inch-thick rounds
- 3 garlic cloves, peeled
- 2 bay leaves
- 1 star anise pod
- 1 cinnamon stick
- ½ cup Sichuan chili flakes
- ⅛ teaspoon table salt

1. Bring oil, shallot, ginger, garlic, bay leaves, star anise, and cinnamon to simmer in small saucepan over medium heat. Reduce heat to low; tiny bubbles should surround aromatics, but aromatics should not fry. Cook until garlic and shallot are golden brown, taking care to maintain gentle bubbling, 45 minutes to 1 hour.

2. Combine Sichuan chili flakes and salt in medium heat-proof bowl. Strain oil mixture through fine-mesh strainer over chili flakes (mixture may bubble). Discard solids in strainer. Let chili oil cool completely, about 1½ hours. Once cool, transfer mixture to airtight container. Store in refrigerator for up to 3 months.

Poultry

Photo: Roast Turkey and Gravy with Herbes de Provence and Lemon

Sautéed Chicken Cutlets

Serves 4 • Total Time: 35 minutes

Why This Recipe Works Sautéed chicken cutlets are a breeze to prepare, but their brief cooking time and lack of skin leaves very little fond behind with which to build a pan sauce. With this in mind, we sought out a sauce that packed big flavor and could be made before the chicken even hit the skillet. Romesco sauce—a thick, coarse Spanish concoction of roasted red peppers, toasted hazelnuts, bread, sherry vinegar, olive oil, smoked paprika, and garlic—was simple to whiz together in a food processor and boasted a bold flavor profile. We browned the cutlets in a hot oiled pan and, in just under 3 minutes, they were ready to be served with either Romesco or one of our other two simple and quick bold sauces (recipes follow).

> *The cutlets will be easier to slice in half if you freeze them for about 15 minutes.*

4 (6- to 8-ounce) boneless, skinless chicken breasts, trimmed, halved horizontally, and pounded ¼ inch thick
1 teaspoon kosher salt
¼ teaspoon pepper
4 teaspoons vegetable oil

Pat cutlets dry with paper towels; sprinkle each side of each cutlet evenly with salt and pepper. Heat 2 teaspoons oil in 12-inch skillet over medium-high heat until just smoking. Place 4 cutlets in skillet and cook, without moving, until browned, about 2 minutes. Flip cutlets and continue to cook

until second sides are opaque, about 30 seconds. Transfer to platter and tent with aluminum foil. Repeat with remaining 4 cutlets and remaining 2 teaspoons oil. Serve.

SAUCES

Romesco Sauce

Makes 1 cup • Total Time: 30 minutes
You will need at least one 12-ounce jar of roasted red peppers for this recipe.

½ slice hearty white sandwich bread, cut into ½-inch pieces
¼ cup hazelnuts, toasted and skinned
2 tablespoons extra-virgin olive oil, divided
2 garlic cloves, sliced thin
1 cup jarred roasted red peppers, rinsed and patted dry
1½ tablespoons sherry vinegar
1 teaspoon honey
½ teaspoon smoked paprika
½ teaspoon table salt
Pinch cayenne pepper

Heat bread, hazelnuts, and 1 tablespoon oil in 12-inch skillet over medium heat; cook, stirring constantly, until bread and hazelnuts are lightly toasted, 2½ to 3 minutes. Add garlic and cook, stirring constantly, until fragrant, about 30 seconds. Transfer bread mixture to food processor and pulse until coarsely chopped, about 5 pulses. Add red peppers, vinegar, honey, paprika, salt, cayenne, and remaining 1 tablespoon oil to processor. Pulse until finely chopped, 5 to 8 pulses. Transfer to bowl and let stand for at least 10 minutes. (Sauce can be refrigerated for up to 2 days.)

Quick Sun-Dried Tomato Sauce

Makes 1 cup • Total Time: 30 minutes
For the best taste and texture, make sure to rinse all the dried herbs off the sun-dried tomatoes.

½ slice hearty white sandwich bread, cut into ½-inch pieces
¼ cup pine nuts
2 tablespoons extra-virgin olive oil, divided
2 garlic cloves, sliced thin
1 small tomato, cored and cut into ½-inch pieces
½ cup oil-packed sun-dried tomatoes, rinsed
2 tablespoons coarsely chopped fresh basil
2 tablespoons balsamic vinegar
½ teaspoon table salt

Heat bread, pine nuts, and 1 tablespoon oil in 12-inch skillet over medium heat; cook, stirring constantly, until bread and pine nuts are lightly toasted, 2½ to 3 minutes. Add garlic and cook, stirring constantly, until fragrant, about 30 seconds. Transfer bread mixture to food processor and pulse until coarsely chopped, about 5 pulses. Add tomato, sun-dried tomatoes, basil, vinegar, salt, and remaining 1 tablespoon oil to processor. Pulse until finely chopped, 5 to 8 pulses. Transfer to bowl and let stand for at least 10 minutes. (Sauce can be refrigerated for up to 2 days.)

Quick Tomatillo Sauce

Makes 1 cup • Total Time: 30 minutes

You will need at least one 15-ounce can of tomatillos for this recipe.

- ½ slice hearty white sandwich bread, cut into ½-inch pieces
- ¼ cup pepitas
- 2 tablespoons extra-virgin olive oil, divided
- 2 garlic cloves, sliced thin
- 1 cup canned tomatillos, rinsed
- 2 tablespoons jarred sliced jalapeños plus 2 teaspoons brine
- 2 tablespoons fresh cilantro leaves
- 1 teaspoon honey
- ½ teaspoon table salt

Heat bread, pepitas, and 1 tablespoon oil in 12-inch skillet over medium heat; cook, stirring constantly, until pepitas and bread are lightly toasted, 2½ to 3 minutes. Add garlic and cook, stirring constantly, until fragrant, about 30 seconds. Transfer bread mixture to food processor and pulse until coarsely chopped, about 5 pulses. Add tomatillos, jalapeños and brine, cilantro, honey, salt, and remaining 1 tablespoon oil to processor. Pulse until finely chopped, 5 to 8 pulses. Transfer to bowl and let stand for at least 10 minutes. (Sauce can be refrigerated for up to 2 days.)

Making Chicken Cutlets

1. Remove tenderloin from underside of breast if necessary. Lay chicken smooth side up on cutting board. To make cutlets, place your hand on top of chicken and carefully slice it in half horizontally.

2. Separate breast to yield 2 cutlets between ³/₈ and ½ inch thick. If necessary, pound to even thickness.

Crispy Pan-Fried Chicken Cutlets

Serves 4 to 6 • Total Time: 40 minutes

Why This Recipe Works Chicken cutlets coated in bread crumbs and pan-fried are a staple weeknight meal: They're quick-cooking and a crowd-pleaser. But the three-step breading process of flour, egg, and crumbs is fussy, so we set out to make a streamlined version inspired by Japanese chicken katsu. We ditched the flour step, which made for a more delicate coating. Instead of using homemade bread crumbs, we swapped in Japanese panko bread crumbs that we poured into a zipper-lock bag and crushed with a rolling pin. To avoid any spotty browning or burned bits of panko with our second batch of cutlets, we discarded the cooking oil from the first batch and started over with fresh oil. Once they were done cooking, we transferred the cutlets to a paper towel–lined rack, which helped wick away excess oil while preventing the underside from turning soggy. To punch up the flavor, we made a tonkatsu-style sauce as well as a garlicky curry sauce.

Be sure to remove any tenderloins from the breasts before halving. The cutlets will be easier to slice in half if you freeze them for about 15 minutes. If you are working with 8-ounce cutlets, the skillet will initially be crowded; the cutlets will shrink slightly as they cook. The first batch of cutlets can be kept warm in a 200-degree oven while the second batch cooks. These cutlets can be sliced into ½-inch-wide strips and served over rice with sauce (recipes follow), in a sandwich, or over a green salad.

2 cups panko bread crumbs

2 large eggs

1 teaspoon table salt

4 (6- to 8-ounce) boneless, skinless chicken breasts, trimmed, halved horizontally, and pounded ¼ inch thick

½ cup vegetable oil, divided

1. Place panko in large zipper-lock bag and finely crush with rolling pin. Transfer crushed panko to shallow dish. Whisk eggs and salt in second shallow dish until well combined.

2. Working with 1 cutlet at a time, dredge cutlet in egg mixture, allowing excess egg to drip off, then coat all sides with panko, pressing gently so crumbs adhere. Transfer cutlet to rimmed baking sheet and repeat with remaining cutlets.

3. Place wire rack in second rimmed baking sheet. Line rack with layer of paper towels. Heat ¼ cup oil and small pinch of panko in 12-inch skillet over medium-high heat. When panko has turned golden brown, place 4 cutlets in skillet. Cook without moving them until bottoms are crispy and deep golden brown, 2 to 3 minutes. Using tongs, carefully flip cutlets and cook on second side until deep golden brown, 2 to 3 minutes. Transfer cutlets to towel-lined rack and season with salt to taste. Wipe out skillet with paper towels. Repeat with remaining ¼ cup oil and 4 cutlets. Serve immediately.

SAUCES

Tonkatsu Sauce

Makes ⅓ cup • Total Time: 5 minutes

You can substitute yellow mustard for the Dijon, but do not use a grainy mustard.

¼ cup ketchup

2 tablespoons Worcestershire sauce

2 teaspoons soy sauce

1 teaspoon Dijon mustard

Whisk all ingredients together in bowl.

Garlic-Curry Sauce

Makes about ½ cup • Total Time: 10 minutes

Full-fat and nonfat yogurt will both work in this recipe.

⅓ cup mayonnaise

¼ cup plain yogurt

2 tablespoons ketchup

2 teaspoons curry powder

1 teaspoon lemon juice

¼ teaspoon minced garlic

Whisk all ingredients together in bowl.

SEASON 11

Pan-Seared Chicken Breasts

Serves 4 • Total Time: 1¼ hours

Why This Recipe Works A boneless, skinless chicken breast doesn't have the bone and skin to protect it from the intensity of a hot pan. Inevitably, it emerges moist in the middle and dry at the edges, with an exterior that's leathery and tough. We wanted a boneless, skinless chicken breast that was every bit as flavorful, moist, and tender as its skin-on counterpart. We utilized a technique that we'd used successfully with steaks, where we gently parcook the meat in the oven and then sear it on the stovetop. First, we salted the chicken to help it retain more moisture as it cooked. To expedite the process we poked holes in the breasts so the salt could reach the interior of the chicken as it parcooked. We then placed the breasts in a baking dish and covered it tightly with foil. In this enclosed environment, any moisture released by the chicken stayed trapped under the foil, keeping the exterior from drying out without becoming so overly wet that it couldn't brown quickly. To achieve a crisp, even crust, we turned to a Chinese cooking technique called velveting, in which meat is dipped in a mixture of oil and cornstarch to create a thin protective layer that keeps the protein moist and tender, even when exposed to ultrahigh heat. We replaced the oil with butter (for flavor) and mixed flour in with the cornstarch to avoid any pasty flavor. The coating helped the chicken make better contact with the hot skillet, creating a thin, browned, crisp veneer that kept the breast's exterior as moist as the interior.

Buy similarly sized chicken breasts. If the breasts include the tenderloin, leave it in place and follow the upper range of time in step 1. For optimal texture, sear chicken immediately after removing it from the oven. Serve with Lemon and Chive Pan Sauce, if desired (recipe follows).

4 (6- to 8-ounce) boneless, skinless chicken breasts, trimmed
1 teaspoon table salt
1 tablespoon vegetable oil
2 tablespoons unsalted butter, melted
1 tablespoon all-purpose flour
1 teaspoon cornstarch
½ teaspoon pepper

1. Adjust oven rack to lower-middle position and heat oven to 275 degrees. Use fork to poke thickest half of each breast 5 or 6 times, then sprinkle each breast with ¼ teaspoon salt. Place chicken, skin side down, in 13 by 9-inch baking dish and cover tightly with foil. Bake until chicken registers 145 to 150 degrees, 30 to 40 minutes.

2. Remove chicken from oven and transfer, skinned side up, to paper towel–lined plate; pat dry. Heat oil in 12-inch skillet over medium-high heat until just smoking. While pan is heating, whisk melted butter, flour, cornstarch, and pepper together in small bowl. Brush tops of chicken with half of butter mixture. Place chicken in skillet, coated side down, and cook until browned, 3 to 4 minutes. While chicken browns, brush second side with remaining butter mixture. Using tongs, flip chicken, reduce heat to medium, and cook until second side is browned and chicken registers 160 to 165 degrees, 3 to 4 minutes. Transfer chicken to platter and let rest while preparing pan sauce. (If not making pan sauce, let chicken rest for 5 minutes before serving.)

ACCOMPANIMENT
Lemon and Chive Pan Sauce
Makes ¾ cup • Total Time: 15 minutes

1 shallot, minced
1 teaspoon all-purpose flour
1 cup chicken broth
1 tablespoon lemon juice
1 tablespoon minced fresh chives
1 tablespoon unsalted butter, chilled

Add shallot to fond in skillet and cook over medium heat until softened, about 2 minutes. Add flour and cook, stirring constantly, for 30 seconds. Add broth, increase heat to medium-high, and bring to simmer, scraping up any browned bits. Simmer rapidly until reduced to ¾ cup, 3 to 5 minutes. Stir in any accumulated chicken juices, return to simmer, and cook for 30 seconds. Off heat, whisk in lemon juice, chives, and butter; season with salt and pepper to taste.

SEASON 15

Crispy-Skinned Chicken Breasts with Vinegar-Pepper Pan Sauce

Serves 2 • Total Time: 55 minutes, plus 1 hour salting

Why This Recipe Works Perfectly cooked chicken with shatteringly crispy, flavorful skin is a rare find, so we set out to develop a foolproof recipe that would work every time. Boning and pounding the chicken breasts was essential to creating a flat, even surface to maximize the skin's contact with the hot pan. We salted the chicken to both season the meat and dry out the skin; poking holes in the skin and the meat allowed the salt to penetrate deeply. Starting the chicken in a cold pan allowed time for the skin to crisp without overcooking the meat. Weighting the chicken for part of the cooking time with a heavy Dutch oven encouraged even contact with the hot pan for all-over crunchy skin. Finally, we created silky, flavorful sauces with a bright, acidic finish, which provided the perfect foil to the skin's richness.

This recipe requires refrigerating the salted meat for at least 1 hour before cooking. Two 10- to 12-ounce chicken breasts are ideal, but three smaller ones can fit in the same pan; the skin will be slightly less crispy. A boning knife or sharp paring knife works best to remove the bones from the breasts. To maintain the crispy skin, spoon the sauce around, not over, the breasts when serving.

Chicken

- 2 (10- to 12-ounce) bone-in split chicken breasts
- 1 teaspoon kosher salt
- ½ teaspoon pepper
- 2 tablespoons vegetable oil

Pan Sauce

- 1 shallot, minced
- 1 teaspoon all-purpose flour
- ½ cup chicken broth
- ¼ cup chopped pickled hot cherry peppers, plus ¼ cup brine
- 1 tablespoon unsalted butter, chilled
- 1 teaspoon minced fresh thyme

1. **For the chicken:** Place 1 chicken breast, skin side down, on cutting board, with ribs facing away from your knife hand. Run tip of knife between breastbone and meat, working from thick end of breast toward thin end. Angling blade slightly and following rib cage, repeat cutting motion several times to remove ribs and breastbone from breast. Find short remnant of wishbone along top edge of breast and run tip of knife along both sides of bone to separate it from meat. Remove tenderloin (reserve for another use) and trim excess fat, taking care not to cut into skin. Repeat with second breast.

2. Using tip of paring knife, poke skin on each breast evenly 30 to 40 times. Turn breasts over and poke thickest half of each breast 5 or 6 times. Cover breasts with plastic wrap and pound thick ends gently with meat pounder until ½ inch thick. Evenly sprinkle each breast with ½ teaspoon kosher salt. Place breasts, skin side up, on wire rack set in rimmed baking sheet, cover loosely with plastic, and refrigerate for at least 1 hour or up to 8 hours.

3. Pat breasts dry with paper towels and sprinkle each breast with ¼ teaspoon pepper. Pour oil in 12-inch skillet and swirl to coat. Place breasts, skin side down, in oil and place skillet over medium heat. Place heavy skillet or Dutch oven on top of breasts. Cook breasts until skin is beginning to brown and meat is beginning to turn opaque along edges, 7 to 9 minutes.

4. Remove weight and continue to cook until skin is well browned and very crispy, 6 to 8 minutes. Flip breasts, reduce heat to medium-low, and cook until second side is lightly browned and meat registers 160 to 165 degrees, 2 to 3 minutes. Transfer breasts to individual plates and let rest while preparing pan sauce.

5. **For the pan sauce:** Pour off all but 2 teaspoons oil from skillet. Return skillet to medium heat and add shallot; cook, stirring occasionally, until shallot is softened, about 2 minutes. Add flour and cook, stirring constantly, for 30 seconds. Increase heat to medium-high; add broth and brine; and bring to simmer, scraping up any browned bits. Simmer until thickened, 2 to 3 minutes. Stir in any accumulated chicken juices; return to simmer and cook for 30 seconds. Remove skillet from heat and whisk in peppers, butter, and thyme; season with salt and pepper to taste. Spoon sauce around breasts and serve.

VARIATIONS

Crispy-Skinned Chicken Breasts with Lemon-Rosemary Pan Sauce

In step 5, increase broth to ¾ cup and substitute 2 tablespoons lemon juice for brine. Omit peppers and substitute rosemary for thyme.

Crispy-Skinned Chicken Breasts with Maple–Sherry Vinegar Pan Sauce

In step 5, substitute 2 tablespoons sherry vinegar for brine, 1 tablespoon maple syrup for peppers, and sage for thyme.

Boning a Split Chicken Breast

1. With chicken breast skin side down, run tip of boning or sharp paring knife between breastbone and meat, working from thick end of breast toward thin end.

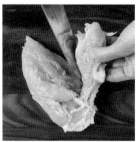

2. Angling blade slightly and following rib cage, repeat cutting motion several times to remove ribs and breastbone from breast.

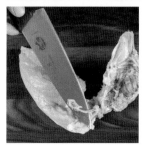

3. Find short remnant of wishbone along top edge of breast and run tip of knife along both sides of bone to separate it from meat.

Skillet-Roasted Chicken Breasts with Garlicky Green Beans

Serves 4 • Total Time: 1¼ hours

Why This Recipe Works This recipe is a twofer from one skillet. First, we seasoned bone-in, skin-on chicken breasts under the skin with salt. We placed them skin side down in a cold skillet and then turned on the heat to slowly render and brown the skin without overcooking the delicate flesh just beneath it. Once the skin was well browned, we flipped the breasts and placed them in a 325-degree oven for about 30 minutes to cook through. While the cooked chicken breasts rested, we added sliced garlic, spicy red pepper flakes, and salt to the skillet and cooked them until the chicken juices reduced and the mixture began to sizzle in the chicken fat and release flavor. We then added green beans to the pan along with a little water, covered the pan, and let the green beans cook through. With the skillet uncovered, the savory, chicken-y liquid thickened to coat the beans. A shower of nutty, salty Parmesan shreds enhanced the rich green beans.

| *Trim excess fatty skin from the thick ends of the breasts.*

> 4 (10- to 12-ounce) bone-in split chicken breasts, trimmed
> 2¼ teaspoons kosher salt, divided
> Vegetable oil spray
> 3 garlic cloves, sliced thin
> ¼ teaspoon red pepper flakes
> 1¼ pounds green beans, trimmed
> ⅓ cup water
> 1½ ounces Parmesan cheese, shredded (½ cup)

1. Adjust oven rack to lower-middle position and heat oven to 325 degrees. Working with 1 breast at a time, use your fingers to carefully separate skin from meat. Peel back skin, leaving skin attached at top and bottom of breast and at ribs. Sprinkle 1½ teaspoons salt evenly over chicken (⅜ teaspoon per breast). Lay skin back in place. Using metal skewer or tip of paring knife, poke 6 to 8 holes in fat deposits in skin of each breast. Spray skin with oil spray.

2. Place chicken, skin side down, in 12-inch ovensafe skillet and set over medium-high heat. Cook, moving chicken as infrequently as possible, until skin is well browned, 7 to 9 minutes.

3. Carefully flip chicken and transfer skillet to oven. Roast until chicken registers 160 degrees, 25 to 30 minutes.

4. Transfer chicken to plate; do not discard liquid in skillet. Add garlic, pepper flakes, and remaining ¾ teaspoon salt to skillet and cook over medium-high heat, stirring occasionally and scraping up any browned bits, until moisture has evaporated and mixture begins to sizzle, 2 to 4 minutes. Add green beans and water and bring to simmer. Cover skillet, reduce heat to medium, and cook until green beans are tender, 8 to 10 minutes, stirring halfway through cooking. Uncover and continue to cook, stirring frequently, until sauce begins to coat green beans, 2 to 4 minutes longer. Add any accumulated chicken juices to skillet and toss to combine. Season with salt to taste. Transfer green beans to serving platter and sprinkle with Parmesan. Top with chicken and serve.

VARIATION

Skillet-Roasted Chicken Breasts with Harissa-Mint Carrots

Substitute 1 thinly sliced shallot for garlic and 2 teaspoons harissa for pepper flakes. Substitute 1½ pounds carrots, peeled and sliced on bias ¼ inch thick, for green beans. Increase salt for vegetables to 1 teaspoon, water to ½ cup, and covered cooking time to 10 to 12 minutes. Add 2 teaspoons lemon juice and 1½ teaspoons chopped fresh mint with accumulated chicken juices. Substitute additional 1½ teaspoons chopped fresh mint for Parmesan.

Chicken Marsala

Serves 4 • **Total Time: 1¼ hours**

Why This Recipe Works Developed in Italy after a successful 19th-century marketing campaign to promote Marsala wine from Sicily, this combination of chicken and mushrooms in wine sauce has become an Italian restaurant staple. Too often, however, the chicken is dry, the mushrooms flabby, and the sauce nondescript. We wanted a failproof recipe. We browned chicken breasts in a skillet to start and kept them warm while we prepared the mushrooms and sauce. The mushrooms went into the skillet next, but the chicken drippings burned. Our solution was to sauté some pancetta before browning the mushrooms, which rendered additional fat as well as added meaty flavor. We preferred sweet (as opposed to dry) Marsala for its depth of flavor and smooth finish. Some lemon juice tempered the Marsala's sweetness, while a little garlic and tomato paste rounded out the flavors. Finally, we whisked butter into the sauce at the end, for a rich finish and beautiful sheen.

> *Our wine of choice for this dish is Sweet Marsala Fine, an imported wine that gives the sauce body, soft edges, and a smooth finish. To make slicing the chicken easier, freeze it for 15 minutes.*

2 tablespoons vegetable oil

1 cup all-purpose flour

4 (5- to 6-ounce) boneless, skinless chicken breasts, tenderloins removed and breasts trimmed

½ teaspoon table salt

½ teaspoon pepper

2½ ounces pancetta (about 3 slices), cut into pieces 1 inch long and ⅛ inch wide

8 ounces white mushrooms, trimmed and sliced (about 2 cups)

1 garlic clove, minced

1 teaspoon tomato paste

1½ cups sweet Marsala

1½ tablespoons lemon juice

4 tablespoons unsalted butter, cut into 4 pieces

2 tablespoons minced fresh parsley

1. Adjust oven rack to lower-middle position, place large ovensafe dinner plate on oven rack, and heat oven to 200 degrees. Heat oil in 12-inch skillet over medium-high heat until shimmering. Meanwhile, place flour in shallow baking dish or pie plate. Halve chicken horizontally, then cover chicken halves with plastic wrap and pound cutlets to even ¼-inch thickness. Pat chicken breasts dry. Sprinkle both sides of breasts with salt and pepper; working with 1 piece at a time, coat both sides with flour. Place 4 floured cutlets in single layer in skillet and cook until golden brown, about 3 minutes. Using tongs, flip cutlets and cook on second side until golden brown and meat feels firm when pressed with your finger, about 3 minutes longer. Transfer chicken to heated plate and return plate to oven while cooking remaining 4 cutlets.

2. Return skillet to low heat and add pancetta; sauté, stirring occasionally and scraping up any browned bits, until pancetta is brown and crisp, about 4 minutes. Using slotted spoon, transfer pancetta to paper towel–lined plate. Add mushrooms and increase heat to medium-high; sauté, stirring occasionally and scraping pan bottom, until liquid released by mushrooms evaporates and mushrooms begin to brown, about 8 minutes. Add garlic, tomato paste, and cooked pancetta; sauté while stirring until tomato paste begins to brown, about 1 minute. Off heat, add Marsala; return pan to high heat and simmer vigorously, scraping up any browned bits, until sauce is slightly syrupy and reduced to about 1¼ cups, about 5 minutes. Off heat, add lemon juice and any accumulated juices from chicken; whisk in butter 1 piece at a time. Season with salt and pepper to taste, and stir in parsley. Pour sauce over chicken and serve immediately.

Next-Level Chicken Piccata

Serves 4 to 6 • **Total Time: 1¼ hours**

Why This Recipe Works Chicken piccata needs little introduction—chicken breasts pounded thin, lightly dusted with flour, pan-seared, and bathed in a lemon-butter pan sauce. We wanted an updated recipe for tender chicken and a complex, lemony sauce. First, we used an innovative approach to butchering and cooking chicken cutlets: We cut each chicken breast in half crosswise, and then halved the thicker portion horizontally to make three similar-size pieces that required only minimal pounding to become cutlets. We salted the cutlets briefly to boost their ability to retain moisture and then lightly coated them in flour, which helped with browning. We seared the cutlets quickly and set them aside while making the sauce. We chose to include both lemon juice and lemon slices in the sauce for complexity and textural appeal. We then returned the cutlets to the pan to cook through and to wash any excess starch into the sauce, eliminating a gummy coating. Briny capers and a few tablespoons of butter finished the sauce, while a sprinkling of parsley added freshness.

> *Serve with buttered pasta, white rice, potatoes, or crusty bread and a simple steamed vegetable.*

Practice Makes Perfect

"This was the very first recipe I developed at America's Test Kitchen. I had just moved to Boston for a test cook position; I was in my twenties and eager to impress. I tested this recipe many more times than I needed to because I was trying to get the hang of things in the test kitchen. I had never worked in a kitchen where you cooked things just to learn. In this kitchen, it was OK to make a mistake. I was very proud when this recipe was published, and I have a framed copy of it as a memento.

I'm also proud to say that this recipe has survived the test of time with my family and friends, who consider it the ultimate Marsala to which all others are measured. One of my friends doubles the sauce because her two sons like to drizzle it over the other things on their dinner plate. The key is that the sauce is made with all wine. It gives the sauce a punchy flavor and gorgeous, glossy appearance."

—Julia

4. Add remaining 1 teaspoon oil and shallot to skillet and cook until softened, 1 minute. Add garlic and cook until fragrant, 30 seconds. Add broth, reserved lemon juice, and reserved lemon slices and bring to simmer, scraping up any browned bits.

5. Add cutlets to sauce and simmer for 4 minutes, flipping halfway through simmering. Transfer cutlets to platter. Sauce should be thickened to consistency of heavy cream; if not, simmer 1 minute longer. Off heat, whisk in butter. Stir in capers and parsley. Season with salt and pepper to taste. Spoon sauce over chicken and serve.

4 (6- to 8-ounce) boneless, skinless chicken breasts, trimmed
2 teaspoons kosher salt
½ teaspoon pepper
2 large lemons
¾ cup all-purpose flour
¼ cup plus 1 teaspoon vegetable oil, divided
1 shallot, minced
1 garlic clove, minced
1 cup chicken broth
3 tablespoons unsalted butter, cut into 6 pieces
2 tablespoons capers, drained
1 tablespoon minced fresh parsley

1. Cut each chicken breast in half crosswise, then cut thick half in half again horizontally, creating 3 cutlets of similar thickness. Place cutlets between sheets of plastic wrap and gently pound to even ½-inch thickness. Place cutlets in bowl and toss with salt and pepper. Set aside for 15 minutes.

2. Halve 1 lemon lengthwise. Trim ends from 1 half, halve lengthwise again, then cut crosswise in ¼-inch-thick slices; set aside. Juice remaining half and whole lemon and set aside 3 tablespoons juice.

3. Spread flour in shallow dish. Working with 1 cutlet at a time, dredge cutlets in flour, shaking gently to remove excess. Place on wire rack set in rimmed baking sheet. Heat 2 tablespoons oil in 12-inch skillet over medium-high heat until just smoking. Place 6 cutlets in skillet, reduce heat to medium, and cook until golden brown on 1 side, 2 to 3 minutes. Flip and cook until golden brown on second side, 2 to 3 minutes. Return cutlets to wire rack. Repeat with 2 tablespoons oil and remaining 6 cutlets.

Best Chicken Parmesan

Serves 4 • Total Time: 1½ hours, plus 20 minutes resting

Why This Recipe Works Classic chicken Parmesan should feature juicy chicken cutlets with a crisp pan-fried breaded coating, complemented by creamy mozzarella and a bright, zesty marinara sauce. But more often it ends up dry and overcooked, with a soggy crust and a chewy mass of cheese. To prevent the cutlets from overcooking, we halved them horizontally and pounded them to an even thickness. Then we salted them for 20 minutes to help them hold on to their moisture. To keep the crust crunchy, we replaced more than half of the sogginess-prone bread crumbs with flavorful grated Parmesan cheese. For a cheese topping that didn't turn chewy, we added some creamy fontina to the usual shredded mozzarella and ran it under the broiler for just 2 minutes to melt and brown. Melting the cheese directly on the fried cutlet formed a barrier between the crispy crust and the tomato sauce.

Our preferred brand of crushed tomatoes is San Merican. This recipe makes enough sauce to top the cutlets as well as four servings of pasta. Serve with pasta and a simple green salad.

Sauce
2 tablespoons extra-virgin olive oil, divided
2 garlic cloves, minced
¾ teaspoon kosher salt
¼ teaspoon dried oregano
   Pinch red pepper flakes
1 (28-ounce) can crushed tomatoes
¼ teaspoon sugar
2 tablespoons coarsely chopped fresh basil

Chicken

- 2 (6- to 8-ounce) boneless, skinless chicken breasts, trimmed, halved horizontally, and pounded ½ inch thick
- 1 teaspoon kosher salt
- 2 ounces whole-milk mozzarella cheese, shredded (½ cup)
- 2 ounces fontina cheese, shredded (½ cup)
- 1 large egg
- 1 tablespoon all-purpose flour
- 1½ ounces Parmesan cheese, grated (¾ cup)
- ½ cup panko bread crumbs
- ½ teaspoon garlic powder
- ¼ teaspoon dried oregano
- ¼ teaspoon pepper
- ⅓ cup vegetable oil
- ¼ cup torn fresh basil

1. For the sauce: Heat 1 tablespoon oil in medium saucepan over medium heat until shimmering. Add garlic, salt, oregano, and pepper flakes; cook, stirring occasionally, until fragrant, about 30 seconds. Stir in tomatoes and sugar; increase heat to high and bring to simmer. Reduce heat to medium-low and simmer until thickened, about 20 minutes. Off heat, stir in basil and remaining 1 tablespoon oil; season with salt and pepper to taste. Cover and keep warm.

2. For the chicken: Sprinkle each side of each cutlet with ⅛ teaspoon salt and let stand at room temperature for 20 minutes. Combine mozzarella and fontina in bowl; set aside.

3. Adjust oven rack 4 inches from broiler element and heat broiler. Whisk egg and flour together in shallow dish or pie plate until smooth. Combine Parmesan, panko, garlic powder, oregano, and pepper in second shallow dish or pie plate. Pat chicken dry with paper towels. Dredge 1 cutlet in egg mixture, allowing excess to drip off. Coat all sides in Parmesan mixture, pressing gently so crumbs adhere. Transfer cutlet to large plate and repeat with remaining cutlets.

4. Heat oil in 10-inch nonstick skillet over medium-high heat until shimmering. Carefully place 2 cutlets in skillet and cook without moving them until bottoms are crispy and deep golden brown, 1½ to 2 minutes. Using tongs, carefully flip cutlets and cook on second side until deep golden brown, 1½ to 2 minutes. Transfer cutlets to paper towel–lined plate and repeat with remaining cutlets.

5. Place cutlets on rimmed baking sheet and sprinkle cheese mixture evenly over cutlets, covering as much surface area as possible. Broil until cheese is melted and beginning to brown, 2 to 4 minutes. Transfer chicken to serving platter and top each cutlet with 2 tablespoons sauce. Sprinkle with basil and serve immediately, passing remaining sauce separately.

Buffalo Chicken Sandwiches

Serves 4 • Total Time: 1 hour, plus 1 hour resting

Why This Recipe Works For a sandwich that combines the spicy appeal of buffalo wings with the crunch of classic fried chicken, we used chicken breasts, the leanness of which allows the fiery hot sauce and tangy blue cheese dressing to shine. We dunked the meat in a generously salted egg mixture, not only to help the breading adhere but also to season the meat and keep it juicy. For the breading, we used all-purpose flour for crunch and added some cornstarch for crispness and baking powder for lightness. We mixed a small amount of buttermilk into the seasoned flour to create a shaggy coating that, after a rest in the refrigerator, adhered well to the chicken. This coating fried up into a satisfying crunchy crust with plenty of surface area for holding the maximum amount of buttery hot sauce, which we cooked down to thicken and intensify it. We spread only enough tangy blue cheese dressing on each sandwich to satisfy tradition and passed the remainder so that true enthusiasts could add extra. Shredded iceberg lettuce provided a cool, juicy contrast to the heat and tang of the chicken and the richness of the blue cheese spread.

Freezing the chicken breasts for 15 minutes will make them easier to halve horizontally. Use a Dutch oven that holds 6 quarts or more. If you prefer less spice, reduce or omit the cayenne in the sauce. An inexpensive Danish blue cheese works well here.

Chicken
- 1 cup all-purpose flour
- ½ cup cornstarch
- 1 teaspoon pepper
- 1 teaspoon cayenne pepper
- 1 teaspoon baking powder
- ¼ cup buttermilk
- 2 large eggs
- 1 teaspoon table salt
- 2 (6- to 8-ounce) boneless, skinless chicken breasts, trimmed, halved horizontally, and pounded ½ inch thick

Buffalo Sauce
- 1 tablespoon unsalted butter
- ½ teaspoon cayenne pepper
- ½ cup Frank's RedHot Original Cayenne Pepper Sauce
- 2 teaspoons cider vinegar

Blue Cheese Spread
- 2 ounces blue cheese, crumbled (½ cup)
- 2 tablespoons mayonnaise
- 2 tablespoons buttermilk
- 1 teaspoon cider vinegar

- 2 quarts vegetable oil for frying
- 4 hamburger buns, toasted if desired
- 2 cups finely shredded iceberg lettuce

1. For the chicken: Set wire rack in rimmed baking sheet. In wide, shallow bowl, whisk together flour, cornstarch, pepper, cayenne, and baking powder. Drizzle buttermilk over flour mixture and mix with your fingers until combined and small clumps form. In medium bowl, whisk together eggs and salt.

2. Working with 1 piece at a time, dip chicken in egg mixture and turn to coat. Lift from egg mixture, allowing excess to drip back into bowl. Coat both sides of chicken in flour mixture, pressing to form thick, bumpy coating. Place on prepared rack. Refrigerate, uncovered, for at least 1 hour or up to 8 hours. While chicken rests, make sauce and blue cheese spread.

3. For the buffalo sauce: Melt butter in small saucepan over medium heat. Add cayenne and cook, stirring constantly, until fragrant, about 30 seconds. Add hot sauce (mixture may sputter) and cook, stirring occasionally, until sauce is thickened and spatula drawn across bottom of pan leaves trail that takes longer than 5 seconds to fill in, 4 to 5 minutes. Remove from heat and stir in vinegar.

4. For the blue cheese spread: In small bowl, mash blue cheese with fork until no pieces larger than ¼ inch remain. Add mayonnaise and continue to mash until incorporated. Stir in buttermilk and vinegar until combined. Refrigerate until needed.

5. Place second wire rack in second rimmed baking sheet. Heat oil in large Dutch oven over medium-high heat to 425 degrees. Carefully transfer all chicken to oil and fry until chicken registers at least 155 degrees, 2 to 3 minutes. Transfer chicken to prepared rack. Using pastry brush, coat top of chicken with half of buffalo sauce.

6. Open buns on cutting board. Transfer 1 chicken piece, sauce side down, to each bun bottom. Brush remaining buffalo sauce over chicken. Top each chicken piece with ½ cup lettuce. Spread each bun top with 2 teaspoons blue cheese spread. Invert bun top onto each sandwich and serve, passing remaining blue cheese spread separately.

Pounding a Chicken Breast

To create chicken breasts of uniform thickness, simply pound thicker ends of breasts to same desired thickness. Though some breasts will still be larger in size, they will cook at same rate.

Braised Chicken Thighs with Fennel, Orange, and Cracked Olives

Serves 4 to 6 • **Total Time: 1½ hours**

Why This Recipe Works For this simple chicken braise, we started by searing bone-in, skin-on thighs to crisp the skin. We then transferred the thighs to the oven where they simmered, skin side up, in a flavorful mix of chicken broth, orange juice, fennel, and Pernod until they reached 195 degrees and turned meltingly tender and juicy. To finish the sauce, we reduced the braising liquid to concentrate its flavors before whisking in a cornstarch slurry to thicken it to a luxurious, velvety consistency. Last-minute additions of olives, orange zest, and minced fennel fronds made for a fragrant finish.

| *Serve with potatoes, rice, or buttered noodles.*

8 (5- to 7-ounce) bone-in chicken thighs, trimmed
1¼ teaspoons table salt
½ teaspoon pepper
1 tablespoon vegetable oil
1 small fennel bulb, finely chopped, plus 2 teaspoons fronds, minced
¼ teaspoon red pepper flakes
1 cup chicken broth
1 cup orange juice
2 tablespoons Pernod
2 teaspoons water
1½ teaspoons cornstarch
2 tablespoons lemon juice
½ teaspoon grated orange zest
18 Castelvetrano olives, pitted and cracked

1. Adjust oven rack to lower-middle position and heat oven to 325 degrees. Pat chicken dry with paper towels and sprinkle both sides with salt and pepper. Heat oil in 12-inch ovensafe skillet over medium heat until shimmering. Add chicken, skin side down, and cook, without moving it, until well browned, about 8 minutes. Using tongs, flip chicken and brown on second side, about 3 minutes. Transfer chicken to large plate.

2. Pour off all but 2 tablespoons fat from skillet. Add chopped fennel and cook, stirring frequently, until lightly browned, about 4 to 5 minutes. Add pepper flakes and cook, stirring constantly, for 1 minute. Add broth, orange juice, and Pernod; bring to simmer, scraping up any browned bits.

Return chicken to skillet skin side up (skin will be above surface of liquid). Transfer skillet to oven and bake, uncovered, until chicken registers 195 degrees, 35 to 40 minutes. Whisk water and cornstarch together in small bowl; set aside.

3. Using tongs, transfer chicken to serving platter and tent with aluminum foil. Place skillet over high heat. Cook, occasionally scraping side of skillet to incorporate fond, until sauce is thickened and reduced to 1½ cups, 8 to 10 minutes. Adjust heat to medium-low. Whisk cornstarch mixture to recombine and then whisk into sauce and simmer until thickened, about 1 minute. Off heat, whisk in lemon juice, orange zest, and olives. Season with salt and pepper to taste. Pour sauce around chicken, top with fennel fronds, and serve.

Filipino Chicken Adobo

Serves 4 • **Total Time: 1¼ hours, plus 30 minutes marinating**

Why This Recipe Works Adobo is the national dish of the Philippines, and chicken adobo is among the most popular versions. The dish consists of chicken simmered in a mixture of vinegar, soy sauce, garlic, bay leaves, and black pepper. Some versions of chicken adobo include coconut milk; we loved how its richness tempered the bracing acidity of the vinegar and masked the briny soy sauce, bringing the sauce into balance. But the fat from the coconut milk and the chicken skin made the sauce somewhat greasy.

To combat this, we borrowed a technique used in French bistros: We placed the meat skin side down in a cold pan and then turned up the heat. As the pan gradually got hotter, the fat under the chicken's skin melted away while the exterior browned.

Light coconut milk can be substituted for regular coconut milk. Serve this dish over rice.

8 (5- to 7-ounce) bone-in chicken thighs, trimmed
⅓ cup soy sauce
1 (13.5-ounce) can coconut milk
¾ cup cider vinegar
8 garlic cloves, peeled
4 bay leaves
2 teaspoons pepper
1 scallion, sliced thin

1. Toss chicken with soy sauce in large bowl. Refrigerate for at least 30 minutes or up to 1 hour.

2. Remove chicken from soy sauce, allowing excess to drip back into bowl. Transfer chicken, skin side down, to 12-inch nonstick skillet; set aside soy sauce.

3. Place skillet over medium-high heat and cook until chicken skin is browned, 7 to 10 minutes. While chicken is browning, whisk coconut milk, vinegar, garlic, bay leaves, and pepper into soy sauce.

4. Transfer chicken to plate and discard fat in skillet. Return chicken to skillet skin side down, add coconut milk mixture, and bring to boil. Reduce heat to medium-low and

simmer, uncovered, for 20 minutes. Flip chicken skin side up and continue to cook, uncovered, until chicken registers 175 degrees, about 15 minutes. Transfer chicken to platter and tent with aluminum foil.

5. Remove bay leaves and skim any fat off surface of sauce. Return skillet to medium-high heat and cook until sauce is thickened, 5 to 7 minutes. Pour sauce over chicken, sprinkle with scallion, and serve.

SEASON 9

Arroz con Pollo

Serves 4 to 6 • Total Time: 2 hours

Why This Recipe Works Arroz con pollo is a popular dish with countless variations throughout Latin America. Many traditional versions require an overnight marinade of the chicken and then a long, slow stewing with rice and vegetables. Could we find a way to achieve similar results in less time? We began by choosing chicken thighs, not only for shopping convenience but also to ensure that all the pieces would cook at the same rate—a problem when using a combination of white and dark meat. We poached the thighs in a broth preseasoned with a sofrito, a classic Latin American mixture of chopped onions and bell peppers. About half an hour before the chicken finished cooking, we added medium-grain rice (which we preferred over long-grain for its creamy texture), stirring it a few times to ensure even cooking. And for maximum flavor, we devised two marinades. Before cooking, we marinated the chicken quickly in garlic, oregano, and distilled white vinegar; after cooking we tossed the cooked chicken with olive oil, vinegar, and cilantro.

Some versions of arroz con pollo have a vibrant orange hue that comes from infusing oil with achiote, a tropical seed. Canned tomato sauce gave our dish a similar color and boosted its savory flavor.

To keep the dish from becoming greasy, remove any visible pockets of waxy yellow fat from the chicken and most of the skin, leaving just enough to protect the meat. To use long-grain rice instead of medium-grain, increase the amount of water added in step 2 from ¼ to ¾ cup and add the additional ¼ cup water in step 3 as needed. When removing the chicken from the bone in step 4, we found it better to use two spoons rather than two forks; forks tend to shred the meat, while spoons pull it apart in chunks.

6 garlic cloves, minced

1¾ teaspoons table salt, divided

1 tablespoon plus 2 teaspoons distilled white vinegar, divided

½ teaspoon dried oregano

½ teaspoon pepper

4 pounds bone-in chicken thighs, trimmed

2 tablespoons extra-virgin olive oil, divided

1 onion, chopped fine

1 small green bell pepper, stemmed, seeded, and chopped fine

¼ teaspoon red pepper flakes

¼ cup minced fresh cilantro, divided

1¾ cups chicken broth

1 (8-ounce) can tomato sauce

¼ cup water, plus extra as needed

3 cups medium-grain rice

½ cup green manzanilla olives, pitted and halved

1 tablespoon capers

½ cup jarred pimentos, cut into 2 by ¼-inch strips

Lemon wedges

1. Adjust oven rack to middle position and heat oven to 350 degrees. Place garlic and 1 teaspoon salt in large bowl; using rubber spatula, mix to make smooth paste. Add 1 tablespoon vinegar, oregano, and pepper to garlic-salt mixture; stir to combine. Place chicken in bowl with marinade. Coat chicken pieces evenly with marinade; set aside for 15 minutes.

2. Heat 1 tablespoon oil in Dutch oven over medium heat until shimmering. Add onion, bell pepper, and pepper flakes; cook, stirring occasionally, until vegetables begin to soften, 4 to 8 minutes. Add 2 tablespoons cilantro; stir to combine. Push vegetables to the sides of pot and increase heat to medium-high. Add chicken to clearing in center of pot, skin side down, in even layer. Cook, without moving chicken, until outer layer of meat becomes opaque, 2 to 4 minutes. (If chicken begins to brown, reduce heat to medium.) Using tongs, flip chicken and cook on second side until opaque, 2 to 4 minutes more. Add broth, tomato sauce, and water; stir to combine. Bring to simmer; cover, reduce heat to medium-low, and simmer for 20 minutes.

3. Add rice, olives, capers, and remaining ¾ teaspoon salt; stir well. Bring to simmer, cover, and transfer pot to oven. After 10 minutes, remove pot from oven and stir chicken and rice once from bottom up. Cover and return pot to oven. After another 10 minutes, stir once more, adding another ¼ cup water if rice appears dry and bottom of pot is beginning to burn. Cover and return pot to oven; cook until rice has absorbed all liquid and is tender but still holds its shape and thickest part of thighs registers 175 degrees, about 10 minutes longer.

4. Using tongs, remove chicken from pot; replace lid and set pot aside. Remove and discard chicken skin; using 2 spoons, pull meat off bones in large chunks. Using your fingers, remove remaining fat and any dark veins from chicken pieces. Place chicken in large bowl and toss with remaining 1 tablespoon oil, remaining 2 teaspoons vinegar, remaining 2 tablespoons cilantro, and pimentos; season with salt and pepper to taste. Place chicken on top of rice, cover, and let stand until warmed through, about 5 minutes. Serve, passing lemon wedges separately.

VARIATION

Arroz con Pollo with Bacon and Roasted Red Peppers

Bacon adds a welcome layer of richness, and red peppers bring subtle sweet flavor and color to this variation. To use long-grain rice, increase the amount of water to ¾ cup in step 2 and the salt added in step 3 to 1 teaspoon.

Substitute 2 teaspoons sweet paprika for oregano and sherry vinegar for white vinegar. Fry 4 ounces (about 4 strips) bacon, cut into ½-inch pieces, in Dutch oven over medium heat until crisp, 6 to 8 minutes. Using slotted spoon, transfer bacon to paper towel–lined plate; pour off all but 1 tablespoon bacon fat. Continue with step 2, substituting 1 small red pepper, chopped fine, and 1 carrot, chopped fine, for green pepper and sautéing vegetables in bacon fat. Continue with recipe, substituting ¼ cup minced fresh parsley leaves for cilantro, omitting olives and capers, and substituting ½ cup roasted red peppers, cut into 2 by ¼-inch strips, for pimentos. Garnish chicken and rice with reserved bacon before serving.

Skillet Jambalaya

Serves 4 to 6 • Total Time: 1½ hours

Why This Recipe Works Jambalaya, a hearty mix of chicken, andouille sausage, shrimp, and rice, is typically made in a Dutch oven and can take at least an hour to prepare. We wanted a quicker, easier version without sacrificing any of the complex flavors of this Creole classic. Using bone-in, skin-on chicken thighs rather than the typical whole cut-up chicken called for in many recipes saved us time and fuss. To mimic long-simmered flavor, we browned the chicken in the skillet, added the sausage, then cooked the vegetables in some of the rendered fat. We then stirred the rice in to coat it with the fat for deep flavor. For our cooking liquid, we relied on chicken broth and clam juice (to complement the shrimp). To prevent the shrimp from overcooking, we cooked it for only a few minutes and allowed it to finish cooking through off the heat (the residual heat is hot enough to cook it through). Entirely made in a skillet, this jambalaya makes a fast and satisfying supper.

> *If you cannot find andouille sausage, either chorizo or linguica can be substituted. For a spicier jambalaya, you can add ¼ teaspoon of cayenne pepper along with the vegetables, and/or serve it with hot sauce.*

1½ pounds bone-in chicken thighs, trimmed
¾ teaspoon table salt, divided
⅛ teaspoon pepper
5 teaspoons vegetable oil, divided
8 ounces andouille sausage, halved lengthwise and sliced into ¼-inch pieces
1 onion, chopped
1 red bell pepper, stemmed, seeded, and chopped
5 garlic cloves, minced
1½ cups long-grain white rice
2½ cups chicken broth
1 (14.5-ounce) can diced tomatoes, drained
1 (8-ounce) bottle clam juice
1 pound large shrimp (31 to 40 per pound), peeled and deveined
2 tablespoons chopped fresh parsley

1. Pat chicken dry with paper towels, then sprinkle with ¼ teaspoon salt and pepper. Heat 2 teaspoons oil in 12-inch nonstick skillet over medium-high heat until just smoking. Carefully lay chicken thighs in skillet, skin side down, and cook until golden, 4 to 6 minutes. Flip chicken over and continue to cook until second side is golden, about 3 minutes. Remove pan from heat and transfer chicken to plate. Using paper towels, remove and discard browned chicken skin.

2. Pour off all but 2 teaspoons fat left in skillet and return to medium-high heat until shimmering. Add andouille and cook until lightly browned, about 3 minutes; transfer sausage to small bowl and set aside.

3. Add remaining 1 tablespoon oil to skillet and return to medium heat until shimmering. Add onion, bell pepper, garlic, and remaining ½ teaspoon salt; cook, scraping up any browned bits, until onion is softened, about 5 minutes. Add rice and cook until edges turn translucent, about 3 minutes. Stir in broth, tomatoes, and clam juice; bring to simmer. Gently nestle chicken and any accumulated juices into rice. Cover; reduce heat to low; and cook until chicken is tender and cooked through, 30 to 35 minutes.

4. Transfer chicken to plate and cover with aluminum foil to keep warm. Stir shrimp and sausage into rice and continue to cook, covered, over low heat for 2 minutes. Remove skillet from heat and let stand, covered, until shrimp are fully cooked and rice is tender, about 5 minutes. Meanwhile, shred chicken into bite-size pieces. Stir parsley and shredded chicken into rice, season with salt and pepper to taste, and serve.

Coq au Vin

Serves 4 • Total Time: 1¾ to 2½ hours

Why This Recipe Works Although conventional recipes for coq au vin take upwards of 3 hours to prepare, we felt that this rustic dish didn't have to be so time-consuming. After all, it's similar to chicken fricassee. We wanted to create a dish with tender, juicy chicken infused with the flavors of red wine, onions, mushrooms, and bacon in under 2 hours. We decided to use chicken parts; this way, we could pick the parts we liked best. If using a mix of dark and white meat, we found it was essential to start the dark before the white, so that all the meat finished cooking at the same time and nothing was overcooked or undercooked. To thicken the stewing liquid, we sprinkled flour over the sautéed vegetables and whisked in butter toward the end of cooking; the butter also provided a nice richness in the sauce. Chicken broth added a savory note to the sauce and gave it some body; an entire bottle of red wine provided a great base of flavor. Tomato paste was a fuss-free way to add extra depth and body to the sauce, while a sprinkling of crisp, salty bacon rounded out the acidity of the wine.

> *Use any $10 bottle of fruity, medium-bodied red wine, such as Pinot Noir, Côtes du Rhône, or Zinfandel. If you use both chicken breasts and thighs/drumsticks, we recommend cutting the breast pieces in half so that each person can have some white meat and dark meat. The breasts and thighs/drumsticks do not cook at the same rate; if using both, note that the breast pieces are added partway through the cooking time. Serve with egg noodles.*

5 slices thick-cut bacon, chopped
   Vegetable oil
4 pounds bone-in, skin-on chicken pieces (split breasts cut in half, drumsticks, and/or thighs)
¾ teaspoon table salt
¾ teaspoon pepper
2 cups frozen pearl onions
10 ounces white mushrooms, trimmed and quartered
2 garlic cloves, minced
1 tablespoon tomato paste
3 tablespoons all-purpose flour
1 (750-ml) bottle medium-bodied red wine
2½ cups chicken broth
1 teaspoon minced fresh thyme or ¼ teaspoon dried
2 bay leaves
2 tablespoons unsalted butter, cut into 2 pieces, chilled
2 tablespoons minced fresh parsley

1. Fry bacon in large Dutch oven over medium heat until crisp, 5 to 7 minutes. Transfer bacon to paper towel–lined plate, leaving fat in pot (you should have about 2 tablespoons; if necessary, add vegetable oil to make this amount). Set aside.

2. Pat chicken dry with paper towels and sprinkle with salt and pepper. Return pot with bacon fat to medium-high heat until shimmering. Brown half of chicken on both sides, 5 to 8 minutes per side, reducing heat if pan begins to scorch. Transfer chicken to plate, leaving fat in pot. Return pot to medium-high heat and repeat with remaining chicken; transfer chicken to plate.

3. Pour off all but 1 tablespoon fat in pot (or add vegetable oil if needed to make this amount). Add onions and mushrooms and cook over medium heat, stirring occasionally, until lightly browned, about 10 minutes. Stir in garlic and tomato paste and cook until fragrant, about 30 seconds. Stir in flour and cook for 1 minute. Stir in wine, broth, thyme, and bay leaves, scraping up any browned bits.

4. Nestle chicken, along with any accumulated juices, into pot and bring to simmer. Cover, turn heat to medium-low, and simmer until chicken is tender and thickest part of breasts registers 160 to 165 degrees, about 20 minutes, or thickest part of thighs and drumsticks registers 175 degrees, about 1 hour. (If using both types of chicken, simmer thighs and drumsticks for 40 minutes before adding breasts.)

5. Transfer chicken to serving dish, tent with aluminum foil, and let rest while finishing sauce. Skim as much fat as possible off surface of sauce and return to simmer until sauce is thickened and measures about 2 cups, about 20 minutes. Off heat, remove bay leaves, whisk in butter, and season with salt and pepper to taste. Pour sauce over chicken, sprinkle with reserved bacon and parsley, and serve.

Chicken with 40 Cloves of Garlic

Serves 4 • Total Time: 2 hours, plus 30 minutes brining

Why This Recipe Works In many versions of chicken with 40 cloves of garlic, the garlic is soft and spreadable, but its flavor is spiritless. The chicken is tender, but the breast meat takes on a dry, chalky quality, and its flavor is washed-out. We wanted to revisit this classic French dish so it would boast well-browned, full-flavored chicken, sweet and nutty garlic, and a savory sauce. Using a cut-up chicken rather than a whole bird ensured that the meat cooked quickly and evenly. We roasted the garlic cloves first to develop their flavor, then added them to the braising liquid. Cooking it all with a pan-roasting/braising technique kept the chicken moist, and finishing the chicken under the broiler made the skin crispy. Shallots and herbs added flavor to the sauce, and several roasted garlic cloves, smashed into a paste, thickened and flavored the sauce.

> *If using a kosher chicken, skip the brining process and begin with step 2. Avoid heads of garlic that have begun to sprout (the green shoots will make the sauce taste bitter). Tie the rosemary and thyme sprigs together with kitchen twine so they will be easy to retrieve from the pan. Serve the dish with slices of crusty baguette; you can spread them with the roasted garlic cloves.*

¼ cup table salt for brining
¾ teaspoon pepper, divided
1 (3½- to 4-pound) whole chicken, cut into 8 pieces (4 breast pieces, 2 drumsticks, 2 thighs)
3 garlic heads, outer papery skins removed, cloves separated and unpeeled
2 shallots, peeled and quartered
1 tablespoon extra-virgin olive oil, divided
½ teaspoon table salt
¾ cup dry vermouth or dry white wine
¾ cup chicken broth
2 sprigs fresh thyme
1 sprig fresh rosemary
1 bay leaf
2 tablespoons unsalted butter

1. Adjust oven rack to middle position and heat oven to 400 degrees. Dissolve ¼ cup salt in 2 quarts cold water in large container; submerge chicken in brine, cover, and refrigerate for 30 minutes. Remove chicken from brine and pat dry with paper towels. Sprinkle both sides of chicken pieces with ½ teaspoon pepper.

2. Meanwhile, combine garlic, shallots, 2 teaspoons oil, salt, and remaining ¼ teaspoon pepper in 9-inch pie plate; cover tightly with aluminum foil and roast until softened and beginning to brown, about 30 minutes, shaking pan once halfway through cooking. Uncover, stir, and continue to roast, uncovered, until browned and fully tender, about 10 minutes longer, stirring once or twice. Remove from oven and increase oven temperature to 450 degrees.

3. Heat remaining 1 teaspoon oil in 12-inch ovensafe skillet over medium-high heat until just smoking. Brown chicken, skin side down, until golden, about 5 minutes; flip chicken pieces and brown until golden on second side, about 4 minutes longer. Transfer chicken to large plate and pour off fat from skillet. Off heat, add vermouth, chicken broth, thyme, rosemary, and bay leaf to pan, scraping up any browned bits. Set skillet over medium heat, add garlic mixture, and return chicken, skin side up, to pan, nestling pieces on top of and between garlic cloves. Place skillet in oven and roast until the thickest part of breasts registers 160 to 165 degrees; remove skillet from oven.

4. Adjust oven rack 6 inches from broiler element and heat broiler. Broil chicken to crisp skin, 3 to 5 minutes. Remove skillet from oven and transfer chicken to serving dish. Transfer 10 to 12 garlic cloves to fine-mesh sieve and reserve. Using slotted spoon, scatter remaining garlic cloves and shallots around chicken; discard herbs. Using rubber spatula, push reserved garlic cloves through sieve and into bowl; discard skins. Add garlic paste to skillet and bring liquid to simmer over medium-high heat, whisking to incorporate garlic. Whisk in butter and season with salt and pepper to taste. Serve chicken, passing sauce separately.

Cutting Up a Whole Chicken

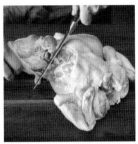

1. Using chef's knife, cut off legs, one at a time, by severing joint between leg and body.

2. Cut each leg into 2 pieces—drumstick and thigh—by slicing through joint that connects them (marked by thick white line of fat).

3. Flip chicken over and remove wings by slicing through each wing joint. Save wings for another purpose.

4. Turn chicken (now without its legs and wings) on its side and, using scissors, remove back from chicken breast.

5. Flip breast skin side down and, using chef's knife, cut it in half through breast plate (marked by thin white line of cartilage), then cut each piece in half again.

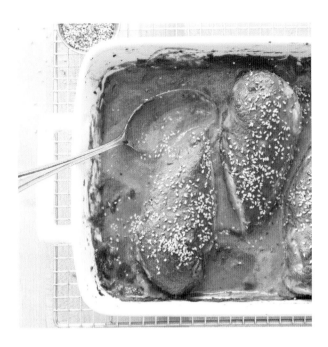

SEASON 16

Chicken in Mole-Poblano Sauce

Serves 4 to 6 • **Total Time: 2½ hours**

Why This Recipe Works The most famous of Mexico's moles, mole poblano often relies on as many as six types of chiles for its deep richness. We pared our recipe down to two: ancho, for a robust chile base; and chipotle, for smoky, intense chile flavor. Using almond butter instead of ground almonds was a simple shortcut that lent a luxurious, velvety texture to the sauce. Just 1 ounce of chocolate added richness and depth but didn't make the sauce taste chocolaty. We added warmth and a touch of sweetness with cinnamon, cloves, and raisins. Sautéing the chiles, chocolate, and spices along with the onion and garlic deepened the flavor of the final sauce. Simmering the mole for just 10 minutes thickened the sauce to the perfect consistency. Bone-in chicken pieces worked perfectly with our mole, and removing the skin kept it from turning soggy in the sauce.

Feel free to substitute ½ teaspoon ground chipotle chile powder or ½ teaspoon minced canned chipotles in adobo sauce for the chipotle chile (we noted little difference in flavor) and add with the cinnamon in step 2. Serve with rice.

2 dried ancho chiles, stemmed, seeded, and torn into ½-inch pieces (½ cup)

½ dried chipotle chile, stemmed, seeded, and torn into ½-inch pieces (scant tablespoon)

3 tablespoons vegetable oil

1 onion, chopped fine

1 ounce bittersweet, semisweet, or Mexican chocolate, chopped coarse

½ teaspoon ground cinnamon

⅛ teaspoon ground cloves

2 garlic cloves, minced

2 cups chicken broth

1 (14.5-ounce) can diced tomatoes, drained

¼ cup raisins

¼ cup almond butter

2 tablespoons sesame seeds, plus extra for garnish, toasted
   Sugar

3½ pounds bone-in chicken pieces (split breasts, drumsticks, and/or thighs), skin removed, trimmed

¼ teaspoon table salt

¼ teaspoon pepper

1. Toast anchos and chipotle in 12-inch skillet over medium heat, stirring frequently, until fragrant, 2 to 6 minutes; transfer to plate. Add oil and onion to now-empty skillet and cook over medium-high heat until softened, 5 to 7 minutes.

2. Stir in chocolate, cinnamon, cloves, and toasted chiles and cook until chocolate is melted and bubbly, about 2 minutes. Stir in garlic and cook until fragrant, about 30 seconds. Stir in broth, tomatoes, raisins, almond butter, and sesame seeds and bring to simmer. Reduce heat to medium and simmer gently, stirring occasionally, until slightly thickened and measures about 3½ cups, about 7 minutes.

3. Transfer mixture to blender and process until smooth, about 20 seconds. Season with salt, pepper, and sugar to taste. (Sauce can be refrigerated for up to 3 days; loosen with water as needed before continuing.)

4. Adjust oven rack to middle position and heat oven to 400 degrees. Pat chicken dry with paper towels and sprinkle with salt and pepper. Arrange chicken in single layer in shallow baking dish and cover with mole sauce, turning to coat chicken evenly. Bake, uncovered, until breasts register 160 degrees, and thighs or drumsticks register 175 degrees, 35 to 45 minutes.

5. Remove chicken from oven, tent with aluminum foil, and let rest for 5 to 10 minutes. Sprinkle with extra sesame seeds and serve.

SEASON 9

French Chicken in a Pot

Serves 4 • Total Time: 2¼ to 2¾ hours, plus 20 minutes resting

Why This Recipe Works Poulet en cocotte (chicken in a pot) is a classic French specialty—at its best, it's a whole chicken baked with root vegetables in a covered pot that delivers incredibly tender and juicy meat. One potential problem is too much moisture in the pot, which washes out the flavor; another pitfall is overcooking. We removed the vegetables—the liquid they released made the pot too steamy—and cooked the chicken by itself. We also tightly sealed the pot with foil before adding the lid. To keep the breast meat from drying out and becoming tough, we cooked the chicken very slowly. After developing the basic technique, we revisited the idea of vegetables, and found that a small amount of potently flavored aromatic vegetables could be added if they were lightly browned with the chicken to erase most of their moisture. Finally, defatting the liquid in the pot rewarded us with a richly flavored sauce.

The cooking times in the recipe are for a 4½- to 5-pound bird. A 3½- to 4½-pound chicken will take about an hour to cook, and a 5- to 6-pound bird will take close to 2 hours. We developed this recipe to work with a 5- to 8-quart Dutch oven with a tight-fitting lid. If using a 5-quart pot, do not cook a chicken larger than 5 pounds. If using a kosher chicken, reduce the amount of table salt to ½ teaspoon. If you choose not to serve the skin with the chicken, simply remove it before carving. The amount of sauce will vary depending on the size of the chicken; season it with about ¼ teaspoon lemon juice for every ¼ cup.

1 (4½- to 5-pound) whole chicken, giblets discarded, wings tucked under back
1 teaspoon table salt
¼ teaspoon pepper
1 tablespoon extra-virgin olive oil
1 small onion, chopped
1 small celery rib, chopped
6 garlic cloves, peeled and trimmed
1 bay leaf
1 sprig fresh rosemary (optional)
½–1 teaspoon lemon juice

1. Adjust oven rack to lowest position and heat oven to 250 degrees. Pat chicken dry with paper towels and sprinkle with salt and pepper.

2. Heat oil in large Dutch oven over medium heat until just smoking. Add chicken, breast side down, and scatter onion, celery, garlic cloves, bay leaf, and rosemary (if using) around chicken. Cook until breast is lightly browned, about 5 minutes. Flip chicken breast side up and continue to cook until chicken and vegetables are well browned, 6 to 8 minutes.

3. Off heat, place large sheet of aluminum foil over pot and cover tightly with lid. Transfer pot to oven and cook until thickest part of breast registers 160 to 165 degrees and thickest part of the thighs registers 175 degrees, 1 hour and 20 minutes to 1 hour and 50 minutes.

4. Remove pot from oven. Transfer chicken to carving board, tent with foil, and let rest for 20 minutes. Strain chicken juices from pot into fat separator, pressing on solids to extract liquid; discard solids (you should have about ¾ cup juices). Let liquid settle for 5 minutes, then pour into saucepan and cook over low heat until hot. Carve chicken, adding any accumulated juices to saucepan. Season sauce with lemon juice to taste. Serve chicken, passing sauce separately.

SEASON 19
Indoor Pulled Chicken

Serves 6 to 8 • **Total Time: 1¼ hours**

Why This Recipe Works Traditional pulled chicken is a true labor of love. We wanted a stovetop version that had the texture and flavor of outdoor slow-smoked pulled chicken but that came together in just a fraction of the time. We started by braising boneless, skinless chicken thighs in a mixture of chicken broth, salt, sugar, molasses, gelatin, and liquid smoke. The liquid smoke simulated the flavor of traditional smoked chicken, while the gelatin and broth mimicked the unctuous texture and intense flavor

of whole chicken parts. To mimic the richness of skin-on chicken, we skipped trimming the fat and added the rendered fat back to the finished chicken. Finally, we mixed the shredded meat with a homemade barbecue sauce.

Do not trim the fat from the chicken thighs; it contributes to the flavor and texture of the pulled chicken. If you don't have 3 tablespoons of fat to add back to the pot in step 3, add melted butter to make up the difference. We like mild molasses in this recipe; do not use blackstrap. Serve the pulled chicken on white bread or hamburger buns with pickles and coleslaw.

1 cup chicken broth
2 tablespoons molasses
1 tablespoon sugar
1 tablespoon liquid smoke, divided
1 teaspoon unflavored gelatin
1 teaspoon table salt
2 pounds boneless, skinless chicken thighs, halved crosswise
1 recipe barbecue sauce (recipes follow)
Hot sauce

1. Bring broth, molasses, sugar, 2 teaspoons liquid smoke, gelatin, and salt to boil in large Dutch oven over high heat, stirring to dissolve sugar. Add chicken and return to simmer. Reduce heat to medium-low; cover; and cook, stirring occasionally, until chicken is easily shredded with fork, about 25 minutes.

2. Transfer chicken to medium bowl and set aside. Strain cooking liquid through fine-mesh strainer set over bowl (do not wash pot). Let liquid settle for 5 minutes; skim fat from surface. Set aside fat and defatted liquid.

3. Using tongs, squeeze chicken until shredded into bite-size pieces. Transfer chicken, 1 cup barbecue sauce, ½ cup reserved defatted liquid, 3 tablespoons reserved fat, and remaining 1 teaspoon liquid smoke to now-empty pot. Cook mixture over medium heat, stirring frequently, until liquid has been absorbed and exterior of meat appears dry, about 5 minutes. Season with salt, pepper, and hot sauce to taste. Serve, passing remaining barbecue sauce separately.

Lexington Vinegar Barbecue Sauce

Makes 2 cups • Total Time: 10 minutes

For a spicier sauce, add hot sauce to taste.

- 1 cup cider vinegar
- ½ cup ketchup
- ½ cup water
- 1 tablespoon sugar
- ¾ teaspoon table salt
- ¾ teaspoon red pepper flakes
- ½ teaspoon pepper

Whisk all ingredients together in bowl.

South Carolina Mustard Barbecue Sauce

Makes 2 cups • Total Time: 10 minutes

You can use either light or dark brown sugar in this recipe.

- 1 cup yellow mustard
- ½ cup distilled white vinegar
- ¼ cup packed brown sugar
- ¼ cup Worcestershire sauce
- 2 tablespoons hot sauce
- 1 teaspoon table salt
- 1 teaspoon pepper

Whisk all ingredients together in bowl.

Sweet and Tangy Barbecue Sauce

Makes 2 cups • Total Time: 10 minutes

We like mild molasses in this recipe.

- 1½ cups ketchup
- ¼ cup molasses
- 2 tablespoons Worcestershire sauce
- 1 tablespoon hot sauce
- ½ teaspoon table salt
- ½ teaspoon pepper

Whisk all ingredients together in bowl.

SEASON 17

Tinga de Pollo

Serves 6 • Total Time: 1¼ hours

Why This Recipe Works Smoky, earthy tinga de pollo is a traditional taco filling that combines shredded chicken meat with a flavorful tomato-chipotle sauce. At first, we poached chicken breast meat separately from the sauce and combined the two only briefly at the end. We realized, though, that we could achieve a deeper flavor by using boneless thighs and cooking them in the spicy, tomatoey sauce. Fire-roasted tomatoes increased the sauce's smokiness, and a little brown sugar and lime juice and zest further boosted the dish's complexity. Simmering the cooked shredded chicken in the sauce for a full 10 minutes before serving gave the sauce a chance to thicken and loosened the chicken's muscle fibers so the sauce could really take hold and cling to the meat, making more cohesive tacos. Final toppings of fresh cilantro, scallions, avocado, crumbled Cotija cheese, and lime juice added the perfect amount of contrasting cool flavors.

If you have a little extra time, homemade tortillas (recipe follows) will take these tacos to the next level. In addition to the Escabeche (recipe follows) and the toppings included here, Mexican crema (or sour cream) and minced onion are also good choices. If you can't find Cotija cheese, substitute feta. The shredded chicken mixture also makes a good topping for tostadas.

Chicken

- 2 pounds boneless, skinless chicken thighs, trimmed
- ½ teaspoon table salt
- ½ teaspoon pepper
- 2 tablespoons vegetable oil, divided
- 1 onion, halved and sliced thin
- 3 garlic cloves, minced
- 1 (14.5-ounce) can fire-roasted diced tomatoes
- ½ cup chicken broth
- 2 tablespoons minced canned chipotle chile in adobo sauce plus 2 teaspoons adobo sauce
- 1 teaspoon ground cumin
- ½ teaspoon brown sugar
- ¼ teaspoon cinnamon
- 1 teaspoon grated lime zest plus 2 tablespoons juice

Tacos

- 12 (6-inch) corn tortillas, warmed
- 1 avocado, halved, pitted, and cut into ½-inch pieces
- 2 ounces Cotija cheese, crumbled (½ cup)
- 6 scallions, minced
  Fresh cilantro leaves
  Lime wedges

1. For the chicken: Pat chicken dry with paper towels and sprinkle with salt and pepper. Heat 1 tablespoon oil in Dutch oven over medium-high heat until shimmering. Add half of chicken and brown on both sides, 3 to 4 minutes per side. Transfer to large plate. Repeat with remaining chicken.

2. Reduce heat to medium, add remaining 1 tablespoon oil to now-empty pot, and heat until shimmering. Add onion and cook, stirring frequently, until browned, about 7 minutes. Add garlic and cook until fragrant, about 1 minute. Add tomatoes and their juice, broth, chipotle and adobo sauce, cumin, sugar, and cinnamon and bring to boil, scraping up any browned bits.

3. Return chicken to pot; reduce heat to medium-low; cover; and simmer until meat registers 195 degrees, about 15 minutes, flipping chicken after 5 minutes. Transfer chicken to cutting board.

4. Transfer cooking liquid to blender and process until smooth, 15 to 30 seconds. Return cooking liquid to pot. When cool enough to handle, use 2 forks to shred chicken into bite-size pieces. Return chicken to pot with cooking liquid. Cook over medium heat, stirring frequently, until sauce is thickened and clings to chicken, about 10 minutes. Stir in lime zest and juice. Season with salt and pepper to taste.

5. For the tacos: Spoon chicken into center of each warm tortilla and serve immediately, passing avocado, Cotija, scallions, cilantro, and lime wedges separately.

Escabeche

Makes 2 cups • Total Time: 20 minutes, plus 30 minutes cooling

For a less spicy pickle, remove the seeds from the jalapeño.

- ½ teaspoon coriander seeds
- ¼ teaspoon cumin seeds
- 1 cup apple cider vinegar
- ½ cup water
- 1½ teaspoons sugar
- ¼ teaspoon table salt
- 1 red onion, halved and sliced thin
- 2 carrots, peeled and sliced thin
- 1 jalapeño, stemmed and sliced thin into rings

Heat coriander seeds and cumin seeds in medium saucepan over medium heat, stirring frequently, until fragrant, about 2 minutes. Add vinegar, water, sugar, and salt and bring to boil, stirring to dissolve sugar and salt. Remove saucepan from heat and add onion, carrots, and jalapeño, pressing to submerge vegetables. Cover and let cool completely, 30 minutes. (Cooled vegetables can be refrigerated for up to 1 week.)

Corn Tortillas

Makes twenty-two 5-inch tortillas
Total Time: 1½ hours

Pressing the dough between a zipper-lock bag that has been cut open at the sides prevents it from sticking to the pie plate. Distribute your weight evenly over the dough when pressing. Using a clear pie plate makes it easy to see the tortilla. A tortilla press, of course, can also be used. You can find masa harina in the international aisle or near the flour.

- 2 cups (8 ounces) masa harina
- 2 teaspoons vegetable oil, divided
- ¼ teaspoon table salt
- 1¼ cups warm water, plus extra as needed

1. Cut sides of sandwich-size zipper-lock bag but leave bottom seam intact so that bag unfolds completely. Place open bag on counter and line large plate with 2 damp dish towels.

2. Mix masa, 1 teaspoon oil, and salt together in medium bowl. Using rubber spatula, stir in warm water to form soft dough. Using your hands, knead dough in bowl, adding extra warm water, 1 tablespoon at a time, until dough is soft and tacky but not sticky (texture is like Play-Doh). Cover dough and set aside for 5 minutes.

3. Meanwhile, heat remaining 1 teaspoon oil in 8-inch nonstick skillet over medium-high heat until shimmering. Using paper towel, wipe out skillet, leaving thin film of oil on bottom. Pinch off 1-ounce piece of dough (about 2 tablespoons) and roll into smooth 1¼-inch ball. Cover remaining dough with damp paper towel. Place ball in center of open bag and fold other side of bag over ball. Using clear pie plate, press down on plastic to flatten ball into 5-inch disk, rotating plastic during pressing to ensure even thickness. Working quickly, gently peel plastic away from tortilla.

4. Carefully place tortilla in skillet and cook, without moving it, until tortilla moves freely when pan is shaken, about 30 seconds. Flip tortilla and cook until edges curl and bottom surface is spotty brown, about 1 minute. Flip tortilla again and continue to cook until bottom surface is spotty brown and puffs up in center, 30 to 60 seconds. Place toasted tortilla between 2 damp dish towels; repeat shaping and cooking with remaining dough. (Cooled tortillas can be transferred to zipper-lock bag and refrigerated for up to 5 days. Reheat before serving.)

SEASON 18

Tamales

Makes 18 tamales • Total Time: 2¼ hours, plus 30 minutes soaking

Why This Recipe Works Tamales are small, moist corn cakes that are stuffed with a variety of fillings, wrapped in corn husks, and steamed. Since they take a lot of time to prepare, they are usually made for holidays and special occasions. We wanted to simplify the process while staying true to the tamales' subtle but hearty flavor and light texture. Although masa dough (made from corn kernels that have been cooked with slaked lime, ground to a flour, and mixed with water) is traditional, it can be difficult to find in some supermarkets. Instead, we turned to widely available masa harina, but found that when used alone, it was too fine-textured and had bland corn flavor. Grits, on the other hand, had a granular texture similar to traditional tamales and didn't sacrifice any of the flavor. Frozen corn added more corn flavor and also some texture. To fold the tamales, most recipes require tying each one closed, a process we found we could do without by simply folding the tamales and placing them with the seam sides facing the edges of a steamer basket. For the filling, hearty chicken thighs worked best for the long cooking time. A combination of dried ancho and New Mexican chiles resulted in a sauce with subtle spice and sweetness. Once cooked, the tamales peeled easily away from the moist rich corn cakes.

We found it easiest to use large corn husks that measure about 8 inches long by 6 inches wide; if the husks are small, you may need to use two per tamale and shingle them as needed to hold all of the filling. You can substitute butter for the lard if desired, but the tamales will have a distinctive buttery flavor. Be sure to use quick, not instant, grits in this recipe. For an accurate measurement of boiling water, bring a full kettle of water to a boil and then measure out the desired amount.

  1 cup plus 2 tablespoons quick grits
1½ cups boiling water
  1 cup (4 ounces) plus 2 tablespoons masa harina
20 large dried corn husks
1½ cups frozen corn, thawed
  6 tablespoons unsalted butter, cut into ½-inch cubes and softened
  6 tablespoons lard, softened
  1 tablespoon sugar
2¼ teaspoons baking powder
  ¾ teaspoon table salt
  1 recipe Red Chile Chicken Filling (recipe follows)

1. Place grits in medium bowl; whisk in boiling water; and let stand until water is mostly absorbed, about 10 minutes. Stir in masa harina; cover; and let cool to room temperature, about 20 minutes. Meanwhile, place husks in large bowl; cover with hot water; and let soak until pliable, about 30 minutes.

2. Process masa dough, corn, butter, lard, sugar, baking powder, and salt in food processor until mixture is light, sticky, and very smooth, about 1 minute, scraping down sides as necessary. Remove husks from water and pat dry with dish towel.

3. Working with 1 husk at a time, lay on counter, cupped side up, with long side facing you and wide end on right side. Spread ¼ cup tamale dough into 4-inch square over bottom right-hand corner, pushing it flush to bottom edge but leaving 1½-inch border at wide edge. Mound scant 2 tablespoons filling in line across center of dough, parallel to bottom edge. Roll husk away from you and over filling, so that dough surrounds filling and forms cylinder. Fold up tapered end, leaving top open, and transfer seam side down to platter.

4. Fit large pot or Dutch oven with steamer basket, removing feet from steamer basket if pot is short. Fill pot with water until it just touches bottom of basket and bring to boil. Gently lay tamales in basket with open ends facing up and seam sides facing down. Cover and steam, checking water level often and adding additional water as needed, until tamales easily come free from husks, about 1 hour. Transfer tamales to large platter. Reheat remaining sauce from filling in covered bowl in microwave, about 30 seconds, and serve with tamales.

Tamales

Red Chile Chicken Filling

Makes enough for 18 tamales • Total Time: 1¼ hours

    4   dried ancho chiles, stemmed, seeded, and
        torn into ½-inch pieces (1 cup)
    4   dried New Mexican chiles, stemmed, seeded,
        and torn into ½-inch pieces (1 cup)
    3   tablespoons vegetable oil
    1   large onion, chopped
    6   garlic cloves, minced
    ¾   teaspoon ground cumin
    ¾   teaspoon dried oregano
    1   teaspoon table salt, divided
    3   cups chicken broth
    ½   teaspoon pepper
    1¼ pounds boneless, skinless chicken thighs, trimmed
    1½ tablespoons cider vinegar
        Sugar

1. Toast anchos and New Mexican chiles in 12-inch skillet over medium heat, stirring frequently, until fragrant, 2 to 6 minutes; transfer to bowl.

2. Heat oil in now-empty skillet over medium heat until shimmering. Add onion and cook until softened, 5 to 7 minutes. Stir in garlic, cumin, oregano, ½ teaspoon salt, and toasted chiles and cook for 30 seconds. Stir in broth and simmer until slightly reduced, about 10 minutes. Transfer mixture to blender and process until smooth, about 20 seconds; return to skillet.

3. Sprinkle chicken with pepper and remaining ½ teaspoon salt, nestle into skillet, and bring to simmer over medium heat. Cover; reduce heat to low; and cook until chicken registers 160 degrees, 20 to 25 minutes.

4. Transfer chicken to carving board and let cool slightly. Using 2 forks, shred chicken into small pieces. Stir vinegar into sauce and season with salt, pepper, and sugar to taste. Toss shredded chicken with 1 cup sauce. Reserve remaining sauce to serve with tamales.

Assembling Tamales

1. Arrange corn husk with long side parallel to counter edge. Spoon scant ¼ cup dough onto center of husk. Spread into 4-inch square, pushing it flush to bottom edge but leaving 1½-inch border at wide end.

2. Place scant 2 tablespoons of filling down center of dough. Roll husk away from you so that dough surrounds filling. It is important to roll tamales tightly so they don't leak while cooking.

3. Fold tapered end of tamale up, leaving top open, and transfer to platter, seam side down. Keeping tamales seam side down means you can skip tedious task of tying each one closed.

SEASON 9

Enchiladas Verdes

Serves 4 to 6 • Total Time: 2 hours, plus 20 minutes cooling

Why This Recipe Works We love the bright taste of enchiladas verdes. For our version, we wanted moist, tender chicken and fresh, citrusy flavors wrapped in soft corn tortillas and topped with just the right amount of melted cheese. The chicken was easy; we poached it in chicken broth enhanced with sautéed onion, garlic, and cumin. The green sauce is based on tomatillos and chiles. Jalapeños and serranos are good for adding heat, but we wanted a more complex herbal flavor, so we opted for poblanos. To get the characteristic char, we tossed the chiles and fresh tomatillos with a little oil and ran them under the broiler. Pulsed in a food processor and thinned with a bit of the broth left from poaching the chicken, the tomatillos and chiles formed a well-seasoned, chunky sauce. To enrich the filling, we liked pepper Jack cheese—and we sprinkled more on top of the dish before baking. To make the tortillas pliable and easy to roll, we sprayed them with vegetable oil spray and baked them for a few minutes. The enchiladas required just a brief stint in the oven to heat through and melt the cheese. Garnished with sour cream, scallions, and radishes, these enchiladas made a satisfying meal.

You can substitute 3 (11-ounce) cans tomatillos, drained and rinsed, for the fresh ones in this recipe. Halve large tomatillos (more than 2 inches in diameter) and place them skin side up for broiling in step 2 to ensure even cooking and charring. If you can't find poblanos, substitute four large jalapeño chiles (with seeds and ribs removed). To increase the spiciness of the sauce, reserve some of the chiles' ribs and seeds and add them to the food processor in step 3.

    4   teaspoons vegetable oil, divided
    1   onion, chopped
    3   garlic cloves, minced, divided
  ½   teaspoon ground cumin
1½   cups chicken broth
    1   pound boneless, skinless chicken breasts, trimmed
1½   pounds tomatillos (16 to 20 medium), husks and
        stems removed, rinsed well and dried
    3   poblano chiles, stemmed, halved, and seeded
1–2   teaspoons sugar
    1   teaspoon table salt
  ½   cup coarsely chopped fresh cilantro
    8   ounces pepper Jack or Monterey Jack cheese,
        grated (2 cups), divided
  12   (6-inch) corn tortillas
    2   scallions, sliced thin
        Thinly sliced radishes
        Sour cream

1. Adjust oven racks to middle and highest positions and heat broiler. Heat 2 teaspoons oil in medium saucepan over medium heat until shimmering; add onion and cook, stirring frequently, until golden, 6 to 8 minutes. Add 2 teaspoons garlic and cumin; cook, stirring frequently, until fragrant, about 30 seconds. Reduce heat to low and stir in broth. Add chicken; cover; and simmer until thickest part of chicken registers 160 to 165 degrees, 15 to 20 minutes, flipping chicken halfway through cooking. Transfer chicken to large bowl and place in refrigerator to cool, about 20 minutes. Remove ¼ cup liquid from saucepan and set aside; discard remaining liquid.

2. Meanwhile, toss tomatillos and poblanos with remaining 2 teaspoons oil; arrange on rimmed baking sheet lined with aluminum foil, with poblanos skin side up. Broil until vegetables blacken and start to soften, 5 to 10 minutes, rotating pan halfway through cooking. Cool for 10 minutes, then remove skin from poblanos (leave tomatillo skins intact). Transfer tomatillos and chiles to food processor. Reduce oven temperature to 350 degrees. Discard foil from baking sheet and set sheet aside for warming tortillas.

3. Add 1 teaspoon sugar, salt, remaining 1 teaspoon garlic, and reserved ¼ cup cooking liquid to food processor; pulse until sauce is somewhat chunky, about 8 pulses. Taste sauce; season with salt and pepper to taste and adjust tartness by stirring in remaining sugar, ½ teaspoon at a time. Set sauce aside (you should have about 3 cups).

4. When chicken is cool, pull into shreds using your hands or 2 forks, then chop into bite-size pieces. Combine chicken with cilantro and 1½ cups pepper Jack; season with salt to taste.

5. Smear bottom of 13 by 9-inch baking dish with ¾ cup tomatillo sauce. Place tortillas in single layer on two baking sheets. Spray both sides of tortillas lightly with vegetable oil spray. Bake until tortillas are soft and pliable, 2 to 4 minutes. Increase oven temperature to 450 degrees. Place warm tortillas on counter and spread ⅓ cup filling down center of each tortilla. Roll each tortilla tightly by hand and place in baking dish, seam side down. Pour remaining tomatillo sauce over top of enchiladas. Use back of a spoon to spread sauce so it coats top of each tortilla. Sprinkle with remaining ½ cup pepper Jack and cover baking dish with foil.

6. Bake enchiladas on middle oven rack until heated through and cheese is melted, 15 to 20 minutes. Uncover, sprinkle with scallions, and serve immediately, passing radishes and sour cream separately.

Oven-Roasted Chicken Thighs

Serves 4 • **Total Time: 55 minutes**

Why This Recipe Works More flavorful and less prone to overcooking than lean breasts, chicken thighs are a perfect weeknight dinner. The only problem is that the layer of fat underneath the skin that helps keep them moist during cooking often leads to flabby skin. To combat this, we cooked the thighs, skin side down, on a preheated baking sheet, until the skin was browned and rendered. We then flipped the thighs over and put them under the broiler briefly to dry and crisp the skin. The result was chicken thighs with succulent and juicy meat under a sheer layer of crackly crisp, deeply browned skin.

For best results, trim all visible fat from the thighs. Use a heavy-duty baking sheet and fully preheat the oven and baking sheet before adding the chicken. The chicken can be served plain or with Roasted Garlic Salsa Verde or Roasted Shallot and Mint Chutney (recipes follow).

8 (6- to 8-ounce) bone-in chicken thighs, trimmed
½ teaspoon table salt
½ teaspoon pepper
  Vegetable oil spray

1. Adjust oven racks to middle and lowest positions, place rimmed baking sheet on lower rack, and heat oven to 450 degrees.

2. Using metal skewer, poke skin side of chicken thighs 10 to 12 times. Sprinkle both sides of thighs with salt and pepper; spray skin lightly with vegetable oil spray. Place thighs skin side down on preheated baking sheet. Return sheet to bottom rack.

3. Roast chicken until skin side is beginning to brown and meat registers 160 degrees, 20 to 25 minutes, rotating pan as needed for even browning. Remove chicken from oven and heat broiler.

4. While broiler heats, flip chicken skin side up. Broil chicken on middle rack until skin is crisp and well browned and meat registers 175 degrees, about 5 minutes, rotating pan as needed for even browning. Transfer chicken to platter and let rest for 5 minutes. Serve.

ACCOMPANIMENTS
Roasted Garlic Salsa Verde
Makes ½ cup • Total Time: 30 minutes

1 garlic head, cloves separated, unpeeled
5 tablespoons extra-virgin olive oil, divided
2 tablespoons lemon juice
1 cup fresh parsley leaves
2 anchovy fillets, rinsed and patted dry
2 tablespoons capers, rinsed
¼ teaspoon table salt
¼ teaspoon red pepper flakes

1. While oven preheats for Oven-Roasted Chicken Thighs, toss garlic cloves and 1 tablespoon oil in bowl. Cover bowl and microwave until garlic is softened, 2 to 5 minutes, stirring once halfway through. Place garlic in center of 12-inch square of aluminum foil. Cover with second 12-inch square of foil; fold edges together to create packet about 7 inches square. Place packet on middle rack of oven for 10 minutes.

2. Remove packet from oven and squeeze garlic cloves out of skins. Process garlic, lemon juice, parsley, anchovies, capers, and salt in food processor until coarsely chopped, about 5 seconds. Add remaining ¼ cup oil and pepper flakes; pulse until combined, scraping bowl as necessary.

Roasted Shallot and Mint Chutney

Makes ½ cup • Total Time: 30 minutes

- 3 shallots, sliced thin
- ¼ cup vegetable oil, divided
- 1 cup fresh mint leaves
- ½ cup fresh cilantro leaves
- 1 jalapeño pepper, stemmed, seeded, and chopped
- 1 tablespoon lime juice
- ½ teaspoon sugar
- ¼ teaspoon table salt

1. While oven preheats for Oven-Roasted Chicken Thighs (page 234), toss shallots and 1 tablespoon oil in bowl. Cover bowl and microwave until shallots have softened, 2 to 5 minutes, stirring once halfway through. Place shallots in center of 12-inch square of aluminum foil. Cover with second 12-inch square of foil; fold edges together to create packet about 7 inches square. Place packet on middle rack of oven for 10 minutes.

2. Remove packet from oven. Process shallots, mint, cilantro, jalapeño, lime juice, sugar, and salt in food processor until finely chopped, about 5 seconds. With food processor running, slowly add remaining 3 tablespoons oil in steady stream until smooth, scraping down bowl as necessary.

SEASON 16

Slow-Roasted Chicken Parts with Shallot-Garlic Pan Sauce

Serves 8 • Total Time: 2¼ hours

Why This Recipe Works Slow roasting keeps chicken nice and juicy, but at a cost: The skin is often a bit flabby, padded with unrendered fat. For ultramoist roast chicken that boasted the shatteringly crisp skin we loved, we bypassed a whole chicken and turned to parts. We seared leg quarters and then split breasts in oil, rendering some of the fat and giving the crisping a head start. We moved the parts to a 250-degree oven, keeping the slower-cooking thighs on the back portion of the wire rack–lined sheet, facing the hotter side of the oven. While the chicken rested, we whisked together a simple pan sauce with butter, shallots, garlic, and coriander, adding a little powdered gelatin and cornstarch to give it the rich body of a jus. Before serving, we gave the skin a final crisping under the broiler.

To serve four people, halve the ingredient amounts.

- 5 pounds bone-in chicken pieces (4 split breasts and 4 leg quarters), trimmed
- 2 teaspoons kosher salt
- ½ teaspoon pepper
- ¼ teaspoon vegetable oil
- 1 tablespoon unflavored gelatin
- 2¼ cups chicken broth
- 2 tablespoons water
- 2 teaspoons cornstarch
- 4 tablespoons unsalted butter, cut into 4 pieces
- 4 shallots, sliced thin
- 6 garlic cloves, sliced thin
- 1 teaspoon ground coriander
- 1 tablespoon minced fresh parsley
- 1½ teaspoons lemon juice

1. Adjust 1 oven rack to lowest position and second rack 8 inches from broiler element. Heat oven to 250 degrees. Line rimmed baking sheet with aluminum foil and place wire rack on top. Sprinkle chicken pieces with salt and pepper (do not pat chicken dry).

2. Heat oil in 12-inch skillet over medium-high heat until shimmering. Place leg quarters skin side down in skillet; cook, turning once, until golden brown on both sides, 5 to 7 minutes total. Transfer to prepared sheet, arranging legs along 1 long side of sheet. Pour off fat from skillet. Place breasts skin side down in skillet; cook, turning once, until golden brown on both sides, 4 to 6 minutes total. Transfer to sheet with legs. Discard fat; do not clean skillet. Place sheet on lower rack, orienting so legs are at back of oven. Roast until breasts register 160 degrees and legs register 175 degrees, 1 hour 25 minutes to 1 hour 45 minutes. Let chicken rest on sheet for 10 minutes.

3. While chicken roasts, sprinkle gelatin over broth in bowl and let sit until gelatin softens, about 5 minutes. Whisk water and cornstarch together in small bowl; set aside.

4. Melt butter in now-empty skillet over medium-low heat. Add shallots and garlic; cook until golden brown and crisp, 6 to 9 minutes. Stir in coriander and cook for 30 seconds. Stir in gelatin mixture, scraping up any browned bits. Bring to simmer over high heat and cook until reduced to 1½ cups, 5 to 7 minutes. Whisk cornstarch mixture to recombine. Whisk into sauce and simmer until thickened, about 1 minute. Off heat, stir in parsley and lemon juice; season with salt and pepper to taste. Cover to keep warm.

5. Heat broiler. Transfer sheet to upper rack and broil chicken until skin is well browned and crisp, 3 to 6 minutes. Serve, passing sauce separately.

GAME CHANGER

Yes, Weeknight Roast Chicken

"Cooking a whole chicken for a weeknight dinner is kind of a tall order, but by harnessing a little thermodynamic science—and a great skillet— you can do it. This recipe is one of my favorites for its brilliance. By preheating a good 12-inch tri-ply clad skillet in the oven, and setting the chicken in its hot interior to roast, breast side up, you can accelerate the cooking time for the dark meat while not overcooking the more delicate white meat. Both light and dark meat cook at the same rate, in a fraction of the usual roasting time for a whole bird, with lovely juicy results. Not only is this a groundbreaking way to roast a chicken, but it also demonstrates that a sturdy, well-designed skillet, with a metal handle that makes it ovensafe, has far more versatility than you might expect in a pan that seems made only for frying on the stovetop. And any time I can wring more value out of my kitchen gear, it underlines my belief that investing in a few good, versatile pieces is worthwhile."

—Lisa

Weeknight Roast Chicken

Serves 4 • **Total Time: 1¼ hours, plus 20 minutes resting**

Why This Recipe Works When done properly, the rich flavor and juicy meat of a roast chicken need little adornment. But the process of preparing and roasting chicken can be surprisingly complicated and time-consuming. And the most time-consuming part is salting or brining the bird, a step that ensures juiciness and well-seasoned meat. We wanted a way to get roast chicken on the table in about an hour without sacrificing flavor. After testing the various components and steps of a typical recipe, we found we could skip trussing and just tie the legs together and tuck the wings underneath. We also discovered we could skip both the V-rack and flipping the chicken by using a preheated skillet and placing the chicken breast side up; this gave the thighs a jumpstart on cooking. Starting the chicken in a 450-degree oven and then turning the oven off while the chicken finished cooking slowed the evaporation of juices, ensuring moist, tender meat.

We prefer to use a 3½- to 4-pound chicken for this recipe; however, this method can be used to cook a larger chicken. If roasting a larger bird, increase the cooking time in step 2 to 35 to 40 minutes. If you choose to serve the chicken with one of the pan sauces that follow, don't wash the skillet after removing the chicken. Prepare the pan sauce while resting the chicken.

  1 tablespoon kosher salt
½ teaspoon pepper
  1 (3½- to 4-pound) whole chicken, giblets discarded
  1 tablespoon extra-virgin olive oil

1. Adjust oven rack to middle position, place 12-inch ovensafe skillet on rack, and heat the oven to 450 degrees. Combine salt and pepper in bowl. Pat chicken dry with paper towels and rub entire surface with oil. Sprinkle evenly all over with salt mixture and rub in mixture with your hands to coat evenly. Tie legs together with twine and tuck wingtips behind back.

2. Transfer chicken, breast side up, to preheated skillet in oven. Roast chicken until thickest part of breasts registers 120 degrees and the thickest part of thighs registers 135 degrees, 25 to 35 minutes. Turn off oven and leave chicken in oven until breasts register 160 degrees and the thighs register 175 degrees, 25 to 35 minutes.

3. Transfer chicken to carving board and let rest, uncovered, for 20 minutes. Carve and serve.

Carving a Whole Roast Chicken

1. Cut chicken where leg meets breast, then pull leg quarter away. Push up on joint, then carefully cut through it to remove leg quarter.

2. Cut through joint that connects drumstick to thigh. Repeat on second side to remove other leg.

3. Cut down along 1 side of breastbone, pulling breast meat away from bone.

4. Remove wing from breast by cutting through wing joint. Slice breast into attractive slices.

Tarragon-Lemon Pan Sauces
Makes ¾ cup • **Total Time: 20 minutes**

  1 shallot, minced
  1 cup chicken broth
  2 teaspoons Dijon mustard
  2 tablespoons unsalted butter
  2 teaspoons chopped fresh tarragon
  2 teaspoons lemon juice

While chicken rests, remove all but 1 tablespoon fat from now-empty skillet using large kitchen spoon, leaving any browned bits and juices in skillet. Place skillet over medium-high heat; add shallot; and cook until softened, about 2 minutes. Stir in broth and mustard, scraping up any browned bits. Cook until reduced to ¾ cup, about 3 minutes. Off heat, whisk in butter, tarragon and lemon juice. Season with pepper to taste; cover and keep warm.

Thyme–Sherry Vinegar Pan Sauce
Makes ¾ cup • Total Time: 20 minutes

- 1 shallot, minced
- 2 garlic cloves, minced
- 2 teaspoons chopped fresh thyme
- 1 cup chicken broth
- 2 teaspoons Dijon mustard
- 2 tablespoons unsalted butter
- 2 teaspoons sherry vinegar

While chicken rests, remove all but 1 tablespoon fat from now-empty skillet, leaving any browned bits and juices in skillet. Place skillet over medium-high heat; add shallot, garlic, and thyme; and cook until softened, about 2 minutes. Stir in broth and mustard, scraping up any browned bits. Cook until reduced to ¾ cup, about 3 minutes. Off heat, whisk in butter and vinegar. Season with pepper to taste; cover and keep warm.

Roast Chicken with Garlic and Lime

Serves 3 to 4 • Total Time: 2 hours, plus 6 hours marinating

Why This Recipe Works This robustly flavored roast chicken is inspired by Peruvian pollo a la brasa, which traditionally cooks on a spit in a wood-fired oven. It is seasoned with garlic, spices, lime, chiles, and huacatay or black mint. We wanted to replicate the chicken using a standard oven. Rubbing a flavorful paste underneath and on top of the skin produced well-seasoned meat and a heady flavor. To this basic paste we added fresh mint (replacing the black mint paste called for in traditional recipes), oregano, pepper, and minced habanero chile for tangy spice, while a little smoked paprika subtly mimicked the smokiness we were missing from the rotisserie. Roasting the chicken vertically allowed it to cook evenly, while using two different oven temperatures helped us achieve both moist meat and well-browned skin.

If habanero chiles are unavailable, 1 tablespoon of minced serrano chile can be substituted. Wear gloves when working with hot chiles. This recipe calls for a vertical poultry roaster. If you don't have one, substitute a 12-ounce

can of beer. Open the can and pour out (or drink) about half of the beer. Spray the can lightly with vegetable oil spray and proceed with the recipe. Serve with Spicy Mayonnaise (recipe follows) and lime wedges.

- ¼ cup fresh mint leaves
- 3 tablespoons extra-virgin olive oil
- 6 garlic cloves, chopped coarse
- 1 tablespoon table salt
- 1 tablespoon pepper
- 1 tablespoon ground cumin
- 1 tablespoon sugar
- 2 teaspoons smoked paprika
- 2 teaspoons dried oregano
- 2 teaspoons finely grated lime zest plus ¼ cup juice (2 limes)
- 1 teaspoon minced habanero chile
- 1 (3½- to 4-pound) whole chicken, giblets discarded
- 1 cup Spicy Mayonnaise

1. Process mint, oil, garlic, salt, pepper, cumin, sugar, paprika, oregano, lime zest and juice, and habanero in blender until smooth paste forms, 10 to 20 seconds. Use your fingers to gently loosen skin covering breast and thighs; place half of paste under skin, directly on meat of breast and thighs. Gently press on skin to distribute paste over meat. Spread entire exterior surface of chicken with remaining paste. Tuck wings behind back. Place chicken in 1-gallon zipper-lock bag and refrigerate for at least 6 hours or up to 24 hours.

2. Adjust oven rack to lowest position and heat oven to 325 degrees. Place vertical roaster on rimmed baking sheet. Slide chicken onto vertical roaster so drumsticks reach down to bottom of roaster, chicken stands upright, and breast is perpendicular to bottom of pan. Roast chicken until skin just begins to turn golden and thickest part of breast registers 140 degrees, 45 to 55 minutes. Carefully remove chicken and pan from oven and increase oven temperature to 500 degrees.

3. Once oven has reached 500 degrees, place 1 cup water in bottom of baking sheet and continue to roast until entire chicken skin is browned and crisp, breast registers 160 degrees, and thighs register 175 degrees, about 20 minutes, rotating pan halfway through roasting. Check chicken halfway through roasting; if top is becoming too dark, place 7-inch square piece of aluminum foil over neck and wingtips of chicken and continue to roast (if pan begins to smoke and sizzle, add additional water to pan).

4. Carefully remove chicken from oven and let rest, still on vertical roaster, for 20 minutes. Using 2 large wads of paper towels, carefully lift chicken off vertical roaster and onto carving board. Carve chicken and serve, passing spicy mayonnaise separately.

Flavoring Roast Chicken

1. Use your fingers to gently loosen chicken skin from over thighs and breast and rub half of paste directly over meat.

2. Spread remaining paste over skin of entire chicken.

3. Place chicken in gallon-size zipper-lock bag; refrigerate for at least 6 or up to 24 hours.

Spicy Mayonnaise

Makes 1 cup • Total Time: 15 minutes

If you have concerns about consuming raw eggs, ¼ cup of an egg substitute can be used in place of the egg.

- 1 large egg
- 2 tablespoons water
- 1 tablespoon minced onion
- 1 tablespoon lime juice
- 1 tablespoon minced fresh cilantro
- 1 tablespoon minced jarred jalapeño chiles
- 1 garlic clove, minced
- 1 teaspoon yellow mustard
- ¼ teaspoon table salt
- 1 cup vegetable oil

Process egg, water, onion, lime juice, cilantro, jalapeños, garlic, mustard, and salt in food processor until combined, about 5 seconds. With machine running, slowly drizzle in oil in steady stream until mayonnaise-like consistency is reached, scraping down bowl as needed.

SEASON 23

Roast Chicken with Quinoa, Swiss Chard, and Lime

Serves 4 • Total Time: 1¾ hours

Why This Recipe Works With no brining, trussing, or flipping required—and a savory side dish that comes together while the bird rests—this might be your new go-to one-pan roast chicken recipe. We roasted the chicken breast side up in a preheated skillet, positioning the legs directly against the hot pan to help them finish cooking at the same time as the quicker-cooking breast. Cutting slits in the skin above and below the thigh allowed juices to drain from the chicken into the skillet, where they browned and developed concentrated flavor. An oven temperature of 400 degrees was hot enough to ensure a moist, deeply bronzed chicken without overreducing the pan juices. While the bird rested, we used the chicken's umami-rich juices as the base for cooking an ultraflavorful grain-and-vegetable side dish.

> *This recipe was developed with Diamond Crystal Kosher Salt; if using Morton Kosher Salt, which is denser, decrease the amount for the chicken to 1¾ teaspoons and the amount for the quinoa to ¼ teaspoon. We like prewashed quinoa; rinsing removes bitter saponins from the surface*

of the quinoa. If you buy unwashed quinoa, rinse it and then spread it out on a clean dish towel to dry for 15 minutes. Rainbow chard is particularly attractive here, but regular chard will also work.

- 1 tablespoon kosher salt, divided
- ½ teaspoon pepper
- 1 (4-pound) whole chicken, giblets discarded
- 1 tablespoon unsalted butter, melted
- ½ teaspoon vegetable oil
- 8 ounces Swiss chard, stems cut into ¼-inch pieces, leaves sliced into ½-inch-wide strips
- ½ small onion, chopped fine
- 1 garlic clove, minced
- ½ teaspoon ground cumin
- ¾ cup prewashed quinoa
- ¾ cup water
- ¼ teaspoon grated lime zest plus 5 teaspoons juice

1. Adjust oven rack to middle position and heat oven to 400 degrees. Stir 2½ teaspoons salt and pepper together in small bowl. Place chicken breast side up on cutting board. Using kitchen shears, thoroughly trim excess fat and skin from cavity. Lift 1 drumstick and use paring knife to cut ½-inch slit in skin where drumstick and thigh meet. Turn chicken on side so breast faces edge of counter. Cut ½-inch slit in skin where top of thigh meets breast. Repeat both cuts on opposite side of chicken. Tuck wingtips behind back. Sprinkle about one-third of salt mixture into cavity. Brush top and sides of chicken with melted butter. Sprinkle remaining salt mixture evenly over all sides of chicken.

2. Heat oil in 12-inch skillet over medium-high heat until shimmering. Place chicken breast side up in skillet; transfer to oven; and roast until thickest part of breast registers 150 to 155 degrees, 1 hour to 1 hour 10 minutes, rotating skillet halfway through roasting. Transfer chicken to carving board and let rest for 15 minutes (chicken temperature will continue to rise as it rests).

3. Meanwhile, pour pan juices into fat separator. Add 2 teaspoons fat to now-empty skillet. Add chard stems and onion and cook over medium-high heat, stirring occasionally, until onion is translucent, about 5 minutes. Add garlic and cumin and cook, stirring constantly, until fragrant, about 30 seconds. Add quinoa and stir until well combined. Stir in ¼ cup defatted pan juices, water, lime juice, and remaining ½ teaspoon salt and bring to simmer. Spread chard leaves in even layer over quinoa; reduce heat to low; cover; and cook until quinoa is just tender and all liquid is absorbed, about 15 minutes.

4. Carve chicken and transfer to platter. Fluff quinoa, stir in lime zest, season with salt to taste, and transfer to bowl. Serve chicken with quinoa.

VARIATIONS

Roast Chicken with Bulgur, Peas, and Mint

Substitute 1 minced shallot for onion and Swiss chard stems and cook until translucent, about 3 minutes. Omit garlic and cumin. Substitute medium-grind bulgur for quinoa. Decrease water to ½ cup. Substitute lemon juice for lime juice. Substitute 1 cup frozen peas for Swiss chard leaves; turn off heat before covering skillet; and let sit until bulgur is just tender and all of liquid is absorbed, about 10 minutes. Substitute 1 tablespoon chopped fresh mint for lime zest.

Roast Chicken with Couscous, Roasted Red Peppers, and Basil

Omit minced garlic and cumin. Substitute 4 thinly sliced garlic cloves for onion and Swiss chard stems and cook over medium-low heat until pale golden brown, about 3 minutes. Substitute couscous for quinoa. Substitute red wine vinegar for lime juice. Substitute ¾ cup jarred roasted red peppers, chopped fine, for Swiss chard leaves; turn off heat before covering skillet; and let sit until couscous is just tender and all of liquid is absorbed, about 10 minutes. Substitute 2 tablespoons chopped fresh basil for lime zest.

Prepping Swiss Chard

To prepare Swiss chard or kale, cut away leafy green portion from either side of stem using chef's knife. Stack several leaves and either slice leaves crosswise or chop them into pieces (as directed in recipe).

Broiled Chicken with Gravy

Serves 4 • **Total Time: 1¾ hours**

Why This Recipe Works We found that the key to getting a whole chicken on the table in a reasonable amount of time was broiling, not roasting. Spatchcocking the chicken kept it flat so that it cooked more evenly under the intense direct heat of the broiler. To get the white meat to finish cooking at the same time as the dark meat, we used a two-pronged approach: A preheated skillet jump-started the cooking of the leg quarters, and starting the chicken under a cold broiler slowed down the cooking of the breast. Because the broiler's heat is more intense than that of the oven, carryover cooking has a bigger impact, so we pulled the chicken from the oven when the breast meat registered 155 degrees instead of 160 degrees. For a gravy that really tasted like the bird, we began by making a full-flavored chicken stock that included the backbone, giblets, and excess skin and fat from the chicken—powerhouses of chicken flavor. Combining the reduced stock with a roux of flour and butter yielded a rich, silky gravy.

If your broiler has multiple settings, choose the highest one. This recipe won't work with a drawer-style broiler. You will need a broiler-safe 12-inch skillet. The backbone and trimmings provide plenty of flavor for the gravy, but if your chicken comes with the giblets and neck, use them as well. Feel free to substitute dry vermouth for the white wine. In step 2, if the skin is dark golden brown but the breast has not yet reached 155 degrees, cover the chicken with foil and continue to broil. Monitor the temperature of the chicken carefully during the final 10 minutes of cooking, because it can quickly overcook.

  1 (4-pound) whole chicken, giblets and
    neck reserved
1½ teaspoons vegetable oil, divided
1½ teaspoons kosher salt, divided
 ½ teaspoon pepper
  4 cups chicken broth, divided
 ½ onion, chopped fine
  1 carrot, peeled and chopped fine
  1 celery rib, chopped fine
  4 sprigs fresh parsley
  2 sprigs fresh thyme
  1 garlic clove, crushed and peeled
 ¼ cup dry white wine
  2 tablespoons unsalted butter
2½ tablespoons all-purpose flour

Spatchcocking a Chicken

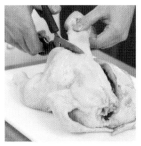

1. Using kitchen shears, cut through bones on either side of backbone and trim any excess fat or skin from chicken, reserving any trimmings.

2. Flip chicken and use heel of your hand to flatten breastbone.

1. Adjust oven rack 12 to 13 inches from broiler element (do not heat broiler). Place chicken breast side down on cutting board. Using kitchen shears, cut through bones on either side of backbone. Cut backbone into 1-inch pieces and reserve. Trim excess fat and skin from chicken and reserve with backbone. Flip chicken and use heel of your hand to press on breastbone to flatten. Using tip of paring knife, poke holes through skin over entire surface of chicken, spacing them approximately ¾ inch apart.

2. Rub ½ teaspoon oil over skin and sprinkle with 1 teaspoon salt and pepper. Flip chicken and sprinkle bone side with remaining ½ teaspoon salt. Flip chicken skin side up, tie legs together with kitchen twine, and tuck wings under breasts. Heat remaining 1 teaspoon oil in broiler-safe 12-inch skillet over high heat until just smoking. Place chicken in skillet, skin side up, and transfer to oven, positioning skillet as close to center of oven as handle allows (turn handle so it points toward 1 of oven's front corners). Turn on broiler and broil chicken for 25 minutes. Rotate skillet by moving handle to opposite front corner of oven and continue to broil until skin is dark golden brown and thickest part of breast registers 155 degrees, 20 to 30 minutes longer.

3. While chicken broils, bring 1 cup broth and reserved giblets, neck, backbone, and trimmings to simmer in large saucepan over high heat. Cook, adjusting heat to maintain vigorous simmer and stirring occasionally, until all liquid evaporates and trimmings begin to sizzle, about 12 minutes. Continue to cook, stirring frequently, until dark fond forms on bottom of saucepan, 2 to 4 minutes longer. Reduce heat to medium. Add onion, carrot, celery, parsley sprigs, thyme sprigs, and garlic to saucepan and cook, stirring frequently, until onion is translucent, 7 to 8 minutes. Stir in wine and bring to simmer, scraping up any browned bits. Add remaining 3 cups broth and bring to simmer over high heat. Adjust heat to maintain simmer and continue to cook, stirring occasionally, until stock (liquid only) is reduced by half, about 20 minutes longer.

4. Strain stock through fine-mesh strainer set over bowl, pressing on solids to extract as much liquid as possible. Melt butter in now-empty saucepan over medium heat. Add flour and cook, stirring constantly, until mixture is deep golden brown, 5 to 8 minutes. Slowly whisk in stock. Increase heat to medium-high and bring to simmer. Simmer until thickened, about 5 minutes.

5. Transfer chicken to carving board and let rest, uncovered, for 15 minutes. While chicken rests, transfer fat and drippings in skillet to small bowl and let sit for 5 minutes. Spoon off fat and discard. Whisk drippings into gravy. Season gravy with salt and pepper to taste. Carve chicken and serve, passing gravy separately.

Chicken Under a Brick with Herb-Roasted Potatoes

Serves 4 • Total Time: 1¾ hours

Why This Recipe Works Cooking a butterflied chicken under a brick in a skillet not only looks cool but also shaves half an hour off the cooking time of a regular roast chicken and produces amazingly crisp skin. The brick helps to keep the chicken flat as it cooks, forcing all of the skin to make contact with the pan. After trying a few recipes, we found that placing several cans in a cast-iron skillet offered a better distribution of weight over the chicken (plus, few people have loose bricks hanging about their kitchen). Also, we found that chickens much larger than 3 pounds were difficult to fit into a 12-inch skillet. When pounded to an even thickness, a superflat chicken cooked evenly, and more of the skin made contact with the pan, thus turning crisp. We cooked the chicken, skin side down, underneath the weighted skillet until it had a beautiful color. We then removed the cans and the cast-iron skillet, flipped the chicken over, and finished it—still in the nonstick skillet—in a 450-degree oven. The hot, dry air of the oven ensured that the skin remained crisp and intact as the meat

finished cooking. We quickly figured out how to include a flavorful side dish of roasted potatoes: We simply threw the potatoes into the pan underneath the browned and seasoned oil–brushed chicken before it went into the oven. While the chicken was resting, the potatoes went back into the oven to finish cooking and pick up some gorgeous color.

Instead of two bricks and a rimmed baking sheet, use a heavy cast-iron skillet loaded with several cans or a large stockpot partially filled with water. Be careful when removing the pan from the oven, as the handle will be hot.

> 1 (3-pound) whole chicken, giblets discarded
> 1¼ teaspoons table salt, divided
> ¾ teaspoon plus ⅛ teaspoon pepper, divided
> 1 teaspoon plus 2 tablespoons vegetable oil, divided
> 2 tablespoons lemon juice, plus 1 lemon, cut into wedges
> 3 garlic cloves, minced
> 1 tablespoon minced fresh thyme, divided
> ⅛ teaspoon red pepper flakes
> 1½ pounds Red Bliss potatoes (small), scrubbed, dried, and cut into ¾ inch pieces
> 1 tablespoon minced fresh parsley

1. Place chicken, breast side down, on cutting board. Using kitchen shears, cut through bones on either side of backbone; discard backbone. Turn chicken breast side up and use palm of your hand to flatten chicken, then pound chicken flat to fairly even thickness. Sprinkle chicken with ½ teaspoon salt and ½ teaspoon pepper.

2. Adjust oven rack to lowest position and heat oven to 450 degrees. Heat 1 teaspoon oil in 12-inch ovensafe non-stick skillet over medium-high heat until just smoking. Swirl skillet to coat evenly with oil. Place chicken, skin side down, in pan and reduce heat to medium. Place weighted skillet or pot on chicken and cook, checking every 5 minutes or so, until evenly browned, about 25 minutes. (After 20 minutes, chicken should be fairly crisp and golden; if not, turn heat up to medium-high and continue to cook until well browned.)

3. Meanwhile, mix lemon juice, garlic, 1½ teaspoons thyme, pepper flakes, ½ teaspoon salt, ¼ teaspoon pepper, and remaining 2 tablespoons oil in small bowl and set aside.

4. Using tongs, carefully transfer chicken, skin side up, to clean plate. Pour off any accumulated fat in pan and add potatoes, sprinkling them with remaining ¼ teaspoon salt, remaining ⅛ teaspoon pepper, and remaining 1½ teaspoons thyme. Place chicken, skin side up, on potatoes and brush skin with reserved thyme–lemon juice mixture.

Learn to Butterfly a Chicken

"This recipe is my absolute number 1, top of the list, GOAT. I know every recipe detail by heart and make it at least every other week. The chicken skin turns out crisp and delicious, and the potatoes take on a schmaltzy caramelization that is nearly impossible to achieve otherwise. Also, you can change up the flavors in the oil (which gets brushed over the chicken in the oven) to suit your mood. The key to the recipe is using a butterflied (aka spatchcocked) chicken. They now sell butterflied chickens at the market, but doing it yourself is easy with a good pair of kitchen shears. Plus, the backbone is perfect for making stock. I save the backbones in the freezer and make a pot of stock when there's enough.

One night, when I was making this recipe and I was a bit tired, I asked my daughter if she had seen the 'chickens'—I meant to say shears. She laughed and the name stuck, so now all shears and scissors are referred to as chickens in my house."

—Julia

5. Transfer pan to oven and roast until thickest part of breast registers 160 degrees, about 10 minutes longer. Transfer chicken to cutting board and let rest for 10 minutes.

6. Return skillet with potatoes to oven and roast until browned and cooked through, about 10 minutes. Using slotted spoon, transfer potatoes to large bowl, leaving fat behind. Toss potatoes with parsley. Cut chicken into pieces. Serve chicken and potatoes immediately with lemon wedges.

SEASON 17

Crisp Roast Butterflied Chicken with Rosemary and Garlic

Serves 4 • Total Time: 1¼ hours

Why This Recipe Works One of the major perks of a butterflied chicken is that it takes considerably less time to cook than a traditional whole bird. Additionally, flattening the chicken encourages crisp skin, since most of the skin is in contact with the hot pan. However, during our testing we found that after initially crisping up, the skin turned soggy as the chicken continued to cook skin side down in its own juices. We set out to produce perfectly cooked chicken with crisp skin that could be on the table in about an hour. We started by heating a cast-iron skillet in a very hot oven. We then put the chicken into the preheated skillet skin side down and cooked it until the skin was golden brown. Flipping the chicken over for the remainder of the cooking time allowed us to take advantage of the hot, dry air of the oven to ensure that the skin remained crisp and intact. A simple mixture of extra-virgin olive oil, rosemary, and garlic brushed on the chicken during roasting elevated the flavor and crisped the skin further. We had four-star, perfectly browned roast chicken with spectacular skin on the table in under an hour. And as a bonus, the butterflied bird was a cinch to carve.

> *Be aware that the chicken may slightly overhang the skillet at first, but once browned it will shrink to fit; do not use a chicken larger than 4 pounds. Serve with lemon wedges.*

2 tablespoons extra-virgin olive oil, divided
1 teaspoon minced fresh rosemary
1 garlic clove, minced
1 (3½- to 4-pound) whole chicken, giblets discarded
½ teaspoon table salt
½ teaspoon pepper

1. Adjust oven rack to lowest position, place 12-inch cast-iron skillet on rack, and heat oven to 500 degrees. Meanwhile, combine 1 tablespoon oil, rosemary, and garlic in bowl; set aside.

2. With chicken breast side down, use kitchen shears to cut through bones on either side of backbone; discard backbone. Flip chicken over, tuck wingtips behind back, and press firmly on breastbone to flatten. Pat chicken dry with paper towels, then rub with remaining 1 tablespoon oil and sprinkle with salt and pepper.

3. When oven reaches 500 degrees, place chicken breast side down in hot skillet. Reduce oven temperature to 450 degrees and roast chicken until well browned, about 30 minutes.

4. Using pot holders, remove skillet from oven. Being careful of hot skillet handle, gently flip chicken breast side up. Brush chicken with oil mixture, return skillet to oven, and continue to roast chicken until breast registers 160 degrees and thighs register 175 degrees, about 10 minutes. Transfer chicken to carving board, tent with aluminum foil, and let rest for 15 minutes. Carve chicken and serve.

Crispy Fried Chicken

Serves 4 to 6 • **Total Time: 1¾ hours, plus 4 hours brining and chilling**

Why This Recipe Works Frying chicken at home is a daunting task, with its messy preparation and spattering hot fat. In the end, the chicken often ends up disappointingly greasy, with a peeling crust and dry, tasteless meat. We wanted fried chicken worthy of the mess and splatter: moist, seasoned meat coated with a delicious crispy mahogany crust. We soaked chicken parts in a seasoned buttermilk brine for ultimate flavor and juiciness. Then we air-dried the brined chicken parts to help ensure a crisp skin. Flour made the crispest coating. We found that peanut oil can withstand the demands of frying and had the most neutral flavor of all the oils we tested. Vegetable oil was a close runner-up. As for frying the chicken, we found that a Dutch oven worked best. With its high sides and lid, the Dutch oven minimized splatters and retained heat which helped the chicken cook through.

> *Avoid using kosher chicken in this recipe or it will be too salty. Maintaining an even oil temperature is key. After the chicken is added to the pot, the temperature will drop dramatically, and most of the frying will be done at about 325 degrees. Use an instant-read thermometer with a high upper range; a clip-on candy/deep-fry thermometer is fine, too, though it can be clipped to the pot only for the uncovered portion of frying.*

Chicken

- ½ cup table salt for brining
- ¼ cup sugar for brining
- 2 tablespoons paprika
- 7 cups buttermilk for brining
- 3 garlic heads, cloves separated and smashed
- 3 bay leaves, crumbled
- 4 pounds bone-in chicken pieces (split breasts cut in half, drumsticks, and/or thighs), trimmed
- 3–4 quarts peanut oil or vegetable oil, for frying

Coating

- 4 cups all-purpose flour
- 1 large egg
- 1 teaspoon baking powder
- ½ teaspoon baking soda
- 1 cup buttermilk

1. For the chicken: Dissolve salt, sugar, and paprika in buttermilk in large container. Add garlic and bay leaves, submerge chicken in brine, cover, and refrigerate for 2 to 3 hours.

2. Remove chicken from brine and place in single layer on wire rack set over rimmed baking sheet. Refrigerate uncovered for 2 hours. (At this point, chicken can be covered with plastic wrap and refrigerated for up to 6 more hours.)

3. Adjust oven rack to middle position and heat oven to 200 degrees. In large Dutch oven, heat 2 inches oil over medium-high heat to 375 degrees.

4. For the coating: Place flour in shallow dish. Whisk egg, baking powder, and baking soda together in medium bowl, then whisk in buttermilk (mixture will bubble and foam). Working with 3 chicken pieces at a time, dredge in flour, shaking off excess, then coat with egg mixture, allowing excess to drip off. Finally, coat with flour again, shake off excess, and return to wire rack.

5. When oil is hot, add half of chicken pieces to pot, skin side down, cover, and fry until deep golden brown, 7 to 11 minutes, adjusting heat as necessary to maintain oil temperature of about 325 degrees. (After 4 minutes, check chicken pieces for even browning and rearrange if some pieces are browning faster than others.) Turn chicken pieces over and continue to cook until thickest part of breasts registers 160 to 165 degrees and thickest part of thighs or drumsticks registers 175 degrees, 6 to 8 minutes. Drain chicken briefly on paper towel–lined plate, then transfer to clean wire rack set in rimmed baking sheet and keep warm in oven.

6. Return oil to 375 degrees (if necessary) over medium-high heat and repeat with remaining chicken pieces. Serve.

You Can, and Should, Fry Chicken at Home

"I LOVE eating at restaurants—I get a break from cooking and I get to eat foods that I wouldn't (or couldn't) make at home. Until I came to ATK as an intern in 2015, I believed that fried foods should only be eaten at restaurants. This recipe changed all of that. It was developed by Andrea Geary, the most meticulous of meticulous test cooks, and it's an absolute gem. This recipe achieves all sorts of culinary gymnastics: The first impression is of the amazing sauce it's coated in: sweet, spicy, salty, savory; it hits all of the pleasure centers in the brain. But then your teeth hit the batter and, remarkably, it's not soggy; an audible crunch gives way to succulent meat within.

There are lots of versions of Korean fried chicken out there but I love Andrea's version because of her attention to detail. It's so precise in the timings, the cut of chicken to use, the balance for that sweet-spicy-savory sauce, exactly how and when you fry, what vessel to use, how much oil, and exactly what temperature it should be. She uses a rack to rest the chicken after the first fry so the outer coating will set evenly before its second fry. Because of this, it stays crunchy even a day after you've drenched it in that glorious sauce. If you follow this recipe to the letter, you will achieve all the hallmarks of this great Korean dish. My one bit of advice: Use a probe thermometer so you can monitor the oil temperature and fry perfectly crisp chicken evermore."

—Joe

Dakgangjeong

Serves 4 to 6 as a main dish
Total Time: 1½ hours

Why This Recipe Works A thin, crispy exterior and a spicy-sweet-salty sauce are the hallmarks of dakgangjeong, Korean fried chicken wings. The biggest challenge is preventing the sauce from destroying the crust. We dunked the wings (which offer a high exterior to interior ratio for maximum crunch and also cook quickly) in a loose batter of flour, cornstarch, and water, which clung nicely to the chicken and fried up brown and crispy. To help the coating withstand a wet sauce, we double-fried the wings, which removed more water from the skin, making the coating extra-crispy. Gochujang, Korean chile paste, gives our sauce the proper spicy, fermented notes, while sugar tempered the heat and garlic and ginger provided depth.

A rasp-style grater makes quick work of turning the garlic into a paste. Gochujang, Korean hot red chile paste, can be found in Asian markets and in some supermarkets. Tailor the heat level of your wings by adjusting its amount. If you can't find gochujang, substitute an equal amount of sriracha and add only 2 tablespoons of water to the sauce. For a complete meal, serve these wings with white rice and a vegetable.

  1 tablespoon toasted sesame oil
  1 teaspoon garlic, minced to paste
  1 teaspoon grated fresh ginger
1¾ cups water, divided
  3 tablespoons sugar
2–3 tablespoons gochujang
  1 tablespoon soy sauce
  2 quarts vegetable oil for frying
  1 cup all-purpose flour
  3 tablespoons cornstarch
  3 pounds chicken wings, cut at joints, wingtips discarded

1. Combine sesame oil, garlic, and ginger in large bowl and microwave until mixture is bubbly and fragrant but not browned, 40 to 60 seconds. Whisk in ¼ cup water, sugar, gochujang, and soy sauce until smooth and set aside.

2. Heat oil in large Dutch oven over medium-high heat to 350 degrees. While oil heats, whisk flour, cornstarch, and remaining 1½ cups water in second large bowl until smooth. Set wire rack in rimmed baking sheet and set aside.

3. Place half of wings in batter and stir to coat. Using tongs, remove wings from batter one at a time, allowing any excess batter to drip back into bowl, and add to hot oil. Increase heat to high and cook, stirring occasionally to prevent wings from sticking, until coating is light golden and beginning to crisp, about 7 minutes. (Oil temperature will drop sharply after adding chicken.) Transfer wings to prepared rack. Return oil to 350 degrees and repeat with remaining wings. Reduce heat to medium and let second batch of chicken rest for 5 minutes.

4. Return oil to 375 degrees. Carefully return all chicken to oil and cook, stirring occasionally, until exterior is deep golden brown and very crispy, about 7 minutes. Transfer to rack and let stand for 2 minutes. Add chicken to reserved sauce and toss until coated. Return chicken to rack and let stand for 2 minutes to allow surface to set. Transfer to platter and serve.

Buffalo Wings

Serves 6 to 8 • Total Time: 1 hour

Why This Recipe Works Buffalo wings are the ultimate bar snack. Great wings boast juicy meat; a crisp coating; and a spicy, slightly sweet, and vinegary sauce. But dry, flabby wings are often the norm and the sauce can be scorchingly hot. We wanted perfectly cooked wings, coated in a well-seasoned sauce. We coated the wings with cornstarch for a supercrisp exterior and deep-fried the wings (rather than roasting, sautéing, or pan-frying them) for the best texture. Then we deepened the flavor of the traditional hot sauce by adding brown sugar and cider vinegar. For heat, we chose Frank's RedHot Original Sauce, which is traditional, but not very spicy, so we added a little Tabasco for even more kick. The fried, unsauced wings can be kept warm in the oven for up to 1½ hours. Toss them with the sauce just before serving.

Frank's RedHot Original Sauce is not terribly spicy. We like to combine it with a more potent hot sauce, such as Tabasco, to bring up the heat. Use a Dutch oven that hold 6 quarts or more for this recipe.

Sauce

- 4 tablespoons unsalted butter
- ½ cup Frank's RedHot Original Sauce
- 2 tablespoons Tabasco or other hot sauce, plus more to taste
- 1 tablespoon packed dark brown sugar
- 2 teaspoons cider vinegar

Wings

- 1–2 quarts peanut oil, for frying
- 3 tablespoons cornstarch
- 1 teaspoon table salt
- 1 teaspoon pepper
- 1 teaspoon cayenne pepper
- 3 pounds chicken wings, cut at joints, wingtips discarded

- 2 carrots, peeled and cut into thin sticks
- 4 celery ribs, cut into thin sticks
  Blue cheese dressing

1. For the sauce: Melt butter in small saucepan over low heat. Whisk in hot sauces, sugar, and vinegar until combined. Remove from heat and set aside.

2. For the wings: Heat oven to 200 degrees. Line baking sheet with paper towels. In large Dutch oven fitted with clip-on candy thermometer, heat 2½ inches oil over medium-high heat to 360 degrees. While oil heats, combine cornstarch, salt, pepper, and cayenne in a small bowl. Dry chicken with paper towels and place pieces in large bowl. Sprinkle spice mixture over wings and toss with rubber spatula until evenly coated. Fry half of chicken wings until golden and crisp, 10 to 12 minutes. With slotted spoon, transfer fried chicken wings to prepared sheet. Keep first batch of chicken warm in oven while frying remaining wings.

3. Pour sauce mixture into large bowl, add chicken wings, and toss until wings are uniformly coated. Serve immediately with carrot and celery sticks and blue cheese dressing on side.

Cutting Up Chicken Wings

1. Cut into skin between larger sections of wing until you hit joint.

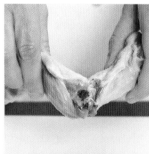

2. Bend back 2 sections to pop and break joint.

3. Cut through skin and flesh to completely separate 2 meaty portions.

4. Hack off wingtip and discard.

Thai Chicken Curry with Potatoes and Peanuts

Serves 4 to 6 • Total Time: 1½ hours

Why This Recipe Works Warm-spiced, savory-sweet massaman curry is a Thai specialty. We set out to create a streamlined version of the traditional recipe. To make a deeply flavorful curry paste, we broiled chiles, garlic, and shallots per tradition, but we replaced the galangal with readily available ginger and traded out toasted, ground whole spices for preground five-spice powder. Coconut milk and lime juice rounded out the flavor of our curry. We stuck with the traditional potatoes, onion, chicken, and peanuts, simmered in the sauce until they were tender. A final garnish of lime zest and cilantro added a splash of color and brightness.

Serve the curry with jasmine rice. The ingredients for the curry paste can be doubled to make extra for future use. Refrigerate the paste for up to one week or freeze it for up to two months.

Curry Paste

- 6 dried New Mexico chiles
- 4 shallots, unpeeled
- 7 garlic cloves, unpeeled
- ½ cup chopped fresh ginger
- ¼ cup water
- 1½ tablespoons lime juice
- 1½ tablespoons vegetable oil
- 1 tablespoon fish sauce
- 1 teaspoon five-spice powder
- ½ teaspoon ground cumin
- ½ teaspoon pepper

Curry

- 1 teaspoon vegetable oil
- 1¼ cups chicken broth
- 1 (13.5-ounce) can coconut milk
- 1 pound Yukon Gold potatoes, unpeeled, cut into ¾-inch pieces
- 1 onion, cut into ¾-inch pieces
- ⅓ cup dry-roasted peanuts
- ¾ teaspoon table salt
- 1 pound boneless, skinless chicken thighs, trimmed and cut into 1-inch pieces
- 2 teaspoons grated lime zest
- ¼ cup chopped fresh cilantro

1. For the curry paste: Adjust oven rack to middle position and heat oven to 350 degrees. Line rimmed baking sheet with aluminum foil. Arrange chiles on prepared sheet and toast until puffed and fragrant, 4 to 6 minutes. Transfer chiles to large plate. Heat broiler.

2. Place shallots and garlic on now-empty foil-lined sheet and broil until softened and skin is charred, 6 to 9 minutes.

3. When cool enough to handle, stem and seed chiles and tear into 1½-inch pieces. Process chiles in blender until finely ground, about 1 minute. Peel shallots and garlic. Add shallots, garlic, ginger, water, lime juice, oil, fish sauce, five-spice powder, cumin, and pepper to blender. Process to smooth paste, scraping down sides of blender jar as needed, 2 to 3 minutes. (You should have 1 cup paste.)

4. For the curry: Heat oil in large saucepan over medium heat until shimmering. Add curry paste and cook, stirring constantly, until paste begins to brown, 2½ to 3 minutes. Stir in broth, coconut milk, potatoes, onion, peanuts, and salt, scraping up any browned bits. Bring to simmer and cook until potatoes are just tender, 12 to 14 minutes.

5. Stir in chicken and continue to simmer until chicken is cooked through, 10 to 12 minutes. Remove pan from heat and stir in lime zest. Serve, passing cilantro separately.

Thai-Style Chicken with Basil

Serves 4 • Total Time: 45 minutes

Why This Recipe Works In Thailand, street vendors have mastered a stir-frying method that uses low flames to produce complex and flavorful dishes such as chicken and basil—chopped pieces of moist chicken in a bright, basil-infused sauce. To create our own version, we started with the aromatics. Because Thai stir-fries are cooked over a lower temperature, the aromatics are added at the very beginning of cooking where they infuse the oil with their flavors. To prevent scorching, we started our aromatics (garlic, chiles, and shallots) in a cold skillet. Since it was time-consuming to chop the chicken by hand, we turned to the food processor. To ensure moist meat, we added fish sauce to the food processor when we ground the chicken and then rested the meat in the refrigerator; the fish sauce acted as a brine, seasoning the chicken and sealing in moisture. For our sauce base, we liked oyster sauce brightened with a dash of white vinegar. We spiced up the flavor of the sauce by adding a reserved tablespoon of the raw garlic-chile mixture at the end of cooking. And for intense, bright basil flavor, we cooked a portion of chopped basil with the garlic, chile, and shallot mixture, and stirred in whole basil leaves just before serving.

Since tolerance for spiciness can vary, we've kept our recipe relatively mild. For a very mild version, remove the seeds and ribs from the chiles. If fresh Thai chiles are unavailable, substitute two serranos or one medium jalapeño. In Thailand, crushed red pepper and sugar are passed at the table, along with extra fish sauce and white vinegar. You do not need to wash the food processor bowl after step 1. Serve with rice and vegetables, if desired.

- 2 cups fresh basil leaves, divided
- 6 green or red Thai chiles, stemmed
- 3 garlic cloves, peeled
- 2 tablespoons fish sauce, divided, plus extra for serving
- 1 tablespoon oyster sauce
- 1 tablespoon sugar, plus extra for serving
- 1 teaspoon distilled white vinegar, plus extra for serving
- 1 pound boneless, skinless chicken breasts, trimmed and cut into 2-inch pieces
- 3 shallots, peeled and sliced thin (about ¾ cup)
- 2 tablespoons vegetable oil
  Red pepper flakes

1. Pulse 1 cup basil leaves, chiles, and garlic in food processor until chopped fine, 6 to 10 pulses, scraping down sides of bowl once during processing. Transfer 1 tablespoon basil mixture to small bowl, stir in 1 tablespoon fish sauce, oyster sauce, sugar, and vinegar and set aside. Transfer remaining basil mixture to 12-inch heavy-bottomed nonstick skillet.

2. Pulse chicken and remaining 1 tablespoon fish sauce in now-empty food processor until meat is chopped into ¼-inch pieces, 6 to 8 pulses. Transfer chicken to medium bowl and refrigerate for 15 minutes.

3. Stir shallots and oil into basil mixture in skillet. Heat mixture over medium-low heat (mixture should start to sizzle after about 1½ minutes; if it doesn't, adjust heat accordingly), stirring constantly, until garlic and shallots are golden brown, 5 to 8 minutes.

4. Add chicken; increase heat to medium; and cook, stirring and breaking up chicken with potato masher or rubber spatula, until only traces of pink remain, 2 to 4 minutes. Add reserved basil–fish sauce mixture and continue to cook, stirring constantly, until chicken is no longer pink, about 1 minute. Stir in remaining 1 cup basil leaves and cook, stirring constantly, until basil is wilted, 30 to 60 seconds. Serve immediately, passing extra fish sauce, sugar, vinegar, and red pepper flakes separately.

Murgh Makhani

Serves 4 to 6 • Total Time: 1 hour

Why This Recipe Works Murgh makhani (butter chicken) should taste rich and creamy but also vibrant and complex, so we started by softening lots of onion, garlic, ginger, and chile in butter followed by aromatic spices such as garam masala, coriander, cumin, and black pepper. Instead of chopped or crushed tomatoes, we opted for a hefty portion of tomato paste and water, which lent the sauce bright acidity, punch, and deep color without making it too liquid-y. A full cup of cream gave the sauce lush, velvety body, and we finished it by whisking in a couple more tablespoons of solid butter for extra richness. To imitate the deep charring produced by a tandoor oven, we broiled chicken thighs coated in yogurt (its milk proteins and lactose brown quickly and deeply) before cutting them into chunks and stirring them into the sauce.

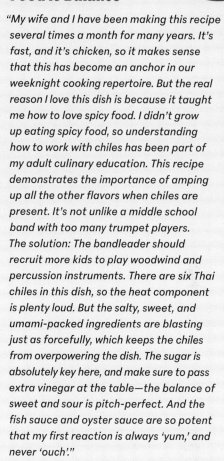

Traditionally, butter chicken is mildly spiced. If you prefer a spicier dish, reserve, mince, and add the ribs and seeds from the chile. Serve with Indian-Style Basmati Rice (recipe follows) and/or warm naan.

 4 tablespoons unsalted butter, cut into 4 pieces and chilled, divided
 1 onion, chopped fine
 5 garlic cloves, minced
 4 teaspoons grated fresh ginger
 1 serrano chile, stemmed, seeded, and minced
 1 tablespoon garam masala
 1 teaspoon ground coriander
 ½ teaspoon ground cumin
 ½ teaspoon pepper
 1½ cups water
 ½ cup tomato paste
 1 tablespoon sugar
 2 teaspoons table salt, divided
 1 cup heavy cream
 2 pounds boneless, skinless chicken thighs, trimmed
 ½ cup plain Greek yogurt
 3 tablespoons chopped fresh cilantro, divided

1. Melt 2 tablespoons butter in large saucepan over medium heat. Add onion, garlic, ginger, and serrano and cook, stirring frequently, until mixture is softened and onion begins to brown, 8 to 10 minutes. Add garam masala, coriander, cumin, and pepper and cook, stirring frequently, until fragrant, about 3 minutes. Add water and tomato paste and whisk until no lumps of tomato paste remain. Add sugar and 1 teaspoon salt and bring to boil. Off heat, stir in cream.

Using immersion blender or blender, process until smooth, 30 to 60 seconds. Return sauce to simmer over medium heat and whisk in remaining 2 tablespoons butter. Remove saucepan from heat and cover to keep warm. (Sauce can be refrigerated for up to 4 days; gently reheat sauce before adding hot chicken.)

2. Adjust oven rack 6 inches from broiler element and heat broiler. Combine chicken, yogurt, and remaining 1 teaspoon salt in bowl and toss well to coat. Using tongs, transfer chicken to wire rack set in aluminum foil–lined rimmed baking sheet. Broil until chicken is evenly charred on both sides and registers 175 degrees, 16 to 20 minutes, flipping chicken halfway through broiling.

3. Let chicken rest for 5 minutes. While chicken rests, warm sauce over medium-low heat. Cut chicken into ¾-inch chunks and stir into sauce. Stir in 2 tablespoons cilantro and season with salt to taste. Transfer to serving dish, sprinkle with remaining 1 tablespoon cilantro, and serve.

ACCOMPANIMENTS
Indian-Style Basmati Rice
Serves 4 to 6 • Total Time: 50 minutes
For basmati rice with a bright yellow color, add ¼ teaspoon of ground turmeric and a pinch of saffron threads with the water in step 3.

 1½ cups basmati rice
 3 tablespoons unsalted butter
 1 teaspoon cumin seeds
 3 green cardamom pods, lightly crushed
 3 whole cloves
 2¼ cups water
 1 cinnamon stick
 1 bay leaf
 1 teaspoon table salt

1. Place rice in fine-mesh strainer and rinse under cold running water until water runs clear. Place strainer over bowl and set aside.

2. Melt butter in medium saucepan over medium heat. Add cumin, cardamom, and cloves and cook, stirring constantly, until fragrant, about 1 minute. Add rice and cook, stirring constantly, until fragrant, about 1 minute.

3. Add water, cinnamon stick, bay leaf, and salt and bring to boil. Reduce heat to low, cover, and simmer until all water is absorbed, about 17 minutes. Let stand, covered, off heat for at least 10 minutes. Discard cardamom, cloves, cinnamon stick, and bay leaf. Fluff rice with fork and serve.

Chicken Biryani

Serves 4 • Total Time: 1¾ hours

Why This Recipe Works In biryani, long-grain basmati rice takes center stage, enriched with butter, saffron, and a variety of fresh herbs and pungent spices and layered with pieces of tender chicken and browned onions. For our recipe, we browned bone-in, skin-on chicken thighs; removed the skin; and layered them with basmati rice, caramelized onions, and a blend of spices. To get the most flavor out of the spices, we tied them into cheesecloth and simmered them in the rice cooking water; we then added some of that water to the biryani. For a finishing touch, we added saffron, currants, and plenty of ginger and chiles.

> *This recipe requires a heavy-bottomed 3½- to 4-quart saucepan about 8 inches in diameter. Do not use a large, wide Dutch oven, as it will adversely affect both the layering of the dish and the final cooking times. For more heat, add the jalapeño seeds and ribs when mincing.*

Yogurt Sauce

- 1 cup whole-milk or low-fat plain yogurt
- 2 tablespoons minced fresh cilantro
- 2 tablespoons minced fresh mint
- 1 garlic clove, minced

Chicken and Rice

- 10 cardamom pods, preferably green, smashed with a chef's knife
- 1 cinnamon stick
- 1 (2-inch) piece fresh ginger, peeled, cut into ½-inch-thick coins, and smashed
- ½ teaspoon cumin seeds
- 3 quarts water
- ¾ teaspoon table salt, divided
- ¼ teaspoon pepper
- 4 (5- to 6-ounce) bone-in chicken thighs, trimmed
- 3 tablespoons unsalted butter
- 2 onions, halved and sliced thin
- 2 jalapeño chiles, stemmed, seeded, and minced
- 4 garlic cloves, minced
- 1¼ cups basmati rice
- ½ teaspoon saffron threads, lightly crumbled
- ¼ cup dried currants or raisins
- 2 tablespoons chopped fresh cilantro
- 2 tablespoons chopped fresh mint

1. For the yogurt sauce: Combine all ingredients in small bowl, season with salt and pepper to taste, and set aside. (Sauce can be refrigerated in airtight container for up to 2 days.)

2. For the chicken and rice: Wrap cardamom pods, cinnamon stick, ginger, and cumin in small piece of cheesecloth and secure with kitchen twine. In 3½- to 4-quart saucepan, bring spice bundle, water, and 1½ teaspoons salt to boil over medium-high heat. Reduce heat to medium and simmer, partially covered, until spices have infused water, at least 15 minutes (but no longer than 30 minutes).

3. Meanwhile, pat chicken thighs dry with paper towels and sprinkle with ¼ teaspoon salt and pepper. Melt butter in 12-inch nonstick skillet over medium-high heat. Add onions and cook, stirring frequently, until soft and dark brown around edges, 10 to 12 minutes. Stir in jalapeños and garlic and cook, stirring frequently, until fragrant, about 2 minutes. Transfer onion mixture to bowl, season with salt to taste, and set aside. Wipe out skillet with wad of paper towels.

4. Place chicken, skin side down, in skillet; return skillet to medium-high heat; and cook until well browned on both sides, 8 to 10 minutes, flipping halfway through. Transfer chicken to plate and discard skin. Tent with aluminum foil to keep warm.

5. If necessary, return spice-infused water to boil over high heat. Add rice and cook, stirring occasionally, for 5 minutes. Drain rice in fine-mesh strainer, reserving ¾ cup cooking liquid; discard spice bundle. Transfer rice to medium bowl and stir in saffron and currants (rice will turn splotchy yellow).

6. Spread half of rice evenly in bottom of saucepan using rubber spatula. Scatter half of onion mixture over rice, then place chicken thighs, skinned side up, on top of onions; add any accumulated juices. Sprinkle evenly with cilantro and mint, scatter remaining onion mixture over herbs, then cover with remaining rice. Pour reserved ¾ cup cooking liquid evenly over rice.

7. Cover saucepan and cook over medium-low heat until rice is tender and chicken registers 175 degrees, about 30 minutes (if large amount of steam is escaping from pot, reduce heat to low).

8. Run heat-resistant rubber spatula around inside rim of saucepan to loosen any affixed rice. Using large serving spoon, spoon biryani into individual bowls, scooping from bottom of the pot. Serve, passing yogurt sauce separately.

SEASON 8

Chicken Tikka Masala

Serves 4 to 6 • Total Time: 1½ hours, plus 30 minutes brining

Why This Recipe Works Chicken tikka masala is arguably the single most popular Indian restaurant dish in the world. Turns out, it's not a traditional Indian dish: It was invented in an Indian restaurant in London. Without historical roots, there is no definitive recipe. We wanted to develop one that would produce moist, tender chunks of chicken in a rich, lightly spiced tomato sauce. To season the chicken, we rubbed it with salt, coriander, cumin, and cayenne. Then we dipped it in yogurt mixed with oil, garlic, and ginger and broiled it. And since large pieces don't dry out as quickly as smaller ones under the broiler, we cooked the chicken breasts whole, cutting them into pieces only after cooking. While the chicken was cooking, we made the sauce using canned crushed tomatoes and cream and added onion, ginger, garlic, chile, and readily available garam masala.

This dish is best when prepared with whole-milk yogurt, but low-fat yogurt can be substituted. For more heat, include the chile seeds and ribs when mincing. Serve with rice pilaf.

Chicken

- 1 teaspoon table salt, divided
- ½ teaspoon ground cumin
- ½ teaspoon ground coriander
- ¼ teaspoon cayenne pepper
- 2 pounds boneless, skinless chicken breasts, trimmed
- 1 cup plain whole-milk yogurt
- 2 tablespoons vegetable oil
- 1 tablespoon minced or grated fresh ginger
- 2 garlic cloves, minced

Sauce

- 3 tablespoons vegetable oil
- 1 onion, chopped fine
- 1 tablespoon garam masala
- 1 tablespoon tomato paste
- 2 garlic cloves, minced
- 2 teaspoons grated fresh ginger
- 1 serrano chile, stemmed, seeded, and minced
- 1 (28-ounce) can crushed tomatoes
- 2 teaspoons sugar
- ½ teaspoon table salt
- ⅔ cup heavy cream
- ¼ cup chopped fresh cilantro

1. For the chicken: Combine ½ teaspoon salt, cumin, coriander, and cayenne in small bowl. Pat chicken dry with paper towels and sprinkle with spice mixture, pressing gently so mixture adheres. Place chicken on plate, cover with plastic wrap, and refrigerate for at least 30 minutes or up to 1 hour. In large bowl, whisk yogurt, oil, ginger, and garlic together and set aside.

2. For the sauce: Heat oil in Dutch oven over medium heat until shimmering. Add onion and cook, stirring frequently, until softened and light golden, 8 to 10 minutes. Stir in garam masala, tomato paste, garlic, ginger, and serrano and cook, stirring frequently, until fragrant, about 3 minutes. Add crushed tomatoes, sugar, and remaining ½ teaspoon salt and bring to a boil. Reduce heat to medium-low, cover, and simmer for 15 minutes, stirring occasionally. Stir in cream and return to simmer. Remove pan from heat and cover to keep warm. (Sauce can be refrigerated in airtight container for up to 4 days and gently reheated before adding hot chicken.)

3. To cook the chicken: While sauce simmers, adjust oven rack 6 inches from broiling element and heat broiler. Line rimmed baking sheet or broiler pan with aluminum foil and set wire rack in sheet.

4. Using tongs, dip chicken into yogurt mixture (chicken should be coated with thick layer of yogurt) and arrange on wire rack. Discard excess yogurt mixture. Broil chicken until lightly charred and chicken registers 160 to 165 degrees, 10 to 18 minutes, flipping chicken halfway through.

5. Let chicken rest for 5 minutes, then cut into 1-inch chunks and stir into warm sauce (do not simmer chicken in sauce). Stir in cilantro, season with salt to taste, and serve.

Chicken Teriyaki

Serves 4 • **Total Time: 1 hour**

Why This Recipe Works Our version of chicken teriyaki started with bone-in chicken thighs, not because we wanted the bones (we promptly removed them), but because we wanted the skin, which protects the meat from the heat of the skillet and adds succulence and meaty flavor. Cutting the thighs into bite-size pieces not only made them easier to eat with chopsticks but also created plenty of surface area for browning and, eventually, for the glaze. A pretreatment with sake boosted savory flavor. Adding cornstarch to the sake had a triple benefit: It formed an extra layer of protection around the chicken, which left it supple; it provided a surface that "grabbed" the glaze; and some of it sloughed off into the glaze, thickening it a bit more. The glaze used plenty of soy sauce for seasoning, sake for savory depth, sugar for sweetness and luster, and a good amount of fresh ginger for brightness.

> *It's worth deboning the chicken thighs here so that you can retain the skin. Boneless, skin-on thighs are a rare find, but if you do find them, buy 1½ pounds for this recipe; do not use skinless thighs, because they'll be less juicy. Use a Frywall or splatter screen if you have one. Inexpensive sake is fine here; it can often be purchased in small cans. We strain the glaze in step 4 to improve its clarity, but you can skip this process if you prefer. Serve with unseasoned short-grain white rice, peppery greens such as watercress or mizuna, and sliced scallions.*

1½–2   pounds bone-in chicken thighs
3½   tablespoons sake, divided
1   tablespoon cornstarch
3   tablespoons soy sauce
1   tablespoon sugar
2   tablespoons grated fresh ginger
2   teaspoons vegetable oil

1. Place 1 chicken thigh skin side down on cutting board. Using sharp paring knife, trim excess skin and fat, leaving enough skin to cover meat. Cut slit along length of thigh bone to expose bone. Using tip of knife, cut/scrape meat from bone. Slip knife under bone to separate bone from meat. Discard bone and trim any remaining cartilage from thigh. Keeping thigh skin side down, cut into 1½-inch pieces, leaving as much skin attached as possible. Transfer to medium bowl and repeat with remaining thighs. Add 1½ tablespoons sake and cornstarch and stir gently until chicken is evenly coated.

2. Combine soy sauce, sugar, and remaining 2 tablespoons sake in small bowl. Microwave until sugar is dissolved, about 30 seconds. Place fine-mesh strainer over bowl containing soy sauce mixture. Add ginger to strainer and press to extract juice. Discard solids, but do not wash strainer.

3. Line large plate with paper towels. Heat oil in 12-inch nonstick skillet over medium heat until shimmering. Place chicken skin side down in skillet (skillet may be very full). Increase heat to medium-high; place Frywall or splatter screen, if using, on skillet; and cook, without moving chicken, until all pieces have ¼- to ½-inch perimeter of white, 6 to 8 minutes. Slide skillet off heat and flip chicken. Return skillet to burner and reduce heat to medium. Continue to cook until chicken is just cooked through, 1 to 2 minutes longer.

4. Remove skillet from heat. Using slotted spoon, transfer chicken to prepared plate. Pour off fat, scrape any browned bits out of skillet, and wipe skillet clean with paper towels. Return chicken to skillet. Add soy sauce mixture and cook over medium heat, stirring frequently, until chicken is thinly coated and sauce has consistency of maple syrup, 1 to 2 minutes. Using slotted spoon, transfer chicken to serving bowl. Pour glaze in skillet through now-empty strainer set over small serving bowl. Drizzle 2 tablespoons glaze over chicken and serve, passing remaining glaze (there will be only a few tablespoons, but it is potent) separately.

Chicken and Sauce

- 1½ pounds boneless, skinless chicken thighs, trimmed and cut into ½-inch pieces
- ¼ cup soy sauce, divided
- 1 tablespoon cornstarch
- 1 tablespoon Chinese rice wine or dry sherry
- ½ teaspoon white pepper
- 1 tablespoon Chinese black vinegar
- 1 tablespoon packed dark brown sugar
- 2 teaspoons toasted sesame oil

Stir-Fry

- 2 tablespoons plus 1 teaspoon vegetable oil, divided
- 3 garlic cloves, minced
- 2 teaspoons grated fresh ginger
- ½ cup dry-roasted peanuts
- 10–15 dried arbol chiles, halved lengthwise and seeded
- 1 teaspoon Sichuan peppercorns, ground coarse
- 2 celery ribs, cut into ½-inch pieces
- 5 scallions, white and light green parts only, cut into ½-inch pieces

1. For the chicken and sauce: Combine chicken, 2 tablespoons soy sauce, cornstarch, rice wine, and white pepper in medium bowl and set aside. Stir vinegar, sugar, oil, and remaining 2 tablespoons soy sauce together in small bowl and set aside.

2. For the stir-fry: Stir 1 tablespoon oil, garlic, and ginger together in second small bowl. Combine peanuts and 1 teaspoon oil in 12-inch nonstick skillet over medium-low heat. Cook, stirring constantly, until peanuts just begin to darken, 3 to 5 minutes. Transfer peanuts to plate and spread into even layer to cool. Return now-empty skillet to medium-low heat. Add remaining 1 tablespoon oil, arbols, and peppercorns and cook, stirring constantly, until arbols begin to darken, 1 to 2 minutes. Add garlic mixture and cook, stirring constantly, until all clumps are broken up and mixture is fragrant, about 30 seconds.

3. Add chicken and spread into even layer. Cover skillet; increase heat to medium-high; and cook, without stirring, for 1 minute. Stir chicken and spread into even layer. Cover and cook, without stirring, for 1 minute. Add celery and cook uncovered, stirring frequently, until chicken is cooked through, 2 to 3 minutes. Add soy sauce mixture and cook, stirring constantly, until sauce is thickened and shiny and coats chicken, 3 to 5 minutes. Stir in scallions and peanuts. Transfer to platter and serve.

Gōngbǎo Jīdīng

Serves 4 to 6 • **Total Time: 45 minutes**

Why This Recipe Works Spicy chiles and tingly Sichuan peppercorns team up with lightly sauced chicken and peanuts to make kung pao chicken that's literally sensational. We started our version by toasting peanuts in a skillet to maximize their crunch. Next we toasted crushed Sichuan peppercorns and arbol chiles that we'd halved lengthwise to release their heat. We stirred in plenty of garlic and ginger and then added marinated diced chicken thighs. We covered the skillet to facilitate quick and even cooking of the chicken. When it was almost cooked through, we added some celery for crisp freshness and then a concentrated sauce mixture that cooked down to a glaze. Stirring in the scallions and toasted peanuts last ensured that they retained their all-important crunch.

Kung pao chicken should be quite spicy. To adjust the heat level, use more or fewer chiles, depending on the size (we used 2-inch-long chiles) and your taste. Have your ingredients prepared and your equipment in place before you begin to cook. Use a spice grinder or mortar and pestle to coarsely grind the Sichuan peppercorns. If Chinese black vinegar is unavailable, substitute sherry vinegar. Serve with white rice and a simple vegetable such as broccoli or bok choy. Do not eat the chiles.

Cast Iron Chicken Pot Pie

Serves 4 to 6 • Total Time: 1½ hours, plus 30 minutes resting

Why This Recipe Works The preparations required for chicken pot pie have largely relegated it to a Sunday treat, but moving this dish to a cast-iron skillet speeds up the process and also improves the results. We started by par-baking the crust separately, which kept it from becoming soggy and ensured that it was done at the same time as the filling. Sautéing the vegetables and aromatics and adding broth created a rich, caramelized base in which we then poached the chicken. Next, we shredded the meat and then stirred it back in with heavy cream, peas, parsley, and dry sherry. We slipped on the parbaked crust and baked the dish for a short time to bring it all together.

You can use our Foolproof All-Butter Dough for Single-Crust Pie or ready-made pie dough in this recipe.

- 1 recipe Foolproof All-Butter Dough for Single-Crust Pie (page 630)
- 1 large egg, lightly beaten with 2 tablespoons water
- 4 tablespoons unsalted butter
- 4 carrots, peeled and sliced ¼ inch thick
- 2 celery ribs, cut into ¼-inch pieces
- 1 onion, chopped fine
- ¼ teaspoon table salt
- ¼ teaspoon pepper
- 1 teaspoon minced fresh thyme or ¼ teaspoon dried
- 6 tablespoons all-purpose flour
- 2 cups chicken broth
- 1½ pounds boneless, skinless chicken breasts, trimmed
- ½ cup frozen peas
- ¼ cup heavy cream
- 3 tablespoons minced fresh parsley
- 1 tablespoon dry sherry

1. Roll dough between 2 sheets of parchment paper into 11-inch circle. Remove top parchment sheet. Fold in outer ½ inch of dough to make 10-inch circle. Using your fingers, crimp edge of dough to make attractive fluted rim. Using paring knife, cut 4 oval-shaped vents, each about 2 inches long and ½ inch wide, in center of dough. Transfer dough, still on parchment, to baking sheet and refrigerate until firm, about 15 minutes.

2. Adjust oven rack to middle position and heat oven to 400 degrees. Brush dough with egg mixture and bake until golden brown, 17 to 20 minutes, rotating sheet halfway through baking. Transfer crust, still on sheet, to wire rack and let cool; do not turn off oven.

3. Heat 10-inch cast-iron skillet over medium heat for 3 minutes. Melt butter in skillet. Add carrots, celery, onion, salt, and pepper and cook until softened and lightly browned, 5 to 7 minutes. Stir in thyme and cook until fragrant, about 30 seconds. Stir in flour and cook for 2 minutes. Slowly whisk in broth, scraping up any browned bits and smoothing out any lumps, and bring to simmer.

4. Pound thicker ends of chicken breasts as needed to create even thickness. Nestle chicken into skillet. Reduce heat to gentle simmer; cover; and cook until chicken registers 160 degrees and sauce has thickened, 10 to 15 minutes, flipping chicken halfway through.

5. Transfer chicken to carving board, let cool slightly, then shred into bite-size pieces using 2 forks. Stir shredded chicken, peas, cream, parsley, and sherry into skillet. Season with salt and pepper to taste.

6. Place parbaked pie crust on top of filling; transfer skillet to oven; and bake until crust is deep golden brown and filling is bubbling, about 10 minutes. Let pot pie cool for 10 minutes before serving.

Shaping a Pot Pie Crust

After folding in outer ½ inch of dough, crimp edge to make attractive fluted rim using index finger of 1 hand and thumb and index finger of other hand.

Roast Turkey and Gravy with Herbes de Provence and Lemon

Serves 10 to 12 • **Total Time: 3½ to 4 hours, plus 24 hours chilling**

Why This Recipe Works For a roast turkey that combines verdant, savory herb flavor in every bite with an easy, reliable roasting method, we started by making a hard-working herb paste that featured delicately floral herbes de Provence and vibrant lemon zest. Adding a generous amount of parsley as well as garlic powder and black pepper gave the paste a complex foundation, and a little vegetable oil made the mixture easy to apply. Applying the paste in three ways—under the skin with salt and sugar before roasting, over the skin in a basting butter, and stirred into the gravy—ensured that it offered bright, savory flavor in every bite. Applying baking powder to the skin before roasting helped it brown deeply. Roasting the bird in a preheated roasting pan set on a baking stone jump-started the cooking of the legs, while covering the breast with a foil shield for part of the time protected the lean breast meat from overcooking. The baking stone also thoroughly reduced and concentrated the pan drippings, so it didn't take long to make a flavorful gravy.

Note that this recipe requires refrigerating the seasoned turkey for at least 24 hours. This recipe was developed using Diamond Crystal Kosher Salt. If you have Morton Kosher Salt, which is denser, reduce the salt in step 2 to 3 tablespoons and rub 1 tablespoon of the herb mixture into each side of the breast, 1½ teaspoons into each leg, and the remainder into the cavity. If using a self-basting turkey (such as a frozen Butterball) or a kosher turkey, omit the salt and sugar; instead, apply 4 teaspoons of the herb paste to each breast side and 2 teaspoons to each leg. When removing the foil in step 5, check the drippings in the roasting pan. If they are very dark or there is no liquid, add ¾ cup of water to the pan. The success of this recipe depends on saturating a baking stone and roasting pan with heat.

Herb Paste

- ¾ cup chopped fresh parsley
- ¼ cup herbes de Provence
- 2 tablespoons vegetable oil
- 2 teaspoons grated lemon zest
- 2 teaspoons garlic powder
- ½ teaspoon pepper

Turkey and Gravy

- ¼ cup kosher salt
- 4 teaspoons sugar
- 1 (12- to 14-pound) turkey, neck and giblets removed and reserved for gravy
- 2½ tablespoons vegetable oil, divided
- 1 teaspoon baking powder
- 2 tablespoons unsalted butter, melted
- 1 small onion, chopped fine
- 1 carrot, peeled and sliced thin
- 5 tablespoons all-purpose flour
- 3¼ cups water
- ¼ cup dry white wine
- 5 sprigs fresh parsley
- 2 bay leaves

1. For the herb paste: Process all ingredients in food processor until finely ground, about 30 seconds, scraping down sides of bowl as necessary.

2. For the turkey and gravy: Combine ¼ cup herb paste, salt, and sugar in bowl. Place turkey, breast side up, on counter. Using your fingers, carefully loosen skin covering breast and leg quarters. Rub 2 tablespoons herb mixture under skin of each side of breast, 4 teaspoons under skin of each leg, and remaining herb mixture inside cavity. Tuck wings behind back and tie legs together with kitchen twine. Place turkey on wire rack set in rimmed baking sheet and refrigerate, uncovered, for at least 24 hours or up to 2 days.

3. At least 30 minutes before roasting turkey, adjust oven rack to lowest position, set baking stone on rack, set roasting pan on baking stone, and heat oven to 500 degrees.

Combine 1½ teaspoons oil and baking powder in small bowl. Pat turkey dry with paper towels. Rub oil mixture evenly over turkey. Cover breast with double layer of aluminum foil.

4. Remove roasting pan from oven. Drizzle remaining 2 tablespoons oil into roasting pan. Place turkey, breast side up, in pan and return pan to oven. Reduce oven temperature to 425 degrees and roast for 45 minutes. Stir 1 tablespoon herb paste into melted butter.

5. Remove turkey from oven. Discard foil and brush herb butter evenly over turkey. Return turkey to oven; reduce oven temperature to 325 degrees; and continue to roast until breast registers 160 degrees and thighs register 175 degrees, 1 to 1½ hours longer.

6. Using spatula, loosen turkey from roasting pan; transfer to carving board and let rest, uncovered, for 45 minutes. While turkey rests, using wooden spoon, scrape up any browned bits from bottom of roasting pan. Strain mixture through fine-mesh strainer set over bowl. Transfer drippings to fat separator and let rest for 10 minutes. Reserve defatted liquid (you should have 1 cup; add water if necessary) and 3 tablespoons fat. Discard remaining fat.

7. Heat reserved fat in large saucepan over medium-high heat until shimmering. Add neck and giblets and cook until well browned, 10 to 12 minutes. Transfer neck and giblets to large plate. Reduce heat to medium; add onion and carrot; and cook, stirring frequently, until vegetables are softened, 5 to 7 minutes. Add flour and cook, stirring constantly, until flour is well coated with fat, about 1 minute. Slowly whisk in defatted liquid and cook until thickened, about 1 minute.

8. Whisk in water, wine, parsley sprigs, and bay leaves. Return neck and giblets to saucepan and bring to simmer. Simmer for 10 minutes. Discard neck. Strain gravy through fine-mesh strainer set over bowl, discarding solids. Stir in remaining herb paste and season with salt and pepper to taste. Transfer to serving bowl. Carve turkey and arrange on serving platter. Serve with gravy.

Applying Herb Paste Under the Skin

Slip your hand between skin and meat to carefully loosen skin. Spread herb paste under skin. During roasting, skin protects herbs from burning.

SEASON 17

Easier Roast Turkey and Gravy

Serves 10 to 12 • Total Time: 3½ to 4 hours, plus 24 hours chilling

Why This Recipe Works To season the meat and help it retain more juices as it cooked, we loosened the skin of the turkey and applied a mixture of salt and sugar to the flesh. We preheated both a baking stone and roasting pan in the oven before placing the turkey in the pan. The stone absorbed heat and delivered it through the pan to the turkey's legs and thighs, which needed to cook to a higher temperature than the delicate breast meat (which we protected with a foil shield). After the leg quarters had gotten a jump start on cooking, we reduced the oven temperature from 425 to 325 degrees and removed the shield to allow the breast to brown while the bird finished cooking. The boost of heat provided by the stone also helped the juices brown and reduce into concentrated drippings that could be turned into a flavorful gravy in the time that the turkey rested.

Note that this recipe requires salting the bird in the refrigerator for 24 to 48 hours. This recipe was developed and tested using Diamond Crystal Kosher Salt. If you have Morton Kosher Salt, which is denser than Diamond Crystal, reduce the salt in step 1 to 3 tablespoons. Rub 1 tablespoon salt mixture into each breast, 1½ teaspoons into each leg, and remainder into cavity. Table salt is too fine and not recommended for this recipe. If you are roasting a kosher or self-basting turkey (such as a frozen Butterball), do not salt it; it already contains a good amount of sodium. The success of this recipe is dependent on saturating the pizza stone and roasting pan with heat. We recommend preheating the stone, pan, and oven for at least 30 minutes.

- 4 teaspoons sugar
- ¼ cup kosher salt
- 1 (12- to 14-pound) turkey, neck and giblets removed and reserved for gravy
- 2½ tablespoons vegetable oil, divided
- 1 teaspoon baking powder
- 1 small onion, chopped fine
- 1 carrot, peeled and sliced thin
- 5 sprigs fresh parsley
- 2 bay leaves
- 5 tablespoons all-purpose flour
- 3¼ cups water
- ¼ cup dry white wine

1. Combine sugar and salt in bowl. With turkey breast side up, use your fingers or handle of wooden spoon to carefully separate skin from thighs and breast. Rub 4 teaspoons salt-sugar mixture under skin of each breast half, 2 teaspoons under skin of each leg, and remaining salt-sugar mixture into cavity. Tie legs together with kitchen twine. Place turkey on rack set in rimmed baking sheet and refrigerate uncovered for 24 to 48 hours.

2. At least 30 minutes before roasting turkey, adjust oven rack to lowest position and set pizza stone on oven rack. Place roasting pan on pizza stone and heat oven to 500 degrees. Combine 1½ teaspoons oil and baking powder in small bowl. Pat turkey dry with paper towels. Rub oil mixture evenly over turkey. Cover turkey breast with double layer of aluminum foil.

3. Remove roasting pan from oven. Place remaining 2 tablespoons oil in roasting pan. Place turkey into pan breast side up and return pan to oven. Reduce oven temperature to 425 degrees and cook for 45 minutes.

4. Remove foil shield, reduce temperature to 325 degrees, and continue to cook until breast registers 160 degrees and thighs register 175 degrees, 1 to 1½ hours longer.

5. Using spatula loosen turkey from roasting pan, transfer to carving board, and let rest uncovered for 45 minutes. While turkey rests, use wooden spoon to scrape any browned bits from bottom of roasting pan. Pour mixture through fine-mesh strainer set in bowl. Transfer drippings to fat separator and let rest 10 minutes. Reserve 3 tablespoons fat and defatted liquid (about 1 cup). Discard remaining fat.

6. Heat reserved fat in large saucepan over medium-high heat until shimmering. Add reserved neck and giblets and cook until well browned, 10 to 12 minutes. Transfer neck and giblets to large plate. Reduce heat to medium; add onion, carrot, parsley, and bay leaves; and cook, stirring frequently, until vegetables are softened, 5 to 7 minutes. Add flour and cook, stirring constantly, until flour is well coated with fat, about 1 minute. Slowly whisk in reserved defatted liquid and cook until thickened, about 1 minute. Whisk in water and wine, return neck and giblets, and bring to simmer. Simmer for 10 minutes. Season with salt and pepper to taste. Discard neck. Strain mixture through fine-mesh strainer and transfer to serving bowl. Carve turkey and arrange on serving platter. Serve with gravy.

GAME CHANGER

A Baking Stone Is the Key to Perfectly Roasted Turkey

"Over all of our turkey recipes, this recipe has become my favorite in terms of both ease and dependable results. While I'm keen to brine a turkey for juicy, seasoned flavor, and I know that flipping a turkey during roasting evens out the usual issue of the internal temperature of the dark meat lagging behind the breast meat (dark meat needs to cook to a higher temp), neither of the methods is without some issue.

With this recipe, there's no need to find space in the fridge for a giant brine bucket. Instead, you salt under the skin of the breast and legs and then let the meat season for a day or so. Easy. But the real game changer is to preheat a baking stone and a heavy-duty roasting pan for at least 30 minutes in a 500-degree oven. At the moment the turkey hits the searing-hot pan, you hear a loud, frantic sizzle—almost like a starting gun signaling that the race between the light and dark meat is off. There's no flipping at all; the baking stone retains and focuses that heat on the dark meat through the entirety of the recipe. The result is that the temps of the drumsticks and thighs reach 175 just as the breast meat arrives at 160. It's roast turkey perfection."

Bridget

1 (5- to 7- pound) bone-in turkey breast
4 teaspoons kosher salt, divided
2 tablespoons unsalted butter, melted
2 teaspoons extra-virgin olive oil, plus extra
  as needed
1 small onion, chopped
1 small carrot, chopped
1 small celery rib, chopped
5 cups water
2 sprigs fresh thyme
1 bay leaf
¼ cup all-purpose flour
¼ cup dry white wine

Roast Whole Turkey Breast with Gravy

Serves 6 to 8 • Total Time: 2½ hours, plus 24 hours salting

Why This Recipe Works For an impressive roast turkey breast, we removed (but did not discard) the backbone so the breast lay flat in the oven for even browning and more stability during carving. Salting the breast for 24 hours seasoned it and helped it retain more juices as it cooked. Brushing the skin with melted butter ensured deep browning and great flavor. Roasting the breast in a 12-inch skillet instead of a roasting pan helped contain drippings underneath the bird so they didn't scorch. Starting the breast at 325 degrees helped gently cook the white meat, while finishing it at 500 degrees ensured that it got deeply bronzed. While the turkey cooked, we used the backbone to make a flavorful stock to use as the base for the gravy, which we built directly in the skillet.

Note that this recipe requires refrigerating the seasoned breast for 24 hours. This recipe was developed using Diamond Crystal Kosher Salt. If you use Morton Kosher Salt, which is denser, reduce the salt in step 2, rubbing 1 teaspoon of salt into each side of the breast and ½ teaspoon into the cavity. If you're using a self-basting (such as a frozen Butterball) or kosher turkey breast, do not salt in step 2. If your turkey breast comes with the back removed, you can skip making the gravy or substitute 1 pound of chicken wings for the turkey back.

1. Place turkey breast on counter skin side down. Using kitchen shears, cut through ribs, following vertical line of fat where breast meets back, from tapered end of breast to wing joint. Using your hands, bend back away from breast to pop shoulder joints out of sockets. Using paring knife, cut through joints between bones to separate back from breast. Reserve back for gravy. Trim excess fat from breast.

2. Place turkey breast, skin side up, on counter. Using your fingers, carefully loosen and separate turkey skin from each side of breast. Peel back skin, leaving it attached at top and center of breast. Rub 1 teaspoon salt onto each side of breast, then place skin back over meat. Rub 1 teaspoon salt onto underside of breast cavity. Place turkey on large plate and refrigerate, uncovered, for 24 hours.

3. Adjust oven rack to middle position and heat oven to 325 degrees. Pat turkey dry with paper towels. Place turkey, skin side up, in 12-inch ovensafe skillet, arranging so narrow end of breast is not touching skillet. Brush melted butter evenly over turkey and sprinkle with remaining 1 teaspoon salt. Roast until thickest part of breast registers 130 degrees, 1 to 1¼ hours.

4. Meanwhile, heat oil in large saucepan over medium-high heat. Add reserved back, skin side down, and cook until well browned, 6 to 8 minutes. Add onion, carrot, and celery and cook, stirring occasionally, until vegetables are softened and lightly browned, about 5 minutes. Add water, thyme sprigs, and bay leaf and bring to boil. Reduce heat to medium-low and simmer for 1 hour. Strain broth through fine-mesh strainer into container. Discard solids; set aside broth (you should have about 4 cups). (Broth can be refrigerated for up to 24 hours.)

5. Remove turkey from oven and increase oven temperature to 500 degrees. When oven reaches 500 degrees, return turkey to oven and roast until skin is deeply browned and thickest part of breast registers 160 degrees, 15 to 30 minutes. Using spatula, loosen turkey from skillet; transfer to carving board and let rest, uncovered, for 30 minutes.

6. While turkey rests, pour off fat from skillet. (You should have about ¼ cup; if not, add extra oil as needed to equal ¼ cup.) Return fat to skillet and heat over medium heat until shimmering. Sprinkle flour evenly over fat and cook, whisking constantly, until flour is coated with fat and browned, about 1 minute. Add wine, whisking to scrape up any browned bits, and cook until wine has evaporated, 1 to 2 minutes. Slowly whisk in reserved broth. Increase heat to medium-high and cook, whisking occasionally, until gravy is thickened and reduced to 2 cups, about 20 minutes. Season with salt and pepper to taste. Carve turkey and serve, passing gravy separately.

Prepping the Turkey Breast

1. Cut through ribs following line of fat where breast meets back, from breast's tapered end to wing joint.

2. Bend back away from breast to pop shoulder joints out of sockets. Cut through joints to remove back.

3. Without backbone in way, it's easy to pull back skin so you can evenly season breast meat.

Porchetta-Style Turkey Breast

Serves 6 to 8 • Total Time: 3½ hours, plus 8 hours salting

Why This Recipe Works For this year's holiday centerpiece, why not trade in the usual whole roast turkey and brown gravy for the prettiest, most flavor-packed piece of white-meat poultry you've ever tasted? Turkey porchetta, or turchetta, is a turkey breast roast that takes its shape and seasonings from the iconic Italian pork roast called porchetta. The boneless, cylindrical roast cooks evenly from end to end and slices beautifully, with bronzed skin that insulates the lean meat to keep it moist and a superflavorful garlic-herb paste that renders gravy totally unnecessary. Instead of starting with a boneless turkey breast, we deboned a crown roast ourselves to keep the skin and meat intact. We tossed the breast halves and tenderloins with the herb-spice paste in a bowl so that, once we wrapped the meat in the skin into a cylinder, the paste was evenly swirled throughout, attractively marbling each slice. Refrigerating the assembled roast for at least 8 hours before cooking allowed the salt in the paste to migrate into the meat, seasoning it and helping it retain its juices during cooking. Starting the roast in a low oven and pulling it out 15 degrees shy of the target temperature meant that carryover cooking could gradually raise its internal temperature to the perfect doneness.

We prefer a natural turkey breast here; if you're using a self-basting breast (such as Butterball) or kosher breast, omit the 4 teaspoons of salt in the herb paste. This recipe was developed using Diamond Crystal Kosher Salt; if you're using Morton Kosher Salt, which is denser, use 1 tablespoon in the herb paste and 1½ teaspoons on the exterior of the roast.

- 1 tablespoon fennel seeds
- 2 teaspoons black peppercorns
- ¼ cup fresh rosemary leaves, chopped
- ¼ cup fresh sage leaves, chopped
- ¼ cup fresh thyme leaves
- 6 garlic cloves, chopped
- 2 tablespoons kosher salt, divided
- 3 tablespoons extra-virgin olive oil
- 1 (7- to 8-pound) bone-in turkey breast
- 2 tablespoons unsalted butter, melted

1. Grind fennel seeds and peppercorns using spice grinder or mortar and pestle until finely ground. Transfer to food processor and add rosemary, sage, thyme, garlic, and 4 teaspoons salt. Pulse mixture until finely chopped, 15 to 20 pulses, scraping down sides of bowl as needed. Add oil and process until paste forms, 20 to 30 seconds. Cut seven 16-inch lengths and one 30-inch length of kitchen twine and set aside. Measure out 20-inch piece of aluminum foil and crumple into loose ball. Uncrumple foil and place on rimmed baking sheet (crinkled foil will insulate bottom of sheet and minimize smoking during final roasting step). Spray wire rack with vegetable oil spray and place on prepared sheet.

2. To remove back, place turkey breast skin side down on cutting board. Using kitchen shears, cut through ribs, following vertical lines of fat where breast meets back, from tapered ends of breast to wing joints. Using your hands, bend back away from breast to pop shoulder joints out of sockets. Using paring knife, cut through joints between bones to separate back from breast.

3. Flip breast skin side up. Starting at tapered side of breast and using your fingers to separate skin from meat, peel skin off breast meat and reserve. Using tip of chef's knife or boning knife, cut along rib cage to remove each breast half completely. Reserve bones for making stock, or discard. Peel tenderloins from underside of each breast and use knife to remove exposed part of white tendon from each tenderloin.

4. Lay 1 breast half on cutting board, smooth side down and with narrow end pointing toward your knife hand. Holding knife parallel to cutting board, slice into breast starting where breast becomes thicker (about halfway along length). Stop ½ inch from edge of breast and open to create 1 long piece of even thickness. Repeat with remaining breast half. Transfer all meat to large bowl. Add herb paste and massage into meat to coat evenly.

5. Pat exterior of skin dry with paper towels and lay flat, exterior side down, on cutting board with long side running parallel to counter. Remove any loose pieces of fat. Lay 1 breast half on 1 side of skin with butterflied end closest to you. Lay second breast half next to first with butterflied end farthest away from you. Spread breast halves slightly apart and lay tenderloins between them with their thin ends overlapping in center.

6. Using skin as aid, fold up each breast half over tenderloins so skin meets directly over tenderloins. Slip one 16-inch length of twine under roast about 2 inches from 1 end and tie into simple knot, pinching skin closed as you tighten. Repeat tying at opposite end. Tie remaining five 16-inch lengths of twine evenly between 2 end pieces. Trim excess twine.

7. Tie 1 end of 30-inch length of twine onto loop farthest from you. Working toward you, loop twine over top and around each successive strand until you get to bottom of roast. Flip roast and continue looping to bottom of roast. Flip roast again and tie off where you started. Sprinkle roast evenly with remaining 2 teaspoons salt; place on prepared rack; and refrigerate, uncovered, for at least 8 hours or up to 2 days.

8. Adjust oven rack to upper-middle position and heat oven to 275 degrees. Brush roast with melted butter. Cook until thickest part of roast registers 125 degrees, 1½ to 1¾ hours. Remove roast from oven and increase oven temperature to 500 degrees. When oven is up to temperature, remove twine from roast; return roast to oven; and cook until skin is browned and roast registers 145 degrees, 15 to 20 minutes.

9. Transfer roast to cutting board, tent with foil, and let rest for 30 minutes. Slice ½ inch thick and serve.

Assembling Turchetta

1. Using kitchen shears, cut through ribs, following vertical lines of fat where breast meets back, from tapered ends of breast to wing joints.

2. Using your hands, bend back away from breast to pop shoulder joints out of sockets.

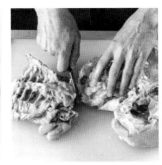

3. Using paring knife, cut through joints between bones to separate back from breast.

4. Starting at tapered side of breast and using your fingers to separate skin from meat, peel skin off breast meat and reserve.

5. Using tip of boning knife or chef's knife, cut along rib cage to remove each breast half completely.

6. Peel tenderloins from underside of each breast and use knife to remove exposed part of white tendon from each tenderloin.

7. Holding knife parallel to cutting board, slice into breast starting where breast becomes thicker (about halfway along length). Stop ½ inch from edge of breast and open to create 1 long piece of even thickness.

8. Massage herb paste into meat. Lay 1 breast half on 1 side of skin with butterflied end closest to you. Lay second breast half next to first with butterflied end farthest away from you. Spread breast halves slightly apart.

9. Lay tenderloins between them with their thin ends overlapping in center.

10. Using skin as an aid, fold each side up over tenderloins so skin meets directly over tenderloins. Slip one 16-inch length of twine under roast about 2 inches from 1 end and tie into simple knot, pinching skin closed as you tighten.

11. Working toward you, loop twine over top and around each successive strand until you get to bottom of roast.

12. Flip roast again and tie off where you started.

Turkey Thigh Confit with Citrus-Mustard Sauce

Serves 6 to 8 • Total Time: 5½ hours, plus 4 days salting

Why This Recipe Works Before refrigeration, confit was used as an effective way to prolong the shelf life of foods, including duck or goose parts. The poultry was cured in salt and then gently poached in its own fat before being buried beneath the fat and stored in an airtight crock. At serving time, all that was needed was a blast of heat to crisp the skin. For silky, supple, evenly seasoned turkey confit, we coated turkey thighs (easier to carve than tendinous drumsticks) in a flavorful paste and let them cure for at least four days. As the thighs sat, the salt, sugar, and some water-soluble compounds in the aromatics gave the turkey a deeply savory flavor. After rinsing away the cure, we oven-poached the thighs in duck fat, eliminating the need to babysit a pot for hours on the stovetop. The thighs could then be refrigerated for up to six days or immediately browned and served with our bright and tangy sauce.

Start this recipe at least five days or up to 12 days before serving (almost all the time is hands-off). The proper measurement of salt is crucial here. Be sure to use table salt, not kosher salt, and to measure it carefully. To ensure proper seasoning, make sure that the total weight of the turkey is within 2 ounces of the 4-pound target weight; do not use enhanced or kosher turkey thighs. Though duck fat is traditional, we found that chicken fat or even vegetable oil will work nicely. Reserve the duck fat or chicken fat and remaining stock in step 5 for further use; used vegetable oil should be discarded. It is convenient to split up the cooking over several days, but if you prefer to do all the cooking in one day, go straight from step 2 to step 5 without letting the turkey cool.

- 3 large onions, chopped coarse (4¾ cups)
- 12 sprigs fresh thyme
- 2½ tablespoons table salt for curing
- 1½ tablespoons sugar
- 1½ teaspoons pepper
- 4 pounds bone-in turkey thighs
- 6 cups duck fat, chicken fat, or vegetable oil for confit
- 1 garlic head, halved crosswise
- 2 bay leaves
- ½ cup orange marmalade
- 2 tablespoons whole-grain mustard
- ¾ teaspoon grated lime zest plus 2 tablespoons juice
- ¼ teaspoon table salt
- ⅛ teaspoon cayenne pepper

GAME CHANGER

A Thermometer Isn't Always Necessary

"Rather than a knife roll, I tote a shallow box from my desk to the kitchen when I cook. My tool kit contains the items I can't do without. There are a couple different knives, a bench scraper, a timer, and my instant-read thermometer. That thermometer is critical for dishes both sweet and savory. But checking for doneness isn't always as simple as looking for a particular number on the thermometer's digital screen. And this turkey confit recipe is a great example of this. Turkey thighs remain tough even after they reach 160 degrees, because the collagen binding the meat fibers together remains intact. It takes time for that collagen to break down, and cooking to higher temperatures doesn't radically speed up the process. It does, however, dry out the meat because the hotter it gets the more moisture is driven off. It takes time for the collagen to transform into gelatin and the temperature of the thighs won't change that. That's why you should reach for a knife or fork when it's time to check for doneness."

—Lan

1. To cure: Process onions, thyme sprigs, 2½ tablespoons salt, sugar, and pepper in food processor until finely chopped, about 20 seconds, scraping down sides of bowl as needed. Spread one-third of mixture evenly in bottom of 13 by 9-inch baking dish. Arrange turkey thighs, skin side up, in single layer in dish. Spread remaining onion mixture evenly over thighs. Wrap dish tightly with plastic wrap and refrigerate for 4 to 6 days (whatever is most convenient).

2. To cook: Adjust oven rack to lower-middle position and heat oven to 200 degrees. Remove thighs from onion mixture and rinse well (if you don't have a garbage disposal, do not allow onion pieces to go down drain). Pat thighs dry with paper towels. Heat fat in large Dutch oven over medium heat to 165 degrees. Off heat, add turkey thighs, skin side down and in single layer, making sure thighs are completely submerged. Add garlic and bay leaves. Transfer to oven, uncovered, and cook until metal skewer inserted straight down into thickest part of largest thigh can be easily

Turkey Thigh Confit with
Citrus-Mustard Sauce

removed without lifting thigh, 4 to 5 hours. (To ensure that oven temperature remains steady, wait at least 20 minutes before retesting if turkey is not done.) Remove from oven.

3. To make ahead: Let turkey cool completely in pot, about 2 hours; cover pot; and refrigerate for up to 6 days.

4. Uncover pot. Heat pot over medium-low heat until fat is melted, about 25 minutes. Increase heat to medium, maintaining bare simmer, and continue to cook until thickest part of largest thigh registers 135 to 140 degrees, about 30 minutes longer. (If turkey has been cooked in vegetable oil, heat pot over medium heat, maintaining bare simmer, until thickest part of largest thigh registers 135 to 140 degrees, about 30 minutes.)

5. To serve: Adjust oven rack to lower-middle position and heat oven to 500 degrees. While oven heats, crumple 20-inch length of aluminum foil into loose ball. Uncrumple foil, place in rimmed baking sheet, and top with wire rack. Using tongs, gently transfer thighs, skin side up, to prepared wire rack, being careful not to tear delicate skin. Set aside. Strain liquid through fine-mesh strainer into large bowl. Working in batches, pour liquid into fat separator, letting

liquid settle for 5 minutes before separating fat from turkey stock. (Alternatively, use bulb baster to extract turkey stock from beneath fat.) Transfer 4 teaspoons turkey stock to small bowl; add marmalade; and microwave until mixture is fluid, about 30 seconds. Stir in mustard, lime zest and juice, salt, and cayenne. Transfer to serving bowl.

6. Transfer thighs to oven and roast until well browned, 12 to 15 minutes. Transfer thighs to cutting board, skin side up, and let rest until just cool enough to handle, about 15 minutes.

7. Flip 1 thigh skin side down. Using tip of paring knife, cut along sides of thighbone, exposing bone. Carefully remove bone and any stray bits of cartilage. Flip thigh skin side up. Using sharp chef's knife, slice thigh crosswise 3/4 inch thick. Transfer to serving platter, skin side up. Repeat with remaining thighs. Serve, passing sauce separately.

Carving Turkey Thighs

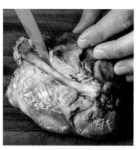

1. Place thigh skin side down. Using tip of paring knife, cut along sides of thighbone, exposing bone.

2. Carefully remove bone and any stray bits of cartilage. Flip thigh skin side up.

3. Using sharp chef's knife, slice thigh crosswise 3/4 inch thick.

Turkey Patty Melts

Makes 4 sandwiches • Total Time: 1 hour

Why This Recipe Works Our ground turkey patty melts started with browning a turkey mixture designed to remain juicy and tender even when pressed into very thin patties and seared. We added onions, water, and baking soda to the skillet; covered it; and allowed the water to lift the fond from the pan and steam the juices from the onion. Then, we removed the lid and continued to cook. The baking soda both tenderized the onions and raised the pH in the pan to promote speedy browning. We boosted the sweetness of the onions with brown sugar and added a splash of balsamic vinegar to give them some tang. We built the melts by layering the onions, patties, and pepper Jack between slices of bread and then gently griddled them until the sandwiches were warmed through, the cheese was melty, and the bread was crisply toasted.

Melty, subtly spicy pepper Jack works well here, but you can use any good melting cheese such as Swiss, Muenster, or American.

1 recipe Ground Turkey Mix (recipe follows)
1 pound onions, halved and sliced thin
1/2 cup water
1 tablespoon plus 4 teaspoons unsalted butter, divided
1/2 teaspoon kosher salt
1/4 teaspoon pepper
　　Pinch baking soda
2 teaspoons balsamic vinegar
1 teaspoon packed brown sugar

8 slices hearty sandwich bread

2 tablespoons Dijon mustard

12 slices pepper Jack cheese (4½ ounces), divided

1. Divide ground turkey mix into 4 equal portions. Shape each portion into thin patties that are ¼ inch larger than slices of bread. Place 2 patties in 12-inch nonstick skillet and cook over medium heat until spotty brown on bottom, about 3 minutes. Flip and cook, pressing down on patties frequently, until second side is lightly browned, about 2 minutes. Transfer to plate. Wipe out skillet and add remaining 2 patties. Repeat cooking process and transfer patties to plate, leaving fat in skillet.

2. Add onions, water, 1 tablespoon butter, salt, pepper, and baking soda and bring to simmer. Cover and cook for 8 minutes. Uncover and continue to cook, stirring occasionally, until onions are well browned, 7 to 10 minutes. Stir in vinegar and sugar.

3. While onions cook, arrange 4 slices of bread on cutting board. Spread 1½ teaspoons mustard on each slice. Top each slice with 1½ slices cheese, breaking up cheese as necessary to keep from hanging over edge. Arrange patties on top of cheese. Divide onions evenly over patties and top with remaining 6 slices cheese and remaining 4 slices bread.

4. In clean, dry skillet, melt 1 teaspoon butter over medium-low heat. Add 2 sandwiches and cook until bottoms are well browned, 4 to 5 minutes, moving sandwiches as needed to ensure even browning. Flip, add 1 teaspoon butter to pan, and continue to cook until second side is well browned, 2 to 3 minutes. Remove sandwiches and repeat with remaining 2 teaspoons butter and remaining 2 sandwiches. Serve.

Ground Turkey Mix

Makes 21 ounces • Total Time: 10 minutes

This mixture can be refrigerated for up to two days or frozen for up to one month.

1 shallot, chopped coarse (⅓ cup)

¼ cup panko bread crumbs

½ teaspoon kosher salt

¼ teaspoon pepper

1 pound 93 percent lean ground turkey

¼ cup milk

2 tablespoons unsalted butter, melted and cooled

1 tablespoon Worcestershire sauce

Process shallot, panko, salt, and pepper in food processor, scraping down sides as necessary, until shallot is finely ground, about 20 seconds. Add turkey, milk, melted butter, and Worcestershire and pulse until just combined, 8 to 12 pulses. Transfer to bowl, cover, and refrigerate until ready to use.

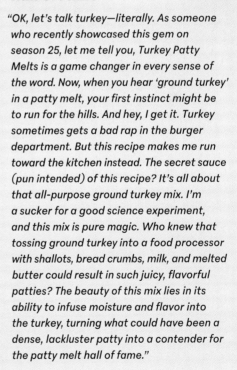

GAME CHANGER

The Patty Melt Hall of Fame

"OK, let's talk turkey—literally. As someone who recently showcased this gem on season 25, let me tell you, Turkey Patty Melts is a game changer in every sense of the word. Now, when you hear 'ground turkey' in a patty melt, your first instinct might be to run for the hills. And hey, I get it. Turkey sometimes gets a bad rap in the burger department. But this recipe makes me run toward the kitchen instead. The secret sauce (pun intended) of this recipe? It's all about that all-purpose ground turkey mix. I'm a sucker for a good science experiment, and this mix is pure magic. Who knew that tossing ground turkey into a food processor with shallots, bread crumbs, milk, and melted butter could result in such juicy, flavorful patties? The beauty of this mix lies in its ability to infuse moisture and flavor into the turkey, turning what could have been a dense, lackluster patty into a contender for the patty melt hall of fame."

— Antoinette

Meat

Photo: Lamb Barbacoa

Smashed Burgers

Serves 2 • **Total Time: 40 minutes**

Why This Recipe Works Smashed burgers trade on one simple truth: Crust is king. These burgers share the same thin, verging-on-well-done profile and all-American array of condiments as typical fast-food burgers, but their big selling point is an ultrabrown, crispy crust. We used commercial ground beef instead of grinding our own because the former is ground finer and thus exposes more myosin, a sticky meat protein that helps the patties hold together when they are smashed. Using a small saucepan to press straight down on the meat ensured that it spread and stuck uniformly to the skillet, which helped guarantee deep browning. We made two smaller patties at a time because they fit nicely inside a burger bun. Sandwiching an ultramelty slice of American cheese between the two patties helped the cheese melt and seep into the meat almost like a rich, salty cheese sauce would. Our creamy, tangy burger sauce added more richness and moisture, and lettuce and thinly sliced tomato provided freshness and acidity.

Do not use a stainless-steel or nonstick skillet here. You can use 85 percent lean ground beef, but 90 percent lean will produce a dry burger. Open a window or turn on your exhaust fan before cooking. Be assertive when pressing the patties. We strongly prefer Kraft Singles here for their meltability. To serve four, double the ingredients for the sauce and burgers and use the same amount of oil; once the burgers are cooked, transfer them to a wire rack set in a rimmed baking sheet, adding cheese to the first four burgers, and keep warm in a 200-degree oven. Place on buns right before serving.

Sauce

- 2 tablespoons mayonnaise
- 1 tablespoon minced shallot
- 1½ teaspoons finely chopped dill pickles plus ½ teaspoon brine
- 1½ teaspoons ketchup
- ⅛ teaspoon sugar
- ⅛ teaspoon pepper

Burgers

- 2 hamburger buns, toasted if desired
- 8 ounces 80 percent lean ground beef
- ¼ teaspoon vegetable oil
- ¼ teaspoon kosher salt, divided

- 2 slices American cheese (2 ounces)
  Bibb lettuce leaves
  Thinly sliced tomato

1. **For the sauce:** Stir all ingredients together in bowl.

2. **For the burgers:** Spread 1 tablespoon sauce on cut side of each bun top. Divide beef into 4 equal pieces (2 ounces each); form into loose, rough balls (do not compress). Place oil in 12-inch cast-iron or carbon-steel skillet. Use paper towel to rub oil into bottom of skillet (reserve paper towel). Heat over medium-low heat for 5 minutes. While skillet heats, wrap bottom and sides of small saucepan with large sheet of aluminum foil, anchoring foil on rim, and place large plate next to cooktop.

3. Increase heat to high. When skillet begins to smoke, place 2 balls about 3 inches apart in skillet. Use bottom of prepared saucepan to firmly smash each ball until 4 to 4½ inches in diameter. Place saucepan on plate next to cooktop. Sprinkle patties with ⅛ teaspoon salt and season with pepper. Cook until at least three-quarters of each patty is no longer pink on top, about 2 minutes (patties will stick to skillet). Use thin metal spatula to loosen patties from skillet. Flip patties and cook for 15 seconds. Slide skillet off heat. Transfer 1 burger to each bun bottom and top each with 1 slice American cheese. Gently scrape any browned bits from skillet, use tongs to wipe with reserved paper towel, and return skillet to heat. Repeat with remaining 2 balls and place burgers on top of cheese. Top with lettuce and tomato. Cap with prepared bun tops. Serve immediately.

Juicy Pub-Style Burgers

Serves 4 • **Total Time: 45 minutes**

Why This Recipe Works Few things are as satisfying as a thick, juicy pub-style burger. But by the time the center of these hefty burgers cooks through, there is often an overcooked band of meat. We wanted a patty that was evenly rosy from center to edge. Grinding our own meat in the food processor was a must (freezing the meat until just firm helped the processor chop it cleanly), and we found that sirloin steak tips were ideal. To give the burgers just enough structure, we cut the meat into small ½-inch chunks before grinding and lightly packed the meat into patties. Melted butter improved their flavor and juiciness. Transferring the burgers from the stovetop to the oven to finish cooking eliminated the overcooked gray zone. For extra pub-style appeal, we came up with flavorful topping combinations to finish off our burgers.

Sticking to the Skillet Is Good

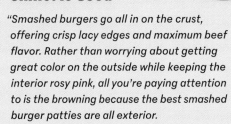

"Smashed burgers go all in on the crust, offering crisp lacy edges and maximum beef flavor. Rather than worrying about getting great color on the outside while keeping the interior rosy pink, all you're paying attention to is the browning because the best smashed burger patties are all exterior.

Early on in recipe development, I found it impossible to produce suitably thin and filigreed patties. I'd heat a small amount of oil in a cast-iron skillet and when it smoked, I smashed a lump of beef into a round. Initially, the patty measured around ⅛ of an inch thick and its edges were appealingly ragged. But as it cooked, it shrank into a disk that was too thick, too narrow, with too-smooth edges. Eventually I realized that the key to that texture I was looking for was to use the oil just as an indicator that my skillet was hot enough to start cooking. When the oil was hot enough to smoke, it needed to be wiped out. This ensured that the beef would stick to the pan until I slid a spatula beneath the patty to flip it over. These patties were crisp at the edges, deeply browned, and supremely beefy. All because I stopped worrying about sticking."

—Lan

Sirloin steak tips are also labeled as "flap meat." When stirring the butter and pepper into the ground meat and shaping the patties, take care not to overwork the meat or the burgers will become dense. For the best flavor, season the burgers aggressively just before cooking. The burgers can be topped as desired. The uncooked patties can be refrigerated for up to 24 hours.

- 2 pounds sirloin steak tips or boneless beef short ribs, trimmed and cut into ½-inch chunks
- 4 tablespoons unsalted butter, melted and cooled slightly
- ½ teaspoon table salt, divided
- 1½ teaspoons pepper, divided
- 1 teaspoon vegetable oil
- 4 large hamburger buns, toasted and buttered
- 1 recipe Pub-Style Burger Sauce (optional; recipe follows)

1. Place beef chunks on baking sheet in single layer. Freeze meat until very firm and starting to harden around edges but still pliable, 15 to 25 minutes.

2. Place one-quarter of meat in food processor and pulse until finely ground into ⅛-inch pieces, about 35 pulses, stopping and redistributing meat around bowl as necessary to ensure beef is evenly ground. Transfer meat to baking sheet by overturning processor bowl and without directly touching meat. Repeat grinding with remaining 3 batches of meat. Spread meat over sheet and inspect carefully, discarding any long strands of gristle or large chunks of hard meat or fat.

3. Adjust oven rack to middle position and heat oven to 300 degrees. Drizzle melted butter over ground meat and add 1 teaspoon pepper. Toss gently with fork to combine. Divide meat into 4 lightly packed balls. Gently flatten into patties ¾ inch thick and about 4½ inches in diameter. Refrigerate patties until ready to cook.

4. Sprinkle 1 side of patties with ¼ teaspoon salt and ¼ teaspoon pepper. Using spatula, flip patties and sprinkle other side with remaining ¼ teaspoon salt and remaining ¼ teaspoon pepper. Heat oil in 12-inch skillet over high heat until just smoking. Using spatula, transfer burgers to skillet and cook without moving for 2 minutes. Using spatula, flip burgers over and cook 2 minutes longer. Transfer patties to rimmed baking sheet and bake until burgers register 125 degrees (for medium-rare), 3 to 5 minutes.

5. Transfer burgers to plate and let rest for 5 minutes. Transfer to buns, top with Pub-Style Burger Sauce, if using, and serve.

Pub-Style Burger Sauce
Makes 1 cup, enough to top 4 burgers
Total Time: 8 minutes

- ¾ cup mayonnaise
- 2 tablespoons soy sauce
- 1 tablespoon packed dark brown sugar
- 1 tablespoon Worcestershire sauce
- 1 tablespoon minced fresh chives
- 1 garlic clove, minced
- ¾ teaspoon pepper

Whisk all ingredients together in bowl.

SEASON 25

Mushroom-Beef Blended Burgers

Serves 4 • Total Time: 35 minutes, plus 20 minutes chilling

Why This Recipe Works This blended burger is a great option for those who want to eat less beef but still want the experience of eating a deeply savory, juicy, meaty-textured patty because it replaces a portion of the beef with mushrooms. Our version started with 12 ounces of inexpensive and readily available white mushrooms.

We processed them to a paste and microwaved the paste to remove enough excess moisture to allow the burgers to cook up juicy but not wet. We then used a food processor to combine the mushroom paste with 80 percent lean ground beef, which was important to ensure that these burgers tasted meaty. (Beef fat contains the aromatic compounds that give the meat its characteristic flavor.) Adding salt to the beef and then mixing it with the mushrooms in a food processor developed a sturdy myosin network that held the patties together. Cooking the patties to 135 to 165 degrees ensured that they had a firm—not floppy—texture.

We strongly prefer 80 percent lean ground beef for this recipe; the fat adds beefy flavor. In step 4, if all of the patties do not fit in the skillet, start by cooking three patties until they shrink slightly, about 2 minutes, before adding the remaining patty. To achieve the tender, cohesive texture of an all-beef burger at your preferred level of doneness, cook these 10 degrees higher than you would an all-beef patty. Serve with your favorite burger toppings.

12 ounces white mushrooms, trimmed
1 pound 80 percent lean ground beef, broken into rough 1½-inch pieces
1¼ teaspoons kosher salt
½–2 teaspoons pepper
1½ teaspoons vegetable oil
4 slices American, Swiss, or cheddar cheese (optional)
4 hamburger buns, toasted

1. Process mushrooms in food processor until smooth paste forms (paste will resemble thick oatmeal), scraping down sides of bowl as needed, about 1 minute. Transfer to large bowl and cover. (Do not wash out processor bowl.)

2. Microwave mushrooms until liquid released begins to boil, about 3 minutes, stirring halfway through microwaving. (Do not walk away during final minute; mushrooms could boil over.) Transfer mushrooms to large fine-mesh strainer set over bowl. Using spatula, press on mushrooms to extract ½ cup liquid (if more than ½ cup is removed, stir extra liquid back into mushrooms). Discard liquid and return mushrooms to bowl. Refrigerate mushrooms until room temperature, about 20 minutes.

3. Return mushrooms to processor bowl. Add beef and salt and process until mixture is uniform and begins to pull away from sides of bowl, about 20 seconds. Divide mixture into 4 equal portions and shape into patties that are 4½ inches in diameter. Sprinkle both sides of each patty with pepper. (Patties can be refrigerated overnight or tightly wrapped and frozen for up to 1 month; if frozen, thaw before cooking.)

Making the Mushroom-Beef Blend

1. Process raw white mushrooms until they form thick paste resembling cooked oatmeal.

2. Microwave mushrooms until their liquid boils, about 3 minutes, then strain off ½ cup of liquid.

3. Process mushrooms with ground beef and salt until mixture pulls away from sides of bowl.

4. Heat oil in 12-inch skillet over medium-high heat until shimmering. Transfer patties to skillet and cook until well browned on both sides and burgers register 135 degrees (for medium-rare) or 155 degrees (for medium-well), 6 to 10 minutes. If using cheese, place 1 slice on each burger 1 minute before burgers finish cooking. Transfer burgers to plate and let rest for 5 minutes, then transfer to buns and serve.

SEASON 20

Classic Sloppy Joes

Serves 4 • Total Time: 45 minutes

Why This Recipe Works This recipe is equally loved by adults and children and will earn Sloppy Joes a regular slot in your weeknight meal rotation. Our objective was to develop a recipe with a balanced, less sweet flavor and much less greasy meat. Treating the ground beef with baking soda (so that it retained more moisture when cooked) and then breaking it down to a fine, uniform texture in the skillet delivered a tender and cohesive mixture. Limiting the aromatics to just onion (also treated with baking soda to soften it) made for a beefier-tasting mixture with a rich, luxurious texture. We made ketchup's flavor more complex by adding vinegar, pepper flakes, and sugar and balanced it out with tomato paste, paprika, and Worcestershire.

Tossing the beef with baking soda in step 1 helps keep it tender and juicy; adding baking soda to the skillet with the onion in step 2 helps the onion break down. You may substitute 90 percent lean ground beef in this recipe, but the cooked mixture will be a bit less tender. Serve the Sloppy Joes with pickle chips, if desired.

> 2 tablespoons water, divided
> ½ teaspoon plus ⅛ teaspoon baking soda, divided
> 1 pound 85 percent lean ground beef
> ½ teaspoon plus ⅛ teaspoon table salt, divided
> 2 teaspoons vegetable oil
> ½ onion, chopped fine
> 2 garlic cloves, minced
> 2 teaspoons packed brown sugar, plus extra for seasoning
> 2 teaspoons paprika
> ¼ teaspoon red pepper flakes
> ¼ cup tomato paste
> ⅓ cup ketchup
> 1 tablespoon red wine vinegar, plus extra for seasoning
> 1 tablespoon Worcestershire sauce
> ½ teaspoon cornstarch
> 4 hamburger buns

1. Combine 1 tablespoon water and ½ teaspoon baking soda in small bowl. In large bowl, toss beef with baking soda mixture and ½ teaspoon salt until thoroughly combined. Set aside.

2. Heat oil in 12-inch nonstick skillet over medium heat until shimmering. Add onion and remaining ⅛ teaspoon baking soda and stir to coat. Cook, stirring occasionally, until onion is softened, 3 to 4 minutes. Add garlic and cook, stirring constantly, until fragrant, about 30 seconds. Stir in sugar, paprika, pepper flakes, and remaining ⅛ teaspoon salt and cook, stirring constantly, until paprika is fragrant, about 1 minute. Add tomato paste and cook, stirring constantly, until paste is rust-colored, 3 to 4 minutes.

3. Add beef and cook, breaking up meat with wooden spoon, until beef is no longer pink, about 5 minutes. Mash beef with potato masher until fine-textured, about 1 minute. Add ketchup, vinegar, and Worcestershire and stir to combine, scraping up any browned bits.

4. Combine cornstarch and remaining 1 tablespoon water in small bowl, then pour cornstarch mixture over beef and stir to incorporate. Cook, stirring constantly, until sauce thickens and coats beef, about 1 minute. Season with salt, extra sugar, and extra vinegar to taste. Spoon beef mixture onto buns and serve.

SEASON 19

Tacos Dorados

Serves 4 • Total Time: 1¾ hours

Why This Recipe Works Frying your own taco shells results in great taste, but the process is messy. Enter tacos dorados, a Mexican preparation in which tortillas are stuffed with a beef filling then folded in half and fried. The tacos are then opened like books and loaded with garnishes. We first tossed ground beef with a bit of baking soda to help it stay juicy before adding it to a savory base of onion, spices, and tomato paste. Next, we stirred in shredded cheddar to make the filling cohesive. To build the tacos, we brushed corn tortillas with oil, warmed them to make them pliable, and stuffed them with the filling. Instead of fussy deep frying, we pan-fried the tacos in two batches until they were crisp and golden.

Arrange the tacos so they face the same direction in the skillet to make them easy to fit and flip. To ensure crispy tacos, cook the tortillas until they are deeply browned. To garnish, open each taco like a book and load it with your preferred toppings; close it to eat.

Upgrading a Classic with One Easy Step

"Sloppy Joes are a carryover from my childhood that still excite me so much. This recipe was probably one of the first things I learned to cook without supervision. It was simple to make with ingredients that you could almost always find in the kitchen of a Midwestern household: ground beef, spices, tomato-based sauce, and hamburger buns.

My uncle always made his barbecue sauce from scratch so that was a definite add. His sauce had the great spiciness and sweetness that I think is the foundation for a good Sloppy Joe sauce and one of the biggest bragging points of this recipe. Another is that all the meat stays in the bun—since I make this recipe for the kids in my family, there's only so much 'sloppy' I want from my Sloppy Joes. Adding baking soda to tenderize meat is a pro tip I've learned since I've worked at ATK and it really does a thing to keep meat tender, not pebbly. This makes for a more sophisticated Sloppy Joe."

— Elle

1 tablespoon water

¼ teaspoon baking soda

12 ounces 90 percent lean ground beef

7 tablespoons vegetable oil, divided

1 onion, chopped fine

1½ tablespoons chili powder

1½ tablespoons paprika

1½ teaspoons ground cumin

1½ teaspoons garlic powder

1 teaspoon table salt

2 tablespoons tomato paste

2 ounces cheddar cheese, shredded (½ cup), plus extra for serving

12 (6-inch) corn tortillas

Shredded iceberg lettuce

Chopped tomato

Sour cream

Pickled jalapeño slices

Hot sauce

Making the Crispiest Tacos

1. Brush corn tortillas with oil; bake until pliable enough to stuff.

2. Stuff warmed tortillas with savory ground beef bound together with melted cheddar cheese.

3. Fry tacos in 2 batches until crispy. (Only ¼ cup of oil is needed for 12 tacos.)

1. Adjust oven rack to middle position and heat oven to 400 degrees. Combine water and baking soda in large bowl. Add beef and mix until thoroughly combined. Set aside.

2. Heat 1 tablespoon oil in 12-inch nonstick skillet over medium heat until shimmering. Add onion and cook, stirring occasionally, until softened, 4 to 6 minutes. Add chili powder, paprika, cumin, garlic powder, and salt and cook, stirring frequently, until fragrant, about 1 minute. Stir in tomato paste and cook until paste is rust-colored, 1 to 2 minutes. Add beef mixture and cook, using wooden spoon to break meat into pieces no larger than ¼ inch, until beef is no longer pink, 5 to 7 minutes. Transfer beef mixture to bowl; stir in cheddar until cheese has melted and mixture is homogeneous. Wipe skillet clean with paper towels.

3. Thoroughly brush both sides of tortillas with 2 tablespoons oil. Arrange tortillas, overlapping, on rimmed baking sheet in 2 rows (6 tortillas each). Bake until tortillas are warm and pliable, about 5 minutes. Remove tortillas from oven and reduce oven temperature to 200 degrees.

4. Place 2 tablespoons filling on 1 side of 1 tortilla. Fold and press to close tortilla (edges will be open, but tortilla will remain folded). Repeat with remaining tortillas and remaining filling. (At this point, filled tortillas can be covered and refrigerated for up to 12 hours.)

5. Set wire rack in second rimmed baking sheet and line rack with double layer of paper towels. Heat remaining ¼ cup oil in now-empty skillet over medium-high heat until shimmering. Arrange 6 tacos in skillet with open sides facing away from you. Cook, adjusting heat so oil actively sizzles and bubbles appear around edges of tacos, until tacos are crispy and deeply browned on 1 side, 2 to 3 minutes. Using tongs and thin spatula, carefully flip tacos. Cook until deeply browned on second side, 2 to 3 minutes, adjusting heat as necessary.

6. Remove skillet from heat and transfer tacos to prepared wire rack. Blot tops of tacos with double layer of paper towels. Place sheet with fried tacos in oven to keep warm. Return skillet to medium-high heat and cook remaining tacos. Serve tacos immediately, passing extra cheddar, lettuce, tomato, sour cream, jalapeños, and hot sauce separately.

SEASON 24

Moussaka

Serves 8 • Total Time: 2½ hours, plus 30 minutes cooling

Why This Recipe Works This iconic casserole has it all: plush vegetables, spiced meat sauce, and a top coat of satiny béchamel. We microwaved the potatoes to help rid them of their raw edge without rendering them greasy or waterlogged, and they retained enough structural integrity to be shingled in the greased baking dish. We skipped the unnecessary fuss of peeling and salting the eggplant and simply cut it into cubes, which we roasted. The eggplant pieces collapsed without turning mushy or stringy and then fit compactly into the baking dish. To make a rich-tasting meat sauce that wouldn't gush from a cut slice, we started with 80 percent lean ground beef and cooked off most of the wine and tomato juice; this ensured that the mixture was tight and concentrated. A low ratio of milk to roux, plus egg yolks and plenty of kasseri cheese, made for a custardy béchamel that baked up thick, lush, and beautifully souffléed.

> *Kasseri is a semifirm Greek sheep's-milk cheese. If it's unavailable, substitute 3 ounces (¾ cup) of shredded provolone and 1½ ounces (¾ cup) of grated Pecorino Romano. We like the richness of whole milk for this dish, but you can substitute 2 percent low-fat; do not use skim. Use a mandoline to quickly slice the potatoes, and use a baking dish that is at least 2¼ inches tall.*

Vegetables

- 3½ pounds eggplant, cut into ¾-inch cubes
- ½ cup plus 2 teaspoons plus 3 tablespoons extra-virgin olive oil, divided
- 2 teaspoons table salt, divided
- ¾ teaspoon pepper, divided
- 1½ pounds Yukon Gold potatoes, unpeeled, sliced crosswise ¼ inch thick

Meat Sauce

- 1 tablespoon extra-virgin olive oil
- 1 onion, chopped fine
- ½ teaspoon table salt
- 4 garlic cloves, minced
- 1 tablespoon tomato paste
- ½ cup dry red wine
- 2 teaspoons paprika
- 2 teaspoons dried oregano
- ½ teaspoon red pepper flakes
- ¼ teaspoon ground cinnamon
- 1 pound 80 percent lean ground beef
- 1 (14.5-ounce) can crushed tomatoes
- 2 teaspoons red wine vinegar

Béchamel

- 6 tablespoons unsalted butter
- ½ cup all-purpose flour
- 2½ cups whole milk
- 4 ounces kasseri cheese, shredded (1 cup)
- ¼ teaspoon table salt
- ⅛ teaspoon ground nutmeg
- 3 large egg yolks, lightly beaten

1. For the vegetables: Adjust oven racks to middle and lower-middle positions and heat oven to 450 degrees. Line 2 rimmed baking sheets with aluminum foil and spray with vegetable oil spray. Divide eggplant evenly between prepared sheets. Toss each batch with ¼ cup oil, ½ teaspoon salt, and ¼ teaspoon pepper until evenly coated, and spread eggplant into single layer. Roast until eggplant is softened and lightly browned, about 30 minutes, switching and rotating sheets halfway through roasting. Transfer sheets to wire racks to cool. Reduce oven temperature to 400 degrees.

2. While eggplant roasts, grease 13 by 9-inch baking dish with 2 teaspoons oil. In medium bowl, toss potatoes with remaining 3 tablespoons oil, 1 teaspoon salt, and ¼ teaspoon pepper. Cover and microwave until potatoes can be easily pierced with tip of paring knife, 8 to 10 minutes, stirring halfway through microwaving. Transfer potatoes, along with any accumulated liquid, to prepared dish and let rest until cool enough to handle, about 15 minutes. Shingle evenly in dish.

3. **For the meat sauce:** Heat oil in Dutch oven over medium heat until shimmering. Add onion and salt and cook, stirring occasionally, until just starting to brown, 6 to 8 minutes. Add garlic and stir constantly until fragrant, about 1 minute. Add tomato paste and cook, stirring frequently, until paste darkens, about 2 minutes. Stir in wine, scraping up any browned bits from bottom of pot. Add paprika, oregano, pepper flakes, and cinnamon and cook, stirring frequently, until wine is almost completely evaporated, 2 to 3 minutes. Add beef; increase heat to medium-high; and cook, breaking up meat with wooden spoon, until no pink remains, 4 to 5 minutes. Add tomatoes and cook, stirring occasionally, until liquid has almost completely evaporated and spoon leaves trail when dragged through sauce, 6 to 8 minutes. Stir in vinegar, cover, and remove from heat.

4. **For the béchamel:** Melt butter in medium saucepan over medium heat. Whisk in flour and cook until golden, about 1 minute. Slowly whisk in milk and cook, whisking constantly, until mixture is thick, smooth, and comes to boil, about 5 minutes. Off heat, whisk in kasseri, salt, and nutmeg. Cover and let stand for 5 minutes. Whisk in egg yolks and cover to keep warm.

5. Cover potatoes with eggplant, lightly pressing into even layer. Spread meat sauce in even layer over eggplant. Top with béchamel. Place dish on rimmed baking sheet and bake on middle rack until top of moussaka is deeply browned in spots and is bubbling at edges, about 30 minutes. Let cool for 30 minutes before serving.

SEASON 25

Keema Aloo

Serves 4 to 6 • Total Time: 1 hour

Why This Recipe Works Keema is a rich and savory spiced ground meat dish that's been a staple of South Asian cuisine for centuries, even gracing the tables of the Turkic sultans and Mughal emperors of the 15th and 16th centuries. Whether it's made with ground goat, lamb, beef, or poultry, the meat is broken into small bits and coated with a complexly spiced, velvety sauce that's rich and savory. Our version features a garam masala, or warming spice mix, comprising whole cinnamon and black and green cardamom as well as ground coriander, cumin, turmeric, and Kashmiri chile powder. We bloomed the whole spices early to coax out their oil-soluble compounds. Then we carefully browned red onion to deepen its flavor before spiking the mixture with garlic and ginger pastes. Next we added 90 percent lean ground beef, and when it sizzled and browned, we stirred in the ground spices in the masala. As soon as these were fragrant, in went ripe tomatoes, pieces of potato, and whole-milk yogurt. The tomatoes broke down as the keema cooked, and the yogurt added subtle richness. Together they created a clingy sauce that flavored every bite of beef and potato.

Have your ingredients in place before you begin to cook. Look for black and green cardamom pods, Kashmiri chile powder, and 4- to 5-inch long green chiles at Indian or Pakistani markets. If you can't find Kashmiri chile powder, toast and grind one large guajillo chile and use 2 teaspoons; if a long green chile is unavailable, substitute a serrano. For a milder keema, omit the fresh chile or use only half of it. A rasp-style grater makes it easy to turn garlic and ginger into pastes. Serve with roti, naan, or basmati rice.

- 2 tablespoons vegetable oil
- 6 black peppercorns
- 4 green cardamom pods
- 2 black cardamom pods
- 1 cinnamon stick
- 1 red onion, halved and sliced thin crosswise
- 1 teaspoon grated garlic
- 1 teaspoon grated fresh ginger
- 1 pound 90 percent lean ground beef
- ¾ teaspoon table salt
- 2 teaspoons ground coriander
- 2 teaspoons Kashmiri chile powder
- ½ teaspoon ground turmeric
- ½ teaspoon ground cumin
- 2 (6-ounce) vine-ripened tomatoes, cored and chopped
- 1 (8-ounce) Yukon Gold potato, peeled and cut into ½-inch pieces
- ¼ cup whole-milk yogurt
- 2 tablespoons water
- 1 long green chile, halved lengthwise (optional)
- ¼ cup chopped fresh cilantro, plus extra for garnish

1. Heat oil in medium saucepan over medium heat until shimmering. Add peppercorns, green and black cardamom pods, and cinnamon stick and cook, stirring occasionally, until fragrant, about 30 seconds. Add onion and cook, stirring occasionally, until onion is browned, 7 to 10 minutes.

A Bounty of Spices Makes Simple Food Sing

"My son, now a teenager, has always been enthralled with spices—he likes mixing his own barbecue rubs, sniffing and tasting each addition as he mixes; adding secret combinations to dips and sauces; and making personalized chai tea blends for each member of the family. So it's only natural that he would be a big fan of keema aloo. Because the ground beef, potato, and savory browned onion dish from the Indian subcontinent comes together so easily, and in a single skillet, it's a terrific choice for weeknights that are busy with homework and sports practices. Just get some basmati rice going in a rice cooker, start to fry the beef, open up the spice cabinet, and a hearty, satisfying dinner is well underway. The masala is particularly fun to make because you get to measure out so many different fragrant, aromatic, warming, and colorful spices: cinnamon, subtly smoky black and minty-piney green cardamom pods, kashmiri chile powder, cumin, golden turmeric, citrusy coriander... The result is deeply satisfying."

Becky

2. Add garlic and ginger and cook, stirring constantly, until fragrant, about 30 seconds. Add beef and salt. Increase heat to medium-high and cook, stirring to break up meat into very small pieces and scraping up any browned bits. Continue to cook, stirring occasionally, until mixture sizzles and bottom of saucepan appears dry, 7 to 12 minutes longer.

3. Add coriander, chile powder, turmeric, and cumin and cook, stirring constantly, until spices are well distributed and fragrant, about 1 minute. Add tomatoes; potato; yogurt; water; and chile, if using, and cook, stirring frequently, until tomatoes release their juice and mixture begins to simmer, about 2 minutes. Adjust heat to maintain gentle simmer. Cover and cook, stirring occasionally, until tomatoes have broken down, potatoes are tender, and wooden spoon scraped across bottom of saucepan leaves clear trail, 12 to 18 minutes. Stir in cilantro and season with salt and pepper to taste. If desired, remove cinnamon stick and cardamom pods. Transfer to serving bowl, garnish with extra cilantro, and serve.

VARIATION
Keema Matar

Omit potato and water. Add 1 cup frozen peas after tomatoes have broken down. Cook for 2 minutes before adding cilantro.

SEASON 14
Cuban-Style Picadillo

Serves 6 • Total Time: 55 minutes

Why This Recipe Works Traditional recipes for this Cuban dish of spiced ground meat, sweet raisins, and briny olives call for hand-chopping or grinding the beef, but we wanted our version to be a quicker option. Store-bought ground beef provided a convenient substitute, and supplementing it with ground pork added a subtle sweetness and complexity. Browning the meat made it tough, so we skipped the extra step and soaked the meat in a mixture of baking soda and water to ensure that it remained tender. Pinching it off into sizable 2-inch chunks before adding it to the pot to simmer also kept it moist. For the spices, we settled on just oregano, cumin, and cinnamon and then bloomed them to heighten their flavor. Beef broth added a savory boost, while drained canned whole tomatoes and white wine provided brightness. Raisins and green olives were a given, but we also liked briny capers and a splash of red wine vinegar.

We prefer this dish prepared with raisins, but they can be replaced with 2 tablespoons of brown sugar added with the broth in step 2. Picadillo is traditionally served with rice and black beans. It can also be topped with chopped parsley, toasted almonds, and/or chopped hard-cooked egg.

  1 pound 85 percent lean ground beef
  1 pound ground pork
  2 tablespoons water
 ½ teaspoon baking soda
 ¾ teaspoon table salt, divided
 ¼ teaspoon pepper
  1 green bell pepper, stemmed, seeded, and cut into 2-inch pieces
  1 onion, halved and cut into 2-inch pieces
  2 tablespoons vegetable oil
  1 tablespoon dried oregano
  1 tablespoon ground cumin
 ½ teaspoon ground cinnamon
  6 garlic cloves, minced
  1 (14.5-ounce) can whole tomatoes, drained and chopped coarse
 ¾ cup dry white wine
 ½ cup beef broth
 ½ cup raisins
  3 bay leaves
 ½ cup pimento-stuffed green olives, chopped coarse
  2 tablespoons capers, rinsed
  1 tablespoon red wine vinegar, plus extra for seasoning

1. Toss beef and pork with water, baking soda, ½ teaspoon salt, and pepper in bowl until thoroughly combined. Set aside for 20 minutes. Meanwhile, pulse bell pepper and onion in food processor until chopped into ¼-inch pieces, about 12 pulses.

2. Heat oil in large Dutch oven over medium-high heat until shimmering. Add chopped vegetables, oregano, cumin, cinnamon, and remaining ¼ teaspoon salt; cook, stirring frequently, until vegetables are softened and beginning to brown, 6 to 8 minutes. Add garlic and cook, stirring constantly, until fragrant, about 30 seconds. Add tomatoes and wine and cook, scraping up any browned bits, until pot is almost dry, 3 to 5 minutes. Stir in broth, raisins, and bay leaves and bring to simmer.

3. Reduce heat to medium-low, add meat mixture in 2-inch chunks to pot, and bring to gentle simmer. Cover and cook, stirring occasionally with 2 forks to break meat chunks into ¼- to ½-inch pieces, until meat is cooked through, about 10 minutes.

4. Discard bay leaves. Stir in olives and capers. Increase heat to medium-high and cook, stirring occasionally, until sauce is thickened and coats meat, about 5 minutes. Stir in vinegar and season with salt, pepper, and extra vinegar to taste. Serve.

VARIATION
Cuban-Style Picadillo with Fried Potatoes

After pulsing vegetables in food processor, toss 1 pound russet potatoes, peeled and cut into ½-inch pieces, with 1 tablespoon vegetable oil in medium bowl. Cover and microwave until potatoes are just tender, 4 to 7 minutes, tossing halfway through microwaving. Line surface of large plate with double layer of coffee filters and lightly spray with vegetable oil spray. Drain potatoes well, transfer to coffee filters, and spread in even layer. Let cool for 10 minutes; proceed with recipe from step 2. After step 3, heat 1 cup vegetable oil in large saucepan over medium-high heat until shimmering. Add cooled potatoes and cook, stirring constantly until deep golden brown, 3 to 5 minutes. Using slotted spoon, transfer potatoes to paper towel–lined plate and set aside. Add potatoes to pot with vinegar in step 4.

SEASON 18

Mapo Tofu

Serves 4 to 6 • **Total Time: 1 hour**

Why This Recipe Works Custardy cubes of tofu and browned ground beef or pork swimming in a glossy red sauce with garlic, ginger, fermented black beans, numbing Sichuan peppercorns, and fiery Sichuan chili powder: The flavors of mapo tofu may be complex, but the preparation is fast and easy. We used cubed soft tofu, poached gently in chicken broth to help the cubes stay intact in the braise. For the sauce base, we used plenty of ginger and garlic, along with four Sichuan pantry powerhouses: doubanjiang (broad bean chili paste), fermented black beans, Sichuan chili powder, and Sichuan peppercorns. In place of the chili oil often called for, we used a generous amount of vegetable oil, extra Sichuan chili powder, and toasted sesame oil. Finally, just the right amount of cornstarch gave the dish a velvety thickness.

Ground pork can be used in place of beef, if desired. Broad bean chili paste (or sauce) is also known as doubanjiang or toban djan; our favorite, Pixian, is available online. Supermarket Lee Kum Kee Chili Bean Sauce is also a good option. If you can't find Sichuan chili powder, an equal amount of gochugaru (Korean red pepper flakes) is a good substitute. In a pinch, use 2½ teaspoons of ancho chile powder and ½ teaspoon of cayenne pepper. If you can't find fermented black beans, you can use an equal amount of fermented black bean paste or sauce or two additional teaspoons of broad bean chili paste. Serve with white rice.

1 tablespoon Sichuan peppercorns
12 scallions
28 ounces soft tofu, cut into ½-inch cubes
2 cups chicken broth
9 garlic cloves, peeled
1 (3-inch) piece ginger, peeled and cut into ¼-inch rounds
⅓ cup doubanjiang (broad bean chili paste)
1 tablespoon fermented black beans
6 tablespoons vegetable oil, divided
1 tablespoon Sichuan chili powder
8 ounces 85 percent lean ground beef
2 tablespoons hoisin sauce
2 teaspoons toasted sesame oil
2 tablespoons water
1 tablespoon cornstarch

1. Place peppercorns in small bowl and microwave until fragrant, 15 to 30 seconds. Let cool completely. Once cool, grind in spice grinder or mortar and pestle (you should have 1½ teaspoons).

2. Using side of chef's knife, lightly crush white parts of scallions, then cut scallions into 1-inch pieces. Place tofu, broth, and scallions in large bowl and microwave, covered, until steaming, 5 to 7 minutes. Let stand while preparing remaining ingredients.

3. Process garlic, ginger, chili paste, and black beans in food processor until coarse paste forms, 1 to 2 minutes, scraping down sides of bowl as needed. Add ¼ cup vegetable oil, chili powder, and 1 teaspoon peppercorns and continue to process until smooth paste forms, 1 to 2 minutes longer. Transfer spice paste to bowl.

4. Heat 1 tablespoon vegetable oil and beef in large saucepan over medium heat; cook, breaking up meat with wooden spoon, until meat just begins to brown, 5 to 7 minutes. Transfer beef to bowl.

5. Add remaining 1 tablespoon vegetable oil and spice paste to now-empty saucepan and cook, stirring frequently, until paste darkens and oil begins to separate from paste, 2 to 3 minutes. Gently pour tofu with broth into saucepan, followed by hoisin, sesame oil, and beef. Cook, stirring gently and frequently, until dish comes to simmer, 2 to 3 minutes. Whisk water and cornstarch together in small bowl. Add cornstarch mixture to saucepan and continue to cook, stirring frequently, until thickened, 2 to 3 minutes longer. Transfer to serving dish, sprinkle with remaining peppercorns, and serve. (Mapo tofu can be refrigerated for up to 24 hours.)

Shepherd's Pie

Serves 4 to 6 • Total Time: 2 hours

Why This Recipe Works Shepherd's pie, a hearty mix of meat, gravy, and mashed potatoes, can take the better part of a day to prepare. And while the dish is indeed satisfying, traditional versions can be very rich. We wanted to scale back its preparation and lighten the dish to make it a part of our dinner rotation. Per other modern recipes, we chose ground beef as our filling over ground lamb. To prevent the beef from turning dry and crumbly, we tossed it with a little baking soda (diluted in water) before browning it. This step raised the pH level of the beef, resulting in more tender meat. An onion and mushroom gravy, spiked with Worcestershire sauce, complemented the beef filling. For the mashed potatoes, we took our cue from an Irish dish called champ and cut way back on the dairy in favor of fresh scallions, which made for a lighter, more flavorful topping that was a good match for the meat filling underneath.

This recipe was developed with 93 percent lean ground beef. Using ground beef with a higher percentage of fat will make the dish too greasy.

1½ pounds 93 percent lean ground beef
2 tablespoons plus 2 teaspoons water, divided
1½ teaspoons table salt, divided, plus salt for cooking potatoes
½ teaspoon pepper, divided
½ teaspoon baking soda
2½ pounds russet potatoes, peeled and cut into 1-inch chunks
4 tablespoons unsalted butter, melted
½ cup milk
1 large egg yolk
8 scallions, green parts only, sliced thin
2 teaspoons vegetable oil
1 onion, chopped
4 ounces white mushrooms, trimmed and chopped
1 tablespoon tomato paste
2 garlic cloves, minced
2 tablespoons Madeira or ruby port
2 tablespoons all-purpose flour
1¼ cups beef broth
2 teaspoons Worcestershire sauce
2 sprigs fresh thyme
1 bay leaf
2 carrots, peeled and chopped
2 teaspoons cornstarch

1. Toss beef with 2 tablespoons water, 1 teaspoon salt, ¼ teaspoon pepper, and baking soda in bowl until thoroughly combined. Let sit for 20 minutes.

2. Meanwhile, place potatoes in medium saucepan; add water to just cover and 1 tablespoon salt. Bring to boil over high heat. Reduce heat to medium-low and simmer until potatoes are soft and tip of paring knife inserted into potato meets no resistance, 8 to 10 minutes. Drain potatoes and return to saucepan. Return saucepan to low heat and cook, shaking pot occasionally, until any surface moisture on potatoes has evaporated, about 1 minute. Remove pan from heat and mash potatoes well with potato masher. Stir in melted butter. Whisk together milk and egg yolk in small bowl, then stir into potatoes. Stir in scallions and season with salt and pepper to taste. Cover and set aside.

3. Heat oil in broiler-safe 10-inch skillet over medium heat until shimmering. Add onion, mushrooms, remaining ½ teaspoon salt, and remaining ¼ teaspoon pepper; cook, stirring occasionally, until vegetables are just starting to soften and dark bits form on bottom of skillet, 4 to 6 minutes. Stir in tomato paste and garlic; cook until bottom of skillet is dark brown, about 2 minutes. Add Madeira and cook, scraping up any browned bits, until evaporated, about 1 minute. Stir in flour and cook for 1 minute. Add broth, Worcestershire, thyme sprigs, bay leaf, and carrots; bring to boil, scraping up any browned bits. Reduce heat to medium-low, add beef in 2-inch pieces to broth, and bring to gentle simmer. Cover and cook until beef is cooked through, 10 to 12 minutes, stirring and breaking up meat chunks with 2 forks halfway

through cooking. Stir cornstarch and remaining 2 teaspoons water together in bowl. Stir cornstarch mixture into filling and continue to simmer for 30 seconds. Discard thyme sprigs and bay leaf. Season with salt and pepper to taste.

4. Adjust oven rack 5 inches from broiler element and heat broiler. Place mashed potatoes in large zipper-lock bag and snip off 1 corner to create 1-inch opening. Pipe potatoes in even layer over filling, making sure to cover entire surface. Smooth potatoes with back of spoon, then use tines of fork to make ridges over surface. Place skillet on rimmed baking sheet and broil until potatoes are golden brown and crusty and filling is bubbly, 10 to 15 minutes. Let cool for 10 minutes before serving.

SEASON 7

Glazed All-Beef Meatloaf

Serves 6 to 8 • **Total Time: 2 hours, plus 20 minutes cooling**

Why This Recipe Works Every all-beef meatloaf we've tasted has had the same problems—chewy texture and uninteresting flavor, making it more of a hamburger in the shape of a log than bona fide meatloaf. In the past, when we wanted a great meatloaf, we turned to a traditional meatloaf mix consisting of beef, pork, and veal. Could we create an all-beef meatloaf to compete with this classic? Supermarkets offer a wide selection of "ground beef," and after testing them alone and in combination we determined that equal parts of chuck (for moisture) and sirloin (for beefy flavor) were best. Beef has a livery taste that we wanted to subdue, and the usual dairy additions to meatloaf didn't work. Chicken broth, oddly enough, neutralized this off-flavor and provided moisture. For additional moisture and richness, we included mild-tasting Monterey Jack cheese, which also helped bind the mixture. To avoid pockets of oozing hot cheese in the meatloaf, we shredded the cheese and froze it briefly. Crushed saltines, our choice for the starchy filler, provided texture, but we felt our meatloaf needed more "sliceability." Surprisingly, gelatin gave us just the smooth, luxurious texture we sought. We seasoned the mixture with onions, celery, garlic (all sautéed), thyme, paprika, soy sauce, and mustard. A traditional ketchup glaze crowned our flavorful all-beef meatloaf.

If you can't find ground chuck and/or sirloin, substitute 85 percent lean ground beef.

Meatloaf

- 3 ounces Monterey Jack cheese, shredded on small holes of box grater (¾ cup)
- 1 tablespoon unsalted butter
- 1 onion, chopped fine
- 1 celery rib, minced
- 2 teaspoons minced fresh thyme
- 1 teaspoon paprika
- 1 garlic clove, minced
- ¼ cup tomato juice
- ½ cup chicken broth
- 2 large eggs
- ½ teaspoon unflavored gelatin
- ⅔ cup crushed saltines
- 2 tablespoons minced fresh parsley
- 1 tablespoon soy sauce
- 1 teaspoon Dijon mustard
- ¾ teaspoon table salt
- ½ teaspoon pepper
- 1 pound 90 percent lean ground sirloin
- 1 pound 80 percent lean ground chuck

Glaze

- ½ cup ketchup
- ¼ cup cider vinegar
- 3 tablespoons packed light brown sugar
- 1 teaspoon hot sauce
- ½ teaspoon ground coriander

1. For the meatloaf: Adjust oven rack to middle position and heat oven to 375 degrees. Spread cheese on plate and place in freezer until ready to use. Set wire rack in rimmed baking sheet. Fold sheet of heavy-duty aluminum foil to form 10 by 6-inch rectangle. Center foil on rack and poke holes in foil with skewer (about half an inch apart). Spray foil with vegetable oil spray.

2. Melt butter in 10-inch skillet over medium-high heat; add onion and celery and cook, stirring occasionally, until beginning to brown, 6 to 8 minutes. Add thyme, paprika, and garlic and cook, stirring, until fragrant, about 1 minute. Reduce heat to low and add tomato juice. Cook, stirring to scrape up any browned bits, until thickened, about 1 minute. Transfer mixture to small bowl and set aside to cool.

3. Whisk broth and eggs together in large bowl until combined. Sprinkle gelatin over liquid and let stand for 5 minutes. Stir in saltines, parsley, soy sauce, mustard, salt, pepper, and onion mixture. Crumble frozen cheese into coarse powder and sprinkle over mixture. Add sirloin and chuck; mix gently with your hands until thoroughly combined, about 1 minute. Transfer meat to foil rectangle and shape into 10 by 6-inch oval about 2 inches high. Smooth top and edges of meatloaf with moistened spatula.

Bake until center of loaf registers 135 to 140 degrees, 55 minutes to 1 hour 5 minutes. Remove meatloaf from oven and heat broiler.

4. For the glaze: While meatloaf cooks, combine glaze ingredients in small saucepan; bring to simmer over medium heat and cook, stirring, until thick and syrupy, about 5 minutes. Spread half of glaze evenly over cooked meatloaf with rubber spatula; place under broiler and cook until glaze bubbles and begins to brown at edges, about 5 minutes. Remove meatloaf from oven and spread evenly with remaining glaze; place back under broiler and cook until glaze is again bubbling and beginning to brown, about 5 minutes more. Let meatloaf cool for about 20 minutes before slicing.

Making a Free-Form Loaf Pan

1. Set wire rack in rimmed baking sheet and top with 10 by 6-inch rectangle of aluminum foil.

2. Using skewer, poke holes in foil, spacing them about half an inch apart.

SEASON 25

Pot Roast with Root Vegetables

Serves 6 • Total Time: 4 to 4½ hours

Why This Recipe Works A good pot roast should always be tender. For a supremely tender pot roast with a spoonable sauce, we cooked ours for 3 to 3½ hours, adding root vegetables partway through. A chuck-eye roast is our favorite cut for pot roast; opening it along its natural seam into two lobes and trimming excess fat eliminated greasiness and promised more thorough seasoning. A stovetop sear created a caramelized exterior before we moved the roast to the oven where it could braise more evenly. To ensure that the vegetables—hearty carrots, potatoes, and parsnips—were perfectly cooked and imbued with beefy flavor by the time the roast was done, we added them directly to the pot partway through the roast's cooking time. By the time the roast emerged, it was so tender a fork met no resistance: Each bite had a silky texture and rich flavor.

> *Use a good-quality medium-bodied wine, such as a Côtes du Rhône or a Pinot Noir.*

- 1 (3½- to 4-pound) boneless beef chuck-eye roast, pulled into 2 pieces at natural seam, trimmed, and tied at 1-inch intervals
- 1 teaspoon table salt
- ½ teaspoon pepper
- 3 tablespoons vegetable oil, divided
- 1 onion, chopped
- 1 celery rib, chopped
- 4 garlic cloves, minced
- 2 teaspoons sugar
- 1 teaspoon fresh minced thyme or ¼ teaspoon dried
- 1 cup chicken broth
- 1 cup beef broth
- 1 cup water
- 1½ pounds carrots, peeled and cut into 3-inch pieces
- 1½ pounds red potatoes, unpeeled, cut into 1½-inch pieces
- 1½ pounds parsnips, peeled and cut into 3-inch pieces
- ⅓ cup red wine

1. Adjust oven rack to lower-middle position and heat oven to 300 degrees. Pat beef dry with paper towels and sprinkle with salt and pepper. Heat 2 tablespoons oil in Dutch oven over medium-high heat until just smoking. Add both beef roasts and brown on all sides, 7 to 10 minutes; transfer to large plate.

2. Add remaining 1 tablespoon oil, onion, and celery to now-empty pot and cook over medium heat until vegetables are softened, 5 to 7 minutes. Stir in garlic, sugar, and thyme and cook until fragrant, about 30 seconds. Stir in broths and water, scraping up any browned bits.

3. Add browned roasts along with any accumulated juices to pot and bring to simmer. Cover, transfer pot to oven, and cook for 2 hours, flipping roasts halfway through cooking.

4. Remove pot from oven. Nestle carrots into pot around meat and sprinkle potatoes and parsnips over top. Return covered pot to oven and cook until meat and vegetables are very tender, 1 to 1½ hours.

5. Remove pot from oven. Transfer roasts to carving board and tent with foil. Transfer vegetables to large bowl and season with salt and pepper to taste; cover to keep warm.

6. Using large spoon, skim any fat from surface of braising liquid. Stir in wine and simmer until sauce measures 2 cups, about 15 minutes. Season with salt and pepper to taste. Transfer vegetables to serving platter. Remove twine from roasts, slice meat against grain ¼ inch thick, and transfer to serving platter. Spoon half of sauce over meat. Serve, passing remaining sauce separately.

SEASON 6

Beef Braised in Barolo

Serves 6 • **Total Time: 4¼ hours**

Why This Recipe Works Italian pot roast is comprised of an inexpensive cut of beef braised in wine. Full-bodied Barolo can be somewhat expensive, so the pot roast has to be special. We wanted tender meat in a rich, savory sauce that would do justice to the wine. A chuck-eye roast can withstand a long braise, but it has a line of fat in the middle that we felt was out of place in this refined dish. Separating one roast into two smaller ones enabled us to discard most of that fat before cooking. We then tied the roasts together and browned them in fat rendered from pancetta. After browning aromatics, we poured a whole bottle of wine into the pot. The Barolo's bold flavor needed tempering, so we added canned diced tomatoes. When the meat was done, we reduced the sauce and strained out the vegetables. The resulting winey sauce was full-flavored and lustrous.

Don't skip tying the roasts—it keeps them intact during the long cooking time. Purchase pancetta that is cut to order, about ¼ inch thick. If pancetta is not available, substitute an equal amount of salt pork (find the meatiest piece possible), cut it into ¼-inch cubes, and boil it in 3 cups of water for about 2 minutes to remove excess salt. After draining, use it as you would pancetta.

1 (3½-pound) boneless beef chuck-eye roast
1 teaspoon table salt
½ teaspoon pepper
4 ounces pancetta, cut into ¼-inch cubes
2 onions, chopped
2 carrots, chopped
2 celery ribs, chopped
1 tablespoon tomato paste
3 garlic cloves, minced
1 tablespoon all-purpose flour
½ teaspoon sugar
1 (750-ml) bottle Barolo wine
1 (14.5-ounce) can diced tomatoes, drained
1 sprig fresh thyme plus 1 teaspoon minced thyme
1 sprig fresh rosemary
10 sprigs fresh parsley

1. Adjust oven rack to middle position and heat oven to 300 degrees. Pull roast apart at its major seams (delineated by lines of fat) into 2 halves. Use knife as necessary. With knife, remove large knobs of fat from each piece, leaving thin layer of fat on meat. Tie 3 pieces of kitchen twine around each piece of meat. Thoroughly pat beef dry with paper towels; sprinkle with salt and pepper. Place pancetta in large Dutch oven; cook over medium heat, stirring occasionally, until browned and crisp, about 8 minutes. Using slotted spoon, transfer pancetta to paper towel–lined plate and reserve. Pour off all but 2 tablespoons of fat; set Dutch oven over medium-high heat and heat fat until just smoking. Add beef to pot and cook until well browned on all sides, about 8 minutes total. Transfer beef to large plate; set aside.

2. Reduce heat to medium; add onions, carrots, celery, and tomato paste to pot and cook, stirring occasionally, until vegetables begin to soften and brown, about 6 minutes. Add garlic, flour, sugar, and reserved pancetta; cook, stirring constantly, until combined and fragrant, about 30 seconds. Add wine and tomatoes, scraping up any browned bits; add thyme sprig, rosemary, and parsley. Return roast and any accumulated juice to pot; increase heat to high and bring liquid to boil, then place large sheet of aluminum foil over pot and cover tightly with lid. Set pot in oven and cook, using tongs to turn beef every 45 minutes, until dinner fork easily slips in and out of meat, about 3 hours.

3. Transfer beef to carving board and tent with foil to keep warm. Allow braising liquid to settle for about 5 minutes, then, using wide shallow spoon, skim fat off surface. Add minced thyme, bring liquid to boil over high heat, and cook, whisking vigorously to help vegetables break down, until mixture is thickened and reduced to about 3½ cups, about 18 minutes. Strain liquid through large fine-mesh strainer, pressing on solids with spatula to extract as much liquid as possible; you should have 1½ cups strained sauce (if necessary, return strained sauce to Dutch oven and reduce to 1½ cups). Discard solids in strainer. Season sauce with salt and pepper to taste.

4. Remove kitchen twine from meat and discard. Using chef's knife or carving knife, slice meat against grain ½ inch thick. Divide meat among warmed bowls or plates; pour about ¼ cup sauce over each portion and serve immediately.

SEASON 9

Slow-Roasted Beef

Serves 6 to 8 • **Total Time: 2¾ to 3¼ hours, plus 18 hours salting**

Why This Recipe Works Roasting inexpensive beef usually yields tough meat best suited for sandwiches. We wanted to take an inexpensive cut and turn it into a tender, rosy, beefy-tasting roast worthy of Sunday dinner. Our favorite cut, the eye round, has good flavor and tenderness and a uniform shape that guarantees even cooking. Next, we chose between the two classic methods for roasting meat—high and fast or low and slow. Low temperature was the way to go. Keeping the meat's internal temperature below 122 degrees as long as possible allowed the meat's enzymes to act as natural tenderizers, breaking down its tough connective tissue (this action stops at 122 degrees). Since most ovens don't heat below 200 degrees, we needed to devise a special method to lengthen this tenderizing period. We roasted the meat at 225 degrees (after searing it to give the meat a crusty exterior) and shut off the oven when the roast reached 115 degrees. The meat stayed below 122 degrees an extra 30 minutes, allowing the enzymes to continue their work before the temperature reached 130 degrees for medium-rare. As for seasoning, we found that salting the meat a full 24 hours before roasting made it even more tender and seasoned the roast throughout.

This recipe requires salting the roast for 18 to 24 hours before cooking. We don't recommend cooking this roast past medium. Open the oven door as little as possible and remove the roast from the oven while taking its temperature. If the roast has not reached the desired temperature in the time specified in step 3, heat the oven to 225 degrees for 5 minutes, shut it off, and continue to cook the roast to the desired temperature. For a smaller (2½- to 3½-pound) roast, reduce the amount of pepper to 1½ teaspoons. For a 4½- to 6-pound roast, cut in half crosswise before cooking to create two smaller roasts. Slice the roast as thin as possible and serve with Horseradish Cream Sauce (recipe follows), if desired.

- 1 (3½- to 4½-pound) boneless eye-round roast, trimmed
- 4 teaspoons kosher salt
- 1 tablespoon plus 2 teaspoons vegetable oil, divided
- 2 teaspoons pepper

1. Sprinkle all sides of roast evenly with salt. Wrap with plastic wrap and refrigerate for 18 to 24 hours.

2. Adjust oven rack to middle position and heat oven to 225 degrees. Pat roast dry with paper towels; rub with 2 teaspoons oil and sprinkle all sides evenly with pepper. Heat remaining 1 tablespoon oil in 12-inch skillet over medium-high heat until just smoking. Sear roast until browned on all sides, 3 to 4 minutes per side. Transfer roast to wire rack set in rimmed baking sheet. Roast until center of roast registers 115 degrees (for medium-rare), 1¼ to 1¾ hours, or 125 degrees (for medium), 1¾ to 2¼ hours.

3. Turn off oven; leave roast in oven, without opening door, until center of roast registers 130 degrees (for medium-rare) or 140 degrees (for medium), 30 to 50 minutes longer. Transfer roast to carving board and let rest for 15 minutes. Slice meat crosswise as thin as possible and serve with sauce, if using.

ACCOMPANIMENT
Horseradish Cream Sauce
Makes 1 cup
Total Time: 10 minutes, plus 30 minutes chilling

- ½ cup heavy cream, chilled
- ½ cup prepared horseradish
- 1 teaspoon table salt
- ⅛ teaspoon pepper

Whisk cream in medium bowl until thickened but not yet holding soft peaks, 1 to 2 minutes. Gently fold in horseradish, salt, and pepper. Transfer to serving bowl and refrigerate for at least 30 minutes or up to 1 hour before serving.

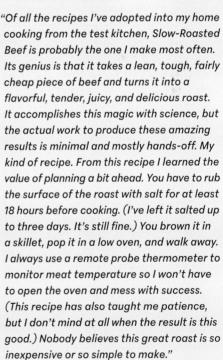

GAME CHANGER

A Tough to Tender Transformation

"Of all the recipes I've adopted into my home cooking from the test kitchen, Slow-Roasted Beef is probably the one I make most often. Its genius is that it takes a lean, tough, fairly cheap piece of beef and turns it into a flavorful, tender, juicy, and delicious roast. It accomplishes this magic with science, but the actual work to produce these amazing results is minimal and mostly hands-off. My kind of recipe. From this recipe I learned the value of planning a bit ahead. You have to rub the surface of the roast with salt for at least 18 hours before cooking. (I've left it salted up to three days. It's still fine.) You brown it in a skillet, pop it in a low oven, and walk away. I always use a remote probe thermometer to monitor meat temperature so I won't have to open the oven and mess with success. (This recipe has also taught me patience, but I don't mind at all when the result is this good.) Nobody believes this great roast is so inexpensive or so simple to make."

— Lisa

Beef Tenderloin with Smoky Potatoes and Persillade Relish

Serves 6 to 8 • Total Time: 2 hours, plus 1 hour resting

Why This Recipe Works For special occasions, few cuts top a beef tenderloin. This elegant roast cooks quickly and serves a crowd, and its rich, buttery slices are fork-tender. We found that a hot oven delivered rich, roasted flavor and perfectly rosy meat without overcooking this lean cut. Tying the roast helped to ensure even cooking. The roast needed company, and small whole red potatoes were a perfect pairing. To punch up the flavor, we tossed the potatoes with smoked paprika, which added a pleasant smokiness to complement our meat, along with garlic and scallions for a deep, flavorful backbone. The tender meat needed a sauce, so we made a simple yet bold persillade relish, which featured parsley, capers, and cornichons.

We prefer to use extra-small red potatoes measuring less than 1 inch in diameter. Larger potatoes can be used, but it may be necessary to return the potatoes to the oven to finish cooking, while the roast is resting in step 5. Center-cut beef tenderloin roasts are sometimes sold as Châteaubriand.

Beef and Potatoes

  1 (3-pound) center-cut beef tenderloin roast, trimmed
3¼ teaspoons kosher salt, divided
1¼ teaspoons pepper, divided
  1 teaspoon baking soda
  3 tablespoons extra-virgin olive oil, divided
  3 pounds extra-small red potatoes, unpeeled
  5 scallions, minced
  4 garlic cloves, minced
  1 tablespoon smoked paprika
  ½ cup water

Persillade Relish

  ¾ cup minced fresh parsley
  ½ cup extra-virgin olive oil
  6 tablespoons minced cornichons plus 1 teaspoon brine
  ¼ cup capers, rinsed and chopped coarse
  3 garlic cloves, minced
  1 scallion, minced
  1 teaspoon sugar
  ¼ teaspoon table salt
  ¼ teaspoon pepper

1. **For the beef and potatoes:** Pat roast dry with paper towels. Combine 2¼ teaspoons salt, 1 teaspoon pepper, and baking soda in small bowl. Rub salt mixture evenly over roast and let stand for 1 hour. After 1 hour, tie roast with kitchen twine at 1½ inch intervals. Adjust oven rack to middle position and heat oven to 425 degrees.

2. Heat 2 tablespoons oil in 16 by 12-inch roasting pan over medium-high heat (over 2 burners, if possible) until shimmering. Add potatoes, scallions, garlic, paprika, remaining 1 teaspoon salt, and remaining ¼ teaspoon pepper and cook until scallions are softened, about 1 minute. Off heat, stir in water, scraping up any browned bits. Transfer roasting pan to oven and roast potatoes for 15 minutes.

3. Brush remaining 1 tablespoon oil over surface of roast. Remove roasting pan from oven, stir potato mixture, and lay beef on top. Reduce oven temperature to 300 degrees. Return pan to oven and roast until beef registers 120 to 125 degrees (for medium-rare), 45 to 55 minutes, rotating roasting pan halfway through cooking.

4. **For the persillade relish:** While beef roasts, combine all ingredients in bowl.

5. Remove pan from oven. Transfer roast to carving board, tent with aluminum foil, and let rest for 15 minutes. Cover potatoes left in pan with foil to keep warm. Remove twine from roast, slice ½ inch thick, and serve with potatoes and persillade relish.

Fennel-Coriander Top Sirloin Roast

Serves 8 to 10 • Total Time: 3 hours, plus 24½ hours brining and resting

Why This Recipe Works Top sirloin offers great beefy flavor and decent tenderness, but this cheap cut has its challenges. Our goal was to figure out how to make it worthy of the holiday table. We began by splitting the roast in half, creating two manageable roasts, salting the halves, and air-drying them in the refrigerator. This seasoned the meat, maximized its juiciness, and dried the surfaces for optimal browning. After 24 hours, we kick-started the browning by quickly searing all sides of the two roasts in a skillet. Tying the roasts with kitchen twine turned the irregularly shaped roasts into two uniform cylinders. To compensate for the meat's leaner makeup, we created a rich, heavily seasoned paste that would further boost browning.

Entertaining Doesn't Have to Be Hard

"I've been making this meal for our family holiday party for years, and it's always a winner because it's impressive, almost completely hands off, and serves a crowd. Plus, the potatoes cook alongside the roast in the oven, which means all you need to add is big salad and dinner is done.

The trick to the beef roast is adding a little baking soda to the seasoning on the meat so that it browns nicely in the oven, omitting the need to wrangle it on the stovetop to get a nice crust. I almost always buy a big, untrimmed tenderloin (weighing 6 pounds or more) still in a cryovac because I don't mind the knife work and I like to use the trimmings for a stir-fry, but there's no shame in ordering it pretrimmed to save time. The flavor of the persillade sauce is pure perfection and tastes great with the beef roast—it is one of my all-time favorite relishes and it can easily be made ahead of time. It's a wonderful thing to have in your repertoire because it tastes good on almost everything from beef to fish to vegetables, and it doesn't require any cooking."

—Julia

We processed garlic, fennel, olive oil, and umami-boosting anchovy fillets to create a spreadable consistency, then added coriander, paprika, and oregano for extra flavor. After applying the spice paste, we roasted the meat in a 225-degree oven for 2 hours. This initial roast cooked the meat to our liking. To give it an attractive browned crust, we removed the roasts from the oven, ramped up the temperature to 500 degrees, and returned them (with twine removed) for a final crisping.

This recipe requires refrigerating the salted meat for at least 24 hours before cooking. The roast, also called a top sirloin roast, top butt roast, center-cut roast, spoon roast, shell roast, or shell sirloin roast, should not be confused with a whole top sirloin butt roast or top loin roast. Do not omit the anchovies; they provide great depth of flavor with no overt fishiness. Monitoring the roast with a meat-probe thermometer is best. If you use an instant-read thermometer, open the oven door as little as possible and remove the roast from the oven to take its temperature.

1   (5- to 6-pound) boneless top sirloin center-cut roast, trimmed
2   tablespoons kosher salt
4   teaspoons plus ¼ cup extra-virgin olive oil, divided
4   garlic cloves, minced
6   anchovy fillets, rinsed and patted dry
2   teaspoons ground fennel
2   teaspoons ground coriander
2   teaspoons paprika
1   teaspoon dried oregano
1   teaspoon pepper

1. Cut roast lengthwise along grain into 2 equal pieces. Rub 1 tablespoon kosher salt over each piece. Transfer to large plate and refrigerate, uncovered, for at least 24 hours or up to 4 days.

2. Adjust oven rack to middle position and heat oven to 225 degrees. Heat 2 teaspoons oil in 12-inch skillet over high heat until just smoking. Brown 1 roast on all sides, 6 to 8 minutes. Return browned roast to plate. Repeat with 2 teaspoons oil and remaining roast. Let cool for 10 minutes.

3. While roasts cool, process garlic, anchovies, fennel, coriander, paprika, oregano, and remaining ¼ cup oil in food processor until smooth paste forms, about 30 seconds, scraping down sides of bowl as needed. Add pepper and pulse to combine, 2 or 3 pulses.

4. Using 5 pieces of kitchen twine per roast, tie each roast crosswise at equal intervals into loaf shape. Transfer roasts to wire rack set in rimmed baking sheet and rub roasts evenly with paste.

5. Roast until meat registers 125 degrees (for medium-rare) or 130 degrees (for medium), 2 to 2¼ hours. Remove roasts from oven, leaving on wire rack, and tent with aluminum foil; let rest for at least 30 minutes or up to 40 minutes.

6. Heat oven to 500 degrees. Remove foil from roasts and cut and discard twine. Return roasts to oven and cook until exteriors of roasts are well browned, 6 to 8 minutes.

7. Transfer roasts to carving board. Slice meat ¼ inch thick. Season with coarse sea salt to taste, and serve.

VARIATION
Rosemary-Garlic Top Sirloin Roast
Omit fennel, coriander, paprika, and oregano. Add 3 tablespoons chopped fresh rosemary to food processor with oil in step 3. Add ¼ teaspoon red pepper flakes with pepper in step 3.

Using a Spice Paste

For roasts lacking a fat cap, cover it in a robustly flavored paste that browns in the oven. It will add a boost of complex flavor, textural contrast, and visual appeal.

Beef Wellington

Serves 8 to 10 • Total Time: 3 hours, plus 13½ hours resting and salting

Why This Recipe Works We developed a failproof process that produces a stunningly beautiful—and delicious—beef Wellington wrapped in buttery pastry and cooked to rosy perfection every time. We first salted beef tenderloin overnight and then slathered it with Dijon mustard before wrapping it in prosciutto spread with a savory mixture of mushrooms, shallots, and garlic known as duxelles. We traded the traditional puff pastry for sturdier, easier-to-work-with pâte brisée, which produces a firm yet flaky and tender crust that slices neatly. Finally, we tackled the biggest challenge of all: producing both a perfectly baked crust and uniformly medium-rare beef. To accomplish this, we roasted the Wellington in a 450-degree oven and removed it when the beef registered a mere 85 degrees. Carryover cooking did the rest of the work, gradually raising the meat's temperature to 130 degrees. A dollop of creamy sauce gives this dish an elegant finish.

> We recommend using a probe thermometer for this recipe. Center-cut beef tenderloin roasts are sometimes sold as Châteaubriand. Request a Châteaubriand from the thicker end of the tenderloin; some butchers refer to this as the "cannon cut." Dry sherry can be substituted for the Madeira. Use packaged prosciutto rather than freshly sliced deli prosciutto, as the slices will be easier to handle. Although the timing for many of the components is flexible, we recommend making the Wellington over a three-day period: Prepare the components on the first day, assemble it on the second day (remember to reserve your leftover egg wash so that you can give the pastry a final coat before roasting it), and bake and serve it on the third day. Serve with Creamy Green Peppercorn Sauce (recipe follows).

Beef

- 1 center-cut beef tenderloin roast, 3 pounds trimmed weight, 12 to 13 inches long and 4 to 4½ inches in diameter
- 1 tablespoon kosher salt
- 1 tablespoon Dijon mustard
- 1 teaspoon pepper

Pastry

- 3¼ cups (17¾ ounces) bread flour
- 22 tablespoons (2¾ sticks) unsalted butter, cut into ½-inch cubes and chilled
- 1 teaspoon table salt
- ½ cup plus 1 tablespoon ice water

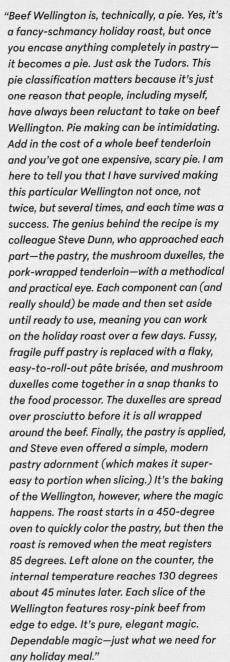

Beef Wellington Is the Sum of Its Parts

"Beef Wellington is, technically, a pie. Yes, it's a fancy-schmancy holiday roast, but once you encase anything completely in pastry—it becomes a pie. Just ask the Tudors. This pie classification matters because it's just one reason that people, including myself, have always been reluctant to take on beef Wellington. Pie making can be intimidating. Add in the cost of a whole beef tenderloin and you've got one expensive, scary pie. I am here to tell you that I have survived making this particular Wellington not once, not twice, but several times, and each time was a success. The genius behind the recipe is my colleague Steve Dunn, who approached each part—the pastry, the mushroom duxelles, the pork-wrapped tenderloin—with a methodical and practical eye. Each component can (and really should) be made and then set aside until ready to use, meaning you can work on the holiday roast over a few days. Fussy, fragile puff pastry is replaced with a flaky, easy-to-roll-out pâte brisée, and mushroom duxelles come together in a snap thanks to the food processor. The duxelles are spread over prosciutto before it is all wrapped around the beef. Finally, the pastry is applied, and Steve even offered a simple, modern pastry adornment (which makes it super-easy to portion when slicing.) It's the baking of the Wellington, however, where the magic happens. The roast starts in a 450-degree oven to quickly color the pastry, but then the roast is removed when the meat registers 85 degrees. Left alone on the counter, the internal temperature reaches 130 degrees about 45 minutes later. Each slice of the Wellington features rosy-pink beef from edge to edge. It's pure, elegant magic. Dependable magic—just what we need for any holiday meal."

—Bridget

Duxelles

- 8 shallots, chopped
- 4 garlic cloves, peeled
- 2 pounds cremini mushrooms, trimmed and quartered, divided
- 8 tablespoons unsalted butter
- ¼ teaspoon pepper
- ⅛ teaspoon table salt
- 1 tablespoon Madeira
- 2 teaspoons minced fresh thyme

Assembly

- 12 slices prosciutto
- 1 large egg plus 1 large yolk

DAY ONE: PREP COMPONENTS

1. For the beef: Sprinkle all sides of beef evenly with salt. Wrap in plastic wrap and refrigerate for at least 12 hours or up to 3 days.

2. For the pastry: Using stand mixer fitted with paddle, mix flour, butter, and salt on medium-low speed until mixture is crumbly and pieces of butter are no larger than peas, 4 to 5 minutes. With mixer running, add ice water in steady stream. Increase speed to medium and continue to mix until smooth dough comes together around paddle, 1 to 3 minutes longer. Transfer dough to lightly floured counter. Remove one-quarter (about 8 ounces) of dough and shape into 6-inch square. Shape remaining dough into 6-inch square. Wrap both pieces in plastic and refrigerate for at least 8 hours or up to 2 days.

3. For the duxelles: Process shallots and garlic in food processor until very finely chopped, about 30 seconds, scraping down sides of bowl as needed. Transfer to small bowl. Pulse half of mushrooms until mushrooms resemble couscous, about 10 pulses, scraping down sides of bowl halfway through processing (do not overprocess). Transfer to large bowl and repeat with remaining mushrooms.

4. Melt butter in 12-inch nonstick skillet over medium-low heat. Add shallot mixture and cook, stirring frequently, until softened, 3 to 5 minutes. Stir in mushrooms, pepper, and salt and cook, stirring occasionally, until liquid given off by mushrooms has evaporated and mushrooms begin to sizzle, about 45 minutes. Add Madeira to mushroom mixture and cook, stirring constantly, until evaporated, about 2 minutes. Off heat, stir in thyme. (If making duxelles ahead, let cool completely and refrigerate in airtight container for up to 3 days.)

DAY TWO: ASSEMBLE

5. To assemble: Overlap 2 or 3 pieces of plastic on counter to form 30-inch square (it's OK if up to 2 inches of plastic hangs off edge of counter). Shingle prosciutto in center of plastic in 2 rows of 6 slices, slightly overlapping to form 14 by 15-inch rectangle, with shorter side parallel to edge of counter. Transfer duxelles to prosciutto and use offset spatula to spread in even layer, leaving 1-inch border of prosciutto on all sides (if duxelles is cold, microwave for 1 minute to soften before spreading).

6. Unwrap beef and pat dry with paper towels. Brush all sides of beef with mustard and sprinkle with pepper. Arrange roast parallel to edge of counter, about one-third of way up duxelles. Using both hands, lift bottom edge of plastic to begin wrapping roast. Continue to roll roast, leaving plastic behind, until roast is completely wrapped in prosciutto. Tuck overhanging slices of prosciutto over each end of roast.

7. Tightly roll roast in plastic and twist plastic tightly at each end to seal. Continue to twist ends of plastic and roll roast on counter until formed into snug cylinder. Refrigerate for at least 30 minutes or up to 2 days before cooking.

8. Line 2 rimmed baking sheets with parchment paper. Roll out larger piece of dough on generously floured counter into 18 by 16-inch rectangle. Drape dough over rolling pin, transfer to prepared sheet, and refrigerate for 15 minutes. Roll smaller piece of dough into 16 by 7-inch rectangle. Transfer to second prepared sheet and refrigerate.

9. Whisk together egg and yolk. Lay large pastry sheet directly on counter with long side parallel to edge of counter. Brush entire surface with egg wash; set aside remaining egg wash. Unwrap beef and place on pastry, arranging it parallel to edge of counter and 2 inches from pastry edge closest to you. Wrap edge of pastry closest to you over beef. Holding edge in place, slowly roll roast away from you, keeping pastry snug to meat, until roast is covered.

10. Allow pastry to overlap by 1 inch and trim away excess. Roll roast so seam is on top. Gently press and pinch overlapping dough to seal. Roll roast so seam is on bottom.

11. To seal ends of roast, tuck sides of pastry tightly against meat as though you are wrapping a present, then fold top of pastry down, pressing snugly.

12. Using rolling pin, roll excess dough at end of roast against counter to make it thinner and longer. Trim rolled end to 2-inch length and tuck under roast. Repeat process on other end of roast. Transfer roast seam side down to lightly greased rimmed baking sheet and refrigerate for at least 15 minutes or up to overnight (if refrigerating longer than 1 hour, wrap in plastic).

13. Transfer smaller rectangle of dough, still on parchment, to counter, with short side parallel to edge of counter. Using ruler and sharp knife or pizza cutter, cut dough lengthwise into ¼-inch-wide strips.

14. Brush top, sides, and ends of roast with some of reserved egg wash; set aside remaining egg wash. Lay strips of dough diagonally across top of roast, leaving ¼ to ½ inch between strips. Gently press strips to adhere to roast and trim excess at each end to ¼ inch. Using bench scraper, tuck ends of strips under roast. Refrigerate roast for at least 10 minutes. (Roast can be loosely covered with plastic and refrigerated for up to 24 hours.)

DAY THREE: BAKE AND SERVE

15. Adjust oven rack to lower-middle position and heat oven to 450 degrees. Brush roast thoroughly with reserved egg wash. Place thermometer probe, if using, through 1 end of roast so tip of probe is positioned at center of roast. Roast until beef registers 85 degrees and crust is well browned and crisp, 40 to 45 minutes. Transfer sheet to wire rack, leaving probe in place to monitor temperature. Let rest, uncovered, until internal temperature reaches 130 degrees, 40 to 45 minutes.

16. To serve: Slide large metal spatula under roast to loosen from sheet. Use both hands to transfer roast to carving board. Using serrated knife, cut roast into 1-inch-thick slices (to keep pastry intact, score through decorative strips before cutting each slice) and serve.

ACCOMPANIMENT
Creamy Green Peppercorn Sauce
Serves 8 to 10 • Total Time: 45 minutes

The sauce can be made as the roast is resting; alternatively, prepare it up to three days ahead and warm it right before serving.

- 2 tablespoons unsalted butter
- ¼ cup jarred green peppercorns
- 2 tablespoons minced shallot
- 1 tablespoon all-purpose flour
- 1½ cups beef broth
- ¼ cup brandy
- 2 tablespoons soy sauce
- 1 cup heavy cream

1. Melt butter in medium saucepan over medium-low heat. Add peppercorns and shallot and cook, stirring frequently, until shallot is softened, 3 to 5 minutes. Add flour and cook, stirring constantly, for 2 minutes. Increase heat to medium and whisk in broth, brandy, and soy sauce. Bring to boil. Cook, whisking occasionally, until mixture is reduced to 1½ cups, 12 to 15 minutes.

2. Add cream and cook, whisking occasionally, until reduced to 2 cups, about 10 minutes. Season with salt and pepper to taste.

Assembling Beef Wellington

1. Lay large pastry sheet directly on counter and brush entire surface of pastry with egg wash.

2. Unwrap beef and place on pastry. Holding edge in place, slowly roll roast keeping pastry snug to meat.

3. With seam on top, gently pinch dough to seal; roll seam to bottom. Tuck sides to seal ends. Brush with egg wash.

4. Lay thin strips of dough diagonally across top of roast, leaving space between strips. Press strips to adhere.

Best Prime Rib

Serves 6 to 8 • Total Time: 4½ to 6¼ hours, plus 24½ hours salting and resting

Why This Recipe Works The perfect prime rib should have a deep-colored, substantial crust encasing a tender, juicy rosy-pink center. To achieve superior results, we cut slits in the layer of fat to help it render efficiently, then salted the roast overnight. The long salting time enhanced the beefy flavor while dissolving some of the proteins, yielding a buttery-tender roast. To further enhance tenderness, we cooked the roast at a very low temperature, which allowed the meat's enzymes to act as natural tenderizers, breaking down its tough connective tissue. A brief stint under the broiler before serving ensured a crisp, flavorful crust.

Look for a roast with an untrimmed fat cap (ideally ½ inch thick). We prefer the flavor and texture of Prime beef, but Choice grade will work as well. Monitoring the roast with a meat-probe thermometer is best. If you use an instant-read thermometer, open the oven door as little as possible and remove the roast from the oven while taking its temperature. If the roast has not reached the correct temperature in the time range specified in step 3, heat the oven to 200 degrees, wait for 5 minutes, then shut it off, and continue to cook the roast until it reaches the desired temperature.

- 1 (7-pound) first-cut beef standing rib roast (3 bones), meat removed from bones, bones reserved
- 2 tablespoons kosher salt
- 2 teaspoons vegetable oil
- 1 teaspoon pepper

1. Using sharp knife, cut through roast's fat cap in 1-inch crosshatch pattern, being careful not to cut into meat. Rub salt over entire roast and into slits. Place meat back on bones (to save space in refrigerator), transfer to large plate, and refrigerate, uncovered, for at least 24 hours or up to 4 days.

2. Adjust oven rack to middle position and heat oven to 200 degrees. Set wire rack in rimmed baking sheet. Heat oil in 12-inch skillet over high heat until just smoking. Sear sides and top of roast (reserving bones) until browned, 6 to 8 minutes total (do not sear side where roast was cut from bones). Place meat back on ribs so bones fit where they were cut and let cool for 10 minutes; tie meat to bones

with 2 lengths of kitchen twine between ribs. Transfer roast, fat side up, to prepared wire rack and sprinkle with pepper. Roast until meat registers 110 degrees, 3 to 4 hours.

3. Turn off oven; leave roast in oven, opening door as little as possible, until meat registers 120 degrees for rare or 125 degrees for medium-rare, 30 minutes to 1¼ hours longer.

4. Remove roast from oven (leave roast on baking sheet), tent with aluminum foil, and let rest for at least 30 minutes or up to 1¼ hours.

5. Adjust oven rack to about 8 inches from broiler element and heat broiler. Remove foil from roast, form into 3-inch ball, and place under ribs to elevate fat cap. Broil until top of roast is well browned and crisp, 2 to 8 minutes.

6. Transfer roast to carving board; cut twine and remove ribs from roast. Slice meat ¾ inch thick. Season with salt to taste, and serve.

Preparing Best Prime Rib

1. Remove ribs to make it easier to sear prime rib in skillet. Run sharp knife down length of bones, following contours as closely as possible to remove ribs.

2. Score fat cap in 1-inch crosshatch pattern to allow salt to contact meat directly and to improve fat rendering and crisping.

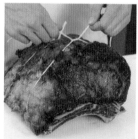

3. After searing meat, place meat back on ribs so bones fit where they were cut and let cool for 10 minutes; tie meat to bones with 2 lengths of kitchen twine between ribs. Bones provide insulation to meat so it cooks evenly.

Modern Beef Burgundy

Serves 6 to 8 • Total Time: 4¾ to 5¼ hours, plus 30 minutes resting

Why This Recipe Works We wanted to update the French classic boeuf bourguignon to have tender braised beef napped with a silky sauce with bold red wine flavor—without all the work that traditional recipes require. To eliminate the time-consuming step of searing the beef, we cooked the stew uncovered in a roasting pan in the oven so that the exposed meat browned as it braised. This method worked so well that we also used the oven, rather than the stovetop, to render the salt pork and to caramelize the traditional mushroom and pearl onion garnish. Salting the beef before cooking and adding some anchovy paste and porcini mushrooms enhanced the meaty savoriness of the dish without making our recipe too fussy.

If the pearl onions have a papery outer coating, remove it by rinsing them in warm water and gently squeezing individual onions between your fingertips. Two minced anchovy fillets can be used in place of the anchovy paste. To save time, salt the meat and let it stand while you prep the remaining ingredients. Serve with mashed potatoes or buttered noodles.

1 (4-pound) boneless beef chuck-eye roast, trimmed and cut into 1½- to 2-inch pieces, scraps reserved

1½ teaspoons table salt

6 ounces salt pork, cut into ¼-inch pieces

3 tablespoons unsalted butter, divided

1 pound cremini mushrooms, trimmed, halved if medium or quartered if large

1½ cups frozen pearl onions, thawed

1 tablespoon sugar

⅓ cup all-purpose flour

4 cups beef broth

1 (750-ml) bottle red Burgundy or Pinot Noir, divided

5 teaspoons unflavored gelatin

1 tablespoon tomato paste

1 teaspoon anchovy paste

2 onions, chopped coarse

2 carrots, peeled and cut into 2-inch lengths

1 garlic head, cloves separated, unpeeled, and crushed

2 bay leaves

½ teaspoon black peppercorns

½ ounce dried porcini mushrooms, rinsed

10 sprigs fresh parsley, plus 3 tablespoons minced

6 sprigs fresh thyme

1. Toss beef and salt together in bowl and let stand at room temperature for 30 minutes.

2. Adjust oven racks to lower-middle and lowest positions and heat oven to 500 degrees. Place salt pork, beef scraps, and 2 tablespoons butter in large roasting pan. Roast on upper rack until well browned and fat has been rendered, 15 to 20 minutes.

3. While salt pork and beef scraps roast, toss remaining 1 tablespoon butter, cremini mushrooms, pearl onions, and sugar together on rimmed baking sheet. Roast on lower rack, stirring occasionally, until moisture released by mushrooms evaporates and vegetables are lightly glazed, 15 to 20 minutes. Transfer vegetables to large bowl, cover, and refrigerate.

4. Remove roasting pan from oven and reduce temperature to 325 degrees. Sprinkle flour over rendered fat and whisk until no dry flour remains. Whisk in broth, 2 cups wine, gelatin, tomato paste, and anchovy paste until combined. Add onions, carrots, garlic, bay leaves, peppercorns, porcini mushrooms, parsley sprigs, and thyme sprigs to pan. Arrange beef in single layer on top of vegetables. Add water as needed to come three-quarters up side of beef (beef should not be submerged). Return roasting pan to oven and cook until meat is tender, 3 to 3½ hours, stirring after 1½ hours and adding water to keep meat at least half-submerged.

5. Using slotted spoon, transfer beef to bowl with cremini mushrooms and pearl onions; cover and set aside. Strain braising liquid through fine-mesh strainer set over large bowl, pressing on solids to extract as much liquid as possible; discard solids. Stir in remaining wine and let cooking liquid settle, 10 minutes. Using wide shallow spoon, skim fat off surface and discard.

6. Transfer liquid to Dutch oven and bring mixture to boil over medium-high heat. Simmer briskly, stirring occasionally, until sauce is thickened to consistency of heavy cream, 15 to 20 minutes. Reduce heat to medium-low, stir in beef and mushroom-onion garnish, cover, and cook until just heated through, 5 to 8 minutes. Season with salt and pepper to taste. Stir in minced parsley and serve. (Stew can be refrigerated for up to 3 days.)

SEASON 6

Onion-Braised Beef Brisket

Serves 6 • **Total Time: 5¾ to 6¼ hours, plus 12 hours chilling**

Why This Recipe Works Brisket is naturally flavorful, but because it is so lean, it requires long, slow braising to become tender—and the result is almost always stringy, dry meat. We wanted a better way to cook brisket so that it remained moist, and we wanted to serve it with a flavorful sauce that would complement the beef. The fat in a piece of brisket is all on the surface; there's no marbling to keep the interior moist. We needed to find a way to get the moisture inside. We tried many different types and amounts of liquids and a variety of cooking vessels and techniques, but no matter what we did, the meat was still dry. Could the answer lie in adding moisture after the long braise? We left the meat in the sauce after cooking it, and after about an hour there was a noticeable difference. Taking this discovery further, we refrigerated the cooked meat and sauce overnight. The meat reabsorbed some of the liquid, becoming moister and easier to carve without shredding. The sauce—based on red wine, chicken broth, and onions—had improved as well; the fat had risen to the surface and congealed, making it easier to remove. All we had to do was reheat the sliced meat in the sauce, and this hearty dish was ready.

This recipe requires a few hours of unattended cooking. It also requires advance preparation. After cooking, the brisket must stand overnight in the braising liquid that later becomes the sauce. Defatting the sauce is essential. If the fat has congealed into a layer on top of the sauce, it can be easily removed while cold. Sometimes, however, fragments of solid fat are dispersed throughout the sauce; in this case, the sauce should be skimmed of fat after reheating. If you prefer a spicy sauce, increase the amount of cayenne to ¼ teaspoon. You will need 18-inch-wide heavy-duty foil for this recipe. If you own an electric knife, it will make easy work of slicing the cold brisket. If you would like to make and serve the brisket on the same day, after removing the brisket from the oven in step 4, reseal

the foil and let the brisket stand at room temperature for an hour. Then transfer the brisket to a carving board and continue with the recipe to strain, defat, and reheat the sauce and slice the meat; because the brisket will still be hot, there will be no need to put it back into the oven once the reheated sauce is poured over it.

- 1 (4- to 5-pound) beef brisket, preferably flat cut
- 1¼ teaspoons table salt, divided
- 1 teaspoon pepper
- 1 teaspoon vegetable oil, plus extra as needed
- 3 large onions (about 2½ pounds), halved and sliced ½ inch thick
- 1 tablespoon packed brown sugar
- 3 garlic cloves, minced
- 1 tablespoon tomato paste
- 1 tablespoon paprika
- ⅛ teaspoon cayenne pepper
- 2 tablespoons all-purpose flour
- 1 cup chicken broth
- 1 cup dry red wine
- 3 bay leaves
- 3 sprigs fresh thyme
- 2 teaspoons cider vinegar

1. Adjust oven rack to lower-middle position and heat oven to 300 degrees. Line 13 by 9-inch baking dish with two 24-inch-long sheets of 18-inch-wide heavy-duty aluminum foil, positioning sheets perpendicular to each other and allowing excess foil to extend beyond edges of pan. Pat brisket dry with paper towels. Place brisket, fat side up, on cutting board; using dinner fork, poke holes in meat through fat layer about 1 inch apart. Sprinkle both sides of brisket with 1 teaspoon salt and pepper.

2. Heat oil in 12-inch skillet over medium-high heat until just smoking. Place brisket, fat side up, in skillet (brisket may climb up sides of skillet); weight brisket with heavy Dutch oven or cast-iron skillet and cook until well browned, about 7 minutes. Remove Dutch oven; using tongs, flip brisket and cook on second side without weight until well browned, about 7 minutes longer. Transfer brisket to platter.

3. Pour off all but 1 tablespoon fat from pan (or, if brisket is lean, add enough oil to fat in skillet to equal 1 tablespoon); stir in onions, sugar, and remaining ¼ teaspoon salt and cook over medium-high heat, stirring occasionally, until onions are softened and golden, 10 to 12 minutes. Add garlic and cook, stirring frequently, until fragrant, about 1 minute; add tomato paste and cook, stirring to combine, until paste darkens, about 2 minutes. Add paprika and cayenne and cook, stirring constantly, until fragrant, about 1 minute. Sprinkle flour over onions and cook, stirring constantly, until well combined, about 2 minutes. Add broth, wine, bay leaves, and thyme, stirring to scrape up any browned bits; bring to simmer and simmer for about 5 minutes to fully thicken.

4. Pour sauce and onions into foil-lined baking dish. Nestle brisket, fat side up, in sauce and onions. Fold foil extensions over and seal (do not tightly crimp foil because it must later be opened to test for doneness). Place in oven and cook until fork can be inserted into and removed from center of brisket with no resistance, 3½ to 4 hours (when testing for doneness, open foil with caution as contents will be steaming). Carefully open foil and let brisket cool at room temperature for 20 to 30 minutes.

5. Transfer brisket to large bowl; set mesh strainer over bowl and strain sauce over brisket. Discard bay leaves and thyme and transfer onions to small bowl. Cover both bowls with plastic wrap, cut vents in plastic with paring knife, and refrigerate overnight.

6. About 45 minutes before serving, adjust oven rack to lower-middle position and heat oven to 350 degrees. While oven heats, transfer cold brisket to carving board. Scrape off and discard any congealed fat from sauce, then transfer sauce to medium saucepan and heat over medium heat until warm, skimming any fat on surface with wide shallow spoon (you should have about 2 cups of sauce without onions; if necessary, simmer sauce over medium-high heat until reduced to 2 cups). While sauce heats, use electric knife, chef's knife, or carving knife to slice brisket against grain ¼ inch thick, trimming and discarding any excess fat, if desired; place slices in 13 by 9-inch baking dish. Stir reserved onions and vinegar into warmed sauce and season with salt and pepper to taste. Pour sauce over brisket slices, cover baking dish with foil, and bake until heated through, 25 to 30 minutes. Serve immediately.

SEASON 16

Ropa Vieja

Serves 6 to 8 • Total Time: 3 hours

Why This Recipe Works Tender yet hearty strands of beef napped with a bright and deeply savory sauce define ropa vieja. For braised and shredded beef dishes, we usually turn to chuck roast and short ribs, but this Cuban specialty calls for thicker, more fibrous shreds, so we used brisket. Slicing the beef into strips made for faster cooking and easy shredding, and a quick sear before braising gave the meat some ultrasavory browning. The accompanying vegetables would get overly soft if braised, so we cooked them ahead of time, browning sliced onions and red bell peppers then using their fond (as well as the beef's) to build the sauce. A fragrant combination of minced anchovies, minced garlic, ground cumin, and dried oregano created the meaty, aromatic base to which we added dry white wine for brightness. After letting the mixture reduce, we added chicken broth, tomato sauce, and bay leaves. We cooked the brisket in this seasoned sauce for 2 hours and it emerged juicy and richly flavored. Green olives are a traditional finishing touch, so we chopped and added them to the sauce while the beef cooled, stirring them in with the cooked onions and peppers. A splash of white wine vinegar made the flavors in our perfectly chewy Cuban shredded beef pop.

Look for a brisket that is 1½ to 2½ inches thick. Serve with steamed white rice and beans. Another good accompaniment is Plátanos Maduros (page 498).

1 (2-pound) beef brisket, fat trimmed to ¼ inch

½ teaspoon table salt

½ teaspoon pepper

5 tablespoons vegetable oil, divided

2 onions, halved and sliced thin

2 red bell peppers, stemmed, seeded, and sliced into ¼-inch-wide strips

2 anchovy fillets, rinsed, patted dry, and minced

4 garlic cloves, minced

2 teaspoons ground cumin

1½ teaspoons dried oregano

½ cup dry white wine

2 cups chicken broth

1 (8-ounce) can tomato sauce

2 bay leaves

¾ cup pitted green olives, chopped coarse

¾ teaspoon white wine vinegar, plus extra for seasoning

1. Adjust oven rack to middle position and heat oven to 300 degrees. Cut brisket against grain into 2-inch-wide strips. Cut any strips longer than 5 inches in half crosswise. Sprinkle beef on all sides with salt and pepper. Heat ¼ cup oil in Dutch oven over medium-high heat until just smoking. Brown beef on all sides, 7 to 10 minutes; transfer to large plate and set aside. Add onions and bell peppers and cook until softened and pan bottom develops fond, 10 to 15 minutes. Transfer vegetables to bowl and set aside. Add remaining 1 tablespoon oil to now-empty pot, then add anchovies, garlic, cumin, and oregano and cook until fragrant, about 30 seconds. Stir in wine, scraping up any browned bits, and cook until mostly evaporated, about 1 minute. Stir in broth, tomato sauce, and bay leaves. Return beef and any accumulated juices to pot and bring to simmer over high heat. Transfer to oven and cook, covered, until beef is just tender, 2 to 2¼ hours, flipping beef halfway through cooking.

2. Transfer beef to cutting board; when cool enough to handle, shred into ¼-inch-thick pieces. Meanwhile, add olives and reserved vegetables to pot and bring to boil over medium-high heat; simmer until thickened and measures 4 cups, 5 to 7 minutes. Stir in beef. Add vinegar. Season with salt, pepper, and extra vinegar to taste; serve.

SEASON 10

Braised Beef Short Ribs

Serves 6 • **Total Time: 3½ hours**

Why This Recipe Works Short ribs have great flavor and luscious texture, but their excess fat can be a problem since so much fat is rendered during the ribs' stint in the oven. Most recipes call for resting them in the braising liquid overnight, so that the fat solidifies into an easy-to-remove layer. However, skimming off such a large amount of fat with a spoon doesn't work well enough. The meat and sauce come out greasy, no matter how diligent one's spoon-wielding. We wanted a silky, grease-free sauce and fork-tender short rib meat. Instead of traditional bone-in short ribs, we used boneless short ribs, which rendered significantly less fat. While we didn't miss much flavor from the bones, we did want the body that the bones' connective tissue added. To solve this, we sprinkled a bit of gelatin into the sauce to restore suppleness. To ramp up the richness of the sauce, we jump-started flavor by reducing wine with browned aromatics before using the liquid to cook the meat. This added the right intensity, but we needed another cup of liquid to keep the meat half-submerged—the right level for braises. More wine yielded too much wine flavor; we used beef broth instead. As for the excess fat, the level was low enough that we could strain and defat the liquid in a fat separator. Reducing the liquid concentrated the flavors and made for a rich, luxurious sauce.

Make sure that the ribs are at least 4 inches long and 1 inch thick. If boneless ribs are unavailable, substitute 7 pounds of bone-in beef short ribs at least 4 inches long with 1 inch of meat above the bone and bone them yourself.

3½ pounds boneless beef short ribs, trimmed

2 teaspoons kosher salt

1 teaspoon pepper

2 tablespoons vegetable oil

2 large onions, sliced thin (about 4 cups)

1 tablespoon tomato paste

6 garlic cloves, peeled

2 cups red wine, such as Cabernet Sauvignon or Côtes du Rhône

1 cup beef broth

4 carrots, peeled and cut crosswise into 2-inch pieces

4 sprigs fresh thyme

1 bay leaf

¼ cup cold water

½ teaspoon unflavored gelatin

1. Adjust oven rack to lower-middle position and heat oven to 300 degrees. Pat beef dry with paper towels and sprinkle with salt and pepper. Heat 1 tablespoon oil in large Dutch oven over medium-high heat until just smoking. Add half of beef and cook, without stirring, until well browned, 4 to 6 minutes. Turn beef and continue to cook on second side until well browned, 4 to 6 minutes longer, reducing heat if fat begins to smoke. Transfer beef to medium bowl. Repeat with remaining 1 tablespoon oil and remaining meat.

2. Reduce heat to medium; add onions; and cook, stirring occasionally, until softened and beginning to brown, 12 to 15 minutes. (If onions begin to darken too quickly, add 1 to 2 tablespoons water to pan.) Add tomato paste and cook, stirring constantly, until it browns on sides and bottom of pan, about 2 minutes. Add garlic and cook until fragrant, about 30 seconds. Increase heat to medium-high, add wine, and simmer, scraping up any browned bits, until reduced by half, 8 to 10 minutes. Add broth, carrots, thyme sprigs, and bay leaf. Add beef and any accumulated juices to pot; cover and bring to simmer. Transfer pot to oven and cook, using tongs to turn meat twice during cooking, until fork slips easily in and out of meat, 2 to 2½ hours.

3. Place water in small bowl and sprinkle gelatin on top; let stand for at least 5 minutes. Using tongs, transfer meat and carrots to serving platter and tent with aluminum foil. Strain cooking liquid through fine-mesh strainer into fat separator or bowl, pressing on solids to extract as much liquid as possible; discard solids. Allow liquid to settle for about 5 minutes and strain off fat. Return cooking liquid to Dutch oven and cook over medium heat until reduced to 1 cup, 5 to 10 minutes. Remove from heat and stir in gelatin mixture; season with salt and pepper to taste. Pour sauce over meat and carrots and serve.

Boning Short Ribs

1. With chef's knife as close as possible to bone, carefully remove meat.

2. Trim excess hard fat and silverskin from both sides of meat.

SEASON 25

Plov

Serves 4 • Total Time: 2¾ hours

Why This Recipe Works This revered beef-and-carrot rice dish from Uzbekistan is worthy of being the centerpiece of the table. The most challenging part of making it is getting the meat to reach perfect tenderness at the same time that the rice finishes cooking. To eliminate tricky timing issues, we removed the beef from the saucepan when it was tender and added it back to the pilaf only when the rice was nearly done. Placing a layer of aluminum foil between the saucepan and the lid ensured a tight seal, so all of the flavorful cooking liquid was retained during the braising step and then absorbed into the rice on the stovetop. A grated carrot added at the beginning of cooking provided sweet, earthy flavor throughout, while larger carrot chunks added with the rice became tender but remained intact. Traditional dried barberries supplied bracing pops of acidity. We simmered a whole head of garlic with the meat and then used it to garnish the platter.

Grate the largest carrot on the large holes of a box grater. You can substitute 1¼ pounds of blade steak, about 1 inch thick, for the boneless short ribs; halve the steak along the central line of connective tissue, and then remove the tissue. Don't substitute bone-in short ribs.

If barberries are unavailable, combine 2 tablespoons of dried currants and 1 tablespoon of lemon juice in a small bowl. Microwave, covered, until very steamy, about 1 minute. Add the currants (and any residual lemon juice) to the plov as directed. Diners can mix individual cloves of the cooked garlic into their pilaf.

    5 carrots, peeled
    1 pound boneless beef short ribs, trimmed
 1½ teaspoons table salt, divided
    1 tablespoon vegetable oil
    2 onions, quartered through root end and
        sliced ¼ inch thick
    2 tablespoons dried barberries, divided
    3 garlic cloves, minced, plus 1 head garlic, outer
        papery skin removed and top ½ inch cut off
    1 tablespoon ground cumin
    2 teaspoons ground coriander
  ½ teaspoon pepper
1¾ cups water
    1 cup basmati rice, rinsed and drained
    2 scallions, sliced thin

1. Adjust oven rack to middle position and heat oven to 350 degrees. Grate largest carrot. Cut remaining 4 carrots into 2 by ½-inch pieces. Pat beef dry with paper towels and sprinkle all over with ½ teaspoon salt. Heat oil in large oven-safe saucepan over medium-high heat until shimmering. Add beef and cook until well browned on all sides, 10 to 12 minutes. Using tongs, transfer beef to bowl.

2. Add onions and remaining 1 teaspoon salt to saucepan. Cover and cook, stirring occasionally and scraping up any browned bits, until onions are soft, about 5 minutes.

Add grated carrot, 1 tablespoon barberries, minced garlic, cumin, coriander, and pepper and cook, stirring constantly, until garlic and spices are fragrant, 1 to 2 minutes. Spread mixture into even layer. Return beef to saucepan, nestling it into vegetables. Add water and any accumulated beef juices. Place garlic head in center of saucepan. Increase heat to high and bring mixture to vigorous simmer. Remove saucepan from heat; place large sheet of aluminum foil over saucepan, crimp tightly to seal, and cover tightly with lid. Transfer saucepan to oven and cook until meat is fork-tender, 1¼ to 1½ hours.

3. Transfer beef and garlic head to cutting board. Stir rice and remaining carrots into cooking liquid (saucepan handle will be hot). Bring to simmer over medium heat. Adjust heat to maintain simmer; replace foil, cover, and cook until liquid level has dropped below rice and rice is half cooked, about 10 minutes. While rice cooks, cut beef into ½-inch cubes. Gently fold beef into rice mixture, making sure to incorporate rice on bottom of saucepan. Replace foil, cover, and continue to cook until rice is tender and moisture is fully absorbed, 10 to 15 minutes longer. (Check rice every 5 minutes by sliding butter knife to bottom of center of saucepan and gently pushing rice aside; if bottom appears to be drying out, reduce heat slightly.)

4. Pile pilaf on platter. Sprinkle with scallions and remaining 1 tablespoon barberries. Garnish with garlic head and serve.

SEASON 16

Simple Pot-au-Feu

Serves 6 to 8 • Total Time: 4½ to 4¾ hours

Why This Recipe Works Pot-au-feu is a French boiled dinner of meltingly tender beef in a flavorful broth with an array of perfectly cooked vegetables. For a pot-au-feu brimming with tradition but suited to today's modern kitchen, we developed a pared-down shopping list. Boneless chuck roast beat out harder-to-find cuts of meat for its relative tenderness and big meaty flavor. Marrow bones gave the broth a buttery, beefy quality when cooked together with the meat, onion, and celery. Gently simmering the broth kept it perfectly clear. We transferred the pot to the oven partially covered to cook low and slow and, in the meantime, stirred together a sauce reminiscent of traditional pot-au-feu accompaniments. The zesty, bright combination of parsley, Dijon, chives, white wine vinegar, minced cornichon pickles, and pepper was deepened with the addition of the soft, beefy marrow extracted from the bones after cooking.

Marrow bones (also called soup bones) can be found in the freezer section or the meat counter at most supermarkets. Use small red potatoes measuring 1 to 2 inches in diameter.

Meat

- 1 (3½- to 4-pound) boneless beef chuck-eye roast, pulled into two pieces at natural seam and trimmed
- 1 tablespoon kosher salt
- 1½ pounds marrow bones
- 1 onion, quartered
- 1 celery rib, sliced thin
- 3 bay leaves
- 1 teaspoon black peppercorns

Parsley Sauce

- ⅔ cup minced fresh parsley
- ¼ cup Dijon mustard
- ¼ cup minced fresh chives
- 3 tablespoons white wine vinegar
- 10 cornichons, minced
- 1½ teaspoons pepper

Vegetables

- 1 pound small red potatoes, unpeeled, halved
- 6 carrots, peeled and halved crosswise, thick halves quartered lengthwise, thin halves halved lengthwise
- 1 pound asparagus, trimmed

1. For the meat: Adjust oven rack to lower-middle position and heat oven to 300 degrees. Sprinkle beef with salt. Using 3 pieces of kitchen twine per piece, tie each into loaf shape for even cooking. Place beef, bones, onion, celery, bay leaves, and peppercorns in Dutch oven. Add 4 cups cold water (water should come halfway up roasts). Bring to simmer over high heat. Partially cover pot and transfer to oven. Cook until beef is fully tender and sharp knife easily slips in and out of meat (meat will not be shreddable), 3¼ to 3¾ hours, flipping beef over halfway through cooking.

2. For the parsley sauce: While beef cooks, combine all ingredients in bowl. Cover and set aside.

3. Remove pot from oven and turn off oven. Transfer beef to large platter, cover tightly with aluminum foil, and return to oven to keep warm. Transfer bones to cutting board and use end of spoon to extract marrow. Mince marrow into paste and add 2 tablespoons to parsley sauce (reserve any remaining marrow for other applications). Using ladle or large spoon, skim fat from surface of broth and discard fat. Strain broth through fine-mesh strainer into large liquid measuring cup; add water to make 6 cups. Return broth to pot. (Meat can be returned to broth, cooled, and refrigerated for up to 2 days. Skim fat from cold broth, then gently reheat and proceed with recipe.)

4. For the vegetables: Add potatoes to broth and bring to simmer over high heat. Reduce heat to medium and simmer for 6 minutes. Add carrots and cook for 10 minutes. Add asparagus and continue to cook until all vegetables are tender, 3 to 5 minutes.

5. Using slotted spoon, transfer vegetables to large bowl. Toss with 3 tablespoons parsley sauce and season with salt and pepper to taste. Season broth with salt to taste.

6. Transfer beef to cutting board, remove twine, and slice against grain ½ inch thick. Arrange servings of beef and vegetables in large, shallow bowls. Dollop beef with parsley sauce, drizzle with ⅓ cup broth, and sprinkle with flake sea salt. Serve, passing remaining parsley sauce and flake sea salt separately.

Pulling Apart a Roast

Pull roast apart at seam to make 2 smaller roasts and trim any large knobs of fat.

Jamaican Pepper Steak

Serves 4 • Total Time: 1¼ hours, plus 1 hour marinating

Why This Recipe Works There's no clearer snapshot of Jamaican Chinese cooking than pepper steak: the beef-and–bell pepper stir-fry lavished with heady seasonings and brown gravy. We briefly soaked the meat in a baking soda solution to raise its pH, which helped it hold on to moisture during cooking. Adding a little cornstarch to the soy sauce marinade sheathed the meat in a thin, protective coating, loosely mimicking Chinese velveting. To cook everything to its precise ideal doneness, we stir-fried in batches—first the steak in two portions, followed by the peppers, then the scallions, and finally the aromatics. The beef browned; the vegetables charred lightly but retained their crisp bite; and the aromatics toasted just enough to turn fragrant. Deglazing the steak fond with a splash of rum released those savory bits for the sauce. Marinating the meat in full-bodied, faintly sweet dark (rather than all-purpose) soy sauce and stirring oyster and Worcestershire sauces in the beef broth captured the savory depth and color that traditional Jamaican browning sauce lends to gravies. We coarsely ground allspice berries, which added far more of the spice's warm, woodsy fragrance than commercial pre-ground allspice would, and the small, well-distributed bits weren't as jarring to bite into as whole berries.

Prepare the vegetables and aromatics while the beef rests. Dark soy sauce is thicker and a bit sweeter than the all-purpose kind; shop for it online or at an Asian market. You can substitute a habanero chile for the Scotch bonnet. We prefer coarsely ground allspice berries (use a spice grinder or mortar and pestle), but ½ teaspoon ground allspice can be used. Serve over rice or rice and peas. If you prefer, you can use a carbon-steel skillet instead of a nonstick skillet.

- 1 (1¼-pound) boneless strip steak, trimmed
- 1 tablespoon water
- ¼ teaspoon baking soda
- 4 teaspoons cornstarch, divided
- 1 tablespoon dark soy sauce
- 1 teaspoon pepper, divided
- ½ teaspoon table salt
- 2 cups beef broth
- 2 tablespoons Worcestershire sauce
- 2 tablespoons oyster sauce
- 1 teaspoon packed brown sugar
- ½ teaspoon garlic powder
- ½ teaspoon onion powder
- 2 tablespoons plus 2 teaspoons vegetable oil, divided
- 2 tablespoons dark rum or brandy
- ½ large red bell pepper, cut into ¼-inch-wide strips
- ½ large yellow bell pepper, cut into ¼-inch-wide strips
- ½ large green bell pepper, cut into ¼-inch-wide strips
- 3 scallions, cut into 2-inch pieces
- 5 garlic cloves, sliced
- 1 teaspoon whole allspice berries, coarsely ground
- ½ teaspoon grated fresh ginger
- ½ teaspoon minced fresh thyme
- ½ teaspoon minced Scotch bonnet chile

1. Slice beef crosswise ¼ inch thick. Cut slices into ¼-inch-thick strips. Combine water and baking soda in medium bowl. Add beef and toss to coat. Let sit at room temperature for 5 minutes.

2. Add 1 teaspoon cornstarch, soy sauce, ½ teaspoon pepper, and salt to beef and toss until well combined. Refrigerate for at least 1 hour or up to 2 hours.

3. Whisk beef broth, Worcestershire, oyster sauce, sugar, garlic powder, onion powder, remaining 1 tablespoon cornstarch, and remaining ½ teaspoon pepper in bowl.

4. Heat 2 teaspoons oil in 12-inch nonstick skillet over medium-high heat until just smoking. Add half of beef in single layer. Cook without stirring for 1 minute. Continue to cook, stirring occasionally, until spotty brown on both sides, about 1 minute longer. Transfer to clean bowl. Repeat with 2 teaspoons oil and remaining beef. Remove now-empty skillet from heat. Add rum and, using spatula, scrape any browned bits from skillet. Transfer any remaining liquid and browned bits to bowl with beef.

5. Return skillet to medium-high heat, add 2 teaspoons oil, and heat until just smoking. Add bell peppers and cook, stirring occasionally, until peppers are spotty brown but still crisp, 2 to 3 minutes. Transfer peppers to bowl with beef.

6. Return skillet to medium-high heat, add remaining 2 teaspoons oil, and heat until just smoking. Add scallions and cook, stirring occasionally, until spotty brown, 1 to 2 minutes. Add garlic, allspice, ginger, thyme, and Scotch bonnet. Cook, stirring frequently, until garlic is lightly browned and fragrant, about 1 minute. Transfer scallion mixture to bowl with beef and peppers.

7. Whisk beef broth mixture to recombine. Add mixture to skillet; reduce heat to medium; and cook, stirring occasionally, until thickened (spatula will start to leave trail that quickly fills in), 4 to 6 minutes. Stir in beef and vegetables and cook until heated through, about 1 minute. Season with salt and pepper to taste. Serve.

GAME CHANGER

Compound Flavors That Don't Quit

"When it comes to the Caribbean and food, most people's first thoughts go towards Jamaica. With mottos such as The Land of Wood and Water and Out of Many One People, you already know that you will undoubtedly encounter cultural fusion in their cuisine. Jamaican Pepper Steak is the model of this experience. Imagine taking everything that you love about Chinese pepper steak and fusing it with the most noted spice blends of Jamaica; with that you get Jamaican Pepper Steak. Peppers that are slightly charred but very much still snappy, tender beef that melts in your mouth, and finally the velvety Jamaican-style gravy that gives you that 'oomph' that Jamaican cuisine is known for. I bring out this dish when I want to impress my Caribbean friends or when I'm simply feeling nostalgic for a childhood favorite with a little kick to it. Like most recipes with this much depth of flavor, it takes a bit of elbow grease to get it done but the result is worth it."

— *Elle*

Steak Frites

Serves 4 • **Total Time: 1½ hours, plus 50 minutes chilling and resting**

Why This Recipe Works Too often, steak frites can miss the mark: The fries are too soggy and the steak just isn't flavorful. To re-create the steak frites of our Parisian dreams, with perfectly cooked steak and fries that were fluffy on the inside and crisp on the outside, we started with high-starch russet potatoes. We found that a double-cooking, blanch-and-fry method yielded the crispiest exterior and fluffiest interior. Cooking small batches of fries and soaking the potatoes in cold water before they were cooked further improved their crispiness, and a "rest" between the first and second frying allowed the fries to develop a thin coating of starch, which made them even crispier. Tossing them with cornstarch made them perfect. We were able to sear four rib-eye steaks at once in a large skillet. Capped with a quick herb butter, the steaks tasted just like the bistro classic.

> *Make sure to dry the potatoes well before tossing them with the cornstarch. For safety, use a Dutch oven with a capacity of at least 7 quarts. A 12-inch skillet is essential for cooking four steaks at once. The recipe can be prepared through step 4 up to 2 hours in advance; shut off the heat under the oil and turn the heat back to medium when you start step 6. The ingredients can be halved to serve two—keep the oil amount the same and forgo blanching and frying the potatoes in batches.*

Herb Butter
- 4 tablespoons unsalted butter, softened
- ½ shallot, minced
- 1 tablespoon minced fresh parsley
- 1 tablespoon minced fresh chives
- 1 garlic clove, minced
- ¼ teaspoon table salt
- ¼ teaspoon pepper

Potatoes and Steak
- 2½ pounds russet potatoes (about 4 large), scrubbed, sides squared off and cut lengthwise into ¼ by ¼-inch fries
- 2 tablespoons cornstarch
- 3 quarts peanut oil
- 1 tablespoon vegetable oil
- 2 (1-pound) boneless rib-eye steaks, cut in half
- ½ teaspoon table salt
- ½ teaspoon pepper

1. For the herb butter: Combine all ingredients in medium bowl.

2. For the potatoes: Rinse cut potatoes in large bowl under cold running water until water turns clear. Cover with cold water and refrigerate for at least 30 minutes or up to 12 hours.

3. Pour off water, spread potatoes onto clean dish towels, and thoroughly dry. Transfer potatoes to large bowl and toss with cornstarch until evenly coated. Transfer potatoes to wire rack set in rimmed baking sheet and let rest until fine white coating forms, about 20 minutes.

4. Meanwhile, heat peanut oil over medium heat to 325 degrees in large, heavy-bottomed Dutch oven fitted with a clip-on candy thermometer.

5. Add half of potatoes, 1 handful at a time, to hot oil and increase heat to high. Fry, stirring with mesh spider or slotted spoon, until potatoes start to turn from white to blond, 4 to 5 minutes. (Oil temperature will drop about 75 degrees during this frying.) Transfer fries to thick paper bag or paper towels. Return oil to 325 degrees and repeat with remaining potatoes. Reduce heat to medium and let fries cool while cooking steaks, at least 10 minutes.

6. For the steak: Heat vegetable oil in 12-inch skillet over medium-high heat until just smoking. Meanwhile, sprinkle steaks with salt and pepper. Lay steaks in pan, leaving ¼ inch between them. Cook, without moving steaks, until well browned, about 4 minutes. Flip steaks and continue to cook until meat registers 120 degrees (for rare to medium-rare), 3 to 7 minutes. Transfer steaks to large plate, top with herb butter, and tent with aluminum foil; let rest while finishing fries.

7. Increase heat under Dutch oven to high and heat oil to 375 degrees. Add half of fries, 1 handful at a time, and fry until golden brown and puffed, 2 to 3 minutes. Transfer to thick paper bag or paper towels. Return oil to 375 degrees and repeat with remaining fries. Season fries with salt to taste, and serve immediately with steaks.

Pan-Seared Strip Steaks

Serves 4 • Total Time: 20 minutes

Why This Recipe Works Pan-searing strip or rib-eye steaks usually leads to a smoky, grease-splattered kitchen—but it doesn't have to. To devise a fast, mess-free method for achieving deeply seared, rosy meat, we started the steaks in a "cold" (not preheated) nonstick skillet over high heat and flipped them every 2 minutes; that way, the meat's temperature increased gradually, allowing a crust to build up on the outside without overcooking the interior. Because we were cooking in a nonstick skillet, it wasn't necessary to lubricate the skillet with oil; plus, the well-marbled meat exuded enough fat to achieve a good sear, and adding more simply encouraged splatter. We started cooking over high heat to burn off moisture and prevent the steaks from steaming but quickly lowered the heat to medium; at this temperature, the meat kept sizzling, but there was no risk of the fat smoking. Before serving, we sliced the steaks and sprinkled them with coarse sea salt so that every bite was well seasoned.

> *This recipe also works with boneless rib-eye steaks of a similar thickness. If you have time, salt the steaks for at least 45 minutes or up to 24 hours before cooking: Sprinkle each of the steaks with 1 teaspoon of kosher salt, refrigerate them, and pat them dry with paper towels before cooking. Serve with Sauce Verte (recipe follows), if desired.*

> 2 (12- to 16-ounce) boneless strip steaks, 1½ inches thick, trimmed
> 1 teaspoon pepper

1. Pat steaks dry with paper towels and sprinkle both sides with pepper. Place steaks 1 inch apart in cold nonstick skillet. Place skillet over high heat and cook steaks for 2 minutes. Flip steaks and cook on second side for 2 minutes. (Neither side of steaks will be browned at this point.)

2. Flip steaks, reduce heat to medium, and continue to cook, flipping steaks every 2 minutes, until browned and meat registers 120 to 125 degrees (for medium-rare), 4 to 10 minutes longer. (Steaks should be sizzling gently; if not, increase heat slightly. Reduce heat if skillet starts to smoke.)

3. Transfer steaks to carving board and let rest for 5 minutes. Slice steaks, season with coarse or flake sea salt to taste, and serve.

VARIATION

Pan-Seared Strip Steak for Two

This recipe also works with a boneless rib-eye steak of a similar thickness. If you have time, salt the steak for at least 45 minutes or up to 24 hours before cooking: Sprinkle the steak with 1 teaspoon of kosher salt, refrigerate it, and pat it dry with paper towels before cooking. Serve with Sauce Verte (recipe follows), if desired.

> 1 (12- to 16-ounce) boneless strip steak, 1½ inches thick, trimmed
> ½ teaspoon pepper

1. Pat steak dry with paper towels and sprinkle both sides with pepper. Place steak in cold nonstick skillet. Place skillet over high heat and cook steak for 2 minutes. Flip steak and cook on second side for 2 minutes. (Neither side of steak will be browned at this point.)

2. Flip steak, reduce heat to medium, and continue to cook, flipping steak every 2 minutes, until browned and meat registers 120 to 125 degrees (for medium-rare), 4 to 10 minutes longer. (Steak should be sizzling gently; if not, increase heat slightly. Reduce heat if skillet starts to smoke.)

3. Transfer steak to carving board and let rest for 5 minutes. Slice steak, season with coarse or flake sea salt to taste, and serve.

ACCOMPANIMENTS

Sauce Verte

Makes ½ cup • Total Time: 10 minutes

The French equivalent of salsa verde, this fresh herb sauce makes a great accompaniment to rich meats, and it comes together in seconds in the food processor. If you like, omit the tarragon and increase the amounts of parsley and mint to ¾ cup each.

- ½ cup fresh parsley leaves
- ½ cup fresh mint leaves
- ½ cup fresh tarragon leaves
- 1 small shallot, chopped
- 1 tablespoon capers, rinsed
- 1 garlic clove, peeled
- 1 anchovy fillet, rinsed and patted dry
- ½ teaspoon kosher salt
- ¼ cup extra-virgin olive oil
- 1 teaspoon finely grated lemon zest plus 1 tablespoon juice

Process parsley, mint, tarragon, shallot, capers, garlic, anchovy, and salt in food processor until coarsely chopped, about 5 seconds. Add oil and lemon zest and juice and process until sauce is uniform, about 5 seconds, scraping down sides of bowl as needed.

Thai Chili Butter

Makes ⅓ cup • Total Time: 25 minutes

If red curry paste isn't available, increase the chili-garlic sauce to 2½ teaspoons.

- 4 tablespoons unsalted butter, softened
- 1 tablespoon chopped fresh cilantro
- 2 teaspoons chili-garlic sauce
- 1½ teaspoons thinly sliced scallion, green part only
- 1 small garlic clove, minced
- ½ teaspoon red curry paste
- 2 teaspoons lime juice

Beat butter vigorously with spoon until soft and fluffy. Add cilantro, chili-garlic sauce, scallion, garlic, and red curry paste; beat to incorporate. Add lime juice, little at a time, beating vigorously between each addition until fully incorporated. Add salt to taste. Spoon dollop over each steak, giving it time to melt before serving.

SEASON 3

Pan-Seared Filet Mignon

Serves 4 • Total Time: 40 minutes

Why This Recipe Works Many cooks feel that filet mignon should be reserved for a celebratory restaurant meal. But we knew we could replicate the best restaurant filet at home, with a rich, brown crust and a tender interior, topped with a quick but luscious pan sauce. For a great crust, we patted the steaks dry before searing them in a very hot skillet. Then we transferred the meat to a hot oven to cook through. Finishing the steak in the oven prevented the richly flavored browned bits in the bottom of the pan from burning and allowed us time to start the sauce, which can be made in minutes while the steaks rest.

If you are making one of the sauces, have all the sauce ingredients ready before searing the steaks, and don't wash the skillet after removing the steaks. Begin the sauce while the steaks are in the oven. To cook six steaks instead of four, use a 12-inch pan and use 6 teaspoons of olive oil.

- 4 (7- to 8-ounce) center-cut filets mignons, 1½ inches thick, trimmed
- 4 teaspoons extra-virgin olive oil
- ½ teaspoon table salt
- ½ teaspoon pepper

1. Adjust oven rack to lower-middle position, place rimmed baking sheet on oven rack, and heat oven to 450 degrees. When oven reaches 450 degrees, heat 12-inch skillet over high heat until just smoking.

2. Meanwhile, pat steaks dry with paper towels; rub each side of steaks with ½ teaspoon oil and sprinkle with salt and pepper. Place steaks in skillet and cook, without moving steaks, until well browned and nice crust has formed, about 3 minutes. Turn steaks with tongs and cook until well browned and nice crust has formed on second side, about 3 minutes longer. Remove pan from heat and use tongs to transfer steaks to hot baking sheet in oven.

3. Roast until center of steaks registers 120 degrees for rare (4 to 5 minutes), 125 degrees for medium-rare (6 to 8 minutes), or 130 degrees for medium (8 to 10 minutes). Transfer steaks to large plate; tent with aluminum foil and let rest for about 10 minutes before serving.

Madeira Pan Sauce with Mustard and Anchovies

Makes ⅔ cup • Total Time: 30 minutes

If you do not have Madeira on hand, sherry makes a fine substitute. The accumulated pan juices from the steaks in the oven are incorporated into the reduction. If the steaks haven't finished cooking once the sauce has reduced, simply set the sauce aside until the steaks (and accumulated juices) are ready.

   1 shallot, minced
   1 cup Madeira
   2 anchovy fillets, minced to paste
   1 tablespoon minced fresh parsley
   1 tablespoon minced fresh thyme
   1 tablespoon Dijon mustard
   1 tablespoon lemon juice
   3 tablespoons unsalted butter, softened

While steaks are in oven, set skillet over medium-low heat; add shallot and cook, stirring constantly, until softened, about 1 minute. Add Madeira, increase heat to high, and scrape up any browned bits. Simmer until liquid is reduced to about ⅓ cup, 6 to 8 minutes. Add accumulated juices from baking sheet and reduce liquid 1 minute longer. Off heat, whisk in anchovies, parsley, thyme, mustard, lemon juice, and butter until butter has melted and sauce is slightly thickened. Season with salt and pepper to taste, spoon sauce over steaks, and serve immediately.

Chimichurri

Makes 1 cup • Total Time: 15 minutes

For best results use flat-leaf parsley.

   1 cup fresh parsley leaves
   5 garlic cloves, peeled
  ½ cup extra-virgin olive oil
  ¼ cup red wine vinegar
   2 tablespoons water
   1 small red onion, chopped fine
   1 teaspoon table salt
  ¼ teaspoon red pepper flakes

Pulse parsley and garlic in food processor until finely chopped, about 20 pulses, scraping down sides of bowl as needed; transfer to medium bowl. Whisk in oil, vinegar, water, onion, salt, and pepper flakes until thoroughly blended. Spoon about 2 tablespoons over each steak and serve. (This sauce tastes best when fresh but can be refrigerated, with plastic wrap pressed directly on surface, for up to 3 days.)

GAME CHANGER

A Ride or Die Technique

"Let's talk about filet mignon. It's the holy grail of steaks—tender, succulent, and worth every penny. But here's the thing: Cooking it perfectly is a whole different story. See, cooking steak can be a high-stakes game. One wrong move and you've turned that beautiful fillet into shoe leather. Luckily, we all have our Pan-Seared Filet Mignon recipe. I'm all about simplicity with a side of flair, and this recipe is simplicity at its finest. It's the little black dress of the culinary world—timeless, elegant, and always a crowd-pleaser. But don't let its simplicity fool you; the real magic is in the technique: this foolproof stove-to-oven method. It's the reason why my filets come out perfectly cooked every single time. Now, let's talk about value—because, let's be real, good meat doesn't come cheap. I'm all for splurging on a nice filet, but wasting $25 on a dinner disaster? Nobody wants that. That's why this recipe is my ride-or-die. It gives me the confidence to cook that pricey filet to perfection every time."

—Antoinette

Steak Tacos

Serves 4 to 6 • Total Time: 55 minutes

Why This Recipe Works Upscale steak tacos usually get their rich, beefy flavor from the grill, but cooking outdoors isn't always possible. We wanted an indoor cooking method that would always yield steak taco meat as tender, juicy, and rich-tasting as the grilled method. We didn't want to use a pricey cut of beef for this recipe, so we explored inexpensive cuts and chose flank steak for its good flavor and ready availability; when sliced against the grain, it can be just as tender as pricier cuts. To add flavor, we poked holes in the meat with a fork and rubbed it with a paste of oil, cilantro, jalapeño, garlic, and scallions; salt helped draw all the flavors into the steak and ensured juiciness. Pan searing, with a sprinkling of sugar to enhance browning, gave us a crust that mimicked the char of the grill. To maximize this effect, we cut the steak into four long pieces, which gave us more sides to brown and turn crispy. For additional flavor, we tossed the cooked steak with some marinade that we had reserved, and garnished the tacos simply with onion, cilantro, and lime wedges. In Mexico, steak tacos are often served with curtido, a relish of pickled vegetables; we devised a quick recipe for pickled onions to accompany our good-as-grilled steak tacos.

Our preferred method for warming tortillas is to place each one over the medium flame of a gas burner until slightly charred, about 30 seconds per side (see page 62). We also like toasting them in a dry skillet over medium-high heat until softened and speckled with brown spots,

20 to 30 seconds per side. For a less spicy dish, remove some or all of the ribs and seeds from the jalapeños before chopping them for the marinade. In addition to the toppings suggested below, try serving the tacos with Sweet and Spicy Pickled Onions (recipe follows), thinly sliced radish or cucumber, or salsa.

Marinade

- ½ cup fresh cilantro leaves
- 3 scallions, roughly chopped
- 1 jalapeño chile, stemmed and roughly chopped
- 3 garlic cloves, roughly chopped
- ½ teaspoon ground cumin
- ¼ cup vegetable oil
- 1 tablespoon lime juice

Steak

- 1 (1½- to 1¾-pound) flank steak, trimmed and cut lengthwise (with grain) into 4 equal pieces
- 1 tablespoon kosher salt
- ½ teaspoon sugar
- ½ teaspoon pepper
- 2 tablespoons vegetable oil

Tacos

- 12 (6-inch) corn tortillas, warmed
  Fresh cilantro leaves
  Minced white onion
  Lime wedges

1. For the marinade: Pulse cilantro, scallions, jalapeño, garlic, and cumin in food processor until finely chopped, 10 to 12 pulses, scraping down sides of bowl as necessary. Add oil and process until mixture is smooth and resembles pesto, about 15 seconds, scraping down sides as necessary. Transfer 2 tablespoons herb paste to medium bowl; whisk in lime juice and set aside.

2. For the steak: Using dinner fork, poke each piece of steak 10 to 12 times on each side. Place in large baking dish; rub all sides of steak pieces evenly with salt and then coat with remaining herb paste. Cover with plastic wrap and refrigerate for at least 30 minutes or up to 1 hour.

3. Scrape herb paste off steak and sprinkle all sides of pieces evenly with sugar and pepper. Heat oil in 12-inch nonstick skillet over medium-high heat until just smoking. Place steak in skillet and cook until well browned, about 3 minutes. Flip steak and sear until second side is well browned, 2 to 3 minutes. Using tongs, stand each piece on cut side and cook, turning as necessary, until all cut sides are well browned and steak registers 125 to 130 degrees, 2 to 7 minutes. Transfer steak to cutting board and let rest for 5 minutes.

4. For the tacos: Slice steak against grain ⅛ inch thick. Transfer sliced steak to bowl with herb paste–lime juice mixture and toss to coat. Season with salt to taste. Spoon small amount of sliced steak into center of each warm tortilla and serve immediately, passing toppings separately.

ACCOMPANIMENT
Sweet and Spicy Pickled Onions
Makes 2 cups
Total Time: 15 minutes, plus 30 minutes cooling
The onions can be refrigerated, tightly covered, for up to one week.

 1 red onion, halved and sliced thin (about 1½ cups)
 1 cup red wine vinegar
 ⅓ cup sugar
 2 jalapeño chiles, stemmed, seeded, and cut into thin rings
 ¼ teaspoon table salt

Place onions in medium heat-resistant bowl. Bring vinegar, sugar, jalapeños, and salt to simmer in small saucepan over medium-high heat, stirring occasionally, until sugar dissolves. Pour vinegar mixture over onions, cover loosely, and let cool to room temperature, about 30 minutes. Once cool, drain and discard the liquid.

SEASON 25

Steak Tips with Mushroom-Onion Gravy

Serves 4 to 6 • **Total Time: 1 hour, plus 30 minutes marinating**

Why This Recipe Works This classic supper promises juicy beef and hearty flavors but often delivers overcooked meat in a generic brown sauce or a greasy, gloppy gravy. To rescue the dish, we started with tender sirloin steak tips. To build flavor without adding any fat, we marinated the tips in a mixture of sugar for sweetness and soy sauce for saltiness. Browning the beef in a skillet leaves behind plenty of flavorful browned bits with which we built a rich gravy. Cremini mushrooms can be used in place of the white mushrooms. This dish can be served over rice or mashed potatoes, or with egg noodles.

> *Steak tips, also known as flap meat, are sold as whole steak, cubes, and strips. To ensure evenly sized chunks, we prefer to purchase whole steak tips and cut them ourselves.*

 1 tablespoon soy sauce
 1 teaspoon sugar
 1½ pounds sirloin steak tips, trimmed and cut into 1½-inch chunks
 1¾ cups beef broth, divided
 ¼ ounce dried porcini mushrooms, rinsed
 ½ teaspoon pepper
 2 tablespoons vegetable oil, divided
 1 pound white mushrooms, trimmed and sliced ¼ inch thick
 ½ teaspoon table salt, divided
 1 large onion, halved and sliced thin
 4 teaspoons all-purpose flour
 1 garlic clove, minced
 ½ teaspoon minced fresh thyme
 1 tablespoon chopped fresh parsley

1. Combine soy sauce and sugar in medium bowl. Add beef, toss well, and marinate for at least 30 minutes or up to 1 hour, tossing once more.

2. Meanwhile, microwave ¼ cup broth and porcini mushrooms in covered bowl until steaming, about 1 minute. Let sit until softened, about 5 minutes. Drain porcini mushrooms in fine-mesh strainer lined with coffee filter, reserve liquid, and mince porcini mushrooms. Set aside porcini mushrooms and liquid.

3. Pat beef dry with paper towels and sprinkle with pepper. Heat 1 tablespoon oil in 12-inch skillet over medium-high heat until just smoking. Add beef and cook until well browned on all sides, 6 to 8 minutes. Transfer to large plate and set aside.

4. Add remaining 1 tablespoon oil to now-empty skillet and heat over medium-high heat. Add white mushrooms, minced porcini mushrooms, and ¼ teaspoon salt; cook, stirring frequently, until all liquid has evaporated and mushrooms start to brown, 7 to 9 minutes, scraping up any browned bits. Add onion and remaining ¼ teaspoon salt; cook, stirring frequently, until onion begins to brown and dark bits form on pan bottom, 6 to 8 minutes longer. Add flour, garlic, and thyme; cook, stirring constantly, until vegetables are coated with flour mixture, about 1 minute. Stir in porcini soaking liquid and remaining 1½ cups broth, scraping up any browned bits, and bring to boil.

5. Nestle beef into mushroom-onion mixture and add any accumulated juices to skillet. Reduce heat to medium-low and simmer until beef registers 130 to 135 degrees (for medium), 3 to 5 minutes, turning beef several times. Season with salt and pepper to taste, sprinkle with parsley, and serve.

SEASON 22

Beef Bulgogi

Serves 4 • **Total Time: 1½ hours**

Why This Recipe Works For our version of bulgogi we first had to pick the best cut of beef. Rib-eye steak offered a nice combination of marbled interior and rich beef flavor. Freezing the meat in pieces firmed it up enough to be shaved superthin. Treating the meat with baking soda helped it stay tender, and because the meat was so thin, we found that there was no need to coat it with a marinade until just before cooking. We paired the marinade's signature sweet flavor with soy sauce, garlic, sesame oil, pepper, and chopped onion, which brought savory undertones but let the delicate flavor of the beef shine through. We cooked the beef in a moderately hot skillet before stirring it until it was fully cooked, which took just a few minutes. Ssamjang, a savory and spicy sauce, and daikon pickles offered heat and textural contrast to the sweet beef. Lettuce leaves, steamed rice, and other sides rounded out the meal.

> *To save time, prepare the pickles and chile sauce while the steak is in the freezer. You can substitute 2 cups of bean sprouts and one cucumber, peeled, quartered lengthwise, seeded, and sliced thin on the bias, for the daikon, if desired. You can find the Korean fermented bean pastes doenjang and gochujang in Asian markets and online. If you can't find them, you can substitute red or white miso for the doenjang and sriracha for the gochujang. You can eat bulgogi as a plated meal with*

> *steamed rice and kimchi or wrap small portions of the beef in lettuce leaves with chile sauce and eat them with your hands.*

Pickles
- 1 cup rice vinegar
- 2 tablespoons sugar
- 1½ teaspoons table salt
- 1 pound daikon radish, peeled and cut into 1½-inch-long matchsticks

Ssamjang
- 4 scallions, white and light green parts only, minced
- ¼ cup doenjang
- 1 tablespoon gochujang
- 1 tablespoon water
- 2 teaspoons sugar
- 2 teaspoons toasted sesame oil
- 1 garlic clove, minced

Beef
- 1 (1¼-pound) boneless rib-eye steak, cut crosswise into 1½-inch-wide pieces and trimmed
- 1 tablespoon water
- ¼ teaspoon baking soda
- ¼ cup chopped onion
- ¼ cup sugar
- 3 tablespoons soy sauce
- 4 garlic cloves, peeled
- 1 tablespoon toasted sesame oil
- ¼ teaspoon pepper
- 2 teaspoons vegetable oil
- 4 scallions, dark green parts only, cut into 1½-inch pieces

1. **For the pickles:** Whisk vinegar, sugar, and salt together in medium bowl. Add daikon and toss to combine. Gently press on daikon to submerge. Cover and refrigerate for at least 30 minutes or up to 24 hours.

2. **For the ssamjang:** Combine all ingredients in small bowl. Cover and set aside. (Sauce can be refrigerated for up to 3 days.)

3. **For the beef:** Place beef on large plate and freeze until very firm, 35 to 40 minutes. Once firm, stand each piece on 1 cut side on cutting board and, using sharp knife, shave beef against grain as thin as possible. (Slices needn't be perfectly intact.) Combine water and baking soda in medium bowl. Add beef and toss to coat. Let sit at room temperature for 5 minutes.

4. Meanwhile, process onion, sugar, soy sauce, garlic, sesame oil, and pepper in food processor until smooth, about 30 seconds, scraping down sides of bowl as needed. Add onion mixture to beef and toss to evenly coat.

5. Heat vegetable oil in 12-inch nonstick skillet over medium-high heat until shimmering. Add beef mixture in even layer and cook, without stirring, until browned on 1 side, about 1 minute. Stir and continue to cook until beef is no longer pink, 3 to 4 minutes longer. Add scallion greens and cook, stirring constantly, until fragrant, about 30 seconds. Transfer to platter. Serve with pickles and chile sauce.

Slicing One Steak into Four Servings

1. Cut rib-eye steak crosswise into 1½-inch-wide pieces. Trim exterior and interior fat. Freeze until very firm to make slicing easier.

2. Stand each piece on cut side to expose grain. Use sharp knife to shave meat as thin as possible against grain.

Braciole

Serves 6 to 8 • Total Time: 4 hours

Why This Recipe Works For our take on these Italian stuffed beef rolls, we chose flank steak rather than top or bottom round (the other common choices) because its loose grain made it easier to pound thin and its higher fat content meant that it emerged from the oven tender and moist. Our filling was on the bold side, with the inclusion of umami-rich ingredients such as prosciutto; anchovies; and fontina, a good melter that also brought much-needed fat to the dish. In addition, a gremolata-inspired mix provided the filling with a jolt of flavor and freshness. Finally, we added beef broth to the tomato sauce to integrate the beef and the sauce into a unified whole.

Cut sixteen 10-inch lengths of kitchen twine before starting the recipe. You can substitute sharp provolone for the fontina, if desired. For the most tender braciole, be sure to roll the meat so that the grain runs parallel to the length of the roll. Serve the braciole and sauce together, with pasta or polenta, or separately, as a pasta course with the sauce followed by the meat.

  7 tablespoons extra-virgin olive oil, divided
10 garlic cloves, minced, divided
  2 teaspoons grated lemon zest
  3 anchovy fillets, rinsed and minced
 ⅓ cup plus 2 tablespoons chopped fresh basil, divided
 ⅓ cup minced fresh parsley
 ⅓ cup grated Pecorino Romano cheese, plus extra for serving
 ⅓ cup plain dried bread crumbs
  3 ounces fontina cheese, shredded (¾ cup)
  1 (2- to 2½-pound) flank steak, trimmed
  8 thin slices prosciutto (4 ounces)
  1 teaspoon kosher salt
 ½ teaspoon pepper
  1 large onion, chopped fine
 ¼ teaspoon red pepper flakes
 ¼ cup tomato paste
 ¾ cup dry red wine
  1 (28-ounce) can crushed tomatoes
  2 cups beef broth

1. Adjust oven rack to lower-middle position and heat oven to 325 degrees. Stir 3 tablespoons oil, half of garlic, lemon zest, and anchovies together in medium bowl. Add ⅓ cup basil, parsley, Pecorino, and bread crumbs and stir to incorporate. Stir in fontina until evenly distributed and set aside filling.

2. Halve steak against grain to create 2 smaller steaks. Lay 1 steak on cutting board with grain running parallel to counter edge. Holding blade of chef's knife parallel to counter, halve steak horizontally to create 2 thin pieces. Repeat with remaining steak. Cover 1 piece with plastic wrap and, using meat pounder, flatten into rough rectangle measuring no more than ¼ inch thick. Repeat pounding with remaining 3 pieces. Cut each piece in half, with grain, to create total of 8 pieces.

3. Lay 4 pieces on cutting board with grain running parallel to counter edge (if 1 side is shorter than the other, place shorter side closer to you). Distribute half of filling evenly over pieces. Top filling on each piece with 1 slice of prosciutto, folding to fit, and press firmly. Keeping filling in place, roll each piece away from you to form tight log. Tie each roll with 2 pieces kitchen twine to secure. Repeat process with remaining steak pieces, filling, and prosciutto. Sprinkle rolls on both sides with salt and pepper.

4. Heat remaining ¼ cup oil in large Dutch oven over medium-high heat until shimmering. Brown rolls on 2 sides, 8 to 10 minutes. Transfer rolls to plate. Add onion to pot and cook, stirring occasionally, until softened and browned, 5 to 7 minutes. Stir in pepper flakes and remaining garlic; cook until fragrant, 30 seconds. Stir in tomato paste and cook until slightly darkened, 3 to 4 minutes. Add wine and cook, scraping up any browned bits. Stir in tomatoes and broth. Return rolls to pot; bring to simmer. Cover and transfer to oven. Braise until meat is fork-tender, 2½ to 3 hours, using tongs to flip rolls halfway through braising.

5. Transfer braciole to serving dish and discard twine. Stir remaining 2 tablespoons basil into tomato sauce and season with salt and pepper to taste. Pour sauce over braciole and serve, passing extra Pecorino separately.

Assembling Braciole

1. Lay 1 steak on cutting board with grain running parallel to counter edge. Slice horizontally to create 2 thin pieces. Repeat with second steak.

2. Cover 1 piece with plastic wrap and pound into rough rectangle measuring about ¼ inch thick. Repeat with remaining 3 pieces.

3. Cut each piece in half, with grain, to create total of 8 pieces.

4. Arrange 4 pieces so grain runs parallel to counter edge. Distribute half of filling over pieces and top with prosciutto slice.

5. Keeping filling in place, roll each piece away from you to form tight log.

6. Tie each roll with 2 pieces kitchen twine to secure. Repeat process with remaining steak pieces, filling, and prosciutto.

Bò Lúc Lắc

Serves 4 • **Total Time: 1 hour**

Why This Recipe Works Bò lúc lắc (shaking beef) is a Vietnamese cross between a beef stir-fry and a watercress salad. We used sirloin steak tips (aka flap meat) for their beefy flavor and pleasant chewy texture. We first marinated the meat in a mixture of soy sauce, fish sauce, and molasses and then reserved the marinade to make the glaze. We coated the meat with oil (to prevent splattering) and then cooked it in two batches to give it ample room in the skillet. True to the dish's name, we shook and stirred the beef to develop good browning and to deglaze the skillet, which prevented the fond from burning. After setting aside the meat, we lightly softened a red onion in butter, added the reserved marinade (along with garlic, water, and cornstarch) to the skillet, and cooked it down to a glossy consistency. We coated the meat with the sauce and then placed it atop the watercress, which we had lightly dressed with a mixture of lime juice and pepper. We used more of the lime juice mixture as a dipping sauce for the meat.

> *Sirloin steak tips are often sold as flap meat. They can be packaged as whole steaks, cubes, or strips. We prefer to buy whole steaks so we can cut our own steak tips. Maggi Seasoning can be used in place of the soy sauce, if desired. Serve with Cơm Đỏ (recipe follows) or steamed white rice.*

4 teaspoons fish sauce

4 teaspoons soy sauce

2 teaspoons molasses

1 pound sirloin steak tips, trimmed and cut into ¾-inch cubes

4 ounces (4 cups) watercress, torn into bite-size pieces

¼ cup lime juice (2 limes)

1 teaspoon pepper

¼ cup water

2 garlic cloves, minced

¾ teaspoon cornstarch

4 teaspoons vegetable oil, divided

1 tablespoon unsalted butter

1 small red onion, sliced thin

1. Whisk fish sauce, soy sauce, and molasses together in medium bowl. Add beef and toss to coat. Let sit at room temperature for 15 minutes. Spread watercress in shallow serving bowl. Combine lime juice and pepper in small bowl and set aside.

2. Using tongs, transfer beef to second medium bowl, letting as much marinade as possible drain back into first bowl. Add water, garlic, and cornstarch to marinade in first bowl and whisk to combine; set aside. Add 2 teaspoons oil to beef and toss to coat.

3. Heat 1 teaspoon oil in 12-inch nonstick skillet over medium-high heat until just smoking. Using tongs, wipe skillet clean with paper towels. Add half of beef to skillet, leaving space between pieces. Cook, swirling skillet gently and occasionally to capture any fond that collects on bottom of skillet, until beef is browned on first side, 3 to 4 minutes. Continue to cook, stirring and shaking skillet frequently, until beef is coated and browned and center is just pink (to check for doneness, remove larger piece and cut in half), 2 to 4 minutes longer. Transfer beef to clean bowl. Wipe skillet clean with wet paper towels and repeat with remaining 1 teaspoon oil and remaining beef.

4. Melt butter in now-empty skillet over medium heat. Add onion and cook, stirring occasionally, until just beginning to soften, about 1 minute. Add reserved marinade and bring to boil. Cook, stirring occasionally, until thickened and glossy, about 2 minutes. Add beef and any accumulated juices and toss to coat. Scatter beef mixture and sauce over watercress. Drizzle 2 teaspoons lime juice mixture over salad. Divide remaining lime juice mixture among small bowls for dipping and serve with salad.

Cơm Đỏ

Serves 4 to 6 • **Total Time: 45 minutes**

Red rice is an ultrasavory Vietnamese dish normally made by stir-frying precooked rice, but we made ours from scratch in one pot, using tomato paste and soy sauce for umami and butter for richness and complexity. We based this recipe on a version made by Vietnamese cooking authority Andrea Nguyen. If jasmine rice is unavailable, substitute another long-grain white rice. Maggi Seasoning can be used in place of the soy sauce, if desired.

1½	cups jasmine rice
2	tablespoons unsalted butter
4	garlic cloves, minced
3	tablespoons tomato paste
1¾	cups water
2	teaspoons soy sauce
½	teaspoon table salt

1. Place rice in fine-mesh strainer and rinse under cold running water until water runs clear. Drain well. Melt butter in medium saucepan over medium-high heat. Add rice and cook, stirring constantly, until grains become chalky and opaque, 1 to 3 minutes. Add garlic and cook, stirring constantly, until fragrant, about 30 seconds. Add tomato paste and cook, stirring constantly, until tomato paste is evenly distributed, about 1 minute.

2. Add water, soy sauce, and salt and bring to boil. Cover, reduce heat to low, and cook until liquid is absorbed and rice is tender, about 20 minutes. Let stand off heat, covered, for 10 minutes. Fluff rice with fork and stir to combine. Serve.

SEASON 23
Stir-Fried Cumin Beef

Serves 4 • **Total Time: 45 minutes**

Why This Recipe Works With roots in Hunan cuisine, cumin beef typically features tender pieces of meat stir-fried with onions and/or peppers and aromatics (garlic and ginger), lightly glossed in a soy sauce–based glaze, seasoned with spices (cumin, Sichuan peppercorns, and dried chiles or chili powder), and finished with cilantro. Before cooking, we briefly treated slices of beefy flank steak with baking soda, which raised the meat's pH so that it stayed moist and tender during cooking. To prevent the meat from overcooking before it browned, we stir-fried it in two batches until its juices reduced to a sticky fond that coated each slice.

Quickly stir-frying sliced onion allowed it to soften but retain a hint of its raw bite and crunch. Grinding whole cumin seeds and Sichuan peppercorns released vibrant aromatic compounds that gave the dish plenty of fragrance, while Sichuan chili powder added moderate heat.

We developed this recipe for a 14-inch wok, but a 12-inch nonstick or carbon-steel skillet can be used instead. You can substitute 1 tablespoon of ground cumin for the cumin seeds. If you can't find Sichuan chili powder, Korean red pepper flakes (gochugaru) are a good substitute. Another alternative is 1¾ teaspoons of ancho chile powder plus ¼ teaspoon of cayenne pepper. There is no substitute for Sichuan peppercorns. We like this stir-fry with steamed white rice and stir-fried baby bok choy.

1	tablespoon water
¼	teaspoon baking soda
1	pound flank steak, trimmed, cut with grain into 2- to 2½-inch-wide strips, each strip sliced against grain ¼ inch thick
4	garlic cloves, minced
1	tablespoon grated fresh ginger
1	tablespoon cumin seeds, ground
2	teaspoons Sichuan chili powder
1¼	teaspoons Sichuan peppercorns, ground
½	teaspoon table salt, divided
1	tablespoon Shaoxing wine or dry sherry
1	tablespoon soy sauce
2	teaspoons molasses
½	teaspoon cornstarch
¼	cup vegetable oil, divided
½	small onion, sliced thin
2	tablespoons coarsely chopped fresh cilantro

1. Combine water and baking soda in medium bowl. Add beef and toss to coat. Let sit at room temperature for 5 minutes.

2. While beef rests, combine garlic and ginger in small bowl. Combine cumin, chili powder, peppercorns, and ¼ teaspoon salt in second small bowl. Add Shaoxing wine, soy sauce, molasses, cornstarch, and remaining ¼ teaspoon salt to beef mixture. Toss until well combined.

3. Heat 1 tablespoon oil in wok over medium-high heat until just smoking. Add half of beef mixture and increase heat to high. Using tongs, toss beef slowly but constantly until exuded juices have evaporated and meat begins to sizzle, 2 to 6 minutes. Transfer to clean bowl. Repeat with 1 tablespoon oil and remaining beef mixture.

4. Heat remaining 2 tablespoons oil in now-empty wok over medium heat until shimmering. Add garlic mixture (oil will splatter) and cook, stirring constantly, until fragrant, 15 to 30 seconds. Add onion and cook, tossing slowly but constantly with tongs, until onion begins to soften, 1 to 2 minutes. Return beef to wok and toss to combine. Sprinkle cumin mixture over beef and toss until onion takes on pale orange color. Transfer to serving platter, sprinkle with cilantro, and serve immediately.

SEASON 23

Stir-Fried Beef and Gai Lan

Serves 4 • Total Time: 55 minutes

Why This Recipe Works Our take on this ever-evolving Chinese American standard features gai lan (Chinese broccoli) and filet mignon. The luxe cut is ideal for the quick, high-heat cooking of stir-frying; is readily available in small portions; and needs only a brief chill in the freezer to firm up for easy slicing. While the meat chilled, we sliced the gai lan stalks thin on the bias and cut the tender leaves into wide ribbons; together, the sweeter-tasting stalks and earthier, pleasantly bitter-tasting blue-green leaves created complexly layered flavor. To avoid sodden leaves, we stir-fried the leaves first, transferred them to a serving dish, and then stir-fried the heartier stalks and the meat with the sauce. Once the sauce thickened, we arranged the beef mixture over the leaves, ensuring that each bite was perfectly sauced.

> *We developed this recipe for a 14-inch wok, but a 12-inch carbon-steel or cast-iron skillet can be used. If gai lan is unavailable, you can use broccolini, substituting the*

> *florets for the gai lan leaves. Do not use standard broccoli. This recipe was developed with Lee Kum Kee oyster sauce. Serve with white rice.*

1   (8-ounce) center-cut filet mignon, trimmed
1   pound gai lan, stalks trimmed
5   teaspoons Shaoxing wine or dry sherry, divided
1   tablespoon soy sauce, divided
2   teaspoons cornstarch, divided
¾   cup chicken broth, divided
2   tablespoons oyster sauce
1½   teaspoons toasted sesame oil, divided
2   tablespoons vegetable oil, divided
1½   teaspoons grated fresh ginger
¾   teaspoon minced garlic, divided

1. Cut beef into 4 equal wedges. Transfer to plate and freeze until very firm, 20 to 25 minutes. While beef freezes, prepare gai lan. Remove leaves, small stems, and florets from stalks; slice leaves crosswise into 1½-inch strips (any florets and stems can go into pile with leaves); and cut stalks on bias into ½-inch-thick pieces. Set aside. When beef is firm, stand 1 piece on its side and slice against grain ¼ inch thick. Repeat with remaining pieces. Transfer to bowl. Add 1 teaspoon Shaoxing wine, 1 teaspoon soy sauce, and 1 teaspoon cornstarch and toss until beef is evenly coated. Set aside.

2. In second bowl, whisk together ½ cup broth, oyster sauce, ½ teaspoon sesame oil, remaining 4 teaspoons Shaoxing wine, remaining 2 teaspoons soy sauce, and remaining 1 teaspoon cornstarch; set aside. In third bowl, combine 4 teaspoons vegetable oil, ginger, and ¼ teaspoon garlic.

3. Heat 1 teaspoon vegetable oil in wok over high heat until just smoking. Add stalks and cook, stirring slowly but constantly, until spotty brown and crisp-tender, 3 to 4 minutes. Transfer to bowl.

4. Add remaining 1 teaspoon sesame oil, remaining 1 teaspoon vegetable oil, and remaining ½ teaspoon garlic to wok and cook, stirring constantly, until garlic is fragrant, about 15 seconds. Add leaves and cook, stirring frequently, until vibrant green, about 1 minute. Add remaining ¼ cup broth and cook, stirring constantly, until broth evaporates, 2 to 3 minutes. Spread evenly on serving dish.

5. Add ginger-garlic mixture to wok and cook, stirring constantly, until fragrant, about 30 seconds. Add beef and cook, stirring slowly but constantly, until no longer pink, about 2 minutes. Return stalks to wok and add oyster sauce mixture. Cook, stirring constantly, until sauce thickens, 30 to 60 seconds. Place mixture on top of leaves. Serve.

Prepping Gai Lan

1. Remove leaves, small stems, and florets from stalks.

2. Slice leaves crosswise into 1½-inch strips.

3. Slice stalks on bias into ½-inch-thick pieces.

Pub-Style Steak and Ale Pie

Serves 6 • **Total Time: 2¾ hours**

Why This Recipe Works Intensely savory steak pie is a classic British comfort food, but making it can be a multi-step procedure. Our streamlined version has all the flavor and texture of the original dish, with less work. We skipped the traditional browning of the meat, which requires working in batches, and browned the mushrooms and onion instead, building a flavorful fond. Adding flour early in the process and limiting the amount of beef broth we added to the pot meant that the gravy formed as the meat cooked so that we could bypass the usual sauce-building steps. To make sure that the limited moisture didn't mean limited flavor, we added bacon, garlic, and thyme. We substituted beer for some of the broth and boosted browning with the addition of a small amount of baking soda. Our sturdy dough included an egg for added structure, which together with sour cream also contributed fat, allowing us to decrease the amount of butter. The resulting dough could be placed over the filling while hot and still bake up flaky and substantial, the perfect complement to the rich filling.

Don't substitute bone-in short ribs; their yield is too variable. Instead, use a 4-pound chuck-eye roast, well trimmed of fat. Use a good-quality beef broth for this recipe; the test kitchen's favorite is Better Than Bouillon Roasted Beef Base. If you don't have a deep-dish pie plate, use an 8 by 8-inch baking dish and roll the pie dough into a 10-inch square. We prefer pale and brown ales for this recipe.

Filling

    3 tablespoons water
    ½ teaspoon baking soda
    3 pounds boneless beef short ribs, trimmed and cut into ¾-inch chunks
    ½ teaspoon table salt
    ½ teaspoon pepper
    2 slices bacon, chopped
    1 pound cremini mushrooms, trimmed and halved if medium or quartered if large
 1½ cups beef broth, divided
    1 large onion, chopped
    1 garlic clove, minced
    ½ teaspoon dried thyme
    ¼ cup all-purpose flour
    ¾ cup beer

Crust

- 1 large egg, lightly beaten, divided
- ¼ cup sour cream, chilled
- 1¼ cups (6¼ ounces) all-purpose flour
- ½ teaspoon table salt
- 6 tablespoons unsalted butter, cut into ½-inch pieces and chilled

1. For the filling: Combine water and baking soda in large bowl. Add beef, salt, and pepper and toss to combine. Adjust oven rack to lower-middle position and heat oven to 350 degrees.

2. Cook bacon in large Dutch oven over high heat, stirring occasionally, until partially rendered but not browned, about 3 minutes. Add mushrooms and ¼ cup broth and stir to coat. Cover and cook, stirring occasionally, until mushrooms are reduced to about half their original volume, about 5 minutes. Add onion, garlic, and thyme and cook, uncovered, stirring occasionally, until onion is softened and fond begins to form on bottom of pot, 3 to 5 minutes. Sprinkle flour over mushroom mixture and stir until all flour is moistened. Cook, stirring occasionally, until fond is deep brown, 2 to 4 minutes. Stir in beer and remaining 1¼ cups broth, scraping up any browned bits. Stir in beef and bring to simmer, pressing as much beef as possible below surface of liquid. Cover pot tightly with aluminum foil, then lid; transfer to oven. Cook for 1 hour.

3. Remove lid and discard foil. Stir filling, cover, return to oven, and continue to cook until beef is tender and liquid is thick enough to coat beef, 15 to 30 minutes longer. Transfer filling to deep-dish pie plate. (Once cool, filling can be covered with plastic wrap and refrigerated for up to 2 days.) Increase oven temperature to 400 degrees.

4. For the crust: While filling is cooking, measure out 2 tablespoons beaten egg and set aside. Whisk remaining egg and sour cream together in bowl. Process flour and salt in food processor until combined, about 3 seconds. Add butter and pulse until only pea-size pieces remain, about 10 pulses. Add half of sour cream mixture and pulse until combined, about 5 pulses. Add remaining sour cream mixture and pulse until dough begins to form, about 10 pulses. Transfer mixture to lightly floured counter and knead briefly until dough comes together. Form into 4-inch disk, wrap in plastic, and refrigerate for at least 1 hour or up to 2 days.

5. Roll dough into 11-inch round on lightly floured counter. Using knife or 1-inch round biscuit cutter, cut round from center of dough. Drape dough over filling (it's OK if filling is hot). Trim overhang to ½ inch beyond lip of plate. Tuck overhang under itself; folded edge should be flush with edge of plate. Crimp dough evenly around edge of plate using your fingers or press with tines of fork to seal. Brush crust with reserved egg. Place pie on rimmed baking sheet. Bake until filling is bubbling and crust is deep golden brown and crisp, 25 to 30 minutes. (If filling has been refrigerated, increase baking time by 15 minutes and cover with foil for last 15 minutes to prevent overbrowning.) Let cool for 10 minutes before serving.

Osso Buco

Serves 6 • Total Time: 3¼ hours

Why This Recipe Works Osso buco, veal shanks braised in a rich sauce until tender, is incredibly rich and hearty. We felt that this time-honored recipe shouldn't be altered much, but we hoped to identify the keys to flavor so that we could perfect it. To serve one shank per person, we searched for medium-size shanks, and we tied them around the equator to keep the meat attached to the bone for an attractive presentation. Most recipes suggest flouring the veal before browning it, but we got better flavor when we simply seared the meat, liberally seasoned with just salt and pepper. Browning in two batches enabled us to deglaze the pan twice, thus enriching the sauce. Celery, onion, and carrots formed the basis of the sauce; for the liquid we used a combination of chicken broth and white wine, along with canned tomatoes. The traditional garnish of gremolata—minced garlic, lemon, and parsley—required no changes; we stirred half into the sauce and sprinkled the rest over individual servings for a fresh burst of citrus flavor.

To keep the meat attached to the bone during the long simmering process, tie a piece of kitchen twine around the thickest portion of each shank before it is browned. Just before serving, taste the liquid and, if it seems too thin, simmer it on the stovetop as you remove the strings from the osso buco and arrange them in individual bowls. Serve with rice or polenta.

Osso Buco

- ¼ cup vegetable oil, divided
- 6 (8- to 10-ounce) veal shanks, 1½ inches thick, patted dry with paper towels and tied with kitchen twine at 1½-inch intervals
- ¾ teaspoon table salt, divided
- ⅜ teaspoon pepper, divided
- 2½ cups dry white wine, divided
- 2 onions, cut into ½-inch pieces
- 2 carrots, cut into ½-inch pieces
- 2 celery ribs, cut into ½-inch pieces
- 6 garlic cloves, minced
- 2 cups chicken broth
- 2 small bay leaves
- 1 (14.5-ounce) can diced tomatoes, drained

Gremolata

- ¼ cup minced fresh parsley
- 3 garlic cloves, minced
- 2 teaspoons grated lemon zest

1. For the osso buco: Adjust oven rack to lower-middle position and heat oven to 325 degrees. Heat 1 tablespoon oil in large Dutch oven over medium-high heat until shimmering. Meanwhile, sprinkle both sides of shanks with ½ teaspoon salt and ½ teaspoon pepper. Place 3 shanks in pan and cook until golden brown on one side, about 5 minutes. Using tongs, flip shanks and cook until golden brown on second side, about 5 minutes longer. Transfer shanks to bowl and set aside. Off heat, add ½ cup wine to Dutch oven, scraping up any browned bits. Pour liquid into bowl with browned shanks. Return pot to medium-high heat, add 1 tablespoon oil, and heat until shimmering. Brown remaining shanks, about 5 minutes for each side. Transfer shanks to bowl. Off heat, add 1 cup wine to pot, scraping up any browned bits. Pour liquid into bowl with shanks.

2. Set pot over medium heat. Add remaining 2 tablespoons oil and heat until shimmering. Add onions, carrots, celery, remaining ¼ teaspoon salt, and remaining ⅛ teaspoon pepper and cook, stirring occasionally, until soft and lightly browned, about 9 minutes. Stir in garlic and cook until fragrant, about 30 seconds. Increase heat to high and stir in broth, remaining 1 cup wine, and bay leaves. Add tomatoes; return veal shanks to pot along with any accumulated juices (liquid should just cover shanks). Bring liquid to simmer. Cover pot and transfer pot to oven. Cook shanks until meat is easily pierced with fork but not falling off bone, about 2 hours. (At this point osso buco can be refrigerated for up to 2 days. Bring to simmer over medium-low heat.)

3. For the gremolata: Combine parsley, garlic, and lemon zest in small bowl. Stir half of gremolata into pot, reserving rest for garnish. Season with salt and pepper to taste. Let osso buco stand, uncovered, for 5 minutes.

4. Using tongs, remove shanks from pot, cut off and discard twine, and place 1 veal shank in each of 6 bowls. Ladle some of braising liquid over each shank and sprinkle each serving with remaining gremolata. Serve immediately.

Pan-Seared Thick-Cut Boneless Pork Chops

Serves 4 • Total Time: 1¼ hours

Why This Recipe Works Searing pork chops in a screaming-hot pan is an obvious way to brown them deeply. What we discovered is that it's also the trick to keeping this lean cut juicy. Superthick pork chops can be hard to find, so we cut them ourselves from a boneless center-cut pork loin roast. To maximize the crust, we avoided brining or salting and patted the chops dry with paper towels so that the exteriors were as dry as possible before the chops went into the pan. We also used a cast-iron skillet, preheated in

a 500-degree oven, and a generous 2 tablespoons of oil to maximize heat transfer to the chops' exteriors. Finally, to keep the interiors juicy, we flipped the chops every 2 minutes and removed them from the pan once they hit 125 degrees, relying on carryover cooking to bring them to the serving temperature of 140 degrees. Our easy no-cook sauces add richness to the lean chops, and a little bit goes a long way.

Look for a pork loin that is 7 to 8 inches long and 3 to 3½ inches in diameter. We strongly prefer using natural pork here. Using pork that is enhanced (injected with a salt solution) will inhibit browning. This recipe works best in a cast-iron skillet, but a 12-inch stainless-steel skillet will work. Serve the chops with one of our sauces (recipes follow), if desired.

- 1 (2½- to 3-pound) boneless center-cut pork loin roast, trimmed
- ½ teaspoon kosher salt
- ½ teaspoon pepper
- 2 tablespoons vegetable oil

1. Adjust oven rack to middle position, place 12-inch cast-iron skillet on rack, and heat oven to 500 degrees. Meanwhile, cut roast crosswise into 4 chops of equal thickness.

2. When oven reaches 500 degrees, pat chops dry with paper towels and sprinkle with salt and pepper. Using pot holders, remove skillet from oven and place over high heat. Being careful of hot skillet handle, add oil and heat until just smoking. Add chops and cook, without moving them, until lightly browned on first side, about 2 minutes. Flip chops and cook until lightly browned on second side, about 2 minutes.

3. Flip chops and continue to cook, flipping every 2 minutes and adjusting heat as necessary if chops brown too quickly or slowly, until exteriors are well browned and meat registers 125 to 130 degrees, 10 to 12 minutes longer. Transfer chops to platter, tent with aluminum foil, and let rest for 15 minutes (temperature will climb to 140 degrees). Serve.

ACCOMPANIMENTS

Roasted Red Pepper–Vinegar Sauce
Makes 1 cup • Total Time: 15 minutes
Red wine vinegar or sherry vinegar can be substituted for the white wine vinegar, if desired.

- ¾ cup jarred roasted red peppers, rinsed and patted dry
- 2 jarred hot cherry peppers, stems removed
- 2 garlic cloves, peeled
- 2 teaspoons dried rosemary, lightly crushed
- 2 anchovy fillets, rinsed and patted dry
- ½ teaspoon table salt
- ⅛ teaspoon pepper
- ¼ cup water
- 2 tablespoons white wine vinegar
- ⅓ cup extra-virgin olive oil
- 2 tablespoons minced fresh parsley

Pulse red peppers, cherry peppers, garlic, rosemary, anchovies, salt, and pepper in food processor until finely chopped, 15 to 20 pulses. Add water and vinegar and pulse briefly to combine. Transfer mixture to medium bowl and slowly whisk in oil until fully incorporated. Stir in parsley.

Mint Persillade
Makes 1 cup • Total Time: 15 minutes
You can substitute 1½ teaspoons of anchovy paste for the fillets, if desired.

- 1 cup fresh mint leaves
- 1 cup fresh parsley leaves
- 3 garlic cloves, peeled
- 3 anchovy fillets, rinsed and patted dry
- 1 teaspoon grated lemon zest plus 1 tablespoon juice
- ½ teaspoon table salt
- ⅛ teaspoon pepper
- ⅓ cup extra-virgin olive oil

Pulse mint, parsley, garlic, anchovies, lemon zest, salt, and pepper in food processor until finely chopped, 15 to 20 pulses. Add lemon juice and pulse briefly to combine. Transfer mixture to medium bowl and slowly whisk in oil until fully incorporated.

A Master Class in Pork Perfection

"Where I grew up, in North Carolina, pork was practically a religion. So, when it comes to pork chops, let's just say I'm no stranger to the game. But mastering that juicy, flavorful chop? That's a whole other ball game. This isn't just a recipe; it's a master class in pork perfection. What I adore about this recipe is its simplicity with a side of sophistication. Sure, anyone can toss a pork chop in a pan, but achieving that juicy center without drying out the edges? That's where the magic lies. And this recipe nails it every single time. But let's talk sauce, shall we? There's this common misconception that sauces are the Everest of cooking—daunting, treacherous, and best left to the pros. But not here. This recipe's sauce is a game changer. It's like the cherry on top of a perfectly cooked chop. It's easy, it's delicious, and it's a revelation. This recipe isn't just about cooking; it's about mastering the fundamentals and then letting your culinary creativity run wild. I love playing with flavors and experimenting in the kitchen. This recipe is the foundation: It gives you the techniques, the confidence, and the know-how to spread your wings and fly."

— Antoinette

Pan-Seared Thick-Cut, Bone-In Pork Chops

Serves 4 • **Total Time: 30 minutes**

Why This Recipe Works If you start with a cold pan and the right cut, you can achieve deeply browned, juicy bone-in pork chops in minutes—without even dirtying your cooktop. This cold-sear method is especially beneficial for leaner cuts that are prone to drying out during a traditional sear. We settled on 1½-inch-thick bone-in rib chops, which were thick enough to build up a browned exterior before cooking through; the bone also helps insulate the meat so it stays nice and juicy. Placing the chops in a cold nonstick skillet over high heat and flipping them every 2 minutes allowed the meat to heat up slowly and evenly and build a crust. The nonstick skillet negated the need for splatter-y, smoky oil.

If you have time, salt the chops for at least 1 hour or up to 24 hours before cooking: Sprinkle each chop with 1½ teaspoons of Diamond Crystal Kosher Salt (if using Morton, which is denser, use only 1⅛ teaspoons), refrigerate them, and pat them dry with paper towels before cooking. If the pork is enhanced (injected with a salt solution), do not salt the chops ahead. Make sure to include the bones when serving; they're great for nibbling. The chops can be served plain or with one of our sauces (recipes follow).

2 (14- to 16-ounce) bone-in pork rib chops, 1½ inches thick, trimmed
½ teaspoon pepper

1. Pat chops dry with paper towels and sprinkle both sides with pepper. Place chops 1 inch apart in cold 12-inch nonstick or carbon-steel skillet, arranging so narrow part of 1 chop is opposite wider part of second. Place skillet over high heat and cook chops for 2 minutes. Flip chops and cook on second side for 2 minutes. (Neither side of chops will be browned at this point.)

2. Flip chops; reduce heat to medium; and continue to cook, flipping chops every 2 minutes, until exterior is well browned and meat registers 140 degrees, 10 to 15 minutes longer. (Chops should be sizzling; if not, increase heat slightly. Reduce heat if skillet starts to smoke.)

3. Transfer chops to carving board and let rest for 5 minutes. Carve meat from bone and slice ½ inch thick. (When carved, meat at tapered end near bone may retain slightly pink hue despite being cooked.) Season meat with coarse or flake sea salt to taste. Serve with bones.

Creamy Apple-Mustard Sauce
Makes ½ cup • Total Time: 10 minutes

¼ cup whole-grain mustard
3 tablespoons unsweetened applesauce
2 tablespoons Dijon mustard
4 teaspoons cider vinegar
1 tablespoon honey
1 tablespoon minced fresh chives (optional)
¼ teaspoon table salt

Stir all ingredients (including chives, if using) in bowl until combined.

Maple Agrodolce
Makes ⅓ cup • Total Time: 20 minutes

¼ cup balsamic vinegar
2 tablespoons maple syrup
2 tablespoons minced shallot
2 tablespoons chopped golden raisins
Pinch red pepper flakes
Pinch table salt

Bring all ingredients to boil in small saucepan over medium heat. Reduce heat to low and simmer until reduced and slightly thickened, 8 to 10 minutes (sauce will continue to thicken as it cools). Cover to keep warm until ready to serve.

Sous Vide Boneless Thick-Cut Pork Chops

Serves 4 • **Total Time: 2¾ to 3¾ hours**

Why This Recipe Works Sous vide pork chops are guaranteed to be uniformly juicy and tender. The temperature-controlled water bath gradually raises the meat to its 140-degree target, maximizing collagen breakdown and minimizing moisture loss for consistently perfect results with practically zero hands-on work. We sealed thick chops in a zipper-lock freezer bag and submerged them in 140-degree water; the meat was cooked through by the 2-hour mark (although it could sit for up to an hour longer with no ill effect). Thoroughly drying the surface of the cooked chops and briefly searing them produced a flavorful brown crust. For a company-worthy dish, we served them with a stir-together roasted red pepper–almond relish.

Flip chops and continue to cook until well browned on second side, 1 to 2 minutes longer. Transfer chops to plate and tent with aluminum foil. Repeat with remaining 1 tablespoon oil and remaining chops. Serve, passing relish separately.

Red Pepper and Almond Relish
Makes ¾ cup • Total Time: 15 minutes
We like Dunbars Sweet Roasted Peppers.

- ½ cup finely chopped jarred roasted red peppers
- ¼ cup slivered almonds, toasted and chopped coarse
- 2 tablespoons extra-virgin olive oil
- 2 tablespoons minced fresh parsley
- 1 tablespoon white wine vinegar
- 1 teaspoon minced fresh oregano
- ¼ teaspoon table salt

Combine all ingredients in bowl.

SEASON 25

Zha Paigu

Serves 4 • Total Time: 1¼ hours, plus 1 hour marinating

Why This Recipe Works Taiwan's zha paigu, or fried pork chops, are meaty, juicy, fragrant with heady five-spice powder, and unsurpassed in their crispiness. We started with bone-in rib chops because they cook up tender and juicy. Pounding the chops ¼ inch thick ensured that they cooked quickly yet still offered plenty of meaty chew. We soaked the chops in a superflavorful marinade of soy sauce, michiu (Taiwanese rice wine), sugar, salt, white pepper, garlic, and five-spice powder. Dipping the marinated chops in beaten egg before dredging them in coarse sweet potato starch created a substantial, shattery crust. Sweet potato starch is a big part of the magic of this dish: It develops an exceptionally crispy crust, especially after the chops are double-fried.

If rib chops are unavailable, blade chops may be used. The bones of the chops are great for nibbling, which is why we include them for serving. Coarse (or "thick") sweet potato starch gives the chops their distinct crunch. You can substitute coarse tapioca starch. We developed this recipe with michiu, Taiwanese rice wine; if it's unavailable, clear rice wine and sake make good substitutes. Fry the chops in a 14-inch wok or a Dutch oven that holds 6 quarts or more. To make paigu fan, serve the chops with white rice; a stir-fried vegetable; a pickled vegetable, such as mustard greens; and Lu Dan (recipe follows).

Buy chops of similar thickness so that they cook at the same rate. If desired, you can sous vide the chops ahead of time; chill them in an ice bath after step 2, and then refrigerate them in their zipper-lock bag for up to three days. To reheat, return the sealed bag to a water bath set to 140°F/60°C for 30 minutes, and then proceed with step 3.

- 4 boneless center-cut pork chops, about 1½ inches thick, trimmed
- 1 teaspoon table salt
- ½ teaspoon pepper
- 6 tablespoons vegetable oil, divided
- 1 recipe Red Pepper and Almond Relish (recipe follows)

1. Using sous vide circulator, bring water to 140°F/60°C in 7-quart container.

2. Sprinkle chops on both sides with salt and pepper. Arrange chops in single layer in 1-gallon zipper-lock freezer bag. Add ¼ cup oil and seal bag, pressing out as much air as possible. Gently lower bag into prepared water bath until chops are fully submerged, and then clip top corner of bag to side of water bath container, allowing remaining air bubbles to rise to top of bag. Reopen 1 corner of zipper, release remaining air bubbles, and reseal bag. Cover and cook for at least 2 hours or up to 3 hours.

3. Transfer chops to paper towel–lined plate and let rest for 5 to 10 minutes. Pat chops dry with paper towels. Heat 1 tablespoon oil in 10-inch skillet over medium-high heat until just smoking. Place 2 chops in skillet and cook until well browned on first side, 1 to 2 minutes, lifting halfway through cooking to redistribute fat underneath each chop.

        1 tablespoon soy sauce
        1 tablespoon michiu
        2 garlic cloves, minced to paste
    1½ teaspoons sugar
    1½ teaspoons water
      ¾ teaspoon five-spice powder
      ½ teaspoon table salt
      ¼ teaspoon white pepper
        2 (8- to 10-ounce) bone-in pork rib chops,
            ¾ to 1 inch thick
        2 large eggs
        1 cup coarse sweet potato starch
        3 cups vegetable oil for frying

1. Whisk soy sauce, michiu, garlic, sugar, water, five-spice powder, salt, and white pepper together in large bowl.

2. Place 1 chop on cutting board; cover with sheet of plastic wrap; and pound to ¼-inch thickness, being careful to avoid bone. Repeat with remaining chop. Add chops to bowl with marinade and toss to evenly coat. Cover and refrigerate for 1 hour or up to 4 hours.

3. Beat eggs in shallow dish. Spread sweet potato starch in second shallow dish. Working with 1 chop at a time, remove from marinade (do not pat dry) and dip into egg, turning to coat well and allowing excess egg to drip back into dish. Coat evenly on all sides with sweet potato starch, pressing on chop to adhere. Transfer chops to rimmed baking sheet.

4. Set wire rack in second rimmed baking sheet. Add oil to wok or large Dutch oven and heat over medium-high heat to 350 degrees. Place 1 chop in oil and cook until just starting to brown on both sides, 1 minute per side. Transfer chop to prepared rack. Return oil to 350 degrees and repeat with remaining chop.

5. Heat oil to 375 degrees. Return 1 chop to oil and cook until golden brown on both sides, about 1 minute per side. Transfer chop to rack. Return oil to 375 degrees and repeat with remaining chop. Let chops rest for 5 minutes. Carve meat from bone and slice ½ inch thick. Serve meat with bones.

ACCOMPANIMENT
Lu Dan
Serves 4 to 6
Total Time: 25 minutes, plus 4 hours marinating
Taiwanese braised eggs ("lu" means "braised," and "dan" means "egg") are eggs cooked or marinated in a soy sauce broth (with spices in northern Taiwan and with fewer or no spices in southern Taiwan). Braised eggs are normally sold in small eateries as an appetizer or as a side dish alongside proteins such as zha paigu; they're also prepared at home. If you don't have a steamer basket, use a spoon or tongs to gently place the eggs in the water. It does not matter if the

eggs are above the water or partially submerged. You can use this method for fewer eggs without altering the timing. You can also double this recipe as long as you use a pot and steamer basket large enough to hold the eggs in a single layer. We developed this recipe with michiu, Taiwanese rice wine; if it's unavailable, clear rice wine and sake make good substitutes. The soy marinade can be reused to marinate up to three batches of eggs; it can be refrigerated for up to one week or frozen for up to one month.

4–6 large eggs
    ¾ cup soy sauce
      1 tablespoon michiu
      1 tablespoon sugar
  1½ teaspoons five-spice powder

1. Bring 1 inch water to rolling boil in medium saucepan over high heat. Place eggs in steamer basket. Transfer basket to saucepan. Cover, reduce heat to medium (small wisps of steam should escape from beneath lid), and cook until eggs reach desired doneness (6½ minutes for soft-cooked eggs or 13 minutes for hard-cooked eggs).

2. When eggs are almost finished cooking, fill large bowl halfway with ice and water. Using tongs or spoon, transfer eggs to ice bath. Discard water in saucepan. Let eggs sit for 15 minutes, then peel eggs. Discard ice bath and wipe out bowl.

3. Meanwhile, combine 2 cups water, soy sauce, michiu, sugar, and five-spice in now-empty saucepan and bring to boil over high heat. Reduce heat to low and simmer for 10 minutes. Remove saucepan from heat and add eggs. Let eggs sit in marinade until cool enough to handle, about 30 minutes.

4. Carefully add eggs and soy sauce mixture to large zipper-lock bag and place bag in now-empty bowl. Press out as much air as possible from bag so eggs are fully submerged in liquid, then seal bag. Refrigerate for at least 4 hours or up to 12 hours (the longer the eggs marinate, the more seasoned they will be). Remove eggs from marinade and serve.

SEASON 25

Spice-Rubbed Pork Roast en Cocotte with Caramelized Onions

Serves 4 to 6 • **Total Time: 1½ hours, plus 20 minutes resting**

Why This Recipe Works Roasting pork en cocotte combines the best of both braising and roasting. We prefer a boneless cut, which fits more easily into the pot. A blade-end loin is a good choice for its flavor and juiciness; a shorter, wider piece is ideal. We tied the meat, for easier browning and more even cooking. To add flavor to the pork, we used a spice rub that combined coriander, paprika, cumin, and anise, a pinch of cayenne for heat, and a touch of brown sugar for sweetness. Caramelized sliced onions provided a sweet contrast to the potent spice rub. Browning the meat on the stovetop, covering the pot, and cooking it slowly in a low oven produced just what we wanted—an incredibly juicy, tender roast.

This recipe works best prepared with a pork roast that is about 7 to 8 inches long and 4 to 5 inches wide. We found that leaving a ¼-inch-thick layer of fat on top of the roast is ideal; if your roast has a thicker fat cap, trim it back to about a ¼-inch thickness. To prevent the spices from burning when browning the pork in step 2, be sure to use medium heat.

1 (2½- to 3-pound) boneless pork loin roast, trimmed and tied at 1½-inch intervals
5 teaspoons ground coriander
2 teaspoons paprika
1 teaspoon table salt
1 teaspoon packed brown sugar
¾ teaspoon ground anise seeds
¾ teaspoon ground cumin
Pinch cayenne pepper
3 tablespoons vegetable oil, divided
2 onions halved and sliced thin
3 garlic cloves, minced
1 tablespoon unsalted butter

1. Adjust oven rack to lowest position and heat oven to 250 degrees. Pat pork dry with paper towels. Toss coriander, paprika, salt, sugar, anise, cumin, and cayenne together in small bowl, then rub mixture evenly over pork.

2. Heat 2 tablespoons oil in large Dutch oven over medium heat until just smoking. Lightly brown pork on all sides, 5 to 7 minutes, reducing heat if pot begins to scorch or spices begin to burn. Transfer pork to large plate.

3. Add remaining 1 tablespoon oil to pot and heat over medium heat until shimmering. Add onions; cover; and cook until softened and wet, about 5 minutes. Remove lid and continue to brown onions, stirring often, until dry and well browned, 10 to 12 minutes. Stir in garlic and cook until fragrant, about 30 seconds.

4. Off heat, nestle pork, along with any accumulated juices, into pot. Place large sheet of aluminum foil over pot and press to seal, then cover tightly with lid. Transfer pot to oven and cook until very center of roast registers 140 to 145 degrees, 35 to 55 minutes.

5. Remove pot from oven. Transfer pork to cutting board; tent with foil; and let rest until center of roast registers 150 degrees, about 20 minutes. Stir butter into onions, season with salt and pepper to taste, and cover to keep warm.

6. Remove twine, slice pork thin, and transfer to serving platter. Spoon onions over pork and serve.

Slow-Roasted Bone-In Pork Rib Roast

Serves 6 to 8 • **Total Time: 3½ to 4½ hours, plus 6½ hours salting and resting**

Why This Recipe Works Some butchers call a center-cut pork rib roast the "pork equivalent of prime rib." Treated right, it can be truly impressive: moist, tender, and full of rich, meaty taste—and for far less money than a prime rib. We set out to make this cut worthy of a holiday table. To start, we pretreated the pork with a salt–brown sugar rub. The salt seasoned the meat and drew moisture into the flesh, helping to keep it juicy. The brown sugar contributed deep molasses notes and a gorgeous mahogany color, which allowed us to skip searing. We also removed the bones from the meat so we could season it from all sides, then tied it back onto the bones to roast. Since heat travels more slowly through bone than through flesh, the bones helped keep the roast moist. And free of bones, the roast was easier to carve. Scoring deep crosshatch marks into the fat helped it melt and baste the meat during roasting. Cooking the roast in a gentle 250-degree oven ensured that the pork was evenly cooked all the way through. We crisped up the fat by blasting it under the broiler. To finish, a classic fruit and herb sauce balanced the meaty roast.

This recipe requires refrigerating the salted meat for at least 6 hours before cooking. For easier carving, ask the butcher to remove the chine bone. Monitoring the roast with an oven probe thermometer is best. If you use an instant-read thermometer, open the oven door as infrequently as possible and remove the roast from the oven while taking its temperature. The sauce may be prepared in advance or while the roast rests in step 3.

- 1 (4- to 5-pound) center-cut bone-in pork rib roast, chine bone removed
- 2 tablespoons packed dark brown sugar
- 1 tablespoon kosher salt
- 1½ teaspoons pepper
- 1 recipe Port Wine–Cherry Sauce (recipe follows)

1. Using sharp knife, remove roast from bones, running knife down length of bones and following contours as closely as possible. Reserve bones. Combine sugar and salt in small bowl. Pat roast dry with paper towels. If necessary, trim thick spots of fat cap to about ¼-inch thickness. Using sharp knife, cut through fat cap in 1-inch crosshatch pattern, being careful not to cut into meat. Rub roast evenly with sugar mixture. Wrap roast and ribs in plastic wrap and refrigerate for at least 6 hours or up to 24 hours.

2. Adjust oven rack to lower-middle position and heat oven to 250 degrees. Sprinkle roast evenly with pepper. Place roast back on ribs so bones fit where they were cut; tie roast to bones with lengths of kitchen twine between ribs. Transfer roast, fat side up, to wire rack set in rimmed baking sheet. Roast until meat registers 145 degrees, 3 to 4 hours.

3. Remove roast from oven (leave roast on sheet), tent with aluminum foil, and let rest for 30 minutes.

4. Adjust oven rack 8 inches from broiler element and heat broiler. Return roast to oven and broil until top of roast is well browned and crispy, 2 to 6 minutes.

5. Transfer roast to carving board; cut twine and remove meat from ribs. Slice meat ¾ inch thick and serve, passing sauce separately.

Port Wine–Cherry Sauce
Makes 1¾ cups • **Total Time: 50 minutes**

- 2 cups tawny port
- 1 cup dried cherries
- ½ cup balsamic vinegar
- 4 sprigs fresh thyme, plus 2 teaspoons minced
- 2 shallots, minced
- ¼ cup heavy cream
- 16 tablespoons unsalted butter, cut into ½-inch pieces and chilled
- 1 teaspoon table salt
- ½ teaspoon pepper

1. Combine port and cherries in bowl and microwave until steaming, 1 to 2 minutes. Cover and let stand until plump, about 10 minutes. Strain port through fine-mesh strainer into medium saucepan, reserving cherries.

2. Add vinegar, thyme sprigs, and shallots to port and bring to boil over high heat. Reduce heat to medium-high and reduce mixture until it measures ¾ cup, 14 to 16 minutes. Add cream and reduce again to ¾ cup, about 5 minutes. Discard thyme sprigs. Off heat, whisk in butter, few pieces at a time, until fully incorporated. Stir in cherries, minced thyme, salt, and pepper. Cover pan and hold, off heat, until serving. Alternatively, let sauce cool completely and refrigerate for up to 2 days. Reheat in small saucepan over medium-low heat, stirring frequently, until warm.

SEASON 18

Porchetta

Serves 8 to 10 • Total Time: 1½ to 2 hours, plus 6 hours 20 minutes chilling and resting

Why This Recipe Works To make porchetta, we opted for easy-to-find pork butt since it offered the right balance of meat and fatty richness. To season and flavor it, we cut slits in the meat, coated it with salt and an intensely flavored paste, and let it sit overnight in the refrigerator. For quicker cooking, we cut and tied the roast into two pieces. We used a two-stage cooking method: First, we covered the pan with foil, which trapped steam to cook the meat evenly and helped to keep the meat moist. We then uncovered the pan and returned it to a hot oven to brown and crisp the baking soda–pasted outer "skin" of the roasts.

> *Pork butt roast is often labeled Boston butt in the supermarket. Look for a roast with a substantial fat cap. If fennel seeds are unavailable, substitute ¼ cup of ground fennel. The porchetta needs to be refrigerated for 6 to 24 hours once it is rubbed with the paste; it is best when it sits for a full 24 hours.*

 3 tablespoons fennel seeds
 ½ cup fresh rosemary leaves (2 bunches)
 ¼ cup fresh thyme leaves (2 bunches)
 12 garlic cloves, peeled
 2 tablespoons plus 1 teaspoon kosher salt, divided
 4 teaspoons pepper, divided
 ½ cup extra-virgin olive oil
 1 (5- to 6-pound) boneless pork butt roast, trimmed
 ¼ teaspoon baking soda

1. Grind fennel seeds in spice grinder or mortar and pestle until finely ground. Transfer ground fennel to food processor and add rosemary, thyme, garlic, 2 teaspoons salt, and 1 tablespoon pepper. Pulse mixture until finely chopped, 10 to 15 pulses. Add oil and process until smooth paste forms, 20 to 30 seconds.

2. Using sharp knife, cut through roast's fat cap in 1-inch crosshatch pattern, being careful not to cut into meat. Cut roast in half with grain into 2 equal pieces.

3. Turn each roast on its side so fat cap is facing away from you, bottom of roast is facing toward you, and newly cut side is facing up. Starting 1 inch from short end of each roast, use boning or paring knife to make slit that starts 1 inch from top of roast and ends 1 inch from bottom, pushing knife completely through roast. Repeat making slits, spaced 1 to 1½ inches apart, along length of each roast, stopping 1 inch from opposite end (you should have 6 to 8 slits, depending on size of roast).

4. Turn each roast so fat cap is facing down. Rub sides and bottom of each roast with 2 teaspoons salt, taking care to work salt into slits from both sides. Rub herb paste onto sides and bottom of each roast, taking care to work paste into slits from both sides. Flip each roast so that fat cap is facing up. Using 3 pieces of kitchen twine per roast, tie each roast into compact cylinder.

5. Combine remaining 1 tablespoon salt, remaining 1 teaspoon pepper, and baking soda in small bowl. Rub fat cap of each roast with salt–baking soda mixture, taking care to work mixture into crosshatches. Transfer roasts to wire rack set in rimmed baking sheet and refrigerate, uncovered, for at least 6 hours or up to 24 hours.

6. Adjust oven rack to middle position and heat oven to 325 degrees. Transfer roasts, fat side up, to large roasting pan, leaving at least 2 inches between roasts. Cover tightly with aluminum foil. Cook until pork registers 180 degrees, 2 to 2½ hours.

7. Remove pan from oven and increase oven temperature to 500 degrees. Carefully remove and discard foil and transfer roasts to large plate. Discard liquid in pan. Line pan with foil. Remove twine from roasts; return roasts to pan, directly on foil; and return pan to oven. Cook until exteriors of roasts are well browned and interiors register 190 degrees, 20 to 30 minutes.

8. Transfer roasts to carving board and let rest for 20 minutes. Slice roasts ½ inch thick, transfer to serving platter, and serve.

SEASON 11

Indoor Pulled Pork with Sweet and Tangy Barbecue Sauce

Serves 6 to 8 • Total Time: 5 hours, plus 2 hours 20 minutes brining and resting

Why This Recipe Works "Indoor barbecue" is usually code for "braised in a Dutch oven with bottled barbecue sauce," which results in mushy meat and candy-sweet sauce. We wanted moist, tender, shreddable meat with deep smoke flavor all the way through, plus a dark, richly seasoned crust, often referred to as bark. With barbecue a good amount of fat is necessary for moisture and flavor, so we chose to use boneless Boston butt because of its high level of marbling. To mimic the moist heat of a covered grill, we came up with a dual cooking method, covering the pork for part of the oven time to speed up cooking and keep it moist and uncovering it for the remainder of the time to help the meat develop a crust. To achieve smoky flavor, we turned to liquid smoke, a natural product derived from condensing the moist smoke of smoldering wood chips. We found that adding it to our brine infused it with smoky flavor. For even more smokiness, we employed a dry rub and a wet rub, which we also fortified with smoky flavorings. Lastly, we developed a classic sweet and tangy sauce to serve alongside our pork, which we flavored with some of the pork's defatted cooking liquid.

Sweet paprika may be substituted for smoked paprika. Covering the pork with parchment and then foil prevents the acidic mustard from eating holes in the foil. Serve the pork on hamburger rolls with pickle chips and thinly sliced onion. In place of the Sweet and Tangy Barbecue Sauce or the variations that follow, you can use 2 cups of your favorite barbecue sauce thinned with ½ cup of the defatted pork cooking liquid in step 5. The shredded and sauced pork can be cooled, tightly covered, and refrigerated for up to 2 days. Reheat it gently before serving.

Pork
- 1 cup table salt for brining
- ½ cup sugar for brining
- 3 tablespoons plus 2 teaspoons liquid smoke, divided
- 1 (5-pound) boneless pork butt roast, cut in half horizontally
- ¼ cup yellow mustard
- 2 tablespoons pepper
- 2 tablespoons smoked paprika
- 2 tablespoons sugar
- 2 teaspoons table salt
- 1 teaspoon cayenne pepper

Sweet and Tangy Barbecue Sauce
- 1½ cups ketchup
- ¼ cup light or mild molasses
- 2 tablespoons Worcestershire sauce
- 1 tablespoon hot sauce
- ½ teaspoon table salt
- ½ teaspoon pepper

1. For the pork: Dissolve 1 cup salt, ½ cup sugar, and 3 tablespoons liquid smoke in 1 gallon cold water in large container. Submerge pork in brine, cover with plastic wrap, and refrigerate for 2 hours.

2. While pork brines, combine mustard and remaining 2 teaspoons liquid smoke in small bowl; set aside. Combine pepper, paprika, sugar, salt, and cayenne in second small bowl; set aside. Adjust oven rack to lower-middle position and heat oven to 325 degrees.

3. Remove pork from brine and dry thoroughly with paper towels. Rub mustard mixture over entire surface of each piece of pork. Sprinkle entire surface of each piece with spice mixture. Place pork on wire rack set in aluminum foil–lined rimmed baking sheet. Place piece of parchment paper over pork, then cover with sheet of foil, sealing edges to prevent moisture from escaping. Roast pork for 3 hours.

4. Remove pork from oven; discard foil and parchment. Carefully pour off liquid in bottom of baking sheet into fat separator and reserve for sauce. Return pork to oven and cook, uncovered, until well browned, tender, and center of roast registers 200 degrees, about 1½ hours. Transfer pork to serving dish, tent with foil, and let rest for 20 minutes.

5. For the sauce: While pork rests, pour ½ cup defatted cooking liquid from fat separator into medium bowl; whisk in sauce ingredients.

6. Using 2 forks, shred pork into bite-size pieces. Toss with 1 cup sauce and season with salt and pepper to taste. Serve, passing remaining sauce separately.

Cutting a Pork Butt in Half

To increase surface area, hold knife parallel to cutting board; press your hand flat against top of pork while cutting horizontally.

Carnitas

Serves 6 • **Total Time: 3 hours**

Why This Recipe Works Spanish for "little meats," carnitas offer fall-apart-tender hunks of pork with lightly crispy, caramelized exteriors. The chunks of meat are often deep-fried in lard or oil. We wanted tender chunks of lightly crisped, caramelized pork, subtly accented with oregano and citrus—without the need for deep frying. Our initial recipe for carnitas started by simmering the meat (we found boneless pork butt had the best flavor) in a seasoned broth in the oven and then sautéing it in some of the rendered fat. The flavor was OK, but too much of the pork flavor was lost when we discarded the cooking liquid. So we reduced the liquid to the consistency of a thick, syrupy glaze that was perfect for coating the meat. Broiled on a rack set over a baking sheet, the glazed meat developed a wonderfully rich flavor, and the rack allowed the excess fat to drip off. We emulated the flavor of the Mexican sour oranges used in traditional carnitas with a mixture of fresh lime and orange juices. Bay leaves and oregano provided aromatic notes, and cumin brought a complementary earthiness.

We like serving carnitas spooned into tacos, but you can also use it as a filling for tamales, enchiladas, and burritos.

1 (3½- to 4-pound) boneless pork butt roast, fat cap trimmed to ⅛ inch thick, cut into 2-inch chunks

1 small onion, halved

2 bay leaves

1 teaspoon dried oregano

1 teaspoon ground cumin

1 teaspoon table salt

½ teaspoon pepper

2 cups water

2 tablespoons lime juice

1 orange, halved

18 (6-inch) corn tortillas, warmed
Lime wedges
Minced white or red onion
Fresh cilantro leaves
Thinly sliced radishes
Sour cream

1. Adjust oven rack to lower-middle position and heat oven to 300 degrees. Combine pork, onion, bay leaves, oregano, cumin, salt, pepper, water, and lime juice in large Dutch oven (liquid should just barely cover meat). Juice orange into medium bowl and remove any seeds (you should have about ⅓ cup juice). Add juice and spent orange halves to pot. Bring mixture to simmer over medium-high heat, stirring occasionally. Cover pot and transfer it to oven; cook until meat is soft and falls apart when prodded with fork, about 2 hours, flipping pieces of meat once during cooking.

2. Remove pot from oven and turn oven to broil. Using slotted spoon, transfer pork to bowl; remove orange halves, onion, and bay leaves from cooking liquid and discard (do not skim fat from liquid). Place pot over high heat (use caution, as handles will be very hot) and simmer liquid, stirring frequently, until thick and syrupy (heat-resistant spatula should leave wide trail when dragged through glaze), 8 to 12 minutes. You should have about 1 cup reduced liquid.

3. Using 2 forks, pull each piece of pork in half. Fold in reduced liquid; season with salt and pepper to taste. Spread pork in even layer on wire rack set in rimmed baking sheet or on broiler pan (meat should cover almost entire surface of rack or broiler pan). Place baking sheet on lower-middle oven rack and broil until top of meat is well browned (but not charred) and edges are slightly crisp, 5 to 8 minutes. Using wide metal spatula, flip pieces of meat and continue to broil until top is well browned and edges are slightly crisp, 5 to 8 minutes longer. Serve immediately with warm tortillas and garnishes.

SEASON 19

Carne Adovada

Serves 6 • **Total Time: 2¾ to 3¼ hours, plus 1½ hours salting and standing**

Why This Recipe Works To make carne adovada, a classic, ultrasimple New Mexican pork braise in a brick-red sauce of chiles, aromatics, and vinegar, we started by cutting boneless pork shoulder into large chunks and salting them (so that they would be well seasoned and retain moisture during cooking). We started with a generous 4 ounces of dried red New Mexican chiles, which are fruity and relatively mild. But rather than toast them, we simply steeped them in water to preserve their bright flavor. When they were pliable, we blended them with aromatics and spices, as well as honey, white vinegar, and just enough of the chile soaking liquid to form a thick paste; when the paste was smooth, we added the remaining water to form a puree, making sure to leave in small bits of chile skin that contributed rustic texture and vibrant flavor. We tossed the pork with the puree in a Dutch oven, then braised it in a low oven until the meat was very tender. A squeeze of lime added brightness and acidity.

> *Pork butt roast is often labeled Boston butt. If you can't find New Mexican chiles, substitute dried California chiles. Dried chiles should be pliable and smell slightly fruity. Kitchen shears can be used to cut them. If you can't find Mexican oregano, substitute Mediterranean oregano.*

Serve with rice and beans, crispy potatoes, or flour tortillas with shredded lettuce and chopped tomato. Alternatively, shred the pork as a filling for tacos and burritos.

1 (3½- to 4-pound) boneless pork butt roast, trimmed and cut into 1½-inch pieces
4 teaspoons kosher salt, divided
4 ounces dried New Mexican chiles, wiped clean, stemmed, seeded, and torn into 1-inch pieces
2 tablespoons honey
2 tablespoons distilled white vinegar
5 garlic cloves, peeled
2 teaspoons dried Mexican oregano
2 teaspoons ground cumin
½ teaspoon cayenne pepper
⅛ teaspoon ground cloves
  Lime wedges

1. Toss pork and 1 tablespoon salt together in bowl; refrigerate for 1 hour.

2. Bring 4 cups water to boil. Place chile pieces in medium bowl. Pour boiling water over chiles, making sure they are completely submerged, and let stand until chiles are softened, 30 minutes. Adjust oven rack to lower-middle position and heat oven to 325 degrees.

3. Drain chiles and reserve 2 cups of soaking liquid (discard remaining soaking liquid). Process chiles, honey, vinegar, garlic, oregano, cumin, cayenne, cloves, and remaining 1 teaspoon salt in blender until chiles are finely ground and thick paste forms, about 30 seconds. With blender running, add 1 cup soaking liquid and blend until puree is smooth, 1½ to 2 minutes, adding up to additional ¼ cup liquid to maintain vortex. Add remaining soaking liquid and continue to blend sauce at high speed, 1 minute longer.

4. Add pork and chile sauce to Dutch oven, stirring to make sure pork is evenly coated. Bring to boil over high heat. Cover pot, transfer to oven, and cook until pork is tender and fork inserted into pork meets little to no resistance, 2 to 2½ hours.

5. Using wooden spoon, scrape any browned bits from sides of pot and stir until pork and sauce are recombined, and sauce is smooth and homogeneous. Let stand, uncovered, for 10 minutes. Season with salt to taste. Serve, passing lime wedges separately.

Goan Pork Vindaloo

Serves 8 • **Total Time: 2½ hours**

Why This Recipe Works Disregard vindaloo's reputation for extreme heat. The word "vindaloo" has evolved to indicate a searingly hot curry because of its adoption into British cuisine, but the original Goan vindaloo is a brightly flavored but relatively mild and more nuanced pork braise that's aromatic with spices. It's made with dried Kashmiri chiles and spices such as cinnamon, cloves, and cardamom. Vindaloo should have a pronounced vinegary tang, but we found that adding the vinegar at the beginning made the meat chalky. We withheld it until halfway through cooking so that we could use less but still enjoy the characteristic acidity. Moving the cooking from the stovetop to the oven made this dish hands-off and foolproof.

Kashmiri chile powder should have a brilliant red hue, a fruity flavor, and a slightly tannic edge, but very little heat. Pork butt roast is often labeled Boston butt. Cider vinegar can be used in place of the coconut vinegar. Traditional Goan vindaloo is not very spicy, but if you prefer more heat, add up to ½ teaspoon of cayenne pepper. Serve with white rice, naan, or Goan pao.

¾ cup water
1 (2-inch) piece ginger, peeled and sliced crosswise ⅛ inch thick
6 garlic cloves
3 tablespoons Kashmiri chile powder
1 tablespoon paprika
1 tablespoon ground cumin
2 teaspoons table salt
1 teaspoon pepper
¼–½ teaspoon cayenne pepper (optional)
½ teaspoon ground cinnamon
½ teaspoon ground cardamom
¼ teaspoon ground cloves
¼ teaspoon ground nutmeg
1 (3- to 3½-pound) boneless pork butt roast, trimmed and cut into 1-inch pieces
1 tablespoon vegetable oil
1 large onion, chopped fine
⅓ cup coconut vinegar

1. Adjust oven rack to middle position and heat oven to 325 degrees. Process water; ginger; garlic; chile powder; paprika; cumin; salt; pepper; cayenne, if using; cinnamon; cardamom; cloves; and nutmeg in blender on low speed until rough paste forms, about 1 minute. Scrape down sides and blend on high speed until paste is smooth, about 1 minute. Place pork in large bowl. Add spice paste and mix thoroughly.

The Magic of Indian Food

"I grew up loving Indian food, but we never cooked it at home, so I figured that making any of those beautiful, perfumed sauces must be quite hard and require some type of alchemy.

In my twenties, when I began to take cooking seriously, I bought a few of Madhur Jaffrey's cookbooks to learn some basic techniques. The thing I found exciting was that her approach was slightly different than the French-based methodology I had learned in culinary school. Aromatics (like garlic and ginger) were often blended with water and added to the pot more than once to achieve layers of flavor. The spices, too, were handled a bit differently and I had to seek some of them out at specialty shops, which was fun. This recipe for vindaloo uses a few of these basic methods, including the opportunity to shop for Kashmiri chile powder if you don't already have it in your pantry. If you're new to cooking Indian food, this recipe is a delicious way to learn."

—Julia

2. Heat oil in Dutch oven over medium heat until shimmering. Add onion and cook, stirring frequently, until soft and golden, 7 to 9 minutes. Add pork mixture and stir to combine. Spread mixture into even layer. Continue to cook until mixture begins to bubble, about 2 minutes longer. Cover pot, transfer to oven, and cook for 40 minutes. Stir in vinegar. Cover, return pot to oven, and cook for 20 minutes. Uncover and cook until fork inserted into pork meets little or no resistance, 20 to 30 minutes longer. Let stand, uncovered, for 10 minutes. Stir and serve. (Pork can be cooked up to 3 days in advance.)

SEASON 19

Chinese-Style Barbecued Spareribs

Serves 6 to 8 as an appetizer or 4 to 6 as a main dish • Total Time: 2¾ hours

Why This Recipe Works Chinese barbecued spareribs have a long history in Chinese cuisine. These ribs are usually marinated for several hours and then slow-roasted and basted repeatedly to build up a thick crust. For a faster version, we skipped both of those steps and instead braised the ribs, which we cut into individual pieces to speed up the cooking process and create more surface area. We also made a highly seasoned liquid, which helped the flavor penetrate the meat thoroughly and quickly. Then we strained, defatted, and reduced the braising liquid to make a full-bodied glaze in which we tossed the ribs before roasting them on a rack in a hot oven to color and crisp their exteriors.

It's not necessary to remove the membrane on the bone side of the ribs. These ribs are chewier than American-style ribs; if you prefer them more tender, cook them for an additional 15 minutes in step 1. Adding water to the baking sheet during roasting helps prevent smoking. Serve the ribs alone as an appetizer or with vegetables and rice as a main course. You can serve the first batch immediately or tent them with foil to keep them warm.

 1 (6-inch) piece fresh ginger, peeled and sliced thin
 8 garlic cloves, peeled
 1 cup honey
 ¾ cup hoisin sauce
 ¾ cup soy sauce
 ½ cup Shaoxing wine or dry sherry
 2 teaspoons five-spice powder
 1 teaspoon red food coloring (optional)
 1 teaspoon white pepper
 2 (2½- to 3-pound) racks St. Louis–style
   spareribs, cut into individual ribs
 2 tablespoons toasted sesame oil

1. Pulse ginger and garlic in food processor until finely chopped, 10 to 12 pulses, scraping down sides of bowl as needed. Transfer ginger-garlic mixture to Dutch oven. Add honey; hoisin; soy sauce; ½ cup water; Shaoxing wine; five-spice powder; food coloring, if using; and white pepper and whisk until combined. Add ribs and stir to coat (ribs will not be fully submerged). Bring to simmer over high heat, then reduce heat to low, cover, and cook for 1¼ hours, stirring occasionally.

2. Adjust oven rack to middle position and heat oven to 425 degrees. Using tongs, transfer ribs to large bowl. Strain braising liquid through fine-mesh strainer set over large container, pressing on solids to extract as much liquid as possible; discard solids. Let cooking liquid settle for 10 minutes. Using wide, shallow spoon, skim fat from surface and discard.

3. Return braising liquid to pot and add sesame oil. Bring to boil over high heat and cook until syrupy and reduced to 2½ cups, 16 to 20 minutes.

4. Set wire rack in aluminum foil–lined rimmed baking sheet and pour ½ cup water into sheet. Transfer half of ribs to pot with braising liquid and toss to coat. Arrange ribs, bone sides up, on prepared rack, letting excess glaze drip off. Roast until edges of ribs start to caramelize, 5 to 7 minutes. Flip ribs and continue to roast until second side starts to caramelize, 5 to 7 minutes longer. Transfer ribs to serving platter; repeat process with remaining ribs. Serve.

Crispy Slow-Roasted Pork Belly

Serves 8 to 10 • Total Time: 4 to 4½ hours, plus 12 hours brining

Why This Recipe Works Pork belly is a boneless cut featuring alternating layers of deeply flavorful, well-marbled meat and buttery fat which, when properly cooked, turn silky and sumptuous, with a crisp crown of skin. To tackle this special cut, we started by scoring the skin and rubbing the meat with a mixture of salt and brown sugar. We then air-dried the belly overnight in the refrigerator to dehydrate the skin. Roasting the pork belly low and slow further dried the skin and broke down the tough collagen, making the meat juicy and supple. We finished by frying the belly skin side down, which caused it to dramatically puff up and crisp. A quick, bracing mustard sauce balanced the richness of the pork belly.

This recipe requires refrigerating the seasoned pork belly for at least 12 hours or up to 24 hours before cooking (a longer time is preferable). Be sure to ask for a flat, rectangular center-cut section of skin-on pork belly that's 1½ inches thick with roughly equal amounts of meat and fat. Serve with white rice and steamed greens or boiled potatoes and salad.

Pork
- 1 (3-pound) skin-on center-cut fresh pork belly, about 1½ inches thick
- 2½ tablespoons kosher salt
- 2 tablespoons packed dark brown sugar
  Vegetable oil

Mustard Sauce
- ⅔ cup Dijon mustard
- ⅓ cup cider vinegar
- ¼ cup packed dark brown sugar
- 1 tablespoon hot sauce
- 1 teaspoon Worcestershire sauce

1. For the pork: Using sharp chef's knife, slice pork belly lengthwise into 3 strips about 2 inches wide, then cut slits, spaced 1 inch apart in crosshatch pattern, in surface fat layer, being careful not to cut into meat. Combine 2 tablespoons salt and sugar in bowl. Rub salt mixture into bottom and sides of pork belly (do not rub into skin). Season skin of each strip evenly with ½ teaspoon salt. Place pork belly, skin side up, in 13 by 9-inch baking dish and refrigerate, uncovered, for at least 12 hours or up to 24 hours.

GAME CHANGER

The Crispy Side of Bacon

"I'm not about to disparage bacon, but, if I'm being totally honest, it's not my favorite way to enjoy pork belly. That distinction goes to fresh pork belly that has been slow-cooked long enough to turn lusciously tender. It's the ultimate pork experience, with its alternating layers of unctuous meat and fat. Not convinced? What if I throw in a light-as-air cap of chicharron-like crispy skin?

I learned so much while developing this recipe. I discovered that in order for pork skin to puff and turn crispy, it first needs to be dehydrated to the right degree, and then rapidly heated to turn the remaining water into steam. And I found that while the science is a little complicated, the kitchen work is straightforward: Salt the belly and let it air-dry in the fridge; slow roast it until the meat turns tender and the skin is dry; and, finally, puff the skin by shallow-frying it in a skillet. I can already hear the crunch."

—Dan

1. Cutting pork belly into 3 strips provides more surface area for seasoning. Smaller pieces of meat and skin also cook more quickly and evenly.

2. Seasoning meat with salt and brown sugar adds flavor, encourages browning, and helps it retain moisture. Sprinkling salt on skin (scored for deeper penetration) helps it dehydrate.

3. Letting seasoned meat sit overnight in refrigerator gives rub time to penetrate. It also dries out surface of skin so that it can crisp.

4. Slow roasting browns meat and further dehydrates skin while converting rigid collagen in both to gelatin. Gelatin keeps meat moist and helps skin puff when crisped.

5. Frying just skin portion of pork belly (start it in cold oil so that all skin heats at same pace) forces its remaining water to evaporate, leaving it puffed up and ultracrisp.

2. Adjust oven rack to middle position and heat oven to 250 degrees. Set wire rack in rimmed baking sheet and spray with vegetable oil spray. Transfer pork belly, skin side up, to wire rack and roast until pork registers 195 degrees and paring knife inserted in pork meets little resistance, 3 to 3½ hours, rotating sheet halfway through roasting.

3. For the mustard sauce: Whisk all ingredients together in bowl; set aside.

4. Transfer pork belly, skin side up, to large plate. (Pork belly can be held at room temperature for up to 1 hour.) Pour fat from sheet into 1-cup liquid measuring cup. Add vegetable oil as needed to equal 1 cup and transfer to 12-inch skillet. Arrange pork belly, skin side down, in skillet (strips can be sliced in half crosswise if skillet won't fit strips whole) and place over medium heat until bubbles form around pork belly. Continue to fry, tilting skillet occasionally to even out hot spots, until skin puffs, crisps, and turns golden, 6 to 10 minutes. Transfer pork belly, skin side up, to carving board and let rest for 5 minutes. Flip pork belly skin side down and slice ½ inch thick (being sure to slice through original score marks). Reinvert slices and serve with sauce.

VARIATION

Crispy Slow-Roasted Pork Belly with Tangy Hoisin Sauce

Omit mustard sauce. Whisk ½ cup hoisin, 4 teaspoons rice vinegar, 1 teaspoon grated fresh ginger, and 2 thinly sliced scallions together in bowl and serve with pork.

SEASON 2

Roast Fresh Ham

Serves 8 to 10 • Total Time: 3½ hours, plus 9 hours brining and standing

Why This Recipe Works Fresh ham is not cured like a Smithfield ham or salted and air-dried like prosciutto. It's not pressed or molded like a canned ham, and it's not smoked like a country ham. In fact, some people think there's no such thing as "fresh" ham. There is—and we wanted to find the best way to cook it for a roasted ham that boasted rich, moist meat and crackling crisp skin. Fresh hams are large, so they're usually cut in half and sold as either the sirloin or the shank end; we chose the latter for its ease of carving. But even cut into these smaller roasts, fresh ham needs a long time in the oven, so the danger is drying out the meat. To prevent this, we brined our ham overnight. A garlic and herb rub added further flavor. We positioned the ham wide cut side down on a rack in a roasting pan; the rack allowed the heat to circulate all around the ham for more even cooking.

A brief roasting at a high temperature followed by longer cooking at a lower temperature produced crunchy skin and succulent meat. The crowning touch was a sweet glaze, which we brushed on periodically while the meat roasted.

> *Fresh ham comes from the pig's hind leg. Because a whole leg is quite large, it is usually cut into two sections. The sirloin, or butt, end is harder to carve than our favorite, the shank end. If you don't have room in your refrigerator, brine the ham in an insulated cooler or a small plastic garbage can; add five or six freezer packs to the brine to keep it well cooled.*

Roast

- 1 (6- to 8-pound) bone-in fresh half ham with skin, preferably shank end, rinsed

Brine

- 3 cups packed brown sugar
- 2 cups table salt
- 2 heads garlic, cloves separated, lightly crushed and peeled
- 10 bay leaves
- ½ cup black peppercorns, crushed

Garlic and Herb Rub

- 1 cup fresh sage leaves
- ½ cup parsley leaves
- ¼ cup extra-virgin olive oil
- 8 garlic cloves, peeled
- ½ tablespoon pepper
- 1½ teaspoons table salt

Glaze

- 1 recipe glaze (recipes follow)

1. For the roast: Using sharp knife, cut through roast's skin and fat cap in 1-inch crosshatch pattern, being careful not to cut into meat.

2. For the brine: In large container, dissolve sugar and 2 cups salt in 2 gallons cold water. Add garlic, bay leaves, and crushed peppercorns. Submerge ham in brine and refrigerate for 8 to 24 hours.

3. Set large disposable aluminum roasting pan on rimmed baking sheet for extra support; set wire rack in roasting pan. Remove ham from brine; rinse under cold water and dry thoroughly with paper towels. Place ham, wide cut side down, on rack. (If using sirloin end, place ham skin side up.) Let ham stand uncovered at room temperature for 1 hour.

4. For the rub: Meanwhile, adjust oven rack to lowest position and heat oven to 500 degrees. Process sage, parsley, oil, garlic, pepper, and salt in food processor until mixture forms smooth paste, about 30 seconds. Rub all sides of ham with paste.

5. Roast ham at 500 degrees for 20 minutes. Reduce oven temperature to 350 degrees and continue to roast, brushing ham with glaze every 45 minutes, until center of ham registers 145 to 150 degrees, about 2½ hours longer. Remove from oven; tent ham with aluminum foil; and let stand until center of ham registers 155 to 160 degrees, 30 to 40 minutes. Carve and serve.

GLAZES
Cider and Brown Sugar Glaze
Makes 1⅓ cups • Total Time: 15 minutes

- 1 cup apple cider
- 2 cups packed brown sugar
- 5 whole cloves

Bring cider, sugar, and cloves to boil in small saucepan over high heat; reduce heat to medium-low and simmer until syrupy and reduced to about 1⅓ cups, 5 to 7 minutes. (Glaze will thicken as it cools between bastings; cook over medium heat for about 1 minute, stirring once or twice, before using.)

Spicy Pineapple-Ginger Glaze
Makes 1⅓ cups • Total Time: 15 minutes

- 1 cup pineapple juice
- 2 cups packed brown sugar
- 1 (1-inch) piece fresh ginger, grated (about 1 tablespoon)
- 1 tablespoon red pepper flakes

Bring pineapple juice, sugar, ginger, and pepper flakes to boil in small saucepan over high heat; reduce heat to medium-low and simmer until syrupy and reduced to about 1⅓ cups, 5 to 7 minutes. (Glaze will thicken as it cools between bastings; cook over medium heat for about 1 minute, stirring once or twice, before using.)

Coca-Cola Glaze with Lime and Jalapeño
Makes 1⅓ cups • Total Time: 15 minutes

  1   cup Coca-Cola
  ¼   cup lime juice (2 limes)
  2   cups packed brown sugar
  2   jalapeño chiles, cut crosswise into
       ¼-inch-thick slices

Bring Coca-Cola, lime juice, sugar, and jalapeños to boil in small nonreactive saucepan over high heat; reduce heat to medium-low and simmer until syrupy and reduced to about 1⅓ cups, 5 to 7 minutes. (Glaze will thicken as it cools between bastings; cook over medium heat for about 1 minute, stirring once or twice, before using.)

Orange, Cinnamon, and Star Anise Glaze
Makes about 1⅓ cups • Total Time: 15 minutes

  1   tablespoon grated orange zest plus
       1 cup juice (2 oranges)
  2   cups packed brown sugar
  4   star anise pods
  1   cinnamon stick

Bring orange juice and zest, sugar, star anise, and cinnamon stick to boil in small nonreactive saucepan over high heat; reduce heat to medium-low and simmer until syrupy and reduced to about 1⅓ cups, 5 to 7 minutes. (Glaze will thicken as it cools between bastings; cook over medium heat for about 1 minute, stirring once or twice, before using.)

SEASON 22
Kimchi Bokkeumbap

Serves 4 to 6 • Total Time: 45 minutes

Why This Recipe Works Iconic, quick-cooking Korean comfort food, kimchi bokkeumbap is typically made with leftover cooked short-grain rice and well-fermented kimchi, but from there the seasonings and additions vary widely from cook to cook. We started by stir-frying some aromatics (chopped onion and sliced scallions) with chopped ham—a popular addition that we liked for its smoky flavor and pleasantly springy texture. Then we

added lots of chopped cabbage kimchi along with some of its savory, punchy juice and a little water and seasoned it with soy sauce, toasted sesame oil, and gochujang to add savoriness, rich nuttiness, and a little more heat. We simmered the cabbage leaves so that they softened a bit; stirred in the rice and cooked the mixture until the liquid had been absorbed; and topped the rice with small strips of gim, sesame seeds, and scallion greens.

This recipe works best with day-old rice; alternatively, cook your rice 2 hours ahead, spread it on a rimmed baking sheet, and let it cool completely before chilling it for 30 minutes. Plain pretoasted seaweed snacks can be substituted for the gim (seaweed paper); omit the toasting in step 1. You'll need at least a 16-ounce jar of kimchi; if it doesn't yield ¼ cup of juice, make up the difference with water. If using soft, well-aged kimchi, omit the water and reduce the cooking time at the end of step 2 to 2 minutes. We developed this recipe with a 12-inch nonstick skillet, but a well-seasoned carbon-steel skillet or 14-inch flat-bottomed wok can be used instead. If desired, top each portion of rice with a fried egg.

  1   (8-inch square) sheet gim
  2   tablespoons vegetable oil, divided
  2   (¼-inch-thick) slices deli ham, cut into
         ¼-inch pieces (about 4 ounces)
  1   large onion, chopped
  6   scallions, white and green parts separated
         and sliced thin on bias
  1¼   cups cabbage kimchi, drained with ¼ cup
         juice reserved, cut into ¼-inch strips
  ¼   cup water
  4   teaspoons soy sauce
  4   teaspoons gochujang

½ teaspoon pepper
3 cups cooked short-grain white rice
4 teaspoons toasted sesame oil
1 tablespoon sesame seeds, toasted

1. Grip gim with tongs and hold 2 inches above low flame on gas burner. Toast gim, turning every 3 to 5 seconds, until gim is aromatic and shrinks slightly, about 20 seconds. (If you do not have a gas stove, toast gim on rimmed baking sheet in 275-degree oven until gim is aromatic and shrinks slightly, 20 to 25 minutes, flipping gim halfway through toasting.) Using kitchen shears, cut gim into four 2-inch-wide strips. Stack strips and cut crosswise into thin strips.

2. Heat 1 tablespoon vegetable oil in 12-inch nonstick skillet over medium-high heat until shimmering. Add ham, onion, and scallion whites and cook, stirring frequently, until onion is softened and ham is beginning to brown at edges, 6 to 8 minutes. Stir in kimchi and reserved juice, water, soy sauce, gochujang, and pepper. Cook, stirring occasionally, until kimchi turns soft and translucent, 4 to 6 minutes.

3. Add rice; reduce heat to medium-low; and cook, stirring and folding constantly until mixture is evenly coated, about 3 minutes. Stir in sesame oil and remaining 1 tablespoon vegetable oil. Increase heat to medium-high and cook, stirring occasionally, until mixture begins to stick to skillet, about 4 minutes. Transfer to serving bowl. Sprinkle with sesame seeds, scallion greens, and gim and serve.

SEASON 22
Shīzi Tóu

Serves 4 to 6 • Total Time: 2 hours

Why This Recipe Works Shīzi tóu, giant lion's head meatballs, are tender-yet-springy pork meatballs from eastern China. For a streamlined approach, we started with commercial ground pork and treated the meat with a baking soda solution before cooking, which helped it retain juices over the relatively long cooking time. We lightly seasoned the meat for a well-rounded savory flavor that still tasted distinctly porky. Beating the pork mixture in a stand mixer caused its sticky proteins to link up into a strong network that trapped fat and moisture, resulting in a texture that was resilient and unctuous. Braising the meatballs in the oven broke down the pork's collagen so that the meatballs were tender. Adding the cabbage for the last 30 minutes of cooking allowed it to soften and absorb the flavor of the broth without turning mushy. Soaking rice vermicelli in just-boiled water softened but did not overcook them.

Fully cooked ground pork may retain a slightly pink hue. Don't be concerned if the meatballs crack while cooking.

¾ teaspoon baking soda
½ teaspoon table salt
2 pounds ground pork
1 large egg, lightly beaten
2 scallions, white parts minced, green parts sliced thin
2 tablespoons soy sauce
2 tablespoons Shaoxing wine
4 teaspoons sugar
2 teaspoons grated fresh ginger
½ teaspoon white pepper
4 cups chicken broth
1 small head napa cabbage (1½ pounds), quartered lengthwise, cored, and cut crosswise into 2-inch pieces
4 ounces rice vermicelli

1. Adjust oven rack to lower-middle position and heat oven to 325 degrees. Whisk baking soda, salt, and 2 tablespoons water together in bowl of stand mixer. Add pork to baking soda mixture and toss to combine. Add egg, scallion whites, soy sauce, Shaoxing wine, sugar, ginger, and white pepper. Fit stand mixer with paddle and beat on medium speed until mixture is well combined and has stiffened and started to pull away from sides of bowl and pork has slightly lightened in color, 45 to 60 seconds. Using your wet hands, form about ½ cup (4½ ounces) pork mixture into 3-inch round meatball; repeat with remaining mixture to form 8 meatballs.

2. Bring broth to boil in large Dutch oven over high heat. Off heat, carefully arrange meatballs in pot (seven around perimeter and one in center; meatballs will not be totally submerged). Cover pot, transfer to oven, and cook for 1 hour.

3. Transfer meatballs to large plate. Add cabbage to pot in even layer and arrange meatballs over cabbage, paler side up. Cover, return pot to oven, and continue to cook until meatballs are lightly browned and cabbage is softened, about 30 minutes longer.

4. While meatballs and cabbage cook, bring 4 quarts water to boil in large pot. Off heat, add vermicelli and let sit, stirring occasionally, until vermicelli is fully tender, 10 to 15 minutes. Drain, rinse with cold water, drain again, and distribute evenly among 4 to 6 large soup bowls.

5. Ladle meatballs, cabbage, and broth into bowls of noodles. Sprinkle with scallion greens and serve.

Cuban-Style Black Beans and Rice

Serves 6 to 8 • **Total Time: 2¼ hours, plus 8 hours soaking**

Why This Recipe Works Beans and rice is a familiar combination the world over, but Cuban black beans and rice is unique in that the rice is cooked in the inky concentrated liquid left over from cooking the beans, which renders the grains just as flavorful. We expanded on this method, simmering a portion of the sofrito (the trio of garlic, bell pepper, and onion) with our beans to infuse them with flavor and then using the liquid to cook our rice and beans. Lightly browning the remaining sofrito vegetables and spices with rendered salt pork added complex, meaty flavor, and finishing the dish in the oven eliminated the crusty bottom that can form when the dish is cooked on the stove.

> *It is important to use lean—not fatty—salt pork. If you can't find it, substitute six slices of bacon. If using bacon, decrease the cooking time in step 4 to 8 minutes. You will need a Dutch oven with a tight-fitting lid for this recipe. For a vegetarian version of this recipe, use water instead of chicken broth, omit the salt pork, add 1 tablespoon tomato paste with the vegetables in step 4, and increase the amount of salt in step 5 to 1½ teaspoons.*

1½ tablespoons table salt for soaking beans
  1 cup dried black beans, picked over and rinsed
  2 cups chicken broth
  2 large green bell peppers, stemmed, seeded, and halved, divided
  1 large onion, halved crosswise, root end left intact, divided

  1 garlic head (5 cloves minced, remaining head halved crosswise with skin left intact)
  2 bay leaves
1½ teaspoons table salt, divided
1½ cups long-grain white rice
  2 tablespoons extra-virgin olive oil, divided
  6 ounces lean salt pork, cut into ¼-inch pieces
  4 teaspoons ground cumin
  1 tablespoon minced fresh oregano
  2 tablespoons red wine vinegar
  2 scallions, sliced thin
    Lime wedges

1. Dissolve 1½ tablespoons salt in 2 quarts cold water in large bowl or container. Add beans and soak at room temperature for at least 8 hours or up to 24 hours. Drain and rinse well.

2. In Dutch oven, stir together drained beans, broth, 2 cups water, 1 bell pepper half, 1 onion half (with root end), halved garlic head, bay leaves, and 1 teaspoon salt. Bring to simmer over medium-high heat, cover, and reduce heat to low. Cook until beans are just soft, 30 to 35 minutes. Using tongs, discard pepper, onion, garlic, and bay leaves. Drain beans in colander set over large bowl, reserving 2½ cups bean cooking liquid. (If you don't have enough bean cooking liquid, add water to equal 2½ cups.) Do not wash Dutch oven.

3. Adjust oven rack to middle position and heat oven to 350 degrees. Place rice in large fine-mesh strainer and rinse under cold running water until water runs clear, about 1½ minutes. Shake strainer vigorously to remove all excess water; set rice aside. Cut remaining peppers and onion into 2-inch pieces and process in food processor until broken into rough ¼-inch pieces, about 8 pulses, scraping down bowl as necessary; set vegetables aside.

4. In now-empty Dutch oven, heat 1 tablespoon oil and salt pork over medium-low heat and cook, stirring frequently, until lightly browned and rendered, 15 to 20 minutes. Add remaining 1 tablespoon oil, chopped bell peppers and onion, cumin, and oregano. Increase heat to medium and continue to cook, stirring frequently, until vegetables are softened and beginning to brown, 10 to 15 minutes longer. Add minced garlic and cook, stirring constantly, until fragrant, about 1 minute. Add rice and stir to coat, about 30 seconds.

5. Stir in beans, reserved bean cooking liquid, vinegar, and remaining ½ teaspoon salt. Increase heat to medium-high and bring to simmer. Cover and transfer to oven. Cook until liquid is absorbed and rice is tender, about 30 minutes. Fluff with fork and let rest, uncovered, for 5 minutes. Serve, passing scallions and lime wedges separately.

SEASON 25

Lamb Barbacoa

Serves 8 • Total Time: 4½ hours, plus 30 minutes resting

Why This Recipe Works Barbacoa is a pit-cooking method traditional to Mexico that produces tender bites of meat and consomé de barbacoa that's flavored by the meat drippings. Our barbacoa begins by coating 1½-inch-thick slabs of lamb or beef in a marinade made by pureeing guajillo chiles with garlic, spices, salt, and vinegar. To mimic a traditional barbacoa setup, we placed the ingredients for consomé de barbacoa in a Dutch oven along with a small ramekin. We placed the meat on a plate on top of the ramekin. After bringing the broth to a simmer on the stove, we covered the pot tightly and placed it in a 325-degree oven, where the meat cooked gently until its collagen broke down and its drippings imbued the broth, beans, and potatoes with a rich savory flavor. We chopped the meat, moistened it with some of the broth, and seasoned it. Then, we served it with corn tortillas; an ancho chile–tomatillo salsa; and lime, cilantro, onion, and radish.

> *Barbacoa is traditionally steamed underground in a pit or in a specially constructed pot. For our barbacoa setup, you'll need a 6-quart or larger round Dutch oven with a tight-fitting lid, a 1½- to 2-inch-tall ramekin, and an 8- to 9-inch-wide heatproof plate. If you prefer a mild salsa, omit the arbol chiles; for a spicier salsa, use two arbols. Because tomatillos can vary in acidity, we adjust the salsa's seasoning with sugar and vinegar. We developed our recipe using lamb, but you can substitute an equivalent weight of boneless beef chuck-eye roast (or boneless leg of goat).*

Lamb and Consomé de Barbacoa
- 6 dried guajillo chiles, stemmed, seeded, and torn into ½-inch pieces (¾ cup)
- 1 (2½- to 3-pound) boneless leg of lamb, fat cap trimmed to ⅛ to ¼ inch
- 6 garlic cloves, peeled, divided
- 5 teaspoons kosher salt, divided
- 2½ teaspoons dried Mexican oregano
- 2 teaspoons cider vinegar
- ½ teaspoon pepper
- 2 whole cloves
- ¼ teaspoon ground cumin
- 1 (15-ounce) can chickpeas, undrained
- 8 ounces red potatoes, unpeeled, cut into ½-inch pieces
- ½ small white onion, halved through root end
- 2 carrots, peeled and halved crosswise
- 2 bay leaves

Spicy Tomatillo Salsa
- 2 dried ancho chiles, stemmed, seeded, and torn into ½-inch pieces (½ cup)
- 6 ounces tomatillos, husks and stems removed, rinsed well and dried
- 1 small plum tomato
- ¼ small white onion, quartered through root end
- 2 garlic cloves, unpeeled
- 1–2 dried arbol chiles, stemmed (optional)
- 1¼ teaspoons kosher salt
- ½–1 teaspoon cider vinegar (optional)
  Pinch to ½ teaspoon sugar (optional)

- 24 (6-inch) corn tortillas, warmed
  Finely chopped white onion
  Thinly sliced radishes
  Fresh cilantro leaves
  Lime wedges

1. For the lamb and consomé de barbacoa: Adjust oven rack to lower-middle position and heat oven to 325 degrees. Toast guajillos in 10-inch cast-iron skillet over medium-high heat, stirring frequently, until fragrant, 2 to 6 minutes. Transfer to bowl (reserve skillet). Add 2 cups hot water to guajillos, making sure they're completely submerged, and let stand until softened, about 20 minutes.

2. Meanwhile, place lamb on cutting board with fat cap facing down. Using sharp knife, trim any pockets of fat and connective tissue from underside of lamb. If lamb is thicker than 1½ inches, cover with plastic wrap and pound until it is no more than 1½ inches thick (thickness does not need to be uniform; some areas may be thinner). Cut lamb crosswise into 3 pieces. Add lamb to large bowl.

8. Peel garlic and trim root end from onion. Add garlic and onion to clean blender along with tomatillos; tomato; arbol chiles, if using; and salt. Drain anchos and reserve ⅔ cup soaking liquid (discard remaining liquid). Add anchos and reserved liquid to blender and process until smooth, 1 to 2 minutes. Transfer to serving bowl and let sit at room temperature so flavors meld, about 30 minutes. Season with salt; vinegar; and sugar, if using, to taste.

9. Transfer lamb to cutting board. Pour accumulated lamb juices from plate into Dutch oven. Remove ramekin and discard onion, carrots, and bay leaves. Bring consomé to simmer over medium heat. Slice lamb crosswise ½ inch thick. Transfer lamb to bowl and add ½ cup consomé. Using tongs, toss meat, breaking it up into bite-size pieces. Season consomé and lamb with salt to taste. Transfer lamb to serving platter. Ladle consomé into individual serving bowls. Serve, passing salsa, warm tortillas, onion, radishes, cilantro, and lime wedges separately.

3. Drain guajillos and reserve ⅔ cup soaking liquid (discard remaining liquid). Process guajillos, reserved liquid, 4 garlic cloves, 1½ tablespoons salt, oregano, vinegar, pepper, cloves, and cumin in blender until smooth, about 3 minutes. Pour chile sauce over lamb and, using tongs, toss until lamb is well coated. Rinse out blender.

4. Place 1½- to 2-inch-tall ramekin right side up in center of Dutch oven. Avoiding ramekin, add 3 cups water, chickpeas and their liquid, potatoes, onion, carrots, bay leaves, remaining 2 garlic cloves, and remaining ½ teaspoon salt. Place 8- to 9-inch-wide plate on top of ramekin.

5. Arrange lamb on plate, placing 2 pieces side by side with third piece on top. Scrape any excess marinade from bowl onto top of meat. Bring to simmer over high heat. Cover tightly with lid and transfer to oven. Cook until paring knife inserted into lamb slides in and out with little resistance, about 3 hours. Let meat rest, covered, for 30 minutes.

6. For the spicy tomatillo salsa: While lamb cooks, toast anchos in now-empty skillet over medium-high heat, stirring frequently, until fragrant, 2 to 6 minutes. Transfer to bowl (reserve skillet). Add 2 cups hot water to anchos, making sure they're completely submerged, and let stand until softened, about 20 minutes.

7. Place tomatillos, tomato, onion, and garlic in skillet and cook over medium-low heat, turning ingredients occasionally. Cook garlic until skins are lightly charred and interior is soft, about 5 minutes. Cook onion until 2 cut sides are lightly charred and onion has softened slightly, 12 to 15 minutes. Cook tomatillos and tomato until exteriors are spotty brown and flesh is soft, 20 to 25 minutes.

Roast Butterflied Leg of Lamb with Coriander, Cumin, and Mustard Seeds

Serves 8 to 10 • Total Time: 2½ hours, plus 1 hour 20 minutes resting

Why This Recipe Works Roast leg of lamb is both delicious and daunting. The usual bone-in or boned, rolled, and tied leg options cook unevenly and are tricky to carve. Choosing a butterflied leg of lamb did away with these problems; we simply pounded it to an even thickness and salted it for an hour to encourage juicy, evenly cooked meat. We first roasted it gently in the oven until it was just medium-rare; we then passed it under the broiler to give it a crisp crust. A standard spice rub scorched under the broiler, so we opted for a spice-infused oil, which seasoned the lamb during cooking and then became a quick sauce for serving.

We prefer the subtler flavor and larger size of lamb labeled "domestic" or "American" for this recipe. The amount of salt (2 tablespoons) in step 1 is for a 6-pound leg. If using a larger leg (7 to 8 pounds), add an additional teaspoon of salt for every pound.

Lamb

- 1 (6- to 8-pound) butterflied leg of lamb
- 2 tablespoons kosher salt
- ⅓ cup vegetable oil
- 3 shallots, sliced thin
- 4 garlic cloves, peeled and smashed
- 1 (1-inch) piece ginger, sliced into ½-inch-thick rounds and smashed
- 1 tablespoon coriander seeds
- 1 tablespoon cumin seeds
- 1 tablespoon mustard seeds
- 3 bay leaves
- 2 (2-inch) strips lemon zest

Sauce

- ⅓ cup chopped fresh mint
- ⅓ cup chopped fresh cilantro
- 1 shallot, minced
- 2 tablespoons lemon juice

1. For the lamb: Place lamb on cutting board with fat cap facing down. Using sharp knife, trim any pockets of fat and connective tissue from underside of lamb. Flip lamb over, trim fat cap so it's between ⅛ and ¼ inch thick, and pound roast to even 1-inch thickness. Cut slits, spaced ½ inch apart, in fat cap in crosshatch pattern, being careful to cut down to but not into meat. Rub salt over entire roast and into slits. Let stand, uncovered, at room temperature for 1 hour.

2. Meanwhile, adjust oven racks 4 to 5 inches from broiler element and to lower-middle position and heat oven to 250 degrees. Stir together oil, shallots, garlic, ginger, coriander seeds, cumin seeds, mustard seeds, bay leaves, and lemon zest on rimmed baking sheet and bake on lower rack until spices are softened and fragrant and shallots and garlic turn golden, about 1 hour. Remove sheet from oven and discard bay leaves.

3. Thoroughly pat lamb dry with paper towels and transfer, fat side up, to sheet (directly on top of spices). Roast on lower rack until lamb registers 120 degrees, 30 to 40 minutes. Remove sheet from oven and heat broiler. Broil lamb on upper rack until surface is well browned and charred in spots and lamb registers 125 degrees, 3 to 8 minutes for medium-rare.

4. Remove sheet from oven and, using 2 pairs of tongs, transfer lamb to carving board (some spices will cling to bottom of roast); tent with aluminum foil and let rest for 20 minutes.

5. For the sauce: Meanwhile, carefully pour pan juices through fine-mesh strainer into medium bowl, pressing on solids to extract as much liquid as possible; discard solids. Stir in mint, cilantro, shallot, and lemon juice. Add any accumulated lamb juices to sauce and season with salt and pepper to taste.

6. With long side facing you, slice lamb with grain into 3 equal pieces. Turn each piece and slice across grain into ¼-inch-thick slices. Serve with sauce. (Briefly warm sauce in microwave if it has cooled and thickened.)

VARIATIONS

Roast Butterflied Leg of Lamb with Coriander, Rosemary, and Red Pepper
Omit cumin and mustard seeds. Toss 6 sprigs fresh rosemary and ½ teaspoon red pepper flakes with oil mixture in step 2. Substitute parsley for cilantro in sauce.

Roast Butterflied Leg of Lamb with Coriander, Fennel, and Black Pepper
Substitute 1 tablespoon fennel seeds for cumin seeds and 1 tablespoon black peppercorns for mustard seeds in step 2. Substitute parsley for mint in sauce.

Fish & Seafood

Photo: Pan-Roasted Halibut Steaks with Chunky Cherry Tomato–Basil Vinaigrette

Pan-Seared Brined Salmon

Serves 4 • **Total Time: 40 minutes**

Why This Recipe Works Harnessing the intense heat of a skillet, you can produce a golden-brown, ultracrisp crust on salmon fillets while keeping their interiors moist. We first brined the fish to season it and to keep it moist. Instead of adding the fish to an already-hot skillet, we placed it in a cold, dry nonstick skillet skin side down and then turned on the heat. The skin protected the fish from drying out while cooking and later was easy to peel off, if desired. Also, because the skin released fat into the pan as it cooked, no extra oil was needed to sear the second side of the fish.

> *To ensure even cooking, buy a whole center-cut fillet and cut it into four pieces. Using skin-on salmon is important here, as we rely on the fat underneath the skin as the cooking medium (as opposed to adding extra oil). It is important to keep the skin on during cooking; once the salmon is cooked, the skin will be easy to remove. If using wild salmon, cook it until it registers 120 degrees. Serve with Mango-Mint Salsa or Cilantro-Mint Chutney (recipes follow), if desired.*

¼ cup table salt for brining
1 (1½- to 2-pound) skin-on salmon fillet, sliced crosswise into 4 equal pieces
½ teaspoon table salt, divided
½ teaspoon pepper, divided
Lemon wedges

1. Dissolve ¼ cup salt in 2 quarts cold water in large container. Submerge salmon in brine and let sit at room temperature for 15 minutes. Remove salmon from brine and pat dry with paper towels.

2. Sprinkle bottom of 12-inch nonstick skillet evenly with ¼ teaspoon salt and ¼ teaspoon pepper. Place fillets, skin side down, in skillet and sprinkle tops of fillets with remaining ¼ teaspoon salt and remaining ¼ teaspoon pepper. Heat skillet over medium-high heat and cook fillets without moving them until fat begins to render, skin begins to brown, and bottom ¼ inch of fillets turns opaque, 6 to 8 minutes.

3. Using tongs and thin spatula, flip fillets and continue to cook without moving them until centers are still translucent when checked with tip of paring knife and register 125 degrees (for medium-rare), 6 to 8 minutes longer. Transfer fillets skin side down to serving platter and let rest for 5 minutes before serving with lemon wedges.

Mango-Mint Salsa

Makes 1 cup • **Total Time: 15 minutes**
Adjust the salsa's heat level by reserving and adding the jalapeño seeds, if desired.

1 mango, peeled, pitted, and cut into ¼-inch pieces
1 shallot, minced
3 tablespoons lime juice (2 limes)
2 tablespoons chopped fresh mint
1 jalapeño chile, stemmed, seeded, and minced
1 tablespoon extra-virgin olive oil
1 garlic clove, minced
½ teaspoon table salt

Combine all ingredients in bowl.

Cilantro-Mint Chutney

Makes 1 cup • **Total Time: 15 minutes**
Adjust the chutney's heat level by reserving and adding the jalapeño seeds, if desired.

2 cups fresh cilantro leaves
1 cup fresh mint leaves
½ cup water
¼ cup sesame seeds, lightly toasted
1 (2-inch) piece ginger, peeled and sliced into ⅛-inch-thick rounds
1 jalapeño chile, stemmed, seeded, and sliced into 1-inch pieces
2 tablespoons vegetable oil
2 tablespoons lime juice
1½ teaspoons sugar
½ teaspoon table salt

Process all ingredients in blender until smooth, about 30 seconds, scraping down sides of jar with spatula after 10 seconds.

Cutting Your Own Fillets

To ensure even cooking, buy a whole center-cut salmon fillet and cut it into 4 even pieces. Cut fillet in half first and then cut each half in half.

The Solution Is a Solution

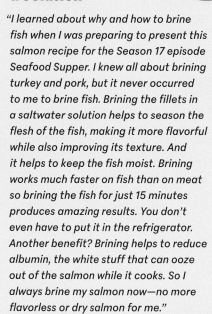

"I learned about why and how to brine fish when I was preparing to present this salmon recipe for the Season 17 episode Seafood Supper. I knew all about brining turkey and pork, but it never occurred to me to brine fish. Brining the fillets in a saltwater solution helps to season the flesh of the fish, making it more flavorful while also improving its texture. And it helps to keep the fish moist. Brining works much faster on fish than on meat so brining the fish for just 15 minutes produces amazing results. You don't even have to put it in the refrigerator. Another benefit? Brining helps to reduce albumin, the white stuff that can ooze out of the salmon while it cooks. So I always brine my salmon now—no more flavorless or dry salmon for me."

—Julia

Saumon aux Lentilles

Serves 4 • Total Time: 1½ hours

Why This Recipe Works For our version of the classic French pairing of salmon and lentils, we started by building a flavorful base for the lentils, gently cooking onion, carrots, and celery in olive oil until soft. Fruity tomato paste and plenty of garlic added even more depth before the lentils and water went in. When the lentils were fully softened and most of the moisture in the pot had either evaporated or been absorbed, we set them aside to focus on the salmon, which we'd briefly brined in a saltwater solution to season the fish and to ensure that it retained plenty of moisture as it cooked. We employed our tried-and-true method of placing the salmon skin side down in a cold nonstick skillet that had been strewn with salt and pepper. As the pan heated up, the salmon released some of the fat just beneath the skin, crisping it, and enabling us to cook the fish without any additional fat. A bit of mustard and sherry vinegar stirred into the lentils brightened their flavor, making them an ideal pairing for the rich fish, and a final addition of extra-virgin olive oil added grassy top notes.

> *To ensure uniform cooking, buy a 1½-pound center-cut salmon fillet and cut it into four pieces. Using skin-on salmon is important here, as we rely on the fat underneath the skin as the cooking medium. If using wild salmon, check for doneness earlier and cook it until it registers 120 degrees. Small, olive-green lentilles du Puy are worth seeking out for their meaty texture, but if you can't find them, substitute another small green lentil. Do not use red or brown lentils.*

Lentils

- 2 tablespoons extra-virgin olive oil, divided
- 1 large onion, chopped fine
- 1 celery rib, chopped fine
- 1 carrot, peeled and chopped fine
- ¾ teaspoon table salt
- 1 tablespoon minced garlic
- 1 tablespoon tomato paste
- ½ teaspoon dried thyme
- ½ teaspoon pepper
- 2½ cups water
- 1 cup dried lentilles du Puy (French green lentils), picked over and rinsed
- 1 tablespoon sherry vinegar, plus extra for seasoning
- 2 teaspoons Dijon mustard

Salmon

- ¼ cup table salt for brining
- 1 (1½- to 2-pound) skin-on salmon fillet, sliced crosswise into 4 equal pieces
- ¾ teaspoon table salt, divided
- ¾ teaspoon pepper, divided

1. For the lentils: Heat 1 tablespoon oil in medium saucepan over medium heat until shimmering. Add onion, celery, carrot, and salt and stir to coat vegetables. Cover and cook, stirring occasionally, until vegetables are softened but not browned, 8 to 10 minutes. Add garlic, tomato paste, thyme, and pepper and cook, stirring constantly, until fragrant, about 2 minutes. Stir in water and lentils. Increase heat and bring to boil. Adjust heat to simmer. Cover and cook, stirring occasionally, until lentils are tender but not mushy and have consistency of thick risotto, 40 to 50 minutes. Remove from heat and keep covered.

2. For the salmon: While lentils are cooking, dissolve ¼ cup salt in 1 quart water in narrow container. Submerge salmon in brine and let stand for 15 minutes. Remove salmon from brine and pat dry with paper towels. Allow to stand while lentils finish cooking.

3. Sprinkle bottom of 12-inch nonstick skillet evenly with ½ teaspoon salt and ½ teaspoon pepper. Place fillets, skin side down, in skillet and sprinkle tops of fillets with remaining ¼ teaspoon salt and remaining ¼ teaspoon pepper. Heat skillet over medium-high heat and cook fillets, without moving them, until fat begins to render, skin begins to brown, and bottom ¼ inch of fillets turns opaque, 6 to 8 minutes.

4. Using tongs and thin spatula, flip fillets and continue to cook without moving them until centers are still translucent when checked with tip of paring knife and register 125 degrees (for medium-rare), 5 to 8 minutes longer. Transfer fillets, skin side up, to clean plate.

5. Warm lentils briefly if necessary. Stir in vinegar, mustard, and remaining 1 tablespoon oil. Season with salt, pepper, and vinegar to taste. Divide lentils among wide, shallow serving bowls. Arrange salmon skin side up on lentils and serve.

Packed with Delicious Protein

"I love athletics, and swimming and running in particular are a big part of my weekly workouts, which is why I enjoy cooking meals that nourish and replenish my body and my taste buds alike. Saumon aux Lentilles is a hearty, protein-packed meal that doesn't disappoint. Tender lentils, flavored with aromatics and pan-seared salmon with a shatteringly crispy skin—what's not to love? The balanced flavors and textures truly makes this a meal worth celebrating.

Sautéing onions, celery, carrots, and garlic creates a flavorful savory base for the lentils. Cooked until tender, but not mushy, the lentils provide a toothsome bite to balance the silky salmon. The cold start cooking technique for the salmon means that the skin cooks up nice and crispy without the need for any added oil. Briefly brining the salmon ensures that it's well seasoned inside, while sprinkling salt and pepper on the skillet before adding the salmon and on top of the salmon fillets ensures that the exterior of the salmon is also well seasoned.

Plating the lentils first and placing a salmon fillet on top of each plate is an elegant way to serve this dish for a dinner party or just a family dinner. With a green salad or any green vegetable, it's a wonderful well-balanced meal."

— Erica

SEASON 25

Crispy Salmon Cakes with Smoked Salmon, Capers, and Dill for Two

Serves 2 • Total Time: 40 minutes

Why This Recipe Works We wanted to give classic New England cod cakes a new spin by swapping in rich, meaty salmon. We were after pure salmon flavor, which was possible with just a few choice ingredients and minimal binder. Fresh salmon easily beat out canned, and we ditched the typical potato binder in favor of mayonnaise and bread crumbs. To chop the salmon, we quickly pulsed 1-inch pieces in the food processor. This gave us both larger chunks for a substantial texture and smaller pieces that helped the cakes hold together. Coating the cakes in ultracrisp panko bread crumbs ensured a good crust. Dijon mustard, shallot, lemon juice, and dill boosted the flavor of the cakes, and a quick tartar sauce completed our dish.

> *Be sure to use raw salmon here; do not substitute cooked salmon. Do not overprocess the salmon in step 2 or the cakes will have a pasty texture. If you purchase skin-on fillets, you can easily remove the skin yourself.*

Tartar Sauce
- ⅓ cup mayonnaise
- 1 tablespoon sweet pickle relish
- 1½ teaspoons capers, rinsed and minced
- 1 teaspoon white wine vinegar
- ¼ teaspoon Worcestershire sauce

Salmon Cakes

- 1 (8-ounce) skinless salmon fillet, cut into 1-inch pieces
- 2 tablespoons plus ½ cup panko bread crumbs, divided
- 2 ounces smoked salmon, finely chopped
- 1 tablespoon chopped fresh dill
- 1 tablespoon mayonnaise
- 1 small shallot, minced
- 2 teaspoons lemon juice
- 1½ teaspoons capers, rinsed and minced
- ½ teaspoon Dijon mustard
- ¼ teaspoon pepper
- ⅛ teaspoon table salt
  Pinch cayenne pepper
- ⅓ cup vegetable oil

1. For the tartar sauce: Whisk all ingredients together in bowl and season with salt and pepper to taste; set aside.

2. For the salmon cakes: Pulse salmon in food processor until there is an even mix of finely minced and coarsely chopped pieces of salmon, about 2 pulses, scraping down sides of bowl as needed.

3. Combine 2 tablespoons panko, smoked salmon, dill, mayonnaise, shallot, lemon juice, capers, mustard, pepper, salt, and cayenne in bowl. Gently fold in processed salmon until just combined.

4. Spread remaining ½ cup panko in shallow dish. Scrape salmon mixture onto small baking sheet. Divide mixture into 4 equal portions and gently flatten each portion into 1-inch-thick patty. Carefully coat each cake with panko, then return to sheet.

5. Line large plate with triple layer of paper towels. Heat oil in 10-inch skillet over medium-high heat until shimmering. Gently place salmon cakes in skillet and cook, without moving, until golden brown and crisp on both sides, 2 to 3 minutes per side. Drain cakes briefly on paper towel–lined plate. Serve with tartar sauce.

Skinning a Salmon Fillet

Insert blade of sharp knife just above skin about 1 inch from end of fillet. Cut through nearest end, away from yourself, keeping blade just above skin. Rotate fish and grab loose skin. Run knife between flesh and skin until skin is completely removed.

SEASON 18

Miso-Marinated Salmon

Serves 4 • Total Time: 30 minutes, plus 6 hours chilling

Why This Recipe Works Miso-marinated salmon promises firm, flavorful fish with a savory-sweet, lacquer-like exterior, but it takes three days to prepare. We wanted to make a dish that pulled back on the traditional approach (and shortened the process) but still achieved the depth of flavor that this dish is known for. And instead of a dense interior, we wanted fish that was silky and moist, contrasting with the texture of the crust. By reducing the marinating to between 6 and 24 hours, we found a window that allowed us to achieve such a goal. A marinade composed of miso, sugar, mirin, and sake allowed for flavor penetration, moisture retention, and better browning by firming up the fish's surface. Broiling the fish at a distance from the heating element allowed the fish to caramelize and cook to tender at the same time.

Note that the fish needs to marinate for at least 6 or up to 24 hours before cooking. Use center-cut salmon fillets of similar thickness. Yellow, red, or brown miso paste can be used instead of white.

- ½ cup white miso paste
- ¼ cup sugar
- 3 tablespoons sake
- 3 tablespoons mirin
- 4 (6- to 8-ounce) skin-on salmon fillets
  Lemon wedges

1. Whisk miso, sugar, sake, and mirin in medium bowl until sugar and miso are dissolved (mixture will be thick). Dip each fillet into miso mixture to evenly coat all flesh sides. Place fish skin side down in baking dish and pour any remaining miso mixture over fillets. Cover with plastic wrap and refrigerate for at least 6 hours or up to 24 hours.

2. Adjust oven rack 8 inches from broiler element and heat broiler. Place wire rack in rimmed baking sheet and cover with aluminum foil. Using your fingers, scrape miso mixture from fillets (do not rinse) and place fish skin side down on foil, leaving 1 inch between fillets.

3. Broil salmon until deeply browned and centers of fillets are still translucent when checked with tip of paring knife and register 125 degrees (for medium-rare), 8 to 12 minutes, rotating sheet halfway through cooking and shielding edges of fillets with foil if necessary. Transfer to platter and serve with lemon wedges.

Glazed Salmon

Serves 4 • Total Time: 30 minutes

Why This Recipe Works The traditional method for glazed salmon calls for broiling, but reaching into a broiling-hot oven every minute to baste the fish is a hassle and, even worse, the fillets often burn if your timing isn't spot-on. We wanted a foolproof method for glazed salmon that was succulent and pink throughout while keeping the slightly crusty, flavorful browned exterior typically achieved with broiling. First we found that reducing the temperature and gently baking the fish, instead of broiling, cooked the salmon perfectly. To rapidly caramelize the exterior of the fillets before they had a chance to toughen, we sprinkled the fillets with sugar and quickly pan-seared each side before transferring them to the oven. To make sure the glaze stayed put, we rubbed the fish with a mixture of cornstarch, brown sugar, and salt before searing.

To ensure uniform pieces of fish that cook at the same rate, buy a whole center-cut fillet and cut it into 4 pieces. Prepare the glaze before you cook the salmon. You will need a 12-inch ovensafe nonstick skillet for this recipe. If your nonstick skillet isn't ovensafe, sear the salmon as directed in step 2, then transfer it to a rimmed baking sheet, glaze it, and bake as directed in step 3.

1 teaspoon light brown sugar
½ teaspoon kosher salt
¼ teaspoon cornstarch
1 (1½- to 2-pound) skin-on salmon fillet, sliced crosswise into 4 equal pieces
1 teaspoon vegetable oil
1 recipe glaze (recipes follow)

1. Adjust oven rack to middle position and heat oven to 300 degrees. Combine brown sugar, salt, and cornstarch in small bowl. Pat fillets dry with paper towels and season with pepper. Sprinkle brown sugar mixture evenly over flesh side of salmon, rubbing to distribute.

2. Heat oil in 12-inch ovensafe nonstick skillet over medium-high heat until just smoking. Place salmon, flesh side down, in skillet and cook until well browned, about 1 minute. Using tongs and thin spatula, carefully flip salmon and cook on skin side for 1 minute.

3. Remove skillet from heat and spoon glaze evenly over salmon fillets. Transfer skillet to oven and cook fillets until centers are still translucent when checked with tip of paring knife and register 125 degrees (for medium-rare), 7 to 10 minutes. Transfer fillets to platter or individual plates and serve.

Pomegranate-Balsamic Glaze

Makes ½ cup • Total Time: 15 minutes

This fruity, tangy glaze is a perfect match for rich salmon.

- 3 tablespoons light brown sugar
- 3 tablespoons pomegranate juice
- 2 tablespoons balsamic vinegar
- 1 tablespoon whole-grain mustard
- 1 teaspoon cornstarch
  Pinch cayenne pepper

Whisk all ingredients together in small saucepan. Bring to boil over medium-high heat; simmer until thickened, about 1 minute. Remove from heat and cover to keep warm.

Hoisin-Ginger Glaze

Makes ½ cup • Total Time: 15 minutes

Toasted sesame oil gives this teriyaki-like glaze rich flavor.

- 2 tablespoons ketchup
- 2 tablespoons hoisin sauce
- 2 tablespoons rice vinegar
- 2 tablespoons packed light brown sugar
- 1 tablespoon soy sauce
- 1 tablespoon toasted sesame oil
- 2 teaspoons chili-garlic sauce
- 1 teaspoon grated fresh ginger

Whisk all ingredients together in small saucepan. Bring to boil over medium-high heat; simmer until thickened, about 3 minutes. Remove from heat and cover to keep warm.

Orange-Miso Glaze

Makes ½ cup • Total Time: 15 minutes

Miso is a fermented soybean paste that adds deep flavor to foods. We prefer milder, white miso here, rather than the strong-flavored red miso.

- 1 teaspoon grated orange zest plus ¼ cup juice
- 2 tablespoons white miso
- 1 tablespoon light brown sugar
- 1 tablespoon rice vinegar
- 1 tablespoon whole-grain mustard
- ¾ teaspoon cornstarch
  Pinch cayenne pepper

Whisk all ingredients together in small saucepan. Bring to boil over medium-high heat; simmer until thickened, about 1 minute. Remove from heat and cover to keep warm.

Soy-Mustard Glaze

Makes ½ cup • Total Time: 15 minutes

Mirin, a sweet Japanese rice wine, can be found in Asian markets and the international section of most supermarkets.

- 3 tablespoons light brown sugar
- 2 tablespoons soy sauce
- 2 tablespoons mirin
- 1 tablespoon sherry vinegar
- 1 tablespoon whole-grain mustard
- 1 tablespoon water
- 1 teaspoon cornstarch
- ⅛ teaspoon red pepper flakes

Whisk all ingredients together in small saucepan. Bring to boil over medium-high heat; simmer until thickened, about 1 minute. Remove from heat and cover to keep warm.

SEASON 19

Roasted Whole Side of Salmon

Serves 8 to 10 • Total Time: 45 minutes, plus 1 hour salting

Why This Recipe Works When it comes to serving a crowd, most cooks turn to a large roast or bird. But salmon is ideal for entertaining, too. We wanted to come up with an approach for a whole roasted fillet that would be evenly moist inside and gorgeously browned on top. To start, we salted it for an hour, which helped the flesh retain moisture and protein. Placing it on a greased aluminum foil sling ensured that it was easy to transfer to a serving platter. We set the salmon on a wire rack set in a rimmed baking sheet to encourage air circulation. Evenly brushing the surface with honey encouraged rapid browning. We preheated the oven to 250 degrees to warm the entire oven, which ensured that cooking happened quickly and evenly. Then, we broiled the fillet until it just began to brown. Last, we again turned the oven heat to 250 degrees to allow the fillet to gently cook through. A squeeze of fresh lemon juice was all it took to temper the richness of the salmon, but a pair of vibrant, no-cook condiments—an arugula-based pesto and a crisp cucumber relish—offered even more dress-up potential.

This recipe requires salting the fish for at least 1 hour. Look for a fillet that is uniformly thick from end to end. The surface will continue to brown after the oven temperature is reduced in step 4; if the surface starts to darken too much before the fillet's center registers 125 degrees, shield the dark portion with aluminum foil.

If using wild salmon, which contains less fat than farmed salmon, remove it from the oven when the center of the fillet registers 120 degrees. Serve as is or with Arugula and Almond Pesto or Cucumber-Ginger Relish (recipes follow).

- 1 (4-pound) skin-on side of salmon, pin bones removed and belly fat trimmed
- 1 tablespoon kosher salt
- 2 tablespoons honey
  Lemon wedges

1. Sprinkle flesh side of salmon evenly with salt and refrigerate, uncovered, for at least 1 hour or up to 4 hours.

2. Adjust oven rack 7 inches from broiler element and heat oven to 250 degrees. Line rimmed baking sheet with aluminum foil and place wire rack in sheet. Fold 18 by 12-inch piece of foil lengthwise to create 18 by 6-inch sling. Place sling on wire rack and spray with vegetable oil spray.

3. Heat broiler. Pat salmon dry with paper towels and place, skin side down, on foil sling. Brush salmon evenly with honey and broil until surface is lightly but evenly browned, 8 to 12 minutes, rotating sheet halfway through broiling.

4. Return oven temperature to 250 degrees and continue to cook until center of fillet is still translucent when checked with tip of paring knife and registers 125 degrees, 10 to 15 minutes longer, rotating sheet halfway through cooking. Using foil sling, transfer salmon to serving platter, then carefully remove foil. Serve with lemon wedges.

ACCOMPANIMENTS
Arugula and Almond Pesto
Makes 1½ cups • Total Time: 15 minutes
For a spicier pesto, reserve, mince, and add the ribs and seeds from the chile. The pesto can be refrigerated for up to 24 hours. If refrigerated, let the pesto sit at room temperature for 30 minutes before serving.

- ¼ cup almonds, lightly toasted
- 4 garlic cloves, peeled
- 4 anchovy fillets, rinsed and patted dry
- 1 serrano chile, stemmed, seeded, and halved lengthwise
- 6 ounces (6 cups) arugula
- ¼ cup lemon juice (2 lemons)
- ¼ cup extra-virgin olive oil
- 1½ teaspoons kosher salt

Process almonds, garlic, anchovies, and serrano in food processor until finely chopped, about 15 seconds, scraping down sides of bowl as needed. Add arugula, lemon juice, oil, and salt and process until smooth, about 30 seconds.

Cucumber-Ginger Relish
Makes 2 cups • Total Time: 15 minutes
For a spicier relish, reserve, mince, and add the chile ribs and seeds. Serve this relish within 30 minutes of assembling it.

- ½ cup rice vinegar
- 6 tablespoons extra-virgin olive oil
- ¼ cup lime juice (2 limes)
- 2 tablespoons whole-grain mustard
- 1 tablespoon grated fresh ginger
- ½ teaspoon kosher salt
- 1 English cucumber, seeded and cut into ¼-inch dice
- 1 cup minced fresh mint
- 1 cup minced fresh cilantro
- 1 serrano chile, stemmed, seeded, and minced

Whisk vinegar, oil, lime juice, mustard, ginger, and salt in bowl until smooth. Add cucumber, mint, cilantro, and serrano and stir to combine.

Removing Pin Bones from Salmon

Drape whole fillet over inverted mixing bowl to help any pin bones protrude. Working from head end to tail end, locate pin bones by running fingers along length of fillet. Use pliers or tweezers to grasp bone and pull slowly but firmly at slight angle.

SEASON 9

Poached Salmon with Herb and Caper Vinaigrette

Serves 4 • Total Time: 45 minutes

Why This Recipe Works For a supple poached salmon accented by the delicate flavor of its poaching liquid, we started with a classic court-bouillon made by boiling water, wine, herbs, vegetables, and aromatics and then straining out the solids. Discarding all those vegetables seemed wasteful so we used less liquid and cut back on the quantity of vegetables and aromatics; shallots, a few herbs, and wine were all we needed to up the flavor. However, the part of the salmon that wasn't submerged in liquid needed to be steamed to cook through, and the low cooking temperature required to poach the salmon evenly didn't create enough steam. Increasing the ratio of wine to water lowered the liquid's boiling point, producing more vapor. Meanwhile, the bottom of the fillets had the opposite problem, overcooking due to direct contact with the pan. Resting the salmon fillets on top of lemon slices provided insulation. For a finishing touch, we reduced the liquid and added olive oil to create an easy sauce.

To ensure uniform pieces of fish that cook at the same rate, buy a whole center-cut fillet and cut it into four pieces. If a skinless whole fillet is unavailable, remove the skin yourself or follow the recipe as directed with a skin-on fillet, adding 3 to 4 minutes to the cooking time in step 2.

2 lemons
1 large shallot, minced (about ¼ cup), divided
2 tablespoons minced fresh parsley, stems reserved
2 tablespoons minced fresh tarragon, stems reserved
½ cup dry white wine
½ cup water
1 (1¾- to 2-pound) skinless salmon fillet, about 1½ inches at the thickest part
2 tablespoons capers, rinsed and chopped coarse
2 tablespoons extra-virgin olive oil
1 tablespoon honey

1. Cut top and bottom off 1 lemon; cut lemon into eight to ten ¼-inch-thick slices. Cut remaining lemon into 8 wedges and set aside. Arrange lemon slices in single layer across bottom of 12-inch skillet. Scatter 2 tablespoons of shallot and herb stems evenly over lemon slices. Add wine and water.

2. Use sharp knife to trim any whitish fat from belly of fillet and cut it into 4 equal pieces. Place salmon fillets in skillet, skinned side down, on top of lemon slices. Set pan over high heat and bring liquid to simmer. Reduce heat to low, cover, and cook until sides of fillets are opaque but center of thickest part of fillets is still translucent (or until thickest part of fillets registers 125 degrees), 11 to 16 minutes. Remove pan from heat and, using spatula, carefully transfer salmon and lemon slices to paper towel–lined plate. Tent with foil.

3. Return pan to high heat and simmer cooking liquid until slightly thickened and reduced to 2 tablespoons, 4 to 5 minutes. Meanwhile, combine remaining shallot, minced herbs, capers, olive oil, and honey in medium bowl. Strain reduced cooking liquid through fine-mesh strainer into bowl with herb-caper mixture, pressing on solids to extract as much liquid as possible. Whisk to combine and season with salt and pepper to taste.

4. Season salmon lightly with salt and pepper. Using spatula, carefully lift and tilt salmon fillets to remove lemon slices. Place salmon on serving platter or individual plates and spoon vinaigrette over top. Serve, with reserved lemon wedges.

Pesce all'Acqua Pazza

Serves 4 • **Total Time: 35 minutes**

Why This Recipe Works Pesca all'acqua pazza, or "fish in crazy water," refers to the centuries-old southern Italian tradition of cooking the day's catch in seawater. Following the lead of modern Italian cooks, we spiked our water-based broth with white wine for brightness and acidity and halved cherry tomatoes for sweetness and pops of color. For the fish, we chose skin-on haddock fillets, which held up nicely during simmering and (due to the abundant collagen in the skin) suffused the broth with rich flavor and body. To ensure perfectly cooked fillets, we poached them over low heat until they were nearly done and then slid the pan off the burner to finish the cooking at a gentler pace. After just a few minutes, the haddock absorbed the heady flavor of the broth and the broth was enriched by the fish.

You may substitute skin-on fillets of other firm, white-fleshed species such as sea bass, branzino, and red snapper. Serve with crusty bread.

1½	pounds skin-on haddock fillets, ¾ to 1 inch thick
1	teaspoon kosher salt, divided
2	tablespoons extra-virgin olive oil
3	garlic cloves, sliced thin
¼	teaspoon crushed red pepper flakes
1	small onion, chopped fine
1	bay leaf
8	ounces cherry or grape tomatoes, halved
1¼	cups water
¼	cup dry white wine
12	parsley stems, plus 3 tablespoons chopped fresh parsley leaves

1. Season fish fillets all over with ½ teaspoon salt and pepper to taste and set aside.

2. Heat oil, garlic, and red pepper flakes in 12-inch skillet over medium heat, stirring constantly, until garlic begins to sizzle gently, 1½ to 2 minutes. Add onion, bay leaf, and remaining ½ teaspoon salt and cook, stirring constantly, until onion just starts to soften, 2 to 3 minutes. Add tomatoes and cook, stirring constantly, until they begin to soften, 2 to 3 minutes. Stir in water, wine, parsley stems and half of chopped parsley and bring to boil. Nestle fillets skin side down in liquid, moving aside solids as much as possible (it's fine if fillets fold over slightly at ends; liquid will not quite cover fillets). Spoon some liquid and solids over fillets.

GAME CHANGER

Find a Friend in Fish Skin

"When it comes to flaky white fish fillets, skinless is often the default. That's fine, of course, but the skin-on haddock fillets we use in our pesce all'acqua pazza reveal the subtle glory of the skin that you may be missing. As the fish cooks, collagen in the skin breaks down to form gelatin, which suffuses the broth with richness, silky body, and extra flavor. In fact, there's often enough gelatin from the skin in the broth that leftovers will set like soft Jell-O when refrigerated. This recipe offers a bonus lesson in carryover cooking. Delicate fish fillets can overcook easily; to avoid that problem, we cook the fish until it's nearly, but not completely, done, and then remove the pan from the heat to allow the pan's residual heat to gently bring the fish to its final temperature. The carefully (and easily) cooked fish is accented by a simple, light, clean-tasting broth with all the right notes from onion, garlic, bay, white wine and a modest quantity of fresh tomato."

—Adam

Chraime

Adjust heat to low, cover, and simmer gently until fillets register 110 at thickest point, 4 to 7 minutes. Remove skillet from heat and let stand, covered, until fish is opaque and just cooked through (fish should register at least 135 degrees), 3 to 7 minutes.

3. Divide fish among 4 shallow soup plates. Remove bay leaf and parsley stems from skillet; stir in remaining parsley. Season broth with salt and pepper to taste. Spoon a portion of broth and solids over each serving of fish and serve immediately.

Chraime

Serves 4 • Total time: 1 hour

Why This Recipe Works This spicy, garlicky, saucy, and aromatic tomato-based fish stew was brought to Israel by Libyan and Moroccan Jewish immigrants and commonly appears on Shabbat, Rosh Hashanah, and Passover tables. Libyan versions typically consist of a fiery sauce of tomato paste, hot peppers, and spices—primarily cumin, caraway, and paprika—while Moroccan versions include more fresh vegetables (tomatoes and bell peppers) along with generous amounts of herbs. Our take paid homage to both: grassy fresh jalapeños and bright Aleppo pepper brought varied heat, and tomato paste and bell pepper provided balancing sweetness. Cherry tomatoes, tossed in almost at the end of cooking, added fresh pops of sweet acidity. Using a spice blend was an easy way to incorporate the dish's varied spices; 1 tablespoon of the Tunisian spice blend tabil added a range of flavors from earthy muskiness to bright citrus notes. A finishing handful of cilantro and a squeeze of lemon balanced all the flavors.

Black sea bass, cod, hake, or pollock can be substituted for the haddock. Thin tail-end fillets can be folded to achieve proper thickness. This dish is typically spicy; for a milder dish, reduce the amount of Aleppo pepper to 1 or 2 teaspoons. Serve with challah, if desired.

3 tablespoons extra virgin olive oil, plus extra for drizzling
1 onion, chopped fine
1 red bell pepper, stemmed, seeded, and chopped
1 jalapeño chile, stemmed, seeded, and minced
¾ teaspoon table salt
¼ cup tomato paste
6 garlic cloves, minced
1 tablespoon tabil (recipe follows)
1 tablespoon ground dried Aleppo pepper
2 teaspoons paprika
¼ teaspoon pepper
1½ cups water
1½ pounds skinless haddock fillets, ½ to ¾ inch thick, cut into 3-inch pieces
10 ounces cherry tomatoes
½ cup chopped fresh cilantro
Lemon wedges

1. Heat oil in 12-inch skillet over medium heat until shimmering. Add onion, bell pepper, jalapeño, and salt and cook until vegetables are softened, 5 to 7 minutes. Stir in tomato paste, garlic, tabil, Aleppo pepper, paprika, and pepper and cook until fragrant, about 30 seconds. Stir in water, scraping up any browned bits, and bring to simmer. Reduce heat to low; cover; and cook until flavors meld, about 15 minutes.

2. Nestle haddock into sauce and spoon some of sauce over fish. Sprinkle tomatoes around haddock and return to simmer. Reduce heat to low; cover; and cook until fish flakes apart when gently prodded with paring knife and registers 135 degrees, 5 to 7 minutes. Season with salt and pepper to taste. Sprinkle with cilantro and drizzle with extra oil. Serve with lemon wedges.

Tabil

Makes ½ cup • Total time: 5 minutes
The word "tabil" is sometimes translated as "coriander," so it's no surprise that coriander is the most prominent ingredient in this Tunisian spice blend. The blend lends dishes a beautiful, complex aroma.

3½ tablespoons coriander seeds
2 tablespoons plus 2 teaspoons caraway seeds
5 teaspoons cumin seeds

Combine all ingredients in bowl. (Tabil can be stored in airtight container at room temperature for up to 1 month.)

Halibut à la Nage with Parsnips and Tarragon

Serves 4 • Total Time: 1¼ hours

Why This Recipe Works Our easy, elegant poached halibut is inspired by the classic French preparation called à la nage, in which fish is delicately cooked and served in a well-seasoned, lightly acidulated broth. For a nontraditional Western European riff, we made a broth infused with parsnip, Parmesan, lemon, vanilla, and tarragon. Gently poaching the fish until it reached 110 degrees, then letting it sit, covered, off the heat, ensured that it came up to temperature (135 degrees) gradually and didn't overshoot the mark. Garnishing the plated fish and broth with a rich, verdant herb oil and additional fresh herbs added pops of flavor and color, not to mention professional-looking polish.

> *For the most vibrant sauce that blends easily, tightly pack the parsley in the measuring cup. Process the oil in a blender; an immersion blender will not process the herbs as finely, producing a paler colored oil. You can substitute other flaky white fish such as cod, haddock, pollock, or hake for the halibut; choose uniformly thick fillets to ensure even cooking.*

Tarragon Oil
- Kosher salt for blanching herbs
- ⅓ cup fresh parsley leaves
- 1 tablespoon fresh tarragon leaves
- ⅓ cup vegetable oil

Fish
- 4 (5- to 6-ounce) skinless halibut fillets, ¾ to 1 inch thick
- 2 teaspoons kosher salt, divided
- 2 cups water
- 6 ounces parsnips, peeled and sliced thin
- 1 shallot, sliced thin
- 1 piece Parmesan cheese rind, about 2½ inches by 1 inch
- 2 (3-inch) strips lemon zest plus 2 teaspoons lemon juice, plus extra juice for seasoning
- ½ teaspoon black peppercorns
- ¼ teaspoon vanilla extract
- 3 sprigs fresh tarragon, plus extra for garnish
- 1 tablespoon whole-grain mustard

1. For the tarragon oil: Bring 6 cups water and 2 teaspoons salt to boil in large saucepan. Add parsley and cook until leaves are tender but still bright green, about 30 seconds. Stir in tarragon, then drain herbs in fine-mesh strainer. Run under cold water until herbs are cool, about 10 seconds. Squeeze dry and transfer to blender. (Reserve strainer.) Add oil and process until herbs are finely ground and oil is bright green, about 2 minutes. (Oil can be refrigerated for up to 24 hours.)

2. For the fish: Sprinkle halibut all over with 1 teaspoon salt and set aside. Add water, parsnips, shallot, cheese rind, lemon zest, 2 teaspoons lemon juice, peppercorns, vanilla, and remaining 1 teaspoon salt to 12-inch skillet and bring to boil over high heat. Adjust heat to maintain gentle simmer, cover, and cook for 25 minutes.

3. Return liquid to boil over medium-high heat. Nestle halibut skinned side down in liquid, moving aside solids as much as possible (liquid will not quite cover fillets). Add tarragon and spoon some liquid over halibut. Reduce heat to low; cover and simmer gently until fish registers 110 degrees at thickest point, 4 to 7 minutes. Let stand off heat, covered, until fish is opaque and just cooked through (fish should register at least 135 degrees), 3 to 7 minutes.

4. Divide halibut among 4 shallow bowls. Season broth with salt and lemon juice to taste. Strain broth into 4-cup liquid measuring cup (you should have about 1⅔ cups broth) and discard solids. Divide broth evenly among bowls. Garnish with tarragon leaves. Top each piece halibut with ¾ teaspoon mustard. At table, drizzle about 1 tablespoon tarragon oil into each bowl. Serve immediately.

Oven-Steamed Fish with Scallions and Ginger

Serves 4 • Total Time: 1 hour

Why This Recipe Works Classic Chinese and French cuisines both use techniques for steaming fish that ensure moist, flavorful results. We borrowed from each approach to come up with an entirely new method that produces fish fillets infused with the flavors of soy sauce, garlic, and ginger. Moving the whole operation to the oven proved to be effective. We spread scallions and ginger over the bottom of a baking pan to infuse the fish with flavor as it steamed. To make removing the steamed fillets easy, we created a foil sling, sprayed it with vegetable oil spray, and placed the fish on it. We poured in a mixture of soy sauce, rice wine, sesame oil, sugar, salt, and white pepper; covered the pan; and placed it in a hot oven. After just 12 minutes the fish was perfectly cooked. To coat the fish in a fragrant sauce all we needed to do was strain the aromatic liquid left behind in the pan and pour it over the fish. Following the Chinese tradition, to finish we sautéed thin matchsticks of ginger in oil and then poured the mixture over the fish; the ginger added a bit of sweet spiciness and some crisp texture. A smattering of cilantro sprigs over the top provided a final, elegant touch.

> *Haddock, red snapper, halibut, and sea bass will also work in this recipe as long as the fillets are about 1 inch thick. If one end of the fillet is thinner, fold it under when placing it in the pan. This recipe works best in a metal baking pan; if using a glass baking dish, add 5 minutes to the cooking time. To ensure that the fish doesn't overcook, remove it from the oven between 125 and 130 degrees; it will continue to cook as it is plated. Serve with steamed rice and vegetables.*

- 8 scallions, trimmed, divided
- 1 (3-inch) piece ginger, peeled, divided
- 3 garlic cloves, sliced thin
- 4 (6-ounce) skinless cod fillets, about 1 inch thick
- 3 tablespoons soy sauce
- 2 tablespoons rice wine or dry sherry
- 1½ teaspoons toasted sesame oil
- 1½ teaspoons sugar
- ¼ teaspoon table salt
- ¼ teaspoon white pepper
- 2 tablespoons vegetable oil
- ⅓ cup cilantro leaves and thin stems

1. Adjust oven rack to middle position and heat oven to 450 degrees. Chop 6 scallions coarse and spread evenly in 13 by 9-inch baking pan. Slice remaining scallions thin on bias, and set aside. Chop 2 inches of ginger coarse and spread in baking pan with scallions. Slice remaining 1 inch of ginger into thin matchsticks and reserve. Sprinkle garlic over scallions and ginger.

2. Fold 18 by 12-inch piece of aluminum foil lengthwise to create 18 by 6-inch sling and spray lightly with vegetable oil spray. Place in pan lengthwise, allowing excess to hang over each end. Arrange fish on sling. If fillets vary in thickness, place thinner fillets in middle and thicker fillets at ends.

3. Whisk soy sauce, rice wine, sesame oil, sugar, salt, and white pepper in small bowl until combined. Pour around fish. Cover pan tightly with aluminum foil. Bake until fish registers 125 to 130 degrees, 12 to 14 minutes.

4. Grasping sling at each end, carefully transfer sling and fish to deep platter. Place spatula at 1 end of fillet to hold in place, and carefully slide foil out from under fish. Pour cooking liquid into fine-mesh strainer set over bowl and press on solids to extract liquid. Discard solids. Pour cooking liquid over fish. Sprinkle remaining scallions over fish. Heat vegetable oil in skillet over high heat until just smoking. Remove from heat and add remaining ginger (ginger will sizzle). Stir until ginger is beginning to brown and crisp. Drizzle oil and ginger over fish. Top with cilantro and serve.

Pan-Roasted Halibut Steaks

Serves 4 to 6 • **Total Time: 40 minutes**

Why This Recipe Works Chefs often choose to braise halibut instead of pan-roasting or sautéing because this moist-heat cooking technique keeps the fish from drying out. The problem is that braising doesn't allow for browning. We didn't want to make any compromises on either texture or flavor, so we set out to develop a technique for pan-roasting halibut that would produce perfectly cooked, moist, and tender fish. Halibut is most frequently sold as steaks, but there is quite a bit of range in size; to ensure that they cooked at the same rate, we chose steaks that were as close in size to each other as possible. We knew we could get a crust on the fish by pan-searing or oven-roasting, but neither technique proved satisfactory. A combination of the two—browning on the stovetop and roasting in the oven—worked best. To be sure the steaks wouldn't overcook, we seared them on one side in a piping-hot skillet and turned them over before placing them in the oven to finish cooking through. When they were done, the steaks were browned but still moist inside. To complement the lean fish, we paired the halibut with a rich flavored butter.

If you plan to serve the fish with the flavored butter or vinaigrette (recipes follow), prepare it before cooking the fish. Even well-dried fish can cause the hot oil in the pan to splatter. You can minimize splattering by laying the halibut steaks in the pan gently and putting the edge closest to you in the pan first so that the far edge falls away from you.

- 2 tablespoons olive oil
- 2 (full) halibut steaks, about 1¼ inches thick and 10 to 12 inches long (about 2½ pounds total), gently rinsed, dried well with paper towels, and trimmed of cartilage at both ends
- ¾ teaspoon table salt
- ¾ teaspoon pepper
- 1 recipe flavored butter or vinaigrette (recipes follow)

1. Adjust oven rack to middle position and heat oven to 425 degrees. When oven reaches 425 degrees, heat oil in 12-inch ovensafe skillet over high heat until oil just begins to smoke.

2. Meanwhile, sprinkle both sides of halibut steaks with salt and pepper. Reduce heat to medium-high and swirl oil in pan to distribute; carefully lay steaks in pan and sear, without moving them, until spotty brown, about 4 minutes.

(If steaks are thinner than 1¼ inches, check browning at 3½ minutes; thicker steaks of 1½ inches may require extra time, so check at 4½ minutes.) Off heat, flip steaks over in pan using 2 thin-bladed metal spatulas.

3. Transfer skillet to oven and roast until steaks reach 140 degrees and fish flakes loosen and flesh is opaque when checked with tip of paring knife, about 9 minutes (thicker steaks may take up to 10 minutes). Remove skillet from oven. Remove skin from cooked steaks and separate each quadrant of meat from bones by slipping spatula or knife gently between them. Transfer fish to warm platter and serve with flavored butter or vinaigrette.

Trimming and Serving Full Halibut Steaks

1. Cut off cartilage at each end of steaks to ensure they will fit neatly in pan and prevent small bones located there from winding up on your plate.

2. Remove skin from cooked steaks and separate quadrants of meat from bone by slipping spatula gently between them.

ACCOMPANIMENTS
Chipotle-Garlic Butter with Lime and Cilantro
Makes ¼ cup • Total Time: 25 minutes

- 4 tablespoons unsalted butter, softened
- 1 medium chipotle chile in adobo sauce, seeded and minced, plus 1 teaspoon adobo sauce
- 2 teaspoons minced fresh cilantro
- 1 garlic clove, minced
- 1 teaspoon honey
- 1 teaspoon grated lime zest
- ½ teaspoon table salt

Beat butter with fork until light and fluffy. Stir in chipotle and adobo sauce, cilantro, garlic, honey, lime zest, and salt until thoroughly combined. Dollop a portion of butter over each piece of hot cooked fish and allow butter to melt. Serve immediately.

Chunky Cherry Tomato–Basil Vinaigrette

Makes 1½ cups • Total Time: 25 minutes

- ½ pint cherry or grape tomatoes, each tomato quartered (about 1 cup)
- ¼ teaspoon table salt
- ¼ teaspoon ground black pepper
- 2 medium shallots, minced (about 6 tablespoons)
- 6 tablespoons extra-virgin olive oil
- 3 tablespoons juice from 1 lemon
- 2 tablespoons minced fresh basil leaves

Mix tomatoes, salt, and pepper in medium bowl; let stand until juicy and seasoned, about 10 minutes. Whisk shallots, oil, lemon juice, and basil together in small bowl; pour vinaigrette over tomatoes and toss to combine. Pour over pieces of hot cooked fish and serve immediately.

Pan-Seared Swordfish Steaks

Serves 4 • Total Time: 30 minutes

Why This Recipe Works Swordfish, unlike silky salmon or flaky halibut, offers a unique dense meatiness, making it an appealing option even for a staunch carnivore. But it isn't that easy to turn out swordfish steaks with a gorgeous brown crust and a tender yet firm interior. Like meats, fish contain enzymes called cathepsins. In the right circumstances, such as slow cooking, the cathepsins will break down the proteins that give swordfish its sturdy texture, rendering the dense steaks mushy. We learned that the key to perfectly cooked swordfish steaks was to cook them quickly in a skillet over high heat, flipping them frequently so that they cooked from both the bottom up and the top down. To keep each bite juicy, we removed the steaks from the heat when they reached 130 degrees and let carryover cooking bring them up to the desired temperature of 140 degrees.

For the best results, purchase swordfish steaks that are ¾ to 1 inch thick. Look for four steaks that weigh 7 to 9 ounces each or two steaks that weigh about 1 pound each. If you purchase the latter, cut them in half to create four steaks. We've found that skin-on swordfish often buckles in the hot skillet. Ask your fishmonger to remove the skin or trim it yourself with a thin, sharp knife. These steaks are great with just a squeeze of lemon or dressed up with a sauce (recipes follow).

- 2 teaspoons vegetable oil
- 2 pounds skinless swordfish steaks, ¾ to 1 inch thick
- 1½ teaspoons kosher salt
- Lemon wedges

1. Heat oil in 12-inch nonstick skillet over medium-high heat until shimmering. While oil heats, pat steaks dry with paper towels and sprinkle on both sides with salt.

2. Place steaks in skillet and cook, flipping every 2 minutes, until golden brown and centers register 130 degrees, 7 to 11 minutes. Transfer to serving platter or individual plates and let rest for 10 minutes. Serve with lemon wedges.

ACCOMPANIMENTS
Caper-Currant Relish

Makes ½ cup • Total Time: 30 minutes

In classic Italian agrodolce style, we balanced sweet currants, salty capers, fresh parsley, and savory garlic in this relish that's perfect for delicately flavored fish and poultry. Golden raisins can be substituted for the currants.

- 3 tablespoons finely chopped fresh parsley
- 3 tablespoons extra-virgin olive oil
- 2 tablespoons capers, rinsed and chopped fine
- 2 tablespoons currants, chopped fine
- 1 garlic clove, minced
- 1 teaspoon grated lemon zest plus 2 tablespoons juice

Combine all ingredients in bowl. Let sit at room temperature for at least 20 minutes before serving.

Spicy Dried Mint–Garlic Sauce

Makes ⅓ cup • **Total Time: 10 minutes**

For this ultragarlicky sauce made with dried mint, we pushed the mint through a strainer to remove any tough stems before moistening the mint powder with bright vinegar and rich olive oil. Plenty of raw garlic added a spicy heat and savory flavor to this simple and surprisingly bold sauce. If you are not using a garlic press, use a fork to bruise the minced garlic when stirring the sauce together.

- 4 teaspoons dried mint
- ¼ cup extra-virgin olive oil
- 2 tablespoons red wine vinegar
- 4 garlic cloves, minced
- ⅛ teaspoon table salt

Place mint in fine-mesh strainer and use spoon to rub mint through strainer into bowl. Discard any solids left in strainer. (You should have about 1 tablespoon mint powder.) Add oil, vinegar, garlic, and salt to mint powder and stir to combine.

Butter-Basted Fish Fillets with Garlic and Thyme

Serves 2 • **Total Time: 30 minutes**

Why This Recipe Works Butter basting, a technique that involves spooning sizzling butter over food as it cooks, is great for mild, flaky fish such as cod, haddock, or snapper. The butter helps cook the top of the fillet as the skillet heats the bottom, allowing you to flip the fish only once during cooking—before the flesh becomes too fragile—so it stays intact. The nutty, aromatic butter, which we enhanced with thyme sprigs and crushed garlic cloves, bathed the fish in savory flavor. We alternated basting with direct-heat cooking on the burner, taking the temperature of the fish so we knew exactly when the fillets were done.

You can substitute red snapper or haddock for the cod. The "skinned" side of a skinless fillet can be identified by its streaky, slightly darker appearance.

- 2 (6-ounce) skinless cod fillets, about 1 inch thick
- ½ teaspoon kosher salt
- ⅛ teaspoon pepper
- 1 tablespoon vegetable oil
- 3 tablespoons unsalted butter, cut into ½-inch cubes
- 2 garlic cloves, crushed and peeled
- 4 sprigs fresh thyme
  Lemon wedges

1. Pat all sides of fillets dry with paper towels. Sprinkle on all sides with salt and pepper. Heat oil in 12-inch nonstick or carbon-steel skillet over medium-high heat until just smoking. Reduce heat to medium and place fillets skinned side down in skillet. Gently press on each fillet with spatula for 5 seconds to ensure good contact with skillet. Cook fillets, without moving them, until underside is light golden brown, 4 to 5 minutes.

2. Using 2 spatulas, gently flip fillets. Cook for 1 minute. Scatter butter around fillets. When butter is melted, tilt skillet slightly toward you so butter pools at front of skillet. Using large spoon, scoop up melted butter and pour over fillets repeatedly for 15 seconds. Place skillet flat on burner and continue to cook 30 seconds longer. Tilt skillet and baste for 15 seconds. Place skillet flat on burner and take temperature of thickest part of each fillet. Continue to alternate basting and cooking until fillets register 130 degrees. Add garlic and thyme sprigs to skillet at 12 o'clock position (butter will spatter). When spattering has subsided, continue basting and cooking until fillets register 140 degrees at thickest point. (Total cooking time will range from 8 to 10 minutes.)

3. Transfer fillets to individual plates. Discard garlic. Top each fillet with thyme sprigs, pour butter over fillets, and serve with lemon wedges.

Pan-Roasted Sea Bass with Green Olive, Almond, and Orange Relish

Serves 4 • **Total Time: 30 minutes**

Why This Recipe Works We set out to develop a foolproof recipe for producing moist, well-browned pan-roasted fish fillets with a bright-meets-briny Greek relish. We chose thick fillets of semifirm sea bass; thinner fish overcooked by the time they achieved a serious sear. We then turned to a common restaurant method to cook the fish: We seared the fillets in a hot pan, flipped them, and then transferred the pan to the oven to finish cooking. Sprinkling the fillets with sugar accelerated browning on the stovetop, shortening the cooking time and thus ensuring that the fish didn't dry out. After a short stay in the oven, the fish emerged well browned, tender, and moist. Creating a complementary relish was as simple as whirling nuts, green olives, and citrus zest in the food processor before stirring in oil and fresh herbs.

Cod and snapper are good substitutes for the sea bass.

A Cheffy Technique That Really Delivers

"Cooking in a restaurant and cooking at home are two very different endeavors. There are times where techniques I've picked up working on the line, like always having a stack of lightweight dish towels within arm's reach, have served me well in my home kitchen. But more often than not, restaurant skills don't translate that well. Case in point: I spent a lot of time making perfect, precise knife cuts and expensive, complicated sauces in professional kitchens. I do neither at home.

But one technique that I'm happy to see jump the professional/home cook line is butter basting. To be fair, it looks very 'cheffy': While searing a piece of fish or meat in a skillet, you drop in a knob of butter and a smattering of aromatics and then repeatedly spoon the hot, foaming mixture over the top of the protein. But it's not just good theater. The butter browns, producing hundreds of new flavor compounds, and it picks up dozens more from the aromatics. When the flavorful hot fat hits the surface of the fish it encourages deep browning. Finally, all it takes to turn this aromatic cooking medium into a luxurious sauce is a squeeze of a lemon and a sprinkle of salt."

—Dan

Relish

- ½ cup pitted brine-cured green olives, chopped coarse
- ½ cup toasted slivered almonds
- 1 small garlic clove, minced
- 1 teaspoon grated zest plus ¼ cup juice from 1 large orange
- ¼ cup extra-virgin olive oil
- ¼ cup minced fresh mint
- 2 teaspoons white wine vinegar
- Cayenne pepper

Sea Bass

- 4 (4- to 6-ounce) skinless sea bass fillets, 1 to 1½ inches thick
- ½ teaspoon sugar
- 1 tablespoon extra-virgin olive oil

1. For the relish: Adjust oven rack to middle position and heat oven to 425 degrees. Pulse olives, nuts, garlic, and orange zest in food processor until finely chopped, 10 to 12 pulses. Transfer to bowl and stir in orange juice, oil, mint, and vinegar. Season with salt and cayenne to taste. Set aside.

2. For the sea bass: Pat sea bass dry with paper towels, season with salt and pepper, and sprinkle sugar evenly on 1 side of each fillet.

3. Heat oil in 12-inch ovensafe skillet over medium-high heat until just smoking. Place sea bass sugared side down in skillet and press lightly to ensure even contact with skillet. Cook until browned on first side, about 2 minutes. Gently flip sea bass using 2 spatulas, transfer skillet to oven, and roast until fish flakes apart when gently prodded with paring knife and registers 140 degrees, 7 to 10 minutes. Serve with relish.

Sautéed Tilapia with Chive-Lemon Miso Butter

Serves 4 • Total Time: 45 minutes

Why This Recipe Works Most tilapia is responsibly raised and features moist, firm flesh with a clean, mild taste. We quickly cooked our tilapia in a nonstick skillet over high heat to maximize flavorful browning without overcooking and drying out the fillets. We found that this fish is firm and resilient enough to cook over aggressive heat without falling apart. Dividing each fillet into a thick and a thin portion and sautéing them separately allowed for more precise cooking and even browning. The fish was top-notch with just a squeeze of lemon but we finished it with a chive-lemon miso butter, which added flavor and richness to this lean fish. We also developed an olive oil–based Cilantro Chimichurri that features fresh cilantro and parsley (recipe follows).

You can use fresh or frozen tilapia in this recipe (if frozen, thaw before cooking). There is no need to take the temperature of the thin halves of the fillets; they will be cooked through by the time they are golden brown. We like the delicate flavor of white miso in this recipe, but red miso can be substituted.

Fish

- 4 (5- to 6-ounce) skinless tilapia fillets
- 1 teaspoon kosher salt
- 2 tablespoons vegetable oil

Chive-Lemon Miso Butter

- 2 tablespoons white miso
- 1 teaspoon grated lemon zest plus 2 teaspoons juice
- ⅛ teaspoon pepper
- 4 tablespoons unsalted butter, softened
- 2 tablespoons minced fresh chives

1. For the fish: Place tilapia on cutting board and sprinkle both sides with salt. Let sit at room temperature for 15 minutes.

2. For the chive-lemon miso butter: While tilapia rests, combine miso, lemon zest and juice, and pepper in small bowl. Add butter and stir until fully incorporated. Stir in chives and set aside.

3. Pat tilapia dry with paper towels. Using seam that runs down middle of fillet as guide, cut each fillet in half lengthwise to create 1 thick half and 1 thin half.

4. Heat oil in 12-inch nonstick skillet over high heat until just smoking. Add thick halves of fillets to skillet. Cook, tilting and gently shaking skillet occasionally to distribute oil, until undersides are golden brown, 2 to 3 minutes. Using thin spatula, flip fillets. Cook until second sides are golden brown and tilapia registers 130 to 135 degrees, 2 to 3 minutes. Transfer tilapia to serving platter. Dot tilapia with two-thirds of miso butter.

5. Return skillet to high heat. When oil is just smoking, add thin halves of fillets and cook until undersides are golden brown, about 1 minute. Flip and cook until second sides are golden brown, about 1 minute. Transfer to serving platter. Top thin halves with remaining miso butter and serve.

Two Fillets Are Better than One

"I thought I'd found the best way to perfectly cook thin white fish fillets from all my years making fish meunière, carefully flipping the fillets using two fish spatulas. But then I tried my colleague Steve Dunn's way of sautéing tilapia. First, instead of brining, the fish is salted for just 15 minutes. But the big trick is to simply cut the fillet down the middle into two pieces. The two sides of the fish, the belly and the back, are different thicknesses. This method cooks the thicker pieces first, and they can be flipped easily with just one fish spatula. Then the thinner belly pieces are quickly cooked. Cooking the halves separately allows me to cook the fish to perfection."

—Bridget

Cilantro Chimichurri

Serves 4

Soaking the dried oregano in hot water and vinegar helps soften it and release its flavor. Top the tilapia with ¼ cup of chimichurri before serving, passing the rest separately.

2	tablespoons hot water
2	tablespoons red wine vinegar
1	teaspoon dried oregano
½	cup minced fresh parsley
¼	cup minced fresh cilantro
3	garlic cloves, minced
1	teaspoon kosher salt
¼	teaspoon red pepper flakes
¼	cup extra-virgin olive oil

Combine hot water, vinegar, and oregano in medium bowl; let stand for 5 minutes. Add parsley, cilantro, garlic, salt, and pepper flakes and stir to combine. Whisk in oil until incorporated.

SEASON 22

Pan-Seared Shrimp with Peanuts, Black Pepper, and Lime

Serves 4 • Total Time: 45 minutes

Why This Recipe Works Shrimp are so small that they tend to overcook before they brown. Briefly salting them helped them retain their moisture, and sprinkling sugar on the shrimp just before searing them boosted browning and underscored their sweetness. We arranged the shrimp in a single layer in a cold skillet so that they made even contact with the surface. They heated up gradually with the skillet, so they didn't buckle and thus browned uniformly; slower searing also created a wider window for ensuring that they didn't overcook. Once the shrimp were spotty brown and pink at the edges, we removed them from the heat and quickly turned each one, letting residual heat gently cook them the rest of the way. A flavorful spice mixture came together quickly in the same pan used to cook the shrimp.

We prefer untreated shrimp; if yours are treated with additives such as sodium tripolyphosphate, skip salting in step 1. You can substitute jumbo shrimp (16 to 20 per pound) for the extra-large shrimp; simply increase the cooking time by 1 to 2 minutes. To use the plain seared shrimp in rice bowls or salads, skip steps 2 and 4.

1½	pounds extra-large shrimp (21 to 25 per pound), peeled, deveined, and tails removed
1	teaspoon kosher salt, divided
2	teaspoons coriander seeds
1	teaspoon black peppercorns
1	teaspoon paprika
1	garlic clove, minced
1⅛	teaspoons sugar, divided
⅛	teaspoon red pepper flakes
4	teaspoons vegetable oil, divided
½	cup fresh cilantro leaves and tender stems, chopped
1	tablespoon lime juice, plus lime wedges for serving
3	tablespoons dry-roasted peanuts, chopped coarse

1. Toss shrimp and ½ teaspoon salt together in bowl; set aside for 15 to 30 minutes.

2. Meanwhile, grind coriander seeds and peppercorns using spice grinder or mortar and pestle until coarsely ground. Transfer to small bowl. Add paprika, garlic, 1 teaspoon sugar, pepper flakes, and remaining ½ teaspoon salt and stir until combined.

3. Pat shrimp dry with paper towels. Add 1 tablespoon oil and remaining ⅛ teaspoon sugar to bowl with shrimp and toss to coat. Add shrimp to cold 12-inch nonstick or well-seasoned carbon-steel skillet in single layer and cook over high heat until undersides of shrimp are spotty brown and edges turn pink, 3 to 4 minutes. Remove skillet from heat. Working quickly, use tongs to flip each shrimp; let stand until second side is opaque, about 2 minutes. Transfer shrimp to platter.

4. Add remaining 1 teaspoon oil to now-empty skillet. Add spice mixture and cook over medium heat until fragrant, about 30 seconds. Off heat, return shrimp to skillet. Add cilantro and lime juice and toss to combine. Transfer to platter; sprinkle with peanuts; and serve, passing lime wedges separately.

VARIATIONS

Pan-Seared Shrimp with Fermented Black Beans, Ginger, and Garlic

Omit spice mixture of coriander seeds, peppercorns, paprika, garlic, 1 teaspoon sugar, ½ teaspoon salt, and red pepper flakes. Omit cilantro, lime, and peanuts. Combine 2 scallion whites, sliced thin; 1 tablespoon fermented black beans, rinsed, drained, and chopped coarse; 1 tablespoon grated fresh ginger; 2 minced garlic cloves; and 1 teaspoon sugar in small bowl. In step 4, add black bean mixture to skillet instead of spice mixture and cook until ginger is just starting to brown, about 45 seconds. Add 2 scallion greens, sliced thin on bias; 1 tablespoon soy sauce; and 2 teaspoons toasted sesame oil to skillet with shrimp.

Pan-Seared Shrimp with Pistachio, Cumin, and Parsley

Omit peppercorns and 1 teaspoon sugar from spice mixture. Substitute 1 teaspoon ground cumin for coriander seeds and cayenne pepper for pepper flakes. Substitute 2 tablespoons extra-virgin olive oil for vegetable oil, adding 1 tablespoon to raw shrimp and using remaining 1 tablespoon to cook spice mixture. Reduce cilantro to ¼ cup and add ¼ cup fresh parsley leaves and tender stems, chopped. Substitute lemon juice for lime juice, omit lime wedges, and substitute ¼ cup coarsely chopped toasted pistachios for peanuts.

Deveining Shrimp

1. After removing shell, use paring knife to make shallow cut along back of shrimp so that vein is exposed.

2. Use tip of knife to lift vein out of shrimp. Discard vein by wiping blade against paper towel.

Garlicky Roasted Shrimp with Parsley and Anise

Serves 4 to 6 • **Total Time: 1 hour**

Why This Recipe Works The flavor of shrimp concentrates through roasting, but it's worth it only if the flesh stays moist and tender. First we chose jumbo-size shrimp, which were the least likely to dry out and overcook. Butterflying the shrimp increased their surface area, giving us more room to add flavor. After brining the shrimp briefly to help them hold on to more moisture, we tossed them in a potent mixture of aromatic spices, garlic, herbs, butter, and oil. Then we roasted them under the broiler to get lots of color as quickly as possible, elevating them on a wire rack so they'd brown all over. To further protect them as they cooked and to produce a more deeply roasted flavor, we left their shells on; the sugar- and protein-rich shells browned quickly in the heat of the oven and transferred flavor to the shrimp itself.

Don't be tempted to use smaller shrimp with this cooking technique; they will be overseasoned and prone to overcook.

¼ cup table salt for brining
2 pounds shell-on jumbo shrimp (16 to 20 per pound)
4 tablespoons unsalted butter, melted
¼ cup vegetable oil
6 garlic cloves, minced
1 teaspoon anise seeds
½ teaspoon red pepper flakes
¼ teaspoon pepper
2 tablespoons minced fresh parsley
Lemon wedges

1. Dissolve salt in 1 quart cold water in large container. Using kitchen shears or sharp paring knife, cut through shell of shrimp and devein but do not remove shell. Using paring knife, continue to cut shrimp ½ inch deep, taking care not to cut in half completely. Submerge shrimp in brine, cover, and refrigerate for 15 minutes.

2. Adjust oven rack 4 inches from broiler element and heat broiler. Combine melted butter, oil, garlic, anise seeds, pepper flakes, and pepper in large bowl. Remove shrimp from brine and pat dry with paper towels. Add shrimp and parsley to butter mixture; toss well, making sure butter mixture gets into interior of shrimp. Arrange shrimp in single layer on wire rack set in rimmed baking sheet.

3. Broil shrimp until opaque and shells are beginning to brown, 2 to 4 minutes, rotating sheet halfway through broiling. Flip shrimp and continue to broil until second side is opaque and shells are beginning to brown, 2 to 4 minutes longer, rotating sheet halfway through broiling. Transfer shrimp to serving platter and serve immediately, passing lemon wedges separately.

VARIATIONS

Garlicky Roasted Shrimp with Cilantro and Lime
Annatto powder, also called achiote, can be found with the Latin American foods at your supermarket. An equal amount of paprika can be substituted.

Omit butter and increase vegetable oil to ½ cup. Omit anise seeds and pepper. Add 2 teaspoons lightly crushed coriander seeds, 2 teaspoons grated lime zest, and 1 teaspoon annatto powder to oil mixture in step 2. Substitute ¼ cup minced fresh cilantro for parsley and lime wedges for lemon wedges.

Garlicky Roasted Shrimp with Cumin, Ginger, and Sesame
Omit butter and increase vegetable oil to ½ cup. Decrease garlic to 2 cloves and omit anise seeds and pepper. Add 2 teaspoons toasted sesame oil, 1½ teaspoons grated fresh ginger, and 1 teaspoon cumin seeds to oil mixture in step 2. Substitute 2 thinly sliced scallion greens for parsley and omit lemon wedges.

SEASON 16

Crispy Salt and Pepper Shrimp

Serves 4 to 6   •   Total Time: 1½ hours

Why This Recipe Works   In this traditional Chinese dish, shell-on shrimp are seasoned and flash-fried until the meat is plump and the shells are as deliciously crispy as fried chicken skin. To keep our shell-on, deep-fried salt and pepper shrimp shells crisp and crunchy rather than tough, we employed several tricks. First, we chose shrimp that were not overly large (31 to 40 per pound), which ensured that the shells were thinner relative to those on more jumbo specimens. Next, we coated them in a thin layer of cornstarch to dry out their shells, which helped make them brittle upon frying. Then we cooked them in small batches in very hot oil, which drove off any remaining water in the shells. To season the shrimp and keep them moist, we tossed them with salt and a little rice wine and let them sit briefly before dredging and frying. For an extra jolt of spiciness, we also dredged and fried a couple of thinly sliced jalapeños. And to give the dish lots of depth, we added black peppercorns, Sichuan peppercorns, cayenne, and sugar to the coating and fried more of the same with ginger and garlic to make a flavorful paste. Finally, we tossed the shrimp in the aromatic paste to unify the dish.

In this recipe the shrimp are meant to be eaten shell and all. To ensure that the shells fry up crisp, avoid using shrimp that are overly large or jumbo. We prefer 31- to 40-count shrimp, but 26- to 30-count may be substituted. Serve with steamed rice.

- 1½ pounds shell-on shrimp (31 to 40 per pound)
- 2 tablespoons Shaoxing wine or dry sherry
- 1½ teaspoons kosher salt, divided
- 2½ teaspoons black peppercorns
- 2 teaspoons Sichuan peppercorns
- 2 teaspoons sugar
- ¼ teaspoon cayenne pepper
- 1 quart vegetable oil, for frying
- 5 tablespoons cornstarch, divided
- 2 jalapeño chiles, stemmed, seeded, and sliced into ⅛-inch-thick rings
- 3 garlic cloves, minced
- 1 tablespoon grated fresh ginger
- 2 scallions, sliced thin on bias
- ¼ head iceberg lettuce, shredded (1½ cups)

1. Adjust oven rack to upper-middle position and heat oven to 225 degrees. Toss shrimp, Shaoxing wine, and 1 teaspoon salt together in large bowl and set aside for 10 to 15 minutes.

2. Grind black peppercorns and Sichuan peppercorns in spice grinder or mortar and pestle until coarsely ground. Transfer peppercorns to small bowl and stir in sugar and cayenne.

3. Heat oil in large Dutch oven over medium heat until oil registers 385 degrees. While oil is heating, drain shrimp and pat dry with paper towels. Transfer shrimp to bowl, add 3 tablespoons cornstarch and 1 tablespoon peppercorn mixture, and toss until well combined.

4. Carefully add one-third of shrimp to oil and fry, stirring occasionally to keep shrimp from sticking together, until light brown, 2 to 3 minutes. Using wire skimmer or slotted spoon, transfer shrimp to paper towel–lined plate. Once paper towels absorb any excess oil, transfer shrimp to wire rack set in rimmed baking sheet and place in oven. Return oil to 385 degrees and repeat in 2 more batches, tossing each batch thoroughly with coating mixture before frying.

5. Toss jalapeño rings and remaining 2 tablespoons cornstarch in medium bowl. Shaking off excess cornstarch, carefully add jalapeño rings to oil and fry until crispy, 1 to 2 minutes. Using wire skimmer or slotted spoon, transfer jalapeño rings to paper towel–lined plate. After frying, reserve 2 tablespoons frying oil.

6. Heat reserved oil in 12-inch skillet over medium-high heat until shimmering. Add garlic, ginger, and remaining peppercorn mixture and cook, stirring occasionally, until mixture is fragrant and just beginning to brown, about 45 seconds. Add shrimp, scallions, and remaining ½ teaspoon salt and toss to coat. Line platter with lettuce. Transfer shrimp to platter, sprinkle with jalapeño rings, and serve immediately.

SEASON 10

Shrimp Tempura

Serves 4 • Total Time: 50 minutes

Why This Recipe Works A few attempts at making tempura made us understand why some Japanese chefs devote their entire careers to this one technique. Success hinges almost entirely on the batter—which is very hard to get right. We wanted perfectly cooked shrimp tempura— light, crisp, and so fresh-tasting that it barely seemed fried. We settled on using the largest shrimp available, since it's easy to overcook small shrimp, and used a large Dutch oven, the test kitchen's preferred deep-frying vessel. Cooking the tempura in 400-degree oil also helped limit grease absorption. To prevent the batter from clumping on the inside curl of the shrimp, we made two shallow cuts on the underside of its flesh. For the batter, we replaced a bit of the flour with cornstarch to improve the structure and lightness. For a super tender coating, we used a combination of seltzer and vodka instead of the traditional tap water.

Do not omit the vodka; it is critical for a crisp coating. For safety, use a Dutch oven with a capacity of at least 7 quarts. Be sure to begin mixing the batter when the oil reaches 385 degrees (the final temperature should reach 400 degrees). It is important to maintain a high oil temperature throughout cooking. If you are unable to find colossal shrimp (8 to 12 per pound), jumbo (16 to 20 per pound) or extra-large (21 to 25 per pound) may be substituted. Fry smaller shrimp in three batches, reducing the cooking time to 1½ to 2 minutes per batch.

3 quarts peanut or vegetable oil

1½ pounds colossal shrimp (8 to 12 per pound), peeled and deveined, tails left on

1½ cups (7½ ounces) all-purpose flour

½ cup (2 ounces) cornstarch

1 cup vodka

1 large egg

1 cup seltzer water

1 recipe Scallion Dipping Sauce (recipe follows)

1. Adjust oven rack to upper-middle position and heat oven to 200 degrees. In large Dutch oven, heat oil over high heat to 385 degrees, 18 to 22 minutes.

2. While oil heats, make 2 shallow cuts about ¼ inch deep and 1 inch apart on underside of each shrimp. Whisk flour and cornstarch together in large bowl. Whisk vodka and egg together in second large bowl, then whisk in seltzer water.

3. When oil reaches 385 degrees, whisk vodka mixture into bowl with flour mixture until just combined (it is OK if small lumps remain). Submerge half of shrimp in batter. Using tongs, remove shrimp from batter one at a time, allowing excess batter to drip off, and carefully place in oil (temperature should now be at 400 degrees). Fry, stirring with chopstick or wooden skewer to prevent sticking, until light brown, 2 to 3 minutes. Using slotted spoon, transfer shrimp to paper towel–lined plate and season with kosher salt. Once paper towels absorb excess oil, transfer shrimp to wire rack set over rimmed baking sheet and place in oven to keep warm.

4. Return oil to 400 degrees, about 4 minutes, then repeat with remaining shrimp. Serve with dipping sauce.

Scallion Dipping Sauce
Makes ¾ cup • Total Time: 10 minutes

¼ cup soy sauce

2 tablespoons rice vinegar

2 tablespoons mirin or sweet sherry

2 tablespoons water

1 teaspoon chili oil (optional)

½ teaspoon toasted sesame oil

1 scallion, minced

Combine all ingredients in small bowl and set aside. (Sauce can be refrigerated in airtight container for up to 24 hours.)

SEASON 11

Greek-Style Shrimp with Tomatoes and Feta

Serves 4 to 6 • Total Time: 1 hour

Why This Recipe Works We can think of few examples where the unlikely combination of seafood and cheese marry as well as in Greece's shrimp saganaki. In this dish, sweet, briny shrimp are covered with a garlic-and-herb-accented tomato sauce and topped with crumbles of creamy, salty feta cheese. We set out to develop a foolproof version of this dish—one that is perfectly cooked and captures the bold and exuberant essence of Greek cuisine. We started with the tomato sauce. Canned diced tomatoes along with sautéed onion and garlic provided our base. Dry white wine added acidity. Ouzo, the slightly sweet anise-flavored Greek liqueur, added welcome complexity when we simmered it in the sauce. While the shrimp are typically layered with the tomato sauce and feta and baked, we found this method lacking. Since this should be a quick and easy dish, we opted to cook the shrimp right in the sauce; adding the shrimp raw to the sauce helped infuse them with the sauce's bright flavor. And for even more flavor, we marinated the shrimp with olive oil, ouzo, garlic, and lemon zest first while we made the sauce. Final touches included a generous sprinkling of feta over the sauced shrimp as well as a scattering of chopped fresh dill.

This recipe works equally well with either jumbo shrimp (16 to 20 per pound) or extra-large shrimp (21 to 25 per pound); the cooking times in step 3 will vary slightly. Serve with crusty bread for soaking up the sauce.

1½ pounds shrimp, peeled and deveined,
   tails left on, if desired
¼ cup extra-virgin olive oil, divided
3 tablespoons ouzo, divided
5 garlic cloves, minced, divided
1 teaspoon grated lemon zest
½ teaspoon table salt, divided
⅛ teaspoon pepper
1 small onion, chopped
½ red bell pepper, chopped
½ green bell pepper, chopped
½ teaspoon red pepper flakes
1 (28-ounce) can diced tomatoes, drained with
   ⅓ cup juice reserved
¼ cup dry white wine
2 tablespoons coarsely chopped fresh parsley
6 ounces feta cheese, preferably sheep's and/or
   goat's milk, crumbled (about 1½ cups)
2 tablespoons chopped fresh dill

1. Toss shrimp, 1 tablespoon oil, 1 tablespoon ouzo, 1 teaspoon garlic, lemon zest, ¼ teaspoon salt, and pepper in small bowl until well combined. Set aside while preparing sauce.

2. Heat 2 tablespoons oil in 12-inch skillet over medium heat until shimmering. Add onion, red and green bell peppers, and remaining ¼ teaspoon salt and stir to combine. Cover skillet and cook, stirring occasionally, until vegetables release their moisture, 3 to 5 minutes. Uncover and continue to cook, stirring occasionally, until moisture cooks off and vegetables have softened, about 5 minutes longer. Add pepper flakes and remaining garlic and cook until fragrant, about 1 minute. Add tomatoes and reserved juice, wine, and remaining 2 tablespoons ouzo; increase heat to medium-high and bring to simmer. Reduce heat to medium and simmer, stirring occasionally, until flavors have melded and sauce is slightly thickened (sauce should not be completely dry), 5 to 8 minutes. Stir in parsley and season with salt and pepper to taste.

3. Reduce heat to medium-low and add shrimp along with any accumulated liquid to pan; stir to coat and distribute evenly. Cover and cook, stirring occasionally, until shrimp are opaque throughout, 6 to 9 minutes for extra-large shrimp or 7 to 11 minutes for jumbo shrimp, adjusting heat as needed to maintain bare simmer. Remove pan from heat and sprinkle evenly with feta. Drizzle remaining 1 tablespoon oil evenly over top and sprinkle with dill. Serve immediately.

Shrimp Scampi

Serves 4 • Total Time: 1¼ hours

Why This Recipe Works Our ultimate shrimp scampi recipe uses a few test kitchen tricks to ensure flavorful and well-cooked shrimp, as well as a creamy and robust sauce to pair them with. First, we brined the shrimp in salt and sugar to season them throughout and to keep them moist and juicy. Then, because sautéing the shrimp led to uneven cooking, we instead poached them in wine, a gentler approach that was more consistent. To get more shrimp flavor into the sauce, we didn't waste the shells; instead, we put them to use as the base of a stock and added wine and thyme. The key was to let it simmer for only 5 minutes, as a longer cooking time resulted in less flavor. For potent but clean garlic flavor, we used a generous amount of sliced, rather than minced, garlic. Just a teaspoon of cornstarch at the end of cooking kept the sauce emulsified and silky.

Extra-large shrimp (21 to 25 per pound) can be substituted for jumbo shrimp. If you use them, reduce the cooking time in step 3 by 1 to 2 minutes. We prefer untreated shrimp, but if your shrimp are treated with sodium or preservatives like sodium tripolyphosphate, skip the brining in step 1 and add ¼ teaspoon of salt to the sauce in step 4. Serve with crusty bread.

- 3 tablespoons table salt for brining
- 2 tablespoons sugar for brining
- 1½ pounds jumbo shrimp (16 to 20 per pound), peeled, deveined, and tails removed, shells reserved
- 2 tablespoons extra-virgin olive oil, divided
- 1 cup dry white wine
- 4 sprigs fresh thyme
- 3 tablespoons lemon juice, plus lemon wedges for serving
- 1 teaspoon cornstarch
- 8 garlic cloves, sliced thin
- ½ teaspoon red pepper flakes
- ¼ teaspoon pepper
- 4 tablespoons unsalted butter, cut into ½-inch pieces
- 1 tablespoon chopped fresh parsley

1. Dissolve salt and sugar in 1 quart cold water in large container. Submerge shrimp in brine, cover, and refrigerate for 15 minutes. Remove shrimp from brine and pat dry with paper towels.

2. Heat 1 tablespoon oil in 12-inch skillet over high heat until shimmering. Add shrimp shells and cook, stirring frequently, until they begin to turn spotty brown and skillet starts to brown, 2 to 4 minutes. Remove skillet from heat and carefully add wine and thyme sprigs. When bubbling subsides, return skillet to medium heat and simmer gently, stirring occasionally, for 5 minutes. Strain mixture through colander set over large bowl. Discard shells and reserve liquid (you should have about ⅔ cup). Wipe out skillet with paper towels.

3. Combine lemon juice and cornstarch in small bowl. Heat remaining 1 tablespoon oil, garlic, pepper flakes, and pepper in now-empty skillet over medium-low heat, stirring occasionally, until garlic is fragrant and just beginning to brown at edges, 3 to 5 minutes. Add reserved wine mixture, increase heat to high, and bring to simmer. Reduce heat to medium, add shrimp, cover, and cook, stirring occasionally, until shrimp are just opaque, 5 to 7 minutes. Remove skillet from heat and, using slotted spoon, transfer shrimp to bowl.

4. Return skillet to medium heat, add lemon juice–cornstarch mixture, and cook until slightly thickened, about 1 minute. Remove from heat and whisk in butter and parsley until combined. Return shrimp and any accumulated juices to skillet and toss to combine. Serve, passing lemon wedges separately.

SEASON 19

Moqueca

Serves 6 • Total Time: 1¼ hours

Why This Recipe Works For a bright, fresh, and filling version of this traditional Brazilian stew, we started with the seafood. Cod and shrimp made for a nice balance of flavor and texture, and both were easy to find. After tossing the seafood with garlic, salt, and pepper, we looked to the other components of the stew. To balance the richness and sweetness of the coconut milk with the flavorful aromatics, we blended the onion, tomatoes, and a portion of the cilantro in the food processor until they had the texture of a slightly chunky salsa, which added body to the stew. We kept the bell peppers diced for contrasting texture and bite. To properly cook the seafood, we brought the broth to a boil to make sure the pot was superhot, added the seafood and lime juice, covered the pot, and removed it from the heat, allowing the seafood to gently cook in the residual heat. To finish our moqueca, we added more cilantro and a couple of tablespoons of homemade pepper sauce, which elevated the stew with its bright, vinegary tang.

Pickled hot cherry peppers are usually sold jarred, next to the pickles or jarred roasted red peppers at the supermarket. Haddock or other firm-fleshed, flaky whitefish may be substituted for cod. We prefer untreated shrimp, but if your shrimp are treated with sodium, do not add salt to the shrimp in step 2. Our favorite coconut milk is made by Aroy-D. Serve with steamed white rice.

Pepper Sauce

- 4 pickled hot cherry peppers (3 ounces)
- ½ onion, chopped coarse
- ¼ cup extra-virgin olive oil
- ⅛ teaspoon sugar

Stew

- 1 pound large shrimp (26 to 30 per pound), peeled, deveined, and tails removed
- 1 pound skinless cod fillets (¾ to 1 inch thick), cut into 1½-inch pieces
- 3 garlic cloves, minced
- 1½ teaspoons table salt, divided
- ¼ teaspoon pepper
- 1 onion, chopped coarse
- 1 (14.5-ounce) can whole peeled tomatoes
- ¾ cup chopped fresh cilantro, divided
- 2 tablespoons extra-virgin olive oil
- 1 red bell pepper, stemmed, seeded, and cut into ½-inch pieces
- 1 green bell pepper, stemmed, seeded, and cut into ½-inch pieces
- 1 (14-ounce) can coconut milk
- 2 tablespoons lime juice

1. For the pepper sauce: Process all ingredients in food processor until smooth, about 30 seconds, scraping down sides of bowl as needed. Season with salt to taste and transfer to separate bowl. Rinse out processor bowl.

2. For the stew: Toss shrimp and cod with garlic, ½ teaspoon salt, and pepper in bowl and set aside. Process onion, tomatoes and their juice, and ¼ cup cilantro in food processor until finely chopped and mixture has texture of pureed salsa, about 30 seconds.

3. Heat oil in large Dutch oven over medium-high heat until shimmering. Add red and green bell peppers and ½ teaspoon salt and cook, stirring frequently, until softened, 5 to 7 minutes. Add onion-tomato mixture and remaining ½ teaspoon salt. Reduce heat to medium and cook, stirring frequently, until puree has reduced and thickened slightly, 3 to 5 minutes (pot should not be dry).

4. Increase heat to high, stir in coconut milk, and bring to boil (mixture should be bubbling across entire surface). Add seafood mixture and lime juice and stir to evenly distribute seafood, making sure all pieces are submerged in liquid. Cover pot and remove from heat. Let stand until shrimp and cod are opaque and just cooked through, 15 minutes.

5. Gently stir in 2 tablespoons pepper sauce and remaining ½ cup cilantro, being careful not to break up cod too much. Season with salt and pepper to taste. Serve, passing remaining pepper sauce separately.

Spanish-Style Toasted Pasta with Shrimp

Serves 4 • Total Time: 1½ hours

Why This Recipe Works Paella may be one of the biggest stars of Spanish cooking, but there's another related dish equally deserving of raves: fideuà. This richly flavored dish swaps the rice for thin noodles that are typically toasted until nut-brown before being cooked in a garlicky, tomatoey stock loaded with seafood. Traditional recipes for fideuà can take several hours to prepare. We wanted to speed up the process but keep the deep flavors of the classic recipes. To replace the slow-cooked fish stock of the classics, we made a quick shrimp stock using the shrimp's shells, a combination of chicken broth and water, and a bay leaf. We also streamlined the sofrito, the aromatic base common in Spanish cooking, by finely mincing the onion and using canned tomatoes (instead of fresh), which helped the recipe components soften and brown more quickly. The final tweak to our recipe was boosting the flavor of the shrimp by quickly marinating them in olive oil, garlic, salt, and pepper.

In step 5, if your skillet is not broiler-safe, once the pasta is tender transfer the mixture to a broiler-safe 13 by 9-inch baking dish lightly coated with olive oil; scatter the shrimp over the pasta and stir them in to partially submerge. Broil and serve as directed. Serve this dish with lemon wedges and Aioli (recipe follows), stirring it into individual portions at the table.

3 tablespoons plus 2 teaspoons extra-virgin olive oil, divided

3 garlic cloves, minced, divided

¾ teaspoon table salt, divided

⅛ plus ½ teaspoon pepper, divided

1½ pounds extra-large shrimp (21 to 25 per pound), peeled and deveined, shells reserved

2¾ cups water

1 cup chicken broth

1 bay leaf

8 ounces spaghettini or thin spaghetti, broken into 1- to 2-inch lengths

1 onion, chopped fine

1 (14.5-ounce) can diced tomatoes, drained and chopped fine

1 teaspoon paprika

1 teaspoon smoked paprika

½ teaspoon anchovy paste

¼ cup dry white wine

1 tablespoon chopped fresh parsley

Lemon wedges

1 recipe Aioli (optional) (recipe follows)

1. Combine 1 tablespoon oil, 1 teaspoon garlic, ¼ teaspoon salt, and ⅛ teaspoon pepper in medium bowl. Add shrimp, toss to coat, and refrigerate until ready to use.

2. Place reserved shrimp shells, water, broth, and bay leaf in medium bowl. Cover and microwave until liquid is hot and shells have turned pink, about 6 minutes. Set aside until ready to use.

3. Toss spaghettini and 2 teaspoons oil in broiler-safe 12-inch skillet until spaghettini is evenly coated. Toast spaghettini over medium-high heat, stirring frequently, until browned and nutty in aroma (spaghettini should be color of peanut butter), 6 to 10 minutes. Transfer spaghettini to bowl. Wipe out skillet with paper towel.

4. Heat remaining 2 tablespoons oil in now-empty skillet over medium-high heat until shimmering. Add onion and ¼ teaspoon salt; cook, stirring frequently, until onion is softened and beginning to brown around edges, 4 to 6 minutes. Add tomatoes and cook, stirring occasionally, until mixture is thick, dry, and slightly darkened in color, 4 to 6 minutes. Reduce heat to medium and add paprika, smoked paprika, anchovy paste, and remaining garlic. Cook until fragrant, about 1½ minutes. Add spaghettini and stir to combine. Adjust oven rack 5 to 6 inches from broiler element and heat broiler.

5. Pour shrimp broth through fine-mesh strainer into skillet. Add wine, remaining ¼ teaspoon salt, and remaining ½ teaspoon pepper and stir well. Increase heat to medium-high and bring to simmer. Cook uncovered, stirring occasionally, until liquid is slightly thickened and spaghettini is just tender,

8 to 10 minutes. Scatter shrimp over spaghettini and stir shrimp into spaghettini to partially submerge. Transfer skillet to oven and broil until shrimp are opaque and surface of spaghettini is dry with crisped, browned spots, 5 to 7 minutes. Remove from oven and let stand, uncovered, for 5 minutes. Sprinkle with parsley and serve immediately, passing lemon wedges and aioli, if using, separately.

VARIATION

Spanish-Style Toasted Pasta with Shrimp and Clams
Reduce shrimp to 1 pound and water to 2½ cups. In step 5, cook pasta until almost tender, about 6 minutes. Scatter 1½ pounds scrubbed littleneck or cherrystone clams over pasta; cover skillet; and cook until clams begin to open, about 3 minutes. Scatter shrimp over pasta, stir to partially submerge shrimp and clams, and proceed with recipe.

ACCOMPANIMENT

Aioli
Makes ¾ cup • Total Time: 10 minutes

2 large egg yolks

4 teaspoons lemon juice

1 garlic clove, minced to paste

¼ teaspoon table salt

⅛ teaspoon sugar

½ cup vegetable oil

¼ cup extra-virgin olive oil

In large bowl, combine egg yolks, lemon juice, garlic, ¼ teaspoon salt, and sugar. Whisking constantly, very slowly drizzle oils into egg mixture until thick and creamy. Season with salt and white pepper to taste.

Snapping Long Strands of Pasta

1. Loosely fold 4 ounces of spaghettini in clean dish towel, keeping pasta flat, not bunched. Position so that 1 to 2 inches of pasta rests on counter and remainder of pasta hangs off edge.

2. Pressing bundle against counter, press down on long end of towel to break strands into pieces, sliding bundle back over edge after each break.

Stir-Fried Shrimp with Snow Peas and Red Bell Pepper in Hot and Sour Sauce

Serves 4 • **Total Time: 40 minutes, plus 30 minutes marinating**

Why This Recipe Works Stir-fries are typically cooked over high heat to sear the food and develop flavor. This works well with chicken, beef, and pork, but delicate shrimp can turn to rubber very quickly. We wanted a stir-fry with plump, juicy, well-seasoned shrimp in a balanced, flavorful sauce. We wondered if browning was really necessary. Abandoning the high-heat method, we turned down the burner to medium-low and gently parcooked a batch of shrimp, removed them from the skillet, then turned up the heat to sear the vegetables, sauté the aromatics, and finish cooking the shrimp with the sauce. This worked beautifully. Reversing the approach—cooking the veggies followed by the aromatics over high heat, then turning the heat down before adding the shrimp—made the process more efficient. We reduced our sweet and spicy sauce so that it tightly adhered to the shellfish.

| *Serve with white rice.*

- 1 pound extra-large shrimp (21 to 25 per pound), peeled, deveined, and tails removed
- 3 tablespoons vegetable oil, divided
- 1 tablespoon grated fresh ginger
- 2 garlic cloves (1 minced, 1 sliced thin)
- ½ teaspoon table salt
- 3 tablespoons sugar
- 3 tablespoons white vinegar
- 1 tablespoon chili-garlic sauce
- 1 tablespoon Shaoxing wine or dry sherry
- 1 tablespoon ketchup
- 2 teaspoons toasted sesame oil
- 2 teaspoons cornstarch
- 1 teaspoon soy sauce
- 1 large shallot, sliced thin (about ⅓ cup)
- 8 ounces snow peas or sugar snap peas, strings removed
- 1 red bell pepper, stemmed, seeded, and cut into ¾-inch dice

1. Combine shrimp with 1 tablespoon vegetable oil, ginger, minced garlic, and salt in medium bowl. Let shrimp marinate at room temperature for 30 minutes.

2. Meanwhile, whisk sugar, vinegar, chili-garlic sauce, Shaoxing wine, ketchup, sesame oil, cornstarch, and soy sauce in small bowl. Combine sliced garlic with shallot in second small bowl.

3. Heat 1 tablespoon vegetable oil in 14-inch flat-bottomed wok or 12-inch nonstick skillet over high heat until just smoking. Add snow peas and bell pepper and cook, tossing slowly but constantly, until vegetables begin to brown, 1½ to 2 minutes. Transfer vegetables to medium bowl.

4. Add remaining 1 tablespoon vegetable oil to now-empty skillet and heat until just smoking. Add garlic-shallot mixture and cook, stirring frequently, until just beginning to brown, about 30 seconds. Reduce heat to medium-low; add shrimp; and cook, stirring frequently, until shrimp are light pink on both sides, 1 to 1½ minutes. Whisk soy sauce mixture to recombine and add to skillet; return to high heat and cook, stirring constantly, until sauce is thickened and shrimp are cooked through, 1 to 2 minutes. Return vegetables to skillet, toss to combine, and serve.

Shrimp Pad Thai

Serves 4 • Total Time: 1½ hours

Why This Recipe Works Thai cuisine is known for its symphony of salty, sweet, and sour flavors, and this hugely popular street food is no different. In our version, we achieved those flavors with a careful balance of fish sauce, sugar, and tamarind juice concentrate. Lime juice squeezed over the finished dish, along with a quick-to-make chile vinegar, added even more tangy kick. Soaking rice noodles in boiling water, versus cooking them in the hot water, prevented the delicate strands from getting too soft. Shrimp and egg bulked up the dish while bean sprouts, scallion greens, and peanuts added crunch. Finally, we pickled regular red radishes in a nod to the traditional addition of preserved daikon, and we created our own faux dried shrimp by microwaving and then frying small pieces of fresh shrimp.

> *Since pad thai cooks very quickly, prepare everything before you begin to cook. Use the time during which the radishes and noodles soak to prepare the other ingredients. We recommend using a tamarind juice concentrate made in Thailand in this recipe. If you cannot find tamarind, substitute 1½ tablespoons lime juice and 1½ tablespoons water and omit the lime wedges.*

Chile Vinegar
- ⅓ cup distilled white vinegar
- 1 serrano chile, stemmed and sliced into thin rings

Stir-Fry
- ½ teaspoon table salt for pickling
- ¼ teaspoon sugar for pickling
- 2 radishes, trimmed and cut into 1½-inch by ¼-inch matchsticks
- 8 ounces (¼-inch-wide) rice noodles
- 3 tablespoons plus 2 teaspoons vegetable oil, divided
- ¼ cup fish sauce
- 3 tablespoons tamarind juice concentrate
- 3 tablespoons plus ⅛ teaspoon sugar, divided
- 1 pound large shrimp (26 to 30 per pound), peeled and deveined
- ⅛ teaspoon table salt
- 4 scallions, white and light green parts minced, dark green parts cut into 1-inch lengths
- 1 garlic clove, minced
- 4 large eggs, beaten
- 4 ounces (2 cups) bean sprouts
- ¼ cup roasted unsalted peanuts, chopped coarse
  Lime wedges

1. For the chile vinegar: Combine vinegar and chile in bowl and let stand at room temperature for at least 15 minutes.

2. For the stir-fry: Combine ¼ cup water, ½ teaspoon salt, and ¼ teaspoon sugar in small bowl. Microwave until steaming, about 30 seconds. Add radishes and let stand for 15 minutes. Drain and pat dry with paper towels.

3. Bring 6 cups water to boil. Place noodles in large bowl. Pour boiling water over noodles. Stir, then let soak until noodles are almost tender, about 8 minutes, stirring once halfway through soaking. Drain noodles and rinse with cold water. Drain noodles well, then toss with 2 teaspoons oil.

4. Combine fish sauce, tamarind concentrate, and 3 tablespoons sugar in bowl and whisk until sugar is dissolved. Set sauce aside.

5. Remove tails from 4 shrimp. Cut shrimp in half lengthwise, then cut each half into ½-inch pieces. Toss shrimp pieces with salt and remaining ⅛ teaspoon sugar. Arrange pieces in single layer on large plate and microwave at 50 percent power until shrimp are dried and have reduced in size by half, 4 to 5 minutes. (Check halfway through microwaving and separate any pieces that may have stuck together.)

6. Heat 2 teaspoons oil in 12-inch nonstick skillet over medium heat until shimmering. Add dried shrimp and cook, stirring frequently, until golden brown and crispy, 3 to 5 minutes. Transfer to large bowl.

7. Heat 1 teaspoon oil in now-empty skillet over medium heat until shimmering. Add minced scallions and garlic and cook, stirring constantly, until garlic is golden brown, about 1 minute. Transfer to bowl with dried shrimp.

8. Heat 2 teaspoons oil in now-empty skillet over high heat until just smoking. Add remaining whole shrimp and spread into even layer. Cook, without stirring, until shrimp turn opaque and brown around edges, 2 to 3 minutes, flipping halfway through cooking. Push shrimp to sides of skillet. Add 2 teaspoons oil to center, then add eggs to center. Using rubber spatula, stir eggs gently and cook until set but still wet. Stir eggs into shrimp and continue to cook, breaking up large pieces of egg, until eggs are fully cooked, 30 to 60 seconds longer. Transfer shrimp-egg mixture to bowl with scallion-garlic mixture and dried shrimp.

9. Heat remaining 2 teaspoons oil in now-empty skillet over high heat until just smoking. Add noodles and sauce and toss with tongs to coat. Cook, stirring and tossing often, until noodles are tender and have absorbed sauce, 2 to 4 minutes. Transfer noodles to bowl with shrimp mixture. Add 2 teaspoons chile vinegar, drained radishes, scallion greens, and bean sprouts and toss to combine.

10. Transfer to platter and sprinkle with peanuts. Serve immediately, passing lime wedges and remaining chile vinegar separately.

Shrimp Salad

Serves 4 • Total Time: 35 minutes

Why This Recipe Works Most shrimp salads drown in a sea of mayonnaise, in part to hide the rubbery, flavorless shrimp. We wanted perfectly cooked shrimp without the extra work of grilling, roasting, or sautéing. And we wanted to coat them with a light yet creamy deli-style dressing. Since overcooking is the cause of rubbery shrimp, we found that starting them in cold water (with lemon, herbs, pepper, sugar, and salt) and then cooking them over gentle heat resulted in tender shrimp. The longer cooking time infused the shrimp with the flavors of the poaching liquid. We didn't want to mask these tender, flavorful shrimp with too much dressing, so we scaled back the mayonnaise to a modest amount. Celery added a nice crunch, and shallot, herbs, and lemon juice perked up and rounded out the flavors.

This recipe can also be prepared with large shrimp (31 to 40 per pound); the cooking time will be 1 to 2 minutes shorter. The shrimp can be cooked up to 24 hours in advance, but hold off on dressing the salad until ready to serve. The recipe can be easily doubled; cook the shrimp in a 7-quart Dutch oven and increase the cooking time to 12 to 14 minutes. Serve the salad spooned over salad greens or on buttered and grilled buns.

1 pound extra-large shrimp (21 to 25 per pound), peeled and deveined

5 tablespoons lemon juice (2 to 3 lemons), spent halves reserved

5 sprigs fresh parsley plus 1 teaspoon minced fresh parsley

3 sprigs fresh tarragon plus 1 teaspoon minced fresh tarragon

1 teaspoon whole black peppercorns

1 tablespoon sugar for cooking shrimp

1 teaspoon table salt for cooking shrimp

¼ cup mayonnaise

1 small celery rib, minced (about ⅓ cup)

1 small shallot, minced (about 1 tablespoon)

1. Combine shrimp, ¼ cup lemon juice, reserved lemon halves, parsley sprigs, tarragon sprigs, whole peppercorns, sugar, and 1 teaspoon salt with 2 cups cold water in medium saucepan. Place saucepan over medium heat and cook shrimp, stirring several times, until pink, firm to touch, and centers are no longer translucent, 8 to 10 minutes (water should be just bubbling around edge of pan and register 165 degrees). Remove pan from heat, cover, and let shrimp sit in broth for 2 minutes.

2. Meanwhile, fill medium bowl with ice water. Drain shrimp into colander and discard lemon halves, herbs, and spices. Immediately transfer shrimp to ice water to stop cooking and chill thoroughly, about 3 minutes. Remove shrimp from ice water and pat dry with paper towels.

3. Whisk together mayonnaise, celery, shallot, remaining 1 tablespoon lemon juice, minced parsley, and minced tarragon in medium bowl. Cut shrimp in half lengthwise and then each half into thirds; add shrimp to mayonnaise mixture and toss to combine. Season with salt and pepper to taste, and serve.

Shrimp Salad with Roasted Red Pepper and Basil

This variation is especially good served over bitter greens.

Omit tarragon sprigs from cooking liquid. Replace celery, minced parsley, and minced tarragon with ⅓ cup thinly sliced jarred roasted red peppers, 2 teaspoons rinsed capers, and 3 tablespoons chopped fresh basil.

Shrimp Salad with Avocado and Orange

Avocado and orange are a refreshing addition to this salad.

Omit tarragon sprigs from cooking liquid. Replace celery, minced parsley, and minced tarragon with 4 halved and thinly sliced radishes; 1 large orange, peeled and cut into ½-inch pieces; ½ ripe avocado, cut into ½-inch pieces; and 2 teaspoons minced fresh mint leaves.

SEASON 11

Pan-Seared Scallops

Serves 4 • Total Time: 40 minutes

Why This Recipes Works For restaurant-style pan-seared scallops with golden-brown crusts and tender interiors, we needed to compensate for the weaker heating power of home stovetops. We started with a nonstick skillet so that the browned bits would form a crust on the fish instead of sticking to the skillet. We waited to add the scallops to the skillet until the oil was beginning to smoke, and we cooked them in two batches to avoid cooling down the pan—both steps in the right direction. But it wasn't until we tried a common restaurant technique—butter basting—that our scallops really improved. We seared the scallops in oil on one side and added butter to the skillet after flipping them. (Butter contains milk proteins and sugars that brown rapidly when heated.) We then spooned the foaming butter over the scallops. Waiting to add the butter ensured that it had just enough time to work its browning magic, but not enough time to burn. These scallops rivaled those made on a powerful restaurant range, golden brown on the outside and juicy on the inside.

We strongly recommend purchasing "dry" scallops, which don't contain chemical additives and taste better than "wet" scallops. Dry scallops will look ivory or pinkish;

wet scallops are bright white. If you can find only wet scallops, soak them in a solution of 1 quart cold water, ¼ cup lemon juice, and 2 tablespoons table salt for 30 minutes before proceeding with step 1, and season the scallops with pepper only in step 2. Prepare the sauce (if serving) while the scallops dry (between steps 1 and 2) and keep it warm while cooking them.

1½ pounds large sea scallops, tendons removed
½ teaspoon table salt
¼ teaspoon pepper
2 tablespoons vegetable oil, divided
2 tablespoons unsalted butter, cut into 2 pieces, divided
Lemon wedges or Lemon Browned Butter Sauce (recipe follows)

1. Place scallops on rimmed baking sheet lined with clean dish towel. Place second clean dish towel on top of scallops and press gently on towel to blot liquid. Let scallops sit at room temperature for 10 minutes while towels absorb moisture.

2. Remove second towel and sprinkle scallops on both sides with salt and pepper. Heat 1 tablespoon oil in 12-inch nonstick skillet over high heat until just smoking. Add half of scallops in single layer, flat side down, and cook, without moving, until well browned, 1½ to 2 minutes.

3. Add 1 tablespoon butter to skillet. Using tongs, flip scallops and continue to cook, using large spoon to baste scallops with melted butter, tilting skillet so butter runs to one side, until sides of scallops are firm and centers are opaque, 30 to 90 seconds longer (remove smaller scallops from the pan as they finish cooking).

4. Transfer scallops to large plate and tent with aluminum foil. Wipe out skillet with paper towels and repeat with remaining 1 tablespoon oil, remaining scallops, and remaining 1 tablespoon butter. Serve immediately with lemon wedges or sauce.

Prepping Scallops

Using your fingers, peel away small, crescent-shaped muscle attached to sides of scallop before cooking.

The Well-Cooked Scallop

"There's something really exciting about a well-cooked scallop. It should be sweet and tender on the inside with a golden, thick crust. I used to think that you needed a superpowerful burner to create this idealized version. That is not so. This recipe teaches you a whole series of steps that mean you can achieve this at home even with an underpowered electric stove: Make sure you use untreated scallops, let them drain on a towel for 10 minutes to draw out their moisture, salt them only at the last minute, use plenty of oil, and start cooking over high heat just as the oil first starts to smoke. That's five steps that every good cook can use to achieve a restaurant-quality sear on a whole variety of foods. Beyond that, it teaches butter basting which also supplies you with a gloriously nutty browned butter sauce for serving. You will feel like a master chef making this dish."

—Joe

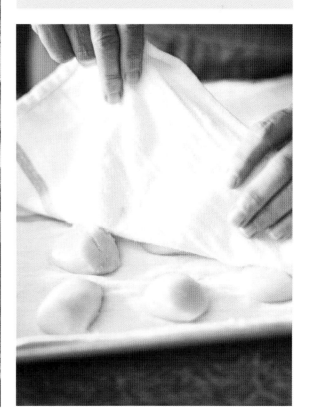

Lemon Browned Butter Sauce

Makes ¼ cup • Total Time: 15 minutes

    4   tablespoons unsalted butter, cut into 4 pieces
    1   small shallot, minced
    1   tablespoon minced fresh parsley
    ½   teaspoon minced fresh thyme
    2   teaspoons lemon juice

Heat butter in small heavy-bottomed saucepan over medium heat and cook, swirling pan constantly, until butter turns dark golden brown and has a nutty aroma, 4 to 5 minutes. Add shallot and cook until fragrant, about 30 seconds. Remove pan from heat and stir in parsley, thyme, and lemon juice. Season with salt and pepper to taste. Cover to keep warm.

SEASON 13

Best Crab Cakes

Serves 4 • Total Time: 1¼ hours, plus 50 minutes soaking and chilling

Why This Recipe Works We wanted to come up with a recipe for crab cakes that were chock-full of sweet, plump meat delicately seasoned and seamlessly held together with a binder that didn't mask the seafood flavor. And we didn't want shopping to be an issue—we wanted our crab cakes to work with either fresh crabmeat or the pasteurized variety found at the supermarket. To highlight and enhance the crabmeat's sweetness, we bound our cakes with a delicate shrimp mousse. Classic components like Old Bay seasoning and lemon juice bolstered the crab's flavor, and panko bread crumbs helped ensure a crisp crust.

> *Either fresh or pasteurized crabmeat can be used in this recipe. With packaged crab, if the meat smells clean and fresh when you first open the package, skip steps 1 and 4 and simply blot away any excess liquid. Serve the crab cakes with lemon wedges.*

    1   pound lump crabmeat, picked over for shells
    1   cup milk
    1½   cups panko bread crumbs, divided
    ¾   teaspoon table salt, divided
    2   celery ribs, chopped
    ½   cup chopped onion
    1   garlic clove, peeled and smashed
    1   tablespoon unsalted butter
    ⅛   teaspoon pepper

    4   ounces shrimp, peeled, deveined, and tails removed
    ¼   cup heavy cream
    2   teaspoons Dijon mustard
    1   teaspoon lemon juice
    ½   teaspoon hot sauce
    ½   teaspoon Old Bay seasoning
    ¼   cup vegetable oil

1. Place crabmeat and milk in bowl, making sure crab is totally submerged. Cover and refrigerate for 20 minutes.

2. Meanwhile, place ¾ cup panko in small zipper-lock bag and finely crush with rolling pin. Transfer crushed panko to 10-inch nonstick skillet and add remaining ¾ cup panko. Toast over medium-high heat, stirring constantly, until golden brown, about 5 minutes. Transfer panko to shallow dish and stir in ¼ teaspoon salt and pepper to taste. Wipe out skillet.

3. Pulse celery, onion, and garlic in food processor until finely chopped, 5 to 8 pulses, scraping down bowl as needed. Transfer vegetables to large bowl. Rinse processor bowl and blade. Melt butter in now-empty skillet over medium heat. Add chopped vegetables, pepper, and remaining ½ teaspoon salt; cook, stirring frequently, until vegetables are softened and all moisture has evaporated, 4 to 6 minutes. Return vegetables to large bowl and let cool to room temperature. Rinse out pan and wipe clean.

4. Drain crabmeat in fine-mesh strainer, pressing firmly to remove milk but being careful not to break up lumps of crabmeat.

5. Pulse shrimp in now-empty food processor until finely ground, 12 to 15 pulses, scraping down bowl as needed. Add cream and pulse to combine, 2 to 4 pulses, scraping down bowl as needed. Transfer shrimp puree to bowl with cooled vegetables. Add mustard, lemon juice, hot sauce, and Old Bay; stir until well combined. Add crabmeat and fold gently with rubber spatula, being careful not to overmix, and break up lumps of crabmeat. Divide mixture into 8 balls and firmly press into ½-inch-thick patties. Place cakes in rimmed baking sheet lined with parchment paper, cover tightly with plastic wrap, and refrigerate for 30 minutes.

6. Coat each cake with panko, firmly pressing to adhere crumbs to exterior. Heat 1 tablespoon oil in now-empty skillet over medium heat until shimmering. Place 4 cakes in skillet and cook without moving them until golden brown, 3 to 4 minutes. Using 2 spatulas, carefully flip cakes. Add 1 tablespoon oil, reduce heat to medium-low, and continue to cook until second side is golden brown, 4 to 6 minutes. Transfer cakes to platter. Wipe out skillet and repeat with remaining 4 cakes and remaining 2 tablespoons oil. Serve immediately.

SEASON 14

Oven-Steamed Mussels

Serves 4 • Total Time 50 minutes

Why This Recipe Works Mussels come in a range of sizes, making it a challenge to cook them evenly. This method guarantees that the mussels cook through at the same rate, even if they are different sizes. First, we moved them from the stovetop to the oven, where the even heat ensured that they cooked through more gently, and we traded the Dutch oven for a large roasting pan so they weren't crowded. Covering the pan with aluminum foil trapped the moisture so the mussels didn't dry out. For a flavorful cooking liquid, we reduced white wine to concentrate its flavor and added thyme, garlic, and red pepper flakes for aromatic complexity. To avoid dirtying another pan, we simply cooked the aromatics and wine on the stovetop in the roasting pan before tossing in our mussels and transferring the pan to the oven. A few pats of butter, stirred in at the end, gave the sauce richness and body.

> *Occasionally, mussels will have a harmless fibrous piece (known as the beard) protruding from between the shells. To remove it, trap the beard between the side of a paring knife and your thumb and pull. The flat surface of the knife gives you leverage to remove the beard. Unopened cooked mussels just need more cooking time. To open them, microwave briefly for 30 seconds or so. Serve mussels with crusty bread to sop up the flavorful broth.*

1 tablespoon extra-virgin olive oil
3 garlic cloves, minced
  Pinch red pepper flakes
1 cup dry white wine
3 sprigs fresh thyme
2 bay leaves
4 pounds mussels, scrubbed and debearded
¼ teaspoon table salt
2 tablespoons unsalted butter, cut into 4 pieces
2 tablespoons minced fresh parsley

1. Adjust oven rack to lowest position and heat oven to 500 degrees. Heat oil, garlic, and pepper flakes in large roasting pan over medium heat; cook, stirring constantly, until fragrant, about 30 seconds. Add wine, thyme sprigs, and bay leaves and bring to boil. Cook until wine is slightly reduced, about 1 minute. Add mussels and salt. Cover pan tightly with aluminum foil and transfer to oven. Cook until most mussels have opened (a few may remain closed), 15 to 18 minutes.

2. Remove pan from oven. Push mussels to sides of pan. Add butter to center and whisk until melted. Discard thyme sprigs and bay leaves, sprinkle parsley over mussels, and toss to combine. Serve immediately.

VARIATIONS

Oven-Steamed Mussels with Tomato and Chorizo
Omit red pepper flakes and increase oil to 3 tablespoons. Heat oil and 12 ounces Spanish-style chorizo sausage, cut into ½-inch pieces, in roasting pan until chorizo starts to brown, about 5 minutes. Add garlic and cook until fragrant, about 30 seconds. Proceed with recipe as directed, adding 1 (28-ounce) can crushed tomatoes to roasting pan before adding mussels and increasing butter to 3 tablespoons.

Oven-Steamed Mussels with Leeks and Pernod

Omit red pepper flakes and increase oil to 3 tablespoons. Heat oil; 1 pound leeks, white and light green parts only, halved lengthwise, sliced thin, and washed thoroughly; and garlic in roasting pan until leeks are wilted, about 3 minutes. Proceed with recipe as directed, omitting thyme sprigs and substituting ½ cup Pernod and ¼ cup water for wine, ¼ cup crème fraîche for butter, and chives for parsley.

Oven-Steamed Mussels with Hard Cider and Bacon

Omit garlic and red pepper flakes. Heat oil and 4 slices thick-cut bacon, cut into ½-inch pieces, in roasting pan until bacon has rendered and is starting to crisp, about 5 minutes. Proceed with recipe as directed, substituting dry hard cider for wine and ¼ cup heavy cream for butter.

SEASON 6

Paella

Serves 6 • Total Time: 2 hours

Why This Recipe Works We wanted a recipe for a stream-lined version of this Spanish classic that still stayed true to the dish's heritage. We started by substituting a Dutch oven for a single-purpose paella pan. Next we pared down our ingredients, dismissing lobster, diced pork, fish, rabbit, and snails. We were left with chorizo, chicken, shrimp, and mussels. We then simplified our sofrito—in this Spanish version, a combination of onions, garlic, and tomatoes—by mincing a can of drained diced tomatoes rather than seeding and grating a fresh tomato. For the rice, we found that we preferred short-grain varieties. Valencia was our favorite, with Italian Arborio a close second. Sautéing the rice in the same pot used to brown the meat and make the sofrito boosted its flavor. For the cooking liquid and seasonings, we chose chicken broth, white wine, saffron, and a bay leaf. Once the rice had absorbed almost all the liquid, we added the mussels, shrimp, and peas to the mix. The result? A colorful, streamlined, yet flavorful rendition of the Spanish classic.

> *Use a Dutch oven that is 11 to 12 inches in diameter with at least a 6-quart capacity. Dry-cured Spanish chorizo is the sausage of choice for paella, but fresh chorizo or linguica is an acceptable substitute. Socarrat, a layer of crusty browned rice that forms on the bottom of the pan, is a traditional part of paella. In our version, socarrat does not develop because most of the cooking is done in the oven. We have provided instructions to develop socarrat in step 5; if you prefer, skip this step and go directly from step 4 to step 6.*

1 pound extra-large shrimp (21 to 25 per pound), peeled and deveined
2 tablespoons extra-virgin olive oil, divided, plus extra as needed
8 garlic cloves, minced, divided
1 teaspoon table salt, divided
½ teaspoon pepper, divided
1 pound boneless, skinless chicken thighs, trimmed and halved crosswise
1 red bell pepper, stemmed, seeded, and cut into ½-inch-wide strips
8 ounces Spanish chorizo, sliced ½ inch thick on bias
1 onion, chopped fine
1 (14.5-ounce) can diced tomatoes, drained, minced, and drained again
2 cups Valencia or Arborio rice
3 cups chicken broth
⅓ cup dry white wine
½ teaspoon saffron threads, crumbled
1 bay leaf
1 dozen mussels, scrubbed and debearded
½ cup frozen peas, thawed
2 tablespoons chopped fresh parsley
Lemon wedges

1. Adjust oven rack to lower-middle position and heat oven to 350 degrees. Toss shrimp, 1 tablespoon oil, 1 teaspoon garlic, ¼ teaspoon salt, and ¼ teaspoon pepper in medium bowl; cover with plastic wrap and refrigerate until needed. Season chicken thighs with ¼ teaspoon salt and remaining ¼ teaspoon pepper; set aside.

2. Heat 2 teaspoons oil in large Dutch oven over medium-high heat until shimmering but not smoking. Add pepper strips and cook, stirring occasionally, until skin begins to blister and turn spotty black, 3 to 4 minutes. Transfer pepper to small plate and set aside.

3. Add remaining 1 teaspoon oil to now-empty Dutch oven; heat oil until shimmering but not smoking. Add chicken pieces in single layer; cook, without moving pieces, until browned, about 3 minutes. Turn pieces and brown on second side, about 3 minutes longer; transfer chicken to medium bowl. Reduce heat to medium and add chorizo to pot; cook, stirring frequently, until deeply browned and fat begins to render, 4 to 5 minutes. Transfer chorizo to bowl with chicken and set aside.

4. Add enough oil to fat in Dutch oven to equal 2 tablespoons; heat over medium heat until shimmering but not smoking. Add onion and cook, stirring frequently, until softened, about 3 minutes; stir in remaining garlic and cook until fragrant, about 1 minute. Stir in tomatoes; cook until mixture begins to darken and thicken slightly, about 3 minutes. Stir in rice and cook until grains are well coated with tomato mixture, 1 to 2 minutes. Stir in chicken broth, wine, saffron, bay leaf, and remaining ½ teaspoon salt. Return chicken and chorizo to pot, increase heat to medium-high, and bring to boil, uncovered, stirring occasionally. Cover pot and transfer it to oven; cook until rice absorbs almost all of liquid, about 15 minutes. Remove pot from oven (close oven door to retain heat). Uncover pot; scatter shrimp over rice, insert mussels, hinged side down, into rice (so they stand upright), arrange bell pepper strips, and scatter peas over top. Cover and return to oven; cook until shrimp are opaque and mussels have opened, 10 to 12 minutes.

5. Optional: If socarrat is desired, set Dutch oven, uncovered, over medium-high heat for about 5 minutes, rotating pot 180 degrees after about 2 minutes for even browning.

6. Let paella stand, covered, for about 5 minutes. Discard any mussels that have not opened and bay leaf, if it can be easily removed. Sprinkle with parsley and serve, passing lemon wedges separately.

Debearding Mussels

If your mussel has a beard (a harmless fibrous piece protruding from between the shells), hold it and use back of paring knife to remove it with a stern yank.

SEASON 4

Indoor Clambake

Serves 4 to 6 • **Total Time: 1¼ hours**

Why This Recipe Works A clambake is perhaps the ultimate seafood meal: clams, mussels, and lobster, nestled with sausage, corn, and potatoes, all steamed together with hot stones in a sand pit by the sea. A genuine clambake is an all-day affair and, of course, requires a beach. But we wanted to re-create the great flavors of the clambake indoors, so we could enjoy this flavorful feast anywhere, without hours of preparation. A large stockpot was our cooking vessel of choice. Many recipes suggest cooking the ingredients separately before adding them to the pot, but we found that with careful layering, we could cook everything in the same pot and have it all finish at the same time. And we didn't need to add water, because the shellfish released enough liquid to steam everything else. Sliced sausage went into the pot first (we liked kielbasa), so that it could sear before the steam was generated. Clams and mussels were next, wrapped in cheesecloth for easy removal. Then in went the potatoes, which would take the longest to cook; they were best placed near the heat source, and we cut them into 1-inch pieces to cook more quickly. Corn, with the husks left on to protect it from seafood flavors and lobster foam, was next, followed by the lobsters. It took less than half an hour for everything to cook—and we had all the elements of a clambake (minus the sand and surf) without having spent all day preparing them.

Choose a large, narrow stockpot in which you can easily layer the ingredients. The recipe can be cut in half and layered in an 8-quart Dutch oven, but it should cook for the same amount of time. We prefer small littlenecks for this recipe. If your market carries larger clams, use 4 pounds. Mussels sometimes contain a small weedy beard between their shells. To remove it easily, trap the beard between the side of a small paring knife and your thumb and pull to remove it. The flat surface of the knife gives you some leverage to remove the beard.

- 2 pounds small littleneck or cherrystone clams, scrubbed
- 2 pounds mussels, scrubbed and debearded
- 1 pound kielbasa, sliced into ⅓-inch-thick rounds
- 1 pound small new or red potatoes, scrubbed and cut into 1-inch pieces
- 6 medium ears corn, silk and all but last layer of husk removed
- 2 (1½-pound) live lobsters
- 8 tablespoons salted butter, melted

1. Place clams and mussels on large piece of cheesecloth and tie ends together to secure; set aside. In heavy-bottomed 12-quart stockpot, layer sliced kielbasa, sack of clams and mussels, potatoes, corn, and lobsters on top of one another. Cover with lid and place over high heat. Cook until potatoes are tender (paring knife can be slipped into and out of center of potato with little resistance), and lobsters are bright red, 17 to 20 minutes.

2. Remove pot from heat and remove lid (watch out for scalding steam). Remove lobsters and set aside until cool enough to handle. Remove corn from pot and peel off husks; arrange ears on large platter. Using slotted spoon, remove potatoes and arrange them on platter with corn. Transfer clams and mussels to large bowl and cut open cheesecloth with scissors. Using slotted spoon, remove kielbasa from pot and arrange it on platter with potatoes and corn. Pour remaining steaming liquid in pot over clams and mussels. Twist and remove lobster tails, claws, and legs (if desired). Arrange lobster parts on platter. Serve immediately with melted butter and napkins.

Removing Lobster Meat from the Shell

1. Once cooked lobster is cool enough to handle, set it on cutting board. Grasp tail with your hand and grab body with your other hand and twist to separate.

2. Lay tail on its side on counter and use both hands to press down on tail until shell cracks.

3. Hold tail, flippers facing you and shell facing down. Pull back on sides to crack open shell and remove meat. Rinse meat under water to remove green tomalley if you wish; pat meat dry with paper-towels and remove dark vein.

4. Twist "arms" to remove both claws and attached "knuckles." Twist knuckle to remove from claw. Break knuckles at joint using back of chef's knife or lobster-cracking tool. Use handle of teaspoon to push out meat.

5. Wiggle hinged portion of each claw to separate. If meat is stuck inside small part, remove it with skewer. Break open claws, cracking 1 side and then flipping them to crack other side, and remove meat.

6. Twist legs to remove them. Lay legs flat on counter. Using rolling pin, start from claw end and roll toward open end, pushing out meat. Stop rolling before reaching end of leg; otherwise, leg can crack and release pieces of shell.

Fisherman's Pie

Serves 4 to 6 • Total Time: 1¾ hours

Why This Recipe Works We hewed close to tradition when selecting the seafood for our Fisherman's Pie, landing on a trio that offered a variety of flavors and textures: flaky, white-fleshed cod; delicate cold-smoked salmon; and snappy jumbo shrimp. A roux-thickened mixture of heavy cream, clam juice, and white wine produced a light, elegant sauce. We kept the flavorings simple, using just leek, thyme, and parsley so as not to overwhelm the delicate fish. Gently simmering the seafood in the sauce on the stovetop before topping it with fluffy mashed potatoes ensured that the seafood would be perfectly cooked.

We use an 8-inch square broiler-safe baking dish for this recipe, but any broiler-safe dish that holds 2 quarts will work here. At the end of step 3, the base for the pie should look quite thick; it will loosen to the perfect consistency as the seafood cooks. We prefer cold-smoked salmon here because it's less likely to overcook, but you can substitute hot-smoked salmon if you prefer it. Making a pattern on the topping not only looks attractive but also provides textural contrast when the pie is broiled.

Topping

- 2 pounds russet potatoes, peeled and cut into 1-inch chunks
  Table salt for cooking potatoes
- 3 tablespoons unsalted butter, cut into 3 pieces
- ⅓ cup heavy cream
- 1 large egg yolk

Filling

- 12 ounces jumbo shrimp (16 to 20 per pound), peeled, deveined, tails removed, and cut in half crosswise
- ¾ teaspoon table salt, divided
- ⅛ teaspoon baking soda
- 4 tablespoons unsalted butter, divided
- 1 leek, white and light-green parts only, halved lengthwise, sliced thin, and washed thoroughly
- 1 teaspoon minced fresh thyme
- ⅓ cup dry white wine or dry vermouth
- 3 tablespoons all-purpose flour
- 2 (8-ounce) bottles clam juice
- ⅔ cup heavy cream
- ¼ teaspoon pepper
- 1 pound skinless cod fillets, cut into 1-inch chunks
- 4 ounces cold-smoked salmon, cut into ½-inch pieces
- ¼ cup minced fresh parsley

1. For the topping: Place potatoes in large saucepan and add water to just cover. Add 1 tablespoon salt and bring to boil over high heat. Reduce heat to maintain simmer and cook until tip of paring knife inserted into potato meets no resistance, 8 to 10 minutes. Drain potatoes and return to saucepan over low heat. Cook, shaking saucepan occasionally, until any surface moisture on potatoes has evaporated, about 1 minute. Off heat, mash potatoes well. Stir in butter until melted. Whisk cream and egg yolk together in bowl; stir into potatoes. Season with salt and pepper to taste. Cover to keep warm and set aside.

2. For the filling: Set 8-inch square broiler-safe baking dish on rimmed baking sheet. Sprinkle shrimp with ¼ teaspoon salt and baking soda in bowl and toss to combine. Refrigerate until needed.

3. Melt 3 tablespoons butter in medium saucepan over medium-low heat. Add leek and thyme and cook, stirring occasionally, until leek is softened, 6 to 7 minutes. Add wine and cook, stirring occasionally, until wine has evaporated, about 5 minutes. Add flour and cook, stirring constantly, for 1 minute. Add clam juice and stir until mixture is smooth. Stir in cream, pepper, and remaining ½ teaspoon salt. Increase heat to medium-high and bring to simmer. Lower heat to maintain simmer and cook, stirring frequently, until mixture resembles thick chowder, 10 to 13 minutes.

4. Stir cod, salmon, and shrimp into sauce and return to simmer. Cover and cook, stirring every 2 minutes and adjusting heat if needed to maintain simmer, until shrimp are opaque and just cooked through, 4 to 6 minutes. Off heat, stir in parsley. Transfer filling to prepared dish.

Clever Choreography Requires Precooking the Chips

"I'm not sure I'd ever been able to recreate a great version of fish and chips at home before we published this recipe. I had a facilities problem: Where pubs usually have multiple fryers going in their kitchens so both the fish and potatoes come out steaming hot, my one-pot home operation meant I had to choose which I didn't mind eating at room temp. Not ideal.

The key to this recipe is thrice cooking the chips. First, the chips are microwaved until just a little tender before cooling to room temperature (essential so they don't overcook). Then the chips get their first dip in the hot oil and stay there until they just begin to turn golden. Once the chips are out, the beer-battered fish gets dipped in an extra coat of seasoned flour and cornstarch for a crust that's both substantial and resistant to sogging out. The fish fries until cooked through and, once removed from the oil, the chips go in for their final flash-fry— just a few minutes."

—Bridget

5. Adjust oven rack 8 inches from broiler element and heat broiler. Spoon topping over filling, starting at edges and working toward center. Smooth with rubber spatula, making sure to seal around edges of dish so no seafood or sauce is exposed. Using back of spoon or tines of fork, make pattern on topping. Melt remaining 1 tablespoon butter and drizzle over topping. Broil pie, still on sheet, until topping is golden brown and crusty and filling is bubbly, 6 to 7 minutes (watch closely). Let cool for 10 minutes before serving.

Fish and Chips

Serves 4 • Total Time: 1¼ hours

Why This Recipe Works Making fish and chips at home can be a hassle and a mess. Plus, by the time the fries finish frying, the fish is cold. We wanted to serve both at their prime. Our first challenge was to create a batter that would protect the fish as it cooked and also provide a crisp contrast. For this, we discovered that a wet batter was best. We liked beer—the traditional choice—as the liquid component. For a crisp coating we used a 3:1 ratio of flour to cornstarch, along with a teaspoon of baking powder. A final layer of flour on top of the battered fish prevented the coating from puffing away from the fish as it cooked. To deliver the fish and fries while both were still hot, we cooked them alternately. First, we precooked the fries in the microwave, which not only lessened cooking time but also removed excess moisture that could diminish crisping. After giving the fries their first fry in hot oil, we battered and fried the fish while the potatoes were draining. Then, as the fish drained, we gave the fries a final fry.

Use a Dutch oven with at least a 7-quart capacity. Serve with traditional malt vinegar or with tartar sauce.

- 3 pounds russet potatoes (about 4 large potatoes), peeled, ends and sides squared off, and cut lengthwise into ½-inch by ½-inch fries
- 3 quarts plus ¼ cup peanut oil or canola oil, divided, for frying
- 1½ cups all-purpose flour
- ½ cup cornstarch
- 2 teaspoons table salt
- ½ teaspoon cayenne pepper
- ½ teaspoon paprika
- ⅛ teaspoon pepper
- 1 teaspoon baking powder
- 1½ pounds cod, hake, or haddock, cut into eight 3-ounce pieces about 1 inch thick
- 1½ cups cold beer, divided

1. Place cut fries in large microwave-safe bowl, toss with ¼ cup oil, and cover with plastic wrap. Microwave on high power until potatoes are partially translucent and pliable but still offer some resistance when pierced with tip of paring knife, 6 to 8 minutes, tossing them with rubber spatula halfway through cooking time. Carefully pull back plastic wrap from side farthest from you and drain potatoes into large mesh strainer set over sink. Rinse well under cold running water. Spread potatoes on few clean dish towels and pat dry. Let rest until fries have reached room temperature, at least 10 minutes or up to 1 hour.

2. While fries cool, whisk flour, cornstarch, salt, cayenne, paprika, and pepper in large bowl; transfer ¾ cup of mixture to rimmed baking sheet. Add baking powder to bowl and whisk to combine.

3. In large Dutch oven heat 2 quarts oil over medium heat to 350 degrees. Add fries to hot oil and increase heat to high. Fry, stirring with a mesh spider or slotted metal spoon, until potatoes turn light golden and just begin to brown at corners, 6 to 8 minutes. Transfer fries to thick paper bag or paper towels to drain.

4. Reduce heat to medium-high, add remaining 1 quart oil, and heat oil to 375 degrees. Meanwhile, thoroughly dry fish with paper towels and dredge each piece in flour mixture on sheet; transfer pieces to wire rack, shaking off any excess flour. Add 1¼ cups beer to flour mixture in bowl and stir until mixture is just combined (batter will be lumpy). Add remaining ¼ cup beer as needed, 1 tablespoon at a time, whisking after each addition, until batter falls from whisk in thin, steady stream and leaves faint trail across surface of batter. Using tongs, dip 1 piece fish in batter and let excess run off, shaking gently. Place battered fish back on sheet with flour mixture and turn to coat both sides. Repeat with remaining fish, keeping pieces in single layer on sheet.

5. When oil reaches 375 degrees, increase heat to high and add battered fish to oil with tongs, gently shaking off any excess flour. Fry, stirring occasionally, until golden brown, 7 to 8 minutes. Transfer fish to thick paper bag or paper towels to drain. Allow oil to return to 375 degrees.

6. Add all of fries back to oil and fry until golden brown and crisp, 3 to 5 minutes. Transfer to fresh paper bag or paper towels to drain. Season fries with salt to taste and serve immediately with fish.

Vegetarian

Photo: Upside-Down Tomato Tart

Unlocking the Mystery of Meatiness

"There's something so satisfying about a meaty bowl of chili. But ground beef isn't actually the main source of its meaty flavor. Stick with me here. Think about beef tartare: It has a delicate flavor. What we think of as meatiness in a bowl of classic chili comes from browning and the other ingredients in the mix. When my colleague Lan Lam developed this recipe, she obviously understood these principles. My home is a mix of meat eaters and vegetarians and we don't agree on much, except that this is the world's best chili. How did Lan satisfy this tough crowd? She got the texture right by relying on nubby bulgur. As for the flavor, this recipe features a powerhouse of umami-packed ingredients— dried shiitake mushrooms, soy sauce, walnuts, tomato paste—to provide the backdrop for the dried chiles and beans (the stars of this dish). And don't underestimate the power of browning 2 pounds of finely chopped onions. Meatiness and meat are not the same thing. Trust me— and my family—on this one."

—Jack

Best Vegetarian Chili

Serves 6 to 8 • Total Time: 4½ hours, plus 1 hour 20 minutes soaking and resting

Why This Recipe Works Vegetarian chilis can be little more than a mishmash of beans and vegetables. To create a robust, complex-flavored chili—not just a bean and vegetable stew—we found vegetarian replacements for the different ways in which meat adds depth and savory flavor to chili. Walnuts, soy sauce, dried shiitake mushrooms, and tomatoes added hearty savoriness. Bulgur filled out the chili, giving it a substantial texture. The added oil and nuts lent a richness to the chili, for full, lingering flavor.

We prefer to use whole dried chiles, but the chili can be prepared with jarred chili powder. If using chili powder, grind the shiitakes and oregano and add them to the pot with ¼ cup of chili powder in step 4. Pinto, black, red kidney, small red, cannellini, or navy beans can be used in this recipe, either a single variety or a combination of beans. For a spicier chili use both jalapeños. Serve with diced avocado, chopped red onion, lime wedges, sour cream, and shredded Monterey Jack or cheddar cheese.

1¼ teaspoons table salt, plus salt for soaking beans
1 pound (2½ cups) dried beans, rinsed and picked over
2 dried ancho chiles
2 dried New Mexico chiles
½ ounce dried shiitake mushrooms, chopped coarse
4 teaspoons dried oregano
½ cup walnuts, toasted
1 (28-ounce) can diced tomatoes, drained with juice reserved
3 tablespoons tomato paste
1–2 jalapeño chiles, stemmed and chopped coarse
6 garlic cloves, minced
3 tablespoons soy sauce
¼ cup vegetable oil
2 pounds onions, chopped fine
1 tablespoon ground cumin
⅔ cup medium-grain bulgur
¼ cup chopped fresh cilantro

1. Bring 4 quarts water, 3 tablespoons salt, and beans to boil in Dutch oven over high heat. Remove pot from heat, cover, and let stand for 1 hour. Drain beans and rinse well.

2. Adjust oven rack to middle position and heat oven to 300 degrees. Arrange ancho and New Mexico chiles on rimmed baking sheet and toast until fragrant and puffed, about 8 minutes. Transfer to plate and let cool, about 5 minutes. Stem and seed toasted chiles. Working in batches, grind toasted chiles, shiitakes, and oregano in spice grinder or with mortar and pestle until finely ground.

3. Process walnuts in food processor until finely ground, about 30 seconds. Transfer to bowl. Process drained tomatoes, tomato paste, jalapeño(s), garlic, and soy sauce in food processor until tomatoes are finely chopped, about 45 seconds, scraping down bowl as needed.

4. Heat oil in Dutch oven over medium-high heat until shimmering. Add onions and salt; cook, stirring occasionally until onions begin to brown, 8 to 10 minutes. Lower heat to medium, add ground chile mixture and cumin, and cook, stirring constantly, until fragrant, about 1 minute. Add rinsed beans and 7 cups water and bring to boil. Cover pot, transfer to oven, and cook for 45 minutes.

5. Remove pot from oven. Stir in bulgur, ground walnuts, tomato mixture, and reserved tomato juice. Return to oven and cook until beans are fully tender, about 2 hours.

6. Remove pot from oven, stir chili well, and let stand, uncovered, for 20 minutes. Stir in cilantro and serve. (Chili can be made up to 3 days in advance.)

Mushroom Bourguignon

Serves 6 to 8 • Total Time: 1¾ hours

Why This Recipe Works Mushrooms are inherently savory; have the ability to build fond, the rich-tasting browned bits that form on a pot's interior surface; and offer a balance of tenderness and resilience that allows them to turn pleasantly supple when simmered without losing structural integrity. For all those reasons, they're great for featuring in a luxurious, wintery braise such as bourguignon. We started with chunks of meaty, satisfying portobellos, while dried porcini offered a heavy-hitting boost of umami. We added plenty of savory supports such as miso, tomato paste, and soy sauce and classic aromatics and herbs such as carrot, shallot, garlic, and thyme. To achieve the French classic's requisite body and gloss while keeping the stew vegan, we made a modified roux with olive oil and flour. A splash of wine at the end of cooking brought brightness to the dish.

Use a good-quality light- to medium-body red wine, such as a Pinot Noir or Grenache. You can substitute dried shiitake mushrooms for the porcini and yellow or red miso for white. Leave the mushroom gills intact; they enhance the stew's color and flavor. Serve the bourguignon over polenta, noodles, or mashed potatoes.

4¾ cups water, divided
¼ cup extra-virgin olive oil, divided
2½ pounds portobello mushroom caps, cut into 1-inch pieces
½ teaspoon table salt
¼ teaspoon pepper
2 carrots, peeled and sliced ¼ inch thick
1 large shallot, chopped
4 garlic cloves, smashed and peeled
3 tablespoons all-purpose flour
1 cup plus 2 tablespoons dry red wine, divided
2 tablespoons white miso
2 tablespoons soy sauce
1 tablespoon tomato paste
6 sprigs fresh thyme
2 bay leaves
1 ounce dried porcini mushrooms, rinsed
1 cup frozen pearl onions, thawed
¼ cup minced fresh parsley

1. Bring ¼ cup water and 2 tablespoons oil to simmer in Dutch oven over medium-high heat. Add portobello mushrooms, salt, and pepper. Cover and cook, stirring occasionally, until mushrooms have released their moisture, about 10 minutes.

2. Uncover and continue to cook, stirring occasionally, until pot is dry and dark fond forms, 10 to 12 minutes longer. Transfer mushrooms to bowl. Add carrots, shallot, and remaining 2 tablespoons oil to pot and cook, stirring frequently, until vegetables start to brown, 3 to 4 minutes. Add garlic and cook for 1 minute. Stir in flour and cook for 30 seconds. Whisk in 1 cup wine.

3. Add miso, soy sauce, tomato paste, and remaining 4½ cups water and whisk to combine. Add thyme sprigs, bay leaves, and porcini mushrooms and bring to boil over high heat. Reduce heat to maintain vigorous simmer and cook, stirring occasionally and scraping bottom of pot to loosen any browned bits, until sauce is reduced and has consistency of heavy cream, about 25 minutes.

4. Strain sauce through fine-mesh strainer set over large bowl, pressing on solids to extract as much liquid as possible; discard solids. You should have 2 cups sauce. (If you have more, return sauce to pot and continue to cook over medium heat until reduced. If you have less, add enough water to yield 2 cups.) Return sauce to pot. Stir in onions, portobello mushrooms, and remaining 2 tablespoons wine. Cover and cook over low heat, stirring occasionally, until onions are tender, about 20 minutes. Stir in parsley. Season with salt and pepper to taste, and serve.

SEASON 22

Chana Masala

Serves 4 to 6 • Total Time: 50 minutes

Why This Recipe Works Chana masala is arguably one of North India's most popular vegetarian dishes, and it can be quick and easy to prepare. We started by using the food processor to grind the aromatic paste that formed the base of our dish. We opted for canned chickpeas because their flavor and texture were nearly indistinguishable from those of chickpeas that were cooked from dried, and we didn't drain them because the canning liquid added body and savory depth to the dish. The canned chickpeas still retained a bit of snap, so we simmered them in the sauce until they turned soft. Adding stronger foundational spices such as cumin, turmeric, and fennel seeds at the beginning of cooking ensured that they permeated the dish, and reserving the sweet, delicate garam masala until near the end preserved its aroma. A generous garnish of chopped onion, sliced chile, and cilantro added so much vibrancy, texture, and freshness that you'd never guess that most of the ingredients in the recipe were from the pantry.

over medium-high heat, stirring frequently, until onion is fully softened and beginning to stick to saucepan, 5 to 7 minutes.

2. While onion mixture cooks, process tomatoes and their juice in now-empty food processor until smooth, about 30 seconds. Add chile powder, cumin, turmeric, and fennel seeds to onion mixture and cook, stirring constantly, until fragrant, about 1 minute. Stir in chickpeas and their liquid and processed tomatoes and bring to boil. Adjust heat to maintain simmer, then cover and simmer for 15 minutes. While mixture cooks, chop reserved onion quarter fine.

3. Stir garam masala and salt into chickpea mixture and continue to cook, uncovered and stirring occasionally, until chickpeas are softened and sauce is thickened, 8 to 12 minutes longer. Season with salt to taste. Transfer to wide, shallow serving bowl. Sprinkle with chopped onion, remaining serranos, and cilantro leaves and serve, passing lime wedges separately.

Because the sodium contents of canned chickpeas and tomatoes vary, we include only a small amount of salt in this recipe; season with additional salt at the end of cooking if needed. If you prefer a spicier dish, leave the seeds in the serrano chiles. If you can't find Kashmiri chile powder, substitute 1 teaspoon paprika. This dish is often paired with bhature, deep-fried breads that puff up as they cook; alternatively, serve it with rice or naan.

1	small red onion, quartered, divided
10	sprigs fresh cilantro, stems and leaves separated
1	(1½-inch) piece ginger, peeled and chopped coarse
2	garlic cloves, chopped coarse
2	serrano chiles, stemmed, halved, seeded, and sliced thin crosswise, divided
3	tablespoons vegetable oil
1	(14.5-ounce) can whole peeled tomatoes
1	teaspoon Kashmiri chile powder
1	teaspoon ground cumin
½	teaspoon ground turmeric
½	teaspoon fennel seeds
2	(15-ounce) cans chickpeas, undrained
1½	teaspoons garam masala
½	teaspoon table salt
	Lime wedges

1. Chop three quarters of onion coarse; reserve remaining quarter for garnish. Cut cilantro stems into 1-inch lengths. Process chopped onion, cilantro stems, ginger, garlic, and half of serranos in food processor until finely chopped, scraping down sides of bowl as necessary, about 20 seconds. Combine onion mixture and oil in large saucepan. Cook

Espinacas con Garbanzos

Serves 4 • Total Time: 40 minutes

Why This Recipe Works Espinacas con garbanzos is a hyper-regional dish—native to Seville with strong Moorish influence—that's substantive and full of flavor. Briefly simmering canned chickpeas (uniformly tender, well sea-soned, and more convenient than dried) in a combination of chicken broth and chickpea canning liquid tenderized them and infused them with savory flavor. A picada (a paste of garlic and bread cooked in plenty of olive oil) thickened and seasoned the sauce. Smoked paprika and Moorish spices such as cumin, cinnamon, and saffron imbued the picada with heady aromas, and tomatoes and vinegar boosted its tang. Thawed frozen chopped spinach was perfect here; already fine and tender, it dispersed beauti-fully throughout the dish and provided plenty of surface area to hold the juices in place.

You can substitute water or chicken broth for the vegetable broth. If using chickpeas that you've cooked from dried, use 3⅓ cups of cooked chickpeas and ⅔ cup of the cooking liquid. Use a fruity, spicy, high-quality olive oil here. Red wine vinegar can be substituted for the sherry vinegar.

3. Stir bread mixture and spinach into chickpeas. Continue to simmer, stirring occasionally, until mixture is thick and stew-like, 5 to 10 minutes longer. Off heat, stir in remaining 2 tablespoons oil. Cover and let stand for 5 minutes. Season with salt and extra vinegar to taste. Transfer to serving bowl and serve with remaining bread.

SEASON 21

Palak Dal

Serves 4 to 6 • Total Time: 1 hour

Why This Recipe Works Dal is an Indian staple that is quick, easy, nourishing, inexpensive, and—most important—incredibly flavorful. Quick-cooking red lentils are the centerpiece of our spinach dal ("palak" means "spinach" in Hindi). Once they had softened, we gave them a vigorous whisk, which transformed them into a rustic, porridge-like stew without requiring us to break out a blender or food processor. Seasoning the lentils with a tadka (whole spices sizzled in ghee with aromatics) right before serving gave the dish loads of complexity, a gorgeous appearance, and an enticing aroma.

For less heat, remove the ribs and seeds of the serrano. Fresh curry leaves add a wonderful aroma to this dal, but if they're unavailable, you can omit them. Yellow mustard seeds can be substituted for brown. Monitor the spices and aromatics carefully during frying, reducing the heat if necessary to prevent scorching. Serve the dal with naan and basmati or another long-grain white rice.

4½	cups water
1½	cups (10½ ounces) dried red lentils, picked over and rinsed
1	tablespoon grated fresh ginger
¾	teaspoon ground turmeric
6	ounces (6 cups) baby spinach
1½	teaspoons table salt
3	tablespoons ghee
1½	teaspoons brown mustard seeds
1½	teaspoons cumin seeds
1	large onion, chopped
15	curry leaves, roughly torn (optional)
6	garlic cloves, sliced
4	whole dried arbol chiles
1	serrano chile, halved lengthwise
1½	teaspoons lemon juice, plus extra for seasoning
⅓	cup chopped fresh cilantro

---

1 loaf crusty bread, divided
2 (15-ounce) cans chickpeas (1 can drained, 1 can undrained)
1½ cups vegetable broth
6 tablespoons extra-virgin olive oil, divided
6 garlic cloves, minced
1 tablespoon smoked paprika
1 teaspoon ground cumin
¼ teaspoon table salt
⅛ teaspoon ground cinnamon
⅛ teaspoon cayenne pepper
1 small pinch saffron
2 small plum tomatoes, halved lengthwise, flesh shredded on large holes of box grater and skins discarded
4 teaspoons sherry vinegar, plus extra for seasoning
10 ounces frozen chopped spinach, thawed and squeezed dry

1. Cut 1½-ounce piece from loaf of bread (thickness will vary depending on size of loaf) and tear into 1-inch pieces. Process in food processor until finely ground (you should have ¾ cup crumbs). Combine chickpeas and broth in large saucepan and bring to boil over high heat. Adjust heat to maintain simmer and cook until level of liquid is just below top layer of chickpeas, about 10 minutes.

2. While chickpeas cook, heat ¼ cup oil in 10-inch nonstick or carbon-steel skillet over medium heat until just shimmering. Add bread crumbs and cook, stirring frequently, until deep golden brown, 3 to 4 minutes. Add garlic, paprika, cumin, salt, cinnamon, cayenne, and saffron and cook until fragrant, 30 seconds. Stir in tomatoes and vinegar; remove from heat.

1. Bring 4½ cups water, lentils, ginger, and turmeric to boil in large saucepan over medium-high heat. Reduce heat to maintain vigorous simmer. Cook, uncovered, stirring occasionally, until lentils are soft and starting to break down, 18 to 20 minutes.

2. Whisk lentils vigorously until coarsely pureed, about 30 seconds. Continue to cook until lentils have consistency of loose polenta or oatmeal, up to 5 minutes longer. Stir in spinach and salt and continue to cook until spinach is fully wilted, 30 to 60 seconds longer. Cover and set aside off heat.

3. Melt ghee in 10-inch skillet over medium-high heat. Add mustard seeds and cumin seeds and cook, stirring constantly, until seeds sizzle and pop, about 30 seconds. Add onion and cook, stirring frequently, until onion is just starting to brown, about 5 minutes. Add curry leaves, if using; garlic; arbols; and serrano and cook, stirring frequently, until onion and garlic are golden brown, 3 to 4 minutes.

4. Add lemon juice to lentils and stir to incorporate. (Dal should have consistency of loose polenta. If too thick, loosen with hot water, adding 1 tablespoon at a time.) Season with salt and extra lemon juice to taste. Transfer dal to serving bowl and spoon onion mixture on top. Sprinkle with cilantro and serve.

Saag Paneer

Serves 4 to 6 • Total Time: 1½ hours, plus 45 minutes resting

Why This Recipe Works Saag paneer, soft cubes of creamy cheese in a spicy pureed spinach sauce, is a popular Indian dish. Even if you've never made cheese at home, our method for making paneer is very simple, and the flavor payoff is well worth the effort. We started our paneer by heating a combination of whole milk and buttermilk, squeezing the curds of moisture, and then weighing the cheese down until it was firm enough to slice. We simply wilted the spinach in the microwave. Mustard greens gave our sauce additional complexity. Canned diced tomatoes brightened the dish, and buttery cashews gave our dish a subtle nutty richness.

To ensure that the cheese is firm, wring it tightly in step 2 and be sure to use two plates that nestle together snugly. Use commercially produced cultured buttermilk in this recipe. We found that some locally produced buttermilks didn't sufficiently coagulate the milk. Serve with basmati rice and/or naan.

Cheese
- 3 quarts whole milk
- 3 cups buttermilk
- 1 tablespoon table salt

Spinach Sauce
- 1 (10-ounce) bag curly-leaf spinach, rinsed
- 12 ounces mustard greens, stemmed and rinsed
- 3 tablespoons unsalted butter
- 1 teaspoon cumin seeds
- 1 teaspoon ground coriander
- 1 teaspoon paprika
- ½ teaspoon ground cardamom
- ¼ teaspoon ground cinnamon
- 1 onion, chopped fine
- ¾ teaspoon table salt
- 3 garlic cloves, minced
- 1 tablespoon grated fresh ginger
- 1 jalapeño chile, stemmed, seeded, and minced
- 1 (14.5-ounce) can diced tomatoes, drained and chopped coarse
- ½ cup roasted cashews, chopped coarse, divided
- 1 cup water
- 1 cup buttermilk
- 3 tablespoons chopped fresh cilantro

1. For the cheese: Line colander with triple layer of cheesecloth and set in sink. Bring milk to boil in Dutch oven over medium-high heat. Whisk in buttermilk and salt, turn off heat, and let stand for 1 minute. Pour milk mixture through cheesecloth and let curds drain for 15 minutes.

2. Pull edges of cheesecloth together to form pouch. Twist edges of cheesecloth together, firmly squeezing out as much liquid as possible from cheese curds. Place taut, twisted cheese pouch between 2 large plates and weigh down top plate with heavy Dutch oven. Set aside at room temperature until cheese is firm and set, at least 45 minutes. Remove cheesecloth and cut cheese into ½-inch pieces. (Left uncut, cheese can be wrapped in plastic wrap and refrigerated for up to 3 days.)

3. For the spinach sauce: Place spinach in large bowl, cover, and microwave until wilted, about 3 minutes. When cool enough to handle, chop enough spinach to measure ⅓ cup and set aside. Transfer remaining spinach to blender and wipe out bowl. Place mustard greens in now-empty bowl, cover, and microwave until wilted, about 4 minutes. When cool enough to handle, chop enough mustard greens to measure ⅓ cup and transfer to bowl with chopped spinach. Transfer remaining mustard greens to blender.

4. Meanwhile, melt butter in 12-inch skillet over medium-high heat. Add cumin seeds, coriander, paprika, cardamom, and cinnamon and cook until fragrant, about 30 seconds. Add onion and salt; cook, stirring frequently, until softened, about 3 minutes. Add garlic, ginger, and jalapeño; cook,

stirring frequently, until lightly browned and just beginning to stick to pan, 2 to 3 minutes. Stir in tomatoes and cook mixture until pan is dry and tomatoes are beginning to brown, 3 to 4 minutes. Remove skillet from heat.

5. Transfer half of onion mixture to blender with greens. Add ¼ cup cashews and water; process until smooth, about 1 minute. Return puree to skillet.

6. Return skillet to medium-high heat, stir in chopped greens and buttermilk, and bring to simmer. Reduce heat to low; cover; and cook until flavors have blended, 5 minutes. Season with salt and pepper to taste. Gently fold in cheese cubes and cook until just heated through, 1 to 2 minutes. Transfer to serving dish, sprinkle with cilantro and remaining ¼ cup cashews, and serve.

Making Paneer

1. Bring milk to boil, curdle it with buttermilk, and let rest for 1 minute off heat. Pour curdled milk through cheesecloth-lined colander; let drain. Twist cheesecloth to squeeze out liquid.

2. Press cheese between plates topped with Dutch oven; let drain until firm. Slice into ½-inch pieces.

SEASON 17

Vegetable Bibimbap with Nurungji

Serves 6 • Total Time: 1½ hours, plus 30 minutes chilling

Why This Recipe Works Bibimbap, an iconic Korean dish with many regional variations, features rice mixed with various toppings. In dolsot bibimbap, the combination of the hot stone bowl called a dolsot and a splash of fragrant sesame oil causes the rice to develop a delicious, crunchy crust called nurungji wherever it touches the dolsot. We wanted to create a bibimbap recipe that could be made without a dolsot but still result in plenty of nurungji. We also wanted to cut down on the sautéing and knife work. First we substituted one cast-iron Dutch oven for a set of stone bowls. To shorten the prep time and simplify the knife work, we made three sautéed vegetable toppings instead of the usual six or more. We also turned the pickles, sauce, and vegetables into make-ahead options. We skipped the traditional step of rinsing the rice before steaming it to save time. A quickly pickled mixture of bean sprouts and cucumbers added crisp brightness.

For a quick dinner, prepare the pickles, chile sauce, and vegetables a day ahead (warm the vegetables to room temperature in the microwave before adding them to the rice). You can also substitute store-bought kimchi for the pickles to save time. The Korean chile paste gochujang is sold in Korean markets and some supermarkets. If you can't find it, an equal amount of sriracha can be substituted.

But because sriracha is more watery than gochujang, omit the water from the chile sauce and stir just 1 table-spoon of sauce into the rice in step 9. For a family-style bibimbap experience, bring the pot to the table before stirring the vegetables into the rice in step 9.

Pickles

- 1 cup cider vinegar
- 2 tablespoons sugar
- 1½ teaspoons table salt
- 1 cucumber, peeled, quartered lengthwise, seeded, and sliced thin on bias
- 4 ounces (2 cups) bean sprouts

Chile Sauce

- ¼ cup gochujang
- 3 tablespoons water
- 2 tablespoons toasted sesame oil
- 1 teaspoon sugar

Rice

- 2½ cups short-grain white rice
- 2½ cups water
- ¾ teaspoon table salt

Vegetables

- ½ cup water
- 3 scallions, minced
- 3 tablespoons soy sauce
- 3 garlic cloves, minced
- 1 tablespoon sugar
- 1 tablespoon vegetable oil, divided
- 3 carrots, peeled and shredded (2 cups)
- 8 ounces shiitake mushrooms, stemmed, caps sliced thin
- 1 (10-ounce) bag curly-leaf spinach, stemmed and chopped coarse

Bibimbap

- 2 tablespoons plus 2 teaspoons vegetable oil, divided
- 1 tablespoon toasted sesame oil
- 4 large eggs

1. For the pickles: Whisk vinegar, sugar, and salt together in medium bowl. Add cucumber and bean sprouts and toss to combine. Gently press on vegetables to submerge. Cover and refrigerate for at least 30 minutes or up to 24 hours.

2. For the chile sauce: Whisk all ingredients together in small bowl. Cover and set aside.

3. For the rice: Bring rice, water, and salt to boil in medium saucepan over high heat. Cover, reduce heat to low, and cook for 7 minutes. Remove rice from heat and let sit, covered, until tender, about 15 minutes.

4. For the vegetables: While rice cooks, stir together water, scallions, soy sauce, garlic, and sugar. Heat 1 teaspoon oil in Dutch oven over high heat until shimmering. Add carrots and stir until coated. Add ⅓ cup scallion mixture and cook, stirring frequently, until carrots are slightly softened and moisture has evaporated, 1 to 2 minutes. Using slotted spoon, transfer carrots to small bowl.

5. Heat 1 teaspoon oil in now-empty pot until shimmering. Add mushrooms and stir until coated with oil. Add ⅓ cup scallion mixture and cook, stirring frequently, until mushrooms are tender and moisture has evaporated, 3 to 4 minutes. Using slotted spoon, transfer mushrooms to second small bowl.

6. Heat remaining 1 teaspoon oil in now-empty pot until shimmering. Add spinach and remaining ⅓ cup scallion mixture and stir to coat spinach. Cook, stirring frequently, until spinach is completely wilted but still bright green, 1 to 2 minutes. Using slotted spoon, transfer spinach to third small bowl. Discard any remaining liquid and wipe out pot with paper towel.

7. For the bibimbap: Heat 2 tablespoons vegetable oil and sesame oil in now-empty pot over high heat until shimmering. Carefully add cooked rice and gently press into even layer. Cook, without stirring, until rice begins to form crust on bottom of pot, about 2 minutes. Using slotted spoon, transfer carrots, spinach, and mushrooms to pot and arrange in piles that cover surface of rice. Reduce heat to low.

8. While crust forms, heat remaining 2 teaspoons vegetable oil in 10-inch nonstick skillet over low heat for 5 minutes. Crack eggs into small bowl. Pour eggs into skillet; cover and cook (about 2 minutes for runny yolks, 2½ minutes for soft but set yolks, and 3 minutes for firmly set yolks). Slide eggs onto vegetables in pot.

9. Drizzle 2 tablespoons chile sauce over eggs. Without disturbing crust, use wooden spoon to stir rice, vegetables, and eggs until combined. Just before serving, scrape large pieces of crust from bottom of pot and stir into rice. Serve in individual bowls, passing pickles and extra chile sauce separately.

SEASON 22

Paella de Verduras

Serves 4 • **Total Time: 1¼ hours**

Why This Recipe Works Rather than using vegetables merely as a flavoring agent, paella de verduras—a common, versatile approach to the beloved rice dish that's prepared throughout Spain—places them front and center. This hearty version features green and butter beans—tributes to the vegetables Valencians often add to paella de verduras—plus chunky cauliflower florets. In lieu of the flavorful fond that lends a meaty backbone to protein-based paellas, we retooled a Spanish sofrito to make a complex and super-savory flavor base: We browned the bell pepper instead of sautéing it, swapped in umami-rich tomato paste for the fresh tomatoes, loaded up on garlic, and omitted the sweet-tasting onion. Mixing in smoked paprika, saffron, and nutty-tasting dry sherry added brightness and depth. To ensure that the rice at the surface of the pan cooked through, we covered the pan for part of the time to trap moist heat, which hydrated the grains. Continuing to cook the rice after the liquid in the pan evaporated created a caramelized, crisp-chewy layer (called a socarrat) that added even more complexity. Letting the paella rest for a few minutes before serving it helped the socarrat firm up enough to release easily from the pan.

If neither Calasparra nor bomba rice is available, use Arborio rice. You can use chicken broth instead of vegetable broth. It's worth seeking out butter beans for their large size; do not substitute small white beans. We've included instructions for creating a socarrat—a chewy, well-browned bottom layer of rice—but it's optional.

3 tablespoons extra-virgin olive oil, divided
8 ounces cauliflower, cut into 2- to 2½-inch florets
¾ teaspoon table salt, divided
6 ounces green beans, trimmed and cut into 2- to 2½-inch pieces
1 red bell pepper, stemmed, seeded, and chopped fine
1 tablespoon tomato paste
3 garlic cloves, minced
1 teaspoon smoked paprika
¼ teaspoon saffron
¼ cup dry sherry
1 cup Calasparra or bomba rice
1 (15-ounce) can butter beans, rinsed
3½ cups vegetable broth
Lemon wedges (optional)

1. Heat 1½ tablespoons oil in 12-inch skillet over medium heat until shimmering. Add cauliflower and ¼ teaspoon salt and cook, stirring frequently, until cauliflower is spotty brown, 3 to 5 minutes. Add green beans and ¼ teaspoon salt. Continue to cook, stirring frequently, until beans are dark green, 2 to 4 minutes. Transfer vegetables to bowl.

2. Heat remaining 1½ tablespoons oil in now-empty skillet over medium heat until shimmering. Add bell pepper and remaining ¼ teaspoon salt and cook, stirring occasionally, until pepper starts to brown, 7 to 10 minutes. Add tomato paste and cook, stirring constantly, until pepper pieces are coated in tomato paste, about 1 minute. Add garlic, smoked paprika, and saffron and cook, stirring constantly until fragrant, about 30 seconds. Stir in sherry and cook, stirring frequently, until excess moisture has evaporated and pepper mixture forms large clumps, 1 to 2 minutes.

3. Add rice and stir until very well combined. Off heat, smooth into even layer. Scatter butter beans evenly over rice. Scatter cauliflower and green beans evenly over butter beans. Gently pour broth all over, making sure rice is fully submerged (it's okay if parts of vegetables aren't submerged).

4. Bring to boil over high heat. Adjust heat to maintain gentle simmer and cook until broth is just below top of rice, 12 to 17 minutes. Cover and cook until rice is cooked through, about 5 minutes. Uncover and cook until rice pops and sizzles and all excess moisture has evaporated (to test, use butter knife to gently push aside some rice and vegetables), 3 to 7 minutes. (If socarrat is desired, continue to cook, rotating skillet one-quarter turn every 20 seconds, until rice at bottom of skillet is well browned and slightly crusty, 2 to 5 minutes.) Let rest off heat for 5 minutes. Serve, passing lemon wedges, if using.

Vegetables and Rice Can Be Company-Worthy

"I've always liked cooking, serving, and eating a wide variety of vegetarian meals, and, over the years, I've enjoyed a tremendous amount of excellent recipes. That said, this Valencian paella de verduras is one of my all-time favorites. It truly has everything going for it: The creamy rice is incredibly satisfying, the flavors are savory and complex, and it's also stunning to look at: Golden-orange, saffron- and smoked paprika–tinted grains of Calasparra rice are punctuated by tender green beans, creamy white cauliflower, and meaty butter beans. (If you make the dish in a paella pan, it becomes even more of a looker.) Dry sherry, garlic, and tomato paste showcase the vegetables with umami depth. The paella also has wonderful textures: The crispy socarrat (a caramelized, crisp-chewy layer of rice at the bottom of the skillet) is a real prize. It's listed as optional in the recipe but I don't recommend skipping it as it beautifully complements the soft creaminess of the rest of the dish. If you're entertaining and want to impress, or simply want a stand-out family meal, I can't recommend this dish highly enough."

—Becky

Stir-Fried Portobellos with Ginger-Oyster Sauce

Serves 3 to 4 • **Total Time: 55 minutes**

Why This Recipe Works We wanted to make a satisfying, filling stir-fry—without meat. We chose meaty portobello mushrooms as the main vegetable. After removing the gills (to keep the mushrooms from tasting leathery and raw), we cut the mushrooms into substantial 2-inch wedges. We cooked the mushrooms over medium-high heat until browned and tender, then added a mixture of broth, soy sauce, and sugar and reduced it to a glaze—this provided an intense flavor boost. For this stir-fry, we bulked up the amount of vegetables in our traditional stir-fries, mixing carrots, snow peas, and napa cabbage. Finally, the sauce—a mixture of broth, oyster sauce, soy sauce, cornstarch, and sesame oil—and a heavy dose of ginger tied the dish together, giving the vegetables great flavor—and nobody missed the meat.

| *Serve with white rice.*

Glaze
- ¼ cup vegetable broth
- 2 tablespoons soy sauce
- 2 tablespoons sugar

Sauce
- 1 cup vegetable broth
- 3 tablespoons vegetarian oyster sauce
- 1 tablespoon soy sauce
- 1 tablespoon cornstarch
- 2 teaspoons toasted sesame oil

Vegetables
- ¼ cup peanut or vegetable oil, divided
- 4 teaspoons minced or grated fresh ginger
- 2 garlic cloves, minced
- 6–8 portobello mushrooms (each 4 to 6 inches), stemmed, gills removed, and cut into 2-inch wedges
- 4 carrots, peeled and sliced ¼ inch thick on bias
- ½ cup vegetable broth
- 3 ounces snow peas, strings removed
- 1 pound napa cabbage (1 small head), cored and cut into ¾-inch strips
- 1 tablespoon sesame seeds, toasted (optional)

1. For the glaze: Combine broth, soy sauce, and sugar in small bowl and set aside.

2. For the sauce: Combine all ingredients in small bowl and set aside.

3. For the vegetables: In small bowl, mix 1 teaspoon oil, ginger, and garlic together; set aside.

4. Heat 3 tablespoons oil in 12-inch nonstick skillet over medium-high heat until shimmering. Add mushrooms and cook without stirring until browned on 1 side, 2 to 3 minutes. Using tongs, flip mushrooms, reduce heat to medium, and cook until second sides are browned and mushrooms are tender, about 5 minutes. Increase heat to medium-high, add glaze, and cook, stirring frequently, until glaze is thick and mushrooms are coated, 1 to 2 minutes. Transfer mushrooms to plate. Rinse skillet clean and wipe dry with paper towels.

5. Add 1 teaspoon oil to skillet and return to high heat until just smoking. Add carrots and cook, stirring frequently, until beginning to brown, 1 to 2 minutes. Add broth, cover, and lower heat to medium. Cook carrots until just tender, 2 to 3 minutes. Uncover and cook until liquid evaporates, about 30 seconds. Transfer carrots to plate with mushrooms.

6. Add remaining 1 teaspoon oil to skillet and return to high heat until just smoking. Add snow peas and cook until spotty brown, about 2 minutes. Add cabbage and cook, stirring frequently, until wilted, about 2 minutes.

7. Clear center of skillet, add ginger mixture, and cook, mashing mixture into pan, until fragrant, 15 to 20 seconds. Stir ginger mixture into vegetables.

8. Stir in mushrooms and carrots. Whisk sauce to recombine, then add to skillet and cook, tossing constantly, until sauce is thickened, 2 to 3 minutes. Transfer to serving platter; sprinkle with sesame seeds, if using; and serve.

VARIATION

Stir-Fried Portobellos with Sweet Chili-Garlic Sauce

Replace sugar in glaze with 2 tablespoons honey. For sauce, omit vegetarian oyster sauce and toasted sesame oil, reduce broth to ¾ cup, increase soy sauce to 3 tablespoons, and add 2 tablespoons honey, 1 tablespoon rice vinegar, and 1 teaspoon sriracha. For vegetables, increase garlic to 4 cloves.

SEASON 25

Make-Ahead Cheese Soufflés

Serves 6 • Total Time: 1¼ hours, plus 1½ hours cooling and chilling

Why This Recipe Works Wouldn't it be nice to produce a batch of rich, cheesy soufflés without having to arrange your schedule around them? With this recipe, it's easily achieved. We began with a standard béchamel sauce and then added plenty of nutty Comté, which we supplemented with Parmesan to add extra-cheesy oomph without a lot of moisture that might otherwise cause the soufflé to collapse. After folding in egg whites that had been whipped to stiff peaks, we portioned the mixture into individual ramekins, which we baked in a water bath until the structure was softly set. The water bath ensured that the soufflés cooked evenly from edge to edge instead of becoming dry and stiff on the sides. When they were cool, we removed them from their ramekins and refrigerated them on a baking sheet. Just before serving, we transferred the baking sheet to a hot oven, where the soufflés became puffy and crisp.

> *You'll need six 4-ounce ramekins for this recipe. Greasing the ramekins generously ensures that the soufflés emerge cleanly. Sharp cheddar, Gruyère, or*

gouda can be substituted for the Comté. The cooled soufflés can be frozen for up to two weeks before the second bake; thaw them at room temperature before baking. Serve the soufflés with Pickled Mustard Seeds (recipe follows) and lightly dressed salad greens, if desired.

- 2 tablespoons unsalted butter
- 3 tablespoons all-purpose flour
- ¼ teaspoon table salt
     Pinch ground nutmeg
- 1 cup milk, divided
- 3 ounces Comté cheese, shredded (¾ cup)
- 1 ounce Parmesan cheese, grated (½ cup)
- 3 large eggs, separated
- 2 teaspoons minced fresh parsley
- ¼ teaspoon cream of tartar

1. Adjust oven rack to middle position and heat oven to 350 degrees. Generously spray six 4-ounce ramekins with vegetable oil spray. Bring kettle of water to boil.

2. Melt butter in medium saucepan over medium heat. Stir in flour, salt, and nutmeg and cook for 1 minute. Add ½ cup milk and whisk until smooth. Whisk in remaining ½ cup milk and cook, whisking constantly, until mixture is thickened and bubbling, about 2 minutes. Off heat, whisk in Comté and Parmesan until melted and smooth (mixture will be thick). Transfer to large bowl and whisk in egg yolks and parsley.

3. Using stand mixer fitted with whisk attachment, whip egg whites and cream of tartar on medium-low speed until foamy, about 1 minute. Increase speed to medium-high and whip until stiff peaks form, about 2 minutes. Gently whisk one-third of whites into cheese mixture. Using rubber spatula, gently fold in remaining whites.

4. Distribute mixture evenly among prepared ramekins and smooth tops. Transfer ramekins to 13 by 9-inch baking pan and add boiling water until it comes halfway up sides of ramekins. Bake until soufflés are puffed and register 170 to 175 degrees, 14 to 17 minutes. Using tongs, transfer ramekins to wire rack and let cool completely, 30 to 40 minutes (soufflés will shrink). While soufflés cool, line rimmed baking sheet with parchment paper and grease parchment lightly.

5. Invert 1 ramekin onto your hand and shake sharply until soufflé releases. Reinvert soufflé onto prepared sheet. Repeat with remaining soufflés. Cover tightly with plastic wrap and refrigerate for at least 1 hour or up to 3 days.

6. Adjust oven rack to middle position and heat oven to 400 degrees. Bake soufflés until puffed and deeply browned, 15 to 18 minutes. While soufflés bake, set out 6 plates. Using thin spatula, transfer 1 soufflé to each plate. Serve immediately.

ACCOMPANIMENT
Pickled Mustard Seeds
Makes ½ cup • Total Time: 50 minutes

With their bright, piquant flavor and caviar-like pop, these seeds make a perfect accompaniment to our Make-Ahead Cheese Soufflés. They are also a great addition to sandwiches, cheese or charcuterie boards, or even a vinaigrette. You can substitute cider vinegar for the white wine vinegar, if desired.

- ½ cup white wine vinegar
- ½ cup water
- ⅓ cup yellow mustard seeds
- 2 tablespoons maple syrup
- ½ teaspoon table salt

1. Whisk all ingredients together in small saucepan and bring to boil over medium-high heat. Lower heat to maintain simmer and cook, stirring frequently, until mustard seeds are swollen and softened and mixture is nearly dry, about 40 minutes (if mixture starts to dry out before mustard seeds have softened, add extra water, 1 tablespoon at a time).

2. Transfer to container and let cool completely. Cover and refrigerate for up to 1 month. Let come to room temperature before serving.

Spinach and Ricotta Gnudi with Tomato-Butter Sauce

Serves 4 • Total Time: 1¼ hours

Why This Recipe Works Pillowy, verdant gnudi are Italian dumplings created from ricotta and greens, delicately seasoned, and bound with egg and flour and/or bread crumbs. The trick to making them well is water management: Both the cheese and the greens are loaded with moisture, much of which needs to be either removed or bound up lest the dough be too difficult to handle or require so much binder that the dumplings are leaden. Some recipes call for draining the cheese for several hours or even overnight; we found that "towel-drying" the ricotta on a paper towel–lined rimmed baking sheet efficiently drained the cheese in just 10 minutes. Using frozen spinach, which readily gives up its water when it thaws, was another time-saver; all we had to do was squeeze it dry. A combination of egg whites, flour, and panko bread crumbs (which lightened the mixture by breaking up the structure) bound the mixture into a light, tender dough. Taking inspiration from both traditional sauces—bright tomato sugo and rich browned butter—we made a hybrid accompaniment by toasting garlic in browning butter and adding halved fresh cherry tomatoes, which collapsed and spilled their bright juices into the rich backdrop.

Ricotta without stabilizers such as locust bean, guar, and xanthan gums drains more readily. You can substitute part-skim ricotta for the whole-milk ricotta. Frozen whole-leaf spinach is easiest to squeeze dry, but frozen chopped spinach will work. Squeezing the spinach should remove ½ to ⅔ cup of liquid; you should have ⅔ cup of finely chopped spinach. Our tomato-butter sauce isn't strictly canonical; if you'd prefer a more traditional accompaniment, try a simple tomato sauce or browned butter and fresh sage. Serve with a simple salad.

Gnudi
- 12 ounces (1½ cups) whole-milk ricotta cheese
- ½ cup all-purpose flour
- 1 ounce Parmesan cheese, grated (½ cup), plus extra for garnishing
- 1 tablespoon panko bread crumbs
- ¾ teaspoon table salt, plus salt for cooking gnudi
- ½ teaspoon pepper
- ¼ teaspoon grated lemon zest
- 10 ounces frozen whole-leaf spinach, thawed and squeezed dry
- 2 large egg whites, lightly beaten

Butter Makes a Deliciously Different Tomato Sauce

"I'm team olive oil all the way. At public events, I'm often asked about my favorite ingredients— the ones I rely on to make my food taste great. My standard response: Maldon sea salt, extra-virgin olive oil, lemons, fresh herbs, and tomato paste. Butter never makes the list. (Don't tell Bridget!)

The test kitchen didn't invent the idea of butter in tomato sauce. I've made Marcella Hazan's famous four-ingredient tomato sauce with butter, onion, and salt. The butter softens the acidity of the canned tomatoes in this delicious sauce, but this recipe always seemed sui generis to me, and not a new way of making tomato sauce. But a few years ago, Lan developed this special but easy recipe for gnudi, and some-where along the way she decided to start her fresh cherry tomato sauce with browned butter. Oh my. As with the Marcella recipe, the butter tames the acidity of the tomatoes. But browning the butter makes this sauce more complex, more savory, and more spectacular. I now use this tomato–browned butter sauce with sautéed chicken cutlets or spooned over poached halibut. Tomatoes can bully milder foods like chicken or fish, and olive oil just amps up their aggressiveness. In contrast, butter brings out their sweet notes and browned butter makes bland foods (yes, I'm looking at you chicken) so much tastier. Can I be on team butter too?"

—Jack

Sauce

- 4 tablespoons unsalted butter
- 3 garlic cloves, sliced thin
- 12 ounces cherry or grape tomatoes, halved
- 2 teaspoons cider vinegar
- ¼ teaspoon table salt
- ¼ teaspoon pepper
- 2 tablespoons shredded fresh basil

1. For the gnudi: Line rimmed baking sheet with double layer of paper towels. Spread ricotta in even layer over towels; set aside and let sit for 10 minutes. Place flour, Parmesan, panko, salt, pepper, and lemon zest in large bowl and stir to combine. Process spinach in food processor until finely chopped, about 30 seconds, scraping down sides of bowl as needed. Transfer spinach to bowl with flour mixture. Grasp paper towels and fold ricotta in half; peel back towels. Rotate sheet 90 degrees and repeat folding and peeling 2 more times to consolidate ricotta into smaller mass. Using paper towels as sling, transfer ricotta to bowl with spinach mixture. Discard paper towels but do not wash sheet. Add egg whites to bowl and mix gently until well combined.

2. Transfer heaping teaspoons of dough to now-empty sheet (you should have 45 to 50 portions). Using your dry hands, gently roll each portion into 1-inch ball.

3. For the sauce: Melt butter in small saucepan over medium heat. Add garlic and cook, swirling saucepan occasionally, until butter is very foamy and garlic is pale golden brown, 2 to 3 minutes. Off heat, add tomatoes and vinegar; cover and set aside.

Managing the Water in Gnudi Making

Ricotta: Spread ricotta in even layer over paper towels; set aside for 10 minutes. Grasp paper towels, fold ricotta in half, and peel back towels. Rotate sheet 90 degrees; repeat folding and peeling to turn ricotta into smaller mass.

Spinach: Divide thawed frozen spinach into 3 or 4 portions. Gather 1 portion in your hands and squeeze out as much liquid as possible. Repeat with remaining portions.

4. Bring 1 quart water to boil in Dutch oven. Add 1½ teaspoons salt. Using spider skimmer or slotted spoon, transfer all gnudi to water. Return water to gentle simmer. Cook, adjusting heat to maintain gentle simmer, for 5 minutes, starting timer once water has returned to simmer (to confirm doneness, cut 1 dumpling in half; center should be firm).

5. While gnudi simmer, add salt and pepper to sauce and cook over medium-high heat, stirring occasionally, until tomatoes are warmed through and slightly softened, about 2 minutes. Divide sauce evenly among 4 bowls. Using spider skimmer or slotted spoon, remove gnudi from pot, drain well, and transfer to bowls with sauce. Garnish with basil and extra Parmesan. Serve immediately.

SEASON 24

White Bean and Mushroom Gratin

Serves 4 to 6 • Total Time: 1½ hours, plus 20 minutes standing

Why This Recipe Works Our complexly flavored vegetarian gratin features creamy white beans, meaty cremini mushrooms, tender carrots, and a crisp layer of bread. The gravy's flavor is created from the fond left by sautéing mushrooms and aromatics and deglazing with nutty dry sherry. Flour and the starchy canned bean liquid thickened the gravy. We baked the gratin in a low oven after topping it with seasoned bread cubes. As it baked, the lower portion of the bread merged with the gratin, creating a lovely soft texture, while the upper portion dried out. Then, using the broiler, we toasted the bread until it was golden brown.

We prefer a round rustic loaf (also known as a boule) with a chewy, open crumb and a sturdy crust for this recipe. Cannellini or navy beans can be used in place of great Northern beans, if desired.

- ½ cup extra-virgin olive oil, divided
- 10 ounces cremini mushrooms, trimmed and sliced ½ inch thick
- ¾ teaspoon table salt
- ½ teaspoon pepper, divided
- 4–5 slices country-style bread, cut into ½-inch cubes (5 cups)
- ¼ cup minced fresh parsley, divided
- 1 cup water
- 1 tablespoon all-purpose flour
- 1 small onion, chopped fine

5 garlic cloves, minced
1 tablespoon tomato paste
1½ teaspoons minced fresh thyme
⅓ cup dry sherry
2 (15-ounce) cans great Northern beans, undrained
3 carrots, peeled, halved lengthwise, and cut into ¾-inch pieces

1. Adjust oven rack to middle position and heat oven to 300 degrees. Heat ¼ cup oil in 12-inch ovensafe skillet over medium-high heat until shimmering. Add mushrooms, salt, and ¼ teaspoon pepper and cook, stirring occasionally, until mushrooms are well browned, 8 to 12 minutes.

2. While mushrooms cook, toss bread, 3 tablespoons parsley, remaining ¼ cup oil, and remaining ¼ teaspoon pepper together in bowl. Set aside. Stir water and flour in second bowl until no lumps of flour remain. Set aside.

3. Reduce heat to medium, add onion to skillet, and continue to cook, stirring frequently, until onion is translucent, 4 to 6 minutes. Reduce heat to medium-low; add garlic, tomato paste, and thyme; and cook, stirring constantly, until bottom of skillet is dark brown, 2 to 3 minutes. Add sherry and cook, scraping up any browned bits.

4. Add beans and their liquid, carrots, and flour mixture. Bring to boil over high heat. Off heat, arrange bread mixture over surface in even layer. Transfer skillet to oven and bake for 40 minutes. (Liquid should have consistency of thin gravy.)

5. Leave skillet in oven and turn on broiler. Broil until crumbs are golden brown, 4 to 7 minutes. Remove gratin from oven and let stand for 20 minutes. Sprinkle with remaining 1 tablespoon parsley; serve.

Roasted Poblano and Black Bean Enchiladas

Serves 4 to 6 • **Total Time: 1¾ hours**

Why This Recipe Works For great vegetarian enchiladas, we wanted a bright sauce featuring sweet-tart tomatillos. We rounded out the sauce with onion, garlic, cilantro, lime juice, and a splash of cream for richness. For the filling, we started with spicy, fruity, roasted poblano chiles. We smashed canned black beans to create a quick "refried" bean base and stirred in a little of the tomatillo sauce, Monterey Jack cheese, and some heady seasonings.

When choosing tomatillos, look for pale-green orbs with firm flesh that fills and splits open the fruit's outer papery husk, which must be removed before cooking. Serve with sour cream, diced avocado, sliced radishes, shredded romaine lettuce, and lime wedges.

1 pound tomatillos, husks and stems removed, rinsed well, dried, and halved
4 poblano chiles, halved, stemmed, and seeded
1 teaspoon plus ¼ cup vegetable oil, divided
2 onions, chopped fine, divided
1 cup fresh cilantro leaves, divided
⅓ cup vegetable broth
¼ cup heavy cream
4 garlic cloves, minced, divided
1 tablespoon lime juice
1¼ teaspoons table salt, divided
1 teaspoon sugar
1 teaspoon chili powder
½ teaspoon ground coriander
½ teaspoon ground cumin
1 (15-ounce) can black beans, rinsed, half of beans mashed smooth
8 ounces Monterey Jack cheese, shredded (2 cups), divided
12 (6-inch) corn tortillas

1. Adjust oven rack 6 inches from broiler element and heat broiler. Line rimmed baking sheet with aluminum foil. Toss tomatillos and poblanos with 1 teaspoon oil. Arrange tomatillos cut side down and poblanos skin side up on prepared sheet. Broil until vegetables are blackened and beginning to soften, 5 to 10 minutes. Let vegetables cool slightly. Remove skins and seeds from poblanos (leave tomatillo skins intact), then chop into ½-inch pieces.

2. Process broiled tomatillos, 1 cup onion, ½ cup cilantro, broth, cream, 1 tablespoon oil, half of garlic, lime juice, 1 teaspoon salt, and sugar in food processor until sauce is smooth, about 2 minutes. Season with salt and pepper to taste.

3. Heat 1 tablespoon oil in 12-inch skillet over medium heat until shimmering. Add remaining onion and remaining ¼ teaspoon salt and cook until softened, 5 to 7 minutes. Stir in chili powder, coriander, cumin, and remaining garlic and cook until fragrant, about 30 seconds. Stir in mashed and whole beans and chopped poblanos and cook until warmed through, about 2 minutes. Transfer mixture to large bowl and let cool slightly. Stir in 1 cup Monterey Jack, ½ cup tomatillo sauce, and remaining ½ cup cilantro. Season with salt and pepper to taste.

4. Adjust oven rack to middle position and heat oven to 400 degrees. Spread ½ cup tomatillo sauce over bottom of 13 by 9-inch baking dish. Brush both sides of tortillas with remaining 2 tablespoons oil. Arrange tortillas, overlapping, on rimmed baking sheet in 2 rows (6 tortillas each). Bake until tortillas are warm and pliable, about 5 minutes.

5. Working with 1 warm tortilla at a time, spread ¼ cup bean-cheese filling across center of tortilla. Roll tortilla tightly around filling and place seam side down in baking dish; arrange enchiladas in 2 rows across width of dish.

6. Pour remaining sauce over top to cover completely and sprinkle remaining 1 cup cheese down center of enchiladas. Cover dish tightly with greased aluminum foil. Bake until enchiladas are heated through and cheese is melted, about 25 minutes. Let cool for 5 minutes before serving.

Eggplant Parmesan

Serves 6 to 8 • **Total Time: 2 hours, plus 30 minutes standing**

Why This Recipe Works Frying the eggplant for eggplant Parm is not only time-consuming but can also make the dish heavy and dull. In hopes of eliminating the grease as well as some prep time, we cooked the eggplant in the oven and looked for other ways to freshen up this Italian classic. We salted and drained the eggplant slices to improve their texture. A traditional bound breading worked best for giving the eggplant a crisp coating. Baking the eggplant on preheated and oiled baking sheets resulted in crisp, golden-brown slices. While the eggplant was in the oven, we made a quick tomato sauce using canned diced tomatoes. We layered the sauce, eggplant, and mozzarella in a baking dish and left the top layer of eggplant mostly unsauced, so that it would crisp up in the oven.

Use kosher salt when salting the eggplant. The coarse grains don't dissolve as readily as the fine grains of regular table salt, so any excess can be easily wiped away. It's necessary to divide the eggplant into two batches when tossing it with the salt. To be time-efficient, use the 30 to 45 minutes during which the salted eggplant sits to prepare the breading.

Eggplant

    2 pounds globe eggplant (2 medium eggplants), cut crosswise into ¼-inch-thick rounds
    1 tablespoon kosher salt, for salting eggplant
    8 slices high-quality white sandwich bread, torn into quarters
    2 ounces Parmesan cheese, grated (1 cup)
 1½ teaspoons pepper, divided
    ¼ teaspoon table salt
    1 cup unbleached all-purpose flour
    4 large eggs
    6 tablespoons vegetable oil

Tomato Sauce

    3 (14.5-ounce) cans diced tomatoes, divided
    2 tablespoons extra-virgin olive oil
    4 garlic cloves, minced
    ¼ teaspoon red pepper flakes
    ½ cup coarsely chopped fresh basil leaves

    8 ounces whole-milk or part-skim mozzarella cheese, shredded (2 cups)
    1 ounce Parmesan cheese, grated (½ cup)
  10 fresh basil leaves, torn, for garnish

1. For the eggplant: Toss half of eggplant slices and 1½ teaspoons kosher salt in a large bowl until combined; transfer salted eggplant to large colander set over bowl. Repeat with remaining eggplant and kosher salt, placing second batch on top of first. Let stand until eggplant releases about 2 tablespoons liquid, 30 to 45 minutes. Spread eggplant slices on triple thickness of paper towels; cover with another triple thickness of paper towels. Press firmly on each slice to remove as much liquid as possible, then wipe off excess salt.

2. While eggplant is draining, adjust oven racks to upper-middle and lower-middle positions, place rimmed baking sheet on each rack, and heat oven to 425 degrees. Process bread in food processor to fine, even crumbs, about 20 to 30 seconds. Transfer crumbs to shallow dish and stir in Parmesan, ½ teaspoon pepper, and salt; set aside. Wipe out workbowl (do not wash) and set aside.

3. Combine flour and remaining 1 teaspoon pepper in large zipper-lock bag; shake to combine. Beat eggs in second shallow dish. Place 8 to 10 eggplant slices in bag with flour; seal bag and shake to coat slices. Remove slices, shaking off excess flour, dip into eggs, let excess egg run off, then coat evenly with bread-crumb mixture; set breaded slices on wire rack set over baking sheet. Repeat with remaining eggplant.

4. Remove preheated baking sheets from oven; add 3 tablespoons vegetable oil to each sheet, tilting to coat evenly with oil. Place half of breaded eggplant slices on each sheet in single layer; bake until eggplant is well browned and crisp, about 30 minutes, switching and rotating baking sheets after 10 minutes, and flipping eggplant slices with wide spatula after 20 minutes. Do not turn off oven.

5. For the tomato sauce: While eggplant bakes, process 2 cans diced tomatoes in food processor until almost smooth, about 5 seconds. Heat olive oil, garlic, and red pepper flakes in large heavy-bottomed saucepan over medium-high heat, stirring occasionally, until fragrant and garlic is light golden, about 3 minutes; stir in processed tomatoes and remaining can of diced tomatoes. Bring sauce to boil, then reduce heat to medium-low and simmer, stirring occasionally, until slightly thickened and reduced, about 15 minutes (you should have about 4 cups). Stir in basil and season with table salt and pepper to taste.

6. To assemble: Spread 1 cup of tomato sauce in bottom of 13 by 9-inch baking dish. Layer in half eggplant slices, overlapping slices to fit; distribute 1 cup more sauce over eggplant; sprinkle with half of mozzarella. Layer in remaining eggplant and dot with 1 cup more sauce, leaving majority of eggplant exposed so it will remain crisp; sprinkle with Parmesan and remaining mozzarella. Bake until bubbling and cheese is browned, 13 to 15 minutes. Let cool for 10 minutes, scatter basil over top, and serve, passing remaining tomato sauce separately.

SEASON 15

Eggplant Involtini

Serves 4 to 6 • Total Time: 1¾ hours

Why This Recipe Works Making eggplant involtini ("little bundles" in Italian) can be a labor-intensive and messy affair, but one bite of the resulting dish—charmingly tidy involtini with homemade tomato sauce and a pleasantly cheesy filling—is enough to realize why it's still made by home cooks. We wanted to see if we could streamline the process and come up with a version of involtini that would emphasize the eggplant and minimize the fuss. First up for fixing: the eggplant. Generally this recipe calls for frying, but in order to fry eggplant, you must first get rid of the excess water or the eggplant will turn mushy and oily. Salting can fix this problem, but it's time-consuming. Instead, we opted for a lighter and more hands-off option: baking. We brushed the planks with oil, seasoned them, and then baked them for 30 minutes. They emerged light brown and tender, with a compact texture that was neither mushy nor sodden. To lighten up our involtini filling, we decreased the amount of ricotta and replaced it with more flavorful Pecorino Romano, and brightened the flavor with a squeeze of lemon juice. To ensure that our filling stayed creamy and didn't toughen up, we added bread crumbs to the mix. We made a bare-bones tomato sauce, then added the eggplant rolls directly to the sauce. Using a skillet meant that we could easily transfer the whole operation to the oven.

Select shorter, wider eggplants for this recipe. Part-skim ricotta may be used, but do not use fat-free ricotta. Serve the eggplant with crusty bread and a salad.

2 large eggplants (1½ pounds each), peeled
6 tablespoons vegetable oil, divided
2 teaspoons kosher salt, divided
½ teaspoon pepper, divided
2 garlic cloves, minced
¼ teaspoon dried oregano
    Pinch red pepper flakes
1 (28-ounce) can whole peeled tomatoes, drained
    with juice reserved, chopped coarse
1 slice hearty white sandwich bread,
    torn into 1-inch pieces
8 ounces (1 cup) whole-milk ricotta cheese
1½ ounces grated Pecorino Romano (¾ cup), divided
¼ cup plus 1 tablespoon chopped fresh basil, divided
1 tablespoon lemon juice

1. Slice each eggplant lengthwise into ½-inch-thick planks (you should have 12 planks). Trim rounded surface from each end piece so it lies flat.

2. Adjust 1 oven rack to lower-middle position and second rack 8 inches from broiler element. Heat oven to 375 degrees. Line 2 rimmed baking sheets with parchment paper and spray generously with vegetable oil spray. Arrange eggplant slices in single layer on prepared sheets. Brush 1 side of eggplant slices with 2½ tablespoons oil and sprinkle with ½ teaspoon salt and ¼ teaspoon pepper. Flip eggplant slices and brush with 2½ tablespoons oil and sprinkle with ½ teaspoon salt and remaining ¼ teaspoon pepper. Bake

until tender and lightly browned, 30 to 35 minutes, switching and rotating sheets halfway through baking. Let cool for 5 minutes. Using thin spatula, flip each slice over. Heat broiler.

3. While eggplant cooks, heat remaining 1 tablespoon oil in 12-inch broiler-safe skillet over medium-low heat until just shimmering. Add garlic, oregano, pepper flakes, and ½ teaspoon salt and cook, stirring occasionally, until fragrant, about 30 seconds. Stir in tomatoes and their juice. Increase heat to high and bring to simmer. Reduce heat to medium-low and simmer until thickened, about 15 minutes. Cover and set aside.

4. Pulse bread in food processor until finely ground, 10 to 15 pulses. Combine bread crumbs, ricotta, ½ cup Pecorino, ¼ cup basil, lemon juice, and remaining ½ teaspoon salt in medium bowl.

5. With widest short sides of eggplant slices facing you, evenly distribute ricotta mixture on bottom third of each slice. Gently roll up each eggplant slice and place seam side down in tomato sauce.

6. Bring sauce to simmer over medium heat. Simmer for 5 minutes. Transfer skillet to oven and broil until eggplant is well browned and cheese is heated through, 5 to 10 minutes. Sprinkle with remaining ¼ cup Pecorino and let stand for 5 minutes. Sprinkle with remaining 1 tablespoon basil and serve.

Alu Parathas

Makes 8 parathas • Total Time: 1½ hours, plus 1 hour 5 minutes cooling and resting

Why This Recipe Works These steamy potato-stuffed Punjabi flatbreads are typically enjoyed as the center of a meal with spicy-sweet mango pickle, cooling raita, or a refreshing tomato salad. We started by making a flavorful potato stuffing of mashed russet potatoes, aromatics, and a bold mix of spices and seeds. Next, we mixed a dough in the food processor, letting it rest for 30 minutes to allow the gluten to relax for easier rolling out. After stuffing the potato balls into rounds of dough, we rolled the packages thin and griddled them in a cast-iron skillet using nutty ghee. Flipping the breads only three times ensured that they stayed pliable while still developing lots of crispy brown spots.

Ghee, kalonji, ajwain, and amchoor can all be purchased at a South Asian market or online. Ajwain has a thyme-like flavor and is often added to fried Indian food to aid digestion; if you can't find it, it's OK to leave it out. If preferred, you can substitute ¼ teaspoon of cayenne pepper for the Thai chile in the stuffing. We strongly recommend weighing the flour for this recipe. Serve the parathas as an entrée with raita, prepared mango pickle, or Tamatya-Kandyachi Koshimbir (recipe follows) for breakfast, lunch, or dinner.

Potato Stuffing

1	pound russet potatoes, peeled and cut into 1-inch pieces
2	tablespoons minced fresh cilantro
1	tablespoon grated fresh ginger
1½	teaspoons amchoor
1	teaspoon ground cumin
¾	teaspoon table salt
1	Thai chile, stemmed and minced
¼	teaspoon kalonji
¼	teaspoon ajwain

Dough

1⅔	cups (8⅓ ounces) all-purpose flour
½	teaspoon table salt
½	teaspoon sugar
2	tablespoons vegetable oil
½	cup plus 1 tablespoon cold water
¼	cup ghee, melted

1. For the potato stuffing: Place potatoes in large saucepan, add cold water to cover by 1 inch, and bring to boil over high heat. Reduce heat to maintain simmer and cook until potatoes are very tender, about 16 minutes. Drain well and process through ricer or mash with potato masher until completely smooth. Set aside and let partially cool, about 20 minutes.

2. Stir cilantro, ginger, amchoor, cumin, salt, Thai chile, kalonji, and ajwain into potatoes. Season with salt to taste. Cover and set aside. (Potato stuffing can be refrigerated for up to 24 hours; let come to room temperature before using.)

3. For the dough: Pulse flour, salt, and sugar in food processor until combined, about 5 pulses. Add oil and pulse until incorporated, about 5 pulses. With processor running, slowly add cold water and process until dough is combined and no dry flour remains, about 30 seconds. Transfer dough to clean counter and knead by hand to form smooth, round ball, about 30 seconds; transfer to bowl, cover with plastic wrap, and let rest for 30 minutes.

GAME CHANGER

Go Ahead. Have Bread and Potatoes for Dinner.

"When I found out that my former colleague Kaumudi Marathé was going to develop a recipe for alu parathas, I was over the moon. I cook a lot of Indian food, and I'm also deeply fond of carbs, so I knew I would love her potato-stuffed flatbreads. They hail from Punjab and are a staple across the northern part of the Indian subcontinent. In India they're served as a main course, accompanied by a simple tomato-onion salad. The combination makes a delightful meal at any time of day, including breakfast.

Making the breads is a bit of a project, but it's well worth it—and fun to do: First, season boiled potatoes with ginger, cilantro, chiles, and aromatic spices: kalonji, ajwain, cumin, and amchoor. Then, make the dough, which comes together easily in the food processor. When you're ready to eat, wrap disks of dough around balls of the potato filling and press them flat. Cook the potato-stuffed breads in nutty ghee until they're pliable but also crisp and browned in spots."

4. Divide potato stuffing into 8 equal portions and roll into balls (they will be about 1½ inches wide); cover with plastic. Divide dough into 8 equal pieces, about 1¾ ounces each, and cover loosely with plastic. Working with 1 piece of dough at a time, form dough pieces into smooth, taut balls. (To round, set piece of dough on unfloured counter. Loosely cup your hand around dough and, without applying pressure to dough, move your hand in small circular motions. Tackiness of dough against counter and circular motion should work dough into smooth ball.) Let dough balls rest, covered, for 15 minutes. While dough balls rest, line rimmed baking sheet with parchment paper.

5. Roll 1 dough ball into 4-inch disk on lightly floured counter. Place 1 stuffing ball in center of dough disk. Gather edges of dough around stuffing to enclose completely; pinch to seal. Place seam side down on lightly floured counter, gently flatten, and lightly and gently roll to even ⅛-inch-thick round (about 8 inches wide). Transfer to prepared sheet and cover loosely with plastic. Repeat with remaining dough balls, stacking parathas between layers of parchment.

6. Heat 10-inch cast-iron skillet over medium heat for 5 minutes, then reduce heat to low. Brush any remaining flour from both sides of 1 paratha, then gently place in hot skillet, being careful not to stretch paratha. Cook until large bubbles begin to form on surface, underside of paratha is light blond, and paratha moves freely in skillet, 30 to 60 seconds. (Paratha may puff.) Using metal spatula, flip paratha; brush with ghee. Cook until underside is spotty brown and moves freely in skillet, 20 to 60 seconds, pressing any puffed edges firmly onto skillet with spatula to ensure even contact.

7. Flip paratha back onto first side. Repeat brushing with ghee, pressing, cooking, and flipping once more until paratha is even more spotty brown on both sides and no longer looks raw, about 30 seconds per side. Transfer cooked paratha to second rimmed baking sheet, let cool slightly, then cover loosely with dish towel.

8. Repeat with remaining parathas, wiping out skillet with paper towels between each paratha and briefly removing skillet from heat if it begins to smoke or if paratha browns too quickly. Serve hot. (Parathas can be stacked between layers of parchment paper, placed in zipper-lock bag, and refrigerated for up to 2 days; to refresh, heat 10-inch cast-iron skillet over medium heat for 5 minutes, then reduce heat to low. Cook paratha until warmed through, flipping 3 times, 10 to 15 seconds per side.)

Tamatya-Kandyachi Koshimbir

Serves 4 • Total Time: 15 minutes

If you are not fond of raw onion, substitute ¼ cup of crushed peanuts.

- 4 large, firm tomatoes, cored and cut into ¼-inch dice
- ½ teaspoon table salt
- 1 Thai green chile, sliced
  Pinch sugar
- 1 large onion, chopped fine
- ¼ teaspoon ground cumin
- 2 tablespoons grated fresh coconut (optional)
- 2 tablespoons finely chopped fresh cilantro (optional)

Stir tomatoes, salt, Thai chile, and sugar together in bowl. Let sit for 5 minutes to allow flavors to meld. Stir in onion and cumin. Serve, garnishing with coconut and cilantro, if using.

Filling Alu Parathas

1. Place stuffing in center of dough.

2. Pinch edges tightly to seal. Turn ball seam side down.

3. To prevent edges from tearing, press gently as you roll. Roll stuffed dough to ⅛-inch-thick 8-inch round.

Grown-Up Grilled Cheese Sandwiches with Cheddar and Shallots

Serves 4 • Total Time: 45 minutes

Why This Recipe Works Melty American cheese on fluffy white bread is a childhood classic, but we wanted a grilled cheese for adults that offered more robust flavor. Aged cheddar gave us the complexity we were after, but it made for a greasy sandwich with a grainy filling. Adding a splash of wine and some Brie helped the aged cheddar melt evenly without separating or becoming greasy. Using a food processor to combine the ingredients ensured our cheese-and-wine mixture was easy to spread. A little bit of shallot ramped up the flavor without detracting from the cheese, and a smear of mustard butter livened up the bread.

For the best flavor, look for a cheddar aged for about one year (avoid cheddar aged for longer; it won't melt well in this recipe). To quickly bring the cheese to room temperature, microwave the pieces until warm, about 30 seconds. The first two sandwiches can be held in a 200-degree oven on a wire rack set in a baking sheet while the second batch cooks.

    7 ounces aged cheddar cheese, cut into 24 equal
       pieces, room temperature
    2 ounces Brie cheese, rind removed
    2 tablespoons dry white wine or dry vermouth
    4 teaspoons minced shallot
    3 tablespoons unsalted butter, softened
    1 teaspoon Dijon mustard
    8 slices hearty white sandwich bread

1. Process cheddar, Brie, and wine in food processor until smooth paste is formed, 20 to 30 seconds. Add shallot and pulse to combine, 3 to 5 pulses. Combine butter and mustard in small bowl.

2. Working on parchment paper–lined counter, divide mustard butter evenly among slices of bread. Spread butter evenly over surface of bread. Flip 4 slices of bread over and spread cheese mixture evenly over slices. Top with remaining 4 slices of bread, buttered sides up.

3. Preheat 12-inch nonstick skillet over medium heat for 2 minutes. (Droplets of water should just sizzle when flicked onto pan.) Place 2 sandwiches in skillet, reduce heat to medium-low, and cook until both sides are crisp and golden brown, 6 to 9 minutes per side, moving sandwiches to ensure even browning. Remove sandwiches from skillet and let stand for 2 minutes before serving. Repeat with remaining 2 sandwiches.

VARIATIONS

Grown-Up Grilled Cheese Sandwiches with Gruyère and Chives

Substitute Gruyère cheese for cheddar, chives for shallot, and rye sandwich bread for white sandwich bread.

Grown-Up Grilled Cheese Sandwiches with Asiago and Dates

Substitute Asiago cheese for cheddar, finely chopped pitted dates for shallot, and oatmeal sandwich bread for white sandwich bread.

Grown-Up Grilled Cheese Sandwiches with Comté and Cornichon

Substitute Comté cheese for cheddar, minced cornichon for shallot, and rye sandwich bread for white sandwich bread.

Grown-Up Grilled Cheese Sandwiches with Robiola and Chipotle

Substitute Robiola cheese, rind removed, for cheddar; ¼ teaspoon minced canned chipotle chile in adobo sauce for shallot; and oatmeal sandwich bread for white sandwich bread.

1. Heat 10-inch nonstick skillet over medium heat until hot, about 2 minutes. Place 1 tortilla in skillet and toast until soft and puffed slightly at the edges, about 2 minutes. Flip tortilla and toast until puffed and slightly browned, 1 to 2 minutes longer. Transfer tortilla to cutting board. Repeat to toast second tortilla while assembling first quesadilla. Sprinkle ¼ cup cheese and half of jalapeños, if using, over half of tortilla, leaving ½-inch border around edge. Fold tortilla in half and press to flatten. Brush top generously with oil, sprinkle lightly with kosher salt, and set aside. Repeat to form second quesadilla.

2. Place both quesadillas in skillet, oiled sides down; cook over medium heat until crisp and well browned, 1 to 2 minutes. Brush tops with oil and sprinkle lightly with kosher salt. Flip quesadillas and cook until second sides are crisp, 1 to 2 minutes. Transfer quesadillas to cutting board; let cool for 3 minutes, halve each quesadilla, and serve.

Cooking Quesadillas

To cook 2 quesadillas at the same time, arrange folded edges at center of 10-inch nonstick skillet.

SEASON 6

Quesadillas

Makes 2 folded 8-inch quesadillas
Total Time: 25 minutes

Why This Recipe Works A traditional quesadilla is meant to be a quick snack, not an overstuffed tortilla with complicated fillings. We wanted a simple toasted tortilla, crisp and hot, filled with just the right amount of cheese. We kept the tortillas crisp by lightly toasting them in a dry skillet. We then filled them with cheese and pickled jalapeños, lightly coated the tortillas with oil, and returned them to the skillet until they were well browned and the cheese was fully melted. Not yet satisfied that our recipe was speedy enough, we made the process even more convenient by switching to 8-inch tortillas and folding them in half around the filling. This allowed us to cook two at one time in the same skillet, and the fold also kept our generous cheese filling from oozing out.

Cooling the quesadillas before cutting and serving them is important; straight from the skillet, the melted cheese will ooze out. Finished quesadillas can be held on a baking sheet in a 200-degree oven for up to 20 minutes.

2 (8-inch) flour tortillas
2 ounces Monterey Jack or cheddar cheese, shredded (½ cup)
1 tablespoon minced pickled jalapeños (optional)
   Vegetable oil for brushing tortillas
   Kosher salt

SEASON 22

Vegan Baja-Style Cauliflower Tacos

Serves 4 to 6 • Total Time: 1 hour

Why This Recipe Works Battered cauliflower bites, drizzled with a cool and creamy sauce, can serve as an incredible vegan stand-in for the fried fish traditionally served in Baja-style tacos. We wanted to avoid the mess of deep frying, so we cut the cauliflower into large florets and roasted it. To boost the cauliflower's flavor, we first dunked the pieces in canned coconut milk seasoned with garlic and spices and then rolled them in a mixture of panko bread crumbs and shredded coconut. Not only did this add richness and tropical flavor, but it also mimicked the crisp exterior texture of batter-fried fish. A bed of

crunchy slaw with juicy mango and spicy jalapeño provided the perfect balance of sweetness and heat. By using equal parts vegan mayonnaise and dairy-free sour cream, plus cilantro, we were able to whip up a vegan crema to top it all off. Just add cerveza and sunshine.

For a spicier slaw, mince and add the jalapeño ribs and seeds. Serve with lime wedges.

3	cups (7½ ounces) coleslaw mix
½	mango, peeled and cut into ¼-inch pieces (¾ cup)
1	tablespoon chopped fresh cilantro
2	tablespoons lime juice
1	tablespoon minced jalapeño chile
1¼	teaspoons table salt, divided
1	cup unsweetened shredded coconut
1	cup panko bread crumbs
1	cup canned coconut milk
1	teaspoon garlic powder
1	teaspoon ground cumin
¼	teaspoon cayenne
½	head cauliflower (1 pound), trimmed and cut into 1-inch pieces
8–12	(6-inch) corn tortillas, warmed
1	recipe Vegan Cilantro Sauce (recipe follows)

1. Adjust oven rack to middle position and heat oven to 450 degrees. Combine coleslaw mix, mango, cilantro, lime juice, jalapeño, and ¼ teaspoon salt in bowl; cover and refrigerate.

2. Spray rimmed baking sheet with vegetable oil spray. Combine coconut and panko in shallow dish. Whisk coconut milk, garlic powder, cumin, cayenne, and

remaining 1 teaspoon salt together in bowl. Add cauliflower to coconut milk mixture; toss to coat well. Working with 1 piece cauliflower at a time, remove from coconut milk, letting excess drip back into bowl, then coat well with coconut-panko mixture, pressing gently to adhere; transfer to prepared sheet.

3. Bake until cauliflower is tender, golden, and crisp, 20 to 25 minutes, flipping cauliflower and rotating sheet halfway through baking.

4. Divide slaw evenly among warm tortillas and top with cauliflower. Drizzle with cilantro sauce and serve.

Vegan Cilantro Sauce

Makes about ¾ cup • Total Time: 5 minutes

We prefer the flavor and texture of Tofutti Better Than Sour Cream. Other dairy-free sour creams will add their distinctive flavor, and you may need to adjust the consistency with water. We strongly prefer our favorite vegan mayonnaise, Just Mayo.

¼	cup vegan mayonnaise
¼	cup dairy-free sour cream
3	tablespoons water
3	tablespoons minced fresh cilantro
¼	teaspoon table salt

Whisk all ingredients together in bowl.

SEASON 22

Pupusas

Makes 8 pupusas • Total Time: 1¼ hours

Why This Recipe Works These savory stuffed corn cakes have a long history in Honduras and El Salvador, where they're made by stuffing cheese, beans, braised meat, or a combination thereof into a ball of corn flour dough called masa. For smooth, well-hydrated dough that was easy to work with and didn't dry out when cooked, we hydrated the masa harina with boiling rather than room-temperature water, which allowed the starches in the flour to absorb it more quickly and completely. Using the proper ratio of masa dough to filling ensured that each bite of pupusa included plenty of melted cheese filling. We pressed the stuffed pupusas into 4-inch disks between sheets of plastic to create a uniform thickness; this size also allowed us to cook four pupusas at once in a 12-inch skillet. The crunch and acidic brightness of curtido and salsa perfectly complemented the tender, savory patties.

For an accurate measurement of boiling water, bring a full kettle of water to a boil and then measure out the desired amount. Properly hydrated masa dough should be tacky, requiring damp hands to keep it from sticking to your palms. If the dough feels the slightest bit dry at any time, knead in warm tap water, 1 teaspoon at a time, until the dough is tacky. An occasional leak while frying the pupusas is to be expected, and the browned cheese is delicious. Feta cheese can be substituted for the cotija; if you can find quesillo, use 10 ounces in place of the cotija and Monterey Jack.

2 cups (8 ounces) masa harina
½ teaspoon table salt
2 cups boiling water, plus warm tap water as needed
2 teaspoons vegetable oil, divided
2 ounces cotija cheese, cut into 2 pieces
8 ounces Monterey Jack cheese, cut into 8 pieces
1 recipe Quick Salsa (recipe follows)
1 recipe Curtido (recipe follows)

1. Using marker, draw 4-inch circle in center of 1 side of 1-quart or 1-gallon zipper-lock bag. Cut open seams along both sides of bag, but leave bottom seam intact so bag opens completely.

2. Mix masa harina and salt together in medium bowl. Add boiling water and 1 teaspoon oil and mix with rubber spatula until soft dough forms. Cover dough and let rest for 20 minutes.

3. While dough rests, line rimmed baking sheet with parchment paper. Process cotija in food processor until cotija is finely chopped and resembles wet sand, about 20 seconds. Add Monterey Jack and process until mixture resembles wet oatmeal, about 30 seconds (it will not form cohesive mass). Remove processor blade. Form cheese mixture into 8 balls, weighing about 1¼ ounces each, and place balls on 1 half of prepared sheet.

4. Knead dough in bowl for 15 to 20 seconds. Test dough's hydration by flattening golf ball–size piece. If cracks larger than ¼ inch form around edges, add warm tap water, 2 teaspoons at a time, until dough is soft and slightly tacky. Transfer dough to counter, shape into large ball, and divide into 8 equal pieces. Using your damp hands, roll 1 dough piece into ball and place on empty half of prepared sheet. Cover with damp dish towel. Repeat with remaining dough pieces.

5. Place open cut bag marked side down on counter. Place 1 dough ball in center of circle. Fold other side of bag over ball. Using glass pie plate or 8-inch square baking dish, gently press dough to 4-inch diameter, using circle drawn on bag as guide. Turn out disk into your palm and place 1 cheese ball in center. Bring sides of dough up around filling and pinch top to seal. Remoisten your hands and roll ball until smooth, smoothing any cracks with your damp fingertip. Return ball to bag and slowly press to 4-inch diameter. Pinch closed any small cracks that form at edges. Return pupusa to sheet and cover with damp dish towel. Repeat with remaining dough and filling.

Shaping Pupusas

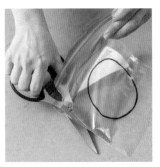   

1. Using marker, draw 4-inch circle in center of 1 side of 1-quart or 1-gallon zipper-lock bag. Cut open seams along both sides of bag, but leave bottom seam intact so bag opens completely.

2. Place open cut bag marked side down on counter. Place dough ball in center of circle. Fold other side of bag over ball. Using glass pie plate, gently press dough to 4-inch diameter.

3. Turn out disk into your palm and place cheese ball in center. Bring sides of dough up around filling; pinch to seal. Remoisten your hands and roll ball, smoothing any cracks with your damp fingertip.

4. Return ball to zipper-lock bag and use pie plate to slowly press to 4-inch diameter. Pinch closed any small cracks that form at edges. Repeat steps 2 through 4 with remaining dough and filling.

6. Heat remaining 1 teaspoon oil in 12-inch nonstick skillet over medium-high heat until shimmering. Wipe skillet clean with paper towels. Carefully lay 4 pupusas in skillet and cook until spotty brown on both sides, 2 to 4 minutes per side. Transfer to platter and repeat with remaining 4 pupusas. Serve warm with salsa and curtido.

Quick Salsa

Serves 4 • Total Time: 10 minutes

For a spicier salsa, add the jalapeño seeds as desired.

- ¼   small red onion
- 2   tablespoons minced fresh cilantro
- ½   small jalapeño chile, seeded and minced
- 1   (14.5-ounce) can diced tomatoes, drained
- 2   teaspoons lime juice, plus extra for seasoning
- 1   small garlic clove, minced
- ¼   teaspoon table salt
  Pinch pepper

Pulse onion, cilantro, and jalapeño in food processor until finely chopped, 5 pulses, scraping down sides of bowl as needed. Add tomatoes, lime juice, garlic, salt, and pepper and process until smooth, 20 to 30 seconds. Season with salt and extra lime juice to taste.

Curtido

Serves 4 • Total Time: 20 minutes, plus 1 hour chilling

For a spicier slaw, add the jalapeño seeds as desired.

- 1   cup cider vinegar
- ½   cup water
- 1   tablespoon sugar
- 1½   teaspoons table salt
- ½   head green cabbage, cored and sliced thin (6 cups)
- 1   onion, sliced thin
- 1   large carrot, peeled and shredded
- 1   jalapeño chile, stemmed, seeded, and minced
- 1   teaspoon dried oregano
- 1   cup chopped fresh cilantro

Whisk vinegar, water, sugar, and salt in large bowl until sugar is dissolved. Add cabbage, onion, carrot, jalapeño, and oregano and toss to combine. Cover and refrigerate for at least 1 hour or up to 24 hours. Toss slaw, then drain. Return slaw to bowl and stir in cilantro.

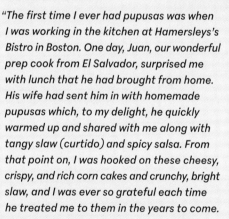

GAME CHANGER

Simply Shaped Corn Cakes

"The first time I ever had pupusas was when I was working in the kitchen at Hamersleys's Bistro in Boston. One day, Juan, our wonderful prep cook from El Salvador, surprised me with lunch that he had brought from home. His wife had sent him in with homemade pupusas which, to my delight, he quickly warmed up and shared with me along with tangy slaw (curtido) and spicy salsa. From that point on, I was hooked on these cheesy, crispy, and rich corn cakes and crunchy, bright slaw, and I was ever so grateful each time he treated me to them in the years to come.

Fast forward 20 years: To say that I was excited when Cook's Illustrated had pupusas on their lineup and was going to develop a recipe is an understatement. Senior editor Steve Dunn did an excellent job developing the recipe, which I can now make and share with my family and friends. It brings back so many fond and delicious memories of my restaurant days and working with my friend Juan."

— *Erin*

Ultimate Veggie Burgers

Makes 12 patties • Total Time: 2½ hours, plus 20 minutes cooling

Why This Recipe Works For veggie burgers with complex, savory flavor and a satisfyingly robust texture good enough to be worth the effort, we used a combination of quick-cooking, meaty lentils and bulgur as the base. As a bonus, these burgers can be made ahead and frozen for a quick weeknight meal. An earthy mix of lentils, bulgur, and panko paired with aromatic onions, celery, leek, and garlic gave these burgers a deeply flavorful base. Cremini mushrooms lent meaty flavor, and a surprising addition of ground cashews amplified the meatiness even more. Pulsing everything in the food processor made for a cohesive and even-textured mix, and mayonnaise provided necessary fat to bind our burgers. After forming the mixture into patties, we seared them in a skillet to develop a crunchy, browned exterior.

Do not confuse bulgur for cracked wheat, which has a much longer cooking time and will not work in this recipe.

¾	cup brown lentils, picked over and rinsed
1	teaspoon table salt, plus salt for cooking lentils and bulgur
¾	cup medium-grind bulgur, rinsed
¼	cup vegetable oil, divided, plus extra as needed
2	onions, chopped fine
1	celery rib, chopped fine
1	small leek, white and light green parts only, halved lengthwise, chopped fine, and washed thoroughly
2	garlic cloves, minced
1	pound cremini or white mushrooms, trimmed and sliced ¼ inch thick
1	cup raw cashews
⅓	cup mayonnaise
2	cups panko bread crumbs
4–12	hamburger buns, toasted if desired

1. Bring 3 cups water, lentils, and 1 teaspoon salt to boil in medium saucepan over high heat. Reduce heat to medium-low and simmer gently, stirring occasionally, until lentils are just beginning to fall apart, about 25 minutes. Drain lentils, spread out over paper towel–lined rimmed baking sheet, and pat dry; let cool to room temperature.

2. Bring 2 cups water and ½ teaspoon salt to boil in small saucepan. Off heat, stir in bulgur, cover, and let sit until tender, 15 to 20 minutes. Drain bulgur, pressing with rubber spatula to remove excess moisture, and transfer to large bowl; let cool slightly.

3. Heat 1 tablespoon oil in 12-inch nonstick skillet over medium-high heat until shimmering. Add onions, celery, leek, and garlic and cook, stirring occasionally, until vegetables begin to brown, about 10 minutes. Spread vegetable mixture onto second rimmed baking sheet.

4. Heat 1 tablespoon oil in now-empty skillet over high heat until shimmering. Add mushrooms and cook, stirring occasionally, until golden brown, about 12 minutes; add to baking sheet with other vegetables and let cool to room temperature, about 20 minutes.

5. Pulse cashews in food processor until finely chopped, about 15 pulses. Stir cashews into bulgur, then stir in cooled lentils, vegetable-mushroom mixture, and mayonnaise. Working in 2 batches, pulse mixture in now-empty food processor until coarsely chopped, 15 to 20 pulses (mixture should be cohesive but roughly textured); transfer to clean bowl.

6. Stir in panko and salt. Divide mixture into 12 equal portions (about ½ cup each), then tightly pack each portion into ½-inch-thick patty. (Patties can be refrigerated for up to 3 days or frozen for up to 1 month. To freeze, transfer patties to 2 parchment paper–lined rimmed baking sheets and freeze until firm, about 1 hour. Stack patties, separated by parchment paper; wrap in plastic.

7. To cook burgers: Heat remaining 2 tablespoons oil in 12-inch nonstick skillet over medium-high heat until shimmering. Place 4 patties in skillet and cook until well browned on first side, about 4 minutes. Using 2 spatulas, gently flip patties and continue to cook until well browned on second side, about 4 minutes, adding extra oil as needed if skillet looks dry. Transfer burgers to platter, wipe skillet clean with paper towels, and repeat with extra oil and remaining patties as desired. (If patties were previously frozen, transfer to wire rack set in rimmed baking sheet and bake in 350-degree oven until heated through, about 10 minutes.) Serve burgers on buns.

Rinsing Grains

We recommend rinsing and draining grains before cooking to remove excess surface starch. Place grain (or rice) in fine-mesh strainer and rinse under cool water until water runs clear, occasionally stirring lightly with your hand. Let drain briefly.

Black Bean Burgers

Serves 6 • Total Time: 1 hour, plus 1 hour resting

Why This Recipe Works As with many meatless patties, black bean burgers often get their structure from fillers that rob them of any trace of black bean flavor. We wanted that key ingredient to shine in our burgers. For convenient and reliable beans, we turned to canned, rinsing and drying them completely to eliminate cohesion-compromising moisture. Eggs and flour served as our binding agents, and adding minced scallions, cilantro, and garlic contributed some personality. We stirred in a couple of spices with major impact—cumin and coriander—plus a hit of hot sauce for zip. In keeping with our Latin American flavor profile, we turned to the bright corn flavor of tortilla chips to build up our burger mix. After blitzing crushed chips in the food processor, we added in the beans and pulsed them into coarsely chopped pieces. We combined the beans with the flour-egg binder and refrigerated the mixture, allowing the starches to absorb some of the eggs' moisture. After an hour, we formed patties and cooked the burgers in an oiled skillet. After a quick browning on each side, these burgers were ready to serve with all of our favorite fixings.

> *When forming the patties it is important to pack them firmly together. Serve the burgers with your favorite toppings or with Chipotle Mayonnaise (recipe follows).*

  2 (15-ounce) cans black beans, rinsed
  2 large eggs
  2 tablespoons all-purpose flour
  4 scallions, minced (¼ cup)
  3 tablespoons minced fresh cilantro
  2 garlic cloves, minced
  1 teaspoon ground cumin
  ½ teaspoon ground coriander
  ¼ teaspoon table salt
  ¼ teaspoon pepper
  1 teaspoon hot sauce (optional)
  1 ounce tortilla chips, crushed coarse (½ cup)
  8 teaspoons vegetable oil, divided
  6 burger buns

1. Line rimmed baking sheet with triple layer of paper towels and spread black beans over towels. Let stand for 15 minutes.

2. Whisk eggs and flour in large bowl until uniform paste forms. Stir in scallions; cilantro; garlic; cumin; coriander; salt; pepper; and hot sauce, if using, until well combined.

3. Process tortilla chips in food processor until finely ground, about 30 seconds. Add black beans and pulse until beans are roughly broken down, about 5 pulses. Transfer black bean mixture to bowl with egg mixture and mix until well combined. Cover and refrigerate for at least 1 hour or up to 24 hours.

4. Divide bean mixture into 6 equal portions. Firmly pack each portion into tight ball, then flatten to 3½-inch patty. (Patties can be wrapped individually in plastic wrap, placed in a zipper-lock bag, and frozen for up to 2 weeks. Thaw patties before cooking.)

5. Heat 2 teaspoons oil in 10-inch nonstick skillet over medium heat until shimmering. Carefully lay 3 patties in skillet and cook until bottoms are well-browned and crisp, about 5 minutes. Flip patties, add 2 teaspoons oil, and cook second sides until well-browned and crisp, 3 to 5 minutes. Transfer patties to buns and repeat with remaining 3 patties and 4 teaspoons oil. Serve.

ACCOMPANIMENT
Chipotle Mayonnaise
Makes about ⅓ cup
Total Time: 10 minutes, plus 1 hour chilling

  3 tablespoons mayonnaise
  3 tablespoons sour cream
  2 teaspoons minced canned chipotle chile in
     adobo sauce
  1 garlic clove, minced
  ⅛ teaspoon table salt

Combine all ingredients. Cover and refrigerate for at least 1 hour.

Falafel

Makes 24 falafel • Total Time: 1¼ hours, plus 8 hours soaking

Why This Recipes Works The best falafel are moist, tender, packed with vibrant fresh herbs and aromatics, and sturdy enough to form and fry. We started by soaking dried chickpeas overnight to soften them slightly and then ground them into coarse bits along with onion, herbs, garlic, and spices. Though many recipes call for mixing starch (flour, cornstarch, or chickpea flour) into the dough, we found success using a technique associated with Asian bread baking called tangzhong, a cooked flour paste. This paste added moisture without making the batter too fragile to form and fry. Adding a bit of baking powder to the dough helped to lighten the fritters as they fried. Frying the fritters at 325 degrees allowed the moist interiors to fully cook through just as the exteriors turned brown and crisp.

This recipe requires that the chickpeas be soaked for at least 8 hours. Use a Dutch oven that holds 6 quarts or more. An equal amount of chickpea flour can be substituted for the all-purpose flour; if using, increase the amount of water to ½ cup in step 4. Do not substitute canned beans or quick-soaked chickpeas. They will make stodgy falafel. Serve the falafel with the tahini sauce as an appetizer or in pita bread with lettuce, chopped tomatoes, chopped cucumbers, fresh cilantro, pickled turnips, and Tomato-Chile Sauce (recipe follows). Serve the first batch of falafel immediately or hold them in a 200-degree oven while the second batch cooks.

Falafel

- 8 ounces dried chickpeas, picked over and rinsed
- ¾ cup fresh cilantro leaves and stems
- ¾ cup fresh parsley leaves
- ½ onion, chopped fine (½ cup)
- 2 garlic cloves, minced
- 1½ teaspoons ground coriander
- 1 teaspoon ground cumin
- 1 teaspoon table salt
- ¼ teaspoon cayenne pepper
- ¼ cup all-purpose flour
- 2 teaspoons baking powder
- 2 quarts vegetable oil for frying

Tahini Sauce

- ⅓ cup tahini
- ⅓ cup plain Greek yogurt
- ¼ cup lemon juice (2 lemons)
- ¼ cup water

1. **For the falafel:** Place chickpeas in large container and cover with 2 to 3 inches of cold water. Let soak at room temperature for at least 8 hours or up to 24 hours. Drain well.

2. **For the tahini sauce:** Whisk tahini, yogurt, and lemon juice in medium bowl until smooth. Whisk in water to thin sauce as desired. Season with salt to taste; set aside. (Sauce can be refrigerated for up to 4 days. Let come to room temperature and stir to combine before serving.)

3. Process cilantro, parsley, onion, garlic, coriander, cumin, salt, and cayenne in food processor for 5 seconds. Scrape down sides of bowl. Continue to process until mixture resembles pesto, about 5 seconds longer. Add chickpeas and pulse 6 times. Scrape down sides of bowl. Continue to pulse until chickpeas are coarsely chopped and resemble sesame seeds, about 6 pulses more. Transfer mixture to large bowl and set aside.

4. Whisk flour and ⅓ cup water in bowl until no lumps remain. Microwave, whisking every 10 seconds, until mixture thickens to stiff, smooth, pudding-like consistency that forms mound when dropped from end of whisk into bowl, 40 to 80 seconds. Stir baking powder into flour paste.

5. Add flour paste to ground chickpea mixture and, using rubber spatula, mix until fully incorporated. Divide mixture into 24 pieces and gently roll into golf ball–size spheres, transferring spheres to parchment paper–lined rimmed baking sheet once they are formed. (Formed falafel can be refrigerated for up to 2 hours.)

6. Heat oil in large Dutch oven over medium-high heat to 325 degrees. Add half of falafel and fry, stirring occasionally, until deep brown, about 5 minutes. Adjust burner, if necessary, to maintain oil temperature of 325 degrees. Using slotted spoon or wire skimmer, transfer to paper towel–lined baking sheet. Return oil to 325 degrees and repeat with remaining falafel. Serve immediately with tahini sauce.

ACCOMPANIMENT
Tomato-Chile Sauce
Makes about 1½ cups • Total Time: 15 minutes

The test kitchen's favorite canned diced tomatoes are made by San Merican.

- 1 (15-ounce) can diced tomatoes, drained
- ½ cup fresh cilantro leaves and stems
- 3 garlic cloves, minced
- 1 tablespoon red pepper flakes
- 1 tablespoon red wine vinegar, plus extra for seasoning
- 1 teaspoon ground cumin
- 1 teaspoon ground coriander
- ¾ teaspoon table salt
- ½ teaspoon smoked paprika
- ⅛ teaspoon sugar
- 2 tablespoons extra-virgin olive oil

Process tomatoes, cilantro, garlic, pepper flakes, vinegar, cumin, coriander, salt, paprika, and sugar in food processor until smooth paste is formed, 20 to 30 seconds. With food processor running, slowly add oil through feed tube until fully incorporated, about 5 seconds. Transfer to bowl and season with salt and vinegar to taste.

SEASON 22
Vospov Kofte

Serves 4 to 6 • Total Time: 1¼ hours, plus 1 hour cooling and chilling

Why This Recipe Works Vospov (red lentil) kofte is the vegetarian analog to chi kofte, the canonical Armenian dish of minced raw beef or lamb that's bound with bulgur, seasoned with tomato paste and spices, formed into logs or balls, served with a mixture of chopped herbs, and eaten inside a shroud of pita or lavash. The meatless version is popular during Lent (as well as on many other occasions during the year when Armenians avoid meat) and is typically served at room temperature with herbs and bread. We opted for a 3:1:1 ratio of water to lentils to bulgur, which yielded a mixture that was tender, moist but not pasty, and

easy to shape. A combination of olive oil and butter enriched the mixture and added complexity and depth, especially since the butter developed nutty flavor as it thoroughly softened the onions and bloomed the spices. For the herb component, we mixed a modest amount of chopped parsley into the kofte and then turned much more of it into a vibrant chopped herb salad along with mint, scallions, Aleppo pepper, sumac, lemon juice, and olive oil.

Fine-grind bulgur (labeled "#1") is ideal here but can be hard to find; if you can't find it, process ¾ cup plus 2 tablespoons of any-size bulgur in a blender until at least half is finely ground, about 2 minutes. If sumac is unavailable, increase the lemon juice to 1 tablespoon and the salt to ½ teaspoon in the salad. We like the gentle heat and raisiny sweetness of Aleppo pepper, but if it's unavailable, substitute ¾ teaspoon paprika and ¼ teaspoon cayenne pepper in the kofte and ⅜ teaspoon paprika and ⅛ teaspoon cayenne pepper in the salad. Serve the kofte on their own or with pita or lavash.

Kofte
- 3 cups water
- 1 cup dried red lentils, picked over and rinsed
- ¼ cup extra-virgin olive oil
- 1¼ teaspoons table salt, divided
- 1 cup fine-grind bulgur
- 4 tablespoons unsalted butter
- 1 onion, chopped fine
- 1 teaspoon ground dried Aleppo pepper
- 1 teaspoon ground cumin
- ¼ teaspoon pepper
- ¼ teaspoon ground allspice
- 2 tablespoons chopped fresh parsley

GAME CHANGER

Ugly Can Be Delicious

"When my wife and I first started entertaining in our twenties, we put a premium on designing menus that were visually appealing. We eat with our eyes, right? Actually, we do not eat with our eyes, and there are lots of other ways to create an aesthetically pleasing atmosphere for a party—lighting, table linens, fancy plates, etc. A lot of delicious food is brown. And a lot of brown food is pretty homely, even ugly. And that's OK. It wasn't until our fifties that we were confident enough to make something like this dish the star at a dinner party. Mujaddara is truly shades of brown. Brown onions. Brown lentils. Rice dyed brown from the spices. The cilantro garnish has a big flavor impact but doesn't change the brown aspect of this dish. But don't worry. Everyone will love the mix of textures—crispy onion, creamy lentils, toothsome rice—and the heady aroma of warm spices.

So don't be afraid to build a special menu around a humble dish like this. Everyone will thank you. And it doesn't hurt to put a gorgeous green salad on the table, too."

—Jack

Salad

- ¾ cup chopped fresh parsley
- 4 scallions, sliced thin
- ¼ cup chopped fresh mint
- 1 tablespoon extra-virgin olive oil
- 2 teaspoons lemon juice
- 1 teaspoon ground sumac
- ½ teaspoon ground dried Aleppo pepper
- ¼ teaspoon table salt

1. For the kofte: Bring water, lentils, oil, and 1 teaspoon salt to boil in large saucepan over high heat. Adjust heat to maintain gentle simmer. Cover and cook, stirring occasionally, until lentils are fully broken down, 20 to 25 minutes. Place bulgur in large bowl.

2. Pour lentil mixture over bulgur, stir until uniform, and set aside. Wipe out saucepan with paper towel. Melt butter in now-empty saucepan over medium-high heat. Add onion, Aleppo pepper, cumin, pepper, allspice, and remaining ¼ teaspoon salt. Cook, stirring frequently, until onion is softened and just beginning to brown, 8 to 10 minutes. Add parsley and onion mixture to lentil mixture and stir until uniform. Let cool completely, 30 to 45 minutes. Refrigerate until stiffened enough to mold, about 30 minutes.

3. Using ¼-cup dry measuring cup sprayed with vegetable oil spray, divide mixture into 16 portions (respray cup if mixture starts to stick). Using your slightly moistened hands, press and roll each portion into 3-inch log. Arrange around perimeter of platter.

4. For the salad: Toss all ingredients together in bowl.

5. Top kofte with salad; serve at room temperature.

SEASON 15

Mujaddara

Serves 4 to 6 • Total Time: 1½ hours

Why This Recipe Works Mujaddara is a hearty, warm-spiced rice and lentil pilaf from the Middle East that contains large brown or green lentils and crispy fried onion strings. We wanted a version of this dish in which all of the elements were cooked perfectly. We found that precooking the lentils and soaking the rice in hot water before combining them ensured that both components cooked evenly. For the crispiest possible onions, we removed some moisture by salting and microwaving them before frying. This allowed

us to pare down the fussy process of batch-frying in several cups of oil to a single batch. And using some of the oil from the onions to dress our pilaf gave it ultrasavory depth.

Large green or brown lentils will work interchangeably in this recipe; do not substitute smaller French lentils. When preparing the Crispy Onions, be sure to reserve 3 tablespoons of the onion cooking oil for cooking the rice and lentils.

Yogurt Sauce

- 1 cup plain whole-milk yogurt
- 2 tablespoons lemon juice
- ½ teaspoon minced garlic
- ½ teaspoon table salt

Rice and Lentils

- 8½ ounces (1¼ cups) green or brown lentils, picked over and rinsed
- 1 teaspoon table salt, plus salt for cooking lentils
- 1¼ cups basmati rice
- 1 recipe Crispy Onions, plus 3 tablespoons reserved oil (recipe follows)
- 3 garlic cloves, minced
- 1 teaspoon ground coriander
- 1 teaspoon ground cumin
- ½ teaspoon ground cinnamon
- ½ teaspoon ground allspice
- ¼ teaspoon pepper
- ⅛ teaspoon cayenne pepper
- 1 teaspoon sugar
- 3 tablespoons minced fresh cilantro

1. For the yogurt sauce: Whisk all ingredients together in bowl. Refrigerate while preparing rice and lentils.

2. For the rice and lentils: Bring lentils, 4 cups water, and 1 teaspoon salt to boil in medium saucepan over high heat. Reduce heat to low and cook until lentils are tender, 15 to 17 minutes. Drain and set aside. While lentils cook, place rice in medium bowl and cover by 2 inches with hot tap water; let stand for 15 minutes.

3. Using your hands, gently swish rice grains to release excess starch. Carefully pour off water, leaving rice in bowl. Add cold tap water to rice and pour off water. Repeat adding and pouring off cold tap water 4 or 5 times, until water runs almost clear. Drain rice in fine-mesh strainer.

4. Heat reserved onion oil, garlic, coriander, cumin, cinnamon, allspice, pepper, and cayenne in Dutch oven over medium heat until fragrant, about 2 minutes. Add rice and cook, stirring occasionally, until edges of rice begin to turn translucent, about 3 minutes. Add 2¼ cups water, sugar, and salt and bring to boil. Stir in lentils, reduce heat to low, cover, and cook until all liquid is absorbed, about 12 minutes.

5. Off heat, remove lid, fold clean dish towel in half, and place over pot; replace lid. Let stand for 10 minutes. Fluff rice and lentils with fork and stir in cilantro and half of crispy onions. Transfer to serving platter, top with remaining crispy onions, and serve, passing yogurt sauce separately.

Crispy Onions

Makes 1½ cups • Total Time: 45 minutes

It is crucial to thoroughly dry the microwaved onions after rinsing. The best way to accomplish this is to use a salad spinner. Reserve 3 tablespoons of oil when draining the onions to use in Mujaddara. Remaining oil may be stored in an airtight container and refrigerated for up to 4 weeks.

- 2 pounds onions, halved and sliced crosswise into ¼-inch-thick pieces
- 2 teaspoons table salt, for salting onions
- 1½ cups vegetable oil

1. Toss onions and salt together in large bowl. Microwave for 5 minutes. Rinse thoroughly, transfer to paper towel–lined baking sheet, and dry well.

2. Heat onions and oil in Dutch oven over high heat, stirring frequently, until onions are golden brown, 25 to 30 minutes. Drain onions in colander set in large bowl. Transfer onions to paper towel–lined baking sheet to drain. Serve.

SEASON 4

Tomato and Mozzarella Tart

Serves 4 to 6 • **Total Time: 1½ hours, plus 30 minutes standing**

Why This Recipe Works Falling somewhere in between pizza and quiche, tomato and mozzarella tart shares the flavors of both but features unique problems. For starters, some sort of pastry crust is required. Second, the moisture in the tomatoes almost guarantees a soggy crust. Third, despite their good looks, tomato tarts often fall short on flavor. We wanted a solid bottom crust and great vine-ripened flavor. Frozen puff pastry was the solution to an easy crust, and prebaking it was a start to solving the problem of sogginess. Sealing the puff pastry shell with an egg wash helped but tomato juice still found its way into the crust. To extract more moisture from the tomatoes

before baking, we sliced and salted them, then pressed them lightly between paper towels. But even with a layer of grated mozzarella cheese between tomatoes and crust, the tart shell still came out a bit soggy. Our breakthrough came when we added a layer of grated nutty Parmesan cheese, which sealed the crust fully and repelled moisture.

> *To keep the frozen dough from cracking, it's best to let it thaw slowly in the refrigerator overnight. For the best flavor, use authentic Parmesan cheese and very ripe, flavorful tomatoes. Fresh mozzarella will make the crust soggy, so be sure to use low-moisture, shrink-wrapped mozzarella.*

- 1 (9 by 9½-inch) sheet frozen puff pastry, thawed
- 1 large egg, lightly beaten
- 1 ounce Parmesan cheese, grated (½ cup)
- 8 ounces plum tomatoes, cored and sliced ¼ inch thick
- ½ teaspoon table salt
- 4 ounces whole-milk mozzarella cheese, shredded (1 cup)
- 2 tablespoons extra-virgin olive oil
- 1 garlic clove, minced
- 2 tablespoons minced fresh basil

1. Adjust oven rack to lowest position and heat oven to 425 degrees. Line large baking sheet with parchment paper. Lay pastry in center of prepared baking sheet. Brush pastry with beaten egg. To form rimmed crust, fold long edges of pastry over by ½ inch, then brush with egg. Fold short edges of pastry over by ½ inch and brush with egg. Use paring knife to cut through folded edges and corner of pastry. Sprinkle Parmesan evenly over crust bottom. Poke dough uniformly with fork. Bake until golden brown and crisp, 15 to 20 minutes. Transfer to wire rack to cool.

2. Meanwhile, spread tomatoes over several layers of paper towels. Sprinkle with salt and let drain for 30 minutes.

3. Sprinkle mozzarella evenly over crust bottom. Press excess moisture from tomatoes, using additional paper towels. Shingle tomatoes evenly over mozzarella. Whisk olive oil and garlic together and drizzle over tomatoes. Bake until shell is deep golden, 10 to 15 minutes.

4. Let cool on wire rack for 5 minutes, then sprinkle with basil. Slide tart onto cutting board, slice into pieces, and serve.

Preparing a Tomato Tart

1. Fold short edges of pastry over by ½ inch and brush with egg. Then fold long edges of pastry over by ½ inch, making sure to keep edges flush and square. Brush with egg.

2. Using paring knife, cut through folded edges and corners of tart shell.

3. After sprinkling bottom of tart with Parmesan, poke dough repeatedly with fork. Bake pastry shell.

4. Sprinkle mozzarella evenly over crust and shingle tomatoes attractively over mozzarella.

Upside-Down Tomato Tart

Serves 4 to 6 • **Total Time: 2¼ hours**

Why This Recipe Works A traditional tarte Tatin is prepared with apples, but here we use the formula for tomatoes. The savory-sweet fruit pairs beautifully with buttery pastry and a tangy-sweet sherry vinegar syrup in lieu of caramel. To ensure a crisp—not soggy—crust, we removed the jelly and seeds from plum tomatoes and then roasted them in the syrup for a full hour, which not only evaporated any excess moisture but also concentrated their fruity taste, gave their edges some flavorful browning, and enhanced their meaty texture. We topped the roasted tomatoes with puff pastry, a convenient alternative to pie or biscuit dough that needed only to be thawed, rolled, and cut before it was ready to go in the oven. After about 30 minutes of baking, the pastry was puffed, crisp, and golden brown.

If you don't have sherry vinegar, cider vinegar is the next best thing. For the proper moisture balance in the tomatoes, use your fingers or a teaspoon to remove as much of the gel and seeds as you can. To thaw frozen puff pastry, let it sit either in the refrigerator for 24 hours or on the counter for 30 minutes to 1 hour. Dimensions of puff pastry sheets vary by brand; if your pastry will accommodate a 10-inch circle, skip the rolling in step 2. This tart is at its best within a couple of hours of baking. Cut the tart into four wedges and serve with salad as a main course or cut it into six wedges and serve as an appetizer.

⅓ cup sherry vinegar
2½ tablespoons sugar
¾ teaspoon table salt, divided
½ teaspoon pepper, divided
1 medium shallot, chopped fine
1 tablespoon unsalted butter
2½ teaspoons minced fresh thyme, divided
2 pounds plum tomatoes (about 10), cored, halved lengthwise, seeds and gel removed
1 sheet puff pastry, thawed but still cool

1. Adjust oven rack to middle position and heat oven to 400 degrees. Bring vinegar, sugar, ½ teaspoon salt, and ¼ teaspoon pepper to simmer in 10-inch ovensafe skillet over medium-high heat, swirling skillet to dissolve sugar. Simmer vigorously, swirling skillet occasionally, until consistency resembles that of maple syrup, about 2 minutes. Add shallot, butter, and 2 teaspoons thyme and whisk until butter is fully incorporated, about 1 minute. Off heat, add tomatoes and toss to coat lightly with syrup. Arrange tomatoes cut sides up in as close to single layer

as possible (some overlap is OK; tomatoes will shrink as they cook) and sprinkle with remaining ¼ teaspoon salt and remaining ¼ teaspoon pepper. Transfer to oven and cook until liquid has evaporated and tomatoes are very lightly browned around edges and softened but not fully collapsed, about 1 hour. While tomatoes are cooking, prepare pastry.

2. On lightly floured counter, roll pastry to 10-inch square. Using plate, bowl, or pot lid as template, cut out 10-inch round. Discard trim. Transfer round to large plate and refrigerate until needed. Remove skillet from oven, and place pastry over tomatoes. Bake until pastry is puffed, crisp, and deep golden brown, about 30 minutes, rotating skillet halfway through baking.

3. Let tart cool for 8 minutes. Run paring knife around edge of crust to loosen and invert plate over skillet. Using pot holders, swiftly and carefully invert tart onto plate (if tomatoes or shallots shift or stick to skillet, arrange with spoon). Let cool for 10 minutes and sprinkle with remaining ½ teaspoon thyme. Serve warm or at room temperature.

SEASON 13

Mushroom and Leek Galette with Gorgonzola

Serves 6 • Total Time: 2 hours, plus 1½ hours chilling

Why This Recipe Works Most vegetable tarts rely on the same pastry dough used for fruit tarts. But vegetable tarts are more prone to leaking liquid into the crust or falling apart when the tart is sliced. We needed a crust that was extra-sturdy and boasted a complex flavor of its own. To increase the flavor of the crust and keep it tender, we swapped out part of the white flour for nutty whole wheat, and we used butter rather than shortening. To punch up its flaky texture and introduce more structure, we gave the crust a series of folds to create numerous interlocking layers. For a filling that was both flavorful and cohesive, we paired mushrooms and leeks with rich, potent binders like Gorgonzola cheese and crème fraîche.

Cutting a few small holes in the dough prevents it from lifting off the pan as it bakes. A pizza stone helps to crisp the crust but is not essential. An overturned baking sheet can be used in place of the pizza stone.

Dough

- 1¼ cups (6¼ ounces) all-purpose flour
- ½ cup (2¾ ounces) whole-wheat flour
- 1 tablespoon sugar
- ¾ teaspoon table salt
- 10 tablespoons unsalted butter, cut into ½-inch pieces and chilled
- 7 tablespoons ice water
- 1 teaspoon distilled white vinegar

Filling

- 1¼ pounds shiitake mushrooms, stemmed and sliced thin
- 5 teaspoons olive oil, divided
- 1 pound leeks, white and light green parts only, sliced ½ inch thick and washed thoroughly (3 cups)
- 1 teaspoon minced fresh thyme
- 2 tablespoons crème fraîche
- 1 tablespoon Dijon mustard

- 3 ounces Gorgonzola cheese, crumbled (¾ cup)
- 1 large egg, lightly beaten
  Kosher salt
- 2 tablespoons minced fresh parsley

1. For the dough: Pulse all-purpose flour, whole-wheat flour, sugar, and salt in food processor until combined, 2 to 3 pulses. Add butter and pulse until it forms pea-size pieces, about 10 pulses. Transfer mixture to medium bowl.

2. Sprinkle water and vinegar over mixture. With rubber spatula, use folding motion to mix until loose, shaggy mass forms with some dry flour remaining (do not overwork). Transfer mixture to center of large sheet of plastic wrap, press gently into rough 4-inch square, and wrap tightly. Refrigerate for at least 45 minutes.

3. Transfer dough to lightly floured counter. Roll into 11 by 8-inch rectangle with short side of rectangle parallel to edge of counter. Using bench scraper, bring bottom third of dough up, then fold upper third over it, folding like business letter into 8 by 4-inch rectangle. Turn dough 90 degrees counterclockwise. Roll out dough again into 11 by 8-inch rectangle and fold into thirds again. Turn dough 90 degrees counterclockwise and repeat rolling and folding into thirds. After last fold, fold dough in half to create 4-inch square. Press top of dough gently to seal. Wrap in plastic and refrigerate for at least 45 minutes or up to 2 days.

4. **For the filling:** Microwave mushrooms in covered bowl until just tender, 3 to 5 minutes. Transfer to colander to drain; return to bowl. Meanwhile, heat 1 tablespoon oil in 12-inch skillet over medium heat until shimmering. Add leeks and thyme, cover, and cook, stirring occasionally, until leeks are tender and beginning to brown, 5 to 7 minutes. Transfer to bowl with mushrooms. Stir in crème fraîche and mustard. Season with salt and pepper to taste. Set aside.

5. Adjust oven rack to lower-middle position, place pizza stone on rack, and heat oven to 400 degrees. Line rimmed baking sheet with parchment paper. Remove dough from refrigerator and let stand at room temperature for 15 to 20 minutes. Roll out on generously floured counter (use up to ¼ cup flour) to 14-inch circle about ⅛ inch thick. (Trim edges as needed to form rough circle.) Transfer dough to prepared baking sheet. With tip of paring knife, cut five ¼-inch circles in dough (one at center and four evenly spaced halfway from center to edge of dough). Brush top of dough with 1 teaspoon oil.

6. Spread half of filling evenly over dough, leaving 2-inch border around edge. Sprinkle with half of Gorgonzola, cover with remaining filling, and top with remaining Gorgonzola. Drizzle remaining 1 teaspoon oil over filling. Gently grasp 1 edge of dough and fold up outer 2 inches over filling. Repeat around circumference of tart, overlapping dough every 2 to 3 inches; gently pinch pleated dough to secure but do not press dough into filling. Brush dough with egg and sprinkle evenly with kosher salt.

7. Lower oven temperature to 375 degrees. Bake until crust is deep golden brown and filling is beginning to brown, 35 to 45 minutes. Let tart cool on baking sheet on wire rack for 10 minutes. Using offset or wide metal spatula, loosen tart from parchment and carefully slide tart off parchment onto cutting board. Sprinkle with parsley, cut into wedges, and serve.

Pleating a Free-Form Tart

Gently grasp 1 edge of dough and make 2-inch-wide fold over filling. Lift and fold another segment of dough over first fold to form pleat. Repeat every 2 to 3 inches.

VARIATIONS

Potato and Shallot Galette with Goat Cheese

Substitute 1 pound Yukon Gold potatoes, sliced ¼ inch thick, for mushrooms and increase microwave cooking time to 4 to 8 minutes. Substitute 4 ounces thinly sliced shallots for leeks and rosemary for thyme. Increase amount of crème fraîche to ¼ cup and substitute ¼ cup chopped pitted kalamata olives and 1 teaspoon finely grated lemon zest for Dijon mustard. Substitute goat cheese for Gorgonzola.

Butternut Squash Galette with Gruyère

If desired, you can substitute rye flour for the whole-wheat flour in this recipe.

1. Microwave 6 ounces baby spinach and ¼ cup water in bowl until spinach is wilted and decreased in volume by half, 3 to 4 minutes. Using pot holders, remove bowl from microwave and keep covered for 1 minute. Carefully remove plate and transfer spinach to colander. Gently press spinach with rubber spatula to release excess liquid. Transfer spinach to cutting board and chop coarse. Return spinach to colander and press again with rubber spatula; set aside.

2. Substitute 1¼ pounds butternut squash, peeled and cut into ½-inch cubes, for mushrooms and increase microwave cooking time to about 8 minutes. Substitute 1 thinly sliced red onion for leeks and ½ teaspoon minced fresh oregano for thyme. Substitute 1 teaspoon sherry vinegar for Dijon mustard and stir reserved spinach and 3 ounces shredded Gruyère cheese into filling along with crème fraîche and vinegar in step 4. Omit Gorgonzola.

SEASON 12

Spanakopita

Serves 6 to 8 • Total Time: 1½ hours

Why This Recipe Works The roots of spinach pie run deep in Greek culture. For our version, we wanted a casserole-style pie with a perfect balance of zesty spinach filling and shatteringly crisp phyllo crust—and we didn't want it to take all day. Using store-bought phyllo dough was an easy time-saver. Among the various spinach options, tasters favored the bold flavor of fresh curly-leaf spinach that had been microwaved, chopped, and squeezed of moisture. Crumbling the feta into fine pieces ensured a salty tang in every bite, while Greek yogurt buffered its assertiveness. We found that Pecorino Romano (a good stand-in for the traditional Greek hard sheep's milk cheese) added complexity to the filling and, when sprinkled between the sheets of phyllo, helped the flaky layers hold together. Using a baking sheet rather than a baking dish allowed excess moisture to easily evaporate, ensuring a crisp crust.

> *It is important to rinse the feta; this step removes some of its salty brine. Full-fat sour cream can be substituted for whole-milk Greek yogurt. Phyllo is also available in 14 by 18-inch sheets; if using, cut them in half to make 14 by 9-inch sheets. Don't thaw the phyllo in the microwave; let it sit in the refrigerator overnight or on the countertop for 4 to 5 hours. The filling can be made up to 24 hours in advance and refrigerated. The assembled, unbaked spanakopita can be frozen on a baking sheet, wrapped well in plastic wrap, or cut in half crosswise and frozen in smaller sections on a plate. To bake, unwrap and increase the baking time by 5 to 10 minutes.*

Filling

1¼	pounds curly-leaf spinach, stemmed
¼	cup water
12	ounces feta cheese, rinsed, patted dry, and crumbled into fine pieces (about 3 cups)
¾	cup whole-milk Greek yogurt
4	scallions, sliced thin
2	large eggs, beaten
¼	cup minced fresh mint leaves
2	tablespoons minced fresh dill leaves
3	medium garlic cloves, minced (about 1 tablespoon)
1	teaspoon grated zest plus 1 tablespoon juice from 1 lemon
1	teaspoon ground nutmeg
½	teaspoon ground black pepper
¼	teaspoon table salt
⅛	teaspoon cayenne pepper

Phyllo Layers

7	tablespoons unsalted butter, melted
8	ounces (14 by 9-inch) phyllo, thawed
1½	ounces Pecorino Romano cheese, grated (¾ cup)
2	teaspoons sesame seeds (optional)

1. For the filling: Place spinach and water in large bowl and cover with large dinner plate. Microwave until spinach is wilted and decreased in volume by half, about 5 minutes. Using pot holders, remove bowl from microwave and keep covered for 1 minute. Carefully remove plate and transfer spinach to colander. Using back of rubber spatula, gently press spinach against colander to release excess liquid. Transfer spinach to cutting board and chop coarse. Transfer the spinach to clean dish towel and squeeze to remove excess water. Place drained spinach in large bowl. Add remaining filling ingredients and mix until thoroughly combined.

2. For the phyllo layers: Adjust oven rack to lower-middle position and heat oven to 425 degrees. Line rimmed baking sheet with parchment paper. Using pastry brush, lightly brush a 14 by 9-inch rectangle in center of parchment with melted butter to cover area same size as phyllo. Lay 1 phyllo sheet on buttered parchment and brush thoroughly with melted butter. Repeat with 9 more phyllo sheets, brushing each with butter (you should have a total of 10 layers of phyllo).

3. Spread spinach mixture evenly over phyllo, leaving ¼-inch border on all sides. Cover spinach with 6 more phyllo sheets, brushing each with butter and sprinkling each with about 2 tablespoons Pecorino cheese. Lay 2 more phyllo sheets on top, brushing each with butter (do not sprinkle these layers with Pecorino).

4. Working from center outward, use palms of your hands to compress layers and press out any air pockets. Using sharp knife, score spanakopita through top 3 layers of phyllo into 24 equal pieces. Sprinkle with sesame seeds, if using. Bake until phyllo is golden and crisp, 20 to 25 minutes. Let cool on baking sheet for 10 minutes or up to 2 hours. Slide spanakopita, still on parchment, onto cutting board. Cut into squares and serve.

Grilling

Photo: Grilled Filets Mignons with Roasted Red Pepper and Smoked Paprika Butter

Tender, Juicy Grilled Burgers

Serves 4 • Total Time: 1¼ hours, plus 1 hour 5 minutes freezing

Why This Recipe Works For us, the ideal burger has an ultracraggy charred crust; a rich, beefy taste; and an interior so juicy and tender that it practically falls apart at the slightest pressure—a particularly difficult achievement when grilling. The problem is that such a burger is pretty hard to come by. While the typical specimen may have a nicely browned crust, it's also heavy and dense, with a pebbly texture that comes from using preground beef. We knew we wanted to grind our own meat to make the ultimate burger. In the test kitchen, we've found it easy to grind meat ourselves with a food processor: We trim gristle and excess fat from the meat, cut the meat into ½-inch pieces, freeze it for about 30 minutes to firm it up so that the blades cut it cleanly, and finally process it in small batches to ensure an even, precise grind. We chose to use beefy steak tips since they are decently tender, require virtually no trimming, and are relatively inexpensive. Adding a bit of butter to the food processor when grinding added richness but not buttery flavor. To form the burgers so that they wouldn't fall apart on the grate but at the same time achieve that essential open texture, we froze them briefly before putting them on the grill. By the time they'd thawed at their centers, they had developed enough crust to ensure that they held together. A few minutes over a hot grill was all our burgers needed to achieve a perfect medium-rare. Whether served with the classic fixings like lettuce and tomato or one of our creamy grilled-vegetable toppings, this grilled burger lives up to our ideal.

This recipe requires freezing the meat twice, for a total of 65 to 80 minutes, before grilling. When stirring the salt and pepper into the ground meat and shaping the patties, take care not to overwork the meat, or the burgers will become dense. Sirloin steak tips are also sold as flap meat. Serve the burgers with your favorite toppings or one of our grilled-vegetable toppings (recipes follow).

1½ pounds sirloin steak tips, trimmed and cut into ½-inch chunks

4 tablespoons unsalted butter, cut into ¼-inch pieces

1 teaspoon kosher salt, divided

1¼ teaspoons pepper, divided

1 (13 by 9-inch) disposable aluminum pan (if using charcoal)

4 hamburger buns

1. Place beef chunks and butter on large plate in single layer. Freeze until meat is very firm and starting to harden around edges but still pliable, about 35 minutes.

2. Place one-quarter of meat and one-quarter of butter cubes in food processor and pulse until finely ground into pieces size of rice grains (about $^1/_{32}$ inch), 15 to 20 pulses, stopping and redistributing meat around bowl as necessary to ensure beef is evenly ground. Transfer meat to baking sheet. Repeat grinding with remaining 3 batches of meat and butter. Spread mixture over sheet and inspect carefully, discarding any long strands of gristle or large chunks of hard meat, fat, or butter.

3. Sprinkle 1 teaspoon pepper and ¾ teaspoon salt over meat and toss gently with fork to combine. Divide meat into 4 balls. Toss each between your hands until uniformly but lightly packed. Gently flatten into patties ¾ inch thick and about 4½ inches in diameter. Using your thumb, make 1-inch-wide by ¼-inch-deep depression in center of each patty. Transfer patties to platter and freeze for 30 to 45 minutes.

4A. For a charcoal grill: Using skewer, poke 12 holes in bottom of disposable pan. Open bottom vent completely and place disposable pan in center of grill. Light large chimney starter two-thirds filled with charcoal briquettes (4 quarts). When top coals are partially covered with ash, pour into disposable pan. Set cooking grate in place, cover, and open lid vent completely. Heat grill until hot, about 5 minutes.

4B. For a gas grill: Turn all burners to high; cover; and heat grill until hot, about 15 minutes. Leave all burners on high.

5. Clean and oil cooking grate. Sprinkle 1 side of patties with ⅛ teaspoon salt and ⅛ teaspoon pepper. Using spatula, flip patties and sprinkle other side with remaining ⅛ teaspoon salt and remaining ⅛ teaspoon pepper. Grill patties (directly over coals if using charcoal), without moving them, until browned and meat easily releases from grate, 4 to 7 minutes. Flip burgers and continue to grill until browned on second side and meat registers 125 degrees (for medium-rare) or 130 degrees (for medium), 4 to 7 minutes longer.

6. Transfer burgers to plate and let rest for 5 minutes. While burgers rest, lightly toast buns on grill, 1 to 2 minutes. Transfer burgers to buns and serve.

Grilled Scallion Topping

Makes ½ cup   •   Total Time: 1 hour

   2 tablespoons sour cream
   2 tablespoons mayonnaise
   2 tablespoons buttermilk
   1 tablespoon cider vinegar
   1 tablespoon minced fresh chives
   2 teaspoons Dijon mustard
   ¼ teaspoon sugar
   ½ teaspoon table salt
   ⅛ teaspoon pepper
  20 scallions
   2 tablespoons vegetable oil

1. Combine sour cream, mayonnaise, buttermilk, vinegar, chives, mustard, sugar, salt, and pepper in medium bowl. Set aside.

2. Toss scallions with oil in large bowl. Grill scallions over hot fire until lightly charred and softened, 2 to 4 minutes per side. Return to bowl and let cool for 5 minutes. Slice scallions thin, then transfer to bowl with reserved sour cream mixture. Toss to combine and season with salt and pepper to taste.

Grilled Shiitake Mushroom Topping

Makes ¾ cup   •   Total Time: 1 hour

    2 tablespoons sour cream
    2 tablespoons mayonnaise
    2 tablespoons buttermilk
    1 tablespoon cider vinegar
    1 tablespoon minced fresh chives
    2 teaspoons Dijon mustard
    ¼ teaspoon sugar
    ½ teaspoon table salt
    ⅛ teaspoon pepper
  8½ ounces shiitake mushrooms, stems removed
    2 tablespoons vegetable oil

1. Combine sour cream, mayonnaise, buttermilk, vinegar, chives, mustard, sugar, salt, and pepper in medium bowl. Set aside.

2. Toss mushrooms with oil in large bowl. Grill mushrooms over hot fire until lightly charred and softened, 2 to 4 minutes per side. Return to bowl and let cool for 5 minutes. Slice mushrooms thin, then transfer to bowl with reserved sour cream mixture. Toss to combine and season with salt and pepper to taste.

Grilled Napa Cabbage and Radicchio Topping

Makes ¾ cup   •   Total Time: 1 hour

   2 tablespoons sour cream
   2 tablespoons mayonnaise
   2 tablespoons buttermilk
   1 tablespoon cider vinegar
   1 tablespoon minced fresh parsley
   2 teaspoons Dijon mustard
   ¼ teaspoon sugar
   ½ teaspoon table salt
   ⅛ teaspoon pepper
   ¼ small head napa cabbage
   ½ small head radicchio, cut into 2 wedges
   2 tablespoons vegetable oil

1. Combine sour cream, mayonnaise, buttermilk, vinegar, parsley, mustard, sugar, salt, and pepper in medium bowl. Set aside.

2. Place cabbage and radicchio wedges on rimmed baking sheet and brush with oil. Grill over hot fire until lightly charred and beginning to wilt, 2 to 4 minutes on each cut side. Return to baking sheet and let cool for 5 minutes. Slice cabbage and radicchio thin, then transfer to bowl with reserved sour cream mixture. Toss to combine and season with salt and pepper to taste.

Grilled Marinated Flank Steak

Serves 4 to 6 • **Total Time: 1 hour, plus 1 hour marinating**

Why This Recipe Works An acidic marinade—such as one made with vinegar—can ruin the texture of flank steak, making the exterior mushy and gray. We wanted an aromatic, acid-free marinade that would boost flavor without over-tenderizing the meat. We knew oil would be a key ingredient because fat carries flavor so well—the challenge was to infuse garlic, shallots, and rosemary into the oil and then into the steak. To do so, we first minced the aromatics and combined them with the oil in a blender to create a marinade paste. Next, we invented a novel "marinating" technique—prick the steak all over with a fork, rub it first with salt and then with the marinade paste, then let it sit for up to 24 hours. After marinating, the paste is wiped off to prevent burning, and the steak is ready for the grill. To grill our steak to perfection, we used a two-level fire (which lets you move the thin part of the steak to the cooler side of the grill once it is done), cooked the steak only to medium-rare to keep it from getting tough, and let the steak rest before slicing to reduce the loss of juices. Our technique was so successful, we created two more marinades—one with garlic, ginger, and sesame and the other with a smoky-spicy kick.

> *Other thin steaks with a loose grain, such as skirt steak or steak tips, can be substituted for the flank steak.*

    1 (2- to 2½-pound) flank steak, trimmed
    1 teaspoon table salt
    1 recipe wet paste marinade (recipes follow)
    ½ teaspoon pepper

1. Pat steak dry with paper towels and place in large baking dish. Using dinner fork, prick steak about 20 times on each side. Rub both sides of steak evenly with salt, then with paste. Cover with plastic wrap and refrigerate for at least 1 hour or up to 24 hours.

2A. For a charcoal grill: Open bottom vent completely. Light large chimney starter filled with charcoal briquettes (6 quarts). When top coals are partially covered with ash, pour two-thirds of coals over half of grill, then pour remaining coals over other half. Set cooking grate in place, cover, and open lid vent completely. Heat grill until hot, about 5 minutes.

2B. For a gas grill: Turn all burners to high; cover; and heat grill until hot, about 15 minutes.

3. Clean and oil cooking grate. Using paper towels, wipe paste off steak and sprinkle with pepper. Place steak on grill (hotter side if using charcoal) and cook (covered if using gas) until well browned on first side, 4 to 6 minutes. Flip steak and cook (covered if using gas) until meat registers 120 to 125 degrees (for medium-rare) or 130 to 135 degrees (for medium), 3 to 6 minutes. If exterior of meat is browned but steak is not yet cooked through, move to cooler side of grill (if using charcoal) or turn down burners (if using gas) and continue to cook to desired doneness.

4. Transfer steak to carving board, tent with aluminum foil, and let rest for 10 minutes. Slice steak against grain on bias ¼ inch thick and serve.

MARINADES
Garlic-Shallot-Rosemary Wet Paste Marinade
Makes ⅔ cup • Total Time: 10 minutes

    6 tablespoons extra-virgin olive oil
    1 shallot, minced
    6 garlic cloves, minced
    2 tablespoons minced fresh rosemary

Process all ingredients in blender until smooth, about 30 seconds, scraping down bowl as needed.

Garlic-Ginger-Sesame Wet Paste Marinade
Makes ⅔ cup • Total Time: 10 minutes

    ¼ cup toasted sesame oil
    3 tablespoons grated fresh ginger
    2 tablespoons vegetable oil
    2 scallions, minced
    3 garlic cloves, minced

Process all ingredients in blender until smooth, about 30 seconds, scraping down bowl as needed.

Garlic-Chile Wet Paste Marinade
Makes ⅔ cup • Total Time: 10 minutes

    6 tablespoons vegetable oil
    6 garlic cloves, minced
    2 scallions, minced
    1 tablespoon minced canned chipotle chile in
       adobo sauce
    1 jalapeño chile, stemmed, seeded, and minced

Process all ingredients in blender until smooth, about 30 seconds, scraping down bowl as needed.

Grilled Strip or Rib-Eye Steaks

Serves 6 • **Total Time: 55 minutes**

Why This Recipe Works Grilled steaks have many tempting qualities—rich, beefy flavor; a thick, caramelized crust; and almost zero prep. But the rendered fat can cause flare-ups, leaving pricey cuts of meat charred and tasting like the inside of a smokestack. We wanted a surefire technique for grilling premium steaks so that they would turn out juicy and tender every time. To get a good crust, a very hot fire was essential. But cooking these thick steaks over consistently high heat led to burned steaks and the dreaded flare-ups from fat dripping down onto the charcoal. The solution was to cook the steaks over a two-level fire, searing them first over high heat and then moving them to the cooler part of the grill to cook through. For strip and rib-eye steaks, lightly oiling the cooking grate was enough to keep them from sticking; we rubbed the lean filets mignons with olive oil to encourage browning. Otherwise, we didn't fuss with our steaks before cooking them—a little salt and pepper was sufficient. To add some richness to our steaks, we topped them with a compound butter before serving.

> *Try to buy steaks of even thickness so they cook at the same rate.*

   4 (12- to 16-ounce) strip or rib-eye steaks, with or without bone, 1¼ to 1½ inches thick, trimmed
   1 teaspoon table salt
  ½ teaspoon pepper

1A. For a charcoal grill: Open bottom vent completely. Light large chimney starter filled with charcoal briquettes (6 quarts). When top coals are partially covered with ash, pour two-thirds of coals over half of grill, then pour remaining coals over other half. Set cooking grate in place, cover, and open lid vent completely. Heat grill until hot, about 5 minutes.

1B. For a gas grill: Turn all burners to high; cover; and heat grill until hot, about 15 minutes. Leave 1 burner on high and turn other burner(s) to medium.

2. Clean and oil cooking grate. Pat steaks dry with paper towels and sprinkle with salt and pepper. Place steaks on grill (hotter side if using charcoal) and cook, uncovered, until well browned on both sides, 4 to 6 minutes, flipping steaks halfway through cooking. Move steaks to cooler side of grill (if using charcoal) or turn all burners to medium (if using gas) and continue to cook until meat registers 115 to 120 degrees (for rare) or 120 to 125 degrees (for medium-rare) 5 to 8 minutes longer.

3. Transfer steaks to serving platter, tent with aluminum foil, and let rest for 10 minutes before serving.

VARIATION
Grilled Filets Mignons
Serves 4 • Total Time: 55 minutes
If the filets are misshapen or unevenly cut, as supermarket steaks sometimes are, tie each one around the center with kitchen twine before grilling. We suggest serving the steaks with one of our flavored butters (recipes follow).

   4 (7- to 8-ounce) center-cut filets mignons, 1½ to 2 inches thick, trimmed
   4 teaspoons extra-virgin olive oil
  ½ teaspoon table salt
  ¼ teaspoon pepper

1A. For a charcoal grill: Open bottom vent completely. Light large chimney starter filled with charcoal briquettes (6 quarts). When top coals are partially covered with ash, pour two-thirds evenly over half of grill, then pour remaining coals over other half. Set cooking grate in place, cover, and open lid vent completely. Heat grill until hot, about 5 minutes.

1B. For a gas grill: Turn all burners to high; cover; and heat grill until hot, about 15 minutes. Leave all burners on high.

2. Meanwhile, pat steaks dry with paper towels and lightly rub with oil. Sprinkle steaks with salt and pepper.

3. Clean and oil cooking grate. Place steaks on grill (hotter side if using charcoal) and cook (covered if using gas) until well browned on both sides, 4 to 6 minutes, flipping halfway through cooking. Move steaks to cooler side of grill (if using charcoal) or turn all burners to medium (if using gas) and continue to cook (covered if using gas), until meat registers 115 to 120 degrees (for rare) or 120 to 125 degrees (for medium-rare), 5 to 9 minutes longer.

4. Transfer steaks to serving platter, tent with aluminum foil, and let rest for 10 minutes before serving.

COMPOUND BUTTERS
Roasted Red Pepper and Smoked Paprika Butter
Makes ¼ cup • Total Time: 25 minutes

    4 tablespoons unsalted butter, softened
    2 tablespoons finely chopped jarred
       roasted red peppers
    1 tablespoon minced fresh thyme
    ¾ teaspoon smoked paprika
    ½ teaspoon table salt
       Pinch pepper

Combine all ingredients in bowl and mix until smooth. While steaks are resting, spoon 1 tablespoon of butter onto each one.

Lemon, Garlic, and Parsley Butter
Makes ¼ cup • Total Time: 25 minutes

    4 tablespoons unsalted butter, softened
    1 tablespoon minced fresh parsley
    1 garlic clove, minced
    ½ teaspoon grated lemon zest
    ½ teaspoon table salt
       Pinch pepper

Combine all ingredients in bowl and mix until smooth. While steaks are resting, spoon 1 tablespoon of butter onto each one.

SEASON 15
Carne Asada

Serves 4 to 6 • Total Time: 55 minutes, plus 45 minutes salting

Why This Recipe Works These days carne asada usually refers to a supercharred, thin steak, but traditionally the dish involves a platter of food. Created around 1940 at the Tampico Club in Mexico City, carne asada is typically served with a bevy of sides. We wanted to stick close to the original while scaling it down for the home cook. A juicy, thin, well-charred steak was a must, and we settled on just a few

extras: a salsa that would complement the meat, some quick refried beans, and simple folded enchiladas. We decided to use skirt steak, since it stayed tender when grilled to medium (the ideal doneness for both adequate charring and tender beef). A rub made with salt and cumin not only added flavor, but the salt dried out the steaks' exteriors to promote browning. For our grill setup, we used a disposable aluminum roasting pan with the bottom removed to corral the coals and ensure high heat for fast browning and char. A smashed clove of garlic rubbed on the steaks after grilling brought a burst of fresh garlic flavor and aroma to the meat, and a squeeze of lime provided fresh citrus flavor.

Two pounds of sirloin steak tips, also sold as flap meat, may be substituted for the skirt steak. Serve with Red Chile Salsa, Simple Refried Beans, and Folded Enchiladas (recipes follow), if desired.

    2 teaspoons kosher salt
    ¾ teaspoon ground cumin
    1 (2-pound) skirt steak, trimmed, pounded ¼ inch
       thick, and cut with grain into 4 equal steaks
    1 (13 by 9-inch) disposable aluminum roasting pan
       (if using charcoal)
    1 garlic clove, peeled and smashed
       Lime wedges

1. Combine salt and cumin in small bowl. Sprinkle salt mixture evenly over both sides of steaks. Transfer steaks to wire rack set in rimmed baking sheet and refrigerate, uncovered, for at least 45 minutes or up to 24 hours. Meanwhile, if using charcoal, use kitchen shears to remove bottom of disposable pan and discard, reserving pan collar.

2A. For a charcoal grill: Open bottom vent completely. Light large chimney starter filled with charcoal briquettes (6 quarts). When top coals are partially covered with ash, place disposable pan collar in center of grill over bottom vent and pour coals into even layer in collar. Set cooking grate in place, cover, and open lid vent completely. Heat grill until hot, about 5 minutes.

2B. For a gas grill: Turn all burners to high; cover; and heat grill until hot, about 15 minutes. Leave all burners on high.

3. Clean and oil cooking grate. Place steaks on grill (if using charcoal, arrange steaks over coals in collar) and cook, uncovered, until well browned on first side, 2 to 4 minutes. Flip steaks and continue to cook until well browned on second side and meat registers 130 degrees, 2 to 4 minutes longer. Transfer steaks to cutting board, tent with aluminum foil, and let rest for 5 minutes.

4. Rub garlic thoroughly over 1 side of steaks. Slice steaks against grain ¼ inch thick and serve with lime wedges.

Simple Refried Beans

Makes 1½ cups • Total Time: 25 minutes

Using the canning liquid from the beans helps develop a creamy texture.

2 slices bacon
1 small onion, chopped fine
2 garlic cloves, minced
1 (15-ounce) can pinto beans
¼ cup water

Cook bacon in 10-inch nonstick skillet over medium-low heat until fat is rendered and bacon crisps, 7 to 10 minutes, flipping bacon halfway through. Remove bacon and reserve for another use. Increase heat to medium, add onion to fat in skillet, and cook until lightly browned, 5 to 7 minutes. Add garlic and cook until fragrant, about 30 seconds. Add beans and their canning liquid and water and bring to simmer. Cook, mashing beans with potato masher, until mixture is mostly smooth, 5 to 7 minutes. Season with kosher salt to taste, and serve.

Red Chile Salsa

Makes 2 cups • Total Time: 15 minutes

Guajillo chiles are tangy with just a bit of heat. Serve the salsa alongside the steak as a dipping sauce.

1¼ ounces dried guajillo chiles, wiped clean
1 (14.5-ounce) can fire-roasted diced tomatoes
¾ cup water
¾ teaspoon table salt
1 garlic clove, peeled and smashed
½ teaspoon distilled white vinegar
¼ teaspoon dried oregano
⅛ teaspoon pepper
Pinch ground cloves
Pinch ground cumin

Toast guajillos in 10-inch nonstick skillet over medium-high heat until softened and fragrant, 1 to 2 minutes per side. Transfer to large plate and, when cool enough to handle, remove stems and seeds. Place guajillos in blender and process until finely ground, 60 to 90 seconds, scraping down sides of blender jar as needed. Add tomatoes and their juice, water, salt, garlic, vinegar, oregano, pepper, cloves, and cumin to blender and process until very smooth, 60 to 90 seconds, scraping down sides of blender jar as needed. (Salsa can be stored in refrigerator for up to 5 days or frozen for up to 1 month.)

Folded Enchiladas

Serves 4 to 6 • Total Time: 30 minutes

Feta cheese can be substituted for the queso fresco. Guajillo chiles are tangy, with just a bit of heat.

⅔ ounce dried guajillo chiles, wiped clean
1 (8-ounce) can tomato sauce
1 cup chicken broth
1 tablespoon vegetable oil
1 garlic clove, peeled and smashed
1 teaspoon distilled white vinegar
¼ teaspoon ground cumin
12 (6-inch) soft corn tortillas
Vegetable oil spray
1 small onion, chopped fine
2 ounces queso fresco, crumbled (½ cup)

1. Toast guajillos in 10-inch nonstick skillet over medium-high heat until softened and fragrant, 1 to 2 minutes per side. Transfer to large plate and, when cool enough to handle, remove stems and seeds. Place guajillos in blender and process until finely ground, 60 to 90 seconds, scraping down sides of blender jar as needed. Add tomato sauce, broth, oil, garlic, vinegar, and cumin to blender and process until very smooth, 60 to 90 seconds, scraping down sides of blender jar as needed. Season with salt to taste.

2. Place 1 cup enchilada sauce in large bowl. Spray both sides of tortillas with oil spray and stack on plate. Microwave, covered, until softened and warm, 60 to 90 seconds. Working with 1 tortilla at a time, dip into sauce in bowl to coat both sides, fold in quarters, and place in 8-inch square baking dish (enchiladas will overlap slightly in dish).

3. When ready to serve, pour remaining sauce evenly over enchiladas. Microwave enchiladas until hot throughout, 3 to 5 minutes. Sprinkle evenly with onion and queso fresco. Serve.

Grilled Boneless Beef Short Ribs

Serves 4 to 6 • **Total Time: 30 minutes, plus 1 hour salting**

Why This Recipe Works The best steaks for searing over hot coals are those that have enough fat and beefy flavor to support the smoky, charred aromas that the meat acquires during grilling. Enter boneless beef short ribs: With their rich marbling and intense, beefy flavor, they can rival a rib eye on the grill—at about half the cost. Instead of flavoring just the surface of the ribs with a marinade, we salted them for an hour to ensure that they were seasoned throughout. We grilled the ribs over high heat, intentionally allowing the drippings to flare up, to impart that charred, savory grill flavor to the meat. Frequent flipping cooked the meat evenly and gently. Finally, we sliced the ribs against the grain so that they were as tender as possible.

> *This recipe was developed using Diamond Crystal kosher salt. If you're using Morton kosher salt, which is denser, use only 1¾ teaspoons of salt. We like these ribs cooked to about 130 degrees (medium). If you prefer them medium-rare, remove the ribs from the grill when they register 125 degrees. Serve with lemon wedges and flake sea salt or with one of our sauces (recipes follow).*

- 2 pounds boneless beef short ribs, trimmed
- 2½ teaspoons kosher salt
- 1 teaspoon pepper

1. Cut ribs into 3- to 4-inch lengths. Sprinkle all sides with salt and pepper. Let sit at room temperature for 1 hour.

2A. For a charcoal grill: Open bottom vent completely. Light large chimney starter mounded with charcoal briquettes (7 quarts). When top coals are partially covered with ash, pour evenly over half of grill. Set cooking grate in place, cover, and open lid vent completely. Heat grill until hot, about 5 minutes.

2B. For a gas grill: Turn all burners to high; cover; and heat grill until hot, about 15 minutes. Turn off 1 burner (if using grill with more than 2 burners, turn off burner farthest from primary burner) and leave other burner(s) on high.

3. Clean and oil cooking grate. Arrange ribs on hotter side of grill. Cook (covered if using gas), flipping ribs every minute, until meat is well browned on all sides and registers

about 130 degrees at thickest part, 8 to 14 minutes. (Ribs will be very pale after first flip but will continue to brown as they cook. This cut can quickly overcook; start checking temperature of smaller ribs after 8 minutes.)

4. Transfer ribs to cutting board, tent with aluminum foil, and let rest for 10 minutes. Slice ribs as thin as possible against grain. (Grain runs diagonally, so as long as you slice lengthwise, you will be cutting against grain.) Serve.

SAUCES

Preserved Lemon–Almond Sauce
Makes 1 cup
Total Time: 10 minutes, plus 15 minutes resting
Sliced almonds provide a delicate crunch; do not substitute slivered or whole almonds.

- 5 tablespoons extra-virgin olive oil, divided
- ¼ cup sliced almonds, chopped
- ½ cup minced fresh parsley
- 2 tablespoons finely chopped preserved lemon plus 2 tablespoons brine
- 2 tablespoons lemon juice
- ¼ teaspoon sugar

Combine 1 tablespoon oil and almonds in 8-inch skillet; toast over medium-high heat, stirring constantly, until almonds are golden brown, 1 to 2 minutes. Immediately transfer to bowl. Stir in parsley, preserved lemon and brine, lemon juice, sugar, and remaining ¼ cup oil. Let sit for 15 minutes. Stir well before using. (Sauce can be refrigerated for up to 24 hours. Let sit at room temperature for 15 minutes before serving.)

Kimchi-Scallion Sauce
Makes 1 cup
Total Time: 10 minutes, plus 15 minutes resting
Cider vinegar or seasoned rice vinegar can be substituted for the unseasoned rice vinegar.

- 6 scallions, sliced thin
- ⅓ cup finely chopped kimchi
- ¼ cup vegetable oil
- 4 teaspoons soy sauce
- 4 teaspoons unseasoned rice vinegar
- ¼ teaspoon sugar

Stir all ingredients together in bowl. Let sit for 15 minutes. Stir well before using. (Sauce can be refrigerated for up to 24 hours. Let sit at room temperature for 15 minutes before serving.)

Grill-Roasted Beef Tenderloin

Serves 4 to 6 • Total Time: 2 hours, plus 20 minutes resting

Why This Recipe Works Grilling is a great way to add flavor that enhances but doesn't overwhelm beef tenderloin's delicate beefiness. Producing deep browning was the first step toward delivering flavor. To do this without overcooking the tenderloin's interior, we rubbed the exterior of the roast with baking soda. This raised the meat's pH, which sped up browning by allowing the Maillard reaction to occur more quickly. "Grilled" flavor also depends on drippings from the food, which hit the coals (charcoal) or heat diffusers (gas), transform into new compounds, vaporize, and then waft up and stick to the meat. Because lean tenderloin produces very little in the way of drippings, we looked to an outside source: bacon. Threading three strips onto a metal skewer and placing the skewer directly over the heat source while the tenderloin cooked, low and slow away from direct heat, allowed the bacon to slowly render and produce the "grilled" flavor the tenderloin needed.

Center-cut beef tenderloin roasts are sometimes sold as Châteaubriand. You will need one metal skewer for this recipe. The bacon will render slowly during cooking, creating a steady stream of smoke that flavors the beef. Serve the roast as is or with Chermoula Sauce (recipe follows).

2¼ teaspoons kosher salt
  1 teaspoon pepper
  2 teaspoons vegetable oil
  1 teaspoon baking soda
  1 (3-pound) center-cut beef tenderloin roast, trimmed and tied at 1½-inch intervals
  3 slices bacon

1. Combine salt, pepper, oil, and baking soda in small bowl. Rub mixture evenly over roast and let stand while preparing grill.

2. Stack bacon slices. Keeping slices stacked, thread metal skewer through bacon 6 or 7 times to create accordion shape. Push stack together to compact into about 2-inch length.

3A. For a charcoal grill: Open bottom vent halfway. Light large chimney starter two-thirds filled with charcoal briquettes (4 quarts). When top coals are partially covered with ash, pour evenly over half of grill. Set cooking grate in place, cover, and open lid vent halfway. Heat grill until hot, about 5 minutes.

3B. For a gas grill: Turn all burners to high; cover; and heat grill until hot, about 15 minutes. Turn primary burner to medium and turn off other burner(s). (Adjust primary burner as necessary to maintain grill temperature of 300 degrees.)

4. Clean and oil cooking grate. Place roast on hotter side of grill and cook until lightly browned on all sides, about 12 minutes. Slide roast to cooler side of grill, arranging so roast is about 7 inches from heat source. Place skewered bacon on hotter side of grill. (For charcoal, place near center of grill, above edge of coals. For gas, place above heat diffuser of primary burner. Bacon should be 4 to 6 inches from roast and drippings should fall on coals or heat diffuser and produce steady stream of smoke and minimal flare-ups. If flare-ups are large or frequent, slide bacon skewer 1 inch toward roast.)

5. Cover and cook until beef registers 120 to 125 degrees (for medium-rare), 50 minutes to 1¼ hours. Transfer roast to carving board, tent with aluminum foil, and let rest for 20 minutes. Discard twine and slice roast ½ inch thick. Serve.

Chermoula Sauce

Makes 1 cup

Total Time: 15 minutes, plus 1 hour resting

To keep the sauce from becoming bitter, whisk in the olive oil by hand.

- ¾ cup fresh cilantro leaves
- 4 garlic cloves, minced
- 1 teaspoon ground cumin
- 1 teaspoon paprika
- ¼ teaspoon cayenne pepper
- ¼ teaspoon table salt
- 3 tablespoons lemon juice
- ½ cup extra-virgin olive oil

Pulse cilantro, garlic, cumin, paprika, cayenne, and salt in food processor until coarsely chopped, about 10 pulses. Add lemon juice and pulse briefly to combine. Transfer mixture to medium bowl and slowly whisk in oil until incorporated and mixture is emulsified. Cover with plastic wrap and let stand at room temperature for at least 1 hour. (Sauce can be refrigerated for up to 2 days; bring to room temperature and rewhisk before serving.)

SEASON 13

Easy Grilled Boneless Pork Chops

Serves 4 to 6 • Total Time: 1 hour, plus 30 minutes brining

Why This Recipe Works Pork chops are a prime candidate for the grill, which can imbue the lean chops with smoky, savory flavor, but too often, the results are disappointing. To produce juicy, well-charred boneless pork chops on the grill, we used a two-pronged approach. We brined the chops to improve their ability to hold on to juices during cooking, provide seasoning throughout, and increase their tenderness. To ensure that we'd get a substantial browned crust before the interior overcooked, we looked to a unique coating of anchovy paste and honey. The anchovies' amino acids couple with the fructose from honey to rapidly begin the flavorful Maillard browning reaction. We developed some complementary relishes using combinations of sweet and savory ingredients to complement the grilled chops.

If your pork is enhanced, do not brine it in step 1. Very finely mashed anchovy fillets (rinsed and dried before mashing) can be used instead of anchovy paste.

- 6 (6- to 8-ounce) boneless pork chops, ¾ to 1 inch thick
- 3 tablespoons table salt for brining
- 1 tablespoon vegetable oil
- 1½ teaspoons honey
- 1 teaspoon anchovy paste
- ½ teaspoon pepper
- 1 recipe relish (optional) (recipes follow)

1. Cut 2 slits about 1 inch apart through outer layer of fat and connective tissue on each chop to prevent buckling. Dissolve salt in 1½ quarts cold water in large container. Submerge chops in brine and let stand at room temperature for 30 minutes.

2. Whisk together oil, honey, anchovy paste, and pepper to form smooth paste. Remove pork from brine and pat dry with paper towels. Using spoon, spread half of oil mixture evenly over 1 side of each chop (about ¼ teaspoon per side).

3A. For a charcoal grill: Open bottom vent completely. Light chimney starter filled with charcoal briquettes (6 quarts). When top coals are partially covered with ash, pour evenly over half of grill. Set cooking grate in place, cover, and open lid vent completely. Heat grill until hot, about 5 minutes.

3B. For a gas grill: Turn all burners to high; cover; and heat grill until hot, about 15 minutes. Leave primary burner on high and turn off other burner(s).

4. Clean and oil cooking grate. Place chops, oiled side down, over hotter part of grill and cook, uncovered, until well browned on first side, 4 to 6 minutes. While chops are grilling, spread remaining oil mixture evenly over second side of chops. Flip chops and continue to cook until chops register 140 degrees, 4 to 6 minutes longer (if chops are well browned but register less than 140 degrees, move to cooler part of grill to finish cooking). Transfer chops to plate and let rest for 5 minutes. Serve with relish, if using.

RELISHES
Onion, Olive, and Caper Relish
Makes 2 cups • Total Time: 25 minutes

- ¼ cup extra-virgin olive oil, divided
- 2 onions, cut into ¼-inch pieces
- 6 garlic cloves, sliced thin
- ½ cup pitted kalamata olives, chopped coarse
- ¼ cup capers, rinsed
- 3 tablespoons balsamic vinegar
- 2 tablespoons minced fresh parsley
- 1 teaspoon minced fresh marjoram
- 1 teaspoon sugar
- ½ teaspoon anchovy paste
- ½ teaspoon pepper
- ¼ teaspoon table salt

Heat 2 tablespoons oil in 10-inch nonstick skillet over medium heat until shimmering. Add onions and cook until softened, about 5 minutes. Stir in garlic and cook until fragrant, about 30 seconds. Transfer onion mixture to medium bowl; stir in remaining 2 tablespoons oil, olives, capers, vinegar, parsley, marjoram, sugar, anchovy paste, pepper, and salt. Serve warm or at room temperature.

Tomato, Fennel, and Almond Relish
Makes 2 cups • Total Time: 30 minutes

- ¼ cup extra-virgin olive oil, divided
- 1 fennel bulb, stalks discarded, bulb halved, cored, and cut into ¼-inch pieces
- 6 garlic cloves, sliced thin
- 2 tomatoes, cored and cut into ½-inch pieces
- ¼ cup green olives, pitted and chopped coarse
- ¼ cup slivered almonds, toasted
- 3 tablespoons minced fresh parsley
- 3 tablespoons sherry vinegar
- 1 teaspoon sugar
- ¾ teaspoon table salt
- ½ teaspoon pepper

Heat 2 tablespoons oil in 10-inch skillet over medium heat until shimmering. Add fennel and cook until slightly softened, about 5 minutes. Stir in garlic and cook until fragrant, about 30 seconds. Stir in tomatoes and continue to cook until tomatoes break down slightly, about 5 minutes. Transfer fennel mixture to medium bowl; stir in remaining 2 table-spoons oil, olives, almonds, parsley, vinegar, sugar, salt, and pepper. Serve warm or at room temperature.

Orange, Jicama, and Pepita Relish
Makes 3 cups • Total Time: 30 minutes

- 1 orange
- ¼ cup extra-virgin olive oil, divided
- 2 jalapeños, stemmed, seeded, and sliced into thin rings
- 3 shallots, sliced thin
- 6 garlic cloves, sliced thin
- 2 cups jicama, peeled and cut into ¼-inch pieces
- ¼ cup pepitas, toasted
- 3 tablespoons chopped fresh cilantro
- 3 tablespoons lime juice (2 limes)
- 1 teaspoon sugar
- ¾ teaspoon table salt
- ½ teaspoon pepper

Cut away peel and pith from orange. Quarter orange, then slice crosswise into ¼-inch-thick pieces. Heat 2 tablespoons oil in 10-inch skillet over medium heat until shimmering. Add jalapeños and shallots and cook until slightly softened, about 5 minutes. Stir in garlic and cook until fragrant, about 30 seconds. Transfer jalapeño-shallot mixture to medium bowl; stir in orange, jicama, pepitas, cilantro, lime juice, sugar, salt, and pepper. Serve warm or at room temperature.

SEASON 15

Garlic–Lime Grilled Pork Tenderloin Steaks

Serves 4 to 6 • Total Time: 1¼ hours, plus 45 minutes marinating

Why This Recipe Works Although pork tenderloin medallions make for a nice presentation and offer lots of surface area to crisp and brown on the grill, they are inherently fussy: They require constant attention lest they overcook or, worse, slip through the grate. We wanted to take the spirit of the medallion approach but find a shape and a technique that, while it reliably delivered a maximum amount of flavorful, nicely browned crust, still kept this lean cut tender. We started by cutting two tenderloin roasts in half and pounding them to an even thickness to make pork tenderloin "steaks." A two-level grill fire, with both hotter and cooler areas, allowed us to sear the steaks on the hotter side and then let them gently finish cooking on the cooler side. We added both bold seasoning and richness through a marinade. Plenty of salt ensured thorough seasoning and tender meat. Oil, lime juice and zest, garlic, fish sauce (which provided a savory boost without tasting fishy), and honey (the sugars in which would encourage browning) rounded out the marinade. We cut crosshatch marks in the steaks, which both made for extra crispy edges and allowed them to absorb even more marinade. A bit of reserved marinade, whisked with some mayo for body and cilantro for freshness, completed our tenderloin steaks.

> *Since marinating is a key step in this recipe, we don't recommend using enhanced pork (injected with a salt solution).*

- 2 (1-pound) pork tenderloins, trimmed
- 1 tablespoon grated lime zest plus ¼ cup juice (2 limes)
- 4 garlic cloves, minced
- 4 teaspoons honey
- 2 teaspoons fish sauce
- ¾ teaspoon table salt
- ½ teaspoon pepper
- ½ cup vegetable oil
- 4 teaspoons mayonnaise
- 1 tablespoon chopped fresh cilantro

1. Slice each tenderloin in half crosswise to create 4 steaks total. Pound each half to ¾-inch thickness. Using sharp knife, cut ⅛-inch-deep slits spaced ½ inch apart in crosshatch pattern on both sides of steaks.

2. Whisk lime zest and juice, garlic, honey, fish sauce, salt, and pepper together in large bowl. Whisking constantly, slowly drizzle oil into lime mixture until smooth and slightly thickened. Transfer ½ cup lime mixture to small bowl and whisk in mayonnaise; set aside sauce. Add steaks to bowl with remaining marinade and toss thoroughly to coat; transfer steaks and marinade to large zipper-lock bag, press out as much air as possible, and seal bag. Let steaks sit at room temperature for 45 minutes.

3A. For a charcoal grill: Open bottom vent completely. Light large chimney starter filled with charcoal briquettes (6 quarts). When top coals are partially covered with ash, pour evenly over half of grill. Set cooking grate in place, cover, and open lid vent completely. Heat grill until hot, about 5 minutes.

3B. For a gas grill: Turn all burners to high; cover; and heat grill until hot, about 15 minutes. Leave primary burner on high and turn off other burner(s).

4. Clean and oil cooking grate. Remove steaks from marinade (do not pat dry) and place over hotter part of grill. Cook, uncovered, until well browned on first side, 3 to 4 minutes. Flip steaks and cook until well browned on second side, 3 to 4 minutes. Transfer steaks to cooler part of grill, with wider end of each steak facing hotter part of grill. Cover and cook until meat registers 140 degrees, 3 to 8 minutes longer (remove steaks as they come to temperature). Transfer steaks to cutting board and let rest for 5 minutes.

5. While steaks rest, microwave reserved sauce until warm, 15 to 30 seconds; stir in cilantro. Slice steaks against grain ½ inch thick. Drizzle with half of sauce; sprinkle with flake sea salt, if desired; and serve, passing remaining sauce separately.

VARIATIONS
Lemon-Thyme Grilled Pork Tenderloin Steaks
Substitute grated lemon zest and juice (2 lemons) for lime zest and juice. Add 1 tablespoon minced fresh thyme to lemon mixture with garlic. Omit cilantro.

Spicy Orange-Ginger Grilled Pork Tenderloin Steaks
Reduce lime zest to 1½ teaspoons and juice to 2 tablespoons. Add 1½ teaspoons grated orange zest plus 2 tablespoons juice, 2 teaspoons grated fresh ginger, and ¼ teaspoon cayenne pepper to lime mixture with garlic.

Grilled Pork Tenderloin with Grilled Pineapple–Red Onion Salsa

Serves 4 to 6 • Total Time: 55 minutes

Why This Recipe Works To produce pork tenderloin with a rich crust and a tender, juicy interior, we used a half-grill fire and seared the roast on the hotter side of the grill. This allowed the exterior to develop flavorful browning before the interior was cooked through. Then we moved the meat to the cooler side of the grill to finish cooking gently. Seasoning the meat with a mixture of salt, cumin, and chipotle chile powder added smoky, savory flavor, and a touch of sugar encouraged browning. To add bright flavor and make the most of the fire, we grilled pineapple and red onion and, while the cooked pork rested, combined them with cilantro, a serrano chile, lime juice, and a bit of reserved spice mixture to make a quick salsa.

We prefer unenhanced pork in this recipe, but enhanced pork (injected with a salt solution) can be used.

Pork
- 1½ teaspoons kosher salt
- 1½ teaspoons sugar
- ½ teaspoon ground cumin
- ½ teaspoon chipotle chile powder
- 2 (12- to 16-ounce) pork tenderloins, trimmed

Salsa
- ½ pineapple, peeled, cored, and cut lengthwise into 6 wedges
- 1 red onion, cut into 8 wedges through root end
- 4 teaspoons extra-virgin olive oil, divided
- ½ cup minced fresh cilantro
- 1 serrano chile, stemmed, seeded, and minced
- 2 tablespoons lime juice, plus extra for seasoning

1. For the pork: Combine salt, sugar, cumin, and chile powder in small bowl. Reserve ½ teaspoon spice mixture. Rub remaining spice mixture evenly over surface of both tenderloins. Transfer to large plate or rimmed baking sheet and refrigerate while preparing grill.

2A. For a charcoal grill: Open bottom vent completely. Light large chimney starter filled with charcoal briquettes (6 quarts). When top coals are partially covered with ash, pour evenly over half of grill. Set cooking grate in place, cover, and open lid vent completely. Heat grill until hot, about 5 minutes.

2B. For a gas grill: Turn all burners to high; cover; and heat grill until hot, about 15 minutes. Leave primary burner on high and turn off other burner(s).

3. Clean and oil cooking grate. Place tenderloins on hotter side of grill. Cover and cook, turning tenderloins every 2 minutes, until well browned on all sides, about 8 minutes.

4. For the salsa: Brush pineapple and onion with 1 teaspoon oil. Move tenderloins to cooler side of grill (6 to 8 inches from heat source) and place pineapple and onion on hotter side of grill. Cover and cook until pineapple and onion are charred on both sides and softened, 8 to 10 minutes, and until pork registers 140 degrees, 12 to 17 minutes, turning tenderloins every 5 minutes. As pineapple and onion and tenderloins reach desired level of doneness, transfer pineapple and onion to plate and transfer tenderloins to carving board. Tent tenderloins with aluminum foil and let rest for 10 minutes.

5. While tenderloins rest, chop pineapple coarse. Pulse pineapple, onion, cilantro, serrano, lime juice, reserved spice mixture, and remaining 1 tablespoon oil in food processor until mixture is roughly chopped, 4 to 6 pulses. Transfer to bowl and season with salt and extra lime juice to taste.

6. Slice tenderloins crosswise ½ inch thick. Serve with salsa.

Pork

- ½ cup packed light brown sugar
- ¼ cup kosher salt
- 1 (3½- to 4-pound) blade-end boneless pork loin roast, trimmed
- 2 cups wood chips
- 1 (13 by 9-inch) disposable aluminum roasting pan (if using charcoal) or 1 (9-inch) disposable aluminum pie plate (if using gas)

Chutney

- ¾ cup dry white wine
- ½ cup dried apricots, diced
- ½ cup dried cherries
- ¼ cup white wine vinegar
- 3 tablespoons water
- 3 tablespoons packed light brown sugar
- 1 shallot, minced
- 2 tablespoons grated fresh ginger
- 1 tablespoon unsalted butter
- 1 tablespoon Dijon mustard
- 1½ teaspoons dry mustard

1. For the pork: Combine sugar and salt in small bowl. Tie roast with twine at 1-inch intervals. Rub sugar-salt mixture over entire surface of roast, making sure roast is evenly coated. Wrap roast tightly in plastic wrap, set in rimmed baking sheet, and refrigerate for at least 6 hours or up to 24 hours.

2. Just before grilling, soak wood chips in water for 15 minutes, then drain. Using large piece of heavy-duty aluminum foil, wrap soaked chips in 8 by 4½-inch foil packet. (Make sure chips do not poke holes in sides or bottom of packet.) Cut 2 evenly spaced 2-inch slits in top of packet.

3A. For a charcoal grill: Open bottom vent halfway. Arrange 25 unlit charcoal briquettes over half of grill and place disposable pan filled with 3 cups water on other side of grill. Light large chimney starter two-thirds filled with charcoal briquettes (4 quarts). When top coals are partially covered with ash, pour evenly over unlit briquettes. Place wood chip packet on coals. Set cooking grate in place, cover, and open lid vent halfway. Heat grill until hot and wood chips are smoking, about 5 minutes. (Adjust top and bottom vents as needed to maintain grill temperature of 300 degrees.)

3B. For a gas grill: Remove cooking grate and place wood chip packet directly on primary burner. Place disposable pie plate filled with 1 inch water directly on other burner(s). Set grate in place; turn all burners to high; cover; and heat grill until hot and wood chips are smoking, about 15 minutes. Turn primary burner to medium and turn off other burner(s). (Adjust primary burner as needed to maintain grill temperature of 300 degrees.)

Smoked Pork Loin with Dried Fruit Chutney

Serves 6 • Total Time: 3 to 3½ hours, plus 6½ hours brining and resting

Why This Recipe Works For a smoky, company-worthy pork roast that cooked in just a couple of hours, we looked to quick-cooking pork loin. Choosing a blade-end roast over a center-cut roast meant more fat and thus more flavor. An overnight rub of salt and brown sugar before grilling helped season the roast, kept it juicy, and delivered a nicely caramelized exterior. Low-and-slow indirect cooking was key for an evenly cooked, tender roast, so we poured lit coals over a layer of unlit coals to create a fire that wouldn't require refueling. Two cups of wood chips (in a single packet) provided just enough smoke to enhance the roast's meaty flavor without overwhelming it. A dried-fruit chutney was the perfect complement to the smoky meat.

A blade roast is our preferred cut, but a center-cut boneless loin roast can also be used. If the pork is enhanced (injected with a salt solution) skip step 1, but season with sugar-salt mixture in step 4. Any variety of wood chip except mesquite will work; we prefer hickory. If you'd like to use wood chunks instead of wood chips when using a charcoal grill, substitute two medium wood chunk(s), soaked in water for 1 hour, for the wood chip packet. To help maintain a constant charcoal grill temperature, do not remove the lid any more than necessary during cooking.

4. Clean and oil cooking grate. Unwrap roast and pat dry with paper towels. Place roast on grill (cooler side if using charcoal), directly over water pan. Cover (position lid vent over roast if using charcoal) and cook until meat registers 140 degrees, 1½ to 2 hours, rotating roast 180 degrees after 45 minutes.

5. For the chutney: Combine wine, apricots, cherries, vinegar, water, sugar, shallot, and ginger in medium saucepan. Bring to simmer over medium heat. Cover and cook until fruit is softened, 10 minutes. Remove lid and reduce heat to medium-low. Add butter, Dijon, and dry mustard and continue to cook until slightly thickened, 4 to 6 minutes. Remove from heat and season with salt to taste. Transfer to bowl and let stand at room temperature.

6. Transfer roast to carving board, tent with foil, and let rest for 30 minutes. Remove and discard twine. Slice ¼ inch thick and serve, passing chutney separately.

SEASON 12

Grilled Bone-In Pork Roast

Serves 6 to 8 • Total Time: 2 hours, plus 6½ hours chilling and resting

Why This Recipe Works Grilling a bulky cut of meat like a pork roast may sound difficult, but we found that a tender, quick-cooking center-cut rib roast and a simple salt rub were all that we needed for a juicy grilled roast with a thick mahogany crust. Scoring the fat on the roast helped the rendered drippings baste the meat during grill-roasting. We grilled the roast over indirect heat (on the cooler side of the grill) so it could cook through slowly, adding a single soaked wood chunk or a small amount of wood chips to the fire for a subtle tinge of smoke flavor. After a little more than an hour on the grill, our roast was tender and juicy, with plenty of rich, deep flavor. For the perfect counterpoint to the roast's richness, we whipped up a fresh orange salsa with bright citrus and fresh herbs, jalapeño, and a warm touch of cumin.

If you buy a blade-end roast (sometimes called a "rib-end roast"), tie it into a uniform shape with kitchen twine at 1-inch intervals; this step is unnecessary with a center-cut roast. For easier carving, ask the butcher to remove the tip of the chine bone and to cut the remainder of the chine bone between each rib. If you'd like to use wood chunks instead of wood chips when using a charcoal grill, substitute one medium wood chunk, soaked in water for 1 hour, for the wood chip packet.

1 (4- to 5-pound) bone-in center-cut pork rib or blade-end roast, tip of chine bone removed, fat trimmed to ¼-inch thickness
4 teaspoons kosher salt
1 cup wood chips
1½ teaspoons pepper
1 recipe Orange Salsa with Cuban Flavors (optional) (recipe follows)

1. Pat roast dry with paper towels. Using sharp knife, cut slits in surface fat layer, spaced 1 inch apart, in crosshatch pattern, being careful not to cut into meat. Sprinkle roast with salt. Wrap with plastic wrap and refrigerate for at least 6 hours or up to 24 hours.

2. Just before grilling, soak wood chips in water for 15 minutes, then drain. Using large piece of heavy-duty aluminum foil, wrap soaked chips in 8 by 4½-inch foil packet. (Make sure chips do not poke holes in sides or bottom of packet.) Cut 2 evenly spaced 2-inch slits in top of packet.

3A. For a charcoal grill: Open bottom vent halfway. Light large chimney starter filled with charcoal briquettes (6 quarts). When top coals are partially covered with ash, pour into steeply banked pile against side of grill. Place wood chip packet on coals. Set cooking grate in place, cover, and open lid vent halfway. Heat grill until hot and wood chips are smoking, about 5 minutes.

3B. For a gas grill: Place wood chip packet over primary burner. Turn all burners to high; cover; and heat grill until hot and wood chips are smoking, about 15 minutes. Turn primary burner to medium-high and turn off other burner(s). (Adjust primary burner as needed during cooking to maintain grill temperature around 325 degrees.)

4. Clean and oil cooking grate. Unwrap roast and season with pepper. Place roast on grate with meat near, but not over, coals and flames and bones facing away from coals and flames. Cover (position lid vent over meat if using charcoal) and cook until meat registers 140 degrees, 1¼ to 1½ hours.

5. Transfer roast to carving board, tent with foil, and let rest for 30 minutes. Carve into thick slices by cutting between ribs. Serve, passing salsa, if using, separately.

ACCOMPANIMENT
Orange Salsa with Cuban Flavors
Makes about 2½ cups • Total Time: 15 minutes
To make this salsa spicier, add the reserved chile seeds.

 ½ teaspoon grated orange zest plus 5 oranges peeled and segmented; each segment quartered crosswise
 ½ cup minced red onion
 1 jalapeño chile, stemmed, seeds reserved, and minced
 2 tablespoons lime juice
 2 tablespoons minced fresh parsley
 1 tablespoon extra-virgin olive oil
 2 teaspoons packed brown sugar
 1½ teaspoons distilled white vinegar
 1½ teaspoons minced fresh oregano
 1 garlic clove, minced
 ½ teaspoon ground cumin
 ½ teaspoon table salt
 ½ teaspoon pepper

Combine all ingredients in medium bowl.

SEASON 8
Kansas City Sticky Ribs

Serves 4 to 6 • Total Time: 3½ hours, plus 1 hour salting and 1 hour cooling

Why This Recipe Works Kansas City ribs are slow-smoked pork ribs slathered in a sauce so thick, sweet, and sticky that you need a case of wet naps to get your hands clean after eating them. But these ribs can take all day to prepare. We knew we could come up with a faster method for Kansas City ribs—one that would produce the same fall-off-the-bone, tender, smoky meat of the long-cooked original recipe. We quickly learned that spareribs, which are well marbled with fat, produce moist, tender ribs, but some racks are so big they barely fit on the grill. We turned to a more manageable cut, referred to as "St. Louis" ribs, which is a narrower, rectangular rack that offers all the taste of whole spareribs without any of the trouble. A spice rub added flavor and encouraged a savory crust on the meat.

We barbecued the ribs, covered with foil, over indirect heat for 4 hours—the foil traps some of the steam over the meat, so that it cooks up tender, not dry. Using wood chips on the grill imparted great smoky flavor to the meat. For sticky, saucy ribs, we brushed the ribs all over with barbecue sauce and finished them in the gentle, even heat of the oven until they were tender and falling off the bone.

We like St. Louis–style racks, but if you can't find them, baby back ribs will work fine; reduce the oven time in step 6 to 1 to 2 hours. If you'd like to use wood chunks instead of wood chips when using a charcoal grill, substitute two medium wood chunks, soaked in water for 1 hour, for the wood chip packets.

Ribs
 3 tablespoons paprika
 2 tablespoons packed brown sugar
 1 tablespoon table salt
 1 tablespoon pepper
 ¼ teaspoon cayenne pepper
 2 (2½- to 3-pound) full racks pork spareribs, trimmed of any large pieces of fat and membrane removed
 2 cups wood chips

Sauce
 1 tablespoon vegetable oil plus more for cooking grate
 1 onion, chopped fine
    Pinch table salt
 4 cups chicken broth
 1 cup root beer
 1 cup cider vinegar
 1 cup dark corn syrup
 ½ cup light or mild molasses
 ½ cup tomato paste
 ½ cup ketchup
 2 tablespoons brown mustard
 1 tablespoon hot sauce
 ½ teaspoon garlic powder
 ¼ teaspoon liquid smoke

Removing the Membrane for Kansas City Ribs

Before cooking, loosen papery membrane with tip of paring knife and, with aid of paper towel, pull it off slowly, all in 1 piece.

1. For the ribs: Combine paprika, sugar, salt, black pepper, and cayenne in bowl. Pat ribs dry with paper towels and rub evenly with spice mixture. Wrap ribs in plastic wrap and let sit at room temperature for at least 1 hour, or refrigerate for up to 24 hours. (If refrigerated, let sit at room temperature for 1 hour before grilling.) Just before grilling, soak wood chips in water for 15 minutes, then drain. Using large piece of heavy-duty aluminum foil, wrap soaked chips in 8 by 4½-inch foil packet. (Make sure chips do not poke holes in sides or bottom of packet.) Cut 2 evenly spaced 2-inch slits in top of packet.

2. For the sauce: Meanwhile, heat oil in large saucepan over medium heat until shimmering. Add onion and salt and cook until softened, 5 to 7 minutes. Whisk in broth, root beer, vinegar, corn syrup, molasses, tomato paste, ketchup, mustard, hot sauce, and garlic powder. Bring sauce to simmer and cook, stirring occasionally, until reduced to 4 cups, about 1 hour. Stir in liquid smoke. Let cool to room temperature and season with salt and pepper to taste. Measure out 1 cup barbecue sauce for cooking; set aside remaining sauce for serving. (Sauce can be refrigerated for up to 4 days.)

3A. For a charcoal grill: Open bottom grill vent halfway. Light large chimney starter three-quarters filled with charcoal briquettes (4½ quarts). When top coals are partially covered with ash, pour into steeply banked pile against side of grill. Place wood chip packet on coals. Set cooking grate in place, cover, and open lid vent halfway. Heat grill until hot and wood chips are smoking, about 5 minutes.

3B. For a gas grill: Remove cooking grate and place wood chip packet directly on primary burner. Set grate in place; turn all burners to high; cover; and heat grill until hot and wood chips are smoking, about 15 minutes. Turn primary burner to medium-high and turn off other burner(s). (Adjust primary burner as needed to maintain grill temperature of 325 degrees.)

4. Clean and oil cooking grate. Place ribs, meat side down, on cooler side of grill; ribs may overlap slightly. Place sheet of foil on top of ribs. Cover (position lid vent over meat if using charcoal) and cook until ribs are deep red and smoky, about 2 hours, flipping and rotating racks halfway through. During final 20 minutes of grilling, adjust oven rack to middle position and heat oven to 250 degrees.

5. Remove ribs from grill, brush evenly with 1 cup sauce reserved for cooking, and wrap tightly with foil. Lay foil-wrapped ribs on rimmed baking sheet and continue to cook in oven until tender and fork inserted into ribs meets no resistance, 1½ to 2½ hours.

6. Remove ribs from oven and let rest, still wrapped, for 30 minutes. Unwrap ribs and brush them thickly with 1 cup sauce set aside for serving. Slice ribs between bones and serve with remaining sauce.

SEASON 11

Memphis-Style Barbecued Spareribs

Serves 4 to 6 • Total Time: 4½ to 5½ hours

Why This Recipe Works Memphis pit masters pride themselves on their all-day barbecued pork ribs with a dark, bark-like crust and distinctive chew. Up for a challenge, we decided to come up with our own version, but one that wouldn't involve tending a grill all day.

After failing to grill the ribs in a reasonable amount of time (less than 7 hours), we opted for a grill-to-oven approach. We started first with the grill. For a fire that would maintain the key amount of indirect heat (roughly 250 to 275 degrees), we turned to a half-grill fire where the hot coals are arranged over half the grill. In addition, we stowed a pan of water underneath the cooking grate on the cooler side of the grill, where it would absorb heat and work to keep the temperature stable, as well as help keep the meat moister. Then we transferred the ribs to a wire rack set over a rimmed baking sheet and cooked them in a moderate oven until tender and thick-crusted. We even mimicked our grill setup by pouring 1½ cups water into the rimmed baking sheet. In all, we'd shaved more than three hours off of our shortest recipe.

> *In the charcoal version, the wood chips are sprinkled over coals. Don't remove the membrane that runs along the bone side of the ribs; it prevents some of the fat from rendering out and is authentic to this style of ribs.*

  1 recipe Spice Rub (recipe follows)
  2 (2½- to 3-pound) racks St. Louis–style spareribs, trimmed
  ½ cup apple juice
  3 tablespoons cider vinegar
  1 (13 by 9-inch) disposable aluminum roasting pan (if using charcoal) or 2 (9-inch) disposable aluminum pie plates (if using gas)
  ¾ cup wood chips, soaked in water for 15 minutes and drained

1. Rub 2 tablespoons spice rub on each side of each rack of ribs. Let ribs sit at room temperature while preparing grill.

2. Combine apple juice and vinegar in small bowl and set aside.

3A. For a charcoal grill: Open bottom vent halfway and evenly space 15 unlit charcoal briquettes on 1 side of grill. Place disposable pan filled with 2 cups water on other side of grill. Light large chimney starter one-third filled with charcoal briquettes (2 quarts). When top coals are partially covered with ash, pour evenly over unlit coals. Sprinkle soaked wood chips over lit coals. Set cooking grate in place, cover, and open lid vent halfway. Heat grill until hot and wood chips are smoking, about 5 minutes.

3B. For a gas grill: Place soaked wood chips in pie plate with ¼ cup water and set over primary burner. Place second pie plate filled with 2 cups water on other burner(s). Turn all burners to high; cover; and heat grill until hot and wood chips are smoking, about 15 minutes. Turn primary burner to medium-high and turn off other burner(s). (Adjust primary burner as needed to maintain grill temperature between 250 to 275 degrees.)

4. Clean and oil cooking grate. Place ribs meat side down on cooler side of grill over water-filled pan. Cover (position lid vent over meat if using charcoal) and cook until ribs

are deep red and smoky, about 1½ hours, brushing with apple juice mixture and flipping and rotating racks halfway through cooking. About 20 minutes before removing ribs from grill, adjust oven rack to lower-middle position and heat oven to 300 degrees.

5. Set wire rack in rimmed baking sheet and transfer ribs to rack. Brush top of each rack with 2 tablespoons apple juice mixture. Pour 1½ cups water into bottom of sheet; roast for 1 hour. Brush ribs with remaining apple juice mixture and continue to cook until meat is tender and registers 195 degrees, 1 to 2 hours. Transfer ribs to cutting board and let rest for 15 minutes. Slice ribs between bones and serve.

Spice Rub
Makes ½ cup • Total Time: 10 minutes
For less spiciness, reduce the amount of cayenne to ½ teaspoon.

  2 tablespoons paprika
  2 tablespoons packed light brown sugar
  1 tablespoon table salt
  2 teaspoons chili powder
 1½ teaspoons pepper
 1½ teaspoons garlic powder
 1½ teaspoons onion powder
 1½ teaspoons cayenne pepper
  ½ teaspoon dried thyme

Combine all ingredients in bowl.

Ribs Unlike Any Other Ribs

"Until I tried rosticciana, ribs always meant one thing to me: a slab of smoky, slow-cooked meat with a fall-off-the-bone texture that's been coated with a flavorful rub or sauce. But these Tuscan grilled pork ribs offer a unique combination of flavors and textures unlike traditional barbecue ribs. Seasoned sparingly with salt and pepper plus a hint of garlic and rosemary, the ribs are grilled quickly over a hot fire until browned and crisp. The result is meat that is succulent and clings to the bone with a satisfying chew. With no smoke, sauce, or spice rubs, the flavor is pure porky goodness. Salting the ribs for an hour before cooking helps them stay juicy over the high heat and cutting them into two-rib sections allows for even seasoning and creates more surface area for flavorful browning. The sweet spot for doneness is between 175 and 185 degrees; in this range the ribs experience some collagen breakdown, which will leave the ribs with a meaty bite, but they aren't cooked long enough to dry out."

– *Keith*

Rosticciana

Serves 4 to 6 • Total Time: 1¼ hours, plus 1 hour salting

Why This Recipe Works With no sauce or spice rub, rosticciana, or Tuscan grilled pork spareribs, are unlike any ribs we've had. Seasoned simply with salt, pepper, and maybe a hint of garlic or rosemary, their preparation aligns with the less-is-more ethos of Tuscan cuisine, where ingredients are seasoned sparingly to allow their natural flavors to shine. The ribs are grilled quickly until the meat is browned and crisp but still succulent. For our version of this dish, we started with two racks of St. Louis–style spareribs. Cutting the ribs into two-rib sections created more surface area for flavorful browning, and salting them an hour prior to grilling ensured that they would be juicy and well seasoned. We grilled the ribs over a medium-hot fire to avoid drying them out and removed them when their temperature reached 175 to 185 degrees—which took only about 20 minutes. Drizzling the pork with a simple vinaigrette balanced its richness without obscuring its flavor.

> *When portioning the meat into two-rib sections, start at the thicker end of the rack. If you are left with a three-rib piece at the tapered end, grill it as such. Take the temperature of the meat between the bones. Since these ribs cook quickly, we like to use the still-hot fire to grill a vegetable. Radicchio's pleasant bitterness and crunch make it a perfect partner for the rich meat (recipe follows).*

Ribs

- 2 (2½- to 3-pound) racks St. Louis–style spareribs, trimmed, membrane removed, and each rack cut into 2-rib sections
- 2 teaspoons kosher salt
- 1 tablespoon vegetable oil
- 1 teaspoon pepper

Vinaigrette

- ¼ cup extra-virgin olive oil
- 2 garlic cloves, minced
- 1 teaspoon finely chopped fresh rosemary
- 2 tablespoons lemon juice

1. For the ribs: Pat ribs dry with paper towels. Rub evenly on both sides with salt and place on wire rack set in rimmed baking sheet. Let sit at room temperature for 1 hour. Brush meat side of ribs with oil and sprinkle with pepper.

2. For the vinaigrette: Combine oil, garlic, and rosemary in small bowl and microwave until fragrant and just starting to bubble, about 30 seconds. Stir in lemon juice and set aside.

3A. For a charcoal grill: Open bottom vent completely. Light large chimney starter filled with charcoal briquettes (6 quarts). When top coals are partially covered with ash, pour evenly over grill. Set cooking grate in place, cover, and open lid vent completely. Heat grill until hot, about 5 minutes.

3B. For a gas grill: Turn all burners to high; cover; and heat grill until hot, about 15 minutes. Turn all burners to medium-high.

4. Clean and oil cooking grate. Place ribs meat side down on grill. Cover and cook until meat side begins to develop spotty browning and light but defined grill marks, 4 to 6 minutes. Flip ribs and cook, covered, until second side is lightly browned, 4 to 6 minutes, moving ribs as needed to ensure even browning. Flip again and cook, covered, until meat side is deeply browned with slight charring and thick ends of ribs register 175 to 185 degrees, 4 to 6 minutes.

5. Transfer ribs to cutting board and let rest for 10 minutes. Cut ribs between bones and serve, passing vinaigrette separately.

ACCOMPANIMENT
Grilled Radicchio

Serves 4 • Total Time: 15 minutes
Turning the wedges during cooking ensures that all sides, including the rounded one, spend time facing the fire.

- 3 heads radicchio (10 ounces each), quartered
- ¼ cup extra-virgin olive oil
- 1 teaspoon table salt
- ½ teaspoon pepper
  Balsamic vinegar

1. Place radicchio on rimmed baking sheet, brush with oil, and sprinkle with salt and pepper.

2. Grill radicchio over medium-hot fire (covered if using gas), turning every 1½ minutes, until edges are browned and wilted but centers are still slightly firm, about 5 minutes. Transfer radicchio to serving dish, drizzle with vinegar, and serve.

Cutting Ribs Two by Two

Starting at thicker end of rack, portion meat into 2-rib sections. If left with 3-rib piece at tapered end of rack, it can be grilled as such.

Bún Chả

Serves 4 to 6 • Total Time: 1¾ hours

Why This Recipe Works Vietnamese bún chả is an ideal one-dish meal, each bite containing an extraordinary balance of smoky, juicy meat; tangy, salty-sweet sauce; cool, tender greens; and delicately springy noodles. We started by boiling dried rice vermicelli, after which we rinsed the noodles well and spread them on a platter to dry. Then we mixed up the bold and zesty sauce known as nước chấm from lime juice, sugar, and fish sauce. To ensure that every drop of the sauce was flavored with garlic and chile, we used a portion of the sugar to help grind the pungent ingredients into a fine paste. Mixing baking soda into ground pork helped the meat retain moisture and brown during the brief grilling time. Per tradition, we also seasoned the pork with shallot, fish sauce, sugar, and pepper. Briefly dunking the grilled patties in the sauce further flavored them, and their meaty char flavors infused the sauce. We then arranged the components separately on platters to allow diners to combine them according to their taste.

Look for dried rice vermicelli in the Asian section of your supermarket. We prefer the more delicate springiness of vermicelli made from 100 percent rice flour to those that include a secondary starch such as cornstarch. If you can find only the latter, just cook them longer—up to 12 minutes. For a less spicy sauce, use only half the Thai chile.

For the cilantro, use the leaves and the thin, delicate stems, not the thicker ones close to the root. To serve, place platters of noodles, salad, sauce, and pork patties on the table and allow diners to combine components to their taste. The sauce is potent, so use it sparingly.

Noodles and Salad

- 8 ounces rice vermicelli
- 1 head Boston lettuce (8 ounces), torn into bite-size pieces
- 1 English cucumber, peeled, quartered lengthwise, seeded, and sliced thin on bias
- 1 cup fresh cilantro leaves and stems
- 1 cup fresh mint leaves, torn if large

Sauce

- 1 small Thai chile, stemmed and minced
- 3 tablespoons sugar, divided
- 1 garlic clove, minced
- ⅔ cup hot water
- 5 tablespoons fish sauce
- ¼ cup lime juice (2 limes)

Pork Patties

- 1 large shallot, minced
- 1 tablespoon fish sauce
- 1½ teaspoons sugar
- ½ teaspoon baking soda
- ½ teaspoon pepper
- 1 pound ground pork

1. For the noodles and salad: Bring 4 quarts water to boil in large pot. Stir in noodles and cook until tender but not mushy, 4 to 12 minutes. Drain noodles and rinse under cold running water until cool. Drain noodles very well, spread on large plate, and let stand at room temperature to dry. Arrange lettuce, cucumber, cilantro, and mint separately on large platter and refrigerate until needed.

2. For the sauce: Using mortar and pestle (or on cutting board using flat side of chef's knife), mash Thai chile, 1 tablespoon sugar, and garlic to fine paste. Transfer to medium bowl and add hot water and remaining 2 tablespoons sugar. Stir until sugar is dissolved. Stir in fish sauce and lime juice. Set aside.

3. For the pork patties: Combine shallot, fish sauce, sugar, baking soda, and pepper in medium bowl. Add pork and mix until well combined. Shape pork mixture into 12 patties, each about 2½ inches wide and ½ inch thick.

4A. For a charcoal grill: Open bottom vent completely. Light large chimney starter filled with charcoal briquettes (6 quarts). When top coals are partially covered with ash, pour over half of grill. Set cooking grate in place, cover, and open lid vent completely. Heat grill until hot, about 5 minutes.

4B. For a gas grill: Turn all burners to high; cover; and heat grill until hot, about 15 minutes. Leave all burners on high.

5. Clean and oil cooking grate. Cook patties (directly over coals if using charcoal; covered if using gas) until well charred, 3 to 4 minutes per side. Transfer grilled patties to bowl with sauce and toss gently to coat. Let stand for 5 minutes.

6. Transfer patties to serving plate, reserving sauce. Serve noodles, salad, sauce, and pork patties separately.

SEASON 14

Grilled Lamb Kofte

Serves 4 to 6 • Total Time: 1½ hours, plus 1 hour chilling

Why This Recipe Works In the Middle East, kebabs called kofte feature ground meat, not chunks, mixed with lots of spices and fresh herbs. For ours, we started with preground lamb for convenience. Kneading the meat ensured the kofte had a sausage-like spring. To help keep the meat firm, we added a small amount of gelatin and then refrigerated it. Ground pine nuts gave the kofte a noticeably richer flavor and added moisture for a perfect texture. Hot smoked paprika, cumin, and cloves contributed warm spice notes, while parsley and mint offered bright, grassy flavors. Adding a little tahini to the tangy garlic and yogurt serving sauce gave it more complexity.

> *You will need 8 (12-inch) metal skewers for this recipe. Serve with rice pilaf or make sandwiches with warm pita bread, sliced red onion, and chopped fresh mint.*

Yogurt-Garlic Sauce
- 1 cup plain whole-milk yogurt
- 2 tablespoons lemon juice
- 2 tablespoons tahini
- 1 garlic clove, minced
- ½ teaspoon table salt

Kofte
- ½ cup pine nuts
- 4 garlic cloves, peeled
- 1½ teaspoons hot smoked paprika
- 1 teaspoon table salt
- 1 teaspoon ground cumin
- ½ teaspoon pepper
- ¼ teaspoon ground coriander
- ¼ teaspoon ground cloves
- ⅛ teaspoon ground nutmeg
- ⅛ teaspoon ground cinnamon
- 1½ pounds ground lamb
- ½ cup grated onion, drained
- ⅓ cup minced fresh parsley
- ⅓ cup minced fresh mint
- 1½ teaspoons unflavored gelatin
- 1 large disposable aluminum roasting pan (if using charcoal)

1. For the yogurt-garlic sauce: Whisk all ingredients together in bowl. Set aside.

2. For the kofte: Process pine nuts, garlic, paprika, salt, cumin, pepper, coriander, cloves, nutmeg, and cinnamon in food processor until coarse paste forms, 30 to 45 seconds. Transfer mixture to large bowl. Add lamb, onion, parsley, mint, and gelatin; knead with your hands until thoroughly combined and mixture feels slightly sticky, about 2 minutes. Divide mixture into 8 equal portions. Shape each portion into 5-inch-long cylinder about 1 inch in diameter. Using 8 (12-inch) metal skewers, thread 1 cylinder onto each skewer, pressing gently to adhere. Transfer skewers to lightly greased baking sheet, cover with plastic wrap, and refrigerate for at least 1 hour or up to 24 hours.

3A. **For a charcoal grill:** Using skewer, poke 12 holes in bottom of disposable pan. Open bottom vent completely and place pan in center of grill. Light large chimney starter filled two-thirds with charcoal briquettes (4 quarts). When top coals are partially covered with ash, pour into pan. Set cooking grate in place, cover, and open lid vent completely. Heat grill until hot, about 5 minutes.

3B. **For a gas grill:** Turn all burners to high; cover; and heat grill until hot, about 15 minutes. Leave all burners on high.

4. Clean and oil cooking grate. Place skewers on grill (directly over coals if using charcoal) at 45-degree angle to grate. Cook (covered if using gas) until browned and meat easily releases from grill, 4 to 7 minutes. Flip skewers and continue to cook until browned on second side and meat registers 160 degrees, about 6 minutes longer. Transfer skewers to platter and serve, passing yogurt-garlic sauce separately.

VARIATION

Grilled Beef Kofte

Substitute 80 percent lean ground beef for lamb. Increase garlic to 5 cloves, paprika to 2 teaspoons, and cumin to 2 teaspoons.

SEASON 18

Grilled Arayes

Serves 4 to 6 • **Total Time: 1½ hours**

Why This Recipe Works Inspired by Middle Eastern arayes, these lamb sandwiches are seasoned with warm spices and herbs, pressed between pita, and grilled. Along with traditional cumin, coriander, and onion, we added lemon zest to our meat mixture as well as cayenne for heat and paprika for its complementary pepper flavor, and bright, aromatic cilantro. The grill helped make the pita bread really crisp, providing contrasting texture to the filling within. We started cooking with the grill lid closed to jump-start the meat and keep the pita from getting dry and tough. The lamb's fat and juices helped turn the bread supercrisp as it cooked. To help balance the richness of the sandwich, we served it with a bright and cooling yogurt-tahini sauce.

You can substitute 85 percent lean ground beef for the ground lamb, if desired. This recipe works best with ¼-inch-thick pitas that are fresh and pliable. To determine which side of the pita is thicker, look closely at the pattern of browning across its surface; the less-fragile side is usually covered with char marks in a dotted-line pattern. Serve with Parsley-Cucumber Salad with Feta, Pomegranate, and Walnuts (recipe follows).

Sauce

- 1 cup plain Greek yogurt
- ½ cup minced fresh mint
- 2 tablespoons lemon juice
- 2 tablespoons tahini
- 2 tablespoons extra-virgin olive oil
- ½ teaspoon table salt

Sandwiches

- 1 onion, cut into 1-inch pieces
- 1 cup fresh cilantro leaves
- ¼ cup extra-virgin olive oil
- 1 tablespoon grated lemon zest plus 3 tablespoons juice
- 1 tablespoon ground coriander
- 1 tablespoon ground cumin
- 1 tablespoon paprika
- 2 teaspoons table salt
- 1½ teaspoons pepper
- ½ teaspoon cayenne pepper
- ¼ teaspoon ground cinnamon
- 2 pounds ground lamb
- 4 (8-inch) pita breads

1. **For the sauce:** Whisk all ingredients together in bowl. Set aside.

2. **For the sandwiches:** Pulse onion and cilantro in food processor until finely chopped, 10 to 12 pulses, scraping down sides of bowl as needed. Transfer mixture to large bowl. Stir in oil, lemon zest and juice, coriander, cumin, paprika, salt, pepper, cayenne, and cinnamon. Add lamb and knead gently with your hands until thoroughly combined.

3. Using kitchen shears, cut around perimeter of each pita and separate into 2 halves. Place 4 thicker halves on counter with interiors facing up. Divide lamb mixture into 4 equal portions and place 1 portion in center of each pita half. Using spatula, gently spread lamb mixture into even layer, leaving ½-inch border around edge. Top each with thinner pita half. Press each sandwich firmly until lamb mixture spreads to ¼ inch from edge of pita. Transfer assembled sandwiches to large plate, cover with plastic wrap, and set aside. (Sandwiches may be held for up to 1 hour before grilling.)

4A. **For a charcoal grill:** Open bottom vent completely. Light large chimney starter two-thirds filled with charcoal briquettes (4 quarts). When top coals are partially covered with ash, spread coals in single layer over bottom of grill. Set cooking grate in place, cover, and open lid vent completely. Heat grill until hot, about 5 minutes.

4B. **For a gas grill:** Turn all burners to high; cover; and heat grill until hot, about 15 minutes. Turn all burners to medium-high.

Moderate Lamb's Flavor Through Addition and Subtraction

"Lamb's assertive flavor is divisive. When simply flavored and roasted, it can be too much for folks who prefer mildly flavored red meat. But even those who are on the fence about lamb love these lamb-wiches. (I wish I could credit the cook who coined this portmanteau.) I'm certain that it's the thoughtful use of spices and the grilling that bring those with hesitance around. Cinnamon, cayenne, and black pepper bring three different types of heat but it's the generous additions of coriander, cumin, paprika, and cinnamon that take center stage. They are enhanced by the lamb's floral flavors and the result is a well-spiced and moderately spicy filling. Lamb's distinctive flavors are found in its fat. During grilling that fat is rendered out. Some of it is captured by the pita and helps the pita crisp as the arayes cook. But a lot of it drips into the grill, which automatically moderates the lamb-iness of this dish. And that's not all. When the fat hits the coals or the baffles over the gas flames, it breaks down, forming new flavor compounds. They waft about the grill and settle onto the arayes, giving them the smoky grill flavor that goes so well with the spices."

—Lan

5. Clean and oil cooking grate. Place sandwiches on grill; cover; and cook until bottoms are evenly browned and edges are starting to crisp, 7 to 10 minutes, moving sandwiches as needed to ensure even cooking. Flip sandwiches; cover grill; and continue to cook until second sides are evenly browned and edges are crisp, 7 to 10 minutes longer. Transfer sandwiches to cutting board and cut each in half crosswise. Transfer sandwiches to platter and serve, passing sauce separately.

ACCOMPANIMENT

Parsley-Cucumber Salad with Feta, Pomegranate, and Walnuts

Serves 4 to 6   •   Total Time: 25 minutes

Use flat-leaf parsley for this salad.

- 1 tablespoon pomegranate molasses
- 1 tablespoon red wine vinegar
- ¼ teaspoon table salt
- ⅛ teaspoon pepper
  Pinch cayenne pepper
- 3 tablespoons extra-virgin olive oil
- 3 cups fresh parsley leaves
- 1 seedless English cucumber, unpeeled, halved lengthwise and sliced thin
- 1 cup walnuts, toasted and chopped coarse
- ½ cup pomegranate seeds
- 4 ounces feta cheese, sliced thin

Whisk molasses, vinegar, salt, pepper, and cayenne together in large bowl. Whisking constantly, add oil in thin stream until fully incorporated. Add parsley and cucumber and toss to coat. Add half of walnuts and half of pomegranate seeds and toss to combine. Season with salt and pepper to taste. Transfer to serving platter and top with feta, remaining walnuts, and remaining pomegranate seeds. Serve.

SEASON 9

Grilled Glazed Bone-In Chicken Breasts

Serves 4   •   Total Time: 1¼ hours, plus 30 minutes brining

Why This Recipe Works We wanted glazed chicken breasts with tender meat and crisp, lacquered skin. Brining the bone-in chicken breasts before grilling helped ensure juicy, well-seasoned meat. For the glazes, we balanced sweet ingredients, such as molasses and sugar, with boldly

flavored ingredients, such as chipotle chiles, ginger, and curry powder. To keep the glazes from burning on the grill, we first seared the breasts over high heat and then moved them to the cool side of the grill, where we brushed them with the glaze in the last few minutes. For extra flavor, we reserved half of the glaze for serving.

If using kosher chicken, do not brine in step 1, and season with salt as well as pepper. Remember to reserve half of the glaze for serving.

- ½ cup table salt for brining
- 4 (10- to 12-ounce) bone-in split chicken breasts, trimmed
- ½ teaspoon pepper
- 1 recipe glaze (recipes follow)

1. Dissolve salt in 2 quarts cold water in large container. Submerge chicken breasts in brine, cover, and refrigerate for 30 minutes to 1 hour. Remove chicken from brine and pat dry with paper towels. Sprinkle chicken with pepper.

2A. For a charcoal grill: Open bottom vent completely. Light large chimney starter filled with charcoal briquettes (6 quarts). When top coals are partially covered with ash, pour evenly over half of grill. Set cooking grate in place, cover, and open lid vent completely. Heat grill until hot, about 5 minutes.

2B. For a gas grill: Turn all burners to high; cover; and heat grill until hot, about 15 minutes. Leave primary burner on high and turn off other burner(s). (Adjust primary burner as needed during cooking to maintain grill temperature of 350 degrees.)

3. Clean and oil cooking grate. Place chicken on hotter side of grill, skin side up, and cook (covered if using gas) until lightly browned on both sides, 6 to 8 minutes, flipping halfway through cooking. Move chicken, skin side down, to cooler side of grill, with thicker end of breasts facing coals and flames. Cover and continue to cook until chicken registers 150 degrees, 15 to 20 minutes longer.

4. Brush bone side of chicken generously with half of glaze; move to hotter side of grill; and cook until browned, 5 to 10 minutes. Brush skin side of chicken with remaining glaze; flip chicken; and continue to cook until chicken registers 160 degrees, 2 to 3 minutes longer.

5. Transfer chicken to serving platter, tent with aluminum foil, and let rest for 5 to 10 minutes before serving, passing reserved glaze separately.

GLAZES

Orange-Chipotle Glaze

Makes ¾ cup • Total Time: 20 minutes
For a spicier glaze, use the greater amount of chipotle chiles.

- 1 teaspoon grated orange zest plus ⅔ cup juice (2 oranges)
- 1–2 tablespoons minced canned chipotle chile in adobo sauce
- 1 small shallot, minced
- 2 teaspoons minced fresh thyme
- 1 tablespoon molasses
- ¾ teaspoon cornstarch

Combine orange zest and juice, chipotle, shallot, and thyme in small saucepan. Whisk in molasses and cornstarch, bring to simmer, and cook over medium heat until thickened, about 5 minutes. Season with salt to taste. Reserve half of glaze for serving and use remaining glaze to brush on chicken.

Soy-Ginger Glaze

Makes ¾ cup • Total Time: 20 minutes
Reduce the amount of salt in the brine to ¼ cup when using this glaze.

- ⅓ cup water
- ¼ cup soy sauce
- 2 tablespoons mirin
- 1 tablespoon grated fresh ginger
- 2 garlic cloves, minced
- 3 tablespoons sugar
- ¾ teaspoon cornstarch
- 2 scallions, minced

Combine water, soy sauce, mirin, ginger, and garlic in small saucepan, then whisk in sugar and cornstarch. Bring to simmer over medium heat and cook until thickened, about 5 minutes; stir in scallions. Reserve half of glaze for serving and use remaining glaze to brush on chicken.

Curry-Yogurt Glaze

Makes ¾ cup • Total Time: 10 minutes

- ¾ cup plain whole-milk yogurt
- 2 garlic cloves, minced
- 2 teaspoons grated fresh ginger
- 2 teaspoons minced fresh cilantro
- ½ teaspoon grated lemon zest
- 1½ teaspoons curry powder
- ½ teaspoon sugar

Whisk all ingredients together in bowl and season with salt and pepper to taste. Reserve half of glaze for serving and use remaining glaze to brush on chicken.

SEASON 19

Best Grilled Chicken Thighs

Serves 4 to 6 • Total Time: 1½ hours

Why This Recipe Works We wanted a recipe that would produce juicy, flavorful grilled chicken thighs that had well-rendered, crispy skin—minus the all-too-frequent inferno. Cooking the chicken over indirect heat for a relatively long time (about 40 minutes), until it registered between 185 to 190 degrees, allowed collagen in the meat to break down into gelatin, which lubricated the meat so that it tasted moist and silky. We also grilled the thighs skin side down for all but the last few minutes of cooking, which thoroughly rendered the fat under the surface of the skin and allowed the collagen in the skin to break down, both of which led to thin, crispy, well-browned skin. For extra flavor, we wanted to coat the chicken with a bold paste and found that spreading two-thirds of the paste on the flesh side of each thigh worked best, as there were lots of nooks and crannies to capture it. We then rubbed the remaining third of the paste over the skin, which seasoned and flavored it without adding so much moisture that crisping was inhibited. The only hitch: If the chicken cooked skin side down the whole time, the paste on the flesh side looked and tasted a bit raw. So after the skin crisped over the hotter side of the grill, we flipped the pieces onto the flesh side for a minute or two to take the raw edge off the paste.

In step 1, the chicken can be refrigerated for up to 2 hours before grilling.

8 (5- to 7-ounce) bone-in chicken thighs, trimmed
½ teaspoon kosher salt
1 recipe spice paste (recipes follow)

1. Place chicken, skin side up, on large plate. Sprinkle skin side with salt and spread evenly with one-third of spice paste. Flip chicken and spread remaining two-thirds of paste evenly over flesh side. Refrigerate while preparing grill.

2A. For a charcoal grill: Open bottom vent halfway. Light large chimney starter mounded with charcoal briquettes (7 quarts). When top coals are partially covered with ash, pour evenly over half of grill. Set cooking grate in place, cover, and open lid vent halfway. Heat grill until hot, about 5 minutes.

2B. For a gas grill: Turn all burners to high; cover; and heat grill until hot, about 15 minutes. Leave primary burner on high and turn off other burner(s). (Adjust primary burner [or, if using 3-burner grill, primary burner and second burner] as needed to maintain grill temperature of 350 degrees.)

3. Clean and oil cooking grate. Place chicken, skin side down, on cooler side of grill. Cover and cook for 20 minutes. Rearrange chicken, keeping skin side down, so that pieces that were positioned closest to edge of grill are now closer to heat source and vice versa. Cover and continue to cook until chicken registers 185 to 190 degrees, 15 to 20 minutes longer.

4. Move all chicken, skin side down, to hotter side of grill and cook until skin is lightly charred, about 5 minutes. Flip chicken and cook until flesh side is lightly browned, 1 to 2 minutes. Transfer to platter, tent with aluminum foil, and let rest for 10 minutes. Serve.

PASTES
Gochujang Paste
Makes ⅓ cup • Total Time: 10 minutes
Gochujang, or Korean red chile paste, can be found in Asian markets or in the Asian section of large supermarkets.

3 tablespoons gochujang
1 tablespoon soy sauce
2 garlic cloves, minced
2 teaspoons sugar
1 teaspoon kosher salt

Combine all ingredients in bowl.

Mustard-Tarragon Paste
Makes ⅓ cup • Total Time: 10 minutes
Rosemary or thyme can be substituted for the tarragon, if desired. When using this paste, we like to serve the chicken with lemon wedges.

3 tablespoons Dijon mustard
5 garlic cloves, minced
1 tablespoon grated lemon zest
2 teaspoons minced fresh tarragon
1½ teaspoons kosher salt
1 teaspoon water
½ teaspoon pepper

Combine all ingredients in bowl.

Garam Masala Paste
Makes ⅓ cup • Total Time: 10 minutes
Adjust the amount of cayenne to suit your taste. When using this paste, we like to serve the chicken with lime wedges.

3 tablespoons vegetable oil
1½ tablespoons garam masala
2 garlic cloves, minced
2 teaspoons grated fresh ginger
2 teaspoons grated lime zest
1¼ teaspoons kosher salt
⅛–¼ teaspoon cayenne pepper

Combine all ingredients in bowl.

Grilled Chicken with Adobo and Sazón

Serves 4 to 6 • Total Time: 1¾ hours, plus 3 hours marinating

Why This Recipe Works This intensely flavored chicken gets its punch from two dried seasonings from the Puerto Rican pantry: adobo, a blend made from granulated garlic, salt, pepper, and oregano; and sazón, a mixture that includes all the ingredients of adobo as well as achiote, dried onion, cumin, and more herbs. We crafted a home-made adobo but used a commercial sazón. Breaking down a chicken gave us proportionately sized legs and breasts, which cooked more evenly, and the grilled backbone to enjoy. After tossing the chicken in oil and vinegar, we rubbed the seasoning over and under the skin as well as into pockets slashed into the legs. Applied after grilling, a punchy marinade added another layer of bright flavor.

> *Look for sazón with culantro and achiote (also called annatto) at the supermarket, and avoid sazón without salt. You can substitute garlic powder for the granulated garlic. Breaking down a whole chicken lets you enjoy the delicacy that is the grilled backbone, but the recipe works fine with 4 to 4½ pounds of bone-in leg quarters and split breasts.*

Adobo and Sazón

    4   teaspoons granulated garlic
 2½   teaspoons commercial sazón
    1   teaspoon table salt
  ½   teaspoon pepper
  ¼   teaspoon dried oregano

Chicken

    1   (4- to 4½-pound) whole chicken, giblets discarded
    5   tablespoons distilled white vinegar, divided
    5   tablespoons extra-virgin olive oil, divided
    6   garlic cloves, minced
  ½   teaspoon table salt
    1   (13 by 9-inch) disposable aluminum roasting pan
  ¼   cup chopped fresh cilantro
  ½   teaspoon pepper

1. For the adobo and sazón: Combine all ingredients in bowl.

2. For the chicken: Place chicken breast side down on cutting board. Using kitchen shears, cut through bones on either side of backbone. Reserve backbone. Using chef's knife, cut through breastbone to split chicken in half.

Big Flavor in Two Steps

"This deeply flavored grilled chicken was created by my friend and colleague David Pazmiño, who based it on his Puerto Rican grandmother's recipe that uses adobo and sazón, two dried savory seasonings that are popular in the Puerto Rican pantry. The chicken parts get their punch from two marinating steps, one before and one after cooking. It starts with tossing the chicken with a combination of adobo, a dried mixture of granulated garlic, salt, black pepper, and oregano; and sazón, which consists of garlic, cumin, dried herbs, achiote, and often MSG. A 3-hour rest with the adobo and sazón allows the salt and the garlic's water-soluble compounds to penetrate the meat, ensuring even seasoning and moisture. After grilling, the chicken gets a second marinade in a punchy mixture made with lots of garlic and chopped cilantro, salt, white vinegar, black pepper, and olive oil. This fresh post-marinade adds a layer of bright, savory flavor, which accentuates the garlicky adobo-sazón blend."

— Keith

3. Working with 1 half of chicken, slice through skin connecting leg quarter to breast, cutting close to leg quarter to ensure skin completely covers breast and rib meat. Leave split breast whole and tuck wing behind back. Flip leg quarter and remove and discard any rib bone connected to thigh bone. Repeat with second half of chicken.

4. Place 1 leg quarter skin side up on cutting board. Using sharp knife, make 3 slashes: 1 across thigh, 1 across joint, and 1 across drumstick (each slash should reach bone). Flip leg quarter and make 1 more diagonal slash across back of drumstick. Repeat with second leg quarter.

5. Toss chicken (including backbone) with 1 tablespoon vinegar and 1 tablespoon oil in large bowl, using your hands to loosen skin from meat. Sprinkle adobo-sazón mixture over chicken pieces. Toss with your hands, rubbing mixture all over chicken, into slashes, and under skin. Cover and refrigerate chicken for at least 3 hours or up to 24 hours.

6A. For a charcoal grill: Open bottom vent completely. Light large chimney starter filled with charcoal briquettes (6 quarts). When top coals are partially covered with ash, pour evenly over half of grill. Set cooking grate in place, cover, and open lid vent completely. Heat grill until hot, about 5 minutes.

6B. For a gas grill: Turn all burners to high; cover; and heat grill until hot, about 15 minutes. Turn primary burner to medium and turn other burner(s) to low. (Adjust primary burner as needed to maintain grill temperature between 400 and 425 degrees.)

7. While grill heats, place garlic on cutting board and sprinkle with salt. Mash to paste with side of knife. (This can also be done using mortar and pestle.) Transfer garlic paste to disposable pan. Add cilantro, pepper, remaining ¼ cup vinegar, and remaining ¼ cup oil and mix to form paste.

8. Clean and oil cooking grate. Place chicken (including backbone) on cooler side of grill, skin side up. Cover and cook until underside of chicken is lightly browned, 15 to 20 minutes. Flip chicken; cover; and continue to cook on cooler side of grill until thickest part of breast registers 150 degrees, 15 to 20 minutes longer. While chicken cooks, place disposable pan with paste on hotter side of grill and heat until liquid begins to simmer and garlic begins to cook, 2 to 3 minutes. Remove disposable pan from grill.

9. Transfer chicken to hotter side of grill, skin side down, and cook (covered if using gas) until skin is well browned, 2 to 3 minutes. As chicken browns, place disposable pan on cooler side of grill.

10. Flip chicken and cook until breasts register 155 degrees and leg quarters register 175 degrees, about 2 to 3 minutes. As chicken reaches temperature, transfer to disposable pan. Once all chicken is in disposable pan, cover with aluminum foil and slide to hotter side of grill. Cook until marinade is sizzling, 3 to 4 minutes. Let stand off heat for 10 minutes.

11. Cut each breast in half crosswise through bone. Cut leg quarters through joint to separate thigh and drumstick. Place chicken, including backbone, on serving platter. Pour marinade from disposable pan into serving bowl. Serve, passing marinade separately.

SEASON 6

Barbecued Pulled Chicken

Serves 6 to 8 • Total Time: 2½ hours

Why This Recipe Works Recipes for pulled chicken sandwiches often rely on boneless breasts and bottled sauce. We wanted to take pulled chicken seriously—using tender, smoky meat pulled off the bone in moist, soft shreds and tossed with a tangy, sweet sauce—but we didn't want to take all day to make it. We chose whole chicken legs for great flavor, low cost, and resistance to overcooking. The legs cooked gently over indirect heat, absorbing plenty of smoke flavor along the way. Cooking the chicken to a higher-than-usual temperature dissolved connective tissue and rendered more fat, making the meat tender and less greasy. We hand-shredded half the cooked chicken and machine-processed the other half for the ideal texture. The chicken then just had to be combined with a tangy barbecue sauce to become truly bun-worthy.

Chicken leg quarters consist of drumsticks attached to thighs; often also attached are backbone sections that must be trimmed away. If you'd like to use wood chunks instead of wood chips when using a charcoal grill, substitute two medium wood chunks, soaked in water for 1 hour, for the wood chip packet. Serve the pulled chicken on hamburger rolls or sandwich bread, with pickles and coleslaw.

Chicken

  2 **cups wood chips, soaked in water for 15 minutes and drained**
  1 **(16 by 12-inch) disposable aluminum roasting pan (if using charcoal)**
  1 **tablespoon vegetable oil**
  8 **(14-ounce) chicken leg quarters, trimmed**
  2 **teaspoons table salt**
  1 **teaspoon pepper**

Sauce

- 1 large onion, quartered
- ¼ cup water
- 1½ cups ketchup
- 1½ cups apple cider
- ¼ cup molasses
- ¼ cup apple cider vinegar, divided
- 3 tablespoons Worcestershire sauce
- 3 tablespoons Dijon mustard
- ½ teaspoon pepper
- 1 tablespoon vegetable oil
- 1½ tablespoons chili powder
- 2 garlic cloves, minced
- ½ teaspoon cayenne pepper
- Hot sauce

1. For the chicken: Using large piece of heavy-duty aluminum foil, wrap soaked chips in 8 by 4½-inch foil packet. (Make sure chips do not poke holes in sides or bottom of packet.) Cut 2 evenly spaced 2-inch slits in top of packet.

2A. For a charcoal grill: Open bottom vent halfway and place disposable pan in center of grill. Light large chimney starter three-quarters filled with charcoal briquettes (4½ quarts). When top coals are partially covered with ash, pour into 2 even piles on either side of pan. Place wood chip packet on 1 pile of coals. Set cooking grate in place, cover, and open lid vent halfway. Heat grill until hot and wood chips are smoking, about 5 minutes.

2B. For a gas grill: Place wood chip packet directly on primary burner. Turn all burners to high; cover; and heat grill until hot and wood chips are smoking, about 15 minutes. Turn all burners to medium. (Adjust burners as needed during cooking to maintain grill temperature between 250 and 300 degrees.)

3. Clean and oil cooking grate. Pat chicken dry with paper towels and sprinkle with salt and pepper. Place chicken in single layer on center of grill (over roasting pan if using charcoal), skin side up, or evenly over grill (if using gas). Cover (position lid vent over meat if using charcoal) and cook until chicken registers 185 degrees, 1 to 1½ hours, rotating chicken pieces halfway through cooking. Transfer chicken to carving board, tent with foil, and let rest until cool enough to handle.

4. For the sauce: Meanwhile, process onion and water in food processor until mixture resembles slush, about 30 seconds. Pass through fine-mesh strainer into liquid measuring cup, pressing on solids with rubber spatula (you should have ¾ cup strained onion juice). Discard solids in strainer.

5. Whisk onion juice, ketchup, cider, molasses, 3 tablespoons vinegar, Worcestershire, mustard, and pepper together in

bowl. Heat oil in large saucepan over medium heat until shimmering. Stir in chili powder, garlic, and cayenne and cook until fragrant, about 30 seconds. Stir in ketchup mixture, bring to simmer, and cook over medium-low heat until slightly thickened, about 15 minutes (you should have about 4 cups of sauce). Transfer 2 cups sauce to serving bowl; leave remaining sauce in saucepan.

6. To serve: Remove and discard skin from chicken legs. Using your fingers, pull meat off bones, separating larger pieces (which should fall off bones easily) from smaller, drier pieces into 2 equal piles.

7. Pulse smaller chicken pieces in food processor until just coarsely chopped, 3 to 4 pulses, stirring chicken with rubber spatula after each pulse. Add chopped chicken to sauce in saucepan. Using your fingers or 2 forks, pull larger chicken pieces into long shreds and add to saucepan. Stir in remaining 1 tablespoon vinegar, cover, and heat chicken over medium-low heat, stirring occasionally, until heated through, about 10 minutes. Add hot sauce to taste, and serve, passing remaining sauce separately.

VARIATION

Barbecued Pulled Chicken for a Crowd
Serves 10 to 12

This technique works best on a charcoal grill. If your gas grill can accommodate more than 8 legs, follow the master recipe, adding as many legs as will fit in a single layer.

Increase amount of charcoal briquettes to 6 quarts. Use 12 chicken legs and slot them into V-shaped roasting rack set on top of cooking grate over disposable aluminum pan. Increase cooking time in step 3 to 1½ to 1¾ hours. In step 5, remove only 1 cup of sauce from saucepan. In step 7, pulse chicken in food processor in 2 batches.

Grilled Chicken Satay

Serves 4 to 6 • Total Time: 1¾ hours

Why This Recipe Works This Malaysian-style chicken satay features pieces of chicken coated in a deeply fragrant paste, skewered, and charred on the grill. We use chicken thighs because they cook up juicy and tender and can stay on the grill long enough to pick up flavorful charring. Cutting the chicken into strips and stretching them between two skewers creates more surface area for the paste to coat and for charring. An aromatic paste of lemongrass, ginger, galangal, garlic, shallots, and spices develops savory character when charred. We use a portion of the paste as the base for a dipping sauce, browning it to soften the aromatics' raw edge and develop savory depth. We then simmer it with ground peanuts, water, tamarind, and sugar to create a subtle, sweet-tangy undertone.

You will need eight 12-inch metal skewers for this recipe. If galangal is unavailable, increase the ginger to one 1½-inch piece. The aromatic paste can also be prepared using a mortar and pestle. For a spicier dish, use the larger amount of red pepper flakes. Lime juice can be substituted for the tamarind paste.

Aromatic Paste

- 2 lemongrass stalks, trimmed to bottom 6 inches
- 3 shallots, chopped (⅔ cup)
- 3 tablespoons water
- 1 tablespoon vegetable oil
- 1 tablespoon packed brown sugar
- 3 garlic cloves, chopped
- 1 (1-inch) piece galangal, peeled and minced
- 1 (1-inch) piece ginger, peeled and sliced into ⅛-inch-thick coins
- 2 teaspoons table salt
- 1 teaspoon ground turmeric
- ½–¾ teaspoon red pepper flakes
- ½ teaspoon ground coriander
- ½ teaspoon ground cumin

Peanut Sauce

- ⅓ cup dry-roasted peanuts
- 2 tablespoons vegetable oil
- ¾ cup water, plus extra as needed
- 1 tablespoon tamarind paste
- 1 tablespoon packed brown sugar

Chicken

- 2 pounds boneless, skinless chicken thighs, trimmed and cut crosswise into 1- to 1½-inch-wide strips
- 2 tablespoons vegetable oil

1. For the aromatic paste: Halve lemongrass lengthwise and, using meat pounder, lightly crush on cutting board to soften. Mince lemongrass and transfer to food processor. Add shallots, water, oil, sugar, garlic, galangal, ginger, salt, turmeric, and pepper flakes and process until uniform paste forms, about 2 minutes, scraping down sides of bowl as necessary. Measure out ⅓ cup paste and set aside. Transfer remaining paste to bowl and stir in coriander and cumin. Cover bowl and microwave paste for 1½ minutes, stirring halfway through microwaving. Transfer bowl to refrigerator and let paste cool while preparing sauce.

2. For the peanut sauce: Place peanuts in now-empty processor and process until coarsely ground, about 15 seconds. Heat oil and reserved ⅓ cup paste in medium saucepan over medium-low heat until fond begins to form on bottom of saucepan and paste starts to darken, about 5 minutes. Stir in water, tamarind, sugar, and ground peanuts and bring to boil, scraping up any browned bits. Reduce heat to maintain gentle simmer and cook, stirring occasionally, until sauce is reduced to about 1 cup, 8 to 10 minutes. Season with salt to taste, cover, and set aside.

3. For the chicken: Add chicken to cooled paste and toss to combine. Thread chicken onto 4 sets of two 12-inch metal skewers. (Hold 2 skewers 1 inch apart and thread chicken onto both skewers at once so strips of chicken are perpendicular to skewers.) Do not crowd skewers; each set of skewers should hold 6 to 8 pieces of chicken. Transfer kebabs to large plate and refrigerate while preparing grill. (Kebabs can be refrigerated for up to 4 hours.)

4A. For a charcoal grill: Open bottom vent completely. Light large chimney starter mounded with charcoal briquettes (7 quarts). When top coals are partially covered with ash, pour evenly over grill. Set cooking grate in place, cover, and open lid vent completely. Heat grill until hot, about 5 minutes.

4B. For a gas grill: Turn all burners to high; cover; and heat grill until hot, about 15 minutes. Turn all burners to medium.

5. Clean and oil cooking grate. Brush both sides of kebabs with oil. Place kebabs on grill and cook (covered if using gas) until browned and char marks appear on first side, about 5 minutes. Using large metal spatula, gently release chicken from grill; flip; and continue to cook until chicken registers 175 to 180 degrees, 3 to 5 minutes longer. Transfer to large platter. Gently reheat peanut sauce, thinning with extra water, 1 tablespoon at a time, to desired consistency. Serve chicken, passing peanut sauce separately.

Grilled Chicken Satay

Pollo a la Brasa

Serves 4 • Total Time: 2½ hours, plus 24 hours marinating

Why This Recipe Works In Peru, maestros polleros, or poultry masters, make the wildly popular chickens known as pollo a la brasa by grill-roasting chickens on rotisseries that spin lazily over crackling wood fires ("brasa" means "ember") to produce meat that's encased in tawny, paper-thin skin and dripping with juices. Our version calls for marinating the bird for 24 hours in a beer-based marinade that also includes ingredients commonly used in pollerías today: soy sauce for salinity; lime juice and mustard for brightness; and garlic, dried thyme, black pepper, and cumin for earthy, savory depth. Instead of a horizontal rotisserie, we used a half-empty beer can to prop the chicken up vertically and then set it in the center of a kettle grill outfitted with a split fire. As it cooked, we rotated the chicken a quarter turn every 15 minutes; about five turns produced remarkably succulent, smoky meat packaged in well rendered, uniformly mahogany skin. We whipped up a pair of bold mayonnaise-based sauces to serve alongside.

Our gas grill instructions are for a three-burner grill. If using a two-burner grill, turn both burners to high and place the wood chips on the primary burner while the grill heats. When the grill is hot, turn the primary burner to medium and turn the secondary burner off; stand the chicken on the cooler side of the grill, about 4 inches from the primary burner, and proceed with the recipe, adjusting the primary burner as needed to maintain 350 to 375 degrees. A rasp-style grater makes quick work of grating the garlic. Inexpensive beer is fine; avoid those with strong hoppy or bitter flavors. Do not use a 16-ounce can; its height will make the chicken less stable. If you'd like to use wood chunks instead of wood chips when using a charcoal grill, substitute one medium wood chunk for the wood chip packet. Serve with french fries and salad and one or both sauces (recipes follow).

1 (12-ounce) can beer, divided
2 tablespoons finely grated garlic
2 tablespoons lime juice
2 tablespoons soy sauce
2 teaspoons table salt
2 teaspoons yellow mustard
1 teaspoon pepper
1 teaspoon dried thyme
1 teaspoon ground cumin
1 (4- to 4½-pound) whole chicken, giblets discarded
1 cup wood chips
1 (13 by 9-inch) disposable aluminum roasting pan

1. Whisk ½ cup beer, garlic, lime juice, soy sauce, salt, mustard, pepper, thyme, and cumin together in liquid measuring cup. Refrigerate remaining beer, still in can, until ready to grill. Using your fingers or handle of wooden spoon, gently loosen skin covering chicken breast and leg quarters. Using paring knife, poke 10 to 15 holes in fat deposits on skin of back. Tuck wingtips underneath chicken.

2. Place chicken in bowl with cavity end facing up. Slowly pour marinade between skin and meat and rub marinade inside cavity, outside skin, and under skin to distribute. Cover and refrigerate for 24 hours, turning chicken halfway through marinating.

3. Using large piece of heavy-duty aluminum foil, wrap wood chips in 8 by 4½-inch foil packet. (Make sure chips do not poke holes in packet.) Cut 2 evenly spaced 2-inch slits in top of packet.

4. Place beer can in large, shallow bowl. Spray can all over with vegetable oil spray. Slide chicken over can so drumsticks reach down to bottom of can and chicken stands upright; set aside at room temperature while preparing grill.

5A. For a charcoal grill: Open bottom vent completely and place disposable pan in center of grill. Light large chimney starter two-thirds filled with charcoal briquettes (4 quarts). When top coals are partially covered with ash, pour into 2 even piles on either side of disposable pan. Place wood chip packet on 1 pile of coals. Set cooking grate in place, cover, and open lid vent completely. Heat grill until hot and wood chips are smoking, about 5 minutes.

5B. **For a gas grill:** Remove cooking grate and place wood chip packet directly on one of outside burners. Set grate in place; turn all burners to high; cover; and heat grill until hot and wood chips are smoking, about 15 minutes. Turn 2 outside burners to medium and turn off center burner. (Adjust outside burners as needed to maintain grill temperature between 350 and 375 degrees.)

6. Clean and oil cooking grate. Transfer chicken with can to center of cooking grate with wings facing piles of coals (or outer burners on gas grill) at 3 and 9 o'clock (ends of drumsticks should rest on grate to help steady bird). Cover grill (with top vent open for charcoal grill) and cook for 15 minutes. Using tongs and wad of paper towels, rotate chicken 90 degrees so wings are at 6 and 12 o'clock. Continue cooking and turning chicken at 15-minute intervals until thickest part of thigh registers 170 to 175 degrees, 1 hour to 1¼ hours longer.

7. With large wad of paper towels in each hand, transfer chicken and can to clean bowl, keeping can upright; let rest for 15 minutes (do not discard paper towels). Using wads of paper towels, carefully lift chicken off can and onto cutting board. Discard can. Carve chicken, transfer to platter, and serve.

SAUCES
Ají Verde
Makes ¾ cup • Total Time: 10 minutes

Zippy ají sauces are mandatory with pollo a la brasa, and they're not just for the chicken: Peruvians also pour them all over the salad and fries that share the plate. Huacatay is a Peruvian herb sometimes called black mint. You can find it jarred in supermarkets or online. If it's unavailable, increase the cilantro to 5 tablespoons.

- ½ cup mayonnaise
- 1 jalapeño chile, stemmed, seeded, and chopped coarse
- 3 tablespoons minced fresh cilantro
- 2 tablespoons grated cotija cheese
- 2 tablespoons lime juice
- 1 tablespoon jarred huacatay paste
- 1 garlic clove, minced

Combine all ingredients in blender and process until smooth, about 1 minute. (Sauce can be refrigerated for up to 1 week.)

Ají Amarillo
Makes ⅔ cup • Total Time: 10 minutes

Ají amarillo paste, made from yellow Peruvian chiles, is available in supermarkets or online. If huacatay paste is unavailable, it can be omitted.

- ½ cup mayonnaise
- 2 tablespoons ají amarillo paste
- 1 tablespoon lime juice
- 1 garlic clove, minced
- 1 teaspoon jarred huacatay paste

Combine all ingredients in blender and process until smooth, about 1 minute. (Sauce can be refrigerated for up to 1 week.)

SEASON 13
Simple Grill-Roasted Turkey

Serves 10 to 12 • Total Time: 3½ to 4 hours, plus 24¾ hours brining and resting

Why This Recipe Works Besides freeing up your oven for other dishes, roasting your turkey out on the grill also means that you don't have to worry about constantly monitoring the bird to ensure a perfectly juicy, tender turkey. To make grilling turkey failproof, we divided our coals into two piles on either side of the grill so that the turkey thighs would receive the highest heat. A combination of lit coals and unlit briquettes yielded a longer-burning fire, making replenishing coals unnecessary. The addition of a pan of water stabilized the temperature inside the grill for even cooking, and a quick salt rub before grilling yielded seasoned meat and crispy skin.

> *Table salt is not recommended for this recipe because it is too fine. If using a kosher or self-basting turkey (such as a frozen Butterball), do not salt it in step 1. Check the wings halfway through roasting; if they are getting too dark, fold a 12 by 8-inch piece of foil in half lengthwise and then again crosswise and slide the foil between the wing and the cooking grate to shield the wings from the flame. As an accompaniment, try our Gravy for Simple Grill-Roasted Turkey (recipe follows).*

Great Grilled Turkey

"I popped this recipe right into my 'Favorites' file on the ATK website, because as soon as I tried it, I knew it was the way I'd be making my holiday turkey forever. I've rarely experienced a recipe that had so much going for it, starting with the most important fact: that it produces a delicious, picture-perfect, golden brown, juicy and perfectly cooked turkey with just the merest hint of smokiness. After a bit of preparation a day or two before you cook, it's mostly hands off, and roasts in less than 3 hours. Because it's outdoors on the grill, you not only free up your oven but you also have the perfect excuse to pop out for fresh air and a bit of peace from a crowded household on the holiday to 'check' the turkey. Full disclosure: This recipe is so simple, you don't really need to check or do anything, as long as you've used a remote probe thermometer. Nothing ever goes wrong. Just enjoy the oohs and aahs when you bring it to the table."

—Lisa

1 (12- to 14-pound) turkey, neck and giblets removed and reserved for gravy

¼ cup plus 1 teaspoon kosher salt, divided

1 teaspoon pepper

1 teaspoon baking powder

1 tablespoon vegetable oil
  Large disposable aluminum roasting pan (if using charcoal) or 2 disposable aluminum pie plates (if using gas)

1. Place turkey breast side down on work surface. Make two 2-inch incisions below each thigh and breast along back of turkey (4 incisions total). Using your fingers or handle of wooden spoon, carefully separate skin from thighs and breast. Rub 4 teaspoons salt evenly inside cavity of turkey, 1 tablespoon salt under skin of each side of breast, and 1 teaspoon salt under skin of each leg.

2. Combine pepper, baking powder, and remaining 1 teaspoon salt in bowl. Pat turkey dry with paper towels and sprinkle surface with pepper mixture; rub in with your hands to coat evenly. Wrap turkey tightly with plastic wrap; refrigerate for at least 24 hours or up to 2 days.

3. Discard plastic. Tuck wings underneath turkey. Using your hands, rub oil evenly over entire surface of turkey.

4A. For a charcoal grill: Open bottom vent halfway and place disposable pan filled with 3 cups water in center of grill. Arrange 1½ quarts unlit charcoal briquettes on either side of pan in even layer. Light large chimney starter two-thirds filled with charcoal briquettes (4 quarts). When top coals are partially covered with ash, pour 2 quarts of lit coals on top of each pile of unlit coals. Set cooking grate in place, cover, and open lid vent halfway. Heat grill until hot, about 5 minutes.

4B. For a gas grill: Place 2 disposable pie plates with 2 cups water in each directly on 1 burner over which turkey will be cooked. Turn all burners to high; cover; and heat grill until hot, about 15 minutes. Turn primary burner (burner opposite pie plates) to medium and turn other burner(s) off. Adjust primary burner as needed to maintain grill temperature of 325 degrees.

5. Clean and oil cooking grate. Place turkey, breast side up, in center of charcoal grill or on cooler side of gas grill, making sure bird is over disposable pans and not over flame. Cover (placing vents over turkey on charcoal grill) and cook until breast registers 160 degrees and thighs/drumsticks register 175 degrees, 2½ to 3 hours, rotating turkey after 1¼ hours if using gas grill.

6. Transfer turkey to carving board and let rest, uncovered, for 45 minutes. Carve turkey and serve.

Gravy for Simple Grill-Roasted Turkey
Makes 6 cups • Total Time: 2½ hours

1 tablespoon vegetable oil
  Reserved turkey neck, cut into 1-inch pieces, and giblets

1 pound onions, chopped coarse, divided

4 cups chicken broth

4 cups beef broth

2 small carrots, peeled and chopped coarse

2 small celery ribs, chopped coarse

6 tablespoons unsalted butter

½ cup all-purpose flour

2 bay leaves

½ teaspoon dried thyme

10 whole black peppercorns

1. Heat oil in Dutch oven over medium-high heat until shimmering. Add turkey neck and giblets; cook, stirring occasionally, until browned, about 5 minutes. Add half of onions and cook, stirring occasionally, until softened, about 3 minutes. Reduce heat to low; cover and cook, stirring occasionally, until turkey parts and onions release their juices, about 20 minutes.

2. Add chicken broth and beef broth; increase heat to high and bring to boil. Reduce heat to low and simmer, uncovered, skimming any scum that rises to surface, until broth is rich and flavorful, about 30 minutes. Strain broth into large bowl (you should have about 8 cups), reserving giblets, if desired; discard neck. Reserve broth. When cool enough to handle, remove gristle from giblets, if using; dice; and set aside. (Broth can be refrigerated for up to 2 days.)

3. Pulse carrots in food processor until broken into rough ¼-inch pieces, about 5 pulses. Add celery and remaining onions; pulse until all vegetables are broken into ⅛-inch pieces, about 5 pulses.

4. Melt butter in now-empty Dutch oven over medium-high heat. Add vegetables and cook, stirring frequently, until softened and well browned, about 10 minutes. Reduce heat to medium; stir in flour and cook, stirring constantly, until thoroughly browned and fragrant, 5 to 7 minutes. Whisking constantly, gradually add reserved broth; bring to boil, skimming off any foam that forms on surface. Reduce heat to medium-low and add bay leaves, thyme, and peppercorns; simmer, stirring occasionally, until thickened and reduced to 6 cups, 30 to 35 minutes.

5. Strain gravy through fine-mesh strainer into clean saucepan, pressing on solids to extract as much liquid as possible; discard solids. Stir in diced giblets, if using. Season with salt and pepper to taste.

Grill-Smoked Salmon

Serves 6 • Total Time: 1¾ hours, plus 1 hour salting

Why This Recipe Works We wanted to capture the intense, smoky flavor of hot-smoked fish and the firm but silky texture of the cold-smoked type, but we also wanted to skip specialized equipment and make this dish less of a project. We quick-cured the fish with a mixture of salt and sugar to draw moisture from the flesh, and we seasoned it inside and out. Cooking it over a gentle fire with ample smoke produced salmon that was sweet, smoky, and tender. Cutting a large fillet into individual portions created more surface area for smoke exposure. Plus, the smaller pieces of salmon were far easier to remove from the grill intact.

Use center-cut salmon fillets of similar thickness so that they cook at the same rate. The best way to ensure uniformity is to buy a 2½- to 3-pound whole center-cut fillet and cut it into six pieces. If you'd like to use wood chunks instead of wood chips when using a charcoal grill, substitute two medium wood chunks, soaked in water for 1 hour, for the wood chip packet. Avoid mesquite wood chunks for this recipe. Serve the salmon with lemon wedges or with our "Smoked Salmon Platter" Sauce or Apple-Mustard Sauce (recipes follow).

- 2 tablespoons sugar
- 1 tablespoon kosher salt
- 6 (6- to 8-ounce) center-cut skin-on salmon fillets
- 2 cups wood chips, half of chips soaked in water for 15 minutes and drained

1. Combine sugar and salt in bowl. Set wire rack in rimmed baking sheet, set salmon on rack, and sprinkle flesh side evenly with sugar mixture. Refrigerate, uncovered, for 1 hour. With paper towels, brush any excess salt and sugar from salmon and blot dry. Return fish on wire rack to refrigerator, uncovered, while preparing grill.

2. Combine soaked and unsoaked chips. Using large piece of heavy-duty aluminum foil, wrap chips in 8 by 4½-inch foil packet. (Make sure chips do not poke holes in sides or bottom of packet.) Cut 2 evenly spaced 2-inch slits in top of packet.

3A. For a charcoal grill: Open bottom vent halfway. Light large chimney starter one-third filled with charcoal briquettes (2 quarts). When top coals are partially covered with ash, pour into steeply banked pile against side of grill. Place wood chip packet on top of coals. Set cooking grate in place, cover, and open lid vent halfway. Heat grill until hot and wood chips are smoking, about 5 minutes.

Think Outside the Box

"The silky texture and smoky flavor of cold-smoked salmon—the thin slices that top bagels with cream cheese—result in large part from two techniques: curing the fish with salt and sugar before it's smoked, and cold-smoking, which is finicky, temperature-sensitive, and impractical for most home cooks. Grill-smoking, however, is well within the reach of home grillers. The genius of this recipe is that it borrows the curing step from cold-smoking, albeit for a much shorter time, before smoking the fish on the grill. Curing the fish for just an hour draws out moisture from the flesh, thus firming it up a little, and seasons it deeply. A gentle two-level fire, with plenty of wood to produce ample smoke, takes care of the rest, and you end up with exceptionally supple, moist, tender, distinctly smoky salmon.

I make this every summer for a group of friends as part of a Scandinavian Midsomer celebration, and every year they rave about it. In fact, one friend professes to dislike all salmon preparations except this one!"

— Adam

3B. For a gas grill: Place wood chip packet directly on primary burner. Turn primary burner to high (leave other burners off); cover; and heat grill until hot and wood chips are smoking, about 15 minutes. Turn primary burner to medium. (Adjust primary burner as needed to maintain grill temperature between 275 to 300 degrees.)

4. Clean and oil cooking grate. Fold piece of heavy-duty foil into 18 by 6-inch rectangle. Place foil rectangle over cooler side of grill and place salmon pieces on foil, spaced at least ½ inch apart. Cover grill (positioning lid vent over fish if using charcoal) and cook until center of thickest part of fillet is still translucent when checked with tip of paring knife and registers 125 degrees (for medium-rare), 30 to 40 minutes. Transfer to platter and serve, or let cool to room temperature.

SAUCES

"Smoked Salmon Platter" Sauce

Makes 1½ cups • Total Time: 10 minutes

This sauce incorporates the three garnishes that are commonly served on a smoked salmon platter—hard-cooked egg, capers, and dill.

- 1 large egg yolk, plus 1 large hard-cooked egg, chopped fine
- 2 teaspoons Dijon mustard
- 2 teaspoons sherry vinegar
- ½ cup vegetable oil
- 2 tablespoons capers, rinsed, plus 1 teaspoon caper brine
- 2 tablespoons minced shallot
- 2 tablespoons minced fresh dill

Whisk egg yolk, mustard, and vinegar together in medium bowl. Whisking constantly, slowly drizzle in oil until emulsified, about 1 minute. Gently fold in capers and brine, hard-cooked egg, shallot, and dill.

Apple-Mustard Sauce

Makes 1½ cups • Total Time: 10 minutes

- 2 Honeycrisp or Granny Smith apples, peeled, cored, and cut into ¼-inch dice
- ¼ cup whole-grain mustard
- 2 tablespoons Dijon mustard
- 2 tablespoons minced fresh chervil or parsley
- 1 tablespoon cider vinegar
- 1 tablespoon honey
- ¼ teaspoon table salt

Combine all ingredients in bowl.

Grilled Whole Trout with Marjoram and Lemon

Serves 4 • Total Time: 1¼ hours

Why This Recipe Works This recipe teaches that whole fish should not be feared, and grill-roasting trout is an immaculate example why. The grill infuses the trout with complementary smoky flavor, and the intense heat crisps the skin beautifully. The dish is simple, because whole trout are almost always sold cleaned, scaled, and gutted. And one fish serves one person for nice portioning. We brush mayonnaise and honey, neither of which you can taste, over the fish to brown it quickly. Fresh marjoram and lemon zest go inside. A concentrated fire, with an aluminum pan to corral the coals and focus their heat, cooks the trout in a flash. To take the temperature, insert the thermometer into the fillets through the opening by the gills.

We prefer marjoram in this recipe, but thyme or oregano can be substituted. Do not flip the fish over in one motion. Instead, use two thin metal spatulas to gently lift the fish from the grate and then slide it from the spatula back onto the grate. The heads can be removed before serving, if desired.

- 2 teaspoons minced fresh marjoram
- 2 teaspoons kosher salt
- 1 teaspoon grated lemon zest, plus lemon wedges for serving
- ½ teaspoon pepper
- 4 (10- to 12-ounce) whole trout, gutted, fins snipped off with scissors
- 2 tablespoons mayonnaise
- ½ teaspoon honey
- 1 (13 by 9-inch) disposable aluminum pan (if using charcoal)

1. Place marjoram, lemon zest, and salt on cutting board and chop until finely minced and well combined. Rinse each fish under cold running water and pat dry with paper towels inside and out. Open up each fish and sprinkle marjoram mixture evenly over flesh of fish. Sprinkle each fish with pepper. Close up fish and let stand for 10 minutes. Stir mayonnaise and honey together. Brush mayonnaise mixture evenly over entire exterior of each fish.

2A. For a charcoal grill: Using kitchen shears, poke twelve ½-inch holes in bottom of disposable pan. Open bottom vent completely and place disposable pan in center of grill.

Light large chimney starter two-thirds filled with charcoal briquettes (4 quarts). When top coals are partially covered with ash, pour into even layer in disposable pan. Set cooking grate over coals with bars parallel to long side of disposable pan, cover, and open lid vent completely. Heat grill until hot, about 5 minutes.

2B. For a gas grill: Turn all burners to high; cover; and heat grill until hot, about 15 minutes. Leave all burners on high.

3. Clean and oil cooking grate. Grill fish (directly over coals if using charcoal and with lid closed if using gas) until skin is browned and beginning to blister, 2 to 4 minutes. Using thin metal spatula, lift bottom of thick backbone edge of fish from cooking grate just enough to slide second thin metal spatula under fish. Remove first spatula, then use it to support raw side of fish as you use second spatula to flip fish over. Grill until second side is browned, beginning to blister, and thickest part of fish registers 130 to 135 degrees, 2 to 4 minutes. Transfer fish to platter and let rest for 5 minutes. Serve with lemon wedges.

VARIATIONS

Grilled Whole Trout with Lime and Coriander
Substitute 1 teaspoon ground coriander for marjoram and lime zest and wedges for lemon zest and wedges.

Grilled Whole Trout with Orange and Fennel
Substitute 1 teaspoon ground fennel for marjoram and orange zest for lemon zest.

Flipping Whole Fish on the Grill

1. Slide spatula scant 1 inch under backbone edge and lift edge up.

2. Slide second spatula under, then remove first spatula, allowing fish to ease onto second spatula.

3. Place first spatula on top of fish, in same direction as second spatula; flip fish so it rests on second spatula, then ease fish onto grill.

SEASON 15

Grilled Fish Tacos

Serves 6 • Total Time: 1¾ hours, plus 30 minutes marinating

Why This Recipe Works For a fish taco with fresh, bold flavors, we fired up the grill. For simplicity, we opted for skinless fillets instead of the traditional whole butterflied fish. Meaty swordfish held up on the grill better than flaky options like hake and cod. A thick paste featuring ancho and chipotle chile powders, oregano, and just a touch of citrus juice developed deep, flavorful charring on the grill without promoting sticking. Refreshing grilled pineapple salsa, avocado, and crunchy iceberg lettuce completed our tacos with flavor and texture contrasts.

Mahi-mahi, tuna, and halibut fillets are all suitable substitutes for the swordfish; to ensure the best results, buy 1-inch-thick fillets and cut them in a similar fashion to the swordfish.

- 3 tablespoons vegetable oil
- 1 tablespoon ancho chile powder
- 2 teaspoons chipotle chile powder
- 1 teaspoon dried oregano
- 1 teaspoon ground coriander
- 2 garlic cloves, minced
- 1 teaspoon table salt
- 2 tablespoons tomato paste
- ½ cup orange juice
- 6 tablespoons lime juice (3 limes)
- 2 pounds skinless swordfish steaks, 1 inch thick, cut lengthwise into 1-inch-wide strips
- 1 pineapple, peeled, quartered lengthwise, cored, and each quarter halved lengthwise
- 1 jalapeño chile
- 18 (6-inch) corn tortillas
- 1 red bell pepper, stemmed, seeded, and cut into ¼-inch pieces
- 2 tablespoons minced fresh cilantro, plus extra for serving
- ½ head iceberg lettuce (4½ ounces), cored and sliced thin
- 1 avocado, halved, pitted, and sliced thin
  Lime wedges

1. Heat 2 tablespoons oil, ancho chile powder, and chipotle chile powder in 8-inch skillet over medium heat, stirring constantly, until fragrant and some bubbles form, 2 to 3 minutes. Add oregano, coriander, garlic, and salt and continue to cook until fragrant, about 30 seconds longer. Add tomato paste and, using spatula, mash tomato paste with spice mixture until combined, about 20 seconds. Stir in orange juice and 2 tablespoons lime juice. Cook, stirring constantly, until thoroughly mixed and reduced slightly, about 2 minutes. Transfer chile mixture to large bowl and cool for 15 minutes.

2. Add swordfish to bowl with chile mixture, and stir gently with rubber spatula to coat fish. Cover and refrigerate for at least 30 minutes or up to 2 hours.

3A. For a charcoal grill: Open bottom vent completely. Light large chimney starter mounded with charcoal briquettes (7 quarts). When top coals are partially covered with ash, pour evenly over grill. Set cooking grate in place, cover, and open lid vent completely. Heat grill until hot, about 5 minutes.

3B. For a gas grill: Turn all burners to high; cover; and heat grill until hot, about 15 minutes. Turn all burners to medium-high.

4. Clean cooking grate, then repeatedly brush grate with well-oiled paper towels until grate is black and glossy, 5 to 10 times. Brush both sides of pineapple with remaining 1 tablespoon oil. Place fish on half of grill. Place pineapple and jalapeño on other half. Cover and cook until fish, pineapple, and jalapeño have begun to brown, 3 to 5 minutes. Using thin spatula, flip fish, pineapple, and jalapeño. Cover and continue to cook until second sides of pineapple and jalapeño are browned and swordfish registers 140 degrees, 3 to 5 minutes. Transfer fish to large platter, flake into pieces, and tent with aluminum foil. Transfer pineapple and jalapeño to cutting board.

5. Clean cooking grate. Place half of tortillas on grill. Grill until softened and speckled with brown spots, 30 to 45 seconds per side. Wrap tortillas in dish towel or foil to keep warm until ready to use. Repeat with remaining tortillas.

6. When cool enough to handle, finely chop pineapple and jalapeño. Transfer to medium bowl and stir in bell pepper, cilantro, and remaining ¼ cup lime juice. Season with salt to taste. Top tortillas with flaked fish, pineapple salsa, lettuce, and avocado. Serve with lime wedges and extra cilantro.

Swoon-Worthy Scallops

"On my first day working on America's Test Kitchen, *the television show, 15 years ago, I was trying to look busy, hiding in the corner, cleaning perfectly clean grills, when someone said, 'Hey! Do you want a scallop?' Keith Dresser appeared carrying a giant plate of the most beautiful grilled scallops I had ever seen, fresh from their on-camera moment. Plump and juicy, sweet and smoky. Perfect golden grill marks stamped on like a brand—I literally swooned.*

Any time I'd attempted to grill scallops before, I ended up with chewy, overcooked blobs. A terrible end for a gorgeous—and expensive— product. As I stuffed my face, Keith explained there's a protein in scallops and fish that fuses to metal grilling grates. He told me they developed a cornstarch slurry to prevent sticking, added a pinch of sugar to promote browning, and threaded the scallops onto two skewers, for easier flipping. These tricks transform the scallop into something I didn't even know was possible, and those scallops are these very scallops right here! They've been a staple for me every summer since. If you love scallops, grilling, and eating outside as much as I do, go make these and have your own swoon session."

—*Hannah*

Grilled Scallops

Serves 4 • **Total Time: 1¼ hours**

Why This Recipe Works In theory, a blazing-hot grill is perfect for cooking scallops with a crisp crust and moist interior, but in practice they're usually rubbery and over-cooked by the time they develop a good sear—and they inevitably stick to the grate. For great grilled scallops, we needed the hottest fire possible. The solution for a char-coal grill was a disposable aluminum pan—it corralled the coals in the center of the grill for a superhot fire that gave us scallops with impressive char and juicy centers. Drying the scallops before cooking helped ensure browning, and threading them onto two side-by-side skewers made them easy to flip. To combat sticking, we lightly coated the scallops in a mixture of flour, cornstarch, oil, and sugar; this allowed them to come off the grill with ease.

We recommend buying "dry" scallops, which don't have additives and taste better than "wet." Dry scallops will look ivory or pinkish; wet scallops are bright white. If using wet scallops, soak them in a solution of 1 quart water, ¼ cup lemon juice, and 2 tablespoons salt for 30 minutes before step 1, and do not season with salt in step 3. You will need eight to twelve 12-inch metal skewers. Serve with a vinaigrette (recipes follow), if desired.

1½ pounds large sea scallops, tendons removed
1 (13 by 9-inch) disposable aluminum roasting pan (if using charcoal)
2 tablespoons vegetable oil, plus extra for cooking grate
1 tablespoon all-purpose flour
1 teaspoon cornstarch
1 teaspoon sugar
1 teaspoon kosher salt
¼ teaspoon pepper
  Lemon wedges

1. Place scallops on rimmed baking sheet lined with clean dish towel. Place second clean dish towel on top of scallops and press gently on towel to blot liquid. Let scallops sit at room temperature, covered with towel, for 10 minutes. Thread 4 to 6 scallops, 1 flat side down, onto 1 skewer and then place second skewer through scallops parallel to and about ¼ inch from first. Return skewered scallops to towel-lined baking sheet; refrigerate, covered with second towel, while preparing grill.

2A. For a charcoal grill: Open bottom vent completely. Light large chimney starter mounded with charcoal bri-quettes (7 quarts). Meanwhile, poke twelve ½-inch holes

in bottom of disposable pan and place in center of grill. When top coals are partially covered with ash, empty coals into pan. Set cooking grate in place, cover, and open lid vent completely. Heat grill until hot, about 5 minutes.

2B. For a gas grill: Turn all burners to high; cover; and heat grill until hot, about 15 minutes.

3. While grill heats, whisk oil, flour, cornstarch, and sugar together in small bowl. Remove towels from scallops. Brush both sides of skewered scallops with oil mixture and sprinkle with salt and pepper.

4. Clean cooking grate, then repeatedly brush grate with well-oiled paper towels until grate is black and glossy, 5 to 10 times.

5. Place skewered scallops directly on grill (directly over coals if using charcoal). Cook (covered if using gas) without moving scallops until lightly browned, 2½ to 4 minutes. Carefully flip skewers and continue to cook until second side of scallops is browned, sides are firm, and centers are opaque, 2 to 4 minutes longer. Serve immediately with lemon wedges.

VINAIGRETTES
Chile-Lime Vinaigrette
Makes 1 cup • **Total Time: 10 minutes**

1 teaspoon grated lime zest plus 3 tablespoons juice (2 limes)
2 tablespoons honey
1 tablespoon sriracha
2 teaspoons fish sauce
½ cup vegetable oil

Whisk lime zest and juice, honey, sriracha, and fish sauce in medium bowl until combined. Whisking constantly, slowly drizzle in oil until emulsified.

Basil Vinaigrette
Makes 1 cup • **Total Time: 10 minutes**

1 cup packed fresh basil leaves
3 tablespoons minced fresh chives
2 tablespoons champagne vinegar
2 garlic cloves, minced
2 teaspoons sugar
1 teaspoon table salt
½ teaspoon pepper
⅔ cup vegetable oil

Pulse basil, chives, vinegar, garlic, sugar, salt, and pepper in blender until roughly chopped, 5 to 7 pulses. With blender running, slowly drizzle in oil until emulsified, scraping down sides of blender jar as needed, about 1 minute.

Grilled Shrimp and Vegetable Kebabs

Serves 4 to 6 • Total Time: 2¼ hours

Why This Recipe Works Combined shrimp and vegetable kebabs are notoriously difficult to cook because the shrimp inevitably overcooks in the time it takes most vegetables to pass from raw to their crisp-tender ideal. As a result, you end up with either overcooked shrimp or undercooked vegetables. This recipe works by pairing slower cooking jumbo shrimp with soft, quick-cooking vegetables. We nestled mushrooms into the curve of the shrimp on the skewer to better insulate the shrimp and extend their cooking time, and we cut the vegetables to mimic the profile of the shrimp, so the entire skewer made contact with the grill, promoting even cooking. Finally, we precooked some vegetables in the microwave before skewering them to give them a head start. Simply seasoning with oil and pepper allowed the kebabs to char beautifully on the grill, and dressing them with a fresh lemon-herb vinaigrette while still hot from the fire finished the dish in style.

> *Small mushrooms about 1¼ to 1½ inches in diameter work best here. If using larger mushrooms, halve them before microwaving. You will need eight 12-inch metal skewers for this recipe.*

Shrimp

- 2 tablespoons table salt for brining
- 2 tablespoons sugar for brining
- 1½ pounds jumbo shrimp (16 to 20 per pound), peeled and deveined
- 3 large red or yellow bell peppers, stemmed, seeded, and cut into ¾-inch-wide by 3-inch-long strips
- ¼ teaspoon plus ⅛ teaspoon table salt, divided
- 24 cremini mushrooms, trimmed
- 12 scallions, cut into 3-inch lengths
- 2 tablespoons vegetable oil
- ¼ teaspoon pepper

Vinaigrette

- ¼ cup lemon juice (2 lemons)
- ¼ cup extra-virgin olive oil
- 2 teaspoons minced fresh thyme
- 1 garlic clove, minced
- ½ teaspoon table salt
- ¼ teaspoon Dijon mustard
- ⅛ teaspoon pepper

1. For the shrimp: Dissolve 2 tablespoons salt and sugar in 1 quart cold water in large container. Submerge shrimp in brine, cover, and refrigerate for 15 minutes. Remove shrimp from brine and pat dry with paper towels.

2. Line large microwave-safe plate with double layer of paper towels. Spread half of bell peppers skin side down in even layer on plate and sprinkle with ⅛ teaspoon salt. Microwave for 2 minutes. Transfer peppers, still on towels, to cutting board and let cool. Repeat with fresh paper towels and remaining bell peppers and ⅛ teaspoon salt.

3. Line second plate with double layer of paper towels. Spread mushrooms in even layer and sprinkle with remaining ⅛ teaspoon salt. Microwave for 3 minutes. Transfer mushrooms, still on towels, to cutting board and let cool.

4. Lay one shrimp on cutting board and run 12-inch metal skewer through center. Thread mushroom onto skewer through sides of cap, pushing so it nestles tightly into curve of shrimp. Follow mushroom with 2 pieces scallion and 2 pieces bell pepper, skewering so vegetables and shrimp form even layer. Repeat shrimp and vegetable sequence two more times. When skewer is full, gently press ingredients so they fit snugly together in center of each skewer. Skewer remaining shrimp and vegetables on 7 more skewers for total of 8 kebabs. Brush each side of kebabs with vegetable oil and sprinkle with pepper.

5A. For a charcoal grill: Open bottom vent completely. Light large chimney starter mounded with charcoal briquettes (7 quarts). When top coals are partially covered with ash, pour evenly over grill. Set cooking grate in place, cover, and open lid vent completely. Heat grill until hot, about 5 minutes.

5B. For a gas grill: Turn all burners to high; cover; and heat grill until hot, about 15 minutes. Leave all burners on high.

6. For the vinaigrette: While grill heats, whisk all ingredients together in bowl.

7. Clean and oil cooking grate. Place kebabs on grill and grill (covered if using gas) until charred, about 2½ minutes. Flip skewers and grill until second side is charred and shrimp are cooked through, 2 to 3 minutes, moving skewers as needed to ensure even cooking. Transfer skewers to serving platter. Rewhisk vinaigrette and drizzle over kebabs. Serve.

SEASON 17

Paella on the Grill

Serves 8 • Total Time: 2¼ hours

Why This Recipe Works Grilling paella lends the dish subtle smoke flavor and a particularly rich crust and makes it a great dish for summer entertaining. In place of a traditional paella pan, we cooked ours in a large, sturdy roasting pan that maximized the amount of socarrat, the prized caramelized rice crust that forms on the bottom of the pan. Building a large (7-quart) fire and fueling it with fresh coals (which ignited during cooking) ensured that the heat output would last throughout cooking, but we also shortened the outdoor cooking time by using roasted red peppers and tomato paste (instead of fresh peppers and tomatoes), making an infused broth with the seasonings, and grilling (rather than searing) the chicken thighs. To ensure that the various components finished cooking at the same time, we staggered the addition of the proteins—first, the chicken thighs, followed by the shrimp, clams, and chorizo. We also deliberately placed the chicken on the perimeter of the pan, where it would finish cooking gently after grilling, and the sausage and seafood in the center, where they were partially submerged in the liquid so that they cooked through; once the liquid reduced, the steam kept them warm.

This recipe was developed with a light-colored 16 by 13.5-inch tri-ply roasting pan; however, it can be made in any heavy roasting pan that measures at least 14 by 11 inches. If your roasting pan is dark in color, the cooking times will be on the lower end of the ranges given. The recipe can also be made in a 15- to 17-inch paella pan. If littlenecks are unavailable, use 1½ pounds shrimp in step 1 and season them with ½ teaspoon salt.

1½ pounds boneless, skinless chicken thighs, trimmed and halved crosswise
1¾ teaspoons table salt, divided
1 teaspoon pepper
12 ounces jumbo shrimp (16 to 20 per pound), peeled and deveined
6 tablespoons extra-virgin olive oil, divided
6 garlic cloves, minced, divided
1¾ teaspoons smoked hot paprika, divided
3 tablespoons tomato paste
4 cups chicken broth
⅔ cup dry sherry
1 (8-ounce) bottle clam juice
Pinch saffron threads (optional)
1 onion, chopped fine
½ cup roasted red peppers, chopped fine
3 cups Arborio rice
1 pound littleneck clams, scrubbed
1 pound Spanish-style chorizo, cut into ½-inch pieces
1 cup frozen peas, thawed
Lemon wedges

1. Place chicken on large plate and sprinkle both sides with 1 teaspoon salt and pepper. Toss shrimp with 1 tablespoon oil, ½ teaspoon garlic, ¼ teaspoon paprika, and ¼ teaspoon salt in bowl until evenly coated. Set aside.

2. Heat 1 tablespoon oil in medium saucepan over medium heat until shimmering. Add remaining garlic and cook, stirring constantly, until garlic sticks to bottom of saucepan and begins to brown, about 1 minute. Add tomato paste and remaining 1½ teaspoons paprika and continue to cook, stirring constantly, until dark brown bits form on bottom of saucepan, about 1 minute. Add broth; sherry; clam juice; and saffron, if using. Increase heat to high and bring to boil. Remove pan from heat and set aside.

3A. For a charcoal grill: Open bottom vent completely. Light large chimney starter mounded with charcoal briquettes (7 quarts). When top coals are partially covered with ash, pour evenly over grill. Using tongs, arrange 20 unlit briquettes evenly over coals. Set cooking grate in place, cover, and open lid vent completely. Heat grill until hot, about 5 minutes.

3B. For a gas grill: Turn all burners to high; cover; and heat grill until hot, about 15 minutes. Leave all burners on high.

4. Clean and oil cooking grate. Place chicken on grill and cook until both sides are lightly browned, 5 to 7 minutes total. Return chicken to plate. Clean cooking grate.

5. Place roasting pan on grill (turning burners to medium-high if using gas) and add remaining ¼ cup oil. When oil begins to shimmer, add onion, red peppers, and remaining ½ teaspoon salt. Cook, stirring frequently, until onion begins to brown, 4 to 7 minutes. Add rice (turning burners to medium if using gas) and stir until grains are well coated with oil.

6. Arrange chicken around perimeter of pan. Pour broth mixture and any accumulated juices from chicken over rice. Smooth rice into even layer, making sure nothing sticks to sides of pan and no rice rests atop chicken. When liquid reaches gentle simmer, place shrimp in center of pan in single layer. Arrange clams in center of pan, evenly distributing with shrimp and pushing hinge sides of clams into rice slightly so they stand up. Distribute chorizo evenly over surface of rice. Cook, moving and rotating pan to maintain gentle simmer across entire surface of pan, until rice is almost cooked through, 12 to 18 minutes. (If using gas, heat can also be adjusted to maintain simmer.)

7. Sprinkle peas evenly over paella; cover grill; and cook until liquid is fully absorbed and rice on bottom of pan sizzles, 5 to 8 minutes. Continue to cook, uncovered, checking frequently, until uniform golden-brown crust forms on bottom of pan, 8 to 15 minutes longer. (Rotate and slide pan around grill as necessary to ensure even crust formation.) Remove from grill, cover with foil, and let stand for 10 minutes. Serve with lemon wedges.

Grilled Halloumi Wraps

Serves 4 • Total Time: 1¼ hours

Why This Recipe Works Firm and easy to brown, halloumi cheese is a natural on the grill. To offset the cheese's salty richness, we combined it with bright, crisp, sumac-spiked onion; smoky grilled bell pepper; and peppery arugula. While the cheese and peppers cooked, we steamed some moistened pitas in a foil packet on the cooler side of the grill so that they would be soft and flexible enough to wrap. For a yogurt spread that was garlicky without being harsh, we combined the garlic with some lemon juice to deactivate its alliinase before combining it with the yogurt.

The saltiness of halloumi varies; for the best results, select a product that has less than 260 milligrams of sodium per serving. Because the cooking time is so brief, using a charcoal grill is impractical here; if you don't have a gas grill, cook the halloumi and bell pepper in a grill pan on the stovetop over medium-high heat, and wrap the moistened pitas in paper towels and warm them in the microwave.

  1 red onion, halved and sliced thin
  3 tablespoons red wine vinegar
  1 tablespoon ground sumac
 ¾ teaspoon table salt, divided
  2 tablespoons lemon juice
  1 garlic clove
 ½ cup plain Greek yogurt
  1 large red bell pepper
  4 (8-inch) pitas, divided
 12 ounces halloumi cheese, sliced crosswise
      ½ inch thick
  1 tablespoon extra-virgin olive oil
 ¼ teaspoon red pepper flakes
  2 ounces (2 cups) arugula

1. Combine onion, vinegar, sumac, and ¼ teaspoon salt in medium bowl. Stir until well combined; set aside. Place lemon juice in small bowl. Mince or grate garlic and add to juice. Add ¼ teaspoon salt and whisk to combine. Whisk in yogurt until smooth.

2. Slice ½ inch from top and bottom of bell pepper. Gently remove stem from top. Twist and pull out core, using knife to loosen at edges if necessary. Cut slit down 1 side of bell pepper. Turn bell pepper skin side down and gently press so it opens to create long strip. Slide knife along insides to remove remaining ribs and seeds.

Halloumi, a Great Non-Melting Cheese

"Halloumi is an ingredient that I have somehow managed to overlook until recently. Last summer while we were filming a recipe segment for Grilled Halloumi Wraps, I was blown away when a tray of the perfectly grilled slices of salty and tender (but not gooey) cheese passed by me only to find that there were extra pieces that 'needed' to be sampled. Three slices later, and after a moment of 'where have you been all of my life' this grilled (or sautéed) slice of pure salty and nutty deliciousness is now on my regular menu rotation.

These wraps are a great option when I'm looking for a fresh, summery meat-free meal, as they're quick to put together and a true crowd pleaser."

— *Erin*

3. Lightly moisten 2 pitas with water. Sandwich remaining pitas between moistened pitas and wrap tightly in lightly greased heavy-duty aluminum foil.

4. Turn all burners on gas grill to high; cover; and heat grill until hot, about 15 minutes. Leave primary burner on high and turn off other burner(s). Clean and oil cooking grate. Arrange halloumi slices and bell pepper pieces, skin side up, on hotter side of grill. Cook, covered, until undersides of cheese and bell pepper are lightly browned, 3 to 5 minutes. Using tongs, flip cheese and bell pepper and continue to cook until second side of cheese and bell pepper are lightly browned, 3 to 5 minutes longer.

5. Meanwhile, place packet of pitas on cooler side of grill. Flip occasionally to heat, about 5 minutes. Transfer cheese and bell pepper to cutting board. Cut bell pepper into ½-inch pieces and transfer to second small bowl. Add oil, pepper flakes, and remaining ¼ teaspoon salt and toss to combine.

6. Lay each warm pita on 12-inch square of foil or parchment paper. Spread each pita with one-quarter of yogurt mixture. Place one-quarter of cheese in middle of each pita. Top with pepper, onion, and arugula. Drizzle with any remaining onion liquid. Roll pita into cylinder. Wrap in foil, cut in half, and serve.

Grilled Corn with Flavored Butter

Serves 4 to 6 • Total Time: 55 minutes

Why This Recipe Works Grilled corn is a go-to summer treat, but we wanted a way to spice it up—literally. To incorporate flavorful herbs and spices into the corn, we found that a two-step approach worked best. First, we brushed the ears with vegetable oil and seared them over a hot grill fire. When the corn had a nice char, we moved the ears to a disposable pan on the grill and added a dollop of butter seasoned with herbs and other aromatic ingredients. The butter infused every kernel with extra flavor, and the disposable pan made the process simple and prevented butter-induced flare-ups on the grill.

Use a disposable aluminum roasting pan that is at least 2¾ inches deep.

1 recipe flavored butter (recipes follow)
1 (13 by 9-inch) disposable aluminum roasting pan
8 ears corn, husks and silk removed
2 tablespoons vegetable oil

1. Place flavored butter in disposable pan. Brush corn evenly with oil and sprinkle with salt and pepper.

2. Grill corn over hot fire, turning occasionally, until lightly charred on all sides, 5 to 9 minutes. Transfer corn to pan and cover tightly with aluminum foil.

3. Place pan on grill and cook, shaking pan frequently, until butter is sizzling, about 3 minutes. Remove pan from grill and carefully remove foil, allowing steam to escape away from you. Serve corn, spooning any butter in pan over individual ears.

Basil and Lemon Butter
Total Time: 20 minutes
Serve with lemon wedges, if desired.

6 tablespoons unsalted butter, softened
2 tablespoons chopped fresh basil
1 tablespoon minced fresh parsley
1 teaspoon grated lemon zest
½ teaspoon table salt
¼ teaspoon pepper

Combine all ingredients in small bowl.

Honey Butter

Total Time: 20 minutes

This butter also works well with cornbread.

- 6 tablespoons unsalted butter, softened
- 2 tablespoons honey
- ½ teaspoon table salt
- ¼ teaspoon red pepper flakes

Combine all ingredients in small bowl.

Cilantro-Chipotle Butter

Total Time: 20 minutes

Serve with orange wedges, if desired.

- 6 tablespoons unsalted butter, softened
- 2 tablespoons minced fresh cilantro
- 1 tablespoon minced fresh parsley
- 1 teaspoon minced canned chipotle chile in adobo sauce
- ½ teaspoon grated orange zest
- ½ teaspoon table salt

Combine all ingredients in small bowl.

New Orleans "Barbecue" Butter

Total Time: 20 minutes

- 6 tablespoons unsalted butter, softened
- 1 garlic clove, minced
- 1 tablespoon Worcestershire sauce
- 1 teaspoon tomato paste
- ½ teaspoon minced fresh rosemary
- ½ teaspoon minced fresh thyme
- ½ teaspoon cayenne pepper

Combine all ingredients in small bowl.

Spicy Old Bay Butter

Total Time: 20 minutes

Serve with lemon wedges, if desired.

- 6 tablespoons unsalted butter, softened
- 1 tablespoon hot sauce
- 1 tablespoon minced fresh parsley
- 1½ teaspoons Old Bay seasoning
- 1 teaspoon grated lemon zest

Combine all ingredients in small bowl.

Grilled Potatoes with Garlic and Rosemary

Serves 4 • Total Time: 50 minutes

Why This Recipe Works We wanted to put a new spin on grilled potatoes by adding rosemary and garlic for a more savory side. To avoid burnt, bitter garlic and charred rosemary, we learned that we needed to introduce the potatoes to a garlic-oil mixture not once, but three times. First we pierced the potatoes, skewered them, brushed on a garlic-rosemary oil, and precooked them in the microwave. We brushed them again with the infused oil before grilling. After grilling, we tossed the potatoes with the oil yet again for serious flavor without any bitterness.

This recipe allows you to grill an entrée while the hot coals burn down in step 4. Once that item is done, start grilling the potatoes. This recipe works best with small potatoes that are about 1½ inches in diameter. If using medium potatoes, 2 to 3 inches in diameter, cut them into quarters. If the potatoes are larger than 3 inches in diameter, cut each potato into eighths. Since the potatoes are first cooked in the microwave, use wooden skewers.

- ¼ cup extra-virgin olive oil
- 9 garlic cloves, minced
- 1 teaspoon chopped fresh rosemary
- 1 teaspoon table salt, divided
- 2 pounds small red potatoes, unpeeled, halved and skewered
- ½ teaspoon pepper
- 2 tablespoons chopped fresh chives

1. Heat oil, garlic, rosemary, and ½ teaspoon salt in small skillet over medium heat until sizzling, about 3 minutes. Reduce heat to medium-low and continue to cook until garlic is light blond, about 3 minutes. Pour mixture through fine-mesh strainer into small bowl; press on solids. Measure 1 tablespoon of solids and 1 tablespoon of oil into large bowl and set aside. Discard remaining solids but reserve remaining oil.

2. Place skewered potatoes in single layer on large plate and poke each potato several times with skewer. Brush with 1 tablespoon of strained oil and sprinkle with ¼ teaspoon salt. Microwave until potatoes offer slight resistance when pierced with paring knife, about 8 minutes, turning halfway through microwaving. Transfer potatoes to baking sheet coated with 1 tablespoon strained oil. Brush with remaining 1 tablespoon strained oil and sprinkle with remaining ¼ teaspoon salt and pepper.

3A. For a charcoal grill: Open bottom vent completely. Light large chimney starter filled with charcoal briquettes (6 quarts). When top coals are partially covered with ash, pour two-thirds evenly over grill, then pour remaining coals over half of grill. Set cooking grate in place, cover, and open lid vent completely. Heat grill until hot, about 5 minutes.

3B. For a gas grill: Turn all burners to high; cover; and heat grill until hot, about 15 minutes. Turn all burners down to medium-high.

4. Clean and oil cooking grate. Place potatoes on grill (hotter side if using charcoal) and cook (covered if using gas) until grill marks appear, 3 to 5 minutes, flipping halfway through cooking. Move potatoes to cooler side of grill (if using charcoal) or turn all burners to medium-low (if using gas). Cover and continue to cook until paring knife slips in and out of potatoes easily, 5 to 8 minutes longer.

5. Remove potatoes from skewers and transfer to bowl with reserved garlic-oil mixture. Add chives, season with salt and pepper to taste, and toss until thoroughly coated. Serve.

VARIATION
Grilled Potatoes with Oregano and Lemon
Reduce garlic to 3 cloves, substitute 2 tablespoons chopped fresh oregano for rosemary, and add 2 teaspoons grated lemon zest to oil in skillet. Substitute 2 teaspoons chopped fresh oregano for chives and add additional 1 teaspoon grated lemon zest to potatoes when they come off grill.

SEASON 2
Grilled Baba Ghanoush

Makes 2 cups • Total Time: 1½ hours, plus 45 minutes chilling

Why This Recipe Works Baba ghanoush showcases eggplant's full potential. We were after a dip that was full of smoky eggplant flavor and brightened with garlic and lemon juice. And one certain way to produce this creation was to start off by grilling our eggplant. For the best flavor, it's imperative to start out with firm, shiny, and unblemished eggplants. We grilled the eggplants directly over a hot fire until they were wrinkled and soft. To avoid a watery texture and any bitterness, we drained the pulp of excess fluid, but didn't bother spending time deseeding the eggplants. We processed the pulp with a modest amount of garlic, tahini paste, and lemon juice for the creaminess and bright flavor that baba ghanoush is known for.

When buying eggplants, select those with shiny, taut, and unbruised skins and an even shape (eggplants with a bulbous shape won't cook evenly). Grill until the eggplant walls have collapsed and the insides feel sloshy when pressed with tongs. We prefer to serve baba ghanoush only lightly chilled; if cold, let it stand at room temperature for about 20 minutes before serving. Baba ghanoush does not keep well, so plan to make it the day you want to serve it. Serve with pita bread, black olives, tomato wedges, or cucumber slices.

2 pounds eggplant, pricked all over with fork
2 tablespoons tahini
1 tablespoon lemon juice
1 tablespoon extra-virgin olive oil, plus extra for serving
1 small garlic clove, minced
¼ teaspoon table salt
¼ teaspoon pepper
2 teaspoons chopped fresh parsley

1A. For a charcoal grill: Open bottom vent completely. Light large chimney starter filled with charcoal briquettes (6 quarts). When top coals are partially covered with ash, pour evenly over grill. Set cooking grate in place, cover, and open lid vent completely. Heat grill until hot, about 5 minutes.

1B. For a gas grill: Turn all burners to high; cover; and heat grill until hot, about 15 minutes. Turn all burners to medium. (Adjust burners as needed to maintain grill temperature of 350 degrees.)

2. Clean and oil cooking grate. Set eggplants on cooking grate and cook until skins darken and wrinkle on all sides and eggplants are uniformly soft when pressed with tongs, about 25 minutes, turning every 5 minutes and reversing direction of eggplants on grill with each turn. Transfer eggplants to rimmed baking sheet and let cool for 5 minutes.

3. Set small colander over bowl. Trim top and bottom off each eggplant. Slit eggplants lengthwise and use spoon to scoop hot pulp from skins; place pulp in colander (you should have about 2 cups packed pulp); discard skins. Let pulp drain for 3 minutes.

4. Transfer pulp to food processor. Add tahini, lemon juice, oil, garlic, salt, and pepper. Pulse until mixture has coarse, choppy texture, about 8 pulses. Season with salt and pepper to taste. Transfer to serving bowl, cover with plastic wrap flush with surface of dip, and refrigerate for 45 minutes to 1 hour. Make trough in center of dip using large spoon and spoon olive oil into it. Sprinkle with parsley and serve.

When It Comes to Grilled Eggplant for Baba, Drain the Swamp!

"It's not an exaggeration to say that almost every time I light the grill, I throw a couple of eggplants on it along with whatever I'm really cooking. I love baba ghanoush and its kin— almost every eggplant-eating region has a dish made from grilled eggplant puree—and during the grilling season I nearly always have one in the fridge for snacking. Eggplant picks up smoky flavor notes from the grill like a champ.

For a dish that's dense and creamy rather than loose and watery, it's very important to drain the cooked eggplant in a colander or strainer before adding the other ingredients. Allowing excess liquid to drain out of the cooked flesh not only facilitates the best possible consistency, it also mitigates the bitterness often associated with eggplant, which helps hallmark seasonings such as lemon, garlic, and tahini shine bright."

—Adam

Sides

Photo: Braised Eggplant with Paprika, Coriander, and Yogurt

Pan-Roasted Asparagus

Serves 3 to 4 • Total Time: 20 minutes

Why This Recipe Works Our simple stovetop method for pan-roasted asparagus delivers crisp, nicely browned spears. We quickly learned to choose thick spears because thinner spears overcooked too quickly. Taking a cue from restaurant chefs who blanch asparagus first, we developed a method to lightly steam and then brown the asparagus in the same skillet. For both flavor and browning, we used olive oil and butter. Positioning half the spears in one direction and the other half in the opposite direction ensured a better fit in the pan. Browning just one side of the asparagus provided a contrast in texture and guaranteed that the asparagus were firm and tender, never limp.

This recipe works best with asparagus that is at least ½ inch thick near the base. If using thinner spears, reduce the covered cooking time to 3 minutes and the uncovered cooking time to 5 minutes. Do not use pencil-thin asparagus; it cannot withstand the heat and overcooks too easily.

- 1 tablespoon olive oil
- 1 tablespoon unsalted butter
- 2 pounds thick asparagus (2 bunches), tough ends trimmed
- ½ lemon (optional)

Trimming Asparagus Spears

1. To remove tough ends, take 1 asparagus spear from bunch and snap off end.

2. Using broken asparagus as guide, trim off ends of remaining spears using chef's knife.

1. Heat oil and butter in 12-inch skillet over medium-high heat. When butter has melted, add half of asparagus to skillet with tips pointed in 1 direction; add remaining asparagus with tips pointed in opposite direction. Using tongs, distribute spears in even layer (spears will not quite fit into single layer); cover and cook until asparagus is bright green and still crisp, about 5 minutes.

2. Uncover and increase heat to high; season asparagus with salt and pepper to taste. Cook until spears are tender and well browned along 1 side, 5 to 7 minutes, using tongs to occasionally move spears from center of pan to edge of pan to ensure all are browned. Transfer asparagus to dish, adjust seasonings with salt and pepper, and squeeze lemon half, if using, over spears. Serve.

Beets with Lemon and Almonds

Serves 4 to 6 • Total Time: 1¼ hours

Why This Recipe Works This streamlined recipe for beets maximizes their sweet, earthy flavor. To achieve our goal, we braised the halved beets on the stovetop in minimal water, reduced the residual cooking liquid, and added light brown sugar and vinegar. This flavor-packed glaze was just thick enough to coat the wedges of peeled beets. For flavor and texture contrast, we added toasted nuts (or pepitas), fresh herbs, and aromatic citrus zest just before serving.

To ensure even cooking, we recommend using beets that are of similar size—roughly 2 to 3 inches in diameter. The beets can be served warm or at room temperature. If serving at room temperature, wait until right before serving to sprinkle on the almonds and herbs.

- 1½ pounds beets, trimmed and halved horizontally
- 1¼ cups water
- ¾ teaspoon table salt, divided
- 3 tablespoons distilled white vinegar
- 1 tablespoon packed light brown sugar
- 1 shallot, sliced thin
- 1 teaspoon grated lemon zest
- ¼ teaspoon pepper
- ½ cup whole almonds, toasted and chopped
- 2 tablespoons chopped fresh mint
- 1 teaspoon chopped fresh thyme

1. Place beets, cut side down, in single layer in 11-inch straight-sided sauté pan or Dutch oven. Add water and ¼ teaspoon salt; bring to simmer over high heat. Reduce heat to low; cover; and simmer until beets are tender and tip of paring knife inserted into beets meets no resistance, 45 to 50 minutes.

2. Transfer beets to cutting board. Increase heat to medium-high and reduce cooking liquid, stirring occasionally, until pan is almost dry, 5 to 6 minutes. Add vinegar and sugar, return to boil, and cook, stirring constantly with heat-resistant spatula, until spatula leaves wide trail when dragged through glaze, 1 to 2 minutes. Remove pan from heat.

3. When beets are cool enough to handle, rub off skins with paper towel or clean dish towel and cut into ½-inch wedges. Add beets, shallot, lemon zest, pepper, and remaining ½ teaspoon salt to glaze and toss to coat. Transfer beets to serving dish; sprinkle with almonds, mint, and thyme; and serve.

VARIATIONS

Beets with Lime and Pepitas

Omit thyme. Substitute lime zest for lemon zest, toasted pepitas for almonds, and cilantro for mint.

Beets with Orange and Walnuts

Substitute orange zest for lemon zest; walnuts, toasted and chopped, for almonds; and parsley for mint.

SEASON 10

Roasted Broccoli

Serves 4 • Total Time: 30 minutes

Why This Recipe Works Roasting can concentrate flavor to turn dull vegetables into something great, but roasting broccoli usually makes for spotty browning and charred, bitter florets. We figured out how to roast broccoli so that it turned out perfectly browned and deeply flavorful every time. To ensure that the broccoli would brown evenly, we cut the crown into uniform wedges that lay flat on the baking sheet, increasing contact with the pan. To promote even cooking of the stem, we sliced away the exterior and cut the stalk into rectangular pieces slightly smaller than the more delicate wedges. Preheating the baking sheet helped the broccoli cook faster, crisping but not charring the florets, while a very hot oven delivered the best browning. Sprinkling a little sugar over the broccoli along with the salt and pepper helped it brown even more deeply. We finally had roasted broccoli with crispy-tipped florets and sweet, browned stems.

GAME CHANGER

Broccoli Love

"This is the recipe that transformed my relationship with green vegetables. Growing up, the only green things I'd eat would be English (obviously) cucumber and green candy. I couldn't stand the sulfurous smell of overcooked vegetables that always seemed to taste like old cabbage. This recipe deeply caramelizes one side of the broccoli through an expert understanding of how to use an oven. Most roasted vegetables are tossed in a little oil, cooked in a 450-degree oven, and turned halfway until crisp at the edges. This recipe starts with a preheated baking sheet, on the bottom rack, and the broccoli is not touched after it goes in. The lowest rack's proximity to the heating element means that direct heat gets focused on one side of the broccoli, turning it tender and sweetly golden brown. The high heat and fast cook time turns the upper side bright green and, as it's not flipped, stays pleasantly crisp-tender. Best of all, it's also the one healthy dish that my veggie-phobic 10-year-old will eat. I love it for that alone."

—Joe

> *It is important to trim away the outer peel from the broccoli stalks; otherwise, they will turn tough when cooked.*

1¾ pounds broccoli (1 large bunch)
3 tablespoons extra-virgin olive oil
½ teaspoon table salt
½ teaspoon sugar
Lemon wedges

1. Adjust oven rack to lowest position, place rimmed baking sheet on rack, and heat oven to 500 degrees. Cut broccoli at juncture of florets and stems; remove outer peel from stalk. Cut stalk into 2- to 3-inch lengths and each length into ½-inch-thick pieces. Cut crowns into 4 wedges (if 3 to 4 inches in diameter) or 6 wedges (if 4 to 5 inches in diameter). Place broccoli in large bowl; drizzle with oil and toss well until evenly coated. Sprinkle with salt and sugar and season with pepper to taste; toss to combine.

2. Carefully remove baking sheet from oven. Working quickly, transfer broccoli to baking sheet and spread into even layer, placing flat sides down. Return baking sheet to oven and roast until stalks are well browned and tender and florets are lightly browned, 9 to 11 minutes. Transfer to dish and serve with lemon wedges.

VARIATION
Roasted Broccoli with Garlic
Add 1 minced garlic clove to oil before drizzling it over broccoli in step 1.

SEASON 13
Roasted Brussels Sprouts

Serves 6 to 8 • Total Time: 45 minutes

Why This Recipe Works Roasting is a simple and quick way to produce brussels sprouts that are well caramelized on the outside and tender on the inside. To ensure that we achieved this balance, we started out roasting the "tiny cabbages" covered with a little bit of water. This created a steamy environment which cooked the vegetables through. We then removed the foil and allowed the exteriors to dry out and caramelize.

> *If you are buying loose brussels sprouts, select those that are about 1½ inches long. Quarter brussels sprouts longer than 2½ inches; don't cut sprouts shorter than 1 inch.*

2¼ pounds brussels sprouts, trimmed and halved
3 tablespoons extra-virgin olive oil
1 tablespoon water
¾ teaspoon table salt
¼ teaspoon pepper

1. Adjust oven rack to upper-middle position and heat oven to 500 degrees. Toss all ingredients in large bowl until sprouts are coated. Transfer sprouts to rimmed baking sheet and arrange cut sides down.

2. Cover baking sheet tightly with aluminum foil and roast for 10 minutes. Remove foil and continue to cook until brussels sprouts are well browned and tender, 10 to 12 minutes longer. Transfer to serving platter, season with salt and pepper to taste, and serve.

VARIATIONS
Roasted Brussels Sprouts with Garlic, Red Pepper Flakes, and Parmesan
While brussels sprouts roast, heat 3 tablespoons extra-virgin olive oil in 8-inch skillet over medium heat until shimmering. Add 2 minced garlic cloves and ½ teaspoon red pepper flakes; cook until garlic is golden and fragrant, about 1 minute. Remove from heat. Toss roasted brussels sprouts with garlic oil and season with salt and pepper to taste. Transfer to platter and sprinkle with ¼ cup grated Parmesan cheese before serving.

Roasted Brussels Sprouts with Bacon and Pecans
While brussels sprouts roast, cook 4 slices bacon in 10-inch skillet over medium heat until crisp, 7 to 10 minutes. Using slotted spoon, transfer bacon to paper towel–lined plate and reserve 1 tablespoon bacon fat. Finely chop bacon. Toss roasted brussels sprouts with 2 tablespoons extra-virgin olive oil, reserved bacon fat, chopped bacon, and ½ cup finely chopped toasted pecans. Season with salt and pepper to taste; transfer to platter and serve.

Roasted Brussels Sprouts with Walnuts and Lemon
Transfer roasted brussels sprouts to platter and toss with 3 tablespoons melted butter, 1 tablespoon lemon juice, and ⅓ cup finely chopped toasted walnuts. Season with salt and pepper to taste, and serve.

GAME CHANGER

Steam and Roast

"I'm convinced that I'm part brussels sprout. The little green orbs are one of my all-time favorite vegetables. I enjoy them in a variety of ways—shredded in salads, roasted, braised, in a hash, creamed in a casserole—the list goes on! This particular recipe is one that I make year-round because it serves a crowd; frees up stove space; and can either be served on its own or, depending on what it's being served with, jazzed up in numerous ways: by adding different nuts, herbs, cheeses, a vinaigrette, or even a simple squeeze of lemon and drizzle of extra-virgin olive oil. With the combo steam-roasting technique, these brussels sprouts are always cooked to perfection, and no matter how I serve them, they're always a dinner winner. I'm proud to say that I have converted many brussels sprouts naysayers over the years with this recipe, including family members."

— Erin

Roasted Carrots

Serves 4 to 6 • Total Time: 1 hour

Why This Recipe Works Roasted carrots should have a pleasingly al dente chew and earthy, sweet flavor. Roasting draws out their natural sugars and intensifies their flavor, but too often carrots shrivel up and turn jerky-like under the high heat of the oven. To compensate for the oven's arid heat, we tried adding liquid to the roasting pan. While our carrots turned out moist, they weren't browned and lacked the intense roasted flavor we wanted. Our science editor then explained that no additional moisture was necessary. While a carrot's hard, woody structure doesn't suggest it, the average carrot is actually 87.5 percent water by weight. For our next test we tossed the carrots with melted butter, spread them onto a baking sheet, and covered the sheet tightly with foil. We roasted the carrots, covered, just until softened; we then removed the foil and continued to roast them to draw out their moisture and brown them. The result? Rich-tasting, tender carrots with a nutty flavor. Best of all, the technique worked just as well when we paired the carrots with other roasted root vegetables such as parsnips, fennel, and shallots.

> *Most bagged carrots come in a variety of sizes and must be cut lengthwise for evenly cooked results. After halving the carrots crosswise, leave small (less than ½ inch in diameter) pieces whole; halve medium pieces (½- to 1-inch diameter) and quarter large pieces (over 1 inch).*

1½ pounds carrots, peeled, halved crosswise, and cut lengthwise if necessary
2 tablespoons unsalted butter, melted
½ teaspoon table salt
¼ teaspoon pepper

1. Adjust oven rack to middle position and heat oven to 425 degrees. Line rimmed baking sheet with parchment paper or aluminum foil. Toss all ingredients in large bowl until carrots are coated. Transfer carrots to prepared baking sheet and spread in single layer.

2. Cover baking sheet tightly with foil and roast for 15 minutes. Remove foil and continue to roast carrots, stirring twice, until well browned and tender, 30 to 35 minutes. Transfer to serving platter, season with salt and pepper to taste, and serve.

VARIATIONS

Roasted Carrots and Fennel with Toasted Almonds and Lemon
Reduce carrots to 1 pound. Add ½ large fennel bulb, cored and sliced ½ inch thick, to bowl with carrots and roast as directed. Toss roasted vegetables with ¼ cup toasted sliced almonds, 2 teaspoons chopped fresh parsley, and 1 teaspoon lemon juice before serving.

Roasted Carrots and Parsnips with Rosemary
Reduce carrots to 1 pound. Add 8 ounces peeled parsnips, cut like carrots, and 1 teaspoon chopped fresh rosemary leaves to bowl with carrots and roast as directed. Toss roasted vegetables with 2 teaspoons chopped fresh parsley before serving.

Buffalo Cauliflower Bites

Serves 4 to 6 • Total Time: 40 minutes

Why This Recipe Works Deemed "better than wings" by anyone who tries them, these crunchy, tangy, spicy cauliflower bites will be the new star of your game day table. The key was to come up with a crunchy coating that would hold up under the buffalo sauce. A mixture of cornstarch and cornmeal gave us an ultracrisp exterior. Because cauliflower is not naturally moist, the mixture didn't adhere; so we dunked the florets in canned coconut milk, which had the right viscosity. Frying helped to achieve an unbelievably crackly crust and tender interior. Since these cauliflower bites are vegan, we developed a ranch dressing that uses a homemade vegan mayonnaise (recipes follow).

We used Frank's RedHot Original Cayenne Pepper Sauce, but other hot sauces can be used. Use a Dutch oven that holds 6 quarts or more for this recipe.

Buffalo Sauce
- ¼ cup coconut oil
- ½ cup hot sauce
- 1 tablespoon packed dark brown sugar
- 2 teaspoons cider vinegar

Cauliflower
- 1–2 quarts peanut or vegetable oil for frying
- ¾ cup cornstarch
- ¼ cup cornmeal
- ½ teaspoon table salt
- ¼ teaspoon pepper
- ⅔ cup canned coconut milk
- 1 tablespoon hot sauce
- 1 pound cauliflower florets, cut into 1½-inch pieces
- 1 recipe Vegan Ranch Dressing (recipe follows)

1. For the buffalo sauce: Melt coconut oil in small saucepan over low heat. Whisk in hot sauce, brown sugar, and vinegar until combined. Remove from heat and cover to keep warm; set aside.

2. For the cauliflower: Line platter with triple layer of paper towels. Add oil to large Dutch oven until it measures about 1½ inches deep and heat over medium-high heat to 400 degrees. While oil heats, combine cornstarch, cornmeal, salt, and pepper in small bowl. Whisk coconut milk and hot sauce together in large bowl. Add cauliflower and toss to coat well. Sprinkle cornstarch mixture over cauliflower; fold with rubber spatula until thoroughly coated.

3. Fry half of cauliflower, adding 1 or 2 pieces to oil at a time, until golden and crisp, gently stirring as needed to prevent pieces from sticking together, about 3 minutes. Using slotted spoon, transfer fried cauliflower to prepared platter.

4. Return oil to 400 degrees and repeat with remaining cauliflower. Transfer ½ cup sauce to clean large bowl, add fried cauliflower, and toss gently to coat. Serve immediately with dressing and remaining sauce.

ACCOMPANIMENTS
Vegan Ranch Dressing
Makes ½ cup • Total Time: 10 minutes
We strongly prefer our favorite vegan mayonnaise, Just Mayo, or our homemade Vegan Mayonnaise (recipe follows).

- ½ cup vegan mayonnaise
- 2 tablespoons unsweetened plain coconut milk yogurt
- 1 teaspoon white wine vinegar
- 1½ teaspoons minced fresh chives
- 1½ teaspoons minced fresh dill
- ¼ teaspoon garlic powder
- ⅛ teaspoon table salt
- ⅛ teaspoon pepper

Whisk all ingredients in bowl until smooth. (Dressing can be refrigerated for up to 4 days.)

Vegan Mayonnaise
Makes 1 cup • Total Time: 15 minutes
Aquafaba, the liquid found in a can of chickpeas, gives our mayo volume and emulsified body without any off-flavors or off-textures.

- ⅓ cup aquafaba
- 1½ teaspoons lemon juice
- ½ teaspoon table salt
- ½ teaspoon sugar
- ½ teaspoon Dijon mustard
- 1¼ cups vegetable oil
- 3 tablespoons extra-virgin olive oil

1. Process aquafaba, lemon juice, salt, sugar, and mustard in food processor for 10 seconds. With processor running, gradually add vegetable oil in slow, steady stream until mixture is thick and creamy, scraping down sides of bowl as needed, about 3 minutes.

2. Transfer mixture to bowl. Whisking constantly, slowly add olive oil until emulsified. If pools of oil form on surface, stop addition of oil and whisk mixture until well combined, then resume adding oil. Mayonnaise should be thick and glossy with no oil pools on surface. (Mayonnaise can be refrigerated for up to 1 week.)

Modern Cauliflower Gratin

Serves 8 to 10 • Total Time: 1¼ hours, plus 20 minutes resting

Why This Recipe Works For a fresh spin on cauliflower gratin, we relied on cauliflower's ability to become an ultra-creamy puree and used it as the base for the sauce. We removed the cores and stems from two heads of cauliflower, steamed them until soft, and then blended them to make the sauce. We cut each head into slabs for a more compact casserole and even cooking. For an efficient cooking setup, we placed the cauliflower cores and stems in water in the bottom of a Dutch oven and set a steamer basket filled with the florets on top. Butter and Parmesan gave the sauce a rich flavor and texture without making it too heavy. Tossing the florets in the sauce before placing them in the dish ensured that they were completely coated. A crisp topping of Parmesan and panko gave the gratin savory crunch, and a sprinkle of chives added color.

When buying cauliflower, look for heads without many leaves. Alternatively, if your cauliflower does have a lot of leaves, buy slightly larger heads—about 2¼ pounds each. This recipe can be halved to serve four to six; cook the cauliflower in a large saucepan and bake the gratin in an 8-inch square baking dish.

2 heads cauliflower (2 pounds each)
3 cups water, plus extra as needed
8 tablespoons unsalted butter, divided
½ cup panko bread crumbs
2 ounces Parmesan cheese, grated (1 cup), divided
2 teaspoons table salt
½ teaspoon pepper
½ teaspoon dry mustard
⅛ teaspoon ground nutmeg
   Pinch cayenne pepper
1 teaspoon cornstarch dissolved in 1 teaspoon water
1 tablespoon minced fresh chives

1. Adjust oven rack to middle position and heat oven to 400 degrees.

2. Pull off outer leaves of 1 head of cauliflower and trim stem. Using paring knife, cut around core to remove; halve core lengthwise and slice thin crosswise. Slice head into ½-inch-thick slabs. Cut stems from slabs to create florets that are about 1½ inches tall; slice stems thin and reserve along with sliced core. Transfer florets to bowl, including any small pieces that may have been created during trimming, and set aside. Repeat with remaining head of cauliflower. (After trimming you should have about 3 cups of sliced stems and cores and 12 cups of florets.)

3. Combine sliced stems and cores, 2 cups florets, and 6 tablespoons butter in Dutch oven and bring to boil over high heat. Place remaining florets in steamer basket (do not rinse bowl). Once mixture is boiling, place steamer basket in pot, cover, and reduce heat to medium. Steam florets in basket until translucent and stem ends can be easily pierced with paring knife, 10 to 12 minutes. Remove steamer basket and drain florets. Re-cover pot; reduce heat to low; and continue to cook stem mixture until very soft, about 10 minutes longer. Transfer drained florets to now-empty bowl.

4. While cauliflower is cooking, melt remaining 2 tablespoons butter in 10-inch skillet over medium heat. Add panko and cook, stirring frequently, until golden brown, 3 to 5 minutes. Transfer to bowl and let cool. Once cool, add ½ cup Parmesan and toss to combine.

5. Transfer stem mixture and cooking liquid to blender and add salt, pepper, mustard, nutmeg, cayenne, and remaining ½ cup Parmesan. Process until smooth and velvety, about 1 minute (puree should be pourable; adjust consistency with additional water as needed). With blender running, add cornstarch slurry. Season with salt and pepper to taste. Pour puree over cauliflower florets and toss gently to evenly coat. Transfer mixture to 13 by 9-inch baking dish (it will be quite loose) and smooth top with spatula.

6. Scatter bread crumb mixture evenly over top. Transfer dish to oven and bake until sauce bubbles around edges, 13 to 15 minutes. Let stand for 20 to 25 minutes. Sprinkle with chives and serve.

Boiled Corn

Makes 6 to 8 ears • **Total Time: 30 minutes**

Why This Recipe Works You might think you don't need a recipe for boiled corn, but it's easy to overcook. For perfectly crisp, juicy corn, we figured out that the ideal doneness range for it is 150 to 170 degrees—when the starches have gelatinized but a minimum amount of the pectin has dissolved. Consistently cooking the corn to that temperature was easy using a sous vide method: Bring water to a boil, drop in the corn, and shut off the heat. The temperature of the water decreased quickly so the corn didn't overcook, while the temperature of the corn increased to the ideal zone.

> *This recipe's success depends on using the proper ratio of hot water to corn. Use a Dutch oven with a capacity of at least 7 quarts and bring the water to a rolling boil. Eight ears of corn can be prepared using this recipe, but let the corn sit for at least 15 minutes before serving. Serve with a flavored salt (recipes follow), if desired.*

　6　ears corn, husks and silk removed
　　　Unsalted butter, softened

1. Bring 4 quarts water to boil in large Dutch oven. Turn off heat, add corn to water, cover, and let stand for at least 10 minutes or up to 30 minutes.

2. Transfer corn to large platter and serve immediately, passing butter, salt, and pepper.

FLAVORED SALTS
Chili-Lime Salt
Makes 3 tablespoons • **Total Time: 5 minutes**
This spice blend can be refrigerated for up to one week.

　2　tablespoons kosher salt
　4　teaspoons chili powder
　¾　teaspoon grated lime zest

Combine salt, chili powder, and lime zest in small bowl.

Pepper-Cinnamon Salt
Makes 2 tablespoons • **Total Time: 5 minutes**
This spice blend can be stored at room temperature for up to one month.

　1　tablespoon kosher salt
　1　tablespoon coarsely ground pepper
　¼　teaspoon ground cinnamon

Combine salt, pepper, and cinnamon in small bowl.

Cumin-Sesame Salt
Makes 3 tablespoons • **Total Time: 10 minutes**
This spice blend can be stored at room temperature for up to one month.

　1　tablespoon cumin seeds
　1　tablespoon sesame seeds
　1　tablespoon kosher salt

Toast cumin seeds and sesame seeds in 8-inch skillet over medium heat, stirring occasionally, until fragrant and sesame seeds are golden brown, 3 to 4 minutes. Transfer mixture to cutting board and let cool for 2 minutes. Mince mixture until well combined. Transfer mixture to small bowl and stir in salt.

Corn Fritters

Makes 12 fritters • **Total Time: 55 minutes**

Why This Recipe Works Less is more when making good corn fritters full of fresh corn flavor. These fritters are light, with crispy exteriors and pillow-soft centers. We minimized the number of fillers we added. We processed some of the kernels to act as a thickener rather than bulk up the batter with more flour or cornmeal. This step also let the fresh corn flavor shine through. Browning the corn puree in a skillet drove off excess moisture and deepened the flavor even more. Adding cayenne, nutty Parmesan cheese, and oniony chives balanced the natural sweetness of the corn, and a touch of cornstarch helped crisp the exterior and provide a textural contrast with the creamy interior.

Serve these fritters as a side dish with steaks, chops, or poultry or as an appetizer with a dollop of sour cream or with Maple-Chipotle Mayonnaise, Red Pepper Mayonnaise, or Basil Mayonnaise (recipes follow).

- 4 ears corn, kernels cut from cobs (3 cups), divided
- 1 teaspoon plus ½ cup vegetable oil, divided
- ⅛ teaspoon plus ¼ teaspoon table salt, divided
- ¼ cup all-purpose flour
- ¼ cup finely minced chives, divided
- 2 tablespoons grated Parmesan cheese
- 1 tablespoon cornstarch
- ⅛ teaspoon pepper
  Pinch cayenne pepper
- 1 large egg, lightly beaten

1. Process 1½ cups corn kernels in food processor to uniformly coarse puree, 15 to 20 seconds, scraping down bowl halfway through processing. Set aside.

2. Heat 1 teaspoon oil in 12-inch nonstick skillet over medium-high heat until shimmering. Add remaining 1½ cups corn kernels and ⅛ teaspoon salt, and cook, stirring frequently, until light golden, 3 to 4 minutes. Transfer to medium bowl.

3. Return skillet to medium heat, add corn puree, and cook, stirring frequently with heatproof spatula, until puree is consistency of thick oatmeal (puree clings to spatula rather than dripping off), about 5 minutes. Transfer puree to bowl with kernels and stir to combine. Rinse skillet and dry with paper towels.

4. Stir flour, 3 tablespoons chives, Parmesan, cornstarch, pepper, cayenne, and remaining ¼ teaspoon salt into corn mixture until well combined. Gently stir in egg until incorporated.

5. Line rimmed baking sheet with paper towels. Heat remaining ½ cup oil in now-empty skillet over medium heat until shimmering. Drop six 2-tablespoon portions batter into skillet. Press with spatula to flatten into 2½- to 3-inch disks. Fry until deep golden brown on both sides, 2 to 3 minutes per side. Transfer fritters to prepared sheet. Repeat with remaining batter.

6. Transfer fritters to large plate or platter, sprinkle with remaining 1 tablespoon chives, and serve immediately.

FLAVORED MAYOS

Maple-Chipotle Mayonnaise

Makes ⅔ cup • Total Time: 5 minutes
For the fullest maple flavor, use maple syrup labeled "Grade A Dark Amber."

- ½ cup mayonnaise
- 1 tablespoon maple syrup
- 1 tablespoon minced canned chipotle chile in adobo sauce
- ½ teaspoon Dijon mustard

Combine all ingredients in small bowl.

Red Pepper Mayonnaise

Makes 1¼ cups
Total Time: 20 minutes, plus 2 hours chilling
Letting the minced garlic sit in the lemon juice mellows its flavor.

- 1½ teaspoons lemon juice
- 1 clove garlic, minced
- ¾ cup jarred roasted red peppers, rinsed and patted dry
- ½ cup mayonnaise
- 2 teaspoons tomato paste

Combine lemon juice and garlic in small bowl and let stand for 15 minutes. Process red peppers, mayonnaise, tomato paste, and lemon juice mixture in food processor until smooth, about 15 seconds, scraping down sides of bowl as needed. Season with salt to taste. Refrigerate until thickened, about 2 hours.

Basil Mayonnaise

Makes ¾ cup • Total Time: 5 minutes
Blue Plate Real Mayonnaise is our favorite mayonnaise. It's one of the top-selling brands in the country, but you'll have to mail-order it unless you live in the South.

- ½ cup mayonnaise
- ½ cup fresh basil leaves
- 1 tablespoon water
- 1 teaspoon lemon juice

Blend mayonnaise, basil, water, and lemon juice in blender until smooth, about 10 seconds, scraping down sides as needed. Transfer to bowl and season with salt and pepper to taste.

Corn Risotto

Serves 6 to 8 • **Total Time: 1 hour**

Why This Recipe Works To make risotto that features truly vibrant corn flavor, we started by blending 3 cups of fresh corn kernels with a little water and the pulpy "milk" we scraped from the cobs to yield a supersweet, bright-tasting puree that infused the rice with corn flavor. Adding the puree near the end of cooking preserved its freshness. The puree also contributed extra liquid as well as naturally occurring cornstarch: The liquid loosened up the risotto to an appropriately fluid consistency (called all'onda in Italian), and the cornstarch gelled and acted like a sauce, making the dish especially creamy. Instead of adding the traditional white wine, which overwhelmed the corn's flavor, we stirred in crème fraîche. The cultured dairy added much subtler acidity, and its flavor and richness underscored the risotto's creamy, luxurious profile.

Serve this risotto as an accompaniment to seared scallops or shrimp or grilled meat. Our favorite arborio rice is RiceSelect, and our favorite supermarket Parmesan cheese is Boar's Head Parmigiano-Reggiano. If crème fraîche is unavailable, you can substitute sour cream. A large ear of corn should yield 1 cup of kernels, but if the ears you find are smaller, buy at least six.

4–6 ears corn, kernels cut from cobs (4 cups), divided, cobs reserved

5½ cups hot water, divided

2 tablespoons unsalted butter

1 shallot, minced

2 teaspoons table salt

1 garlic clove, minced

½ teaspoon pepper

1½ cups arborio rice

3 sprigs fresh thyme

1 ounce Parmesan cheese, grated (½ cup)

¼ cup crème fraîche

2 tablespoons chopped fresh chives

½ teaspoon lemon juice

1. Stand 1 reserved corn cob on end on cutting board and firmly scrape downward with back of butter knife to remove any pulp remaining on cob. Repeat with remaining reserved cobs. Transfer pulp to blender. Add 3 cups corn kernels.

2. Process corn and pulp on low speed until thick puree forms, about 30 seconds. With blender running, add ½ cup hot water. Increase speed to high and continue to process until smooth, about 3 minutes longer. Pour puree into fine-mesh strainer set over large liquid measuring cup or bowl. Using back of ladle or rubber spatula, push puree through strainer, extracting as much liquid as possible (you should have about 2 cups corn liquid). Discard solids.

3. Melt butter in large Dutch oven over medium heat. Add shallot, salt, garlic, and pepper and cook, stirring frequently, until softened but not browned, about 1 minute. Add rice and thyme sprigs and cook, stirring frequently, until grains are translucent around edges, 2 to 3 minutes.

4. Stir in 4½ cups hot water. Reduce heat to medium-low, cover, and simmer until liquid is slightly thickened and rice is just al dente, 16 to 19 minutes, stirring twice during cooking.

5. Add corn liquid and continue to cook, stirring gently and constantly, until risotto is creamy and thickened but not sticky, about 3 minutes longer (risotto will continue to thicken as it sits). Stir in Parmesan and remaining 1 cup corn kernels. Cover pot and let stand off heat for 5 minutes. Stir in crème fraîche, chives, and lemon juice. Discard thyme sprigs and season with salt and pepper to taste. Adjust consistency with remaining ½ cup hot water as needed. Serve immediately.

Braised Eggplant with Paprika, Coriander, and Yogurt

Serves 4 to 6 • **Total Time: 50 minutes**

Why This Recipe Works Braised eggplant develops a meltingly tender, creamy texture, yet the pieces remain meaty and intact. Eggplant is easy to prep and mild in flavor, with extremely porous flesh that soaks up seasonings. We cut the eggplant into slim wedges, making sure that each piece had some skin attached to it, which gave it structural integrity even after the flesh became tender. We braised the eggplant in a single batch in a skillet. As the eggplant cooked, its uniquely air-filled flesh collapsed and became denser and firmer. We cooked the eggplant until it softened and the savory braising liquid—made with tomato paste, garlic, and a mix of warm spices—reduced to a thick sauce. We served our eggplant and sauce with a drizzle of cool yogurt and a refreshing sprinkle of cilantro.

Large globe and Italian eggplants disintegrate when braised, so do not substitute a single 1- to 1¼-pound eggplant here. You can substitute 1 to 1¼ pounds of long, slim Chinese or Japanese eggplants if they are available; cut them as directed.

2   (8- to 10-ounce) globe or Italian eggplants
3   tablespoons vegetable oil
2   garlic cloves, minced
1   tablespoon tomato paste
2   teaspoons paprika
1   teaspoon table salt
1   teaspoon ground coriander
½   teaspoon sugar
½   teaspoon ground cumin
½   teaspoon ground cinnamon
½   teaspoon ground nutmeg
½   teaspoon ground ginger
2¾   cups water
⅓   cup plain whole-milk yogurt
2   tablespoons minced fresh cilantro

1. Trim ½ inch from top and bottom of 1 eggplant. Halve eggplant crosswise. Cut each half lengthwise into 2 pieces. Cut each piece into ¾-inch-thick wedges. Repeat with remaining eggplant.

2. Heat oil in 12-inch nonstick skillet over medium heat until shimmering. Add garlic and cook, stirring constantly, until fragrant, about 30 seconds. Add tomato paste, paprika, salt, coriander, sugar, cumin, cinnamon, nutmeg, and ginger and cook, stirring constantly, until mixture starts to darken, 1 to 2 minutes. Spread eggplant evenly in skillet (pieces will not form single layer). Pour water over eggplant. Increase heat to high and bring to boil. Reduce heat to maintain gentle boil. Cover and cook until eggplant is soft and has decreased in volume enough to form single layer on bottom of skillet, about 15 minutes, gently shaking skillet to settle eggplant halfway through cooking (some pieces will remain opaque).

3. Uncover and continue to cook, swirling skillet occasionally, until liquid is thickened and reduced to just a few tablespoons, 12 to 14 minutes longer. Off heat, season with salt and pepper to taste. Transfer to platter, drizzle with yogurt, sprinkle with cilantro, and serve.

VARIATION
Braised Eggplant with Soy, Garlic, and Ginger
Serves 4 to 6 • Total Time: 50 minutes

1½   cups water
¼   cup Shaoxing wine or dry sherry
2   tablespoons soy sauce
4   teaspoons sugar
2   teaspoons broad bean chili paste
1   teaspoon cornstarch
2   (8- to 10-ounce) globe or Italian eggplants
1   tablespoon vegetable oil
1   garlic clove, minced
1   teaspoon grated fresh ginger
½   teaspoon toasted sesame oil
2   scallions, sliced thin on bias

1. Whisk water, Shaoxing wine, soy sauce, sugar, chili paste, and cornstarch in medium bowl until sugar is dissolved. Trim ½ inch from top and bottom of 1 eggplant. Halve eggplant crosswise. Cut each half lengthwise into 2 pieces. Cut each piece into ¾-inch-thick wedges. Repeat with remaining eggplant.

2. Heat vegetable oil in 12-inch nonstick skillet over medium heat until shimmering. Add garlic and ginger and cook, stirring constantly, until fragrant, about 30 seconds. Spread eggplant evenly in skillet (pieces will not form single layer). Pour Shaoxing wine mixture over eggplant. Increase heat to high and bring to boil. Reduce heat to maintain gentle boil. Cover and cook until eggplant is soft and has decreased in volume enough to form single layer on bottom of skillet, about 15 minutes, gently shaking skillet to settle eggplant halfway through cooking (some pieces will remain opaque).

3. Uncover and continue to cook, swirling skillet occasionally, until liquid is thickened and reduced to just a few tablespoons, 12 to 14 minutes longer. Transfer to platter, drizzle with sesame oil, sprinkle with scallions, and serve.

Skillet-Charred Green Beans with Crispy Bread Crumb Topping

Serves 4 • **Total Time: 40 minutes**

Why This Recipe Works Sichuan cooks have a method for preparing green beans called dry frying, which is a two-step process where the beans are deep-fried, and then stir-fried with aromatics and maybe a little ground pork. We love this dish and wanted to re-create what we love about it—deeply browned, blistered green beans with a satisfying chew and concentrated flavor—without the deep frying. The secret, we learned, to truly charred beans was to steam the beans first (which we did in the microwave to keep things easy and avoid having to wash out the skillet before cooking them, as steaming them leaves a residue in the pan). Then we charred them in a skillet with just a couple tablespoons of hot oil. We didn't stir the beans for the first few minutes so that they developed deep color and flavor on one side; then we tossed them in the pan so that they blistered all over. Once they were charred, we seasoned them with a crispy bread crumb topping, which offered great contrast to their tender chew.

> *Microwave thinner, more tender beans for 6 to 8 minutes and thicker, tougher beans for 10 to 12 minutes. To make the beans without a microwave, bring ¼ cup of water to a boil in a skillet over high heat. Add the beans, cover, and cook for 5 minutes. Transfer the beans to a paper towel–lined plate to drain and wash the skillet before proceeding with the recipe.*

2 tablespoons panko bread crumbs
3 tablespoons vegetable oil, divided
¾ teaspoon kosher salt
¼ teaspoon pepper
¼ teaspoon red pepper flakes
1 pound green beans, trimmed

1. Process panko in spice grinder or mortar and pestle until uniformly ground to medium-fine consistency that resembles couscous. Transfer panko to 12-inch skillet, add 1 tablespoon oil, and stir to combine. Cook over medium-low heat, stirring frequently, until light golden brown, 5 to 7 minutes. Remove skillet from heat; add salt, pepper, and pepper flakes; and stir to combine. Transfer panko mixture to bowl and set aside. Wash out skillet thoroughly and dry with paper towels.

Smart Cooks Use Their Microwave

"Microwaves are fine for reheating leftovers, but no serious cooking gets done in them, right? Well, in the test kitchen we cook a lot of veggies (greens beans, eggplant, and mushrooms) at least partially in the microwave. You know I love veggies and I now 'fry' sliced shallots in the microwave; less oil and less mess. I also microwave eggplant before sautéing or frying it. This dehydrates it so it absorbs less oil and browns faster.

In this recipe, the microwave partially cooks the beans; this allows you to crank the heat on the stove and really char them. Without microwaving the beans first, they would burn on the outside and still be raw inside.

I regularly toast nuts, shredded coconut, and bread crumbs in the microwave. And I will only temper chocolate in the microwave.

Pro tip: Learn how to use the power level button. Many of our recipes call for cooking at 50 percent power, which slows things down and reduces uneven cooking."

—*Jack*

2. Rinse green beans but do not dry. Place in medium bowl, cover, and microwave until tender, 6 to 12 minutes, stirring every 3 minutes. Using tongs, transfer green beans to paper towel–lined plate and let drain.

3. Heat remaining 2 tablespoons oil in now-empty skillet over high heat until just smoking. Add green beans in single layer. Cook, without stirring, until green beans begin to blister and char, 4 to 5 minutes. Toss green beans and continue to cook, stirring occasionally, until green beans are softened and charred, 4 to 5 minutes longer. Using tongs, transfer green beans to serving bowl, leaving any excess oil in skillet. Sprinkle with panko mixture and toss to coat. Serve.

SEASON 25

Ultimate Green Bean Casserole

Serves 10 to 12 • Total Time: 3½ hours

Why This Recipe Works For many, a green bean casserole is a holiday tradition—but this classic dish can all too often turn out bland and uninspired. We wanted to update this casserole and turn it into a side to get excited about. The first step was using fresh green beans rather than frozen or canned. Next, in place of the usual canned cream of mushroom soup, we made a mushroom variation of the classic French velouté sauce (a savory sauce made by combining stock with a roux of flour and fat). Ultimately, we found that the canned onions couldn't be entirely replaced in our green bean casserole recipe without sacrificing the level of convenience we thought appropriate to the dish, but we masked their commercial flavor in the crispy topping with the addition of freshly made buttered bread crumbs.

The components of the casserole can be prepared ahead of time. Store the bread crumb topping in an airtight container in the refrigerator for up to two days and combine with the onions just before cooking. Combine the beans and cooled sauce in a baking dish, cover with plastic wrap, and refrigerate for up to 24 hours. To serve, remove the plastic wrap and heat the casserole in a 425-degree oven for 10 minutes, then add the topping and bake as directed. This recipe can be halved and baked in a 2-quart (or 8-inch square) baking dish. If making a half batch, reduce the cooking time of the sauce in step 3 to about 6 minutes (until the sauce measures about 1¾ cups) and the baking time in step 4 to 10 minutes.

Topping
- 4 slices hearty white sandwich bread, torn into quarters
- 2 tablespoons unsalted butter, softened
- ¼ teaspoon table salt
- ⅛ teaspoon pepper
- 1 (6-ounce) can fried onions (3 cups)

Green Beans and Sauce
- 2 pounds green beans, trimmed and halved crosswise
- ¾ teaspoon table salt, plus salt for cooking green beans
- 3 tablespoons unsalted butter
- 1 pound white mushrooms, trimmed and broken into ½-inch pieces
- 3 garlic cloves, minced
- ⅛ teaspoon pepper
- 3 tablespoons all-purpose flour
- 1½ cups chicken broth
- 1½ cups heavy cream

1. For the topping: Pulse bread, butter, salt, and pepper in food processor until mixture resembles coarse crumbs, about 10 pulses. Transfer to large bowl and toss with onions; set aside.

2. For the green beans and sauce: Adjust oven rack to middle position and heat oven to 425 degrees. Line baking sheet with paper towels. Fill large bowl halfway with ice and water. Bring 4 quarts water to boil in Dutch oven. Add green beans and 2 tablespoons salt and cook until bright green and crisp-tender, about 6 minutes. Drain green beans and transfer to ice bath to cool. Drain again, then spread green beans on prepared sheet and let dry.

3. Melt butter in now-empty pot over medium-high heat. Add mushrooms, garlic, pepper, and salt and cook until mushrooms release their moisture and liquid evaporates, about 6 minutes. Add flour and cook for 1 minute, stirring constantly. Stir in broth and bring to simmer, stirring constantly. Add cream, reduce heat to medium, and simmer until sauce is thickened and reduced to 3½ cups, about 12 minutes. Season with salt and pepper to taste.

4. Add green beans to sauce and stir until evenly coated. Spread in even layer in 3-quart (or 13 by 9-inch) baking dish. Sprinkle with topping and bake until topping is golden brown and sauce is bubbling around edges, about 15 minutes. Serve immediately.

To make ahead: Bread crumb topping can be refrigerated for up to 2 days. After green beans and sauce are transferred to baking dish in step 4, wrap dish tightly in plastic wrap and refrigerate for up to 24 hours. To serve, remove plastic and bake casserole in 425-degree oven for 10 minutes, then sprinkle with topping and bake as directed.

SEASON 20

Sautéed Mushrooms with Red Wine and Rosemary

Serves 4 • Total Time: 35 minutes

Why This Recipe Works These deeply flavored mushrooms are a game changer—they make a fantastic side dish or a topping for steak, polenta, or crostini. And it is a counterintuitive trick—starting by adding water, not oil—that makes all the difference. Usually, sautéing mushrooms means piling them in a skillet slicked with oil and waiting patiently for them to release their moisture, which then must evaporate before the mushrooms can brown. We accelerated this process by adding a little water to the pan to steam the mushrooms, which allowed them to release their moisture more quickly. The added benefit of steaming them was that the collapsed mushrooms didn't absorb much oil; in fact, ½ teaspoon of oil was enough to prevent sticking and encourage browning. And because we used so little fat to sauté the mushrooms, we were able to sauce them with a butter-based reduction without making them overly rich. Adding broth to the sauce and simmering the mixture ensured that the butter emulsified, creating a flavorful glaze that clung to the mushrooms.

> *Use one variety of mushroom or a combination. Stem and halve portobello mushrooms and cut each half crosswise into ½-inch pieces. Trim white or cremini mushrooms;*

quarter them if large or medium or halve them if small. Tear trimmed oyster mushrooms into 1- to 1½-inch pieces. Stem shiitake mushrooms; quarter large caps and halve small caps. Cut trimmed maitake (hen-of-the-woods) mushrooms into 1- to 1½-inch pieces. You can substitute vegetable broth for the chicken broth, if desired.

  1¼ pounds mushrooms
  ¼ cup water
  ½ teaspoon vegetable oil
  1 tablespoon unsalted butter
  1 shallot, minced
  1 teaspoon finely chopped fresh rosemary
  ¼ teaspoon table salt
  ¼ teaspoon pepper
  ¼ cup red wine
  1 tablespoon cider vinegar
  ½ cup chicken broth

1. Cook mushrooms and water in 12-inch nonstick skillet over high heat, stirring occasionally, until skillet is almost dry and mushrooms begin to sizzle, 4 to 8 minutes. Reduce heat to medium-high. Add oil and toss until mushrooms are evenly coated. Continue to cook, stirring occasionally, until mushrooms are well browned, 4 to 8 minutes longer. Reduce heat to medium.

2. Push mushrooms to sides of skillet. Add butter to center. When butter has melted, add shallot, rosemary, salt, and pepper to center and cook, stirring constantly, until aromatic, about 30 seconds. Add wine and vinegar and stir mixture into mushrooms. Cook, stirring occasionally, until liquid has evaporated, 2 to 3 minutes. Add broth and cook, stirring occasionally, until glaze is reduced by half, about 3 minutes. Season with salt and pepper to taste, and serve.

Beer-Battered Onion Rings with Jalapeño Dipping Sauce

Serves 6   •   Total Time: 1¼ hours

Why This Recipe Works For crisp, flavorful onion rings we started by adding a bit of flavor to the onions themselves by coating them lightly with a mixture of confectioners' sugar, salt, and onion powder. A bit of cornstarch helped absorb any moisture the salt drew out of the onions as they awaited coating and frying. For the batter, we used a combination of all-purpose flour, which clings and browns nicely, and cornstarch, which doesn't brown or cling as well as the flour but crisps beautifully. Cold beer provided plenty of bubbles to lighten the batter, and a hefty dose of baking powder boosted those bubbles even more. Cutting the onions to a ½-inch thickness and cooking them briefly in 375-degree oil ensured that the inner onion softened perfectly as the batter crisped, producing onion rings that were easy to bite through without experiencing the dreaded "onion escape." These rings were great on their own, but a cool, creamy, jalapeño-spiked sauce made a complementary accompaniment.

> *Use a Dutch oven that holds 6 quarts or more. We like large yellow onions here, about 1 pound each, but sweet onions such as Vidalia or Walla Walla can be used. If using sweet onions, which are smaller and flatter, do not trim the ends (trimming will reduce the yield too much), and increase the salt to 2 teaspoons. We like an inexpensive lager for this recipe, but nonalcoholic beer works well too.*

Sauce

- ½ cup mayonnaise
- 3 tablespoons ketchup
- 2 tablespoons minced jarred jalapeño chiles, plus 1 tablespoon brine
- ½ teaspoon granulated sugar
- ¼ teaspoon cayenne pepper

Onion Rings

- 2 quarts vegetable oil for frying
- 2 teaspoons plus 3 tablespoons cornstarch, divided
- 1 tablespoon confectioners' sugar
- 1½ teaspoons table salt
- 1 teaspoon onion powder
- 2 large yellow onions, peeled
- 2 cups (10 ounces) all-purpose flour
- 2 teaspoons baking powder
- 2 cups cold beer

1. For the sauce: Whisk all ingredients in bowl until combined. Refrigerate until needed.

2. For the onion rings: Heat oil in large Dutch oven over medium-high heat to 380 degrees. While oil heats, combine 2 teaspoons cornstarch, sugar, salt, and onion powder in small bowl.

3. Adjust oven rack to middle position and heat oven to 200 degrees. Set wire rack in rimmed baking sheet and line with triple layer of paper towels. With sharp knife, remove ½-inch slice from each end of 1 onion and save for other use. Cut onion crosswise into ½-inch-thick rounds. Repeat with remaining onion. Separate onion rounds into rings, saving 3 innermost layers of each round for other use. Transfer rings to bowl. Sprinkle with 1 tablespoon confectioners' sugar mixture and toss to coat.

4. Whisk flour, baking powder, remaining 3 tablespoons cornstarch, and remaining 1½ tablespoons sugar mixture in medium bowl to combine. Whisk in beer until almost smooth (small lumps are OK). Add one-quarter of rings to batter and stir to coat. Using your fingers or tongs, transfer rings to oil one at a time until surface of oil is covered. Fry rings, turning occasionally and adjusting heat to keep oil temperature between 360 and 375, until deep golden brown and crisp, about 4 minutes. Transfer rings to prepared rack and place in oven. Return oil to 380 degrees and repeat with remaining onion rings and batter. Serve with sauce.

Plátanos Maduros

Serves 6 to 8 • Total Time: 30 minutes

Why This Recipe Works In Cuban restaurants, rich, meaty dishes are often accompanied by plátanos maduros, or fried sweet plantains. This savory-sweet side features thick, soft slices of very ripe plantains that are fried in oil to create a caramel-like browned crust encasing a soft, sweet interior; a sprinkling of salt balances the sweetness. We deep-fried our plantains and stirred the slices occasionally so that they would brown evenly.

| *Make sure to use plantains that are very ripe and black.*

3 cups vegetable oil for frying
5 very ripe black plantains (8½ ounces each), peeled and sliced on bias into ½-inch pieces

Heat oil in medium saucepan over medium-high heat until it registers 350 degrees. Carefully add one-third of plantains and cook until dark brown on both sides, 3 to 5 minutes, stirring occasionally. Using wire skimmer or slotted spoon, transfer plantains to wire rack set in rimmed baking sheet. (Do not place plantains on paper towel or they will stick.) Season with kosher salt to taste. Repeat with remaining plantains in 2 more batches. Serve immediately.

Rajas Poblanas con Crema

Serves 4 to 6 • Total Time: 50 minutes

Why This Recipe Works Rajas poblanas con crema is a Mexican favorite that features tender strips of roasted chiles and sliced onion cooked with crema. We started our recipe by broiling poblanos until they were completely charred and then wrapping them in foil to steam. This imbued the chiles with smoky flavor and made them easy to peel. White onion gently cooked in butter added a bit of sweetness, and garlic contributed savoriness. Just under a cup of Mexican crema made the dish creamy, lightly salty, and tangy and balanced the mild heat of the poblanos without overpowering them.

| *Cooking times will vary depending on the broiler, so watch the chiles carefully. Mexican crema (or crema mexicana) can be found in the dairy section of the grocery store.*

If you don't have crema, substitute heavy cream. Rajas con crema is a versatile dish that can be enjoyed alongside grilled meat or fish, rice, or beans or as a filling for tacos or quesadillas.

1 pound (3 to 4) poblano chiles, stemmed, halved, and seeded
2 tablespoons unsalted butter
½ white onion, sliced through root end ¼ inch thick
2 garlic cloves, minced
½ teaspoon table salt
¼ teaspoon pepper
¾ cup Mexican crema

1. Line rimmed baking sheet with aluminum foil. Arrange poblanos skin side up on prepared sheet and press to flatten. Adjust oven rack 3 to 4 inches from broiler element and heat broiler. Broil until skin is puffed and most of surface is well charred, 5 to 10 minutes, rotating sheet halfway through broiling.

2. Using tongs, pile poblanos in center of foil. Gather foil over poblanos and crimp to form pouch. Let steam for 10 minutes. Open foil packet carefully and spread out poblanos. When cool enough to handle, peel poblanos (it's OK if some bits of skin remain intact) and discard skins. Slice lengthwise into ½-inch-thick strips. (Rajas can be refrigerated for up to 3 days.)

3. Melt butter in 12-inch nonstick skillet over medium heat. Add onion and cook, stirring occasionally, until onion has softened and edges are just starting to brown, 6 to 8 minutes. Add garlic and cook until fragrant, about 30 seconds. Add rajas, salt, and pepper and cook until warmed through, about 1 minute. Add crema and cook, stirring gently but frequently, until crema has thickened and clings to vegetables, 2 to 3 minutes. Serve immediately.

VARIATION
Rajas Poblanas con Crema y Elote
Add ¾ cup fresh or frozen corn to skillet with rajas in step 3.

Peeling a Broiled Chile

A blackened chile develops charry flavor compounds that linger on the flesh, imbuing it with smokiness. When stripping away the skin, don't be tempted to rinse off stray bits that cling to the flesh—or you'll wash away flavor.

Rajas Poblanas con Crema y Elote

2. Remove potatoes from oven and brush tops and sides with oil. Return potatoes to oven and continue to bake for 10 minutes.

3. Remove potatoes from oven and, using paring knife, make 2 slits, forming X, in each potato. Using clean dish towel, hold ends and squeeze slightly to push flesh up and out. Season with salt and pepper to taste. Serve immediately.

TOPPINGS

Creamy Egg Topping

Makes 1 cup • Total Time: 10 minutes

3	Easy-Peel Hard-Cooked Eggs (page 27), chopped
¼	cup sour cream
1½	tablespoons minced cornichons
1	tablespoon minced fresh parsley
1	tablespoon Dijon mustard
1	tablespoon capers, rinsed and minced
1	tablespoon minced shallot

Stir all ingredients together and season with salt and pepper to taste.

Herbed Goat Cheese Topping

Makes ¾ cup • Total Time: 10 minutes

Our favorite goat cheese is Laura Chenel's Original Fresh Goat Cheese Log.

4	ounces goat cheese, softened
2	tablespoons extra-virgin olive oil
2	tablespoons minced fresh parsley
1	tablespoon minced shallot
½	teaspoon grated lemon zest

Mash goat cheese with fork. Stir in oil, parsley, shallot, and lemon zest. Season with salt and pepper to taste.

Smoked Trout Topping

Makes 1 cup • Total Time: 10 minutes

We prefer trout for this recipe, but any hot-smoked fish, such as salmon or bluefish, can be substituted.

5	ounces smoked trout, chopped
⅓	cup crème fraîche
2	tablespoons minced fresh chives
4	teaspoons minced shallot
1¼	teaspoons grated lemon zest plus ¾ teaspoon juice

Stir all ingredients together and season with salt and pepper to taste.

SEASON 17

Best Baked Potatoes

Serves 4 • Total Time: 1½ hours

Why This Recipe Works For baked potatoes with an evenly fluffy interior, their center should reach an ideal doneness temperature of 205 degrees. Baking them in a hot (450-degree) oven prevented a leathery "pellicle" or film from forming underneath the peel. To season the potato skin, we coated the potatoes in salty water before baking them. We also achieved a crisp skin by painting the potatoes with vegetable oil once they were cooked through and then baking the potatoes for an additional 10 minutes.

> *Open up the potatoes immediately after removing them from the oven in step 3 so that steam can escape. Top them as desired, or with one of our toppings (recipes follow).*

	Table salt for salting potatoes
4	(7- to 9-ounce) russet potatoes, unpeeled, each lightly pricked with fork in 6 places
1	tablespoon vegetable oil

1. Adjust oven rack to middle position and heat oven to 450 degrees. Dissolve 2 tablespoons salt in ½ cup water in large bowl. Place potatoes in bowl and toss so exteriors of potatoes are evenly moistened. Transfer potatoes to wire rack set in rimmed baking sheet and bake until center of largest potato registers 205 degrees, 45 minutes to 1 hour.

Make-Ahead Mashed Potatoes

Serves 8 to 10 • Total Time: 1 hour 20 minutes

Why This Recipe Works Mashed potatoes are a must-have at a holiday dinner, but as a side dish they need to be quick and easy enough to leave plenty of time for preparing the main event. We wanted a recipe for mashed potatoes that we could make in advance (up to two days ahead of time)—but one that also yielded fluffy and flavorful potatoes. For light and smooth potatoes, we used high-starch russets; gave them a head start in the microwave; and finished them in the oven, where the dry heat cooked off their excess moisture. We then beat the potatoes in a stand mixer to remove every lump before stirring in a generous amount of heavy cream and butter. To serve, all we needed to do was pull the potatoes from the fridge and zap them in the microwave.

We prefer to buy loose potatoes rather than bagged potatoes, as their quality is far superior. Be sure to bake the potatoes until they are completely tender; err on the side of overbaking rather than underbaking. The texture of the mash will be quite loose after you introduce the remaining ½ cup of cream in step 5; the potatoes will thicken once refrigerated and reheated. This recipe can be easily halved to serve four to six, but the mixing times in step 4 may be slightly shorter.

- 5   pounds russet potatoes, unpeeled
- 3   cups heavy cream, hot, divided
- 8   tablespoons unsalted butter, melted
- 2   teaspoons table salt

1. Adjust oven rack to middle position and heat oven to 450 degrees.

2. Pierce skins of potatoes all over with fork. Microwave for 16 minutes, turning over potatoes halfway through microwaving. Transfer potatoes directly to oven rack and bake, flipping halfway through baking, until paring knife slides easily in and out of potatoes, about 30 minutes (do not underbake).

3. Remove potatoes from oven and cut each potato in half lengthwise. Using oven mitt or folded dish towel to hold hot potatoes, scoop out all flesh from each potato half into medium bowl. Using fork, potato masher, or rubber spatula, mash flesh into small pieces.

4. Transfer half of potatoes to bowl of stand mixer fitted with paddle. Beat on high speed until smooth, about 30 seconds. Gradually add remaining potatoes and continue beating, scraping down bowl as needed, until completely smooth and no lumps remain, 1 to 2 minutes.

5. Remove bowl from mixer. Using rubber spatula, gently fold in 2 cups cream until combined, followed by melted butter and salt. Gently fold in ½ cup cream until combined, then gently fold in remaining ½ cup cream (potatoes will be quite loose).

6. Transfer mashed potatoes to large bowl and cover bowl tightly with plastic wrap. Refrigerate for up to 2 days.

7. When ready to serve, evenly poke small holes in plastic with tip of knife and microwave until potatoes are hot, about 14 minutes, stirring halfway through microwaving. Season with salt and pepper to taste, and serve.

Aligot

Serves 6 • Total Time: 45 minutes

Why This Recipe Works Aligot is French cookery's intensely rich, cheesy take on mashed potatoes. These potatoes get their elastic, satiny texture through prolonged, vigorous stirring—which can easily go awry and lead to a gluey, sticky mess. We wanted to create cheesy, garlicky mashed potatoes with a smooth, elastic texture and the same signature stretch as the French original. After making aligot with different potatoes, we found medium-starch Yukon Golds to be the clear winner, yielding a puree with a mild, buttery flavor and a light, creamy consistency. We boiled the potatoes, then used a food processor to "mash" them. Traditional aligot uses butter and crème fraîche to add flavor and creaminess and loosen the texture before mixing in the cheese. But crème fraîche isn't always easy to find, so we substituted whole milk, which provided depth without going overboard. For the cheese, a combination of mild mozzarella and nutty Gruyère proved just right. As for the stirring, we needed to monitor the consistency closely: too much stirring and the aligot turned rubbery, too little and the cheese didn't marry with the potatoes for that essential elasticity.

The finished potatoes should have a smooth and slightly elastic texture. White cheddar can be substituted for the Gruyère. For richer, stretchier aligot, double the mozzarella.

  2 pounds Yukon Gold potatoes, peeled, cut into ½-inch-thick slices, rinsed well, and drained
1½ teaspoons table salt, plus salt for cooking potatoes
  6 tablespoons unsalted butter
  2 garlic cloves, minced
1–1½ cups whole milk
  4 ounces mozzarella cheese, shredded (1 cup)
  4 ounces Gruyère cheese, shredded (1 cup)

1. Place potatoes and 1 tablespoon salt in large saucepan; add water to cover by 1 inch. Partially cover saucepan with lid and bring to boil over high heat. Reduce heat to medium-low and simmer until potatoes are tender and just break apart when poked with fork, 12 to 17 minutes. Drain potatoes and dry saucepan.

2. Add potatoes, butter, garlic, and salt to food processor. Pulse until butter is melted and incorporated, about 10 pulses. Add 1 cup milk and continue to process until potatoes are smooth and creamy, about 20 seconds, scraping down sides of bowl halfway through.

3. Return potato mixture to saucepan and set over medium heat. Stir in mozzarella and Gruyère 1 cup at a time, until incorporated. Continue to cook potatoes, stirring vigorously, until cheese is fully melted and mixture is smooth and elastic, 3 to 5 minutes. If mixture is difficult to stir and seems thick, stir in 2 tablespoons milk at a time (up to ½ cup) until potatoes are loose and creamy. Season with salt and pepper to taste. Serve immediately.

SEASON 11

Crispy Smashed Potatoes

Serves 4 to 6 • Total Time: 1 hour

Why This Recipe Works Crispy smashed potatoes deliver the best of both worlds: mashed potato creaminess and the crackling-crisp crust of roasted potatoes. Typically, skin-on spuds are parcooked in water. Once squashed, the potatoes are oiled and either pan-fried on the stovetop or roasted in the oven to render the roughened edges browned and crispy and the interior flesh creamy. But we found that parcooking the potatoes in water diluted their flavor. To fix the flavor problem and streamline cooking, we turned to one pan—a baking sheet. Its roomy surface allowed us to prepare all the potatoes at once rather than in batches. We spread them out on the sheet, added a little water, covered the pan, and baked them until tender. To smash all the potatoes at once, we used a second sheet, which we pressed firmly on top of the pan of parcooked potatoes. To crisp the potatoes we simply coated the baking sheet and drizzled the broken spuds with olive oil.

This recipe is designed to work with potatoes that are 1½ to 2 inches in diameter; don't use potatoes that are over 2 inches. Remove the potatoes from the baking sheet as soon as they are done browning—they will toughen if left on the sheet for too long. A potato masher can also be used to "smash" the potatoes.

  2 pounds small red potatoes, unpeeled
  6 tablespoons extra-virgin olive oil, divided
  1 teaspoon chopped fresh thyme

1. Adjust oven racks to top and lowest positions and heat oven to 500 degrees. Spread potatoes on rimmed baking sheet, pour ¾ cup water into baking sheet, and wrap tightly with aluminum foil. Cook on bottom rack until skewer or paring knife slips in and out of potatoes easily, 25 to 30 minutes (poke skewer through foil to test). Remove foil and let cool for 10 minutes. If any water remains on pan, blot dry with paper towel.

2. Drizzle 3 tablespoons oil over potatoes and roll to coat. Space potatoes evenly on sheet. Place second baking sheet on top; press down uniformly on sheet until potatoes are roughly ⅓ to ½ inch thick. Sprinkle with thyme and season with salt and pepper to taste; drizzle evenly with remaining 3 tablespoons oil. Roast potatoes on top rack for 15 minutes. Transfer potatoes to bottom rack and continue to roast until well browned, 20 to 30 minutes. Serve immediately.

Making Smashed Potatoes

After rolling cooled, oven-steamed potatoes in olive oil, space them evenly on baking sheet and place second baking sheet on top; press down uniformly on baking sheet until potatoes are roughly ⅓ to ½ inch thick.

SEASON 12

Simplified Potato Galette

Serves 6 to 8 • Total Time: 1½ hours

Why This Recipe Works Pommes Anna, the classic French potato cake (or galette) in which thinly sliced potatoes are tossed with butter, tightly shingled in a skillet, and cooked slowly on the stovetop, delivers showstopping results, but it requires so much labor and time that we don't make it very often. We wanted a potato galette with a crisp, deeply bronzed crust encasing a creamy center that tasted of earthy potatoes and sweet butter—and we wanted one we could make on a weeknight. We started by neatly arranging just the first layer of potatoes in the skillet and then casually packed the rest of the potatoes into the pan; once the galette was inverted onto the plate, only the tidy layer was visible. We swapped the traditional cast-iron skillet for a nonstick pan and achieved superior browning by starting the galette on the stovetop before transferring it to the

bottom rack of the oven. For a galette that held together but wasn't gluey, we rinsed the potatoes to rid them of excess starch, and we incorporated a little cornstarch for just the right amount of adhesion. And in lieu of occasionally tamping down on the galette during cooking as in traditional recipes, we simply filled a cake pan with pie weights and set it on the galette for a portion of the baking time. A bit of fresh rosemary added another layer of earthy flavor.

For the potato cake to hold together, it is important to slice the potatoes no more than ⅛ inch thick and to make sure the slices are thoroughly dried before assembling the cake. Use a mandoline slicer or the slicing attachment of a food processor to slice the potatoes uniformly thin. A pound of dried beans, rice, or coins can be substituted for the pie weights. You will need a 10-inch ovensafe nonstick skillet for this recipe.

2½ pounds Yukon Gold potatoes, unpeeled, sliced ⅛ inch thick
5 tablespoons unsalted butter, melted, divided
1 tablespoon cornstarch
1½ teaspoons chopped fresh rosemary leaves (optional)
1 teaspoon table salt
½ teaspoon pepper

1. Adjust oven rack to lowest position and heat oven to 450 degrees. Place potatoes in large bowl and fill with cold water. Using your hands, swirl to remove excess starch, drain, then spread potatoes onto dish towels and dry thoroughly.

2. Whisk 4 tablespoons melted butter; cornstarch; rosemary, if using; salt; and pepper together in large bowl. Add dried potatoes and toss to thoroughly coat.

Place remaining 1 tablespoon butter in 10-inch ovensafe nonstick skillet and swirl to coat. Place 1 potato slice in center of skillet, then overlap slices in circle around center slice, followed by outer circle of overlapping slices. Gently place remaining sliced potatoes on top of first layer, arranging so they form even thickness.

3. Place skillet over medium-high heat and cook until sizzling and potatoes around edge of skillet start to turn translucent, about 5 minutes. Spray 12-inch square of aluminum foil with vegetable oil spray. Place foil, sprayed side down, on top of potatoes. Place 9-inch cake pan on top of foil and fill with 2 cups pie weights. Firmly press down on cake pan to compress potatoes. Transfer skillet to oven and bake for 20 minutes.

4. Remove cake pan and foil from skillet. Continue to bake until potatoes are tender when paring knife is inserted in center, 20 to 25 minutes. Return skillet to stovetop and cook over medium heat, gently shaking pan, until galette releases from sides of pan, 2 to 3 minutes.

5. Invert galette onto cutting board. Using serrated knife, gently cut into wedges and serve immediately.

Inverting a Galette

1. Using spatula, loosen galette and slide it out of skillet onto large plate.

2. Gently place cutting board over galette. (Do not use an overly heavy board, which may crush the cake.)

3. Flip plate over so board is on bottom. Remove plate; galette is now ready to be sliced and served.

Easier French Fries

Serves 4 • Total Time: 35 minutes

Why This Recipe Works We challenged ourselves to devise a streamlined recipe for crisp, golden fries without the usual work. We began with an unorthodox procedure of starting the cut potatoes in a few cups of cold oil. To our surprise, the fries were pretty good, if a little dry. When we swapped russets, which are fairly dry, for Yukon Golds, which have more water and less starch, the fries came out creamy and smooth inside and crisp outside. Leaving the fries undisturbed for 15 minutes, then stirring them, kept them from sticking or breaking apart. Thinner batons were also less likely to stick. These fries have all the qualities of classic french fries, without all the bother.

> *Use a Dutch oven that holds 6 quarts or more. For those who like it, flavoring the oil with bacon fat gives the fries a mild meaty flavor. This recipe will not work with sweet potatoes or russets. Serve with dipping sauces (recipes follow), if desired.*

2½ pounds Yukon Gold potatoes, unpeeled, sides squared off, cut lengthwise into ¼-inch by ¼-inch batons
6 cups peanut or vegetable oil for frying
¼ cup bacon fat, strained (optional)

1. Combine potatoes; oil; and bacon fat, if using, in large Dutch oven. Cook over high heat until oil has reached rolling boil, about 5 minutes. Continue to cook, without stirring, until potatoes are pale golden and exteriors are beginning to crisp, about 15 minutes.

2. Using tongs, stir potatoes, gently scraping up any that stick, and continue to cook, stirring occasionally, until golden and crisp, 5 to 10 minutes longer. Using spider skimmer or slotted spoon, transfer fries to thick paper bag or paper towels. Season with salt to taste; serve immediately.

DIPPING SAUCES
Chive and Black Pepper Dipping Sauce
Makes ½ cup • Total Time: 5 minutes

5 tablespoons mayonnaise
3 tablespoons sour cream
2 tablespoons chopped fresh chives
1½ teaspoons lemon juice
¼ teaspoon table salt
¼ teaspoon pepper

Whisk all ingredients together in small bowl.

Cold Oil Makes Deep Frying a Breeze

"With a growing teenage boy in the house, I get a lot of requests for french fries. Before I found this recipe, honoring those requests was, to be honest, a bit of a drag. Peeling, cutting, rinsing, and drying the potatoes; heating gobs of oil; double frying; and draining the fries added up to a bit of a project. With this revolutionary recipe, everything changed. If my son gets a hankering for french fries, I simply start slicing (you don't even need to bother peeling the potatoes; simply scrub them clean). Once the spuds are cut into long, thin strips, the only tasks left are to put them in a pot, pour in oil (you only need half the amount of traditional recipes), and turn on the burner. You need to stay in the kitchen to monitor progress and (very) occasionally stir, but that's it. These fries practically make themselves. And if you've ever had freshly made fries (lay them out on a paper bag to catch excess grease), salty and straight from the oil, you know what a treat they are."

—Becky

Belgian-Style Dipping Sauce

Makes ½ cup • Total Time: 5 minutes

 5 tablespoons mayonnaise
 3 tablespoons ketchup
 2 tablespoons chopped fresh chives
½–¾ teaspoon Tabasco sauce
 ¼ teaspoon table salt

Whisk all ingredients together in small bowl.

Cutting Potatoes for French Fries

1. Square off potato by cutting ¼-inch-thick slice from each of its 4 long sides.

2. Cut potato lengthwise into ¼-inch-thick planks.

3. Stack 3 or 4 planks and cut into ¼-inch-thick batons. Repeat with remaining planks.

Crispy Potato Latkes

Serves 4 to 6 • Total Time: 1¼ hours

Why This Recipe Works We wanted latkes that were light, not greasy, with buttery soft interiors and crisp outer crusts. We started with high-starch russet potatoes, shredded them, mixed them with some grated onion, and then wrung out the mixture in a dish towel to rid it of

excess moisture, which would prevent the latkes from crisping. To ensure that the latkes' centers were cooked before their crusts were too dark, we parcooked the potato-onion mixture in the microwave. This step also caused the starches in the potatoes to coalesce, further inhibiting the release of the potatoes' moisture when frying. We tossed the mixture with beaten egg to help bind the cakes and pan-fried them in just ¼ inch of oil. With the excess water taken care of, our latkes crisped up beautifully and absorbed minimal oil.

We prefer shredding the potatoes on the large holes of a box grater, but you can also use the large shredding disk of a food processor; cut the potatoes into 2-inch lengths first so you are left with short shreds. Serve with applesauce, sour cream, or gravlax.

 2 pounds russet potatoes, unpeeled, shredded
½ cup grated onion
 1 teaspoon table salt
 2 large eggs, lightly beaten
 2 teaspoons minced fresh parsley
¼ teaspoon pepper
  Vegetable oil

1. Adjust oven rack to middle position, place rimmed baking sheet on rack, and heat oven to 200 degrees. Toss potatoes, onion, and salt in bowl. Place half of potato mixture in center of clean dish towel. Gather ends together and twist tightly to drain as much liquid as possible, reserving liquid in liquid measuring cup. Transfer drained potato mixture to second bowl and repeat process with remaining potato mixture. Set potato liquid aside and let stand so starch settles to bottom, at least 5 minutes.

2. Cover potato mixture and microwave until just warmed through but not hot, 1 to 2 minutes, stirring mixture with fork every 30 seconds. Spread potato mixture evenly over second rimmed baking sheet and let cool for 10 minutes. Don't wash out bowl.

3. Pour off water from reserved potato liquid, leaving potato starch in measuring cup. Add eggs and stir until smooth. Return cooled potato mixture to bowl. Add parsley, pepper, and potato starch mixture and toss until evenly combined.

4. Set wire rack in clean rimmed baking sheet and line with triple layer of paper towels. Heat ¼-inch depth of oil in 12-inch skillet over medium-high heat until shimmering but not smoking (350 degrees). Place ¼-cup mound of potato mixture in oil and press with nonstick spatula into ⅓-inch-thick disk. Repeat until 5 latkes are in pan. Cook, adjusting heat so fat bubbles around latke edges, until golden brown on bottom, about 3 minutes. Turn and continue cooking until golden brown on second side, about 3 minutes longer. Drain on paper towels and transfer to baking sheet in oven. Repeat with remaining potato mixture, adding oil to maintain ¼-inch depth and returning oil to 350 degrees between batches. Season with salt and pepper to taste; serve immediately.

To make ahead: Cooled latkes can be covered loosely with plastic wrap and held at room temperature for up to 4 hours. Alternatively, they can be frozen on baking sheet until firm, transferred to zipper-lock bag, and frozen for up to 1 month. Reheat latkes in 375-degree oven until crisp and hot, 3 minutes per side for room-temperature latkes and 6 minutes per side for frozen latkes.

SEASON 15

Thick-Cut Sweet Potato Fries

Serves 4 to 6 • Total Time: 1¼ hours

Why This Recipe Works For thick-cut sweet potato fries with crispy exteriors and creamy interiors, we took a cue from commercial frozen fries and dunked the potato wedges in a slurry of water and cornstarch. Blanching the potatoes with salt and baking soda before dipping them in the slurry helped the coating stick to the potatoes, giving the fries a super-crunchy crust that stayed crispy. To keep the fries from sticking to the pan, we used a nonstick skillet, which had the added benefit of allowing us to use less oil. For a finishing touch to complement the natural sweetness of the fries, we made a spicy mayo-based dipping sauce.

Use a Dutch oven that holds 6 quarts or more. If your sweet potatoes are shorter than 4 inches in length, do not cut the wedges crosswise. Leftover frying oil may be saved for further use; strain the cooled oil into an airtight container and store it in a cool, dark place for up to one month or in the freezer for up to two months. We like these fries with our Spicy Fry Sauce (recipe follows), but they are also good served plain.

½ cup cornstarch
　Kosher salt, for cooking potatoes
1 teaspoon baking soda
3 pounds sweet potatoes, peeled and cut into ¾-inch-thick wedges, wedges cut in half crosswise
3 cups peanut or vegetable oil for frying

1. Adjust oven rack to middle position and heat oven to 200 degrees. Set wire rack in rimmed baking sheet. Whisk cornstarch and ½ cup cold water together in large bowl.

2. Bring 2 quarts water, ¼ cup salt, and baking soda to boil in Dutch oven. Add potatoes and return to boil. Reduce heat to simmer and cook until exteriors turn slightly mushy (centers will remain firm), 3 to 5 minutes. Whisk cornstarch slurry to recombine. Using spider skimmer or slotted spoon, transfer potatoes to bowl with slurry.

3. Using rubber spatula, fold potatoes with slurry until slurry turns light orange, thickens to paste, and clings to potatoes.

4. Heat oil in 12-inch nonstick skillet over high heat to 325 degrees. Using tongs, carefully add one-third of potatoes to oil, making sure that potatoes aren't touching one another. Fry until crispy and lightly browned, 7 to 10 minutes, using tongs to flip potatoes halfway through frying (adjust heat as necessary to maintain oil temperature between 280 and 300 degrees). Using spider skimmer or slotted spoon, transfer fries to prepared wire rack (fries that stick together can be separated with tongs or forks). Season with salt to taste and transfer to oven to keep warm. Return oil to 325 degrees and repeat with remaining potatoes in 2 batches. Serve immediately.

ACCOMPANIMENT
Spicy Fry Sauce
Makes ½ cup • Total Time: 5 minutes

For a less spicy version, use only 2 teaspoons of chili-garlic sauce. The sauce can be made up to four days in advance and stored, covered, in the refrigerator.

- 6 tablespoons mayonnaise
- 1 tablespoon chili-garlic sauce
- 2 teaspoons distilled white vinegar

Whisk all ingredients together in small bowl.

SEASON 15
Roasted Butternut Squash with Browned Butter and Hazelnuts

Serves 4 to 6 • Total Time: 1½ hours

Why This Recipe Works Taking a cue from famed chef Yotam Ottolenghi, we sought to create a savory recipe for roasted butternut squash that was simple yet presentation-worthy. We chose to peel the squash thoroughly to remove not only the tough outer skin but also the rugged fibrous layer of white flesh just beneath, ensuring supremely tender squash. To encourage the squash slices to caramelize, we used a hot 425-degree oven, placed the squash on the lowest oven rack, and increased the baking time to evaporate the water. We also swapped in melted butter for olive oil to promote the flavorful Maillard reaction. Finally, we selected a mix of toppings that added crunch, creaminess, brightness, and visual appeal.

For plain roasted squash, omit the topping. This dish can be served warm or at room temperature. For the best texture, it's important to remove the fibrous flesh just below the squash's skin.

Squash
- 1 large (2½- to 3-pound) butternut squash
- 3 tablespoons unsalted butter, melted
- ½ teaspoon table salt
- ½ teaspoon pepper

Topping
- 3 tablespoons unsalted butter, cut into 3 pieces
- ⅓ cup hazelnuts, toasted, skinned, and chopped coarse
- 1 tablespoon water
- 1 tablespoon lemon juice
- Pinch table salt
- 1 tablespoon minced fresh chives

1. For the squash: Adjust oven rack to lowest position and heat oven to 425 degrees. Using sharp vegetable peeler or chef's knife, remove skin and fibrous threads from squash just below skin (peel until squash is completely orange with no white flesh remaining, roughly ⅛ inch deep). Halve squash lengthwise and scrape out seeds. Place squash, cut side down, on cutting board and slice crosswise ½ inch thick.

2. Toss squash with melted butter, salt, and pepper until evenly coated. Arrange squash on rimmed baking sheet in single layer. Roast squash until side touching sheet toward back of oven is well browned, 25 to 30 minutes. Rotate sheet and continue to bake until side touching sheet toward back of oven is well browned, 6 to 10 minutes. Remove squash from oven and use metal spatula to flip each piece. Continue to roast until squash is very tender and side touching sheet is browned, 10 to 15 minutes longer.

3. For the topping: While squash roasts, melt butter with hazelnuts in 8-inch skillet over medium-low heat. Cook, stirring frequently, until butter and hazelnuts are brown and fragrant, about 2 minutes. Immediately remove skillet from heat and stir in water (butter will foam and sizzle). Let cool for 1 minute; stir in lemon juice and salt.

4. Transfer squash to large serving platter. Spoon butter mixture evenly over squash. Sprinkle with chives and serve.

VARIATIONS

Roasted Butternut Squash with Radicchio and Parmesan

Omit topping. Whisk 1 tablespoon sherry vinegar, ½ teaspoon mayonnaise, and pinch salt together in small bowl; gradually whisk in 2 tablespoons extra-virgin olive oil until smooth. Before serving, drizzle vinaigrette over squash and sprinkle with ½ cup coarsely shredded radicchio; ½ ounce Parmesan cheese, shaved into thin strips; and 3 tablespoons toasted pine nuts.

Roasted Butternut Squash with Goat Cheese, Pecans, and Maple

Omit topping. Stir 2 tablespoons maple syrup and pinch cayenne pepper together in small bowl. Before serving, drizzle maple mixture over squash and sprinkle with ⅓ cup crumbled goat cheese; ⅓ cup pecans, toasted and chopped coarse; and 2 teaspoons fresh thyme leaves.

Roasted Butternut Squash with Tahini and Feta

Omit topping. Whisk 1 tablespoon tahini, 1 tablespoon extra-virgin olive oil, 1½ teaspoons lemon juice, 1 teaspoon honey, and pinch salt together in small bowl. Before serving, drizzle tahini mixture over squash and sprinkle with ¼ cup finely crumbled feta cheese; ¼ cup shelled pistachios, toasted and chopped fine; and 2 tablespoons chopped fresh mint.

SEASON 20

Best Summer Tomato Gratin

Serves 6 to 8 • **Total Time: 1¾ hours**

Why This Recipe Works A summer tomato gratin should burst with concentrated, bright tomato flavor and contrasting firm texture from the bread, but most recipes lead to mushy results. Starting our gratin on the stovetop initiated the breakdown of the tomatoes, drove off some moisture that would otherwise have sogged out the bread, and

shortened the overall cooking time. We finished the dish in the dry, even heat of the oven. Toasting large cubes of crusty artisan-style baguette ensured that the bread didn't get too soggy once combined with the tomatoes. After toasting the bread, we added garlic and then coarsely chopped tomatoes, a small amount of sugar, and salt and pepper. Just before moving the skillet to the oven, we folded in most of the toasted bread and scattered the remainder over the top along with some Parmesan to create a crusty, savory topping that contrasted with the custardy interior. A scattering of fresh basil provided color and bright flavor.

For the best results, use the ripest in-season tomatoes you can find. Supermarket vine-ripened tomatoes will work, but the gratin won't be as flavorful as one made with locally grown tomatoes. Do not use plum tomatoes, which contain less juice than regular round tomatoes and will result in a dry gratin. For the bread, we prefer a crusty baguette with a firm, chewy crumb. You can serve the gratin hot, warm, or at room temperature.

- 6 tablespoons extra-virgin olive oil, divided
- 6 ounces crusty baguette, cut into ¾-inch cubes (4 cups)
- 3 garlic cloves, sliced thin
- 3 pounds tomatoes, cored and cut into ¾-inch pieces
- 2 teaspoons sugar
- 1 teaspoon table salt
- 1 teaspoon pepper
- 1½ ounces Parmesan cheese, grated (¾ cup)
- 2 tablespoons chopped fresh basil

1. Adjust oven rack to middle position and heat oven to 350 degrees. Heat ¼ cup oil in 12-inch ovensafe skillet over medium-low heat until shimmering. Add bread and stir to coat. Cook, stirring constantly, until bread is browned and toasted, about 5 minutes. Transfer bread to bowl.

2. Return now-empty skillet to low heat and add remaining 2 tablespoons oil and garlic. Cook, stirring constantly, until garlic is golden at edges, 30 to 60 seconds. Add tomatoes, sugar, salt, and pepper and stir to combine. Increase heat to medium-high and cook, stirring occasionally, until tomatoes have started to break down and have released enough juice to be mostly submerged, 8 to 10 minutes.

3. Remove skillet from heat and gently stir in 3 cups bread until completely moistened and evenly distributed. Using spatula, press down on bread until completely submerged. Arrange remaining 1 cup bread evenly over surface, pressing to partially submerge. Sprinkle evenly with Parmesan.

4. Bake until top of gratin is deeply browned, tomatoes are bubbling, and juice has reduced, 40 to 45 minutes; after 30 minutes, run spatula around edge of skillet to loosen crust and release any juice underneath. (Gratin will appear loose and jiggle around outer edges but will thicken as it cools.)

5. Remove skillet from oven and let sit for 15 minutes. Sprinkle gratin with basil and serve.

SEASON 23

Briam

Serves 8 • Total Time: 1½ hours, plus 20 minutes cooling

Why This Recipe Works Here's the magic of Greek briam: A rainbow of summer produce—tomatoes, zucchini, bell peppers, onions, and potatoes—enters the oven simply sliced, seasoned, and bathed in garlic-infused olive oil and emerges as a meltingly soft and velvety mélange in which each vegetable is an amplified version of itself. We sliced our vegetables ¼ inch thick and strategically layered them in a 13 by 9-inch baking dish, with the potatoes serving as a sturdy base and the tomatoes an attractive, browned top. Loosely covering the dish with aluminum foil for the first 30 minutes of cooking allowed just the right amount of moisture to evaporate, hyperconcentrating the vegetables' flavor. We then removed the foil to encourage browning. Warm, room temperature, or chilled, briam makes for a hearty vegetarian meal, especially when accompanied by crusty bread and a slice of feta cheese.

Use small or medium zucchini, which contain more flesh and fewer seeds, for this recipe. We prefer local seasonal tomatoes here, but supermarket tomatoes will work; plum tomatoes are too dry for this dish. High-quality olive oil is vital. Some oil will pool in the bottom of the baking dish; spoon it over the portioned briam or sop it up with bread. Briam is usually served with crusty bread and feta cheese, but it can also be served over pasta or rice or alongside meat or fish. Serve this dish warm, at room temperature, or chilled.

- 1 pound Yukon Gold potatoes, peeled and sliced crosswise ¼ inch thick
- ⅔ cup extra-virgin olive oil, divided
- 6 garlic cloves (3 minced, 3 sliced thin)
- 1¼ teaspoons table salt, divided
- 1 onion, halved and sliced through root end ¼ inch thick, divided
- 1 teaspoon pepper, divided
- 1 teaspoon dried oregano, divided
- 1 green bell pepper, stemmed, seeded, and cut into 2-inch-long matchsticks
- 12 ounces zucchini (2 small), sliced crosswise ¼ inch thick
- 1½ pounds tomatoes (3 large), cored and sliced ¼ inch thick
- ¼ cup chopped fresh parsley

1. Adjust oven rack to middle position and heat oven to 400 degrees. Place potatoes, ⅓ cup oil, minced garlic, and ½ teaspoon salt in 13 by 9-inch baking dish and toss to combine thoroughly. Spread into even layer. Scatter half of onion slices over potatoes. Sprinkle with ½ teaspoon pepper and ½ teaspoon oregano.

2. Scatter bell pepper over surface, followed by remaining onion, sliced garlic, ¼ teaspoon salt, ¼ teaspoon pepper, and remaining ½ teaspoon oregano. Arrange zucchini in single layer. Top with tomato slices, overlapping pieces slightly so they cover entire surface (it should be snug). Pour remaining ⅓ cup oil evenly over tomatoes and sprinkle with remaining ½ teaspoon salt and remaining ¼ teaspoon pepper.

3. Cover dish loosely with aluminum foil, leaving sides open so moisture can escape. Bake for 30 minutes. Remove foil and bake until potatoes can be easily pierced with tip of paring knife and tomatoes have collapsed slightly and started to brown at edges, 40 to 50 minutes. Let cool for at least 20 minutes. Sprinkle parsley over top and serve.

Briam

Kousa Mihshi

Serves 4 to 6 • **Total Time: 2¼ hours**

Why This Recipe Works Kousa mihshi, which translates as "stuffed squash" in Arabic, consists of hollowed-out zucchini stuffed with a mixture of spiced ground lamb and rice called hashweh. The squash is slowly braised in cinnamon-accented tomato sauce until the meat is succulent, the rice tender, and the zucchini is yielding but not mushy. Soaking the rice for 10 minutes before combining it with the lamb ensured that the grains cooked evenly and thoroughly. Browning the stuffing and breaking it up with the back of a spatula created small, distinct pieces that packed lightly into the squash cavities. To give the sauce a meaty underpinning, we sautéed the aromatics in the fatty juices we drained from the lamb.

For this recipe, you'll need an apple corer that removes only the core but does not create wedges; the small end of a melon baller or a long handled bar spoon is also helpful. We like ground lamb here, but you can substitute 90 percent lean ground beef, if preferred. Select zucchini that are similarly sized to ensure even cooking; and to make them easier to core, choose the straightest ones you can find. Use fresh, in-season tomatoes for the best flavor.

Hashweh
- ½ cup long-grain white rice
- 8 ounces ground lamb
- 2 tablespoons extra-virgin olive oil, divided
- 1 teaspoon table salt
- ½ teaspoon pepper
- ¼ teaspoon ground cinnamon

Sauce
- 2 tablespoons extra-virgin olive oil
- ½ teaspoon pepper
- ¼ teaspoon ground cinnamon
- 1 small onion, chopped coarse
- 2 garlic cloves, minced
- 2 pounds tomatoes, cored and chopped coarse
- 2 tablespoons tomato paste
- 2 teaspoons cider vinegar
- 1 teaspoon table salt

Zucchini
- 6 zucchini (6 to 7 inches long and at least 1½ inches wide)
- 2 tablespoons extra-virgin olive oil
- ¼ cup fresh parsley leaves
- 2 cups plain whole-milk yogurt

1. For the hashweh: Place rice in fine-mesh strainer and rinse under cold running water until water runs clear. Place rice in bowl and cover with 2 cups hot water; let stand for 10 minutes. Drain rice in now-empty strainer and return to bowl (do not wash strainer). Add lamb, 1 tablespoon oil, salt, pepper, and cinnamon and mix until rice is well dispersed. Heat remaining 1 tablespoon oil in 12-inch nonstick skillet over medium-high heat until shimmering. Add lamb mixture to skillet (do not wash bowl) and, using heat-resistant spatula, mash to thin layer. Cook, stirring constantly and breaking up meat with side of spatula, until meat is almost cooked through but still slightly pink, 3 to 4 minutes. Transfer mixture to now-empty strainer set over bowl. Return juices and fat to skillet. Transfer lamb mixture to now-empty bowl and, using fork, break up mixture until meat is reduced to pieces no larger than ¼ inch.

2. For the sauce: Add oil to juices and fat in skillet and heat over medium-low heat until sizzling. Stir in pepper and cinnamon and cook until just fragrant, about 30 seconds. Add onion and garlic and cook, stirring occasionally, until very soft and light golden, 7 to 9 minutes.

3. Transfer onion mixture to food processor. Add tomatoes, tomato paste, vinegar, and salt to processor and process until smooth, 1½ to 2 minutes. Transfer tomato mixture to now-empty skillet. Bring to boil over medium-high heat. Reduce heat to simmer and cook, uncovered and stirring occasionally, until sauce is thickened and heat-resistant spatula dragged across bottom of skillet leaves trail, 25 to 30 minutes. While sauce cooks, prepare zucchini.

4. For the zucchini: Remove stem end of 1 zucchini and discard. Holding zucchini with 1 hand, insert apple corer into stemmed end and press and turn until cutting end of corer is about ½ inch from bottom of zucchini (or as far as corer will go), being careful not to damage walls of zucchini. (If stemmed end is too narrow to accommodate corer without damaging walls, remove additional inch of stemmed end.) Remove corer. Using melon baller or long-handled bar spoon, scoop out any remaining core in pieces until farthest part of hollow is ½ inch from bottom of zucchini. Repeat with remaining zucchini. Rinse hollows and drain zucchini on dish towel.

5. Hold 1 zucchini stemmed side up on counter. Using your hand or small spoon, drop small portions of stuffing into hollow, tapping bottom of zucchini on counter to settle stuffing, until it is ½ inch from top of zucchini. Do not compact stuffing. Repeat with remaining zucchini and stuffing.

6. Remove sauce from heat. Gently arrange stuffed zucchini in single layer in skillet. Return skillet to medium-high heat and bring to boil. Adjust heat to maintain low simmer, cover, and cook for 20 minutes (small wisps of steam should escape from beneath skillet lid, but sauce should not boil). Turn zucchini over gently. Cover and continue to simmer until rice and meat are fully cooked and zucchini are tender but not mushy, 20 to 25 minutes longer. Drizzle zucchini and sauce with oil; sprinkle with parsley; and serve, passing yogurt separately.

Coring Zucchini

1. Core zucchini with apple corer, pressing apple corer into squash as far down as it will go.

2. Scoop out more pieces of core using melon baller or long-handled bar spoon until hollow is ½ inch from bottom.

3. Rinse cavity to remove seeds and debris clinging to walls. Let zucchini drain on dish towel.

Walkaway Ratatouille

Serves 6 to 8 • Total Time: 2 hours

Why This Recipe Works Classic ratatouille recipes call for cutting vegetables into small pieces, labor- and time-intensive pretreatments such as salting and/or pressing the vegetables to remove excess moisture, and cooking them in batches on the stovetop. Our secret to great yet easy ratatouille? "Overcook" some of the vegetables, barely cook the others—and let the oven do the work. Our streamlined recipe started by sautéing onions and aromatics and then adding chunks of eggplant and tomatoes before moving the pot to the oven, where the dry, ambient heat thoroughly evaporated moisture, concentrated flavors, and caramelized some of the veggies. After 45 minutes, the tomatoes and eggplant became meltingly soft and could be mashed into a thick, silky sauce. Zucchini and bell peppers went into the pot last so that they retained some texture. Finishing the dish with fresh herbs, a splash of sherry vinegar, and a drizzle of extra-virgin olive oil tied everything together.

This dish is best prepared using ripe, in-season tomatoes. If good tomatoes are not available, substitute one 28-ounce can of whole peeled tomatoes that have been drained, rinsed, and chopped coarse. Ratatouille can be served as an accompaniment to meat or fish. It can also be served on its own with crusty bread, topped with an egg, or over pasta or rice. This dish can be served warm, at room temperature, or chilled.

1/3 cup plus 1 tablespoon extra-virgin olive oil
2 large onions, cut into 1-inch pieces
8 large garlic cloves, peeled and smashed
1¾ teaspoons table salt, divided
¾ teaspoon pepper, divided
1½ teaspoons herbes de Provence
¼ teaspoon red pepper flakes
1 bay leaf
1½ pounds eggplant, peeled and cut into
1-inch pieces
2 pounds plum tomatoes, peeled and
chopped coarse
2 small zucchini, halved lengthwise and
cut into 1-inch pieces
1 red bell pepper, stemmed, seeded,
and cut into 1-inch pieces
1 yellow bell pepper, stemmed, seeded,
and cut into 1-inch pieces
2 tablespoons chopped fresh basil, divided
1 tablespoon minced fresh parsley
1 tablespoon sherry vinegar

1. Adjust oven rack to middle position and heat oven to 400 degrees. Heat oil in Dutch oven over medium-high heat until shimmering. Add onions, garlic, 1 teaspoon salt, and ¼ teaspoon pepper and cook, stirring occasionally, until onions are starting to soften and have become translucent, about 10 minutes. Add herbes de Provence, pepper flakes, and bay leaf and cook, stirring frequently, for 1 minute. Stir in eggplant and tomatoes. Sprinkle with ½ teaspoon salt and ¼ teaspoon pepper and stir to combine. Transfer pot to oven and cook, uncovered, until vegetables are very tender and spotty brown, 40 to 45 minutes.

2. Remove pot from oven and, using potato masher or heavy wooden spoon, smash and stir eggplant mixture until broken down into sauce-like consistency. Stir in zucchini, bell peppers, remaining ¼ teaspoon salt, and remaining ¼ teaspoon pepper and return to oven. Cook, uncovered, until zucchini and peppers are just tender, 20 to 25 minutes.

3. Remove pot from oven, cover, and let stand until zucchini is translucent and easily pierced with tip of paring knife, 10 to 15 minutes. Using wooden spoon, scrape any browned bits from sides of pot and stir back into ratatouille. Stir in 1 tablespoon basil, parsley, and vinegar. Season with salt and pepper to taste. Transfer to large platter, drizzle with remaining 1 tablespoon oil, sprinkle with remaining 1 tablespoon basil, and serve.

Perfect Roasted Root Vegetables

Serves 6 • Total Time: 1¼ hours

Why This Recipe Works Roasted root vegetables develop complex flavors with just a quick toss in oil, salt, and pepper and a stint in a hot oven—until you try to roast different vegetables at the same time. We wanted a medley of vegetables that would cook through evenly. The trick was to carefully prep each vegetable according to how long it took to cook through. With each vegetable cut into the right size and shape, we could roast them together in one batch for uniformly tender results. To speed up the roasting, we briefly microwaved the vegetables and then placed them on a preheated baking sheet to jump-start the browning. A fruity salsa garnish and a rich bacon topping gave us some flavorful seasoning options.

Use turnips that are roughly 2 to 3 inches in diameter. Instead of sprinkling the roasted vegetables with chopped herbs, try garnishing them with one of our toppings (recipes follow).

1 celery root (14 ounces), peeled
4 carrots, peeled and cut into 2½-inch lengths, halved or quartered lengthwise if necessary to create pieces ½ to 1 inch in diameter
12 ounces parsnips, peeled and sliced on bias 1 inch thick
5 ounces small shallots, peeled
1 teaspoon kosher salt
12 ounces turnips, peeled, halved horizontally, and each half quartered
3 tablespoons vegetable oil
2 tablespoons chopped fresh parsley, tarragon, or chives

1. Adjust oven rack to middle position, place rimmed baking sheet on rack, and heat oven to 425 degrees. Cut celery root into ¾-inch-thick rounds. Cut each round into ¾-inch-thick planks about 2½ inches in length.

2. Place celery root, carrots, parsnips, and shallots in large bowl, sprinkle with salt and season with pepper to taste, and toss to combine. Cover bowl and microwave until small pieces of carrot are just pliable enough to bend, 8 to 10 minutes, stirring once halfway through microwaving. Drain vegetables well. Return vegetables to bowl, add turnips and oil, and toss to coat.

3. Working quickly, remove baking sheet from oven and carefully transfer vegetables to baking sheet; spread into even layer. Roast for 25 minutes.

4. Using thin metal spatula, stir vegetables and spread into even layer. Rotate pan and continue to roast until vegetables are golden brown and celery root is tender when pierced with tip of paring knife, 15 to 25 minutes longer. Transfer to platter, sprinkle with parsley, and serve.

ACCOMPANIMENTS
Bacon-Shallot Topping
Makes ½ cup • Total Time: 25 minutes

    4 slices bacon, cut into ¼-inch pieces
    ¼ cup water
    2 tablespoons minced shallot
    1 tablespoon sherry vinegar
    2 tablespoons minced fresh chives

Bring bacon and water to boil in 8-inch skillet over high heat. Reduce heat to medium and cook until water has evaporated and bacon is crisp, about 10 minutes. Transfer bacon to paper towel–lined plate and pour off all but ½ teaspoon fat from skillet. Add shallot and cook, stirring frequently, until softened, 2 to 4 minutes. Remove pan from heat and add vinegar. Transfer shallot mixture to bowl and stir in bacon and chives. Sprinkle over vegetables before serving.

Orange-Parsley Salsa
Makes ½ cup
Total Time: 20 minutes, plus 30 minutes resting

    ¼ cup slivered almonds
    ¼ teaspoon ground cumin
    ¼ teaspoon ground coriander
    1 orange
    ½ cup fresh parsley leaves, minced
    2 garlic cloves, minced
    2 teaspoons extra-virgin olive oil
    1 teaspoon cider vinegar
    ¼ teaspoon kosher salt

1. Toast almonds in 10-inch skillet over medium-high heat until fragrant and golden brown, 5 to 6 minutes. Add cumin and coriander; continue to toast, stirring constantly, until fragrant, about 45 seconds. Immediately transfer to bowl.

2. Cut away peel and pith from orange. Use paring knife to slice between membranes to release segments. Cut segments into ¼-inch pieces. Stir orange pieces, parsley, garlic, oil, vinegar, and salt into almond mixture. Let stand for 30 minutes. Spoon over vegetables before serving.

SEASON 17
Chelow ba Tahdig

Serves 6 • Total Time: 1½ hours

Why This Recipe Works This classic Iranian dish takes rice to a whole new level, marrying light and fluffy steamed rice (chelow) with a golden-brown, crispy crust known as tahdig. Rinsing the rice and then soaking it for 15 minutes in hot salted water produced fluffy grains. Parboiling the rice and then steaming it to finish cooking was also essential to creating the best texture for the rice and the crunchy crust. Wrapping the lid with a towel absorbed extra moisture and thereby ensured fluffiness. Combining a portion of the rice with yogurt, oil, and saffron water created a nicely browned, flavorful crust, while chunks of butter added before steaming enriched the steamed rice portion and more saffron water added bright yellow color to some of the rice. The yogurt also made the tahdig easier to remove from the pot, as did brushing the bottom of the pot with a little extra oil and letting the pot rest on a damp towel after cooking.

Plain Greek yogurt will also work here. For the best results, use a Dutch oven with a bottom diameter between 8½ and 10 inches. If you own a nonstick pot, this is a good place to use it. Skip oiling the pot in step 3 and omit 1 tablespoon of oil in step 4. It is important not to overcook the rice during the parboiling step, as it will continue to cook during steaming. Begin checking the rice at the lower end of the given time range. Do not skip placing the pot on a damp towel in step 7—doing so will help free the crust from the pot. Serve this dish alongside stews or grilled meats.

¼ teaspoon saffron threads, crumbled
 2 cups basmati rice
    Table salt for soaking and cooking rice
 5 tablespoons vegetable oil, divided
¼ cup plain yogurt
 2 tablespoons unsalted butter, cut into 8 cubes

1. Stir saffron threads in ⅓ cup water. Place rice in large fine-mesh strainer and rinse under cold running water until water runs clear. Place rice and 1 tablespoon salt in medium bowl and cover with 4 cups hot tap water. Stir gently to dissolve salt; let stand for 15 minutes. Drain rice in fine-mesh strainer.

2. Bring 8 cups water to boil in large Dutch oven over high heat. Add rice and 2 tablespoons salt. Boil briskly until rice is mostly tender with slight bite in center and grains are floating toward top of pot, 3 to 5 minutes.

3. Drain rice in fine-mesh strainer and rinse with cold water to stop cooking, about 30 seconds. Rinse and dry pot well to remove any residual starch. Brush bottom and 1 inch up sides of pot with 1 tablespoon oil.

4. Combine yogurt, 1 tablespoon saffron water, 2 cups parcooked rice, and remaining ¼ cup oil in medium bowl. Stir until rice is evenly coated. Spread yogurt-rice mixture evenly over bottom of prepared pot, packing it down well.

5. Mound remaining rice in center of pot on top of yogurt-rice base (it should look like cone or small hill). Poke 8 equally spaced holes through rice mound but not into yogurt-rice base. Place 1 butter cube in each hole. Drizzle remaining saffron water over rice mound.

6. Wrap pot lid with clean dish towel and cover pot tightly, making sure towel is secure on top of lid and away from heat. Cook over medium-high heat until rice on bottom is crackling and steam is coming from sides of pot, 8 to 10 minutes, rotating pot halfway through for even cooking.

7. Reduce heat to medium-low and continue to cook until rice is tender and fluffy, 30 to 35 minutes longer. Remove covered pot from heat and place on damp dish towel set in rimmed baking sheet; let stand for 5 minutes.

8. Gently fluff rice and spoon onto serving platter. Using thin metal spatula, loosen edges of crust from pot, then break crust into large pieces. Transfer pieces to serving platter, arranging evenly around rice. Serve.

SEASON 11

Almost Hands-Free Risotto with Parmesan and Herbs

Serves 6 • Total Time: 1 hour

Why This Recipe Works Classic risotto can demand half an hour of stovetop tedium for the best creamy results. Our goal was 5 minutes of stirring, tops. First, we chose to cook our risotto in a Dutch oven rather than a saucepan. A Dutch oven's thick, heavy bottom, deep sides, and tight-fitting lid are made to trap and distribute heat as evenly as possible. Typical recipes dictate adding the broth in small increments after the wine has been absorbed (and stirring constantly after each addition), but we added most of the broth at once. Then we covered the pan and simmered the rice until almost all the broth had been absorbed, stirring just twice during this time. After adding the second and final addition of broth, we stirred the pot for just a few minutes to ensure that the bottom didn't cook more quickly than the top, and then turned off the heat. Without

sitting over a direct flame, the sauce turned out perfectly creamy and the rice was thickened, velvety, and just barely chewy. To finish, we simply stirred in butter, herbs, and a squeeze of lemon juice to brighten the flavors.

This more hands-off method does require precise timing, so we strongly recommend using a timer. The consistency of risotto is largely a matter of personal taste; if you prefer a brothy risotto, add extra broth in step 4. This makes a great side dish for braised meats.

   5 cups chicken broth
1½ cups water
   4 tablespoons unsalted butter, divided
   1 large onion, chopped fine
 ¾ teaspoon table salt
   1 garlic clove, minced
   2 cups arborio rice
   1 cup dry white wine
   2 ounces Parmesan cheese, grated (1 cup)
   2 tablespoons minced fresh parsley
   2 tablespoons minced fresh chives
   1 teaspoon lemon juice

1. Bring broth and water to boil in large saucepan over high heat. Reduce heat to medium-low to maintain gentle simmer.

2. Melt 2 tablespoons butter in Dutch oven over medium heat. Add onion and salt and cook, stirring frequently, until onion is softened but not browned, 5 to 7 minutes. Add garlic and stir until fragrant, about 30 seconds. Add rice and cook, stirring frequently, until grains are translucent around edges, about 3 minutes.

3. Add wine and cook, stirring constantly, until fully absorbed, 2 to 3 minutes. Stir 5 cups hot broth mixture into rice; reduce heat to medium-low; cover; and simmer until almost all liquid has been absorbed and rice is just al dente, 16 to 19 minutes, stirring twice during cooking.

4. Add ¾ cup broth mixture and stir gently and constantly until risotto becomes creamy, about 3 minutes. Stir in Parmesan. Remove pot from heat, cover, and let stand for 5 minutes. Stir in parsley, chives, lemon juice, and remaining 2 tablespoons butter. Season with salt and pepper to taste. If desired, add up to ½ cup remaining broth mixture to loosen texture of risotto. Serve immediately.

SEASON 18

Parmesan Farrotto

Serves 6 • **Total Time: 1¼ hours**

Why This Recipe Works Italian farrotto is a risotto-style dish made with farro in place of rice. Although the method is similar, farro's more robust, nutty flavor gives the dish new dimension. But because much of farro's starch is trapped inside the outer bran, achieving a creamy, velvety consistency can be a challenge. We found that cracking about half the farro in a blender was the key to freeing enough starch from the grains to create a creamy, risotto-like consistency. Adding most of the liquid up front and cooking the farrotto in a lidded Dutch oven helped the grains cook evenly and meant we didn't have to stir constantly—just twice before stirring in the flavorings. We created a variation with mushrooms, which could turn this simple side into a satisfying main course.

We prefer the flavor and texture of whole farro. Do not use quick-cooking or pearled farro. The consistency of farrotto is a matter of personal taste; if you prefer a looser texture, add more of the hot broth mixture in step 6.

1½ cups whole farro
   3 cups chicken broth
   3 cups water
   4 tablespoons unsalted butter, divided
 ½ onion, chopped fine
   1 garlic clove, minced
   2 teaspoons minced fresh thyme
   1 teaspoon table salt
 ¾ teaspoon pepper
   2 ounces Parmesan cheese, grated (1 cup)
   2 tablespoons minced fresh parsley
   2 teaspoons lemon juice

1. Pulse farro in blender until about half of grains are broken into smaller pieces, about 6 pulses.

2. Bring broth and water to boil in large saucepan over high heat. Reduce heat to medium-low to maintain gentle simmer.

3. Melt 2 tablespoons butter in large Dutch oven over medium-low heat. Add onion and cook, stirring frequently, until softened, 3 to 4 minutes. Add garlic and stir until fragrant, about 30 seconds. Add farro and cook, stirring frequently, until grains are lightly toasted, about 3 minutes.

4. Stir 5 cups hot broth mixture into farro mixture; reduce heat to low; cover; and cook until almost all liquid has been absorbed and farro is just al dente, about 25 minutes, stirring twice during cooking.

5. Add thyme, salt, and pepper and continue to cook, stirring constantly, until farro becomes creamy, about 5 minutes.

6. Off heat, stir in Parmesan, parsley, lemon juice, and remaining 2 tablespoons butter. Season with salt and pepper to taste. Adjust consistency with remaining hot broth mixture as needed. Serve immediately.

VARIATION
Mushroom Farrotto
Serves 6 • Total Time: 1¼ hours

1½ cups whole farro
 ¾ ounce dried porcini mushrooms, rinsed
  6 cups water, divided
  4 tablespoons unsalted butter, divided
 12 ounces cremini mushrooms, trimmed and sliced thin
1½ teaspoons table salt, divided
 ½ onion, chopped fine
  1 garlic clove, minced
  2 teaspoons minced fresh thyme
 ¾ teaspoon pepper
1½ ounces Parmesan cheese, grated (¾ cup)
  2 tablespoons minced fresh chives
  2 teaspoons sherry vinegar

1. Pulse farro in blender until about half of grains are broken into smaller pieces, about 6 pulses.

2. Microwave porcini mushrooms and 1 cup water in covered bowl until steaming, about 1 minute. Let sit until softened, about 5 minutes. Drain mushrooms in fine-mesh strainer lined with coffee filter set over large saucepan. Chop porcini mushrooms fine.

3. Add remaining 5 cups water to liquid in saucepan and bring to boil over high heat. Reduce heat to medium-low to maintain gentle simmer.

4. Melt 2 tablespoons butter in large Dutch oven over medium-low heat. Add cremini mushrooms and ½ teaspoon salt and cook, stirring frequently, until moisture released by mushrooms evaporates and pan is dry, 4 to 5 minutes. Add onion and chopped porcini mushrooms and continue to cook until onion has softened, 3 to 4 minutes. Add garlic and stir until fragrant, about 30 seconds. Add farro and cook, stirring frequently, until grains are lightly toasted, about 3 minutes.

5. Stir 5 cups hot water into farro; reduce heat to low; cover; and cook until almost all liquid has been absorbed and farro is just al dente, about 25 minutes, stirring twice during cooking.

6. Add thyme, pepper, and remaining 1 teaspoon salt and continue to cook, stirring constantly, until farro becomes creamy, about 5 minutes.

7. Off heat, stir in Parmesan, chives, vinegar, and remaining 2 tablespoons butter. Season with salt and pepper to taste. Adjust consistency with remaining hot water as needed. Serve immediately.

Tabbouleh

Serves 4 • **Total Time: 20 minutes, plus
2 hours salting, soaking, and resting**

Why This Recipe Works Tabbouleh has long been a meze
staple in the Middle East, but these days it can be found in
virtually every American supermarket. To make tabbouleh,
chopped fresh parsley and mint, tomatoes, onion, and bits
of nutty bulgur are tossed with lemon and olive oil for a
refreshing appetizer or side dish. We wanted our recipe to
feature a generous amount of parsley as well as a decent
amount of bulgur. A high ratio of chopped parsley to
chopped mint emphasized the bright, peppery parsley but
didn't overpower the other ingredients. Soaking the bulgur
in lemon juice infused it with ample flavor, and some olive
oil tempered the tartness of the citrus. To avoid soggy
tabbouleh we salted the tomatoes; but rather than throw
out the exuded liquid, we added it to the bulgur-soaking
liquid. Two sliced scallions rounded out the mix.

*Serve the salad with the crisp inner leaves of romaine
lettuce and wedges of pita.*

  3   medium round tomatoes, cored and
       cut into ½-inch pieces
  ½   teaspoon table salt, divided
  ½   cup medium-grind bulgur
  ¼   cup lemon juice (2 lemons), divided
  6   tablespoons extra-virgin olive oil
  ⅛   teaspoon cayenne pepper
  1½ cups chopped fresh parsley
  ½   cup chopped fresh mint
  2   scallions, sliced thin

1. Toss tomatoes and ¼ teaspoon salt in large bowl.
Transfer to fine-mesh strainer, set strainer in bowl, and
let stand for 30 minutes, tossing occasionally.

2. Rinse bulgur in fine-mesh strainer under cold running
water. Drain well and transfer to second bowl. Stir in
2 tablespoons lemon juice and 2 tablespoons juice from
draining tomatoes. Let stand until grains are beginning
to soften, 30 to 40 minutes.

3. Whisk oil, cayenne, remaining 2 tablespoons lemon
juice, and remaining ¼ teaspoon salt together in large
bowl. Add drained tomatoes, soaked bulgur, parsley, mint,
and scallions; toss gently to combine. Cover and let stand
at room temperature until flavors have blended and bulgur
is tender, about 1 hour. Toss to recombine, season with salt
and pepper to taste, and serve immediately.

New England Baked Beans

Serves 4 to 6 • **Total Time: 4 hours,
plus 8 hours brining**

Why This Recipe Works For a pot of classic New England
baked beans, we made a few tweaks while keeping the
traditional flavor. Brining the beans overnight jump-started
hydration and softened their skins, so they cooked in the
oven with few blowouts. Uncovering the pot for the last hour
of cooking ensured that the liquid reduced sufficiently to
coat the beans in a rich, molasses-based sauce, while salt
pork added meatiness.

*You'll get fewer blowouts if you soak the beans overnight,
but you can quick-salt-soak your beans. In step 1,
combine the salt, water, and beans in a large Dutch oven
and bring them to a boil over high heat. Remove the pot
from the heat, cover it, and let it stand for 1 hour. Drain
and rinse the beans and proceed with the recipe.*

  1½ tablespoons table salt for brining
  1   pound (2½ cups) dried navy beans,
       picked over and rinsed
  6   ounces salt pork, rinsed and cut into 3 pieces
  1   onion, halved
  ½   cup molasses
  2   tablespoons packed dark brown sugar
  1   tablespoon soy sauce
  2   teaspoons dry mustard
  ½   teaspoon pepper
  ¼   teaspoon table salt
  1   bay leaf

1. Dissolve 1½ tablespoons salt in 2 quarts cold water in large container. Add beans and let soak at room temperature for at least 8 hours or up to 24 hours. Drain and rinse well.

2. Adjust oven rack to lower-middle position and heat oven to 300 degrees. Combine beans, salt pork, onion, molasses, sugar, soy sauce, mustard, pepper, salt, bay leaf, and 4 cups water in large Dutch oven. (Liquid should cover beans by about ½ inch. Add more water if necessary.) Bring to boil over high heat. Cover pot, transfer to oven, and cook until beans are softened and bean skins curl up and split when you blow on them, about 2 hours. (After 1 hour, stir beans and check amount of liquid. Liquid should just cover beans. Add water if necessary.)

3. Remove lid and continue to cook until beans are fully tender, browned, and slightly crusty on top, about 1 hour longer. (Liquid will reduce slightly below top layer of beans.)

4. Remove pot from oven, cover, and let stand for 5 minutes. Using wooden spoon or rubber spatula, scrape any browned bits from sides of pot and stir into beans. Discard onion and bay leaf. (Salt pork can be eaten, if desired.) Let beans stand, uncovered, until liquid has thickened slightly and clings to beans, 10 to 15 minutes, stirring once halfway through. Season with salt and pepper to taste, and serve. (Beans can be refrigerated for up to 4 days.)

SEASON 23

Red Lentil Kibbeh

Serves 4 to 6 • Total Time: 1¼ hours

Why This Recipe Works Kibbeh is a popular Middle Eastern dish made from bulgur, onions, spices, and, typically, ground meat. During Lent, however, this meal is often prepared with lentils. We wanted to develop this flavor-packed mixture into something that could be served either on its own with Bibb lettuce and yogurt or as a showstopping addition to a larger spread. We chose red lentils for their vibrant hue and enhanced both their color and flavor with two red pastes: Tomato paste brought sweetness and an umami quality, and harissa, a smoky, spicy chile paste, added complexity. We gave the bulgur a head start before adding the quick-cooking lentils to the same saucepan. Fresh lemon juice and parsley balanced the deep flavors.

This kibbeh would go great on a meze platter alongside baba ghanoush, hummus, nuts, pickled radishes, and/or pita. You can use our homemade harissa (recipe follows) or store-bought; note that spiciness can vary greatly by brand. If your harissa is spicy, omit the cayenne.

3 tablespoons extra-virgin olive oil, divided
1 onion, chopped fine
1 red bell pepper, stemmed, seeded, and chopped fine
1 teaspoon table salt
2 tablespoons harissa
2 tablespoons tomato paste
½ teaspoon cayenne pepper (optional)
1 cup medium-grind bulgur
4 cups water
¾ cup dried red lentils, picked over and rinsed
½ cup chopped fresh parsley
2 tablespoons lemon juice
1 head Bibb lettuce (8 ounces), leaves separated
½ cup plain yogurt
  Lemon wedges

1. Heat 1 tablespoon oil in large saucepan over medium heat until shimmering. Add onion, bell pepper, and salt and cook until softened, about 5 minutes. Stir in harissa; tomato paste; and cayenne, if using, and cook, stirring frequently, until fragrant, about 1 minute.

2. Stir in bulgur and water and bring to simmer. Reduce heat to low; cover; and simmer gently until bulgur is barely tender, about 8 minutes. Stir in lentils; cover; and continue to cook, stirring occasionally, until lentils and bulgur are tender, 8 to 10 minutes.

3. Off heat, lay clean dish towel underneath lid and let mixture sit for 10 minutes. Stir in 1 tablespoon oil, parsley, and lemon juice and stir vigorously until mixture is cohesive. Season with salt and pepper to taste. Transfer to platter and drizzle with remaining 1 tablespoon oil. Spoon kibbeh into lettuce leaves and drizzle with yogurt. Serve with lemon wedges.

Harissa

Makes ½ cup

Total Time: 10 minutes, plus 20 minutes cooling

This spicy, aromatic chile paste is used both as an ingredient and as a condiment throughout North Africa; use it to enliven vegetables, eggs, lamb, soups, and more. If you can't find Aleppo pepper, substitute ¾ teaspoon of paprika and ¾ teaspoon of finely chopped red pepper flakes.

6 tablespoons extra-virgin olive oil
6 garlic cloves, minced
2 tablespoons paprika
1 tablespoon ground coriander
1 tablespoon ground dried Aleppo pepper
1 teaspoon ground cumin
¾ teaspoon caraway seeds
½ teaspoon table salt

Combine all ingredients in bowl and microwave until bubbling and very fragrant, about 1 minute, stirring halfway through microwaving; let cool completely. (Harissa can be refrigerated for up to 4 days.)

SEASON 25

Rustic Bread Stuffing with Cranberries and Walnuts

Serves 6 to 8 • Total Time: 1½ hours

Why This Recipe Works A lighter, more loosely textured stuffing is a welcome addition to the various hefty, moist side dishes that dominate the holiday meal. With this recipe, we steered away from the usual custardy stuffing by eliminating the eggs and cutting back on the broth. We swapped the usual cubes of toasted white sandwich bread for torn chunks of baguette, which retained some crispness and chew through cooking. In homage to traditional stuffing flavors, we stirred in sautéed onions, celery, dried cranberries, and sage.

Baguettes from the bakery section of the supermarket, which have a slightly soft crust, work well in this recipe. The weight should be listed on the wrapper. To make the stuffing ahead, wrap it with plastic wrap immediately after transferring it to the baking dish, and refrigerate it for up to 24 hours. Add 5 minutes to the baking time.

3 tablespoons unsalted butter, divided
2 baguettes (10 ounces each), bottom crust and ends trimmed and discarded
3 tablespoons extra-virgin olive oil

2 cups chicken broth
3 celery ribs, cut into ½-inch pieces
1 teaspoon table salt
¼ teaspoon pepper
2 large onions, cut into ½-inch pieces
½ cup dried cranberries
3 tablespoons chopped fresh sage
3 tablespoons chopped fresh parsley
¼ cup walnuts, toasted and chopped coarse

1. Adjust oven rack to upper-middle position and heat oven to 450 degrees. Grease 13 by 9-inch baking dish with 1 tablespoon butter and set aside. Tear baguettes into bite-size pieces (you should have about 12 cups) and spread into even layer on rimmed baking sheet. Drizzle with oil and toss with spatula until oil is well distributed. Toast in oven for 5 minutes. Stir bread, then continue to toast until edges are lightly browned and crisped, about 5 minutes longer. Transfer sheet to wire rack. Drizzle broth over bread and stir to combine.

2. Melt remaining 2 tablespoons butter in 10-inch skillet over medium heat. Add celery, salt, and pepper. Cook, stirring frequently, until celery begins to soften, 3 to 5 minutes. Add onions and cook until vegetables are soft but not browned, about 8 minutes. Add cranberries and sage and cook until fragrant, about 1 minute.

3. Add vegetable mixture to bread and toss with spatula until well combined. Transfer stuffing mixture to prepared dish and spread into even layer. Bake for 20 minutes. Stir with spatula, turning crisp edges into middle, and spread into even layer. Continue to bake until top is crisp and brown, about 10 minutes longer. Stir in parsley, sprinkle with walnuts, and serve.

Bread & Pizza

Photo: Popovers

Cream Biscuits

Makes 8 biscuits • Total Time: 35 minutes

Why This Recipe Works With a high rise, light texture, and rich flavor, fresh-from-the-oven biscuits tend to disappear quicker than cookies. We wanted to make great biscuits that eliminated the strenuous step of cutting butter into flour or the messy move of rolling out dough time and again to get every last piece into a round. We started with a basic combination of heavy cream, flour, baking powder, and salt. Instead of cutting butter into flour, we included a generous amount of heavy cream in our biscuits, which gave them a lighter and more tender texture. Kneading for just 30 seconds was enough to get our dough smooth and uniform. And we used an extra bit of cream to soak up all the last bits of flour in the bowl. To enhance the light flavor of our biscuits, we added a small amount of sugar. Although it is easy enough to pat out this dough and cut it into rounds with a biscuit cutter, we devised a strategy of simply pressing the dough into an 8-inch cake pan, turning out the dough, and then slicing it into wedges.

> *Bake the biscuits immediately after cutting them; letting them stand for any length of time can decrease the leavening power and thereby prevent the biscuits from rising properly in the oven.*

> 2 **cups (10 ounces) all-purpose flour**
> 2 **teaspoons sugar**
> 2 **teaspoons baking powder**
> ½ **teaspoon table salt**
> 1½ **cups heavy cream, divided**

1. Adjust oven rack to upper-middle position and heat oven to 425 degrees. Line large rimmed baking sheet with parchment paper. Whisk flour, sugar, baking powder, and salt together in medium bowl.

2. Add 1¼ cups cream to flour mixture and stir with wooden spoon until dough forms, about 30 seconds. Transfer dough to lightly floured work surface, leaving all dry, floury bits behind in the bowl. Add remaining ¼ cup cream, 1 tablespoon at a time, to bowl, mixing with wooden spoon after each addition, until all loose flour is just moistened; add these moistened bits to dough. Knead dough briefly just until smooth, about 30 seconds.

3. Pat dough into ¾-inch-thick circle or press it into 8-inch cake pan and turn it out onto lightly floured surface. Cut biscuits into rounds using 2½-inch biscuit cutter or into 8 wedges using knife. Place rounds or wedges on prepared sheet and bake until golden brown, about 15 minutes. Serve immediately.

VARIATIONS

Cream Biscuits with Fresh Herbs
Use the herb of your choice in this variation.
Add 2 tablespoons minced fresh herbs to flour mixture in step 1. Proceed as directed.

Cheddar Biscuits
Add ½ cup shredded sharp cheddar cheese to flour mixture in step 1. Increase baking time to 18 minutes.

Ultimate Flaky Buttermilk Biscuits

Makes 9 biscuits • Total Time: 1¾ hours, plus 30 minutes resting

Why This Recipe Works For the ultimate flaky biscuits with innumerable, ethereally thin layers, we grated the butter so that it would be evenly distributed in the flour mixture, which we learned was key for ideal flakiness. Freezing the butter prior to grating ensured that it stayed in individual pieces throughout the mixing and shaping process. Using a higher-protein all-purpose flour (such as King Arthur) provided the right amount of structure for flakiness (rather than fluffiness, which you'd get with a lower-protein flour) without toughness, while buttermilk gave the biscuits tang and sugar lent complexity. To produce the maximum

number of layers, we rolled out and folded the dough like a letter five times. Cutting the biscuits into squares was easy and avoided any wasted scraps (or tough rerolls). And finally, we learned that letting the dough rest for 30 minutes and trimming away the edges ensured that the biscuits rose up tall in the oven.

We prefer King Arthur all-purpose flour for this recipe, but other brands will work. Use sticks of butter. In hot or humid environments, chill the flour mixture, grater, and work bowls before use. The dough will start out very crumbly and dry in pockets but will be smooth by the end of the folding process; do not be tempted to add extra buttermilk. Flour the counter and the top of the dough as needed to prevent sticking, but be careful not to incorporate large pockets of flour into the dough when folding.

- 3 cups (15 ounces) King Arthur all-purpose flour
- 2 tablespoons sugar
- 4 teaspoons baking powder
- ½ teaspoon baking soda
- 1½ teaspoons table salt
- 16 tablespoons (2 sticks) unsalted butter, frozen for 30 minutes, divided
- 1¼ cups buttermilk, chilled

1. Line rimmed baking sheet with parchment paper and set aside. Whisk flour, sugar, baking powder, baking soda, and salt together in large bowl. Coat sticks of butter in flour mixture, then grate 7 tablespoons from each stick on large holes of box grater directly into flour mixture. Toss gently to combine. Set aside remaining 2 tablespoons butter.

2. Add buttermilk to flour mixture and fold with spatula until just combined (dough will look dry). Transfer dough to liberally floured counter. Dust surface of dough with flour; using your floured hands, press dough into rough 7-inch square.

3. Roll dough into 12 by 9-inch rectangle with short side parallel to edge of counter. Starting at bottom of dough, fold into thirds like business letter, using bench scraper or metal spatula to release dough from counter. Press top of dough firmly to seal folds. Turn dough 90 degrees clockwise. Repeat rolling into 12 by 9-inch rectangle, folding into thirds, and turning clockwise 4 more times, for total of 5 sets of folds. After last set of folds, roll dough into 8½-inch square about 1 inch thick. Transfer dough to prepared sheet, cover with plastic wrap, and refrigerate for 30 minutes. Adjust oven rack to upper-middle position and heat oven to 400 degrees.

4. Transfer dough to lightly floured cutting board. Using sharp, floured chef's knife, trim ¼ inch of dough from each side of square and discard. Cut remaining dough into 9 squares, flouring knife after each cut. Arrange biscuits at least 1 inch apart on sheet. Melt reserved butter; brush tops of biscuits with melted butter.

5. Bake until tops are golden brown, 22 to 25 minutes, rotating sheet halfway through baking. Transfer biscuits to wire rack and let cool for 15 minutes before serving.

SEASON 22

Popovers

Makes 6 popovers • Total Time: 1 hour

Why This Recipe Works The ideal popover is crisp and well browned on the outside and hollow on the inside, with inner walls that are lush and custardy. Bread flour gave our batter extra gluten-forming proteins so that it was stretchy enough to accommodate the expanding steam within the popover. Though many recipes call for preheating the popover pan to jump-start the "pop," we found it equally effective to warm the batter instead by adding heated milk. Lightly greasing the cold cups of the popover pan allowed the batter to "climb" the sides of the cups for bases that were full and round instead of shrunken. Most recipes call for lowering the oven temperature after the popovers reach their maximum height to prevent the outsides from burning, but we found that zeroing in on the ideal baking temperature ensured a perfect bake inside and out, with less fuss.

This batter comes together quickly, so start heating your oven before gathering your ingredients and equipment. Our recipe works best in a 6-cup popover pan, but you can substitute a 12-cup muffin tin, distributing the batter evenly among the 12 cups; start checking these smaller popovers after 25 minutes. Whole or skim milk can be used in place of the low-fat milk. We strongly recommend weighing the flour for this recipe. Do not open the oven during the first 30 minutes of baking; if possible, use the oven window and light to monitor the popovers.

1¼ cups (6¾ ounces) bread flour
¾ teaspoon table salt
1½ cups 2 percent low-fat milk, heated to 110 to 120 degrees
3 large eggs
Salted butter

1. Adjust oven rack to middle position and heat oven to 400 degrees. Lightly spray cups of popover pan with vegetable oil spray. Using paper towel, wipe out cups, leaving thin film of oil on bottom and sides.

2. Whisk together flour and salt in 8-cup liquid measuring cup or medium bowl. Add milk and eggs and whisk until mostly smooth (some small lumps are OK). Distribute batter evenly among prepared cups in popover pan. Bake until popovers are lofty and deep golden brown all over, 40 to 45 minutes. Serve hot, passing butter separately. (Leftover popovers can be stored in zipper-lock bag at room temperature for up to 2 days; reheat directly on middle rack of 300-degree oven for 5 minutes.)

SEASON 21

Piadine

Makes 4 flatbreads • Total time: 40 minutes, plus 30 minutes resting

Why This Recipe Works Meet piadine: the rustic, tender-chewy rounds from Emilia-Romagna, tailor-made for filling with cured meat, cheese, and/or vegetables, that are made without yeast, lengthy rising times, or even your oven. For chewy-tender piadine with an open crumb, we added baking powder to the dough, as well as ample amounts of fat and water that diluted the gluten strands, keeping the dough soft and pliable without making it too rich. Rolling the dough into 9-inch rounds made for substantial breads that fit perfectly in a cast-iron pan, which we preheated thoroughly so that they would brown quickly without drying out.

We use pantry-friendly vegetable oil because the Italian flatbreads it makes are similar in flavor and texture to those made with traditional lard. If you'd prefer to use lard, increase the amount to ¼ cup to account for its lower density. Do not substitute butter or olive oil; their flavors are obtrusive here. A nonstick skillet can be used in place of cast iron; increase the heat to medium-high and preheat the empty skillet with ½ teaspoon of oil until shimmering; wipe out the oil before proceeding with the recipe.

2 cups (10 ounces) all-purpose flour
¾ teaspoon baking powder
½ teaspoon table salt
3 tablespoons vegetable oil
¾ cup water

1. Process flour, baking powder, and salt in food processor until combined, about 5 seconds. Add oil and process until no visible bits of fat remain, about 10 seconds. With processor running, slowly add water; process until most of dough forms soft, slightly tacky ball that clears sides of workbowl, 30 to 60 seconds (there may be small bits of loose dough).

2. Transfer dough to counter and gently knead until smooth, about 15 seconds. Divide dough into 4 equal pieces and shape each into ball. Working with 1 dough ball at a time, place ball seam side down on clean counter and, using your cupped hand, drag in small circles until ball is taut and smooth. Cover dough balls loosely with plastic wrap. Let rest for 30 minutes.

3. Pat 1 dough ball into 5-inch disk on lightly floured counter (keep remaining dough balls covered). Roll disk into 9-inch round, flouring counter as needed to prevent sticking. Repeat with remaining dough balls.

4. Heat 12-inch cast-iron skillet over medium heat until drop of water dripped onto surface sizzles immediately, about 3 minutes. Prick 1 dough round all over with fork, then carefully place in skillet. Cook until underside is spotty brown, 1 to 2 minutes, using fork to pop any large bubbles that form. Flip round and cook until second side is spotty brown, 1 to 2 minutes (flatbread should still be pliable). Transfer piadina to plate, gently fold in half, and cover with clean dish towel to keep warm. Repeat with remaining dough rounds, stacking piadine and re-covering with towel as they finish. Serve warm. (Piadine can be stored in zipper-lock bag for up to 2 days. Reheat in cast-iron skillet over medium-high heat for 20 to 30 seconds per side, until warmed through.)

GAME CHANGER

Flatbread on the Fly

"If you love the idea of freshly baked homemade bread (just like me), but find yourself constantly short on time to make it (yep, guilty as charged), then piadine are your saving grace. Translated as 'little plates,' these rustic flatbreads hail from Emilia-Romagna (although they've gained popularity across Italy). Our recipe stays true to the traditional flatbread, crafted from flour, salt, fat, and water. To achieve chewy-tender piadine that stay pliable, we add a generous amount of fat (for the best flavor I recommend using lard) and water, which helps to soften the gluten structure. We also add a touch of baking powder to the dough. The chemical leavener creates a more open, bread-like crumb that keeps the bread from becoming too dense. Rolled into 9-inch rounds, the breads are cooked in a hot cast-iron skillet, ensuring attractive spotty browning without drying out.

Once baked, piadine can be eaten on their own or cut into wedges to accompany a meal, but they really shine when they are folded over and filled like a sandwich. My favorite is thinly sliced mortadella, a sprinkling of baby arugula, and a drizzle of aged balsamic vinegar, but there are limitless possibilities."

— Keith

Pão de Queijo

Makes 8 rolls • Total Time: 1¼ hours, plus 2 hours resting

Why This Recipe Works Pão de queijo are traditional Brazilian rolls made using a classic French pate a choux dough. Comprised of butter, water, flour, and eggs, choux pastry relies on steam rather than chemical leavening agents to create rise; this type of dough is used for items both sweet (éclairs, profiteroles) and savory (Parisian gnocchi, gougères). But in developing our own recipe for this bread, many of the recipes we tried baked up with a too-gooey interior. So we played with the hydration level until we nailed our favorite version. At 91 percent hydration (most recipes have hydration levels well over 100 percent, which makes them more of a batter than a dough), our rolls baked up crackly on the outsides, bready just under the crusts, and gooey at the very centers. As an added bonus, these little rolls are gluten-free.

    3 cups tapioca starch
    2¼ teaspoons kosher salt, divided
    ¼ teaspoon baking powder
    ⅔ cup plus 2 tablespoons whole milk
    ½ cup vegetable oil
    1½ tablespoons unsalted butter
    3 large eggs, divided
    3½ ounces Parmesan cheese, finely grated (1¾ cups)
    3½ ounces Pecorino Romano, finely grated (1¾ cups)
    1 teaspoon water

1. Using stand mixer fitted with paddle, mix tapioca starch, 2 teaspoons salt, and baking powder on low speed until combined, about 30 seconds.

2. Combine milk, oil, and butter in medium saucepan and bring to boil over high heat. With mixer running on low speed, working quickly, pour milk mixture over tapioca mixture and continue to mix on low speed until all ingredients are incorporated, about 3 minutes longer.

3. Add 2 eggs and mix on low speed until dough comes together, turns shiny and sticky, and clings to sides of bowl, about 8 minutes, scraping down paddle and bowl halfway through mixing.

4. Add Parmesan and Pecorino and mix on low speed until cheeses are incorporated, 30 to 60 seconds. Mix with rubber spatula to ensure mixture is fully incorporated. Remove bowl from stand mixer and press plastic wrap directly onto surface of dough. Refrigerate for at least 2 hours or overnight.

5. Adjust oven rack to middle position and heat oven to 450 degrees. Stack 2 baking sheets and line top sheet with parchment paper. Divide dough into 8 balls (about 3½ ounces each). To form rolls, lightly dampen your hands with water and roll balls between your palms until smooth. Evenly space rolls on prepared sheet.

6. Whisk remaining egg, water, and remaining ¼ teaspoon salt together in small bowl. Brush egg mixture over tops of rolls. Place rolls in oven and immediately reduce oven temperature to 375 degrees. Bake for 20 minutes. Rotate sheet and continue to bake until rolls are deep golden brown and outer crusts are dry and crunchy, about 20 minutes longer. Transfer rolls to serving platter and let cool for 5 minutes. Serve.

Southern Cornbread

**Makes one 8-inch loaf
Total Time: 55 minutes**

Why This Recipe Works Classic Southern cornbread is made in a ripping-hot skillet greased with bacon fat, which causes it to develop a thin, crispy crust as the bread bakes. The resulting bread is moist and tender, with the aroma of toasted corn and the subtle flavor of dairy. Traditionally, Southern-style cornbread is made from white cornmeal and has only trace amounts of sugar and flour. We wanted to perfect the proportions of ingredients and come up with our own crusty, savory Southern-style cornbread baked in a cast-iron skillet. Departing from tradition, we chose yellow cornmeal over white—cornbreads made with yellow cornmeal consistently had a more potent corn flavor than those made with white cornmeal. We chose a rustic method to incorporate the cornmeal—combining part of the cornmeal with boiling water to create a cornmeal "mush." Cornbread that started with some mush had the most corn flavor, and it also produced a fine, moist crumb. We then stirred the buttermilk and egg into the mush before adding the remaining cornmeal and other dry ingredients. As for sugar, a small amount enhanced the natural sweetness of the corn. Finally, we poured the batter into a hot, greased cast-iron skillet to bake until crusty and fragrant.

Cornmeal mush of just the right texture is essential to this bread. Make sure that the water is at a rapid boil when it is added to the cornmeal. And for an accurate measurement of boiling water, bring a kettle of water to a boil, then measure out the desired amount. Though we prefer to make cornbread in a preheated cast-iron skillet, a 9-inch round cake pan or 9-inch square baking pan, greased lightly with butter and not preheated, will also produce acceptable results if you double the recipe and bake the bread for 25 minutes.

  4 teaspoons bacon drippings or vegetable oil
  1 cup (5 ounces) yellow cornmeal, preferably stone-ground, divided
  2 teaspoons sugar
  1 teaspoon baking powder
  ½ teaspoon table salt
  ¼ teaspoon baking soda
  ⅓ cup boiling water
  ¾ cup buttermilk
  1 large egg, lightly beaten

1. Adjust oven rack to lower-middle position and heat oven to 450 degrees. Add bacon drippings to 8-inch cast-iron skillet and place skillet in heating oven. Whisk ⅔ cup cornmeal, sugar, baking powder, salt, and baking soda together in small bowl; set aside.

2. Place remaining ⅓ cup cornmeal in medium bowl, add boiling water, and stir to make stiff mush. Whisk in buttermilk gradually, breaking up lumps until smooth, then whisk in egg.

3. When oven is preheated and skillet is very hot, add dry ingredients to cornmeal mush and stir until just moistened. Carefully remove skillet from oven (skillet handle will be hot). Pour hot bacon fat from pan into batter and stir to incorporate, then quickly pour batter into heated skillet. Bake until golden brown, about 20 minutes. Invert cornbread onto wire rack and let cool for 5 minutes; serve.

SEASON 22

Irish Brown Soda Bread

Makes one 8-inch loaf
Total Time: 1¼ hours, plus 1 hour cooling

Why This Recipe Works Robust, moist, and permeated with wheaty sweetness, Irish brown soda bread combines a high proportion of whole-wheat flour with extra wheat germ and bran to produce a rustic loaf with nutty flavor and an appropriately coarse crumb. We balanced the strong wheat flavor with white flour and a touch of sugar. The addition of baking powder guaranteed a nicely risen loaf, while baking soda lent the characteristic mineral-y tang that it gives to soda breads. Acidic buttermilk also contributed welcome flavor. To produce a loaf with pleasing stature, we baked the soft dough in a cake pan.

Our favorite whole-wheat flour is King Arthur Premium. To ensure the best flavor, use fresh whole-wheat flour. Wheat bran can be found at natural foods stores or in the baking aisle of your supermarket. This bread is best when served on the day it is made, but leftovers can be wrapped in plastic wrap for up to two days.

  2 cups (11 ounces) whole-wheat flour
  1 cup (5 ounces) all-purpose flour
  1 cup wheat bran
  ¼ cup wheat germ
  2 teaspoons sugar
  1½ teaspoons baking powder
  1½ teaspoons baking soda
  1 teaspoon table salt
  2 cups buttermilk

Extra Wheat Bran and Germ Makes a Better Soda Bread

"Soda bread has always been one of my favorite quick breads to make. It's a dump-and-stir operation—no mixer necessary—and its free-form shape only adds to its rustic appeal. I've made more than a few of the refined versions that use white flour and contain dried fruits, lots of sugar, butter, and cream; these are more like giant scones, really. The more rustic brown versions, however, always came out heavy and dense: loaves to be endured rather than enjoyed.

My colleague Andrea Geary worked on this winning recipe. One of her main goals was to replicate the flavor of the lovely loaves found in Ireland, which use a coarse flour that contains much more visible wheat bran than most American whole-wheat flour. Her solution was to fortify an American whole-wheat flour with extra bran as well as extra wheat germ for a distinct whole-meal flavor. To offset the denseness that usually accompanies such hearty loaves, the whole-wheat flour is cut with some white flour. While baking soda does its traditional job of reacting with the acidic buttermilk and raising the loaf, a little baking powder is called in to assist in the operation. Just a wee bit of sugar helps enhance the wheaty flavor.

I started making this bread several years ago for a St. Patrick's dinner, but it's in constant rotation now. I can attest that there few things better in the morning than a slice of toasted Irish brown soda bread, slathered with salted, golden Irish butter."

—Bridget

1. Adjust oven rack to middle position and heat oven to 375 degrees. Lightly grease 8-inch round cake pan. Whisk whole-wheat flour, all-purpose flour, wheat bran, wheat germ, sugar, baking powder, baking soda, and salt together in medium bowl.

2. Add buttermilk and stir with rubber spatula until all flour is moistened and dough forms soft, ragged mass. Transfer dough to counter and gently shape into 6-inch round (surface will be craggy). Using serrated knife, cut ½-inch-deep cross about 5 inches long on top of loaf. Transfer to prepared pan. Bake until loaf is lightly browned and center registers 185 degrees, 40 to 45 minutes, rotating pan halfway through baking.

3. Invert loaf onto wire rack. Reinvert loaf and let cool for at least 1 hour. Slice and serve.

SEASON 15

British-Style Currant Scones

Makes 12 scones • Total Time: 55 minutes

Why This Recipe Works Compared to American scones, British scones are lighter, fluffier, and less sweet; perfect for serving with butter and jam. Rather than leaving pieces of cold butter in the dry ingredients as we would with American scones, we thoroughly worked in softened butter until it was fully integrated. This protected some of the flour granules from moisture, which in turn limited gluten development and kept the crumb tender and cakey. For a higher rise, we added more than the usual amount of leavening and started the scones in a 500-degree oven to boost their lift before turning the temperature down. We brushed some reserved milk and egg on top for enhanced browning, and added currants for tiny bursts of fruit flavor throughout.

We prefer whole milk in this recipe, but low-fat milk can be used. The dough will be quite soft and wet; dust your work surface and your hands liberally with flour. For a tall, even rise, use a sharp-edged biscuit cutter and push straight down; do not twist the cutter. These scones are best served fresh, but leftover scones may be stored in the freezer and reheated in a 300-degree oven for 15 minutes before serving. Serve these scones with jam as well as salted butter or clotted cream.

3 cups (15 ounces) all-purpose flour

⅓ cup (2⅓ ounces) sugar

2 tablespoons baking powder

½ teaspoon table salt

8 tablespoons unsalted butter, cut into ½-inch pieces and softened

¾ cup dried currants

1 cup whole milk

2 large eggs

1. Adjust oven rack to upper-middle position and heat oven to 500 degrees. Line rimmed baking sheet with parchment paper. Pulse flour, sugar, baking powder, and salt in food processor until combined, about 5 pulses. Add butter and pulse until fully incorporated and mixture looks like very fine crumbs with no visible butter, about 20 pulses. Transfer mixture to large bowl and stir in currants.

2. Whisk milk and eggs together in second bowl. Set aside 2 tablespoons milk mixture. Add remaining milk mixture to flour mixture and, using rubber spatula, fold together until almost no dry bits of flour remain.

3. Transfer dough to well-floured counter and gather into ball. With your floured hands, knead until surface is smooth and free of cracks, 25 to 30 times. Press gently to form disk. Using floured rolling pin, roll disk into 9-inch round, about 1 inch thick. Using floured 2½-inch round cutter, stamp out 8 rounds, recoating cutter with flour if it begins to stick. Arrange scones on prepared sheet. Gather dough scraps, form into ball, and knead gently until surface is smooth. Roll dough to 1-inch thickness and stamp out 4 rounds. Discard remaining dough.

4. Brush tops of scones with reserved milk mixture. Reduce oven temperature to 425 degrees and bake scones until risen and golden brown, 10 to 12 minutes, rotating sheet halfway through baking. Transfer scones to wire rack and let cool for at least 10 minutes. Serve scones warm or at room temperature.

SEASON 10

Blueberry Muffins

Makes 12 muffins • Total Time: 1½ hours

Why This Recipe Works These muffins have an intense blueberry flavor that will shine through whether you use freshly picked wild berries or supermarket berries. To intensify the blueberry in our muffins, we tried combining blueberry jam with supermarket blueberries, but the jam made them too sweet. To solve this, we made our own low-sugar berry jam by simmering fresh blueberries with a bit of sugar. Adding our cooled jam to the batter along with uncooked berries gave us the best of both worlds: intense blueberry flavor and the liquid burst that only fresh berries could provide. We found that the quick-bread method—whisking together eggs and sugar before adding milk and melted butter, and then gently folding in the dry ingredients— produced a hearty, substantial crumb that could support a generous amount of fruit. An equal amount of butter and oil gave our muffins just the right combination of buttery flavor and moist, tender texture. For added richness, we swapped the whole milk for buttermilk. Finally, a sprinkling of lemon-scented sugar provided a pleasant crunch.

▎ *For finely grated lemon zest, use a rasp-style grater.*

Lemon-Sugar Topping

⅓ cup (2⅓ ounces) sugar

1½ teaspoons finely grated lemon zest

Muffins

10 ounces (2 cups) blueberries, divided

1 teaspoon plus 1⅛ cups (8 ounces) sugar, divided

2½ cups (12½ ounces) all-purpose flour

2½ teaspoons baking powder

1 teaspoon table salt

2 large eggs

4 tablespoons unsalted butter, melted and cooled slightly

4 tablespoons vegetable oil

1 cup buttermilk

1½ teaspoons vanilla extract

1. **For the topping:** Stir sugar and lemon zest in small bowl until combined and set aside.

2. **For the muffins:** Adjust oven rack to upper-middle position and heat oven to 425 degrees. Spray 12-cup muffin tin with vegetable oil spray. Bring 1 cup blueberries and 1 teaspoon sugar to simmer in small saucepan over medium heat. Cook, mashing berries with spoon several times and stirring frequently, until berries have broken down and mixture is thickened and reduced to ¼ cup, about 6 minutes. Transfer to small bowl and let cool to room temperature, 10 to 15 minutes.

3. Whisk flour, baking powder, and salt together in large bowl. Whisk remaining 1⅛ cups sugar and eggs in medium bowl until thick and homogeneous, about 45 seconds. Slowly whisk in melted butter and oil until combined. Whisk in buttermilk and vanilla until combined. Using rubber spatula, fold egg mixture and remaining 1 cup blueberries into flour mixture until just moistened. (Batter will be very lumpy with few spots of dry flour; do not overmix.)

4. Using ⅓-cup measure or an ice cream scoop, divide batter equally among prepared muffin cups (batter should completely fill cups and mound slightly). Spoon 1 teaspoon of cooked berry mixture into center of each mound of batter. Using chopstick or skewer, gently swirl berry filling into batter using figure-eight motion. Sprinkle lemon sugar evenly over muffins.

5. Bake until muffin tops are golden and just firm, 17 to 19 minutes, rotating muffin tin halfway through baking. Let muffins cool in muffin tin on wire rack for 5 minutes. Remove muffins from muffin tin and let cool for 5 minutes before serving.

Savory Corn Muffins

Makes 12 muffins   •   Total Time: 1 hour

Why This Recipe Works For a corn muffin with great cornmeal flavor and proper muffin structure, we used a ratio of 2 parts cornmeal to 1 part flour for the former's big flavor and the latter's gluten-forming power. Cutting back on sugar promised a perfectly savory muffin, but we needed to keep a few tablespoons of the sweet stuff in order to boost the batter's moisture retention. To make up for the moisture that extra sugar normally provides, we used a mix of milk, butter, and sour cream for the right amount of water and fat. We incorporated extra liquid into the batter by precooking a portion of the cornmeal with additional milk to make a polenta-like porridge. With this technique, we were able to add nearly double the liquid in the batter, promising a supermoist crumb while still allowing the batter to rise into a pretty dome.

Don't use coarse-ground or white cornmeal.

2	cups (10 ounces) cornmeal, divided
1	cup (5 ounces) all-purpose flour
1½	teaspoons baking powder
1	teaspoon baking soda
1¼	teaspoons table salt
1¼	cups whole milk
1	cup sour cream
8	tablespoons unsalted butter, melted and cooled slightly
3	tablespoons sugar
2	large eggs, beaten

1. Adjust oven rack to upper-middle position and heat oven to 425 degrees. Spray 12-cup muffin tin with vegetable oil spray. Whisk 1½ cups cornmeal, flour, baking powder, baking soda, and salt together in medium bowl.

2. Combine milk and remaining ½ cup cornmeal in large bowl. Microwave milk-cornmeal mixture for 1½ minutes. Whisk thoroughly and continue to microwave, whisking every 30 seconds, until thickened to batter-like consistency (whisk will leave channel in bottom of bowl that slowly fills in), 1 to 3 minutes longer. Whisk in sour cream, melted butter, and sugar until combined. Whisk in eggs until combined. Fold in flour mixture until thoroughly combined. Using portion scoop or large spoon, divide batter evenly among prepared muffin cups (about ½ cup batter per cup; batter will mound slightly above rim).

3. Bake until tops are golden brown and toothpick inserted in center comes out clean, 13 to 17 minutes, rotating muffin tin halfway through baking. Let muffins cool in muffin tin on wire rack for 5 minutes. Remove muffins from muffin tin and let cool for 5 minutes before serving.

VARIATION

Savory Corn Muffins with Rosemary and Black Pepper

Whisk in 1 tablespoon minced fresh rosemary and 1½ teaspoons pepper with eggs.

SEASON 11

Ultimate Banana Bread

Makes one 9-inch loaf • Total Time: 2½ hours

Why This Recipe Works Recipes for ultimate banana bread abound, but because they include an overload of bananas for flavor, the bread's texture is often soggy. We wanted a moist, not mushy, loaf that tasted of banana through and through. We needed to use a generous amount of bananas, but we needed to rid them of excess moisture. To do this, we zapped them in the microwave then drained the now-pulpy fruit and mixed it into the batter. We reduced the flavorful liquid and added it to the batter as well. Like a mock extract, our reduction infused the bread with ripe, intense banana flavor. With the flavor problem solved, a few tweaks completed the recipe: We exchanged the granulated sugar for light brown sugar, finding that the molasses notes better complemented the bananas. Swapping out the oil for the richness of butter improved the loaf further. We also added toasted walnuts to the batter; their crunch provided a pleasing contrast to the moist crumb. To add a little embellishment to the crust, we sliced a banana and shingled it on top of the batter. A final sprinkle of sugar helped the banana slices caramelize and gave the loaf an enticingly crisp, crunchy top.

Be sure to use very ripe, heavily speckled (or even black) bananas in this recipe. This recipe can be made using five thawed frozen bananas; since they release a lot of liquid naturally, they can bypass the microwaving in step 2 and go directly into the fine-mesh strainer. Do not use a thawed frozen banana in step 4; it will be too soft to slice. Instead, simply sprinkle the top of the loaf with sugar. The test kitchen's preferred loaf pan measures 8½ by 4½ inches; if you use a 9 by 5-inch loaf pan, start checking for doneness 5 minutes earlier than advised in the recipe. The texture is best when the loaf is eaten fresh, but it can be cooled completely and stored, covered tightly with plastic wrap, for up to three days.

1¾ cups (8¾ ounces) all-purpose flour

1 teaspoon baking soda

½ teaspoon table salt

6 large very ripe bananas (about 2¼ pounds), peeled, divided

8 tablespoons unsalted butter, melted and cooled slightly

2 large eggs

¾ cup packed (5¼ ounces) light brown sugar

1 teaspoon vanilla extract

½ cup walnuts, toasted and chopped coarse (optional)

2 teaspoons granulated sugar

1. Adjust oven rack to middle position and heat oven to 350 degrees. Spray 8½ by 4½-inch loaf pan with vegetable oil spray. Whisk flour, baking soda, and salt together in large bowl.

2. Place 5 bananas in a microwave-safe bowl; cover with plastic wrap and cut several steam vents in plastic with paring knife. Microwave on high power until bananas are soft and have released their liquid, about 5 minutes. Transfer bananas to fine-mesh strainer placed over medium bowl and allow to drain, stirring occasionally, for 15 minutes (you should have ½ to ¾ cup liquid).

3. Transfer liquid to medium saucepan and cook over medium-high heat until reduced to ¼ cup, about 5 minutes. Return drained bananas to bowl. Stir reduced liquid into bananas and mash them with potato masher until fairly smooth. Whisk in melted butter, eggs, brown sugar, and vanilla.

4. Pour banana mixture into flour mixture and stir until just combined with some streaks of flour remaining. Gently fold in walnuts, if using. Scrape batter into prepared pan. Slice remaining 1 banana diagonally into ¼-inch-thick slices. Shingle banana slices on top of either side of loaf, leaving 1½-inch-wide space down center to ensure even rise. Sprinkle granulated sugar evenly over loaf.

5. Bake until toothpick inserted in center of loaf comes out clean, 55 minutes to 1¼ hours. Let cool in pan on wire rack for 15 minutes, then remove from pan and continue to cool on wire rack. Serve warm or at room temperature.

Shingling the Loaf

Layer thin banana slices on either side of loaf to add even more banana flavor. To ensure even rise, leave 1½-inch-wide space down center.

Easy Sandwich Bread

Makes 1 loaf • Total Time: 1¾ hours, plus 2 hours 20 minutes rising and cooling

Why This Recipe Works A freshly baked loaf of bread is one of life's great pleasures. But most people don't have 4 hours to devote to mixing dough, waiting for it to rise, kneading, shaping, and baking. Could we find a quicker way? We started with basic batter bread, which relies on a high hydration level and a single rise, but falls short on flavor. Adding melted butter was a good start toward a tastier loaf, and substituting some whole-wheat flour provided nutty depth. Swapping the rest of the all-purpose flour for bread flour lent better structure. We also traded 1 tablespoon of honey for sugar, which contributed complexity and encouraged browning. Two 20-minute proofs were enough for flavor development. Adding salt only after the initial rise allowed the bread to rise high. An egg wash before baking and a brush of melted butter provided a shiny, tender crust.

The test kitchen's preferred loaf pan measures 8½ by 4½ inches; if using a 9 by 5-inch pan, check for doneness 5 minutes early. To prevent the loaf from deflating as it rises, do not let the batter come in contact with the plastic wrap. This loaf is best eaten the day it is made, but leftovers may be wrapped in plastic wrap and stored for up to two days at room temperature or frozen for up to one month.

2 cups (11 ounces) bread flour
6 tablespoons (2 ounces) whole-wheat flour
2¼ teaspoons instant or rapid-rise yeast
1¼ cups plus 2 tablespoons warm water (120 degrees), divided
3 tablespoons unsalted butter, melted, divided
1 tablespoon honey
¾ teaspoon table salt
1 large egg, lightly beaten with 1 teaspoon water and pinch table salt

1. In bowl of stand mixer, whisk bread flour, whole-wheat flour, and yeast together. Add 1¼ cups warm water, 2 tablespoons melted butter, and honey. Fit stand mixer with paddle and mix on low speed for 1 minute. Increase speed to medium and mix for 2 minutes. Scrape down bowl and paddle with greased rubber spatula. Continue to mix 2 minutes longer. Remove bowl and paddle from mixer. Scrape down bowl and paddle, leaving paddle in batter. Cover with plastic wrap and let batter rise in warm place until doubled in size, about 20 minutes.

2. Adjust oven rack to lower-middle position and heat oven to 375 degrees. Spray 8½ by 4½-inch loaf pan with vegetable oil spray. Dissolve salt in remaining 2 tablespoons warm water. When batter has doubled, attach bowl and paddle to mixer. Add salt-water mixture and mix on low speed until water is mostly incorporated, about 40 seconds. Increase speed to medium and mix until thoroughly combined, about 1 minute, scraping down paddle if necessary. Transfer batter to prepared pan and smooth surface with greased rubber spatula. Cover and leave in warm place until batter reaches ½ inch below edge of pan, 15 to 20 minutes. Uncover and let rise until center of batter is level with edge of pan, 5 to 10 minutes longer.

3. Gently brush top of risen loaf with egg mixture. Bake until deep golden brown and loaf registers 208 to 210 degrees, 40 to 45 minutes. Using clean dish towels, carefully invert bread onto wire rack. Reinvert loaf and brush top and sides with remaining 1 tablespoon melted butter. Let cool completely before slicing.

SEASON 14

No-Knead Brioche

Makes 2 loaves • Total Time: 1¾ hours, plus 19½ to 20 hours rising and cooling

Why This Recipe Works The average brioche recipe is 50 percent butter, and the high fat content can make the brioche incredibly tender—or it can cause the dough to separate into a greasy mess. We made brioche not only a simple process but a failproof one by eliminating the hassle of adding softened butter to the dough little by little. Instead, we melted the butter and added it directly to the eggs. Then we dispensed with the stand mixer and opted for an equally effective no-knead approach that lets time do most of the work: An overnight rest in the fridge developed both structure and flavor. We used two simple loaf pans and then, to build structure and ensure a fine, even crumb, we shaped the dough into four balls before placing two in each pan. The dough can also be divided to make brioche buns or traditionally shaped loaves using fluted brioche molds.

> *High-protein King Arthur Bread Flour works best with this recipe, though other bread flours will suffice. If you don't have a baking stone, bake the bread on a preheated rimmed baking sheet.*

3¼ cups (17¾ ounces) bread flour
2¼ teaspoons instant or rapid-rise yeast
1½ teaspoons salt
 7 large eggs (1 lightly beaten with pinch salt)
½ cup water, room temperature
⅓ cup (2⅓ ounces) sugar
16 tablespoons unsalted butter, melted and cooled slightly

1. Whisk flour, yeast, and salt together in large bowl. Whisk 6 eggs, water, and sugar together in medium bowl until sugar has dissolved. Whisk in melted butter until smooth. Add egg mixture to flour mixture and stir with wooden spoon until uniform mass forms and no dry flour remains, about 1 minute. Cover bowl with plastic wrap and let stand for 10 minutes.

2. Holding edge of dough with your fingertips, fold dough over itself by gently lifting and folding edge of dough toward middle. Turn bowl 45 degrees; fold again. Turn bowl and fold dough 6 more times (total of 8 folds). Cover with plastic and let rise for 30 minutes. Repeat folding and rising every 30 minutes, 3 more times. After fourth set of folds, cover bowl tightly with plastic and refrigerate for at least 16 hours or up to 48 hours.

3. Transfer dough to well-floured counter and divide into 4 pieces. Working with 1 piece of dough at a time, pat dough into 4-inch disk. Working around circumference of dough, fold edges of dough toward center until ball forms. Flip dough over and, without applying pressure, move your hands in small circular motions to form dough into smooth, taut round. (If dough sticks to your hands, lightly dust top of dough with flour.) Repeat with remaining dough. Cover dough rounds loosely with plastic and let rest for 5 minutes.

4. Grease two 8½ by 4½-inch loaf pans. After 5 minutes, flip each dough ball so seam side is facing up, pat into 4-inch disk, and repeat rounding step. Place 2 rounds, seam side down, side by side into prepared pans and press gently into corners. Cover loaves loosely with plastic and let rise at room temperature until almost doubled in size (dough should rise to about ½ inch below top edge of pan), 1½ to 2 hours. Thirty minutes before baking, adjust oven rack to middle position, place baking stone on rack, and heat oven to 350 degrees.

5. Remove plastic and brush loaves gently with remaining 1 egg beaten with salt. Set loaf pans on stone and bake until golden brown and internal temperature registers 190 degrees, 35 to 45 minutes, rotating pans halfway through baking. Transfer pans to wire rack and let cool for 5 minutes. Remove loaves from pans, return to wire rack, and let cool completely before slicing and serving, about 2 hours.

Challah

Makes 1 loaf • Total Time: 1¾ hours, plus 7 hours rising and cooling

Why This Recipe Works To make challah dough that was moist but malleable, we combined a short rest during kneading with a long fermentation; this built a sturdy but stretchy gluten network that made the dough easy to handle. We also employed a Japanese dough-mixing technique called tangzhong, incorporating a cooked flour-water paste that bound up water in the dough so that it was moist but not sticky. Ample amounts of oil and eggs made the baked bread plush. Pointing the four dough strands in different directions, rather than lining them up parallel to one another, made them easier to keep track of during braiding. Brushing an egg wash—lightly salted to make the eggs more fluid—over the braided dough encouraged rich browning as the loaf baked.

> *We strongly recommend weighing the flour for this recipe. This dough will be firmer and drier than most bread doughs, which makes it easy to braid. Some friction is necessary for rolling and braiding the ropes, so resist the urge to dust your counter with flour. If your counter is too narrow to stretch the ropes, slightly bend the pieces at the 12 o'clock and 6 o'clock positions. Bake this loaf on two nested baking sheets to keep the bottom of the loaf from getting too dark.*

Flour Paste
- ½ cup water
- 3 tablespoons bread flour

Dough
- 1 large egg plus 2 large yolks
- ¼ cup water
- 2 tablespoons vegetable oil
- 2¾ cups (15⅛ ounces) bread flour
- 1¼ teaspoons instant or rapid-rise yeast
- ¼ cup (1¾ ounces) sugar
- 1 teaspoon table salt
- Vegetable oil spray

Egg Wash
- 1 large egg
- Pinch table salt
- 1 tablespoon sesame seeds or poppy seeds (optional)

1. For the flour paste: Whisk water and flour in small bowl until no lumps remain. Microwave, whisking every 20 seconds, until mixture thickens to stiff, smooth, pudding-like consistency that forms mound when dropped from end of whisk into bowl, 40 to 80 seconds.

2. For the dough: In bowl of stand mixer, whisk flour paste, egg and yolks, water, and oil until well combined. Add flour and yeast. Fit mixer with dough hook and mix on low speed until all flour is moistened, 3 to 4 minutes. Let stand for 20 minutes.

3. Add sugar and salt and mix on medium speed for 9 minutes (dough will be quite firm and dry). Transfer dough to counter and lightly spray now-empty mixer bowl with oil spray. Knead dough briefly to form ball and return it to prepared bowl. Lightly spray dough with oil spray and cover bowl with plastic wrap. Let dough rise until about doubled in volume, about 1½ hours.

4. Line rimmed baking sheet with parchment paper and nest in second rimmed baking sheet. Transfer dough to counter and press into 8-inch square, expelling as much air as possible. Cut dough in half lengthwise to form 2 rectangles. Cut each rectangle in half lengthwise to form 4 equal strips of dough. Roll 1 strip of dough into 16-inch rope. Continue rolling, tapering ends, until rope is 18 inches long. Repeat with remaining dough strips. Arrange ropes in plus-sign shape, with 4 ends overlapping in center by ½ inch. Firmly press center of cross into counter to seal ropes to each other and to counter.

5. Lift rope at 12 o'clock, bring over center, and place in 5 o'clock position. Lift rope at 6 o'clock, bring over center, and place in 12 o'clock position.

6. Lift rope at 9 o'clock, bring over center, and place in 4 o'clock position. Lift rope at 3 o'clock and, working toward yourself, bring over braid and place in 8 o'clock position. Adjust ropes so they are at 12, 3, 6, and 9 o'clock positions.

7. Repeat steps 5 and 6, working toward yourself, until you can no longer braid. Loaf will naturally list to 1 side.

8. Pinch ends of ropes together and tuck both ends under braid. Carefully transfer braid to prepared sheets. Cover loosely with plastic and let rise until dough does not spring back fully when gently pressed with your knuckle, about 3 hours.

9. For the egg wash: Thirty minutes before baking, adjust oven rack to middle position and heat oven to 350 degrees. Whisk together egg and salt. Brush loaf with egg wash and sprinkle with sesame seeds, if using. Bake until loaf is deep golden brown and registers at least 195 degrees, 35 to 40 minutes. Let cool on sheets for 20 minutes. Transfer loaf to wire rack and let cool completely before slicing, about 2 hours.

Braiding Challah

1. Arrange ropes in plus-sign shape, with 4 ends overlapping in center by ½ inch. Firmly press center of cross into counter to seal ropes to each other and to counter.

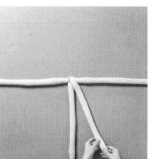

2. Lift rope at 12 o'clock, bring over center, and place in 5 o'clock position.

3. Lift rope at 6 o'clock, bring over center, and place in 12 o'clock position.

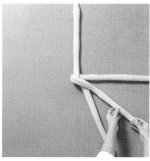

4. Lift rope at 9 o'clock, bring over center, and place in 4 o'clock position.

5. Lift rope at 3 o'clock and, working toward yourself, bring over braid and place in 8 o'clock position.

6. Adjust ropes so they are at 12, 3, 6, and 9 o'clock positions. Repeat steps 2 through 6.

7. Continue braiding, working toward yourself, until you can no longer braid. Loaf will naturally list to 1 side.

8. Pinch ends of ropes together. Tuck both ends under braid.

Rosemary Focaccia

Makes two 9-inch round loaves
Total Time: 1½ hours, plus 10½ hours rising and cooling

Why This Recipe Works Most focaccia in the States is heavy, thick, and strewn with pizza-like toppings. We wanted a lighter loaf, airy on the inside and topped with just a smattering of herbs. To start, we focused on flavor. To get the benefits of a long fermentation with minimal effort, many bakers use a "pre-ferment" (also known as a "sponge" or "starter" or, in Italian, "biga"): a mixture of flour, water, and yeast that rests before being incorporated into the dough. We followed suit, but the interiors of the loaves weren't as tender and airy as we wanted. We wondered if our stand mixer was developing too much gluten (the network of proteins that give bread its structure). We tried a more gentle approach, where a high hydration level (the weight of the water in relation to the weight of the flour) and a long autolyse (the dough resting process) take advantage of the enzymes naturally present in the wheat to produce the same effect as kneading. Our loaves were now light and airy, but squat. To improve the structure, we turned the dough at regular intervals while it proofed. To hasten gluten development and shorten our proofing time, we held back the salt when mixing our dough, adding it later. For a crisp crust, we oiled the baking pans and added coarse salt for flavor and crunchy texture.

> *If you don't have a baking stone, bake the bread on an overturned, preheated rimmed baking sheet set on the upper-middle oven rack.*

Biga
- ½ cup (2½ ounces) all-purpose flour
- ⅓ cup (2⅔ ounces) warm water (100–110 degrees)
- ¼ teaspoon instant or rapid-rise yeast

Dough
- 2½ cups (12½ ounces) all-purpose flour
- 1¼ cups (10 ounces) warm water (100–110 degrees)
- 1 teaspoon instant or rapid-rise yeast
- 1 tablespoon kosher salt, divided
- ¼ cup extra-virgin olive oil
- 2 tablespoons chopped fresh rosemary

1. For the biga: Combine flour, water, and yeast in large bowl and stir with wooden spoon until uniform mass forms and no dry flour remains, about 1 minute. Cover bowl tightly with plastic wrap and let stand at room temperature (about 70 degrees) at least 8 hours or up to 24 hours. Use immediately or store in refrigerator for up to 3 days (allow to stand at room temperature for 30 minutes before proceeding with recipe).

2. For the dough: Stir flour, water, and yeast into biga with wooden spoon until uniform mass forms and no dry flour remains, about 1 minute. Cover with plastic wrap and let rise at room temperature for 15 minutes.

3. Sprinkle 2 teaspoons salt over dough; stir into dough until thoroughly incorporated, about 1 minute. Cover with plastic wrap and let rise at room temperature for 30 minutes. Spray rubber spatula or bowl scraper with vegetable oil spray; fold partially risen dough over itself by gently lifting and folding the edge of the dough toward the middle. Turn bowl 90 degrees; fold again. Turn bowl and fold dough 6 more times (total of 8 turns). Cover with plastic wrap and let rise for 30 minutes. Repeat folding, turning, and rising 2 more times, for a total of three 30-minute rises. Meanwhile, adjust oven rack to upper-middle position, place baking stone on the rack, and heat oven to 500 degrees, at least 30 minutes before baking.

4. Gently transfer dough to lightly floured work surface. Lightly dust top of dough with flour and divide it in half. Shape each piece of dough into 5-inch round by gently tucking under edges. Coat two 9-inch round cake pans with 2 tablespoons olive oil each. Sprinkle each pan with ½ teaspoon kosher salt. Place round of dough in 1 pan, top side down; slide dough around pan to coat bottom and sides, then flip dough over. Repeat with second piece of dough and second pan. Cover pans with plastic wrap and let rest for 5 minutes.

5. Using your fingertips, press dough out toward edges of pan, taking care not to tear it. (If dough resists stretching, let it relax for 5 to 10 minutes before trying to stretch it again.) Using dinner fork, poke entire surface of dough 25 to 30 times, popping any large bubbles. Sprinkle rosemary evenly over top of dough. Let dough rest in pan until slightly bubbly, 5 to 10 minutes.

6. Place pans on baking stone and lower oven temperature to 450 degrees. Bake until tops are golden brown, 25 to 28 minutes, switching placement of pans halfway through baking time. Transfer pans to wire rack and let cool for 5 minutes. Remove loaves from pans and place on wire rack. Brush tops with any oil remaining in pans. Let cool for 30 minutes before serving. (Focaccia can be stored for up to 2 days at room temperature or frozen for 2 months.)

Making Focaccia

1. Fold partially risen dough over itself by gently lifting and folding edge of dough toward middle. Turn bowl 90 degrees; fold again. Turn bowl and fold dough 6 more times (for total of 8 turns).

2. Cover with plastic wrap and let rise for 30 minutes. Repeat turning, folding, and rising 2 more times, for total of three 30-minute rises.

3. Divide dough in half and gently shape halves into rounds. Place in oiled, salted pans, then coat with oil and salt and flip. Cover with plastic wrap and let rest for 5 minutes.

4. Using your fingertips, press dough out toward edges, taking care not to tear it. (If dough resists let it relax and try again.) With dinner fork, poke dough surface 25 to 30 times. Sprinkle rosemary over top. Let dough rest in pans until slightly bubbly.

Fluffy Dinner Rolls

Makes 12 rolls • Total Time: 1¾ hours, plus 2 hours 5 minutes rising and cooling

Why This Recipe Works Moist, fluffy American dinner rolls are great when fresh but lose those qualities as they sit. We took a classic dinner roll recipe and applied a Japanese bread-making method called tangzhong, which adds extra moisture to the dough in the form of a flour paste. The added liquid extends the rolls' shelf life—they maintain their fluffy texture for more than a day. To support the weight of the extra moisture, we built a strong gluten structure by changing the mixing method—adding a resting period and withholding the butter until the gluten was established. The shaping method was also important. Flattening each portion of dough and rolling it up in a spiral organized the gluten strands into coiled layers, which baked up into feathery sheets.

> *We strongly recommend weighing the flour for the dough. The slight tackiness of the dough aids in flattening and stretching it in step 5, so do not dust your counter with flour. This recipe requires letting the dough rest for at least 2 hours before baking. The rolls can be made a day ahead. To refresh them before serving, wrap them in aluminum foil and heat them in a 350-degree oven for 15 minutes.*

Flour Paste
- ½ cup water
- 3 tablespoons bread flour

Dough
- ½ cup cold milk
- 1 large egg
- 2 cups (11 ounces) bread flour
- 1½ teaspoons instant or rapid-rise yeast
- 2 tablespoons sugar
- 1 teaspoon table salt
- 4 tablespoons unsalted butter, softened, plus ½ tablespoon, melted

1. For the flour paste: Whisk water and flour in small bowl until no lumps remain. Microwave, whisking every 20 seconds, until mixture thickens to stiff, smooth, pudding-like consistency that forms mound when dropped from end of whisk into bowl, 40 to 80 seconds.

2. For the dough: In bowl of stand mixer, whisk flour paste and milk together until smooth. Add egg and whisk until incorporated. Add flour and yeast. Fit stand mixer with dough hook and mix on low speed until all flour is moistened, 1 to 2 minutes. Let stand for 15 minutes.

3. Add sugar and salt and mix on medium-low speed for 5 minutes. With mixer running, add softened butter, 1 tablespoon at a time. Continue to mix on medium-low speed 5 minutes longer, scraping down dough hook and sides of bowl occasionally (dough will stick to bottom of bowl).

4. Transfer dough to very lightly floured counter. Knead briefly to form ball and transfer, seam side down, to lightly greased bowl; lightly coat surface of dough with vegetable oil spray and cover with plastic wrap. Let rise until doubled in volume, about 1 hour.

5. Grease 9-inch round cake pan and set aside. Transfer dough to counter. Press dough gently but firmly to expel all air. Pat and stretch dough to form 8 by 9-inch rectangle with short side facing you. Cut dough lengthwise into 4 equal strips and cut each strip crosswise into 3 equal pieces. Working with 1 piece at a time, stretch and press dough gently to form 8 by 2-inch strip. Starting on short side, roll dough to form snug cylinder and arrange shaped rolls seam side down in prepared pan, placing 10 rolls around edge of pan, pointing inward, and remaining 2 rolls in center. Cover with plastic and let rise until doubled, 45 minutes to 1 hour.

6. When rolls are nearly doubled, adjust oven rack to lowest position and heat oven to 375 degrees. Bake rolls until deep golden brown, 25 to 30 minutes. Let rolls cool in pan on wire rack for 3 minutes; invert rolls onto rack, then reinvert. Brush tops and sides of rolls with melted butter. Let rolls cool for at least 20 minutes before serving.

Homemade Naan

Makes 4 pieces • Total Time: 1½ hours, plus 16 hours chilling

Why This Recipe Works We wanted a light and tender naan that could be made at home without a tandoor. We started with a moist dough with a fair amount of fat, which created a soft bread that was pleasantly chewy, but the real secret was the cooking method. While we thought a grill or preheated pizza stone would be the best cooking method, we discovered that they cooked the bread unevenly. A much better option was a covered skillet. The skillet delivered heat to the bottom and the top of the bread, producing naan that were nicely charred but still moist.

This recipe works best with a high-protein all-purpose flour such as King Arthur brand. Do not use nonfat yogurt in this recipe. A 12-inch nonstick skillet may be used in place of the cast-iron skillet. For efficiency, stretch the next ball of dough while each naan is cooking.

½ cup ice water
⅓ cup plain whole-milk yogurt
3 tablespoons plus 1 teaspoon vegetable oil, divided
1 large egg yolk
2 cups (10 ounces) all-purpose flour
1¼ teaspoons sugar
½ teaspoon instant or rapid-rise yeast
1¼ teaspoons table salt
1½ tablespoons unsalted butter, melted

1. In measuring cup or small bowl, combine water, yogurt, 3 tablespoons oil, and egg yolk. Process flour, sugar, and yeast in food processor until combined, about 2 seconds. With processor running, slowly add water mixture; process until dough is just combined and no dry flour remains, about 10 seconds. Let dough stand for 10 minutes.

2. Add salt to dough and process until dough forms satiny, sticky ball that clears sides of workbowl, 30 to 60 seconds. Transfer dough to lightly floured work surface and knead until smooth, about 1 minute. Shape dough into tight ball and place in large, lightly oiled bowl. Cover tightly with plastic wrap and refrigerate for 16 to 24 hours.

3. Adjust oven rack to middle position and heat oven to 200 degrees. Place heatproof plate on rack. Transfer dough to lightly floured work surface and divide into 4 equal pieces. Shape each piece into smooth, tight ball. Place dough balls on lightly oiled baking sheet, at least 2 inches apart; cover loosely with plastic coated with vegetable oil spray. Let stand for 15 to 20 minutes.

4. Transfer 1 ball to lightly floured work surface and sprinkle with flour. Using your hands and rolling pin, press and roll piece of dough into 9-inch round of even thickness, sprinkling dough and work surface with flour as needed to prevent sticking. Using fork, poke entire surface of round 20 to 25 times. Heat remaining 1 teaspoon oil in 12-inch cast-iron skillet over medium heat until shimmering. Wipe oil out of skillet completely with paper towels. Mist top of dough lightly with water. Place dough in pan, moistened side down; mist top surface of dough with water; and cover. Cook until bottom is browned in spots across surface, 2 to 4 minutes. Flip naan, cover, and continue to cook on second side until lightly browned, 2 to 3 minutes. (If naan puffs up, gently poke with fork to deflate.) Flip naan, brush top with about 1 teaspoon melted butter, transfer to plate in oven, and cover plate tightly with aluminum foil. Repeat rolling and cooking remaining 3 dough balls. Once last naan is baked, serve immediately.

VARIATION
Quicker Homemade Naan
Total Time: 1½ hours, plus 1½ hours resting
This variation, which can be prepared in about 2 hours, forgoes the overnight rest, but the dough may be a little harder to roll out.

After shaping dough in step 2, let dough rise at room temperature for 30 minutes. After 30 minutes, fold partially risen dough over itself 8 times by gently lifting and folding edge of dough toward middle, turning bowl 90 degrees after each fold. Cover with plastic wrap and let rise for 30 minutes. Repeat folding, turning, and rising 1 more time, for total of three 30-minute rises. After last rise, proceed with recipe from step 3.

New York Bagels

Makes 8 bagels   •   Total Time: 2¼ hours, plus 17 hours rising and chilling

Why This Recipe Works For the chewy center and crackly-crisp shell of a New York bagel, we needed to take the obvious steps—mixing flour, water, yeast, and salt; shaping the dough into rings; letting the rings proof—and add some extra at-home finesse. For a fine, uniform crumb with plenty of chew, the dough's gluten network needed tightening. Mixing vital wheat gluten with bread flour elevated the gluten, and ice water kept the dough cool during mixing. Dissolving malt syrup in the water ahead of time infused the dough with distinct malty flavor. Flattening, rolling, and twisting the dough into a compact spiral stressed it, eliminating air pockets and promising a bagel with substantial chew. After the bagels proofed in the refrigerator, we boiled them in an alkaline mixture of water, sugar, and baking soda to wake up the yeast and cook some of the surface starches for a glossy, crisp crust. Preheating a baking stone in the oven created a hearth-like cooking environment while the bagels boiled. We arranged them on a wire rack–lined rimmed baking sheet and placed the sheet directly on the baking stone. Before leaving the bagels to bake, we poured boiling water into the bottom of the sheet for plenty of steam. A flip halfway through baking ensured even browning.

This recipe requires refrigerating the shaped bagels for 16 to 24 hours before baking them. This recipe works best with King Arthur bread flour, although other bread flours will work. Vital wheat gluten and malt syrup are available in most supermarkets in the baking and syrup aisles, respectively. If you cannot find malt syrup, substitute 4 teaspoons of molasses. The bagels are best eaten within a day of baking; fully cooled bagels can be transferred to heavy-duty zipper-lock bags and frozen for up to one month.

1	cup plus 2 tablespoons ice water (9 ounces)
2	tablespoons malt syrup
2⅔	cups (14⅔ ounces) bread flour
4	teaspoons vital wheat gluten
2	teaspoons instant or rapid-rise yeast
2	teaspoons table salt
¼	cup (1¼ ounces) cornmeal
¼	cup (1¾ ounces) sugar
1	tablespoon baking soda

1. Stir ice water and malt syrup in 2-cup liquid measuring cup until malt syrup has fully dissolved. Process flour, wheat gluten, and yeast in food processor until combined, about 2 seconds. With processor running, slowly add ice water mixture; process until dough is just combined and no dry flour remains, about 20 seconds. Let dough stand for 10 minutes.

2. Add salt to dough and process, stopping processor and redistributing dough as needed, until dough forms shaggy mass that clears sides of workbowl (dough may not form one single mass), 45 to 90 seconds. Transfer dough to unfloured counter and knead until smooth, about 1 minute. Divide dough into 8 equal pieces (3½ ounces each) and cover loosely with plastic wrap.

3. Working with 1 piece of dough at a time and keeping remaining pieces covered, form dough pieces into smooth, taut rounds. (To round, set piece of dough on unfloured counter. Loosely cup your hand around dough and, without applying pressure to dough, move your hand in small circular motions. Tackiness of dough against counter and circular motion should work dough into smooth, even ball, but if dough sticks to your hands, lightly dust your fingers with flour.) Let dough balls rest on counter, covered, for 15 minutes.

4. Sprinkle rimmed baking sheet with cornmeal. Working with 1 dough ball at a time and keeping remaining pieces covered, coat dough balls lightly with flour and then, using your hands and rolling pin, pat and roll dough balls into 5-inch rounds. Starting with edge of dough farthest from you, roll into tight cylinder. Starting at center of cylinder and working toward ends, gently and evenly roll and stretch dough into 8- to 9-inch-long rope. Do not taper ends. Rolling ends of dough under your hands in opposite directions, twist rope to form tight spiral. Without unrolling spiral, wrap rope around your fingers, overlapping ends of dough by about 2 inches under your palm, to create ring shape. Pinch ends of dough gently together. With overlap under your palm, press and roll seam using circular motion on counter to fully seal. Transfer rings to prepared sheet and cover loosely with plastic, leaving at least 1 inch between bagels. Let bagels stand at room temperature for 1 hour. Cover sheet tightly with plastic and refrigerate for at least 16 hours or up to 24 hours.

5. One hour before baking, adjust oven rack to upper-middle position, place baking stone on rack, and heat oven to 450 degrees.

6. Bring 4 quarts water, sugar, and baking soda to boil in large Dutch oven. Set wire rack in rimmed baking sheet and spray rack with vegetable oil spray.

7. Transfer 4 bagels to boiling water and cook for 20 seconds. Using wire skimmer or slotted spoon, flip bagels over and cook 20 seconds longer. Using wire skimmer or slotted spoon, transfer bagels to prepared wire rack, with corn-meal side facing down. Repeat with remaining 4 bagels.

8. Place sheet with bagels on preheated baking stone and pour ½ cup boiling water into bottom of sheet. Bake until tops of bagels are beginning to brown, 10 to 12 minutes. Using metal spatula, flip bagels and continue to bake until golden brown, 10 to 12 minutes longer. Remove sheet from oven and let bagels cool on wire rack for at least 15 minutes. Serve warm or at room temperature.

ACCOMPANIMENT
Bagel Toppings
Place ½ cup poppy seeds, sesame seeds, caraway seeds, dehydrated onion flakes, dehydrated garlic flakes, or coarse/pretzel salt in small bowl. Press tops of just-boiled bagels (side without cornmeal) gently into topping and return to wire rack, topping side up.

Shaping Bagels like a Pro

1. Pat and roll dough ball (lightly coated with flour) with rolling pin into 5-inch round. Roll into tight cylinder, starting with far side of dough.

2. Roll and stretch dough into 8- to 9-inch-long rope, starting at center of cylinder (don't taper ends). Twist rope to form tight spiral by rolling ends of dough under hands in opposite directions.

3. Wrap rope around your fingers, overlapping ends by 2 inches, to create ring. Pinch ends together. Press and roll seam (positioned under your palm) using circular motion on counter to fully seal.

New York Bagels

Laugenbrezeln

Makes 6 pretzels • Total Time: 2¾ hours, plus 3 hours 10 minutes rising, resting, and chilling

Why This Recipe Works Making pretzels the way German bakers do combines science and arts and crafts with a frisson of (manageable) risk. The process is fun; the payoff is spectacular. For pretzels that were sturdy and chewy, we started with bread flour, which contains more gluten-forming proteins than all-purpose flour, and we added just enough water to make a malleable dough that would stick to itself when knotted. Rolling out each portion of dough with a rolling pin removed most air bubbles, ensuring that the crumb would be even and fine. We shaped the pretzels in stages, giving the dough short rests to keep the gluten relaxed so that our pretzels would remain large and elegant instead of small and chunky. A quick dip in either a room-temperature lye solution or a simmering baking soda solution accelerated the Maillard reaction, breaking up proteins on the surface of the pretzel so that they interacted more readily with sugars for quick and deep browning during the brief, hot bake.

Dipping pretzels in a lye solution before baking gives them their characteristic flavor and texture, but lye is caustic and can be dangerous if used incorrectly. (Lye-dipped pretzels are perfectly safe to eat after baking; the heat of the oven neutralizes the alkali.) If dipping in lye, you must read "Working with Lye Safely" before proceeding. Alternatively, use the baking soda dip. Food-safe lye and pretzel salt are available at specialty baking shops and online. Kosher salt can be substituted for the pretzel salt, but it will melt more easily. We strongly recommend measuring the flour by weight. This is a great place to use a silicone baking mat, or you can line your baking sheet with parchment paper and coat it very generously with vegetable oil spray. Eat the pretzels plain or like the Germans do: sliced horizontally and spread with butter.

2⅓ cups (12¾ ounces) bread flour
   1 teaspoon table salt
   1 teaspoon instant or rapid-rise yeast
   1 cup room temperature water
   2 tablespoons unsalted butter, softened
 40 grams lye crystals or ½ cup baking soda
      Pretzel salt

1. Combine flour, table salt, and yeast in bowl of stand mixer and stir to combine. Add water and butter. Fit mixer with dough hook and mix on low speed until all flour is moistened, about 1 minute. Increase speed to medium-low and continue to mix until dough is smooth and elastic, about 6 minutes longer, scraping down bowl and dough hook halfway through mixing. Shape dough into ball and transfer to lightly greased bowl. Cover and let rise until almost doubled in size, about 1 hour.

2. Divide dough into 6 equal portions. Working with 1 piece of dough at a time, form into smooth balls. Cover with damp dish towel and let rest for 10 minutes. While dough rests, line rimmed baking sheet with parchment paper.

3. Place 1 dough ball seam side up on unfloured counter and flatten with your hand, pressing out as much air as possible. Using rolling pin, roll out dough to expel remaining air. Stretch and pat dough into roughly 8 by 4-inch rectangle with short side parallel to edge of counter. Starting at short side farthest away from you, roll dough into tight cylinder. Pinch seam to seal. Roll cylinder into 9-inch rope and place under damp dish towel. Repeat with remaining dough balls.

4. Working from center outward, roll first 9-inch rope into 28-inch rope, expelling any lingering air pockets as you go. Shape rope into inverted U with ends facing toward you. Cross rope ends once, and then again. Lift ends and attach them to other side of inverted U at about 10 o'clock and 2 o'clock. Press ends firmly into body of pretzel. Transfer to prepared sheet. Repeat with remaining 9-inch ropes. If pretzels have contracted, stretch each gently and return to sheet. Let sit for 10 minutes, uncovered. Cover with plastic wrap and refrigerate for at least 2 hours or up to 24 hours.

Working with Lye Safely

Dipping the dough in a lye solution gives traditional German pretzels their characteristic salinity, chew, and smooth mahogany exterior; but the strong alkali (sodium hydroxide) is corrosive and can burn your skin, so it must be handled with caution. (Don't worry about eating it: Baking neutralizes lye and makes it perfectly safe to consume.) Follow this guide to make your experience safe and comfortable.

LYE-DIPPING STATION SETUP
Work in a well-ventilated room, on a stable and roomy counter near an empty sink, if possible. Do not use lye around small children or pets.

KEY SUPPLIES
- Food-grade lye (also known as sodium hydroxide), available at baking shops or online
- Long sleeves with long rubber gloves (such as for dish washing; before wearing, blow up each glove like a balloon to ensure that there are no holes)
- Eyeglasses or safety goggles
- Digital scale that measures in grams
- Rags in case of spills or drips
- Counter protection (plastic wrap or large plastic bag)

METHOD
1. Cover counter with plastic wrap or large plastic bag. Put on rubber gloves, making sure no skin on your arms is showing. Put on eyeglasses or safety goggles.

2. Measure out exactly 40 grams of lye crystals into small bowl on scale. Set aside small bowl with lye crystals. Cover container of lye crystals and store in safe location per package instructions.

3. Place large bowl on scale. Add 1,000 grams cold water to large bowl. Add reserved 40 grams lye crystals to water and whisk gently to dissolve. Order of operations is important: Always add lye to water instead of adding water to lye. (Lye solution in bowl will heat up slightly and will give off some vapors, which are barely noticeable, but it's not advisable to put your face directly over solution.) Rinse whisk well with cool water. Remove scale.

4. Set wire rack in rimmed baking sheet and place to right of lye solution. Unwrap sheet of chilled pretzels, place to left of lye solution, and proceed with recipe. (Clear counter while pretzels bake.)

CLEANUP
1. Still wearing gloves and eyewear, transfer bowl of lye solution to sink.

2. Run cold water into bowl in gentle stream to dilute solution. Pour solution down drain. Flush drain and rinse bowl and sink thoroughly with plenty of cold water.

3. Rinse rimmed baking sheets and wire rack with plenty of cold water. Dispose of plastic wrap or plastic bag on counter. Rinse gloves before removing. Once gloves are off, remove eyewear.

IF YOUR SKIN TOUCHES LYE
Avoid touching anything but the pretzels while working with the lye solution. Before touching something else, rinse your gloved hands with cool water and dry them with rags.

If you get lye solution on your skin: Rinse your skin immediately with cool running water for 15 minutes.

If you touch lye crystals: Brush them off with a dry cloth, and then rinse your skin with cool running water for 10 minutes.

5. Adjust oven rack to middle position and heat oven to 475 degrees. Line second rimmed baking sheet with silicone baking mat or parchment. If using parchment, spray very generously with vegetable oil spray.

6A. For the lye dip: Set up station as directed in "Working with Lye Safely." Grasp 1 pretzel with your gloved hands, pinching where ends meet body of pretzel, and transfer gently, presentation side down, to prepared lye bath. Let pretzel soak for 15 seconds, pressing occasionally to submerge. Using your gloved hands, grasp pretzel gently where ends meet body of pretzel and transfer, presentation side up, to prepared wire rack. Repeat with remaining pretzels. With your gloved hands, transfer pretzels to silicone-lined sheet.

6B. For the baking soda dip: Set wire rack in third rimmed baking sheet. Dissolve baking soda in 8 cups water in Dutch oven and bring to boil over medium-high heat. Reduce heat to simmer. Grasp 1 pretzel with your hands, pinching where ends meet body of pretzel, and transfer gently, presentation side down, to simmering water. Cook for 30 seconds, pressing occasionally with slotted spatula to submerge. Carefully flip pretzel with spatula, then lift with spatula and transfer to prepared wire rack. Repeat with remaining pretzels. Transfer pretzels to silicone-lined sheet.

7. Sprinkle pretzels evenly with pretzel salt. Bake until deeply browned, about 12 minutes. Transfer to second wire rack and let cool for at least 5 minutes before serving.

Doing the Twist

1. After making inverted U with dough rope, cross rope ends once, and then again.

2. Lift ends and attach them to curve of inverted U at about 10 o'clock and 2 o'clock. Press ends firmly into body of pretzel.

Stollen

Makes 2 loaves • Total Time: 1¾ hours, plus 15½ hours rising and cooling

Why This Recipe Works Stollen is a rich, sweet yeasted bread served at Christmas throughout Germany and Austria. Unlike most breads, stollen improves over time, so you can enjoy it bit by bit or make extra loaves to give as gifts. We wanted our stollen to feature both dried and candied fruits as well as almonds and heady spirits. We enriched the dough with milk, brandy, egg, and butter, melting the butter before stirring it in to produce the short crumb we wanted. To make the traditional marzipan core, we softened our almond filling with butter and water and scented it with a pinch of nutmeg before shaping it into a rectangle and sealing it inside the dough.

We do not recommend mixing this dough by hand. If the dough becomes too soft to work with at any point, refrigerate it until it's firm enough to handle easily. The texture and flavor of stollen improves over time; the bread is best eaten two weeks after baking.

Filling
- 1 tube (7 ounces) almond paste, cut into 4 pieces
- 1 tablespoon unsalted butter, softened
- 1 tablespoon water
- Pinch nutmeg

Dough
- 1 cup raisins
- ½ cup (4 ounces) brandy
- ½ cup chopped candied lemon peel
- ½ cup chopped candied orange peel
- ½ cup slivered almonds, toasted
- 3½ cups (17½ ounces) all-purpose flour
- 4 teaspoons instant or rapid-rise yeast
- 1¼ teaspoons table salt
- 1 cup (8 ounces) whole milk, room temperature
- 10 tablespoons unsalted butter, melted, divided
- ½ cup (3½ ounces) granulated sugar
- 1 large egg, room temperature
- 1 teaspoon vanilla extract
- Confectioners' sugar

1. For the filling: Using stand mixer fitted with paddle, beat almond paste, butter, water, and nutmeg on medium speed until smooth, about 1 minute. Transfer to bowl, cover, and refrigerate until ready to use.

2. **For the dough:** Microwave raisins and brandy in covered bowl until steaming, about 1 minute. Let sit until raisins have softened, about 15 minutes. Drain raisins and reserve brandy. Combine raisins, candied lemon peel, candied orange peel, and almonds in bowl.

3. Whisk flour, yeast, and salt together in clean, dry mixer bowl. Whisk milk, 8 tablespoons melted butter, granulated sugar, egg, vanilla, and reserved brandy in 4-cup liquid measuring cup until sugar has dissolved. Using paddle on low speed, slowly add milk mixture to flour mixture and mix until cohesive dough starts to form and no dry flour remains, about 2 minutes, scraping down bowl as needed. Slowly add fruit mixture and mix until incorporated, about 30 seconds. Transfer dough to lightly greased large bowl or container, cover tightly with plastic wrap, and refrigerate for at least 12 hours or up to 24 hours.

4. Stack 2 rimmed baking sheets, line with aluminum foil, and spray with vegetable oil spray. Transfer filling to well-floured counter, divide in half, and press each half into 7 by 2-inch rectangle; set aside.

5. Transfer dough to well-floured counter, divide in half, and cover loosely with greased plastic. Using your well-floured hands, press 1 piece of dough into 10 by 8-inch rectangle (keep remaining piece covered), with short side parallel to counter edge. Place 1 piece of filling across top edge of dough, leaving 2-inch border at top. Fold dough away from you over filling until folded edge is snug against filling and dough extends 2 inches beyond top edge.

6. Fold top 2 inches of dough back toward center of loaf. Pinch side seams together to seal. Repeat with remaining dough and filling. Transfer loaves to prepared sheet, spaced about 4 inches apart. Cover loosely with greased plastic and let rest for 30 minutes.

7. Adjust oven rack to middle position and heat oven to 350 degrees. Bake until golden brown and loaves register 190 to 195 degrees, 40 to 45 minutes, rotating sheet halfway through baking. Brush loaves with remaining 2 tablespoons melted butter and dust liberally with confectioners' sugar. Transfer to wire rack and let cool completely, about 3 hours. Dust with additional confectioners' sugar before serving. (Stollen can be wrapped in plastic wrap and stored at room temperature for up to 1 month.)

Shaping Stollen

1. Working with 1 piece of dough at a time, press into 10 by 8-inch rectangle, with short side parallel to counter edge.

2. Place 1 piece of filling across top edge of dough, leaving 2-inch border at top. Fold dough away from you over filling until folded edge is snug against filling and dough extends 2 inches beyond top edge.

3. Fold top 2 inches of dough back toward center of loaf. Pinch side seams together to seal.

Softer, More Tender Sticky Buns Start with a Paste

"My dad's sweet tooth could win awards and one of his favorite treats is the sticky bun. I myself was never a fan. Hear me out: The versions I grew up eating had tough edges that forced me to peel it away like a banana until I reached the tender center. No thanks. I'll just stick with my coffee.

A few Christmases ago, my dad asked for sticky buns. As a former sticky bun doubter, I begrudgingly agreed. But as a former pastry chef, I was intrigued by this recipe. Why? The flour and water paste. This magical, pudding-like goo was the answer to all my doubts. It made the dough soft and easy to work with. It also trapped water, steaming the buns from the inside out. Talk about a two for one deal. Flipping out the baked buns on Christmas morning was Instagrammable. The gooey pecan topping slowly dripped down the sides. As we pulled them apart they were as plush as a pillow, light and fluffy from end to end. After one bite I smiled like a giddy child. I felt proud to call myself an official sticky bun fan. And impressed with my dad, who ate three."

—Sam

Perfect Sticky Buns

Makes 12 buns • Total Time: 2¼ hours, plus 2 hours 20 minutes rising

Why This Recipe Works We wanted a sticky bun that fulfilled its promise of being both soft and sticky. To make a soft, tender, and moist sticky bun, we added a cooked flour-and-water paste (called a tangzhong) to the dough. The paste traps water, so the dough isn't sticky or difficult to work with, and the increased hydration converts to steam during baking, which makes the buns fluffy. The added water also keeps the crumb moist and tender. To ensure that the soft bread wouldn't collapse under the weight of the topping, we strengthened the crumb by adding a resting period and withholding the sugar and salt until the gluten was firmly established. Dark corn syrup plus water was the key to a gooey, sticky topping that was substantial enough to sit atop the buns without sinking in.

> *These buns take about 4 hours to make from start to finish. For dough that is easy to work with and produces light, fluffy buns, we strongly recommend that you measure the flour for the dough by weight. The slight tackiness of the dough aids in flattening and stretching it in step 6, so resist the urge to use a lot of dusting flour. Rolling the dough cylinder tightly in step 7 will result in misshapen rolls; keep the cylinder a bit slack. Bake these buns in a metal, not glass or ceramic, baking pan. We like dark corn syrup and pecans here, but light corn syrup may be used, and the nuts may be omitted, if desired.*

Flour Paste

- ⅔ cup water
- ¼ cup (1⅓ ounces) bread flour

Dough

- ⅔ cup milk
- 1 large egg plus 1 large yolk
- 2¾ cups (15⅛ ounces) bread flour
- 2 teaspoons instant or rapid-rise yeast
- 3 tablespoons granulated sugar
- 1½ teaspoons table salt
- 6 tablespoons unsalted butter, softened

Topping

- 6 tablespoons unsalted butter, melted
- ½ cup packed (3½ ounces) dark brown sugar
- ¼ cup (1¾ ounces) granulated sugar
- ¼ cup dark corn syrup
- ¼ teaspoon table salt
- 2 tablespoons water
- 1 cup pecans, toasted and chopped (optional)

Filling

- ¾ cup packed (5¼ ounces) dark brown sugar
- 1 teaspoon ground cinnamon

1. For the flour paste: Whisk water and flour in small bowl until no lumps remain. Microwave, whisking every 25 seconds, until mixture thickens to stiff, smooth, pudding-like consistency that forms mound when dropped from end of whisk into bowl, 50 to 75 seconds.

2. For the dough: In bowl of stand mixer, whisk flour paste and milk until smooth. Add egg and yolk and whisk until incorporated. Add flour and yeast. Fit stand mixer with dough hook and mix on low speed until all flour is moistened, 1 to 2 minutes. Let stand for 15 minutes. Add sugar and salt and mix on medium-low speed for 5 minutes. Stop mixer and add butter. Continue to mix on medium-low speed for 5 minutes longer, scraping down dough hook and sides of bowl halfway through (dough will stick to bottom of bowl).

3. Transfer dough to lightly floured counter. Knead briefly to form ball and transfer seam side down to lightly greased bowl; lightly coat surface of dough with vegetable oil spray and cover bowl with plastic wrap. Let dough rise until just doubled in volume, 40 minutes to 1 hour.

4. For the topping: While dough rises, grease 13 by 9-inch metal baking pan. Whisk melted butter, brown sugar, granulated sugar, corn syrup, and salt in medium bowl until smooth. Add water and whisk until incorporated. Pour mixture into prepared pan and tilt pan to cover bottom. Sprinkle evenly with pecans, if using.

5. For the filling: Stir sugar and cinnamon in small bowl until thoroughly combined; set aside.

6. Turn out dough onto lightly floured counter. Press dough gently but firmly to expel air. Working from center toward edge, pat and stretch dough to form 18 by 15-inch rectangle with long edge nearest you. Sprinkle filling over dough, leaving 1-inch border along top edge; smooth filling into even layer with your hand, then gently press mixture into dough to adhere.

7. Beginning with long edge nearest you, roll dough into cylinder, taking care not to roll too tightly. Pinch seam to seal and roll cylinder seam side down. Mark gently with knife to create 12 equal portions. To slice, hold strand of dental floss taut and slide underneath cylinder, stopping at first mark. Cross ends of floss over each other and pull. Slice cylinder into 12 portions and transfer, cut sides down, to prepared baking pan. Cover tightly with plastic wrap and let rise until buns are puffy and touching one another, 40 minutes to 1 hour. (Buns may be refrigerated immediately after shaping for up to 14 hours. To bake, remove baking pan from refrigerator and let sit until buns are puffy and touching one another, 1 to 1½ hours.) Meanwhile, adjust oven racks to lowest and lower-middle positions. Place rimmed baking sheet on lower rack to catch any drips and heat oven to 375 degrees.

8. Bake buns on upper rack until golden brown, about 20 minutes. Tent with aluminum foil and bake until center of dough registers at least 200 degrees, 10 to 15 minutes longer. Let buns cool in pan on wire rack for 5 minutes. Place rimmed baking sheet over buns and carefully invert. Using spoon, scoop any glaze from baking pan onto buns. Let cool for at least 10 minutes longer before serving.

Rolling Dough for Sticky Buns

Because these sticky buns bake up so soft and fluffy, it's important to roll dough loosely when forming cylinder in step 7. If rolled too tightly, buns will expand upward.

SEASON 23

Kanelbullar

Makes 12 buns • Total Time: 2 hours, plus 2 hours chilling and rising

Why This Recipe Works The Swedish cinnamon buns known as kanelbullar are soft and fluffy, with lightly crisp swirled edges, and are filled with buttery cinnamon sugar and suffused with cardamom. They're a favorite feature of fika, the daily social ritual of sharing coffee and a snack with friends or colleagues. For our version of this iconic sweet, we started by incorporating a tangzhong (a cooked paste of flour and milk) into the dough. The paste helped lock in moisture so our high-hydration dough was workable and not too sticky. The water in the dough converted to steam during baking, which made the buns fluffy and light. Refrigerating the dough allowed the flour to fully absorb moisture and the butter to firm up, making the dough easier to handle, and preshaping it in a baking pan made it easier to roll out later. Starting with a long strip of dough was important when shaping each bun. Instead of stretching, we cut each strip almost in half and then opened it up to a 2-foot length. Shaping the buns loosely gave them the space to expand during baking without becoming misshapen.

We strongly recommend using a scale to measure the flour. It's well worth seeking out cardamom seeds at a South Asian market or online. Alternatively, crack open whole green cardamom pods and remove the seeds yourself. Coarsely grind the seeds using a spice grinder or mortar and pestle. Swedish pearl sugar is available online; you can substitute turbinado sugar (sometimes sold as Sugar in the Raw) if you prefer, though it may soften on the buns during storage.

Flour Paste
¾ cup milk
¼ cup (1⅓ ounces) bread flour

Dough
½ cup milk, chilled
2 cups (11 ounces) bread flour
1 tablespoon instant or rapid-rise yeast
¼ cup (1¾ ounces) granulated sugar
1 teaspoon table salt
6 tablespoons unsalted butter, cut into 6 pieces and softened
2 teaspoons cardamom seeds, ground coarse

Filling
¾ cup (5¼ ounces) granulated sugar
6 tablespoons unsalted butter, softened
2 tablespoons ground cinnamon
1 tablespoon bread flour
¼ teaspoon table salt

1 large egg beaten with 1 tablespoon water and pinch table salt
¼ cup Swedish pearl sugar

1. **For the flour paste:** Whisk milk and flour in small bowl until no lumps remain. Microwave, whisking every 20 seconds, until mixture has thick, stiff consistency, 1 to 2 minutes.

2. **For the dough:** In bowl of stand mixer, whisk flour paste and milk until smooth. Add flour and yeast. Fit mixer with dough hook and mix on low speed until all flour is moistened, 1 to 2 minutes (dough will look quite dry). Let stand for 15 minutes. Add sugar and salt and mix on medium-low speed for 5 minutes. Stop mixer and add butter and cardamom. Continue to mix on medium-low speed 5 minutes longer, scraping down dough hook and sides of bowl halfway through mixing (dough may stick to bottom of bowl but should clear sides).

3. Lightly grease 13 by 9-inch baking pan. Transfer dough to prepared pan (scrape bowl but do not wash). Flip dough, then press and stretch dough until it reaches edges of pan. Cover with plastic wrap and refrigerate for 1 hour. While dough chills, make filling.

4. **For the filling:** Add all ingredients to now-empty mixer bowl. Fit mixer with paddle and mix on low speed until fully combined, about 1 minute.

5. Line 18 by 13-inch rimmed baking sheet with parchment paper. Transfer dough to well-floured counter. Roll dough into 18 by 10-inch rectangle, with shorter side parallel to edge of counter. Using offset spatula, spread filling over lower two-thirds of rectangle, going all the way to edges

(if filling is too stiff to spread, transfer to smaller bowl and microwave for 5 to 10 seconds). Fold upper third of dough over middle third. Fold lower third over middle third to create 10 by 6-inch rectangle. Roll into 12-inch square.

6. Cut dough into twelve 1-inch strips. Cut each strip in half lengthwise, leaving it attached at very top (each strip will look like a pair of legs). Extend 1 strip to 24-inch length, but do not stretch. Starting at 1 end, wrap strip around tips of your first 3 fingers, loosely coiling strands side by side along length of your fingers. Continue to wrap loosely until you have just 4 to 6 inches left. Use your thumb to pin dough to side of bundle closest to you, then loop remaining strip over bundle. Transfer to prepared sheet, tucking end of strip under bun. Repeat with remaining strips. Cover sheet with plastic or damp dish towel. Let sit until slightly puffed, about 1 hour.

7. About 15 minutes before baking, adjust oven rack to middle position and heat oven to 425 degrees. Brush buns with egg mixture (you won't need all of it) and sprinkle 1 teaspoon pearl sugar on top of each bun. Bake until buns are golden brown and register at least 200 degrees, 13 to 17 minutes, rotating sheet halfway through baking. Transfer buns, still on sheet, to wire rack and let sit for 5 minutes. Use spatula to transfer buns to wire rack (some filling may leak out and form crisp frill around bun). Let cool for at least 10 minutes before serving. (Buns can be cooled completely and stored in zipper-lock bag at room temperature for up to 2 days or frozen for up to 2 weeks.)

Shaping Kanelbullar

   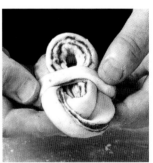

1. Starting at 1 end, wrap strip around tips of your first 3 fingers, coiling strands side by side along length of your fingers.

2. Continue to wrap loosely until you have just 4 to 6 inches left.

3. Use your thumb to pin dough to side of bundle closest to you.

4. Loop remaining strip over bundle and tuck into underside of bun.

Thin-Crust Pizza

Serves 4 to 6 • Total Time: 2¼ hours, plus 25 hours chilling and rising

Why This Recipe Works With home ovens that reach only 500 degrees and dough that's difficult to stretch thin, even the savviest cooks can struggle to produce parlor-quality pizza. We were in pursuit of a simple-to-make pizza with a New York–style crust: thin, crisp, and spottily charred on the exterior, tender yet chewy within. High-protein bread flour gave us a chewy, nicely tanned pizza crust and the right ratio of flour to water to yeast gave us dough that was easy to stretch and retained moisture as it baked. We kneaded the dough in a food processor then let it proof in the refrigerator for 24 hours to develop its flavors. After we shaped and topped the pizza, it went onto a blazing hot baking stone to cook. Placing the stone near the top of the oven was a surprising improvement, allowing the top of the pizza to brown as well as the bottom. In minutes we had a pizza with everything in sync: a thoroughly crisp, browned crust with a slightly chewy texture.

If you don't own a baking stone, bake the pizzas on a rimless or overturned baking sheet that has been preheated just like the pizza stone. If you don't own a pizza peel, stretch the dough on a large sheet of lightly floured parchment paper, transfer to a rimless or overturned baking sheet, and slide the pizza with the parchment onto the hot pizza stone. You can shape the second dough round while the first pizza bakes, but don't add the toppings until just before baking. It's important to use ice water in the dough to prevent it from overheating in the food processor. Semolina flour is ideal for dusting the peel; use it in place of bread flour if you have it. The sauce will yield more than needed in the recipe; extra sauce can be refrigerated for up to one week or frozen for up to one month.

Dough

- 3 cups (16½ ounces) bread flour
- 2 teaspoons sugar
- ½ teaspoon instant or rapid-rise yeast
- 1⅓ cups ice water
- 1 tablespoon vegetable oil
- 1½ teaspoons table salt

Sauce

- 1 (28-ounce) can whole tomatoes, drained
- 1 tablespoon extra-virgin olive oil
- 2 garlic cloves, minced
- 1 teaspoon red wine vinegar
- 1 teaspoon table salt
- 1 teaspoon dried oregano
- ¼ teaspoon pepper

- 1 ounce Parmesan cheese, grated fine (½ cup), divided
- 8 ounces whole-milk mozzarella, shredded (2 cups), divided

1. For the dough: Pulse flour, sugar, and yeast in food processor (fitted with dough blade, if possible) until combined, about 5 pulses. With food processor running, slowly add water; process until dough is just combined and no dry flour remains, about 10 seconds. Let dough sit for 10 minutes.

2. Add oil and salt to dough and process until dough forms satiny, sticky ball that clears sides of bowl, 30 to 60 seconds. Transfer dough to lightly oiled work surface and knead briefly by hand until smooth, about 1 minute. Shape dough into tight ball and place in large, lightly oiled bowl; cover bowl tightly with plastic wrap and refrigerate for at least 24 hours or up to 3 days.

3. For the sauce: Process all ingredients in clean bowl of food processor until smooth, about 30 seconds. Transfer to bowl and refrigerate until ready to use.

4. One hour before baking, adjust oven rack to upper-middle position (rack should be 4 to 5 inches from broiler), set baking stone on rack, and heat oven to 500 degrees. Transfer dough to clean work surface and divide in half. With your cupped palms, form each half into smooth, tight ball. Place balls of dough on lightly greased baking sheet, spacing them at least 3 inches apart; cover loosely with greased plastic wrap and let sit for 1 hour.

5. Coat 1 ball of dough generously with flour and place on well-floured work surface (keep other ball covered). Use your fingertips to gently flatten dough into 8-inch disk, leaving 1 inch of outer edge slightly thicker than center. Using your hands, gently stretch disk into 12-inch round, working along edges and giving disk quarter turns. Transfer dough to well-floured pizza peel and stretch into 13-inch round. Using back of spoon or ladle, spread ½ cup tomato sauce in thin layer over surface of dough, leaving ¼-inch border around edge. Sprinkle ¼ cup Parmesan evenly over the sauce, followed by 1 cup of mozzarella. Slide pizza carefully onto baking stone and bake until crust is well browned and cheese is bubbly and beginning to brown, 10 to 12 minutes, rotating pizza halfway through baking. Transfer pizza to a wire rack and let cool for 5 minutes before slicing and serving. Repeat step 5 to shape, top, and bake second pizza.

Great Homemade Pizza Starts in the Fridge

"I lived in Boston's North End for several years—an area rich in Italian culture and food—and I became absolutely spoiled for great pizza. After I moved to the 'burbs I tried making pizzas at home. They were meh: bready, kind of tough, kind of bland; definitely not like those blistered and bubbled, flavorful, Neapolitan-style, thin-crust pizzas I missed so much.

Enter this recipe, which improved my pizza-making abilities one hundredfold. The two main keys are time and temperature. Extending the amount of time that the dough spends in the initial proofing stage means the resulting baked crust will be exponentially more flavorful and have that bubbled texture. To extend this time, one must keep the dough cold at all times, which means using ice water to make the dough, blitzing the dough ingredients together at rapid speed in a food processor (instead of a mixer), and moving the dough to the refrigerator for three days. In the cold environment, favorable flavor compounds develop and off-flavors are kept at bay.

I also learned that positioning and heating a pizza stone on the top oven rack is the best way to mimic the hot, reflective heat found in commercial pizza (deck) ovens. That tip alone has changed the way I make pizzas of any kind."

—Bridget

Pizza al Taglio with Arugula and Fresh Mozzarella

Serves 4 to 6 • Total Time: 1½ hours, plus 18 hours chilling and rising

Why This Recipe Works Tender and airy yet substantial, this Roman pie is often topped like an open-faced sandwich. Roman pizzerias adorn it in a variety of ways and display it behind glass cases, where it is sold by the length and cut with scissors ("al taglio" means "by the cut"). It's also one of the easiest pizzas you'll ever make. Our dough contains lots of water and olive oil for a tender and airy crust with a crisp, light underside. Because the dough is so wet, we folded it by hand (rather than employ a stand mixer) to develop gluten. We placed the dough in a baking pan to proof overnight in the refrigerator to develop flavor and allow the dough to relax for easy stretching. We then coated the top of the dough with olive oil and turned it out onto a baking sheet. We stretched it to the edges of the sheet and allowed it to proof for an hour until it was bubbly and risen. Finally, we added the sauce and baked the pizza on the lowest rack of a 450-degree oven until the bottom was evenly browned and crisp before adding the toppings.

The dough for this pizza requires a 16- to 24-hour rest in the refrigerator. You'll get the crispest texture by using high-protein King Arthur bread flour, but other bread flours will also work. For the best results, weigh your flour and water. The bread flour should weigh 14⅔ ounces regardless of which brand of flour is used. Anchovies give the sauce depth, so don't omit them; they won't make the sauce taste fishy. Use the large holes of a box grater to shred the Parmesan.

Dough

- 2⅔ cups (14⅔ ounces) bread flour
- 1 teaspoon instant or rapid-rise yeast
- 1½ cups (12 ounces) water, room temperature
- 2 tablespoons extra-virgin olive oil
- 1¼ teaspoons table salt
- Vegetable oil spray

Sauce

- 1 (14.5-ounce) can whole peeled tomatoes, drained
- 1 tablespoon extra-virgin olive oil
- 2 anchovy fillets, rinsed
- 1 teaspoon dried oregano
- ½ teaspoon table salt
- ¼ teaspoon red pepper flakes

Topping

- ¼ cup extra-virgin olive oil, divided
- 4 ounces (4 cups) baby arugula
- 8 ounces fresh mozzarella cheese, torn into bite-size pieces (about 2 cups)
- 1½ ounces Parmesan cheese, shredded (½ cup)

1. For the dough: Whisk flour and yeast together in medium bowl. Add room-temperature water and oil and stir with wooden spoon until shaggy mass forms and no dry flour remains. Cover bowl with plastic wrap and let sit for 10 minutes. Sprinkle salt over dough and mix until fully incorporated. Cover bowl with plastic and let dough rest for 20 minutes.

2. Using your wet hands, fold dough over itself by gently lifting and folding edge of dough toward middle. Turn bowl 90 degrees; fold again. Turn bowl and fold dough 4 more times (total of 6 turns). Cover bowl with plastic and let dough rest for 20 minutes. Repeat folding technique, turning bowl each time, until dough tightens slightly, 3 to 6 turns total. Cover bowl with plastic and let dough rest for 10 minutes.

3. Spray bottom of 13 by 9-inch baking pan liberally with oil spray. Transfer dough to prepared pan and spray top of dough lightly with oil spray. Gently press dough into 10 by 7-inch oval of even thickness. Cover pan tightly with plastic and refrigerate for at least 16 hours or up to 24 hours.

4. For the sauce: While dough rests, process all ingredients in blender until smooth, 20 to 30 seconds. Transfer sauce to bowl, cover, and refrigerate until needed. (Sauce can be refrigerated for up to 2 days.)

5. For the topping: Brush top of dough with 2 tablespoons oil. Spray rimmed baking sheet (including rim) with oil spray. Invert prepared sheet on top of pan and flip, allowing dough to fall onto sheet (you may need to lift pan and nudge dough at 1 end to release). Using your fingertips, gently dimple dough into even thickness and stretch toward edges of sheet to form 15 by 11-inch oval. Spray top of dough lightly with oil spray, cover loosely with plastic, and let rest until slightly puffy, 1 to 1¼ hours.

6. Thirty minutes before baking, adjust oven rack to lowest position and heat oven to 450 degrees. Just before baking, use your fingertips to gently dimple dough into even thickness, pressing into corners of sheet. Using back of spoon or ladle, spread ½ cup sauce in even layer over surface of dough. (Remaining sauce can be frozen for up to 2 months.)

7. Drizzle 1 tablespoon oil over top of sauce and use back of spoon to spread evenly over surface. Transfer sheet to oven and bake until bottom of crust is evenly browned and top is lightly browned in spots, 20 to 25 minutes, rotating sheet halfway through baking. Transfer sheet to wire rack and let cool for 5 minutes. Run knife around rim of sheet to loosen pizza. Transfer pizza to cutting board and cut into 8 rectangles. Toss arugula with remaining 1 tablespoon oil in bowl. Top pizza with arugula, followed by mozzarella and Parmesan, and serve.

VARIATIONS

Pizza al Taglio with Potatoes and Soppressata

Decrease oil in topping to 3 tablespoons and omit arugula, mozzarella, and Parmesan. After spreading sauce over dough, lay 6 ounces thinly sliced soppressata in even layer over sauce, followed by 10 ounces thinly sliced provolone. Toss 1 pound peeled and thinly sliced small Yukon Gold potatoes with ½ teaspoon pepper and remaining 1 tablespoon oil. Starting in 1 corner, shingle potatoes to form even row across bottom of pizza, overlapping each slice by about one-quarter. Continue to layer potatoes in rows, overlapping each row by about one-quarter. Bake pizza as directed until bottom of crust is evenly browned and potatoes are browned around edges. Sprinkle pizza with 2 teaspoons chopped fresh parsley before serving.

Pizza al Taglio with Prosciutto and Figs

Omit sauce ingredients as well as arugula, mozzarella, and Parmesan in topping. Spread remaining 2 tablespoons oil evenly over dough. Bake pizza as directed until bottom of crust is evenly browned and top is lightly browned in spots. Let pizza cool, then cut as directed. Top slices of pizza with 4 ounces thinly sliced prosciutto, followed by 8 thinly sliced figs and 2 ounces thinly shaved ricotta salata.

Folding Dough

1. To fold dough in on itself, grasp section of dough with your wet fingertips and gently lift.

2. Place edge down in middle of dough. Rotate bowl 90 degrees and repeat for total of 6 turns.

SEASON 21

Cast Iron Pan Pizza

Serves 4 • **Total Time: 1¼ hours, plus 14 hours chilling and rising**

Why This Recipe Works This pizza recipe is dead simple: no rolling, stretching, or baking stone required. The crumb is thick, plush, and encased in a golden, crispy crust. We started with an easy stir-together dough of bread flour, salt, yeast, and warm water; the warm water jump-started yeast activity so that the crumb was open and light. Instead of kneading the dough, we let it rest overnight in the refrigerator. During this rest, the dough's gluten strengthened enough for the crust to support the toppings but still have a tender crumb. Baking the pie in a generously oiled cast-iron skillet "fried" the outside of the crust. We also moved the skillet to the stove for the last few minutes of cooking to crisp up the underside of the crust. For the crispy cheese edge known as frico, we pressed shredded Monterey Jack cheese around the edge of the dough and up the sides of the skillet. For the sauce, we crushed canned whole tomatoes by hand and then pureed them in the food processor with classic seasonings—no cooking required.

> *This pizza bakes in a 12-inch cast-iron skillet. Weigh the flour and water for the best results. Use a block cheese, not fresh mozzarella, for this recipe. Avoid preshredded cheese; it contains added starch, which gives the melted cheese a drier, chewier texture.*

Dough

- 2 cups (11 ounces) bread flour
- 1 teaspoon table salt
- 1 teaspoon instant or rapid-rise yeast
- 1 cup (8 ounces) warm water (105 to 110 degrees)
  Vegetable oil spray

Sauce

- 1 (14.5-ounce) can whole peeled tomatoes
- 1 teaspoon extra-virgin olive oil
- 1 garlic clove, minced
- ¼ teaspoon sugar
- ¼ teaspoon table salt
- ¼ teaspoon dried oregano
  Pinch red pepper flakes

Pizza

- 3 tablespoons extra-virgin olive oil
- 4 ounces Monterey Jack cheese, shredded (1 cup)
- 7 ounces whole-milk mozzarella cheese, shredded (1¾ cups)

1. For the dough: Using wooden spoon or spatula, stir flour, salt, and yeast together in bowl. Add warm water and mix until most of flour is moistened. Using your hands, knead dough in bowl until dough forms sticky ball, about 1 minute. Spray 9-inch pie plate or cake pan with oil spray. Transfer dough to prepared plate and press into 7- to 8-inch disk. Spray top of dough with oil spray. Cover tightly with plastic wrap and refrigerate for 12 to 24 hours.

2. For the sauce: Place tomatoes in fine-mesh strainer and crush with your hands. Drain well, then transfer to food processor. Add oil, garlic, sugar, salt, oregano, and pepper flakes and process until smooth, about 30 seconds. (Sauce can be refrigerated for up to 3 days.)

3. For the pizza: Two hours before baking, remove dough from refrigerator and let sit at room temperature for 30 minutes.

4. Coat bottom of 12-inch cast-iron skillet with oil. Transfer dough to prepared skillet and use your fingertips to flatten dough until it is ⅛ inch from edge of skillet. Cover tightly with plastic and let rest until slightly puffy, about 1½ hours.

5. Thirty minutes before baking, adjust oven rack to lowest position and heat oven to 400 degrees. Spread ½ cup sauce evenly over top of dough, leaving ½-inch border (save remaining sauce for another use). Sprinkle Monterey Jack evenly over border. Press Monterey Jack into side of skillet, forming ½- to ¾-inch-tall wall. (Not all cheese will stick to side of skillet.) Evenly sprinkle mozzarella over sauce. Bake until cheese at edge of skillet is well browned, 25 to 30 minutes.

6. Transfer skillet to stovetop and let sit until sizzling stops, about 3 minutes. Run butter knife around rim of skillet to loosen pizza. Using thin metal spatula, gently lift edge of pizza and peek at underside to assess browning. Cook pizza over medium heat until bottom crust is well browned, 2 to 5 minutes (skillet handle will be hot). Using 2 spatulas, transfer pizza to wire rack and let cool for 10 minutes. Slice and serve.

GAME CHANGER

A No-Knead Pizza Dough

"If you love pizza but aren't sure you're ready to commit to kneading and stretching dough, then this is the pizza for you. In fact, it's fine if you don't own a pizza stone or steel, or a peel. You could even skip the pizza wheel and slice this with a knife.

Pan pizzas feature a thick crust with an open and airy crumb. And getting that crumb doesn't require a mixer or food processor or knowing how to knead dough. Just combine the ingredients, making sure there aren't any dry pockets of flour and then pop the dough into the fridge. The work of developing a gluten network literally happens overnight. Gluten is responsible for the open, focaccia-like interior and appealing chew of a pizza's crust. Traditionally, kneading the dough creates that critical gluten network. But that structure can be created passively too. Given plenty of water and time, a gluten network forms naturally. You can take advantage of this if you're willing to put in 15 minutes of work the night before you want pizza. After the dough is stirred together, preshape it by pressing it into a disk before popping it into the fridge. Then the next day, you just let it warm up, top as desired, and you'll be digging into a slice half an hour later."

—Lan

Cast Iron Pan Pizza

Cookies

Photo: Big and Chewy Oatmeal-Raisin Cookies

Perfect Chocolate Chip Cookies

Makes 16 large cookies • Total Time: 1 hour, plus 20 minutes cooling

Why This Recipe Works Rich and buttery, with their soft cores and crispy edges, chocolate chip cookies are the American cookie-jar standard. Since Nestlé first began printing the recipe for Toll House cookies on the back of chocolate chip bags in 1939, generations of bakers have packed them into lunches and taken them to potlucks. But we wondered if this was really the best that a chocolate chip cookie could be. We wanted something more than the standard bake sale offering; we wanted a moist and chewy cookie with crisp edges and deep notes of toffee and butterscotch to balance its sweetness. Melting the butter before combining it with the other ingredients gave us the chewy texture we wanted, and browning a portion of it added nutty flavor. Upping the brown sugar enhanced chewiness, while a combination of one whole egg and one egg yolk gave us supremely moist cookies. For the crisp edges and deep toffee flavor, we allowed the sugar to dissolve and rest in the melted butter. We baked the cookies until golden brown and just set, but still soft in the center. The resulting cookies were crisp, chewy, and gooey with chocolate and boasted a complex medley of sweet, buttery, caramel, and toffee flavors.

Avoid using a nonstick skillet to brown the butter; the dark color of the nonstick coating makes it difficult to gauge when the butter is browned. Use fresh, moist brown sugar instead of hardened brown sugar, which will make the cookies dry. This recipe works with light brown sugar, but the cookies will be less full-flavored. If you're using smaller baking sheets, put fewer cookies on each sheet and bake them in batches.

1¾ cups (8¾ ounces) all-purpose flour
½ teaspoon baking soda
14 tablespoons unsalted butter, divided
¾ cup packed (5¼ ounces) dark brown sugar
½ cup (3½ ounces) granulated sugar
1 teaspoon table salt
2 teaspoons vanilla extract
1 large egg plus 1 large yolk
1¼ cups (7½ ounces) semisweet chocolate chips or chunks
¾ cup chopped pecans or walnuts, toasted (optional)

1. Adjust oven rack to middle position and heat oven to 375 degrees. Line 2 rimmed baking sheets with parchment paper. Whisk flour and baking soda together in medium bowl; set aside.

2. Melt 10 tablespoons butter in 10-inch skillet over medium-high heat, about 2 minutes. Continue cooking, stirring and scraping constantly with rubber spatula until milk solids are dark golden brown and butter has nutty aroma, 1 to 3 minutes. Immediately transfer browned butter to large heatproof bowl. Add remaining 4 tablespoons butter and stir until completely melted.

3. Add brown sugar, granulated sugar, salt, and vanilla to melted butter; whisk until fully incorporated. Add whole egg and egg yolk; whisk until mixture is smooth and no sugar lumps remain, about 30 seconds. Let mixture stand for 3 minutes, then whisk for 30 seconds. Repeat process of resting and whisking 2 more times until mixture is thick, smooth, and shiny. Using rubber spatula, stir in flour mixture until just combined, about 1 minute. Stir in chocolate chips and nuts, if using, giving dough final stir to ensure that no flour pockets remain.

4. Divide dough into 16 equal pieces, about 3 tablespoons each. Using your hands, roll dough into balls and space about 2 inches apart on prepared sheets.

5. Bake cookies, 1 sheet at a time, until golden brown and still puffy and edges have begun to set but centers are still soft, 10 to 14 minutes, rotating sheet halfway through baking. Transfer sheet to wire rack; let cool completely before serving.

Crispy Chocolate Chip Cookies

Makes 48 cookies • Total Time: 1 hour, plus 20 minutes cooling

Why This Recipe Works Too often, thin and crispy chocolate chip cookies are brittle and crumbly or tough and lacking flavor. We wanted cookies that were thin and packed a big crunch without breaking teeth or shattering into a million pieces when eaten. And they had to have the simple, gratifying flavors of deeply caramelized sugar and rich butter. For cookies with a notable butterscotch flavor and sufficient crunch, we turned to a combination of light brown sugar and white sugar. Next we focused on the thickness of our cookies. When butter is creamed with sugar, air cells are created in the batter; these cells expand during baking, leading to cookies that rise—and cookies with height were not what we wanted. So we used melted butter and milk to create a batter that would spread (not rise) in the oven, resulting in cookies with the perfect thin crispiness. A bit of baking soda and corn syrup promoted maximum browning and caramelization, and vanilla and salt gave our cookies the best flavor.

> *The dough, en masse or shaped into balls and wrapped well, can be refrigerated for up to two days or frozen for up to one month; bring it to room temperature before baking.*

1½ cups (7½ ounces) all-purpose flour
¾ teaspoon baking soda
¼ teaspoon table salt
8 tablespoons unsalted butter, melted and cooled
½ cup (3½ ounces) granulated sugar
⅓ cup packed (2⅓ ounces) light brown sugar
2 tablespoons light corn syrup
1 large egg yolk
2 tablespoons milk
1 tablespoon vanilla extract
¾ cup (4½ ounces) semisweet chocolate chips

1. Adjust oven rack to middle position and heat oven to 375 degrees. Line 2 rimmed baking sheets with parchment paper. Whisk flour, baking soda, and salt together in medium bowl; set aside.

2. In stand mixer fitted with paddle, beat melted butter, granulated sugar, brown sugar, and corn syrup at low speed until thoroughly blended, about 1 minute. Add egg yolk, milk, and vanilla; mix until fully incorporated and smooth, about 1 minute, scraping down bowl and beater as needed. With mixer still running on low, slowly add dry ingredients and mix until just combined. Do not overbeat. Add chocolate chips and mix until evenly distributed throughout batter, about 5 seconds.

3. Divide dough into 48 equal pieces, about 1 tablespoon each. Using your hands, roll dough into balls and space about 2 inches apart on prepared sheets. Bake, 1 sheet at a time, until cookies are deep golden brown and flat, about 12 minutes, rotating sheet halfway through baking.

4. Let cookies cool on sheets for 3 minutes, then transfer to wire rack and let cool completely before serving.

Chocolate Chip Cookie Ice Cream Sandwiches

Makes 12 sandwiches • Total Time: 1½ hours, plus 9 hours cooling and chilling

Why This Recipe Works The stars of this updated nostalgic treat are the thin, rich chocolate chip cookies we engineered for just the right texture and pliability to make them the perfect partner for the ice cream. We found that making a moister cookie was key, so we replaced the white sugar in our favorite chocolate chip cookie recipe with dark brown sugar, since the molasses it contains is a source of both water and simple sugars (glucose and fructose) that are hygroscopic—that is, very effective at attracting water. (It also added appealing toffee-like notes to the cookies.) The brown sugar boosted the dough's water content and ability to retain water. This dough was encouragingly moist, and the frozen cookies noticeably more tender, though still harder than we wanted. So next we went straight to the source and added various amounts of water along with the egg and vanilla. Ultimately, we settled on 2 tablespoons of water, which, when combined with a good 8 hours in the freezer, made for cookies that were sturdy enough to sandwich the ice cream, but tender enough to bite through with just a hint of snap. Browning all of the butter maximized the amount of browned flecks and aromatic compounds that make its flavor rich and round, and we upped the amount of vanilla and salt. The resulting cookies boasted big toffee-like, hazelnut-y richness even after spending hours in the freezer. Using mini chips added delicately crunchy bursts of chocolate.

These sandwiches should be made at least 8 hours before serving. We prefer the deeper flavor of dark brown sugar here, but light brown will also work. Use your favorite ice cream. If using a premium brand such as Ben and Jerry's or Häagen-Dazs, which tend to be harder when frozen, let the ice cream soften slightly in the refrigerator before scooping. If you have it, a #16 scoop works well for portioning the ice cream. We like these sandwiches with chocolate chips pressed into the sides, but the garnish is optional.

10 tablespoons unsalted butter
¾ cup (5¼ ounces) dark brown sugar
¾ teaspoon table salt
1 cup plus 2 tablespoons (5⅔ ounces) all-purpose flour
¼ teaspoon baking soda
1 large egg
2 tablespoons water
2 teaspoons vanilla extract
½ cup (3 ounces) mini semisweet chocolate chips, plus 1 cup for optional garnish
3 pints ice cream

1. Adjust oven rack to middle position and heat oven to 325 degrees. Melt butter in 10-inch skillet over medium-high heat, about 2 minutes. Continue cooking, stirring and scraping constantly with rubber spatula until milk solids are dark golden brown and butter has nutty aroma, 1 to 3 minutes. Immediately transfer to large heatproof bowl. Whisk in sugar and salt until fully incorporated and let mixture cool for 10 minutes. Meanwhile, line 2 rimmed baking sheets with parchment paper. Stir flour and baking soda together in bowl; set aside.

2. Add egg, water, and vanilla to browned butter mixture and whisk until smooth, about 30 seconds. Using rubber spatula, stir in flour mixture until combined. Stir in ½ cup chocolate chips. (Dough will be very soft.)

3. Using 1-tablespoon measure or #60 scoop, space 12 mounds of dough evenly on each prepared sheet. Bake, 1 sheet at a time, until cookies are puffed and golden brown, 9 to 12 minutes, rotating sheet halfway through baking. Let cookies cool on sheet for 5 minutes, then transfer to wire rack and let cool completely. Place 1 sheet, without discarding parchment, in freezer.

4. Place 4 cookies upside down on work surface. Quickly deposit 2-inch-tall and 2-inch-wide scoop of ice cream onto center of each cookie. Place 1 cookie from rack, right side up, on top of each scoop. Gently press and twist each sandwich between your hands until ice cream spreads to edges (this doesn't have to be perfect; ice cream can be neatened after chilling). Transfer sandwiches to sheet in freezer. Repeat with remaining cookies and ice cream. Place 1 cup chocolate chips, if using, in shallow bowl or pie plate.

5. Remove first 4 sandwiches from freezer. Hold 1 sandwich at a time over bowl of chips and gently press chips into sides with your other hand, neatening ice cream if needed. Return garnished sandwiches to freezer, and repeat with remaining 8 sandwiches in 2 batches. Freeze sandwiches for at least 8 hours before serving. (For longer storage, wrap each sandwich tightly with plastic wrap. Transfer wrapped sandwiches to zipper-lock bag and freeze for up to 2 months.)

GAME CHANGER

For Softer Frozen Cookies, Just Add Water

"'Sometimes all you need is a little water' is something that my first chef once told me as she adjusted the consistency of a pasta dish that I was making. She was referring to the fact that I didn't need more stock or butter or cheese but I've found this sentiment to be true time and again. The most surprising example was these ice cream sandwiches.

During recipe testing, my team endured sample after sample of sandwiches featuring cookies so firm that ice cream would squish out as we tried to take a bite. Everyone worried about cracking a tooth or wearing ice cream to the meeting after my tasting. We tossed around all sorts of ideas for modifying the texture of the cookies but none worked. It was when I bit into a sandwich that had been in the freezer for 24 hours that I began to understand. It had clearly absorbed water from the ice cream and softened slightly. So, I tried adding more water to the dough. Counterintuitive as it seems, adding water to this frozen treat was the key to softening the texture. That's because sugar dissolves in the water, preventing it from freezing."

—Lan

Big and Chewy Oatmeal-Raisin Cookies

Makes 18 large cookies
Total Time: 1 hour, plus 30 minutes cooling

Why This Recipe Works Big, moist, and craggy, oatmeal-raisin cookies are so good and so comforting, but also so hard to get just right. Too often, they have textural issues and other times the flavor is off, with cookies that lack any sign of oatiness. For an oversize, chewy cookie with buttery oat flavor, we discovered three key changes that made a significant difference. First, we substituted baking powder for baking soda, which gave the dough more lift and made the cookies less dense and a bit chewier. Second, we eliminated the cinnamon recommended in lots of recipes; by taking away the cinnamon, we revealed more oat flavor. We wanted some spice, however, and chose nutmeg, which has a cleaner, subtler flavor that we like with oats. Finally, we increased the sugar in our cookies, and this made a huge difference in terms of texture and moistness.

> *If you prefer a less sweet cookie, you can reduce the granulated sugar to ¾ cup, but you will lose some crispness. Do not overbake these cookies. The edges should be brown, but the rest of the cookie should be very light in color.*

- 1½ cups (7½ ounces) all-purpose flour
- ½ teaspoon table salt
- ½ teaspoon baking powder
- ¼ teaspoon freshly grated nutmeg
- 16 tablespoons unsalted butter, softened
- 1 cup packed (7 ounces) light brown sugar
- 1 cup (7 ounces) granulated sugar
- 2 eggs
- 3 cups (9 ounces) old-fashioned rolled oats
- 1½ cups (7½ ounces) raisins (optional)

1. Adjust oven racks to upper-middle and lower-middle positions and heat oven to 350 degrees. Line 2 large baking sheets with parchment paper. Whisk flour, salt, baking powder, and nutmeg together in medium bowl; set aside.

2. Using stand mixer fitted with paddle, beat butter, brown sugar, and granulated sugar at medium speed until light and fluffy, about 2 minutes. Add eggs, one at a time, and mix until combined, about 30 seconds.

3. Decrease speed to low and slowly add dry ingredients until combined, about 30 seconds. Mix in oats and raisins, if using, until just incorporated.

4. Divide dough into 18 equal pieces, generous 2 tablespoons each. Using your hands, roll them into balls and space about 2 inches apart on prepared sheets.

5. Bake until cookies turn golden brown around edges, 22 to 25 minutes, switching and rotating sheets halfway through baking. Let cookies cool on sheets for 2 minutes, then transfer to wire rack and let cool completely before serving.

VARIATION
Big and Chewy Oatmeal-Date Cookies
Substitute 1½ cups chopped dates for raisins.

SEASON 8
Brown Sugar Cookies

Makes 24 cookies • Total Time: 1¼ hours, plus 20 minutes cooling

Why This Recipe Works Simple sugar cookies, while classic, can seem too basic—even dull—at times. We wanted to turn up the volume on the sugar cookie by switching out the granulated sugar in favor of brown sugar. We had a clear vision of this cookie. It would be oversized, with a crackling crisp exterior and a chewy interior, and it would scream "brown sugar." We wanted butter for optimal flavor, but the traditional creaming method (creaming softened butter with sugar until fluffy, beating in an egg, and then adding the dry ingredients) gave us a cakey texture. Cutting the butter into the flour produced crumbly cookies. What worked was first melting the butter. We then tweaked the amount of eggs, dark brown sugar, flour, and leavener to give us a good cookie, but we wanted even more brown sugar flavor. We made progress by rolling the dough balls in a combination of brown and granulated sugar and adding a healthy amount of vanilla and table salt. But our biggest success came from an unlikely refinement. Browning the melted butter added a complex nuttiness that made a substantial difference.

Avoid using a nonstick skillet to brown the butter. The dark color of the nonstick coating makes it difficult to gauge when the butter is sufficiently browned. Use fresh brown sugar, as hardened brown sugar will make the cookies too dry. Achieving the proper texture—crisp at the edges and chewy in the middle—is critical to this recipe. Because the cookies are so dark, it's hard to judge doneness by color. Instead, gently press halfway between the edge and center of the cookie. When it's done, it will form an indentation with slight resistance. Check early and err on the side of underdone.

- 14 tablespoons unsalted butter, divided
- 1¾ cups packed (12¼ ounces) dark brown sugar, plus ¼ cup for rolling
- ¼ cup granulated sugar
- 2 cups plus 2 tablespoons (10⅔ ounces) all-purpose flour
- ½ teaspoon baking soda
- ¼ teaspoon baking powder
- ½ teaspoon table salt
- 1 large whole egg plus 1 large egg yolk
- 1 tablespoon vanilla extract

1. Melt 10 tablespoons butter in 10-inch skillet over medium-high heat, about 2 minutes. Continue cooking, stirring and scraping constantly with rubber spatula until milk solids are dark golden brown and butter has nutty aroma, 1 to 3 minutes. Immediately transfer to large heat-proof bowl. Stir remaining 4 tablespoons butter into hot butter to melt; set aside for 15 minutes.

2. Meanwhile, adjust oven rack to middle position and heat oven to 350 degrees. Line 2 large baking sheets with parchment paper. In shallow dish, mix ¼ cup brown sugar and granulated sugar, rubbing mixture between your fingers until well combined; set aside. Whisk flour, baking soda, and baking powder together in medium bowl; set aside.

3. Add remaining 1¾ cups brown sugar and salt to bowl with cooled butter; mix until no sugar lumps remain, about 30 seconds. Scrape down bowl with rubber spatula; add egg, egg yolk, and vanilla and mix until fully incorporated, about 30 seconds. Scrape down the bowl. Add flour mixture and mix until just combined, about 1 minute. Give dough final stir to ensure that no flour pockets remain and ingredients are evenly distributed.

4. Divide dough into 24 equal pieces, about 2 tablespoons each. Using your hands, roll them into balls. Working in batches, drop 12 dough balls into baking dish with sugar mixture and toss to coat. Space dough balls about 2 inches apart on prepared sheet; repeat with second batch of 12.

5. Bake 1 sheet at a time until cookies are browned and still puffy and edges have begun to set but centers are still soft (cookies will look raw between cracks and seem underdone), 12 to 14 minutes, rotating sheet halfway through baking. Do not overbake.

6. Let cookies cool on sheet for 5 minutes, then transfer to wire rack and let cool completely before serving.

SEASON 3

Molasses Spice Cookies

Makes 22 cookies • **Total Time: 1¼ hours, plus 20 minutes cooling**

Why This Recipe Works Molasses spice cookies are often disappointing: They can be dry and cakey without the requisite chew, or they might be timidly flavored with molasses and scantily spiced. We wanted to create the ultimate molasses spice cookie—soft, chewy, and gently spiced with deep, dark molasses flavor. We also wanted it to have the traditional cracks and crinkles so characteristic of these charming cookies. We started with all-purpose flour and butter for full, rich flavor. Using just the right amount of molasses and brown sugar and flavoring the cookies with a combination of vanilla, ginger, cinnamon, cloves, black pepper, and allspice gave these spiced cookies the warm tingle that we were after. We found that to keep the cookies mild, using a light or mild molasses was imperative; but if it's a stronger flavor you want, dark molasses is in order. We pulled the cookies from the oven when they still looked a bit underdone; residual heat finished the baking and kept the cookies chewy and moist.

GAME CHANGER

Always, Always, Always Underbake Your Cookies

"For me, cookie perfection starts with chewiness. Shortbread aside, I have never understood the appeal of a crisp cookie. There's something so utterly comforting about a cookie that gives away with the gentlest bite. And the absolute enemy of chewiness is overbaking. Because these cookies have so many lovely cracks, I finally understood just how much underbaking is necessary to achieve my desired texture. It's just fine—in fact, it's ideal—to remove the baking sheet from the oven when the cookies look decidedly underdone. After 5 minutes of 'cooling' on the still-hot baking sheet, residual heat will have finished the job and the cookies will have the ideal chewy texture. The cookies will firm up further when they reach room temperature. But I like to eat these spiced treats with big molasses flavor when they are still warm from the oven, the point at which they are no longer molten and are at their maximum chewiness."

—Jack

For best flavor, make sure that your spices are fresh. Light or mild molasses gives the cookies a milder flavor; for a stronger flavor, use dark molasses. Either way, measure molasses in a liquid measure. If you find that the dough sticks to your palms as you shape the balls, moisten your hands occasionally in a bowl filled with cold tap water and shake off the excess. Bake the cookies one sheet at a time; if baked two sheets at a time, the cookies started on the bottom rack won't develop attractive crackly tops. Remove the cookies from the oven when they still look slightly raw and underbaked.

⅓ cup (2⅓ ounces) granulated sugar, plus ½ cup for rolling
2¼ cups (11¼ ounces) all-purpose flour
1 teaspoon baking soda
1½ teaspoons ground cinnamon
1½ teaspoons ground ginger
½ teaspoon ground cloves
¼ teaspoon ground allspice
¼ teaspoon pepper
¼ teaspoon table salt
12 tablespoons unsalted butter, softened
⅓ cup packed (2⅓ ounces) dark brown sugar
1 large egg yolk
1 teaspoon vanilla extract
½ cup light or dark molasses

1. Adjust oven rack to middle position and heat oven to 375 degrees. Line 2 large baking sheets with parchment paper. Place ½ cup granulated sugar in shallow dish; set aside.

2. Whisk flour, baking soda, cinnamon, ginger, cloves, allspice, pepper, and salt together in medium bowl; set aside.

3. Using stand mixer fitted with paddle, beat butter, brown sugar, and remaining ⅓ cup granulated sugar on medium-high speed until light and fluffy, about 3 minutes. Decrease speed to medium-low and add egg yolk and vanilla; increase speed to medium and beat until incorporated, about 20 seconds. Decrease speed to medium-low and add molasses; beat until fully incorporated, about 20 seconds, scraping down bowl once with rubber spatula. Decrease speed to low and add flour mixture; beat until just incorporated, about 30 seconds, scraping down bowl once. Give dough final stir to ensure that no flour pockets remain. (Dough will be soft.)

4. Divide dough into 22 equal pieces, about 1 tablespoon each. Using your hands, roll them into balls. Working in batches of five, drop dough balls into baking dish with sugar and roll to coat. Space dough balls about 2 inches apart on prepared sheets.

5. Bake cookies, 1 sheet at a time, until cookies are browned, still puffy, and edges have begun to set but centers are still soft (cookies will look raw between cracks and seem underdone), about 11 minutes, rotating sheet halfway through baking. Do not overbake.

6. Let cookies cool on sheets for 5 minutes, then transfer cookies to wire rack and let cool completely before serving.

VARIATION

Molasses Spice Cookies with Dark Rum Glaze
If the glaze is too thick to drizzle, whisk in up to an additional ½ tablespoon rum.

Whisk 1 cup (4 ounces) confectioners' sugar and 2½ tablespoons dark rum together in medium bowl until smooth. Drizzle or spread glaze using back of spoon on cooled cookies. Allow glazed cookies to dry for at least 15 minutes.

SEASON 15

Chocolate Crinkle Cookies

Makes 22 cookies • Total Time: 1¼ hours, plus 20 minutes cooling

Why This Recipe Works Rolled in powdered sugar before going in the oven, chocolate crinkle cookies (aka earthquakes) form dark chocolaty fissures that break through the bright white surface during baking. When done well, they're eye-catching, with an irresistible deep chocolaty richness. But too often, these cookies turn out tooth-achingly sweet, with just a couple of gaping cracks instead of a crackly surface. We wanted a cookie with deep chocolate flavor and only enough sweetness to balance the chocolate's bitterness; a moist and tender—but not gooey—interior; and plenty of small irregular crinkly fissures breaking through a bright-white surface. For the best chocolate flavor, we used a combination of unsweetened chocolate and cocoa powder, which got an additional flavor boost from espresso powder. Using brown sugar instead of granulated lent a more complex, tempered sweetness with a bitter molasses edge that complemented the chocolate. A combination of baking powder and baking soda gave us cookies with the right amount of lift and spread and contributed to a crackly surface. But the real key was rolling the cookies in granulated sugar before the traditional powdered sugar. It not only helped produce the perfect crackly exterior by creating a "shell" that broke into numerous fine fissures as the cookie rose and spread, but it also helped the powdered sugar coating stay in place for chocolate crinkle cookies that lived up to their name.

The Ultimate Chocolate Experience

"Although this recipe was developed about a decade ago, I remember the details clearly. The test cook had baked five published recipes, and the results were disappointing to say the least. There were two clear camps: Those in the first looked perfect, but lacked true chocolate flavor. Those in the second were soft, chocolatey, and delicious, but failed miserably in appearance. The cook masterfully tested each variable until she reached her goal in creating the perfect cookie with a striking 'crinkly' surface; a pillowy, yet crisp-around-the-edges texture; and deep, dark chocolate flavor. This cookie is a true crowd pleaser and has since been my go-to recipe for entertaining, gifting, or any time that I have a craving for an ultimate chocolate experience."

— Erin

Both natural and Dutch-processed cocoa will work in this recipe.

1 cup (5 ounces) all-purpose flour
½ cup (1½ ounces) unsweetened cocoa powder
1 teaspoon baking powder
¼ teaspoon baking soda
½ teaspoon table salt
1½ cups packed (10½ ounces) brown sugar
3 large eggs
4 teaspoons instant espresso powder (optional)
1 teaspoon vanilla extract
4 ounces unsweetened chocolate, chopped
4 tablespoons unsalted butter
½ cup (3½ ounces) granulated sugar
½ cup (2 ounces) confectioners' sugar

1. Adjust oven rack to middle position and heat oven to 325 degrees. Line 2 baking sheets with parchment paper. Whisk flour, cocoa, baking powder, baking soda, and salt together in medium bowl; set aside.

2. Whisk brown sugar; eggs; espresso powder, if using; and vanilla together in large bowl. Microwave chocolate and butter in bowl at 50 percent power, stirring occasionally, until melted, 2 to 3 minutes.

3. Whisk chocolate mixture into egg mixture until combined. Fold in flour mixture until no dry streaks remain. Let dough sit at room temperature for 10 minutes.

4. Place granulated sugar and confectioners' sugar in 2 separate shallow dishes. Divide dough into equal pieces, about 2 tablespoons each. Using your hands, roll into balls (or use #30 scoop). Drop balls of dough into granulated sugar and roll to coat. Transfer balls to confectioners' sugar and roll to coat. Evenly space dough balls on prepared sheets, 11 dough balls per sheet.

5. Bake cookies, 1 sheet at a time, until cookies are puffed and cracked and edges have begun to set but centers are still soft (cookies will look raw between cracks and will seem underdone), about 12 minutes, rotating sheet halfway through baking. Let cool completely on baking sheet before serving.

Speculoos

Makes 32 cookies • Total Time: 1¼ hours, plus 1 hour 50 minutes chilling and cooling

Why This Recipe Works The enthusiasm for these humble cookies is understandable: Speculoos boast warm spice notes, nuanced caramel flavor, and a crisp, open texture that crumbles easily. Imagine something between a delicate graham cracker and a hard gingersnap that nearly melts in your mouth. The widely available packaged version of these Belgian treats, Biscoff cookies, gained a huge following when Delta Airlines started giving them away during flights. We aimed to create a homemade version that mimicked their caramel taste but improved the spice flavor. To achieve the appropriate texture, we rolled the dough thin so it would bake up dry and crisp, used only enough sugar to lightly sweeten the dough since sugar is hygroscopic and makes cookies moist, and added baking powder along with the usual baking soda to produce an open, airy crumb. For a subtle caramel taste, we chose turbinado sugar rather than molasses-based brown sugar or traditional Belgian brown sugar. To nail the spice flavor, we used a large amount of cinnamon along with small amounts of cardamom and cloves for complexity.

For the proper flavor, we strongly recommend using turbinado sugar (commonly sold as Sugar in the Raw). If you can't find it, use ¾ cup plus 2 tablespoons (6 ounces) of packed light brown sugar and skip the sugar grinding in step 2. In step 3, use a rolling pin and a combination of rolling and a smearing motion to form the rectangle. If the dough spreads beyond the rectangle, trim it and use the scraps to fill in the corners; then, replace the parchment and continue to roll. Do not use cookie molds or an embossed rolling pin for the speculoos; they will not hold decorations.

1½ cups (7½ ounces) all-purpose flour
5 teaspoons ground cinnamon
1 teaspoon ground cardamom
¼ teaspoon ground cloves
¼ teaspoon baking soda
¼ teaspoon baking powder
¼ teaspoon table salt
¾ cup (6 ounces) turbinado sugar
8 tablespoons unsalted butter, cut into ½-inch pieces and chilled
1 large egg

1. Whisk flour, cinnamon, cardamom, cloves, baking soda, baking powder, and salt together in bowl. Using pencil and ruler, draw 12 by 10-inch rectangle in center of each of 2 large sheets of parchment paper, crisscrossing lines at corners. (Use crisscrosses to help line up top and bottom sheets as dough is rolled.)

2. Process sugar in food processor for 30 seconds (some grains will be smaller than granulated sugar; others will be larger). Add butter and process until uniform mass forms and no large pieces of butter are visible, about 30 seconds, scraping down sides of bowl as needed. Add egg and process until smooth and paste-like, about 10 seconds, scraping down sides of bowl as needed. Add flour mixture and process until no dry flour remains but mixture remains crumbly, about 30 seconds, scraping down sides of bowl as needed.

3. Transfer dough to bowl and knead gently with spatula until uniform and smooth, about 10 seconds. Place 1 piece of parchment on counter with pencil side facing down (you should be able to see rectangle through paper). Place dough in center of marked rectangle and press into 9 by 6-inch rectangle. Place second sheet of parchment over dough, with pencil side facing up, so dough is in center of marked rectangle. Using pencil marks as guide, use rolling pin and bench scraper to shape dough into 12 by 10-inch rectangle of even ⅜-inch thickness. Transfer dough with parchment to rimmed baking sheet. Refrigerate until dough is firm, at least 1½ hours (or freeze for 30 minutes). (Rolled dough can be wrapped in plastic wrap and refrigerated for up to 5 days.)

4. Adjust oven racks to upper-middle and lower-middle positions and heat oven to 300 degrees. Line 2 rimless baking sheets with parchment. Transfer chilled dough to counter. Gently peel off top layer of parchment from dough. Using fluted pastry wheel (or sharp knife or pizza cutter) and ruler, trim off rounded edges of dough that extend over marked edges of 12 by 10-inch rectangle. Cut dough lengthwise into 8 equal strips about 1¼ inches wide. Cut each strip crosswise into 4 equal pieces about 3 inches long. Transfer cookies to prepared sheets, spacing them at least ½ inch apart. Bake until cookies are lightly and evenly browned, 30 to 32 minutes, switching and rotating sheets halfway through baking. Let cookies cool completely on sheets before serving. (Cookies can be stored at room temperature for up to 3 weeks.)

VARIATION
Speculoos with Almonds
Once dough has been rolled into rectangle in step 3, gently peel off top layer of parchment. Sprinkle ½ cup sliced almonds evenly over dough. Using rolling pin, gently press almonds into dough. Return parchment to dough, flip dough over, and transfer with parchment to sheet. Proceed with recipe as directed.

SEASON 19
Easy Holiday Sugar Cookies

Makes 40 cookies • Total Time: 1¾ hours, plus 3 hours 20 minutes chilling, cooling, and drying

Why This Recipe Works Our holiday roll-and-cut sugar cookies taste as great as they are easy to make. For a crisp and sturdy texture with no hint of graininess, we made superfine sugar by grinding granulated sugar briefly in the food processor, and we added small amounts of baking powder and baking soda to the dough. A touch of almond extract, added along with the usual vanilla, made these cookies taste more interesting without giving them overt almond flavor. We skipped creaming softened butter and sugar in favor of whizzing cold butter with sugar in the food processor, which let the dough come together in just minutes. The just-made dough was cold enough to be rolled out immediately, and we chilled it after rolling. For an even, golden color; minimal browning; and a crisp, crunchy texture from edge to edge, we baked the cookies at a gentle 300 degrees on a rimless cookie sheet (to promote air circulation) on the oven's lower-middle rack.

For the dough to have the proper consistency when rolling, make sure to use cold butter directly from the refrigerator. In step 3, use a rolling pin and a combination of rolling and a pushing or smearing motion to form the soft dough into an oval. A rimless cookie sheet helps achieve evenly baked cookies; if you do not have one, use an overturned rimmed baking sheet. Dough scraps can be combined and rerolled once, though the cookies will be slightly less tender. If desired, stir 1 or 2 drops of food coloring into the icing. For a pourable icing, whisk in milk, 1 teaspoon at a time, until the desired consistency is reached. You can also decorate the shapes with sanding sugar or sprinkles before baking.

Cookies

- 1 large egg
- 1 teaspoon vanilla extract
- ¾ teaspoon table salt
- ¼ teaspoon almond extract
- 2½ cups (12½ ounces) all-purpose flour
- ¼ teaspoon baking powder
- ¼ teaspoon baking soda
- 1 cup (7 ounces) granulated sugar
- 16 tablespoons unsalted butter, cut into ½-inch pieces and chilled

Royal Icing

- 2⅔ cups (10⅔ ounces) confectioners' sugar
- 2 large egg whites
- ½ teaspoon vanilla extract
- ⅛ teaspoon table salt

1. For the cookies: Whisk egg, vanilla, salt, and almond extract together in small bowl. Whisk flour, baking powder, and baking soda together in second bowl.

2. Process sugar in food processor until finely ground, about 30 seconds. Add butter and process until uniform mass forms and no large pieces of butter are visible, about 30 seconds, scraping down sides of bowl as needed. Add egg mixture and process until smooth and paste-like, about 10 seconds. Add flour mixture and process until no dry flour remains but mixture remains crumbly, about 30 seconds, scraping down sides of bowl as needed.

3. Turn out dough onto counter and knead gently by hand until smooth, about 10 seconds. Divide dough in half. Place 1 piece of dough in center of large sheet of parchment paper and press into 9 by 7-inch oval. Place second large sheet of parchment over dough and roll dough into 14 by 10-inch oval of even ⅛-inch thickness. Transfer dough with parchment to rimmed baking sheet. Repeat pressing and rolling with second piece of dough, then stack on top of first piece on sheet. Refrigerate until dough is firm, at least 1½ hours (or freeze for 30 minutes). (Rolled dough can be wrapped in plastic wrap and refrigerated for up to 5 days.)

4. Adjust oven rack to lower-middle position and heat oven to 300 degrees. Line rimless baking sheet with parchment. Working with 1 piece of rolled dough, gently peel off top layer of parchment. Replace parchment, loosely covering dough. (Peeling off parchment and returning it will make cutting and removing cookies easier.) Turn over dough and parchment and gently peel off and discard second piece of parchment. Using cookie cutter, cut dough into shapes. Transfer shapes to prepared sheet, spacing them about ½ inch apart. Bake until cookies are lightly and evenly browned around edges, 14 to 17 minutes, rotating sheet halfway through baking. Let cookies cool on sheet for 5 minutes, then transfer to wire rack and let cool completely. Repeat cutting and baking with remaining dough. (Dough scraps can be patted together, rerolled, and chilled once before cutting and baking.)

5. For the royal icing: Using stand mixer fitted with whisk attachment, whip all ingredients on medium-low speed until combined, about 1 minute. Increase speed to medium-high and whip until glossy, soft peaks form, 3 to 4 minutes, scraping down bowl as needed.

6. Spread icing onto cooled cookies. Let icing dry completely, about 1½ hours, before serving.

VARIATION
Easy Holiday Cocoa Sugar Cookies
Reduce vanilla extract to ½ teaspoon and substitute 1½ teaspoons espresso powder for almond extract. Add ⅓ cup (1 ounce) Dutch-processed cocoa powder to flour mixture in step 1.

Baci di Dama

Makes 32 sandwich cookies
Total Time: 1¼ hours, plus 1 hour cooling

Why This Recipe Works These tiny Italian hazelnut-chocolate sandwich cookies are typically made from a very rich, fragile dough that easily softens and crumbles when you roll it. Reducing the amount of butter and nuts in the dough made it firmer but still plenty rich and tender. We left bits of skin on the nuts to help firm up the dough and add complex flavor and attractive color. Instead of scooping and weighing dozens of individual pieces of dough, we found that it was much faster and easier to press the dough into a parchment paper–lined square baking pan, briefly freeze it to firm it up, and cut a "portion grid" into the resulting dough block. Melting dark chocolate in the microwave and letting it cool and thicken slightly before spooning it onto the inverted cookies ensured that it didn't drip off the sides. We gently pressed the second cookie on top to spread the filling just to the edges and then let the cookies rest for 15 minutes before serving to allow the chocolate to set.

> *Toast the hazelnuts on a rimmed baking sheet in a 325-degree oven until fragrant, 13 to 15 minutes, shaking the sheet halfway through toasting. To skin them, gather the warm hazelnuts in a dish towel and rub to remove some of the skins. A square-cornered metal baking pan works best for shaping the dough. If using a baking dish with rounded corners, be sure to square the corners of the dough before portioning. We prefer Ghirardelli 60% Cacao Bittersweet Chocolate Premium Baking Bar for this recipe.*

¾ cup hazelnuts, toasted and partially skinned
⅔ cup (3⅓ ounces) all-purpose flour
⅓ cup (2⅓ ounces) sugar
⅛ teaspoon table salt
6 tablespoons unsalted butter, cut into ½-inch pieces and chilled
2 ounces bittersweet chocolate, chopped

1. Adjust oven rack to middle position and heat oven to 325 degrees. Line 2 rimmed baking sheets with parchment paper. Line bottom of 8-inch square baking pan with parchment. Process hazelnuts, flour, sugar, and salt in food processor until hazelnuts are very finely ground, 20 to 25 seconds. Add butter and pulse until dough just comes together, 20 to 25 pulses.

Assembling Baci di Dama

1. To make quick work of assembling sandwich cookies, invert every other row of cookies.

2. Spoon melted chocolate onto centers of inverted cookies.

3. Top with remaining cookies.

2. Transfer dough to counter, knead briefly to form smooth ball, place in prepared pan, and press into even layer that covers bottom of pan. Freeze for 10 minutes. Run knife or bench scraper between dough and edge of pan to loosen. Turn out dough onto counter and discard parchment. Cut dough into 64 squares (8 rows by 8 rows). Roll dough squares into balls and evenly space 32 dough balls on each prepared sheet. Bake, 1 sheet at a time, until cookies look dry and are fragrant (cookies will settle but not spread), about 20 minutes, rotating sheet halfway through baking. Transfer sheet to wire rack and let cookies cool completely.

3. Microwave chocolate in small bowl at 50 percent power, stirring every 20 seconds, until melted, 1 to 2 minutes. Let chocolate cool at room temperature until it is slightly thickened and registers 80 degrees, about 10 minutes. Invert half of cookies on each sheet. Using ¼-teaspoon measure, spoon chocolate onto flat surfaces of all inverted cookies. Top with remaining cookies, pressing lightly to adhere. Let chocolate set for at least 15 minutes before serving. (Cookies can be stored in airtight container at room temperature for up to 10 days.)

SEASON 24

Alfajores de Maicena

Makes 24 cookies
Total Time: 1 hour, plus 2 hours chilling

Why This Recipe Works Beloved across Latin America, alfajores de maicena are buttery sandwich cookies that are often filled with the region's caramelized milk jam, dulce de leche. In this version, cornstarch in the dough leads to the characteristically crumbly, melt-in-the-mouth texture. Some recipes call for cornstarch alone, but we found the resulting cookies too fragile. Instead, we used slightly more cornstarch than flour by volume in our dough for powdery-soft cookies with enough structure to hold together when we filled them. Plenty of butter contributed additional tenderness and rich flavor. We opted for yolks instead of whole eggs, since the proteins in the whites would bind the dough and make the cookies less delicate. To provide contrast to the sweetness of the filling, we used only a modest amount of sugar in the dough. For the filling, we took a common shortcut and turned to the commercial kind. Nestlé La Lechera Dulce de Leche is thickened with agar-agar, so it is thick enough to keep its shape rather than oozing out from between the cookies. Doctoring it with a little vanilla and salt enhanced its complexity.

It's essential to buy the Nestlé La Lechera brand of canned dulce de leche, or the filling won't have the right consistency. Look for it near the sweetened condensed milk in the supermarket. You can also make your own filling by following the electric pressure cooker instructions in our recipe for Dulce de Leche (recipe follows). The brandy complements the flavors of the vanilla and lemon zest, but you can omit it, if preferred. Alfajores are fragile, so we've designed this recipe to make a few extra cookies in case some break. Coconut is a customary garnish, but you can also simply sift confectioners' sugar over the cookies before serving. Refrigerate any leftover dulce de leche in an airtight container for up to one month.

Filling
- 2 (13.4-ounce) cans Nestlé La Lechera Dulce de Leche
- 1 teaspoon vanilla extract
- ¼ teaspoon table salt

Cookies
- 1½ cups (6 ounces) cornstarch
- 1⅓ cups (6⅔ ounces) all-purpose flour
- 1 teaspoon baking powder
- ¼ teaspoon table salt
- 16 tablespoons unsalted butter, softened
- ½ cup (3½ ounces) sugar
- 3 large egg yolks
- 1 tablespoon brandy (optional)
- 1 teaspoon grated lemon zest
- 1 teaspoon vanilla extract
- 1 cup (3 ounces) unsweetened shredded coconut

1. For the filling: Transfer dulce de leche to medium bowl. Stir in vanilla and salt until thoroughly incorporated. Cover and refrigerate until mixture is completely chilled, at least 2 hours.

2. For the cookies: While filling chills, whisk cornstarch, flour, baking powder, and salt together in medium bowl. Using stand mixer fitted with paddle, beat butter and sugar on medium-high speed until pale and fluffy, 2 to 3 minutes. Add egg yolks; brandy, if using; lemon zest; and vanilla and beat until combined. Add cornstarch mixture; reduce speed to low; and mix until dough is smooth, scraping down bowl as needed.

3. Divide dough in half. Place 1 piece of dough in center of large sheet of parchment paper and press with your hand to ½-inch thickness. Place second large sheet of parchment over dough and roll dough to ¼-inch thickness. Using your flat hand on parchment, smooth out wrinkles on both sides. Transfer dough with parchment to rimmed baking sheet. Repeat pressing, rolling, and smoothing second piece of dough, then stack on top of first piece on sheet. Freeze until dough is firm, about 30 minutes.

4. Adjust oven racks to upper-middle and lower-middle positions and heat oven to 350 degrees. Transfer 1 piece of dough to counter. Peel off top layer of parchment and replace loosely. Flip dough and parchment. Peel away second piece of parchment and place on rimmed baking sheet. Using 2-inch round cutter, cut dough into rounds. Transfer rounds to prepared sheet, spaced about ½ inch apart. Repeat with remaining dough and second rimmed baking sheet. Reroll, chill, and cut scraps until you have 26 rounds on each sheet.

5. Bake until tops are set but still pale and bottoms are light golden, 10 to 12 minutes, switching and rotating sheets halfway through baking. Let cookies cool on sheets for 5 minutes, then carefully transfer to wire rack and let cool completely.

6. To assemble, place half of cookies upside down on counter. Place about 2 teaspoons filling on each upside-down cookie. Hold 1 topped cookie on fingers of 1 hand. Place second, untopped cookie on top of filling, right side up, and press gently with fingers of your other hand until filling spreads to edges. Repeat with remaining cookies.

7. Place coconut in small bowl. Working with 1 cookie at a time, roll sides of cookies in coconut, pressing gently to help coconut adhere to exposed filling. Serve immediately or refrigerate in airtight container for up to 5 days. Allow refrigerated cookies to sit out at room temperature for 10 minutes before serving.

Dulce de Leche

Makes 3⅓ cups • Total Time: 2½ hours

This recipe can be made in the oven or in an electric pressure cooker to produce slightly different consistencies. Dulce de leche cooked in the oven will be thick but pourable when warm—perfect for drizzling over pancakes, waffles, or ice cream or as a milky sweetener for coffee. Made in a multicooker, it will be thick enough to fill cookies (such as alfajores) or cakes or to spread on toast; note that you'll need a rack that fits inside your multicooker model.

- 2 (14-ounce) cans sweetened condensed milk
- 1 teaspoon vanilla extract
- ¼ teaspoon table salt

1A. For the oven: Adjust oven rack to middle position and heat oven to 350 degrees. Pour condensed milk into 13 by 9-inch baking pan. Cover pan tightly with aluminum foil. Pour 1 inch boiling water into large roasting pan and carefully set baking pan inside (water should come about halfway up sides of baking pan). Bake, topping up roasting pan with boiling water every 45 minutes, until condensed milk is brown and has jiggly, flan-like consistency, 2¼ to 2½ hours.

1B. For the multicooker: Set rack into 6- or 8-quart multicooker and add 8 cups water. If using a 6-quart multicooker use only 6 cups water (or bowl will float). Pour condensed milk into 8-inch-diameter stainless-steel bowl. Cover tightly with foil; set on rack. Lock lid into place and close pressure-release valve. Select high pressure-cook function and cook for 1 hour. Turn off multicooker and quick-release pressure. Carefully remove lid, allowing steam to escape away from you.

2. Carefully transfer cooked condensed milk (it will look broken and grainy) to fine-mesh strainer set over bowl. Stir and press solids with back of small ladle or spoon. Stir in vanilla and salt. Transfer to airtight container. (Dulce de leche can be refrigerated for up to 2 weeks.)

Filling a Sandwich Cookie

Press down gently on top cookie to ensure that dulce de leche is flush with rim of cookies so it can capture embellishments such as shredded coconut.

Crescent-Shaped Rugelach with Raisin-Walnut Filling

Makes 32 cookies • Total Time: 2 hours, plus 50 minutes freezing and cooling

Why This Recipe Works Part cookie, part pastry, rugelach are a traditional Jewish party snack. Their tight curls can contain a variety of bounteous sweet fillings, from nuts and jam to dried fruit and even chocolate. The dough is made with tangy cream cheese and bakes up tender and flaky; however, many rugelach doughs are sticky and hard to work with, so solving this problem was our first order of business. We started by adding more flour to the dough than traditional recipes call for, which helped make it more workable. A couple tablespoons of sour cream in addition to the cream cheese gave the cookies more tang and tenderized them further. For the filling, we settled on a generous combination of apricot preserves, raisins, and walnuts. To abate leaking, we finely chopped the nuts; smaller pieces were less likely to tear the dough. We also processed the preserves in a food processor to eliminate any large chunks.

Dough

- 2¼ cups (11¼ ounces) all-purpose flour
- 1½ tablespoons sugar
- ¼ teaspoon table salt
- 16 tablespoons unsalted butter, chilled and cut into ¼-inch pieces
- 8 ounces cream cheese, chilled and cut into ½-inch chunks
- 2 tablespoons sour cream

Fruit Filling

- 1 cup (7 ounces) sugar
- 1 tablespoon ground cinnamon
- ⅔ cup apricot preserves, processed briefly in food processor until smooth
- 1 cup raisins, preferably golden
- 2 cups walnuts, chopped fine

Glaze

- 2 large egg yolks
- 2 tablespoons milk

1. For the dough: Pulse flour, sugar, and salt in food processor until combined, about 3 pulses. Add butter, cream cheese, and sour cream; pulse until dough comes together in small, uneven pebbles the size of cottage cheese curds, about 16 pulses. Transfer dough to counter, press into 9 by 6-inch log, and divide log into 4 equal pieces. Form each piece into 4½ by ¾-inch disk. Place each disk between 2 sheets plastic wrap and roll into 8½-inch circle. Stack dough circles, between pieces of parchment paper, on plate; freeze for 30 minutes.

2. For the fruit filling: Meanwhile, combine sugar and cinnamon in small bowl; set aside. Line 2 rimmed baking sheets with parchment. Working with 1 dough circle at a time, remove dough from freezer and spread with 2½ tablespoons preserves. Sprinkle 2 tablespoons cinnamon sugar, ¼ cup raisins, and ½ cup walnuts over preserves and pat down gently with your fingers. Cut circle into 8 wedges. Roll each wedge into crescent shape; space crescents 2 inches apart on prepared sheets. Repeat with remaining dough rounds. Freeze crescents on sheets for 15 minutes. (To make ahead, cover baking sheet loosely with plastic and freeze crescents until firm, about 1¼ hours. Once frozen, transfer crescents to airtight container or zipper-lock bag and freeze for up to 6 weeks. To bake frozen rugelach, place on parchment-lined baking sheets and glaze and bake immediately, increasing baking time by 6 to 7 minutes.)

3. For the glaze: Adjust oven racks to upper-middle and lower-middle positions and heat oven to 375 degrees. Whisk egg yolks and milk in bowl. Brush crescents with glaze. Bake until rugelach are pale golden and slightly puffy, 21 to 23 minutes, switching and rotating sheets halfway through baking. Sprinkle each cookie with scant teaspoon cinnamon sugar. Transfer rugelach to wire rack with metal spatula and let cool completely before serving. (Rugelach can be stored at room temperature for up to 4 days.)

Meringue Christmas Trees

Makes about 50 cookies • Total Time: 1¾ hours, plus 1 hour 20 minutes cooling

Why This Recipe Works This standout holiday cookie pairs crisp, sweet meringue with milk chocolate kisses and colorful, festive decorations for a showstopping treat that resembles a miniature trimmed Christmas tree. We whipped egg whites to stiff peaks and then incorporated green food coloring before piping the glossy mixture onto baking sheets using a pastry bag fitted with a star tip. To trim the tree with colorful "lights" and "ornaments," we chose multicolor nonpareils and yellow sugar stars, but you can decorate however you like. To finish, we cut a small hole in the bottom of each tree and snugly affixed a Hershey's Kiss (with the help of some melted chocolate) to serve as the trunk of our tree.

> *You'll need a 12-ounce bag of Hershey's Kisses for this recipe (you'll have a few left over). If baking on a humid day, let the meringues cool in a turned-off oven for an additional hour without opening the door and then immediately seal them in an airtight container. We used 9 drops of food coloring; for a lighter or darker green, use 8 or 10 drops.*

¾ cup (5¼ ounces) granulated sugar
2 teaspoons cornstarch
4 large egg whites
¾ teaspoon vanilla extract
8–10 drops green food coloring
⅛ teaspoon table salt
Sugar stars
Multicolored nonpareils
62 Hershey's Kisses, unwrapped
Confectioners' sugar

1. Adjust oven racks to upper-middle and lower-middle positions and heat oven to 225 degrees. Line 2 baking sheets with parchment paper. Combine granulated sugar and cornstarch in small bowl. Using stand mixer fitted with whisk attachment, whip egg whites, vanilla, food coloring, and salt on medium-low speed until foamy, about 1 minute. Increase speed to medium-high and whip whites to soft, billowy mounds, about 1 minute. Gradually add sugar mixture and whip until glossy, stiff peaks form, 2 to 3 minutes.

2. Working quickly, fill pastry bag fitted with ¼- to ⅝-inch star tip with meringue. Pipe 1-inch-wide stars, spaced 1 inch apart, on prepared sheets. Top each star with another smaller star; then pipe even smaller star on top (trees should be 1½ inches tall). Place sugar star on top of each tree and sprinkle nonpareils around sides.

3. Bake meringues for 1 hour, switching and rotating sheets halfway through baking. Turn off oven and let meringues cool in oven for at least 1 hour. Transfer sheets to wire rack and let meringues cool completely.

4. Microwave 12 candies at 50 percent power until melted, 1 to 2 minutes. Using paring knife, gently cut small hole in bottom of each tree. Press tips of remaining candies into melted chocolate and then snugly into each hole. Dust trees with confectioners' sugar before serving.

Chewy Brownies

**Makes 24 brownies
Total Time: 1 hour, plus 2½ hours cooling**

Why This Recipe Works Our goal was clear: a homemade brownie with chewiness to rival the boxed-mix standard—but flush with a rich, deep chocolate flavor. Boxed brownie mixes derive their chewy texture from the right combination of saturated (solid) and unsaturated (liquid) fats: Unsaturated vegetable oil and powdered solid fat combine in a ratio designed to deliver maximum chew. To get the same chew, we tested and tested until we finally homed in on the ratio that produced the chewiest brownie. To combat greasiness, we replaced some of the oil with egg yolks, whose emulsifiers prevented fat from separating and leaking out during baking. We focused on flavor next. Unsweetened chocolate contains a similar ratio of saturated and unsaturated fat to butter, so we replaced some of the butter with unsweetened chocolate, thereby providing more chocolate flavor.

Espresso powder improved the chocolate taste as well. And finally, folding in bittersweet chocolate chunks just before baking gave our chewy, fudgy brownies gooey pockets of melted chocolate.

For an accurate measurement of boiling water, bring a full kettle of water to a boil, then measure out the desired amount. For the chewiest texture, it is important to let the brownies cool thoroughly before cutting. If your baking dish is glass, let the brownies cool for 10 minutes, then remove them promptly from the pan (otherwise, the superior heat retention of glass can lead to overbaking). While any high-quality chocolate can be used, our preferred brand of bittersweet chocolate is Ghirardelli 60% Cacao Bittersweet Chocolate Premium Baking Bar. Our preferred brand of unsweetened chocolate is Baker's.

⅓ cup (1 ounce) Dutch-processed cocoa powder
1½ teaspoons instant espresso powder (optional)
½ cup plus 2 tablespoons boiling water
2 ounces unsweetened chocolate, chopped fine
½ cup plus 2 tablespoons vegetable oil
4 tablespoons unsalted butter, melted
2 large eggs plus 2 large yolks
2 teaspoons vanilla extract
2½ cups (17½ ounces) sugar
1¾ cups (8¾ ounces) all-purpose flour
¾ teaspoon table salt
6 ounces bittersweet chocolate, cut into ½-inch pieces

1. Adjust oven rack to lowest position and heat oven to 350 degrees. Make foil sling for 13 by 9-inch baking pan by folding 2 long sheets of aluminum foil; first sheet should be 13 inches wide and second sheet should be 9 inches wide. Lay sheets of foil in pan perpendicular to each other, with extra foil hanging over edges of pan. Push foil into corners and up sides of pan, smoothing foil flush to pan. Lightly spray foil with vegetable oil spray.

2. Whisk cocoa; espresso powder, if using; and boiling water in large bowl until smooth. Add unsweetened chocolate and whisk until chocolate is melted. Whisk in oil and melted butter. (Mixture may look curdled.) Add eggs and yolks and vanilla and continue to whisk until smooth and homogeneous. Whisk in sugar until fully incorporated. Add flour and salt and mix with rubber spatula until combined. Fold in bittersweet chocolate pieces.

3. Scrape batter into prepared pan and bake until toothpick inserted halfway between edge and center comes out with few moist crumbs attached, 30 to 35 minutes. Transfer pan to wire rack and let cool for 1½ hours.

4. Loosen edges with paring knife. Using foil overhang, lift brownies out of pan. Return brownies to wire rack and let cool completely. Cut into 2-inch squares and serve. (Brownies can be stored in airtight container at room temperature for up to 4 days.)

Making a Foil Sling

1. Place 2 sheets of aluminum foil perpendicular to each other in baking pan, with extra foil hanging over edges of pan. Push foil into corners and up sides of pan, smoothing out any wrinkles in foil.

2. After brownies or bars have baked and cooled, use foil sling to lift and transfer them to cutting board before cutting into squares.

Caramel

- 6 tablespoons heavy cream
- ¼ teaspoon table salt
- ¼ cup water
- 2 tablespoons light corn syrup
- 1¼ cups (8¾ ounces) sugar
- 2 tablespoons unsalted butter
- 1 teaspoon vanilla extract

Brownies

- 8 tablespoons unsalted butter, cut into 8 pieces
- 4 ounces bittersweet chocolate, chopped
- 2 ounces unsweetened chocolate, chopped
- ¾ cup (3¾ ounces) all-purpose flour
- ½ teaspoon baking powder
- 2 large eggs, room temperature
- 1 cup (7 ounces) sugar
- 2 teaspoons vanilla extract
- ¼ teaspoon table salt
- ⅔ cup chopped pecans, plus 25 toasted pecan halves, divided
- ⅓ cup (2 ounces) semisweet chocolate chips (optional)

SEASON 25

Ultimate Turtle Brownies

Makes 25 brownies • Total Time: 1¾ hours, plus 3½ hours cooling and chilling

Why This Recipe Works Dark chocolate brownies, rich caramel, and crunchy pecans—this irresistible combination featured in turtle brownies is hard to beat. But many recipes for this treat call for box mixes and jarred caramel sauce; unsurprisingly, these shortcuts yield lackluster and sickly sweet results. For brownies reminiscent of the classic turtle candy, we started with a basic recipe: Whole eggs, a modest amount of flour, and baking powder gave us brownies with a structure that was partway between cakey and chewy—perfect for supporting a blanket of caramel. A combination of bittersweet and unsweetened chocolate struck just the right balance. Garnishing each brownie with a pecan half made them look like turtles, but they didn't taste like turtles until we stirred chopped pecans into the brownie batter as well. We wanted a thick, shiny caramel that wouldn't drip off the brownies, but that also wouldn't tug at our teeth. Caramel made with cream, butter, and sugar was pleasantly chewy and gooey, and a little corn syrup prevented it from crystallizing. Swirling some caramel into the batter and pouring more over the top ensured plenty of rich, gooey caramel in every bite.

> *If the caramel is too cool to be fluid, reheat it in the microwave. Be sure to use a metal baking pan and not a glass baking dish in this recipe.*

1. For the caramel: Combine cream and salt in small bowl; stir well to dissolve salt. Combine water and corn syrup in medium saucepan; pour sugar into center of saucepan, taking care not to let sugar granules touch sides of saucepan. Gently stir with spatula to moisten sugar thoroughly. Cover and bring to boil over medium-high heat and cook, covered and without stirring, until sugar is completely dissolved and liquid is clear, 3 to 5 minutes. Uncover and continue to cook, without stirring, until bubbles show faint golden color, 3 to 5 minutes longer. Reduce heat to medium-low and continue to cook, swirling saucepan occasionally, until caramel is light amber and registers about 360 degrees, 1 to 3 minutes longer. Off heat, carefully add cream mixture to center of saucepan; stir (mixture will bubble and steam vigorously) until cream is fully incorporated and bubbling subsides. Stir in butter and vanilla until combined. Transfer caramel to liquid measuring cup or bowl; set aside.

2. For the brownies: Adjust oven rack to lower-middle position and heat oven to 325 degrees. Make foil sling for 9-inch square baking pan by folding 2 long sheets of aluminum foil so each is 9 inches wide. Lay sheets of foil in pan perpendicular to each other, with extra foil hanging over edges of pan. Push foil into corners and up sides of pan, smoothing foil flush to pan. Grease foil.

3. Microwave butter, bittersweet chocolate, and unsweetened chocolate in bowl at 50 percent power, stirring occasionally, until melted and smooth, 2 to 4 minutes; set aside and let cool slightly. Meanwhile, whisk flour and baking powder together in second bowl; set aside.

Whisk eggs in large bowl to combine; add sugar, vanilla, and salt and whisk until incorporated. Add cooled chocolate mixture to egg mixture and whisk until combined. Using rubber spatula, stir in flour mixture until almost combined. Stir in chopped pecans and chocolate chips, if using, until incorporated and no flour streaks remain.

4. Spread half of brownie batter in even layer in prepared pan. Using greased ¼-cup dry measuring cup, drizzle ¼ cup caramel over batter. Using spoon, dollop remaining batter in large mounds over caramel layer and spread into even layer. Drizzle another ¼ cup caramel over top. Using butter knife, swirl brownie batter through caramel. Bake until toothpick inserted in center comes out with few moist crumbs attached, 35 to 40 minutes, rotating pan halfway through baking. Let brownies cool completely in pan on wire rack, about 1½ hours.

5. Heat remaining caramel (you should have about ¾ cup) in microwave until warm and pourable but still thick (do not boil), 45 to 60 seconds, stirring once or twice; pour caramel over brownies. Spread caramel to cover surface. Refrigerate brownies, uncovered, for 2 hours.

6. Using foil overhang, lift brownies out of pan, loosening sides with paring knife if needed, and transfer to cutting board. Using chef's knife, cut brownies into 25 pieces. Press pecan half onto surface of each brownie. Serve chilled or at room temperature. (Brownies can be refrigerated for up to 3 days.)

SEASON 22

Browned Butter Blondies

Makes 24 blondies
Total Time: 1¼ hours, plus 2 hours cooling

Why This Recipe Works For a blondie that's chewy but not too sweet, we found that you can't simply swap in a cookie dough or brownie batter. Using melted rather than creamed butter made for a blondie that was dense and chewy instead of cakey. To boost the blondie's flavor with nutty complexity, we browned the butter first. Brown sugar was a must for its underlying caramel notes, and its moistness contributed to a chewy texture. To tone down the sweetness, we replaced a portion of the sugar with corn syrup. A full 2 tablespoons of vanilla brought more complexity to the bars, and a generous amount of salt in the batter and sprinkled on top brought all the flavors into focus. Chopped pecans and milk chocolate chips complemented the butterscotch flavor without overwhelming it.

We developed this recipe using a metal baking pan; using a glass baking dish may cause the blondies to overbake. Toast the pecans on a rimmed baking sheet in a 350-degree oven until fragrant, 8 to 12 minutes, stirring them halfway through.

2¼ cups (11¼ ounces) all-purpose flour
1¼ teaspoons table salt
½ teaspoon baking powder
12 tablespoons unsalted butter
1¾ cups packed (12¼ ounces) light brown sugar
3 large eggs
½ cup corn syrup
2 tablespoons vanilla extract
1 cup pecans, toasted and chopped coarse
½ cup (3 ounces) milk chocolate chips
¼–½ teaspoon flake sea salt, crumbled (optional)

1. Adjust oven rack to middle position and heat oven to 350 degrees. Make foil sling for 13 by 9-inch baking pan by folding 2 long sheets of aluminum foil; first sheet should be 13 inches wide and second sheet should be 9 inches wide. Lay sheets of foil in pan perpendicular to each other, with extra foil hanging over edges of pan. Push foil into corners and up sides of pan, smoothing foil flush to pan. Lightly spray foil with vegetable oil spray.

2. Whisk flour, table salt, and baking powder together in medium bowl.

3. Heat butter in 10-inch skillet over medium-high heat until melted, about 2 minutes. Continue cooking, stirring and scraping constantly with rubber spatula until milk solids are dark golden brown and butter has nutty aroma, 1 to 3 minutes. Immediately transfer to large heatproof bowl.

4. Add sugar to hot butter and whisk until combined. Add eggs, corn syrup, and vanilla and whisk until smooth. Using rubber spatula, stir in flour mixture until fully incorporated. Stir in pecans and chocolate chips. Transfer batter to prepared pan; using spatula, spread batter into corners of pan and smooth surface. Sprinkle with sea salt, if using. Bake until top is deep golden brown and springs backs when lightly pressed, 35 to 40 minutes, rotating pan halfway through baking (blondies will firm as they cool).

5. Let blondies cool completely in pan on wire rack, about 2 hours. Using foil overhang, lift blondies out of pan and transfer to cutting board. Remove foil. Cut into 24 bars and serve. (Blondies can be wrapped tightly in plastic wrap and stored at room temperature for up to 5 days.)

Browned Butter Blondies

Millionaire's Shortbread

Makes 40 cookies • Total Time: 1½ hours, plus 1¾ hours cooling

Why This Recipe Works Millionaire's shortbread has a lot going for it: a crunchy shortbread base topped with a chewy, caramel-like layer, all covered in shiny, snappy chocolate. We wanted foolproof methods for producing all three layers. We started by making a quick pat-in-the-pan short-bread with melted butter. Sweetened condensed milk was important to the creaminess of the middle layer, but we needed to add a little heavy cream to keep it from sepa-rating. Gently heating the chocolate in the microwave and stirring in grated chocolate created a firm top layer, which made a suitably elegant finish for this rich yet refined cookie.

> *For a caramel filling with the right texture, monitor the temperature with an instant-read thermometer. We prefer Ghirardelli 60% Cacao Bittersweet Chocolate Premium Baking Bar for this recipe. Grating a portion of the chocolate is important for getting the chocolate to set properly; the small holes on a box grater work well for this task. Stir often while melting the chocolate and don't overheat it.*

Crust

2½ cups (12½ ounces) all-purpose flour
½ cup (3½ ounces) granulated sugar
¾ teaspoon table salt
16 tablespoons unsalted butter, melted

Filling

1 (14-ounce) can sweetened condensed milk
1 cup packed (7 ounces) brown sugar
½ cup heavy cream
½ cup corn syrup
8 tablespoons unsalted butter
½ teaspoon table salt

Chocolate

8 ounces bittersweet chocolate (6 ounces chopped fine, 2 ounces grated)

1. For the crust: Adjust oven rack to lower-middle position and heat oven to 350 degrees. Make foil sling for 13 by 9-inch baking pan by folding 2 long sheets of aluminum foil; first sheet should be 13 inches wide and second sheet should be 9 inches wide. Lay sheets of foil in pan perpendicular to each other, with extra foil hanging over edges of pan. Push foil into corners and up sides of pan, smoothing foil flush to pan. Combine flour, sugar, and salt in medium bowl. Add melted butter and stir with rubber spatula until flour is evenly moist-ened. Crumble dough evenly over bottom of prepared pan. Using your fingertips and palm of your hand, press and smooth dough into even thickness. Using fork, pierce dough at 1-inch intervals. Bake until light golden brown and firm to touch, 25 to 30 minutes. Transfer pan to wire rack. Using sturdy metal spatula, press on entire surface of warm crust to compress (this will make finished bars easier to cut). Let crust cool until it is just warm, at least 20 minutes.

2. For the filling: Stir all ingredients together in large, heavy-bottomed saucepan. Cook over medium heat, stirring frequently, until mixture registers between 236 and 239 degrees (temperature will fluctuate), 16 to 20 minutes. Pour over crust and spread to even thickness (mixture will be very hot). Let cool completely, about 1½ hours.

3. For the chocolate: Microwave chopped chocolate in bowl at 50 percent power, stirring every 15 seconds, until melted but not much warmer than body temperature (check by holding in palm of your hand), 1 to 2 minutes. Add grated chocolate and stir until smooth, returning to microwave for no more than 5 seconds at a time to finish melting if necessary. Spread chocolate evenly over surface of filling. Refrigerate shortbread until chocolate is just set, about 10 minutes.

4. Using foil overhang, lift shortbread out of pan and transfer to cutting board; discard foil. Using serrated knife and gentle sawing motion, cut shortbread in half crosswise to create two 9 by 6½-inch rectangles. Cut each rectangle in half to make four 9 by 3½-inch strips. Cut each strip crosswise into 10 equal pieces and serve. (Shortbread can be stored at room temperature, between layers of parchment, for up to 1 week.)

Extraordinary Confections Don't Always Require Extraordinary Work

"I had millionaire's shortbread for the first time during a family visit to Scotland many years ago and immediately thought I had come across pastry perfection. The layers of crisp shortbread, burnished toffee, and tempered, dark chocolate were in perfect balance. Such creations usually require attention and patience, which can be frustrating for the home baker.

This recipe masterfully breaks down each of the components, always with simplicity as the driving force. The shortbread crust is a melted butter, pat-in-the-pan affair. The toffee uses a little corn syrup to stave off that insidious enemy of caramel-work: crystallization. Even the method of tempering chocolate to achieve a thin, snappy veneer gets a makeover. Instead of a thermometer, bench scrapers, and a slab of marble, a microwave oven re-creates that tempering magic in minutes.

With all of these recipe modifications, one might think that the result would be a magnificent mire of mediocrity. Not so. I'd say that those smart simplifications made this shortbread a billion times better."

—Bridget

SEASON 2

Raspberry Squares

Makes 25 squares • Total Time: 1½ hours, plus 1½ hours cooling

Why This Recipe Works Raspberry squares are one of the best, and easiest, bar cookies to prepare, especially since the filling is ready-made (a jar of raspberry preserves). But sometimes the proportions are uneven, leaving you feeling parched from too much sandy crust, or puckered up from an overload of tart filling. We were after a buttery, tender, golden brown crust and crumb topping with just the right amount of sweet and tart raspberry preserves in the middle.

For the tender, almost (but not quite) sandy crumb, we had to get the right combination of ingredients, especially the butter and sugar. Too much butter made the raspberry squares greasy, but too little left them on the dry side. We found that equal amounts of white and light brown sugar made for a deeper flavor than white alone; oats and nuts made a subtle contribution to flavor while also adding some textural interest. For a golden brown bottom crust, we prebaked it before layering it with raspberry preserves and sprinkling on the top crust, which was a small amount of the reserved bottom crust mixture.

For a nice presentation, trim ¼ inch off the outer rim of the uncut baked block. The outside edges of all cut squares will then be neat.

1½   cups (7½ ounces) all-purpose flour

1¼   cups (3¾ ounces) quick oats

½   cup pecans or almonds, chopped fine

⅓   cup (2⅓ ounces) granulated sugar

⅓   cup packed (2⅓ ounces) light brown sugar

¼   teaspoon baking soda

¼   teaspoon table salt

12   tablespoons unsalted butter, cut into 12 pieces and softened

1   cup raspberry preserves

1. Adjust oven rack to lower-middle position and heat oven to 350 degrees. Make foil sling for 9-inch square baking pan by folding 2 long sheets of aluminum foil so each is 9 inches wide. Lay sheets of foil in pan perpendicular to each other, with extra foil hanging over edges of pan. Push foil into corners and up sides of pan, smoothing foil flush to pan. Spray with vegetable oil spray.

2. Whisk flour, oats, pecans, granulated sugar, brown sugar, baking soda, and salt together in large bowl. Using stand mixer fitted with paddle, beat flour mixture and butter at low speed until well blended and mixture resembles wet sand, about 2 minutes.

3. Transfer two-thirds of mixture to prepared pan. Press crumbs evenly and firmly into bottom of pan. Bake until just starting to brown, about 20 minutes. Using rubber spatula, spread preserves evenly over hot crust; sprinkle remaining flour mixture evenly over preserves. Bake until bubbling around edges and top is golden brown, about 30 minutes, rotating pan halfway through baking. Let cool completely in pan on wire rack. Using foil overhang, lift bars out of pan and transfer to cutting board. Cut bars into 25 squares and serve.

SEASON 19

Best Lemon Bars

Makes 12 bars • Total Time: 1 hour, plus 1½ hours cooling time

Why This Recipe Works For the lemoniest lemon bars with a sweet-tart flavor, a silky-smooth filling, and a crisp, well-browned crust, we started at the bottom. Our pat-in-the-pan crust is made with melted—not cold—butter and can therefore be stirred together instead of requiring a food processor. For a truly crisp texture, we used granulated sugar instead of the usual confectioners' sugar and baked the crust until it was dark golden brown to ensure that it retained its crispness even after we topped it with

the lemon filling. We cooked our lemon filling on the stove to shorten the oven time and keep it from curdling or browning at the edges when it baked. A combination of lemon juice and lemon zest provided complex flavor and aroma, and a unique ingredient—cream of tartar (tartaric acid)—gave the bars a bold sharpness and bright, lingering finish.

| *Do not substitute bottled lemon juice for fresh here.*

Crust

1   cup (5 ounces) all-purpose flour

¼   cup (1¾ ounces) granulated sugar

½   teaspoon table salt

8   tablespoons unsalted butter, melted

Filling

1   cup (7 ounces) granulated sugar

2   tablespoons all-purpose flour

2   teaspoons cream of tartar

¼   teaspoon table salt

3   large eggs plus 3 large yolks

2   teaspoons grated lemon zest plus ⅔ cup juice (4 lemons)

4   tablespoons unsalted butter, cut into 8 pieces

    Confectioners' sugar (optional)

1. For the crust: Adjust oven rack to middle position and heat oven to 350 degrees. Make foil sling for 8-inch square baking pan by folding 2 long sheets of aluminum foil so each is 8 inches wide. Lay sheets of foil in pan perpendicular to each other, with extra foil hanging over edges of pan. Push foil into corners and up sides of pan, smoothing foil flush to pan.

2. Whisk flour, sugar, and salt together in bowl. Add melted butter and stir until combined. Transfer mixture to prepared pan and press into even layer over entire bottom of pan (do not wash bowl). Bake crust until dark golden brown, 19 to 24 minutes, rotating pan halfway through baking.

Patting Crust into the Pan

Stir melted butter into mixture of flour, sugar, and salt. Press dough into pan in even layer.

Pay Attention to Proportion

"Many of my colleagues adore lemon. The brighter and more pucker-inducing the lemon flavor the better. In fact, one person confessed that their benchmark for a great lemon bar is 'It's so tart it makes my forehead break into a sweat.' During recipe development, I found that no matter how much I increased the lemon juice, they clamored for more. The only problem was the more juice I used, the more egg or flour or butter I needed to add to keep the bars sliceable. Which in turn, muted the lemon flavor. I spun in circles for a few days, testing other thickening methods. None panned out and it wasn't until someone suggested adding ground up sour candies that I realized that I needed a dry acid. Luckily, most bakers have a dry acid in their pantry: cream of a tartar, aka tartaric acid. A couple teaspoons amped up the tang without messing with the texture. This satisfied the lemonheads in the crowd but left me with a problem. My bars were too tart for me. The solution was to change the ratio of lemon curd to crust. Increasing the amount of crust slightly ensured that there was enough buttery shortbread crust to temper the curd's brightness."

— *Lan*

Pecans Are the "Main Character"

"Having pies for dessert is a common practice in
my household. I grew up eating and loving pies,
pecan being my favorite. What I didn't eat
much of was cookie bars and, with my Southern-
groomed palate, for years they weren't even on
my radar—until I made Ultranutty Pecan Bars for
ATK TV season 17. I think I thought making bars
like blondies and the like were too complicated
when pies were simply 'stir and dump' if you will.
Turns out that pecans really shine in this recipe
and I mean, they are the main character here.
The thing I loved most about pecan pie was the
toastiness of the pecans layered on top;
my least favorite part sometimes was the
extremely sugary filling but those pecans made
it all better. I think my lesson here was that I
could reimagine the filling stance and give the
pecans all the space to develop into layers of
toasted (some chewy and some crunchy)
cookie bar that welp, literally raised the bar."

– Elle

3. For the filling: While crust bakes, whisk sugar, flour, cream of tartar, and salt together in now-empty bowl. Whisk in eggs and yolks until no streaks of egg remain. Whisk in lemon zest and juice. Transfer mixture to saucepan and cook over medium-low heat, stirring constantly, until mixture thickens and registers 160 degrees, 5 to 8 minutes. Off heat, stir in butter. Strain filling through fine-mesh strainer set over bowl.

4. Pour filling over hot crust and tilt pan to spread evenly. Bake until filling is set and barely jiggles when pan is shaken, 8 to 12 minutes. (Filling around perimeter of pan may be slightly raised.) Let bars cool completely in pan about 1½ hours. Using foil overhang, lift bars out of pan and transfer to cutting board. Cut into bars, wiping knife clean between cuts as necessary. Before serving, dust bars with confectioners' sugar, if using.

Ultranutty Pecan Bars

Makes 24 bars • Total Time: 1 hour, plus 1½ hours cooling

Why This Recipe Works Pecan bars usually are more about the custardy filling than the pecans but we wanted a bar cookie that emphasized the star ingredient. We increased the amount of pecans to a full pound and tossed them in a thick mixture of brown sugar, corn syrup, and melted butter for a filling that spread itself evenly in the heat of the oven. Using so many nuts gave these pecan bars a variety of textures; some parts were chewy and some crunchy—a quality we enjoyed. Instead of making a crust using cold butter in a food processor, we found that melted butter helped form an easy press-in crust. And after we eliminated the wet filling, we discovered the crust also didn't need parbaking. A final sprinkling of flaky sea salt elevated the flavor and appearance of this nutty treat.

It is important to use pecan halves, not pieces. The edges of the bars will be slightly firmer than the center. If desired, trim ¼ inch from the edges before cutting into bars. Toast the pecans on a rimmed baking sheet in a 350-degree oven until fragrant, 8 to 12 minutes, shaking the sheet halfway through.

Crust
- 1¾ cups (8¾ ounces) all-purpose flour
- 6 tablespoons (2⅔ ounces) granulated sugar
- ½ teaspoon table salt
- 8 tablespoons unsalted butter, melted

Topping
- ¾ cup packed (5¼ ounces) light brown sugar
- ½ cup light corn syrup
- 7 tablespoons unsalted butter, melted and hot
- 1 teaspoon vanilla extract
- ½ teaspoon table salt
- 4 cups (1 pound) pecan halves, toasted
- ½ teaspoon flake sea salt (optional)

1. For the crust: Adjust oven rack to lowest position and heat oven to 350 degrees. Make foil sling for 13 by 9-inch baking pan by folding 2 long sheets of aluminum foil; first sheet should be 13 inches wide and second sheet should be 9 inches wide. Lay sheets of foil in pan perpendicular to each other, with extra foil hanging over edges of pan. Push foil into corners and up sides of pan, smoothing foil flush to pan. Lightly spray foil with vegetable oil spray.

2. Whisk flour, sugar, and salt together in medium bowl. Add melted butter and stir with wooden spoon until dough begins to form. Using your hands, continue to combine until no dry flour remains and small portion of dough holds together when squeezed in palm of your hand. Evenly scatter tablespoon-size pieces of dough over surface of pan. Using your fingertips and palm of your hand, press and smooth dough into even thickness in bottom of pan.

3. For the topping: Whisk sugar, corn syrup, melted butter, vanilla, and salt in medium bowl until smooth (mixture will look separated at first), 20 seconds. Fold pecans into sugar mixture until nuts are evenly coated.

4. Pour topping over crust. Using spatula, spread topping over crust, pushing to edges and into corners (there will be bare patches). Bake until topping is evenly distributed and rapidly bubbling across entire surface, 23 to 25 minutes.

5. Transfer pan to wire rack and lightly sprinkle with flake sea salt, if using. Let bars cool completely in pan, about 1½ hours. Using foil overhang, lift bars out of pan and transfer to cutting board. Cut into 24 bars and serve. (Bars can be stored at room temperature for up to 5 days.)

Toasting Nuts

Spread nuts in single layer on rimmed baking sheet and toast in 350-degree oven until fragrant and slightly darkened, 8 to 12 minutes, shaking sheet halfway through baking.

Cakes & More

Photo: French Apple Cake

The Elegant Crowd Pleaser

"I love entertaining but I really love hosting afternoon tea or coffee and cake. It became a way of life for me, especially when I lived abroad. I have a plethora of cakes in my recipe canon, and olive oil cake fits in perfectly because it is light and plush, elegant but simple, and subtly sweet to complement just about anything else that fills the table. A few pantry staples are all you need to whip up a cake, and thanks to the olive oil it stays moist and fresh for days, making it a make-ahead staple. The plush, fine crumb isn't overly sweet and the contrast of the crackly sugar topping balances the bite. It's delicious enough on its own but its elegant simplicity makes it the perfect vehicle to top with fresh cream or seasonal berries. Besides the incredible taste, I absolutely love how pantry-friendly this recipe is. Without even looking into my kitchen cupboards, I know that I already have all of the ingredients on hand to make this cake on a moment's notice, just in time for tea."

— Erica

Olive Oil Cake

Serves 8 to 10 • Total Time: 1½ hours, plus 1½ hours cooling

Why This Recipe Works Our popular olive oil cake has a light yet plush crumb, with a subtle but noticeable olive oil flavor. Whipping the sugar with whole eggs, rather than just the whites, produced a fine texture that was airy but sturdy enough to support the olive oil–rich batter. To emphasize the defining flavor, we opted for a good-quality extra-virgin olive oil and accentuated its fruitiness with a tiny bit of lemon zest. Sugar created a crackly topping that added a touch of sweetness and sophistication.

For the best flavor, use fresh high-quality extra-virgin olive oil. If your springform pan is prone to leaking, place a rimmed baking sheet on the oven floor to catch any drips. Leftover cake can be wrapped in plastic wrap and stored at room temperature for up to three days.

- 1¾ cups (8¾ ounces) all-purpose flour
- 1 teaspoon baking powder
- ¾ teaspoon table salt
- 3 large eggs
- 1¼ cups (8¾ ounces) plus 2 tablespoons sugar, divided
- ¼ teaspoon grated lemon zest
- ¾ cup extra-virgin olive oil
- ¾ cup milk

1. Adjust oven rack to middle position and heat oven to 350 degrees. Grease 9-inch springform pan. Whisk flour, baking powder, and salt together in bowl.

2. Using stand mixer fitted with whisk attachment, whip eggs on medium speed until foamy, about 1 minute. Add 1¼ cups sugar and lemon zest; increase speed to high; and whip until mixture is fluffy and pale yellow, about 3 minutes. Reduce speed to medium and, with mixer running, slowly pour in oil. Mix until oil is fully incorporated, about 1 minute. Add half of flour mixture and mix on low speed until incorporated, about 1 minute, scraping down bowl as needed. Add milk and mix until combined, about 30 seconds. Add remaining flour mixture and mix until just incorporated, about 1 minute, scraping down bowl as needed.

3. Transfer batter to prepared pan; sprinkle remaining 2 tablespoons sugar over entire surface. Bake until cake is deep golden brown and toothpick inserted in center comes out with few crumbs attached, 40 to 45 minutes. Transfer pan to wire rack and let cool for 15 minutes. Remove side of pan and let cake cool completely, about 1½ hours. Cut into wedges and serve.

Cider-Glazed Apple Bundt Cake

Serves 12 to 16 • Total Time: 2 hours, plus 2½ hours cooling

Why This Recipe Works We were able to pack the equivalent of 4½ pounds of fruit into our apple cake and its glaze with the help of a Bundt pan. This specialty pan is a practical vessel for baking moist cakes: The central hole allows heat to reach the center of the batter, which would remain dense and underbaked by the time the exterior was cooked through if baked in a conventional round cake pan. An apple cider reduction bolstered the apple flavor of our cake without making the crumb dense or soggy. Mixing the reduced apple cider into the batter, brushing it onto the cake, and using it to flavor the icing drizzled on top provided layers of pervasive apple flavor. Being selective with our spices—opting for just cinnamon and allspice—and using a light hand allowed the true apple flavor to shine.

For the sake of efficiency, we recommend that you begin boiling the cider before assembling the rest of the ingredients. Reducing the cider to exactly 1 cup is important to the success of this recipe. If you accidentally overreduce the cider, make up the difference with water. Spray the pan well in step 1 to prevent sticking. If you don't have nonstick baking spray with flour, mix 1 tablespoon melted butter and 1 tablespoon flour into a paste and brush inside the pan. We like the tartness of Granny Smith apples in this recipe, but any variety of apple will work. You may shred the apples with the large shredding disk of a food processor or with the large holes of a box grater.

- 4 cups apple cider
- 3¾ cups (18¾ ounces) all-purpose flour
- 1½ teaspoons table salt
- 1½ teaspoons baking powder
- ½ teaspoon baking soda
- ¾ teaspoon ground cinnamon
- ¼ teaspoon ground allspice
- ¾ cup (3 ounces) confectioners' sugar
- 16 tablespoons unsalted butter, melted
- 1½ cups packed (10½ ounces) dark brown sugar
- 3 large eggs
- 2 teaspoons vanilla extract
- 1½ pounds Granny Smith apples, peeled, cored, and shredded (3 cups)

Marbled Blueberry Bundt Cake

Serves 12 • Total Time: 2¼ hours, plus 3 hours cooling

Why This Recipe Works Switching from flavor-packed wild Maine blueberries to oversized, bland cultivated blueberries wreaks havoc in a cake. The berries refuse to stay suspended in the batter and burst into bland, soggy pockets in the heat of the oven. We solved these problems by pureeing the fruit, seasoning it with sugar and lemon, and bumping up its natural pectin content with low-sugar pectin for a thickened, fresh-tasting filling that could be marbled throughout the cake.

Spray the pan well in step 1 to prevent sticking. If you don't have nonstick baking spray with flour, mix 1 tablespoon melted butter and 1 tablespoon flour into a paste and brush inside the pan. For fruit pectin we recommend Sure-Jell for Less or No Sugar Needed Recipes. Ball Fruit Pectin will not work. If using frozen berries, thaw them before blending in step 3. This cake can be served plain or with Lemon Glaze or Cinnamon Whipped Cream (recipes follow).

1. Boil cider in 12-inch skillet over high heat until reduced to 1 cup, 20 to 25 minutes. While cider is reducing, adjust oven rack to middle position and heat oven to 350 degrees. Heavily spray 12-cup nonstick Bundt pan with baking spray with flour. Whisk flour, salt, baking powder, baking soda, cinnamon, and allspice in large bowl until combined. Place confectioners' sugar in small bowl.

2. Add 2 tablespoons reduced cider to confectioners' sugar and whisk to form smooth icing. Cover icing with plastic wrap and set aside. Pour ½ cup reduced cider into second large bowl. Set remaining 6 tablespoons reduced cider aside to brush over baked cake.

3. Add melted butter, brown sugar, eggs, and vanilla to ½ cup cider reduction and whisk until smooth. Pour cider mixture over flour mixture and stir with rubber spatula until almost fully combined (some streaks of flour will remain). Stir in apples and any accumulated juices until evenly distributed. Transfer mixture to prepared Bundt pan and smooth top. Bake until skewer inserted in center of cake comes out clean, 55 minutes to 1 hour 5 minutes.

4. Transfer pan to wire rack set in rimmed baking sheet. Brush exposed surface of cake lightly with 1 tablespoon reserved cider reduction. Let cake cool for 10 minutes. Invert cake onto wire rack. Brush top and sides with remaining 5 tablespoons reserved cider reduction. Let cake for cool 20 minutes. Stir icing to loosen and drizzle over cake. Let cake cool completely, at least 2 hours, before serving. (Leftover cake may be wrapped loosely and stored at room temperature for up to 3 days.)

Cake
- 3 cups (15 ounces) all-purpose flour
- 1½ teaspoons baking powder
- ¾ teaspoon baking soda
- 1 teaspoon table salt
- ½ teaspoon ground cinnamon
- ¾ cup buttermilk
- 2 teaspoons grated lemon zest, plus 3 tablespoons juice
- 2 teaspoons vanilla extract
- 3 large eggs, plus 1 large yolk, room temperature
- 18 tablespoons (2¼ sticks) unsalted butter, softened
- 2 cups (14 ounces) sugar

Filling
- ¾ cup (5¼ ounces) sugar
- 3 tablespoons low- or no-sugar-needed fruit pectin
  Pinch table salt
- 10 ounces (2 cups) fresh or thawed frozen blueberries
- 1 teaspoon grated lemon zest, plus 1 tablespoon juice

1. For the cake: Adjust oven rack to lower-middle position and heat oven to 325 degrees. Heavily spray 12-cup non-stick Bundt pan with baking spray with flour. Whisk flour, baking powder, baking soda, salt, and cinnamon together in large bowl. Whisk buttermilk, lemon zest and juice, and vanilla together in medium bowl. Gently whisk eggs and yolk to combine in third bowl.

2. Using stand mixer fitted with paddle, beat butter and sugar on medium-high speed until pale and fluffy, about 3 minutes, scraping down bowl as needed. Reduce speed to medium and beat in half of eggs until incorporated, about 15 seconds. Repeat with remaining eggs, scraping down bowl after incorporating. Reduce speed to low and add one-third of flour mixture, followed by half of buttermilk mixture, mixing until just incorporated after each addition, about 5 seconds. Repeat using half of remaining flour mixture and all of remaining buttermilk mixture. Scrape down bowl, add remaining flour mixture, and mix at medium-low speed until batter is thoroughly combined, about 15 seconds. Remove bowl from mixer and fold batter once or twice with rubber spatula to incorporate any remaining flour. Cover bowl with plastic wrap and set aside while preparing filling (batter will inflate a bit).

3. For the filling: Whisk sugar, pectin, and salt together in small saucepan. Process blueberries in blender until mostly smooth, about 1 minute. Transfer ¼ cup puree and lemon zest to saucepan with sugar mixture and stir to thoroughly combine. Heat sugar-blueberry mixture over medium heat until just simmering, about 3 minutes, stirring frequently to dissolve sugar and pectin. Transfer mixture to medium

bowl and let cool for 5 minutes. Add remaining puree and lemon juice to cooled mixture and whisk to combine. Let sit until slightly set, about 8 minutes.

4. Spoon half of batter into prepared pan and smooth top. Using back of spoon, create ½-inch-deep channel in center of batter. Spoon half of filling into channel. Using butter knife or small offset spatula, thoroughly swirl filling into batter (there should be no large pockets of filling remaining). Repeat swirling step with remaining batter and filling.

5. Bake until top is golden brown and skewer inserted in center comes out with no crumbs attached, 1 hour to 1 hour 10 minutes. Let cake cool in pan on wire rack for 10 minutes, then invert cake directly onto wire rack. Let cake cool completely, at least 3 hours, before serving.

TOPPINGS
Lemon Glaze
Makes 2 cups • Total Time: 5 minutes, plus 3 hours setting

- 3–4 tablespoons lemon juice (2 lemons)
- 2 cups (8 ounces) confectioners' sugar

1. While cake is baking, whisk 3 tablespoons lemon juice and sugar until smooth, gradually adding more lemon juice as needed until glaze is thick but still pourable (mixture should leave faint trail across bottom of mixing bowl when drizzled from whisk).

2. After cake has been removed from pan and inverted onto wire rack set in baking sheet, pour half of glaze over warm cake and let cool for 1 hour. Pour remaining glaze evenly over cake and continue to let cool to room temperature, at least 2 hours.

Cinnamon Whipped Cream
Makes 2 cups • Total Time: 5 minutes
For the best texture, whip the cream until soft peaks just form. Do not overwhip.

- 1 cup heavy cream
- 2 tablespoons confectioners' sugar
- ¼ teaspoon ground cinnamon
  Pinch table salt

Using stand mixer fitted with whisk attachment, whip all ingredients on medium-low speed until foamy, about 1 minute. Increase speed to high and whip until soft peaks form, 1 to 3 minutes.

Lemon Pound Cake

Makes one 8-inch loaf
Total Time: 1¾ hours, plus 1 hour cooling

Why This Recipe Works Pound cakes often turn out spongy, rubbery, heavy, and dry—and lemon pound cakes often lack true lemon flavor. We wanted to produce a superior pound cake (fine-crumbed, rich, moist, and buttery) while making the process as simple and foolproof as possible. After less-than-successful results with a stand mixer and a hand mixer, we turned to the food processor to mix our cake. It ensured a perfect emulsification of the eggs, sugar, and melted butter (we found that a blender worked, too). Cake flour produced a tender crumb, but our cake was still a bit heavy. We fixed matters with the addition of baking powder, which increased lift and produced a consistent, fine crumb. Finally, in addition to mixing lemon zest into the cake batter, we glazed the finished cake with lemon sugar syrup—but first we poked holes all over the cake to ensure that the tangy, sweet glaze infused the cake with a blast of bright lemon flavor.

> *You can use a blender instead of a food processor to mix the batter. To add the butter, remove the center cap of the lid so it can be drizzled into the whirling blender with minimal splattering. This batter looks almost like a thick pancake batter and is very fluid.*

Cake
- 1½ cups (6 ounces) cake flour
- 1 teaspoon baking powder
- ½ teaspoon table salt
- 16 tablespoons unsalted butter, melted
- 1¼ cups (8¾ ounces) sugar
- 2 tablespoons grated lemon zest plus 2 teaspoons juice
- 4 large eggs, room temperature
- 1½ teaspoons vanilla extract

Glaze
- ½ cup (3½ ounces) sugar
- ¼ cup lemon juice (2 lemons)

1. For the cake: Adjust oven rack to middle position and heat oven to 350 degrees. Grease and flour 8½ by 4½-inch loaf pan. In medium bowl, whisk together flour, baking powder, and salt; set aside.

2. In food processor, pulse sugar and lemon zest until combined, about 5 pulses. Add lemon juice, eggs, and vanilla; process until combined, about 5 seconds. Whisk melted butter thoroughly to reincorporate any separated milk solids. With machine running, add melted butter through feed tube in steady stream (this should take about 20 seconds). Transfer mixture to large bowl. Sift flour mixture over egg mixture in 3 additions, whisking gently after each addition until just combined.

3. Pour batter into prepared pan and bake for 15 minutes. Reduce oven temperature to 325 degrees and continue to bake until deep golden brown and toothpick inserted in center comes out clean, about 35 minutes, rotating pan halfway through baking. Let cool in pan for 10 minutes, then turn onto wire rack. Poke top and sides of cake throughout with toothpick. Let cake cool completely, at least 1 hour. (Cooled cake can be wrapped tightly in plastic wrap and stored at room temperature for up to 5 days.)

4. For the glaze: While cake is cooling, bring sugar and lemon juice to boil in small saucepan, stirring occasionally to dissolve sugar. Reduce heat to low and simmer until thickened slightly, about 2 minutes. Brush top and sides of cake with glaze and let cool to room temperature before serving.

Pear-Walnut Upside-Down Cake

Serves 8 to 10 • **Total Time: 2 hours, plus 2 hours cooling**

Why This Recipe Works Pears have a subtle floral flavor and graceful shape, but their popularity in desserts has always been a distant second to apples. We wanted to create an elegant cake that really showcased the pears. We settled on Bosc pears, which have dense flesh and hold their shape after baking; cutting the pears into wedges allowed them to be baked raw. For the cake, we opted for a walnut-based version, which was light but sturdy, earthy-tasting, and not too sweet. Lining the cake pan with parchment and removing the cake from the pan after 15 minutes allowed the top to set while preventing the bottom from steaming and turning soggy.

We strongly recommend baking this cake in a light-colored cake pan with sides that are at least 2 inches tall. If using a dark-colored pan, start checking for doneness at 1 hour, and note that the cake may dome in the center and the topping may become too sticky. Serve with crème fraîche or lightly sweetened whipped cream.

Topping

- 4 tablespoons unsalted butter, melted
- ½ cup packed (3½ ounces) dark brown sugar
- 2 teaspoons cornstarch
- ⅛ teaspoon table salt
- 3 ripe but firm Bosc pears (8 ounces each)

Cake

- 1 cup walnuts, toasted
- ½ cup (2½ ounces) all-purpose flour
- ½ teaspoon table salt
- ¼ teaspoon baking powder
- ⅛ teaspoon baking soda
- 3 large eggs
- 1 cup (7 ounces) granulated sugar
- 4 tablespoons unsalted butter, melted
- ¼ cup vegetable oil

1. For the topping: Adjust oven rack to middle position and heat oven to 300 degrees. Grease 9-inch round cake pan and line bottom with parchment paper. Pour melted butter over bottom of pan and swirl to evenly coat. Combine sugar, cornstarch, and salt in bowl and sprinkle over butter.

2. Peel, halve, and core pears. Set aside 1 pear half and reserve for other use. Cut remaining 5 pear halves into 4 wedges each. Arrange pears in circular pattern around cake pan with tapered ends pointing inward. Arrange 2 smallest pear wedges in center.

3. For the cake: Pulse walnuts, flour, salt, baking powder, and baking soda in food processor until walnuts are finely ground, 8 to 10 pulses. Transfer walnut mixture to bowl.

4. Process eggs and sugar in now-empty processor until very pale yellow, about 2 minutes. With processor running, add melted butter and oil in steady stream until incorporated. Add walnut mixture and pulse to combine, 4 or 5 pulses. Pour batter evenly over pears (some pear may show through; cake will bake up over fruit).

5. Bake until center of cake is set and bounces back when gently pressed and toothpick inserted in center comes out clean, 1 hour 10 minutes to 1¼ hours, rotating pan after 40 minutes. Let cake cool in pan on wire rack for 15 minutes. Carefully run paring knife or offset spatula around sides of pan. Invert cake onto wire rack set in rimmed baking sheet; discard parchment. Let cake cool completely, about 2 hours. Transfer to serving platter, cut into wedges, and serve.

Unmolding an Upside-Down Cake

Lining pan with parchment paper ensures that fruit releases cleanly. Let cake rest in pan for just 15 minutes before turning it out onto wire rack.

French Apple Cake

Serves 8 to 10 • Total Time: 2¼ hours, plus 2 hours cooling

Why This Recipe Works For our own version of this classic French dessert, we wanted the best of both worlds: a dessert with a custardy, apple-rich base beneath a light, cake-like topping. To ensure that the apple slices softened fully, we microwaved them briefly to break the enzyme responsible for firming up pectin. And to create two differently textured layers from one batter, we divided the batter and added egg yolks to one part to make the custardy base and added flour to the rest to form the cake layer above it.

> *The microwaved apples should be pliable but not completely soft when cooked. To test for doneness, take one apple slice and try to bend it. If it snaps in half, it's too firm; microwave it for an additional 30 seconds and test again. If Calvados is unavailable, 1 tablespoon of apple brandy or white rum can be substituted.*

1½ pounds Granny Smith apples, peeled, cored, cut into 8 wedges, and sliced ⅛ inch thick crosswise
1 tablespoon Calvados
1 teaspoon lemon juice
1 cup (5 ounces) plus 2 tablespoons all-purpose flour, divided
1 cup (7 ounces) plus 1 tablespoon granulated sugar, divided
2 teaspoons baking powder
½ teaspoon table salt
1 large egg plus 2 large yolks
1 cup vegetable oil
1 cup whole milk
1 teaspoon vanilla extract
Confectioners' sugar

1. Adjust oven rack to lower-middle position and heat oven to 325 degrees. Spray 9-inch springform pan with vegetable oil spray. Place prepared pan on rimmed baking sheet lined with aluminum foil. Place apple slices in microwave-safe pie plate; cover; and microwave until apples are pliable and slightly translucent, about 3 minutes. Toss apple slices with Calvados and lemon juice and let cool for 15 minutes.

2. Whisk 1 cup flour, 1 cup granulated sugar, baking powder, and salt together in bowl. Whisk egg, oil, milk, and vanilla in second bowl until smooth. Add dry ingredients to wet ingredients and whisk until just combined. Transfer 1 cup batter to separate bowl and set aside.

3. Add egg yolks to remaining batter and whisk to combine. Using spatula, gently fold in cooled apples. Transfer batter to prepared pan; using offset spatula, spread batter evenly to pan edges, gently pressing on apples to create even, compact layer, and smooth surface.

4. Whisk remaining 2 tablespoons flour into reserved batter. Pour over batter in pan, spread batter evenly to pan edges, and smooth surface. Sprinkle remaining 1 tablespoon granulated sugar evenly over cake. Bake until center of cake is set, toothpick inserted in center comes out clean, and top is golden brown, about 1¼ hours. Let cake cool in pan on wire rack for 5 minutes. Run thin knife around edge of pan to loosen cake, then let cool completely, 2 to 3 hours. Remove sides of pan and slide thin metal spatula between cake bottom and pan bottom to loosen, then slide cake onto platter. Dust cake lightly with confectioners' sugar before serving.

Carrot Layer Cake

Serves 10 to 12 • Total Time: 1½ hours, plus 1½ hours cooling and chilling

Why This Recipe Works This American classic has a lot going for it: moist cake, delicate spices, tangy cream cheese frosting. But its presentation could use some refinement. We wanted to reengineer humble carrot cake as a four-tier, nut-crusted confection that could claim its place among the most glamorous desserts. To start, we found that baking this cake in a half sheet pan meant that it baked and cooled in far less time than a conventional layer cake, and—cut into quarters—it produced four thin, level layers that did not require splitting or trimming. Extra baking soda raised the pH of the batter, ensuring that the coarsely shredded carrots softened during the shortened baking time. Buttermilk powder in the frosting reinforced the tangy flavor of the cream cheese.

Shred the carrots on the large holes of a box grater or in a food processor fitted with the shredding disk. Do not substitute liquid buttermilk for the buttermilk powder. To ensure the proper spreading consistency for the frosting, use cold cream cheese. If your baked cake is of an uneven thickness, adjust the orientation of the layers as they are stacked to produce a level cake. Assembling this cake on a cardboard cake round trimmed to about an 8 by 6-inch rectangle makes it easy to press the pecans onto the sides of the frosted cake.

Cake

1¾ cups (8¾ ounces) all-purpose flour
2 teaspoons baking powder
1 teaspoon baking soda
1½ teaspoons ground cinnamon
¾ teaspoon ground nutmeg
½ teaspoon table salt
¼ teaspoon ground cloves
1¼ cups packed (8¾ ounces) light brown sugar
¾ cup vegetable oil
3 large eggs
1 teaspoon vanilla extract
2⅔ cups shredded carrots (4 carrots)
⅔ cup dried currants

Frosting

3 cups (12 ounces) confectioners' sugar
16 tablespoons unsalted butter, softened
⅓ cup buttermilk powder
2 teaspoons vanilla extract
¼ teaspoon table salt
12 ounces cream cheese, chilled and cut into 12 equal pieces
2 cups (8 ounces) pecans, toasted and chopped coarse

1. For the cake: Adjust oven rack to middle position and heat oven to 350 degrees. Grease 18 by 13-inch rimmed baking sheet, line with parchment paper, and grease parchment. Whisk flour, baking powder, baking soda, cinnamon, nutmeg, salt, and cloves together in large bowl.

2. Whisk sugar, oil, eggs, and vanilla in second bowl until mixture is smooth. Stir in carrots and currants. Add flour mixture and fold with rubber spatula until mixture is just combined.

3. Transfer batter to prepared sheet and smooth surface with offset spatula. Bake until center of cake is firm to touch, 15 to 18 minutes. Let cool in pan on wire rack for 5 minutes. Invert cake onto wire rack (do not remove parchment), then reinvert onto second wire rack. Let cake cool completely, about 30 minutes.

4. For the frosting: Using stand mixer fitted with paddle, beat sugar, butter, buttermilk powder, vanilla, and salt on low speed until smooth, about 2 minutes, scraping down bowl as needed. Increase speed to medium-low; add cream cheese, 1 piece at a time; and mix until smooth, about 2 minutes.

5. Transfer cooled cake to cutting board, parchment side down. Using sharp chef's knife, cut cake and parchment in half crosswise, then lengthwise into 4 even quarters.

6. Place 8 by 6-inch cardboard rectangle on cake platter. Place 1 cake layer, parchment side up, on cardboard and carefully remove parchment. Using offset spatula, spread ⅔ cup frosting evenly over top, right to edge of cake. Repeat with 2 more layers of cake, pressing lightly to adhere and frosting each layer with ⅔ cup frosting. Top with last cake layer and spread 1 cup frosting evenly over top. Spread remaining frosting evenly over sides of cake. (It's fine if some crumbs show through frosting on sides, but if you go back to smooth top of cake, be sure that spatula is free of crumbs.)

7. Hold cake with your hand and gently press chopped pecans onto sides with your other hand. Chill for at least 1 hour before serving. (Frosted cake can be refrigerated for up to 24 hours before serving.)

Best Almond Cake

Serves 8 to 10 • Total time: 1¾ hours, plus 2 hours cooling

Why This Recipe Works Simple, rich almond cake makes a sophisticated dessert, but traditional European versions can be heavy and dense. For a slightly cakier version with plenty of nutty flavor, we swapped out traditional almond paste for toasted, blanched sliced almonds and added a bit of almond extract for extra depth. Lemon zest in the batter provided citrusy brightness. For a lighter crumb, we increased the flour slightly and added baking powder. Making the batter in a food processor broke down some of the protein structure in the eggs, ensuring that the cake had a level, not domed, top. We swapped some butter for oil and lowered the oven temperature to produce an evenly baked, moist cake. For a finishing touch, we topped the cake with sliced almonds and lemon-infused sugar.

If you can't find blanched sliced almonds, grind slivered almonds for the batter and use unblanched sliced almonds for the topping. Serve plain or with Orange Crème Fraîche (recipe follows).

- 1½ cups (5¼ ounces) plus ⅓ cup blanched sliced almonds, toasted, divided
- ¾ cup (3¾ ounces) all-purpose flour
- ¾ teaspoon table salt
- ¼ teaspoon baking powder
- ⅛ teaspoon baking soda
- 4 large eggs
- 1¼ cups (8¾ ounces) plus 2 tablespoons sugar, divided
- 1 tablespoon plus ½ teaspoon grated lemon zest (2 lemons), divided
- ¾ teaspoon almond extract
- 5 tablespoons unsalted butter, melted
- ⅓ cup vegetable oil

1. Adjust oven rack to middle position and heat oven to 300 degrees. Grease 9-inch round cake pan and line with parchment paper. Pulse 1½ cups almonds, flour, salt, baking powder, and baking soda in food processor until almonds are finely ground, 5 to 10 pulses. Transfer almond mixture to bowl.

2. Process eggs, 1¼ cups sugar, 1 tablespoon lemon zest, and almond extract in now-empty processor until very pale yellow, about 2 minutes. With processor running, add melted butter and oil in steady stream, until incorporated. Add almond mixture and pulse to combine, 4 or 5 pulses. Transfer batter to prepared pan.

3. Using your fingers, combine remaining 2 tablespoons sugar and remaining ½ teaspoon lemon zest in small bowl until fragrant, 5 to 10 seconds. Sprinkle top of cake evenly with remaining ⅓ cup almonds followed by sugar-zest mixture.

4. Bake until center of cake is set and bounces back when gently pressed and toothpick inserted in center comes out clean, 55 minutes to 1 hour 5 minutes, rotating pan after 40 minutes. Let cake cool in pan on wire rack for 15 minutes. Run paring knife around sides of pan. Invert cake onto greased wire rack, discard parchment, and reinvert cake onto second wire rack. Let cake cool completely, about 2 hours. Cut into wedges and serve. (Store cake in plastic wrap at room temperature for up to 3 days.)

ACCOMPANIMENT
Orange Crème Fraîche
Makes 2 cups
Total Time: 10 minutes, plus 1 hour chilling

- 2 oranges
- 1 cup crème fraîche
- 2 tablespoons sugar
- ⅛ teaspoon salt

Grate 1 teaspoon zest from 1 orange. Cut away peel and pith from oranges. Slice between membranes to release segments and cut segments into ¼-inch pieces. Combine orange pieces and zest, crème fraîche, sugar, and salt in bowl and mix well. Refrigerate for 1 hour.

Financiers

Makes 24 cakes • Total Time: 40 minutes, plus 20 minutes cooling

Why This Recipe Works It is said that financiers were created in the late 19th century by a pâtissier whose shop was located near the Paris stock exchange as treats for bankers to enjoy on the go. Making these elegant little cakes requires only six ingredients and they bake in less than 15 minutes. For financiers with complex almond flavor and contrasting textures, we started by spraying a mini-muffin tin with baking spray with flour. The flour in the spray helped the sides of the cakes rise along with the center, preventing doming. We then stirred together almond flour, sugar, all-purpose flour, and egg whites. We opted for granulated sugar, which doesn't totally dissolve in the egg whites, to ensure a pleasantly coarse texture. Once these ingredients were whisked together, it was just a matter of

stirring in nutty browned butter and baking the cakes. These two-bite treats were easy to customize so we created a variety of add-ins including fresh fruit, dark chocolate chunks, citrus zest, warm spices, and several types of nuts.

> *You'll need a 24-cup mini-muffin tin for this recipe. Because egg whites can vary in size, measuring the whites by weight or volume is essential. Baking spray with flour ensures that the cakes bake up with appropriately flat tops; we don't recommend substituting vegetable oil spray in this recipe. To enjoy the crisp edges of the cakes, eat them on the day they're baked; store leftovers in an air-tight container at room temperature for up to three days.*

- 5 tablespoons unsalted butter
- ¾ cup (3 ounces) finely ground almond flour
- ½ cup plus 1 tablespoon (4 ounces) sugar
- 2 tablespoons all-purpose flour
- ⅛ teaspoon table salt
- ⅓ cup (3 ounces) egg whites (3 to 4 large eggs)

1. Adjust oven rack to middle position and heat oven to 375 degrees. Generously spray 24-cup mini-muffin tin with baking spray with flour. Melt butter in 10-inch skillet over medium-high heat. Cook, stirring and scraping skillet constantly with rubber spatula, until milk solids are dark golden brown and butter has nutty aroma, 1 to 3 minutes. Immediately transfer butter to heatproof bowl.

2. Whisk almond flour, sugar, all-purpose flour, and salt together in second bowl. Add egg whites. Using rubber spatula, stir until combined, mashing any lumps against side of bowl until mixture is smooth. Stir in butter until incorporated. Distribute batter evenly among prepared muffin cups (cups will be about half full).

3. Bake until edges are well browned and tops are golden, about 14 minutes, rotating muffin tin halfway through baking. Remove tin from oven and immediately invert wire rack on top of tin. Invert rack and tin; carefully remove tin. Turn cakes right side up and let cool for at least 20 minutes before serving.

VARIATIONS
Fresh Fruit Financiers

Place 1 small raspberry on its side on top of each cake (do not press into batter). Or pit 1 small firm plum, peach, apricot, or nectarine and cut into 6 wedges. Slice each wedge crosswise ¼ inch thick. Shingle 2 slices on top of each cake (do not press into batter) before baking.

Chocolate Chunk Financiers

Place one ½-inch dark chocolate chunk on top of each cake (do not press into batter) before baking.

GAME CHANGER

Two-Bite Treats

"I love making financiers. These mini cakes feature delightfully crunchy shells, unveiling the richness of nutty browned butter and toasted almonds. Inside, they're moist with a subtle chew. Absolutely delicious, their true magic lies in their simplicity—just six ingredients. While simple to make, each ingredient has a distinct role and the ratios of those ingredients are the key to the best texture. Almond flour takes the lead, infusing the batter with a rich, nutty flavor. But almond flour alone often makes a dry cake. In addition to the almond flour, a small amount of all-purpose flour provides protein and starch, aiding moisture retention from the egg whites. Sugar contributes to the crackly exterior and crisp shell, characteristic of a good financier. The ratio of sugar to egg whites is also important, providing the requisite chew without being too sweet. As a bonus, these treats can be customized with various add-ins like nuts, chocolate, and fresh berries and stone fruits. So good."

— Keith

Citrus or Spice Financiers

Add ¾ teaspoon grated citrus zest or ¼ teaspoon ground cinnamon, ginger, or cardamom to the batter.

Nut Financiers

Sprinkle lightly toasted sliced almonds on top of batter. Or substitute ¾ cup (3 ounces) shelled untoasted pistachios, hazelnuts, pecans, or whole unblanched almonds for almond flour. Process nuts and all-purpose flour in food processor until finely ground, about 1 minute, scraping down sides of bowl twice during processing.

SEASON 10

Coconut Layer Cake

Serves 10 to 12 • **Total Time: 2 hours, plus 2 hours cooling**

Why This Recipe Works Our coconut cake is perfumed inside and out with the cool, subtle essence of coconut. Its layers of snowy white cake are moist and tender, with a delicate, yielding crumb, and the icing is a silky, gently sweetened coat covered with a deep drift of downy coconut. For this type of cake, we found a traditional butter cake to be best. To infuse the cake with maximum coconut flavor, we relied on coconut extract and cream of coconut in the cake and the buttercream icing. We coated the cake with a generous amount of toasted shredded coconut for textural interest and a final dose of flavor.

> *Be sure to use cream of coconut (such as Coco López), and not coconut milk here. One 15-ounce can of cream of coconut is enough for both the cake and the frosting.*

Cake

- 1 large egg plus 5 large whites
- ¾ cup cream of coconut
- ¼ cup water
- 1 teaspoon coconut extract
- 1 teaspoon vanilla extract
- 2¼ cups (9 ounces) cake flour
- 1 cup (7 ounces) granulated sugar
- 1 tablespoon baking powder
- ¾ teaspoon table salt
- 12 tablespoons unsalted butter, cut into 12 pieces and softened
- 2 cups (6 ounces) sweetened shredded coconut

Frosting

- 4 large egg whites
- 1 cup (7 ounces) granulated sugar
  Pinch table salt

- 1 pound (4 sticks) unsalted butter, each stick cut into 6 pieces and softened
- ¼ cup cream of coconut
- 1 teaspoon coconut extract
- 1 teaspoon vanilla extract

1. For the cake: Adjust oven rack to lower-middle position and heat oven to 325 degrees. Grease two 9-inch round cake pans, line with parchment paper, grease parchment, and flour pans. Whisk egg and whites together in 4-cup liquid measuring cup. Whisk in cream of coconut, water, coconut extract, and vanilla.

2. Using stand mixer fitted with paddle, mix flour, sugar, baking powder, and salt on low speed until combined. Add butter, 1 piece at a time, until only pea-size pieces remain, about 1 minute. Add half of egg mixture, increase speed to medium-high, and beat until light and fluffy, about 1 minute. Reduce speed to medium-low, add remaining egg mixture, and beat until incorporated, about 30 seconds. Give batter final stir by hand.

3. Divide batter evenly between prepared pans and smooth tops with rubber spatula. Gently tap pans on counter to settle batter. Bake until toothpick inserted in center comes out clean, about 30 minutes, switching and rotating pans halfway through baking.

4. Let cakes cool in pans on wire rack for 10 minutes. Remove cakes from pans, discarding parchment, and let cool completely on rack, about 2 hours. (Cake layers can be stored at room temperature for up to 24 hours or frozen up to 1 month; defrost cakes at room temperature.) Meanwhile spread shredded coconut on rimmed baking sheet and toast in oven until shreds are mix of golden brown and white, 15 to 20 minutes, stirring 2 or 3 times; let cool.

5. For the frosting: Combine egg whites, sugar, and salt in bowl of stand mixer and set over medium saucepan filled with 1 inch barely simmering water, making sure that water does not touch bottom of bowl. Cook, whisking constantly, until mixture is opaque and registers 120 degrees, about 2 minutes.

6. Remove bowl from heat and transfer to stand mixer fitted with whisk attachment. Whip egg white mixture on high speed until glossy, sticky, and barely warm (80 degrees), about 7 minutes. Reduce speed to medium-high and whip in butter, 1 piece at a time, followed by cream of coconut, coconut extract, and vanilla, scraping down bowl as needed. Continue to whip until combined, about 1 minute.

7. Using long serrated knife, cut 1 horizontal line around sides of each layer; then, following scored lines, cut each layer into 2 even layers.

8. Line edges of cake platter with 4 strips of parchment to keep platter clean. Place 1 cake layer on platter. Spread ¾ cup frosting evenly over top, right to edge of cake. Repeat with 2 more cake layers, pressing lightly to adhere and spreading ¾ cup frosting evenly over each layer. Top with remaining cake layer and spread remaining frosting evenly over top and sides of cake. Sprinkle top of cake evenly with toasted coconut, then gently press remaining toasted coconut onto sides. Carefully remove parchment strips before serving. (Frosted cake can be refrigerated for up to 24 hours. Bring to room temperature before serving.)

Lining Cake Pans

1. Trace outline of bottom of pan onto sheet of parchment paper. Cut out outline, cutting on inside of line so that round fits snugly inside pan.

2. Fit trimmed piece of parchment into pan.

Chocolate Sheet Cake with Milk Chocolate Frosting

Serves 12 • Total Time: 1 hour, plus 1 hour cooling

Why This Recipe Works For a simple cake that boasted deep chocolate flavor and color, we used a combination of Dutch-processed cocoa and melted bittersweet chocolate; the cocoa offered pure, assertive chocolate flavor while the chocolate contributed complexity as well as fat and sugar. Neutral-tasting oil allowed the chocolate flavor to shine. To minimize cleanup, we mixed the wet and dry ingredients directly into the saucepan where we'd melted the chocolate with cocoa and milk. A milk chocolate ganache frosting contrasted nicely with the deeper flavor of the cake. To make the ganache thick, rich, and creamy, we added plenty of softened butter to the warm chocolate-cream mixture, refrigerated the frosting to cool it quickly so that it would spread nicely, and gave it a quick whisk to smooth it out and lighten its texture.

While any high-quality chocolate can be used here, our preferred bittersweet chocolate is Ghirardelli 60% Cacao Bittersweet Chocolate Premium Baking Bar, and our favorite milk chocolate is Endangered Species Chocolate Smooth + Creamy Milk Chocolate. We recommend making this cake with a Dutch-processed cocoa powder; our favorite is from Droste. Using a natural cocoa powder will result in a drier cake.

Cake

- 1½ cups (10½ ounces) granulated sugar
- 1¼ cups (6¼ ounces) all-purpose flour
- ½ teaspoon baking soda
- ½ teaspoon table salt
- 1 cup whole milk
- 8 ounces bittersweet chocolate, chopped fine
- ¾ cup (2¼ ounces) Dutch-processed cocoa powder
- ⅔ cup vegetable oil
- 4 large eggs
- 1 teaspoon vanilla extract

Frosting

- 1 pound milk chocolate, chopped
- ⅔ cup heavy cream
- 16 tablespoons unsalted butter, cut into 16 pieces and softened

1. For the cake: Adjust oven rack to middle position and heat oven to 325 degrees. Lightly spray 13 by 9-inch baking pan with vegetable oil spray. Whisk sugar, flour, baking soda, and salt together in medium bowl; set aside.

2. Combine milk, chocolate, and cocoa in large saucepan. Place saucepan over low heat and cook, whisking frequently, until chocolate is melted and mixture is smooth. Remove from heat and let cool slightly, about 5 minutes. Whisk oil, eggs, and vanilla into chocolate mixture (mixture may initially look curdled) until smooth and homogeneous. Add sugar mixture and whisk until combined, making sure to scrape corners of saucepan.

3. Transfer batter to prepared pan; bake until firm in center when lightly pressed and toothpick inserted in center comes out with few crumbs attached, 30 to 35 minutes, rotating pan halfway through baking. Let cake cool completely in pan on wire rack before frosting, 1 to 2 hours.

4. For the frosting: While cake is baking, combine chocolate and cream in large heatproof bowl set over saucepan filled with 1 inch barely simmering water, making sure that water does not touch bottom of bowl. Whisk mixture occasionally until chocolate is uniformly smooth and glossy, 10 to 15 minutes. Remove bowl from saucepan. Add butter, whisking once or twice to break up pieces. Let mixture stand for 5 minutes to finish melting butter, then whisk until completely smooth. Refrigerate frosting, without stirring, until cooled and thickened, 30 minutes to 1 hour.

5. Once cool, whisk frosting until smooth. (Whisked frosting will lighten in color slightly and should hold its shape on whisk.) Spread frosting evenly over top of cake. Cut cake into squares and serve out of pan. (Leftover cake can be refrigerated in airtight container for up to 2 days.)

Ultimate Chocolate Cupcakes with Ganache Filling

Makes 12 cupcakes • Total Time: 1 hour, plus 1 hour 50 minutes chilling and cooling

Why This Recipe Works Chocolate cupcakes pose a unique challenge: If the cupcakes are packed with chocolate flavor they are often too crumbly to be eaten out of hand, but achieving the right structure can mean sacrificing rich chocolate flavor. We wanted a chocolate cupcake that had it all. We started by making cupcakes using our favorite chocolate cake recipe. Tasters liked the chocolate flavor, but their crumbly texture made the cupcakes impossible to eat without a fork. Substituting bread flour—which is specifically engineered for gluten development—for the all-purpose flour resulted in cupcakes that were markedly less crumbly, but not tough. To intensify the chocolate flavor we mixed the cocoa with hot coffee and also replaced the butter with more neutral-flavored vegetable oil. For a final chocolate burst, we spooned ganache onto the cupcakes before baking, which gave them a truffle-like center. A velvety buttercream with just enough sweetness crowned the cakes perfectly.

> *Use a high-quality bittersweet or semisweet chocolate for this recipe, such as one of the test kitchen's favorite baking chocolates, Ghirardelli 60% Cacao Bittersweet Chocolate. Though we highly recommend the ganache filling, you can omit it for a more traditional cupcake.*

Ganache Filling

- 2 ounces bittersweet chocolate, chopped fine
- ¼ cup heavy cream
- 1 tablespoon confectioners' sugar

Chocolate Cupcakes

- 3 ounces bittersweet chocolate, chopped fine
- ⅓ cup (1 ounce) Dutch-processed cocoa powder
- ¾ cup hot coffee
- ¾ cup (4⅛ ounces) bread flour
- ¾ cup (5¼ ounces) granulated sugar
- ½ teaspoon table salt
- ½ teaspoon baking soda
- 6 tablespoons vegetable oil
- 2 large eggs
- 2 teaspoons distilled white vinegar
- 1 teaspoon vanilla extract
- 1 recipe Creamy Chocolate Frosting (recipe follows)

1. **For the ganache filling:** Place chocolate, cream, and confectioners' sugar in medium bowl. Microwave until mixture is warm to touch, 20 to 30 seconds. Whisk mixture until smooth, then refrigerate until just chilled, no longer than 30 minutes.

2. **For the cupcakes:** Adjust oven rack to middle position and heat oven to 350 degrees. Line 12-cup muffin tin with baking cup liners. Place chocolate and cocoa in medium bowl. Pour hot coffee over mixture and whisk until smooth. Refrigerate until completely cool, about 20 minutes. Whisk flour, granulated sugar, salt, and baking soda together in medium bowl and set aside.

3. Whisk oil, eggs, vinegar, and vanilla into cooled chocolate-cocoa mixture until smooth. Add flour mixture and whisk until smooth.

4. Divide batter evenly among muffin tin cups. Place 1 slightly rounded teaspoon of ganache filling on top of each cupcake. Bake until cupcakes are set and just firm to touch, 17 to 19 minutes. Let cupcakes cool in muffin tin on wire rack until cool enough to handle, about 10 minutes. Carefully lift each cupcake from muffin tin and set on wire rack. Let cool completely before frosting, about 1 hour.

5. **To frost:** Mound 2 to 3 tablespoons of frosting on center of each cupcake. Use small icing spatula or butter knife to ice each cupcake. (Cupcakes can be made up to 24 hours in advance and stored unfrosted in airtight container.)

Creamy Chocolate Frosting
Makes 2¼ cups

Cool the chocolate to between 85 and 100 degrees before adding it to the frosting. If the frosting seems too soft after adding the chocolate, chill it briefly in the refrigerator and then rewhip it until creamy.

- ⅓ cup (2⅓ ounces) sugar
- 2 large egg whites
  Pinch table salt
- 12 tablespoons unsalted butter, cut into 12 pieces and softened
- 6 ounces bittersweet chocolate, melted and cooled
- ½ teaspoon vanilla extract

1. Combine sugar, egg whites, and salt in bowl of stand mixer, then place bowl over pan of simmering water. Whisking gently but constantly, heat mixture until slightly thickened and foamy and registers 150 degrees, 2 to 3 minutes.

2. Using whisk attachment, whip mixture on medium speed in stand mixer until it reaches consistency of shaving cream and is slightly cooled, 1 to 2 minutes. Add butter, 1 piece at a time, until smooth and creamy. (Frosting may look curdled after half of butter has been added; it will smooth with additional butter.) Once all butter is added, add cooled melted chocolate and vanilla and mix until combined. Increase mixer speed to medium-high and beat until light, fluffy, and thoroughly combined, about 30 seconds, scraping beater and sides of bowl with rubber spatula as necessary. (Frosting can be made up to 24 hours in advance and refrigerated in airtight container. When ready to frost, microwave briefly until just slightly softened, 5 to 10 seconds. Once warmed, stir until creamy.)

SEASON 23

Choux au Craquelin

Makes 24 choux • Total Time: 1¾ hours, plus 3 hours chilling and cooling

Why This Recipe Works Choux au craquelin are airy, crispy shells that encase smooth, lush pastry cream. We began our recipe by making the pastry cream, which we reinforced with a little extra flour so that it could be lightened with whipped cream later on. While it chilled and set, we mixed the craquelin dough—a simple combination of flour, butter, and sugar—and rolled it into a thin sheet from which we cut 24 disks before freezing the dough. For the shells, incorporating both milk and water ensured that our puffs baked up crisp and browned nicely, and using the food processor made it easy to incorporate eggs into the choux paste. Before sliding the piped mounds of batter into the oven, we topped them with slim disks of the craquelin dough, which transformed into crackly shells as the puffs baked. Slitting the baked puffs released steam before we returned them to the oven (now turned off) for 45 minutes to ensure crispness.

> *You'll need a 2-inch round cutter, a pastry bag, and two pastry tips—one with a ¼-inch round opening and one with a ½-inch round opening—for this recipe. If desired, this recipe can be made over two days: Make the pastry cream and craquelin on day 1 and the puffs on day 2. We strongly recommend measuring the flour by weight. We prefer whole milk in the pastry cream, but you can use low-fat milk; do not use skim milk. Use a mixer to whip the cream if you prefer.*

Pastry Cream
- 2½ cups whole milk, divided
- ⅔ cup (3⅓ ounces) all-purpose flour
- ½ cup (3½ ounces) granulated sugar
- ¼ teaspoon table salt
- 6 large egg yolks
- 4 tablespoons unsalted butter, cut into 4 pieces and chilled
- 1 tablespoon vanilla extract

Craquelin
- 6 tablespoons unsalted butter, softened
- ½ cup packed (3½ ounces) light brown sugar
- ¾ cup (3¾ ounces) all-purpose flour
  Pinch table salt

Choux
- 2 large eggs plus 1 large white
- 6 tablespoons water
- 5 tablespoons unsalted butter, cut into ½-inch pieces
- 2 tablespoons milk
- 1½ teaspoons granulated sugar
- ¼ teaspoon table salt
- ½ cup (2½ ounces) all-purpose flour

- 1 cup heavy cream

1. For the pastry cream: Heat 2 cups milk in medium saucepan over medium heat until just simmering. Meanwhile, whisk flour, sugar, and salt in medium bowl until combined. Add egg yolks and remaining ½ cup milk to flour mixture and whisk until smooth. Remove saucepan from heat and, whisking constantly, slowly add ½ cup milk to yolk mixture to temper. Whisking constantly, add tempered yolk mixture to milk in saucepan.

2. Return saucepan to medium heat and cook, whisking constantly, until mixture thickens slightly, about 1 minute. Reduce heat to medium-low and continue to simmer, whisking constantly, for 8 minutes longer. Increase heat to medium and cook, whisking vigorously, until very thick (mixture dripped from whisk should mound on surface), 1 to 2 minutes. Off heat, whisk in butter and vanilla until butter is melted and incorporated. Transfer to wide bowl. Press lightly greased parchment paper directly on surface and refrigerate until set, at least 2 hours or up to 24 hours.

3. For the craquelin: Mix butter and sugar in medium bowl until combined. Mix in flour and salt. Transfer mixture to large sheet of parchment and press into 6-inch square. Cover with second piece of parchment and roll dough into 13 by 9-inch rectangle (it's fine to trim and patch dough to achieve correct dimensions). Remove top piece of parchment and use 2-inch round cutter to cut 24 circles. Leaving circles and trim in place, replace top parchment and transfer to rimless baking sheet. Freeze until firm, at least 30 minutes or up to 2 days.

4. For the choux: Adjust oven rack to middle position and heat oven to 400 degrees. Spray rimmed baking sheet with vegetable oil spray and dust lightly and evenly with flour, discarding any excess. Using 2-inch round cutter, mark 24 circles on sheet. Fit pastry bag with ½-inch round tip. Beat eggs and white together in 2-cup liquid measuring cup.

5. Bring water, butter, milk, sugar, and salt to boil in small saucepan over medium heat, stirring occasionally. Off heat, stir in flour until incorporated. Return saucepan to low heat and cook, stirring constantly and using smearing motion, until mixture looks like shiny, wet sand, about 3 minutes (mixture should register between 175 and 180 degrees).

6. Immediately transfer hot mixture to food processor and process for 10 seconds to cool slightly. With processor running, add beaten eggs in steady stream and process until incorporated, about 30 seconds. Scrape down sides of bowl and continue to process until smooth, thick, sticky paste forms, about 30 seconds longer.

7. Fill pastry bag with warm mixture and pipe into 1½-inch-wide mounds on prepared sheet, using circles as guide. Using small, thin spatula, transfer 1 frozen craquelin disk to top of each mound. Bake for 15 minutes; then, without opening oven door, reduce oven temperature to 350 degrees and continue to bake until golden brown and firm, 7 to 10 minutes longer.

8. Remove sheet from oven and cut ¾-inch slit into side of each pastry with paring knife to release steam. Return pastries to oven, turn off oven, and prop open oven door with handle of wooden spoon. Let pastries dry until center is mostly dry and surface is crisp, about 45 minutes. Transfer pastries to wire rack and let cool completely.

Forming Choux au Craquelin

1. Cook choux paste and pipe into mounds on sheet, using circles as guide.

2. Top choux mounds with frozen craquelin disks. Bake pastries.

3. Pipe filling into buns until cream just starts to appear around opening.

9. Fit pastry bag with ¼-inch round tip. In large bowl, whisk cream to stiff peaks. Gently whisk pastry cream until smooth. Fold pastry cream into whipped cream until combined. Transfer one-third of mixture to pastry bag. To fill choux buns, insert pastry tip ¾ inch into opening and squeeze gently until cream just starts to appear around opening, about 2 tablespoons cream per bun. Refill bag as needed. Serve. (Choux are best eaten up to 2 hours after filling. Leftovers can be refrigerated for up to 3 days but will soften over time.)

VARIATIONS
Colorful Choux au Craquelin
Substitute granulated sugar for brown sugar in craquelin. Add gel or paste food coloring to craquelin dough until desired color is achieved.

Mocha Choux au Craquelin
Add 5 teaspoons instant espresso powder to hot milk for pastry cream. Decrease flour in craquelin to ⅔ cup and add 1 tablespoon unsweetened cocoa powder.

SEASON 20
Torta Caprese

Serves 12 to 14 • Total Time: 1½ hours, plus 2 hours 20 minutes cooling

Why This Recipe Works This torte, a classic dessert along the Amalfi Coast, is a showstopper that packs in all the richness and depth of flourless chocolate cake. It features finely ground almonds in the batter that subtly break up the fudgy crumb, making it lighter and less cloying to eat. Our version contains melted butter and bittersweet chocolate as well as vanilla, cocoa powder, and salt to boost the chocolate's complexity. Instead of grinding almonds in a food processor, we used commercial almond flour (commercial "almond meal," which may or may not be made from skin-on nuts, also works well). All flourless cakes are aerated with whipped eggs instead of chemical leaveners, and we found that whipping the whites and yolks separately in a stand mixer, each with half the sugar, created strong, stable egg foams that lightened the rich, heavy batter and prevented it from collapsing after baking.

For the best results, use a good-quality bittersweet chocolate and Dutch-processed cocoa here. We developed this recipe using our favorite bittersweet chocolate, Ghirardelli 60% Cacao Bittersweet Chocolate Premium Baking Bar, and our favorite Dutch-processed cocoa, Droste Cacao. Either almond flour or almond meal will work in this recipe; we used Bob's Red Mill.

Serve with lightly sweetened whipped cream or with Amaretto Whipped Cream or Orange Whipped Cream (recipes follow).

- 12 tablespoons unsalted butter, cut into 12 pieces
- 6 ounces bittersweet chocolate, chopped
- 1 teaspoon vanilla extract
- 4 large eggs, separated
- 1 cup (7 ounces) granulated sugar, divided
- 2 cups (7 ounces) almond flour
- 2 tablespoons Dutch-processed cocoa powder
- ½ teaspoon table salt
-    Confectioners' sugar (optional)

1. Adjust oven rack to middle position and heat oven to 325 degrees. Lightly spray 9-inch springform pan with vegetable oil spray.

2. Microwave butter and chocolate in medium bowl at 50 percent power, stirring often, until melted, 1½ to 2 minutes. Stir in vanilla and set aside.

3. Using stand mixer fitted with whisk attachment, whip egg whites on medium-low speed until foamy, about 1 minute. Increase speed to medium-high and continue to whip, slowly adding ½ cup granulated sugar, until whites are glossy and thick and hold stiff peaks, about 4 minutes longer. Transfer whites to large bowl.

4. Add egg yolks and remaining ½ cup granulated sugar to now-empty mixer bowl and whip on medium-high speed until thick and pale yellow, about 3 minutes, scraping down bowl as necessary. Add chocolate mixture and mix on medium speed until incorporated, about 15 seconds. Add almond flour, cocoa, and salt and mix until incorporated, about 30 seconds.

5. Remove bowl from mixer and stir few times with large rubber spatula, scraping bottom of bowl to ensure almond flour is fully incorporated. Add one-third of whipped whites to bowl, return bowl to mixer, and mix on medium speed until no streaks of white remain, about 30 seconds, scraping down bowl halfway through mixing. Transfer batter to bowl with remaining whites. Using large rubber spatula, gently fold whites into batter until no streaks of white remain. Pour batter into prepared pan, smooth top with spatula, and place pan on rimmed baking sheet.

6. Bake until toothpick inserted in center comes out with few moist crumbs attached, about 50 minutes, rotating pan halfway through baking. Let cake cool in pan on wire rack for 20 minutes. Remove side of pan and let cake cool completely, about 2 hours. (Cake can be wrapped in plastic wrap and stored at room temperature for up to 3 days.)

Two Chocolates Are Better Than One

"Our recipe for this Italian flourless chocolate cake falls in line with many other ATK recipes for chocolate confections in which we strive for a resonant, well-rounded chocolate flavor. A surefire path is to use chocolate in several forms; here we opt for a good-quality bittersweet, along with Dutch-processed cocoa powder. Some vanilla, and, of course, a little salt, deepens the chocolate's impact further.

Generally I'm disinclined toward flourless chocolate cakes because I find the texture to be simply too much: too dense; too buttery with no flour to mitigate it; and too fudgy, to the point of cloying. But the torta caprese beats those pitfalls. It's somewhat lighter because it includes some almond flour (or meal), which breaks up the usual density of a flourless chocolate cake. Don't get me wrong; this torta caprese is still rich, fudgy, and oh-so-satisfying, but it's not overwhelming."

—Adam

7. Dust top of cake with confectioners' sugar, if using. Using offset spatula, transfer cake to serving platter. Cut into wedges and serve.

Amaretto Whipped Cream

Makes 2 cups • Total Time: 5 minutes

For the best results, chill the bowl and the whisk attachment before whipping the cream.

1 cup heavy cream, chilled
2 tablespoons Amaretto
1 tablespoon confectioners' sugar

Using stand mixer fitted with whisk attachment, whip all ingredients on medium-low speed until foamy, about 1 minute. Increase speed to high and whip until soft peaks form, 1 to 3 minutes.

Orange Whipped Cream

Makes 2 cups • Total Time: 5 minutes

You can substitute Grand Marnier for the Cointreau, if desired.

1 cup heavy cream, chilled
2 tablespoons Cointreau
1 tablespoon confectioners' sugar
¼ teaspoon grated orange zest

Using stand mixer fitted with whisk attachment, whip all ingredients on medium-low speed until foamy, about 1 minute. Increase speed to high and whip until soft peaks form, 1 to 3 minutes.

SEASON 10

Triple-Chocolate Mousse Cake

Serves 12 to 16 • Total Time: 1¾ hours, plus 3½ hours cooling and chilling

Why This Recipe Works Triple-chocolate mousse cake is a truly decadent dessert. Most times, though, the mousse texture is exactly the same from one layer to the next and the flavor is so overpoweringly rich it's hard to finish more than a few forkfuls. We set out to tweak this showy confection. By finessing one layer at a time, starting with the dark chocolate base and building to the top white chocolate tier, we aimed to create a triple-decker that was incrementally lighter in texture—and richness. For simplicity's sake, we decided to build the whole dessert, layer by layer, in the same springform pan. For a base layer that had the heft to support the upper two tiers, we chose flourless chocolate cake instead of the typical mousse. Folding egg whites into the batter helped lighten the cake without affecting its structural integrity. For the middle layer, we started with a traditional chocolate mousse, but the texture seemed too heavy when combined with the cake, so we removed the eggs and cut back on the chocolate a bit—this resulted in the lighter, creamier layer we desired. And for the crowning layer to our cake, we made an easy white chocolate mousse by folding whipped cream into melted white chocolate—and to prevent the soft mousse from oozing during slicing, we added a little gelatin to the mix.

This recipe requires a springform pan at least 3 inches high. It is imperative that the layers are made in sequential order. Let the base cool completely before topping it with the middle layer. We recommend Ghirardelli 60% Cacao Bittersweet Chocolate Premium Baking Bar for the base and middle layers. Our preferred brand of white chocolate is Ghirardelli Classic White Baking Chips. For the best results, chill the mixer bowl before whipping the heavy cream. The entire cake can be made through step 8 and refrigerated up to a day in advance; leave it out at room temperature for up to 45 minutes before releasing it from the cake pan and serving. For neater slices, use a cheese wire or dip your knife in hot water before cutting each slice.

Bottom Layer

6 tablespoons unsalted butter, cut into 6 pieces, plus extra for greasing pan
7 ounces bittersweet chocolate, chopped fine
¾ teaspoon instant espresso powder
4 large eggs, separated
1½ teaspoons vanilla extract
Pinch table salt
⅓ cup packed (about 2½ ounces) light brown sugar, crumbled with your fingers to remove lumps, divided

Middle Layer

2 tablespoons cocoa powder, preferably Dutch-processed
5 tablespoons hot water
7 ounces bittersweet chocolate, chopped fine
1½ cups heavy cream, chilled
1 tablespoon granulated sugar
⅛ teaspoon table salt

Top Layer

- ¾ teaspoon powdered gelatin
- 1 tablespoon water
- 6 ounces white chocolate chips
- 1½ cups heavy cream, chilled, divided
  Shaved chocolate or cocoa powder
  for serving (optional)

1. For the bottom layer: Adjust oven rack to middle position and heat oven to 325 degrees. Butter bottom and sides of 9½-inch springform pan. Melt butter, chocolate, and espresso powder in large heatproof bowl set over saucepan filled with 1 inch of barely simmering water, stirring occasionally until smooth. Remove from heat and let mixture cool slightly, about 5 minutes. Whisk in egg yolks and vanilla; set aside.

2. Using stand mixer fitted with whisk attachment, beat egg whites and salt at medium speed until frothy, about 30 seconds. Add half of sugar and beat until combined, about 15 seconds. Add remaining sugar and beat at high speed until soft peaks form when whisk is lifted, about 1 minute longer, scraping down sides of bowl halfway through. Using whisk, fold one-third of beaten egg whites into chocolate mixture to lighten. Using rubber spatula, fold in remaining egg whites until no white streaks remain. Carefully transfer batter to prepared springform pan, gently smoothing top with offset spatula.

3. Bake until cake has risen, is firm around edges, and center has just set but is still soft (center of cake will spring back after pressing gently with your finger), 13 to 18 minutes. Transfer cake to wire rack and let cool completely, about 1 hour. (Cake will collapse as it cools.) Do not remove cake from pan.

4. For the middle layer: Combine cocoa powder and hot water in small bowl; set aside. Melt chocolate in large heatproof bowl set over saucepan filled with 1 inch of barely simmering water, stirring occasionally until smooth. Remove from heat and let cool slightly, 2 to 5 minutes.

5. Using clean, dry mixer bowl and whisk attachment, whip cream, granulated sugar, and salt at medium speed until mixture begins to thicken, about 30 seconds. Increase speed to high and whip until soft peaks form when whisk is lifted, 15 to 60 seconds.

6. Whisk cocoa powder mixture into melted chocolate until smooth. Using whisk, fold one-third of whipped cream into chocolate mixture to lighten. Using rubber spatula, fold in remaining whipped cream until no white streaks remain.

Spoon mousse into springform pan over cooled cake and gently tap pan on counter 3 times to remove any large air bubbles; gently smooth top with offset spatula. Wipe inside edge of pan with damp cloth to remove any drips. Refrigerate cake at least 15 minutes while preparing top layer.

7. For the top layer: In small bowl, sprinkle gelatin over water; let stand for at least 5 minutes. Place white chocolate in medium bowl. Bring ½ cup cream to simmer in small saucepan over medium-high heat. Remove from heat; add gelatin mixture and stir until fully dissolved. Pour cream mixture over white chocolate and whisk until chocolate is melted and mixture is smooth, about 30 seconds. Let cool to room temperature, stirring occasionally, 5 to 8 minutes (mixture will thicken slightly).

8. Using clean, dry mixer bowl and whisk attachment, whip remaining 1 cup cream at medium speed until it begins to thicken, about 30 seconds. Increase speed to high and whip until soft peaks form when whisk is lifted, 15 to 60 seconds. Using whisk, fold one-third of whipped cream into white chocolate mixture to lighten. Using rubber spatula, fold remaining whipped cream into white chocolate mixture until no white streaks remain. Spoon white chocolate mousse into pan over middle layer. Smooth top with offset spatula. Return cake to refrigerator and chill until set, at least 2½ hours.

9. To serve: If using, garnish top of cake with chocolate curls or dust with cocoa. Run thin knife between cake and side of springform pan; remove side of pan. Run cleaned knife along outside of cake to smooth sides. Cut into slices and serve.

Tiramisu

Serves 10 to 12 • Total Time: 45 minutes, plus 6 hours chilling

Why This Recipe Works There's a reason restaurant menus (Italian or not) offer tiramisu. Delicate ladyfingers soaked in a spiked coffee mixture layered with a sweet, creamy filling make an irresistible combination. Preparing tiramisu, however, can be labor-intensive. Some versions are overly rich, with ladyfingers that turn soggy. We wanted to avoid these issues and find a streamlined approach—one that highlighted the luxurious combination of flavors and textures that have made this dessert so popular. Instead of hauling out a double boiler to make the fussy custard-based filling (called zabaglione), we simply whipped egg yolks, sugar, salt, rum, and mascarpone together. Salt heightened the filling's subtle flavors. To lighten the filling, we found that whipped cream comple-mented the mascarpone's flavor better than whipped egg whites. For the coffee soaking mixture, we combined strong brewed coffee and espresso powder (along with more rum). To moisten the ladyfingers so that they were neither too dry nor too saturated, we dropped them one at a time into the spiked coffee mixture and rolled them over to moisten the other side for just a couple of seconds. For the best flavor and texture, we discovered that it was important to allow the tiramisu to chill in the refrigerator for at least 6 hours.

Brandy and even whiskey can stand in for the dark rum. The test kitchen prefers a tiramisu with a pronounced rum flavor; for a less potent rum flavor, halve the amount of rum added to the coffee mixture in step 1. Do not allow the mascarpone to warm to room temperature before using it; it has a tendency to break if allowed to do so.

2½ cups strong brewed coffee, room temperature
9 tablespoons dark rum, divided
1½ tablespoons instant espresso powder
6 large egg yolks, room temperature
⅔ cup (4⅔ ounces) sugar
¼ teaspoon table salt
1½ pounds mascarpone (generous 3 cups)
¾ cup heavy cream, chilled
14 ounces (42 to 60, depending on size) dried ladyfingers
3½ tablespoons cocoa powder, preferably Dutch-processed, divided
¼ cup grated semisweet or bittersweet chocolate (optional)

1. Stir together coffee, 5 tablespoons rum, and espresso powder in wide bowl or baking dish until espresso dissolves; set aside.

2. Using stand mixer fitted with whisk attachment, beat egg yolks at low speed until just combined. Add sugar and salt and beat at medium-high speed until pale yellow, 1½ to 2 minutes, scraping down sides of bowl with rubber spatula once or twice. Add remaining ¼ cup rum and beat at medium speed until just combined, 20 to 30 seconds; scrape bowl. Add mascarpone and beat at medium speed until no lumps remain, 30 to 45 seconds, scraping down sides of bowl once or twice. Transfer mixture to large bowl and set aside.

3. In now-empty mixer bowl, beat cream at medium speed until frothy, 1 to 1½ minutes. Increase speed to high and continue to beat until cream holds stiff peaks, 1 to 1½ min-utes longer. Using rubber spatula, fold one-third of whipped cream into mascarpone mixture to lighten, then gently fold in remaining whipped cream until no white streaks remain. Set mascarpone mixture aside.

4. Working with one at a time, drop half of ladyfingers into coffee mixture, roll, remove, and transfer to 13 by 9-inch glass or ceramic baking dish. (Do not submerge ladyfingers in coffee mixture; entire process should take no longer than 2 to 3 seconds for each cookie.) Arrange soaked cookies in single layer in baking dish, breaking or trimming ladyfingers as needed to fit neatly into dish.

5. Spread half of mascarpone mixture over ladyfingers; use rubber spatula to spread mixture to sides and into corners of dish and smooth the surface. Place 2 tablespoons cocoa in fine-mesh strainer and dust cocoa over mascarpone.

6. Repeat dipping and arrangement of ladyfingers; spread remaining mascarpone mixture over ladyfingers and dust with remaining 1½ tablespoons cocoa. Wipe edges of dish with dry paper towel. Cover with plastic wrap and refrigerate for 6 to 24 hours. Sprinkle with grated chocolate, if using; cut into pieces and serve chilled.

7. To make ahead: The tiramisu can be made up to 24 hours in advance.

VARIATION
Tiramisu with Cooked Eggs
Total Time: 1 hour, plus 6 hours chilling
This recipe involves cooking the yolks in a double boiler, which requires a little more effort and makes for a slightly thicker mascarpone filling, but the results are just as good as with our traditional method. You will need an additional ⅓ cup heavy cream.

After beating egg yolks, sugar, and salt until pale yellow in step 2, add ⅓ cup cream and beat at medium speed until just combined, 20 to 30 seconds; scrape bowl. Set bowl with yolk mixture over medium saucepan containing 1 inch gently simmering water; cook, constantly scraping along bottom and sides of bowl with heat-resistant rubber spatula, until mixture coats back of spoon and registers 160 degrees, 4 to 7 minutes. Remove from heat and stir vigorously to cool slightly, then set aside to cool to room temperature, about 15 minutes. Whisk in remaining ¼ cup rum until combined. Transfer bowl to stand mixer fitted with whisk attachment, add mascarpone, and beat at medium speed until no lumps remain, 30 to 45 seconds. Transfer mixture to large bowl and set aside. Continue with recipe from step 3, using the full ¾ cup cream specified.

SEASON 16
Foolproof New York Cheesecake

Serves 12 to 16 • Total Time: 4½ to 5 hours, plus 9 hours cooling, chilling, and resting

Why This Recipe Works Our original New York Cheesecake had a luxurious texture and brown surface, but some ovens produced inconsistent cakes. To revise our recipe for everyone's ovens, we first created a pastry–graham cracker hybrid crust that wouldn't become soggy. Pulsing graham crackers, sugar, flour, and salt with melted butter coated the starches, making a crisp crust. Straining and resting the filling released bubble-producing air pockets. New York–style cheesecakes usually start in a hot oven so that a burnished outer skin and puffy rim develops before the temperature is dropped, but we found the time it took for the oven temperature to change varied. We flipped the order, baking at a low temperature to set the filling and then removing it before ramping up the oven's heat. Once the oven hit 500 degrees, we put the cheesecake on the upper rack to brown. This cheesecake would now have the same texture, flavor, and appearance no matter what oven was used.

> *This cheesecake takes up to 14 hours to make (including chilling), so we recommend making it the day before serving. An accurate oven thermometer and instant-read thermometer are essential. To ensure proper baking, check that the oven thermometer is holding steady at 200 degrees and refrain from frequently taking the temperature of the cheesecake (unless it is within a few degrees of 165, allow 20 minutes between checking). Keep a close eye on the cheesecake in step 5 to prevent overbrowning.*

Crust
- 6 whole graham crackers, broken into pieces
- ⅓ cup packed (2⅓ ounces) dark brown sugar
- ½ cup (2½ ounces) all-purpose flour
- ¼ teaspoon table salt
- 7 tablespoons unsalted butter, melted, divided

Filling
- 2½ pounds cream cheese, softened
- 1½ cups (10½ ounces) granulated sugar, divided
- ⅛ teaspoon table salt
- ⅓ cup sour cream
- 2 teaspoons lemon juice
- 2 teaspoons vanilla extract
- 6 large eggs plus 2 large yolks

1. **For the crust:** Adjust oven racks to upper-middle and lower-middle positions and heat oven to 325 degrees. Process cracker pieces and sugar in food processor until finely ground, about 30 seconds. Add flour and salt and pulse to combine, 2 pulses. Add 6 tablespoons melted butter and pulse until crumbs are evenly moistened, about 10 pulses. Brush bottom of 9-inch springform pan with ½ tablespoon melted butter. Using your hands, press crumb mixture evenly into pan bottom. Using flat bottom of measuring cup or ramekin, firmly pack crust into pan. Bake on lower-middle rack until fragrant and beginning to brown around edges, about 13 minutes. Transfer to rimmed baking sheet and set aside to cool completely. Reduce oven temperature to 200 degrees.

2. **For the filling:** Using stand mixer fitted with paddle, beat cream cheese, ¾ cup sugar, and salt at medium-low speed until combined, about 1 minute. Beat in remaining ¾ cup sugar until combined, about 1 minute. Scrape beater and bowl well; add sour cream, lemon juice, and vanilla and beat at low speed until combined, about 1 minute. Add egg yolks and beat at medium-low speed until thoroughly combined, about 1 minute. Scrape bowl and beater. Add whole eggs two at a time, beating until thoroughly combined, about 30 seconds after each addition. Pour filling through fine-mesh strainer set in large bowl, pressing against strainer with rubber spatula or back of ladle to help filling pass through strainer.

3. Brush sides of springform pan with remaining ½ tablespoon melted butter. Pour filling into crust and set aside for 10 minutes to allow air bubbles to rise to top. Gently draw tines of fork across surface of cake to pop air bubbles that have risen to surface.

4. When oven thermometer reads 200 degrees, bake cheesecake on lower rack until center registers 165 degrees, 3 to 3½ hours. Remove cake from oven and increase oven temperature to 500 degrees.

5. When oven is at 500 degrees, bake cheesecake on upper rack until top is evenly browned, 4 to 12 minutes. Let cool for 5 minutes; run paring knife between cheesecake and side of springform pan. Let cheesecake cool until barely warm, 2½ to 3 hours. Wrap tightly in plastic wrap and refrigerate until cold and firmly set, at least 6 hours.

6. To unmold cheesecake, remove side of pan. Slide thin metal spatula between crust and pan bottom to loosen, then slide cheesecake onto serving plate. Let cheesecake sit at room temperature for about 30 minutes. To slice, dip sharp knife in very hot water and wipe dry between cuts. Serve. (Leftovers can be refrigerated for up to 4 days.)

Spiced Pumpkin Cheesecake

Serves 12 • Total Time: 3 hours, plus 8¼ hours cooling, chilling, and resting

Why This Recipe Works Pumpkin cheesecake is a welcome alternative to traditional pumpkin pie, but the ideal pumpkin cheesecake is elusive: It's often either too dry and dense or soft and mousse-like, while the flavor veers from too tangy to overspiced to bland. We wanted a pumpkin cheesecake with a velvety texture that balanced the flavor of sweet, earthy pumpkin with tangy cream cheese and just enough spice, and a crisp, buttery, cookie-crumb crust. For a cookie crust that complemented the pumpkin flavor, we spiced up a graham cracker crust with ginger, cinnamon, and cloves. Blotting canned pumpkin puree with paper towels remove its excess moisture, creating a smooth and creamy texture. For dairy, we liked heavy cream, not sour cream, for added richness. We also preferred white sugar to brown, which tended to overpower the pumpkin flavor. Whole eggs, vanilla, salt, lemon juice, and a moderate blend of spices rounded out our cake. And to further ensure a smooth, velvety texture, we baked the cheesecake in a water bath in a moderate oven.

> *Be sure to buy unsweetened canned pumpkin, not pumpkin pie filling, which is preseasoned and sweetened. For neater slices, clean the knife thoroughly between slices.*

Crust

  8 whole graham crackers, broken into 1-inch pieces
  7 tablespoons unsalted butter, melted, divided
  3 tablespoons sugar
 ½ teaspoon ground ginger
 ½ teaspoon ground cinnamon
 ¼ teaspoon ground cloves

Filling

  1 (15-ounce) can pumpkin puree
1⅓ cups (9⅓ ounces) sugar
  1 teaspoon ground cinnamon
 ½ teaspoon ground ginger
 ¼ teaspoon ground nutmeg
 ¼ teaspoon ground cloves
 ¼ teaspoon ground allspice
 ½ teaspoon table salt
1½ pounds cream cheese, softened
  1 tablespoon lemon juice
  1 tablespoon vanilla extract
  5 large eggs, room temperature
  1 cup heavy cream

Pumpkin for Non-Pumpkin Lovers

"I remember this recipe being developed in the test kitchen 20 years ago. At the time, I didn't think it was going to be something I would ever make because I'm not a huge pumpkin fan. Boy was I wrong. I've since made this cheesecake every Thanksgiving since I've been married—it's one of the few dishes that is requested every year (that, and my killer gravy).

The cool thing about this recipe is that it uses canned pumpkin. You'd think that taking the time to cook down a fresh pumpkin into a puree would yield a better flavor (I've tried this myself) but it doesn't. You actually have to work pretty hard to get fresh pumpkin to taste as good, and I don't think that's time well spent, especially on such a busy holiday. The graham cracker crust is the other star of this dish because it stays crisp, which is rare for a cheesecake. They usually wind up being pretty soggy. Both major brands of graham crackers work well here but I've noticed that the size of their cookies are slightly different, so don't be shy to pull out a scale to weigh here."

—Julia

1. **For the crust:** Adjust oven rack to middle position and heat oven to 325 degrees. Process graham cracker pieces in food processor to fine, even crumbs, about 30 seconds. Sprinkle 6 tablespoons melted butter, sugar, and spices over crumbs and pulse to incorporate. Sprinkle mixture into 9-inch springform pan. Press crumbs firmly into even layer using bottom of measuring cup. Bake crust until fragrant and beginning to brown, 10 to 15 minutes. Let crust cool to room temperature, about 30 minutes. Once cool, wrap outside of pan with 2 sheets of heavy-duty aluminum foil and set in large roasting pan lined with dish towel. Bring kettle of water to boil.

2. **For the filling:** Line rimmed baking sheet with triple layer of paper towels. Spread pumpkin on paper towels in even layer. Press with second triple layer of paper towels to wick away moisture. Whisk sugar, spices, and salt together in small bowl.

3. Using stand mixer fitted with paddle, beat cream cheese on medium-low speed until smooth, about 1 minute. Scrape down bowl and beaters as needed.

4. Beat in half of sugar mixture until incorporated, about 1 minute. Beat in remaining sugar mixture until incorporated, about 1 minute. Beat in dried pumpkin, lemon juice, and vanilla until incorporated, about 1 minute. Beat in eggs, one at a time, until combined, about 1 minute. Beat in heavy cream until incorporated, about 1 minute.

5. Being careful not to disturb baked crust, brush inside of springform pan with remaining 1 tablespoon melted butter. Carefully pour filling into pan. Set roasting pan, with cheesecake, on oven rack and pour boiling water into roasting pan until it reaches about halfway up sides of pan. Bake cheesecake until center registers 150 degrees, about 1½ hours.

6. Let cheesecake cool in roasting pan for 45 minutes, then transfer to wire rack and let cool until barely warm, 2½ to 3 hours, running knife around edge of cake every hour or so. Wrap pan tightly in plastic wrap and refrigerate until cold, about 3 hours.

7. To unmold cheesecake, wrap wet, hot dish towel around cake pan and let sit for 1 minute. Remove side of pan and carefully slide cake onto cake platter. Let cheesecake sit at room temperature for 30 minutes before serving.

Double-Apple Bread Pudding

Serves 6 • Total Time: 1½ hours, plus 1½ hours cooling and soaking

Why This Recipe Works Granny Smith apples bring tangy freshness to a bread pudding that's rich with creamy custard. For a bread pudding that was chock-full of apple flavor, we combined the bright Grannies with cubes of toasted challah and a rich custard laced with autumnal spices. Parcooking the apples in a little water, butter, and sugar prior to combining them with the bread and custard not only helped achieve the perfect texture but also created a fruity apple liquid that we used to boost the flavor of the custard. Toasting the challah bread cubes ensured that they soaked up the maximum amount of custard, giving the pudding a light and fluffy texture. Finally, reserving some of the toasted bread cubes and coating them in melted butter and sugar created a quasi-streusel topping that added crunch to the lush pudding.

If you can't find challah, substitute a firm high-quality sandwich bread such as Arnold Country Style White Bread or Pepperidge Farm Farmhouse Hearty White Bread. We like the brightness of Granny Smith apples here, but you can use another firm, tart apple variety. Use a glass or ceramic baking dish. In step 3, you may not need all the milk. Serve with whipped cream or vanilla ice cream, if desired.

10 ounces challah, cut into ½-inch cubes (6 cups)
2 tablespoons unsalted butter, plus
1½ tablespoons melted
½ cup packed (3½ ounces) brown sugar, divided,
plus 1½ tablespoons
⅓ cup water
2 large Granny Smith apples (8 ounces each),
peeled, cored, and cut into ½-inch pieces
1 cup milk
¾ teaspoon ground cinnamon
½ teaspoon vanilla extract
¼ teaspoon ground nutmeg
¼ teaspoon table salt
2 large eggs
1¼ cups heavy cream

1. Adjust oven rack to middle position and heat oven to 325 degrees. Spread bread cubes in single layer on rimmed baking sheet. Bake, tossing occasionally, until just dry, about 15 minutes. Let bread cubes cool for about 15 minutes; measure out ¾ cup and set aside.

2. Melt 2 tablespoons butter in 10-inch skillet over medium heat. Add ¼ cup sugar and water and whisk until sugar dissolves. Stir in apples, increase heat to medium-high, and bring to simmer. Cover and cook, stirring occasionally, for 4 minutes. Uncover and continue to cook until apples are translucent and just tender, about 4 minutes longer.

3. Drain apples in fine-mesh strainer set over 2-cup liquid measuring cup, pressing gently to remove as much juice as possible. Set aside apples. Add enough milk to juice to yield 1¼ cups liquid.

4. Combine ¼ cup sugar, cinnamon, vanilla, nutmeg, and salt in large bowl. Whisk in eggs. Whisk in cream and milk-juice mixture until combined. Gently stir in apples. Add remaining 5¼ cups bread cubes and toss to coat. Transfer mixture to 8-inch square baking dish and gently press down with spatula. Let soak for 30 minutes, pressing bread cubes into custard halfway through soaking.

5. Toss reserved bread cubes with remaining 1½ table-spoons sugar in separate bowl. Use your fingers to crush bread to create mix of small and large pieces. Add melted butter and toss to combine. Press bread cubes into custard once more and sprinkle bread topping evenly over soaked bread mixture. Place dish on rimmed baking sheet and bake until bread pudding is golden brown and center registers 160 to 165 degrees, 1 hour to 1 hour 5 minutes. Transfer to wire rack and let cool until pudding is set and just warm, about 45 minutes. Serve.

Chocolate-Raspberry Trifle

Serves 12 to 16 • Total Time: 2 hours, plus 10½ hours cooling and chilling

Why This Recipe Works For a showstopper chocolate-raspberry trifle that tasted as good as it looked, we started by making our chocolate custard so that it could chill and set while we prepared the other components. Using a moderate amount of bittersweet chocolate in combination with Dutch-processed cocoa powder and instant espresso powder helped achieve maximum chocolate flavor and a silky-smooth texture. Tender but resilient chiffon cake remained intact in the trifle even after it absorbed the surrounding moisture, and its vegetable oil–enriched crumb stayed softer in this chilled dessert than butter cake would. It baked and cooled quickly in a rimmed baking sheet and was easy to cut into flat, even squares for arranging in the trifle bowl. We mashed half of the raspberries so that their juice—thickened by a brief simmer—helped the trifle components meld. A bit of rum drizzled on each layer of cake added a festive touch. Crowned with billowy whipped cream and (optional) sprinkles, this dessert is fit for the glitziest occasion.

To use frozen raspberries, thaw them first and include the juice. Assemble the trifle (except for the top cream layer) at least 6 hours or up to two days before serving. Use a glass bowl (preferably with straight sides) with at least a 3½-quart capacity. To really dress up the trifle, top it with whole raspberries and decorative chocolate triangles sparkling with luster dust (recipe follows).

Custard

2 teaspoons vanilla extract
½ teaspoon instant espresso powder
½ cup (3½ ounces) sugar
3 tablespoons cornstarch
2 tablespoons Dutch-processed cocoa powder
¼ teaspoon table salt
3 cups whole milk, divided
3 large egg yolks (reserve whites for cake)
4 ounces bittersweet chocolate, chopped fine
5 tablespoons unsalted butter, cut into 5 pieces

Raspberry Filling

1 pound (3¼ cups) raspberries, divided
3 tablespoons sugar
1 teaspoon cornstarch
Pinch table salt

Cake

- 1⅓ cups (5⅓ ounces) cake flour
- ¾ cup (5¼ ounces) sugar
- 1½ teaspoons baking powder
- ¼ teaspoon table salt
- ⅓ cup vegetable oil
- ¼ cup water
- 2 large eggs, separated, plus 3 large whites (reserved from custard)
- 2 teaspoons vanilla extract
- ¼ teaspoon cream of tartar

Whipped Cream

- 2 cups heavy cream, divided
- 4 teaspoons sugar, divided
- 6 tablespoons rum, divided

Sprinkles (optional)

1. For the custard: Combine vanilla and espresso powder in small bowl and set aside. Whisk sugar, cornstarch, cocoa, and salt together in large saucepan. Whisk in ½ cup milk and egg yolks until fully incorporated, making sure to scrape corners of saucepan. Whisk in remaining 2½ cups milk until incorporated.

2. Whisk gently over medium heat until mixture is thickened and bubbling over entire surface, 5 to 8 minutes. Cook 30 seconds longer, remove from heat, add chocolate and butter, and whisk until melted and incorporated. Whisk in vanilla mixture.

3. Pour custard through fine-mesh strainer into wide, shallow bowl. Press lightly greased parchment paper against surface of custard and refrigerate until cool, at least 4 hours or up to 2 days.

4. For the raspberry filling: Place half of raspberries, sugar, cornstarch, and salt in medium saucepan. Place remaining raspberries in large bowl. Using potato masher, thoroughly mash raspberries in saucepan. Cook over medium heat, stirring frequently, until sugar is dissolved and mixture is thick and bubbling, 3 to 5 minutes. Pour over raspberries in bowl and stir to combine. Set aside.

5. For the cake: Adjust oven rack to middle position and heat oven to 350 degrees. Lightly grease 18 by 13-inch rimmed baking sheet, line with parchment, and lightly grease parchment. Whisk flour, sugar, baking powder, and salt together in medium bowl. Whisk oil, water, egg yolks, and vanilla into flour mixture until smooth batter forms.

6. Using stand mixer fitted with whisk attachment, whip 5 egg whites and cream of tartar on medium-low speed until foamy, about 1 minute. Increase speed to medium-high

and whip until soft peaks form, 2 to 3 minutes. Transfer one-third of whites to batter; whisk gently until mixture is lightened. Using rubber spatula, gently fold remaining whites into batter.

7. Pour batter into prepared sheet; spread evenly. Bake until cake springs back when pressed lightly in center, 10 to 13 minutes.

8. Transfer cake to wire rack; let cool for 5 minutes. Run knife around edge of sheet, then invert cake onto rack. Remove parchment, then re-invert cake onto second wire rack. Let cool completely, at least 30 minutes.

9. For the whipped cream: Using clean, dry mixer bowl and whisk attachment, whip 1 cup cream and 2 teaspoons sugar on medium-low speed until foamy, about 45 seconds. Increase speed to high and whip until soft peaks form, about 1 minute. Trim ¼ inch off each side of cake; discard trimmings. Cut cake into 24 equal pieces (each piece about 2½ inches square). Briefly whisk custard until smooth.

10. Spoon ½ cup raspberry mixture into trifle bowl and spread over bottom. Tear 1 cake square into 4 pieces and pile in center of bowl. Shingle 10 cake squares, fallen-domino-style, around bottom of trifle, placing edges against bowl wall. Tear another cake square into 4 pieces and fill in center. Drizzle 3 tablespoons rum evenly over cake. Spoon half of custard over cake and spread evenly. Spoon whipped cream over custard and spread evenly. Spoon remaining raspberry mixture over cream and spread evenly.

11. Repeat layering with remaining 12 cake squares, pressing firmly but gently on cake to remove any gaps in layers. Sprinkle with remaining 3 tablespoons rum and spread remaining custard over soaked cake. Cover trifle with plastic wrap and refrigerate for at least 6 hours or up to 2 days.

12. Using stand mixer fitted with whisk attachment, whip remaining 1 cup cream and remaining 2 teaspoons sugar on medium-low speed until foamy, about 45 seconds. Increase speed to high and whip until soft peaks form, about 1 minute. Spread or pipe cream over top of trifle. Decorate with sprinkles, if using, and serve.

ACCOMPANIMENT
DIY Chocolate Decorations
Makes 4 ounces • Total Time: 20 minutes

Our chocolate decorations add height and a touch of elegance to our Chocolate-Raspberry Trifle, but they can also be used on cakes or to adorn plated desserts. We started by melting 3 ounces of finely chopped chocolate, and then we stirred in an additional ounce of finely grated chocolate to seed the chocolate with beta crystals, the ones that give tempered chocolate its snappy texture and attractive sheen. We spread the chocolate thinly on a sheet of parchment and let it start to set up just slightly before cutting it into the desired shapes, as fully set chocolate is brittle and likely to crack when cut.

Cut the chocolate into triangles when it has just turned matte but is not yet fully hardened. Luster dust is a fine, edible, iridescent powder that gives sweets a little extra finesse. It can be found at cake decorating shops or online. The chocolate decorations can be wrapped well and refrigerated for up to one week.

4 ounces bittersweet chocolate (3 ounces chopped fine, 1 ounce grated)
Gold luster dust (optional)

1. Invert rimmed baking sheet and top with sheet of parchment paper. Tape parchment to sheet. Microwave chopped chocolate in bowl at 50 percent power, stirring every 30 seconds, until melted but not much warmer than body temperature (check by holding bowl in palm of your hand), 2 to 3 minutes. Add grated chocolate and stir until smooth, returning to microwave for no more than 5 seconds at a time to finish melting if necessary.

2. Spread chocolate thinly and evenly over prepared parchment to form rough 8 by 12-inch rectangle. Refrigerate until surface of chocolate just turns matte, 1 to 2 minutes. Using tip of sharp knife, cut half of chocolate into tall, slim triangles. Refrigerate until fully hardened, about 10 minutes. Brush triangles with luster dust, if using. Break remaining chocolate into 1-inch shards. Refrigerate until needed.

SEASON 14
Best Butterscotch Pudding

Serves 8 • Total Time: 50 minutes, plus 3 hours chilling

Why This Recipe Works For butterscotch pudding with rich, bittersweet flavor, we made butterscotch sauce by cooking butter, brown and white sugar, corn syrup, lemon juice, and salt together into a dark caramel. Because making caramel can be finicky—it can go from caramelized to burnt in a matter of seconds—we used a two-step process that gave us a larger window in which to gauge the doneness of the caramel. We first brought the mixture to a rolling boil and then we reduced the heat to a low simmer where it slowly came up to temperature and we could stop the cooking at just the right moment. To turn our butterscotch into pudding, we ditched the classical (yet time-consuming) tempering method in favor of a revolutionary technique that calls for pouring the boiling caramel sauce directly over the thickening agents (egg yolks and cornstarch thinned with a little milk). The result is the sophisticated bittersweet flavor of traditional butterscotch with less mess and fuss.

When taking the temperature of the caramel in step 1, tilt the pan and move the thermometer back and forth to equalize hot and cool spots. Work quickly when pouring the caramel mixture over the egg mixture in step 4 to ensure proper thickening. Serve the pudding with lightly sweetened whipped cream.

12 tablespoons unsalted butter, cut into ½-inch pieces
½ cup (3½ ounces) granulated sugar
½ cup packed (3½ ounces) dark brown sugar
¼ cup water
2 tablespoons light corn syrup
1 teaspoon lemon juice
¾ teaspoon table salt
1 cup heavy cream, divided
2¼ cups whole milk, divided
4 large egg yolks
¼ cup (1 ounce) cornstarch
2 teaspoons vanilla extract
1 teaspoon dark rum

1. Bring butter, granulated sugar, brown sugar, water, corn syrup, lemon juice, and salt to boil in large saucepan over medium heat, stirring occasionally to dissolve sugar and melt butter. Once mixture is at full rolling boil, cook, stirring occasionally, for 5 minutes (caramel will register about 240 degrees). Immediately reduce heat to medium-low and simmer gently (caramel should maintain steady stream of lazy bubbles—if not, adjust heat accordingly), stirring frequently, until mixture is color of dark peanut butter, 12 to 16 minutes longer (caramel will register about 300 degrees and should have slight burnt smell).

2. Remove pan from heat; carefully pour ¼ cup cream into caramel mixture and swirl to incorporate (mixture will bubble and steam); let bubbling subside. Whisk vigorously and scrape corners of pan until mixture is completely smooth, at least 30 seconds. Return pan to medium heat and gradually whisk in remaining ¾ cup cream until smooth. Whisk in 2 cups milk until mixture is smooth, making sure to scrape corners and edges of pan to remove any remaining bits of caramel.

3. Meanwhile, microwave remaining ¼ cup milk until simmering, 30 to 45 seconds. Whisk egg yolks and cornstarch in large bowl until smooth. Gradually whisk in hot milk until smooth; set aside (do not refrigerate).

4. Return saucepan to medium-high heat and bring mixture to full rolling boil, whisking frequently. Once mixture is boiling rapidly and beginning to climb toward top of pan, immediately pour into bowl with yolk mixture in 1 motion (do not add gradually). Whisk thoroughly for 10 to 15 seconds (mixture will thicken after a few seconds). Whisk in vanilla and rum. Spray piece of parchment paper with vegetable oil spray and press on surface of pudding. Refrigerate until cold and set, at least 3 hours. Whisk pudding until smooth before serving.

Classic Crème Brûlée

Serves 8 • Total Time: 1¼ hours, plus 2 hours cooling and 4½ hours chilling

Why This Recipe Works Crème brûlée is all about the contrast between the crisp sugar crust and the silky custard underneath. But too often the crust is either skimpy or rock-hard and the custard is heavy and tasteless. Because crème brûlée requires so few ingredients, we knew that finding just the right technique would be key in creating the quintessential version of this elegant dessert. The texture of the custard should not be firm but rather soft and supple. The secret, we found, is using egg yolks—and lots of them—rather than whole eggs. Heavy cream gave the custard a luxurious richness. Sugar, a vanilla bean, and a pinch of salt were the only other additions. Despite

instructions in many recipes to use scalded cream, we found that this technique was more likely to result in overcooked custard, so we thought we would leave the ingredients cold. The downside, however, was that we needed heat to extract flavor from the vanilla bean and dissolve the sugar. Our compromise was to heat only half of the cream with the sugar and vanilla bean and add the remaining cream cold, which worked perfectly. For the crust, we used crunchy turbinado sugar, which was easy to spread on the baked and chilled custards. A propane or butane torch worked better than the broiler for caramelizing the sugar, and because the blast of heat inevitably warms the custard beneath the crust, we chilled our crèmes brûlées once more before serving.

Separate the eggs and whisk the yolks after the cream has finished steeping; if left to sit, the surface of the yolks will dry and form a film. A vanilla bean gives the custard the deepest flavor, but 2 teaspoons of vanilla extract, whisked into the yolks in step 4, can be used instead. The best way to judge doneness is with an instant-read thermometer. While we prefer turbinado or Demerara sugar for the caramelized sugar crust, regular granulated sugar will work, too, but use only 1 scant teaspoon for each ramekin. It's important to use 6-ounce ramekins.

1 vanilla bean
4 cups heavy cream, divided
⅔ cup (4⅔ ounces) granulated sugar
   Pinch table salt
12 large egg yolks
8 teaspoons turbinado or Demerara sugar

1. Adjust oven rack to lower-middle position and heat oven to 300 degrees.

2. Cut vanilla bean in half lengthwise. Using tip of paring knife, scrape out seeds. Combine vanilla bean and seeds, 2 cups cream, granulated sugar, and salt in medium saucepan. Bring cream mixture to boil over medium heat, stirring occasionally to dissolve sugar. Off heat, let steep for 15 minutes.

3. Meanwhile, place dish towel in bottom of large baking dish or roasting pan; set eight 6-ounce ramekins on towel (they should not touch). Bring kettle of water to boil.

4. After cream mixture has steeped, stir in remaining 2 cups cream. Whisk egg yolks in large bowl until uniform. Whisk about 1 cup cream mixture into yolks until combined; repeat with another 1 cup cream mixture. Add remaining cream mixture and whisk until evenly colored and thoroughly combined. Strain mixture through fine-mesh strainer into large bowl; discard solids in strainer. Divide mixture evenly among ramekins.

5. Set baking dish on oven rack. Taking care not to splash water into ramekins, pour enough boiling water into dish to reach two-thirds up sides of ramekins. Bake until centers of custards are just barely set and register 170 to 175 degrees, 30 to 35 minutes, checking temperature about 5 minutes before recommended minimum time.

6. Transfer ramekins to wire rack and let cool completely, about 2 hours. Set ramekins on baking sheet, cover tightly with plastic wrap, and refrigerate until cold, at least 4 hours.

7. Uncover ramekins; if condensation has collected on custards, blot moisture from tops of custards with paper towel. Sprinkle each with about 1 teaspoon turbinado sugar; tilt and tap each ramekin to distribute sugar evenly, dumping out excess sugar. Ignite torch and caramelize sugar, keeping torch flame 2 inches above sugar and slowly sweeping flame across sugar, starting at perimeter and moving toward middle, until sugar is bubbling and deep golden brown. Refrigerate ramekins, uncovered, to rechill, 30 to 45 minutes; serve.

VARIATION
Espresso Crème Brûlée
Place ¼ cup espresso beans in zipper-lock bag and crush lightly with rolling pin or meat pounder until coarsely cracked. Follow recipe for Classic Crème Brûlée, substituting cracked espresso beans for vanilla bean and whisking 1 teaspoon vanilla extract into egg yolks in step 4 before adding cream.

SEASON 15

Latin Flan

Serves 8 to 10 • Total Time: 2 hours, plus 12 hours cooling and chilling

Why This Recipe Works The Latin style of this baked custard isn't light and quivering like its European counterparts. It is far richer and more densely creamy, with a texture somewhere between pudding and cheesecake. It also boasts a more deeply caramelized, toffee-like flavor. We got to work on a version that was as dense and rich-tasting as it was creamy. The custard gets its thick, luxurious texture from canned milk—evaporated as well as sweetened condensed. But we realized that the high protein content of canned milk products was contributing to a stiff texture. Removing one egg from the mix helped, but not enough. To further improve creaminess, we added ½ cup of fresh milk. Wrapping the cake pan in foil before baking prevented a skin from forming on top, and reducing the oven temperature ensured that the custard baked evenly. Switching from a shallow cake pan to a loaf pan produced a gorgeous, tall flan less likely to crack. Adding a bit of water to the warm caramel and letting the baked flan sit overnight helped more of the caramel to come out of the dish, creating a substantial layer of gooey caramel.

This recipe should be made at least one day before serving. We recommend an 8½ by 4½-inch loaf pan for this recipe. If your pan is 9 by 5 inches, begin checking for doneness at 1 hour 15 minutes. You may substitute 2 percent milk for the whole milk, but do not use skim milk. Serve the flan on a platter with a raised rim to contain the liquid caramel.

2/3 cup (4²/₃ ounces) sugar

¼ cup water plus 2 tablespoons warm tap water, divided

2 large eggs plus 5 large yolks

1 (14-ounce) can sweetened condensed milk

1 (12-ounce) can evaporated milk

½ cup whole milk

1½ tablespoons vanilla extract

½ teaspoon table salt

1. Stir together sugar and ¼ cup water in medium heavy saucepan until sugar is completely moistened. Bring to boil over medium-high heat, 3 to 5 minutes, and cook without stirring until mixture begins to turn golden, another 1 to 2 minutes. Gently swirling pan, continue to cook until sugar is the color of peanut butter, 1 to 2 minutes. Remove from heat and swirl pan until sugar is reddish-amber and fragrant, 15 to 20 seconds. Carefully swirl in remaining 2 tablespoons warm tap water until incorporated; mixture will bubble and steam. Pour caramel into 8½ by 4½-inch loaf pan; do not scrape out saucepan. Set loaf pan aside.

2. Adjust oven rack to middle position and heat oven to 300 degrees. Line bottom of 13 by 9-inch baking pan with dish towel, folding towel to fit smoothly, and set aside. Bring 2 quarts water to boil.

3. Whisk eggs and yolks until combined. Add sweetened condensed milk, evaporated milk, whole milk, vanilla, and salt and whisk until incorporated. Strain mixture through fine-mesh strainer into prepared loaf pan.

4. Cover loaf pan tightly with aluminum foil and place in prepared baking pan. Place baking pan in oven and carefully pour boiling water into pan. Bake until center of custard jiggles slightly when shaken and custard registers 180 degrees, 1¼ to 1½ hours. Remove foil and leave custard in water bath until loaf pan has cooled to room temperature. Wrap loaf pan tightly with plastic wrap and chill overnight or up to 4 days.

5. To unmold, slide paring knife around edges of pan. Invert serving platter on top of pan and turn pan and platter over. When flan is released, remove loaf pan. Use rubber spatula to scrape residual caramel onto flan. Slice and serve. Leftover flan may be covered loosely and refrigerated for up to 4 days.

VARIATIONS
Coffee Flan
Whisk 4 teaspoons of instant espresso powder into egg-milk mixture until dissolved.

Orange-Cardamom Flan
Whisk 2 tablespoons grated orange zest and ¼ teaspoon ground cardamom into egg-milk mixture before straining.

Chocolate Pots de Crème

Serves 8 • Total Time: 40 minutes, plus 4 hours 50 minutes cooling, chilling, and standing

Why This Recipe Works Classic pots de crème is a decadent dessert with a satiny texture and intense chocolate flavor. It can be finicky and laborious, requiring a hot water bath that threatens to splash the custards every time the pan is moved. In addition, the individual custards don't always cook at the same rate. Our user-friendly recipe eradicates those problems.

First we moved the dish out of the oven, concentrating on an unconventional approach in which the custard is cooked on the stovetop in a saucepan and then poured into ramekins. Our next challenge was developing the right amount of richness and body, which we did by choosing a combination of heavy cream and half-and-half, along with egg yolks only, for maximum richness. For intense chocolate flavor, we focused on bittersweet chocolate—and a lot of it. Our chocolate content was at least 50 percent more than in any other recipe we had encountered.

We prefer pots de crème made with 60 percent bittersweet chocolate (our favorite brand is Ghirardelli Bittersweet Chocolate), but 70 percent bittersweet chocolate can also be used. If using a 70 percent bittersweet chocolate, reduce the amount of chocolate to 8 ounces. An instant-read thermometer is the most reliable way to judge when the custard has reached the proper temperature. However, you can also judge the progress of the custard by its thickness. Dip a wooden spoon into the custard and run your finger across the back. The custard is ready when it coats the spoon and a line drawn maintains neat edges. The pots de crème (minus the whipped cream garnish) can be covered tightly with plastic wrap and refrigerated for up to three days.

Pots de Crème
10 ounces bittersweet chocolate, chopped fine

5 large egg yolks

5 tablespoons (2¼ ounces) sugar

¼ teaspoon table salt

1½ cups heavy cream

¾ cup half-and-half

1 tablespoon vanilla extract

½ teaspoon instant espresso powder mixed with 1 tablespoon water

GAME CHANGER

The Power of Espresso Powder

"This recipe has a very special place in my heart. Not only is it deeply, deeply chocolaty and satisfying, but it also plays a part in some of my favorite memories over my years of working in the test kitchen. When I wrote a tasting story about dark chocolate several years ago, I made this recipe with every one of the chocolate brands in our lineup. The stampede to the table when I called around the company asking for tasters was impressive. Everyone was bubbly and happy, unlike when we taste more, shall we say, 'difficult' ingredient lineups like vinegar or vegan mayonnaise. It also reminds me of a time I was asked to judge a chocolate dessert contest in Boston, and I realized that far too many chocolate desserts have no actual chocolate flavor. If blindfolded, all you'd detect is sweetness. From this recipe, I first learned to enhance the nuances of chocolate flavor with a bit of instant espresso powder. And I saw that here, as usual, ATK test cooks go above and beyond: This recipe packs in 50 percent more chocolate than is typical. Trust me, you'll never be in doubt of its rich chocolate deliciousness."

—Lisa

Whipped Cream and Garnish

- ½ cup heavy cream, chilled
- 2 teaspoons sugar
- ½ teaspoon vanilla extract
  Cocoa, for dusting (optional)
  Chocolate shavings, for sprinkling (optional)

1. For the pots de crème: Place chocolate in medium heatproof bowl; set fine-mesh strainer over bowl and set aside.

2. Whisk egg yolks, sugar, and salt in medium bowl until combined, then whisk in heavy cream and half-and-half. Transfer mixture to medium saucepan. Cook mixture over medium-low heat, stirring constantly and scraping bottom of pot with wooden spoon, until it is thickened and silky and registers 175 to 180 degrees, 8 to 12 minutes. (Do not let custard overcook or simmer.)

3. Immediately pour custard through strainer over chocolate. Let mixture stand to melt chocolate, about 5 minutes. Whisk gently until smooth, then whisk in vanilla and dissolved espresso. Divide mixture evenly among eight 5-ounce ramekins. Gently tap ramekins against counter to remove any air bubbles.

4. Let pots de crème cool to room temperature, then cover with plastic wrap and refrigerate until chilled, at least 4 hours or up to 3 days. Before serving, let pots de crème stand at room temperature for 20 to 30 minutes.

5. For the whipped cream and garnish: Using stand mixer fitted with whisk attachment, whip cream, sugar, and vanilla on medium-low speed until small bubbles form, about 30 seconds. Increase speed to medium-high and continue to whip mixture until it thickens and forms stiff peaks, about 1 minute. Dollop each pot de crème with about 2 tablespoons of whipped cream and garnish with cocoa and/or chocolate shavings, if using. Serve.

VARIATION
Milk Chocolate Pots de Crème

Milk chocolate behaves differently in this recipe than bittersweet chocolate, and more of it must be used to ensure that the custard sets. And because of the increased amount of chocolate, it's necessary to cut back on the amount of sugar so that the custard is not overly sweet.

Substitute 12 ounces milk chocolate for 10 ounces bittersweet chocolate. Reduce amount of sugar to 2 tablespoons.

Chocolate Semifreddo

Serves 12 • Total Time: 1 hour, plus 6 hours chilling

Why This Recipe Works Semifreddo, a classic Italian dessert that's often described as a frozen mousse, typically starts with a custard base. For a chocolate semifreddo that was rich and creamy, we started by preparing a custard-style base of whole eggs, sugar, cream, and water directly on the stovetop (rather than over a fussy water bath). We conveniently melted the chocolate by straining the hot custard directly over it. To ensure a rich, creamy, and sliceable semifreddo that was also cold and refreshing, we had to balance fat and water: Using whole eggs instead of yolks and cutting the cream in the custard base with a bit of water were key. Garnishing the semifreddo with a sweet cherry sauce and crunchy candied nuts added contrast and made for an elegant presentation. Semifreddo can sit out of the freezer without melting, making it ideal for serving to company.

The semifreddo needs to be frozen for at least 6 hours before serving. We developed this recipe with our favorite dark chocolate, Ghirardelli 60% Cacao Bittersweet Chocolate Premium Baking Bar. Do not whip the heavy cream until the chocolate mixture has cooled. If the semifreddo is difficult to release from the pan, run a thin offset spatula around the edges of the pan or carefully run the sides of the pan under hot water for 5 to 10 seconds. If frozen overnight, the semifreddo should be tempered before serving for the best texture. To temper, place slices on individual plates or a large tray and refrigerate for 30 minutes. Serve the semifreddo as is or with our Cherry Sauce (recipe follows). For some crunch, sprinkle each serving with Quick Candied Nuts (recipe follows).

- 8 ounces bittersweet chocolate, chopped fine
- 1 tablespoon vanilla extract
- ½ teaspoon instant espresso powder
- 3 large eggs
- 5 tablespoons (2¼ ounces) sugar
- ¼ teaspoon table salt
- 2 cups heavy cream, chilled, divided
- ¼ cup water

1. Lightly spray loaf pan with vegetable oil spray and line with plastic wrap, leaving 3-inch overhang on all sides. Place chocolate in large heatproof bowl; set fine-mesh strainer over bowl and set aside. Stir vanilla and espresso powder in small bowl until espresso powder is dissolved.

2. Whisk eggs, sugar, and salt in medium bowl until combined. Heat ½ cup cream (keep remaining 1½ cups chilled) and water in medium saucepan over medium heat until simmering. Slowly whisk hot cream mixture into egg mixture until combined. Return mixture to saucepan and cook over medium-low heat, stirring constantly and scraping bottom of saucepan with rubber spatula, until mixture is very slightly thickened and registers 160 to 165 degrees, about 5 minutes. Do not let mixture simmer.

3. Immediately pour mixture through strainer set over chocolate. Let mixture stand to melt chocolate, about 5 minutes. Whisk until chocolate is melted and smooth, then whisk in vanilla-espresso mixture. Let chocolate mixture cool completely, about 15 minutes.

4. Using stand mixer fitted with whisk attachment, beat remaining 1½ cups cream on low speed until bubbles form, about 30 seconds. Increase speed to medium and beat until whisk leaves trail, about 30 seconds. Increase speed to high and continue to beat until nearly doubled in volume and whipped cream forms soft peaks, 30 to 45 seconds longer.

5. Whisk one-third of whipped cream into chocolate mixture. Using rubber spatula, gently fold remaining whipped cream into chocolate mixture until incorporated and no streaks of whipped cream remain. Transfer mixture to prepared pan and spread evenly with rubber spatula. Fold overhanging plastic over surface. Freeze until firm, at least 6 hours.

6. When ready to serve, remove plastic from surface and invert pan onto serving plate. Remove plastic and smooth surface with spatula as necessary. Dip slicing knife in very hot water and wipe dry. Slice semifreddo ¾ inch thick,

transferring slices to individual plates and dipping and wiping knife after each slice. Serve immediately. (Semifreddo can be wrapped tightly in plastic wrap and frozen for up to 2 weeks.)

ACCOMPANIMENTS

Cherry Sauce

Makes 2 cups
Total Time: 20 minutes, plus 20 minutes cooling
This recipe was developed with frozen cherries. Do not thaw the cherries before using. Water can be substituted for the kirsch, if desired.

    12 ounces frozen sweet cherries
    ¼   cup (1¾ ounces) sugar
    2   tablespoons kirsch
    1½ teaspoons cornstarch
    1   tablespoon lemon juice

1. Combine cherries and sugar in bowl and microwave for 1½ minutes. Stir, then continue to microwave until sugar is mostly dissolved, about 1 minute longer. Combine kirsch and cornstarch in small bowl.

2. Drain cherries in fine-mesh strainer set over small saucepan. Return cherries to bowl and set aside.

3. Bring juice in saucepan to simmer over medium-high heat. Stir in kirsch mixture and bring to boil. Boil, stirring occasionally, until mixture has thickened and appears syrupy, 1 to 2 minutes. Remove saucepan from heat and stir in cherries and lemon juice. Let sauce cool completely before serving. (Sauce can be refrigerated for up to 1 week.)

Quick Candied Nuts

Makes ½ cup
Total Time: 50 minutes, plus 20 minutes cooling
We like this recipe prepared with shelled pistachios, walnut or pecan halves, roasted cashews, salted or unsalted peanuts, and sliced almonds. If you want to make a mixed batch, cook the nuts individually and then toss to combine once you've chopped them.

    ½   cup nuts
    1   tablespoon sugar
    1   tablespoon hot water
    ⅛   teaspoon table salt

1. Adjust oven rack to middle position and heat oven to 350 degrees. Spread nuts in single layer on rimmed baking sheet and toast until fragrant and slightly darkened, 8 to 12 minutes, shaking sheet halfway through toasting. Transfer nuts to plate and let cool for 10 to 15 minutes. Do not wash sheet.

2. Line now-empty sheet with parchment paper. Whisk sugar, hot water, and salt in large bowl until sugar is mostly dissolved. Add nuts and stir to coat. Spread nuts on prepared sheet in single layer and bake until nuts are crisp and dry, 10 to 12 minutes.

3. Transfer sheet to wire rack and let nuts cool completely, about 20 minutes. Transfer nuts to cutting board and chop as desired. (Nuts can be stored at room temperature for up to 1 week.)

Lemon Posset with Berries

Serves 6 • **Total Time: 35 minutes, plus 3 hours 20 minutes cooling and chilling**

Why This Recipe Works Lemon posset is a lush pudding with clean citrus flavor. This classic English dessert is exceptionally easy to make: There are no temperamental egg yolks or add-ins needed to help the mixture thicken or set or to interfere with the bright taste of citrus. We found that using just the right proportions of sugar and lemon juice—along with a generous amount of lemon zest—was the key to custard with a smooth, luxurious consistency and a bright enough flavor to balance the richness of the cream. For an optimally dense, firm set, we reduced the cream-sugar mixture to 2 cups before adding the lemon juice, which in turn caused the mixture to solidify. Letting the warm mixture rest for 20 minutes before straining allowed the flavors to meld and ensured a silky-smooth consistency. We topped the posset with fresh berries for textural contrast and to keep it from feeling overly rich.

This dessert requires portioning into individual servings. Reducing the cream mixture to exactly 2 cups creates the best consistency. Transfer the liquid to a 2-cup heatproof liquid measuring cup once or twice during boiling to monitor the amount. Do not leave the cream unattended, as it can boil over easily.

  2 cups heavy cream
 ²/₃ cup (4²/₃ ounces) sugar
  1 tablespoon grated lemon zest plus
     6 tablespoons juice (2 lemons)
 1½ cups (7½ ounces) blueberries or raspberries

1. Combine cream, sugar, and lemon zest in medium saucepan and bring to boil over medium heat. Continue to boil, stirring frequently to dissolve sugar. If mixture begins to boil over, briefly remove from heat. Cook until mixture is reduced to 2 cups, 8 to 12 minutes.

2. Remove saucepan from heat and stir in lemon juice. Let sit until mixture is cooled slightly and skin forms on top, about 20 minutes. Strain through fine-mesh strainer into bowl; discard zest. Divide mixture evenly among 6 individual ramekins or serving glasses.

3. Refrigerate, uncovered, until set, at least 3 hours. Once chilled, possets can be wrapped in plastic wrap and refrigerated for up to 2 days. Unwrap and let sit at room temperature for 10 minutes before serving. Garnish with berries and serve.

Make-Ahead Chocolate Soufflés

Serves 6 to 8 • **Total time: 45 minutes, plus 3 hours freezing**

Why This Recipe Works To eliminate the anxiety of making chocolate soufflé, we found a way to make it in advance. We wanted the chocolate to be front and center, so we used a base of egg yolks beaten with sugar, with no flour or milk to mute the chocolate flavor. Instead of an equal number of egg yolks and whites, we found that two extra whites lightened and lifted our chocolaty base. Now that we had the flavor and texture we wanted, it was time to address the problem of making the soufflé ahead of time. To our amazement, the answer was simple: freezing. Adding a little confectioners' sugar to the egg whites stabilized them so they held up in the freezer, and individual ramekins produced better results than a single large soufflé dish. Now we could make our dinner party dessert in advance, confident that we could pull perfectly risen, rich chocolate soufflés from the oven at the end of the meal.

> *This technique only works for the individual chocolate soufflés, which can be made and frozen for at least 3 hours and up to one month before baking. If you are microwave oriented, melt the chocolate at 50 percent power for 3 minutes, stirring in the butter after 2 minutes.*

Ramekin Preparation
- 2 tablespoons unsalted butter, softened
- 2 tablespoons granulated sugar

Soufflés
- 8 ounces bittersweet or semisweet chocolate, chopped coarse
- 4 tablespoons unsalted butter, cut into ½-inch pieces
- 1 tablespoon Grand Marnier
- ½ teaspoon vanilla extract
- ⅛ teaspoon table salt
- 6 large eggs, separated, plus 2 large whites
- ⅓ cup (2⅓ ounces) granulated sugar
- ¼ teaspoon cream of tartar
- 2 tablespoons confectioners' sugar

1. For the ramekins: Coat inside of eight 8-ounce ramekins with softened butter, then coat inside of each dish evenly with sugar. Refrigerate until ready to use.

2. For the soufflés: Melt chocolate and butter in medium heatproof bowl set over saucepan filled with 1 inch of barely simmering water, stirring frequently until smooth. Remove from heat and stir in Grand Marnier, vanilla, and salt; set aside.

3. Using stand mixer fitted with whisk attachment, whip egg yolks and granulated sugar at medium speed until mixture triples in volume and is thick and pale yellow, 3 to 8 minutes. Fold yolk mixture into chocolate mixture.

4. Using clean, dry mixer bowl and whisk attachment, whip egg whites at medium-low speed until frothy, 1 to 2 minutes. Add cream of tartar, increase mixer speed to medium-high, and whip until soft peaks form, 1 to 2 minutes. Add confectioners' sugar and continue to whip until stiff peaks form, 2 to 4 minutes (do not overwhip). Whisk last few strokes by hand, making sure to scrape any unwhipped whites from bottom of bowl.

5. Vigorously stir one-quarter of whipped egg whites into chocolate mixture. Gently fold remaining whites into chocolate mixture until just incorporated. Carefully spoon

mixture into prepared ramekins almost to rim, wiping excess filling from rims with wet paper towel. If making foil collar for ramekins, see below. (To serve right away, bake as directed in step 7, reducing baking time to 12 to 15 minutes.)

6. To store: Cover each ramekin tightly with plastic wrap and then foil and freeze for at least 3 hours or up to 1 month. (Do not thaw before baking.)

7. To bake and serve: Adjust oven rack to lower-middle position and heat oven to 400 degrees. Unwrap frozen ramekins and spread them out on baking sheet. Bake soufflés until fragrant, fully risen, and exterior is set but interior is still a bit loose and creamy, about 25 minutes. (To check interior, use 2 spoons to pull open top of one and peek inside.) Serve immediately.

VARIATION
Make-Ahead Mocha Soufflés
Add 1 tablespoon instant coffee or espresso powder dissolved in 1 tablespoon hot water to melted chocolate with vanilla in step 2.

Making a Foil Collar

Placing a foil collar around ramekins yields higher rise and flatter top. After filling ramekins, secure strip of oiled foil around ramekins so it extends 2 inches above rim. If needed, you can tape collar to dish to prevent it from slipping.

Pavlova with Fruit and Whipped Cream

Serves 10 • Total Time: 2 to 2½ hours, plus 1½ hours cooling

Why This Recipe Works Pavlova is a gorgeous dessert featuring crisp-shelled meringue piled with whipped cream and fresh fruit. For a foolproof pavlova, we switched from the typical French meringue—which requires precise timing when adding sugar to egg whites—to a Swiss meringue, which is made by dissolving the sugar in the egg whites as they are heated over a water bath and then whipping the mixture to stiff peaks. Cornstarch and vinegar produced a meringue that was marshmallowy within, with a slight chew at the edge; plenty of sugar ensured a crisp exterior. We shaped the meringue into a wide disk, baked it, and let it dry in a turned-off oven. Whipped cream and fresh fruit balanced the meringue's sweetness and made for a beautiful presentation. Letting the meringue sit before serving helped soften the crust for neater slices.

> *Because eggs can vary in size, measuring the egg whites by weight or volume is essential to ensure that you are working with the correct ratio of egg whites to sugar. Open the oven door as infrequently as possible while the meringue is inside. Do not worry if the meringue cracks; it is part of the dessert's charm. The inside of the meringue will remain soft.*

Meringue

1½ cups (10½ ounces) sugar
¾ cup (6 ounces) egg whites (5 to 7 large eggs)
1½ teaspoons distilled white vinegar
1½ teaspoons cornstarch
1 teaspoon vanilla extract

Whipped Cream

2 cups heavy cream, chilled
2 tablespoons sugar

1 recipe fruit topping (recipes follow)

1. For the meringue: Adjust oven rack to middle position and heat oven to 250 degrees. Using pencil, draw 10-inch circle in center of 18 by 13-inch piece of parchment paper.

2. Combine sugar and egg whites in bowl of stand mixer; place bowl over saucepan filled with 1 inch simmering water, making sure that water does not touch bottom of bowl. Whisking gently but constantly, heat until sugar is dissolved and mixture registers 160 to 165 degrees, 5 to 8 minutes.

3. Fit stand mixer with whisk attachment and whip mixture on high speed until meringue forms stiff peaks, is smooth and creamy, and is bright white with sheen, about 4 minutes (bowl may still be slightly warm to touch). Stop mixer and scrape down bowl with spatula. Add vinegar, cornstarch, and vanilla and whip on high speed until combined, about 10 seconds.

4. Spoon about ¼ teaspoon meringue onto each corner of rimmed baking sheet. Press parchment, marked side down, onto sheet to secure. Pile meringue in center of circle on parchment. Using circle as guide, spread and smooth meringue with back of spoon or spatula from center outward, building 10-inch disk that is slightly higher around edges. Finished disk should measure about 1 inch high with ¼-inch depression in center.

5. Bake meringue until exterior is dry and crisp and meringue releases cleanly from parchment when gently lifted at edge with thin metal spatula, 1 to 1½ hours. Meringue should be quite pale (a hint of creamy color is OK). Turn off oven, prop door open with wooden spoon, and let meringue cool in oven for 1½ hours. Remove from oven and let cool completely before topping, about 15 minutes. (Cooled meringue can be wrapped tightly in plastic wrap and stored at room temperature for up to 1 week.)

6. For the whipped cream: Whip cream and sugar in chilled bowl of stand mixer fitted with whisk attachment on low speed until small bubbles form, about 30 seconds. Increase speed to medium and whip until whisk leaves trail, about 30 seconds. Increase speed to high and continue to whip until cream is smooth, thick, and nearly doubled in volume, about 20 seconds longer for soft peaks. If necessary, finish whipping by hand to adjust consistency.

7. Carefully peel meringue away from parchment and place on large serving platter. Spoon whipped cream into center of meringue. Top whipped cream with fruit topping. Let stand for at least 5 minutes or up to 1 hour, then slice and serve.

VARIATION

Individual Pavlovas with Fruit and Whipped Cream

Adjust oven racks to upper-middle and lower-middle positions and heat oven to 250 degrees. In step 4, spoon about ¼ teaspoon meringue onto each corner of 2 rimmed baking sheets. Line sheets with parchment paper. Spoon heaping ½ cup meringue into 5 evenly spaced piles on each sheet. Spread each meringue pile with back of spoon to form 3½-inch disk with slight depression in center. Decrease baking time in step 5 to 50 minutes. Top each meringue with ½ cup whipped cream, followed by ½ cup fruit topping.

TOPPINGS

Orange, Cranberry, and Mint Topping

Makes 4½ cups   •   Total Time: 25 minutes, plus 1½ hours cooling and resting

You can substitute tangelos or Cara Cara oranges for the navel oranges, if desired. Valencia or blood oranges can also be used, but since they are smaller, increase the number of oranges to six.

- 1½ cups (10½ ounces) sugar, divided
- 6 ounces (1½ cups) frozen cranberries
- 5 navel oranges
- ⅓ cup chopped fresh mint, plus 10 small mint leaves

1. Bring 1 cup sugar and 1 cup water to boil in medium saucepan over medium heat, stirring to dissolve sugar.

Off heat, stir in cranberries. Let cranberries and syrup cool completely, about 30 minutes. (Cranberries in syrup can be refrigerated for up to 24 hours.)

2. Place remaining ½ cup sugar in shallow dish. Drain cranberries, discarding syrup. Working in 2 batches, roll ½ cup cranberries in sugar and transfer to large plate or tray. Let stand at room temperature to dry, about 1 hour.

3. Cut away peel and pith from oranges. Cut each orange into quarters from pole to pole, then cut crosswise into ¼-inch-thick pieces (you should have 3 cups). Just before serving, toss oranges with non-sugared cranberries and chopped mint in bowl until combined. Using slotted spoon, spoon fruit in even layer over pavlova. Garnish with sugared cranberries and mint leaves. Before serving, drizzle pavlova slices with any juice from bowl.

Mango, Kiwi, and Blueberry Topping

Makes 5 cups   •   Total Time: 15 minutes, plus 30 minutes resting

Do not use frozen blueberries in this recipe.

- 3 large mangos, peeled, pitted, and cut into ½-inch pieces (3 cups)
- 2 kiwis, peeled, quartered lengthwise, and sliced crosswise ¼ inch thick (about 1 cup)
- 5 ounces (1 cup) blueberries
- 1 tablespoon sugar

Toss all ingredients together in large bowl. Set aside for 30 minutes. Using slotted spoon, spoon fruit in even layer over pavlova. Before serving, drizzle pavlova slices with any juice from bowl.

Making a Stunning Pavlova

1. Whip 160-degree mixture of egg whites and sugar until stiff, glossy, and pure white, then add vinegar, cornstarch, and vanilla.

2. Scoop meringue onto parchment and spread and smooth into 10-inch disk. Use back of spoon to create rim around edge.

3. Bake for 1 hour, then turn off oven and prop door open for 1½ hours, at which point meringue will be dry and crisp and lift cleanly from parchment.

4. Let topped pavlova sit briefly so meringue softens for neater slicing. To slice, use serrated knife to make single decisive downward stroke. (Do not use sawing motion.)

Sweet Cream Ice Cream

Sweet Cream Ice Cream

Makes 1 quart • Total Time: 20 minutes, plus 8 hours 20 minutes cooling and chilling

Why This Recipe Works Sweet cream ice cream is the most basic of ice cream flavors. It doesn't contain vanilla or eggs—just milk, heavy cream, and sugar—so the sweet dairy flavor really shines. The key to a great ice cream is controlling the size of the ice crystals formed during freezing; the smaller the ice crystals, the smoother the ice cream feels on the tongue. To ensure a creamy, smooth consistency, we added milk powder, cornstarch, and corn syrup to our sweet cream base. The milk powder replaced a portion of the liquid milk in the mix, decreasing the amount of freezable water, and it also trapped some of the water so that it couldn't freeze (cornstarch performed this function, too). Like sugar, the corn syrup kept a portion of the water from freezing. But because corn syrup is less sweet than sugar, it provided the same textural benefits without making the ice cream too sweet.

> *This recipe can be used to make sweet cream ice cream or used as a base for making other flavors (recipes follow). If using a canister-style ice cream maker, be sure to freeze the empty canister for at least 24 hours (or preferably 48 hours) before churning. For self-refrigerating ice cream makers, prechill the canister by running the maker for 5 to 10 minutes before pouring in the base. We prefer Carnation Instant Nonfat Dry Milk. Some base may stick to the bottom of the saucepan when pouring it into the strainer in step 3; simply scrape it into the strainer with the rest of the base and press it through with a spatula. This ice cream can be frozen for up to five days. You can make Quick Candied Nuts (page 621) as a topping.*

½ cup plus ⅓ cup nonfat dry milk powder
⅓ cup (2⅓ ounces) sugar
¼ teaspoon kosher salt
1½ cups whole milk, divided
1½ cups heavy cream
¼ cup corn syrup
5 teaspoons cornstarch

1. Whisk milk powder, sugar, and salt together in small bowl. Whisk 1¼ cups milk, cream, corn syrup, and sugar mixture together in large saucepan. Cook over medium-high heat, whisking frequently to dissolve sugar and break up any clumps, until tiny bubbles form around edge of saucepan and mixture registers 190 degrees, 5 to 7 minutes.

2. Meanwhile, whisk cornstarch and remaining ¼ cup milk together in small bowl.

3. Reduce heat to medium. Whisk cornstarch mixture to recombine, then whisk into milk mixture in saucepan. Cook, constantly scraping bottom of saucepan with rubber spatula, until mixture thickens, about 30 seconds. Immediately pour ice cream base through fine-mesh strainer into large bowl; let cool until no longer steaming, about 20 minutes. Cover bowl; transfer to refrigerator; and chill until base registers 40 degrees, at least 6 hours. (Base can be chilled overnight. Alternatively, base can be chilled to 40 degrees in about 1½ hours by placing bowl in ice bath of 6 cups ice, ½ cup water, and ⅓ cup table salt.)

4. Churn base in ice cream maker until mixture resembles thick soft serve and registers 21 degrees, about 30 minutes. Transfer ice cream to airtight container, pressing firmly to remove air pockets; freeze until firm, at least 2 hours. Serve.

VARIATIONS

Vanilla Bean Sweet Cream Ice Cream

In step 1, process milk with 1 vanilla bean, cut in half lengthwise and then cut crosswise into 3 pieces, in blender on high speed until vanilla bean is reduced to specks, about 1 minute. Do not strain. Proceed with recipe, whisking vanilla milk with cream, corn syrup, and sugar mixture.

White Coffee Chip Sweet Cream Ice Cream

At end of step 1, stir 2 cups whole dark-roast coffee beans into milk mixture, cover, and let steep for 1 hour. Using slotted spoon, discard coffee beans. Return mixture to 190 degrees over medium-high heat and proceed with step 2, whisking extra ½ cup milk (for total of ¾ cup milk) into cornstarch. Before churning base, microwave 4 ounces finely chopped bittersweet chocolate in bowl, stirring frequently, until melted, about 2 minutes; set aside and let cool. Churn base as directed; when base registers 21 degrees, with maker running, slowly drizzle chocolate into ice cream and continue to churn until incorporated, 1 to 2 minutes longer. Proceed with recipe.

Strawberry Ripple Sweet Cream Ice Cream

While base chills, combine 6 ounces hulled fresh strawberries, ½ cup plus 1 tablespoon sugar, and 1 cup (½ ounce) freeze-dried strawberries in blender; process on high speed until smooth, about 1 minute. Transfer to airtight container and refrigerate until ready to use. In step 4, when base registers 21 degrees, spread one-quarter of base on bottom of airtight container and top with ¼ cup strawberry mixture. Repeat 3 more times, then proceed with recipe.

Pies & Fruit Desserts

Photo: Easy Strawberry Shortcakes for Two

Foolproof All-Butter Dough for Single-Crust Pie

Makes one 9-inch single crust
Total Time: 35 minutes, plus 2 hours chilling

Why This Recipe Works This is now our go-to pie dough: It's supremely supple and extremely easy to roll out. Even better, it bakes up buttery, tender, and flaky. How did we do it? First, we used the food processor to coat two-thirds of the flour with butter, creating a water-resistant paste-like mixture. Next, we broke that dough into pieces, coated the pieces with the remaining flour, and tossed in grated butter. By doing this, we ensured that the water we folded in was absorbed only by the dry flour that coated the butter-flour chunks. Since gluten can develop only when flour is hydrated, the resulting crust was supertender but had enough structure to support flakes. After a 2-hour chill, the dough was completely hydrated and easy to roll out.

Be sure to weigh the flour. This dough will be more moist than most pie doughs, but it will absorb a lot of excess moisture as it chills. Roll out the dough on a well-floured counter.

  10 tablespoons unsalted butter, chilled, divided
1¼ cups (6¼ ounces) all-purpose flour, divided
   1 tablespoon sugar
 ½ teaspoon table salt
 ¼ cup ice water, divided

1. Grate 2 tablespoons butter on large holes of box grater and place in freezer. Cut remaining 8 tablespoons butter into ½-inch cubes.

2. Pulse ¾ cup flour, sugar, and salt in food processor until combined, 2 pulses. Add cubed butter and process until homogeneous paste forms, about 30 seconds. Using your hands, carefully break paste into 2-inch pieces and redistribute evenly around processor blade. Add remaining ½ cup flour and pulse until mixture is broken into pieces no larger than 1 inch (most pieces will be much smaller), 4 or 5 pulses. Transfer mixture to medium bowl. Add grated butter and toss until butter pieces are separated and coated with flour.

3. Sprinkle 2 tablespoons ice water over mixture. Toss with rubber spatula until mixture is evenly moistened. Sprinkle remaining 2 tablespoons ice water over mixture and toss to combine. Press dough with spatula until dough sticks together. Transfer dough to sheet of plastic wrap. Draw edges of plastic over dough and press firmly on sides and top to form compact, fissure-free mass. Wrap in plastic and form into 5-inch disk. Refrigerate dough for at least 2 hours or up to 2 days. Let chilled dough sit on counter to soften slightly, about 10 minutes, before rolling. (Dough, wrapped tightly in plastic, can be frozen for up to 1 month. If frozen, let dough thaw completely on counter before rolling.)

VARIATION
Foolproof Whole-Wheat Dough for Single-Crust Pie
Substitute ¾ cup (4⅛ ounces) whole-wheat flour for first addition of all-purpose flour, using ½ cup all-purpose flour (2½ ounces) for second addition of flour.

Mixing All-Butter Pie Dough

1. To make flour and butter paste, process most of flour (and sugar and salt) and cubed butter until homogeneous paste forms, about 30 seconds.

2. To add more flour, carefully separate paste into 2-inch chunks and redistribute evenly around processor blade, then pulse in remaining flour.

3. Transfer mixture to bowl. Add frozen grated butter and gently toss to coat butter shreds with flour.

4. Using rubber spatula, mix in ice water in 2 additions to form wet, sticky dough. Transfer to plastic wrap, press into disk, and refrigerate.

Foolproof All-Butter Dough for Single-Crust Pie

Foolproof All-Butter Dough for Double-Crust Pie

Makes one 9-inch double crust
Total Time: 35 minutes, plus 2 hours chilling

Why This Recipe Works Be sure to weigh the flour for this recipe. This dough will be more moist than most pie doughs, but as it chills it will absorb a lot of excess moisture. Roll the dough on a well-floured counter. If your recipe requires rolling your dough piece(s) to a rectangle after chilling, as when making a lattice top for a pie, form the dough into a 5-inch square instead of a disk.

> 20 tablespoons (2½ sticks) unsalted butter, chilled, divided
> 2½ cups (12½ ounces) all-purpose flour, divided
> 2 tablespoons sugar
> 1 teaspoon table salt
> ½ cup ice water, divided

1. Grate 4 tablespoons butter on large holes of box grater and place in freezer. Cut remaining 16 tablespoons butter into ½-inch cubes.

2. Pulse 1½ cups flour, sugar, and salt in food processor until combined, 2 pulses. Add cubed butter and process until homogeneous paste forms, 40 to 50 seconds. Using your hands, carefully break paste into 2-inch pieces and redistribute evenly around processor blade. Add remaining 1 cup flour and pulse until mixture is broken into pieces no larger than 1 inch (most pieces will be much smaller), 4 or 5 pulses. Transfer mixture to medium bowl. Add grated butter and toss until butter pieces are separated and coated with flour.

3. Sprinkle ¼ cup ice water over mixture. Toss with rubber spatula until mixture is evenly moistened. Sprinkle remaining ¼ cup ice water over mixture and toss to combine. Press dough with spatula until dough sticks together. Use spatula to divide dough into 2 portions. Transfer each portion to sheet of plastic wrap. Working with 1 portion at a time, draw edges of plastic over dough and press firmly on sides and top to form compact, fissure-free mass. Wrap in plastic and form into 5-inch disk (or square). Repeat with remaining portion; refrigerate dough for at least 2 hours or up to 2 days. Let chilled dough sit on counter to soften slightly, about 10 minutes, before rolling. (Dough, wrapped tightly in plastic, can be frozen for up to 1 month. If frozen, let dough thaw completely on counter before rolling.)

Foolproof Whole-Wheat Dough for Double-Crust Pie
Substitute 1½ cups (8¼ ounces) whole-wheat flour for first addition of all-purpose flour, using 1 cup all-purpose flour (5 ounces) for second addition of flour.

Graham Cracker Crust

Makes enough for one 9-inch pie
Total Time: 40 minutes, plus 30 minutes cooling

Why This Recipe Works Saving time is always a good idea—just as long as you're not sacrificing quality. But while store-bought graham cracker pie crusts are tempting (all you have to do is fill, chill, then serve), they taste stale and bland. We wanted a fresh-tasting homemade crust that wasn't too sweet, with a crisp texture. Turns out, a classic graham cracker crust couldn't be easier to make: We combined crushed crumbs with a little butter and sugar to bind them, then used a measuring cup or flat-bottomed glass to pack the crumbs into the pie plate. Producing a perfect graham cracker crust has a lot to do with the type of graham crackers used. After experimenting with the three leading brands, we discovered subtle but distinct differences among them and found that these differences carried over into crumb crusts made with each kind of cracker. Here in the test kitchen, we prefer Nabisco Original Graham Crackers for their hearty molasses flavor.

> *We don't recommend using store-bought graham cracker crumbs here as they can often be stale. Be sure to note whether the crust needs to be warm or cool before filling (the pie recipes will specify) and plan accordingly.*

Making a Graham Cracker Crust

Press crumb mixture firmly and evenly across bottom of pie plate, using bottom of dry measuring cup. Tightly pack crumbs against sides of pie plate, using your thumb and measuring cup simultaneously.

8 whole graham crackers, broken into 1-inch pieces

5 tablespoons unsalted butter, melted and cooled

3 tablespoons sugar

1. Adjust oven rack to middle position and heat oven to 325 degrees. Process graham cracker pieces in food processor to fine, even crumbs, about 30 seconds. Sprinkle butter and sugar over crumbs and pulse to incorporate, about 5 pulses.

2. Sprinkle mixture into 9-inch pie plate. Use bottom of dry measuring cup to press crumbs into even layer on bottom and sides of pie plate. Bake until crust is fragrant and beginning to brown, 13 to 18 minutes. Following particular pie recipe, use crust while it is still warm or let it cool completely.

SEASON 2
Classic Tart Dough

Makes enough for one 9-inch tart
Total Time: 20 minutes, plus 1 hour chilling

Why This Recipe Works The problem with most tarts is the crust: It's usually either too tough or too brittle. While regular pie crust is tender and flaky, tart crust should be fine-textured, buttery-rich, crisp, and crumbly—it is often described as shortbread-like. We set out to achieve the perfect tart dough, one that we could use in several of our tart recipes. Using a full stick of butter made tart dough that tasted great and was easy to handle, yet still had a delicate crumb. Instead of using the hard-to-find superfine sugar and pastry flour that many other recipes call for, we used confectioners' sugar and all-purpose flour for a crisp texture. Rolling the dough and fitting it into the tart pan was easy, and we had ample dough to patch any holes.

> *Tart crust is sweeter, crisper, and less flaky than pie crust—it is more similar in texture to a cookie. The dough, wrapped tightly in plastic wrap, can be refrigerated for up to two days or frozen for up to one month. If frozen, let the dough thaw completely on the counter before rolling it out.*

1 large egg yolk

1 tablespoon heavy cream

½ teaspoon vanilla extract

1¼ cups (6¼ ounces) all-purpose flour

⅔ cup (2⅔ ounces) confectioners' sugar

¼ teaspoon table salt

8 tablespoons unsalted butter, cut into ¼-inch pieces and chilled

1. Whisk egg yolk, cream, and vanilla together in small bowl. Process flour, sugar, and salt in food processor until combined, about 5 seconds. Scatter butter pieces over top and pulse until mixture resembles coarse cornmeal, about 15 pulses.

2. With machine running, add egg mixture through feed tube and continue to process until dough just comes together around processor blade, about 12 seconds.

3. Turn dough onto sheet of plastic wrap and flatten into 6-inch disk. Wrap dough tightly in plastic wrap and refrigerate for 1 hour. Before rolling dough out, let it sit on counter to soften slightly, about 10 minutes.

Making a Tart Shell

1. After rolling dough out into 11-inch circle on lightly floured counter, wrap it loosely around rolling pin and unroll dough over 9-inch tart pan with removable bottom.

2. Lifting edge of dough, gently ease dough into pan. Press dough into corners and fluted sides of pan.

3. Run rolling pin over top of tart pan to remove any excess dough and make clean edge.

4. If parts of edge are too thin, reinforce them by pressing in some of excess dough. If edge is too thick, press some of dough up over edge of pan and trim it away.

Classic Apple Pie

Serves 8 • Total Time: 2¼ hours, plus 5½ hours chilling and cooling

Why This Recipe Works It is difficult to produce an apple pie with a filling that is tart as well as sweet and juicy. We wanted to develop a classic apple pie recipe—one with the clean, bright taste of apples that could be made year-round, with supermarket apples. To arrive at the tartness and texture we were after, we had to use two kinds of apples in our pie, Granny Smith and McIntosh. The Grannies were tart and kept their shape during cooking; the Macs added flavor, and their tendency to become mushy was a virtue, providing a juicy base for the Grannies. While many bakers add butter to their apple pie fillings, we found that it dulled the fresh taste of the apples, so we did without it. Lemon juice, however, was essential, counterbalancing the sweetness of the apples. To give the apples the upper hand, we settled on modest amounts of cinnamon, nutmeg, and allspice.

> *This pie is best eaten when cooled to room temperature, or even the next day. Serve with vanilla ice cream or lightly sweetened whipped cream.*

1 recipe Foolproof All-Butter Dough for Double-Crust Pie (page 632)
¾ cup (5¼ ounces) plus 1 tablespoon sugar, divided
2 tablespoons all-purpose flour
1 teaspoon grated lemon zest plus 1 tablespoon juice
¼ teaspoon table salt
¼ teaspoon ground nutmeg
¼ teaspoon ground cinnamon
⅛ teaspoon ground allspice
2 pounds firm McIntosh apples, peeled, cored, and sliced ¼ inch thick
1½ pounds Granny Smith apples, peeled, cored, and sliced ¼ inch thick
1 large egg white, lightly beaten

1. Roll 1 disk of dough into 12-inch circle on well-floured counter. Roll dough loosely around rolling pin and gently unroll it onto 9-inch pie plate, leaving at least 1-inch overhang around edge. Ease dough into plate by gently lifting edge of dough with your hand while pressing into plate bottom with your other hand. Wrap dough-lined plate loosely in plastic wrap and refrigerate until dough is firm, about 30 minutes. Roll other disk of dough into 12-inch circle on well-floured counter, then transfer to parchment paper–lined baking sheet; cover with plastic and refrigerate for 30 minutes.

2. Adjust oven rack to lowest position and heat oven to 500 degrees. Mix ¾ cup sugar, flour, lemon zest, salt, nutmeg, cinnamon, and allspice together in large bowl. Add lemon juice and apples and toss until combined. Spread apples with their juice into dough-lined pie plate, mounding them slightly in middle.

3. Roll remaining dough round loosely around rolling pin and gently unroll it onto filling. Trim overhang to ½ inch beyond lip of plate. Pinch edges of top and bottom crusts firmly together. Tuck overhang under itself; folded edge

Rolling Double-Crust Pie Dough

1. Roll 1 disk of dough into 12-inch circle on floured counter.

2. Loosely roll dough around rolling pin and gently unroll it onto 9-inch pie plate, letting excess dough hang over edge.

3. Ease dough into plate by gently lifting edge of dough with your hand while pressing into plate bottom with your other hand. Leave any dough that overhangs plate in place.

4. Fill dough-lined plate; loosely roll remaining dough round around rolling pin and gently unroll it onto filling.

should be flush with edge of plate. Crimp dough evenly around edge of plate using your fingers. Cut four 2-inch slits in top of dough. Brush surface with beaten egg white and sprinkle with remaining 1 tablespoon sugar.

4. Place pie on rimmed baking sheet; reduce oven temperature to 425 degrees; and bake until crust is golden, about 25 minutes. Reduce oven temperature to 375 degrees, rotate sheet, and continue to bake until juices are bubbling and crust is deep golden brown, 35 to 45 minutes longer. Let pie cool on wire rack until filling has set, about 4 hours. Serve.

VARIATIONS

Apple Pie with Crystallized Ginger

Add 3 tablespoons chopped crystallized ginger to filling with lemon juice and apples.

Apple Pie with Dried Fruit

Toss 1 cup raisins, dried sweet cherries, or dried cranberries with lemon juice plus 1 tablespoon applejack, brandy, or cognac. Add dried fruit and liquid to filling with apples.

Apple Pie with Fresh Cranberries

Increase sugar in filling to 1 cup (7 ounces). Add 1 cup fresh or frozen cranberries to filling with lemon juice and apples.

Salted Caramel Apple Pie

Serves 8 • Total Time: 1¾ hours, plus 30 minutes chilling and 4 hours cooling

Why This Recipe Works This stunning pie recalls the flavors of caramel apples at a county fair but looks like an edible bouquet. Rather than stewing the apples beneath a top crust, we used apple slices as a fancy garnish topping a caramel custard pie. We made the salted caramel filling by whisking basic custard components into homemade caramel. A surprising ingredient—white miso—deepened the caramel flavor dramatically and prevented our filling from being too sweet. To adorn the custard, we softened thin apple slices with sugar and a little lemon juice so they could be formed into beautiful roses that gave our pie showstopping visual appeal.

Carefully tilt the saucepan to pool the caramel to get a more consistent temperature reading. For best results, use a mandoline to slice the apples paper-thin.

  1 recipe Foolproof All-Butter Dough for Single-Crust Pie (page 630)
1½ cups (10½ ounces) plus 2 tablespoons sugar, divided
  3 large eggs
  ¼ cup (1 ounce) cornstarch
  2 tablespoons white miso
  ½ teaspoon vanilla extract
  ¼ teaspoon table salt
  2 tablespoons water
  1 cup heavy cream, divided
1½ cups whole milk
  3 Fuji, Gala, or Golden Delicious apples, cored, quartered, and sliced very thin lengthwise
  2 tablespoons lemon juice
     Flake sea salt

1. Roll dough into 12-inch circle on well-floured counter. Roll dough loosely around rolling pin and unroll it onto 9-inch pie plate, leaving at least 1-inch overhang around edge. Ease dough into plate by gently lifting edge of dough with your hand while pressing into plate bottom with your other hand.

2. Trim overhang to ½ inch beyond lip of plate. Tuck overhang under itself; folded edge should be flush with edge of plate. Crimp dough evenly around edge of plate using your fingers. Refrigerate dough-lined plate until dough is firm, about 30 minutes. Adjust oven rack to middle position and heat oven to 350 degrees.

3. Line chilled pie shell with double layer of aluminum foil, covering edges to prevent burning, and fill with pie weights. Bake on foil-lined rimmed baking sheet until pie dough looks dry and is light in color, 25 to 30 minutes, rotating sheet halfway through baking. Remove weights and foil, rotate sheet, and continue to bake crust until deep golden brown, 10 to 15 minutes longer. Transfer sheet to wire rack. (Crust must still be warm when filling is added.)

4. While shell is baking, whisk ¾ cup sugar, eggs, corn-starch, miso, vanilla, and table salt together in bowl; set aside. Bring ¾ cup sugar and water to boil in large sauce-pan over medium-high heat. Cook, without stirring, until mixture is straw-colored, 4 to 6 minutes. Reduce heat to low and continue to cook, swirling saucepan occasionally, until caramel is amber-colored and registers 360 to 370 degrees, 2 to 5 minutes.

5. Off heat, carefully stir in ¼ cup cream; mixture will bubble and steam. Whisk vigorously, being sure to scrape corners of saucepan, until mixture is completely smooth, at least 30 seconds. Gradually whisk in remaining ¾ cup cream and milk, then bring to simmer over medium heat. Slowly whisk 1 cup hot caramel mixture into egg mixture to temper, then slowly whisk tempered egg mixture into

remaining caramel mixture in saucepan. Cook, whisking constantly, until mixture is thickened and bubbling and registers 180 degrees, 4 to 6 minutes (mixture should have consistency of thick pudding). Strain mixture through fine-mesh strainer into clean bowl.

6. With pie still on sheet, pour filling into warm crust, smoothing top with clean spatula into even layer. Bake until center of pie registers 160 degrees, 14 to 18 minutes. Let pie cool completely on wire rack, about 4 hours.

7. Before serving, combine apple slices, lemon juice, and remaining 2 tablespoons sugar in bowl. Microwave until apples are pliable, about 2 minutes, stirring halfway through microwaving. Drain apples, then transfer to paper towel–lined sheet and pat dry with paper towels. Shingle 5 apple slices, peel side out, overlapping each slice by about ½ inch on cutting board or counter. Starting at 1 end, roll up slices to form rose shape; place in center of pie. Repeat, arranging apple roses decoratively over top of pie. Sprinkle with sea salt and serve.

Making Apple Rosettes

1. Combine apple slices, 2 tablespoons sugar, and lemon juice in bowl. Microwave until apples are pliable, about 2 minutes, stirring halfway through microwaving.

2. Drain apples and pat dry with paper towels. Shingle 5 apple slices, peel side out, overlapping each slice by about ½ inch.

3. Starting at 1 end, roll up slices to form rose shape.

Skillet Apple Pie

Serves 6 to 8 • Total Time: 1¼ hours, plus 30 minutes chilling

Why This Recipe Works Who says a pie needs to bake in a special plate—or even have a bottom crust? We wanted to expand the definition of perfect apple pie: It can come in a skillet, and it can be just about the easiest pie you can make. Unlike the filling for a double-crust pie, the filling for a skillet apple pie can be saucy. Apple cider provided resonant apple flavor and, when thickened with cornstarch, it yielded a juicy filling with just the right body. We used ⅓ cup of maple syrup to further sweeten the filling, and it complemented the natural sweetness of the apples without being cloying. Working in a heavy skillet allowed us to sauté the apples just long enough to caramelize them before we transferred the dough-topped pie to the oven for 20 minutes, where the crust developed a lovely deep-brown hue. Cutting the dough into six pieces prior to baking allowed the crust to develop multiple crisp, flaky edges that contrasted with the saucy, caramelized, and tender apples.

> *If your skillet is not ovensafe, precook the apples and stir in the cider mixture as instructed, then transfer the apples to a 13 by 9-inch baking dish. Roll out the dough to a 13 by 9-inch rectangle and cut the crust and bake as instructed. If you do not have apple cider, reduced apple juice may be used as a substitute: Simmer 1 cup apple juice in a small saucepan over medium heat until reduced to ½ cup (about 10 minutes). Serve the pie warm or at room temperature with vanilla ice cream or whipped cream. Use a combination of sweet, crisp apples such as Golden Delicious and firm, tart apples such as Cortland or Empire.*

Crust

- 1 cup (5 ounces) all-purpose flour
- 1 tablespoon sugar
- ½ teaspoon table salt
- 2 tablespoons vegetable shortening, chilled
- 6 tablespoons unsalted butter, cut into ¼-inch pieces and chilled
- 3–4 tablespoons ice water

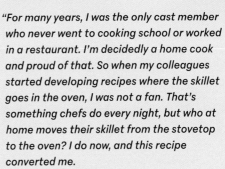

GAME CHANGER

Your Skillet Belongs in the Oven

"For many years, I was the only cast member who never went to cooking school or worked in a restaurant. I'm decidedly a home cook and proud of that. So when my colleagues started developing recipes where the skillet goes in the oven, I was not a fan. That's something chefs do every night, but who at home moves their skillet from the stovetop to the oven? I do now, and this recipe converted me.

A warning up front: The handle will be screaming-hot when the pan comes out of the oven. But there's a simple solve. Slide an oven mitt over the handle as the skillet cools. Even if you forget that the handle is hot, your hand will be protected. So why bother with this chef-y technique? The stovetop heats from the bottom and gets things going quickly. In this recipe, the apples soften on the stovetop, and you control just how much the juices are reduced. No more soupy apple pie! The oven is great for even heat, so once the apple filling is good to go, add the pie dough and slide the skillet into the oven to get the crust evenly baked and crisp.

Once I started making this recipe—which is much, much simpler than classic apple pie— I became more comfortable with other stovetop-oven recipes. Start a skillet filled with steaks or chops in a low oven to cook the meat evenly from edge to edge, and then blast the pan on the stovetop to develop a browned crust. Or make an easy ziti by cooking the pasta right in the sauce, top with cheese, and move the pan into a hot oven to create a bubbly browned crust.

Maybe I am a chef after all?"

—*Jack*

Filling

½	cup apple cider
⅓	cup maple syrup
2	tablespoons lemon juice
2	teaspoons cornstarch
⅛	teaspoon ground cinnamon (optional)
2	tablespoons unsalted butter
2½	pounds sweet and tart apples, peeled, cored, and cut into ½-inch-thick wedges
1	large egg white, lightly beaten
2	teaspoons sugar

1. For the crust: Pulse flour, sugar, and salt in food processor until combined, about 4 pulses. Add shortening and pulse until mixture has texture of coarse sand, about 10 pulses. Sprinkle butter pieces over flour mixture and pulse until mixture is pale yellow and resembles coarse crumbs, with butter bits no larger than small peas, about 10 pulses. Transfer mixture to medium bowl.

2. Sprinkle 3 tablespoons ice water over mixture. With rubber spatula, use folding motion to mix, pressing down on dough until dough is slightly tacky and sticks together, adding up to 1 tablespoon more ice water if dough does not come together. Flatten dough into 4-inch disk. Wrap disk in plastic wrap and refrigerate for at least 1 hour or up to 2 days. Let dough stand at room temperature for 15 minutes before rolling.

3. For the filling: Adjust oven rack to upper-middle position (between 7 and 9 inches from the heating element) and heat oven to 500 degrees. Whisk cider; syrup; lemon juice; cornstarch; and cinnamon, if using, in medium bowl until smooth. Melt butter in 12-inch ovensafe skillet over

medium-high heat. Add apples and cook, stirring 2 or 3 times, until apples begin to caramelize, about 5 minutes. (Do not fully cook apples.) Remove pan from heat, add cider mixture, and gently stir until apples are well coated. Set aside to cool slightly.

4. To assemble and bake: Roll dough out on lightly floured counter to 11-inch circle. Roll dough loosely around rolling pin and unroll over apple filling. Brush dough with egg white and sprinkle with sugar. With sharp knife, gently cut dough into 6 pieces by making 1 vertical cut followed by 2 evenly spaced horizontal cuts (perpendicular to first cut). Bake until apples are tender and crust is deep golden brown, about 20 minutes, rotating skillet halfway through baking. Let pie cool for 15 minutes and serve.

SEASON 9

Blueberry Pie

Serves 8 • Total Time: 2½ hours, plus 4¾ hours chilling and cooling

Why This Recipe Works The best blueberry pie has a firm, glistening filling full of fresh, bright flavor and still-plump berries. Since too much thickener can make the filling unappealingly dense, we favored tapioca to thicken our pie because it didn't mute the fresh blueberry flavor as cornstarch and flour did. But too much tapioca produced a stiff, congealed mass. Cooking and reducing half of the berries helped us cut down on the tapioca required, as did adding a peeled and grated Granny Smith apple. Apples are high in pectin, a type of carbohydrate that acts as a thickener when cooked. Combined with a modest 2 tablespoons of tapioca, the apple thickened the filling to a soft, even consistency. The crust posed a much simpler challenge. As with all of our fruit pies, baking on a rimmed baking sheet on the bottom oven rack produced a crisp, golden bottom crust. And we found a fast alternative to a lattice top in a small biscuit cutter, which we used to cut out circles in the top crust before transferring the dough onto the pie. This easy top crust vented the steam from the berries as successfully as a classic lattice top.

This recipe was developed using fresh blueberries, but unthawed frozen blueberries will work as well. In step 3, cook half the frozen berries over medium-high heat, without mashing, until reduced to 1¼ cups, 12 to 15 minutes. Grind the tapioca to a powder in a spice grinder or mini food processor. If using pearl tapioca, reduce the amount to 5 teaspoons. Serve with vanilla ice cream or lightly sweetened whipped cream.

1 recipe Foolproof All-Butter Dough for Double-Crust Pie (page 632)

6 cups (30 ounces) blueberries, divided

1 Granny Smith apple, peeled, cored, and shredded on large holes of box grater

¾ cup (5¼ ounces) sugar

2 tablespoons instant tapioca, ground

2 teaspoons grated lemon zest plus 2 teaspoons juice
Pinch table salt

2 tablespoons unsalted butter, cut into ¼-inch pieces

1 large egg white, lightly beaten

1. Roll 1 disk of dough into 12-inch circle on well-floured counter. Roll dough loosely around rolling pin and gently unroll it onto 9-inch pie plate, leaving at least 1-inch overhang around edge. Ease dough into plate by gently lifting edge of dough with your hand while pressing into plate bottom with your other hand. Wrap dough-lined plate loosely in plastic and refrigerate until dough is firm, about 30 minutes.

2. Roll other disk of dough into 12-inch circle on well-floured counter. Use 1¼-inch round biscuit cutter to cut round from center of dough. Cut 6 more rounds from dough, 1½ inches from edge of center hole and equally spaced around center hole. Transfer dough to parchment-lined baking sheet; cover with plastic wrap and refrigerate for 30 minutes.

3. Place 3 cups blueberries in medium saucepan and set over medium heat. Using potato masher, mash berries several times to release juices. Continue to cook, stirring frequently and mashing occasionally, until about half of berries have broken down and mixture is thickened and reduced to 1½ cups, about 8 minutes. Let cool slightly.

4. Adjust oven rack to lowest position and heat oven to 400 degrees.

5. Place shredded apple in clean dish towel and wring dry. Transfer apple to large bowl and stir in cooked blueberries, remaining 3 cups uncooked blueberries, sugar, tapioca, lemon zest and juice, and salt until combined. Spread mixture into dough-lined pie plate and scatter butter pieces over top.

6. Roll remaining dough round loosely around rolling pin and gently unroll it onto filling. Trim overhang to ½ inch beyond lip of plate. Pinch edges of top and bottom crusts firmly together. Tuck overhang under itself; folded edge should be flush with edge of plate. Crimp dough evenly around edge of plate using your fingers. Brush surface with egg white.

7. Place pie on aluminum foil–lined rimmed baking sheet and bake until crust is golden, about 25 minutes. Reduce oven temperature to 350 degrees, rotate sheet, and continue to bake until juices are bubbling and crust is deep golden brown, 35 to 50 minutes longer. Let pie cool on wire rack until filling has set, about 4 hours. Serve.

SEASON 11

Sweet Cherry Pie

Serves 8 • Total Time: 2 hours, plus 4 hours 50 minutes chilling, freezing, and cooling

Why This Recipe Works Great cherry pie is typically made with sour cherries because their soft, juicy flesh and bright, punchy flavor isn't dulled by oven heat or sugar. But cherry season is cruelly short and chances are the cherries that are available are the sweet variety. Sweet cherries have mellower flavors and meaty, firm flesh—traits that make them ideal for eating straight off the stem but don't translate well to baking. We wanted a recipe for sweet cherry pie with all the intense, jammy flavor and softened but still intact fruit texture of the best sour cherry pie. To mimic the bright, tart flavor of a sour cherry pie filling, we supplemented sweet cherries with chopped plums, which are tart and helped tame the cherries' sweet flavor. To fix the texture problem, we cut the cherries in half to expose their sturdy flesh. This step encouraged the cherries to soften and give up their juices. A splash of bourbon and lemon juice also offset the sweetness and added flavorful depth. To keep the filling juicy, rather than dry, we switched out the typical lattice pie crust in favor of a traditional top crust, which prevented any moisture from evaporating.

The tapioca should be measured first, then ground in a coffee grinder or food processor for 30 seconds. If you are using frozen fruit, measure it frozen, but let it thaw before filling the pie. If not, you run the risk of partially cooked fruit and undissolved tapioca.

1 recipe Foolproof All-Butter Dough for Double-Crust Pie (page 632)

2 red plums, halved and pitted

2 pounds pitted sweet cherries or 6 cups pitted frozen cherries, halved, divided

½ cup (3½ ounces) sugar

2 tablespoons instant tapioca, ground

1 tablespoon lemon juice

2 teaspoons bourbon (optional)

⅛ teaspoon table salt

⅛ teaspoon ground cinnamon (optional)

2 tablespoons unsalted butter, cut into ¼-inch pieces

1 large egg, lightly beaten with 1 teaspoon water

1. Roll 1 disk of dough into 12-inch circle on well-floured counter. Roll dough loosely around rolling pin and gently unroll it onto 9-inch pie plate, leaving at least 1-inch overhang around edge. Ease dough into plate by gently lifting edge of dough with your hand while pressing into plate bottom with your other hand. Wrap dough-lined plate loosely in plastic and refrigerate until dough is firm, about 30 minutes. Roll other disk of dough into 12-inch circle on well-floured counter, then transfer to parchment paper–lined baking sheet; cover with plastic and refrigerate for 30 minutes.

2. Adjust oven rack to lowest position and heat oven to 400 degrees. Process plums and 1 cup halved cherries in food processor until smooth, about 1 minute, scraping down sides of bowl as necessary. Strain puree through fine-mesh strainer into large bowl, pressing on solids to extract liquid; discard solids. Stir in remaining 5 cups halved cherries; sugar; tapioca; lemon juice; bourbon, if using; salt; and cinnamon, if using, into puree; let stand for 15 minutes.

3. Transfer cherry mixture, including juices, to dough-lined plate. Scatter butter pieces over fruit. Roll remaining dough round loosely around rolling pin and gently unroll it onto filling. Trim overhang to ½ inch beyond lip of plate. Pinch edges of top and bottom crusts firmly together. Tuck overhang under itself; folded edge should be flush with edge of plate. Crimp dough evenly around edge of plate using your fingers. Cut eight 1-inch slits in top of dough. Brush dough with egg wash. Freeze pie for 20 minutes.

4. Place pie on rimmed baking sheet and bake for 30 minutes. Reduce oven temperature to 350 degrees and continue to bake until juices bubble and crust is deep golden brown, 35 to 50 minutes longer.

5. Let pie cool on wire rack until filling has set, about 4 hours, before serving.

SEASON 22

Fresh Peach Pie

Serves 8 • Total Time: 2 hours, plus 4½ hours macerating, freezing, chilling, and cooling

Why This Recipe Works Juicy summer peaches produce the best pies. To control the moisture, we macerated the peaches to draw out some of their juices and then added a measured amount back to the filling. Cornstarch and pectin helped hold the fruit filling together without making it gluey or bouncy, and mashing some of the peaches helped make neat, attractive slices. A buttery, tender lattice-top crust allowed moisture to evaporate and made for an impressive presentation.

If your peaches are too soft to withstand the pressure of a peeler, cut a shallow X in the bottom of the fruit, blanch them in a pot of simmering water for 15 seconds, and then shock them in a bowl of ice water before peeling. For fruit pectin we recommend both Sure-Jell for Less or No Sugar Needed Recipes and Ball RealFruit Low or No-Sugar Needed Pectin.

3 pounds peaches, peeled, quartered, and pitted, each quarter cut into thirds

½ cup (3½ ounces) plus 3 tablespoons sugar, divided

1 teaspoon grated lemon zest plus 1 tablespoon juice

⅛ teaspoon table salt

2 tablespoons low- or no-sugar-needed fruit pectin

¼ teaspoon ground cinnamon

Pinch ground nutmeg

1 recipe Pie Dough for Lattice-Top Pie (recipe follows)

1 tablespoon cornstarch

1. Toss peaches, ½ cup sugar, lemon zest and juice, and salt in medium bowl. Let stand at room temperature for at least 30 minutes or up to 1 hour. Combine pectin, cinnamon, nutmeg, and 2 tablespoons sugar in small bowl and set aside.

2. Remove dough from refrigerator. Before rolling out dough, let it sit on counter to soften slightly, about 10 minutes. Roll 1 disk of dough into 12-inch circle on lightly floured counter. Transfer to parchment paper–lined baking sheet. With pizza wheel, fluted pastry wheel, or paring knife, cut round into ten 1¼-inch-wide strips. Freeze strips on sheet until firm, about 30 minutes.

3. Adjust oven rack to lowest position, place rimmed baking sheet on rack, and heat oven to 425 degrees. Roll other disk of dough into 12-inch circle on lightly floured counter. Loosely roll dough around rolling pin and gently unroll it onto 9-inch pie plate, letting excess dough hang over edge. Ease dough into plate by gently lifting edge of dough with your hand while pressing into plate bottom with your other hand. Leave any dough that overhangs plate in place. Wrap dough-lined pie plate loosely in plastic wrap and refrigerate until dough is firm, about 30 minutes.

4. Meanwhile, transfer 1 cup peach mixture to small bowl and mash with fork until coarse paste forms. Drain remaining peach mixture through colander set in large bowl. Transfer peach juice to liquid measuring cup (you should have about ½ cup liquid; if liquid measures more than ½ cup, discard remainder). Return peach pieces to bowl and toss with cornstarch. Transfer peach juice to 12-inch skillet, add pectin mixture, and whisk until combined. Cook over medium heat, stirring occasionally, until slightly thickened and pectin is dissolved (liquid should become less cloudy), 3 to 5 minutes. Remove skillet from heat, add peach pieces and peach paste, and toss to combine.

5. Transfer peach mixture to dough-lined pie plate. Remove dough strips from freezer; if too stiff to be workable, let stand at room temperature until malleable and softened slightly but still very cold. Lay 2 longest strips across center of pie perpendicular to each other. Using 4 shortest strips, lay 2 strips across pie parallel to 1 center strip and 2 strips parallel to other center strip, near edges of pie; you should have 6 strips in place. Using remaining 4 strips, lay each one across pie parallel and equidistant from center and edge strips. If dough becomes too soft to work with, refrigerate pie and dough strips until dough firms up.

6. Trim overhang to ½ inch beyond lip of pie plate. Press edges of bottom crust and lattice strips together and fold under. Folded edge should be flush with edge of pie plate. Crimp dough evenly around edge of pie using your fingers. Using spray bottle, evenly mist lattice with water and sprinkle with remaining 1 tablespoon sugar.

7. Place pie on rimmed baking sheet and bake until crust is set and begins to brown, about 25 minutes. Reduce oven temperature to 375 degrees, rotate sheet, and continue to bake until crust is deep golden brown and filling is bubbly at center, 30 to 40 minutes longer. Let pie cool on wire rack for 3 hours before serving.

Pie Dough for Lattice-Top Pie
Makes enough for one 9-inch pie
Total Time: 20 minutes, plus 1 hour chilling

3 cups (15 ounces) all-purpose flour

2 tablespoons sugar

1 teaspoon salt

7 tablespoons vegetable shortening, cut into ½-inch pieces and chilled

10 tablespoons unsalted butter, cut into ¼-inch pieces and frozen for 30 minutes

10–12 tablespoons ice water

1. Process flour, sugar, and salt in food processor until combined, about 5 seconds. Scatter shortening over top and process until mixture resembles coarse cornmeal, about 10 seconds. Scatter butter over top and pulse until mixture resembles coarse crumbs, about 10 pulses. Transfer to bowl.

2. Sprinkle 5 tablespoons ice water over flour mixture. With rubber spatula, use folding motion to evenly combine water and flour mixture. Sprinkle 5 tablespoons ice water over mixture and continue using folding motion to combine until small portion of dough holds together when squeezed in palm of your hand, adding up to 2 tablespoons remaining ice water if necessary. (Dough should feel quite moist.) Turn out dough onto clean, dry counter and gently press together into cohesive ball. Divide dough into 2 even pieces and flatten each into 4-inch disk. Wrap disks tightly in plastic wrap and refrigerate for 1 hour or up to 2 days.

Building a "No-Weave" Lattice Top

1. Roll dough into 12-inch circle, transfer to parchment paper–lined baking sheet, and cut into ten 1¼-inch-wide strips with a fluted pastry wheel, pizza wheel, or paring knife. Freeze for 30 minutes.

2. Lay 2 longest strips perpendicular to each other across center of pie to form cross. Place 4 shorter strips along edges of pie, parallel to center strips.

3. Lay 4 remaining strips between each edge strip and center strip. Trim off excess lattice ends, press edges of bottom crust and lattice strips together, and fold under.

Triple Berry Slab Pie with Ginger-Lemon Streusel

Serves 18 to 24 • **Total Time: 2 hours, plus 2½ hours chilling and cooling**

Why This Recipe Works Our berry slab pie is guaranteed to elicit oohs and aahs before the first slice is even cut. And no one will know it's a cinch to prepare. We started by tossing no-prep berries—blueberries, raspberries, and blackberries—with sugar, lemon zest, and tapioca for the filling. Instead of applying a top crust, which would hide the beautiful berry hues and trap moisture, we sprinkled on a streusel that we flavored liberally with more lemon zest as well as some crystallized ginger; the topping added fresh and zingy pops of flavor to the sweet, bright berries peeking through.

You will need one 18 by 13-inch rimmed baking sheet for this recipe. You can toss the berry mixture in step 5 in two bowls if it doesn't fit in one.

1 recipe Slab Pie Dough (recipe follows)

Streusel
1½ cups (7½ ounces) all-purpose flour
½ cup packed (3½ ounces) light brown sugar
½ cup crystallized ginger, chopped fine
¼ cup (1¾ ounces) granulated sugar
1 tablespoon ground ginger
1 teaspoon grated lemon zest
¼ teaspoon table salt
10 tablespoons unsalted butter, melted and cooled

Filling
1 cup (7 ounces) granulated sugar
6 tablespoons instant tapioca, ground
1 teaspoon grated lemon zest
¼ teaspoon table salt
1¼ pounds (4 cups) blackberries
1¼ pounds (4 cups) blueberries
1¼ pounds (4 cups) raspberries

1. Line rimmed baking sheet with parchment paper. Roll each dough square into 16 by 11-inch rectangle on floured counter; stack on prepared sheet, separated by second sheet of parchment. Cover loosely with plastic wrap and refrigerate until dough is firm but still pliable, about 10 minutes.

Triple Berry Slab Pie with
Ginger-Lemon Streusel

2. Using parchment as sling, transfer chilled dough rectangles to counter; discard parchment. Wipe sheet clean with paper towels and spray with vegetable oil spray. Starting at short side of 1 dough rectangle, loosely roll around rolling pin, then gently unroll over half of long side of prepared sheet, leaving about 2 inches of dough overhanging 3 edges. Repeat with second dough rectangle, unrolling it over empty side of sheet and overlapping first dough piece by ½ inch.

3. Ease dough into sheet by gently lifting edges of dough with your hand while pressing into sheet bottom with your other hand. Brush overlapping edge of dough rectangles with water and press to seal. Trim overhang to ½ inch beyond edge of sheet. Tuck overhang under itself; folded edge should rest on edge of sheet. Crimp dough evenly around edge of sheet. Cover loosely with plastic and refrigerate until firm, about 30 minutes.

4. For the streusel: Meanwhile, adjust oven racks to lower-middle and lowest positions and heat oven to 375 degrees. Combine flour, brown sugar, crystallized ginger, granulated sugar, ground ginger, lemon zest, and salt in bowl. Stir in melted butter until mixture is completely moistened; let sit for 10 minutes.

5. For the filling: Whisk sugar, tapioca, lemon zest, and salt together in large bowl. Add blackberries, blueberries, and raspberries and toss gently to combine. Spread berry mixture evenly over chilled dough-lined sheet. Sprinkle streusel evenly over fruit, breaking apart any large chunks. Place large sheet of aluminum foil directly on lower rack (to catch any bubbling juices). Place pie on upper rack and

bake until crust and streusel are deep golden brown and juices are bubbling, 45 minutes to 1 hour, rotating sheet halfway through baking. Let pie cool on wire rack until filling has set, about 2 hours. Serve.

Slab Pie Dough
Makes one 18 by 13-inch single crust
Total Time: 30 minutes, plus 2 hours chilling

This dough is very workable, which makes it ideal for rolling into large rectangles that fit into a baking sheet to make this large-scale pie. Be sure to weigh the flour for this recipe. In the mixing stage, this dough will be moister than most pie doughs, but as it chills it will absorb much of the excess moisture. Be sure to roll the dough on a well-floured counter.

- 24 **tablespoons (3 sticks) unsalted butter, divided**
- 2¾ **cups (13¾ ounces) all-purpose flour, divided**
- 2 **tablespoons sugar**
- 1 **teaspoon table salt**
- ½ **cup ice water, divided**

1. Grate 5 tablespoons butter on large holes of box grater and place in freezer. Cut remaining 19 tablespoons butter into ½-inch cubes.

2. Pulse 1¾ cups flour, sugar, and salt in food processor until combined, 2 pulses. Add cubed butter and process until homogeneous paste forms, 40 to 50 seconds. Using your hands, carefully break paste into 2-inch chunks and redistribute evenly around processor blade. Add remaining 1 cup flour and pulse until mixture is broken into pieces no larger than 1 inch (most pieces will be much smaller), 4 to 5 pulses.

Fitting Slab Pie Dough into a Baking Sheet

1. Starting at short side of 1 piece of dough, roll loosely around rolling pin, then gently unroll over half of long side of sheet, leaving about 2 inches of dough overhanging 3 edges of sheet.

2. Repeat with second piece of dough, overlapping first piece of dough by ½ inch in center of sheet.

3. Ease dough into sheet by gently lifting edges of dough with your hand while pressing into sheet bottom with your other hand.

4. Brush edge where doughs overlap with water, pressing to seal.

Transfer mixture to bowl. Add grated butter and toss until butter pieces are separated and coated with flour.

3. Sprinkle ¼ cup ice water over mixture. Toss with rubber spatula until mixture is evenly moistened. Sprinkle remaining ¼ cup ice water over mixture and toss to combine. Press dough with spatula until dough sticks together. Using spatula, divide dough into 2 equal portions. Transfer each portion to sheet of plastic wrap. Working with 1 portion at a time, draw edges of plastic over dough and press firmly on sides and top to form compact, fissure-free mass. Wrap in plastic and form into 5 by 6-inch rectangle. Refrigerate dough for at least 2 hours or up to 2 days. Let chilled dough sit on counter to soften slightly, about 10 minutes, before rolling. (Wrapped dough can be frozen for up to 1 month. If frozen, let dough thaw completely on counter before rolling.)

Fruit Hand Pies

Makes 8 hand pies • Total Time: 1½ hours, plus 1 hour 20 minutes chilling and cooling

Why This Recipe Works Hand pies treat you to the pleasures of sugar-crusted pastry and vibrant, jewel-toned fruit without a plate and fork. The dough needs a little extra structure, so we made rough puff: a type of pastry dough that contains more gluten than most pie pastry and comes together by working cold butter into the flour mixture and then rolling out and folding the dough a few times to create flaky layers. Frozen fruit saved us loads of prep work; plus, it tastes at least as good as most fresh fruit because it's picked and frozen at its peak. Crushing a portion of the fruit with the sugar made a pulpy mash that filled in gaps between the chunks and released juice that gelled lightly when cooked with a little cornstarch. Plenty of lemon (or lime) juice added acidity and oomph. Making square parcels minimized dough waste and maximized efficiency on the assembly line. Rolling, filling, and sealing the dough using the same process we came up with to make hand-cut ravioli produced tidy, airtight packages. We briefly chilled the assembled pies to help them maintain their sharp, clean edges. Trimming the pastry edges with a fluted pastry wheel or decorating them with the tines of a fork or a serrated knife added visual appeal. Cutting distinctive vents—a series of slashes or a simple pattern on the top of the dough—made it easy to identify different fruit fillings. A sprinkle of demerara sugar on the top of each pie added a hint of sweetness and shimmer.

Be sure to have the filling ready before you start this recipe. We strongly recommend weighing the flour here. If you're baking only one sheet of hand pies, adjust the oven rack to the middle position.

- 2½ cups (12½ ounces) all-purpose flour
- 2 tablespoons granulated sugar
- 1 teaspoon plus pinch table salt, divided
- 20 tablespoons (2½ sticks) unsalted butter, halved lengthwise and chilled
- ¾ cup ice water
- 1 large egg
- 1 recipe hand pie filling (recipes follow)
- 2 tablespoons demerara or turbinado sugar (optional)

1. Place flour, granulated sugar, and 1 teaspoon salt in 1-gallon, heavy-duty zipper-lock bag. Seal and shake well to combine. Add butter to bag and shake to coat with flour mixture. Seal bag, pressing out as much air as possible. Set rolling pin over lowest portion of bag and, using rocking motion, flatten butter beneath pin into large flakes. Working in sections, move pin up bag and flatten remaining butter. Shake bag to mix. Roll over bag with pin, shaking bag occasionally to mix, until flour becomes very pale yellow and almost all of butter is incorporated. Transfer mixture to large bowl (use rubber spatula or bench scraper to scrape any remaining butter and flour mixture from bag). Add ice water and toss with rubber spatula until just combined (mixture will be tacky). Transfer dough to floured counter. With your floured hands, press dough into rough 8-inch square.

2. Roll dough into 15 by 10-inch rectangle with short side parallel to edge of counter, flouring counter and dough as needed. Starting at top of dough, fold into thirds like business letter, using bench scraper or metal spatula to release dough from counter. Turn dough 90 degrees and repeat rolling and folding. Divide dough in half crosswise. Wrap each half tightly in plastic wrap and refrigerate for at least 1 hour or up to 2 days.

3. Adjust oven racks to upper-middle and lower-middle positions and heat oven to 400 degrees. In small bowl, beat egg and remaining pinch salt until well combined. Line 2 rimmed baking sheets with parchment paper.

4. On lightly floured counter, roll 1 piece of dough into 17 by 9-inch rectangle with short side parallel to edge of counter. Roll dough loosely around rolling pin, turn 90 degrees, and arrange on counter so long side is parallel to edge of counter. If dough has contracted, roll again briefly to achieve 17 by 9-inch dimensions. Using pastry brush, apply 1-inch-wide band of egg wash horizontally across center of dough. Apply 1-inch-wide strip of egg wash to edges of lower half of dough. Apply 1-inch-wide bands of egg wash vertically to divide bottom half of dough into 4 equal squares.

5. Place 2 tablespoons filling into each square, being careful to keep filling clear of egg wash. Using spoon, shape filling into rough squares. Using pizza cutter or sharp knife, cut dough at center points between filling to create 4 pieces. Leaving pieces in place but working with 1 piece at a time, gently fold dough over, aligning top edge with bottom edge. Use your fingers to gently press dough layers together, working out as much air as possible. Trim ¼ inch of dough from ragged and folded sides of each pie. Arrange pies on prepared sheet, leaving at least ¾ inch between them.

6. Repeat steps 4 and 5 with remaining dough and filling. Cut 1-inch vent on top of each pie. Transfer pies to refrigerator to chill for 15 minutes. (Pies can be frozen on baking sheets until solid, at least 4 hours, and then transferred to airtight container and frozen for up to 6 weeks. Transfer to parchment paper–lined rimmed baking sheets and thaw in refrigerator for 2 hours before proceeding with step 7.)

7. Brush tops of pies with egg wash and sprinkle with demerara sugar, if using. Bake until dark golden brown, 20 to 25 minutes, switching and rotating sheets halfway through baking. Let cool for 20 minutes; serve warm.

Assembling Hand Pies

1. Roll 1 piece of dough into 17 by 9-inch rectangle. Brush 4 squares onto bottom of dough with egg wash. Add 2 tablespoons filling to each square, spreading up to (but not on) grid lines. Cut dough between filling to create 4 even pieces.

2. Fold 1 piece of dough over itself, aligning top and bottom edges. Seal edges with your fingers, pressing out as much air as possible. Repeat with remaining 3 pieces.

3. Trim ¼ inch from ragged and folded sides of pies.

FILLINGS

Cherry Hand Pie Filling

Makes 1¼ cups • Total Time: 20 minutes,
plus 1½ hours chilling

Use your choice of sweet or sour cherries here. You can substitute 10 ounces (2 cups) of fresh pitted cherries for the frozen cherries. Do not use canned cherries.

- 10 ounces frozen cherries, thawed, juice reserved, cut into approximate ½-inch pieces
- ⅓ cup (2⅓ ounces) sugar
- ⅛ teaspoon table salt
- 2 tablespoons lemon juice
- 4 teaspoons cornstarch
- ⅛ teaspoon almond extract

1. Combine cherries and reserved juice, sugar, and salt in medium saucepan. Using potato masher, crush one-third of cherries. Cook over medium heat, stirring occasionally, until sugar is dissolved, about 5 minutes.

2. Stir lemon juice and cornstarch in small bowl until well combined. Add mixture to saucepan and cook, stirring constantly, until mixture comes to simmer and juice thickens, 30 to 60 seconds. Transfer to bowl and refrigerate until fully cooled, about 1½ hours. Stir in almond extract.

Peach Hand Pie Filling

Makes 1¼ cups • Total Time: 20 minutes,
plus 1½ hours chilling

You can substitute 10 ounces (2 cups) of fresh peaches, nectarines, plums, or apricots for the frozen peaches. Don't use canned fruit.

- 10 ounces frozen sliced peaches, thawed, juice reserved, cut into approximate ½-inch pieces
- ⅓ cup (2⅓ ounces) sugar
- ⅛ teaspoon table salt
- ¼ teaspoon grated lemon zest plus 2 tablespoons juice
- 4 teaspoons cornstarch

1. Combine peaches and reserved juice, sugar, and salt in medium saucepan. Using potato masher, crush one-third of peaches. Cook over medium heat, stirring occasionally, until sugar is dissolved, about 5 minutes.

2. Stir lemon juice and cornstarch in small bowl until well combined. Add mixture to saucepan and cook, stirring constantly, until mixture comes to simmer and juice thickens, 30 to 60 seconds. Transfer to bowl and refrigerate until fully cooled, about 1½ hours. Stir in lemon zest.

Pineapple Hand Pie Filling

Makes 1¼ cups • Total Time: 20 minutes,
plus 1½ hours chilling

You can substitute 10 ounces (2 cups) of fresh pineapple for the frozen pineapple. Don't use canned pineapple.

- 10 ounces frozen pineapple chunks, thawed, juice reserved, cut into approximate ½-inch pieces
- ⅓ cup (2⅓ ounces) sugar
- ⅛ teaspoon table salt
- 2 tablespoons lime juice
- 4 teaspoons cornstarch
- ¼ teaspoon ground cinnamon

1. Combine pineapple and reserved juice, sugar, and salt in medium saucepan. Using potato masher, crush one-third of pineapple. Cook over medium heat, stirring occasionally, until sugar is dissolved, about 5 minutes.

2. Stir lime juice and cornstarch in small bowl until well combined. Add mixture to saucepan and cook, stirring constantly, until mixture comes to simmer and juice thickens, 30 to 60 seconds. Transfer to bowl and refrigerate until fully cooled, about 1½ hours. Stir in cinnamon.

SEASON 3

Ultimate Lemon Meringue Pie

Serves 8 • Total Time: 2 hours,
plus 3½ hours chilling and cooling

Why This Recipe Works Most everybody loves lemon meringue pie—at least the bottom half of it. On any given day the meringue can shrink, bead, puddle, deflate, burn, sweat, break down, or turn rubbery. We wanted a pie with a crisp, flaky crust and a rich filling that would balance the airy meringue, with clear lemon flavor. The filling should be soft but not runny; firm enough to cut but not stiff and gelatinous. Most important, we wanted a meringue that didn't break down and puddle on the bottom or "tear" on top. The puddling underneath the meringue is from undercooking while the beading on top of the pie is from overcooking. We discovered that if the filling is piping hot when the meringue is applied, the underside of the meringue will not undercook; if the oven temperature is relatively low, the top of the meringue won't overcook.

Baking the pie in a relatively cool oven also produced the best-looking, most evenly baked meringue. To further stabilize the meringue and keep it from weeping (even on hot, humid days), we beat in a small amount of cornstarch.

Make the pie crust, let it cool, and then begin work on the filling. As soon as the filling is made, cover it with plastic wrap to keep it hot and then start working on the meringue topping. You want to add hot filling to the pie crust, apply the meringue topping, and then quickly get the pie into the oven.

1 recipe Foolproof All-Butter Dough for Single-Crust Pie (page 630)

Filling

1½ cups water
1 cup (7 ounces) sugar
¼ cup (1 ounce) cornstarch
⅛ teaspoon table salt
6 large egg yolks
1 tablespoon grated lemon zest plus ½ cup juice (3 lemons)
2 tablespoons unsalted butter, cut into 2 pieces

Meringue

⅓ cup water
1 tablespoon cornstarch
4 large egg whites
½ teaspoon vanilla extract
¼ teaspoon cream of tartar
½ cup (3½ ounces) sugar

1. Roll dough into 12-inch circle on well-floured counter. Roll dough loosely around rolling pin and unroll it onto 9-inch pie plate, leaving at least 1-inch overhang around edge. Ease dough into plate by gently lifting edge of dough with your hand while pressing into plate bottom with your other hand. Trim overhang to ½ inch beyond lip of plate. Tuck overhang under itself; folded edge should be flush with edge of plate. Crimp dough evenly around edge of plate using your fingers. Refrigerate dough-lined plate until dough is firm, about 30 minutes. Adjust oven rack to middle position and heat oven to 375 degrees.

2. Line chilled pie shell with double layer of aluminum foil and fill with pie weights. Bake until pie dough looks dry and is light in color, 25 to 30 minutes. Remove weights and foil and continue to bake crust until deep golden brown, 10 to 12 minutes longer. Let crust cool completely. Reduce oven temperature to 325 degrees.

3. For the filling: Bring water, sugar, cornstarch, and salt to simmer in large saucepan over medium heat, whisking constantly. When mixture starts to turn translucent, whisk in egg yolks, two at a time. Whisk in lemon zest and juice and butter. Return mixture to brief simmer, then remove pan from heat. Lay sheet of plastic wrap directly on surface of filling to keep warm and prevent skin from forming.

4. For the meringue: Bring water and cornstarch to simmer in small saucepan and cook, whisking occasionally, until thickened and translucent, 1 to 2 minutes. Set aside off heat to cool slightly.

5. Using stand mixer fitted with whisk attachment, whip egg whites, vanilla, and cream of tartar on medium-low speed until foamy, about 1 minute. Increase speed to medium-high and beat in sugar, 1 tablespoon at a time, until incorporated and mixture forms soft, billowy mounds. Add cornstarch mixture, 1 tablespoon at a time, and continue to beat to glossy, stiff peaks, 2 to 3 minutes.

6. Meanwhile, remove plastic wrap from filling and return to very low heat during last minute or so of beating meringue (to ensure filling is hot).

7. Pour warm filling into pie crust. Using rubber spatula, immediately distribute meringue evenly around edge and then center of pie, attaching meringue to pie crust to prevent shrinking. Use back of spoon to create attractive swirls and peaks in meringue. Bake until meringue is golden brown, about 20 minutes. Let pie cool on wire rack until filling has set, about 2 hours. Serve.

Key Lime Pie

Serves 8 • Total Time: 1¼ hours, plus 4 hours cooling and chilling

Why This Recipe Works We wanted to serve classic key lime pie with a fresh flavor and silky filling. Traditional key lime pie is usually not baked; instead, the combination of egg yolks, lime juice, and sweetened condensed milk firms up when chilled because the juice's acidity causes the proteins in the eggs and milk to bind. Although we suspected that the sweetened condensed milk was guilty of giving key lime pies their "off" flavor, we found that the real culprit was the lime juice—bottled, reconstituted lime juice, that is. When we substituted the juice and zest from fresh limes, the pie became a very different experience: pungent and refreshing, cool and yet creamy. We also discovered that while the pie filling will set without baking (most recipes call only for mixing and then chilling), it set more nicely after being baked for only 15 minutes. We tried other, more dramatic departures from the "classic" recipe—folding in egg whites, substituting heavy cream for condensed milk—but they didn't work. Just our two seemingly minor adjustments to the recipe made all the difference.

We found that tasters could not tell the difference between pies made with regular supermarket limes (called Persian limes) and true key limes. Since Persian limes are easier to find and juice, we recommend them. You need to make the filling first, then prepare the crust.

Pie

- 4 large egg yolks
- 4 teaspoons grated lime zest plus ½ cup juice (4 limes)
- 1 (14-ounce) can sweetened condensed milk
- 1 recipe Graham Cracker Crust (page 632)

Topping (optional)

- 1 cup heavy cream, chilled
- ¼ cup (1 ounce) confectioners' sugar

1. For the pie: Whisk egg yolks and lime zest in medium bowl until mixture has light green tint, about 2 minutes. Whisk in condensed milk until smooth, then whisk in lime juice. Cover mixture and set aside at room temperature until thickened, about 30 minutes.

2. Meanwhile, prepare and bake crust. Transfer pie plate to wire rack and leave oven at 325 degrees. (Crust must still be warm when filling is added.)

3. Pour thickened filling into warm pie crust. Bake pie until center is firm but jiggles slightly when shaken, 15 to 20 minutes. Let pie cool slightly on wire rack, about 1 hour, then cover loosely with plastic wrap and refrigerate until filling is chilled and set, about 3 hours.

4. For the topping, if using: Before serving, using stand mixer fitted with whisk attachment, whip cream and sugar on medium-low speed until foamy, about 1 minute. Increase speed to high and whip until soft peaks form, 1 to 3 minutes. Spread whipped cream attractively over top of pie and serve.

Perfect Pecan Pie

Serves 8 • Total Time: 2½ hours, plus 6 hours chilling and cooling

Why This Recipe Works Pecan pies can be overwhelmingly sweet, with no real pecan flavor. And they too often turn out curdled and separated. What's more, the weepy filling makes the bottom crust soggy and leathery. The fact that the crust usually seems underbaked to begin with doesn't help matters. We wanted to create a recipe for a not-too-sweet pie with a smooth-textured filling and a properly baked bottom crust. We tackled this pie's problems by using brown sugar and reducing the amount, which helped bring out the pecan flavor. We also partially baked the crust, which kept it crisp. We found that it's important to add the

Perfect Pecan Pie

hot filling to a warm pie crust as this helps keep the crust from getting soggy. In addition, we discovered that simulating a double boiler when you're melting the butter and making the filling is an easy way to maintain gentle heat, which helps ensure that the filling doesn't curdle.

The crust must still be warm when the filling is added. To serve the pie warm, cool it thoroughly so that it sets completely, then warm it in a 250-degree oven for about 15 minutes and slice. Serve with vanilla ice cream or lightly sweetened whipped cream.

- 1 recipe Foolproof All-Butter Dough for Single-Crust Pie (page 630)
- 6 tablespoons unsalted butter, cut into 1-inch pieces
- 1 cup packed (7 ounces) dark brown sugar
- ½ teaspoon table salt
- 3 large eggs
- ¾ cup light corn syrup
- 1 tablespoon vanilla extract
- 2 cups whole pecans (8 ounces), toasted and chopped into small pieces

1. Roll dough into 12-inch circle on well-floured counter. Roll dough loosely around rolling pin and unroll it onto 9-inch pie plate, leaving at least 1-inch overhang around edge. Ease dough into plate by gently lifting edge of dough with your hand while pressing into plate bottom with your other hand. Trim overhang to ½ inch beyond lip of plate. Tuck overhang under itself; folded edge should be flush with edge of plate. Crimp dough evenly around edge of plate using your fingers. Refrigerate dough-lined plate until dough is firm, about 30 minutes. Adjust oven racks to middle and lower-middle positions and heat oven to 375 degrees.

2. Line chilled pie shell with double layer of aluminum foil and fill with pie weights. Bake on upper rack until pie dough looks dry and is light in color, 25 to 30 minutes. Transfer pie plate to wire rack and remove weights and foil. Reduce oven temperature to 275 degrees. (Crust must still be warm when filling is added.)

3. Melt butter in heatproof bowl set in skillet of water maintained at just below simmer. Remove bowl from skillet and stir in sugar and salt until butter is absorbed. Whisk in eggs, then corn syrup and vanilla until smooth. Return bowl to hot water and stir until mixture is shiny and hot to touch and registers 130 degrees. Off heat, stir in pecans.

4. Pour pecan mixture into warm pie crust. Bake pie on lower rack until filling looks set but yields like Jell-O when gently pressed with back of spoon, 50 minutes to 1 hour. Let pie cool on wire rack until filling has firmed up, at least 4 hours; serve at room temperature or slightly warm.

Crimping a Single-Crust Pie Dough

For fluted edge, use your index finger and your other index finger and thumb to create fluted ridges perpendicular to edge of pie plate.

Lemon–Olive Oil Tart

Serves 8 • **Total Time: 1¼ hours, plus 2 hours cooling**

Why This Recipe Works A unique ingredient is the key to this simple, elegant, and brightly flavored tart. Most lemon tarts feature butter in the crust and the filling, but here we used extra-virgin olive oil. It made the crust a snap: We just mixed the flour, sugar, and salt with the oil and a little water until a soft dough formed; crumbled it into the tart pan; pressed it into the sides and bottom; and baked it right away—no rolling or chilling required. The filling got plenty of structure from the protein in the eggs, so using olive oil didn't compromise its firmness or sliceability. The olive oil did, however, allow the lemons' acidity to come to the fore in a way that butter doesn't, so we could use a bit less juice and still enjoy plenty of bright lemon flavor.

You'll need a 9-inch tart pan with a removable bottom for this recipe. For the best flavor, use a fresh, high-quality extra-virgin olive oil. Make sure that all your metal equipment—saucepan, strainer, and whisk—is nonreactive, or the filling may have a metallic flavor.

Crust

- 1½ cups (7½ ounces) all-purpose flour
- 5 tablespoons (2¼ ounces) sugar
- ½ teaspoon table salt
- ½ cup extra-virgin olive oil
- 2 tablespoons water

Filling

- 1 cup (7 ounces) sugar
- 2 tablespoons all-purpose flour
- ¼ teaspoon table salt
- 3 large eggs plus 3 large yolks
- 1 tablespoon grated lemon zest plus ½ cup juice (3 lemons)
- ¼ cup extra-virgin olive oil

1. For the crust: Adjust oven rack to middle position and heat oven to 350 degrees. Whisk flour, sugar, and salt together in bowl. Add oil and water and stir until uniform dough forms. Using your hands, crumble three-quarters of dough over bottom of 9-inch tart pan with removable bottom. Press dough to even thickness in bottom of pan. Crumble remaining dough and scatter evenly around edge of pan, then press crumbled dough into fluted sides of pan. Press dough to even thickness. Bake on rimmed baking sheet until crust is deep golden brown and firm to touch, 30 to 35 minutes, rotating sheet halfway through baking. Transfer sheet to wire rack. (Tart shell must still be warm when filling is added.)

2. For the filling: About 5 minutes before crust is finished baking, whisk sugar, flour, and salt in medium saucepan until combined. Whisk in eggs and yolks until no streaks of egg remain, then whisk in lemon zest and juice. Cook over medium-low heat, whisking constantly and scraping corners of saucepan, until mixture thickens slightly and registers 160 degrees, 5 to 8 minutes.

3. Off heat, whisk in oil until incorporated. Strain curd through fine-mesh strainer into bowl. Pour curd into warm tart shell.

4. Bake until filling is set and barely jiggles when pan is shaken, 8 to 12 minutes. Let tart cool completely on sheet on wire rack, about 2 hours. Remove outer ring of tart pan, slide thin metal spatula between tart and tart pan bottom, and carefully slide tart onto serving platter or cutting board. Serve. (Leftovers can be wrapped loosely in plastic wrap and refrigerated for up to 3 days.)

SEASON 22

Cranberry Curd Tart with Almond Crust

Serves 8 • Total Time: 1½ hours, plus 4 hours resting

Why This Recipe Works Our cranberry curd tart showcases cranberries' bold flavor and brilliant color while making use of their ample pectin content. Quickly simmering the cranberry filling softened the berries and released their acids and pectin, and immediately pureeing the berries with egg yolks and cornstarch allowed the berries' heat to cook the eggs and thicken the cornstarch. The combination of almond flour and cornstarch kept our press-in crust both sturdy and gluten-free. Pureeing butter into the cooled filling, straining it, and pouring the mixture over the baked crust prevented the filling from developing a thick, rubbery skin. We whisked up a whipped cream topping stabilized by a small amount of the pectin-rich puree, which meant that the topping could be piped onto the tart hours in advance without breaking or weeping.

You'll need a 9-inch tart pan with a removable bottom for this recipe. We strongly recommend weighing the almond flour and cornstarch for the crust. If preferred, you can use a stand mixer or hand mixer to whip the cream in step 4. The tart crust will be firm if you serve the tart on the day that it's made; if you prefer a more tender crust, make the tart through step 3 up to two days ahead.

Filling
- 1 pound (4 cups) fresh or frozen cranberries
- 1¼ cups (8¾ ounces) plus 1 tablespoon sugar, divided
- ½ cup water
  Pinch table salt
- 3 large egg yolks
- 2 teaspoons cornstarch
- 4 tablespoons unsalted butter, cut into 4 pieces and softened

Crust
- 1 cup (4 ounces) almond flour
- ½ cup (2 ounces) cornstarch
- ⅓ cup (2⅓ ounces) sugar
- ½ teaspoon table salt
- 6 tablespoons unsalted butter, melted and cooled
- ¾ teaspoon almond extract

- 1 cup heavy cream

1. For the filling: Bring cranberries, 1¼ cups sugar, water, and salt to boil in medium saucepan over medium-high heat, stirring occasionally. Adjust heat to maintain very gentle simmer. Cover and cook until all cranberries have burst and started to shrivel, about 10 minutes. While cranberries cook, whisk egg yolks and cornstarch in bowl until smooth. Transfer hot cranberry mixture to food processor. Immediately add yolk mixture and process until smooth (small flecks of cranberry skin will be visible), about 1 minute, scraping down sides of bowl as necessary. Let mixture cool in processor bowl until skin forms and mixture registers 120 to 125 degrees, 45 minutes to 1 hour. While mixture cools, make crust.

2. For the crust: Adjust oven rack to middle position and heat oven to 350 degrees. Whisk flour, cornstarch, sugar, and salt in bowl until well combined. Add melted butter and almond extract and stir with wooden spoon until uniform dough forms. Crumble two-thirds of mixture over bottom of 9-inch tart pan with removable bottom. Press dough to even thickness in bottom of pan. Crumble remaining dough and scatter evenly around edge of pan. Press crumbled dough into sides of pan. Press edges to even thickness. Place pan on rimmed baking sheet and bake until crust is golden brown, about 20 minutes, rotating pan halfway through baking.

3. Add softened butter to cranberry puree and process until fully combined, about 30 seconds. Strain mixture through fine-mesh strainer set over bowl, pressing on solids with rubber spatula to extract puree. Transfer 2 tablespoons puree to medium bowl, then stir in cream and remaining 1 tablespoon sugar. Cover and refrigerate. Transfer remaining puree to crust (it's OK if crust is still warm) and smooth into even layer. Let tart sit at room temperature for at least 4 hours. (Cover tart with large bowl and refrigerate after 4 hours if making ahead.)

Piping Decorative Designs

All of these designs require holding the filled pastry bag at a 90-degree angle about ½ inch above the tart.

Confetti Border: Squeeze pastry bag fitted with ¾- to 1-inch round tip to create 1-inch dots around perimeter (8 to 12 in total). With each dot, stop squeezing and pull bag straight up to create peak. Fill in empty areas with smaller dots.

Zigzag Border: Squeeze pastry bag fitted with ½- to ¾-inch round tip to pipe 1- to 1½-inch-wide, slightly overlapped zigzag pattern around tart perimeter.

Simple Swirls Border: Squeeze pastry bag fitted with ½- to ¾-inch star tip, moving tip in tight circle. When circle is complete, stop piping and pull bag straight up to create swirl. Repeat at regular intervals around tart perimeter.

4. Whisk cream mixture until stiff peaks form, 1 to 3 minutes. Transfer to pastry bag fitted with pastry tip. Pipe decorative border around edge of tart. Transfer any remaining whipped cream to small serving bowl.

5. To serve: Remove outer metal ring of tart pan. Slide thin metal spatula between tart and pan bottom to loosen tart. Carefully slide tart onto serving platter. Slice into wedges, wiping knife clean between cuts if necessary, and serve, passing extra whipped cream separately. (Leftovers can be covered and refrigerated for up to 3 days.)

SEASON 6

Free-Form Summer Fruit Tart

Serves 6 • Total Time: 2¼ hours, plus 1¾ hours chilling and cooling

Why This Recipe Works What we wanted was a simpler fruit pie: a buttery, flaky crust paired with juicy summer fruit. A free-form tart (a single layer of pie dough folded up around fresh fruit) seemed the obvious solution. Without the support of a pie plate, tender crusts are prone to leak juice, resulting in soggy bottoms. For our crust, we used a high proportion of butter to flour, which provided buttery flavor and tender texture without compromising the structure. We then turned to a French technique in pastry making called fraisage. To begin, butter is only partially cut into the dry ingredients. Then, the cook presses the barely mixed dough firmly against the counter. As a result, the chunks of butter are pressed into long, thin sheets that create lots of flaky layers when the dough is baked. We rolled the dough into a 12-inch circle for a crust that was thick enough to contain a lot of fruit but thin enough to bake evenly and thoroughly. We placed the fruit in the middle, then lifted the dough up and back over the fruit and pleated it loosely to allow for shrinkage.

The dough, wrapped tightly in plastic wrap, can be refrigerated for up to two days or frozen for up to one month. If frozen, let the dough thaw completely on the counter before rolling it out. Though we prefer a tart made with a mix of stone fruits and berries, you can use only one type of fruit if you prefer. Taste the fruit before adding sugar to it; use the lesser amount if the fruit is very sweet, more if it is tart. However much sugar you use, do not add it to the fruit until you are ready to fill and form the tart. Serve with vanilla ice cream, lightly sweetened whipped cream, or crème fraîche.

Rustic Tart Dough

- 1½ cups (7½ ounces) all-purpose flour
- ½ teaspoon table salt
- 10 tablespoons unsalted butter, cut into ½-inch pieces and chilled
- 4–6 tablespoons ice water

Filling

- 1 pound peaches, nectarines, apricots, or plums, pitted and sliced into ½-inch-thick wedges
- 5 ounces (1 cup) blueberries, raspberries, or blackberries
- 3–5 tablespoons plus 1 tablespoon sugar, divided

1. For the rustic tart dough: Process flour and salt in food processor until combined, about 3 seconds. Scatter butter pieces over top and pulse until mixture resembles coarse bread crumbs and butter pieces are about size of small peas, about 10 pulses. Continue to pulse, adding water through feed tube 1 tablespoon at a time, until dough begins to form small curds that hold together when pinched with your fingers (dough will be crumbly), about 10 pulses.

2. Turn dough crumbs out onto lightly floured counter and gather into rectangular-shaped pile. Starting at farthest end, use heel of your hand to smear small amount of dough against counter. Continue to smear dough until all crumbs have been worked. Gather smeared crumbs together in another rectangular-shaped pile and repeat process. Flatten dough into 6-inch disk, wrap it tightly in plastic wrap, and refrigerate for 1 hour. Before rolling dough out, let it sit on counter to soften slightly, about 10 minutes.

3. Roll dough into 12-inch circle between 2 large sheets of floured parchment paper. Slide dough, still between parchment, onto rimmed baking sheet and refrigerate until firm, about 20 minutes.

4. For the filling: Adjust oven rack to middle position and heat oven to 375 degrees. Gently toss peaches, blueberries, and sugar together in large bowl. Remove top sheet of parchment from dough. Mound fruit in center of dough, leaving 2½-inch border around edge. Fold 2 inches of dough up over fruit, leaving ½-inch border between fruit and edge of tart shell, pleating it every 2 to 3 inches as needed; gently pinch pleated dough to secure, but do not press dough into fruit. Working quickly, brush dough with water and sprinkle evenly with remaining 1 tablespoon sugar.

5. Bake tart until crust is deep golden brown and fruit is bubbling, about 1 hour, rotating baking sheet halfway through.

6. Let tart cool on baking sheet on wire rack for 10 minutes, then use parchment to gently transfer tart to wire rack. Use metal spatula to loosen tart from parchment and remove parchment. Let tart cool on rack until juices have thickened, about 25 minutes. Serve warm or at room temperature.

Using Fraisage to Mix Dough

1. Starting at 1 end of rectangular pile of dough, smear small amount of dough against counter with heel of your hand. Repeat this process (called fraisage) until rest of buttery crumbs have been worked.

2. Gather smeared bits into another rectangular pile and repeat smearing process until all of crumbs have been worked again. This second time won't take as long and will result in large flakes of dough.

Fresh Fruit Tart with Pastry Cream

Serves 8 to 10 • Total Time: 1¾ hours, plus 4½ hours chilling, freezing, and cooling

Why This Recipe Works Fresh fruit tarts usually offer dazzling beauty and little else. We set out to create a buttery, crisp crust filled with rich, lightly sweetened pastry cream, topped with fresh, glistening fruit. We started with our classic tart dough and baked it until golden brown. We then filled the crust with pastry cream, made with half-and-half enriched with butter and thickened with just enough cornstarch to keep its shape without becoming gummy. For the fruit, we chose a combination of sliced kiwi, raspberries, and blueberries. We found that it was important not to wash the berries, as washing causes them to bruise and bleed and makes for a less than attractive tart. The finishing touch: a drizzle with a jelly glaze for a glistening presentation.

You will need a 9-inch tart pan with a removable bottom for this recipe. The pastry cream can be made a day or two in advance, but do not fill the prebaked tart shell until just before serving. Once filled, the tart should be topped with fruit, glazed, and served within half an hour or so. Don't wash the berries or they will lose their flavor and shape.

Pastry Cream
- 2 cups half-and-half
- ½ cup (3½ ounces) sugar, divided
  Pinch table salt
- 5 large egg yolks
- 3 tablespoons cornstarch
- 4 tablespoons unsalted butter, cut into 4 pieces
- 1½ teaspoons vanilla extract

Tart Shell and Fruit
- 1 recipe Classic Tart Dough (page 633)
- 2 large kiwis, peeled, halved lengthwise, and sliced ⅜ inch thick
- 10 ounces (2 cups) raspberries
- 5 ounces (1 cup) blueberries
- ½ cup red currant or apple jelly

1. **For the pastry cream:** Bring half-and-half, 6 tablespoons sugar, and salt to simmer in medium saucepan over medium-high heat, stirring occasionally.

2. As half-and-half mixture begins to simmer, whisk egg yolks, cornstarch, and remaining 2 tablespoons sugar in medium bowl until smooth. Slowly whisk 1 cup simmering half-and-half mixture into yolks to temper, then slowly whisk tempered yolks back into simmering saucepan. Reduce heat to medium and cook, whisking vigorously, until mixture is thickened and few bubbles burst on surface, about 30 seconds.

3. Off heat, stir in butter and vanilla. Transfer mixture to medium bowl; lay sheet of plastic wrap directly on surface; and refrigerate pastry cream until chilled and firm, about 3 hours.

4. **For the tart shell and fruit:** Roll dough out into 11-inch circle on lightly floured counter. Wrap it loosely around rolling pin and unroll dough over 9-inch tart pan with removable bottom. Lifting edge of dough, gently ease dough into pan. Press dough into corners and fluted sides of pan. Run rolling pin over top of tart pan to remove any excess dough and make clean edge. (If parts of edge are too thin, reinforce them by pressing in some of excess dough. If edge is too thick, press some of dough up over edge of pan and trim it away.) Set tart pan on large plate and freeze tart shell for 30 minutes.

5. Adjust oven rack to middle position and heat oven to 375 degrees. Set tart pan on rimmed baking sheet. Press double layer of aluminum foil into frozen tart shell and over edges of pan and fill with pie weights. Bake until tart shell is golden brown and set, about 30 minutes, rotating sheet halfway through baking.

6. Carefully remove weights and foil and continue to bake tart shell until it is fully baked and golden, 5 to 10 minutes longer. Transfer tart shell on sheet to wire rack and let cool completely, about 1 hour.

7. Spread chilled pastry cream evenly over bottom of cooled tart shell. Shingle kiwi slices around edge of tart, then arrange 3 rows of raspberries inside kiwi. Finally, arrange mound of blueberries in center.

8. Melt jelly in small saucepan over medium-high heat, stirring occasionally to smooth out any lumps. Using pastry brush, dab melted jelly over fruit. To serve, remove outer metal ring of tart pan, slide thin metal spatula between tart and tart pan bottom, and carefully slide tart onto serving platter or cutting board.

VARIATION
Mixed Berry Tart with Pastry Cream
Omit kiwi and add 2 cups extra berries (including blackberries or quartered strawberries). Combine berries in large plastic bag and toss them gently to mix. Carefully spread berries in even layer over tart. Glaze and serve as directed.

SEASON 21
Peach Tarte Tatin

Serves 8 • Total Time: 1½ hours, plus 40 minutes resting

Why This Recipe Works The classic tarte Tatin is an upside-down caramelized apple tart. We wanted to create a peach version, but simply swapping fruits produced a cloying tart that was awash in juice. To make wetter, sweeter, more fragile peaches work, we had to tweak the recipe. We started by layering butter, a small amount of sugar, salt, and peaches in a cool skillet. After cooking the filling on the stovetop until the peach juice was deeply browned, we removed the skillet from the heat, slid a pie pastry disk on top, and baked it. When the crust was browned and crisp, we let the tart cool for 20 minutes before pouring off the excess juice and inverting the tart onto a platter. Reducing the juice with a bit of bourbon and then brushing the mixture back over the peaches gave this tart extra flavor and shine while supporting its cohesiveness.

Chill the dough for at least 1 hour before rolling it. We like using firm peaches in this recipe because they are easier to peel and retain their shape when cooked; yellow peaches are also preferable to white peaches. When you're pouring off the liquid in step 4, the peaches may shift in the skillet; shaking the skillet will help redistribute them. Serve the tart with lightly sweetened whipped cream, if desired.

1 recipe Foolproof All-Butter Dough for Single-Crust Pie (page 630)
3 tablespoons unsalted butter, softened
½ cup (3½ ounces) plus 2 tablespoons sugar, divided
¼ teaspoon table salt
2 pounds ripe but firm peaches, peeled, pitted, and quartered
1 tablespoon bourbon (optional)

1. Invert rimmed baking sheet and place sheet of parchment paper or waxed paper on top. Roll dough into 10-inch circle on lightly floured counter. Loosely roll dough around rolling pin and gently unroll it onto prepared sheet. Working around circumference, fold ½ inch of dough under itself and pinch to create 9-inch round with raised rim. Cut three 2-inch slits in center of dough and refrigerate until needed.

2. Adjust oven rack to middle position and heat oven to 400 degrees. Smear butter over bottom of 10-inch oven-safe skillet. Sprinkle ½ cup sugar over butter and shake skillet to distribute sugar in even layer. Sprinkle salt over sugar. Arrange peaches in circular pattern around edge of skillet, nestling fruit snugly. Tuck remaining peaches into center, squeezing in as much fruit as possible (it is not necessary to maintain circular pattern in center).

3. Place skillet over high heat and cook, without stirring fruit, until juice is released and turns from pink to deep amber, 8 to 12 minutes. (If necessary, adjust skillet's placement on burner to even out hot spots and encourage even browning.) Remove skillet from heat. Carefully slide prepared dough over fruit, making sure dough is centered and does not touch edge of skillet. Brush dough lightly with water and sprinkle with remaining 2 tablespoons sugar. Bake until crust is very well browned, 30 to 35 minutes. Transfer skillet to wire rack set in rimmed baking sheet and let cool for 20 minutes.

4. Place inverted plate on top of crust. With your hand firmly securing plate, carefully tip skillet over bowl to drain juice (skillet handle may still be hot). When all juice has been transferred to bowl, return skillet to wire rack, remove plate, and shake skillet firmly to redistribute peaches. Carefully invert tart onto plate, then slide tart onto wire rack. (If peaches have shifted during unmolding, gently nudge them back into place with spoon.)

5. Pour juice into now-empty skillet (handle may be hot). Stir in bourbon, if using, and cook over high heat, stirring constantly, until mixture is dark and thick and starting to smoke, 2 to 3 minutes. Return mixture to bowl and let cool until mixture is consistency of honey, 2 to 3 minutes. Brush mixture over peaches. Let tart cool for at least 20 minutes. Cut into wedges and serve.

Milk Chocolate Crémeux Tart

Serves 8 to 10 • **Total Time: 1½ hours, plus 3 hours 40 minutes freezing, cooling, and chilling**

Why This Recipe Works Chocolate crémeux, whose name translates from French as "creamy," is silkier than a ganache yet denser than a mousse. It's a delicate filling that pairs perfectly with a crisp, cookie-like tart shell. Instead of chilling the dough after mixing, we sped up the usual process by rolling out the just-mixed dough between layers of parchment until it was very thin and then freezing it, so it was ready to shape after only 30 minutes. Cutting the dough into one large round and a few strips allowed us to assemble the tart shell quickly and neatly. Milk chocolate that we blended with custard instead of cream formed the base of our crémeux filling, a perfect match for our thin pâte sucrée tart shell. Butter enhanced the filling's silky, sliceable texture.

You will need a 9-inch tart pan with a removable bottom for this recipe. The tart shell can be baked up to two days ahead; let it cool, wrap it tightly, and store it at room temperature. This recipe was developed using Endangered Species Smooth + Creamy Milk Chocolate, which has a high cacao content. If you'll be using another brand, consider adding the optional tablespoon of cocoa powder

for a darker milk chocolate flavor. Avoid chocolate chips, which sometimes contain additives to hinder melting. If desired, serve with unsweetened whipped cream or fruit.

Pâte Sucrée Tart Shell
    1 large egg
    1 teaspoon vanilla extract
 1½ cups (7½ ounces) all-purpose flour
 ⅔ cup (2⅔ ounces) confectioners' sugar
 ¼ teaspoon table salt
    8 tablespoons unsalted butter, cut into
        ½-inch pieces and chilled

Milk Chocolate Filling
    1 cup half-and-half
    4 large egg yolks
    1 tablespoon unsweetened cocoa powder (optional)
 ⅜ teaspoon table salt
  12 ounces milk chocolate, chopped fine
 1½ teaspoons vanilla extract
  10 tablespoons unsalted butter, melted and hot

1. **For the pâte sucrée tart shell:** Whisk egg and vanilla together in 1-cup liquid measuring cup; set aside. Pulse flour, sugar, and salt in food processor until combined, 2 pulses. Scatter butter over flour mixture; process until mixture looks like very fine crumbs with no pieces of butter visible, about 20 seconds. With processor running, add egg mixture and continue to process until dough just forms mass, about 18 seconds longer.

2. Transfer dough to center of 18 by 12-inch piece of parchment paper. Place second sheet of parchment on top of dough and press with your hand to ½-inch thickness. Using rolling pin, roll out dough so it nearly reaches edges of parchment. Using your flat hand on parchment, smooth out wrinkles on both sides. Transfer dough with parchment to baking sheet and freeze until firm, about 30 minutes.

3. Place dough and parchment on counter and peel away top layer of parchment. Replace top layer of parchment, flip dough and parchment, and peel away second piece of parchment. Invert 9-inch metal tart ring on left half of dough and press to cut out circle (leave circle on parchment). Using paring knife and ruler, cut right half of dough lengthwise into 1-inch-wide strips. Place removable bottom in tart pan. Lift dough round (if necessary, use thin spatula to loosen) and fit into bottom of tart pan, pressing edges of dough firmly into corners (it's OK if some dough smears up sides of tart pan). Lift strips and fit into sides of pan, overlapping strips only slightly. Trim final strip to fit. (Dough scraps can be sprinkled with sugar and baked as cook's treat.) If at any point dough becomes too soft to manipulate, freeze for 15 minutes.

A Very Streamlined and French Tart

"I love to entertain and I love to serve this luxurious, and foolproof, chocolate tart for dessert. It is simple to make, even if you are a novice baker. The tart dough comes together quickly in the food processor and the just-mixed dough is easy to roll out. Freezing the rolled-out dough is so much easier than trying to roll out a chunk of cold dough. And how you fit the delicate dough into a tart pan is really clever. You use the pan like a giant cookie cutter to cut out a fluted base that fits right into the bottom of the pan. Then you build the thin sides with the excess strips of dough along the edges of the pan. Baking melds the dough into a tidy thin crust.

The cookie-like shell holds a wealth of milk chocolate filling that is something between a dense ganache and an airy mousse. It starts with a quick custard rich with egg yolks and half-and-half to which you add two of my favorite ingredients: chopped chocolate and melted butter. Once the shell is filled, into the fridge it goes. This tart serves up to 10 people because a small wedge is all you need. This dessert is like my friends—very classy."

— Elle

4. Freeze tart shell until very firm, about 20 minutes. While tart shell chills, adjust oven rack to middle position and heat oven to 350 degrees.

5. Hold paring knife parallel to counter and shave off any excess dough to force dough into flutes for clean edge. Spray large sheet of heavy-duty aluminum foil with vegetable oil spray. Place foil sprayed side down in tart shell and smooth gently along bottom and sides. Fill with pie weights. Bake on rimmed baking sheet until tart shell is golden and set, about 30 minutes, rotating sheet halfway through baking. Remove foil and weights and continue to bake tart shell until fully baked and golden brown, about 10 minutes longer. Transfer sheet to wire rack and let cool completely, about 30 minutes.

6. For the milk chocolate filling: Place fine-mesh strainer over medium bowl. Whisk half-and-half; egg yolks; cocoa, if using; and salt in medium saucepan until combined. Cook mixture over medium-low heat, stirring constantly and scraping bottom of saucepan with heatproof spatula, until mixture is thickened and silky and registers 170 to 175 degrees, 5 to 7 minutes. Remove from heat. Working quickly, whisk in chocolate and vanilla until smooth. Add melted butter and whisk gently until incorporated. Pour mixture into prepared strainer and transfer strained mixture to cooled tart shell. Let cool completely, about 20 minutes, then refrigerate until filling is set, at least 2 hours or up to 24 hours.

7. Remove outer ring from tart pan. Insert thin metal spatula between crust and pan bottom to loosen tart; slide tart onto serving platter. Cut into wedges and serve. (Leftovers can be wrapped loosely and refrigerated for up to 3 days.)

Creating an Ultraslim Tart Shell

1. Using tart pan like giant cookie cutter, cut out fluted base and fit it into bottom of pan.

2. Fit excess strips of dough along sides of pan to create thin, elegant sides. Trim top to force dough into flutes for pretty and clean edge.

Apple Galette

Serves 10 to 12 • **Total Time: 2 hours**

Why This Recipe Works The French tart known as an apple galette should have a flaky crust and a layer of shingled caramelized apples. But it's challenging to make a crust strong enough to hold the apples and still be eaten out of hand—most recipes create a tough, bland crust. Choosing the right flour put us on the right track. All-purpose flour contained too much gluten; it made the pastry tough. Lower-protein pastry flour created a flaky and sturdy pastry. As pastry flour is hard to find, we mixed regular all-purpose flour with instant flour (Wondra). Technique also proved to be important. We used the French fraisage method of blending butter into dough (see page 655). We found that any thinly sliced apple would work, although we slightly preferred Granny Smith.

Wondra is an instant flour sold in canisters in the baking aisle. The galette can be made without Wondra, using 2 cups unbleached all-purpose flour and 2 tablespoons cornstarch; however, you might have to increase the amount of ice water. The dough, wrapped tightly in plastic wrap, can be refrigerated for up to two days or frozen for up to one month. If frozen, let the dough thaw completely on the counter before rolling out. Serve with ice cream, whipped cream, or crème fraîche.

Dough

- 1½ cups (7½ ounces) all-purpose flour
- ½ cup (2½ ounces) Wondra flour
- ½ teaspoon table salt
- ½ teaspoon sugar
- 12 tablespoons unsalted butter, cut into ¼-inch pieces and chilled
- 7–9 tablespoons ice water

Topping

- 1½ pounds Granny Smith apples, peeled, cored, and sliced ⅛ inch thick
- 2 tablespoons unsalted butter, cut into ¼-inch pieces
- ¼ cup (1¾ ounces) sugar
- 3 tablespoons apple jelly

1. For the dough: Process all-purpose flour, Wondra, salt, and sugar in food processor until combined, about 5 seconds. Scatter butter pieces over top and pulse until mixture resembles coarse cornmeal, about 15 pulses. Continue to pulse, adding water through feed tube 1 tablespoon at a time until dough begins to form small curds that hold together when pinched with your fingers (dough will be crumbly), about 10 pulses.

2. Turn dough crumbs onto lightly floured counter and gather into rectangular-shaped pile. Starting at farthest end, use heel of your hand to smear small amount of dough against counter. Continue to smear dough until all crumbs have been worked. Gather smeared crumbs together in another rectangular-shaped pile and repeat process. Press dough into 4-inch square, wrap it tightly in plastic wrap, and refrigerate for 1 hour. Before rolling dough out, let it sit on counter to soften slightly, about 10 minutes.

3. Adjust oven rack to middle position and heat oven to 400 degrees. Cut piece of parchment to measure exactly 16 by 12 inches. Roll dough out over parchment, dusting with flour as needed, until it just overhangs parchment. Trim edges of dough even with parchment. Roll outer 1 inch of dough up to create ½-inch-thick border. Slide parchment with dough onto rimmed baking sheet.

4. For the topping: Starting in 1 corner of tart, shingle apple slices onto crust in tidy diagonal rows, overlapping them by a third. Dot with butter and sprinkle evenly with sugar. Bake tart until bottom is deep golden brown and apples have caramelized, 45 minutes to 1 hour, rotating sheet halfway through baking.

5. Melt jelly in small saucepan over medium-high heat, stirring occasionally to smooth out any lumps. Brush glaze over apples and let tart cool slightly on sheet for 10 minutes. Slide tart onto large platter or cutting board and slice tart in half lengthwise, then crosswise into square pieces. Serve warm or at room temperature.

Preparing Apple Galette

1. Cut piece of parchment paper to measure exactly 16 by 12 inches, then roll dough out on top of parchment until it just overhangs edge and is about ⅛ inch thick.

2. Trim dough so that edges are even with parchment. (We use parchment as a guide to cut a perfectly even rectangle of dough from which we can make a large thin crust.)

3. Roll up 1 inch of each edge to create ½-inch-thick border. (This border is decorative and helps keep the apple slices in place.)

4. Slide parchment and dough onto rimmed baking sheet. Starting in 1 corner, shingle apple slices in tidy rows on diagonal over dough, overlapping each row by a third.

Easy Apple Strudel

Serves 6 • Total Time: 55 minutes, plus 40 minutes cooling

Why This Recipe Works Apple strudel, lightly spiced apples in a thin, flaky pastry, is meant to be savored by the forkful. We wanted all the flavor and charm of this apple dessert, but we didn't want to bother with the hours of preparation the paper-thin dough requires. So we simplified this classic dessert while keeping the rich apple filling and as much of the crisp, flaky texture as possible. Replacing homemade strudel dough with purchased phyllo dough made for a crust with perfect flaky layers in a fraction of the time. We brushed the phyllo sheets with melted butter to keep them crisp and flaky. A combination of Golden Delicious and McIntosh apples, sliced thin, gave us a filling with layered apple flavor and just the right texture. A small amount of bread crumbs, browned in butter, thickened the filling without weighing it down. Golden raisins, plumped with Calvados (apple brandy), added a sophisticated, fruity dimension to the apple filling; for brightness and to lighten the filling, we added in fresh lemon juice. We found that the phyllo on most strudels, including this one, curled and shattered as it cooled; sprinkling sugar between the layers of phyllo "glued" them together in the oven and prevented this.

The best ways to thaw the phyllo are in the refrigerator overnight or at room temperature for 3 to 4 hours; it doesn't defrost well in the microwave. Make sure that the phyllo sheets you use for the strudel are not badly torn. If they have small cuts or tears in the same location (sometimes an entire package sustains cuts in the same spot), when forming the strudel, flip alternating layers so that the cuts will not line up, thereby creating a weak spot that can cause the strudel to burst during baking. To make the fresh bread crumbs, process one slice of high-quality white sandwich bread in a food processor until fine, 20 to 30 seconds. Serve the strudel warm with Tangy Whipped Cream (recipe follows) or regular whipped cream.

- ½ cup golden raisins
- 2 tablespoons Calvados or apple cider
- 8 tablespoons unsalted butter, divided
- ¼ cup fresh bread crumbs
- 1 pound Golden Delicious apples, peeled, cored, and sliced ¼ inch thick
- 1 medium McIntosh apple, peeled, cored, and sliced ¼ inch thick

- 6 tablespoons (2⅔ ounces) granulated sugar, divided
- ⅓ cup finely chopped walnuts, toasted (optional)
- 1 teaspoon lemon juice
- ¼ teaspoon ground cinnamon
- ⅛ teaspoon table salt
- 10 (14 by 9-inch) phyllo sheets, thawed
- 1½ teaspoons confectioners' sugar

1. Adjust oven rack to lower-middle position and heat oven to 475 degrees. Line rimmed baking sheet with parchment paper. Bring raisins and Calvados to simmer in small saucepan over medium heat. Cover, remove from heat, and let stand until needed.

2. Combine 1 tablespoon butter and bread crumbs in 8-inch skillet and cook over medium heat, stirring frequently, until golden brown, about 2 minutes. Transfer bread crumbs to large bowl.

3. Drain off and discard any remaining liquid from raisins. Toss raisins; bread crumbs; apples; ¼ cup granulated sugar; walnuts, if using; lemon juice; cinnamon; and salt in large bowl to combine.

4. Melt remaining 7 tablespoons butter in now-empty skillet. Place large sheet of parchment horizontally on counter. Lay 1 sheet phyllo on left side of parchment, then brush with melted butter and sprinkle with ½ teaspoon granulated sugar. Place another sheet of phyllo on right side of parchment, overlapping sheets by 1 inch, then brush with more butter and sprinkle with sugar. Repeat this process with remaining 8 sheets phyllo, butter, and sugar.

Mound filling along bottom edge of phyllo, leaving 2½-inch border on bottom and 2-inch border on sides. Fold dough on sides over apples. Fold dough on bottom over apples and continue to roll dough around filling to form strudel.

5. Place strudel, seam side down, on prepared sheet; brush with remaining butter and sprinkle with remaining 1 teaspoon sugar. Cut four 1-inch crosswise vents into top of strudel and bake until golden brown, 15 minutes. Transfer sheet to wire rack and let cool until warm, about 40 minutes.

6. Dust strudel with confectioners' sugar before serving; slice with serrated knife and serve warm or at room temperature.

Assembling Easy Apple Strudel

1. Brush 1 sheet of phyllo with melted butter and sprinkle with granulated sugar. Place another sheet of phyllo next to it, overlapping sheets. Brush with more butter and sprinkle with sugar. Repeat this process 4 times.

2. Mound filling along bottom edge of phyllo, leaving 2½-inch border on bottom and 2-inch border on sides.

3. Fold dough on sides over apples. Fold dough on bottom over apples and continue to roll dough around filling to form strudel.

4. After strudel has been assembled and rolled, gently lay it seam side down on prepared baking sheet.

Tangy Whipped Cream

Makes 2 cups • Total Time: 5 minutes

Adding sour cream to whipped cream mimics the pleasantly tart flavor of the rich French-style whipped cream, crème fraîche.

    1 cup heavy cream
    ½ cup sour cream
    1 tablespoon sugar
    1 teaspoon vanilla extract

Using stand mixer fitted with whisk attachment, whip all ingredients on medium-low speed until frothy, about 1 minute. Increase speed to high and whip until soft peaks form, 1 to 3 minutes.

SEASON 11

Skillet Apple Crisp

Serves 6 to 8 • Total Time: 1¼ hours

Why This Recipe Works Apple crisp needs to live up to its crisp moniker. We wanted an exemplary apple crisp—a lush (but not mushy) sweet-tart apple filling covered with truly crisp morsels of buttery, sugary topping. For apple crisp, we prefer crisp apples such as Golden Delicious, because they turn tender yet not mushy. But the problem with these apples is that their mellow flesh lacks fruity punch and they tend to cook unevenly. Stirring the fruit helped solve the problem but reaching into a hot oven to stir bubbling fruit was a hassle. Instead, we softened the fruit on the stovetop—in a skillet. The shallow, flared shape of the skillet also encouraged evaporation, browning, and better flavor overall. For even more intense fruity depth we added apple cider, which we first reduced to a syrupy consistency. As for the topping, we added brown sugar to white to play up the apples' caramel notes. Rolled oats contributed a pleasant chew and chopped pecans improved the crunch factor and added rich flavor. We then slid the skillet into the oven for a quick browning and to finish cooking the apples.

> *If your skillet is not ovensafe, prepare the recipe through step 3 and then transfer the filling to a 13 by 9-inch baking dish. Top the filling as directed and bake for an additional 5 minutes. We like Golden Delicious apples here, but any sweet, crisp apple such as Honeycrisp or Braeburn can be used. Do not use Granny Smith apples. While old-fashioned oats are preferable, quick-cooking oats can be substituted. Serve the apple crisp warm or at room temperature with vanilla ice cream or whipped cream.*

12 to 14 minutes. (Do not fully cook apples.) Remove pan from heat and gently stir in cider mixture until apples are coated.

4. Sprinkle topping evenly over fruit, breaking up any large chunks. Place skillet on rimmed baking sheet and bake until fruit is tender and topping is deep golden brown, 15 to 20 minutes. Let cool on wire rack until warm, at least 15 minutes, and serve.

SEASON 23

Apple-Blackberry Betty

Serves 6 to 8 • Total Time: 1½ hours, plus 20 minutes cooling

Why This Recipe Works An apple Betty is like an apple crisp, but instead of a crumbly butter-sugar-flour topping, it features slightly sweetened bread crumbs both above and below the apples. A combination of Granny Smith and Golden Delicious apples mixed with just ⅓ cup of brown sugar gave our Betty a sweet-tart flavor while blackberries added bursts of wine-like acidity. Vanilla and a touch of nutmeg added subtle depth. Two tablespoons of water mixed into the apples created steam in the oven to jump-start the cooking, ensuring that the apples would be luxuriously soft. Bread crumbs made from white sandwich bread, enriched with butter and brown sugar and pressed into the bottom of the baking dish, accommodated any excess moisture shed by the apples as they cooked, while the bread crumbs on the top turned crisp and brown.

You can substitute another soft, enriched bread such as challah or brioche for the sandwich bread; be sure to use 10 ounces. We call for a mix of Golden Delicious and Granny Smith apples here, but feel free to substitute a sweet variety and a tart variety of your choice. You can substitute raspberries or blueberries for the blackberries, and it's fine to use frozen berries; alternatively, you can omit the berries. We like the flavor of nutmeg here, but substitute ½ teaspoon of ground cinnamon if you prefer it. This dessert is best served freshly baked and warm, but you can cover any leftovers tightly with foil and refrigerate them for up to two days; warm them before serving.

10 ounces hearty white sandwich bread, cut into 1-inch pieces
½ cup packed (3½ ounces) plus ⅓ cup packed (2⅓ ounces) light brown sugar, divided
¾ teaspoon table salt, divided
6 tablespoons unsalted butter, melted

Topping
¾ cup (3¾ ounces) all-purpose flour
¾ cup pecans, chopped fine
¾ cup (2¼ ounces) old-fashioned rolled oats
½ cup packed (3½ ounces) light brown sugar
¼ cup (1¾ ounces) granulated sugar
½ teaspoon ground cinnamon
½ teaspoon table salt
8 tablespoons unsalted butter, melted

Filling
3 pounds Golden Delicious apples, peeled, cored, halved, and cut into ½-inch-thick wedges
¼ cup (1¾ ounces) granulated sugar
¼ teaspoon ground cinnamon (optional)
1 cup apple cider
2 teaspoons lemon juice
2 tablespoons unsalted butter

1. For the topping: Adjust oven rack to middle position and heat oven to 450 degrees. Combine flour, pecans, oats, brown sugar, granulated sugar, cinnamon, and salt in medium bowl. Stir in melted butter until mixture is thoroughly moistened and crumbly. Set aside while preparing fruit filling.

2. For the filling: Toss apples; sugar; and cinnamon, if using, together in large bowl; set aside. Bring cider to simmer in 12-inch ovensafe skillet over medium heat; cook until reduced to ½ cup, about 5 minutes. Transfer reduced cider to bowl or liquid measuring cup; stir in lemon juice and set aside.

3. Melt butter in now-empty skillet over medium heat. Add apple mixture and cook, stirring frequently, until apples are beginning to soften and become translucent,

1½ pounds Golden Delicious apples, peeled, cored, and cut into ½-inch pieces
1 pound Granny Smith apples, peeled, cored, and cut into ½-inch pieces
2 tablespoons water
1 teaspoon vanilla extract
¼ teaspoon ground nutmeg
3¾ ounces (¾ cup) blackberries, berries larger than ¾ inch cut in half crosswise
Vanilla ice cream or sweetened whipped cream

1. Adjust oven racks to upper-middle and lower-middle positions and heat oven to 375 degrees. Pulse bread in food processor until coarsely ground, about 15 pulses. Add ½ cup sugar and ½ teaspoon salt and pulse to combine, about 5 pulses. Drizzle with melted butter and pulse until evenly distributed, about 5 pulses. Scatter 2½ cups bread crumb mixture in 8-inch square baking dish. Press gently to create even layer.

2. Combine apples, water, vanilla, nutmeg, remaining ⅓ cup sugar, and remaining ¼ teaspoon salt in bowl. Pile apple mixture atop bread crumb mixture in dish and spread and press into even layer. Sprinkle blackberries over apples (dish will be very full). Distribute remaining bread crumb mixture evenly over blackberries and press lightly to form uniform layer. Cover tightly with aluminum foil. (Uncooked Betty can be refrigerated for up to 2 days.) Place on rimmed baking sheet and bake on lower rack until apples are soft, 1 hour to 1 hour 10 minutes.

3. Remove foil and transfer dish (still on sheet) to upper rack. Bake until crumbs on top are crisp and well browned, about 15 minutes. Transfer to wire rack and let cool for at least 20 minutes. Serve with ice cream.

Sour Cherry Cobbler

Serves 12 • Total Time: 1¼ hours

Why This Recipe Works Many cherry cobblers are no more than canned pie filling topped with dry, heavy biscuits. We wanted a filling that highlighted the unique, sweet-tart flavor of sour cherries and, on top, we wanted a tender, feather-light biscuit crust. Because fresh sour cherries are so hard to find most of the year, we picked jarred Morello cherries—easy to find and available year-round. Embellishing the cherries with cherry juice, cinnamon, and vanilla was a≈step in the right direction but the filling still tasted a bit flat, so we switched out some of the juice for red wine and replaced the vanilla with almond extract. The resulting sauce was better, but a little thin. A small amount of cornstarch thickened the filling nicely. As for the biscuits, we favored buttermilk biscuits, which have a light and fluffy texture. To ensure nicely browned biscuits that didn't become soggy over the filling, we parbaked them on their own ahead of time, then slid the biscuits over the warm cherry filling and put it in the oven to finish cooking.

Use the smaller amount of sugar in the filling if you prefer your fruit desserts on the tart side and the larger amount if you like them sweet. Serve with vanilla ice cream or lightly sweetened whipped cream.

Biscuit Topping
2 cups (10 ounces) all-purpose flour
½ cup (3½ ounces) sugar, divided
½ teaspoon baking powder
½ teaspoon baking soda
½ teaspoon table salt
6 tablespoons unsalted butter, cut into ½-inch pieces and chilled
1 cup buttermilk

Filling
8 cups jarred Morello cherries from 4 (24-ounce) jars, drained, 2 cups juice reserved
¾–1 cup (5¼ to 7 ounces) sugar
3 tablespoons plus 1 teaspoon cornstarch
Pinch table salt
1 cup dry red wine
1 cinnamon stick
¼ teaspoon almond extract

1. Adjust oven rack to middle position and heat oven to 425 degrees. Line rimmed baking sheet with parchment paper.

2. For the biscuit topping: Pulse flour, 6 tablespoons sugar, baking powder, baking soda, and salt in food processor until combined, about 3 pulses. Sprinkle butter pieces over top and pulse until mixture resembles coarse meal, about 15 pulses. Transfer mixture to large bowl; add buttermilk and stir with rubber spatula until combined. Using greased ¼-cup measure, space 12 biscuits 1½ inches apart on prepared sheet. Sprinkle biscuits evenly with remaining 2 tablespoons sugar and bake until lightly browned, about 15 minutes, rotating sheet halfway through baking. (Do not turn oven off.)

3. For the filling: Meanwhile, arrange drained cherries in even layer in 13 by 9-inch baking dish. Combine sugar, cornstarch, and salt in medium saucepan. Stir in reserved cherry juice and wine and add cinnamon stick; cook over medium-high heat, stirring frequently, until mixture simmers and thickens, about 5 minutes. Discard cinnamon stick, stir in almond extract, and pour hot liquid over cherries in baking dish.

4. To bake: Arrange hot biscuits in 3 rows of 4 biscuits over warm filling. Bake cobbler until filling is bubbling and biscuits are deep golden brown, about 10 minutes. Transfer baking dish to wire rack and let cool for 10 minutes; serve.

VARIATION
Fresh Sour Cherry Cobbler
Total Time: 1½ hours, plus 30 minutes standing
Morello or Montmorency cherries can be used in this cobbler made with fresh sour cherries. Do not use sweet Bing cherries. If the cherries do not release enough juice after 30 minutes in step 1, add cranberry juice to make up the difference.

1¼ cups (8¾ ounces) sugar
3 tablespoons plus 1 teaspoon cornstarch
   Pinch table salt
4 pounds fresh sour cherries, pitted, juice from pitting reserved
1 cup dry red wine
   Cranberry juice, as needed
1 recipe Biscuit Topping (page 665)
1 cinnamon stick
¼ teaspoon almond extract

1. Whisk sugar, cornstarch, and salt together in large bowl; add cherries and toss well to combine. Pour wine over cherries; let stand for 30 minutes. Drain cherries in colander set over medium bowl. Combine drained and reserved juices (from pitting cherries); you should have 3 cups (if not, add cranberry juice to make this amount).

2. Meanwhile, prepare and bake biscuit topping.

3. Arrange drained cherries in even layer in 13 by 9-inch baking dish. Bring juices and cinnamon stick to simmer in medium saucepan over medium-high heat, stirring frequently, until mixture thickens, about 5 minutes. Discard cinnamon stick, stir in almond extract, and pour hot juices over cherries in baking dish.

4. Arrange hot biscuits in 3 rows of 4 biscuits over warm filling. Bake cobbler until filling is bubbling and biscuits are deep golden brown, about 10 minutes. Transfer baking dish to wire rack and let cool for 10 minutes; serve.

SEASON 16
Cherry Clafouti

Serves 6 to 8 • Total Time: 1¼ hours, plus 25 minutes cooling

Why This Recipe Works For a clafouti that featured juicy cherries in every bite (and no pits to get in the way, as most traditional recipes have), we pitted and halved the cherries. To concentrate their flavor and prevent excess moisture from leaking into the custard, we roasted them in a hot oven for 15 minutes and then tossed them with a couple of teaspoons of absorbent flour. To recover the slightly spicy, floral flavor the pits contributed, we added ⅛ teaspoon of cinnamon to the flour. We found that too much flour made the custard too bready, whereas an excess of dairy made it too loose. Ultimately, we settled on a moderate amount of each for a tender yet slightly resilient custard void of pastiness. Switching from a casserole dish to a preheated 12-inch skillet gave us better browning and made the

custard easy to slice and serve. A last-minute sprinkle of granulated sugar added a touch of sweetness and a delicate crunch.

We prefer whole milk in this recipe, but 1 or 2 percent low-fat milk may be substituted. Do not substitute frozen cherries for the fresh cherries.

- 1½ pounds fresh sweet cherries, pitted and halved
- 1 teaspoon lemon juice
- 2 teaspoons plus ½ cup (2½ ounces) all-purpose flour, divided
- ⅛ teaspoon ground cinnamon
- 4 large eggs
- ⅔ cup (4⅔ ounces) plus 2 teaspoons sugar, divided
- 2½ teaspoons vanilla extract
- ¼ teaspoon table salt
- 1 cup heavy cream
- ⅔ cup whole milk
- 1 tablespoon unsalted butter

1. Adjust oven racks to upper-middle and lowest positions; place 12-inch ovensafe skillet on lower rack and heat oven to 425 degrees. Line rimmed baking sheet with aluminum foil and place cherries, cut side up, on sheet. Roast cherries on upper rack until just tender and cut sides look dry, about 15 minutes. Transfer cherries to medium bowl, toss with lemon juice, and let cool 5 for minutes. Combine 2 teaspoons flour and cinnamon in small bowl; dust flour mixture evenly over cherries and toss to coat thoroughly.

2. While cherries roast, whisk eggs, ⅔ cup sugar, vanilla, and salt in large bowl until smooth and pale, about 1 minute. Whisk in remaining ½ cup flour until smooth. Whisk in cream and milk until incorporated.

3. Remove skillet (skillet handle will be hot) from oven and set on wire rack. Add butter and swirl to coat bottom and sides of skillet (butter will melt and brown quickly). Pour batter into skillet and place cherries evenly over top (some will sink). Transfer skillet to lower rack and bake until clafouti puffs and surface is golden brown (edges will be dark brown) and center registers 195 degrees, 18 to 22 minutes, rotating skillet halfway through baking. Transfer skillet to wire rack and let cool for 25 minutes. Sprinkle evenly with remaining 2 teaspoons sugar. Slice into wedges and serve.

SEASON 25

Easy Strawberry Shortcakes for Two

Serves 2 • **Total Time: 40 minutes, plus 45 minutes sitting and cooling**

Why This Recipe Works Our ideal strawberry shortcakes are tender, flaky biscuits topped with juicy strawberries and a dollop of whipped cream. And because they're assembled individually, they're an ideal dessert for two. Because the fruit isn't cooked, fresh, ripe berries are essential. Slicing most of the strawberries made for an attractive presentation, while crushing a portion of them helped unify the sliced fruit and prevented it from sliding off the biscuits. We used all-purpose flour for tender, cakey biscuits; an egg and some half-and-half contributed richness. With such a small amount of dough, we found it best to shape the biscuits by hand (rather than stamp them out) to ensure that none went to waste. Fresh blueberries, raspberries, or halved blackberries can be substituted for some or all of the strawberries. Fresh fruit is key to the success of these shortcakes; do not substitute frozen strawberries.

Fruit
- 10 ounces strawberries, hulled (2 cups), divided
- 5 teaspoons sugar

Biscuits
- ⅔ cup (3⅓ ounces) all-purpose flour
- 2 tablespoons sugar, divided
- 1 teaspoon baking powder
- ⅛ teaspoon table salt
- 4 tablespoons unsalted butter, cut into ½-inch pieces and chilled
- 2 tablespoons half-and-half
- 1 large egg, lightly beaten, plus 1 large white, lightly beaten

- 1 recipe Whipped Cream (recipe follows)

1. **For the fruit:** Crush ¾ cup strawberries in medium bowl with potato masher. Slice remaining 1¼ cups strawberries. Stir sliced strawberries and sugar into crushed strawberries. Set aside until sugar has dissolved and strawberries are juicy, at least 30 minutes or up to 2 hours.

2. **For the biscuits:** Meanwhile, adjust oven rack to middle position and heat oven to 425 degrees. Line rimmed baking sheet with parchment paper. Process flour, 5 teaspoons sugar, baking powder, and salt in food processor until combined, about 5 seconds. Scatter butter over top and pulse until mixture resembles coarse cornmeal, about 15 pulses. Transfer mixture to medium bowl.

3. In separate bowl, whisk half-and-half and whole egg together, then stir into flour mixture with rubber spatula until large clumps form. Turn dough and any floury bits onto lightly floured counter and knead lightly until dough comes together (do not overwork dough). Divide dough into 2 even pieces, then, with your well-floured hands, shape each into 2½-inch round, about 1 inch thick.

4. Arrange biscuits on prepared sheet. Brush tops with egg white and sprinkle evenly with remaining 1 teaspoon sugar. Bake biscuits until golden brown, 10 to 12 minutes, rotating sheet halfway through baking. Transfer biscuits to wire rack and let cool for 15 minutes.

5. To assemble, split each biscuit in half and place bottoms on individual serving plates. Spoon strawberries over each bottom, dollop with whipped cream, and cap with biscuit tops. Serve immediately.

Whipped Cream

Makes ¾ cup • **Total Time: 5 minutes**

The whipped cream can be refrigerated in a fine-mesh strainer set over a small bowl, wrapped tightly with plastic wrap, for up to 8 hours.

- ⅓ cup heavy cream, chilled
- 1 teaspoon sugar
- ¼ teaspoon vanilla extract

Using hand mixer set at medium-low speed, beat cream, sugar, and vanilla in medium bowl until foamy, about 1 minute. Increase speed to high and beat until soft peaks form, 1 to 3 minutes.

Summer Berry Trifle

Serves 12 to 16 • **Total Time: 2 hours, plus 8½ hours chilling and cooling**

Why This Recipe Works Trifles usually look a lot better than they taste because busy cooks simplify the complicated preparation by subbing in shortcut ingredients like store-bought cake and pudding from a box. We wanted to streamline, but not shortchange, the components so that the entire trifle could be made from scratch in just a few hours. We added a little extra flour to a classic chiffon cake so we could bake it in an 18 by 13-inch sheet, which baked and cooled much more quickly than the traditional tall chiffon cake, and we prevented our pastry cream from turning runny during assembly by adding a little extra cornstarch. We mashed one-third of the berries so their juices would provide moisture to the cake. A bit of cream sherry added a sophisticated layer of flavor.

> *For the best texture, this trifle should be assembled at least 6 hours before serving. Use a glass bowl with at least a 3½-quart capacity; straight sides are preferable.*

Pastry Cream
- 3½ cups whole milk, divided
- 1 cup (7 ounces) sugar
- 6 tablespoons cornstarch
  Pinch table salt
- 5 large egg yolks (reserve whites for cake)
- 4 tablespoons unsalted butter, cut into ½-inch pieces and chilled
- 4 teaspoons vanilla extract

Cake

1⅓ cups (5⅓ ounces) cake flour
¾ cup (5¼ ounces) sugar
1½ teaspoons baking powder
¼ teaspoon table salt
⅓ cup vegetable oil
¼ cup water
1 large egg
2 teaspoons vanilla extract
5 large egg whites (reserved from pastry cream)
¼ teaspoon cream of tartar

Fruit Filling

1½ pounds strawberries, hulled and cut into ½-inch pieces (4 cups), reserving 3 halved for garnish, divided
12 ounces (2⅓ cups) blackberries, large berries halved crosswise, reserving 3 whole for garnish, divided
12 ounces (2⅓ cups) raspberries, reserving 3 for garnish, divided
¼ cup (1¾ ounces) sugar
½ teaspoon cornstarch
Pinch table salt

Whipped Cream

1 cup heavy cream
1 tablespoon sugar
1 tablespoon plus ½ cup cream sherry, divided

1. For the pastry cream: Heat 3 cups milk in medium saucepan over medium heat until just simmering. Meanwhile, whisk sugar, cornstarch, and salt together in medium bowl. Whisk remaining ½ cup milk and egg yolks into sugar mixture until smooth. Remove milk from heat and, whisking constantly, slowly add 1 cup to sugar mixture to temper. Whisking constantly, return tempered sugar mixture to milk in saucepan.

2. Return saucepan to medium heat and cook, whisking constantly, until mixture is very thick and bubbles burst on surface, 4 to 7 minutes. Remove saucepan from heat; whisk in butter and vanilla until butter is melted and incorporated. Strain pastry cream through fine-mesh strainer set over medium bowl. Press lightly greased parchment paper directly on surface and refrigerate until set, at least 2 hours or up to 24 hours.

3. For the cake: Adjust oven rack to middle position and heat oven to 350 degrees. Lightly grease 18 by 13-inch rimmed baking sheet, line with parchment, and lightly grease parchment. Whisk flour, sugar, baking powder, and salt together in medium bowl. Whisk oil, water, egg, and vanilla into flour mixture until smooth batter forms.

4. Using stand mixer fitted with whisk attachment, whip egg whites and cream of tartar on medium-low speed until foamy, about 1 minute. Increase speed to medium-high and whip until soft peaks form, 2 to 3 minutes. Transfer one-third of whipped egg whites to batter; whisk gently until mixture is lightened. Using rubber spatula, gently fold remaining egg whites into batter.

5. Pour batter into prepared sheet; spread evenly. Bake until top is golden brown and cake springs back when pressed lightly in center, 13 to 16 minutes.

6. Transfer cake to wire rack; let cool for 5 minutes. Run knife around edge of sheet, then invert cake onto wire rack. Carefully remove parchment, then reinvert cake onto second wire rack. Let cool completely, at least 30 minutes.

7. For the fruit filling: Place 1½ cups strawberries, 1 cup blackberries, 1 cup raspberries, sugar, cornstarch, and salt in medium saucepan. Place remaining berries (except those reserved for garnish) in large bowl; set aside. Using potato masher, thoroughly mash berries in saucepan. Cook over medium heat until sugar is dissolved and mixture is thick and bubbling, 4 to 7 minutes. Pour over berries in bowl and stir to combine. Set aside.

8. For the whipped cream: Using stand mixer fitted with whisk attachment, whip cream, sugar, and 1 tablespoon sherry on medium-low speed until foamy, about 1 minute. Increase speed to high and whip until soft peaks form, 1 to 2 minutes.

9. Trim ¼ inch off each side of cake; discard trimmings. Using serrated knife, cut cake into 24 equal pieces (each piece about 2½ inches square).

10. Briefly whisk pastry cream until smooth. Spoon ¾ cup pastry cream into trifle bowl; spread over bottom. Shingle 12 cake pieces, fallen-domino-style, around bottom of trifle, placing 10 pieces against dish wall and 2 remaining pieces in center. Drizzle ¼ cup sherry evenly over cake. Spoon half of berry mixture evenly over cake, making sure to use half of liquid. Using back of spoon, spread half of remaining pastry cream over berries, then spread half of whipped cream over pastry cream (whipped cream layer will be thin). Repeat layering with remaining 12 cake pieces, sherry, berries, pastry cream, and whipped cream. Cover bowl with plastic wrap and refrigerate for at least 6 hours or up to 36 hours. Garnish top of trifle with reserved berries and serve.

Berry Fool

Serves 6 • Total Time: 45 minutes, plus 2 hours chilling

Why This Recipe Works Fruit fool is made by folding pureed stewed fruit—traditionally gooseberries—into sweet custard. Modern recipes skip the custard and use whipped cream. But whipped cream blunts the fruit flavor and is too light and insubstantial, and it can turn the dessert soupy. We wanted intense fruitiness and rich body—and to use raspberries or strawberries. Gooseberries are naturally high in pectin; when exposed to heat, sugar, and acid, pectin breaks down and causes fruit to thicken, which makes gooseberries ideal for fruit fool. Raspberries and strawberries are low in pectin, so our first challenge was to thicken the fruit properly. To do so we opted for a modest amount of gelatin, softening it first in some uncooked berry puree and then combining the softened mixture with some heated puree to help melt and distribute the gelatin. The result? A smooth, thickened puree with intense fruit flavor. We liked the ease of whipped cream for the base, but to make it richer and sturdier we added some sour cream; this mixture was airy yet substantial with the right touch of richness and tangy undertone. For even more fruit flavor, we layered the fruit puree and cream base with fresh berries that had been macerated in sugar. Topping the dessert with crumbled sweet wheat crackers added a pleasant, nutty contrast.

Blueberries or blackberries can be substituted for raspberries in this recipe. You may also substitute frozen fruit for fresh, but there will be a slight compromise in texture. If using frozen fruit, reduce the amount of sugar in the puree by 1 tablespoon. The thickened fruit puree can be made up to 4 hours in advance; just make sure to whisk it well in step 4 to break up any clumps before combining it with the whipped cream. For the best results, chill your beater and bowl before whipping the cream. We like the granular texture and nutty flavor of Carr's Whole Wheat Crackers, but graham crackers or gingersnaps will also work.

2	pounds strawberries, hulled (6 cups), divided
12	ounces (2¼ cups) raspberries, divided
¾	cup (5¼ ounces) sugar, divided
2	teaspoons unflavored gelatin
1	cup heavy cream
¼	cup sour cream
½	teaspoon vanilla extract
4	Carr's Whole Wheat Crackers, crushed fine (about ¼ cup)
6	sprigs fresh mint (optional)

1. Process 3 cups strawberries, 1 cup raspberries, and ½ cup sugar in food processor until the mixture is completely smooth, about 1 minute. Strain berry puree through fine-mesh strainer into 4-cup liquid measuring cup (you should have about 2½ cups puree; reserve any excess for another use). Transfer ½ cup puree to small bowl and sprinkle gelatin over top; stir until gelatin is incorporated and let stand for at least 5 minutes. Heat remaining 2 cups puree in small saucepan over medium heat until it begins to bubble, 4 to 6 minutes. Off heat, stir in gelatin mixture until dissolved. Transfer gelatin-puree mixture to medium bowl, cover with plastic wrap, and refrigerate until cold, about 2 hours.

2. Meanwhile, chop remaining strawberries into rough ¼-inch pieces. Toss strawberries, remaining raspberries, and 2 tablespoons sugar together in medium bowl. Set aside for 1 hour.

3. Place cream, sour cream, vanilla, and remaining 2 tablespoons sugar in chilled bowl of stand mixer. Fit mixer with paddle and beat on low speed until bubbles form, about 30 seconds. Increase mixer speed to medium and continue beating until beaters leave trail, about 30 seconds. Increase mixer speed to high; continue beating until mixture has nearly doubled in volume and holds stiff peaks, about 30 seconds. Transfer ⅓ cup whipped cream mixture to small bowl and set aside.

4. Remove thickened berry puree from refrigerator and whisk until smooth. With mixer running at medium speed, slowly add two-thirds of puree to remaining whipped cream mixture; mix until incorporated, about 15 seconds. Using spatula, gently fold in remaining thickened puree, leaving streaks of puree.

5. Transfer uncooked berries to fine-mesh strainer; shake gently to remove any excess juice. Divide two-thirds of berries evenly among 6 tall parfait or sundae glasses. Divide creamy berry mixture evenly among the glasses, followed by remaining uncooked berries. Top each glass with reserved plain whipped cream mixture. Sprinkle with crushed crackers and garnish with mint sprigs, if using. Serve immediately.

Crepes with Sugar and Lemon

Serves 4 • Total Time: 50 minutes

Why This Recipe Works A crepe is nothing but a thin pancake cooked quickly on each side and wrapped around a sweet or savory filling, but it has a reputation for being difficult. We wanted an easy method for crepes that were thin and delicate yet rich and flavorfully browned in spots.

Finding the perfect ratio of milk to flour and sugar gave us rich-tasting, lightly sweet pancakes. We were surprised to find that neither the type of flour nor the mixing method seemed to matter, and a plain old 12-inch nonstick skillet worked as well as a specialty crepe pan. What does matter is heating the pan properly (over low heat for at least 10 minutes), using the right amount of batter (we settled on ¼ cup), and flipping the crepe at precisely the right moment, when the edges appear dry, matte, and lacy. To transform our perfectly cooked crepes into decadent desserts, we whipped up a few sweet fillings: the simple classic of sugar and lemon; a decadent chocolate and orange filling; and a banana and Nutella filling sure to please kids and adults alike.

> *The crepes will give off steam as they cook, but if at any point the skillet begins to smoke, remove it from the heat immediately and turn down the heat. Stacking the crepes on a wire rack allows excess steam to escape so they won't stick together. To allow for practice, the recipe yields 10 crepes; only eight are needed for the filling.*

½ teaspoon vegetable oil
1 cup (5 ounces) all-purpose flour
1 teaspoon sugar, plus 8 teaspoons for sprinkling
¼ teaspoon table salt
1½ cups whole milk
3 large eggs
2 tablespoons unsalted butter, melted and cooled
Lemon wedges

1. Heat oil in 12-inch nonstick skillet over low heat for at least 10 minutes.

2. While skillet is heating, whisk flour, 1 teaspoon sugar, and salt together in medium bowl. In separate bowl, whisk together milk and eggs. Add half of milk mixture to dry ingredients and whisk until smooth. Add melted butter and whisk until incorporated. Whisk in remaining milk mixture until smooth.

3. Using paper towel, wipe out skillet, leaving thin film of oil on bottom and sides of pan. Increase heat to medium and let skillet heat for 1 minute. After 1 minute, test heat of skillet by placing 1 teaspoon batter in center; cook for 20 seconds. If mini crepe is golden brown on bottom, skillet is properly heated; if it is too light or too dark, adjust heat accordingly and retest.

4. Pour ¼ cup batter into far side of pan and tilt and shake gently until batter evenly covers bottom of pan. Cook crepe without moving until top surface is dry and edges are starting to brown, loosening crepe from side of pan with rubber spatula, about 25 seconds. Gently slide spatula underneath edge of crepe, grasp edge with your fingertips, and flip crepe. Cook until second side is lightly spotted, about 20 seconds. Transfer cooked crepe to wire rack, inverting so spotted side is facing up. Return pan to heat and heat for 10 seconds before repeating with remaining batter. As crepes are done, stack on wire rack.

5. Transfer stack of crepes to large plate and invert second plate over crepes. Microwave until crepes are warm, 30 to 45 seconds (45 to 60 seconds if crepes have cooled completely). Remove top plate and wipe dry with paper towel.

Sprinkle half of top crepe with 1 teaspoon sugar. Fold unsugared bottom half over sugared half, then fold into quarters. Transfer sugared crepe to second plate. Continue with remaining crepes and remaining sugar. Serve immediately, passing lemon wedges separately.

VARIATIONS

Crepes with Chocolate and Orange

Omit 8 teaspoons sugar for sprinkling and lemon wedges. Using your fingertips, rub 1 teaspoon finely grated orange zest into ¼ cup sugar. Stir in 2 ounces finely grated bitter-sweet chocolate. In step 5, sprinkle 1½ tablespoons chocolate-orange mixture over half of each crepe. Fold crepes into quarters. Serve immediately.

Crepes with Bananas and Nutella

Omit 8 teaspoons sugar for sprinkling and lemon wedges. In step 5, spread 2 teaspoons Nutella over half of each crepe, followed by eight to ten ¼-inch-thick banana slices. Fold crepes into quarters. Serve immediately.

Making a Crepe

1. Pour ¼ cup batter into far side of skillet.

2. Tilt and shake skillet gently until batter evenly covers bottom of skillet.

3. Gently slide rubber spatula underneath edge of crepe, grasp edge with your fingertips, and flip crepe.

SEASON 5

Caramelized Pears with Blue Cheese and Black Pepper–Caramel Sauce

Serves 6 • Total Time: 35 minutes

Why This Recipe Works Pears and blue cheese are a classic combination, but we upped the flavor ante with another component—caramel. We had encountered this triple play in restaurants, where a caramel sauce is draped over seared pears, and a modest amount of pungent blue cheese provides a nice contrast to the dessert's sweetness. We decided to adapt this dish so it would be easy for the home cook to get it just right (meaning no mushy pears and no sticky, overcooked caramel). To streamline the recipe, we cooked the pears right in the caramel sauce, instead of separately, saving some time. We brought water and sugar (the basis for caramel sauce) to a boil in a skillet and slid the pears into the hot mixture to cook in the browning caramel. We added cream to the pan to transform the sticky sugar syrup into a smooth sauce that clung lightly to the pears. After removing the pears, we were able to season the sauce left in the skillet with just the right amount of black pepper and salt. For an attractive presentation, we stood the pears upright on a plate (we had already trimmed the bottom off each pear for a flat base) and drizzled the caramel sauce around them, then added wedges of strong blue cheese—the perfect foil to the sweet caramel.

Any type of pear can be used in this recipe, but the pears must be firm to withstand the heat. If desired, the pears can be served upright on a large platter instead of on individual plates, with the warm caramel sauce and the blue cheese passed separately. Many pepper mills do not have a sufficiently coarse setting; in that case, crush peppercorns with the back of a heavy pan or a rolling pin.

⅓ cup water

⅔ cup (4⅔ ounces) sugar

3 ripe but firm pears (7 to 8 ounces each), halved, cored, and ¼ inch trimmed off bottom

⅔ cup heavy cream

¼ teaspoon black peppercorns, crushed

3 ounces strong blue cheese (such as Stilton), cut into 6 wedges

GAME CHANGER

Sophistication Doesn't Need to Be Fussy

"My family and I once took a trip to Disney World and dined at the California Grill. The fine dining menu was full of intriguing accompaniments, but what really stood out was a surprising salad component: caramelized blue cheese. I've always understood the beauty behind sweet and salty, but blue cheese? Really? After one bite, I immediately confirmed. Yes, really.

This elegant pear dessert brings me right back to that Orlando 'aha' moment. As the caramel begins bubbling away, the pears are added to cook until golden, tender, and infused with the sauce. The buttery caramel gets finished with just the right amount of black pepper to wake up your tastebuds. A hunk of strong blue cheese served alongside brings a humble funk that perfectly complements the dish. It almost makes you want to put your pinky out. You don't have to, of course. The sophistication is in the taste, not the execution. It's quick and easy enough to throw together for a weeknight treat. Disney's known as 'the happiest place on earth,' but they just might relinquish the title to this dish from the comfort of your own home."

—Sam

1. Pour water into 12-inch nonstick skillet, then pour sugar into center of pan, being careful not to let it hit sides of pan. Bring to boil over high heat, stirring occasionally, until sugar is fully dissolved and liquid is bubbling. Add pears to skillet, cut side down, cover, reduce heat to medium-high, and cook until pears are almost tender and paring knife inserted into center of pears meets slight resistance, 13 to 15 minutes.

2. Uncover, reduce heat to medium, and cook until sauce is golden brown and cut sides of pears are beginning to brown, 3 to 5 minutes. Pour heavy cream around pears and cook, shaking pan until sauce is smooth and deep caramel color and cut sides of pears are golden brown, 3 to 5 minutes.

3. Off heat, transfer pears, cut side up, to wire rack set over rimmed baking sheet and let cool slightly. Season sauce left in pan with salt to taste and stir in crushed peppercorns, then transfer it to small bowl.

4. Carefully (pears will still be hot) stand each pear half upright on individual plate and place wedge of blue cheese beside it. Drizzle caramel sauce over plate and pear. Serve immediately.

to spoon over the berries. Finally, we sprinkled the custard with a mixture of brown and white sugar before broiling for a crackly, caramelized crust.

When making the zabaglione, make sure to cook the egg mixture in a glass bowl over water that is barely simmering; glass conducts heat more evenly and gently than metal. If the heat is too high, the yolks around the edges of the bowl will start to scramble. Constant whisking is required. Do not use frozen berries for this recipe. You will need four shallow 6-inch gratin dishes, but a broiler-safe pie plate or gratin dish can be used instead. To prevent scorching, pay close attention to the gratins when broiling.

SEASON 10

Individual Fresh Berry Gratins with Zabaglione

Serves 4 • Total Time: 50 minutes

Why This Recipe Works Gratins can be very humble or they can be a bit more sophisticated, as when they are topped with the foamy Italian custard called zabaglione. Ideally, the process for making zabaglione transforms egg yolks into a thick, creamy custard. But this tricky topping can be easy to overcook, so we wanted a foolproof method. We chose to make individual gratins—perfect for entertaining—featuring raspberries, strawberries, blueberries, and blackberries. We tossed the berries with sugar and a pinch of salt to draw out their juices and let the mixture sit while we prepared the custard. To prevent scrambled eggs we kept the heat low, and for the right texture we didn't stop whisking when soft peaks formed; instead we waited until the custard became slightly thicker. Zabaglione made with the traditional Marsala wine was a bit sweet on top of the berries. A crisp, dry Sauvignon Blanc allowed the berries to shine; however, with that change our zabaglione was almost runny. Carefully folding a few tablespoons of whipped cream into the cooked and slightly cooled zabaglione base thickened it just enough

Berry Mixture
- 2¼ cups (11 ounces) raspberries, blueberries, and/or blackberries
- ¾ cup (4 ounces) strawberries, hulled and halved lengthwise if small or quartered if large
- 2 teaspoons granulated sugar
  Pinch table salt

Zabaglione
- 3 large egg yolks
- 3 tablespoons granulated sugar, divided
- 3 tablespoons dry white wine
- 2 teaspoons packed light brown sugar
- 3 tablespoons heavy cream, chilled

1. For the berry mixture: Toss berries, strawberries, sugar, and salt together in medium bowl. Divide berry mixture evenly among 4 shallow 6-ounce gratin dishes set on rimmed baking sheet; set aside.

2. For the zabaglione: Whisk egg yolks, 2 tablespoons plus 1 teaspoon granulated sugar, and wine in medium glass bowl until sugar is dissolved, about 1 minute. Set bowl over saucepan of barely simmering water and cook, whisking constantly, until mixture is frothy. Continue to cook, whisking constantly, until mixture is slightly thickened, creamy, and glossy, 5 to 10 minutes (mixture will form loose mounds when dripped from whisk). Remove bowl from saucepan and whisk constantly for 30 seconds to cool slightly. Transfer bowl to refrigerator and chill until egg mixture is completely cool, about 10 minutes.

3. Meanwhile, adjust oven rack 6 inches from broiler element and heat broiler. Combine brown sugar and remaining 2 teaspoons granulated sugar in small bowl.

4. Whisk heavy cream in large bowl until it holds soft peaks, 30 to 90 seconds. Using rubber spatula, gently fold whipped cream into cooled egg mixture. Spoon zabaglione over berries and sprinkle sugar mixture evenly on top; let stand at room temperature for 10 minutes, until sugar dissolves.

5. Broil gratins until sugar is bubbly and caramelized, 1 to 4 minutes. Serve immediately.

VARIATION
Individual Fresh Berry Gratins with Lemon Zabaglione
Substitute 1 tablespoon lemon juice for 1 tablespoon wine and add 1 teaspoon grated zest to yolk mixture in step 2.

SEASON 24
Khao Niaow Ma Muang

Serves 6 • Total Time: 1 hour, plus 1 hour soaking

Why This Recipe Works Consisting of thick, golden slices of mango; subtly sweet, coconut-flavored sticky rice; a salty coconut sauce; and crunchy toasted mung beans, this classic Thai dish is a delicate balancing act of flavors and textures. We started with the sticky rice, which needs to be rinsed well to remove excess starch and then soaked for at least 1 hour to hydrate before it is steamed. Wrapping the rice in a wet dish towel prevented it from sticking while it steamed in a bamboo steamer basket. We poured warm, lightly sweetened coconut milk over the hot, tender-chewy rice, which made it glossy and rich. We then made a salted coconut sauce lightly thickened with cornstarch to balance out the rice and the thick slices of very sweet, ripe Ataulfo mango that we served alongside. A topping of toasted mung beans added crunch.

Thai sticky rice (also labeled "glutinous" or "sweet") is available online and at Asian markets. Do not substitute other rice such as sushi or arborio. The quality of coconut milk matters here; our favorite brand is Aroy-D. Shake the coconut milk well before opening. Do not use light coconut milk. The mangos are ready to use when their skins have turned yellow, they're a bit wrinkly and spotty, and they yield to gentle pressure. Make the mung beans while the rice soaks. Though they won't offer the same crunch, toasted white or black sesame seeds can be substituted for the mung beans. This dish can be served warm or at room temperature as dessert or a snack.

1 cup Thai sticky rice
1 (14-ounce) can coconut milk, divided
¼ cup (1¾ ounces) sugar
¼ teaspoon plus ⅛ teaspoon table salt, divided
½ teaspoon cornstarch
3 very ripe Ataulfo mangos, peeled, pitted, and sliced crosswise into ½-inch-thick slices
  Toasted Mung Beans (recipe follows)

1. Place rice in fine-mesh strainer and rinse under cold running water until water runs clear. Place rinsed rice in medium heatproof bowl and cover with several inches cold water. Let rice stand for at least 1 hour or up to 24 hours. Drain rice well in fine-mesh strainer. Rinse bowl in which rice soaked.

2. Bring 4 cups water to boil in 14-inch flat-bottomed wok or 12-inch skillet over high heat. Meanwhile, line steamer basket with clean, damp dish towel. Transfer rice to center of towel and pat rice in even layer. Fold overhang over rice to form bundle and cover with steamer lid. Set steamer in wok and reduce heat to maintain simmer (small wisps of steam should escape from beneath lid). Steam rice until translucent, tender but still chewy, 20 to 25 minutes (check rice by carefully unwrapping bundle; taste rice from center of pile).

3. While rice steams, combine 1 cup coconut milk, sugar, and ¼ teaspoon salt in small saucepan over medium heat and cook, stirring frequently, until sugar dissolves. Remove from heat and cover to keep warm.

4. Transfer rice to cleaned bowl. Working quickly, pour coconut milk mixture over top (it will look like too much liquid). Stir gently to combine; cover; and let stand until liquid is absorbed, about 15 minutes.

5. Meanwhile, rinse saucepan and add remaining coconut milk and remaining ⅛ teaspoon salt. Bring to simmer over medium heat. Combine 1 teaspoon water and cornstarch in small bowl, stirring until cornstarch is dissolved. Stir cornstarch mixture into coconut milk and cook, stirring constantly, until sauce is slightly thickened, 1 to 2 minutes. Remove from heat and set aside. (Cooled sauce may be refrigerated overnight. Bring to room temperature before serving.)

6. When ready to serve, divide coconut rice among serving plates. Arrange sliced mango alongside (½ mango per person). Spoon sauce over rice. Sprinkle mung beans over sauce and rice and serve.

Toasted Mung Beans
Makes ¼ cup • **Total Time: 30 minutes**
Yellow mung beans are made from whole mung beans that have been hulled and split, resulting in a delicate lentil-like legume. The toasted beans are a classic topping to Khao Niaow Ma Muang. For our recipe, we quickly softened the beans by soaking them in boiling water. After draining and patting them dry, we cooked the beans in an unoiled skillet until they were just starting to brown, which dried them out and gave them a delicate, crunchy texture.

1. Bring 1 cup water to boil in small saucepan. Remove from heat; add 2 tablespoons yellow mung beans; cover and set aside until beans have softened, about 10 minutes.

2. Drain beans and transfer to paper towel–lined plate, spreading into even layer. Let stand at least 5 minutes to dry. Add beans to small skillet and place over medium-high heat.

3. Cook, stirring frequently, until mung beans are just starting to turn lightly golden, 5 to 7 minutes. Transfer to bowl and let cool completely before using. (Toasted mung beans can be stored in airtight container at room temperature for 1 week.)

Honeydew, Mango, and Blueberries with Lime-Ginger Reduction

Makes 6 cups • **Total Time: 40 minutes**

Why This Recipe Works Cut-up fresh fruit is a nice dessert or addition to a brunch, but it can be a little boring. Yogurt-based sauces mask the fresh flavors of the fruit, and sweet syrups make the fruit too dessert-y. Looking for a lighter, more flavorful alternative, we adapted a French dressing called a gastrique, a reduction of an acidic liquid with sugar that usually accompanies savory dishes made with fruit. It's a simple technique, and our experiments with reducing different types of acid—wine, citrus juice, and balsamic vinegar—were an unqualified success. We were able to use additional flavorings in the dressing, such as spices, extracts, and citrus zests, that would complement the flavors of the fruit. Served at room temperature or chilled, fresh fruit bathed in a light dressing is delicious and easy to make.

Be sure to zest one of the limes before juicing. Cantaloupe can be used in place of honeydew, although the color contrast with the mango won't be as vivid.

1 tablespoon grated lime zest plus
   1 cup juice (8 limes)
¼ cup (1¾ ounces) sugar
   Pinch table salt
1 tablespoon minced fresh ginger
1 tablespoon lemon juice
2 cups 1-inch honeydew melon pieces
1 mango, peeled, pitted, and cut into
   ½-inch pieces (1½ cups)
10 ounces (2 cups) blueberries

1. Simmer lime juice, sugar, and salt in small saucepan over high heat until syrupy, honey-colored, and reduced to ¼ cup, about 15 minutes. Off heat, stir in lime zest, ginger, and lemon juice; steep for 1 minute to blend flavors and strain.

2. Combine melon, mango, and blueberries in medium bowl; pour warm dressing over fruit and toss to coat. Serve at room temperature, or cover with plastic wrap, refrigerate for up to 4 hours, and serve chilled.

Fresh Fruit with French Flair

"I am not ashamed to say that I could eat this fruit salad every day for the rest of my life. The trick of using a lime-ginger reduction, or gastrique, makes it endlessly lively and complex for such a simple combination of fruit. Its tart, sweet, tangy sauce enhances all of the natural flavors of the melon, mango, and blueberries and takes the whole dish to the next level. I loved tasting this recipe when Erin McMurrer was developing it, and it's become one of my favorite dishes to contribute for potlucks and parties, because everyone seems to feel the same way I do about it. Once, I brought it to a brunch and the kids of the family literally swiped the whole bowl and hid on the staircase to eat it all, before anyone else got the seconds they were looking for. I couldn't really blame them. I'm just glad I saved some at home for myself to eat later!"

—Lisa

Nutritional Information for Our Recipes

To calculate the nutritional values of our recipes per serving, we used The Food Processor SQL by ESHA research. When using this program, we entered all the ingredients, using weights wherever possible. We also used our preferred brands in these analyses. Any ingredient listed as "optional" was excluded from the analyses. If there is a range in the serving size, we used the highest number of servings to calculate nutritional values. We did not include additional salt or pepper for food that's seasoned to taste.

	Calories	Total Fat (G)	Sat Fat (G)	Chol (MG)	Sodium (MG)	Total Carb (G)	Dietary Fiber (G)	Total Sugars (G)	Protein (G)
Appetizers & Drinks									
Classic Guacamole	124	11	2	0	205	7	5	1	2
Ultracreamy Hummus	218	12	1	0	287	23	7	4	8
Baharat-Spiced Beef Topping for Hummus	90	7	2	15	160	1	0	0	5
Spiced Walnut Topping for Hummus	190	19	3	0	170	3	1	1	1
Curry Deviled Eggs with Easy-Peel Hard-Cooked Eggs	120	10	3	190	125	1	0	0	6
Bacon and Chive Deviled Eggs	70	6	2	95	115	0	0	0	4
Easy-Peel Hard-Cooked Eggs	72	5	2	186	71	0	0	0	6
Spanish Tortilla with Roasted Red Peppers and Peas	486	31	6	372	754	35	5	4	17
Spanish Tortilla with Chorizo and Scallions	527	35	8	390	791	34	4	2	20
Garlic Mayonnaise	104	12	1	18	34	0	0	0	0
Cheesy Nachos with Guacamole and Salsa	630	45	18	86	647	38	7	4	22
One-Minute Salsa	30	0	0	0	570	7	0	3	1
Albóndigas en Salsa de Almendras	90	7	2	20	140	2	0	0	4
Crispy Cacio e Pepe Bites	70	3.5	1	5	90	8	0	1	1
Frico	222	14	8	4	669	2	0	0	20
Baked Brie en Croûte	119	8	4	41	159	7	0	4	6
Bouyourdi	154	14	5	29	379	3	1	1	5
Pa amb Tomàquet	208	8	1	0	332	28	2	4	6
Congyóubing	313	20	2	0	296	30	1	1	4
Pakoras	172	12	1	0	213	14	2	2	4
Carrot-Tamarind Chutney	69	0	0	0	211	17	2	11	1
Gỏi Cuốn	604	21	4	98	771	76	5	8	28
Nước Chấm	54	0	0	0	1769	13	0	11	1
Lumpiang Shanghai with Seasoned Vinegar	390	31	6	66	378	16	1	1	13
Banana Ketchup	30	1	0	0	45	5	0	3	0
Cóctel de Camarón	166	6	1	119	832	15	15	8	15
Roasted Oysters on the Half Shell with Mustard Butter	249	14	7	125	243	10	0	0	19
Rhode Island–Style Fried Calamari	633	40	3	267	650	44	3	3	24
Quick Marinara Sauce	93	7	1	0	185	8	2	5	2
Spicy Mayonnaise	403	45	7	23	524	1	1	0	0
Gravlax	110	5	1	20	1140	6	0	6	8
Spiced Pecans with Rum Glaze	210	19	2.5	5	220	7	2	5	2
Holiday Eggnog	166	8	4	123	106	13	0	13	6
ATK 25	160	0	0	0	5	15	0	10	0
New Englander	80	0	0	0	35	22	1	20	0
New Englander with Vodka	150	0	0	0	35	22	1	20	0
Fresh Margaritas	271	0	0	0	33	26	0	24	0
Rosé Sangria	206	0	0	0	10	26	1	22	0
Simple Syrup	290	0	0	0	4	75	0	75	0
Sangria	299	0	0	0	9	33	2	26	1

	Calories	Total Fat (G)	Sat Fat (G)	Chol (MG)	Sodium (MG)	Total Carb (G)	Dietary Fiber (G)	Total Sugars (G)	Protein (G)
Eggs & Breakfast									
Perfect Scrambled Eggs	189	14	6	385	277	2	0	1	13
Scrambled Eggs with Asparagus, Smoked Salmon, and Chives	262	20	5	375	385	3	1	1	17
Scrambled Eggs with Pinto Beans and Cotija Cheese	385	23	6	379	540	23	6	1	22
Scrambled Eggs with Shiitake Mushrooms and Feta Cheese	288	22	6	380	402	8	2	3	16
Xīhóngshì Chǎo Jīdàn	296	22	4	372	765	11	4	8	14
Breakfast Tacos: Scrambled Eggs	180	13	5	380	340	1	0	0	13
Breakfast Tacos: Migas	260	17	4	255	360	17	1	3	12
Sautéed Poblanos, Beans, and Corn	110	3	0	0	240	17	4	2	4
Salsa Roja	17	0	0	0	190	4	1	2	1
Fluffy Omelets	386	27	13	413	587	8	1	3	28
Asparagus and Smoked Salmon Filling	60	3	0	5	170	5	2	3	5
Mushroom Filling	45	2	0	0	151	5	1	3	2
Artichoke and Bacon Filling	160	12	4	20	390	9	5	2	6
French Omelets	383	31	15	603	421	1	0	1	23
Broccoli and Feta Frittata	237	16	6	390	463	5	1	2	17
Asparagus and Goat Cheese Frittata	239	16	6	382	496	5	2	2	18
Chorizo and Potato Frittata	314	19	6	391	533	16	2	2	18
Shiitake Mushroom Frittata with Pecorino Romano	264	17	7	391	508	8	2	3	20
Huevos Rancheros	266	16	2	186	679	22	5	7	10
Refried Beans	90	3.5	1	5	290	10	3	1	4
Eggs Benedict with Perfect Poached Eggs and Foolproof Hollandaise	593	40	20	644	784	28	3	2	32
Çılbır	188	14	8	211	311	3	0	3	12
Soft-Cooked Eggs	72	5	2	186	71	0	0	0	6
Soft-Cooked Eggs with Salad	347	30	6	372	474	6	1	3	14
Soft-Cooked Eggs with Sautéed Mushrooms	302	23	5	372	664	9	1	3	17
Soft-Cooked Eggs with Steamed Asparagus	335	26	6	378	683	8	4	4	20
Green Shakshuka	473	34	8	377	990	22	6	4	22
Microwave-Fried Garlic	40	3	0	0	0	4	0	0	1
Simple Cheese Quiche	195	16	8	151	254	5	0	3	9
Breakfast Strata with Spinach and Gruyère	500	34	19	272	642	22	2	6	23
French Toast	380	20	10	175	420	35	1	18	9
Easy Pancakes	349	14	2	68	398	46	1	10	9
Orange-Almond Butter	110	11	7	30	35	2	0	1	0
Ginger-Molasses Butter	110	11	7	30	35	1	0	1	0
Deluxe Blueberry Pancakes	448	10	5	68	670	76	3	20	14
100 Percent Whole-Wheat Pancakes	148	7	1	26	167	19	2	4	5
German Pancake	520	19	10	311	440	65	2	18	19
Brown Sugar–Apple Topping	169	6	4	15	78	31	4	25	0
Buttermilk Waffles	550	22	6	125	630	65	0	13	18
Yeasted Waffles	333	17	10	94	315	36	1	5	8
Liège Waffles	436	19	11	71	266	60	1	31	7
Crepes with Berries and Apricot Beurre Monté	536	36	21	225	395	41	3	11	12
Congee	134	4	0	1	205	21	0	1	3
Easy-Peel Jammy Eggs	70	5	2	185	70	0	0	0	6
Microwave-Fried Shallots	30	2	0	0	2	2	0	1	0
Ten-Minute Steel-Cut Oatmeal	74	1	0	0	156	14	2	0	3
Apple-Cinnamon Steel-Cut Oatmeal	239	12	2	3	315	30	3	13	6
Carrot-Spice Steel-Cut Oatmeal	284	11	2	3	495	44	4	25	6
Almond Granola with Dried Fruit	337	18	1	0	77	41	6	16	8
Spiced Walnut Granola with Dried Apple	330	20	2	0	85	35	5	14	6
Hazelnut Granola with Dried Pear	356	20	2	0	77	43	6	22	7
Pecan-Orange Granola with Dried Cranberries	372	22	2	0	76	44	5	23	5

	Calories	Total Fat (G)	Sat Fat (G)	Chol (MG)	Sodium (MG)	Total Carb (G)	Dietary Fiber (G)	Total Sugars (G)	Protein (G)
Soups & Stews									
Classic Chicken Noodle Soup	561	37	10	179	765	11	1	2	44
Tortilla Soup	481	29	10	75	1261	29	6	4	30
Best Chicken Stew	491	22	8	194	1128	25	3	6	40
Chicken and Sausage Gumbo	493	22	6	169	1024	30	2	4	42
White Chicken Chili	475	19	5	109	491	31	6	4	46
Beef and Vegetable Soup	335	12	5	74	1444	27	6	9	31
Best Beef Stew	587	29	11	139	1171	24	4	4	47
Alcatra	505	18	6	112	951	11	2	3	56
Carbonnade à la Flamande	606	29	10	180	898	28	4	10	58
Best Ground Beef Chili	323	17	6	62	613	21	7	3	22
Simple Beef Chili with Kidney Beans	398	19	6	62	624	34	10	11	27
Chile Verde con Cerdo	373	23	7	100	892	12	3	7	30
Caldo Verde	347	19	5	40	1110	32	5	4	13
Jamaican Stew Peas with Spinners	512	21	14	48	1108	50	16	4	34
Hot Ukrainian Borscht	333	18	4	53	871	25	5	9	19
New England Clam Chowder	370	22	12	75	640	29	1	3	15
Cioppino	553	29	7	120	1341	18	4	6	46
Cataplana	516	21	6	198	2170	20	4	7	57
Guay Tiew Tom Yum Goong	526	24	3	131	1783	52	4	18	30
Nam Prik Pao	76	6	0	0	160	5	1	3	1
Broccoli-Cheese Soup	184	11	6	28	767	12	4	3	12
Silky Butternut Squash Soup	331	20	12	53	698	38	5	5	5
Super Greens Soup with Lemon-Tarragon Cream	172	11	4	15	936	17	4	3	5
Cauliflower Soup	188	16	10	41	886	11	4	4	4
Wild Rice and Mushroom Soup	248	12	7	32	883	27	2	3	8
Best French Onion Soup	505	23	13	65	1685	51	6	14	26
Ultimate Cream of Tomato Soup	360	24	14	67	312	28	5	15	7
Soupe au Pistou	328	18	4	8	1067	31	7	4	13
Black Bean Soup	477	11	2	13	1233	68	15	7	29
Acquacotta	451	21	4	42	1237	51	11	9	17
Hearty Ham and Split Pea Soup with Potatoes	620	20	6	110	2590	55	17	10	55
Harira	363	13	2	4	1136	49	10	10	16
Red Lentil Soup with Warm Spices	320	10	5	25	777	42	6	5	17
Quinoa and Vegetable Stew	337	17	5	21	949	38	7	5	13
Quinoa and Vegetable Stew with Eggs	310	13	2	140	630	38	7	5	12
Pasta e Piselli	459	17	5	22	747	57	6	8	19
Hong Kong–Style Wonton Noodle Soup	329	13	4	112	617	28	1	1	22
Vegetable Broth Base	10	0	0	0	380	2	0	1	0
Chicken Broth	45	0	0	5	436	1	0	0	9
Pressure-Cooker Chicken Broth	45	0	0	5	436	1	0	0	9
Salads									
Foolproof Vinaigrette	93	10	1	0	38	0	0	0	0
Foolproof Lemon Vinaigrette	93	10	1	0	36	0	0	0	0
Foolproof Balsamic-Mustard Vinaigrette	98	10	1	0	33	1	0	1	0
Foolproof Walnut Vinaigrette	94	10	1	0	38	0	0	0	0
Foolproof Herb Vinaigrette	94	10	1	0	40	0	0	0	0
Lao Hu Cai	60	4	1	0	181	5	1	2	2
Kale Caesar Salad	315	22	5	20	591	16	5	3	14
Horiatiki Salata	398	33	11	50	1008	17	4	8	11
Mediterranean Chopped Salad	387	23	7	33	860	33	10	8	15
Salade Lyonnaise	295	25	7	209	426	5	3	1	13
Perfect Poached Eggs	145	10	3	372	251	1	0	0	13
Salade Niçoise	822	57	10	298	1319	40	7	8	41
Salad Niçoise for Four	824	57	10	298	1339	40	7	9	41

	Calories	Total Fat (G)	Sat Fat (G)	Chol (MG)	Sodium (MG)	Total Carb (G)	Dietary Fiber (G)	Total Sugars (G)	Protein (G)
Salads (cont.)									
Classic Tuna Salad	279	23	4	42	387	1	0	1	17
Tuna Salad with Balsamic Vinegar and Grapes	246	14	2	31	433	13	2	9	19
Curried Tuna Salad with Apples and Currants	322	23	4	42	401	13	2	9	17
Tuna Salad with Lime and Horseradish	285	23	4	42	434	3	1	1	17
Classic Chicken Salad	305	18	3	104	424	3	1	1	30
Waldorf Chicken Salad	387	25	4	104	517	9	2	5	32
Curried Chicken Salad with Cashews	399	24	4	104	186	13	1	7	33
Chicken Salad with Red Grapes and Smoked Almonds	600	41	5	135	550	14	4	8	45
Panzanella	489	29	4	0	769	49	4	9	10
Fattoush	315	25	3	0	635	23	4	5	5
Beet Salad with Spiced Yogurt and Watercress	212	13	3	8	580	19	5	13	9
Beet Salad with Goat Cheese and Arugula	194	11	5	14	494	16	5	11	9
Broccoli Salad with Creamy Avocado Dressing	225	14	2	0	423	25	7	13	6
Brussels Sprouts Salad with Warm Mustard Vinaigrette	233	15	1	0	441	21	7	7	7
Brussels Sprout Salad with Warm Bacon Vinaigrette	201	12	4	19	418	15	5	4	11
Creamy Buttermilk Coleslaw	140	10	2	9	356	11	3	7	2
Esquites	183	12	4	18	265	16	2	5	6
Pai Huang Gua	61	3	0	0	493	9	1	4	2
Green Bean Salad with Cherry Tomatoes and Feta	160	12	3	11	459	11	4	5	4
Green Bean Salad with Shallot, Mustard, and Tarragon	102	7	1	0	307	9	3	4	2
French Potato Salad	191	9	1	0	397	25	3	2	3
All-American Potato Salad	221	13	2	62	272	22	3	3	4
Watermelon Salad with Cotija and Serrano Chiles	155	8	3	15	457	17	1	13	6
Cantaloupe Salad with Olives and Red Onion	58	1	0	0	268	13	2	10	1
Honeydew Salad with Peanuts and Lime	149	4	1	0	473	28	3	22	4
Cool and Creamy Macaroni Salad	413	27	4	14	224	35	2	2	6
Antipasto Pasta Salad	686	42	13	72	1690	51	4	5	26
Chilled Soba Noodles with Cucumber, Snow Peas, and Radishes	215	6	1	0	620	34	1	2	8
Lentil Salad with Olives, Mint, and Feta	276	15	3	6	952	27	5	2	11
Lentil Salad with Spinach, Walnuts, and Parmesan Cheese	318	18	3	5	981	27	5	2	14
Lentil Salad with Hazelnuts and Goat Cheese	310	19	3	4	941	27	5	2	13
Lentil Salad with Carrots and Cilantro	244	12	2	0	914	26	5	2	10
Wheat Berry Salad with Radicchio, Dried Cherries, and Pecans	263	15	3	4	195	30	5	6	6
Pasta, Noodles & Dumplings									
Pasta with Garlic and Oil	458	18	4	8	258	59	3	2	15
Pasta Cacio e Uova	177	15	5	82	353	1	0	0	10
Fresh Pasta Without a Machine	280	11	3	245	30	35	0	0	0
Walnut Cream Sauce	327	29	8	31	214	6	2	2	9
Pasta with Burst Cherry Tomato Sauce and Fried Caper Crumbs	417	19	5	12	573	53	4	6	10
Marinara Sauce	128	7	1	0	306	13	6	9	2
Meatless "Meat" Sauce with Chickpeas and Mushrooms	176	10	1	0	523	20	5	7	6
Pasta alla Norma	738	23	6	32	1284	112	11	16	25
Pasta with Pesto, Potatoes, and Green Beans	617	28	7	19	603	75	6	5	18
Pasta alla Trapanese	476	19	4	8	419	61	4	4	16
Pasta e Ceci	534	20	5	15	923	67	13	10	22
Linguine allo Scoglio	696	18	3	256	1163	69	3	3	55
Rigatoni with Beef and Onion Ragu	495	15	6	60	766	59	5	9	26

	Calories	Total Fat (G)	Sat Fat (G)	Chol (MG)	Sodium (MG)	Total Carb (G)	Dietary Fiber (G)	Total Sugars (G)	Protein (G)
Pasta, Noodles & Dumplings (cont.)									
Pasta with Rustic Slow-Simmered Tomato Sauce with Meat	850	29	9	195	1350	98	1	10	44
Ragu alla Bolognese	774	38	13	171	660	54	4	6	43
Weeknight Tagliatelle with Bolognese Sauce	748	34	13	86	1046	66	4	6	35
Pork, Fennel, and Lemon Ragu with Pappardelle	610	29	13	104	744	52	4	6	34
Spaghetti and Meatballs	979	63	8	87	881	74	6	9	32
Italian-Style Turkey Meatballs	380	22	6	127	646	16	3	7	31
Foolproof Spaghetti Carbonara	867	38	16	221	1087	88	4	4	41
Potato Gnocchi with Browned Butter and Sage Sauce	663	18	10	103	986	111	7	3	16
Gorgonzola Cream Sauce	378	34	22	101	535	3	0	2	11
Parmesan Sauce with Pancetta and Walnuts	238	22	7	90	264	3	1	1	9
Porcini Mushroom Broth	110	9	1	0	200	3	1	1	1
Baked Manicotti	760	41	23	175	1077	54	5	7	44
Baked Ziti	502	25	13	100	892	45	4	8	26
Skillet Lasagna	463	25	6	34	668	33	6	10	26
Spinach Lasagna	605	32	19	119	819	46	4	10	34
Pastitsio	541	27	13	101	801	45	3	12	28
Stovetop Macaroni and Cheese	563	28	14	70	656	52	2	5	26
Pasta alla Zozzona	550	27	10	143	726	50	3	5	26
Pappardelle with Duck and Chestnut Ragu	1336	78	25	227	1484	105	1	5	40
Fresh Pappardelle	380	16	4	370	50	43	0	0	13
Japchae	315	21	6	41	1147	20	5	11	16
Beef Ho Fun	247	7	1	50	378	34	2	2	12
Dan Dan Mian	788	36	7	136	677	88	6	4	28
Chinese Pork Dumplings	74	3	1	6	93	8	1	1	3
Shu Mai	342	9	2	93	617	39	2	1	23
Quick Chili Oil	90	10	1	0	10	1	0	0	0
Har Gow	73	1	0	13	43	13	0	0	1
Chili Oil	90	10	1	0	50	1	1	0	0
Poultry									
Sautéed Chicken Cutlets	281	10	1	145	474	0	0	0	45
Romesco Sauce	140	12	1	0	142	7	1	4	2
Quick Sun-Dried Tomato Sauce	224	20	2	0	204	11	2	3	3
Quick Tomatillo Sauce	133	11	2	0	135	6	1	3	3
Crispy Pan-Fried Chicken Cutlets	418	24	2	159	436	14	1	1	34
Tonkatsu Sauce	25	0	0	0	330	5	0	4	0
Garlic-Curry Sauce	103	10	2	6	131	2	0	2	1
Pan-Seared Chicken Breasts	374	18	7	168	669	5	0	1	46
Lemon and Chive Pan Sauce	150	12	7	30	570	9	0	2	2
Crispy-Skinned Chicken Breasts with Vinegar-Pepper Pan Sauce	615	29	7	245	1105	12	3	4	73
with Lemon-Rosemary Pan Sauce	618	29	7	246	1098	12	2	4	74
with Maple–Sherry Vinegar Pan Sauce	640	29	7	245	1056	18	3	9	73
Skillet-Roasted Chicken Breasts with Garlicky Green Beans	552	20	5	240	1162	11	4	5	79
Skillet-Roasted Chicken Breasts with Harissa-Mint Carrots	515	16	2	228	1239	18	5	9	72
Chicken Marsala	549	26	7	124	922	29	2	4	40
Next-Level Chicken Piccata	391	20	5	113	592	19	2	2	33
Best Chicken Parmesan	671	44	12	165	948	25	5	10	45
Buffalo Chicken Sandwiches	1054	71	11	189	1425	65	3	6	38
Braised Chicken Thighs with Fennel, Orange, and Cracked Olives	421	30	8	157	746	6	1	2	28
Filipino Chicken Adobo	750	60	29	233	1376	8	1	0	44

	Calories	Total Fat (G)	Sat Fat (G)	Chol (MG)	Sodium (MG)	Total Carb (G)	Dietary Fiber (G)	Total Sugars (G)	Protein (G)
Poultry (cont.)									
Arroz con Pollo	890	40	10	194	1353	87	2	3	42
Arroz con Pollo with Bacon and Roasted Red Peppers	939	44	12	207	1385	88	3	4	45
Skillet Jambalaya	430	13	3	185	1220	43	1	4	35
Coq au Vin	780	28	10	255	1190	19	1	6	74
Chicken with 40 Cloves of Garlic	980	54	16	305	840	14	1	2	97
Chicken in Mole-Poblano Sauce	844	57	14	201	1114	28	5	17	56
French Chicken in a Pot	883	64	18	338	1220	4	1	1	68
Indoor Pulled Chicken	160	4.5	1	105	480	6	0	5	23
Lexington Vinegar Barbecue Sauce	35	0	0	0	380	7	0	6	0
South Carolina Mustard Barbecue Sauce	60	1	0	0	810	10	2	8	1
Sweet and Tangy Barbecue Sauce	90	0	0	0	720	23	0	20	0
Tinga de Pollo	456	21	5	153	869	32	8	4	37
Escabeche	20	0	0	0	100	4	1	2	0
Corn Tortillas	41	1	0	0	28	8	1	0	1
Tamales	889	21	6	45	777	155	15	8	26
Red Chile Chicken Filling	99	5	1	31	232	7	1	3	8
Enchiladas Verdes	500	25	8	90	840	40	4	11	32
Oven-Roasted Chicken Thighs	665	52	13	272	938	1	0	0	46
Roasted Garlic Salsa Verde	180	17	2	2	185	6	1	0	2
Roasted Shallot and Mint Chutney	154	14	1	0	156	7	2	2	1
Slow-Roasted Chicken Parts with Shallot-Garlic Pan Sauce	708	50	16	230	889	7	1	2	56
Weeknight Roast Chicken	731	53	17	232	1204	5	1	1	56
Tarragon-Lemon Pan Sauce	60	6	4	15	200	2	0	1	0
Thyme–Sherry Vinegar Pan Sauce	60	6	4	15	200	2	0	1	1
Roast Chicken with Garlic and Lime	771	56	14	225	771	8	2	3	57
Spicy Mayonnaise	129	14	1	12	50	0	0	0	0
Roast Chicken with Quinoa, Swiss Chard, and Lime	830	52	15	239	1403	24	4	1	63
with Bulgur, Peas, and Mint	823	51	15	239	1325	28	5	3	63
with Couscous, Roasted Red Peppers, and Basil	827	50	15	239	1324	28	2	1	62
Broiled Chicken with Gravy	864	57	18	254	1287	17	1	5	65
Chicken Under a Brick with Herb-Roasted Potatoes	847	53	13	225	1139	32	4	2	60
Crisp Roast Butterflied Chicken with Rosemary and Garlic	686	50	13	217	1010	1	0	0	54
Crispy Fried Chicken	790	34	7	125	940	73	1	14	45
Dakgangjeong	941	72	11	252	608	28	1	7	43
Buffalo Wings	613	55	15	148	651	7	1	3	22
Thai Chicken Curry with Potatoes and Peanuts	448	26	14	73	697	34	5	9	24
Thai-Style Chicken with Basil	337	12	1	124	916	16	2	9	41
Murgh Makhani	451	30	16	210	780	12	2	8	34
Indian-Style Basmati Rice	223	6	4	15	333	38	1	0	3
Chicken Biryani	688	35	13	169	2359	64	5	9	31
Chicken Tikka Masala	470	27	9	146	945	19	4	12	39
Chicken Teriyaki	505	35	9	194	820	7	0	3	34
Gōngbǎo Jīdīng	338	18	3	107	715	17	3	8	29
Cast Iron Chicken Pot Pie	368	18	9	148	754	20	3	5	31
Roast Turkey and Gravy with Herbes de Provence and Lemon	597	27	7	256	1366	7	1	2	76
Easier Roast Turkey and Gravy	700	29	7	325	1670	5	0	2	99
Roast Whole Turkey Breast with Gravy	548	26	8	207	1221	6	1	1	68
Porchetta-Style Turkey Breast	694	36	10	256	1032	4	2	0	85
Turkey Thigh Confit with Citrus-Mustard Sauce	1803	169	56	315	1253	30	3	19	46
Turkey Patty Melts	259	14	7	59	381	19	2	5	15
Ground Turkey Mix	170	11	4	67	244	4	0	1	15

	Calories	Total Fat (G)	Sat Fat (G)	Chol (MG)	Sodium (MG)	Total Carb (G)	Dietary Fiber (G)	Total Sugars (G)	Protein (G)
Meat									
Smashed Burgers	619	43	15	104	710	27	1	5	30
Juicy Pub-Style Burgers	722	47	21	207	667	23	1	3	50
Pub-Style Burger Sauce	323	33	5	17	746	5	0	4	1
Mushroom-Beef Blended Burgers	560	36	14	108	635	26	2	5	33
Classic Sloppy Joes	447	21	7	77	859	37	2	13	27
Tacos Dorados	640	41	8	65	970	49	3	7	26
Moussaka	735	51	18	152	1218	44	10	15	26
Keema Aloo	233	13	4	50	378	12	3	3	17
Keema Matar	288	21	6	55	401	10	3	4	16
Cuban-Style Picadillo	518	34	11	106	820	19	4	12	29
Cuban-Style Picadillo with Fried Potatoes	929	74	14	106	1089	33	5	12	31
Mapo Tofu	383	28	4	28	391	16	2	5	20
Shepherd's Pie	605	34	14	133	1137	48	5	6	28
Glazed All-Beef Meatloaf	364	19	9	145	539	17	1	10	31
Pot Roast with Root Vegetables	570	27	12	137	1319	38	7	9	42
Beef Braised in Barolo	680	36	15	174	1344	16	4	7	51
Slow-Roasted Beef	270	9	3	115	680	0	0	0	45
Horseradish Cream Sauce	77	7	5	22	93	3	1	2	1
Beef Tenderloin with Smoky Potatoes and Persillade Relish	542	29	6	103	947	31	4	3	41
Fennel-Coriander Top Sirloin Roast	430	23	5	140	890	1	1	0	51
Rosemary-Garlic Top Sirloin Roast	430	23	5	140	890	1	0	0	51
Beef Wellington	686	42	24	165	789	49	3	6	30
Creamy Green Peppercorn Sauce	126	11	7	33	254	2	0	1	2
Best Prime Rib	520	27	10	185	870	0	0	0	64
Modern Beef Burgundy	763	47	20	168	1389	23	3	6	48
Onion-Braised Beef Brisket	530	13	5	195	1320	25	4	11	68
Ropa Vieja	471	37	11	109	666	9	2	4	23
Braised Beef Short Ribs	590	32	12	155	990	8	1	3	52
Plov	570	26	10	83	1001	59	5	9	26
Simple Pot-au-Feu	1199	105	10	130	1200	20	5	5	41
Jamaican Pepper Steak	462	24	7	106	975	14	2	4	41
Steak Frites	1644	139	40	179	1449	58	5	2	47
Pan-Seared Strip Steaks	240	9	3	90	95	0	0	0	39
Pan-Seared Strip Steak for Two	120	4.5	1.5	45	50	0	0	0	20
Sauce Verte	150	14	2	0	230	3	1	1	1
Thai Chili Butter	105	12	7	31	5	1	0	0	0
Pan-Seared Filet Mignon	549	41	16	175	506	0	0	0	41
Madeira Pan Sauce with Mustard and Anchovies	130	9	5	24	85	6	1	3	1
Chimichurri	172	18	3	0	131	2	1	0	1
Steak Tacos	440	26	5	84	470	23	3	1	29
Sweet and Spicy Pickled Onions	45	0	0	0	95	11	1	10	0
Steak Tips with Mushroom-Onion Gravy	336	21	7	88	691	9	2	4	27
Beef Bulgogi	560	36	13	93	997	32	3	25	28
Braciole	491	28	9	111	896	17	3	7	38
Bò Lúc Lắc	341	24	9	96	835	7	1	4	24
Cơm Đỏ	213	4	2	10	307	39	1	1	4
Stir-Fried Cumin Beef	346	24	5	77	404	7	1	3	25
Stir-Fried Beef and Gai Lan	419	27	8	120	633	4	0	1	36
Pub-Style Steak and Ale Pie	890	61	28	239	879	35	2	3	49
Osso Buco	467	21	3	136	216	14	3	6	38
Pan-Seared Thick-Cut Boneless Pork Chops	546	38	11	153	744	1	0	0	48
Roasted Red Pepper–Vinegar Sauce	184	18	3	2	243	4	1	2	1
Mint Persillade	185	19	3	3	147	4	2	0	2
Pan-Seared Thick-Cut, Bone-In Pork Chops	272	14	5	110	88	0	0	0	33
Creamy Apple-Mustard Sauce	144	3	0	0	1030	28	4	23	4
Maple Agrodolce	115	0	0	0	87	28	1	24	1

	Calories	Total Fat (G)	Sat Fat (G)	Chol (MG)	Sodium (MG)	Total Carb (G)	Dietary Fiber (G)	Total Sugars (G)	Protein (G)
Meat (cont.)									
Sous Vide Boneless Thick-Cut Pork Chops	530	43	9	100	720	0	0	0	36
Red Pepper and Almond Relish	118	11	1	0	89	3	1	1	2
Zha Paigu	588	40	6	159	518	32	0	2	23
Lu Dan	155	6	2	233	2715	3	0	0	12
Spice-Rubbed Pork Roast en Cocotte with Caramelized Onions	389	24	7	117	473	4	1	1	38
Slow-Roasted Bone-In Pork Rib Roast	200	7	2	75	500	4	0	3	30
Port Wine–Cherry Sauce	363	26	16	69	265	26	1	19	1
Porchetta	469	35	10	118	634	4	2	0	34
Indoor Pulled Pork with Sweet and Tangy Barbecue Sauce	550	20	7	152	881	39	2	34	52
Carnitas	743	40	14	187	1163	38	6	3	57
Carne Adovada	438	27	9	134	1106	9	1	7	38
Goan Pork Vindaloo	311	20	6	87	586	7	2	1	26
Chinese-Style Barbecued Spareribs	700	21	6	200	2540	62	0	51	61
Crispy Slow-Roasted Pork Belly	237	15	5	67	327	3	0	3	21
with Tangy Hoisin Sauce	740	73	26	100	1090	9	0	6	21
Roast Fresh Ham	340	19	5	120	660	2	0	0	39
Cider and Brown Sugar Glaze	180	0	0	0	15	46	0	45	0
Spicy Pineapple-Ginger Glaze	180	0	0	0	15	47	0	45	0
Coca-Cola Glaze with Lime and Jalapeño	180	0	0	0	15	47	0	46	0
Orange, Cinnamon, and Star Anise Glaze	180	0	0	0	15	46	0	45	43
Kimchi Bokkeumbap	250	10	1	10	690	34	2	3	8
Shīzi Tóu	570	35	13	145	1079	27	2	7	34
Cuban-Style Black Beans and Rice	307	22	7	18	596	22	5	3	8
Lamb Barbacoa	546	22	8	83	888	57	11	6	32
Roast Butterflied Leg of Lamb with Coriander, Cumin, and Mustard Seeds	440	22	6	175	330	1	1	0	56
with Coriander, Rosemary, and Red Pepper	440	22	6	175	330	1	1	0	56
with Coriander, Fennel, and Black Pepper	440	22	6	175	330	1	1	0	56
Fish & Seafood									
Pan-Seared Brined Salmon	415	27	6	109	467	1	0	0	41
Mango-Mint Salsa	97	4	1	0	279	17	2	13	1
Cilantro-Mint Chutney	146	12	1	0	242	9	3	2	3
Saumon aux Lentilles	615	30	6	94	1044	38	7	4	48
Crispy Salmon Cakes with Smoked Salmon, Capers, and Dill for Two	1014	90	11	87	736	21	2	5	31
Miso-Marinated Salmon	510	24	5	95	1040	28	0	22	38
Glazed Salmon	506	31	7	109	556	12	0	9	41
Pomegranate-Balsamic Glaze	70	0	0	0	95	15	0	14	0
Hoisin-Ginger Glaze	40	1	0	0	420	10	0	8	0
Orange-Miso Glaze	40	0	0	0	330	7	0	5	1
Soy-Mustard Glaze	70	0	0	0	550	13	0	12	1
Roasted Whole Side of Salmon	390	24	6	100	433	4	0	3	37
Arugula and Almond Pesto	80	8	1	0	230	2	1	1	2
Cucumber-Ginger Relish	110	11	2	0	160	2	1	1	1
Poached Salmon with Herb and Caper Vinaigrette	567	36	7	117	794	12	2	6	45
Pesce all'Acqua Pazza	221	8	1	92	814	5	1	2	29
Chraime	280	12	2	92	999	14	4	7	31
Tabil	20	1	0	0	0	3	2	0	1
Halibut à la Nage with Parsnips and Tarragon	367	21	2	76	835	13	2	4	31
Oven-Steamed Fish with Scallions and Ginger	262	10	1	73	758	8	1	3	32
Pan-Roasted Halibut Steaks	238	14	6	87	382	2	0	1	26
Chipotle-Garlic Butter with Lime and Cilantro	112	11	7	30	215	3	0	2	0
Chunky Cherry Tomato–Basil Vinaigrette	130	14	2	0	99	2	1	1	0

	Calories	Total Fat (G)	Sat Fat (G)	Chol (MG)	Sodium (MG)	Total Carb (G)	Dietary Fiber (G)	Total Sugars (G)	Protein (G)
Fish & Seafood (cont.)									
Pan-Seared Swordfish Steaks	348	17	4	150	537	0	0	0	45
Caper-Currant Relish	215	20	3	0	210	9	2	6	1
Spicy Dried Mint–Garlic Sauce	190	20	3	0	85	2	0	0	0
Butter-Basted Fish Fillets with Garlic and Thyme	366	26	11	119	491	3	1	0	31
Pan-Roasted Sea Bass with Green Olive, Almond, and Orange Relish	399	29	4	61	471	6	3	2	29
Sautéed Tilapia with Chive-Lemon Miso Butter	332	22	9	108	439	3	1	1	33
Cilantro Chimichurri	130	14	2	0	290	2	0	0	0
Pan-Seared Shrimp with Peanuts, Black Pepper, and Lime	239	9	1	274	450	4	1	2	36
Pan-Seared Shrimp with Fermented Black Beans, Ginger, and Garlic	225	8	1	274	581	3	0	2	35
Pan-Seared Shrimp with Pistachio, Cumin, and Parsley	255	11	2	274	454	4	1	1	36
Garlicky Roasted Shrimp with Parsley and Anise	265	19	6	211	858	3	0	0	21
Garlicky Roasted Shrimp with Cilantro and Lime	282	20	2	191	857	3	1	0	21
Garlicky Roasted Shrimp with Cumin, Ginger, and Sesame	291	22	2	191	857	2	0	0	21
Crispy Salt and Pepper Shrimp	290	20	2	145	500	10	0	2	16
Shrimp Tempura	750	31	3	280	270	53	0	0	30
Scallion Dipping Sauce	24	1	0	0	584	1	0	0	1
Greek-Style Shrimp with Tomatoes and Feta	338	18	6	216	824	10	4	5	30
Shrimp Scampi	371	20	9	245	969	14	1	7	24
Moqueca	419	29	15	154	916	12	3	5	32
Spanish-Style Toasted Pasta with Shrimp	504	16	3	215	1439	54	5	6	34
Spanish-Style Toasted Pasta with Shrimp and Clams	657	20	3	236	1680	59	5	6	58
Aioli	132	15	2	31	43	0	0	0	0
Stir-Fried Shrimp with Snow Peas and Red Bell Pepper in Hot and Sour Sauce	302	14	1	183	543	20	2	15	25
Shrimp Pad Thai	594	23	3	369	1731	59	3	9	37
Shrimp Salad	224	12	2	188	386	7	1	4	23
Shrimp Salad with Roasted Red Pepper and Basil	222	12	2	188	397	7	1	4	23
Shrimp Salad with Avocado and Orange	282	16	2	188	541	14	3	8	24
Pan-Seared Scallops	232	14	4	56	668	6	0	0	21
Lemon Browned Butter Sauce	105	12	7	31	2	1	0	0	0
Best Crab Cakes	451	26	8	186	795	23	2	5	31
Oven-Steamed Mussels	526	19	6	142	1303	20	1	1	54
Oven-Steamed Mussels with Tomato and Chorizo	876	51	16	203	2339	36	4	9	69
Oven-Steamed Mussels with Leeks and Pernod	646	23	5	135	1471	35	2	5	56
Oven-Steamed Mussels with Hard Cider and Bacon	614	30	9	163	1523	20	0	1	59
Paella	674	23	6	225	1328	67	4	5	48
Indoor Clambake	905	42	17	469	2996	38	3	6	93
Fisherman's Pie	587	32	19	245	1097	34	2	3	39
Fish and Chips	1060	62	5	75	800	83	4	2	40

	Calories	Total Fat (G)	Sat Fat (G)	Chol (MG)	Sodium (MG)	Total Carb (G)	Dietary Fiber (G)	Total Sugars (G)	Protein (G)
Vegetarian									
Best Vegetarian Chili	439	14	1	0	1252	66	16	10	20
Mushroom Bourguignon	172	8	1	0	568	17	3	5	7
Chana Masala	291	11	1	0	576	39	11	8	11
Espinacas con Garbanzos	571	28	4	3	908	62	17	12	21
Palak Dal	273	8	4	16	348	40	7	4	14
Saag Paneer	540	30	15	71	2121	47	6	38	27
Vegetable Bibimbap with Nurungji	591	20	3	124	1163	86	4	12	15
Paella de Verduras	517	14	3	6	804	78	9	9	19
Stir-Fried Portobellos with Ginger-Oyster Sauce	297	19	2	0	1095	26	5	11	9
Stir-Fried Portobellos with Sweet Chili-Garlic Sauce	316	17	1	0	1182	37	5	22	9

	Calories	Total Fat (G)	Sat Fat (G)	Chol (MG)	Sodium (MG)	Total Carb (G)	Dietary Fiber (G)	Total Sugars (G)	Protein (G)
Vegetarian (cont.)									
Make-Ahead Cheese Soufflés	215	15	8	130	292	6	0	2	13
Pickled Mustard Seeds	296	12	1	0	723	36	4	27	9
Spinach and Ricotta Gnudi with Tomato-Butter Sauce	407	26	15	85	727	26	3	3	20
White Bean and Mushroom Gratin	428	20	3	0	757	49	9	6	15
Roasted Poblano and Black Bean Enchiladas	521	30	12	50	820	47	11	8	20
Eggplant Parmesan	479	27	8	122	918	41	9	10	21
Eggplant Involtini	330	23	6	36	1020	22	9	10	12
Alu Parathas	490	21	0	33	561	68	3	2	9
Tamatya-Kandyachi Koshimbir	51	1	1	0	300	10	3	6	2
Grown-Up Grilled Cheese Sandwiches with Cheddar and Shallots	492	32	18	86	703	30	2	4	21
with Gruyère and Chives	495	31	18	92	733	28	2	4	24
with Asiago and Dates	497	28	16	71	964	33	3	7	27
with Comté and Cornichon	490	32	18	86	703	30	2	4	21
with Robiola and Chipotle	489	32	18	86	705	30	2	4	21
Quesadillas	230	12	6	25	500	20	0	1	10
Vegan Baja-Style Cauliflower Tacos	438	28	17	7	643	45	8	12	8
Vegan Cilantro Sauce	205	20	5	23	323	3	0	2	3
Pupusas	490	26	14	65	577	44	4	0	22
Quick Salsa	20	0	0	0	156	5	2	3	1
Curtido	58	0	0	0	466	11	3	7	1
Ultimate Veggie Burgers	383	15	2	3	411	52	5	6	13
Black Bean Burgers	373	11	2	62	531	52	11	4	16
Chipotle Mayonnaise	63	7	1	6	55	0	0	0	0
Falafel	440	35	4	5	570	34	1	2	11
Tomato-Chile Sauce	117	10	1	0	381	8	4	4	2
Vospov Kofte	379	20	7	20	548	42	8	2	12
Mujaddara	875	58	5	5	783	75	8	10	16
Crispy Onions	100	5	0	0	100	13	2	6	1
Tomato and Mozzarella Tart	381	27	10	58	444	19	1	2	17
Upside-Down Tomato Tart	97	4	2	5	311	15	2	10	2
Mushroom and Leek Galette with Gorgonzola	507	31	16	97	613	48	6	7	13
Potato and Shallot Galette with Goat Cheese	533	32	17	98	541	52	5	5	13
Butternut Squash Galette with Gruyère	496	30	16	99	588	48	5	5	12
Spanakopita	402	28	16	128	888	22	3	1	18

	Calories	Total Fat (G)	Sat Fat (G)	Chol (MG)	Sodium (MG)	Total Carb (G)	Dietary Fiber (G)	Total Sugars (G)	Protein (G)
Grilling									
Tender, Juicy Grilled Burgers	590	38	17	163	532	22	1	3	38
Grilled Scallion Topping	153	14	2	7	243	6	2	3	2
Grilled Shiitake Mushroom Topping	150	14	2	7	214	5	2	2	2
Grilled Napa Cabbage and Radicchio Topping	138	14	2	7	200	3	1	1	1
Grilled Marinated Flank Steak	250	13	5	105	470	0	0	0	32
Garlic-Shallot-Rosemary Wet Paste Marinade	130	14	2	0	0	2	0	0	0
Garlic-Ginger-Sesame Wet Paste Marinade	130	14	1.5	0	0	1	0	0	0
Garlic-Chile Wet Paste Marinade	130	14	1	0	25	2	0	0	0
Grilled Strip or Rib-Eye Steaks	713	51	21	247	163	0	0	0	58
Grilled Filets Mignons	549	41	16	175	506	0	0	0	41
Roasted Red Pepper and Smoked Paprika Butter	106	12	7	31	52	1	0	0	0
Lemon, Garlic, and Parsley Butter	103	12	7	31	37	0	0	0	0
Carne Asada	294	19	8	97	357	0	0	0	30
Simple Refried Beans	250	9	3	13	487	32	9	2	13
Red Chile Salsa	23	0	0	0	183	5	2	3	1
Folded Enchiladas	214	9	2	8	364	29	5	4	7

	Calories	Total Fat (G)	Sat Fat (G)	Chol (MG)	Sodium (MG)	Total Carb (G)	Dietary Fiber (G)	Total Sugars (G)	Protein (G)
Grilling (*cont.*)									
Grilled Boneless Beef Short Ribs	364	29	12	110	353	0	0	0	26
Preserved Lemon–Almond Sauce	128	13	2	0	3	2	1	1	1
Kimchi-Scallion Sauce	90	9	1	0	218	1	0	0	1
Grill-Roasted Beef Tenderloin	420	21	7	160	680	1	0	0	53
Chermoula Sauce	167	18	3	0	71	2	0	0	0
Easy Grilled Boneless Pork Chops	482	29	7	128	659	9	1	5	43
Onion, Olive, and Caper Relish	125	10	2	0	234	8	1	4	1
Tomato, Fennel, and Almond Relish	140	12	2	0	256	7	3	4	2
Orange, Jicama, and Pepita Relish	139	12	2	0	154	8	2	4	2
Garlic-Lime Grilled Pork Tenderloin Steaks	411	28	4	111	490	6	1	5	36
Lemon-Thyme Grilled Pork Tenderloin Steaks	411	28	4	111	491	6	1	5	36
Spicy Orange-Ginger Grilled Pork Tenderloin Steaks	413	28	4	111	492	7	1	5	36
Grilled Pork Tenderloin with Grilled Pineapple–Red Onion Salsa	239	8	3	86	549	14	2	10	29
Smoked Pork Loin with Dried Fruit Chutney	600	22	8	155	2960	45	0	37	48
Grilled Bone-In Pork Roast	459	27	9	125	833	12	3	9	40
Orange Salsa with Cuban Flavors	51	1	0	0	118	10	2	7	1
Kansas City Sticky Ribs	1100	65	20	210	2370	86	2	80	43
Memphis-Style Barbecued Spareribs	780	62	20	210	1410	10	1	7	42
Spice Rub	68	3	0	0	14	11	5	3	3
Rosticciana	1246	109	33	333	965	1	0	0	65
Grilled Radicchio	170	14	2	0	45	9	2	1	3
Bún Chả	403	17	6	54	1641	45	3	10	18
Grilled Lamb Kofte	470	39	13	88	496	8	2	3	24
Grilled Beef Kofte	441	35	10	86	472	9	2	3	25
Grilled Arayes	725	55	19	117	680	26	5	4	34
Parsley-Cucumber Salad with Feta, Pomegranate, and Walnuts	270	24	5	15	290	11	3	6	7
Grilled Glazed Bone-In Chicken Breasts	220	5	1	135	450	0	0	0	42
Orange-Chipotle Glaze	40	0	0	0	0	10	0	8	1
Soy-Ginger Glaze	60	0	0	0	920	11	0	9	2
Curry-Yogurt Glaze	35	1.5	1	5	20	4	0	3	2
Best Grilled Chicken Thighs	360	27	7	155	220	0	0	0	27
Gochujang Paste	30	0	0	0	520	7	0	4	1
Mustard-Tarragon Paste	15	0	0	0	460	1	0	0	0
Garam Masala Paste	60	7	0.5	0	230	1	0	0	0
Grilled Chicken with Adobo and Sazón	584	44	11	164	738	3	0	0	41
Barbecued Pulled Chicken	230	6	1	45	1800	32	1	26	10
Barbecued Pulled Chicken for a Crowd	650	21	5	360	2130	32	1	26	77
Grilled Chicken Satay	385	22	3	142	589	14	2	7	33
Pollo a la Brasa	760	50	14	246	1374	6	1	0	63
Ají Verde	144	16	3	10	146	1	0	0	1
Ají Amarillo	200	22	3	11	167	0	0	0	0
Simple Grill-Roasted Turkey	517	21	5	251	1150	2	0	0	76
Gravy for Simple Grill-Roasted Turkey	144	9	4	33	230	11	1	3	7
Grill-Smoked Salmon	429	27	6	109	471	4	0	4	40
"Smoked Salmon Platter" Sauce	192	20	2	62	109	1	0	0	2
Apple-Mustard Sauce	55	1	0	0	188	12	2	9	1
Grilled Whole Trout with Marjoram and Lemon	496	25	5	187	752	2	0	1	62
Grilled Whole Trout with Lime and Coriander	497	25	5	187	753	2	1	1	62
Grilled Whole Trout with Orange and Fennel	496	25	5	187	753	2	0	1	62
Grilled Fish Tacos	575	22	4	100	1135	62	10	20	36
Grilled Scallops	540	45	3	41	668	12	1	3	21
Chile-Lime Vinaigrette	290	28	2	0	190	11	0	9	0
Basil Vinaigrette	344	37	2	0	132	3	0	2	0

	Calories	Total Fat (G)	Sat Fat (G)	Chol (MG)	Sodium (MG)	Total Carb (G)	Dietary Fiber (G)	Total Sugars (G)	Protein (G)
Grilling (cont.)									
Grilled Shrimp and Vegetable Kebabs	285	15	2	183	739	16	2	6	26
Paella on the Grill	813	31	8	205	1350	76	4	5	53
Grilled Halloumi Wraps	437	25	13	80	1188	36	5	6	20
Grilled Corn with Flavored Butter	262	18	8	31	366	26	3	9	5
Basil and Lemon Butter	154	17	11	46	56	0	0	0	0
Honey Butter	185	17	11	46	74	9	0	9	0
Cilantro-Chipotle Butter	154	17	11	46	55	0	0	0	0
New Orleans "Barbecue" Butter	159	17	11	46	69	2	0	1	0
Spicy Old Bay Butter	155	17	11	46	98	1	0	0	0
Grilled Potatoes with Garlic and Rosemary	336	17	2	0	587	42	5	2	5
Grilled Potatoes with Oregano and Lemon	335	17	2	0	586	43	6	2	5
Grilled Baba Ghanoush	67	4	1	0	80	8	4	4	2
Sides									
Pan-Roasted Asparagus	104	7	2	7	394	7	4	3	5
Beets with Lemon and Almonds	134	6	0	0	447	17	5	11	5
Beets with Lime and Pepitas	124	5	1	0	440	15	4	10	5
Beets with Orange and Walnuts	130	7	1	0	441	16	4	11	4
Roasted Broccoli	161	11	2	0	357	14	5	4	6
Roasted Broccoli with Garlic	140	11	1.5	0	330	9	3	3	3
Roasted Brussels Sprouts	101	5	1	0	314	12	5	3	4
Roasted Brussels Sprouts with Garlic, Red Pepper Flakes, and Parmesan	165	12	2	3	338	12	5	3	6
Roasted Brussels Sprouts with Bacon and Pecans	230	19	3	`0	370	13	6	3	7
Roasted Brussels Sprouts with Walnuts and Lemon	172	13	4	11	342	13	5	3	5
Roasted Carrots	81	4	2	10	276	11	3	5	1
Roasted Carrots and Fennel with Toasted Almonds and Lemon	97	6	3	10	267	11	4	5	2
Roasted Carrots and Parsnips with Rosemary	94	4	2	10	277	14	4	5	1
Buffalo Cauliflower Bites	570	53	19	0	690	25	2	4	2
Vegan Ranch Dressing	90	10	1	0	120	0	0	0	0
Vegan Mayonnaise	180	20	2	0	75	0	0	0	0
Modern Cauliflower Gratin	199	14	8	35	493	12	4	4	9
Boiled Corn	98	3	1	3	241	19	2	6	3
Chili-Lime Salt	5	0	0	0	1200	1	1	0	0
Pepper-Cinnamon Salt	5	0	0	0	560	1	0	0	0
Cumin-Sesame Salt	15	1	0	0	560	1	0	0	0
Corn Fritters	116	8	1	17	102	9	1	2	2
Maple-Chipotle Mayonnaise	142	15	2	8	133	2	0	2	0
Red Pepper Mayonnaise	42	4	1	2	38	1	0	0	0
Basil Mayonnaise	67	7	1	4	56	0	0	0	0
Corn Risotto	273	8	4	18	683	44	3	5	8
Braised Eggplant with Paprika, Coriander, and Yogurt	98	8	1	2	423	7	3	4	2
Braised Eggplant with Soy, Garlic, and Ginger	72	3	0	0	298	9	2	5	1
Skillet-Charred Green Beans with Crispy Bread Crumb Topping	135	11	1	0	293	9	3	4	2
Ultimate Green Bean Casserole	300	23	14	45	490	18	2	5	4
Sautéed Mushrooms with Red Wine and Rosemary	97	4	2	9	199	9	2	5	6
Beer-Battered Onion Rings with Jalapeño Dipping Sauce	684	48	4	8	577	53	2	6	6
Plátanos Maduros	321	23	1	0	403	31	2	17	1
Rajas Poblanas con Crema	191	15	8	41	316	14	2	8	4
Rajas Poblanas con Crema y Elote	213	15	8	41	317	19	3	9	4

	Calories	Total Fat (G)	Sat Fat (G)	Chol (MG)	Sodium (MG)	Total Carb (G)	Dietary Fiber (G)	Total Sugars (G)	Protein (G)
Sides (*cont.*)									
Best Baked Potatoes	167	4	0	0	537	31	2	1	4
Creamy Egg Topping	83	6	2	147	152	2	0	1	5
Herbed Goat Cheese Topping	137	13	5	13	132	1	0	0	5
Smoked Trout Topping	82	5	2	19	244	2	0	1	7
Make-Ahead Mashed Potatoes	505	35	22	105	722	44	3	4	7
Aligot	465	30	18	94	650	31	3	4	20
Crispy Smashed Potatoes	237	14	2	0	384	27	3	1	3
Simplified Potato Galette	177	7	5	19	301	26	3	1	3
Easier French Fries	599	43	8	2	759	50	6	2	6
Chive and Black Pepper Dipping Sauce	144	16	3	12	107	1	0	0	0
Belgian-Style Dipping Sauce	138	14	2	7	224	4	0	3	0
Crispy Potato Latkes	172	4	1	62	429	29	2	2	6
Thick-Cut Sweet Potato Fries	554	36	6	0	638	55	7	9	4
Spicy Fry Sauce	101	11	2	6	83	0	0	0	0
Roasted Butternut Squash with Browned Butter and Hazelnuts	187	16	8	31	224	11	2	2	2
Roasted Butternut Squash with Radicchio and Parmesan	169	14	5	17	246	10	2	2	2
Roasted Butternut Squash with Goat Cheese, Pecans, and Maple	170	12	5	20	245	15	2	6	3
Roasted Butternut Squash with Tahini and Feta	173	13	5	21	253	13	3	3	3
Best Summer Tomato Gratin	239	14	4	9	507	20	3	7	9
Briam	319	25	3	0	504	24	4	6	4
Kousa Mihshi	613	39	12	57	1357	48	7	21	22
Walkaway Ratatouille	178	11	2	0	752	19	6	9	3
Perfect Roasted Root Vegetables	180	8	1	0	588	28	7	10	3
Bacon-Shallot Topping	80	7	2.5	10	125	1	0	0	2
Orange-Parsley Salsa	161	12	1	0	243	13	4	7	4
Chelow ba Tahdig	368	16	3	12	236	50	1	1	5
Almost Hands-Free Risotto with Parmesan and Herbs	491	16	9	37	1056	62	3	3	18
Parmesan Farrotto	364	16	9	41	770	38	5	5	19
Mushroom Farrotto	319	14	8	33	892	38	6	5	15
Tabbouleh	277	21	3	0	446	22	5	3	4
New England Baked Beans	580	24	8	24	923	74	12	29	19
Red Lentil Kibbeh	264	8	2	3	460	40	7	5	11
Harissa	208	21	3	0	75	5	3	1	1
Rustic Bread Stuffing with Cranberries and Walnuts	380	15	4	13	528	54	4	13	11
Bread & Pizza									
Cream Biscuits	270	160	10	50	182	26	1	2	4
Cream Biscuits with Fresh Herbs	270	16	10	50	184	26	1	2	5
Cheddar Biscuits	303	19	12	59	201	27	1	2	6
Ultimate Flaky Buttermilk Biscuits	378	21	13	56	285	41	1	5	6
Popovers	188	5	2	100	278	26	1	3	9
Piadine	351	11	1	0	294	54	2	0	7
Pão de Queijo	560	35	13	130	845	39	0	2	24
Southern Cornbread	956	31	10	210	1176	143	6	21	24
Irish Brown Soda Bread	255	2	1	2	397	52	8	5	11
British-Style Currant Scones	270	9	5	53	210	41	1	12	6
Blueberry Muffins	313	10	3	42	274	52	1	28	5

	Calories	Total Fat (G)	Sat Fat (G)	Chol (MG)	Sodium (MG)	Total Carb (G)	Dietary Fiber (G)	Total Sugars (G)	Protein (G)
Bread & Pizza (*cont.*)									
Savory Corn Muffins	276	14	8	65	237	33	1	6	5
Savory Corn Muffins with Rosemary and Black Pepper	277	14	8	65	238	33	1	6	5
Ultimate Banana Bread	344	15	7	62	263	50	3	24	6
Easy Sandwich Bread	220	5	3	35	250	35	2	2	7
No-Knead Brioche	264	14	8	112	185	27	1	4	7
Challah	299	8	1	47	243	48	2	6	9
Rosemary Focaccia	170	4.5	0.5	0	95	26	0	0	4
Fluffy Dinner Rolls	162	6	3	28	140	23	1	3	4
Homemade Naan	216	9	2	30	167	28	1	1	4
Quicker Homemade Naan	216	9	2	30	167	28	1	1	4
New York Bagels	253	1	0	0	478	52	2	10	8
Bagel Toppings	45	3.5	0	0	0	2	2	0	2
Laugenbrezeln	254	5	3	10	153	44	2	0	8
Stollen	335	13	5	30	181	48	3	22	6
Perfect Sticky Buns	375	19	8	47	262	46	2	17	7
Kanelbullar	319	13	8	49	226	45	2	22	6
Thin-Crust Pizza	523	18	8	38	746	67	5	8	23
Pizza al Taglio with Arugula and Fresh Mozzarella	613	34	10	43	664	55	4	3	23
Pizza al Taglio with Potatoes and Soppressata	770	42	14	56	1121	68	5	3	30
Pizza al Taglio with Prosciutto and Figs	465	19	3	13	519	58	3	6	14
Cast Iron Pan Pizza	713	38	15	68	784	62	4	3	30
Cookies									
Perfect Chocolate Chip Cookies	314	18	9	50	155	37	2	23	3
Crispy Chocolate Chip Cookies	65	3	2	9	34	9	0	6	1
Chocolate Chip Cookie Ice Cream Sandwiches	467	24	14	70	238	60	2	38	6
Big and Chewy Oatmeal-Raisin Cookies	311	12	7	45	90	50	2	30	4
Big and Chewy Oatmeal-Date Cookies	310	12	7	45	86	50	3	32	4
Brown Sugar Cookies	220	7	4	33	88	36	1	18	3
Molasses Spice Cookies	159	7	4	25	88	24	1	12	2
Molasses Spice Cookies with Dark Rum Glaze	186	7	4	25	89	29	1	18	2
Chocolate Crinkle Cookies	155	6	3	31	96	24	2	17	3
Speculoos	74	3	2	13	34	11	0	5	1
Speculoos with Almonds	83	4	2	13	34	11	1	5	1
Easy Holiday Sugar Cookies	125	5	3	17	67	19	0	12	1
Easy Holiday Cocoa Sugar Cookies	126	5	3	17	67	20	0	12	1
Baci di Dama	267	19	7	23	39	24	2	13	4
Alfajores de Maicena	272	13	8	52	109	35	1	20	4
Dulce de Leche	107	3	2	11	66	18	0	18	3
Crescent-Shaped Rugelach with Raisin-Walnut Filling	223	14	6	34	47	24	1	13	3
Meringue Christmas Trees	75	4	2	0	12	11	1	10	1
Chewy Brownies	299	15	5	43	98	41	2	30	3
Ultimate Turtle Brownies	230	13	6	31	64	28	1	23	2
Browned Butter Blondies	186	10	5	39	104	21	1	10	3
Millionaire's Shortbread	187	11	7	25	91	22	1	15	2
Raspberry Squares	180	8	4	15	42	26	1	12	2
Best Lemon Bars	258	13	8	77	166	34	1	22	3
Ultranutty Pecan Bars	268	21	6	19	115	20	2	10	3

	Calories	Total Fat (G)	Sat Fat (G)	Chol (MG)	Sodium (MG)	Total Carb (G)	Dietary Fiber (G)	Total Sugars (G)	Protein (G)
Cakes & More									
Olive Oil Cake	372	18	3	58	237	47	1	28	5
Cider-Glazed Apple Bundt Cake	401	15	9	75	359	62	2	30	6
Marbled Blueberry Bundt Cake	500	19	11	93	375	78	2	49	6
Lemon Glaze	70	0	0	0	0	19	0	19	0
Cinnamon Whipped Cream	55	5	3	17	13	1	0	1	0
Lemon Pound Cake	488	25	15	154	231	61	0	44	5
Pear-Walnut Upside-Down Cake	382	24	7	80	195	39	3	28	5
French Apple Cake	411	24	2	21	208	46	2	31	3
Carrot Layer Cake	811	54	18	116	454	78	4	56	8
Best Almond Cake	405	25	5	90	217	40	3	28	8
Orange Crème Fraîche	66	4	2	13	36	7	1	6	1
Financiers	81	4	2	6	18	10	0	9	1
Fresh Fruit Financiers	60	4	1.5	5	20	6	1	5	1
Chocolate Chunk Financiers	250	16	9	7	24	23	3	16	3
Citrus or Spice Financiers	60	4	1.5	5	20	6	0	5	1
Nut Financiers	80	6	2	5	20	7	1	5	2
Coconut Layer Cake	782	53	36	127	361	73	1	55	6
Chocolate Sheet Cake with Milk Chocolate Frosting	782	53	25	128	221	75	4	56	9
Ultimate Chocolate Cupcakes with Ganache Filling	434	29	14	67	190	44	2	33	5
Creamy Chocolate Frosting	190	15	9	30	20	15	0	12	1
Choux au Craquelin	195	13	8	94	78	15	0	7	4
Colorful Choux au Craquelin	209	13	8	94	78	19	0	10	4
Mocha Choux au Craquelin	194	13	8	94	79	15	0	7	4
Torta Caprese	310	22	9	79	107	26	2	22	6
Amaretto Whipped Cream	68	6	4	19	5	2	0	2	0
Orange Whipped Cream	65	6	4	19	5	1	0	1	0
Triple-Chocolate Mousse Cake	464	38	23	126	82	32	2	29	6
Tiramisu	485	31	17	239	285	38	1	16	9
Tiramisu with Cooked Eggs	508	34	19	246	287	38	1	16	9
Foolproof New York Cheesecake	515	38	22	206	353	36	0	27	9
Spiced Pumpkin Cheesecake	437	31	18	148	318	35	1	27	7
Double-Apple Bread Pudding	446	28	16	156	334	40	3	16	10
Chocolate-Raspberry Trifle	471	28	14	120	191	48	3	34	7
DIY Chocolate Decorations	136	9	5	0	3	18	2	15	1
Best Butterscotch Pudding	413	33	20	178	267	27	0	23	5
Classic Crème Brûlée	576	50	30	410	63	27	0	26	7
Espresso Crème Brûlée	581	50	30	413	67	27	0	26	8
Latin Flan	252	7	4	62	223	39	0	39	7
Coffee Flan	252	7	4	62	223	39	0	39	7
Orange-Cardamom Flan	253	7	4	62	223	39	0	39	7
Chocolate Pots de Crème	476	38	23	190	112	35	2	31	6
Milk Chocolate Pots de Crème	515	40	24	200	142	33	1	29	7
Chocolate Semifreddo	267	21	13	91	79	19	1	17	3
Cherry Sauce	126	0	0	0	3	28	1	26	1
Quick Candied Nuts	111	9	1	0	54	7	1	4	3
Lemon Posset with Berries	382	29	18	90	22	31	1	28	3
Make-Ahead Chocolate Soufflés	309	19	11	157	102	31	2	28	7
Make-Ahead Mocha Soufflés	320	20	11	160	105	33	0	27	7
Pavlova with Fruit and Whipped Cream	300	17	11	55	40	34	0	34	3
Individual Pavlovas with Fruit and Whipped Cream	300	17	11	55	40	34	0	34	3
Orange, Cranberry, and Mint Topping	160	0	0	0	0	41	2	36	1
Mango, Kiwi, and Blueberry Topping	80	0.5	0	0	0	21	2	18	1
Sweet Cream Ice Cream	314	21	13	68	147	27	0	25	6
Vanilla Bean Sweet Cream Ice Cream	316	21	13	68	147	27	0	25	6
White Coffee Chip Sweet Cream Ice Cream	425	25	16	68	153	45	1	33	8
Strawberry Ripple Sweet Cream Ice Cream	283	14	9	45	98	37	0	35	4

	Calories	Total Fat (G)	Sat Fat (G)	Chol (MG)	Sodium (MG)	Total Carb (G)	Dietary Fiber (G)	Total Sugars (G)	Protein (G)
Pies & Fruit Desserts									
Foolproof All-Butter Dough for Single-Crust Pie	210	14	9	40	150	18	0	2	2
Foolproof Whole-Wheat Dough for Single-Crust Pie	210	14	9	40	150	19	2	2	3
Foolproof All-Butter Dough for Double-Crust Pie	410	28	18	75	290	35	0	3	5
Foolproof Whole-Wheat Dough for Double-Crust Pie	420	28	28	75	290	37	3	3	6
Graham Cracker Crust	100	7	4.5	20	20	7	0	6	0
Classic Tart Dough	230	12	8	55	75	26	0	9	3
Classic Apple Pie	617	31	14	46	376	82	6	44	5
Apple Pie with Crystallized Ginger	619	31	14	46	376	83	6	44	5
Apple Pie with Dried Fruit	684	30	14	45	377	99	7	57	5
Apple Pie with Fresh Cranberries	630	28	18	100	380	89	3	49	6
Salted Caramel Apple Pie	386	15	9	108	514	58	2	50	6
Skillet Apple Pie	333	15	8	31	157	47	5	26	3
Blueberry Pie	644	34	16	77	324	76	4	35	6
Sweet Cherry Pie	557	34	16	77	326	54	2	17	6
Fresh Peach Pie	152	1	0	0	51	36	3	31	2
Pie Dough for Lattice-Top Pie	420	24	11	40	290	42	0	3	5
Triple Berry Slab Pie with Ginger-Lemon Streusel	373	18	11	47	168	50	5	22	4
Slab Pie Dough	283	20	13	52	145	23	1	2	3
Fruit Hand Pies	420	28	18	100	320	35	0	3	5
Cherry Hand Pie Filling	60	0	0	0	75	15	1	13	0
Peach Hand Pie Filling	50	0	0	0	35	13	1	11	0
Pineapple Hand Pie Filling	60	0	0	0	35	14	1	9	0
Ultimate Lemon Meringue Pie	3813	177	82	1351	1957	516	7	328	51
Key Lime Pie	421	23	13	153	142	48	1	40	7
Perfect Pecan Pie	668	42	13	108	347	72	3	52	7
Lemon–Olive Oil Tart	443	22	3	70	247	57	1	33	6
Cranberry Curd Tart with Almond Crust	547	34	17	141	180	59	4	45	5
Free-Form Summer Fruit Tart	382	20	12	51	198	48	3	19	5
Fresh Fruit Tart with Pastry Cream	430	22	13	165	110	54	3	33	6
Mixed Berry Tart with Pastry Cream	430	22	13	165	110	54	4	33	6
Peach Tarte Tatin	161	6	3	11	88	28	2	25	1
Milk Chocolate Crémeux Tart	537	36	22	163	201	46	2	26	8
Apple Galette	311	17	10	43	122	39	2	14	3
Easy Apple Strudel	252	13	6	23	104	35	3	24	2
Tangy Whipped Cream	159	16	10	50	14	3	0	3	1
Skillet Apple Crisp	475	22	10	38	156	68	6	45	4
Apple-Blackberry Betty	269	11	6	23	390	39	6	18	5
Sour Cherry Cobbler	324	6	4	16	210	61	3	37	4
Fresh Sour Cherry Cobbler	348	6	4	16	210	67	3	44	4
Cherry Clafouti	326	15	9	132	128	42	2	33	6
Easy Strawberry Shortcakes for Two	714	42	25	204	388	75	4	35	11
Whipped Cream	52	5	3	17	4	1	0	1	0
Summer Berry Trifle	420	19	8	113	163	55	4	38	7
Berry Fool	349	18	10	50	49	48	7	36	4
Crepes with Sugar and Lemon	305	13	7	164	240	35	2	6	12
Crepes with Chocolate and Orange	415	17	9	164	241	54	2	26	12
Crepes with Bananas and Nutella	534	21	14	164	251	75	5	33	14
Caramelized Pears with Blue Cheese and Black Pepper–Caramel Sauce	280	14	9	41	394	38	3	32	4
Individual Fresh Berry Gratins with Zabaglione	185	8	4	150	48	24	6	19	4
Individual Fresh Berry Gratins with Lemon Zabaglione	183	8	4	150	48	25	6	19	4
Khao Niaow Ma Muang	396	15	13	0	157	64	3	32	6
Toasted Mung Beans	45	0	0	0	2	8	2	1	3
Honeydew, Mango, and Blueberries with Lime-Ginger Reduction	160	0	0	0	20	40	1	35	0

Conversions & Equivalents

Some say cooking is a science and an art. We would say that geography has a hand in it, too. Flour milled in the United Kingdom and elsewhere will feel and taste different from flour milled in the United States. So, while we cannot promise that the loaf of bread you bake in Canada or England will taste the same as a loaf baked in the States, we can offer guidelines for converting weights and measures. We also recommend that you rely on your instincts when making our recipes. Refer to the visual cues provided. If the dough hasn't "come together in a ball," as described, you may need to add more flour—even if the recipe doesn't tell you so. You be the judge.

The recipes in this book were developed using standard U.S. measures following U.S. government guidelines. The charts below offer equivalents for U.S. and metric measures. All conversions are approximate and have been rounded up or down to the nearest whole number.

EXAMPLES:

1 teaspoon = 4.929 milliliters, rounded up to 5 milliliters
1 ounce = 28.349 grams, rounded down to 28 grams

Volume Conversions

U.S.	METRIC
1 teaspoon	5 milliliters
2 teaspoons	10 milliliters
1 tablespoon	15 milliliters
2 tablespoons	30 milliliters
¼ cup	59 milliliters
⅓ cup	79 milliliters
½ cup	118 milliliters
¾ cup	177 milliliters
1 cup	237 milliliters
1¼ cups	296 milliliters
1½ cups	355 milliliters
2 cups (1 pint)	473 milliliters
2½ cups	591 milliliters
3 cups	710 milliliters
4 cups (1 quart)	0.946 liter
1.06 quarts	1 liter
4 quarts (1 gallon)	3.8 liters

Weight Conversions

OUNCES	GRAMS
½	14
¾	21
1	28
1½	43
2	57
2½	71
3	85
3½	99
4	113
4½	128
5	142
6	170
7	198
8	227
9	255
10	283
12	340
16 (1 pound)	454

Conversions for Common Baking Ingredients

Because measuring by weight is far more accurate than measuring by volume, and thus more likely to achieve reliable results, in our recipes we provide ounce measures in addition to cup measures for many ingredients. Refer to the chart below to convert these measures into grams.

INGREDIENT	OUNCES	GRAMS
Flour		
1 cup all-purpose flour*	5	142
1 cup cake flour	4	113
1 cup whole-wheat flour	5½	156
Sugar		
1 cup granulated (white) sugar	7	198
1 cup packed brown sugar (light or dark)	7	198
1 cup confectioners' sugar	4	113
Cocoa Powder		
1 cup cocoa powder	3	85
Butter†		
4 tablespoons (½ stick, or ¼ cup)	2	57
8 tablespoons (1 stick, or ½ cup)	4	113
16 tablespoons (2 sticks, or 1 cup)	8	227

* U.S. all-purpose flour, the most frequently used flour in this book, does not contain leaveners, as some European flours do. These leavened flours are called self-rising or self-raising. If you are using self-rising flour, take this into consideration before adding leavening to a recipe.

† In the United States, butter is sold both salted and unsalted. We generally recommend unsalted butter. If you are using salted butter, take this into consideration before adding salt to a recipe.

Oven Temperature

FAHRENHEIT	CELSIUS	GAS MARK
225	105	¼
250	120	½
275	135	1
300	150	2
325	165	3
350	180	4
375	190	5
400	200	6
425	220	7
450	230	8
475	245	9

Converting Temperatures from an Instant-Read Thermometer

We include doneness temperatures in many of the recipes in this book. We recommend an instant-read thermometer for the job. Refer to the table above to convert Fahrenheit degrees to Celsius. Or, for temperatures not represented in the chart, use this simple formula:

Subtract 32 degrees from the Fahrenheit reading, then divide the result by 1.8 to find the Celsius reading.

EXAMPLE:
"Roast chicken until thighs register 175 degrees."

TO CONVERT:
175°F − 32 = 143°
143° ÷ 1.8 = 79.44°C, rounded down to 79°C

Index

Note: Page references in *italics* indicate photographs. (v) indicates recipe has variations.

C

Cabbage
Chinese Pork Dumplings, 200–201, *201*
Creamy Buttermilk Coleslaw, 148, *148*
Curtido, 415, *415*
Grilled Napa, and Radicchio Topping, 431
Hot Ukrainian Borscht, *88,* 107–8
Shīzi Tóu, *339,* 339–40
shredding, 148
Stir-Fried Portobellos with Ginger-Oyster
Sauce (v), *400,* 400–401
see also Kimchi

Cakes
Almond, Best, *596, 597*
Apple, French, *594, 594*
Apple Bundt, Cider-Glazed, 589–90, *590*
Blueberry Bundt, Marbled, 590–91, *591*
Chocolate Sheet, with Milk Chocolate
Frosting, *600,* 600–601
Coconut Layer, *599,* 599–600
Financiers (v), 597–98, *598*
Foolproof New York Cheesecake,
609, 609–10
Lemon Pound, *592, 592*
lining cake pans for, 600
Olive Oil, *588,* 589
Pear-Walnut Upside-Down, 593, *593*
Spiced Pumpkin Cheesecake, 610–12, *611*
Torta Caprese, 604–6, *605*
Triple-Chocolate Mousse, 606–7, *607*
Ultimate Chocolate Cupcakes with
Ganache Filling, 601–2, *602*
Calamari, Rhode Island–Style Fried,
44–47, *46*
Caldo Verde, 105, *105*
Cơm Đỏ, 316
Cantaloupe Salad with Olives and
Red Onion, 154

Caper(s)
-Currant Relish, 361
Onion, and Olive Relish, 440
Persillade Relish, 290
Tartar Sauce, *349,* 349–50
Carbonnade à la Flamande, 98–100, *100*

Cardamom
Kanelbullar, *550,* 550–51
-Orange Flan, 618
Speculoos (v), 568–69
Carne Adovada, *331,* **331–32**
Carne Asada, 434–35, *435*
Carnitas, *330,* **330–31**

Carrot(s)
Beef and Vegetable Stew, 96, *96*
Best Beef Stew, *97,* 97–98
Best Chicken Stew, *92, 93*
and Cilantro, Lentil Salad with, 158
Escabeche, 229
Harissa-Mint, Skillet-Roasted Chicken
Breasts with, 213
Layer Cake, 594–95, *595*
Perfect Roasted Root Vegetables,
514–15, *515*
Plov, 301–2, *302*

Carrot(s) (*cont.*)
Pot Roast with Root Vegetables,
286–87, *287*
Roasted (v), 486, *486*
Simple Pot-au-Feu, 302–3, *303*
-Spice Steel-Cut Oatmeal, 86
-Tamarind Chutney, *37,* 38
Vegetable Bibimbap with Nurungji,
396–98, *397*
Cashews, Curried Chicken Salad with, 142
Cataplana, 110, *110*

Cauliflower
Bites, Buffalo, 486–87, *487*
Gratin, Modern, 488, *488*
Paella de Verduras, 398, *399*
Soup, 116, *117*
Tacos, Vegan Baja-Style, 412–13, *413*
Challah, *536,* **536–37**

Champagne
ATK 25, 49–51, *50*
Chana Masala, 392–93, *393*

Cheddar
Biscuits, 524
Broccoli-Cheese Soup, 112–14, *113*
Cheesy Nachos with Guacamole and
Salsa, 30, *30*
and Shallots, Grown-Up Grilled Cheese
Sandwiches with (v), 411, *411*
Simple Cheese Quiche, 74, *74*
Stovetop Macaroni and Cheese, 191, *191*
Tacos Dorados, 276–79, *278*

Cheese
Aligot, 501–2
Antipasto Pasta Salad, 156
Baked Brie en Croûte, *22,* 33–34
Baked Manicotti, *185,* 185–86
Baked Ziti, 186, *187*
Best Chicken Parmesan, 216–17, *217*
Blue, and Black Pepper–Caramel Sauce,
Caramelized Pears with, 672–74, *673*
Breakfast Strata with Spinach and
Gruyère, 75, *75*
Buffalo Chicken Sandwiches, 217–18, *218*
Butternut Squash Galette with Gruyère,
426
Cast Iron Pan Pizza, 555–56, *557*
Cotija, and Pinto Beans, Scrambled
Eggs with, 60
Croutons, 119, *119*
Eggplant Involtini, 407–8, *408*
Eggplant Parmesan, 406–7, *407*
Enchiladas Verdes, 232–33, *233*
Esquites, 149, *149*
Folded Enchiladas, 435
Frico, 33, *33*
Gorgonzola-Cream Sauce, 184
Grilled Halloumi Wraps, 474–76, *475*
Grown-Up Grilled, Sandwiches with
Cheddar and Shallots (v), 411, *411*
Mushroom and Leek Galette with
Gorgonzola (v), *424,* 425–26
Pizza al Taglio with Arugula and Fresh
Mozzarella (v), *554,* 554–55
Pupusas, 413–15, *415*

Cheese (*cont.*)
Quesadillas, 412, *412*
Roasted Poblano and Black Bean
Enchiladas, 405–6, *406*
Saag Paneer, 395–96
Skillet Lasagna, 188, *188*
Soufflés, Make-Ahead, *401,* 401–2
Spinach and Ricotta Gnudi with
Tomato-Butter Sauce, 402–4, *403*
Spinach Lasagna, 188–89, *189*
Stovetop Macaroni and, 191, *191*
Thin-Crust Pizza, 552, *553*
Tomato and Mozzarella Tart, *422,* 422–23
Turkey Patty Melts, 268–69, *269*
Watermelon Salad with Cotija and
Serrano Chiles (v), 152–54, *154*
see also Cheddar; Cream cheese; Feta;
Goat Cheese; Parmesan; Pecorino

Cheesecake
New York, Foolproof, *609,* 609–10
Spiced Pumpkin, 610–12, *611*
Chelow ba Tahdig, 515–16, *516*
Chermoula Sauce, *438,* **439**

Cherry(ies)
Apple Pie with Dried Fruit, 635
Clafouti, 666–67, *667*
Dried, Radicchio, and Pecans, Wheat
Berry Salad with, 158, *159*
Hand Pie Filling, 647
-Port Wine Sauce, 327–28
Sauce, 621, *621*
Sour, Cobbler (v), 665–66, *666*
Sweet, Pie, 639–40, *640*
Chestnut and Duck Ragu, Pappardelle with,
194, **194–95**

Chicken
with 40 Cloves of Garlic, *224,* 224–25
Adobo, Filipino, 219–20, *220*
Arroz con Pollo (v), 220–21, *221*
Barbecued Grilled (v), 458–59, *459*
Biryani, *253,* 253–54
breast, pounding, 218
breast, split, boning, 212
Breasts, Crispy-Skinned, with Vinegar-
Pepper Pan Sauce (v), *211,* 211–12
Breasts, Grilled Glazed Bone-In,
454, 454–55
Breasts, Pan-Seared, *210,* 210–11
Breasts, Skillet-Roasted, with Garlicky
Green Beans (v), 213, *213*
Under a Brick with Herb-Roasted
Potatoes, 242–44, *243*
Broiled, with Gravy, 241–42
Broth (v), 130, *131*
Buffalo Wings, 247–48, *248*
Chili, White, 94–95, *95*
Coq au Vin, 223, *223*
Crisp Roast Butterflied, with Rosemary
and Garlic, 244, *244*
Crispy Fried, 245, *245*
Curry, Thai, with Potatoes and Peanuts,
249, *249*
Cutlets, Crispy Pan-Fried, 209, *209–10*
cutlets, preparing, 209

N

Naan, Homemade (v), 540–41, *541*
Nachos, Cheesy, with Guacamole and Salsa, 30, *30*
Nam Prik Pao, 112
New Englander (v), 51
Noodle(s)
  Beef Ho Fun, 198, *198*
  Bún Chả, *450*, 450–51
  Chicken Soup, Classic, 90, *90*
  Chilled Soba, with Cucumber, Snow Peas, and Radishes, 156–57, *157*
  Dan Dan Mian, *199*, 199–200
  Gỏi Cuốn, 38–41, *39*
  Guay Tiew Tom Yum Goong, *111*, 111–12
  Japchae, 196, *197*
  Shīzi Tóu, *339*, 339–40
  Shrimp Pad Thai, *376*, 376–77
  Wonton Soup, Hong Kong–Style, 128–29, *129*
Nuóc Chấm, *39*, 41
Nutella and Bananas, Crepes with, 672
Nut(s)
  Financiers, *598*, 599
  Quick Candied, *621*, 621–22
  toasting, 585
  see also specific nuts

O

Oats
  Almond Granola with Dried Fruit (v), 86, *87*
  Big and Chewy Oatmeal-Raisin Cookies (v), *558*, 563–64
  Ten-Minute Steel-Cut Oatmeal (v), 85–86
Oils
  Chili, *204*, 205
  Chili, Quick, 203
  Tarragon, 358
  see also Olive Oil
Old Bay Butter, Spicy, 477
Olive Oil
  Cake, *588*, 589
  –Lemon Tart, *652*, 652–53
Olive(s)
  Cracked, Fennel, and Orange, Braised Chicken Thighs with, 219, *219*
  Cuban-Style Picadillo (v), *282*, 282–83
  Green, Almond, and Orange Relish, 364
  Horiatiki Salata, *136*, 136–37
  Mint, and Feta, Lentil Salad with (v), 157–58
  Onion, and Caper Relish, 440
  and Red Onion, Cantaloupe Salad with, 154
  Ropa Vieja, *299*, 299–300
  Salade Niçoise, 138–39, *139*

Omelets
  Fluffy, *64*, 64–65
  French, *65*, 65–66
  Spanish Tortilla with Roasted Red Peppers and Peas (v), 28–30, *29*
Onion(s)
  Alcatra, 98, *99*
  and Beef Ragu, Pasta with, 173–74, *174*
  Best Beef Stew, *97*, 97–98
  -Braised Beef Brisket, *298*, 298–99
  Caramelized, Spice-Rubbed Pork Roast en Cocotte with, *326*
  Carbonnade à la Flamande, 98–100, *100*
  Chicken Biryani, *253*, 253–54
  Crispy, 422
  Escabeche, 229
  Mujaddara, *420*, 421–22
  -Mushroom Gravy, Steak Tips with, *311*, 311–12
  Olive, and Caper Relish, 440
  Pakoras, *37*, 37–38
  Red, and Olives, Cantaloupe Salad with, 154
  Red, –Grilled Pineapple Salsa, *442*, 442
  Rings, Beer-Battered, with Jalapeño Dipping Sauce, *497*, 497
  Soup, Best French, 118–19, *119*
  Sweet and Spicy Pickled, *310*, 311
  Tamatya-Kandyachi Koshimbir, *409*, 410
  Turkey Patty Melts, 268–69, *269*
  Ultimate Green Bean Casserole, *495*, 495–96
Orange(s)
  -Almond Butter, 77
  and Avocado, Shrimp Salad with, 378
  -Cardamom Flan, 618
  -Chipotle Glaze, 455
  and Chocolate, Crepes with, 672
  Cinnamon, and Star Anise Glaze, 338
  Cranberry, and Mint Pavlova Topping, 625
  Crème Fraîche, 597
  Fennel, and Cracked Olives, Braised Chicken Thighs with, 219, *219*
  and Fennel, Grilled Whole Trout with, 468
  -Ginger Grilled Pork Tenderloin Steaks, Spicy, 441
  Green Olive, and Almond Relish, 364
  Jicama, and Pepita Relish, 440
  -Miso Glaze, 352
  -Parsley Salsa, 515
  -Pecan Granola with Dried Cranberries, 86
  Salsa with Cuban Flavors, 445
  Sangria, 54, *55*
  and Walnuts, Beets with, 483
  Whipped Cream, 606
Oregano and Lime, Grilled Potatoes with, 478
Osso Buco, 319–20, *320*
Oysters on the Half Shell, Roasted, with Mustard Butter, 44, *45*

P

Pa amb Tomàquet, 35, *35*
Pad Thai, Shrimp, *376*, 376–77
Paella, *382*, 382–83
  de Verduras, 398, *399*
  on the Grill, *473*, 473–74
Pai Huang Gua, 149–50
Pakoras, *37*, 37–38
Palak Dal, 394–95, *395*
Pancakes
  Blueberry, Deluxe, *78*, 79
  Cōngyóubǐng, *36*, 36–37
  Easy, 77
  German, *80*, 80–81
  100 Percent Whole-Wheat, 79–80
  see also Crepes
Pancetta
  Salade Lyonnaise, 137–38, *138*
  and Walnuts, Parmesan Sauce with, 184
Paneer, Saag, 395–96
Panzanella, 143
Pão de Queijo, *528*, 528
Paprika
  Harissa, 521
  Smoked, and Roasted Red Pepper Butter, *428*, 434
  Spice Rub, 447
Parathas, Alu, 408–10, *409*
Parmesan
  Baked Manicotti, *185*, 185–86
  Baked Ziti, 186, *187*
  Best Summer Tomato Gratin, *509*, 509–10
  Broccoli-Cheese Soup, 112–14, *113*
  Brussels Sprouts Salad with Warm Bacon Vinaigrette, 146
  Cheese, Spinach, and Walnuts, Lentil Salad with, 158
  Chicken, Best, 216–17, *217*
  Eggplant, 406–7, *407*
  Farrotto (v), 517–18
  Fluffy Omelets, *64*, 64–65
  and Herbs, Almost Hands-Free Risotto with, 516–17, *517*
  Kale Caesar Salad, *132*, 135–36
  Make-Ahead Cheese Soufflés, *401*, 401–2
  Modern Cauliflower Gratin, *488*, 488
  Pão de Queijo, *528*, 528
  Pasta Cacio e Uova, 162, *163*
  Pistou, 121
  and Radicchio, Roasted Butternut Squash with, 509
  Red Pepper Flakes, and Garlic, Roasted Brussels Sprouts with, 484
  Sauce with Pancetta and Walnuts, 184
  Spinach Lasagna, 188–89, *189*
  Thin-Crust Pizza, 552, *553*
  Tomato and Mozzarella Tart, *422*, 422–23
Parsley
  Caper-Currant Relish, 361
  Chimichurri, 309, *309*
  Cilantro Chimichurri, *365*, 366
  -Cucumber Salad with Feta, Pomegranate, and Walnuts, *453*, 454

V

Vanilla Bean Sweet Cream Ice Cream, 627

Veal
   Osso Buco, 319–20, *320*
   Ragu alla Bolognese, 175–76, *176*
   Skillet Lasagna, 188, *188*

Vegetable(s)
   and Beef Stew, 96, *96*
   Bibimbap with Nurungji, 396–98, *397*
   Broth Base, 130
   and Quinoa Stew (v), 127, *127*
   Root, Perfect Roasted, 514–15, *515*
   Root, Pot Roast with, 286–87, *287*
   see also specific vegetables

Veggie Burgers, Ultimate, 416

Vinaigrettes
   Basil, 471
   Chile-Lime, *470*, 471
   Chunky Cherry Tomato–Basil, *344*, 361
   Foolproof (v), 134, *135*
   for Rosticciana, *448*, 449

Vinegar
   Banana Ketchup, 43
   Barbecue Sauce, Lexington, 228
   Cranberry Shrub Syrup, 51
   Filipino Chicken Adobo, 219–20, *220*
   Maple Agrodolce, 323
   –Roasted Red Pepper Sauce, 321
   Seasoned, Lumpiang Shanghai with, *41*, 41–43

Vodka, New Englander with, 51

Vospov Kofte, *419*, 419–20

W

Waffles
   Buttermilk, *81*, 81–82
   Liège, 82–83, *83*
   Yeasted, 82

Waldorf Chicken Salad, 142

Walnut(s)
   Best Vegetarian Chili, *390*, 391
   and Cranberries, Rustic Bread Stuffing with, 521, *521*

Walnut(s) (*cont.*)
   Cream Sauce, 165
   Easy Apple Strudel, *662*, 662–63
   Granola, Spiced, with Dried Apple, 86
   and Lemon, Roasted Brussels Sprouts with, 484
   and Orange, Beets with, 483
   and Pancetta, Parmesan Sauce with, 184
   -Pear Upside-Down Cake, 593, *593*
   -Raisin Filling, Crescent-Shaped Rugelach with, 574, *574*
   Topping for Hummus, Spiced, 26
   Waldorf Chicken Salad, 142

Walnut Vinaigrette, Foolproof, 134

Watercress
   Bò Lúc Lắc, *315*, 315–16
   Brussels Sprouts Salad with Warm Mustard Vinaigrette (v), 146, *147*
   and Spiced Yogurt, Beet Salad with (v), *144*, 144–45

Watermelon Salad with Cotija and Serrano Chiles (v), 152–54, *154*

Wheat Berry Salad with Radicchio, Dried Cherries, and Pecans, 158, *159*

Whipped Cream, 668
   Amaretto, 606
   Cinnamon, 591
   and Fruit, Pavlova with (v), *624*, 624–25
   Orange, 606
   Tangy, 663

Whole-Wheat Dough for Double-Crust Pie, Foolproof, 632

Whole-Wheat Dough for Single-Crust Pie, Foolproof, 630

Whole-Wheat Pancakes, 100 Percent, 79–80

Wild Rice and Mushroom Soup, 116–18, *118*

Wine
   ATK 25, 49–51, *50*
   Chicken Marsala, 214, *215*
   Madeira Pan Sauce with Mustard and Anchovies, 309
   Port, –Cherry Sauce, 327–28
   Rosé Sangria, 53, *53*
   see also Red Wine

Wonton Noodle Soup, Hong Kong–Style, 128–29, *129*

Wraps, Grilled Halloumi, 474–76, *475*

X

Xīhóngshì Chǎo Jīdàn, 61, *61*

Y

Yogurt
   Çılbır, *70*, 71
   -Curry Glaze, 455
   Garlic-Curry Sauce, 210
   -Garlic Sauce, 451, *451*
   Kousa Mihshi, *512*, 512–13
   Paprika, and Coriander, Braised Eggplant with (v), *480*, 493
   Sauce, 253, 421
   Spiced, and Watercress, Beet Salad with (v), *144*, 144–45
   Tahini Sauce, 418

Z

Zabaglione, Individual Fresh Berry Gratins with (v), *674*, 674–75

Zha Paigu, 324–26, *325*

Zucchini
   Briam, 510, *511*
   coring, 513
   Kousa Mihshi, *512*, 512–13
   Soupe au Pistou, 121–22
   Walkaway Ratatouille, *513*, 513–14

Library of Congress Cataloging-in-Publication Data has been applied for.

ISBN 978-1-954210-92-9

AMERICA'S TEST KITCHEN
21 Drydock Avenue, Boston, MA 02210

Printed in Canada
10 9 8 7 6 5 4 3 2 1

Distributed by: Penguin Random House Publisher Services, tel: 800-733-3000

Front Cover Cast Photography: Joseph Keller

Support for the America's Test Kitchen television series has been provided by our sponsors:

Sur la table

Editorial Director, Books: Adam Kowit

Executive Food Editor: Dan Zuccarello

Executive Managing Editor: Debra Hudak

Test Cooks: Olivia Counter, Laila Ibrahim, José Maldonado, and David Yu

Assistant Editor: Julia Arwine

Additional Editorial Support: Elizabeth Wray Emery, Sara Mayer, April Poole, Cheryl Redmond, and Vicki Rowland

Design Director: Lindsey Timko Chandler

Art Director: Katie Barranger

Designers: Allison Boales and Jen Kanavos Hoffman

Photography Director: Julie Bozzo Cote

Senior Photography Producer: Meredith Mulcahy

Senior Staff Photographers: Steve Klise and Daniel J. van Ackere

Staff Photographer: Kritsada Panichgul

Additional Photography: Beth Fuller, Joseph Keller, Elisabeth O'Donnell, Carl Tremblay, and Kevin White

Food Styling: Sheila Jarnes, Catrine Kelty, Chantal Lambeth, Kendra McKnight, Ashley Moore, Marie Piraino, Mary Jane Sawyer, Elle Simone Scott, Kendra Smith, Sally Staub, and Christine Tobin

Illustrations: Sophie Greenspan

Project Manager, Books: Katie Kimmerer

Senior Print Production Specialist: Lauren Robbins

Production and Imaging Coordinator: Amanda Yong

Production and Imaging Specialists: Tricia Neumyer, Dennis Noble, and Chloe Petraske

Copyeditor: Cheryl Redmond

Proofreader: Ann-Marie Imbornoni

Indexer: Elizabeth Parson

Chief Executive Officer: Dan Suratt

Chief Creative Officer: Jack Bishop

Executive Editorial Directors: Julia Collin Davison and Bridget Lancaster

Senior Director, Book Sales: Emily Logan